The Book of (Kinda) Complete English Poetry: For Readings*

Volume one

by Hudson Tarasiuk

*According to Moby Words II SINGLE.TXT

A, a's, a/c, a1, aa, aaa, aah, aahed, aahing, aahs, aal, aalii, aaliis, aals, aam, aardvark, aardvarks, aardwolf, aardwolves, aargh, aaron, aaronic, aarrgh, aarrghh, aas, aasvogel, aasvogels, ab, aba, abac, abaca, abacas, abacate, abacaxi, abacay, abaci, abacinate, abacination, abacisci, abaciscus, abacist, aback, abacli, abacot, abacterial, abactinal, abactinally, abaction, abactor, abaculi, abaculus, abacus, abacuses, abada, abaddon, abadejo, abadengo, abadia, abaff, abaft, abaisance, abaised, abaiser, abaisse, abaissed, abaka, abakas, abalation, abalienate, abalienated, abalienating, abalienation, abalone, abalones, abamp, abampere, abamperes, abamps, aband, abandon, abandonable, abandoned, abandonedly, abandonee, zabandoner, abandoners, abandoning, abandonment, abandonments, abandons, abandum, abanet, abanga, abannition, abapical, abaptiston, abaptistum, abarthrosis, abarticular, abarticulation, abas, abase, abased, abasedly, abasedness, abasement, abasements, abaser, abasers, abases, abash, abashed, abashedly, abashedness, abashes, abashing, abashless, abashlessly, abashment, abashments, abasia, abasias, abasic, abasing, abasio, abask, abassi, abastard, abastardize, abastral, abatable, abatage, abate, abated, abatement, abatements, abater, abaters, abates, abatic, abating, abatis, abatised, abatises, abatjour, abatjours, abaton, abator, abators, abattage, abattis, abattised, abattises, abattoir, abattoirs, abattu, abattue, abature, abaue, abave, abaxial, abaxile, abay, abayah, abaze, abb, abba, abbacies, abbacomes, abbacy, abbandono, abbas, abbasi, abbasid, abbassi, abbate, abbatial, abbatical, abbatie, abbaye, abbe, abbes, abbess, abbesses, abbest, abbevillian, abbey, abbey's, abbeys, abbeystead, abbeystede, abboccato, abbogada, abbot, abbot's, abbotcies, abbotcy, abbotnullius, abbotric, abbots, abbotship, abbotships, abbott, abbozzo, abbr, abbrev, abbreviatable, abbreviate, abbreviated, abbreviately, abbreviates, abbreviating, abbreviation, abbreviations, abbreviator, abbreviators, abbreviatory, abbreviature, abbroachment, abby, abc, abcess, abcissa, abcoulomb, abd, abdal, abdali, abdaria, abdat, abdest, abdicable, abdicant, abdicate, abdicated, abdicates, abdicating, abdication, abdications, abdicative, abdicator, abditive, abditory, abdom, abdomen, abdomen's, abdomens, abdomina, abdominal, abdominales, abdominalia, abdominalian, abdominally, abdominals, abdominoanterior, abdominocardiac, abdominocentesis, abdominocystic, abdominogenital, abdominohysterectomy, abdominohysterotomy, abdominoposterior, abdominoscope, abdominoscopy, abdominothoracic, abdominous, abdominovaginal, abdominovesical, abduce, abduced, abducens, abducent, abducentes, abduces, abducing, abduct, abducted, abducting, abduction, abduction's, abductions, abductor, abductor's, abductores, abductors, abducts, abeam, abear, abearance, abecedaire, abecedaria, abecedarian, abecedarians, abecedaries, abecedarium, abecedarius, abecedary, abed, abede, abedge, abegge, abeigh, abel, abele, abeles, abelian, abelite, abelmosk, abelmosks, abelmusk, abeltree, abend, abends, abenteric, abepithymia, aberdavine, aberdeen, aberdevine, aberduvine, abernethy, aberr, aberrance, aberrancies, aberrancy, aberrant, aberrantly, aberrants, aberrate, aberrated, aberrating, aberration, aberrational, aberrations, aberrative, aberrator, aberrometer, aberroscope, aberuncate, aberuncator, abesse, abessive, abet, abetment, abetments, abets, abettal, abettals, abetted, abetter, abetters, abetting, abettor, abettors, abevacuation, abey, abeyance, abeyances, abeyancies, abeyancy, abeyant, abfarad, abfarads, abhenries, abhenry, abhenrys, abhinaya, abhiseka, abhominable, abhor, abhorred, abhorrence, abhorrences, abhorrency, abhorrent, abhorrently, abhorrer, abhorrers, abhorrible, abhorring, abhors, abib, abichite, abidal, abidance, abidances, abidden, abide, abided, abider, abiders, abides, abidi, abiding, abidingly, abidingness, abiegh, abience, abient, abietate, abietene, abietic, abietin, abietineous, abietinic, abietite, abigail, abigails, abigailship, abigeat, abigei, abigeus, abilao, abilene, abiliment, abilitable, abilities, ability, ability's, abilla, abilo, abime, abintestate, abiogeneses, abiogenesis, abiogenesist, abiogenetic, abiogenetical, abiogenetically, abiogenist, abiogenous, abiogeny, abiological, abiologically, abiology, abioses, abiosis, abiotic, abiotical, abiotically, abiotrophic, abiotrophy, abir, abirritant, abirritate, abirritated, abirritating, abirritation, abirritative, abiston, abit, abiuret, abject, abjectedness, abjection, abjections, abjective, abjectly, abjectness, abjoint, abjudge, abjudged, abjudging, abjudicate, abjudicated, abjudicating, abjudication, abjudicator, abjugate, abjunct, abjunction, abjunctive, abjuration, abjurations, abjuratory, abjure, abjured, abjurement, abjurer, abjurers, abjures, abjuring, abkar, abkari, abkary, abl, ablach, ablactate, ablactated, ablactating, ablactation, ablaqueate, ablare, ablastemic, ablastin, ablastous, ablate, ablated, ablates, ablating, ablation, ablations, ablatitious, ablatival, ablative, ablatively, ablatives, ablator, ablaut, ablauts, ablaze, able, ableeze, ablegate, ablegates, ablegation, ablend, ableness, ablepharia, ablepharon, ablepharous, ablepsia, ablepsy, ableptical, ableptically, abler, ables, ablesse, ablest, ablet, ablewhackets, ablings, ablins, ablock, abloom, ablow, ablude, abluent, abluents, ablush, ablute, abluted, ablution, ablutionary, ablutions, abluvion, ably, abmho, abmhos, abmodalities, abmodality, abn, abnegate, abnegated, abnegates, abnegating, abnegation, abnegations, abnegative, abnegator, abnegators, abner, abnerval, abnet, abneural, abnormal, abnormalcies, abnormalcy, abnormalise, abnormalised, abnormalising, abnormalism, abnormalist, abnormalities, abnormality, abnormalize, abnormalized, abnormalizing, abnormally, abnormalness, abnormals, abnormities, abnormity, abnormous, abnumerable, abo, aboard, aboardage, abococket, abodah, abode, abode's, aboded, abodement, abodes, aboding, abody, abogado, abogados, abohm, abohms, aboideau, aboideaus, aboideaux, aboil, aboiteau, aboiteaus, aboiteaux, abolete, abolish, abolishable, abolished, abolisher, abolishers, abolishes, abolishing, abolishment, abolishment's, abolishments, abolition, abolitionary, abolitionise, abolitionised, abolitionising, abolitionism, abolitionist, abolitionists, abolitionize, abolitionized, abolitionizing, abolla, abollae, aboma, abomas, abomasa, abomasal, abomasi, abomasum, abomasus, abomasusi, abominability, abominable, abominableness, abominably, abominate, abominated, abominates, abominating, abomination, abominations, abominator, abominators, abomine, abondance, abonne, abonnement, aboon, aborad, aboral, aborally, abord, aboriginal, aboriginality, aboriginally, aboriginals, aboriginary, aborigine, aborigine's, aborigines, aborning, aborsement, aborsive, abort, aborted, aborter, aborters, aborticide, abortient, abortifacient, abortin, aborting, abortion, abortion's, abortional, abortionist, abortionists, abortions, abortive, abortively, abortiveness, abortogenic, aborts, abortus, abortuses, abos, abote, abouchement, aboudikro, abought, aboulia, aboulias, aboulic, abound, abounded, abounder, abounding, aboundingly, abounds, about, abouts, above, aboveboard, abovedeck, aboveground, abovementioned, aboveproof, aboves, abovesaid, abovestairs, abow, abox, abp, abr, abracadabra, abrachia, abrachias, abradable, abradant, abradants, abrade, abraded, abrader, abraders, abrades, abrading, abraham, abraid, abranchial, abranchialism, abranchian, abranchiate, abranchious, abrasax, abrase, abrased, abraser, abrash, abrasing, abrasiometer, abrasion, abrasion's, abrasions, abrasive, abrasively, abrasiveness, abrasives, abrastol, abraum, abraxas, abray, abrazite, abrazitic, abrazo, abrazos, abreact, abreacted, abreacting, abreaction, abreactions, abreacts, abreast, abreed, abrege, abreid, abrenounce, abrenunciate, abrenunciation, abreption, abret, abreuvoir, abri, abrico, abricock, abricot, abridgable, abridge, abridgeable, abridged, abridgedly, abridgement, abridgements, abridger, abridgers, abridges, abridging, abridgment, abridgments, abrim, abrin, abrine, abris, abristle, abroach, abroad, abrocome, abrogable, abrogate, abrogated, abrogates, abrogating, abrogation, abrogations, abrogative, abrogator, abrogators, abronia, abrood, abrook, abrosia, abrosias, abrotanum, abrotin, abrotine, abrupt, abruptedly, abrupter, abruptest, abruptio, abruption, abruptiones, abruptly, abruptness, abs, absampere, absarokite, abscam, abscess, abscessed, abscesses, abscessing, abscession, abscessroot, abscind, abscise, abscised, abscises, abscising, abscisins, abscision, absciss, abscissa, abscissa's, abscissae, abscissas, abscisse, abscissin, abscission, abscissions, absconce, abscond, absconded, abscondedly, abscondence, absconder, absconders, absconding, absconds, absconsa, abscoulomb, abscound, absee, abseil, abseiled, abseiling, abseils, absence, absence's, absences, absent, absentation, absented, absentee, absentee's, absenteeism, absentees, absenteeship, absenter, absenters, absentia, absenting, absently, absentment, absentminded, absentmindedly, absentmindedness, absentness, absents, absey, absfarad, abshenry, absinth, absinthe, absinthes, absinthial, absinthian, absinthiate, absinthiated, absinthiating, absinthic, absinthiin, absinthin, absinthine, absinthism, absinthismic, absinthium, absinthol, absinthole, absinths, absis, absist, absistos, absit, absmho, absohm, absoil, absolent, absolute, absolutely, absoluteness, absoluter, absolutes, absolutest, absolution, absolutions, absolutism, absolutist, absolutista, absolutistic, absolutistically, absolutists, absolutive, absolutization, absolutize, absolutory, absolvable, absolvatory, absolve, absolved, absolvent, absolver, absolvers, absolves, absolving, absolvitor, absolvitory, absonant, absonous, absorb, absorbability, absorbable, absorbance, absorbancy, absorbant, absorbed, absorbedly, absorbedness, absorbefacient, absorbencies, absorbency, absorbent, absorbents, absorber, absorbers, absorbing, absorbingly, absorbition, absorbs, absorbtion, absorpt, absorptance, absorptiometer, absorptiometric, absorption, absorption's, absorptional, absorptions, absorptive, absorptively, absorptiveness, absorptivity, absquatulate, absquatulation, abstain, abstained, abstainer, abstainers, abstaining, abstainment, abstains, abstemious, abstemiously, abstemiousness, abstention, abstentionism, abstentionist, abstentions, abstentious, absterge, absterged, abstergent, absterges, absterging, absterse, abstersion, abstersive, abstersiveness, abstertion, abstinence, abstinency, abstinent, abstinential, abstinently, abstort, abstr, abstract, abstractable, abstracted, abstractedly, abstractedness, abstracter, abstracters, abstractest, abstracting, abstraction, abstraction's, abstractional, abstractionism, abstractionist, abstractionists, abstractions, abstractitious, abstractive, abstractively, abstractiveness, abstractly, abstractness, abstractor, abstractor's, abstractors, abstracts, abstrahent, abstrict, abstricted, abstricting, abstriction, abstricts, abstrude, abstruse, abstrusely, abstruseness, abstrusenesses, abstruser, abstrusest, abstrusion, abstrusities, abstrusity, absume, absumption, absurd, absurder, absurdest, absurdism, absurdist, absurdities, absurdity, absurdity's, absurdly, absurdness, absurds, absurdum, absvolt, abt, abterminal, abthain, abthainrie, abthainry, abthanage, abtruse, abu, abubble, abucco, abuilding, abuleia, abulia, abulias, abulic, abulomania, abulyeit, abumbral, abumbrellar, abuna, abundance, abundances, abundancy, abundant, abundantly, abune, abura, aburabozu, aburagiri, aburban, aburst, aburton, abusable, abusage, abuse, abused, abusedly, abusee, abuseful, abusefully, abusefulness, abuser, abusers, abuses, abush, abusing, abusion, abusious, abusive, abusively, abusiveness, abut, abutilon, abutilons, abutment, abutments, abuts, abuttal, abuttals, abutted, abutter, abutter's, abutters, abutting, abuzz, abv, abvolt, abvolts, abwab, abwatt, abwatts, aby, abye, abyes, abying, abys, abysm, abysmal, abysmally, abysms, abyss, abyss's, abyssa, abyssal, abysses, abyssinia, abyssinian, abyssinians, abyssobenthonic, abyssolith, abyssopelagic, abyssus, ac, acacatechin, acacatechol, acacetin, acacia, acacias, acaciin, acacin, acacine, acad, academe, academes, academia, academial, academian, academias, academic, academical, academically, academicals, academician, academicians, academicianship, academicism, academics, academie, academies, academise, academised, academising, academism, academist, academite, academization, academize, academized, academizing, academy, academy's, acadia, acadialite, acadian, acaena, acajou, acajous, acalculia, acale, acaleph, acalepha, acalephae, acalephan, acalephe, acalephes, acalephoid, acalephs, acalycal, acalycine, acalycinous, acalyculate, acalyptrate, acampsia, acana, acanaceous, acanonical, acanth, acantha, acanthaceous, acanthad, acanthi, acanthial, acanthin, acanthine, acanthion, acanthite, acanthocarpous, acanthocephalan, acanthocephalous, acanthocladous, acanthodean, acanthodian, acanthoid, acanthological, acanthology, acantholysis, acanthoma, acanthomas, acanthon, acanthophorous, acanthopod, acanthopodous, acanthopomatous, acanthopore, acanthopteran, acanthopterous, acanthopterygian, acanthoses, acanthosis, acanthotic, acanthous, acanthus, acanthuses, acanthuthi, acapnia, acapnial, acapnias, acappella, acapsular, acapu, acapulco, acara, acarari, acardia, acardiac, acardite, acari, acarian, acariasis, acariatre, acaricidal, acaricide, acarid, acaridae, acaridan, acaridans, acaridean, acaridomatia, acaridomatium, acarids, acariform, acarine, acarines, acarinosis, acarocecidia, acarocecidium, acarodermatitis, acaroid, acarol, acarologist, acarology, acarophilous, acarophobia, acarotoxic, acarpellous, acarpelous, acarpous, acarus, acast, acatalectic, acatalepsia, acatalepsy, acataleptic, acatallactic, acatamathesia, acataphasia, acataposis, acatastasia, acatastatic, acate, acategorical, acater, acatery, acates, acatharsia, acatharsy, acatholic, acaudal, acaudate, acaudelescent, acaulescence, acaulescent, acauline, acaulose, acaulous, acc, acca, accable, accademia, accadian, acce, accede, acceded, accedence, acceder, acceders, accedes, acceding, accel, accelerable, accelerando, accelerant, accelerate, accelerated, acceleratedly, accelerates, accelerating, acceleratingly, acceleration, accelerations, accelerative, accelerator, acceleratorh, accelerators, acceleratory, accelerograph, accelerometer, accelerometer's, accelerometers, accend, accendibility, accendible, accensed, accension, accensor, accent, accented, accenting, accentless, accentor, accentors, accents, accentuable, accentual, accentuality, accentually, accentuate, accentuated, accentuates, accentuating, accentuation, accentuator, accentus, accept, acceptability, acceptable, acceptableness, acceptably, acceptance, acceptance's, acceptances, acceptancies, acceptancy, acceptant, acceptation, acceptavit, accepted, acceptedly, acceptee, acceptees, accepter, accepters, acceptilate, acceptilated, acceptilating, acceptilation, accepting, acceptingly, acceptingness, acception, acceptive, acceptor, acceptor's, acceptors, acceptress, accepts, accerse, accersition, accersitor, access, accessability, accessable, accessaries, accessarily, accessariness, accessary, accessaryship, accessed, accesses, accessibility, accessible, accessibleness, accessibly, accessing, accession, accession's, accessional, accessioned, accessioner, accessioning, accessions, accessit, accessive, accessively, accessless, accessor, accessor's, accessorial, accessories, accessorii, accessorily, accessoriness, accessorius, accessoriusorii, accessorize, accessorized, accessorizing, accessors, accessory, accessory's, acciaccatura, acciaccaturas, acciaccature, accidence, accidencies, accidency, accident, accidental, accidentalism, accidentalist, accidentality, accidentally, accidentalness, accidentals, accidentarily, accidentary, accidented, accidential, accidentiality, accidently, accidents, accidia, accidie, accidies, accinge, accinged, accinging, accipenser, accipient, accipiter, accipitral, accipitrary, accipitrine, accipter, accise, accismus, accite, acclaim, acclaimable, acclaimed, acclaimer, acclaimers, acclaiming, acclaims, acclamation, acclamations, acclamator, acclamatory, acclimatable, acclimatation, acclimate, acclimated, acclimatement, acclimates, acclimating, acclimation, acclimatisable, acclimatisation, acclimatise, acclimatised, acclimatiser, acclimatising, acclimatizable, acclimatization, acclimatize, acclimatized, acclimatizer, acclimatizes, acclimatizing, acclimature, acclinal, acclinate, acclivities, acclivitous, acclivity, acclivous, accloy, accoast, accoil, accolade, accoladed, accolades, accolated, accolent, accoll, accolle, accolled, accollee, accombination, accommodable, accommodableness, accommodate, accommodated, accommodately, accommodateness, accommodates, accommodating, accommodatingly, accommodatingness, accommodation, accommodational, accommodationist, accommodations, accommodative, accommodatively, accommodativeness, accommodator, accommodators, accomodate, accompanable, accompanied, accompanier, accompanies, accompaniment, accompaniment's, accompanimental, accompaniments, accompanist, accompanist's, accompanists, accompany, accompanying, accompanyist, accomplement, accompletive, accompli, accomplice, accomplices, accompliceship, accomplicity, accomplis, accomplish, accomplishable, accomplished, accomplisher, accomplishers, accomplishes, accomplishing, accomplishment, accomplishment's, accomplishments, accomplisht, accompt, accord, accordable, accordance, accordances, accordancy, accordant, accordantly, accordatura, accordaturas, accordature, accorded, accorder, accorders, according, accordingly, accordion, accordion's, accordionist, accordionists, accordions, accords, accorporate, accorporation, accost, accostable, accosted, accosting, accosts, accouche, accouchement, accouchements, accoucheur, accoucheurs, accoucheuse, accoucheuses, accounsel, account, accountability, accountable, accountableness, accountably, accountancy, accountant, accountant's, accountants, accountantship, accounted, accounter, accounters, accounting, accountment, accountrement, accounts, accouple, accouplement, accourage, accourt, accouter, accoutered, accoutering, accouterment, accouterments, accouters, accoutre, accoutred, accoutrement, accoutrements, accoutres, accoutring, accoy, accoyed, accoying, accra, accrease, accredit, accreditable, accreditate, accreditation, accreditations, accredited, accreditee, accrediting, accreditment, accredits, accrementitial, accrementition, accresce, accrescence, accrescendi, accrescendo, accrescent, accretal, accrete, accreted, accretes, accreting, accretion, accretion's, accretionary, accretions, accretive, accriminate, accroach, accroached, accroaching, accroachment, accroides, accruable, accrual, accruals, accrue, accrued, accruement, accruer, accrues, accruing, acct, accts, accubation, accubita, accubitum, accubitus, accueil, accultural, acculturate, acculturated, acculturates, acculturating, acculturation, acculturational, acculturationist, acculturative, acculturize, acculturized, acculturizing, accum, accumb, accumbency, accumbent, accumber, accumulable, accumulate, accumulated, accumulates, accumulating, accumulation, accumulations, accumulativ, accumulative, accumulatively, accumulativeness, accumulator, accumulator's, accumulators, accupy, accur, accuracies, accuracy, accurate, accurately, accurateness, accurre, accurse, accursed, accursedly, accursedness, accursing, accurst, accurtation, accus, accusable, accusably, accusal, accusals, accusant, accusants, accusation, accusation's, accusations, accusatival, accusative, accusatively, accusativeness, accusatives, accusator, accusatorial, accusatorially, accusatory, accusatrix, accusatrixes, accuse, accused, accuser, accusers, accuses, accusing, accusingly, accusive, accusor, accustom, accustomation, accustomed, accustomedly, accustomedness, accustoming, accustomize, accustomized, accustomizing, accustoms, ace, ace's, aceacenaphthene, aceanthrene, aceanthrenequinone, acecaffin, acecaffine, aceconitic, aced, acedia, acediamin, acediamine, acedias, acediast, acedy, aceite, aceituna, aceldama, aceldamas, acellular, acemila, acenaphthene, acenaphthenyl, acenaphthylene, acenesthesia, acensuada, acensuador, acentric, acentrous, aceologic, aceology, acephal, acephala, acephalan, acephali, acephalia, acephaline, acephalism, acephalist, acephalocyst, acephalous, acephalus, acepots, acequia, acequiador, acequias, aceraceous, acerate, acerated, acerathere, aceratosis, acerb, acerbate, acerbated, acerbates, acerbating, acerber, acerbest, acerbic, acerbically, acerbities, acerbitude, acerbity, acerbityacerose, acerbly, acerbophobia, acerdol, aceric, acerin, acerli, acerola, acerolas, acerose, acerous, acerra, acertannin, acerval, acervate, acervately, acervatim, acervation, acervative, acervose, acervuli, acervuline, acervulus, aces, acescence, acescency, acescent, acescents, aceship, acesodyne, acesodynous, acestoma, aceta, acetable, acetabula, acetabular, acetabularia, acetabuliferous, acetabuliform, acetabulous, acetabulum, acetabulums, acetacetic, acetal, acetaldehydase, acetaldehyde, acetaldehydrase, acetaldol, acetalization, acetalize, acetals, acetamid, acetamide, acetamidin, acetamidine, acetamido, acetamids, acetaminol, acetaminophen, acetanilid, acetanilide, acetanion, acetaniside, acetanisidide, acetanisidine, acetannin, acetarious, acetars, acetarsone, acetary, acetate, acetated, acetates, acetation, acetazolamide, acetbromamide, acetenyl, acethydrazide, acetiam, acetic, acetification, acetified, acetifier, acetifies, acetify, acetifying, acetimeter, acetimetric, acetimetry, acetin, acetine, acetins, acetite, acetize, acetla, acetmethylanilide, acetnaphthalide, acetoacetanilide, acetoacetate, acetoacetic, acetoamidophenol, acetoarsenite, acetobacter, acetobenzoic, acetobromanilide, acetochloral, acetocinnamene, acetoin, acetol, acetolysis, acetolytic, acetometer, acetometric, acetometrical, acetometrically, acetometry, acetomorphin, acetomorphine, acetonaemia, acetonaemic, acetonaphthone, acetonate, acetonation, acetone, acetonemia, acetonemic, acetones, acetonic, acetonitrile, acetonization, acetonize, acetonuria, acetonurometer, acetonyl, acetonylacetone, acetonylidene, acetophenetide, acetophenetidin, acetophenetidine, acetophenin, acetophenine, acetophenone, acetopiperone, acetopyrin, acetopyrine, acetosalicylic, acetose, acetosity, acetosoluble, acetostearin, acetothienone, acetotoluid, acetotoluide, acetotoluidine, acetous, acetoveratrone, acetoxim, acetoxime, acetoxyl, acetoxyls, acetoxyphthalide, acetphenetid, acetphenetidin, acetract, acettoluide, acetum, aceturic, acetyl, acetylacetonates, acetylacetone, acetylamine, acetylaminobenzene, acetylaniline, acetylasalicylic, acetylate, acetylated, acetylating, acetylation, acetylative, acetylator, acetylbenzene, acetylbenzoate, acetylbenzoic, acetylbiuret, acetylcarbazole, acetylcellulose, acetylcholine, acetylcholinesterase, acetylcholinic, acetylcyanide, acetylenation, acetylene, acetylenediurein, acetylenic, acetylenogen, acetylenyl, acetylfluoride, acetylglycin, acetylglycine, acetylhydrazine, acetylic, acetylid, acetylide, acetyliodide, acetylizable, acetylization, acetylize, acetylized, acetylizer, acetylizing, acetylmethylcarbinol, acetylperoxide, acetylphenol, acetylphenylhydrazine, acetylrosaniline, acetyls, acetylsalicylate, acetylsalicylic, acetylsalol, acetyltannin, acetylthymol, acetyltropeine, acetylurea, ach, achaenocarp, achaetous, achafe, achage, achalasia, achape, achaque, achar, acharne, acharnement, acharya, achate, achates, achatour, ache, acheat, achech, acheck, ached, acheer, acheilary, acheilia, acheilous, acheiria, acheirous, acheirus, achene, achenes, achenia, achenial, achenium, achenocarp, achenodia, achenodium, acher, acheron, acheronian, acherontic, aches, achesoun, achete, acheulean, acheweed, achier, achiest, achievability, achievable, achieve, achieved, achievement, achievement's, achievements, achiever, achievers, achieves, achieving, achigan, achilary, achill, achillea, achillean, achilleas, achillein, achilleine, achilles, achillize, achillobursitis, achillodynia, achilous, achime, achimenes, achiness, achinesses, aching, achingly, achiote, achiotes, achira, achirite, achkan, achlamydate, achlamydeous, achlorhydria, achlorhydric, achlorophyllous, achloropsia, achluophobia, achoke, acholia, acholias, acholic, acholous, acholuria, acholuric, achondrite, achondritic, achondroplasia, achondroplastic, achoo, achor, achordal, achordate, achras, achree, achroacyte, achrodextrin, achrodextrinase, achroglobin, achroiocythaemia, achroiocythemia, achroite, achroma, achromacyte, achromasia, achromat, achromate, achromatic, achromatically, achromaticity, achromatin, achromatinic, achromatisation, achromatise, achromatised, achromatising, achromatism, achromatizable, achromatization, achromatize, achromatized, achromatizing, achromatocyte, achromatolysis, achromatope, achromatophil, achromatophile, achromatophilia, achromatophilic, achromatopia, achromatopsia, achromatopsy, achromatosis, achromatous, achromats, achromaturia, achromia, achromic, achromobacter, achromoderma, achromophilous, achromotrichia, achromous, achronical, achronism, achronychous, achroodextrin, achroodextrinase, achroous, achropsia, achtehalber, achtel, achtelthaler, achter, achterveld, achuete, achy, achylia, achylous, achymia, achymous, acichlorid, acichloride, acicula, aciculae, acicular, acicularity, acicularly, aciculas, aciculate, aciculated, aciculum, aciculums, acid, acidaemia, acidanthera, acidemia, acidemias, acider, acidhead, acidheads, acidic, acidiferous, acidifiable, acidifiant, acidific, acidification, acidified, acidifier, acidifiers, acidifies, acidify, acidifying, acidimeter, acidimetric, acidimetrical, acidimetrically, acidimetry, acidite, acidities, acidity, acidize, acidized, acidizing, acidly, acidness, acidnesses, acidogenic, acidoid, acidology, acidolysis, acidometer, acidometry, acidophil, acidophile, acidophilic, acidophilous, acidophilus, acidoproteolytic, acidoses, acidosis, acidosteophyte, acidotic, acidproof, acids, acidulant, acidulate, acidulated, acidulates, acidulating, acidulation, acidulent, acidulous, acidulously, acidulousness, aciduria, acidurias, aciduric, acidy, acidyl, acier, acierage, acierate, acierated, acierates, acierating, acieration, acies, aciform, aciliate, aciliated, acinaceous, acinaces, acinacifoliate, acinacifolious, acinaciform, acinacious, acinacity, acinar, acinarious, acinary, acinetae, acinetan, acinetarian, acinetic, acinetiform, acinetinan, acing, acini, acinic, aciniform, acinose, acinotubular, acinous, acinuni, acinus, acipenser, acipenserid, acipenserine, acipenseroid, aciurgy, ack, ackee, ackees, acker, ackey, ackeys, ackman, ackmen, acknew, acknow, acknowing, acknowledge, acknowledgeable, acknowledged, acknowledgedly, acknowledgement, acknowledgements, acknowledger, acknowledgers, acknowledges, acknowledging, acknowledgment, acknowledgment's, acknowledgments, acknown, ackton, aclastic, acle, acleidian, acleistocardia, acleistous, aclidian, aclinal, aclinic, acloud, aclu, aclydes, aclys, acmaesthesia, acmatic, acme, acmes, acmesthesia, acmic, acmite, acne, acned, acneform, acneiform, acnemia, acnes, acnodal, acnode, acnodes, acoasm, acoasma, acocantherin, acock, acockbill, acocotl, acoelomate, acoelomatous, acoelomous, acoelous, acoenaesthesia, acoin, acoine, acold, acologic, acology, acolous, acoluthic, acolyctine, acolyte, acolytes, acolyth, acolythate, acolytus, acoma, acomia, acomous, aconative, acondylose, acondylous, acone, aconelline, aconic, aconin, aconine, aconital, aconite, aconites, aconitia, aconitic, aconitin, aconitine, aconitum, aconitums, acontia, acontium, aconuresis, acool, acop, acopic, acopon, acopyrin, acopyrine, acor, acorea, acoria, acorn, acorn's, acorned, acorns, acorus, acosmic, acosmism, acosmist, acosmistic, acost, acotyledon, acotyledonous, acouasm, acouchi, acouchy, acoumeter, acoumetry, acounter, acouometer, acouophonia, acoup, acoupa, acoupe, acousma, acousmas, acousmata, acousmatic, acoustic, acoustical, acoustically, acoustician, acousticolateral, acousticophobia, acoustics, acoustoelectric, acpt, acquaint, acquaintance, acquaintance's, acquaintances, acquaintanceship, acquaintanceships, acquaintancy, acquaintant, acquainted, acquaintedness, acquainting, acquaints, acquent, acquereur, acquest, acquests, acquiesce, acquiesced, acquiescement, acquiescence, acquiescency, acquiescent, acquiescently, acquiescer, acquiesces, acquiescing, acquiescingly, acquiesence, acquiet, acquirability, acquirable, acquire, acquired, acquirement, acquirements, acquirenda, acquirer, acquirers, acquires, acquiring, acquisible, acquisita, acquisite, acquisited, acquisition, acquisition's, acquisitional, acquisitions, acquisitive, acquisitively, acquisitiveness, acquisitor, acquisitum, acquist, acquit, acquital, acquitment, acquits, acquittal, acquittals, acquittance, acquitted, acquitter, acquitting, acquophonia, acracy, acraein, acraldehyde, acrania, acranial, acraniate, acrasia, acrasias, acrasin, acrasins, acraspedote, acrasy, acratia, acraturesis, acrawl, acraze, acre, acre's, acreable, acreage, acreages, acreak, acream, acred, acreman, acremen, acres, acrestaff, acrid, acridan, acridane, acrider, acridest, acridian, acridic, acridid, acridin, acridine, acridines, acridinic, acridinium, acridities, acridity, acridly, acridness, acridone, acridonium, acridophagus, acridyl, acriflavin, acriflavine, acrimonies, acrimonious, acrimoniously, acrimoniousness, acrimony, acrindolin, acrindoline, acrinyl, acrisia, acrisy, acrita, acritan, acrite, acritical, acritochromacy, acritol, acritude, acrity, acroaesthesia, acroama, acroamata, acroamatic, acroamatical, acroamatics, acroanesthesia, acroarthritis, acroasis, acroasphyxia, acroataxia, acroatic, acrobacies, acrobacy, acrobat, acrobat's, acrobatholithic, acrobatic, acrobatical, acrobatically, acrobatics, acrobatism, acrobats, acroblast, acrobryous, acrobystitis, acrocarpous, acrocentric, acrocephalia, acrocephalic, acrocephalous, acrocephaly, acrochordon, acrock, acroconidium, acrocontracture, acrocoracoid, acrocyanosis, acrocyst, acrodactyla, acrodactylum, acrodermatitis, acrodont, acrodontism, acrodonts, acrodrome, acrodromous, acrodynia, acroesthesia, acrogamous, acrogamy, acrogen, acrogenic, acrogenous, acrogenously, acrogens, acrography, acrogynae, acrogynous, acrolein, acroleins, acrolith, acrolithan, acrolithic, acroliths, acrologic, acrologically, acrologies, acrologism, acrologue, acrology, acromania, acromastitis, acromegalia, acromegalic, acromegalies, acromegaly, acromelalgia, acrometer, acromia, acromial, acromicria, acromimia, acromioclavicular, acromiocoracoid, acromiodeltoid, acromiohumeral, acromiohyoid, acromion, acromioscapular, acromiosternal, acromiothoracic, acromonogrammatic, acromphalus, acromyodian, acromyodic, acromyodous, acromyotonia, acromyotonus, acron, acronal, acronarcotic, acroneurosis, acronic, acronical, acronically, acronichal, acronichally, acronomy, acronyc, acronycal, acronycally, acronych, acronychal, acronychally, acronychous, acronyctous, acronym, acronym's, acronymic, acronymically, acronymize, acronymized, acronymizing, acronymous, acronyms, acronyx, acrook, acroparalysis, acroparesthesia, acropathology, acropathy, acropetal, acropetally, acrophobia, acrophonetic, acrophonic, acrophonically, acrophonies, acrophony, acropodia, acropodium, acropoleis, acropolis, acropolises, acropolitan, acropore, acrorhagus, acrorrheuma, acrosarc, acrosarca, acrosarcum, acroscleriasis, acroscleroderma, acroscopic, acrose, acrosome, acrosomes, acrosphacelus, acrospire, acrospired, acrospiring, acrospore, acrosporous, across, acrostic, acrostical, acrostically, acrostichal, acrostichic, acrostichoid, acrosticism, acrostics, acrostolia, acrostolion, acrostolium, acrotarsial, acrotarsium, acroteleutic, acroter, acroteral, acroteria, acroterial, acroteric, acroterion, acroterium, acroterteria, acrotic, acrotism, acrotisms, acrotomous, acrotrophic, acrotrophoneurosis, acryl, acrylaldehyde, acrylate, acrylates, acrylic, acrylics, acrylonitrile, acrylyl, act, acta, actability, actable, actaeon, acted, actg, actification, actifier, actify, actin, actinal, actinally, actinautographic, actinautography, actine, actinenchyma, acting, actings, actinia, actiniae, actinian, actinians, actiniarian, actinias, actinic, actinical, actinically, actinide, actinides, actiniferous, actiniform, actinine, actiniochrome, actiniohematin, actinism, actinisms, actinium, actiniums, actinobaccilli, actinobacilli, actinobacillosis, actinobacillotic, actinobacillus, actinoblast, actinobranch, actinobranchia, actinocarp, actinocarpic, actinocarpous, actinochemical, actinochemistry, actinocrinid, actinocrinite, actinocutitis, actinodermatitis, actinodielectric, actinodrome, actinodromous, actinoelectric, actinoelectrically, actinoelectricity, actinogonidiate, actinogram, actinograph, actinographic, actinography, actinoid, actinoids, actinolite, actinolitic, actinologous, actinologue, actinology, actinomere, actinomeric, actinometer, actinometers, actinometric, actinometrical, actinometricy, actinometry, actinomorphic, actinomorphous, actinomorphy, actinomyces, actinomycese, actinomycesous, actinomycestal, actinomycetal, actinomycete, actinomycetous, actinomycin, actinomycoma, actinomycosis, actinomycosistic, actinomycotic, actinon, actinoneuritis, actinons, actinophone, actinophonic, actinophore, actinophorous, actinophryan, actinopod, actinopraxis, actinopteran, actinopterous, actinopterygian, actinopterygious, actinoscopy, actinosoma, actinosome, actinost, actinostereoscopy, actinostomal, actinostome, actinotherapeutic, actinotherapeutics, actinotherapy, actinotoxemia, actinotrichium, actinotrocha, actinouranium, actinozoal, actinozoan, actinozoon, actins, actinula, actinulae, action, action's, actionability, actionable, actionably, actional, actionary, actioner, actiones, actionist, actionize, actionized, actionizing, actionless, actions, actious, activable, activate, activated, activates, activating, activation, activations, activator, activator's, activators, active, actively, activeness, actives, activin, activism, activisms, activist, activist's, activistic, activists, activital, activities, activity, activity's, activize, activized, activizing, actless, actomyosin, acton, actor, actor's, actorish, actors, actorship, actory, actos, actress, actress's, actresses, actressy, acts, actu, actual, actualisation, actualise, actualised, actualising, actualism, actualist, actualistic, actualities, actuality, actualization, actualize, actualized, actualizes, actualizing, actually, actualness, actuals, actuarial, actuarially, actuarian, actuaries, actuary, actuaryship, actuate, actuated, actuates, actuating, actuation, actuator, actuator's, actuators, actuose, acture, acturience, actus, actutate, acuaesthesia, acuate, acuating, acuation, acuchi, acuclosure, acuductor, acuerdo, acuerdos, acuesthesia, acuities, acuity, aculea, aculeae, aculeate, aculeated, aculei, aculeiform, aculeolate, aculeolus, aculeus, acumble, acumen, acumens, acuminate, acuminated, acuminating, acumination, acuminose, acuminous, acuminulate, acupress, acupressure, acupunctuate, acupunctuation, acupuncturation, acupuncturator, acupuncture, acupunctured, acupuncturing, acupuncturist, acupuncturists, acurative, acus, acusection, acusector, acushla, acustom, acutance, acutances, acutangular, acutate, acute, acutely, acutenaculum, acuteness, acuter, acutes, acutest, acutiator, acutifoliate, acutilingual, acutilobate, acutiplantar, acutish, acutograve, acutonodose, acutorsion, acxoyatl, acy, acyanoblepsia, acyanopsia, acyclic, acyclically, acyesis, acyetic, acyl, acylal, acylamido, acylamidobenzene, acylamino, acylase, acylate, acylated, acylates, acylating, acylation, acylogen, acyloin, acyloins, acyloxy, acyloxymethane, acyls, acyrological, acyrology, acystia, ad, adactyl, adactylia, adactylism, adactylous, adad, adage, adages, adagial, adagietto, adagiettos, adagio, adagios, adagissimo, adagy, adalat, adalid, adam, adamance, adamances, adamancies, adamancy, adamant, adamantean, adamantine, adamantinoma, adamantly, adamantness, adamantoblast, adamantoblastoma, adamantoid, adamantoma, adamants, adamas, adambulacral, adamellite, adamine, adamite, adams, adamsite, adamsites, adance, adangle, adansonia, adapid, adapt, adaptability, adaptable, adaptableness, adaptably, adaptation, adaptation's, adaptational, adaptationally, adaptations, adaptative, adapted, adaptedness, adapter, adapters, adapting, adaption, adaptional, adaptionism, adaptions, adaptitude, adaptive, adaptively, adaptiveness, adaptivity, adaptometer, adaptor, adaptorial, adaptors, adapts, adar, adarbitrium, adarme, adarticulation, adat, adati, adatis, adatom, adaty, adaunt, adaw, adawe, adawlut, adawn, adaxial, aday, adays, adazzle, adc, adcon, adcons, adcraft, add, adda, addability, addable, addax, addaxes, addda, addebted, added, addedly, addeem, addend, addenda, addends, addendum, addendums, adder, adderbolt, adderfish, adders, adderspit, adderwort, addibility, addible, addice, addicent, addict, addicted, addictedness, addicting, addiction, addiction's, addictions, addictive, addictively, addictiveness, addictives, addicts, addiment, adding, addio, addis, addison, addita, additament, additamentary, additiment, addition, addition's, additional, additionally, additionary, additionist, additions, addititious, additive, additive's, additively, additives, additivity, additory, additum, additur, addle, addlebrain, addlebrained, addled, addlehead, addleheaded, addleheadedly, addleheadedness, addlement, addleness, addlepate, addlepated, addlepatedness, addleplot, addles, addling, addlings, addlins, addn, addnl, addoom, addorsed, addossed, addr, address, addressability, addressable, addressed, addressee, addressee's, addressees, addresser, addressers, addresses, addressful, addressing, addressor, addrest, adds, adduce, adduceable, adduced, adducent, adducer, adducers, adduces, adducible, adducing, adduct, adducted, adducting, adduction, adductive, adductor, adductors, adducts, addulce, ade, adead, adeem, adeemed, adeeming, adeems, adeep, adelantado, adelantados, adelante, adelarthrosomatous, adelaster, adeling, adelite, adelocerous, adelocodonic, adelomorphic, adelomorphous, adelopod, adelphic, adelphogamy, adelpholite, adelphophagy, adelphous, ademonist, adempt, adempted, ademption, aden, adenalgia, adenalgy, adenase, adenasthenia, adendric, adendritic, adenectomies, adenectomy, adenectopia, adenectopic, adenemphractic, adenemphraxis, adenia, adeniform, adenin, adenine, adenines, adenitis, adenitises, adenization, adenoacanthoma, adenoblast, adenocancroid, adenocarcinoma, adenocarcinomas, adenocarcinomata, adenocarcinomatous, adenocele, adenocellulitis, adenochondroma, adenochondrosarcoma, adenochrome, adenocyst, adenocystoma, adenocystomatous, adenodermia, adenodiastasis, adenodynia, adenofibroma, adenofibrosis, adenogenesis, adenogenous, adenographer, adenographic, adenographical, adenography, adenohypersthenia, adenohypophyseal, adenohypophysial, adenohypophysis, adenoid, adenoidal, adenoidectomies, adenoidectomy, adenoidism, adenoiditis, adenoids, adenoliomyofibroma, adenolipoma, adenolipomatosis, adenologaditis, adenological, adenology, adenolymphocele, adenolymphoma, adenoma, adenomalacia, adenomas, adenomata, adenomatome, adenomatous, adenomeningeal, adenometritis, adenomycosis, adenomyofibroma, adenomyoma, adenomyxoma, adenomyxosarcoma, adenoncus, adenoneural, adenoneure, adenopathy, adenopharyngeal, adenopharyngitis, adenophlegmon, adenophore, adenophoreus, adenophorous, adenophthalmia, adenophyllous, adenophyma, adenopodous, adenosarcoma, adenosarcomas, adenosarcomata, adenosclerosis, adenose, adenoses, adenosine, adenosis, adenostemonous, adenotome, adenotomic, adenotomy, adenotyphoid, adenotyphus, adenous, adenoviral, adenovirus, adenoviruses, adenyl, adenylic, adenylpyrophosphate, adenyls, adephaga, adephagan, adephagia, adephagous, adeps, adept, adepter, adeptest, adeption, adeptly, adeptness, adepts, adeptship, adequacies, adequacy, adequate, adequately, adequateness, adequation, adequative, adermia, adermin, adermine, adesmy, adespota, adespoton, adessenarian, adessive, adeste, adet, adeuism, adevism, adfected, adffroze, adffrozen, adfiliate, adfix, adfluxion, adfreeze, adfreezing, adfroze, adfrozen, adglutinate, adhaka, adhamant, adharma, adherant, adhere, adhered, adherence, adherences, adherency, adherend, adherends, adherent, adherent's, adherently, adherents, adherer, adherers, adheres, adherescence, adherescent, adhering, adhesion, adhesional, adhesions, adhesive, adhesive's, adhesively, adhesivemeter, adhesiveness, adhesives, adhibit, adhibited, adhibiting, adhibition, adhibits, adhocracy, adhort, adiabat, adiabatic, adiabatically, adiabolist, adiactinic, adiadochokinesia, adiadochokinesis, adiadokokinesi, adiadokokinesia, adiagnostic, adiamorphic, adiamorphism, adiantiform, adiantum, adiaphanous, adiaphanousness, adiaphon, adiaphonon, adiaphora, adiaphoral, adiaphoresis, adiaphoretic, adiaphorism, adiaphorist, adiaphoristic, adiaphorite, adiaphoron, adiaphorous, adiaphory, adiapneustia, adiate, adiated, adiathermal, adiathermancy, adiathermanous, adiathermic, adiathetic, adiating, adiation, adibasi, adicity, adience, adient, adieu, adieus, adieux, adighe, adight, adigranth, adinidan, adinole, adinvention, adion, adios, adipate, adipescent, adiphenine, adipic, adipinic, adipocele, adipocellulose, adipocere, adipoceriform, adipocerite, adipocerous, adipocyte, adipofibroma, adipogenic, adipogenous, adipoid, adipolysis, adipolytic, adipoma, adipomata, adipomatous, adipometer, adiponitrile, adipopectic, adipopexia, adipopexic, adipopexis, adipose, adiposeness, adiposes, adiposis, adiposities, adiposity, adiposogenital, adiposuria, adipous, adipsia, adipsic, adipsous, adipsy, adipyl, adit, adital, aditio, adits, aditus, adj, adjacence, adjacencies, adjacency, adjacent, adjacently, adjag, adject, adjection, adjectional, adjectitious, adjectival, adjectivally, adjective, adjective's, adjectively, adjectives, adjectivism, adjectivitis, adjiga, adjiger, adjoin, adjoinant, adjoined, adjoinedly, adjoiner, adjoining, adjoiningness, adjoins, adjoint, adjoints, adjourn, adjournal, adjourned, adjourning, adjournment, adjournments, adjourns, adjoust, adjt, adjudge, adjudgeable, adjudged, adjudger, adjudges, adjudging, adjudgment, adjudicata, adjudicate, adjudicated, adjudicates, adjudicating, adjudication, adjudication's, adjudications, adjudicative, adjudicator, adjudicators, adjudicatory, adjudicature, adjugate, adjument, adjunct, adjunct's, adjunction, adjunctive, adjunctively, adjunctly, adjuncts, adjuration, adjurations, adjuratory, adjure, adjured, adjurer, adjurers, adjures, adjuring, adjuror, adjurors, adjust, adjustability, adjustable, adjustably, adjustage, adjustation, adjusted, adjuster, adjusters, adjusting, adjustive, adjustment, adjustment's, adjustmental, adjustments, adjustor, adjustor's, adjustores, adjustoring, adjustors, adjusts, adjutage, adjutancies, adjutancy, adjutant, adjutants, adjutantship, adjutator, adjute, adjutor, adjutorious, adjutory, adjutrice, adjutrix, adjuvant, adjuvants, adjuvate, adlay, adlegation, adlegiare, adlerian, adless, adlet, adlumidin, adlumidine, adlumin, adlumine, adm, adman, admarginate, admass, admaxillary, admeasure, admeasured, admeasurement, admeasurer, admeasuring, admedial, admedian, admen, admensuration, admerveylle, admetus, admi, admin, adminicle, adminicula, adminicular, adminiculary, adminiculate, adminiculation, adminiculum, administer, administerd, administered, administerial, administering, administerings, administers, administrable, administrant, administrants, administrate, administrated, administrates, administrating, administration, administration's, administrational, administrationist, administrations, administrative, administratively, administrator, administrator's, administrators, administratorship, administratress, administratrices, administratrix, adminstration, admirability, admirable, admirableness, admirably, admiral, admiral's, admirals, admiralship, admiralships, admiralties, admiralty, admirance, admiration, admirations, admirative, admiratively, admirator, admire, admired, admiredly, admirer, admirers, admires, admiring, admiringly, admissability, admissable, admissibility, admissible, admissibleness, admissibly, admission, admission's, admissions, admissive, admissively, admissory, admit, admits, admittable, admittance, admittances, admittatur, admitted, admittedly, admittee, admitter, admitters, admittible, admitting, admitty, admix, admixed, admixes, admixing, admixt, admixtion, admixture, admixtures, admonish, admonished, admonisher, admonishes, admonishing, admonishingly, admonishment, admonishment's, admonishments, admonition, admonition's, admonitioner, admonitionist, admonitions, admonitive, admonitively, admonitor, admonitorial, admonitorily, admonitory, admonitrix, admortization, admov, admove, admrx, adnascence, adnascent, adnate, adnation, adnations, adnephrine, adnerval, adnescent, adneural, adnex, adnexa, adnexal, adnexed, adnexitis, adnexopexy, adnominal, adnominally, adnomination, adnoun, adnouns, adnumber, ado, adobe, adobes, adobo, adobos, adod, adolesce, adolesced, adolescence, adolescency, adolescent, adolescent's, adolescently, adolescents, adolescing, adolf, adolph, adon, adonai, adonic, adonidin, adonin, adonis, adonises, adonist, adonite, adonitol, adonize, adonized, adonizing, adoors, adoperate, adoperation, adopt, adoptabilities, adoptability, adoptable, adoptant, adoptative, adopted, adoptedly, adoptee, adoptees, adopter, adopters, adoptian, adoptianism, adoptianist, adopting, adoption, adoption's, adoptional, adoptionism, adoptionist, adoptions, adoptious, adoptive, adoptively, adopts, ador, adorability, adorable, adorableness, adorably, adoral, adorally, adorant, adoration, adoratory, adore, adored, adorer, adorers, adores, adoring, adoringly, adorn, adornation, adorned, adorner, adorners, adorning, adorningly, adornment, adornment's, adornments, adorno, adornos, adorns, adorsed, ados, adosculation, adossed, adossee, adoulie, adown, adoxaceous, adoxies, adoxography, adoxy, adoze, adp, adpao, adposition, adpress, adpromission, adpromissor, adrad, adradial, adradially, adradius, adread, adream, adreamed, adreamt, adrectal, adrenal, adrenalcortical, adrenalectomies, adrenalectomize, adrenalectomized, adrenalectomizing, adrenalectomy, adrenalin, adrenaline, adrenalize, adrenally, adrenalone, adrenals, adrench, adrenergic, adrenin, adrenine, adrenitis, adreno, adrenochrome, adrenocortical, adrenocorticosteroid, adrenocorticotrophic, adrenocorticotrophin, adrenocorticotropic, adrenolysis, adrenolytic, adrenomedullary, adrenosterone, adrenotrophin, adrenotropic, adrent, adret, adriatic, adrift, adrip, adrogate, adroit, adroiter, adroitest, adroitly, adroitness, adroop, adrop, adrostal, adrostral, adrowse, adrue, adry, ads, adsbud, adscendent, adscititious, adscititiously, adscript, adscripted, adscription, adscriptitious, adscriptitius, adscriptive, adscripts, adsessor, adsheart, adsignification, adsignify, adsmith, adsmithing, adsorb, adsorbability, adsorbable, adsorbate, adsorbates, adsorbed, adsorbent, adsorbents, adsorbing, adsorbs, adsorption, adsorptive, adsorptively, adsorptiveness, adspiration, adstipulate, adstipulated, adstipulating, adstipulation, adstipulator, adstrict, adstringe, adsum, adterminal, adtevac, aduana, adular, adularescence, adularescent, adularia, adularias, adulate, adulated, adulates, adulating, adulation, adulator, adulators, adulatory, adulatress, adulce, adullamite, adult, adult's, adulter, adulterant, adulterants, adulterate, adulterated, adulterately, adulterateness, adulterates, adulterating, adulteration, adulterator, adulterators, adulterer, adulterer's, adulterers, adulteress, adulteresses, adulteries, adulterine, adulterize, adulterous, adulterously, adulterousness, adultery, adulthood, adulticidal, adulticide, adultlike, adultly, adultness, adultoid, adultress, adults, adumbral, adumbrant, adumbrate, adumbrated, adumbrates, adumbrating, adumbration, adumbrations, adumbrative, adumbratively, adumbrellar, adunation, adunc, aduncate, aduncated, aduncity, aduncous, adure, adurent, adusk, adust, adustion, adustiosis, adustive, adv, advance, advanceable, advanced, advancedness, advancement, advancement's, advancements, advancer, advancers, advances, advancing, advancingly, advancive, advantage, advantaged, advantageous, advantageously, advantageousness, advantages, advantaging, advect, advected, advecting, advection, advectitious, advective, advects, advehent, advena, advenae, advene, advenience, advenient, advent, advential, adventism, adventist, adventists, adventitia, adventitial, adventitious, adventitiously, adventitiousness, adventive, adventively, adventry, advents, adventual, adventure, adventured, adventureful, adventurement, adventurer, adventurers, adventures, adventureship, adventuresome, adventuresomely, adventuresomeness, adventuresomes, adventuress, adventuresses, adventuring, adventurish, adventurism, adventurist, adventuristic, adventurous, adventurously, adventurousness, adverb, adverb's, adverbial, adverbiality, adverbialize, adverbially, adverbiation, adverbless, adverbs, adversa, adversant, adversaria, adversarial, adversaries, adversariness, adversarious, adversary, adversary's, adversative, adversatively, adverse, adversed, adversely, adverseness, adversifoliate, adversifolious, adversing, adversion, adversities, adversity, adversive, adversus, advert, adverted, advertence, advertency, advertent, advertently, adverting, advertisable, advertise, advertised, advertisee, advertisement, advertisement's, advertisements, advertiser, advertisers, advertises, advertising, advertizable, advertize, advertized, advertizement, advertizer, advertizes, advertizing, adverts, advice, adviceful, advices, advisability, advisable, advisableness, advisably, advisal, advisatory, advise, advised, advisedly, advisedness, advisee, advisee's, advisees, advisement, advisements, adviser, advisers, advisership, advises, advising, advisive, advisiveness, adviso, advisor, advisor's, advisories, advisorily, advisors, advisory, advisy, advitant, advocaat, advocacies, advocacy, advocate, advocated, advocates, advocateship, advocatess, advocating, advocation, advocative, advocator, advocatory, advocatress, advocatrice, advocatrix, advoke, advolution, advoteresse, advowee, advowry, advowsance, advowson, advowsons, advoyer, advt, adward, adwesch, ady, adynamia, adynamias, adynamic, adynamy, adyta, adyton, adytta, adytum, adz, adze, adzer, adzes, adzooks, ae, aecia, aecial, aecidia, aecidial, aecidioform, aecidiospore, aecidiostage, aecidium, aeciospore, aeciostage, aeciotelia, aecioteliospore, aeciotelium, aecium, aedeagal, aedeagi, aedeagus, aedegi, aedes, aedicula, aediculae, aedicule, aedile, aediles, aedileship, aedilian, aedilic, aedilitian, aedilities, aedility, aedine, aedoeagi, aedoeagus, aedoeology, aefald, aefaldness, aefaldy, aefauld, aegagri, aegagropila, aegagropilae, aegagropile, aegagropiles, aegagrus, aegean, aegemony, aeger, aegerian, aegeriid, aegicrania, aegilops, aegir, aegirine, aegirinolite, aegirite, aegis, aegises, aegisthus, aegithognathism, aegithognathous, aegophony, aegritude, aegrotant, aegrotat, aegyptilla, aegyrite, aeipathy, aelodicon, aeluroid, aelurophobe, aelurophobia, aeluropodous, aenach, aenean, aeneas, aeneid, aeneolithic, aeneous, aeneus, aenigma, aenigmatite, aeolharmonica, aeolian, aeolic, aeolid, aeolight, aeolina, aeoline, aeolipile, aeolipyle, aeolist, aeolistic, aeolodicon, aeolodion, aeolomelodicon, aeolopantalon, aeolotropic, aeolotropism, aeolotropy, aeolsklavier, aeolus, aeon, aeonial, aeonian, aeonic, aeonicaeonist, aeonist, aeons, aepyornis, aeq, aequor, aequoreal, aequorin, aequorins, aer, aerage, aeraria, aerarian, aerarium, aerate, aerated, aerates, aerating, aeration, aerations, aerator, aerators, aerenchyma, aerenterectasia, aerial, aerial's, aerialist, aerialists, aeriality, aerially, aerialness, aerials, aeric, aerical, aerides, aerie, aeried, aerier, aeries, aeriest, aerifaction, aeriferous, aerification, aerified, aerifies, aeriform, aerify, aerifying, aerily, aeriness, aero, aeroacoustic, aerobacter, aerobacteriological, aerobacteriologically, aerobacteriologist, aerobacteriology, aerobacters, aeroballistic, aeroballistics, aerobate, aerobated, aerobatic, aerobatics, aerobating, aerobe, aerobee, aerobes, aerobia, aerobian, aerobic, aerobically, aerobics, aerobiologic, aerobiological, aerobiologically, aerobiologist, aerobiology, aerobion, aerobiont, aerobioscope, aerobiosis, aerobiotic, aerobiotically, aerobious, aerobium, aeroboat, aerobranchiate, aerobus, aerocamera, aerocar, aerocartograph, aerocartography, aerocolpos, aerocraft, aerocurve, aerocyst, aerodermectasia, aerodone, aerodonetic, aerodonetics, aerodontalgia, aerodontia, aerodontic, aerodrome, aerodromes, aerodromics, aeroduct, aeroducts, aerodynamic, aerodynamical, aerodynamically, aerodynamicist, aerodynamics, aerodyne, aerodynes, aeroelastic, aeroelasticity, aeroelastics, aeroembolism, aeroenterectasia, aerofoil, aerofoils, aerogel, aerogels, aerogen, aerogene, aerogenes, aerogenesis, aerogenic, aerogenically, aerogenous, aerogeography, aerogeologist, aerogeology, aerognosy, aerogram, aerogramme, aerograms, aerograph, aerographer, aerographic, aerographical, aerographics, aerographies, aerography, aerogun, aerohydrodynamic, aerohydropathy, aerohydroplane, aerohydrotherapy, aerohydrous, aeroides, aerolite, aerolites, aerolith, aerolithology, aeroliths, aerolitic, aerolitics, aerologic, aerological, aerologies, aerologist, aerologists, aerology, aeromaechanic, aeromagnetic, aeromancer, aeromancy, aeromantic, aeromarine, aeromechanic, aeromechanical, aeromechanics, aeromedical, aeromedicine, aerometeorograph, aerometer, aerometric, aerometry, aeromotor, aeron, aeronat, aeronaut, aeronautic, aeronautical, aeronautically, aeronautics, aeronautism, aeronauts, aeronef, aeroneurosis, aeronomer, aeronomic, aeronomical, aeronomics, aeronomies, aeronomist, aeronomy, aeropathy, aeropause, aeroperitoneum, aeroperitonia, aerophagia, aerophagist, aerophagy, aerophane, aerophilatelic, aerophilatelist, aerophilately, aerophile, aerophilia, aerophilic, aerophilous, aerophobia, aerophobic, aerophone, aerophor, aerophore, aerophoto, aerophotography, aerophotos, aerophysical, aerophysicist, aerophysics, aerophyte, aeroplane, aeroplaner, aeroplanes, aeroplanist, aeroplankton, aeropleustic, aeroporotomy, aeropulse, aerosat, aerosats, aeroscepsis, aeroscepsy, aeroscope, aeroscopic, aeroscopically, aeroscopy, aerose, aerosiderite, aerosiderolite, aerosinusitis, aerosol, aerosolization, aerosolize, aerosolized, aerosolizing, aerosols, aerospace, aerosphere, aerosporin, aerostat, aerostatic, aerostatical, aerostatics, aerostation, aerostats, aerosteam, aerotactic, aerotaxis, aerotechnical, aerotechnics, aerotherapeutics, aerotherapy, aerothermodynamic, aerothermodynamics, aerotonometer, aerotonometric, aerotonometry, aerotow, aerotropic, aerotropism, aeroview, aeroyacht, aeruginous, aerugo, aerugos, aery, aes, aesc, aeschylean, aeschylus, aeschynite, aeschynomenous, aesculaceous, aesculapian, aesculapius, aesculetin, aesculin, aesir, aesop, aesopian, aestethic, aesthesia, aesthesics, aesthesis, aesthesodic, aesthete, aesthetes, aesthetic, aesthetic's, aesthetical, aesthetically, aesthetician, aestheticism, aestheticist, aestheticize, aesthetics, aesthiology, aesthophysiology, aestival, aestivate, aestivated, aestivates, aestivating, aestivation, aestivator, aestive, aestuary, aestuate, aestuation, aestuous, aesture, aestus, aet, aetat, aethalia, aethalioid, aethalium, aetheling, aetheogam, aetheogamic, aetheogamous, aether, aethereal, aethered, aetheric, aethers, aethogen, aethon, aethrioscope, aetiogenic, aetiological, aetiologically, aetiologies, aetiologist, aetiologue, aetiology, aetiophyllin, aetiotropic, aetiotropically, aetites, aetosaur, aetosaurian, aettekees, aevia, aeviternal, aevum, af, aface, afaced, afacing, afaint, afar, afara, afars, afb, afd, afdecho, afear, afeard, afeared, afebrile, afer, afernan, afetal, aff, affa, affability, affable, affableness, affably, affabrous, affair, affair's, affaire, affaires, affairs, affaite, affamish, affatuate, affect, affectability, affectable, affectate, affectation, affectation's, affectationist, affectations, affected, affectedly, affectedness, affecter, affecters, affectibility, affectible, affecting, affectingly, affection, affection's, affectional, affectionally, affectionate, affectionately, affectionateness, affectioned, affectionless, affections, affectious, affective, affectively, affectivity, affectless, affectlessness, affector, affects, affectual, affectum, affectuous, affectus, affeeble, affeer, affeerer, affeerment, affeeror, affeir, affenpinscher, affenspalte, affere, afferent, afferently, affettuoso, affettuosos, affiance, affianced, affiancer, affiances, affiancing, affiant, affiants, affich, affiche, affiches, afficionado, affidare, affidation, affidavit, affidavit's, affidavits, affidavy, affied, affies, affile, affiliable, affiliate, affiliated, affiliates, affiliating, affiliation, affiliations, affinage, affinal, affination, affine, affined, affinely, affines, affing, affinitative, affinitatively, affinite, affinities, affinition, affinitive, affinity, affinity's, affirm, affirmable, affirmably, affirmance, affirmant, affirmation, affirmation's, affirmations, affirmative, affirmatively, affirmativeness, affirmatives, affirmatory, affirmed, affirmer, affirmers, affirming, affirmingly, affirmly, affirms, affix, affixable, affixal, affixation, affixed, affixer, affixers, affixes, affixial, affixing, affixion, affixment, affixt, affixture, afflate, afflated, afflation, afflatus, afflatuses, afflict, afflicted, afflictedness, afflicter, afflicting, afflictingly, affliction, affliction's, afflictionless, afflictions, afflictive, afflictively, afflicts, affloof, afflue, affluence, affluency, affluent, affluently, affluentness, affluents, afflux, affluxes, affluxion, affodill, afforce, afforced, afforcement, afforcing, afford, affordable, afforded, affording, affords, afforest, afforestable, afforestation, afforestational, afforested, afforesting, afforestment, afforests, afformative, affranchise, affranchised, affranchisement, affranchising, affrap, affray, affrayed, affrayer, affrayers, affraying, affrays, affreight, affreighter, affreightment, affret, affrettando, affreux, affricate, affricated, affricates, affrication, affricative, affriended, affright, affrighted, affrightedly, affrighter, affrightful, affrightfully, affrighting, affrightingly, affrightment, affrights, affront, affronted, affrontedly, affrontedness, affrontee, affronter, affronting, affrontingly, affrontingness, affrontive, affrontiveness, affrontment, affronts, affronty, afft, affuse, affusedaffusing, affusion, affusions, affy, affydavy, affying, afghan, afghanets, afghani, afghanis, afghanistan, afghans, afgod, afibrinogenemia, aficionada, aficionadas, aficionado, aficionados, afield, afikomen, afire, aflagellar, aflame, aflare, aflat, aflatoxin, aflatus, aflaunt, afley, aflicker, aflight, afloat, aflow, aflower, afluking, aflush, aflutter, afoam, afocal, afoot, afore, aforegoing, aforehand, aforementioned, aforenamed, aforesaid, aforethought, aforetime, aforetimes, aforeward, afortiori, afoul, afounde, afraid, afraidness, afray, afreet, afreets, afresca, afresh, afret, afrete, africa, african, africander, africanist, africans, afright, afrikaans, afrikaner, afrit, afrite, afrits, afro, afront, afrormosia, afros, afrown, aft, aftaba, after, afteract, afterage, afterattack, afterband, afterbay, afterbeat, afterbirth, afterbirths, afterblow, afterbodies, afterbody, afterbrain, afterbreach, afterbreast, afterburner, afterburners, afterburning, aftercare, aftercareer, aftercast, aftercataract, aftercause, afterchance, afterchrome, afterchurch, afterclap, afterclause, aftercome, aftercomer, aftercoming, aftercooler, aftercost, aftercourse, aftercrop, aftercure, afterdamp, afterdate, afterdated, afterdays, afterdeal, afterdeath, afterdeck, afterdecks, afterdinner, afterdischarge, afterdrain, afterdrops, aftereffect, aftereffects, afterend, aftereye, afterfall, afterfame, afterfeed, afterfermentation, afterform, afterfriend, afterfruits, afterfuture, aftergame, aftergas, afterglide, afterglow, afterglows, aftergo, aftergood, aftergrass, aftergrave, aftergrief, aftergrind, aftergrowth, afterguard, afterguns, afterhand, afterharm, afterhatch, afterheat, afterhelp, afterhend, afterhold, afterhope, afterhours, afterimage, afterimages, afterimpression, afterings, afterking, afterknowledge, afterlife, afterlifetime, afterlight, afterlives, afterloss, afterlove, aftermark, aftermarket, aftermarriage, aftermass, aftermast, aftermath, aftermaths, aftermatter, aftermeal, aftermilk, aftermost, afternight, afternoon, afternoon's, afternoons, afternose, afternote, afteroar, afterpain, afterpains, afterpart, afterpast, afterpeak, afterpiece, afterplanting, afterplay, afterpotential, afterpressure, afterproof, afterrake, afterreckoning, afterrider, afterripening, afterroll, afters, afterschool, aftersend, aftersensation, aftershaft, aftershafted, aftershave, aftershaves, aftershine, aftership, aftershock, aftershocks, aftersong, aftersound, afterspeech, afterspring, afterstain, afterstate, afterstorm, afterstrain, afterstretch, afterstudy, aftersupper, afterswarm, afterswarming, afterswell, aftertan, aftertask, aftertaste, aftertastes, aftertax, afterthinker, afterthought, afterthoughted, afterthoughts, afterthrift, aftertime, aftertimes, aftertouch, aftertreatment, aftertrial, afterturn, aftervision, afterwale, afterwar, afterward, afterwards, afterwash, afterwhile, afterwisdom, afterwise, afterwit, afterwitted, afterword, afterwork, afterworking, afterworld, afterwort, afterwrath, afterwrist, afteryears, aftmost, aftosa, aftosas, aftward, aftwards, afunction, afunctional, afwillite, ag, aga, agabanee, agacant, agacante, agacella, agacerie, agad, agada, agadic, again, againbuy, againsay, against, againstand, againward, agal, agalactia, agalactic, agalactous, agalawood, agalaxia, agalaxy, agalite, agalloch, agallochs, agallochum, agallop, agalma, agalmatolite, agalwood, agalwoods, agama, agamas, agamemnon, agamete, agametes, agami, agamian, agamic, agamically, agamid, agamis, agamist, agammaglobulinemia, agammaglobulinemic, agamobia, agamobium, agamogenesis, agamogenetic, agamogenetically, agamogony, agamoid, agamont, agamospermy, agamospore, agamous, agamy, aganglionic, aganippe, agapae, agapai, agapanthus, agapanthuses, agape, agapeic, agapeically, agapetae, agapeti, agapetid, agaphite, agar, agaric, agaricaceae, agaricaceous, agaricic, agariciform, agaricin, agaricine, agaricinic, agaricoid, agarics, agarita, agaroid, agarose, agaroses, agars, agarwal, agas, agasp, agast, agastric, agastroneuria, agata, agate, agatelike, agates, agateware, agathin, agathism, agathist, agathodaemon, agathodaemonic, agathodemon, agathokakological, agathology, agatiferous, agatiform, agatine, agatize, agatized, agatizes, agatizing, agatoid, agaty, agave, agaves, agavose, agaze, agazed, agba, agcy, age, ageable, aged, agedly, agedness, agednesses, agee, ageing, ageings, ageism, ageisms, ageist, ageists, agelast, ageless, agelessly, agelessness, agelong, agen, agencies, agency, agency's, agend, agenda, agenda's, agendaless, agendas, agendum, agendums, agene, agenes, ageneses, agenesia, agenesias, agenesic, agenesis, agenetic, agenize, agenized, agenizes, agenizing, agennesis, agennetic, agent, agent's, agentess, agential, agenting, agentival, agentive, agentives, agentries, agentry, agents, agentship, ageometrical, ager, agerasia, ageratum, ageratums, agers, ages, aget, agete, ageusia, ageusic, ageustia, aggadic, aggelation, aggenerate, agger, aggerate, aggeration, aggerose, aggers, aggest, aggie, aggies, aggiornamenti, aggiornamento, agglomerant, agglomerate, agglomerated, agglomerates, agglomeratic, agglomerating, agglomeration, agglomerations, agglomerative, agglomerator, agglutinability, agglutinable, agglutinant, agglutinate, agglutinated, agglutinates, agglutinating, agglutination, agglutinationist, agglutinations, agglutinative, agglutinatively, agglutinator, agglutinin, agglutinins, agglutinize, agglutinogen, agglutinogenic, agglutinoid, agglutinoscope, agglutogenic, aggrace, aggradation, aggradational, aggrade, aggraded, aggrades, aggrading, aggrammatism, aggrandise, aggrandised, aggrandisement, aggrandiser, aggrandising, aggrandizable, aggrandize, aggrandized, aggrandizement, aggrandizements, aggrandizer, aggrandizers, aggrandizes, aggrandizing, aggrate, aggravable, aggravate, aggravated, aggravates, aggravating, aggravatingly, aggravation, aggravations, aggravative, aggravator, aggregable, aggregant, aggregate, aggregated, aggregately, aggregateness, aggregates, aggregating, aggregation, aggregational, aggregations, aggregative, aggregatively, aggregator, aggregatory, aggrege, aggress, aggressed, aggresses, aggressing, aggression, aggression's, aggressionist, aggressions, aggressive, aggressively, aggressiveness, aggressivity, aggressor, aggressors, aggrievance, aggrieve, aggrieved, aggrievedly, aggrievedness, aggrievement, aggrieves, aggrieving, aggro, aggros, aggroup, aggroupment, aggry, aggur, agha, aghanee, aghas, aghast, aghastness, agible, agilawood, agile, agilely, agileness, agilities, agility, agillawood, agilmente, agin, aging, agings, aginner, aginners, agio, agios, agiotage, agiotages, agism, agisms, agist, agistator, agisted, agister, agisting, agistment, agistor, agists, agit, agitability, agitable, agitant, agitate, agitated, agitatedly, agitates, agitating, agitation, agitational, agitationist, agitations, agitative, agitato, agitator, agitator's, agitatorial, agitators, agitatrix, agitprop, agitpropist, agitprops, agitpunkt, agkistrodon, agla, aglaia, aglance, aglaozonia, aglare, agleaf, agleam, aglee, aglet, aglethead, aglets, agley, aglimmer, aglint, aglisten, aglitter, aglobulia, aglobulism, aglossal, aglossate, aglossia, aglow, aglucon, aglucone, aglutition, agly, aglycon, aglycone, aglycones, aglycons, aglycosuric, aglyphodont, aglyphous, agma, agmas, agmatine, agmatology, agminate, agminated, agnail, agnails, agname, agnamed, agnat, agnate, agnates, agnathia, agnathic, agnathostomatous, agnathous, agnatic, agnatical, agnatically, agnation, agnations, agnean, agneau, agneaux, agnel, agnification, agnition, agnize, agnized, agnizes, agnizing, agnoiology, agnoites, agnomen, agnomens, agnomical, agnomina, agnominal, agnomination, agnosia, agnosias, agnosis, agnostic, agnostic's, agnostical, agnostically, agnosticism, agnostics, agnosy, agnus, agnuses, ago, agog, agoge, agogic, agogics, agoho, agoing, agomensin, agomphiasis, agomphious, agomphosis, agon, agonal, agone, agones, agonia, agoniada, agoniadin, agoniatite, agonic, agonied, agonies, agonise, agonised, agonises, agonising, agonisingly, agonist, agonistarch, agonistic, agonistical, agonistically, agonistics, agonists, agonium, agonize, agonized, agonizedly, agonizer, agonizes, agonizing, agonizingly, agonizingness, agonothet, agonothete, agonothetic, agons, agony, agora, agorae, agoramania, agoranome, agoranomus, agoraphobia, agoraphobiac, agoraphobic, agoras, agorot, agoroth, agos, agostadero, agouara, agouta, agouti, agouties, agoutis, agouty, agpaite, agpaitic, agr, agrace, agrafe, agrafes, agraffe, agraffee, agraffes, agrah, agral, agramed, agrammaphasia, agrammatica, agrammatical, agrammatism, agrammatologia, agranulocyte, agranulocytosis, agranuloplastic, agrapha, agraphia, agraphias, agraphic, agraria, agrarian, agrarianism, agrarianize, agrarianly, agrarians, agravic, agre, agreat, agreation, agreations, agree, agreeability, agreeable, agreeableness, agreeably, agreed, agreeing, agreeingly, agreement, agreement's, agreements, agreer, agreers, agrees, agregation, agrege, agreges, agreing, agremens, agrement, agrements, agrest, agrestal, agrestial, agrestian, agrestic, agrestical, agrestis, agria, agrias, agribusiness, agribusinesses, agric, agricere, agricole, agricolist, agricolite, agricolous, agricultor, agricultural, agriculturalist, agriculturalists, agriculturally, agriculture, agriculturer, agricultures, agriculturist, agriculturists, agrief, agrimonies, agrimony, agrimotor, agrin, agriological, agriologist, agriology, agrionid, agriot, agriotype, agrise, agrised, agrising, agrito, agritos, agroan, agrobacterium, agrobiologic, agrobiological, agrobiologically, agrobiologist, agrobiology, agrodolce, agrogeological, agrogeologically, agrogeology, agrologic, agrological, agrologically, agrologies, agrologist, agrology, agrom, agromania, agromyzid, agron, agronome, agronomial, agronomic, agronomical, agronomically, agronomics, agronomies, agronomist, agronomists, agronomy, agroof, agrope, agrosteral, agrosterol, agrostis, agrostographer, agrostographic, agrostographical, agrostographies, agrostography, agrostologic, agrostological, agrostologist, agrostology, agrote, agrotechny, agrotype, aground, agrufe, agruif, agrypnia, agrypniai, agrypnias, agrypnode, agrypnotic, agsam, agst, agt, agtbasic, agua, aguacate, aguada, aguador, aguaji, aguamas, aguamiel, aguara, aguardiente, aguavina, ague, aguelike, agueproof, agues, agueweed, agueweeds, aguey, aguglia, aguilarite, aguilawood, aguilt, aguinaldo, aguinaldos, aguirage, aguise, aguish, aguishly, aguishness, agujon, agunah, agura, aguroth, agush, agust, agy, agyiomania, agynarious, agynary, agynic, agynous, agyrate, agyria, agyrophobia, ah, aha, ahaaina, ahab, ahamkara, ahankara, ahartalav, ahaunch, ahchoo, ahead, aheap, aheight, ahem, ahems, ahey, ahi, ahimsa, ahimsas, ahind, ahint, ahistoric, ahistorical, ahluwalia, ahmadi, ahmedi, aho, ahold, aholds, aholt, ahong, ahorse, ahorseback, ahoy, ahs, ahsan, ahu, ahuaca, ahuatle, ahuehuete, ahull, ahum, ahungered, ahungry, ahunt, ahura, ahurewa, ahush, ahuula, ahwal, ahypnia, ai, aiblins, aichmophobia, aid, aidable, aidance, aidant, aide, aided, aider, aiders, aides, aidful, aiding, aidless, aidman, aidmanmen, aidmen, aids, aiel, aiery, aiger, aigialosaur, aiglet, aiglets, aiglette, aigre, aigremore, aigret, aigrets, aigrette, aigrettes, aiguelle, aiguellette, aiguiere, aiguille, aiguilles, aiguillesque, aiguillette, aiguilletted, aik, aikane, aikido, aikidos, aikinite, aikona, aikuchi, ail, ailantery, ailanthic, ailanthus, ailanthuses, ailantine, ailanto, aile, ailed, aileron, ailerons, ailette, ailing, aillt, ailment, ailment's, ailments, ails, ailsyte, ailuro, ailuroid, ailuromania, ailurophile, ailurophilia, ailurophilic, ailurophobe, ailurophobia, ailurophobic, ailweed, aim, aimable, aimak, aimara, aimed, aimer, aimers, aimful, aimfully, aiming, aimless, aimlessly, aimlessness, aims, aimworthiness, ain, ain't, ainaleh, aine, ainee, ainhum, ainoi, ains, ainsell, ainsells, aint, ainu, ainus, aioli, aiolis, aion, aionial, air, airable, airampo, airan, airbag, airbags, airbill, airbills, airboat, airboats, airborn, airborne, airbound, airbrained, airbrasive, airbrick, airbrush, airbrushed, airbrushes, airbrushing, airburst, airbursts, airbus, airbuses, airbusses, aircheck, airchecks, aircoach, aircoaches, aircraft, aircraftman, aircraftmen, aircrafts, aircraftsman, aircraftsmen, aircraftswoman, aircraftswomen, aircraftwoman, aircrew, aircrewman, aircrewmen, aircrews, airdate, airdates, airdock, airdrome, airdromes, airdrop, airdropped, airdropping, airdrops, aire, aired, airedale, airedales, airer, airers, airest, airfare, airfares, airfield, airfield's, airfields, airflow, airflows, airfoil, airfoils, airframe, airframes, airfreight, airfreighter, airglow, airglows, airgraph, airgraphics, airhead, airheads, airier, airiest, airiferous, airified, airify, airily, airiness, airinesses, airing, airings, airish, airless, airlessly, airlessness, airlift, airlift's, airlifted, airlifting, airlifts, airlight, airlike, airline, airliner, airliners, airlines, airling, airlock, airlock's, airlocks, airmail, airmailed, airmailing, airmails, airman, airmanship, airmark, airmarker, airmass, airmen, airmobile, airmonger, airn, airns, airohydrogen, airometer, airpark, airparks, airphobia, airplane, airplane's, airplaned, airplaner, airplanes, airplaning, airplanist, airplay, airplays, airplot, airport, airport's, airports, airpost, airposts, airproof, airproofed, airproofing, airproofs, airs, airscape, airscapes, airscrew, airscrews, airshed, airsheds, airsheet, airship, airship's, airships, airsick, airsickness, airsome, airspace, airspaces, airspeed, airspeeds, airstream, airstrip, airstrip's, airstrips, airt, airted, airth, airthed, airthing, airths, airtight, airtightly, airtightness, airtime, airtimes, airting, airts, airview, airward, airwards, airwash, airwave, airwaves, airway, airway's, airwaybill, airwayman, airways, airwise, airwoman, airwomen, airworthier, airworthiest, airworthiness, airworthy, airy, ais, aischrolatreia, aiseweed, aisle, aisled, aisleless, aisles, aisling, aisteoir, aistopod, ait, aitch, aitchbone, aitches, aitchless, aitchpiece, aitesis, aith, aithochroi, aitiology, aition, aitiotropic, aitis, aits, aiver, aivers, aivr, aiwain, aiwan, aizle, aizoaceous, ajaja, ajangle, ajar, ajari, ajava, ajax, ajee, ajenjo, ajhar, ajimez, ajitter, ajiva, ajivas, ajivika, ajog, ajoint, ajonjoli, ajoure, ajourise, ajowan, ajowans, ajuga, ajugas, ajutment, ak, aka, akaakai, akala, akalimba, akamai, akamatsu, akan, akaroa, akasa, akasha, akazga, akazgin, akazgine, akcheh, ake, akeake, akebi, aked, akee, akees, akehorne, akeki, akela, akelas, akeley, akemboll, akenbold, akene, akenes, akenobeite, akepiro, akepiros, aker, akerite, aketon, akey, akhara, akhoond, akhrot, akhund, akhundzada, akhyana, akia, akimbo, akin, akindle, akinesia, akinesic, akinesis, akinete, akinetic, aking, akkadian, akmite, akmudar, akmuddar, aknee, aknow, ako, akoasm, akoasma, akolouthia, akoluthia, akonge, akov, akpek, akra, akre, akroasis, akrochordite, akron, akroter, akroteria, akroterial, akroterion, akrteria, aktiebolag, aku, akuammin, akuammine, akule, akund, akvavit, akvavits, al, ala, alabama, alabamian, alabamians, alabamide, alabamine, alabandine, alabandite, alabarch, alabaster, alabastoi, alabastos, alabastra, alabastrian, alabastrine, alabastrites, alabastron, alabastrons, alabastrum, alabastrums, alablaster, alacha, alachah, alack, alackaday, alacran, alacreatine, alacreatinin, alacreatinine, alacrify, alacrious, alacriously, alacrities, alacritous, alacrity, alada, aladdin, alae, alagao, alagarto, alagau, alahee, alai, alaihi, alaite, alala, alalia, alalite, alaloi, alalonga, alalunga, alalus, alambique, alameda, alamedas, alamiqui, alamire, alamo, alamodality, alamode, alamodes, alamonti, alamort, alamos, alamosite, alamoth, alan, aland, alands, alane, alang, alange, alangin, alangine, alani, alanin, alanine, alanines, alanins, alannah, alans, alant, alantic, alantin, alantol, alantolactone, alantolic, alants, alanyl, alanyls, alap, alapa, alar, alares, alarge, alarm, alarmable, alarmclock, alarmed, alarmedly, alarming, alarmingly, alarmingness, alarmism, alarmisms, alarmist, alarmists, alarms, alarum, alarumed, alaruming, alarums, alary, alas, alasas, alaska, alaskaite, alaskan, alaskans, alaskas, alaskite, alastor, alastors, alastrim, alate, alated, alatern, alaternus, alation, alations, alaudine, alaund, alaunt, alay, alazor, alb, alba, albacea, albacora, albacore, albacores, albahaca, alban, albania, albanian, albanians, albanite, albany, albarco, albardine, albarelli, albarello, albarellos, albarium, albas, albaspidin, albata, albatas, albation, albatross, albatrosses, albe, albedo, albedograph, albedometer, albedos, albee, albeit, alberca, albergatrice, alberge, alberghi, albergo, alberich, albert, alberta, albertin, albertite, alberttype, albertustaler, albertype, albescence, albescent, albespine, albespyne, albeston, albetad, albicans, albicant, albication, albicore, albicores, albiculi, albification, albificative, albified, albiflorous, albify, albifying, albigenses, albin, albinal, albines, albiness, albinic, albinism, albinisms, albinistic, albino, albinoism, albinos, albinotic, albinuria, albion, albite, albites, albitic, albitical, albitite, albitization, albitophyre, albizia, albizias, albizzia, albizzias, albocarbon, albocinereous, albocracy, albolite, albolith, albopannin, albopruinose, alborada, alborak, alboranite, albricias, albronze, albs, albuginea, albugineous, albugines, albuginitis, albugo, album, albumean, albumen, albumeniizer, albumenisation, albumenise, albumenised, albumeniser, albumenising, albumenization, albumenize, albumenized, albumenizer, albumenizing, albumenoid, albumens, albumimeter, albumin, albuminate, albuminaturia, albuminiferous, albuminiform, albuminimeter, albuminimetry, albuminiparous, albuminise, albuminised, albuminising, albuminization, albuminize, albuminized, albuminizing, albuminocholia, albuminofibrin, albuminogenous, albuminoid, albuminoidal, albuminolysis, albuminometer, albuminometry, albuminone, albuminorrhea, albuminoscope, albuminose, albuminosis, albuminous, albuminousness, albumins, albuminuria, albuminuric, albuminurophobia, albumoid, albumoscope, albumose, albumoses, albumosuria, albums, albuquerque, alburn, alburnous, alburnum, alburnums, albus, albutannin, alc, alcabala, alcade, alcades, alcahest, alcahests, alcaic, alcaiceria, alcaics, alcaid, alcaide, alcaides, alcalde, alcaldes, alcaldeship, alcaldia, alcali, alcaligenes, alcalizate, alcamine, alcanna, alcantara, alcapton, alcaptonuria, alcargen, alcarraza, alcatras, alcavala, alcayde, alcaydes, alcazaba, alcazar, alcazars, alcazava, alce, alcelaphine, alcestis, alchem, alchemic, alchemical, alchemically, alchemies, alchemise, alchemised, alchemising, alchemist, alchemister, alchemistic, alchemistical, alchemistry, alchemists, alchemize, alchemized, alchemizing, alchemy, alchera, alcheringa, alchimy, alchitran, alchochoden, alchornea, alchymies, alchymy, alcibiades, alcid, alcidine, alcids, alcine, alclad, alcmene, alco, alcoate, alcogel, alcogene, alcohate, alcohol, alcohol's, alcoholate, alcoholature, alcoholdom, alcoholemia, alcoholic, alcoholic's, alcoholically, alcoholicity, alcoholics, alcoholimeter, alcoholisation, alcoholise, alcoholised, alcoholising, alcoholism, alcoholist, alcoholizable, alcoholization, alcoholize, alcoholized, alcoholizing, alcoholmeter, alcoholmetric, alcoholomania, alcoholometer, alcoholometric, alcoholometrical, alcoholometry, alcoholophilia, alcohols, alcoholuria, alcoholysis, alcoholytic, alconde, alcoothionic, alcoran, alcornoco, alcornoque, alcosol, alcove, alcove's, alcoved, alcoves, alcovinometer, alcumy, alcyon, alcyonacean, alcyonarian, alcyone, alcyonic, alcyoniform, alcyonium, alcyonoid, ald, aldamin, aldamine, aldane, alday, aldazin, aldazine, aldea, aldeament, aldebaran, aldebaranium, aldehol, aldehydase, aldehyde, aldehydes, aldehydic, aldehydine, aldehydrol, aldeia, alden, alder, alderflies, alderfly, alderliefest, alderling, alderman, alderman's, aldermanate, aldermancy, aldermaness, aldermanic, aldermanical, aldermanity, aldermanlike, aldermanly, aldermanries, aldermanry, aldermanship, aldermen, aldern, alders, alderwoman, alderwomen, aldide, aldim, aldime, aldimin, aldimine, aldine, alditol, aldm, aldoheptose, aldohexose, aldoketene, aldol, aldolase, aldolases, aldolization, aldolize, aldolized, aldolizing, aldols, aldononose, aldopentose, aldose, aldoses, aldoside, aldosterone, aldosteronism, aldoxime, aldrin, aldrins, ale, aleak, aleatoric, aleatory, alebench, aleberry, alebush, alec, alecithal, alecithic, alecize, aleconner, alecost, alecs, alectoria, alectoriae, alectoridine, alectorioid, alectoromachy, alectoromancy, alectoromorphous, alectoropodous, alectryomachy, alectryomancy, alectryon, alecup, alee, alef, alefnull, alefs, aleft, alefzero, alegar, alegars, aleger, alehoof, alehouse, alehouses, aleikoum, aleikum, aleiptes, aleiptic, aleknight, alem, alemana, alemannic, alembic, alembicate, alembicated, alembics, alembroth, alemite, alemmal, alemonger, alen, alencon, alencons, alenge, alength, alentours, alenu, aleph, alephs, alephzero, alepidote, alepine, alepole, alepot, alerce, alerion, alerse, alert, alerta, alerted, alertedly, alerter, alerters, alertest, alerting, alertly, alertness, alerts, ales, alesan, aleshot, alestake, aletap, aletaster, alethic, alethiologic, alethiological, alethiologist, alethiology, alethopteis, alethopteroid, alethoscope, aletocyte, alette, aleucaemic, aleucemic, aleukaemic, aleukemic, aleuritic, aleuromancy, aleurometer, aleuron, aleuronat, aleurone, aleurones, aleuronic, aleurons, aleuroscope, aleut, aleutian, aleutians, aleutite, alevin, alevins, alew, alewhap, alewife, alewives, alexander, alexanders, alexandria, alexandrian, alexandrine, alexandrines, alexandrite, alexia, alexias, alexic, alexin, alexine, alexines, alexinic, alexins, alexipharmacon, alexipharmacum, alexipharmic, alexipharmical, alexipyretic, alexiteric, alexiterical, aleyard, aleyrodid, alezan, alf, alfa, alfaje, alfaki, alfakis, alfalfa, alfalfas, alfaqui, alfaquin, alfaquins, alfaquis, alfarga, alfas, alfenide, alferes, alferez, alfet, alfilaria, alfileria, alfilerilla, alfilerillo, alfin, alfiona, alfione, alfoncino, alfonsin, alfonso, alforge, alforja, alforjas, alfred, alfresco, alfridaric, alfridary, alg, alga, algae, algaecide, algaeological, algaeologist, algaeology, algaesthesia, algaesthesis, algal, algalia, algarad, algarde, algaroba, algarobas, algarot, algarroba, algarrobilla, algarrobin, algas, algate, algates, algazel, algebra, algebra's, algebraic, algebraical, algebraically, algebraist, algebraists, algebraization, algebraize, algebraized, algebraizing, algebras, algebrization, algedo, algedonic, algedonics, algefacient, algeria, algerian, algerians, algerienne, algerine, algerines, algerita, algerite, algesia, algesic, algesimeter, algesiometer, algesireceptor, algesis, algesthesis, algetic, algic, algicidal, algicide, algicides, algid, algidities, algidity, algidness, algiers, algific, algin, alginate, alginates, algine, alginic, algins, alginuresis, algiomuscular, algist, algivorous, algocyan, algodon, algodoncillo, algodonite, algoesthesiometer, algogenic, algoid, algol, algolagnia, algolagnic, algolagnist, algolagny, algological, algologically, algologies, algologist, algology, algometer, algometric, algometrical, algometrically, algometry, algonkian, algonquian, algonquians, algonquin, algonquins, algophagous, algophilia, algophilist, algophobia, algor, algorism, algorismic, algorisms, algorist, algoristic, algorithm, algorithm's, algorithmic, algorithmically, algorithms, algors, algosis, algous, algovite, algraphic, algraphy, alguacil, alguazil, alguifou, algum, algums, alhacena, alhagi, alhambra, alhambresque, alhandal, alhenna, alhet, alia, aliamenta, alias, aliased, aliases, aliasing, alibangbang, alibi, alibi's, alibied, alibies, alibiing, alibility, alibis, alible, alicant, alice, alichel, alicoche, alictisal, alicula, aliculae, alicyclic, alidad, alidada, alidade, alidades, alidads, alien, alien's, alienabilities, alienability, alienable, alienage, alienages, alienate, alienated, alienates, alienating, alienation, alienator, aliency, aliene, aliened, alienee, alienees, aliener, alieners, alienicola, alienicolae, alienigenate, aliening, alienism, alienisms, alienist, alienists, alienize, alienly, alienness, alienor, alienors, aliens, alienship, aliesterase, aliet, aliethmoid, aliethmoidal, alif, alife, aliferous, aliform, alifs, aligerous, alight, alighted, alighten, alighting, alightment, alights, align, aligned, aligner, aligners, aligning, alignment, alignments, aligns, aligreek, alii, aliipoe, alike, alikeness, alikewise, alilonghi, alima, alimenation, aliment, alimental, alimentally, alimentariness, alimentary, alimentation, alimentative, alimentatively, alimentativeness, alimented, alimenter, alimentic, alimenting, alimentive, alimentiveness, alimentotherapy, aliments, alimentum, alimonied, alimonies, alimony, alin, alinasal, aline, alineation, alined, alinement, aliner, aliners, alines, alingual, alining, alinit, alinota, alinotum, alintatao, aliofar, alioth, alipata, aliped, alipeds, aliphatic, alipin, aliptae, alipteria, alipterion, aliptes, aliptic, aliptteria, aliquant, aliquid, aliquot, aliquots, alisanders, aliseptal, alish, alisier, alisma, alismaceous, alismad, alismal, alismoid, aliso, alison, alisonite, alisos, alisp, alispheno, alisphenoid, alisphenoidal, alist, alit, alite, aliter, alitrunk, aliturgic, aliturgical, ality, aliunde, alive, aliveness, alives, alivincular, aliya, aliyah, aliyahaliyahs, aliyas, aliyos, aliyoth, alizarate, alizari, alizarin, alizarine, alizarins, aljama, aljamado, aljamia, aljamiado, aljamiah, aljoba, aljofaina, alk, alkahest, alkahestic, alkahestica, alkahestical, alkahests, alkalamide, alkalemia, alkalescence, alkalescency, alkalescent, alkali, alkali's, alkalic, alkalies, alkaliferous, alkalifiable, alkalified, alkalifies, alkalify, alkalifying, alkaligen, alkaligenous, alkalimeter, alkalimetric, alkalimetrical, alkalimetrically, alkalimetry, alkalin, alkaline, alkalinisation, alkalinise, alkalinised, alkalinising, alkalinities, alkalinity, alkalinization, alkalinize, alkalinized, alkalinizes, alkalinizing, alkalinuria, alkalis, alkalisable, alkalisation, alkalise, alkalised, alkaliser, alkalises, alkalising, alkalizable, alkalizate, alkalization, alkalize, alkalized, alkalizer, alkalizes, alkalizing, alkaloid, alkaloid's, alkaloidal, alkaloids, alkalometry, alkalosis, alkalous, alkamin, alkamine, alkanal, alkane, alkanes, alkanet, alkanethiol, alkanets, alkanna, alkannin, alkanol, alkapton, alkaptone, alkaptonuria, alkaptonuric, alkargen, alkarsin, alkarsine, alkatively, alkedavy, alkekengi, alkene, alkenes, alkenna, alkenyl, alkermes, alkide, alkies, alkin, alkine, alkines, alkitran, alkool, alkoxid, alkoxide, alkoxy, alkoxyl, alky, alkyd, alkyds, alkyl, alkylamine, alkylamino, alkylarylsulfonate, alkylate, alkylated, alkylates, alkylating, alkylation, alkylbenzenesulfonate, alkylbenzenesulfonates, alkylene, alkylic, alkylidene, alkylize, alkylogen, alkylol, alkyloxy, alkyls, alkyne, alkynes, all, all'antica, all'italiana, all'ottava, allabuta, allachesthesia, allactite, allaeanthus, allagite, allagophyllous, allagostemonous, allah, allah's, allalinite, allamonti, allamoth, allamotti, allan, allanite, allanites, allanitic, allantiasis, allantochorion, allantoic, allantoid, allantoidal, allantoidean, allantoides, allantoidian, allantoin, allantoinase, allantoinuria, allantois, allantoxaidin, allanturic, allargando, allassotonic, allative, allatrate, allay, allayed, allayer, allayers, allaying, allayment, allays, allbone, allecret, allect, allectory, allegata, allegate, allegation, allegation's, allegations, allegator, allegatum, allege, allegeable, alleged, allegedly, allegement, alleger, allegers, alleges, allegheny, allegiance, allegiance's, allegiances, allegiancy, allegiant, allegiantly, allegiare, alleging, allegoric, allegorical, allegorically, allegoricalness, allegories, allegorisation, allegorise, allegorised, allegoriser, allegorising, allegorism, allegorist, allegorister, allegoristic, allegorists, allegorization, allegorize, allegorized, allegorizer, allegorizing, allegory, allegory's, allegresse, allegretto, allegretto's, allegrettos, allegro, allegro's, allegros, allele, alleles, alleleu, allelic, allelism, allelisms, allelocatalytic, allelomorph, allelomorphic, allelomorphism, allelopathy, allelotropic, allelotropism, allelotropy, alleluia, alleluiah, alleluias, alleluiatic, alleluja, allelvia, allemand, allemande, allemandes, allemands, allemontite, allen, allenarly, allene, alleniate, allentando, allentato, aller, allergen, allergenic, allergenicity, allergens, allergia, allergic, allergies, allergin, allergins, allergist, allergists, allergology, allergy, allergy's, allerion, allesthesia, allethrin, alleve, alleviant, alleviate, alleviated, alleviater, alleviaters, alleviates, alleviating, alleviatingly, alleviation, alleviations, alleviative, alleviator, alleviators, alleviatory, alley, alley's, alleyed, alleyite, alleys, alleyway, alleyway's, alleyways, allez, allgood, allgovite, allhallows, allheal, allheals, alliable, alliably, alliaceous, alliage, alliance, alliance's, allianced, alliancer, alliances, alliancing, alliant, allicampane, allice, allicholly, alliciency, allicient, allicin, allicins, allicit, allied, allies, alligate, alligated, alligating, alligation, alligations, alligator, alligator's, alligatored, alligatorfish, alligatorfishes, alligatoring, alligators, allineate, allineation, allis, allision, alliteral, alliterate, alliterated, alliterates, alliterating, alliteration, alliteration's, alliterational, alliterationist, alliterations, alliterative, alliteratively, alliterativeness, alliterator, allituric, allium, alliums, allivalite, allmouth, allmouths, allness, allo, alloantibody, allobar, allobaric, allobars, allobrogical, allocability, allocable, allocaffeine, allocatable, allocate, allocated, allocatee, allocates, allocating, allocation, allocations, allocator, allocator's, allocators, allocatur, allocheiria, allochetia, allochetite, allochezia, allochiral, allochirally, allochiria, allochlorophyll, allochroic, allochroite, allochromatic, allochrous, allochthon, allochthonous, allocinnamic, alloclase, alloclasite, allocochick, allocrotonic, allocryptic, allocthonous, allocute, allocution, allocutive, allocyanine, allod, allodelphite, allodesmism, allodge, allodia, allodial, allodialism, allodialist, allodiality, allodially, allodian, allodiaries, allodiary, allodies, allodification, allodium, allods, allody, alloeosis, alloeostropha, alloeotic, alloerotic, alloerotism, allogamies, allogamous, allogamy, allogene, allogeneic, allogeneity, allogeneous, allogenic, allogenically, allograft, allograph, allographic, alloimmune, alloiogenesis, alloiometric, alloiometry, alloisomer, alloisomeric, alloisomerism, allokinesis, allokinetic, allokurtic, allolalia, allolalic, allomerism, allomerization, allomerize, allomerized, allomerizing, allomerous, allometric, allometry, allomorph, allomorphic, allomorphism, allomorphite, allomucic, allonge, allonges, allonomous, allonym, allonymous, allonymously, allonyms, alloo, allopalladium, allopath, allopathetic, allopathetically, allopathic, allopathically, allopathies, allopathist, allopaths, allopathy, allopatric, allopatrically, allopatry, allopelagic, allophanamid, allophanamide, allophanate, allophanates, allophane, allophanic, allophite, allophone, allophones, allophonic, allophonically, allophore, allophyle, allophylian, allophylic, allophytoid, alloplasm, alloplasmatic, alloplasmic, alloplast, alloplastic, alloplasty, alloploidy, allopolyploid, allopolyploidy, allopsychic, allopurinol, alloquial, alloquialism, alloquy, allorhythmia, allorrhyhmia, allorrhythmic, allosaur, allose, allosematic, allosome, allosteric, allosterically, allosyndesis, allosyndetic, allot, alloted, allotee, allotelluric, allotheism, allotheist, allotheistic, allothigene, allothigenetic, allothigenetically, allothigenic, allothigenous, allothimorph, allothimorphic, allothogenic, allothogenous, allotment, allotment's, allotments, allotransplant, allotransplantation, allotriodontia, allotriomorphic, allotriophagia, allotriophagy, allotriuria, allotrope, allotropes, allotrophic, allotropic, allotropical, allotropically, allotropicity, allotropies, allotropism, allotropize, allotropous, allotropy, allotrylic, allots, allottable, allotted, allottee, allottees, allotter, allotters, allottery, allotting, allotype, allotypes, allotypic, allotypical, allotypically, allotypies, allotypy, allover, allovers, allow, allowable, allowableness, allowably, allowance, allowance's, allowanced, allowances, allowancing, allowed, allowedly, allower, allowing, allows, alloxan, alloxanate, alloxanic, alloxans, alloxantin, alloxuraemia, alloxuremia, alloxuric, alloxy, alloxyproteic, alloy, alloy's, alloyage, alloyed, alloying, alloys, allozooid, allround, alls, allseed, allseeds, allspice, allspices, allthing, allthorn, alltud, allude, alluded, alludes, alluding, allumette, allumine, alluminor, allurance, allure, allured, allurement, allurements, allurer, allurers, allures, alluring, alluringly, alluringness, allusion, allusion's, allusions, allusive, allusively, allusiveness, allusory, allutterly, alluvia, alluvial, alluvials, alluviate, alluviation, alluvio, alluvion, alluvions, alluvious, alluvium, alluviums, alluvivia, alluviviums, allwhere, allwhither, allwork, ally, allyic, allying, allyl, allylamine, allylate, allylation, allylene, allylic, allyls, allylthiourea, allyou, alma, almacantar, almacen, almacenista, almaciga, almacigo, almadia, almadie, almagest, almagests, almagra, almah, almahs, almain, almaine, almanac, almanac's, almanacs, almander, almandine, almandines, almandite, almanner, almas, alme, almeh, almehs, almeidina, almemar, almemars, almemor, almendro, almendron, almeries, almeriite, almery, almes, almice, almicore, almight, almightily, almightiness, almighty, almique, almirah, almistry, almner, almners, almochoden, almocrebe, almogavar, almohad, almoign, almoin, almon, almonage, almond, almond's, almondlike, almonds, almondy, almoner, almoners, almonership, almoning, almonries, almonry, almose, almost, almous, alms, almsdeed, almsfolk, almsful, almsgiver, almsgiving, almshouse, almshouses, almsman, almsmen, almsmoney, almswoman, almswomen, almucantar, almuce, almuces, almud, almude, almudes, almuds, almuerzo, almug, almugs, almury, almuten, aln, alnage, alnager, alnagership, alnath, alnein, alnico, alnicoes, alniresinol, alniviridol, alnoite, alnuin, alnus, alo, alocasia, alochia, alod, aloddia, alodia, alodial, alodialism, alodialist, alodiality, alodially, alodialty, alodian, alodiaries, alodiary, alodies, alodification, alodium, alody, aloe, aloed, aloedary, aloelike, aloemodin, aloeroot, aloes, aloesol, aloeswood, aloetic, aloetical, aloewood, aloft, alogia, alogian, alogical, alogically, alogism, alogotrophy, alogy, aloha, alohas, aloid, aloin, aloins, aloisiite, aloma, alomancy, alone, alonely, aloneness, along, alongships, alongshore, alongshoreman, alongside, alongst, aloof, aloofe, aloofly, aloofness, aloose, alop, alopathic, alopecia, alopecias, alopecic, alopecist, alopecoid, alopekai, alopeke, alophas, alorcinic, alose, alouatte, aloud, alouette, alouettes, alout, alow, alowe, aloyau, aloysia, alp, alpaca, alpacas, alpargata, alpasotes, alpax, alpeen, alpen, alpenglow, alpenhorn, alpenhorns, alpenstock, alpenstocker, alpenstocks, alpestral, alpestrian, alpestrine, alpha, alphabet, alphabet's, alphabetarian, alphabetary, alphabeted, alphabetic, alphabetical, alphabetically, alphabetics, alphabetiform, alphabeting, alphabetisation, alphabetise, alphabetised, alphabetiser, alphabetising, alphabetism, alphabetist, alphabetization, alphabetize, alphabetized, alphabetizer, alphabetizers, alphabetizes, alphabetizing, alphabetology, alphabets, alphameric, alphamerical, alphamerically, alphanumeric, alphanumerical, alphanumerically, alphanumerics, alphas, alphatoluic, alphenic, alpheus, alphin, alphitomancy, alphitomorphous, alphol, alphonsin, alphonsine, alphorn, alphorns, alphos, alphosis, alphosises, alphyl, alphyls, alphyn, alpieu, alpigene, alpine, alpinely, alpinery, alpines, alpinesque, alpinia, alpinism, alpinisms, alpinist, alpinists, alpist, alpiste, alps, alqueire, alquier, alquifou, alraun, alreadiness, already, alright, alrighty, alroot, alruna, alrune, als, alsatia, alsatian, alsbachite, alsifilm, alsike, alsikes, alsinaceous, alsmekill, also, alsoon, alstonidine, alstonine, alstonite, alsweill, alswith, alt, altaian, altaic, altair, altaite, altaltissimo, altar, altar's, altarage, altared, altarist, altarlet, altarpiece, altarpieces, altars, altarwise, altazimuth, alter, alterability, alterable, alterableness, alterably, alterant, alterants, alterate, alteration, alteration's, alterations, alterative, alteratively, altercate, altercated, altercating, altercation, altercation's, altercations, altercative, altered, alteregoism, alteregoistic, alterer, alterers, altering, alterity, alterius, alterman, altern, alternacy, alternamente, alternance, alternant, alternariose, alternat, alternate, alternated, alternately, alternateness, alternater, alternates, alternating, alternatingly, alternation, alternationist, alternations, alternative, alternatively, alternativeness, alternatives, alternativity, alternativo, alternator, alternator's, alternators, alterne, alternifoliate, alternipetalous, alternipinnate, alternisepalous, alternity, alternize, alterocentric, alters, alterum, altesse, alteza, altezza, althaea, althaeas, althaein, althea, altheas, althein, altheine, althing, althionic, altho, althorn, althorns, although, altify, altigraph, altilik, altiloquence, altiloquent, altimeter, altimeters, altimetrical, altimetrically, altimetry, altimettrically, altin, altincar, altingiaceous, altininck, altiplanicie, altiplano, altiscope, altisonant, altisonous, altissimo, altitonant, altitude, altitudes, altitudinal, altitudinarian, altitudinous, alto, alto's, altocumulus, altogether, altogetherness, altoist, altometer, altos, altostratus, altoun, altrices, altricial, altropathy, altrose, altruism, altruisms, altruist, altruistic, altruistically, altruists, alts, altschin, altumal, altun, alture, altus, aludel, aludels, alula, alulae, alular, alulet, alum, alumbloom, alumbrado, alumen, alumetize, alumian, alumic, alumiferous, alumin, alumina, aluminaphone, aluminas, aluminate, alumine, alumines, aluminic, aluminide, aluminiferous, aluminiform, aluminise, aluminised, aluminish, aluminising, aluminite, aluminium, aluminize, aluminized, aluminizes, aluminizing, aluminoferric, aluminographic, aluminography, aluminose, aluminosilicate, aluminosis, aluminosity, aluminothermic, aluminothermics, aluminothermy, aluminotype, aluminous, alumins, aluminum, aluminums, aluminyl, alumish, alumite, alumium, alumna, alumna's, alumnae, alumnal, alumni, alumniate, alumnus, alumohydrocalcite, alumroot, alumroots, alums, alumstone, alundum, aluniferous, alunite, alunites, alunogen, alupag, alure, alurgite, alushtite, aluta, alutaceous, alvar, alvearies, alvearium, alveary, alveated, alvelos, alveloz, alveola, alveolae, alveolar, alveolariform, alveolarly, alveolars, alveolary, alveolate, alveolated, alveolation, alveole, alveolectomy, alveoli, alveoliform, alveolite, alveolitis, alveoloclasia, alveolocondylean, alveolodental, alveololabial, alveololingual, alveolonasal, alveolosubnasal, alveolotomy, alveolus, alveus, alvia, alviducous, alvine, alvite, alvus, alw, alway, always, alwise, alwite, aly, alycompaine, alymphia, alymphopotent, alypin, alypine, alypum, alysson, alyssum, alyssums, alytarch, alzheimer, am, ama, amaas, amabile, amability, amable, amacratic, amacrinal, amacrine, amadan, amadavat, amadavats, amadelphous, amadou, amadous, amaga, amah, amahs, amain, amaine, amaist, amaister, amakebe, amal, amala, amalaita, amalaka, amalekite, amalett, amalg, amalgam, amalgam's, amalgamable, amalgamate, amalgamated, amalgamater, amalgamates, amalgamating, amalgamation, amalgamationist, amalgamations, amalgamative, amalgamatize, amalgamator, amalgamators, amalgamist, amalgamization, amalgamize, amalgams, amalic, amaltas, amamau, amande, amandin, amandine, amang, amani, amania, amanita, amanitas, amanitin, amanitine, amanitins, amanori, amanous, amant, amantadine, amante, amantillo, amanuenses, amanuensis, amapa, amar, amaracus, amarant, amarantaceous, amaranth, amaranthaceous, amaranthine, amaranthoid, amaranths, amarantine, amarantite, amarelle, amarelles, amarettos, amarevole, amargosa, amargoso, amargosos, amarillo, amarillos, amarin, amarine, amaritude, amarity, amarna, amaroid, amaroidal, amarthritis, amarvel, amaryllid, amaryllidaceous, amaryllideous, amaryllis, amaryllises, amas, amasesis, amass, amassable, amassed, amasser, amassers, amasses, amassette, amassing, amassment, amassments, amasthenic, amastia, amasty, amate, amated, amaterialistic, amateur, amateur's, amateurish, amateurishly, amateurishness, amateurism, amateurs, amateurship, amathophobia, amati, amating, amatito, amative, amatively, amativeness, amatol, amatols, amatorial, amatorially, amatorian, amatories, amatorio, amatorious, amatory, amatrice, amatungula, amaurosis, amaurotic, amaut, amaxomania, amay, amaze, amazed, amazedly, amazedness, amazeful, amazement, amazer, amazers, amazes, amazia, amazing, amazingly, amazon, amazon's, amazonian, amazonite, amazons, amazonstone, amb, amba, ambach, ambage, ambages, ambagiosity, ambagious, ambagiously, ambagiousness, ambagitory, ambalam, amban, ambar, ambaree, ambarella, ambari, ambaries, ambaris, ambary, ambas, ambash, ambassade, ambassador, ambassador's, ambassadorial, ambassadorially, ambassadors, ambassadorship, ambassadorships, ambassadress, ambassage, ambassiate, ambassy, ambatch, ambatoarinite, ambay, ambe, ambeer, ambeers, amber, amberfish, amberfishes, ambergrease, ambergris, amberies, amberiferous, amberina, amberite, amberjack, amberjacks, amberlike, amberoid, amberoids, amberous, ambers, ambery, ambiance, ambiances, ambicolorate, ambicoloration, ambidexter, ambidexterities, ambidexterity, ambidexterous, ambidextral, ambidextrous, ambidextrously, ambidextrousness, ambience, ambiences, ambiency, ambiens, ambient, ambients, ambier, ambigenal, ambigenous, ambigu, ambiguities, ambiguity, ambiguity's, ambiguous, ambiguously, ambiguousness, ambilaevous, ambilateral, ambilateralaterally, ambilaterality, ambilaterally, ambilevous, ambilian, ambilogy, ambiopia, ambiparous, ambisextrous, ambisexual, ambisexualities, ambisexuality, ambisinister, ambisinistrous, ambisporangiate, ambisyllabic, ambit, ambital, ambitendencies, ambitendency, ambitendent, ambition, ambition's, ambitioned, ambitioning, ambitionist, ambitionless, ambitionlessly, ambitions, ambitious, ambitiously, ambitiousness, ambits, ambitty, ambitus, ambivalence, ambivalency, ambivalent, ambivalently, ambiversion, ambiversive, ambivert, ambiverts, amble, ambled, ambleocarpus, ambler, amblers, ambles, ambling, amblingly, amblosis, amblotic, amblyacousia, amblyaphia, amblychromatic, amblygeusia, amblygon, amblygonal, amblygonite, amblyocarpous, amblyope, amblyopia, amblyopic, amblyoscope, amblypod, amblypodous, amblystegite, ambo, amboceptoid, amboceptor, ambodexter, amboina, amboinas, ambolic, ambomalleal, ambon, ambones, ambonite, ambos, ambosexous, ambosexual, amboyna, amboynas, ambracan, ambrain, ambreate, ambreic, ambrein, ambrette, ambrettolide, ambries, ambrite, ambroid, ambroids, ambrology, ambrose, ambrosia, ambrosiac, ambrosiaceous, ambrosial, ambrosially, ambrosian, ambrosias, ambrosiate, ambrosin, ambrosine, ambrosterol, ambrotype, ambry, ambsace, ambsaces, ambulacra, ambulacral, ambulacriform, ambulacrum, ambulance, ambulance's, ambulanced, ambulancer, ambulances, ambulancing, ambulant, ambulante, ambulantes, ambulate, ambulated, ambulates, ambulating, ambulatio, ambulation, ambulative, ambulator, ambulatoria, ambulatorial, ambulatories, ambulatorily, ambulatorium, ambulatoriums, ambulators, ambulatory, ambulia, ambuling, ambulomancy, amburbial, ambury, ambuscade, ambuscaded, ambuscader, ambuscades, ambuscading, ambuscado, ambuscadoed, ambuscados, ambush, ambushed, ambusher, ambushers, ambushes, ambushing, ambushlike, ambushment, ambustion, amchoor, amdahl, amdt, ame, ameba, amebae, ameban, amebas, amebean, amebian, amebiasis, amebic, amebicidal, amebicide, amebid, amebiform, amebobacter, amebocyte, ameboid, ameboidism, amebous, amebula, ameed, ameen, ameer, ameerate, ameerates, ameers, ameiosis, ameiotic, amel, amelanchier, ameland, amelcorn, amelcorns, amelet, amelia, amelification, ameliorable, ameliorableness, ameliorant, ameliorate, ameliorated, ameliorates, ameliorating, amelioration, ameliorations, ameliorativ, ameliorative, amelioratively, ameliorator, amelioratory, amellus, ameloblast, ameloblastic, amelu, amelus, amen, amenability, amenable, amenableness, amenably, amenage, amenance, amend, amendable, amendableness, amendatory, amende, amended, amender, amenders, amending, amendment, amendment's, amendments, amends, amene, amenia, amenities, amenity, amenorrhea, amenorrheal, amenorrheic, amenorrho, amenorrhoea, amenorrhoeal, amenorrhoeic, amens, ament, amenta, amentaceous, amental, amentia, amentias, amentiferous, amentiform, aments, amentula, amentulum, amentum, amenty, amenuse, amerce, amerceable, amerced, amercement, amercements, amercer, amercers, amerces, amerciable, amerciament, amercing, america, america's, american, american's, americana, americanism, americanisms, americanist, americanization, americanize, americanized, americanizes, americanizing, americans, americanum, americanumancestors, americas, americium, amerikani, amerind, amerindian, amerindians, amerinds, amerism, ameristic, amerveil, amesace, amesaces, amesite, amess, ametabola, ametabole, ametabolia, ametabolian, ametabolic, ametabolism, ametabolous, ametaboly, ametallous, amethodical, amethodically, amethyst, amethystine, amethystlike, amethysts, ametoecious, ametria, ametrometer, ametrope, ametropia, ametropic, ametrous, amex, amgarn, amhar, amharic, amherstite, amhran, ami, amia, amiability, amiable, amiableness, amiably, amiant, amianth, amianthiform, amianthine, amianthoid, amianthoidal, amianthus, amiantus, amiantuses, amias, amic, amicabilities, amicability, amicable, amicableness, amicably, amical, amice, amiced, amices, amici, amicicide, amicous, amicrobic, amicron, amicronucleate, amictus, amicus, amid, amidase, amidases, amidate, amidated, amidating, amidation, amide, amides, amidic, amidid, amidide, amidin, amidine, amidins, amidmost, amido, amidoacetal, amidoacetic, amidoacetophenone, amidoaldehyde, amidoazo, amidoazobenzene, amidoazobenzol, amidocaffeine, amidocapric, amidocyanogen, amidofluorid, amidofluoride, amidogen, amidogens, amidoguaiacol, amidohexose, amidoketone, amidol, amidols, amidomyelin, amidon, amidone, amidophenol, amidophosphoric, amidoplast, amidoplastid, amidopyrine, amidosuccinamic, amidosulphonal, amidothiazole, amidoxime, amidoxy, amidoxyl, amidrazone, amids, amidship, amidships, amidst, amidstream, amidulin, amidward, amie, amies, amiga, amigas, amigo, amigos, amil, amildar, amimia, amimide, amin, aminase, aminate, aminated, aminating, amination, aminded, amine, amines, amini, aminic, aminish, aminities, aminity, aminization, aminize, amino, aminoacetal, aminoacetanilide, aminoacetic, aminoacetone, aminoacetophenetidine, aminoacetophenone, aminoacidemia, aminoaciduria, aminoanthraquinone, aminoazo, aminoazobenzene, aminobarbituric, aminobenzaldehyde, aminobenzamide, aminobenzene, aminobenzine, aminobenzoic, aminocaproic, aminodiphenyl, aminoethionic, aminoformic, aminogen, aminoglutaric, aminoguanidine, aminoid, aminoketone, aminolipin, aminolysis, aminolytic, aminomalonic, aminomyelin, aminopeptidase, aminophenol, aminopherase, aminophylline, aminoplast, aminoplastic, aminopolypeptidase, aminopropionic, aminopurine, aminopyrine, aminoquin, aminoquinoline, aminosis, aminosuccinamic, aminosulphonic, aminothiophen, aminotransferase, aminotriazole, aminovaleric, aminoxylol, amins, amir, amiral, amirate, amirates, amiray, amire, amirs, amirship, amis, amish, amiss, amissibility, amissible, amissing, amission, amissness, amit, amitate, amitie, amities, amitoses, amitosis, amitotic, amitotically, amitriptyline, amitrole, amitroles, amitular, amity, amixia, amla, amlacra, amlet, amli, amlikar, amlong, amma, amman, ammelide, ammelin, ammeline, ammeos, ammer, ammeter, ammeters, ammi, ammiaceous, ammine, ammines, ammino, amminochloride, amminolysis, amminolytic, ammiolite, ammiral, ammites, ammo, ammobium, ammocete, ammocetes, ammochaeta, ammochaetae, ammochryse, ammocoete, ammocoetes, ammocoetid, ammocoetiform, ammocoetoid, ammodyte, ammodytoid, ammonal, ammonals, ammonate, ammonation, ammonia, ammoniac, ammoniacal, ammoniacs, ammoniacum, ammoniaemia, ammonias, ammoniate, ammoniated, ammoniating, ammoniation, ammonic, ammonical, ammoniemia, ammonification, ammonified, ammonifier, ammonifies, ammonify, ammonifying, ammoniojarosite, ammonion, ammonionitrate, ammonite, ammonites, ammonitic, ammoniticone, ammonitiferous, ammonitoid, ammonium, ammoniums, ammoniuret, ammoniureted, ammoniuria, ammonization, ammono, ammonobasic, ammonocarbonic, ammonocarbonous, ammonoid, ammonoidean, ammonoids, ammonolitic, ammonolyses, ammonolysis, ammonolytic, ammonolyze, ammonolyzed, ammonolyzing, ammophilous, ammoresinol, ammoreslinol, ammos, ammotherapy, ammu, ammunition, amn't, amnemonic, amnesia, amnesiac, amnesiacs, amnesias, amnesic, amnesics, amnestic, amnestied, amnesties, amnesty, amnestying, amnia, amniac, amniatic, amnic, amninia, amninions, amnioallantoic, amniocentesis, amniochorial, amnioclepsis, amniomancy, amnion, amnionate, amnionia, amnionic, amnions, amniorrhea, amnios, amniota, amniote, amniotes, amniotic, amniotin, amniotitis, amniotome, amobarbital, amober, amobyr, amoeba, amoeba's, amoebae, amoebaea, amoebaean, amoebaeum, amoebalike, amoeban, amoebas, amoebean, amoebeum, amoebian, amoebiasis, amoebic, amoebicidal, amoebicide, amoebid, amoebiform, amoebocyte, amoeboid, amoeboidism, amoebous, amoebula, amoibite, amoinder, amok, amoke, amoks, amole, amoles, amolilla, amolish, amollish, amomal, amomum, among, amongst, amontillado, amontillados, amor, amora, amorado, amoraic, amoraim, amoral, amoralism, amoralist, amorality, amoralize, amorally, amoret, amoretti, amoretto, amorettos, amorini, amorino, amorism, amorist, amoristic, amorists, amorite, amornings, amorosa, amorosity, amoroso, amorous, amorously, amorousness, amorph, amorpha, amorphi, amorphia, amorphic, amorphinism, amorphism, amorphophyte, amorphotae, amorphous, amorphously, amorphousness, amorphozoa, amorphus, amorphy, amort, amortisable, amortise, amortised, amortises, amortising, amortissement, amortisseur, amortizable, amortization, amortize, amortized, amortizement, amortizes, amortizing, amos, amosite, amotion, amotions, amotus, amouli, amount, amounted, amounter, amounters, amounting, amounts, amour, amouret, amourette, amourist, amours, amovability, amovable, amove, amoved, amoving, amowt, amp, ampalaya, ampalea, ampangabeite, amparo, ampasimenite, ampassy, ampelidaceous, ampelideous, ampelite, ampelitic, ampelographist, ampelography, ampelograpny, ampelopsidin, ampelopsin, ampelopsis, ampelotherapy, amper, amperage, amperages, ampere, amperemeter, amperes, amperometer, amperometric, ampersand, ampersand's, ampersands, ampery, amphanthia, amphanthium, ampheclexis, ampherotokous, ampherotoky, amphetamine, amphetamines, amphi, amphiarthrodial, amphiarthroses, amphiarthrosis, amphiaster, amphib, amphibali, amphibalus, amphibia, amphibial, amphibian, amphibian's, amphibians, amphibichnite, amphibiety, amphibiological, amphibiology, amphibion, amphibiontic, amphibiotic, amphibious, amphibiously, amphibiousness, amphibium, amphiblastic, amphiblastula, amphiblestritis, amphibole, amphiboles, amphibolia, amphibolic, amphibolies, amphiboliferous, amphiboline, amphibolite, amphibolitic, amphibological, amphibologically, amphibologies, amphibologism, amphibology, amphibolostylous, amphibolous, amphiboly, amphibrach, amphibrachic, amphibryous, amphicarpia, amphicarpic, amphicarpium, amphicarpogenous, amphicarpous, amphicarpus, amphicentric, amphichroic, amphichrom, amphichromatic, amphichrome, amphichromy, amphicoelian, amphicoelous, amphicome, amphicondylous, amphicrania, amphicreatinine, amphicribral, amphictyon, amphictyonian, amphictyonic, amphictyonies, amphictyons, amphictyony, amphicyrtic, amphicyrtous, amphicytula, amphid, amphide, amphidesmous, amphidetic, amphidiarthrosis, amphidiploid, amphidiploidy, amphidisc, amphidiscophoran, amphidisk, amphidromia, amphidromic, amphierotic, amphierotism, amphigaean, amphigam, amphigamous, amphigastria, amphigastrium, amphigastrula, amphigean, amphigen, amphigene, amphigenesis, amphigenetic, amphigenous, amphigenously, amphigonia, amphigonic, amphigonium, amphigonous, amphigony, amphigoric, amphigories, amphigory, amphigouri, amphigouris, amphikaryon, amphikaryotic, amphilogism, amphilogy, amphimacer, amphimictic, amphimictical, amphimictically, amphimixes, amphimixis, amphimorula, amphimorulae, amphineurous, amphinucleus, amphion, amphioxi, amphioxis, amphioxus, amphioxuses, amphipeptone, amphiphithyra, amphiphloic, amphiplatyan, amphiploid, amphiploidy, amphipneust, amphipneustic, amphipod, amphipoda, amphipodal, amphipodan, amphipodiform, amphipodous, amphipods, amphiprostylar, amphiprostyle, amphiprotic, amphipyrenin, amphirhinal, amphirhine, amphisarca, amphisbaena, amphisbaenae, amphisbaenas, amphisbaenian, amphisbaenic, amphisbaenid, amphisbaenoid, amphisbaenous, amphiscians, amphiscii, amphispermous, amphisporangiate, amphispore, amphistomatic, amphistome, amphistomoid, amphistomous, amphistylar, amphistylic, amphistyly, amphitene, amphithalami, amphithalamus, amphithalmi, amphitheater, amphitheater's, amphitheatered, amphitheaters, amphitheatral, amphitheatre, amphitheatric, amphitheatrical, amphitheatrically, amphitheccia, amphithecia, amphithecial, amphithecium, amphithect, amphithere, amphithura, amphithuron, amphithurons, amphithurthura, amphithyra, amphithyron, amphithyrons, amphitokal, amphitokous, amphitoky, amphitriaene, amphitricha, amphitrichate, amphitrichous, amphitrite, amphitron, amphitropal, amphitropous, amphitryon, amphiuma, amphivasal, amphivorous, amphodarch, amphodelite, amphodiplopia, amphogenic, amphogenous, amphogeny, ampholyte, ampholytic, amphopeptone, amphophil, amphophile, amphophilic, amphophilous, amphora, amphorae, amphoral, amphoras, amphore, amphorette, amphoric, amphoricity, amphoriloquy, amphoriskoi, amphoriskos, amphorophony, amphorous, amphoteric, amphotericin, ampicillin, ampitheater, ample, amplect, amplectant, ampleness, ampler, amplest, amplex, amplexation, amplexicaudate, amplexicaul, amplexicauline, amplexifoliate, amplexus, amplexuses, ampliate, ampliation, ampliative, application, amplicative, amplidyne, amplifiable, amplificate, amplification, amplifications, amplificative, amplificator, amplificatory, amplified, amplifier, amplifiers, amplifies, amplify, amplifying, amplitude, amplitude's, amplitudes, amplitudinous, amply, ampollosity, ampongue, ampoule, ampoule's, ampoules, amps, ampul, ampulate, ampulated, ampulating, ampule, ampules, ampulla, ampullaceous, ampullae, ampullar, ampullary, ampullate, ampullated, ampulliform, ampullitis, ampullosity, ampullula, ampullulae, ampuls, amputate, amputated, amputates, amputating, amputation, amputational, amputations, amputative, amputator, amputee, amputees, ampyces, ampyx, ampyxes, amra, amreeta, amreetas, amrelle, amrit, amrita, amritas, amsath, amsel, amsonia, amsterdam, amt, amtman, amtmen, amtrac, amtrack, amtracks, amtracs, amtrak, amu, amuck, amucks, amugis, amuguis, amula, amulae, amulas, amulet, amuletic, amulets, amulla, amunam, amurca, amurcosity, amurcous, amus, amusable, amuse, amused, amusedly, amusee, amusement, amusement's, amusements, amuser, amusers, amuses, amusette, amusia, amusias, amusing, amusingly, amusingness, amusive, amusively, amusiveness, amutter, amuyon, amuyong, amuze, amuzzle, amvis, amy, amyatonic, amyctic, amydon, amyelencephalia, amyelencephalic, amyelencephalous, amyelia, amyelic, amyelinic, amyelonic, amyelotrophy, amyelous, amygdal, amygdala, amygdalaceous, amygdalae, amygdalase, amygdalate, amygdale, amygdalectomy, amygdales, amygdalic, amygdaliferous, amygdaliform, amygdalin, amygdaline, amygdalinic, amygdalitis, amygdaloid, amygdaloidal, amygdalolith, amygdaloncus, amygdalopathy, amygdalothripsis, amygdalotome, amygdalotomy, amygdonitrile, amygdophenin, amygdule, amygdules, amyl, amylaceous, amylamine, amylan, amylase, amylases, amylate, amylemia, amylene, amylenes, amylenol, amylic, amylidene, amyliferous, amylin, amylo, amylocellulose, amyloclastic, amylocoagulase, amylodextrin, amylodyspepsia, amylogen, amylogenesis, amylogenic, amylogens, amylohydrolysis, amylohydrolytic, amyloid, amyloidal, amyloidoses, amyloidosis, amyloids, amyloleucite, amylolysis, amylolytic, amylom, amylome, amylometer, amylon, amylopectin, amylophagia, amylophosphate, amylophosphoric, amyloplast, amyloplastic, amyloplastid, amylopsase, amylopsin, amylose, amyloses, amylosis, amylosynthesis, amyls, amylum, amylums, amyluria, amynodont, amyosthenia, amyosthenic, amyotaxia, amyotonia, amyotrophia, amyotrophic, amyotrophy, amyous, amyrin, amyris, amyrol, amyroot, amyxorrhea, amyxorrhoea, amzel, an, an'a, an't, ana, anabaena, anabaenas, anabantid, anabaptism, anabaptist, anabaptist's, anabaptists, anabaptize, anabaptized, anabaptizing, anabas, anabases, anabasin, anabasine, anabasis, anabasse, anabata, anabathmoi, anabathmos, anabathrum, anabatic, anaberoga, anabia, anabibazon, anabiosis, anabiotic, anableps, anablepses, anabo, anabohitsite, anabolic, anabolin, anabolism, anabolite, anabolitic, anabolize, anaboly, anabong, anabranch, anabrosis, anabrotic, anacahuita, anacahuite, anacalypsis, anacampsis, anacamptic, anacamptically, anacamptics, anacamptometer, anacanth, anacanthine, anacanthous, anacara, anacard, anacardiaceous, anacardic, anacatadidymus, anacatharsis, anacathartic, anacephalaeosis, anacephalize, anacharis, anachoret, anachorism, anachromasis, anachronic, anachronical, anachronically, anachronism, anachronism's, anachronismatical, anachronisms, anachronist, anachronistic, anachronistical, anachronistically, anachronize, anachronous, anachronously, anachueta, anacid, anacidity, anack, anaclasis, anaclastic, anaclastics, anaclete, anacletica, anacleticum, anaclinal, anaclisis, anaclitic, anacoenoses, anacoenosis, anacolutha, anacoluthia, anacoluthic, anacoluthically, anacoluthon, anacoluthons, anacoluttha, anaconda, anacondas, anacoustic, anacreontic, anacrisis, anacrogynae, anacrogynous, anacromyodian, anacrotic, anacrotism, anacruses, anacrusis, anacrustic, anacrustically, anaculture, anacusia, anacusic, anacusis, anadem, anadems, anadenia, anadesm, anadicrotic, anadicrotism, anadidymus, anadiplosis, anadipsia, anadipsic, anadrom, anadromous, anaematosis, anaemia, anaemias, anaemic, anaemotropy, anaeretic, anaerobation, anaerobe, anaerobes, anaerobia, anaerobian, anaerobic, anaerobically, anaerobies, anaerobion, anaerobiont, anaerobiosis, anaerobiotic, anaerobiotically, anaerobious, anaerobism, anaerobium, anaerophyte, anaeroplastic, anaeroplasty, anaesthatic, anaesthesia, anaesthesiant, anaesthesiologist, anaesthesiology, anaesthesis, anaesthetic, anaesthetically, anaesthetics, anaesthetist, anaesthetization, anaesthetize, anaesthetized, anaesthetizer, anaesthetizing, anaesthyl, anaetiological, anagalactic, anagap, anagenesis, anagenetic, anagenetical, anagennesis, anagep, anagignoskomena, anaglyph, anaglyphic, anaglyphical, anaglyphics, anaglyphoscope, anaglyphs, anaglyphy, anaglypta, anaglyptic, anaglyptical, anaglyptics, anaglyptograph, anaglyptographic, anaglyptography, anaglypton, anagnorises, anagnorisis, anagnost, anagnostes, anagoge, anagoges, anagogic, anagogical, anagogically, anagogics, anagogies, anagogy, anagram, anagram's, anagrammatic, anagrammatical, anagrammatically, anagrammatise, anagrammatised, anagrammatising, anagrammatism, anagrammatist, anagrammatization, anagrammatize, anagrammatized, anagrammatizing, anagrammed, anagramming, anagrams, anagraph, anagua, anagyrin, anagyrine, anahao, anahau, anaheim, anakinesis, anakinetic, anakinetomer, anakinetomeric, anakoluthia, anakrousis, anaktoron, anal, analabos, analagous, analav, analcime, analcimes, analcimic, analcimite, analcite, analcites, analcitite, analecta, analectic, analects, analemma, analemmas, analemmata, analemmatic, analepses, analepsis, analepsy, analeptic, analeptical, analgen, analgene, analgesia, analgesic, analgesics, analgesis, analgesist, analgetic, analgia, analgias, analgic, analgize, analities, anality, analkalinity, anallagmatic, anallagmatis, anallantoic, anallantoidean, anallergic, anally, analog, analoga, analogal, analogia, analogic, analogical, analogically, analogicalness, analogice, analogies, analogion, analogions, analogise, analogised, analogising, analogism, analogist, analogistic, analogize, analogized, analogizing, analogon, analogous, analogously, analogousness, analogs, analogue, analogue's, analogues, analogy, analogy's, analphabet, analphabete, analphabetic, analphabetical, analphabetism, analysability, analysable, analysand, analysands, analysation, analyse, analysed, analyser, analysers, analyses, analysing, analysis, analyst, analyst's, analysts, analyt, analytic, analytical, analytically, analyticities, analyticity, analytics, analytique, analyzability, analyzable, analyzation, analyze, analyzed, analyzer, analyzers, analyzes, analyzing, anam, anama, anamesite, anametadromous, anamirtin, anamite, anammonid, anammonide, anamneses, anamnesis, anamnestic, anamnestically, anamnionic, anamniote, anamniotic, anamorphic, anamorphism, anamorphoscope, anamorphose, anamorphoses, anamorphosis, anamorphote, anamorphous, anan, anana, ananaplas, ananaples, ananas, ananda, anandrarious, anandria, anandrious, anandrous, ananepionic, anangioid, anangular, ananias, anankastic, ananke, anankes, ananter, anantherate, anantherous, ananthous, ananthropism, ananym, anapaest, anapaestic, anapaestical, anapaestically, anapaests, anapaganize, anapaite, anapanapa, anapeiratic, anapes, anapest, anapestic, anapestically, anapests, anaphalantiasis, anaphase, anaphases, anaphasic, anaphia, anaphora, anaphoral, anaphoras, anaphoria, anaphoric, anaphorical, anaphorically, anaphrodisia, anaphrodisiac, anaphroditic, anaphroditous, anaphylactic, anaphylactically, anaphylactin, anaphylactogen, anaphylactogenic, anaphylactoid, anaphylatoxin, anaphylaxis, anaphyte, anaplasia, anaplasis, anaplasm, anaplasmoses, anaplasmosis, anaplastic, anaplasty, anapleroses, anaplerosis, anaplerotic, anapnea, anapneic, anapnoeic, anapnograph, anapnoic, anapnometer, anapodeictic, anapophyses, anapophysial, anapophysis, anapsid, anapsidan, anapterygote, anapterygotism, anapterygotous, anaptotic, anaptychi, anaptychus, anaptyctic, anaptyctical, anaptyxes, anaptyxis, anaqua, anarcestean, anarch, anarchal, anarchial, anarchic, anarchical, anarchically, anarchies, anarchism, anarchist, anarchist's, anarchistic, anarchists, anarchize, anarcho, anarchoindividualist, anarchosocialist, anarchosyndicalism, anarchosyndicalist, anarchs, anarchy, anarcotin, anareta, anaretic, anaretical, anargyroi, anargyros, anarithia, anarithmia, anarthria, anarthric, anarthropod, anarthropodous, anarthrosis, anarthrous, anarthrously, anarthrousness, anartismos, anarya, anas, anasarca, anasarcas, anasarcous, anaschistic, anaseismic, anaspadias, anaspalin, anaspid, anastalsis, anastaltic, anastases, anastasimon, anastasimos, anastasis, anastate, anastatic, anastigmat, anastigmatic, anastomos, anastomose, anastomosed, anastomoses, anastomosing, anastomosis, anastomotic, anastrophe, anastrophy, anat, anatabine, anatase, anatases, anatexes, anatexis, anathem, anathema, anathemas, anathemata, anathematic, anathematical, anathematically, anathematisation, anathematise, anathematised, anathematiser, anathematising, anathematism, anathematization, anathematize, anathematized, anathematizer, anathematizes, anathematizing, anatheme, anathemize, anatifa, anatifae, anatifer, anatiferous, anatine, anatira, anatman, anatocism, anatolian, anatomic, anatomical, anatomically, anatomicals, anatomicobiological, anatomicochirurgical, anatomicomedical, anatomicopathologic, anatomicopathological, anatomicophysiologic, anatomicophysiological, anatomicosurgical, anatomies, anatomiless, anatomisable, anatomisation, anatomise, anatomised, anatomiser, anatomising, anatomism, anatomist, anatomists, anatomizable, anatomization, anatomize, anatomized, anatomizer, anatomizes, anatomizing, anatomopathologic, anatomopathological, anatomy, anatopism, anatosaurus, anatox, anatoxin, anatoxins, anatreptic, anatripsis, anatripsology, anatriptic, anatron, anatropal, anatropia, anatropous, anatta, anatto, anattos, anaudia, anaudic, anaunter, anaunters, anauxite, anaxagorean, anaxagorize, anaxial, anaximandrian, anaxon, anaxone, anay, anazoturia, anba, anbury, anc, ancestor, ancestor's, ancestorial, ancestorially, ancestors, ancestral, ancestrally, ancestress, ancestresses, ancestrial, ancestrian, ancestries, ancestry, anchietin, anchietine, anchieutectic, anchimonomineral, anchises, anchithere, anchitherioid, anchoic, anchor, anchorable, anchorage, anchorage's, anchorages, anchorate, anchored, anchorer, anchoress, anchoresses, anchoret, anchoretic, anchoretical, anchoretish, anchoretism, anchorets, anchorhold, anchoring, anchorite, anchorites, anchoritess, anchoritic, anchoritical, anchoritically, anchoritish, anchoritism, anchorless, anchorlike, anchorman, anchormen, anchors, anchorwise, anchory, anchoveta, anchovies, anchovy, anchusa, anchusas, anchusin, anchusine, anchusins, anchylose, anchylosed, anchylosing, anchylosis, anchylotic, ancien, ancience, anciency, anciennete, anciens, ancient, ancienter, ancientest, ancientism, anciently, ancientness, ancientry, ancients, ancienty, ancile, ancilia, ancilla, ancillae, ancillaries, ancillary, ancillas, ancille, ancipital, ancipitous, ancistrocladaceous, ancistrodon, ancistroid, ancle, ancodont, ancoly, ancome, ancon, ancona, anconad, anconagra, anconal, anconas, ancone, anconeal, anconei, anconeous, ancones, anconeus, anconitis, anconoid, ancony, ancor, ancora, ancoral, ancraophobia, ancre, ancress, ancresses, ancylopod, ancylose, ancylostome, ancylostomiasis, ancyroid, and, and/or, anda, andabata, andabatarian, andabatism, andalusite, andamenta, andamento, andamentos, andante, andantes, andantini, andantino, andantinos, andean, anders, anderson, anderun, andes, andesine, andesinite, andesite, andesites, andesitic, andesyte, andesytes, andia, anding, andirin, andirine, andiroba, andiron, andirons, andor, andorite, andoroba, andorra, andouille, andouillet, andouillette, andradite, andragogy, andranatomy, andrarchy, andre, andrena, andrenid, andrew, andrewartha, andrewsite, andric, andrite, androcentric, androcephalous, androcephalum, androclclinia, androcles, androclinia, androclinium, androclus, androconia, androconium, androcracy, androcratic, androcyte, androdioecious, androdioecism, androdynamous, androeccia, androecia, androecial, androecium, androgametangium, androgametophore, androgamone, androgen, androgenesis, androgenetic, androgenic, androgenous, androgens, androginous, androgone, androgonia, androgonial, androgonidium, androgonium, andrographolide, androgyn, androgynal, androgynary, androgyne, androgyneity, androgynia, androgynic, androgynies, androgynism, androgynous, androgynus, androgyny, android, androidal, androides, androids, androkinin, androl, androlepsia, androlepsy, andromache, andromania, andromed, andromeda, andromedotoxin, andromonoecious, andromonoecism, andromorphous, andron, andronitis, andropetalar, andropetalous, androphagous, androphobia, androphonomania, androphore, androphorous, androphorum, androphyll, androseme, androsin, androsphinges, androsphinx, androsphinxes, androsporangium, androspore, androsterone, androtauric, androtomy, ands, andvari, ane, anear, aneared, anearing, anears, aneath, anecdota, anecdotage, anecdotal, anecdotalism, anecdotalist, anecdotally, anecdote, anecdote's, anecdotes, anecdotic, anecdotical, anecdotically, anecdotist, anecdotists, anecdysis, anechoic, anelace, anelastic, anelasticity, anele, anelectric, anelectrode, anelectrotonic, anelectrotonus, aneled, aneles, aneling, anelytrous, anematize, anematized, anematizing, anematosis, anemia, anemias, anemic, anemically, anemious, anemobiagraph, anemochord, anemochore, anemochoric, anemochorous, anemoclastic, anemogram, anemograph, anemographic, anemographically, anemography, anemologic, anemological, anemology, anemometer, anemometer's, anemometers, anemometric, anemometrical, anemometrically, anemometrograph, anemometrographic, anemometrographically, anemometry, anemonal, anemone, anemones, anemonin, anemonol, anemony, anemopathy, anemophile, anemophilous, anemophily, anemoscope, anemoses, anemosis, anemotactic, anemotaxis, anemotropic, anemotropism, anencephalia, anencephalic, anencephalotrophia, anencephalous, anencephalus, anencephaly, anend, anenergia, anenst, anent, anenterous, anepia, anepigraphic, anepigraphous, anepiploic, anepithymia, anerethisia, aneretic, anergia, anergias, anergic, anergies, anergy, anerly, aneroid, aneroidograph, aneroids, anerotic, anerythroplasia, anerythroplastic, anes, anesis, anesone, anesthesia, anesthesiant, anesthesimeter, anesthesiologies, anesthesiologist, anesthesiologists, anesthesiology, anesthesiometer, anesthesis, anesthetic, anesthetic's, anesthetically, anesthetics, anesthetist, anesthetists, anesthetization, anesthetize, anesthetized, anesthetizer, anesthetizes, anesthetizing, anesthyl, anestri, anestrous, anestrus, anet, anethene, anethol, anethole, anetholes, anethols, anetic, anetiological, aneuch, aneuploid, aneuploidy, aneuria, aneuric, aneurilemmic, aneurin, aneurine, aneurism, aneurismal, aneurismally, aneurismatic, aneurisms, aneurysm, aneurysmal, aneurysmally, aneurysmatic, aneurysms, anew, anfeeld, anfract, anfractuose, anfractuosity, anfractuous, anfractuousness, anfracture, anga, angakok, angakoks, angakut, angaralite, angareb, angareeb, angarep, angaria, angarias, angariation, angaries, angary, angas, angekkok, angekok, angekut, angel, angel's, angelate, angeldom, angeleen, angeles, angelet, angeleyes, angelfish, angelfishes, angelhood, angelic, angelica, angelical, angelically, angelicalness, angelicas, angelicic, angelicize, angelicness, angelico, angelim, angelin, angelina, angeline, angelinformal, angelique, angelito, angelize, angelized, angelizing, angellike, angelocracy, angelographer, angelolater, angelolatry, angelologic, angelological, angelology, angelomachy, angelon, angelophanic, angelophany, angelot, angels, angelship, angelus, angeluses, anger, angered, angering, angerless, angerly, angers, angevin, angeyok, angia, angiasthenia, angico, angiectasis, angiectopia, angiemphraxis, angiitis, angild, angili, angilo, angina, anginal, anginas, anginiform, anginoid, anginophobia, anginose, anginous, angioasthenia, angioataxia, angioblast, angioblastic, angiocardiographic, angiocardiographies, angiocardiography, angiocarditis, angiocarp, angiocarpian, angiocarpic, angiocarpous, angiocarpy, angiocavernous, angiocholecystitis, angiocholitis, angiochondroma, angioclast, angiocyst, angiodermatitis, angiodiascopy, angioelephantiasis, angiofibroma, angiogenesis, angiogenic, angiogeny, angioglioma, angiogram, angiograph, angiographic, angiography, angiohemophilia, angiohyalinosis, angiohydrotomy, angiohypertonia, angiohypotonia, angioid, angiokeratoma, angiokinesis, angiokinetic, angioleucitis, angiolipoma, angiolith, angiology, angiolymphitis, angiolymphoma, angioma, angiomalacia, angiomas, angiomata, angiomatosis, angiomatous, angiomegaly, angiometer, angiomyocardiac, angiomyoma, angiomyosarcoma, angioneoplasm, angioneurosis, angioneurotic, angionoma, angionosis, angioparalysis, angioparalytic, angioparesis, angiopathy, angiophorous, angioplany, angioplasty, angioplerosis, angiopoietic, angiopressure, angiorrhagia, angiorrhaphy, angiorrhea, angiorrhexis, angiosarcoma, angiosclerosis, angiosclerotic, angioscope, angiosis, angiospasm, angiospastic, angiosperm, angiospermal, angiospermatous, angiospermic, angiospermous, angiosperms, angiosporous, angiostegnosis, angiostenosis, angiosteosis, angiostomize, angiostomy, angiostrophy, angiosymphysis, angiotasis, angiotelectasia, angiotenosis, angiotensin, angiotensinase, angiothlipsis, angiotome, angiotomy, angiotonase, angiotonic, angiotonin, angiotribe, angiotripsy, angiotrophic, angiport, angkhak, anglaise, angle, angleberry, angled, angledog, angledozer, anglehook, anglemeter, anglepod, anglepods, angler, anglers, angles, anglesite, anglesmith, angletouch, angletwitch, anglewing, anglewise, angleworm, angleworms, angliae, anglian, anglians, anglican, anglicanism, anglicanisms, anglicans, anglice, anglicisation, anglicism, anglicisms, anglicist, anglicization, anglicize, anglicized, anglicizes, anglicizing, anglify, anglimaniac, angling, anglings, anglish, anglo, angloid, angloman, anglomania, anglophil, anglophile, anglophiles, anglophilia, anglophiliac, anglophilic, anglophilism, anglophily, anglophobe, anglophobes, anglophobia, anglophobic, anglos, ango, angoise, angola, angolan, angolans, angolar, angor, angora, angoras, angostura, angrier, angriest, angrily, angriness, angrite, angry, angst, angster, angstrom, angstroms, angsts, anguid, anguiform, anguille, anguilliform, anguilloid, anguillule, anguine, anguineal, anguineous, anguiped, anguis, anguish, anguished, anguishes, anguishful, anguishing, anguishous, anguishously, angula, angular, angulare, angularia, angularities, angularity, angularization, angularize, angularly, angularness, angulate, angulated, angulately, angulateness, angulates, angulating, angulation, angulatogibbous, angulatosinuous, angule, anguliferous, angulinerved, angulodentate, angulometer, angulose, angulosity, angulosplenial, angulous, angulus, anguria, angus, anguses, angust, angustate, angustia, angusticlave, angustifoliate, angustifolious, angustirostrate, angustisellate, angustiseptal, angustiseptate, angustura, angwantibo, angwich, anhaematopoiesis, anhaematosis, anhaemolytic, anhalamine, anhaline, anhalonidine, anhalonin, anhalonine, anhalouidine, anhang, anharmonic, anhedonia, anhedonic, anhedral, anhedron, anhelation, anhele, anhelose, anhelous, anhematopoiesis, anhematosis, anhemitonic, anhemolytic, anhidrosis, anhidrotic, anhima, anhinga, anhingas, anhistic, anhistous, anhungered, anhungry, anhyd, anhydraemia, anhydraemic, anhydrate, anhydrated, anhydrating, anhydration, anhydremia, anhydremic, anhydric, anhydride, anhydrides, anhydridization, anhydridize, anhydrite, anhydrization, anhydrize, anhydroglocose, anhydromyelia, anhydrosis, anhydrotic, anhydrous, anhydrously, anhydroxime, anhysteretic, ani, anicca, aniconic, aniconism, anicular, anicut, anidian, anidiomatic, anidiomatical, anidrosis, aniente, anientise, anigh, anight, anights, anil, anilao, anilau, anile, anileness, anilic, anilid, anilide, anilidic, anilidoxime, aniliid, anilin, anilinctus, aniline, anilines, anilingus, anilinism, anilino, anilinophile, anilinophilous, anilins, anilities, anility, anilla, anilopyrin, anilopyrine, anils, anim, anima, animability, animable, animableness, animacule, animadversal, animadversion, animadversional, animadversions, animadversive, animadversiveness, animadvert, animadverted, animadverter, animadverting, animadverts, animal, animal's, animala, animalcula, animalculae, animalcular, animalcule, animalcules, animalculine, animalculism, animalculist, animalculous, animalculum, animalhood, animalian, animalic, animalier, animalillio, animalisation, animalise, animalised, animalish, animalising, animalism, animalist, animalistic, animalities, animality, animalivore, animalivorous, animalization, animalize, animalized, animalizing, animallike, animally, animalness, animals, animando, animant, animas, animastic, animastical, animate, animate, animated, animatedly, animately, animateness, animater, animaters, animates, animating, animatingly, animation, animations, animatism, animatist, animatistic, animative, animato, animatograph, animator, animator's, animators, anime, animes, animetta, animi, animikite, animine, animis, animism, animisms, animist, animistic, animists, animize, animized, animo, animose, animoseness, animosities, animosity, animoso, animotheism, animous, animus, animuses, anion, anion's, anionic, anionically, anionics, anions, aniridia, anis, anisado, anisal, anisalcohol, anisaldehyde, anisaldoxime, anisamide, anisandrous, anisanilide, anisanthous, anisate, anisated, anischuria, anise, aniseed, aniseeds, aniseikonia, aniseikonic, aniselike, aniseroot, anises, anisette, anisettes, anisic, anisidin, anisidine, anisidino, anisil, anisilic, anisobranchiate, anisocarpic, anisocarpous, anisocercal, anisochromatic, anisochromia, anisocoria, anisocotyledonous, anisocotyly, anisocratic, anisocycle, anisocytosis, anisodactyl, anisodactyle, anisodactylic, anisodactylous, anisodont, anisogamete, anisogametes, anisogametic, anisogamic, anisogamous, anisogamy, anisogenous, anisogeny, anisognathism, anisognathous, anisogynous, anisoiconia, anisoin, anisokonia, anisol, anisole, anisoles, anisoleucocytosis, anisomelia, anisomelus, anisomeric, anisomerous, anisometric, anisometrope, anisometropia, anisometropic, anisomyarian, anisomyodian, anisomyodous, anisopetalous, anisophyllous, anisophylly, anisopia, anisopleural, anisopleurous, anisopod, anisopodal, anisopodous, anisopogonous, anisopteran, anisopterous, anisosepalous, anisospore, anisostaminous, anisostemonous, anisosthenic, anisostichous, anisostomous, anisotonic, anisotropal, anisotrope, anisotropic, anisotropical, anisotropically, anisotropies, anisotropism, anisotropous, anisotropy, anisoyl, anisum, anisuria, anisyl, anisylidene, anither, anitinstitutionalism, anitos, anitrogenous, anjan, ankara, ankaramite, ankaratrite, ankee, anker, ankerhold, ankerite, ankerites, ankh, ankhs, ankle, ankle's, anklebone, anklebones, anklejack, ankles, anklet, anklets, anklong, anklung, ankus, ankuses, ankush, ankusha, ankushes, ankylenteron, ankyloblepharon, ankylocheilia, ankylodactylia, ankylodontia, ankyloglossia, ankylomele, ankylomerism, ankylophobia, ankylopodia, ankylopoietic, ankyloproctia, ankylorrhinia, ankylos, ankylosaur, ankylosaurus, ankylose, ankylosed, ankyloses, ankylosing, ankylosis, ankylostoma, ankylostomiasis, ankylotia, ankylotic, ankylotome, ankylotomy, ankylurethria, ankyroid, anlace, anlaces, anlage, anlagen, anlages, anlas, anlases, anlaut, anlaute, anlet, anlia, anmia, ann, anna, annabergite, annal, annale, annalia, annaline, annalism, annalist, annalistic, annalistically, annalists, annalize, annals, annaly, annamese, annapolis, annary, annas, annat, annates, annats, annatto, annattos, anne, anneal, annealed, annealer, annealers, annealing, anneals, annect, annectant, annectent, annection, annelid, annelida, annelidan, annelidian, annelidous, annelids, annelism, anneloid, annerodite, annerre, annet, annex, annexa, annexable, annexal, annexation, annexational, annexationism, annexationist, annexations, annexe, annexed, annexer, annexes, annexing, annexion, annexionist, annexitis, annexive, annexment, annexure, anni, annicut, annidalin, annie, annihil, annihilability, annihilable, annihilate, annihilated, annihilates, annihilating, annihilation, annihilationism, annihilationist, annihilationistic, annihilationistical, annihilative, annihilator, annihilators, annihilatory, annist, annite, anniv, anniversalily, anniversaries, anniversarily, anniversariness, anniversary, anniversary's, anniverse, anno, annodated, annominate, annomination, annona, annonaceous, annonce, annot, annotate, annotated, annotater, annotates, annotating, annotation, annotations, annotative, annotatively, annotativeness, annotator, annotators, annotatory, annotine, annotinous, annotto, announce, announceable, announced, announcement, announcement's, announcements, announcer, announcers, announces, announcing, annoy, annoyance, annoyance's, annoyancer, annoyances, annoyed, annoyer, annoyers, annoyful, annoying, annoyingly, annoyingness, annoyment, annoyous, annoyously, annoys, annual, annualist, annualize, annualized, annually, annuals, annuary, annuation, annueler, annueller, annuent, annuisance, annuitant, annuitants, annuities, annuity, annul, annular, annularity, annularly, annulary, annulata, annulate, annulated, annulately, annulation, annulations, annule, annuler, annulet, annulets, annulettee, annuli, annulism, annullable, annullate, annullation, annulled, annuller, annulli, annulling, annulment, annulment's, annulments, annuloid, annuloida, annulosa, annulosan, annulose, annuls, annulus, annuluses, annum, annumerate, annunciable, annunciade, annunciate, annunciated, annunciates, annunciating, annunciation, annunciations, annunciative, annunciator, annunciators, annunciatory, annus, anoa, anoas, anobing, anocarpous, anocathartic, anociassociation, anociation, anocithesia, anococcygeal, anodal, anodally, anode, anode's, anodendron, anodes, anodic, anodically, anodine, anodization, anodize, anodized, anodizes, anodizing, anodon, anodontia, anodos, anodyne, anodynes, anodynia, anodynic, anodynous, anoegenetic, anoesia, anoesis, anoestrous, anoestrum, anoestrus, anoetic, anogenic, anogenital, anoia, anoil, anoine, anoint, anointed, anointer, anointers, anointing, anointment, anointments, anoints, anole, anoles, anoli, anolian, anolyte, anolytes, anomal, anomalies, anomaliflorous, anomaliped, anomalipod, anomalism, anomalist, anomalistic, anomalistical, anomalistically, anomalocephalus, anomaloflorous, anomalogonatous, anomalonomy, anomaloscope, anomalotrophy, anomalous, anomalously, anomalousness, anomalure, anomaly, anomaly's, anomer, anomia, anomic, anomie, anomies, anomite, anomocarpous, anomodont, anomoeomery, anomophyllous, anomorhomboid, anomorhomboidal, anomouran, anomphalous, anomural, anomuran, anomurous, anomy, anon, anonaceous, anonad, anonang, anoncillo, anonol, anonychia, anonym, anonyma, anonyme, anonymities, anonymity, anonymous, anonymously, anonymousness, anonyms, anonymuncule, anoopsia, anoopsias, anoperineal, anophele, anopheles, anopheline, anophoria, anophthalmia, anophthalmos, anophyte, anopia, anopias, anopisthograph, anopisthographic, anopisthographically, anoplocephalic, anoplonemertean, anoplothere, anoplotherioid, anoplotheroid, anopluriform, anopsia, anopsias, anopsy, anopubic, anorak, anoraks, anorchi, anorchia, anorchism, anorchous, anorchus, anorectal, anorectic, anorectous, anoretic, anorexia, anorexiant, anorexias, anorexic, anorexics, anorexies, anorexigenic, anorexy, anorgana, anorganic, anorganism, anorganology, anormal, anormality, anorn, anorogenic, anorth, anorthic, anorthite, anorthitic, anorthitite, anorthoclase, anorthographic, anorthographical, anorthographically, anorthography, anorthophyre, anorthopia, anorthoscope, anorthose, anorthosite, anoscope, anoscopy, anosmatic, anosmia, anosmias, anosmic, anosognosia, anosphrasia, anosphresia, anospinal, anostosis, anoterite, another, another's, anotherguess, anotherkins, anotia, anotropia, anotta, anotto, anotus, anounou, anour, anoura, anoure, anourous, anova, anovesical, anovulant, anovular, anovulatory, anoxaemia, anoxaemic, anoxemia, anoxemias, anoxemic, anoxia, anoxias, anoxic, anoxidative, anoxybiosis, anoxybiotic, anoxyscope, anquera, anre, ans, ansa, ansae, ansar, ansarian, ansate, ansated, ansation, anschauung, anschluss, anserated, anserin, anserine, anserines, anserous, ansi, anspessade, anstoss, anstosse, ansu, ansulate, answer, answerability, answerable, answerableness, answerably, answered, answerer, answerers, answering, answeringly, answerless, answerlessly, answers, ant, ant's, anta, antacid, antacids, antacrid, antadiform, antae, antaean, antaeus, antagonisable, antagonisation, antagonise, antagonised, antagonising, antagonism, antagonisms, antagonist, antagonist's, antagonistic, antagonistical, antagonistically, antagonists, antagonizable, antagonization, antagonize, antagonized, antagonizer, antagonizes, antagonizing, antagony, antal, antalgesic, antalgic, antalgics, antalgol, antalkali, antalkalies, antalkaline, antalkalis, antambulacral, antanacathartic, antanaclasis, antanagoge, antanemic, antapex, antapexes, antaphrodisiac, antaphroditic, antapices, antapocha, antapodosis, antapology, antapoplectic, antarala, antaranga, antarchism, antarchist, antarchistic, antarchistical, antarchy, antarctic, antarctica, antarctical, antarctically, antares, antarthritic, antas, antasphyctic, antasthenic, antasthmatic, antatrophic, antbird, antdom, ante, anteact, anteal, anteambulate, anteambulation, anteater, anteater's, anteaters, antebaptismal, antebath, antebellum, antebrachia, antebrachial, antebrachium, antebridal, antecabinet, antecaecal, antecardium, antecavern, antecedal, antecedaneous, antecedaneously, antecede, anteceded, antecedence, antecedency, antecedent, antecedent's, antecedental, antecedently, antecedents, antecedes, anteceding, antecell, antecessor, antechamber, antechambers, antechapel, antechoir, antechoirs, antechurch, anteclassical, antecloset, antecolic, antecommunion, anteconsonantal, antecornu, antecourt, antecoxal, antecubital, antecurvature, anted, antedate, antedated, antedates, antedating, antedawn, antediluvial, antediluvially, antediluvian, antedonin, antedorsal, anteed, antefact, antefebrile, antefix, antefixa, antefixal, antefixes, anteflected, anteflexed, anteflexion, antefurca, antefurcae, antefurcal, antefuture, antegarden, antegrade, antehall, antehistoric, antehuman, antehypophysis, anteing, anteinitial, antejentacular, antejudiciary, antejuramentum, antelabium, antelation, antelegal, antelocation, antelope, antelope's, antelopes, antelopian, antelopine, antelucan, antelude, anteluminary, antemarginal, antemarital, antemask, antemedial, antemeridian, antemetallic, antemetic, antemillennial, antemingent, antemortal, antemortem, antemundane, antemural, antenarial, antenatal, antenatalitial, antenati, antenatus, antenave, antenna, antenna's, antennae, antennal, antennariid, antennary, antennas, antennate, antennifer, antenniferous, antenniform, antennula, antennular, antennulary, antennule, antenodal, antenoon, antenumber, antenuptial, anteoccupation, anteocular, anteopercle, anteoperculum, anteorbital, antepagment, antepagmenta, antepagments, antepalatal, antepartum, antepaschal, antepaschel, antepast, antepasts, antepatriarchal, antepectoral, antepectus, antependia, antependium, antependiums, antepenuit, antepenult, antepenultima, antepenultimate, antepenults, antephialtic, antepileptic, antepirrhema, antepone, anteporch, anteport, anteportico, anteporticoes, anteporticos, anteposition, anteposthumous, anteprandial, antepredicament, antepredicamental, antepreterit, antepretonic, anteprohibition, anteprostate, anteprostatic, antepyretic, antequalm, antereformation, antereformational, anteresurrection, anterethic, anterevolutional, anterevolutionary, antergic, anteri, anteriad, anterin, anterior, anteriority, anteriorly, anteriorness, anteriors, anterioyancer, anteroclusion, anterodorsal, anteroexternal, anterofixation, anteroflexion, anterofrontal, anterograde, anteroinferior, anterointerior, anterointernal, anterolateral, anterolaterally, anteromedial, anteromedian, anteroom, anterooms, anteroparietal, anteroposterior, anteroposteriorly, anteropygal, anterospinal, anterosuperior, anteroventral, anteroventrally, antes, antescript, antesignani, antesignanus, antespring, antestature, antesternal, antesternum, antesunrise, antesuperior, antetemple, antethem, antetype, antetypes, antevenient, anteversion, antevert, anteverted, anteverting, anteverts, antevocalic, antewar, anthdia, anthecological, anthecologist, anthecology, anthela, anthelae, anthelia, anthelices, anthelion, anthelions, anthelix, anthelminthic, anthelmintic, anthem, anthem's, anthema, anthemas, anthemata, anthemed, anthemene, anthemia, antheming, anthemion, anthemis, anthems, anthemwise, anthemy, anther, antheral, antherid, antheridia, antheridial, antheridiophore, antheridium, antherids, antheriferous, antheriform, antherine, antherless, antherogenous, antheroid, antherozoid, antherozoidal, antherozooid, antherozooidal, anthers, antheses, anthesis, anthesterin, anthesterol, antheximeter, anthill, anthills, anthine, anthobian, anthobiology, anthocarp, anthocarpous, anthocephalous, anthocerote, anthochlor, anthochlorine, anthoclinium, anthocyan, anthocyanidin, anthocyanin, anthodia, anthodium, anthoecological, anthoecologist, anthoecology, anthogenesis, anthogenetic, anthogenous, anthography, anthoid, anthokyan, anthol, antholite, anthological, anthologically, anthologies, anthologion, anthologise, anthologised, anthologising, anthologist, anthologists, anthologize, anthologized, anthologizer, anthologizes, anthologizing, anthology, antholysis, anthomania, anthomaniac, anthomedusan, anthomyiid, anthony, anthood, anthophagous, anthophagy, anthophile, anthophilian, anthophilous, anthophobia, anthophore, anthophorous, anthophyllite, anthophyllitic, anthophyte, anthorine, anthos, anthosiderite, anthotaxis, anthotaxy, anthotropic, anthotropism, anthoxanthin, anthozoa, anthozoan, anthozoic, anthozooid, anthozoon, anthracaemia, anthracemia, anthracene, anthraceniferous, anthraces, anthrachrysone, anthracia, anthracic, anthraciferous, anthracin, anthracite, anthracitic, anthracitiferous, anthracitious, anthracitism, anthracitization, anthracitous, anthracnose, anthracnosis, anthracocide, anthracoid, anthracolithic, anthracomancy, anthracomartian, anthracometer, anthracometric, anthraconecrosis, anthraconite, anthracosilicosis, anthracosis, anthracothere, anthracotic, anthracoxen, anthracyl, anthradiol, anthradiquinone, anthraflavic, anthragallol, anthrahydroquinone, anthralin, anthramin, anthramine, anthranil, anthranilate, anthranilic, anthranol, anthranone, anthranoyl, anthranyl, anthraphenone, anthrapurpurin, anthrapyridine, anthraquinol, anthraquinone, anthraquinonyl, anthrarufin, anthrasilicosis, anthratetrol, anthrathiophene, anthratriol, anthrax, anthraxolite, anthraxylon, anthribid, anthrohopobiological, anthroic, anthrol, anthrone, anthrop, anthrophore, anthropic, anthropical, anthropobiologist, anthropobiology, anthropocentric, anthropocentrically, anthropocentricity, anthropocentrism, anthropoclimatologist, anthropoclimatology, anthropocosmic, anthropodeoxycholic, anthropogenesis, anthropogenetic, anthropogenic, anthropogenist, anthropogenous, anthropogeny, anthropogeographer, anthropogeographic, anthropogeographical, anthropogeography, anthropoglot, anthropogony, anthropographic, anthropography, anthropoid, anthropoidal, anthropoidea, anthropoidean, anthropoids, anthropol, anthropolater, anthropolatric, anthropolatry, anthropolite, anthropolith, anthropolithic, anthropolitic, anthropologic, anthropological, anthropologically, anthropologies, anthropologist, anthropologist's, anthropologists, anthropology, anthropomancy, anthropomantic, anthropomantist, anthropometer, anthropometric, anthropometrical, anthropometrically, anthropometrist, anthropometry, anthropomophitism, anthropomorph, anthropomorphic, anthropomorphical, anthropomorphically, anthropomorphisation, anthropomorphise, anthropomorphised, anthropomorphising, anthropomorphism, anthropomorphisms, anthropomorphist, anthropomorphite, anthropomorphitic, anthropomorphitical, anthropomorphitism, anthropomorphization, anthropomorphize, anthropomorphized, anthropomorphizing, anthropomorphological, anthropomorphologically, anthropomorphology, anthropomorphosis, anthropomorphotheist, anthropomorphous, anthropomorphously, anthroponomical, anthroponomics, anthroponomist, anthroponomy, anthroponym, anthropopathia, anthropopathic, anthropopathically, anthropopathism, anthropopathite, anthropopathy, anthropophagi, anthropophagic, anthropophagical, anthropophaginian, anthropophagism, anthropophagist, anthropophagistic, anthropophagit, anthropophagite, anthropophagize, anthropophagous, anthropophagously, anthropophagus, anthropophagy, anthropophilous, anthropophobia, anthropophuism, anthropophuistic, anthropophysiography, anthropophysite, anthropopsychic, anthropopsychism, anthroposcopy, anthroposociologist, anthroposociology, anthroposomatology, anthroposophic, anthroposophical, anthroposophist, anthroposophy, anthropoteleoclogy, anthropoteleological, anthropotheism, anthropotheist, anthropotheistic, anthropotomical, anthropotomist, anthropotomy, anthropotoxin, anthropozoic, anthropurgic, anthroropolith, anthroxan, anthroxanic, anthryl, anthrylene, anththeridia, anthurium, anthypnotic, anthypophora, anthypophoretic, anti, antiabolitionist, antiabortion, antiabrasion, antiabrin, antiabsolutist, antiacid, antiadiaphorist, antiaditis, antiadministration, antiae, antiaesthetic, antiager, antiagglutinant, antiagglutinating, antiagglutination, antiagglutinative, antiagglutinin, antiaggression, antiaggressionist, antiaggressive, antiaggressively, antiaggressiveness, antiaircraft, antialbumid, antialbumin, antialbumose, antialcoholic, antialcoholism, antialcoholist, antialdoxime, antialexin, antialien, antiamboceptor, antiamusement, antiamylase, antianaphylactogen, antianaphylaxis, antianarchic, antianarchist, antiangular, antiannexation, antiannexationist, antianopheline, antianthrax, antianthropocentric, antianthropomorphism, antiantibody, antiantidote, antiantienzyme, antiantitoxin, antianxiety, antiaphrodisiac, antiaphthic, antiapoplectic, antiapostle, antiaquatic, antiar, antiarin, antiarins, antiaristocracies, antiaristocracy, antiaristocrat, antiaristocratic, antiaristocratical, antiaristocratically, antiarrhythmic, antiars, antiarthritic, antiascetic, antiasthmatic, antiastronomical, antiatheism, antiatheist, antiatheistic, antiatheistical, antiatheistically, antiatom, antiatoms, antiatonement, antiattrition, antiauthoritarian, antiauthoritarianism, antiautolysin, antiauxin, antibacchic, antibacchii, antibacchius, antibacterial, antibacteriolytic, antiballistic, antiballooner, antibalm, antibank, antibaryon, antibasilican, antibenzaldoxime, antiberiberin, antibias, antibibliolatry, antibigotry, antibilious, antibiont, antibiosis, antibiotic, antibiotically, antibiotics, antibishop, antiblack, antiblackism, antiblastic, antiblennorrhagic, antiblock, antiblue, antibodies, antibody, antiboss, antiboxing, antibrachial, antibreakage, antibridal, antibromic, antibubonic, antibug, antiburgher, antibusing, antic, antic's, antica, anticachectic, antical, anticalcimine, anticalculous, anticalligraphic, antically, anticamera, anticancer, anticancerous, anticapital, anticapitalism, anticapitalist, anticapitalistic, anticapitalistically, anticapitalists, anticar, anticardiac, anticardium, anticarious, anticarnivorous, anticaste, anticatalase, anticatalyst, anticatalytic, anticatalytically, anticatalyzer, anticatarrhal, anticathexis, anticathode, anticatholic, anticausotic, anticaustic, anticensorial, anticensorious, anticensoriously, anticensoriousness, anticensorship, anticentralism, anticentralist, anticentralization, anticephalalgic, anticeremonial, anticeremonialism, anticeremonialist, anticeremonially, anticeremonious, anticeremoniously, anticeremoniousness, antichamber, antichance, anticheater, antichlor, antichlorine, antichloristic, antichlorotic, anticholagogue, anticholinergic, anticholinesterase, antichoromanic, antichorus, antichreses, antichresis, antichretic, antichrist, antichristian, antichristianism, antichristianity, antichristianly, antichrists, antichrome, antichronical, antichronically, antichronism, antichthon, antichthones, antichurch, antichurchian, antichymosin, anticipant, anticipatable, anticipate, anticipated, anticipates, anticipating, anticipatingly, anticipation, anticipations, anticipative, anticipatively, anticipator, anticipatorily, anticipators, anticipatory, anticity, anticivic, anticivil, anticivilian, anticivism, anticize, antick, anticked, anticker, anticking, anticks, antickt, anticlactic, anticlassical, anticlassicalism, anticlassicalist, anticlassically, anticlassicalness, anticlassicism, anticlassicist, anticlastic, anticlergy, anticlerical, anticlericalism, anticlericalist, anticlimactic, anticlimactical, anticlimactically, anticlimax, anticlimaxes, anticlinal, anticline, anticlines, anticlinoria, anticlinorium, anticlnoria, anticlockwise, anticlogging, anticly, anticnemion, anticness, anticoagulan, anticoagulant, anticoagulants, anticoagulate, anticoagulating, anticoagulation, anticoagulative, anticoagulator, anticoagulin, anticodon, anticogitative, anticoincidence, anticold, anticolic, anticombination, anticomet, anticomment, anticommercial, anticommercialism, anticommercialist, anticommercialistic, anticommerciality, anticommercially, anticommercialness, anticommunism, anticommunist, anticommunistic, anticommunistical, anticommunistically, anticommunists, anticommutative, anticompetitive, anticomplement, anticomplementary, anticomplex, anticonceptionist, anticonductor, anticonfederationism, anticonfederationist, anticonfederative, anticonformist, anticonformities, anticonformity, anticonscience, anticonscription, anticonscriptive, anticonservatism, anticonservative, anticonservatively, anticonservativeness, anticonstitution, anticonstitutional, anticonstitutionalism, anticonstitutionalist, anticonstitutionally, anticontagion, anticontagionist, anticontagious, anticontagiously, anticontagiousness, anticonvellent, anticonvention, anticonventional, anticonventionalism, anticonventionalist, anticonventionally, anticonvulsant, anticonvulsive, anticor, anticorn, anticorona, anticorrosion, anticorrosive, anticorrosively, anticorrosiveness, anticorrosives, anticorset, anticosine, anticosmetic, anticosmetics, anticouncil, anticourt, anticourtier, anticous, anticovenanter, anticovenanting, anticreation, anticreational, anticreationism, anticreationist, anticreative, anticreatively, anticreativeness, anticreativity, anticreator, anticreep, anticreeper, anticreeping, anticrepuscular, anticrepuscule, anticrisis, anticritic, anticritical, anticritically, anticriticalness, anticritique, anticrochet, anticrotalic, anticryptic, anticryptically, antics, anticularia, anticult, anticum, anticus, anticyclic, anticyclical, anticyclically, anticyclogenesis, anticyclolysis, anticyclone, anticyclones, anticyclonic, anticyclonically, anticynic, anticynical, anticynically, anticynicism, anticytolysin, anticytotoxin, antidactyl, antidancing, antidecalogue, antideflation, antidemocracies, antidemocracy, antidemocrat, antidemocratic, antidemocratical, antidemocratically, antidemoniac, antidepressant, antidepressants, antidepressive, antiderivative, antidetonant, antidetonating, antidiabetic, antidiastase, antidicomarianite, antidictionary, antidiffuser, antidinic, antidiphtheria, antidiphtheric, antidiphtherin, antidiphtheritic, antidisciplinarian, antidisestablishmentarian, antidisestablishmentarianism, antidiuretic, antidivine, antidivorce, antidogmatic, antidogmatical, antidogmatically, antidogmatism, antidogmatist, antidomestic, antidomestically, antidominican, antidora, antidoron, antidotal, antidotally, antidotary, antidote, antidote's, antidoted, antidotes, antidotical, antidotically, antidoting, antidotism, antidraft, antidrag, antidromal, antidromic, antidromically, antidromous, antidromy, antidrug, antiduke, antidumping, antidynamic, antidynastic, antidynastical, antidynastically, antidynasty, antidyscratic, antidysenteric, antidysuric, antiecclesiastic, antiecclesiastical, antiecclesiastically, antiecclesiasticism, antiedemic, antieducation, antieducational, antieducationalist, antieducationally, antieducationist, antiegoism, antiegoist, antiegoistic, antiegoistical, antiegoistically, antiegotism, antiegotist, antiegotistic, antiegotistical, antiegotistically, antiejaculation, antielectron, antielectrons, antiemetic, antiemperor, antiempiric, antiempirical, antiempirically, antiempiricism, antiempiricist, antiendotoxin, antiendowment, antienergistic, antient, antienthusiasm, antienthusiast, antienthusiastic, antienthusiastically, antienvironmentalism, antienvironmentalist, antienvironmentalists, antienzymatic, antienzyme, antienzymic, antiepicenter, antiepileptic, antiepiscopal, antiepiscopist, antiepithelial, antierosion, antierosive, antierysipelas, antiestablishment, antiethnic, antieugenic, antievangelical, antievolution, antievolutional, antievolutionally, antievolutionary, antievolutionist, antievolutionistic, antiexpansion, antiexpansionism, antiexpansionist, antiexporting, antiexpressionism, antiexpressionist, antiexpressionistic, antiexpressive, antiexpressively, antiexpressiveness, antiextreme, antieyestrain, antiface, antifaction, antifame, antifanatic, antifascism, antifascist, antifascists, antifat, antifatigue, antifebrile, antifebrin, antifederal, antifederalism, antifederalist, antifelon, antifelony, antifeminism, antifeminist, antifeministic, antiferment, antifermentative, antiferroelectric, antiferromagnet, antiferromagnetic, antiferromagnetism, antifertility, antifertilizer, antifeudal, antifeudalism, antifeudalist, antifeudalistic, antifeudalization, antifibrinolysin, antifibrinolysis, antifideism, antifire, antiflash, antiflattering, antiflatulent, antiflux, antifoam, antifoaming, antifoggant, antifogmatic, antiforeign, antiforeignism, antiformant, antiformin, antifouler, antifouling, antifowl, antifreeze, antifreezes, antifreezing, antifriction, antifrictional, antifrost, antifundamentalism, antifundamentalist, antifungal, antifungin, antigalactagogue, antigalactic, antigambling, antiganting, antigay, antigen, antigen's, antigene, antigenes, antigenic, antigenically, antigenicity, antigens, antighostism, antigigmanic, antiglare, antiglobulin, antiglyoxalase, antignostic, antignostical, antigod, antigone, antigonococcic, antigonorrheic, antigorite, antigovernment, antigovernmental, antigovernmentally, antigraft, antigrammatical, antigrammatically, antigrammaticalness, antigraph, antigraphy, antigravitate, antigravitation, antigravitational, antigravitationally, antigravity, antigropelos, antigrowth, antiguggler, antigun, antigyrous, antihalation, antiharmonist, antihectic, antihelices, antihelix, antihelixes, antihelminthic, antihemagglutinin, antihemisphere, antihemoglobin, antihemolysin, antihemolytic, antihemophilic, antihemorrhagic, antihemorrheidal, antihero, antiheroes, antiheroic, antiheroism, antiheterolysin, antihidrotic, antihierarchal, antihierarchic, antihierarchical, antihierarchically, antihierarchies, antihierarchism, antihierarchist, antihierarchy, antihistamine, antihistamines, antihistaminic, antihistorical, antiholiday, antihormone, antihuff, antihum, antihuman, antihumanism, antihumanist, antihumanistic, antihumbuggist, antihunting, antihydrophobic, antihydropic, antihydropin, antihygienic, antihygienically, antihylist, antihypertensive, antihypertensives, antihypnotic, antihypnotically, antihypochondriac, antihypophora, antihysteric, antiinflammatories, antiinflammatory, antiinstitutionalist, antiinstitutionalists, antiinsurrectionally, antiinsurrectionists, antijam, antikathode, antikenotoxin, antiketogen, antiketogenesis, antiketogenic, antikinase, antiking, antikings, antiknock, antiknocks, antilabor, antilaborist, antilacrosse, antilacrosser, antilactase, antilapsarian, antilapse, antileague, antileak, antileft, antilegalist, antilegomena, antilemic, antilens, antilepsis, antileptic, antilepton, antilethargic, antileukemic, antileveling, antilevelling, antiliberal, antiliberalism, antiliberalist, antiliberalistic, antiliberally, antiliberalness, antiliberals, antilibration, antilife, antilift, antilipase, antilipoid, antiliquor, antilithic, antilitter, antiliturgic, antiliturgical, antiliturgically, antiliturgist, antiliturgy, antilles, antilobium, antiloemic, antilog, antilogarithm, antilogarithmic, antilogarithms, antilogic, antilogical, antilogies, antilogism, antilogistic, antilogistically, antilogous, antilogs, antilogy, antiloimic, antilopine, antiloquy, antilottery, antiluetic, antiluetin, antilynching, antilysin, antilysis, antilyssic, antilytic, antimacassar, antimacassars, antimachination, antimachine, antimachinery, antimagistratical, antimagnetic, antimalaria, antimalarial, antimale, antimallein, antiman, antimaniac, antimaniacal, antimark, antimartyr, antimask, antimasker, antimasks, antimason, antimasque, antimasquer, antimasquerade, antimaterialism, antimaterialist, antimaterialistic, antimaterialistically, antimatrimonial, antimatrimonialist, antimatter, antimechanism, antimechanist, antimechanistic, antimechanistically, antimechanization, antimediaeval, antimediaevalism, antimediaevalist, antimediaevally, antimedical, antimedically, antimedication, antimedicative, antimedicine, antimedieval, antimedievalism, antimedievalist, antimedievally, antimelancholic, antimellin, antimeningococcic, antimensia, antimension, antimensium, antimephitic, antimere, antimeres, antimerger, antimerging, antimeric, antimerism, antimeristem, antimesia, antimeson, antimetabole, antimetabolite, antimetathesis, antimetathetic, antimeter, antimethod, antimethodic, antimethodical, antimethodically, antimethodicalness, antimetrical, antimetropia, antimetropic, antimiasmatic, antimicrobial, antimicrobic, antimilitarism, antimilitarist, antimilitaristic, antimilitaristically, antimilitary, antiministerial, antiministerialist, antiministerially, antiminsia, antiminsion, antimiscegenation, antimissile, antimission, antimissionary, antimissioner, antimitotic, antimixing, antimnemonic, antimodel, antimodern, antimodernism, antimodernist, antimodernistic, antimodernization, antimodernly, antimodernness, antimonarch, antimonarchal, antimonarchally, antimonarchial, antimonarchic, antimonarchical, antimonarchically, antimonarchicalness, antimonarchism, antimonarchist, antimonarchistic, antimonarchists, antimonarchy, antimonate, antimonial, antimoniate, antimoniated, antimonic, antimonid, antimonide, antimonies, antimoniferous, antimonious, antimonite, antimonium, antimoniuret, antimoniureted, antimoniuretted, antimonopolism, antimonopolist, antimonopolistic, antimonopolization, antimonopoly, antimonous, antimonsoon, antimony, antimonyl, antimoral, antimoralism, antimoralist, antimoralistic, antimorality, antimosquito, antimusical, antimusically, antimusicalness, antimycotic, antimystic, antimystical, antimystically, antimysticalness, antimysticism, antimythic, antimythical, antinarcotic, antinarcotics, antinarrative, antinational, antinationalism, antinationalist, antinationalistic, antinationalistically, antinationalists, antinationalization, antinationally, antinatural, antinaturalism, antinaturalist, antinaturalistic, antinaturally, antinaturalness, antinegro, antinegroism, antineologian, antineoplastic, antinephritic, antinepotic, antineuralgic, antineuritic, antineurotoxin, antineutral, antineutralism, antineutrality, antineutrally, antineutrino, antineutrinos, antineutron, antineutrons, anting, antinganting, antings, antinial, antinicotine, antinihilism, antinihilist, antinihilistic, antinion, antinodal, antinode, antinodes, antinoise, antinome, antinomian, antinomianism, antinomians, antinomic, antinomical, antinomies, antinomist, antinomy, antinoness, antinormal, antinormality, antinormalness, antinosarian, antinovel, antinovelist, antinovels, antinucleon, antinucleons, antinuke, antiodont, antiodontalgic, antiopelmous, antiophthalmic, antiopium, antiopiumist, antiopiumite, antioptimism, antioptimist, antioptimistic, antioptimistical, antioptimistically, antioptionist, antiorgastic, antiorthodox, antiorthodoxly, antiorthodoxy, antioxidant, antioxidants, antioxidase, antioxidizer, antioxidizing, antioxygen, antioxygenating, antioxygenation, antioxygenator, antioxygenic, antiozonant, antipacifism, antipacifist, antipacifistic, antipacifists, antipapacy, antipapal, antipapalist, antipapism, antipapist, antipapistic, antipapistical, antiparabema, antiparabemata, antiparagraphe, antiparagraphic, antiparallel, antiparallelogram, antiparalytic, antiparalytical, antiparasitic, antiparasitical, antiparasitically, antiparastatitis, antiparliament, antiparliamental, antiparliamentarian, antiparliamentarians, antiparliamentarist, antiparliamentary, antiparliamenteer, antipart, antiparticle, antiparticles, antipass, antipasti, antipastic, antipasto, antipastos, antipatharian, antipathetic, antipathetical, antipathetically, antipatheticalness, antipathic, antipathies, antipathist, antipathize, antipathogen, antipathogene, antipathogenic, antipathy, antipatriarch, antipatriarchal, antipatriarchally, antipatriarchy, antipatriot, antipatriotic, antipatriotically, antipatriotism, antipedal, antipeduncular, antipellagric, antipendium, antipepsin, antipeptone, antiperiodic, antiperistalsis, antiperistaltic, antiperistasis, antiperistatic, antiperistatical, antiperistatically, antipersonnel, antiperspirant, antiperspirants, antiperthite, antipestilence, antipestilent, antipestilential, antipestilently, antipetalous, antipewism, antiphagocytic, antipharisaic, antipharmic, antiphase, antiphilosophic, antiphilosophical, antiphilosophically, antiphilosophies, antiphilosophism, antiphilosophy, antiphlogistian, antiphlogistic, antiphlogistin, antiphon, antiphona, antiphonal, antiphonally, antiphonaries, antiphonary, antiphoner, antiphonetic, antiphonic, antiphonical, antiphonically, antiphonies, antiphonon, antiphons, antiphony, antiphrases, antiphrasis, antiphrastic, antiphrastical, antiphrastically, antiphthisic, antiphthisical, antiphylloxeric, antiphysic, antiphysical, antiphysically, antiphysicalness, antiphysician, antipill, antiplague, antiplanet, antiplastic, antiplatelet, antipleion, antiplenist, antiplethoric, antipleuritic, antiplurality, antipneumococcic, antipodagric, antipodagron, antipodal, antipode, antipode's, antipodean, antipodeans, antipodes, antipodic, antipodism, antipodist, antipoetic, antipoetical, antipoetically, antipoints, antipolar, antipole, antipolemist, antipoles, antipolitical, antipolitically, antipolitics, antipollution, antipolo, antipolygamy, antipolyneuritic, antipool, antipooling, antipope, antipopery, antipopes, antipopular, antipopularization, antipopulationist, antipopulism, antiportable, antiposition, antipot, antipoverty, antipragmatic, antipragmatical, antipragmatically, antipragmaticism, antipragmatism, antipragmatist, antiprecipitin, antipredeterminant, antiprelate, antiprelatic, antiprelatism, antiprelatist, antipreparedness, antiprestidigitation, antipriest, antipriestcraft, antipriesthood, antiprime, antiprimer, antipriming, antiprinciple, antiprism, antiproductionist, antiproductive, antiproductively, antiproductiveness, antiproductivity, antiprofiteering, antiprogressive, antiprohibition, antiprohibitionist, antiprojectivity, antiprophet, antiprostate, antiprostatic, antiprotease, antiproteolysis, antiproton, antiprotons, antiprotozoal, antiprudential, antipruritic, antipsalmist, antipsoric, antipsychiatry, antipsychotic, antiptosis, antipudic, antipuritan, antiputrefaction, antiputrefactive, antiputrescent, antiputrid, antipyic, antipyics, antipyonin, antipyresis, antipyretic, antipyretics, antipyrin, antipyrine, antipyrotic, antipyryl, antiq, antiqua, antiquarian, antiquarian's, antiquarianism, antiquarianize, antiquarianly, antiquarians, antiquaries, antiquarism, antiquarium, antiquartan, antiquary, antiquate, antiquated, antiquatedness, antiquates, antiquating, antiquation, antique, antique's, antiqued, antiquely, antiqueness, antiquer, antiquers, antiques, antiquing, antiquist, antiquitarian, antiquities, antiquity, antiquum, antirabic, antirabies, antiracemate, antiracer, antirachitic, antirachitically, antiracial, antiracially, antiracing, antiracism, antiradiant, antiradiating, antiradiation, antiradical, antiradicalism, antiradically, antiradicals, antirailwayist, antirape, antirational, antirationalism, antirationalist, antirationalistic, antirationality, antirationally, antirattler, antireacting, antireaction, antireactionaries, antireactionary, antireactive, antirealism, antirealist, antirealistic, antirealistically, antireality, antirebating, antirecruiting, antired, antiredeposition, antireducer, antireducing, antireduction, antireductive, antireflexive, antireform, antireformer, antireforming, antireformist, antireligion, antireligionist, antireligiosity, antireligious, antireligiously, antiremonstrant, antirennet, antirennin, antirent, antirenter, antirentism, antirepublican, antirepublicanism, antireservationist, antiresonance, antiresonator, antirestoration, antireticular, antirevisionist, antirevolution, antirevolutionaries, antirevolutionary, antirevolutionist, antirheumatic, antiricin, antirickets, antiriot, antiritual, antiritualism, antiritualist, antiritualistic, antirobin, antiroll, antiromance, antiromantic, antiromanticism, antiromanticist, antiroyal, antiroyalism, antiroyalist, antirrhinum, antirumor, antirun, antirust, antirusts, antis, antisabbatarian, antisacerdotal, antisacerdotalist, antisag, antisaloon, antisalooner, antisavage, antiscabious, antiscale, antisceptic, antisceptical, antiscepticism, antischolastic, antischolastically, antischolasticism, antischool, antiscia, antiscians, antiscience, antiscientific, antiscientifically, antiscii, antiscion, antiscolic, antiscorbutic, antiscorbutical, antiscriptural, antiscripturism, antiscrofulous, antiseismic, antiselene, antisemite, antisemitic, antisemitism, antisensitivity, antisensitizer, antisensitizing, antisensuality, antisensuous, antisensuously, antisensuousness, antisepalous, antisepsin, antisepsis, antiseptic, antiseptical, antiseptically, antisepticise, antisepticised, antisepticising, antisepticism, antisepticist, antisepticize, antisepticized, antisepticizing, antiseptics, antiseption, antiseptize, antisera, antiserum, antiserums, antiserumsera, antisex, antisexist, antiship, antishipping, antisialagogue, antisialic, antisiccative, antisideric, antisilverite, antisimoniacal, antisine, antisiphon, antisiphonal, antiskeptic, antiskeptical, antiskepticism, antiskid, antiskidding, antislavery, antislaveryism, antislickens, antislip, antismog, antismoking, antismut, antisnapper, antisnob, antisocial, antisocialist, antisocialistic, antisocialistically, antisociality, antisocially, antisolar, antisophism, antisophist, antisophistic, antisophistication, antisophistry, antisoporific, antispace, antispadix, antispasis, antispasmodic, antispasmodics, antispast, antispastic, antispectroscopic, antispeculation, antispermotoxin, antispiritual, antispiritualism, antispiritualist, antispiritualistic, antispiritually, antispirochetic, antisplasher, antisplenetic, antisplitting, antispreader, antispreading, antisquama, antisquatting, antistadholder, antistadholderian, antistalling, antistaphylococcic, antistat, antistate, antistater, antistatic, antistatism, antistatist, antisteapsin, antisterility, antistes, antistimulant, antistimulation, antistock, antistreptococcal, antistreptococcic, antistreptococcin, antistreptococcus, antistrike, antistriker, antistrophal, antistrophe, antistrophic, antistrophically, antistrophize, antistrophon, antistrumatic, antistrumous, antisubmarine, antisubstance, antisudoral, antisudorific, antisuffrage, antisuffragist, antisun, antisupernatural, antisupernaturalism, antisupernaturalist, antisupernaturalistic, antisurplician, antisymmetric, antisymmetrical, antisymmetry, antisyndicalism, antisyndicalist, antisyndication, antisynod, antisyphilitic, antitabetic, antitabloid, antitangent, antitank, antitarnish, antitarnishing, antitartaric, antitax, antitaxation, antiteetotalism, antitegula, antitemperance, antitetanic, antitetanolysin, antithalian, antitheft, antitheism, antitheist, antitheistic, antitheistical, antitheistically, antithenar, antitheologian, antitheological, antitheologizing, antitheology, antithermic, antithermin, antitheses, antithesis, antithesism, antithesize, antithet, antithetic, antithetical, antithetically, antithetics, antithrombic, antithrombin, antithyroid, antitintinnabularian, antitobacco, antitobacconal, antitobacconist, antitonic, antitorpedo, antitoxic, antitoxin, antitoxin's, antitoxine, antitoxins, antitrade, antitrades, antitradition, antitraditional, antitraditionalist, antitraditionally, antitragal, antitragi, antitragic, antitragicus, antitragus, antitrinitarian, antitrismus, antitrochanter, antitropal, antitrope, antitropic, antitropical, antitropous, antitropy, antitrust, antitruster, antitrypsin, antitryptic, antitubercular, antituberculin, antituberculosis, antituberculotic, antituberculous, antitumor, antitumoral, antiturnpikeism, antitussive, antitwilight, antitypal, antitype, antitypes, antityphoid, antitypic, antitypical, antitypically, antitypous, antitypy, antityrosinase, antiuating, antiunion, antiunionist, antiuratic, antiurease, antiusurious, antiutilitarian, antiutilitarianism, antivaccination, antivaccinationist, antivaccinator, antivaccinist, antivariolous, antivenefic, antivenene, antivenereal, antivenin, antivenine, antivenins, antivenom, antivenomous, antivermicular, antivibrating, antivibrator, antivibratory, antivice, antiviral, antivirotic, antivirus, antivitalist, antivitalistic, antivitamin, antivivisection, antivivisectionist, antivivisectionists, antivolition, antiwar, antiwarlike, antiwaste, antiwear, antiwedge, antiweed, antiwhite, antiwhitism, antiwit, antiworld, antixerophthalmic, antizealot, antizoea, antizymic, antizymotic, antjar, antler, antlered, antlerite, antlerless, antlers, antlia, antliate, antlike, antling, antlion, antlions, antlophobia, antluetic, antocular, antodontalgic, antoeci, antoecian, antoecians, antoinette, antoniniani, antoninianus, antonio, antonomasia, antonomastic, antonomastical, antonomastically, antonomasy, antonovics, antony, antonym, antonymic, antonymies, antonymous, antonyms, antonymy, antorbital, antozone, antozonite, antproof, antra, antral, antralgia, antre, antrectomy, antres, antrin, antritis, antrocele, antronasal, antrophore, antrophose, antrorse, antrorsely, antroscope, antroscopy, antrotome, antrotomy, antrotympanic, antrotympanitis, antroversion, antrovert, antrum, antrums, antrustion, antrustionship, ants, antship, antshrike, antsier, antsiest, antsigne, antsy, antthrush, antu, antwerp, antwise, anubin, anubing, anucleate, anucleated, anukabiet, anuloma, anunder, anura, anural, anuran, anurans, anureses, anuresis, anuretic, anuria, anurias, anuric, anurous, anury, anus, anuses, anusim, anusvara, anutraminosa, anvasser, anvil, anvil's, anviled, anviling, anvilled, anvilling, anvils, anvilsmith, anviltop, anviltops, anxieties, anxietude, anxiety, anxiolytic, anxious, anxiously, anxiousness, any, anybodies, anybody, anybody'd, anybodyd, anyhow, anymore, anyone, anyplace, anything, anythingarian, anythingarianism, anythings, anytime, anyway, anyways, anywhen, anywhence, anywhere, anywhereness, anywheres, anywhither, anywhy, anywise, anywither, anzac, aob, aogiri, aoli, aonach, aonian, aor, aorist, aoristic, aoristically, aorists, aorta, aortae, aortal, aortarctia, aortas, aortectasia, aortectasis, aortic, aorticorenal, aortism, aortitis, aortoclasia, aortoclasis, aortographic, aortographies, aortography, aortoiliac, aortolith, aortomalacia, aortomalaxis, aortopathy, aortoptosia, aortoptosis, aortorrhaphy, aortosclerosis, aortostenosis, aortotomy, aosmic, aouad, aouads, aoudad, aoudads, ap, apa, apabhramsa, apace, apache, apaches, apachism, apachite, apadana, apaesthesia, apaesthetic, apaesthetize, apaestically, apagoge, apagoges, apagogic, apagogical, apagogically, apagogue, apaid, apair, apaise, apalit, apanage, apanaged, apanages, apanaging, apandry, apanthropia, apanthropy, apar, aparaphysate, aparavidya, apardon, aparejo, aparejos, aparithmesis, apart, apartado, apartheid, aparthrosis, apartment, apartment's, apartmental, apartments, apartness, apasote, apass, apast, apastra, apastron, apasttra, apatan, apatetic, apathaton, apatheia, apathetic, apathetical, apathetically, apathia, apathic, apathies, apathism, apathist, apathistical, apathize, apathogenic, apathy, apatite, apatites, apatosaurus, apay, ape, apeak, apectomy, aped, apedom, apeek, apehood, apeiron, apeirophobia, apelet, apelike, apeling, apelles, apellous, apeman, apennines, apenteric, apepsia, apepsinia, apepsy, apeptic, aper, aperch, apercu, apercus, aperea, aperient, aperients, aperies, aperiodic, aperiodically, aperiodicity, aperispermic, aperistalsis, aperitif, aperitifs, aperitive, apers, apersee, apert, apertion, apertly, apertness, apertometer, apertum, apertural, aperture, apertured, apertures, aperu, aperulosid, apery, apes, apesthesia, apesthetic, apesthetize, apetalies, apetaloid, apetalose, apetalous, apetalousness, apetaly, apex, apexed, apexes, apexing, aph, aphacia, aphacial, aphacic, aphaeresis, aphaeretic, aphagia, aphagias, aphakia, aphakial, aphakic, aphanesite, aphaniptera, aphanipterous, aphanisia, aphanisis, aphanite, aphanites, aphanitic, aphanitism, aphanophyre, aphanozygous, aphasia, aphasiac, aphasiacs, aphasias, aphasic, aphasics, aphasiology, aphelia, aphelian, aphelilia, aphelilions, aphelion, apheliotropic, apheliotropically, apheliotropism, aphemia, aphemic, aphengescope, aphengoscope, aphenoscope, apheresis, apheretic, apheses, aphesis, apheta, aphetic, aphetically, aphetism, aphetize, aphicidal, aphicide, aphid, aphid's, aphides, aphidian, aphidians, aphidicide, aphidicolous, aphidid, aphidious, aphidivorous, aphidlion, aphidolysin, aphidophagous, aphidozer, aphids, aphilanthropy, aphis, aphislion, aphizog, aphlaston, aphlebia, aphlogistic, aphnology, aphodal, aphodi, aphodian, aphodus, apholate, apholates, aphonia, aphonias, aphonic, aphonics, aphonous, aphony, aphoria, aphorise, aphorised, aphoriser, aphorises, aphorising, aphorism, aphorism's, aphorismatic, aphorismer, aphorismic, aphorismical, aphorismos, aphorisms, aphorist, aphoristic, aphoristical, aphoristically, aphorists, aphorize, aphorized, aphorizer, aphorizes, aphorizing, aphotaxis, aphotic, aphototactic, aphototaxis, aphototropic, aphototropism, aphrasia, aphrite, aphrizite, aphrodesiac, aphrodisia, aphrodisiac, aphrodisiacal, aphrodisiacs, aphrodisian, aphrodisiomania, aphrodisiomaniac, aphrodisiomaniacal, aphrodite, aphroditic, aphroditous, aphrolite, aphronia, aphronitre, aphrosiderite, aphtha, aphthae, aphthic, aphthitalite, aphthoid, aphthong, aphthongal, aphthongia, aphthonite, aphthous, aphydrotropic, aphydrotropism, aphyllies, aphyllose, aphyllous, aphylly, aphyric, apiaceous, apian, apiararies, apiarian, apiarians, apiaries, apiarist, apiarists, apiary, apiator, apicad, apical, apically, apices, apicial, apician, apicifixed, apicilar, apicillary, apicitis, apickaback, apickback, apickpack, apicoectomy, apicolysis, apicula, apicular, apiculate, apiculated, apiculation, apiculi, apicultural, apiculture, apiculturist, apiculus, apiece, apieces, apigenin, apii, apiin, apikores, apikoros, apikorsim, apilary, apili, apimania, apimanias, apinch, aping, apinoid, apio, apiocrinite, apioid, apioidal, apiol, apiole, apiolin, apiologies, apiologist, apiology, apionol, apiose, apiphobia, apis, apish, apishamore, apishly, apishness, apism, apitong, apitpat, apium, apivorous, apjohnite, apl, aplace, aplacental, aplacophoran, aplacophorous, aplanat, aplanatic, aplanatically, aplanatism, aplanogamete, aplanospore, aplasia, aplasias, aplastic, aplenty, aplite, aplites, aplitic, aplobasalt, aplodiorite, aplomb, aplombs, aplome, aploperistomatous, aplostemonous, aplotaxene, aplotomy, aplustra, aplustre, aplustria, apnea, apneal, apneas, apneic, apneumatic, apneumatosis, apneumonous, apneusis, apneustic, apnoea, apnoeal, apnoeas, apnoeic, apoaconitine, apoapsides, apoapsis, apoatropine, apobiotic, apoblast, apocaffeine, apocalypse, apocalypses, apocalypst, apocalypt, apocalyptic, apocalyptical, apocalyptically, apocalypticism, apocalyptism, apocalyptist, apocamphoric, apocarp, apocarpies, apocarpous, apocarps, apocarpy, apocatastasis, apocatastatic, apocatharsis, apocathartic, apocenter, apocentre, apocentric, apocentricity, apocha, apochae, apocholic, apochromat, apochromatic, apochromatism, apocinchonine, apocodeine, apocopate, apocopated, apocopating, apocopation, apocope, apocopes, apocopic, apocrenic, apocrine, apocrisiary, apocrustic, apocryph, apocrypha, apocryphal, apocryphalist, apocryphally, apocryphalness, apocryphate, apocryphon, apocynaceous, apocyneous, apocynthion, apocynthions, apocyte, apod, apodal, apodan, apodedeipna, apodeictic, apodeictical, apodeictically, apodeipna, apodeipnon, apodeixis, apodema, apodemal, apodemas, apodemata, apodematal, apodeme, apodia, apodiabolosis, apodictic, apodictical, apodictically, apodictive, apodioxis, apodixis, apodoses, apodosis, apodous, apods, apodyteria, apodyterium, apoembryony, apoenzyme, apofenchene, apoferritin, apogaeic, apogaic, apogalacteum, apogamic, apogamically, apogamies, apogamous, apogamously, apogamy, apogeal, apogean, apogee, apogees, apogeic, apogenous, apogeny, apogeotropic, apogeotropically, apogeotropism, apogonid, apograph, apographal, apographic, apographical, apoharmine, apohyal, apoikia, apoious, apoise, apojove, apokatastasis, apokatastatic, apokrea, apokreos, apolar, apolarity, apolaustic, apolegamic, apolitical, apolitically, apollinarian, apollinian, apollo, apollonian, apollonicon, apollos, apollyon, apolog, apologal, apologer, apologete, apologetic, apologetical, apologetically, apologetics, apologia, apologiae, apologias, apological, apologies, apologise, apologised, apologiser, apologising, apologist, apologist's, apologists, apologize, apologized, apologizer, apologizers, apologizes, apologizing, apologs, apologue, apologues, apology, apology's, apolousis, apolune, apolunes, apolusis, apolysis, apolytikion, apomecometer, apomecometry, apometabolic, apometabolism, apometabolous, apometaboly, apomict, apomictic, apomictical, apomictically, apomicts, apomixes, apomixis, apomorphia, apomorphin, apomorphine, aponeurology, aponeurorrhaphy, aponeuroses, aponeurosis, aponeurositis, aponeurotic, aponeurotome, aponeurotomy, aponia, aponic, aponogetonaceous, apoop, apopemptic, apopenptic, apopetalous, apophantic, apophasis, apophatic, apophlegm, apophlegmatic, apophlegmatism, apophonia, apophonic, apophonies, apophony, apophorometer, apophthegm, apophthegmatic, apophthegmatical, apophthegmatist, apophyeeal, apophyge, apophyges, apophylactic, apophylaxis, apophyllite, apophyllous, apophysary, apophysate, apophyseal, apophyses, apophysial, apophysis, apophysitis, apoplasmodial, apoplastogamous, apoplectic, apoplectical, apoplectically, apoplectiform, apoplectoid, apoplex, apoplexies, apoplexious, apoplexy, apopyle, apoquinamine, apoquinine, aporetic, aporetical, aporhyolite, aporia, aporiae, aporias, aporobranchian, aporose, aporphin, aporphine, aporrhaoid, aporrhea, aporrhegma, aporrhiegma, aporrhoea, aport, aportlast, aportoise, aposafranine, aposaturn, aposaturnium, aposelene, aposematic, aposematically, aposepalous, aposia, aposiopeses, aposiopesis, aposiopestic, aposiopetic, apositia, apositic, aposoro, aposporic, apospories, aposporogony, aposporous, apospory, apostacies, apostacize, apostacy, apostasies, apostasis, apostasy, apostate, apostates, apostatic, apostatical, apostatically, apostatise, apostatised, apostatising, apostatism, apostatize, apostatized, apostatizes, apostatizing, apostaxis, apostem, apostemate, apostematic, apostemation, apostematous, aposteme, aposteriori, aposthia, aposthume, apostil, apostille, apostils, apostle, apostle's, apostlehood, apostles, apostleship, apostleships, apostoile, apostolate, apostoless, apostoli, apostolian, apostolic, apostolical, apostolically, apostolicalness, apostolicism, apostolicity, apostolize, apostrophal, apostrophation, apostrophe, apostrophes, apostrophi, apostrophic, apostrophied, apostrophise, apostrophised, apostrophising, apostrophize, apostrophized, apostrophizes, apostrophizing, apostrophus, apostume, apotactite, apotelesm, apotelesmatic, apotelesmatical, apothec, apothecal, apothecarcaries, apothecaries, apothecary, apothecaryship, apothece, apotheces, apothecia, apothecial, apothecium, apothegm, apothegmatic, apothegmatical, apothegmatically, apothegmatist, apothegmatize, apothegms, apothem, apothems, apotheose, apotheoses, apotheosis, apotheosise, apotheosised, apotheosising, apotheosize, apotheosized, apotheosizing, apothesine, apothesis, apothgm, apotihecal, apotome, apotracheal, apotropaic, apotropaically, apotropaion, apotropaism, apotropous, apoturmeric, apotype, apotypic, apout, apoxesis, apozem, apozema, apozemical, apozymase, app, appair, appal, appalachia, appalachian, appalachians, appale, appall, appalled, appalling, appallingly, appallingness, appallment, appalls, appalment, appaloosa, appaloosas, appals, appalto, appanage, appanaged, appanages, appanaging, appanagist, appar, apparail, apparance, apparat, apparatchik, apparatchiki, apparatchiks, apparation, apparats, apparatus, apparatuses, apparel, appareled, appareling, apparelled, apparelling, apparelment, apparels, apparence, apparencies, apparency, apparens, apparent, apparentation, apparentement, apparentements, apparently, apparentness, apparition, apparition's, apparitional, apparitions, apparitor, appartement, appassionata, appassionatamente, appassionate, appassionato, appast, appaume, appaumee, appay, appd, appeach, appeacher, appeachment, appeal, appealability, appealable, appealed, appealer, appealers, appealing, appealingly, appealingness, appeals, appear, appearance, appearanced, appearances, appeared, appearer, appearers, appearing, appears, appeasable, appeasableness, appeasably, appease, appeased, appeasement, appeasements, appeaser, appeasers, appeases, appeasing, appeasingly, appeasive, appel, appellability, appellable, appellancy, appellant, appellant's, appellants, appellate, appellation, appellational, appellations, appellative, appellatived, appellatively, appellativeness, appellatory, appellee, appellees, appellor, appellors, appels, appenage, append, appendage, appendage's, appendaged, appendages, appendalgia, appendance, appendancy, appendant, appendectomies, appendectomy, appended, appendence, appendency, appendent, appender, appenders, appendical, appendicalgia, appendicate, appendice, appendiceal, appendicectasis, appendicectomies, appendicectomy, appendices, appendicial, appendicious, appendicitis, appendicle, appendicocaecostomy, appendicostomy, appendicular, appendicularian, appendiculate, appendiculated, appending, appenditious, appendix, appendix's, appendixed, appendixes, appendixing, appendorontgenography, appendotome, appends, appennage, appense, appentice, appenzell, apperceive, apperceived, apperceiving, apperception, apperceptionism, apperceptionist, apperceptionistic, apperceptive, apperceptively, appercipient, appere, apperil, appersonation, appersonification, appert, appertain, appertained, appertaining, appertainment, appertains, appertinent, appertise, appestat, appestats, appet, appete, appetence, appetencies, appetency, appetent, appetently, appetibility, appetible, appetibleness, appetiser, appetising, appetisse, appetit, appetite, appetite's, appetites, appetition, appetitional, appetitious, appetitive, appetitiveness, appetitost, appetize, appetized, appetizement, appetizer, appetizers, appetizing, appetizingly, appinite, appl, applanate, applanation, applaud, applaudable, applaudably, applauded, applauder, applauders, applauding, applaudingly, applauds, applause, applauses, applausive, applausively, apple, apple's, appleberry, appleblossom, applecart, appled, appledrane, appledrone, applegrower, applejack, applejohn, applemonger, applenut, appleringie, appleringy, appleroot, apples, applesauce, applesnits, applewife, applewoman, applewood, appliable, appliableness, appliably, appliance, appliance's, appliances, appliant, applicabilities, applicability, applicable, applicableness, applicably, applicancy, applicant, applicant's, applicants, applicate, application, application's, applications, applicative, applicatively, applicator, applicator's, applicatorily, applicators, applicatory, applied, appliedly, applier, appliers, applies, appling, applique, appliqued, appliqueing, appliques, applosion, applosive, applot, applotment, apply, applying, applyingly, applyment, appmt, appoggiatura, appoggiaturas, appoggiature, appoint, appointable, appointe, appointed, appointee, appointee's, appointees, appointer, appointers, appointing, appointive, appointively, appointment,

appointment's, appointments, appointor, appoints, appomattox, apport, apportion, apportionable, apportionate, apportioned, apportioner, apportioning, apportionment, apportionments, apportions, apposability, apposable, appose, apposed, apposer, apposers, apposes, apposing, apposiopestic, apposite, appositely, appositeness, apposition, appositional, appositionally, appositions, appositive, appositively, apppetible, appraisable, appraisal, appraisal's, appraisals, appraise, appraised, appraisement, appraiser, appraisers, appraises, appraising, appraisingly, appraisive, apprecate, appreciable, appreciably, appreciant, appreciate, appreciated, appreciates, appreciating, appreciatingly, appreciation, appreciational, appreciations, appreciativ, appreciative, appreciatively, appreciativeness, appreciator, appreciatorily, appreciators, appreciatory, appredicate, apprehend, apprehendable, apprehended, apprehender, apprehending, apprehendingly, apprehends, apprehensibility, apprehensible, apprehensibly, apprehension, apprehension's, apprehensions, apprehensive, apprehensively, apprehensiveness, apprend, apprense, apprentice, apprenticed, apprenticehood, apprenticement, apprentices, apprenticeship, apprenticeships, apprenticing, appress, appressed, appressor, appressoria, appressorial, appressorium, apprest, appreteur, appreve, apprise, apprised, appriser, apprisers, apprises, apprising, apprizal, apprize, apprized, apprizement, apprizer, apprizers, apprizes, apprizing, appro, approach, approachability, approachabl, approachable, approachableness, approached, approacher, approachers, approaches, approaching, approachless, approachment, approbate, approbated, approbating, approbation, approbations, approbative, approbativeness, approbator, approbatory, approprompt, approof, appropinquate, appropinquation, appropinquity, appropre, appropriable, appropriament, appropriate, appropriated, appropriately, appropriateness, appropriates, appropriating, appropriation, appropriations, appropriative, appropriativeness, appropriator, appropriator's, appropriators, approvability, approvable, approvableness, approvably, approval, approval's, approvals, approvance, approve, approved, approvedly, approvedness, approvement, approver, approvers, approves, approving, approvingly, approx, approximable, approximal, approximant, approximants, approximate, approximated, approximately, approximates, approximating, approximation, approximations, approximative, approximatively, approximativeness, approximator, appt, apptd, appui, appulse, appulses, appulsion, appulsive, appulsively, appunctuation, appurtenance, appurtenances, appurtenant, apr, apractic, apraxia, apraxias, apraxic, aprendiz, apres, apreynte, apricate, aprication, aprickle, apricot, apricot's, apricots, april, apriori, apriorism, apriorist, aprioristic, aprioristically, apriority, apritif, aproctia, aproctous, apron, apron's, aproned, aproneer, apronful, aproning, apronless, apronlike, aprons, apronstring, apropos, aprosexia, aprosopia, aprosopous, aproterodont, aprowl, apse, apselaphesia, apselaphesis, apses, apsid, apsidal, apsidally, apsides, apsidiole, apsinthion, apsis, apsychia, apsychical, apt, aptate, apter, apteral, apteran, apteria, apterial, apterium, apteroid, apterous, apterygial, apterygote, apterygotous, apteryla, apteryx, apteryxes, aptest, aptitude, aptitudes, aptitudinal, aptitudinally, aptly, aptness, aptnesses, aptote, aptotic, apts, aptyalia, aptyalism, aptychus, apulmonic, apulse, apurpose, apx, apyonin, apyrase, apyrases, apyrene, apyretic, apyrexia, apyrexial, apyrexy, apyrotype, apyrous, aq, aqua, aquabelle, aquabib, aquacade, aquacades, aquacultural, aquaculture, aquadag, aquaduct, aquaducts, aquae, aquaemanale, aquaemanalia, aquafer, aquafortis, aquafortist, aquage, aquagreen, aquake, aqualung, aqualunger, aquamanale, aquamanalia, aquamanile, aquamaniles, aquamanilia, aquamarine, aquamarines, aquameter, aquanaut, aquanauts, aquaphobia, aquaplane, aquaplaned, aquaplaner, aquaplanes, aquaplaning, aquapuncture, aquaregia, aquarelle, aquarelles, aquarellist, aquaria, aquarial, aquarian, aquarians, aquariia, aquariist, aquariiums, aquarist, aquarists, aquarium, aquariums, aquarius, aquarter, aquas, aquascope, aquascutum, aquashow, aquate, aquatic, aquatical, aquatically, aquatics, aquatile, aquatint, aquatinta, aquatinted, aquatinter, aquatinting, aquatintist, aquatints, aquation, aquativeness, aquatone, aquatones, aquavalent, aquavit, aquavits, aqueduct, aqueduct's, aqueducts, aqueity, aquench, aqueoglacial, aqueoigneous, aqueomercurial, aqueous, aqueously, aqueousness, aquerne, aquiclude, aquicolous, aquicultural, aquiculture, aquiculturist, aquifer, aquiferous, aquifers, aquifoliaceous, aquiform, aquifuge, aquila, aquilawood, aquilege, aquilegia, aquilia, aquiline, aquilinity, aquilino, aquilon, aquinas, aquincubital, aquincubitalism, aquintocubital, aquintocubitalism, aquiparous, aquiver, aquo, aquocapsulitis, aquocarbonic, aquocellolitis, aquopentamminecobaltic, aquose, aquosity, aquotization, aquotize, ar, ar'n't, ara, arab, arab's, araba, araban, arabana, arabesk, arabesks, arabesque, arabesquely, arabesquerie, arabesques, arabia, arabian, arabians, arabic, arabica, arabicize, arability, arabin, arabine, arabinic, arabinose, arabinosic, arabinoside, arabis, arabist, arabit, arabite, arabitol, arabiyeh, arabize, arabized, arabizes, arabizing, arable, arables, arabs, araby, araca, aracanga, aracari, arace, araceous, arach, arache, arachic, arachide, arachidic, arachidonic, arachin, arachis, arachnactis, arachne, arachnean, arachnephobia, arachnid, arachnid's, arachnidan, arachnidial, arachnidism, arachnidium, arachnids, arachnism, arachnitis, arachnoid, arachnoidal, arachnoidea, arachnoidean, arachnoiditis, arachnological, arachnologist, arachnology, arachnophagous, arachnopia, arad, aradid, arado, araeometer, araeostyle, araeosystyle, araeotic, arage, aragonite, aragonitic, aragonspath, araguane, araguato, araignee, arain, araire, araise, arak, arakawaite, arake, araks, aralia, araliaceous, araliad, aralie, aralkyl, aralkylated, aramaean, aramaic, aramayoite, aramid, aramids, aramina, araneid, araneidal, araneidan, araneids, araneiform, aranein, araneologist, araneology, araneose, araneous, aranga, arango, arangoes, arank, aranzada, arapahite, arapaho, arapahos, arapaima, arapaimas, araphorostic, araphostic, araponga, arapunga, arar, arara, araracanga, ararao, ararauna, arariba, araroba, ararobas, araru, arase, arati, aratinga, aration, aratory, araucanian, araucaria, araucarian, arawak, arawakan, arayne, arb, arba, arbacia, arbacin, arbalest, arbalester, arbalestre, arbalestrier, arbalests, arbalist, arbalister, arbalists, arbalo, arbalos, arber, arbinose, arbiter, arbiter's, arbiters, arbith, arbitrable, arbitrage, arbitrager, arbitragers, arbitrages, arbitrageur, arbitragist, arbitral, arbitrament, arbitraments, arbitraries, arbitrarily, arbitrariness, arbitrary, arbitrate, arbitrated, arbitrates, arbitrating, arbitration, arbitrational, arbitrationist, arbitrations, arbitrative, arbitrator, arbitrator's, arbitrators, arbitratorship, arbitratrix, arbitre, arbitrement, arbitrer, arbitress, arbitry, arblast, arboloco, arbor, arbor's, arboraceous, arboral, arborary, arborator, arborea, arboreal, arboreally, arborean, arbored, arboreous, arborer, arbores, arborescence, arborescent, arborescently, arboresque, arboret, arboreta, arboretum, arboretums, arborical, arboricole, arboricoline, arboricolous, arboricultural, arboriculture, arboriculturist, arboriform, arborise, arborist, arborists, arborization, arborize, arborized, arborizes, arborizing, arboroid, arborolater, arborolatry, arborous, arbors, arborvitae, arborvitaes, arborway, arbory, arbota, arbour, arboured, arbours, arbovirus, arbs, arbtrn, arbuscle, arbuscles, arbuscula, arbuscular, arbuscule, arbust, arbusta, arbusterin, arbusterol, arbustum, arbutase, arbute, arbutean, arbutes, arbutin, arbutinase, arbutus, arbutuses, arc, arca, arcabucero, arcade, arcade's, arcaded, arcades, arcadia, arcadian, arcadians, arcadias, arcading, arcadings, arcady, arcae, arcana, arcanal, arcane, arcanist, arcanite, arcanum, arcate, arcato, arcature, arcatures, arcboutant, arccos, arccosine, arced, arcella, arces, arceuthobium, arcform, arch, archabomination, archae, archaean, archaecraniate, archaeocyte, archaeogeology, archaeographic, archaeographical, archaeography, archaeohippus, archaeol, archaeolater, archaeolatry, archaeolith, archaeolithic, archaeologer, archaeologian, archaeologic, archaeological, archaeologically, archaeologist, archaeologist's, archaeologists, archaeology, archaeomagnetism, archaeopteryx, archaeornis, archaeostoma, archaeostomatous, archaeotherium, archaeus, archagitator, archai, archaic, archaical, archaically, archaicism, archaicness, archaise, archaised, archaiser, archaises, archaising, archaism, archaisms, archaist, archaistic, archaists, archaize, archaized, archaizer, archaizes, archaizing, archangel, archangel's, archangelic, archangelical, archangels, archangelship, archantagonist, archanthropine, archantiquary, archapostate, archapostle, archarchitect, archarios, archartist, archbanc, archbancs, archband, archbeacon, archbeadle, archbishop, archbishopess, archbishopric, archbishoprics, archbishopry, archbishops, archbotcher, archboutefeu, archbuffoon, archbuilder, archchampion, archchaplain, archcharlatan, archcheater, archchemic, archchief, archchronicler, archcity, archconfraternities, archconfraternity, archconsoler, archconspirator, archcorrupter, archcorsair, archcount, archcozener, archcriminal, archcritic, archcrown, archcupbearer, archd, archdapifer, archdapifership, archdeacon, archdeaconate, archdeaconess, archdeaconries, archdeaconry, archdeacons, archdeaconship, archdean, archdeanery, archdeceiver, archdefender, archdemon, archdepredator, archdespot, archdetective, archdevil, archdiocesan, archdiocese, archdioceses, archdiplomatist, archdissembler, archdisturber, archdivine, archdogmatist, archdolt, archdruid, archducal, archduchess, archduchesses, archduchies, archduchy, archduke, archdukedom, archdukes, archduxe, arche, archeal, archean, archearl, archebanc, archebancs, archebiosis, archecclesiastic, archecentric, arched, archegay, archegone, archegonia, archegonial, archegoniate, archegoniophore, archegonium, archegony, archeion, archelogy, archelon, archemastry, archemperor, archencephalic, archenemies, archenemy, archengineer, archenia, archenteric, archenteron, archeocyte, archeol, archeolithic, archeologian, archeologic, archeological, archeologically, archeologist, archeology, archeopteryx, archeostome, archeozoic, archer, archeress, archerfish, archerfishes, archeries, archers, archership, archery, arches, archespore, archespores, archesporia, archesporial, archesporium, archespsporia, archest, archetto, archettos, archetypal, archetypally, archetype, archetypes, archetypic, archetypical, archetypically, archetypist, archeunuch, archeus, archexorcist, archfelon, archfiend, archfiends, archfire, archflamen, archflatterer, archfoe, archfool, archform, archfounder, archfriend, archgenethliac, archgod, archgomeral, archgovernor, archgunner, archhead, archheart, archheresy, archheretic, archhost, archhouse, archhumbug, archhypocrisy, archhypocrite, archiater, archibenthal, archibenthic, archibenthos, archiblast, archiblastic, archiblastoma, archiblastula, archical, archicantor, archicarp, archicerebra, archicerebrum, archichlamydeous, archicleistogamous, archicleistogamy, archicoele, archicontinent, archicyte, archicytula, archidiaconal, archidiaconate, archididascalian, archididascalos, archidome, archidoxis, archie, archiepiscopacy, archiepiscopal, archiepiscopality, archiepiscopally, archiepiscopate, archiereus, archigaster, archigastrula, archigenesis, archigonic, archigonocyte, archigony, archiheretical, archikaryon, archil, archilithic, archilla, archilochian, archilowe, archils, archilute, archimage, archimagus, archimandrite, archimandrites, archimedean, archimedes, archimime, archimorphic, archimorula, archimperial, archimperialism, archimperialist, archimperialistic, archimpressionist, archin, archine, archines, archineuron, archinfamy, archinformer, arching, archings, archipallial, archipallium, archipelagian, archipelagic, archipelago, archipelagoes, archipelagos, archiphoneme, archipin, archiplasm, archiplasmic, archiprelatical, archipresbyter, archipterygial, archipterygium, archisperm, archisphere, archispore, archistome, archisupreme, archisymbolical, archisynagogue, archit, architect, architect's, architective, architectonic, architectonically, architectonics, architectress, architects, architectural, architecturalist, architecturally, architecture, architecture's, architectures, architecturesque, architecure, architis, architraval, architrave, architraved, architraves, architricline, architypographer, archival, archivault, archive, archived, archiver, archivers, archives, archiving, archivist, archivists, archivolt, archizoic, archjockey, archking, archknave, archleader, archlecher, archlet, archleveler, archlexicographer, archliar, archlute, archly, archmachine, archmagician, archmagirist, archmarshal, archmediocrity, archmessenger, archmilitarist, archmime, archminister, archmock, archmocker, archmockery, archmonarch, archmonarchist, archmonarchy, archmugwump, archmurderer, archmystagogue, archness, archnesses, archocele, archocystosyrinx, archology, archon, archons, archonship, archonships, archont, archontate, archontic, archoplasm, archoplasma, archoplasmic, archoptoma, archoptosis, archorrhagia, archorrhea, archostegnosis, archostenosis, archosyrinx, archoverseer, archpall, archpapist, archpastor, archpatriarch, archpatron, archphilosopher, archphylarch, archpiece, archpilferer, archpillar, archpirate, archplagiarist, archplagiary, archplayer, archplotter, archplunderer, archplutocrat, archpoet, archpolitician, archpontiff, archpractice, archprelate, archprelatic, archprelatical, archpresbyter, archpresbyterate, archpresbytery, archpretender, archpriest, archpriesthood, archpriestship, archprimate, archprince, archprophet, archprotopope, archprototype, archpublican, archpuritan, archradical, archrascal, archreactionary, archrebel, archregent, archrepresentative, archrobber, archrogue, archruler, archsacrificator, archsacrificer, archsaint, archsatrap, archscoundrel, archseducer, archsee, archsewer, archshepherd, archsin, archsnob, archspirit, archspy, archsteward, archswindler, archsynagogue, archt, archtempter, archthief, archtraitor, archtreasurer, archtreasurership, archturncoat, archtyrant, archurger, archvagabond, archvampire, archvestryman, archvillain, archvillainy, archvisitor, archwag, archway, archways, archwench, archwife, archwise, archworker, archworkmaster, archy, arciferous, arcifinious, arciform, arcing, arcked, arcking, arclength, arclike, arco, arcocentrous, arcocentrum, arcograph, arcose, arcosolia, arcosoliulia, arcosolium, arcs, arcsin, arcsine, arcsines, arctan, arctangent, arctation, arctian, arctic, arctically, arctician, arcticize, arcticized, arcticizing, arcticologist, arcticology, arctics, arcticward, arcticwards, arctiid, arctitude, arctogaeal, arctoid, arctoidean, arcturus, arcual, arcuale, arcualia, arcuate, arcuated, arcuately, arcuation, arcubalist, arcubalister, arcubos, arcula, arculite, arcus, arcuses, ardass, ardassine, ardeb, ardebs, ardeid, ardelio, ardella, ardellae, ardencies, ardency, ardennite, ardent, ardently, ardentness, arder, ardilla, ardish, ardisia, arditi, ardito, ardoise, ardor, ardors, ardour, ardours, ardri, ardrigh, ardu, arduinite, arduous, arduously, arduousness, ardure, ardurous, are, area, area's, areach, aread, aready, areae, areal, areality, areally, arear, areas, areason, areasoner, areaway, areaways, areawide, areca, arecaceous, arecaidin, arecaidine, arecain, arecaine, arecas, areche, arecolidin, arecolidine, arecolin, arecoline, ared, areek, areel, arefact, arefaction, arefy, areg, aregenerative, aregeneratory, areic, areito, aren, aren't, arena, arena's, arenaceous, arenae, arenaria, arenariae, arenarious, arenas, arenation, arend, arendalite, arendator, areng, arenicole, arenicolite, arenicolor, arenicolous, arenilitic, arenite, arenites, arenoid, arenose, arenosity, arenous, arent, arenulous, areocentric, areographer, areographic, areographical, areographically, areography, areola, areolae, areolar, areolas, areolate, areolated, areolation, areole, areoles, areolet, areologic, areological, areologically, areologies, areologist, areology, areometer, areometric, areometrical, areometry, areopagist, areopagite, areopagitic, areopagus, areopagy, areostyle, areosystyle, areotectonics, arere, arerola, areroscope, ares, arest, aret, aretaics, aretalogy, arete, aretes, arethusa, arethusas, arette, arew, arf, arfillite, arfvedsonite, arg, argaile, argal, argala, argalas, argali, argalis, argals, argan, argand, argans, argasid, argeers, argel, argema, argemone, argemony, argenol, argent, argental, argentamid, argentamide, argentamin, argentamine, argentan, argentarii, argentarius, argentate, argentation, argenteous, argenter, argenteum, argentic, argenticyanide, argentide, argentiferous, argentin, argentina, argentine, argentinean, argentineans, argentines, argentinitrate, argentino, argention, argentite, argentojarosite, argentol, argentometer, argentometric, argentometrically, argentometry, argenton, argentoproteinum, argentose, argentous, argentry, argents, argentum, argentums, argh, arghan, arghel, arghool, arghoul, argify, argil, argillaceous, argillic, argilliferous, argillite, argillitic, argilloarenaceous, argillocalcareous, argillocalcite, argilloferruginous, argilloid, argillomagnesian, argillous, argils, argin, arginase, arginases, argine, arginine, argininephosphoric, arginines, argive, argle, arglebargle, arglebargled, arglebargling, argled, argles, argling, argo, argol, argolet, argoletier, argols, argon, argonaut, argonautic, argonautid, argonauts, argonon, argons, argos, argosies, argosine, argosy, argot, argotic, argots, arguable, arguably, argue, argued, arguendo, arguer, arguers, argues, argufied, argufier, argufiers, argufies, argufy, argufying, arguing, arguitively, argument, argument's, argumenta, argumental, argumentation, argumentatious, argumentative, argumentatively, argumentativeness, argumentator, argumentatory, argumentive, arguments, argumentum, argus, arguses, argusfish, argusfishes, arguta, argutation, argute, argutely, arguteness, argyle, argyles, argyll, argylls, argyranthemous, argyranthous, argyria, argyric, argyrite, argyrocephalous, argyrodite, argyrose, argyrosis, argyrythrose, arhar, arhat, arhats, arhatship, arhythmia, arhythmic, arhythmical, arhythmically, aria, ariadne, arian, arianism, arianist, arianists, arias, aribin, aribine, ariboflavinosis, aricin, aricine, arid, arider, aridest, aridge, aridian, aridities, aridity, aridly, aridness, aridnesses, ariegite, ariel, ariels, arienzo, aries, arietate, arietation, arietinous, arietta, ariettas, ariette, ariettes, aright, arightly, arigue, ariki, aril, ariled, arillary, arillate, arillated, arilled, arilli, arilliform, arillode, arillodes, arillodium, arilloid, arillus, arils, ariolate, ariole, ariose, ariosi, arioso, ariosos, ariot, aripple, arisaid, arisard, arise, arised, arisen, ariser, arises, arish, arising, arisings, arist, arista, aristae, aristarch, aristarchies, aristarchy, aristas, aristate, ariste, aristeia, aristippus, aristo, aristocracies, aristocracy, aristocrat, aristocrat's, aristocratic, aristocratical, aristocratically, aristocraticalness, aristocraticism, aristocraticness, aristocratism, aristocrats, aristodemocracies, aristodemocracy, aristodemocratical, aristogenesis, aristogenetic, aristogenic, aristogenics, aristoi, aristolochia, aristolochiaceous, aristolochin, aristolochine, aristological, aristologist, aristology, aristomonarchy, aristorepublicanism, aristos, aristotelean, aristotelian, aristotle, aristotype, aristulate, arite, arith, arithmancy, arithmetic, arithmetical, arithmetically, arithmetician, arithmeticians, arithmetics, arithmetization, arithmetizations, arithmetize, arithmetized, arithmetizes, arithmic, arithmocracy, arithmocratic, arithmogram, arithmograph, arithmography, arithmomancy, arithmomania, arithmometer, arithromania, arizona, arizonan, arizonans, arizonian, arizonians, arizonite, arjun, ark, arkansan, arkansans, arkansas, arkansawyer, arkansite, arkie, arkite, arkose, arkoses, arkosic, arks, arksutite, arkwright, arle, arlequinade, arles, arless, arling, arlington, arloup, arm, armada, armadas, armadilla, armadillo, armadillos, armageddon, armagnac, armagnacs, armament, armament's, armamentaria, armamentarium, armamentary, armaments, armangite, armaria, armarian, armaries, armariolum, armarium, armariumaria, armary, armature, armatured, armatures, armaturing, armband, armbands, armbone, armchair, armchair's, armchaired, armchairs, armed, armenia, armeniaceous, armenian, armenians, armenite, armer, armers, armet, armets, armful, armfuls, armgaunt, armguard, armhole, armholes, armhoop, armied, armies, armiferous, armiger, armigeral, armigeri, armigero, armigeros, armigerous, armigers, armil, armill, armilla, armillae, armillaria, armillary, armillas, armillate, armillated, armine, arming, armings, arminian, armipotence, armipotent, armisonant, armisonous, armistice, armistices, armit, armitas, armless, armlessly, armlessness, armlet, armlets, armlike, armload, armloads, armlock, armlocks, armoire, armoires, armomancy, armoniac, armonica, armonicas, armor, armorbearer, armored, armorer, armorers, armorial, armorially, armorials, armorica, armorican, armoried, armories, armoring, armorist, armorless, armorplated, armorproof, armors, armorwise, armory, armour, armourbearer, armoured, armourer, armourers, armouries, armouring, armours, armoury, armozeen, armozine, armpad, armpiece, armpit, armpit's, armpits, armplate, armrack, armrest, armrests, arms, armscye, armseye, armsful, armsize, armstrong, armure, armures, army, army's, armyworm, armyworms, arn, arna, arnatta, arnatto, arnattos, arnberry, arnee, arnement, arni, arnica, arnicas, arnold, arnotta, arnotto, arnottos, arnut, aroar, aroast, arock, aroeira, aroid, aroideous, aroids, aroint, arointed, arointing, aroints, arolia, arolium, arolla, aroma, aromacity, aromadendrin, aromal, aromas, aromata, aromatic, aromatical, aromatically, aromaticity, aromaticness, aromatics, aromatise, aromatised, aromatiser, aromatising, aromatitae, aromatite, aromatites, aromatization, aromatize, aromatized, aromatizer, aromatizing, aromatophor, aromatophore, aromatous, aroon, aroph, arose, around, arousable, arousal, arousals, arouse, aroused, arousement, arouser, arousers, arouses, arousing, arow, aroxyl, aroynt, aroynted, aroynting, aroynts, arpanet, arpeggiando, arpeggiated, arpeggiation, arpeggio, arpeggio's, arpeggioed, arpeggios, arpen, arpens, arpent, arpenteur, arpents, arquated, arquebus, arquebuses, arquebusier, arquerite, arquifoux, arr, arracach, arracacha, arrace, arrach, arrack, arracks, arrage, arragonite, arrah, arraign, arraignability, arraignable, arraignableness, arraigned, arraigner, arraigning, arraignment, arraignment's, arraignments, arraigns, arrame, arrand, arrange, arrangeable, arranged, arrangement, arrangement's, arrangements, arranger, arrangers, arranges, arranging, arrant, arrantly, arrantness, arras, arrased, arrasene, arrases, arrastra, arrastre, arratel, arrau, array, arrayal, arrayals, arrayan, arrayed, arrayer, arrayers, arraying, arrayment, arrays, arrear, arrearage, arrearages, arrears, arrect, arrectary, arrector, arrendation, arrendator, arrenotokous, arrenotoky, arrent, arrentable, arrentation, arreption, arreptitious, arrest, arrestable, arrestant, arrestation, arrested, arrestee, arrestees, arrester, arresters, arresting, arrestingly, arrestive, arrestment, arrestor, arrestor's, arrestors, arrests, arret, arretez, arrgt, arrha, arrhal, arrhenal, arrhenoid, arrhenotokous, arrhenotoky, arrhinia, arrhizal, arrhizous, arrhythmia, arrhythmias, arrhythmic, arrhythmical, arrhythmically, arrhythmous, arrhythmy, arri, arriage, arriba, arribadas, arricci, arricciati, arricciato, arricciatos, arriccio, arriccioci, arriccios, arride, arrided, arridge, arriding, arrie, arriere, arriero, arrimby, arris, arrises, arrish, arrisways, arriswise, arrivage, arrival, arrival's, arrivals, arrivance, arrive, arrived, arrivederci, arrivederla, arriver, arrivers, arrives, arriving, arrivism, arrivisme, arrivist, arriviste, arrivistes, arroba, arrobas, arrode, arrogance, arrogancy, arrogant, arrogantly, arrogantness, arrogate, arrogated, arrogates, arrogating, arrogatingly, arrogation, arrogations, arrogative, arrogator, arrojadite, arrondi, arrondissement, arrondissements, arrope, arrosion, arrosive, arround, arrouse, arrow, arrowbush, arrowed, arrowhead, arrowhead's, arrowheaded, arrowheads, arrowing, arrowleaf, arrowless, arrowlet, arrowlike, arrowplate, arrowroot, arrowroots, arrows, arrowsmith, arrowstone, arrowweed, arrowwood, arrowworm, arrowy, arroya, arroyo, arroyos, arroyuelo, arroz, arrtez, arrythmia, arrythmic, arrythmical, arrythmically, ars, arsanilic, arse, arsedine, arsefoot, arsehole, arsenal, arsenal's, arsenals, arsenate, arsenates, arsenation, arseneted, arsenetted, arsenfast, arsenferratose, arsenhemol, arseniasis, arseniate, arsenic, arsenical, arsenicalism, arsenicate, arsenicated, arsenicating, arsenicism, arsenicize, arsenicked, arsenicking, arsenicophagy, arsenics, arsenide, arsenides, arseniferous, arsenillo, arseniopleite, arseniosiderite, arsenious, arsenism, arsenite, arsenites, arsenium, arseniuret, arseniureted, arseniuretted, arsenization, arseno, arsenobenzene, arsenobenzol, arsenobismite, arsenoferratin, arsenofuran, arsenohemol, arsenolite, arsenophagy, arsenophen, arsenophenol, arsenophenylglycin, arsenopyrite, arsenostyracol, arsenotherapy, arsenotungstates, arsenotungstic, arsenous, arsenoxide, arsenyl, arses, arsesmart, arsheen, arshin, arshine, arshins, arsine, arsines, arsinic, arsino, arsis, arsle, arsmetik, arsmetrik, arsmetrike, arsmetry, arsnicker, arsoite, arson, arsonate, arsonation, arsonic, arsonist, arsonists, arsonite, arsonium, arsono, arsonous, arsons, arsonvalization, arsphenamine, arsyl, arsylene, arsyversy, art, art's, artaba, artabe, artal, artar, artarin, artarine, artcraft, arte, artefac, artefact, artefacts, artel, artels, artemia, artemis, artemisia, artemisic, artemisin, artemon, arter, arteria, arteriac, arteriae, arteriagra, arterial, arterialisation, arterialise, arterialised, arterialising, arterialization, arterialize, arterialized, arterializing, arterially, arterials, arteriarctia, arteriasis, arteriectasia, arteriectasis, arteriectomy, arteriectopia, arteried, arteries, arterin, arterioarctia, arteriocapillary, arteriococcygeal, arteriodialysis, arteriodiastasis, arteriofibrosis, arteriogenesis, arteriogram, arteriograph, arteriographic, arteriography, arteriolar, arteriole, arteriole's, arterioles, arteriolith, arteriology, arteriioloscleroses, arteriolosclerosis, arteriomalacia, arteriometer, arteriomotor, arterionecrosis, arteriopalmus, arteriopathy, arteriophlebotomy, arterioplania, arterioplasty, arteriopressor, arteriorenal, arteriorrhagia, arteriorrhaphy, arteriorrhexis, arterioscleroses, arteriosclerosis, arteriosclerotic, arteriospasm, arteriostenosis, arteriostosis, arteriostrepsis, arteriosympathectomy, arteriotome, arteriotomies, arteriotomy, arteriotrepsis, arterious, arteriovenous, arterioversion, arterioverter, arteritis, artery, artery's, arterying, artesian, artesonado, artesonados, artful, artfully, artfulness, artha, arthel, arthemis, arthogram, arthra, arthragra, arthral, arthralgia, arthralgic, arthrectomies, arthrectomy, arthredema, arthrempyesis, arthresthesia, arthritic, arthritical, arthritically, arthriticine, arthritics, arthritides, arthritis, arthritism, arthrobacterium, arthrobranch, arthrobranchia, arthrocace, arthrocarcinoma, arthrocele, arthrochondritis, arthroclasia, arthrocleisis, arthroclisis, arthroderm, arthrodesis, arthrodia, arthrodiae, arthrodial, arthrodic, arthrodiran, arthrodire, arthrodirous, arthrodymic, arthrodynia, arthrodynic, arthroempyema, arthroempyesis, arthroendoscopy, arthrogastran, arthrogenous, arthrography, arthrogryposis, arthrolite, arthrolith, arthrolithiasis, arthrology, arthromeningitis, arthromere, arthromeric, arthrometer, arthrometry, arthron, arthroncus, arthroneuralgia, arthropathic, arthropathology, arthropathy, arthrophlogosis, arthrophyma, arthroplastic, arthroplasty, arthropleura, arthropleure, arthropod, arthropod's, arthropodal, arthropodan, arthropodous, arthropods, arthropody, arthropomatous, arthropterous, arthropyosis, arthrorheumatism, arthrorrhagia, arthrosclerosis, arthroses, arthrosia, arthrosis, arthrospore, arthrosporic, arthrosporous, arthrosteitis, arthrosterigma, arthrostome, arthrostomy, arthrosynovitis, arthrosyrinx, arthrotome, arthrotomies, arthrotomy, arthrotrauma, arthrotropic, arthrotyphoid, arthrous, arthroxerosis, arthrozoan, arthrozoic, arthur, arthurian, artiad, artic, artichoke, artichoke's, artichokes, article, article's, articled, articles, articling, articulability, articulable, articulacy, articulant, articular, articulare, articularly, articulars, articulary, articulata, articulate, articulated, articulately, articulateness, articulates, articulating, articulation, articulationes, articulationist, articulations, articulative, articulator, articulatorily, articulators, articulatory, articulite, articulus, artier, artiest, artifact, artifact's, artifactitious, artifacts, artifactual, artifactually, artifex, artifice, artificer, artificers, artificership, artifices, artificial, artificialism, artificialities, artificiality, artificialize, artificially, artificialness, artificious, artilize, artiller, artilleries, artillerist, artillerists, artillery, artilleryman, artillerymen, artilleryship, artily, artiness, artinesses, artinite, artiodactyl, artiodactylous, artiphyllous, artisan, artisan's, artisanal, artisanry, artisans, artisanship, artist, artist's, artistdom, artiste, artistes, artistess, artistic, artistical, artistically, artistries, artistry, artists, artize, artless, artlessly, artlessness, artlet, artlike, artly, artmobile, artocarpad, artocarpeous, artocarpous, artolater, artolatry, artophagous, artophophoria, artophoria, artophorion, artotype, artotypy, artotyrite, artou, arts, artsman, artsy, artus, artware, artwork, artworks, arty, aru, arugola, arugolas, arugula, arugulas, arui, aruke, arum, arumin, arumlike, arums, arundiferous, arundinaceous, arundineous, arupa, arusa, arusha, aruspex, aruspice, aruspices, aruspicy, arustle, arval, arvejon, arvel, arvicole, arvicoline, arvicolous, arviculture, arvo, arvos, arx, ary, aryan, aryanize, aryans, aryballi, aryballoi, aryballoid, aryballos, aryballus, arybballi, aryepiglottic, aryepiglottidean, aryl, arylamine, arylamino, arylate, arylated, arylating, arylation, arylide, aryls, arytenoepiglottic, arytenoid, arytenoidal, arythmia, arythmias, arythmic, arythmical, arythmically, arzan, arzrunite, arzun, as, asaddle, asafetida, asafoetida, asak, asale, asamblea, asana, asap, asaphia, asaphid, asaprol, asarabacca, asarin, asarite, asaron, asarone, asarota, asarotum, asarta, asarum, asarums, asb, asbest, asbestic, asbestiform, asbestine, asbestinize, asbestoid, asbestoidal, asbestos, asbestoses, asbestosis, asbestous, asbestus, asbestuses, asbolan, asbolane, asbolin, asboline, asbolite, ascan, ascape, ascare, ascared, ascariasis, ascaricidal, ascaricide, ascarid, ascarides, ascaridiasis, ascaridol, ascaridole, ascarids, ascaris, ascaron, ascebc, ascelli, ascellus, ascence, ascend, ascendable, ascendance, ascendancy, ascendant, ascendantly, ascendants, ascended, ascendence, ascendency, ascendent, ascender, ascenders, ascendible, ascending, ascendingly, ascends, ascenseur, ascension, ascensional, ascensionist, ascensions, ascensive, ascensor, ascent, ascents, ascertain, ascertainability, ascertainable, ascertainableness, ascertainably, ascertained, ascertainer, ascertaining, ascertainment, ascertains, ascescency, ascescent, asceses, ascesis, ascetic, ascetic's, ascetical, ascetically, asceticism, ascetics, aschaffite, ascham, ascher, aschistic, asci, ascian, ascians, ascicidia, ascidia, ascidian, ascidians, ascidiate, ascidicolous, ascidiferous, ascidiform, ascidiia, ascidioid, ascidiozooid, ascidium, asciferous, ascigerous, ascii, ascill, ascitan, ascitb, ascite, ascites, ascitic, ascitical, ascititious, asclent, asclepiad, asclepiadaceous, asclepiadeous, asclepias, asclepidin, asclepidoid, asclepin, asclepius, ascocarp, ascocarpous, ascocarps, ascogenous, ascogone, ascogonia, ascogonial, ascogonidia, ascogonidium, ascogonium, ascolichen, ascoma, ascomata, ascomycetal, ascomycete, ascomycetes, ascomycetous, ascon, asconia, asconoid, ascophore, ascophorous, ascorbate, ascorbic, ascospore, ascosporic, ascosporous, ascot, ascots, ascribable, ascribe, ascribed, ascribes, ascribing, ascript, ascription, ascriptions, ascriptitii, ascriptitious, ascriptitius, ascriptive, ascrive, ascry, ascula, asculae, ascus, ascyphous, asdic, asdics, ase, asea, asearch, asecretory, aseethe, aseismatic, aseismic, aseismicity, aseitas, aseity, aselar, aselgeia, asellate, aselline, asellus, asem, asemasia, asemia, asemic, asepalous, asepses, asepsis, aseptate, aseptic, aseptically, asepticism, asepticize, asepticized, asepticizing, aseptify, aseptol, aseptolin, asexual, asexualisation, asexualise, asexualised, asexualising, asexuality, asexualization, asexualize, asexualized, asexualizing, asexually, asexuals, asfast, asfetida, asg, asgard, asgd, asgmt, ash, ashake, ashame, ashamed, ashamedly, ashamedness, ashamnu, ashanti, ashberry, ashcake, ashcan, ashcans, ashed, ashen, asher, asherah, asherahs, asheries, asherim, ashery, ashes, ashet, ashfall, ashier, ashiest, ashily, ashimmer, ashine, ashiness, ashing, ashipboard, ashiver, ashkenazi, ashkey, ashkoko, ashlar, ashlared, ashlaring, ashlars, ashler, ashlered, ashlering, ashlers, ashless, ashling, ashman, ashmen, ashore, ashot, ashpan, ashpit, ashplant, ashplants, ashraf, ashrafi, ashram, ashrama, ashrams, ashstone, ashthroat, ashtoreth, ashtray, ashtray's, ashtrays, ashur, ashvamedha, ashweed, ashwort, ashy, asia, asialia, asian, asians, asiarch, asiatic, asiaticism, aside, asidehand, asiden, asideness, asiderite, asides, asideu, asiento, asilid, asimen, asimmer, asinego, asinegoes, asinine, asininely, asininities, asininity, asiphonate, asiphonogama, asitia, ask, askable, askance, askant, askapart, askar, askarel, askari, askaris, asked, asker, askers, askeses, askesis, askew, askewgee, askewness, askile, asking, askingly, askings, askip, asklent, askoi, askos, askoye, asks, aslake, aslant, aslantwise, aslaver, asleep, aslop, aslope, aslumber, asmack, asmalte, asmear, asmile, asmodeus, asmoke, asmolder, asniffle, asnort, asoak, asocial, asok, asoka, asomatophyte, asomatous, asonant, asonia, asop, asor, asouth, asp, aspace, aspalathus, aspalax, asparagic, asparagin, asparagine, asparaginic, asparaginous, asparagus, asparaguses, asparagyl, asparamic, asparkle, aspartame, aspartate, aspartic, aspartokinase, aspartyl, aspca, aspect, aspect's, aspectable, aspectant, aspection, aspects, aspectual, aspen, aspens, asper, asperate, asperated, asperates, asperating, asperation, aspergation, asperge, asperger, asperges, asperggilla, asperggilli, aspergil, aspergill, aspergilla, aspergilli, aspergilliform, aspergillin, aspergilloses, aspergillosis, aspergillum, aspergillums, aspergillus, asperifoliate, asperifolious, asperite, asperities, asperity, asperly, aspermatic, aspermatism, aspermatous, aspermia, aspermic, aspermous, aspern, asperness, asperous, asperously, aspers, asperse, aspersed, asperser, aspersers, asperses, aspersing, aspersion, aspersion's, aspersions, aspersive, aspersively, aspersoir, aspersor, aspersoria, aspersorium, aspersoriums, aspersors, aspersory, asperuloside, asperulous, asphalt, asphalted, asphaltene, asphalter, asphaltic, asphalting, asphaltite, asphaltlike, asphalts, asphaltum, asphaltus, aspheric, aspherical, aspheterism, aspheterize, asphodel, asphodels, asphyctic, asphyctous, asphyxia, asphyxial, asphyxiant, asphyxias, asphyxiate, asphyxiated, asphyxiates, asphyxiating, asphyxiation, asphyxiative, asphyxiator, asphyxied, asphyxies, asphyxy, aspic, aspics, aspiculate, aspiculous, aspidate, aspide, aspidiaria, aspidinol, aspidistra, aspidistras, aspidium, aspidobranchiate, aspidomancy, aspidospermine, aspiquee, aspirant, aspirant's, aspirants, aspirata, aspiratae, aspirate, aspirated, aspirates, aspirating, aspiration, aspiration's, aspirations, aspirator, aspirators, aspiratory, aspire, aspired, aspiree, aspirer, aspirers, aspires, aspirin, aspiring, aspiringly, aspiringness, aspirins, aspis, aspises, aspish, asplanchnic, asplenioid, asplenium, asporogenic, asporogenous, asporous, asport, asportation, asporulate, aspout, asprawl, aspread, asprete, aspring, asprout, asps, aspy, asquare, asquat, asqueal, asquint, asquirm, asrama, asramas, ass, ass's, assacu, assafetida, assafoetida, assagai, assagaied, assagaiing, assagais, assahy, assai, assail, assailability, assailable, assailableness, assailant, assailant's, assailants, assailed, assailer, assailers, assailing, assailment, assails, assais, assalto, assam, assamar, assamese, assapan, assapanic, assapanick, assarion, assart, assary, assassin, assassin's, assassinate, assassinated, assassinates, assassinating, assassination, assassinations, assassinative, assassinator, assassinatress, assassinist, assassins, assate, assation, assauagement, assault, assaultable, assaulted, assaulter, assaulters, assaulting, assaultive, assaults, assausive, assaut, assay, assayable, assayed, assayer, assayers, assaying, assays, assbaa, asse, asseal, assecuration, assecurator, assecure, assecution, assedat, assedation, assegai, assegaied, assegaiing, assegaing, assegais, asseize, asself, assembl, assemblable, assemblage, assemblage's, assemblages, assemblagist, assemblance, assemble, assembled, assemblee, assemblement, assembler, assemblers, assembles, assemblies, assembling, assembly, assembly's, assemblyman, assemblymen, assemblywoman, assemblywomen, assent, assentaneous, assentation, assentatious, assentator, assentatorily, assentatory, assented, assenter, assenters, assentient, assenting, assentingly, assentive, assentiveness, assentor, assentors, assents, asseour, assert, asserta, assertable, assertative, asserted, assertedly, asserter, asserters, assertible, asserting, assertingly, assertion, assertion's, assertional, assertions, assertive, assertively, assertiveness, assertor, assertorial, assertorially, assertoric, assertorical, assertorically, assertorily, assertors, assertory, assertress, assertrix, asserts, assertum, asserve, asservilize, asses, assess, assessable, assessably, assessed, assessee, assesses, assessing, assession, assessionary, assessment, assessment's, assessments, assessor, assessorial, assessors, assessorship, assessory, asset, asset's, asseth, assets, assever, asseverate, asseverated, asseverates, asseverating, asseveratingly, asseveration, asseverations, asseverative, asseveratively, asseveratory, assewer, asshead, assheadedness, asshole, assholes, assi, assibilate, assibilated, assibilating, assibilation, assidaean, assident, assidual, assidually, assiduate, assiduities, assiduity, assiduous, assiduously, assiduousness, assiege, assientist, assiento, assiette, assify, assign, assignability, assignable, assignably, assignat, assignation, assignations, assignats, assigned, assignee, assignee's, assignees, assigneeship, assigner, assigners, assigning, assignment, assignment's, assignments, assignor, assignors, assigns, assilag, assimilability, assimilable, assimilate, assimilated, assimilates, assimilating, assimilation, assimilationist, assimilations, assimilative, assimilativeness, assimilator, assimilatory, assimulate, assinego, assinuate, assis, assisa, assise, assish, assishly, assishness, assisi, assist, assistance, assistances, assistant, assistant's, assistanted, assistants, assistantship, assistantships, assisted, assistency, assister, assisters, assistful, assisting, assistive, assistless, assistor, assistors, assists, assith, assize, assized, assizement, assizer, assizes, assizing, asslike, assman, assmanship, assn, assobre, assoc, associability, associable, associableness, associate, associated, associatedness, associates, associateship, associating, association, associational, associationalism, associationalist, associationism, associationist, associationistic, associations, associative, associatively, associativeness, associativity, associator, associator's, associators, associatory, associe, assoil, assoiled, assoiling, assoilment, assoils, assoilzie, assoin, assoluto, assonance, assonanced, assonances, assonant, assonantal, assonantic, assonantly, assonants, assonate, assoria, assort, assortative, assortatively, assorted, assortedness, assorter, assorters, assorting, assortive, assortment, assortment's, assortments, assorts, assot, asssembler, asst, assuade, assuagable, assuage, assuaged, assuagement, assuagements, assuager, assuages, assuaging, assuasive, assubjugate, assuefaction, assuetude, assumable, assumably, assume, assumed, assumedly, assument, assumer, assumers, assumes, assuming, assumingly, assumingness, assummon, assumpsit, assumpt, assumption, assumption's, assumptions, assumptious, assumptiousness, assumptive, assumptively, assumptiveness, assurable, assurance, assurance's, assurances, assurant, assurate, assurd, assure, assured, assuredly, assuredness, assureds, assurer, assurers, assures, assurge, assurgency, assurgent, assuring, assuringly, assuror, assurors, asswage, asswaged, asswages, asswaging, assyntite, assyria, assyrian, assyrians, assyriologist, assyriology, assyth, assythment, ast, asta, astable, astacian, astalk, astarboard, astare, astart, astarte, astasia, astasias, astate, astatic, astatically, astaticism, astatine, astatines, astatize, astatized, astatizer, astatizing, astay, asteam, asteatosis, asteep, asteer, asteism, astel, astelic, astely, aster, aster's, asteraceous, astereognosis, asteria, asteriae, asterial, asterias, asteriated, asterikos, asterin, asterioid, asterion, asteriscus, asteriscuses, asterisk, asterisk's, asterisked, asterisking, asteriskless, asteriskos, asterisks, asterism, asterismal, asterisms, asterite, asterixis, astern, asternal, asternia, asteroid, asteroid's, asteroidal, asteroidean, asteroids, asterophyllite, asterospondylic, asterospondylous, asters, astert, asterwort, asthamatic, asthenia, asthenias, asthenic, asthenical, asthenics, asthenies, asthenobiosis, asthenobiotic, asthenolith, asthenology, asthenope, asthenophobia, asthenopia, asthenopic, asthenosphere, astheny, asthma, asthmas, asthmatic, asthmatical, asthmatically, asthmatics, asthmatoid, asthmogenic, asthore, asthorin, astichous, astigmat, astigmatic, astigmatical, astigmatically, astigmatism, astigmatizer, astigmatometer, astigmatometry, astigmatoscope, astigmatoscopies, astigmatoscopy, astigmia, astigmias, astigmic, astigmism, astigmometer, astigmometry, astigmoscope, astilbe, astint, astipulate, astipulation, astir, astite, astogeny, astomatal, astomatous, astomia, astomous, astond, astone, astoned, astonied, astonies, astonish, astonished, astonishedly, astonisher, astonishes, astonishing, astonishingly, astonishingness, astonishment, astonishments, astony, astonying, astoop, astor, astore, astound, astoundable, astounded, astounding, astoundingly, astoundment, astounds, astr, astrachan, astracism, astraddle, astraea, astraean, astraeid, astraeiform, astragal, astragalar, astragalectomy, astragali, astragalocalcaneal, astragalocentral, astragalomancy, astragalonavicular, astragaloscaphoid, astragalotibial, astragals, astragalus, astrain, astrakanite, astrakhan, astral, astrally, astrals, astrand, astraphobia, astrapophobia, astray, astre, astream, astrean, astrer, astrict, astricted, astricting, astriction, astrictive, astrictively, astrictiveness, astricts, astride, astrier, astriferous, astrild, astringe, astringed, astringence, astringency, astringent, astringently, astringents, astringer, astringes, astringing, astrion, astrionics, astroalchemist, astrobiological, astrobiologically, astrobiologies, astrobiologist, astrobiologists, astrobiology, astroblast, astrobotany, astrochemist, astrochemistry, astrochronological, astrocompass, astrocyte, astrocytic, astrocytoma, astrocytomas, astrocytomata, astrodiagnosis, astrodome, astrodynamic, astrodynamics, astrofel, astrofell, astrogate, astrogated, astrogating, astrogation, astrogational, astrogator, astrogeny, astrogeologist, astrogeology, astroglia, astrognosy, astrogonic, astrogony, astrograph, astrographer, astrographic, astrography, astrohatch, astroid, astroite, astrol, astrolabe, astrolabes, astrolabical, astrolater, astrolatry, astrolithology, astrolog, astrologaster, astrologe, astrologer, astrologers, astrologian, astrologic, astrological, astrologically, astrologist, astrologistic, astrologists, astrologize, astrologous, astrology, astromancer, astromancy, astromantic, astromeda, astrometeorological, astrometeorologist, astrometeorology, astrometer, astrometric, astrometrical, astrometry, astron, astronaut, astronaut's, astronautic, astronautical, astronautically, astronautics, astronauts, astronavigation, astronavigator, astronomer, astronomer's, astronomers, astronomic, astronomical, astronomically, astronomics, astronomien, astronomize, astronomy, astrophel, astrophil, astrophobia, astrophotographer, astrophotographic, astrophotography, astrophotometer, astrophotometrical, astrophotometry, astrophyllite, astrophysical, astrophysicist, astrophysicists, astrophysics, astroscope, astroscopy, astrose, astrospectral, astrospectroscopic, astrosphere, astrospherecentrosomic, astrotheology, astructive, astrut, astucious, astuciously, astucity, astute, astutely, astuteness, astutious, astyanax, astylar, astyllen, asuang, asudden, asunder, aswail, aswarm, aswash, asway, asweat, aswell, asweve, aswim, aswing, aswirl, aswithe, aswoon, aswooned, aswough, asyla, asylabia, asyle, asyllabia, asyllabic, asyllabical, asylum, asylums, asymbiotic, asymbolia, asymbolic, asymbolical, asymmetral, asymmetranthous, asymmetric, asymmetrical, asymmetrically, asymmetries, asymmetrocarpous, asymmetry, asymptomatic, asymptomatically, asymptote, asymptote's, asymptotes, asymptotic, asymptotical, asymptotically, asymtote, asymtotes, asymtotic, asymtotically, asynapsis, asynaptic, asynartete, asynartetic, async, asynchronism, asynchronisms, asynchronous, asynchronously, asynchrony, asyndesis, asyndeta, asyndetic, asyndetically, asyndeton, asyndetons, asynergia, asynergy, asyngamic, asyngamy, asyntactic, asyntrophy, asystematic, asystole, asystolic, asystolism, asyzygetic, at, atabal, atabals, atabeg, atabek, atabrine, atacamite, atactic, atactiform, atafter, ataghan, ataghans, atake, atalanta, atalantis, atalaya, atalayas, ataman, atamans, atamasco, atamascos, atame, atangle, atap, atar, ataractic, ataraxia, ataraxias, ataraxic, ataraxics, ataraxies, ataraxy, atatschite, ataunt, ataunto, atavi, atavic, atavism, atavisms, atavist, atavistic, atavistically, atavists, atavus, ataxaphasia, ataxia, ataxiagram, ataxiagraph, ataxiameter, ataxiaphasia, ataxias, ataxic, ataxics, ataxies, ataxinomic, ataxite, ataxonomic, ataxophemia, ataxy, atazir, atbash, atchison, ate, atebrin, atechnic, atechnical, atechny, ated, atees, ateeter, atef, ateknia, atelectasis, atelectatic, ateleiosis, atelene, ateleological, atelestite, atelets, atelic, atelier, ateliers, ateliosis, ateliotic, atellan, atelo, atelocardia, atelocephalous, ateloglossia, atelognathia, atelomitic, atelomyelia, atelophobia, atelopodia, ateloprosopia, atelorachidia, atelostomia, ately, atemoya, atemporal, aterian, ates, ateuchi, ateuchus, athalamous, athalline, athamantin, athamaunte, athanasia, athanasian, athanasies, athanasy, athanor, athapaskan, athar, athbash, athecate, atheism, atheisms, atheist, atheist's, atheistic, atheistical, atheistically, atheisticalness, atheisticness, atheists, atheize, atheizer, athel, athelia, atheling, athelings, athematic, athena, athenaeum, athenaeums, athenee, atheneum, atheneums, athenian, athenians, athenor, athens, atheological, atheologically, atheology, atheous, athericeran, athericerous, atherine, athermancy, athermanous, athermic, athermous, atherogenesis, atherogenic, atheroma, atheromas, atheromasia, atheromata, atheromatosis, atheromatous, atheroscleroses, atherosclerosis, atherosclerotic, atherosclerotically, athetesis, atheticize, athetize, athetized, athetizing, athetoid, athetoids, athetosic, athetosis, athetotic, athing, athink, athirst, athlete, athlete's, athletehood, athletes, athletic, athletical, athletically, athleticism, athletics, athletism, athletocracy, athlothete, athlothetes, athodyd, athodyds, athogen, athold, athonite, athort, athrepsia, athreptic, athrill, athrive, athrob, athrocyte, athrocytosis, athrogenic, athrong, athrough, athumia, athwart, athwarthawse, athwartship, athwartships, athwartwise, athymia, athymic, athymy, athyreosis, athyria, athyrid, athyroid, athyroidism, athyrosis, atilt, atimon, atimy, ating, atinga, atingle, atinkle, atip, atiptoe, atis, atlanta, atlantad, atlantal, atlantean, atlantes, atlantic, atlantis, atlantite, atlantoaxial, atlantodidymus, atlantomastoid, atlantoodontoid, atlantosaurus, atlas, atlases, atlatl, atlatls, atle, atlee, atli, atloaxoid, atloid, atloidean, atloidoaxoid, atm, atma, atman, atmans, atmas, atmiatrics, atmiatry, atmid, atmidalbumin, atmidometer, atmidometry, atmo, atmocausis, atmocautery, atmoclastic, atmogenic, atmograph, atmologic, atmological, atmologist, atmology, atmolyses, atmolysis, atmolyzation, atmolyze, atmolyzer, atmometer, atmometric, atmometry, atmophile, atmos, atmosphere, atmosphere's, atmosphered, atmosphereful, atmosphereless, atmospheres, atmospheric, atmospherical, atmospherically, atmospherics, atmospherium, atmospherology, atmostea, atmosteal, atmosteon, atocha, atocia, atokal, atoke, atokous, atole, atoll, atoll's, atolls, atom, atom's, atomatic, atomechanics, atomerg, atomic, atomical, atomically, atomician, atomicism, atomicity, atomics, atomies, atomiferous, atomisation, atomise, atomised, atomises, atomising, atomism, atomisms, atomist, atomistic, atomistical, atomistically, atomistics, atomists, atomity, atomization, atomize, atomized, atomizer, atomizers, atomizes, atomizing, atomology, atoms, atomy, atonable, atonal, atonalism, atonalist, atonalistic, atonality, atonally, atone, atoneable, atoned, atonement, atonements, atoneness, atoner, atoners, atones, atonia, atonic, atonicity, atonics, atonies, atoning, atoningly, atony, atop, atopen, atophan, atopic, atopies, atopite, atopy, atour, atoxic, atoxyl, atpoints, atrabilaire, atrabilar, atrabilarian, atrabilarious, atrabile, atrabiliar, atrabiliarious, atrabiliary, atrabilious, atrabiliousness, atracheate, atragene, atrail, atrament, atramental, atramentary, atramentous, atraumatic, atrazine, atrazines, atrede, atremate, atrematous, atremble, atren, atrenne, atrepsy, atreptic, atresia, atresias, atresic, atresy, atretic, atreus, atria, atrial, atrible, atrichia, atrichic, atrichosis, atrichous, atrickle, atrienses, atriensis, atriocoelomic, atrioporal, atriopore, atrioventricular, atrip, atrium, atriums, atroce, atroceruleous, atroceruleus, atrocha, atrochal, atrochous, atrocious, atrociously, atrociousness, atrocities, atrocity, atrocity's, atrocoeruleus, atrolactic, atropaceous, atropal, atropamine, atrophia, atrophias, atrophiated, atrophic, atrophied, atrophies, atrophoderma, atrophous, atrophy, atrophying, atropia, atropic, atropin, atropine, atropines, atropinism, atropinization, atropinize, atropins, atropism, atropisms, atropos, atropous, atrorubent, atrosanguineous, atroscine, atrous, atry, atrypoid, atsara, att, atta, attababy, attabal, attaboy, attacca, attacco, attach, attachable, attachableness, attache, attached, attachedly, attacher, attachers, attaches, attacheship, attaching, attachment, attachment's, attachments, attack, attackable, attacked, attacker, attackers, attacking, attackingly, attackman, attacks, attacolite, attacus, attagal, attagen, attaghan, attagirl, attain, attainability, attainable, attainableness, attainably, attainder, attainders, attained, attainer, attainers, attaining, attainment, attainment's, attainments, attainor, attains, attaint, attainted, attainting, attaintment, attaints, attainture, attal, attaleh, attame, attapulgite, attar, attargul, attars, attask, attaste, attatched, attatches, atte, atteal, attemper, attemperament, attemperance, attemperate, attemperately, attemperation, attemperator, attempered, attempering, attempers, attempre, attempt, attemptability, attemptable, attempted, attempter, attempters, attempting, attemptive, attemptless, attempts, attend, attendance, attendance's, attendances, attendancy, attendant, attendant's, attendantly, attendants, attended, attendee, attendee's, attendees, attender, attenders, attending, attendingly, attendment, attendress, attends, attensity, attent, attentat, attentate, attention,

attention's, attentional, attentionality, attentions, attentive, attentively, attentiveness, attently, attenuable, attenuant, attenuate, attenuated, attenuates, attenuating, attenuation, attenuations, attenuative, attenuator, attenuator's, attenuators, atter, attercop, attercrop, atterminal, attermine, attermined, atterminement, attern, atterr, atterrate, attery, attest, attestable, attestant, attestation, attestations, attestative, attestator, attested, attester, attesters, attesting, attestive, attestor, attestors, attests, attic, attic's, attice, atticism, atticisms, atticist, atticists, atticize, atticized, atticizing, atticomastoid, attics, attid, attidae, attila, attinge, attingence, attingency, attingent, attirail, attire, attired, attirement, attirer, attires, attiring, attitude, attitude's, attitudes, attitudinal, attitudinarian, attitudinarianism, attitudinise, attitudinised, attitudiniser, attitudinising, attitudinize, attitudinized, attitudinizer, attitudinizes, attitudinizing, attitudist, attle, attn, attntrp, attollent, attomy, attorn, attornare, attorned, attorney, attorney's, attorneydom, attorneyism, attorneys, attorneyship, attorning, attornment, attorns, attouchement, attour, attourne, attract, attractability, attractable, attractableness, attractance, attractancy, attractant, attractants, attracted, attracter, attractile, attracting, attractingly, attraction, attraction's, attractionally, attractions, attractive, attractively, attractiveness, attractivity, attractor, attractor's, attractors, attracts, attrahent, attrap, attrectation, attrib, attributable, attributal, attribute, attributed, attributer, attributes, attributing, attribution, attributional, attributions, attributive, attributively, attributiveness, attributives, attributor, attrist, attrite, attrited, attriteness, attriting, attrition, attritional, attritive, attritus, attriutively, attroopment, attroupement, attry, attune, attuned, attunely, attunement, attunes, attuning, atturn, atty, atua, atule, atumble, atune, atveen, atwain, atweel, atween, atwin, atwind, atwirl, atwist, atwitch, atwite, atwitter, atwixt, atwo, atypic, atypical, atypicality, atypically, atypy, auantic, aubade, aubades, aubain, aubaine, aube, aubepine, auberge, auberges, aubergine, aubergiste, aubergistes, aubin, aubretia, aubretias, aubrieta, aubrietas, aubrietia, aubrite, auburn, auburns, aubusson, auca, auchenia, auchenium, auchlet, aucht, auckland, auctary, auction, auctionary, auctioned, auctioneer, auctioneer's, auctioneers, auctioning, auctions, auctor, auctorial, auctorizate, auctors, aucuba, aucubas, aucupate, aud, audace, audacious, audaciously, audaciousness, audacities, audacity, audad, audads, audibility, audible, audibleness, audibles, audibly, audience, audience's, audiencer, audiences, audiencia, audiencier, audient, audients, audile, audiles, auding, audings, audio, audioemission, audiogenic, audiogram, audiogram's, audiograms, audiological, audiologies, audiologist, audiologist's, audiologists, audiology, audiometer, audiometers, audiometric, audiometrically, audiometries, audiometrist, audiometry, audion, audiophile, audiophiles, audios, audiotape, audiotapes, audiotypist, audiovisual, audiovisuals, audiphone, audit, auditable, audited, auditing, audition, audition's, auditioned, auditioning, auditions, auditive, auditives, auditor, auditor's, auditoria, auditorial, auditorially, auditories, auditorily, auditorium, auditoriums, auditors, auditorship, auditory, auditotoria, auditress, audits, auditual, audivise, audiviser, audivision, audubon, auf, aufait, aufgabe, aufklarung, auftakt, aug, auganite, auge, augean, augelite, augen, augend, augends, auger, auger's, augerer, augers, auget, augh, aught, aughtlins, aughts, augite, augites, augitic, augitite, augitophyre, augment, augmentable, augmentation, augmentationer, augmentations, augmentative, augmentatively, augmented, augmentedly, augmenter, augmenters, augmenting, augmentive, augmentor, augments, augrim, augur, augural, augurate, auguration, augure, augured, augurer, augurers, augurial, auguries, auguring, augurous, augurs, augurship, augury, august, augusta, augustal, augustan, auguste, auguster, augustest, augustin, augustine, augustinian, augustly, augustness, auh, auhuhu, auk, auklet, auklets, auks, auksinai, auksinas, auksinu, aul, aula, aulacocarpous, aulae, aularian, aulas, auld, aulder, auldest, auldfarrantlike, auletai, aulete, auletes, auletic, auletrides, auletris, aulic, aulical, aulicism, aullay, auloi, aulophobia, aulophyte, aulos, aulostomid, aulu, aum, aumaga, aumail, aumakua, aumbries, aumbry, aumery, aumil, aumildar, aummbulatory, aumoniere, aumous, aumrie, auncel, aune, aunt, aunt's, aunter, aunters, aunthood, aunthoods, auntie, aunties, auntish, auntlier, auntliest, auntlike, auntly, auntre, auntrous, aunts, auntsary, auntship, aunty, aupaka, aura, aura's, aurae, aural, aurally, auramin, auramine, aurang, aurantia, aurantiaceous, aurantium, aurar, auras, aurata, aurate, aurated, aureal, aureate, aureately, aureateness, aureation, aurei, aureity, aurelia, aurelian, aurene, aureola, aureolae, aureolas, aureole, aureoled, aureoles, aureolin, aureoline, aureoling, aureomycin, aureous, aureously, aures, auresca, aureus, auribromide, auric, aurichalcite, aurichalcum, aurichloride, aurichlorohydric, auricle, auricled, auricles, auricomous, auricula, auriculae, auricular, auriculare, auriculares, auricularia, auriculariae, auricularian, auricularias, auricularis, auricularly, auriculars, auriculas, auriculate, auriculated, auriculately, auriculo, auriculocranial, auriculoid, auriculoparietal, auriculotemporal, auriculoventricular, auriculovertical, auricyanhydric, auricyanic, auricyanide, auride, auriferous, aurifex, aurific, aurification, aurified, auriflamme, auriform, aurify, aurifying, auriga, aurigal, aurigation, aurigerous, aurignacian, aurigo, aurigraphy, aurilave, aurin, aurinasal, aurine, auriphone, auriphrygia, auriphrygiate, auripigment, auripuncture, aurir, auris, auriscalp, auriscalpia, auriscalpium, auriscope, auriscopic, auriscopically, auriscopy, aurist, aurists, aurite, aurited, aurivorous, auroauric, aurobromide, auroch, aurochloride, aurochs, aurochses, aurocyanide, aurodiamine, auronal, aurophobia, aurophore, aurora, aurorae, auroral, aurorally, auroras, aurore, aurorean, aurorium, aurotellurite, aurothiosulphate, aurothiosulphuric, aurous, aurrescu, aurulent, aurum, aurums, aurung, aurure, auryl, auscult, auscultascope, auscultate, auscultated, auscultates, auscultating, auscultation, auscultations, auscultative, auscultator, auscultatory, auscultoscope, ausform, ausformed, ausforming, ausforms, ausgespielt, auslander, auslaut, auslaute, auspex, auspicate, auspicated, auspicating, auspice, auspices, auspicial, auspicious, auspiciously, auspiciousness, auspicy, aussie, aussies, austausch, austemper, austenite, austenitic, austenitize, austenitized, austenitizing, auster, austere, austerely, austereness, austerer, austerest, austerities, austerity, austerus, austin, austral, australasian, australene, australia, australian, australians, australis, australite, australoid, australopithecine, australorp, austria, austrian, austrians, austrine, austringer, austrium, austroasiatic, austromancy, austronesian, ausu, ausubo, ausubos, autacoid, autacoidal, autacoids, autaesthesy, autallotriomorphic, autantitypy, autarch, autarchic, autarchical, autarchically, autarchies, autarchist, autarchy, autarkic, autarkical, autarkically, autarkies, autarkik, autarkikal, autarkist, autarky, aute, autechoscope, autecious, auteciously, auteciousness, autecism, autecisms, autecologic, autecological, autecologically, autecologist, autecology, autecy, autem, autere, auteur, auteurism, autexousy, auth, authentic, authentical, authentically, authenticalness, authenticatable, authenticate, authenticated, authenticates, authenticating, authentication, authentications, authenticator, authenticators, authenticities, authenticity, authenticly, authenticness, authigene, authigenetic, authigenic, authigenous, author, author's, authorcraft, authored, authoress, authoresses, authorhood, authorial, authorially, authoring, authorisable, authorisation, authorise, authorised, authoriser, authorish, authorising, authorism, authoritarian, authoritarianism, authoritarianisms, authoritarians, authoritative, authoritatively, authoritativeness, authorities, authority, authority's, authorizable, authorization, authorization's, authorizations, authorize, authorized, authorizer, authorizers, authorizes, authorizing, authorless, authorling, authorly, authors, authorship, authotype, autism, autisms, autist, autistic, auto, auto's, autoabstract, autoactivation, autoactive, autoaddress, autoagglutinating, autoagglutination, autoagglutinin, autoalarm, autoalkylation, autoallogamous, autoallogamy, autoanalysis, autoanalytic, autoantibody, autoanticomplement, autoantitoxin, autoasphyxiation, autoaspiration, autoassimilation, autobahn, autobahnen, autobahns, autobasidia, autobasidiomycetous, autobasidium, autobiographal, autobiographer, autobiographers, autobiographic, autobiographical, autobiographically, autobiographies, autobiographist, autobiography, autobiography's, autobiology, autoblast, autoboat, autoboating, autobolide, autobus, autobuses, autobusses, autocab, autocade, autocades, autocall, autocamp, autocamper, autocamping, autocar, autocarist, autocarp, autocarpian, autocarpic, autocarpous, autocatalepsy, autocatalyses, autocatalysis, autocatalytic, autocatalytically, autocatalyze, autocatharsis, autocatheterism, autocephalia, autocephalic, autocephality, autocephalous, autocephaly, autoceptive, autochanger, autochemical, autocholecystectomy, autochrome, autochromy, autochronograph, autochthon, autochthonal, autochthones, autochthonic, autochthonism, autochthonous, autochthonously, autochthonousness, autochthons, autochthony, autochton, autocide, autocinesis, autoclasis, autoclastic, autoclave, autoclaved, autoclaves, autoclaving, autocoder, autocoenobium, autocoherer, autocoid, autocoids, autocollimate, autocollimation, autocollimator, autocollimators, autocolony, autocombustible, autocombustion, autocomplexes, autocondensation, autoconduction, autoconvection, autoconverter, autocopist, autocoprophagous, autocorrelate, autocorrelation, autocorrosion, autocosm, autocracies, autocracy, autocrat, autocrat's, autocratic, autocratical, autocratically, autocraticalness, autocrator, autocratoric, autocratorical, autocratrix, autocrats, autocratship, autocremation, autocriticism, autocross, autocue, autocycle, autocystoplasty, autocytolysis, autocytolytic, autodecomposition, autodecrement, autodecremented, autodecrements, autodepolymerization, autodermic, autodestruction, autodetector, autodiagnosis, autodiagnostic, autodiagrammatic, autodial, autodialed, autodialer, autodialers, autodialing, autodialled, autodialling, autodials, autodidact, autodidactic, autodidactically, autodidacts, autodifferentiation, autodiffusion, autodigestion, autodigestive, autodrainage, autodrome, autodynamic, autodyne, autodynes, autoecholalia, autoecic, autoecious, autoeciously, autoeciousness, autoecism, autoecous, autoecy, autoed, autoeducation, autoeducative, autoelectrolysis, autoelectrolytic, autoelectronic, autoelevation, autoepigraph, autoepilation, autoerotic, autoerotically, autoeroticism, autoerotism, autoette, autoexcitation, autofecundation, autofermentation, autofluorescence, autoformation, autofrettage, autogamic, autogamies, autogamous, autogamy, autogauge, autogeneal, autogeneses, autogenesis, autogenetic, autogenetically, autogenic, autogenies, autogenous, autogenously, autogenuous, autogeny, autogiro, autogiros, autognosis, autognostic, autograft, autografting, autogram, autograph, autographal, autographed, autographer, autographic, autographical, autographically, autographing, autographism, autographist, autographometer, autographs, autography, autogravure, autogyro, autogyros, autoharp, autoheader, autohemic, autohemolysin, autohemolysis, autohemolytic, autohemorrhage, autohemotherapy, autoheterodyne, autoheterosis, autohexaploid, autohybridization, autohypnosis, autohypnotic, autohypnotically, autohypnotism, autohypnotization, autoicous, autoignition, autoimmune, autoimmunities, autoimmunity, autoimmunization, autoimmunize, autoimmunized, autoimmunizing, autoincrement, autoincremented, autoincrements, autoindex, autoindexing, autoinduction, autoinductive, autoinfection, autoinfusion, autoing, autoinhibited, autoinoculable, autoinoculation, autointellectual, autointoxicant, autointoxication, autoionization, autoirrigation, autoist, autojigger, autojuggernaut, autokinesis, autokinesy, autokinetic, autokrator, autolaryngoscope, autolaryngoscopic, autolaryngoscopy, autolater, autolatry, autolavage, autolesion, autolimnetic, autolith, autolithograph, autolithographer, autolithographic, autolithography, autoloader, autoloaders, autoloading, autological, autologist, autologous, autology, autoluminescence, autoluminescent, autolysate, autolyse, autolysin, autolysis, autolytic, autolyzate, autolyze, autolyzed, autolyzes, autolyzing, automa, automacy, automaker, automan, automania, automanipulation, automanipulative, automanual, automat, automata, automatable, automate, automated, automates, automatic, automatical, automatically, automaticity, automatics, automatictacessing, automation, automatism, automatist, automative, automatization, automatize, automatized, automatizes, automatizing, automatograph, automaton, automatonlike, automatons, automatonta, automatontons, automatous, automats, automechanical, automechanism, automelon, automen, autometamorphosis, autometric, autometry, automobile, automobile's, automobiled, automobiles, automobiling, automobilism, automobilist, automobilistic, automobilists, automobility, automolite, automonstration, automorph, automorphic, automorphically, automorphism, automotive, automotor, automower, autompne, automysophobia, autonavigator, autonavigator's, autonavigators, autonegation, autonephrectomy, autonephrotoxin, autonetics, autoneurotoxin, autonitridation, autonoetic, autonomasy, autonomic, autonomical, autonomically, autonomies, autonomist, autonomize, autonomous, autonomously, autonomousness, autonomy, autonym, autooxidation, autoparasitism, autopathic, autopathography, autopathy, autopelagic, autopepsia, autophagi, autophagia, autophagous, autophagy, autophobia, autophoby, autophon, autophone, autophonoscope, autophonous, autophony, autophotoelectric, autophotograph, autophotometry, autophthalmoscope, autophyllogeny, autophyte, autophytic, autophytically, autophytograph, autophytography, autopilot, autopilot's, autopilots, autopista, autoplagiarism, autoplasmotherapy, autoplast, autoplastic, autoplastically, autoplasties, autoplasty, autopneumatic, autopoint, autopoisonous, autopolar, autopolo, autopoloist, autopolyploid, autopolyploidy, autopore, autoportrait, autoportraiture, autopositive, autopotamic, autopotent, autoprogressive, autoproteolysis, autoprothesis, autopsic, autopsical, autopsied, autopsies, autopsist, autopsy, autopsychic, autopsychoanalysis, autopsychology, autopsychorhythmia, autopsychosis, autopsying, autoptic, autoptical, autoptically, autopticity, autoput, autopyotherapy, autor, autoracemization, autoradiogram, autoradiograph, autoradiographic, autoradiography, autorail, autoreduction, autoreflection, autoregenerator, autoregressive, autoregulation, autoregulative, autoregulatory, autoreinfusion, autoretardation, autorhythmic, autorhythmus, autoriser, autorotate, autorotation, autorotational, autoroute, autorrhaphy, autos, autoschediasm, autoschediastic, autoschediastical, autoschediastically, autoschediaze, autoscience, autoscope, autoscopic, autoscopy, autosender, autosensitization, autosensitized, autosepticemia, autoserotherapy, autoserum, autosexing, autosight, autosign, autosite, autositic, autoskeleton, autosled, autoslip, autosomal, autosomally, autosomatognosis, autosomatognostic, autosome, autosomes, autosoteric, autosoterism, autospore, autosporic, autospray, autostability, autostage, autostandardization, autostarter, autostethoscope, autostoper, autostrada, autostradas, autostylic, autostylism, autostyly, autosuggest, autosuggestibility, autosuggestible, autosuggestion, autosuggestionist, autosuggestions, autosuggestive, autosuppression, autosymbiontic, autosymbolic, autosymbolical, autosymbolically, autosymnoia, autosyn, autosyndesis, autota, autotelegraph, autotelic, autotelism, autotetraploid, autotetraploidy, autothaumaturgist, autotheater, autotheism, autotheist, autotherapeutic, autotherapy, autothermy, autotimer, autotomic, autotomies, autotomise, autotomised, autotomising, autotomize, autotomized, autotomizing, autotomous, autotomy, autotoxaemia, autotoxemia, autotoxic, autotoxication, autotoxicity, autotoxicosis, autotoxin, autotoxis, autotractor, autotransformer, autotransfusion, autotransplant, autotransplantation, autotrepanation, autotriploid, autotriploidy, autotroph, autotrophic, autotrophically, autotrophy, autotropic, autotropically, autotropism, autotruck, autotuberculin, autoturning, autotype, autotypes, autotyphization, autotypic, autotypies, autotypography, autotypy, autourine, autovaccination, autovaccine, autovalet, autovalve, autovivisection, autoxeny, autoxidation, autoxidator, autoxidizability, autoxidizable, autoxidize, autoxidizer, autozooid, autre, autrefois, autumn, autumn's, autumnal, autumnally, autumnian, autumnity, autumns, autunite, autunites, auturgy, aux, auxamylase, auxanogram, auxanology, auxanometer, auxeses, auxesis, auxetic, auxetical, auxetically, auxetics, auxil, auxiliar, auxiliaries, auxiliarly, auxiliary, auxiliate, auxiliation, auxiliator, auxiliatory, auxilium, auxillary, auxilytic, auximone, auxin, auxinic, auxinically, auxins, auxoaction, auxoamylase, auxoblast, auxobody, auxocardia, auxochrome, auxochromic, auxochromism, auxochromous, auxocyte, auxoflore, auxofluor, auxograph, auxographic, auxohormone, auxology, auxometer, auxospore, auxosubstance, auxotonic, auxotox, auxotroph, auxotrophic, auxotrophy, av, ava, avadana, avadavat, avadavats, avadhuta, avahi, avail, availabile, availabilities, availability, available, availableness, availably, availed, availer, availers, availing, availingly, availment, avails, aval, avalanche, avalanched, avalanches, avalanching, avale, avalent, avalon, avalvular, avance, avania, avanious, avant, avantage, avanters, avantgarde, avantlay, avanturine, avanyu, avaram, avaremotemo, avarice, avarices, avaricious, avariciously, avariciousness, avaritia, avascular, avast, avatar, avatara, avatars, avaunt, avdp, ave, avell, avellan, avellane, avellaneous, avellano, avelonge, aveloz, avenaceous, avenage, avenalin, avenant, avenary, avener, avenery, avenge, avenged, avengeful, avengement, avenger, avengeress, avengers, avenges, avenging, avengingly, avenida, aveniform, avenin, avenine, avenolith, avenous, avens, avenses, aventail, aventails, aventayle, aventine, aventre, aventure, aventurin, aventurine, avenue, avenue's, avenues, aveny, aver, avera, average, averaged, averagely, averageness, averager, averages, averaging, averah, averia, averil, averin, averish, averment, averments, avern, avernal, avernus, averrable, averral, averred, averrer, averring, averroist, averruncate, averruncation, averruncator, avers, aversant, aversation, averse, aversely, averseness, aversion, aversion's, aversions, aversive, avert, avertable, averted, avertedly, averter, avertible, avertiment, avertin, averting, avertive, averts, aves, avesta, avestan, avestruz, aveugle, avg, avgas, avgases, avgasses, aviador, avian, avianization, avianize, avianized, avianizes, avianizing, avians, aviararies, aviaries, aviarist, aviarists, aviary, aviate, aviated, aviates, aviatic, aviating, aviation, aviational, aviations, aviator, aviator's, aviatorial, aviatoriality, aviators, aviatory, aviatress, aviatrice, aviatrices, aviatrix, aviatrixes, avichi, avicide, avick, avicolous, avicular, avicularia, avicularian, avicularium, aviculture, aviculturist, avid, avidin, avidins, avidious, avidiously, avidities, avidity, avidly, avidness, avidnesses, avidous, avidya, avie, aview, avifauna, avifaunae, avifaunal, avifaunally, avifaunas, avifaunistic, avigate, avigation, avigator, avigators, avijja, avilaria, avile, avilement, avilion, avine, aviolite, avion, avionic, avionics, avions, avirulence, avirulent, avis, avision, aviso, avisos, avital, avitaminoses, avitaminosis, avitaminotic, avitic, avives, avizandum, avn, avo, avocado, avocadoes, avocados, avocat, avocate, avocation, avocation's, avocational, avocationally, avocations, avocative, avocatory, avocet, avocets, avodire, avodires, avogadrite, avogadro, avogram, avoid, avoidable, avoidably, avoidance, avoidances, avoidant, avoided, avoider, avoiders, avoiding, avoidless, avoidment, avoids, avoir, avoirdupois, avoke, avolate, avolation, avolitional, avondbloem, avos, avoset, avosets, avouch, avouchable, avouched, avoucher, avouchers, avouches, avouching, avouchment, avoue, avour, avoure, avourneen, avouter, avoutry, avow, avowable, avowableness, avowably, avowal, avowals, avowance, avowant, avowe, avowed, avowedly, avowedness, avower, avowers, avowing, avowries, avowry, avows, avowter, avoy, avoyer, avoyership, avulse, avulsed, avulses, avulsing, avulsion, avulsions, avuncular, avunculate, avunculize, avyayibhava, avys, aw, awa, awabi, awacs, awaft, awag, await, awaited, awaiter, awaiters, awaiting, awaits, awakable, awake, awakeable, awaked, awaken, awakenable, awakened, awakener, awakeners, awakening, awakeningly, awakenings, awakenment, awakens, awakes, awaking, awakings, awald, awalim, awalt, awane, awanting, awanyu, awapuhi, award, awardable, awarded, awardee, awardees, awarder, awarders, awarding, awardment, awards, aware, awaredom, awareness, awarn, awarrant, awaruite, awash, awaste, awat, awatch, awater, awave, away, awayness, awaynesses, aways, awber, awd, awe, awearied, aweary, aweather, aweband, awed, awedly, awedness, awee, aweek, aweel, aweigh, aweing, aweless, awelessness, awes, awesome, awesomely, awesomeness, awest, awestricken, awestrike, awestruck, aweto, awfu, awful, awfuller, awfullest, awfully, awfulness, awhape, awheel, awheft, awhet, awhile, awhir, awhirl, awide, awiggle, awikiwiki, awin, awing, awingly, awink, awiwi, awk, awkly, awkward, awkwarder, awkwardest, awkwardish, awkwardly, awkwardness, awl, awl's, awless, awlessness, awls, awlwort, awlworts, awm, awmbrie, awmous, awn, awned, awner, awning, awning's, awninged, awnings, awnless, awnlike, awns, awny, awoke, awoken, awol, awols, awonder, awork, aworry, aworth, awreak, awreck, awrist, awrong, awry, awunctive, ax, axal, axanthopsia, axbreaker, axe, axebreaker, axed, axel, axels, axeman, axemaster, axemen, axenic, axenically, axer, axerophthol, axers, axes, axfetch, axhammer, axhammered, axhead, axial, axialities, axiality, axially, axiate, axiation, axiferous, axiform, axifugal, axil, axile, axilemma, axilemmas, axilemmata, axilla, axillae, axillant, axillar, axillaries, axillars, axillary, axillas, axils, axin, axine, axing, axiniform, axinite, axinomancy, axiolite, axiolitic, axiological, axiologically, axiologies, axiologist, axiology, axiom, axiom's, axiomatic, axiomatical, axiomatically, axiomatization, axiomatization's, axiomatizations, axiomatize, axiomatized, axiomatizes, axiomatizing, axioms, axion, axiopisty, axis, axised, axises, axisymmetric, axisymmetrical, axisymmetrically, axisymmetry, axite, axites, axle, axle's, axled, axles, axlesmith, axletree, axletrees, axlike, axmaker, axmaking, axman, axmanship, axmaster, axmen, axminster, axodendrite, axofugal, axogamy, axoid, axoidean, axolemma, axolotl, axolotl's, axolotls, axolysis, axometer, axometric, axometry, axon, axon's, axonal, axone, axonemal, axoneme, axonemes, axones, axoneure, axoneuron, axonic, axonolipous, axonometric, axonometry, axonophorous, axonost, axons, axopetal, axophyte, axoplasm, axoplasmic, axoplasms, axopodia, axopodium, axospermous, axostyle, axotomous, axseed, axseeds, axstone, axtree, axunge, axweed, axwise, axwort, ay, ayacahuite, ayah, ayahausca, ayahs, ayahuasca, ayapana, ayatollah, ayatollahs, aye, ayegreen, ayelp, ayen, ayenbite, ayens, ayenst, ayes, ayield, ayin, ayins, ayless, aylet, ayllu, aymara, ayme, ayne, ayond, ayont, ayous, ayre, ayrshire, ays, ayu, ayudante, ayuntamiento, ayuntamientos, ayurveda, ayurvedas, ayuyu, aywhere, az, azadirachta, azadrachta, azafran, azafrin, azalea, azalea's, azaleamum, azaleas, azan, azans, azarole, azaserine, azathioprine, azazel, azedarac, azedarach, azelaic, azelate, azeotrope, azeotropic, azeotropism, azeotropy, azide, azides, azido, aziethane, azilut, azimene, azimethylene, azimide, azimin, azimine, azimino, aziminobenzene, azimuth, azimuth's, azimuthal, azimuthally, azimuths, azine, azines, azinphosmethyl, aziola, azlactone, azlon, azlons, azo, azobacter, azobenzene, azobenzil, azobenzoic, azobenzol, azoblack, azoch, azocochineal, azocoralline, azocorinth, azocyanide, azocyclic, azodicarboxylic, azodiphenyl, azodisulphonic, azoeosin, azoerythrin, azofication, azofier, azoflavine, azoformamide, azoformic, azofy, azogallein, azogreen, azogrenadine, azohumic, azoic, azoimide, azoisobutyronitrile, azole, azoles, azolitmin, azomethine, azon, azonal, azonaphthalene, azonic, azonium, azons, azoology, azoospermia, azoparaffin, azophen, azophenetole, azophenine, azophenol, azophenyl, azophenylene, azophosphin, azophosphore, azoprotein, azores, azorite, azorubine, azosulphine, azosulphonic, azotaemia, azotate, azote, azotea, azoted, azotemia, azotemias, azotemic, azotenesis, azotes, azotetrazole, azoth, azothionium, azoths, azotic, azotin, azotine, azotise, azotised, azotises, azotising, azotite, azotize, azotized, azotizes, azotizing, azotobacter, azotoluene, azotometer, azotorrhea, azotorrhoea, azotous, azoturia, azoturias, azovernine, azox, azoxazole, azoxime, azoxine, azoxonium, azoxy, azoxyanisole, azoxybenzene, azoxybenzoic, azoxynaphthalene, azoxyphenetole, azoxytoluidine, azrael, aztec, azteca, aztecan, aztecs, azthionium, azulejo, azulejos, azulene, azuline, azulite, azulmic, azumbre, azure, azurean, azured, azureness, azureous, azures, azurine, azurite, azurites, azurmalachite, azurous, azury, azygobranchiate, azygomatous, azygos, azygoses, azygosperm, azygospore, azygote, azygous, azyme, azymite, azymous, b, b'hoy, b's, b/l, b/s, ba, baa, baaed, baahling, baaing, baal, baalim, baalism, baalisms, baals, baar, baas, baaskaap, baaskaaps, baaskap, bab, baba, babacoote, babai, babajaga, babakoto, babas, babasco, babassu, babassus, babasu, babaylan, babaylanes, babbage, babbie, babbishly, babbit, babbitt, babbitted, babbitter, babbitting, babbittry, babbitts, babblative, babble, babbled, babblement, babbler, babblers, babbles, babblesome, babbling, babblingly, babblings, babblish, babblishly, babbly, babbool, babbools, babby, babcock, babe, babe's, babehood, babel, babel's, babelet, babelike, babels, babery, babes, babeship, babesia, babesias, babesiasis, babesiosis, babiche, babiches, babied, babies, babillard, babingtonite, babion, babirousa, babiroussa, babirusa, babirusas, babirussa, babis, babish, babished, babishly, babishness, babka, babkas, bablah, bable, babloh, baboen, baboo, baboodom, babooism, babool, babools, baboon, baboonery, baboonish, baboonroot, baboons, baboos, baboosh, baboot, babouche, babracot, babroot, babu, babudom, babuina, babuism, babul, babuls, baburd, babus, babushka, babushkas, baby, babydom, babyfied, babyhood, babyhoods, babyhouse, babying, babyish, babyishly, babyishness, babyism, babylike, babylon, babylonia, babylonian, babylonians, babylonish, babyolatry, babysat, babyship, babysit, babysitter, babysitting, bac, bacaba, bacach, bacalao, bacalaos, bacao, bacauan, bacbakiri, bacca, baccaceous, baccae, baccalaurean, baccalaureat, baccalaureate, baccalaureates, baccalaureus, baccar, baccara, baccaras, baccarat, baccarats, baccare, baccate, baccated, bacchae, bacchanal, bacchanalia, bacchanalian, bacchanalianism, bacchanalianly, bacchanalias, bacchanalism, bacchanalization, bacchanalize, bacchanals, bacchant, bacchante, bacchantes, bacchantic, bacchants, bacchar, baccharis, baccharoid, baccheion, bacchiac, bacchian, bacchic, bacchii, bacchiuchii, bacchius, bacchus, baccies, bacciferous, bacciform, baccilla, baccilli, baccillla, baccillum, baccivorous, baccy, bach, bach's, bacharach, bache, bached, bachel, bachelor, bachelor's, bachelordom, bachelorette, bachelorhood, bachelorism, bachelorize, bachelorlike, bachelorly, bachelors, bachelorship, bachelorwise, bachelry, baches, baching, bacilary, bacile, bacillar, bacillariaceous, bacillary, bacillemia, bacilli, bacillian, bacillicidal, bacillicide, bacillicidic, bacilliculture, bacilliform, bacilligenic, bacilliparous, bacillite, bacillogenic, bacillogenous, bacillophobia, bacillosis, bacilluria, bacillus, bacin, bacitracin, back, backache, backache's, backaches, backaching, backachy, backadation, backage, backare, backarrow, backarrows, backband, backbar, backbear, backbearing, backbeat, backbeats, backbencher, backbenchers, backbend, backbend's, backbends, backberand, backberend, backbit, backbite, backbiter, backbiters, backbites, backbiting, backbitingly, backbitten, backblocks, backblow, backboard, backboards, backbone, backbone's, backboned, backboneless, backbonelessness, backbones, backbrand, backbreaker, backbreaking, backcap, backcast, backcasts, backchain, backchat, backchats, backcloth, backcomb, backcountry, backcourt, backcourtman, backcross, backdate, backdated, backdates, backdating, backdoor, backdown, backdrop, backdrop's, backdrops, backed, backen, backened, backening, backer, backers, backet, backfall, backfatter, backfield, backfields, backfill, backfilled, backfiller, backfilling, backfills, backfire, backfired, backfires, backfiring, backflap, backflash, backflip, backflow, backflowing, backfold, backframe, backfriend, backfurrow, backgame, backgammon, backgeared, background, background's, backgrounds, backhand, backhanded, backhandedly, backhandedness, backhander, backhanding, backhands, backhatch, backhaul, backhauled, backhauling, backhauls, backheel, backhoe, backhoes, backhooker, backhouse, backhouses, backie, backiebird, backing, backings, backjaw, backjoint, backland, backlands, backlash, backlashed, backlasher, backlashes, backlashing, backless, backlet, backliding, backlighting, backlings, backlins, backlist, backlists, backlit, backlog, backlog's, backlogged, backlogging, backlogs, backlotter, backmost, backoff, backorder, backout, backouts, backpack, backpack's, backpacked, backpacker, backpackers, backpacking, backpacks, backpedal, backpedaled, backpedaling, backpiece, backplane, backplane's, backplanes, backplate, backpointer, backpointer's, backpointers, backrest, backrests, backrope, backropes, backrun, backrush, backrushes, backs, backsaw, backsaws, backscatter, backscattered, backscattering, backscatters, backscraper, backscratcher, backscratching, backseat, backseats, backset, backsets, backsetting, backsettler, backsey, backsheesh, backshift, backshish, backside, backsides, backsight, backsite, backslap, backslapped, backslapper, backslappers, backslapping, backslaps, backslash, backslashes, backslid, backslidden, backslide, backslided, backslider, backsliders, backslides, backsliding, backslidingness, backspace, backspaced, backspacefile, backspacer, backspaces, backspacing, backspang, backspear, backspeer, backspeir, backspier, backspierer, backspin, backspins, backsplice, backspliced, backsplicing, backspread, backspringing, backstab, backstabbed, backstabber, backstabbing, backstaff, backstage, backstair, backstairs, backstamp, backstay, backstays, backster, backstick, backstitch, backstitched, backstitches, backstitching, backstone, backstop, backstopped, backstopping, backstops, backstrap, backstrapped, backstreet, backstretch, backstretches, backstring, backstrip, backstroke, backstroked, backstrokes, backstroking, backstromite, backswept, backswimmer, backswing, backsword, backswording, backswordman, backswordmen, backswordsman, backtack, backtalk, backtender, backtenter, backtrace, backtrack, backtracked, backtracker, backtrackers, backtracking, backtracks, backtrail, backtrick, backup, backups, backus, backveld, backvelder, backwall, backward, backwardation, backwardly, backwardness, backwards, backwash, backwashed, backwasher, backwashes, backwashing, backwater, backwater's, backwatered, backwaters, backway, backwind, backwinded, backwinding, backwood, backwoods, backwoodser, backwoodsiness, backwoodsman, backwoodsmen, backwoodsy, backword, backworm, backwort, backwrap, backwraps, backy, backyard, backyard's, backyarder, backyards, baclava, baclin, bacon, baconer, baconian, baconize, bacons, baconweed, bacony, bacquet, bact, bacteraemia, bacteremia, bacteremic, bacteria, bacteriaceous, bacteriaemia, bacterial, bacterially, bacterian, bacteric, bactericholia, bactericidal, bactericidally, bactericide, bactericides, bactericidin, bacterid, bacteriemia, bacteriform, bacterin, bacterins, bacterioagglutinin, bacterioblast, bacteriochlorophyll, bacteriocidal, bacteriocin, bacteriocyte, bacteriodiagnosis, bacteriofluorescin, bacteriogenic, bacteriogenous, bacteriohemolysin, bacterioid, bacterioidal, bacteriol, bacteriologic, bacteriological, bacteriologically, bacteriologies, bacteriologist, bacteriologists, bacteriology, bacteriolysin, bacteriolysis, bacteriolytic, bacteriolyze, bacteriopathology, bacteriophage, bacteriophages, bacteriophagia, bacteriophagic, bacteriophagous, bacteriophagy, bacteriophobia, bacterioprecipitin, bacterioprotein, bacteriopsonic, bacteriopsonin, bacteriopurpurin, bacteriorhodopsin, bacterioscopic, bacterioscopical, bacterioscopically, bacterioscopist, bacterioscopy, bacteriosis, bacteriosolvent, bacteriostasis, bacteriostat, bacteriostatic, bacteriostatically, bacteriotherapeutic, bacteriotherapy, bacteriotoxic, bacteriotoxin, bacteriotropic, bacteriotropin, bacteriotrypsin, bacterious, bacteririum, bacteritic, bacterium, bacteriuria, bacterization, bacterize, bacterized, bacterizing, bacteroid, bacteroidal, bacteroides, bactetiophage, bactriticone, bactritoid, bacubert, bacula, bacule, baculere, baculi, baculiferous, baculiform, baculine, baculite, baculitic, baculiticone, baculoid, baculum, baculums, baculus, bacury, bad, badan, badarrah, badass, badassed, badasses, badaud, badaxe, badchan, baddeleyite, badder, badderlocks, baddest, baddie, baddies, baddish, baddishly, baddishness, baddock, baddy, bade, badenite, badge, badged, badgeless, badgeman, badgemen, badger, badger's, badgerbrush, badgered, badgerer, badgering, badgeringly, badgerlike, badgerly, badgers, badgerweed, badges, badging, badgir, badhan, badiaga, badian, badigeon, badinage, badinaged, badinages, badinaging, badiner, badinerie, badineur, badious, badju, badland, badlands, badling, badly, badman, badmash, badmen, badminton, badmouth, badmouthed, badmouthing, badmouths, badness, badnesses, badrans, bads, bae, baedeker, baedekers, bael, baetuli, baetulus, baetyl, baetylic, baetylus, baetzner, bafaro, baff, baffed, baffeta, baffies, baffing, baffle, baffled, bafflement, bafflements, baffleplate, baffler, bafflers, baffles, baffling, bafflingly, bafflingness, baffs, baffy, baft, bafta, baftah, bag, bag's, baga, bagani, bagass, bagasse, bagasses, bagataway, bagatelle, bagatelle's, bagatelles, bagatine, bagattini, bagattino, bagel, bagel's, bagels, bagful, bagfuls, baggage, baggageman, baggagemaster, baggager, baggages, baggala, bagganet, bagge, bagged, bagger, bagger's, baggers, baggie, baggier, baggies, baggiest, baggily, bagginess, bagging, baggings, baggit, baggy, baggyrinkle, baggywrinkle, bagh, baghdad, baghla, baghouse, bagie, bagio, bagios, bagle, bagleaves, baglike, bagmaker, bagmaking, bagman, bagmen, bagne, bagnes, bagnet, bagnette, bagnio, bagnios, bagnut, bago, bagonet, bagong, bagoong, bagpipe, bagpipe's, bagpiped, bagpiper, bagpipers, bagpipes, bagpiping, bagplant, bagpod, bagpudding, bagrationite, bagre, bagreef, bagroom, bags, bagsful, bagtikan, baguet, baguets, baguette, baguettes, baguio, baguios, bagwash, bagwig, bagwigged, bagwigs, bagwoman, bagwomen, bagwork, bagworm, bagworms, bagwyn, bah, bahada, bahadur, bahadurs, bahai, bahamas, bahamian, bahamians, bahan, bahar, bahawder, bahay, bahera, bahiaite, bahisti, bahnung, baho, bahoe, bahoo, baht, bahts, bahur, bahut, bahuts, bahuvrihi, bahuvrihis, bai, baidak, baidar, baidarka, baidarkas, baiginet, baign, baignet, baigneuse, baigneuses, baignoire, baikalite, baikerinite, baikerite, baikie, bail, bailable, bailage, baile, bailed, bailee, bailees, bailer, bailers, bailey, baileys, bailiaries, bailiary, bailie, bailieries, bailiery, bailies, bailieship, bailiff, bailiff's, bailiffry, bailiffs, bailiffship, bailiffwick, bailing, bailiwick, bailiwicks, bailli, bailliage, baillie, baillone, bailment, bailments, bailo, bailor, bailors, bailout, bailouts, bailpiece, bails, bailsman, bailsmen, bailwood, bain, bainie, bainite, baioc, baiocchi, baiocco, bairagi, bairam, bairdi, bairn, bairnie, bairnish, bairnishness, bairnlier, bairnliest, bairnliness, bairnly, bairns, bairnteam, bairnteem, bairntime, bairnwort, baisemain, baister, bait, baited, baiter, baiters, baitfish, baith, baiting, baits, baittle, baitylos, baiza, baizas, baize, baized, baizes, baizing, baja, bajada, bajan, bajarigar, bajocco, bajochi, bajoire, bajonado, bajra, bajree, bajri, bajulate, bajury, baka, bakal, bake, bakeapple, bakeboard, baked, bakehead, bakehouse, bakehouses, bakelite, bakelize, bakemeat, bakemeats, baken, bakeout, bakeoven, bakepan, baker, bakerdom, bakeress, bakeries, bakerite, bakerless, bakerlike, bakerly, bakers, bakersfield, bakership, bakery, bakery's, bakes, bakeshop, bakeshops, bakestone, bakeware, bakie, baking, bakingly, bakings, baklava, baklavas, baklawa, baklawas, bakli, bakra, baksheesh, baksheeshes, bakshi, bakshis, bakshish, bakshished, bakshishes, bakshishing, baktun, baku, bakula, bakupari, bal, balaam, balabos, balachan, balachong, balaclava, balada, baladine, balaenid, balaenoid, balaenoidean, balafo, balagan, balaghat, balaghaut, balai, balalaika, balalaika's, balalaikas, balance, balanceable, balanced, balancedness, balancelle, balanceman, balancement, balancer, balancers, balances, balancewise, balancing, balander, balandra, balandrana, balaneutics, balangay, balanic, balanid, balaniferous, balanism, balanite, balanitis, balanoblennorrhea, balanocele, balanoid, balanophoraceous, balanophore, balanophorin, balanoplasty, balanoposthitis, balanopreputial, balanops, balanorrhagia, balant, balantidial, balantidiasis, balantidic, balantidiosis, balao, balaos, balaphon, balarao, balas, balases, balat, balata, balatas, balate, balatong, balatron, balatronic, balatte, balau, balausta, balaustine, balaustre, balayeuse, balboa, balboas, balbriggan, balbusard, balbutiate, balbutient, balbuties, balche, balcon, balcone, balconet, balconette, balconied, balconies, balcony, balcony's, bald, baldacchini, baldacchino, baldachin, baldachined, baldachini, baldachino, baldachinos, baldachins, baldakin, baldaquin, baldberry, baldcrown, balded, balden, balder, balderdash, baldest, baldfaced, baldhead, baldheaded, baldheads, baldicoot, balding, baldish, baldling, baldly, baldmoney, baldmoneys, baldness, baldnesses, baldoquin, baldpate, baldpated, baldpatedness, baldpates, baldrib, baldric, baldrick, baldricked, baldricks, baldrics, baldricwise, balds, balducta, balductum, baldy, bale, baleare, balebos, baled, baleen, baleens, balefire, balefires, baleful, balefully, balefulness, balei, baleise, baleless, baler, balers, bales, balestra, balete, balewort, baleys, bali, balian, balibago, balibuntal, balibuntl, balimbing, baline, balinese, baling, balinger, balinghasay, balisaur, balisaurs, balisier, balistarii, balistarius, balister, balistid, balistraria, balita, balitao, baliti, balize, balk, balkan, balkanization, balkanize, balkanized, balkanizing, balkans, balked, balker, balkers, balkier, balkiest, balkily, balkiness, balking, balkingly, balkish, balkline, balklines, balks, balky, ball, ballad, ballad's, ballade, balladeer, balladeers, ballader, balladeroyal, ballades, balladic, balladical, balladier, balladise, balladised, balladising, balladism, balladist, balladize, balladized, balladizing, balladlike, balladling, balladmonger, balladmongering, balladries, balladromic, balladry, ballads, balladwise, ballahoo, ballahou, ballam, ballan, ballant, ballarag, ballard, ballas, ballast, ballast's, ballastage, ballasted, ballaster, ballastic, ballasting, ballasts, ballat, ballata, ballate, ballaton, ballatoon, ballbuster, ballcarrier, balldom, balldress, balled, baller, ballerina, ballerina's, ballerinas, ballerine, ballers, ballet, ballet's, balletic, balletically, balletomane, balletomanes, balletomania, ballets, ballett, ballfield, ballflower, ballgame, ballgames, ballgown, ballgown's, ballgowns, ballhawk, ballhawks, ballhooter, balli, balliage, ballies, balling, ballised, ballism, ballismus, ballist, ballista, ballistae, ballistic, ballistically, ballistician, ballisticians, ballistics, ballistite, ballistocardiogram, ballistocardiograph, ballistocardiographic, ballistocardiography, ballistophobia, ballium, ballmine, ballo, ballock, ballocks, balloen, ballogan, ballon, ballone, ballones, ballonet, ballonets, ballonette, ballonne, ballonnes, ballons, balloon, balloonation, ballooned, ballooner, ballooners, balloonery, balloonet, balloonfish, balloonfishes, balloonflower, balloonful, ballooning, balloonish, balloonist, balloonlike, balloons, ballot, ballot's, ballotade, ballotage, ballote, balloted, balloter, balloters, balloting, ballotist, ballots, ballottable, ballottement, ballottine, ballottines, ballow, ballpark, ballpark's, ballparks, ballplayer, ballplayer's, ballplayers, ballpoint, ballpoints, ballproof, ballroom, ballroom's, ballrooms, balls, ballsier, ballsiest, ballstock, ballsy, ballup, ballute, ballutes, ballweed, bally, ballyhack, ballyhoo, ballyhooed, ballyhooer, ballyhooing, ballyhoos, ballyrag, ballyragged, ballyragging, ballyrags, ballywack, ballywrack, balm, balm's, balmacaan, balmier, balmiest, balmily, balminess, balmlike, balmonies, balmony, balmoral, balmorals, balms, balmy, balnea, balneae, balneal, balneary, balneation, balneatory, balneographer, balneography, balneologic, balneological, balneologist, balneology, balneophysiology, balneotechnics, balneotherapeutics, balneotherapia, balneotherapy, balneum, balon, balonea, baloney, baloneys, baloo, balopticon, balotade, balourdise, balow, balr, bals, balsa, balsam, balsamaceous, balsamation, balsameaceous, balsamed, balsamer, balsamic, balsamical, balsamically, balsamiferous, balsamina, balsaminaceous, balsamine, balsaming, balsamitic, balsamiticness, balsamize, balsamo, balsamous, balsamroot, balsams, balsamum, balsamweed, balsamy, balsas, balsawood, baltei, balter, baltetei, balteus, baltheus, baltic, baltimore, baltimorite, balu, baluchi, baluchithere, baluchitheria, baluchitherium, balun, balushai, baluster, balustered, balusters, balustrade, balustrade's, balustraded, balustrades, balustrading, balut, balwarra, balza, balzarine, bam, bamah, bambacciata, bamban, bambini, bambino, bambinos, bambocciade, bambochade, bamboche, bamboo, bamboos, bamboozle, bamboozled, bamboozlement, bamboozler, bamboozlers, bamboozles, bamboozling, bamboula, bambuco, bambuk, bambusa, bammed, bamming, bamoth, bams, ban, ban's, banaba, banago, banagos, banak, banakite, banal, banalities, banality, banalize, banally, banalness, banana, banana's, bananaquit, bananas, bananist, bananivorous, banat, banate, banatite, banausic, banbury, banc, banca, bancal, bancales, bancha, banchi, banco, bancos, bancus, band, banda, bandage, bandaged, bandager, bandagers, bandages, bandaging, bandagist, bandaid, bandaite, bandaka, bandala, bandalore, bandana, bandanaed, bandanas, bandanna, bandannaed, bandannas, bandar, bandarlog, bandbox, bandboxes, bandboxical, bandboxy, bandcase, bandcutter, bande, bandeau, bandeaus, bandeaux, banded, bandel, bandelet, bandelette, bandeng, bander, banderilla, banderillas, banderillero, banderilleros, banderlog, banderol, banderole, banderoled, banderoles, banderoling, banderols, banders, bandersnatch, bandfile, bandfiled, bandfiling, bandfish, bandgap, bandh, bandhava, bandhook, bandhu, bandi, bandicoot, bandicoots, bandicoy, bandido, bandidos, bandie, bandied, bandies, bandikai, bandiness, banding, bandit, bandit's, banditism, banditries, banditry, bandits, banditti, bandle, bandleader, bandless, bandlessly, bandlessness, bandlet, bandlimit, bandlimited, bandlimiting, bandlimits, bandman, bandmaster, bandmasters, bando, bandobust, bandog, bandogs, bandoleer, bandoleered, bandoleers, bandolerismo, bandolero, bandoleros, bandolier, bandoliered, bandoline, bandon, bandonion, bandora, bandoras, bandore, bandores, bandos, bandpass, bandrol, bands, bandsaw, bandsawed, bandsawing, bandsawn, bandsman, bandsmen, bandspreading, bandstand, bandstand's, bandstands, bandster, bandstop, bandstring, bandura, bandurria, bandurrias, bandwagon, bandwagon's, bandwagons, bandwidth, bandwidths, bandwork, bandworm, bandy, bandyball, bandying, bandylegged, bandyman, bane, baneberries, baneberry, baned, baneful, banefully, banefulness, banes, banewort, bang, banga, bangalay, bangalow, bangboard, bange, banged, banger, bangers, banghy, bangiaceous, banging, bangkok, bangkoks, bangladesh, bangle, bangle's, bangled, bangles, bangling, bangos, bangs, bangster, bangtail, bangtailed, bangtails, bangup, bangy, bani, bania, banian, banians, banig, banilad, baning, banish, banished, banisher, banishers, banishes, banishing, banishment, banishments, banister, banister's, banisterine, banisters, baniwa, baniya, banjara, banjo, banjo's, banjoes, banjoist, banjoists, banjore, banjorine, banjos, banjuke, banjulele, bank, bankable, bankbook, bankbooks, bankcard, bankcards, banked, banker, bankera, bankerdom, bankeress, bankers, banket, bankfull, banking, bankings, bankman, bankmen, banknote, banknotes, bankrider, bankroll, bankrolled, bankroller, bankrolling, bankrolls, bankrupcy, bankrupt, bankruptcies, bankruptcy, bankruptcy's, bankrupted, bankrupting, bankruptism, bankruptlike, bankruptly, bankrupts, bankruptship, bankrupture, banks, bankshall, banksia, banksias, bankside, banksides, banksman, banksmen, bankweed, banky, banlieu, banlieue, bannack, bannat, banned, banner, banner's, bannered, bannerer, banneret, bannerets, bannerette, bannerfish, bannerless, bannerlike, bannerline, bannerman, bannermen, bannerol, bannerole, bannerols, banners, bannerwise, bannet, bannets, bannimus, banning, bannister, bannisters, bannition, bannock, bannocks, banns, bannut, banovina, banque, banquet, banqueted, banqueteer, banqueteering, banqueter, banqueters, banqueting, banquetings, banquets, banquette, banquettes, banquo, bans, bansalague, bansela, banshee, banshee's, banshees, banshie, banshies, banstickle, bant, bantam, bantamize, bantams, bantamweight, bantamweights, bantay, bantayan, banteng, banter, bantered, banterer, banterers, bantering, banteringly, banters, bantery, bantin, banting, bantingize, bantings, bantling, bantlings, bantu, bantus, banty, banus, banuyo, banxring, banya, banyan, banyans, banzai, banzais, baobab, baobabs, bap, baphomet, bapistery, bapt, baptise, baptised, baptises, baptisia, baptisias, baptising, baptism, baptism's, baptismal, baptismally, baptisms, baptist, baptist's, baptisteries, baptistery, baptistic, baptistries, baptistry, baptistry's, baptists, baptizable, baptize, baptized, baptizee, baptizement, baptizer, baptizers, baptizes, baptizing, bar, bar's, bara, barabara, barabbas, barabora, barad, baradari, baragnosis, baragouin, baragouinish, baraita, barajillo, baraka, baralipton, baramin, barandos, barangay, barani, bararesque, bararite, barasingha, barat, barathea, baratheas, barathra, barathron, barathrum, barato, baratte, barauna, baraza, barb, barba, barbacan, barbacou, barbadoes, barbados, barbal, barbaloin, barbar, barbara, barbaralalia, barbaresque, barbarian, barbarian's, barbarianism, barbarianize, barbarianized, barbarianizing, barbarians, barbaric, barbarical, barbarically, barbarious, barbariousness, barbarisation, barbarise, barbarised, barbarising, barbarism, barbarisms, barbarities, barbarity, barbarization, barbarize, barbarized, barbarizes, barbarizing, barbarous, barbarously, barbarousness, barbary, barbas, barbasco, barbascoes, barbascos, barbastel, barbastelle, barbate, barbated, barbatimao, barbe, barbeau, barbecue, barbecued, barbecueing, barbecuer, barbecues, barbecuing, barbed, barbedness, barbeiro, barbel, barbeled, barbell, barbell's, barbellate, barbells, barbellula, barbellulae, barbellulate, barbels, barbeque, barbequed, barbequing, barber, barbera, barbered, barberess, barberfish, barbering, barberish, barberite, barbermonger, barbero, barberries, barberry, barbers, barbershop, barbershops, barbery, barbes, barbet, barbets, barbette, barbettes, barbican, barbicanage, barbicans, barbicel, barbicels, barbierite, barbigerous, barbing, barbion, barbita, barbital, barbitalism, barbitals, barbiton, barbitone, barbitos, barbituism, barbiturate, barbiturates, barbituric, barbiturism, barble, barbless, barblet, barbola, barbone, barbotine, barbotte, barbouillage, barboy, barbre, barbs, barbu, barbudo, barbudos, barbula, barbulate, barbule, barbules, barbulyie, barbut, barbute, barbuts, barbwire, barbwires, barcarole, barcaroles, barcarolle, barcas, barcella, barcelona, barcelonas, barchan, barchans, barche, barcolongo, barcone, bard, bard's, bardane, bardash, bardcraft, barde, barded, bardee, bardel, bardelle, bardes, bardess, bardic, bardie, bardier, bardiest, bardiglio, bardily, bardiness, barding, bardings, bardish, bardism, bardlet, bardlike, bardling, bardo, bardocucullus, bardolater, bardolatry, bards, bardship, bardy, bare, bareback, barebacked, bareboat, bareboats, barebone, bareboned, barebones, bareca, bared, barefaced, barefacedly, barefacedness, barefisted, barefit, barefoot, barefooted, barege, bareges, barehanded, barehead, bareheaded, bareheadedness, bareka, bareknuckle, bareknuckled, barelegged, barely, barenecked, bareness, barenesses, barer, bares, baresark, baresarks, baresma, barest, baresthesia, baret, baretta, barf, barfed, barff, barfing, barfish, barflies, barfly, barfly's, barfs, barful, barfy, bargain, bargainable, bargained, bargainee, bargainer, bargainers, bargaining, bargainor, bargains, bargainwise, bargander, barge, bargeboard, barged, bargee, bargeer, bargees, bargeese, bargehouse, bargelike, bargelli, bargello, bargellos, bargeload, bargeman, bargemaster, bargemen, bargepole, barger, barges, bargestone, bargh, bargham, barghest, barghests, barging, bargir, bargoose, barguest, barguests, barhal, barhop, barhopped, barhopping, barhops, bari, baria, bariatrician, bariatrics, baric, barid, barie, barih, barile, barilla, barillas, baring, bariolage, baris, barish, barit, barite, baritenor, barites, baritonal, baritone, baritone's, baritones, barium, bariums, bark, barkan, barkantine, barkary, barkbound, barkcutter, barked, barkeep, barkeeper, barkeepers, barkeeps, barken, barkened, barkening, barkentine, barkentines, barker, barkers, barkery, barkevikite, barkevikitic, barkey, barkhan, barkier, barkiest, barking, barkingly, barkle, barkless, barklyite, barkometer, barkpeel, barkpeeler, barkpeeling, barks, barksome, barkstone, barky, barlafumble, barlafummil, barleduc, barleducs, barless, barley, barleybird, barleybrake, barleybreak, barleycorn, barleyhood, barleymow, barleys, barleysick, barling, barlock, barlow, barlows, barly, barm, barmaid, barmaids, barman, barmaster, barmbrack, barmcloth, barmecidal, barmecide, barmen, barmfel, barmie, barmier, barmiest, barming, barmkin, barmote, barms, barmskin, barmy, barmybrained, barn, barn's, barnabas, barnabite, barnaby, barnacle, barnacled, barnacles, barnacling, barnage, barnard, barnbrack, barndoor, barney, barneys, barnful, barnhardtite, barnier, barniest, barnlike, barnman, barnmen, barns, barnstorm, barnstormed, barnstormer, barnstormers, barnstorming, barnstorms, barnumize, barny, barnyard, barnyard's, barnyards, barocco, baroclinicity, baroclinity, barocyclonometer, barodynamic, barodynamics, barognosis, barogram, barograms, barograph, barographic, barographs, baroi, baroko, barolo, barology, baromacrometer, barometer, barometer's, barometers, barometric, barometrical, barometrically, barometrograph, barometrography, barometry, barometz, baromotor, baron, baron's, baronage, baronages, baronduki, baroness, baronesses, baronet, baronetage, baronetcies, baronetcy, baroneted, baronethood, baronetical, baroneting, baronetise, baronetised, baronetising, baronetize, baronetized, baronetizing, baronets, baronetship, barong, barongs, baroni, baronial, baronies, baronize, baronized, baronizing, baronne, baronnes, baronries, baronry, barons, baronship, barony, barony's, barophobia, baroque, baroquely, baroqueness, baroques, baroreceptor, baroscope, baroscopic, baroscopical, barosinusitis, barosinusitus, barosmin, barostat, baroswitch, barotactic, barotaxis, barotaxy, barothermogram, barothermograph, barothermohygrogram, barothermohygrograph, baroto, barotrauma, barotraumas, barotraumata, barotropic, barotropy, barouche, barouches, barouchet, barouchette, baroxyton, barpost, barquantine, barque, barquentine, barques, barquest, barquette, barr, barra, barrabkie, barrable, barrabora, barracan, barrace, barrack, barracked, barracker, barracking, barracks, barraclade, barracoon, barracouta, barracoutas, barracuda, barracudas, barracudina, barrad, barragan, barrage, barrage's, barraged, barrages, barraging, barragon, barramunda, barramundas, barramundi, barramundies, barramundis, barranca, barrancas, barranco, barrancos, barrandite, barras, barrat, barrater, barraters, barrator, barrators, barratries, barratrous, barratrously, barratry, barre, barred, barrel, barrel's, barrelage, barreled, barreler, barrelet, barreleye, barreleyes, barrelfish, barrelfishes, barrelful, barrelfuls, barrelhead, barrelhouse, barrelhouses, barreling, barrelled, barrelling, barrelmaker, barrelmaking, barrels, barrelsful, barrelwise, barren, barrener, barrenest, barrenly, barrenness, barrens, barrenwort, barrer, barrera, barres, barret, barretor, barretors, barretries, barretry, barrets, barrette, barretter, barrettes, barricade, barricade's, barricaded, barricader, barricaders, barricades, barricading, barricado, barricadoed, barricadoes, barricadoing, barricados, barrico, barricoes, barricos, barrier, barrier's, barriers, barriguda, barrigudo, barrigudos, barrikin, barriness, barring, barringer, barrio, barrios, barrister, barristerial, barristers, barristership, barristress, barroom, barrooms, barrow, barrowcoat, barrowful, barrowist, barrowman, barrows, barrulee, barrulet, barrulety, barruly, barry, bars, barse, barsom, barspoon, barstool, barstools, bart, bartend, bartended, bartender, bartender's, bartenders, bartending, bartends, barter, bartered, barterer, barterers, bartering, barters, barth, barthian, barthite, bartholinitis, bartholomew, bartisan, bartisans, bartizan, bartizaned, bartizans, bartlett, bartletts, barton, bartram, bartree, bartsia, baru, barukhzy, baruria, barvel, barvell, barwal, barware, barwares, barway, barways, barwin, barwing, barwise, barwood, barycenter, barycentre, barycentric, barye, baryecoia, baryes, baryglossia, barylalia, barylite, baryon, baryonic, baryons, baryphonia, baryphonic, baryphony, barysilite, barysphere, baryta, barytas, baryte, barytes, barythymia, barytic, barytine, barytocalcite, barytocelestine, barytocelestite, baryton, barytone, barytones, barytons, barytophyllite, barytostrontianite, barytosulphate, bas, basad, basal, basale, basalia, basally, basalt, basaltes, basaltic, basaltiform, basaltine, basaltoid, basalts, basaltware, basan, basanite, basaree, basat, bascinet, basculation, bascule, bascules, bascunan, base, baseball, baseball's, baseballdom, baseballer, baseballs, baseband, baseboard, baseboard's, baseboards, baseborn, basebred, baseburner, basecoat, basecourt, based, basehearted, baseheartedness, baselard, baseless, baselessly, baselessness, baselevel, baselike, baseline, baseline's, baseliner, baselines, basella, basellaceous, basely, baseman, basemen, basement, basement's, basementless, basements, basementward, basename, baseness, basenesses, basenet, basenji, basenjis, baseplate, baseplug, basepoint, baser, baserunning, bases, basest, bash, bashalick, bashara, bashaw, bashawdom, bashawism, bashaws, bashawship, bashed, basher, bashers, bashes, bashful, bashfully, bashfulness, bashibazouk, bashing, bashless, bashlik, bashlyk, bashlyks, bashment, bashyle, basial, basialveolar, basiarachnitis, basiarachnoiditis, basiate, basiated, basiating, basiation, basibranchial, basibranchiate, basibregmatic, basic, basic's, basically, basicerite, basichromatic, basichromatin, basichromatinic, basichromiole, basicities, basicity, basicranial, basics, basicytoparaplastin, basidia, basidial, basidigital, basidigitale, basidigitalia, basidiocarp, basidiogenetic, basidiolichen, basidiomycete, basidiomycetes, basidiomycetous, basidiophore, basidiospore, basidiosporous, basidium, basidorsal, basifacial, basification, basified, basifier, basifiers, basifies, basifixed, basifugal, basify, basifying, basigamous, basigamy, basigenic, basigenous, basiglandular, basigynium, basihyal, basihyoid, basil, basilar, basilard, basilary, basilateral, basilect, basileis, basilemma, basileus, basilian, basilic, basilica, basilicae, basilical, basilicalike, basilican, basilicas, basilicate, basilicock, basilicon, basilics, basilidan, basilinna, basiliscan, basiliscine, basilisk, basilisks, basilissa, basils, basilweed, basilysis, basilyst, basimesostasis, basin, basin's, basinal, basinasal, basinasial, basined, basinerved, basinet, basinets, basinful, basing, basinlike, basins, basioccipital, basion, basions, basiophitic, basiophthalmite, basiophthalmous, basiotribe, basiotripsy, basiparachromatin, basiparaplastin, basipetal, basipetally, basiphobia, basipodite, basipoditic, basipterygial, basipterygium, basipterygoid, basiradial, basirhinal, basirostral, basis, basiscopic, basisidia, basisolute, basisphenoid, basisphenoidal, basitemporal, basitting, basiventral, basivertebral, bask, baske, basked, basker, basket, basket's, basketball, basketball's, basketballer, basketballs, basketful, basketfuls, basketing, basketlike, basketmaker, basketmaking, basketries, basketry, baskets, basketware, basketweaving, basketwoman, basketwood, basketwork, basketworm, basking, basks, basnat, basnet, basocyte, basoid, basommatophorous, bason, basophil, basophile, basophilia, basophilic, basophilous, basophils, basophobia, basos, basote, basotho, basque, basqued, basques, basquine, bass, bass's, bassan, bassanello, bassanite, bassara, bassarid, bassarisk, basses, basset, basseted, basseting, bassetite, bassets, bassetta, bassette, bassetted, bassetting, bassi, bassia, bassie, bassine, bassinet, bassinet's, bassinets, bassing, bassirilievi, bassist, bassists, bassly, bassness, bassnesses, basso, basson, bassoon, bassoonist, bassoonists, bassoons, bassorin, bassos, bassus, basswood, basswoods, bassy, bast, basta, bastant, bastard, bastard's, bastarda, bastardice, bastardies, bastardisation, bastardise, bastardised, bastardising, bastardism, bastardization, bastardizations, bastardize, bastardized, bastardizes, bastardizing, bastardliness, bastardly, bastardry, bastards, bastardy, baste, basted, basten, baster, basters, bastes, basti, bastian, bastide, bastile, bastiles, bastille, bastilles, bastillion, bastiment, bastinade, bastinaded, bastinades, bastinading, bastinado, bastinadoed, bastinadoes, bastinadoing, basting, bastings, bastion, bastion's, bastionary, bastioned, bastionet, bastions, bastite, bastnaesite, bastnasite, basto, baston, bastonet, bastonite, basts, basural, basurale, basuto, basyl, bat, bat's, bataan, batable, batad, batakan, bataleur, batamote, batara, batarde, batardeau, batata, batatilla, batavian, batboy, batboys, batch, batched, batcher, batchers, batches, batching, bate, batea, bateau, bateaux, bated, bateful, batel, bateleur, batell, bateman, batement, bater, bates, batete, batfish, batfishes, batfowl, batfowled, batfowler, batfowling, batfowls, batful, bath, bathe, batheable, bathed, bather, bathers, bathes, bathetic, bathetically, bathflower, bathhouse, bathhouses, bathic, bathinette, bathing, bathkol, bathless, bathman, bathmat, bathmats, bathmic, bathmism, bathmotropic, bathmotropism, bathochromatic, bathochromatism, bathochrome, bathochromic, bathochromy, bathoflore, bathofloric, batholite, batholith, batholithic, batholiths, batholitic, bathomania, bathometer, bathometry, bathool, bathophobia, bathorse, bathos, bathoses, bathrobe, bathrobe's, bathrobes, bathroom, bathroom's, bathroomed, bathrooms, bathroot, baths, bathtub, bathtub's, bathtubful, bathtubs, bathukolpian, bathukolpic, bathvillite, bathwater, bathwort, bathyal, bathyanesthesia, bathybian, bathybic, bathybius, bathycentesis, bathychrome, bathycolpian, bathycolpic, bathycurrent, bathyesthesia, bathygraphic, bathyhyperesthesia, bathyhypesthesia, bathyl, bathylimnetic, bathylite, bathylith, bathylithic, bathylitic, bathymeter, bathymetric, bathymetrical, bathymetrically, bathymetry, bathyorographical, bathypelagic, bathyplankton, bathyscape, bathyscaph, bathyscaphe, bathyscaphes, bathyseism, bathysmal, bathysophic, bathysophical, bathysphere, bathyspheres, bathythermogram, bathythermograph, batidaceous, batik, batiked, batiker, batiking, batiks, bating, batino, batiste, batistes, batitinan, batlan, batler, batlet, batlike, batling, batlon, batman, batmen, batoid, baton, baton's, batoneer, batonist, batonistic, batonne, batonnier, batons, batoon, batophobia, batrachia, batrachian, batrachians, batrachiate, batrachite, batrachoid, batrachophagous, batrachophobia, batrachoplasty, batrachotoxin, bats, batsman, batsmanship, batsmen, batster, batswing, batt, batta, battable, battailant, battailous, battalia, battalias, battalion, battalion's, battalions, battarism, battarismus, batteau, batteaux, batted, battel, batteled, batteler, batteling, battels, battement, battements, batten, battened, battener, batteners, battening, battens, batter, batterable, battercake, batterdock, battered, batterer, batterfang, batterie, batteried, batteries, battering, batterman, batters, battery, battery's, batteryman, batteuse, battier, batties, battiest, battik, battiks, battiness, batting, battings, battish, battle, battled, battledore, battledored, battledores, battledoring, battlefield, battlefield's, battlefields, battlefront, battlefront's, battlefronts, battleful, battleground, battleground's, battlegrounds, battlement, battlement's, battlemented, battlements, battlepiece, battleplane, battler, battlers, battles, battleship, battleship's, battleships, battlesome, battlestead, battlewagon, battleward, battlewise, battling, battological, battologise, battologised, battologising, battologist, battologize, battologized, battologizing, battology, batton, batts, battu, battue, battues, batture, battuta, battutas, battute, battuto, battutos, batty, battycake, batukite, batule, batuque, batwing, batwoman, batwomen, batyphone, batz, batzen, baubee, baubees, bauble, bauble's, baublery, baubles, baubling, bauch, bauchle, bauckie, bauckiebird, baud, baudekin, baudekins, baudery, baudrons, baudronses, bauds, baufrey, bauge, bauhinia, bauhinias, bauk, baul, bauld, baulea, bauleah, baulk, baulked, baulkier, baulkiest, baulking, baulks, baulky, baume, baumhauerite, baumier, baun, bauno, bauson, bausond, bauta, bautta, bauxite, bauxites, bauxitic, bauxitite, bavardage, bavarian, bavarois, bavaroise, bavaroy, bavary, bavenite, bavette, baviaantje, bavian, baviere, bavin, bavoso, baw, bawarchi, bawbee, bawbees, bawble, bawcock, bawcocks, bawd, bawdier, bawdies, bawdiest, bawdily, bawdiness, bawdric, bawdrick, bawdrics, bawdries, bawdry, bawds, bawdship, bawdstrot, bawdy, bawdyhouse, bawdyhouses, bawhorse, bawke, bawl, bawled, bawler, bawlers, bawley, bawling, bawls, bawly, bawn, bawneen, bawrel, baws'nt, bawsint, bawsunt, bawtie, bawties, bawty, baxter, baxtone, bay, baya, bayadeer, bayadeers, bayadere, bayaderes, bayal, bayamo, bayamos, bayano, bayard, bayardly, bayards, bayberries, bayberry, baybolt, baybush, baycuru, bayed, bayesian, bayeta, bayete, baygall, bayhead, baying, bayish, bayldonite, baylet, baylike, bayman, baymen, bayness, bayok, bayonet, bayonet's, bayoneted, bayoneteer, bayoneting, bayonets, bayonetted, bayonetting, bayong, bayou, bayou's, bayous, bays, baysmelt, baysmelts, baywood, baywoods, bayz, bazaar, bazaar's, bazaars, bazar, bazars, baze, bazoo, bazooka, bazookaman, bazookamen, bazookas, bazoos, bazzite, bb, bbl, bbls, bbs, bcd, bcf, bch, bchs, bd, bde, bdellatomy, bdellid, bdellium, bdelliums, bdelloid, bdellometer, bdellotomy, bdellovibrio, bdft, bdl, bdle, bdls, bdrm, bds, be, beach, beachboy, beachboys, beachcomb, beachcomber, beachcombers, beachcombing, beachdrops, beached, beacher, beaches, beachfront, beachhead, beachhead's, beachheads, beachie, beachier, beachiest, beaching, beachlamar, beachless, beachman, beachmaster, beachmen, beachside, beachward, beachwear, beachy, beacon, beacon's, beaconage, beaconed, beaconing, beaconless, beacons, beaconwise, bead, beaded, beader, beadeye, beadeyes, beadflush, beadhouse, beadhouses, beadier, beadiest, beadily, beadiness, beading, beadings, beadle, beadle's, beadledom, beadlehood, beadleism, beadlery, beadles, beadleship, beadlet, beadlike, beadman, beadmen, beadroll, beadrolls, beadrow, beads, beadsman, beadsmen, beadswoman, beadswomen, beadwork, beadworks, beady, beagle, beagle's, beagles, beagling, beak, beaked, beaker, beakerful, beakerman, beakermen, beakers, beakful, beakhead, beakier, beakiest, beakiron, beakless, beaklike, beaks, beaky, beal, beala, bealach, bealing, beallach, bealtared, beam, beamage, beambird, beamed, beamer, beamers, beamfilling, beamful, beamhouse, beamier, beamiest, beamily, beaminess, beaming, beamingly, beamish, beamishly, beamless, beamlet, beamlike, beamman, beamroom, beams, beamsman, beamsmen, beamster, beamwork, beamy, bean, beanbag, beanbags, beanball, beanballs, beancod, beaned, beaner, beaneries, beaners, beanery, beanfeast, beanfeaster, beanfest, beanfield, beanie, beanier, beanies, beaniest, beaning, beanlike, beano, beanos, beanpole, beanpoles, beans, beansetter, beanshooter, beanstalk, beanstalks, beant, beanweed, beany, beaproned, bear, bearability, bearable, bearableness, bearably, bearance, bearbaiter, bearbaiting, bearbane, bearberries, bearberry, bearbind, bearbine, bearbush, bearcat, bearcats, bearcoot, beard, bearded, beardedness, bearder, beardfish, beardfishes, beardie, bearding, beardless, beardlessness, beardlike, beardom, beards, beardtongue, beardy, beared, bearer, bearers, bearess, bearfoot, bearfoots, bearherd, bearhide, bearhound, bearhug, bearhugs, bearing, bearings, bearish, bearishly, bearishness, bearleap, bearlet, bearlike, bearm, bearnaise, bearpaw, bears, bearship, bearskin, bearskins, beartongue, bearward, bearwood, bearwoods, bearwort, beast, beastbane, beastdom, beasthood, beastie, beasties, beastily, beastings, beastish, beastishness, beastlier, beastliest, beastlike, beastlily, beastliness, beastling, beastlings, beastly, beastman, beasts, beastship, beat, beata, beatable, beatably, beatae, beatas, beatee, beaten, beater, beaterman, beatermen, beaters, beath, beati, beatific, beatifical, beatifically, beatificate, beatification, beatified, beatifies, beatify, beatifying, beatille, beatinest, beating, beatings, beatitude, beatitude's, beatitudes, beatles, beatless, beatnik, beatnik's, beatnikism, beatniks, beatrice, beats, beatster, beatus, beatuti, beau, beau's, beauclerk, beaucoup, beaued, beauetry, beaufet, beaufin, beaufort, beaugregories, beaugregory, beauing, beauish, beauism, beaujolais, beaume, beaumont, beaupere, beaupers, beaus, beauseant, beauship, beausire, beaut, beauteous, beauteously, beauteousness, beauti, beautician, beauticians, beautied, beauties, beautification, beautifications, beautified, beautifier, beautifiers, beautifies, beautiful, beautifully, beautifulness, beautify, beautifying, beautihood, beautiless, beauts, beauty, beauty's, beautydom, beautyship, beaux, beauxite, beaver, beaver's, beaverboard, beavered, beaverette, beaveries, beavering, beaverish, beaverism, beaverite, beaverize, beaverkin, beaverlike, beaverpelt, beaverroot, beavers, beaverskin, beaverteen, beaverwood, beavery, beback, bebait, beballed, bebang, bebannered, bebar, bebaron, bebaste, bebat, bebathe, bebatter, bebay, bebeast, bebed, bebeerin, bebeerine, bebeeru, bebeerus, bebelted, bebilya, bebite, bebization, beblain, beblear, bebled, bebleed, bebless, beblister, beblood, beblooded, beblooding, bebloods, bebloom, beblot, beblotch, beblubber, beblubbered, bebog, bebop, bebopper, beboppers, bebops, beboss, bebotch, bebothered, bebouldered, bebrave, bebreech, bebrine, bebrother, bebrush, bebump, bebusy, bebuttoned, bec, becafico, becall, becalm, becalmed, becalming, becalmment, becalms, became, becap, becapped, becapping, becaps, becard, becarpet, becarpeted, becarpeting, becarpets, becarve, becasse, becassine, becassocked, becater, because, beccabunga, beccaccia, beccafico, beccaficoes, beccaficos, becchi, becco, becense, bechained, bechalk, bechalked, bechalking, bechalks, bechamel, bechamels, bechance, bechanced, bechances, bechancing, becharm, becharmed, becharming, becharms, bechase, bechatter, bechauffeur, beche, becheck, becher, bechern, bechic, bechignoned, bechirp, becircled, becivet, beck, becked, beckelite, becker, becket, beckets, beckett, becking, beckiron, beckon, beckoned, beckoner, beckoners, beckoning, beckoningly, beckons, becks, beclad, beclamor, beclamored, beclamoring, beclamors, beclamour, beclang, beclap, beclart, beclasp, beclasped, beclasping, beclasps, beclatter, beclaw, beclip, becloak, becloaked, becloaking, becloaks, beclog, beclogged, beclogging, beclogs, beclose, beclothe, beclothed, beclothes, beclothing, becloud, beclouded, beclouding, beclouds, beclout, beclown, beclowned, beclowning, beclowns, becluster, becobweb, becoiffed, becollier, becolme, becolor, becombed, become, becomed, becomes, becometh, becoming, becomingly, becomingness, becomings, becomma, becompass, becompliment, becoom, becoresh, becost, becousined, becovet, becoward, becowarded, becowarding, becowards, becquerelite, becram, becramp, becrampon, becrawl, becrawled, becrawling, becrawls, becreep, becrime, becrimed, becrimes, becriming, becrimson, becrinolined, becripple, becrippled, becrippling, becroak, becross, becrowd, becrowded, becrowding, becrowds, becrown, becrush, becrust, becrusted, becrusting, becrusts, becry, becudgel, becudgeled, becudgeling, becudgelled, becudgelling, becudgels, becuffed, becuiba, becumber, becuna, becurl, becurry, becurse, becursed, becurses, becursing, becurst, becurtained, becushioned, becut, bed, bed's, bedabble, bedabbled, bedabbles, bedabbling, bedad, bedaff, bedaggered, bedaggle, bedamn, bedamned, bedamning, bedamns, bedamp, bedangled, bedare, bedark, bedarken, bedarkened, bedarkening, bedarkens, bedash, bedaub, bedaubed, bedaubing, bedaubs, bedawee, bedawn, beday, bedaze, bedazed, bedazement, bedazzle, bedazzled, bedazzlement, bedazzles, bedazzling, bedazzlingly, bedboard, bedbug, bedbug's, bedbugs, bedcap, bedcase, bedchair, bedchairs, bedchamber, bedclothes, bedclothing, bedcord, bedcover, bedcovers, beddable, bedded, bedder, bedder's, bedders, bedding, beddingroll, beddings, bede, bedead, bedeaf, bedeafen, bedeafened, bedeafening, bedeafens, bedebt, bedeck, bedecked, bedecking, bedecks, bedecorate, bedeen, bedegar, bedeguar, bedehouse, bedehouses, bedel, bedell, bedells, bedels, bedelve, bedeman, bedemen, beden, bedene, bedesman, bedesmen, bedeswoman, bedeswomen, bedevil, bedeviled, bedeviling, bedevilled, bedevilling, bedevilment, bedevils, bedew, bedewed, bedewer, bedewing, bedewoman, bedews, bedfast, bedfellow, bedfellows, bedfellowship, bedflower, bedfoot, bedfordshire, bedframe, bedframes, bedgery, bedgoer, bedgown, bedgowns, bediademed, bediamonded, bediaper, bediapered, bediapering, bediapers, bedight, bedighted, bedighting, bedights, bedikah, bedim, bedimmed, bedimming, bedimple, bedimpled, bedimples, bedimplies, bedimpling, bedims, bedin, bedip, bedirt, bedirter, bedirtied, bedirties, bedirty, bedirtying, bedismal, bedivere, bedizen, bedizened, bedizening, bedizenment, bedizens, bedkey, bedlam, bedlamer, bedlamise, bedlamised, bedlamising, bedlamism, bedlamite, bedlamitish, bedlamize, bedlamized, bedlamizing, bedlamp, bedlamps, bedlams, bedlar, bedless, bedlids, bedlight, bedlike, bedmaker, bedmakers, bedmaking, bedman, bedmate, bedmates, bednighted, bednights, bedoctor, bedog, bedolt, bedot, bedote, bedotted, bedouin, bedouins, bedouse, bedown, bedoyo, bedpad, bedpan, bedpans, bedplate, bedplates, bedpost, bedpost's, bedposts, bedquilt, bedquilts, bedrabble, bedrabbled, bedrabbling, bedraggle, bedraggled, bedragglement, bedraggles, bedraggling, bedrail, bedrails, bedral, bedrape, bedraped, bedrapes, bedraping, bedravel, bedread, bedrel, bedrench, bedrenched, bedrenches, bedrenching, bedress, bedribble, bedrid, bedridden, bedriddenness, bedrift, bedright, bedrip, bedrite, bedrivel, bedriveled, bedriveling, bedrivelled, bedrivelling, bedrivels, bedrizzle, bedrock, bedrock's, bedrocks, bedroll, bedrolls, bedroom, bedroom's, bedrooms, bedrop, bedrown, bedrowse, bedrug, bedrugged, bedrugging, bedrugs, beds, bedscrew, bedsheet, bedsheets, bedsick, bedside, bedsides, bedsit, bedsite, bedsitter, bedsock, bedsonia, bedsonias, bedsore, bedsores, bedspread, bedspread's, bedspreads, bedspring, bedspring's, bedsprings, bedstaff, bedstand, bedstands, bedstaves, bedstead, bedstead's, bedsteads, bedstock, bedstraw, bedstraws, bedstring, bedswerver, bedtick, bedticking, bedticks, bedtime, bedtimes, bedub, beduchess, beduck, beduin, beduins, beduke, bedull, bedumb, bedumbed, bedumbing, bedumbs, bedunce, bedunced, bedunces, bedunch, bedunping, bedung, bedur, bedusk, bedust, bedward, bedwards, bedwarf, bedwarfed, bedwarfing, bedwarfs, bedwarmer, bedway, bedways, bedwell, bedye, bee, beearn, beeball, beebee, beebees, beebread, beebreads, beech, beechdrops, beechen, beecher, beeches, beechier, beechiest, beechnut, beechnuts, beechwood, beechwoods, beechy, beedged, beedi, beedom, beef, beefalo, beefaloes, beefalos, beefburger, beefburgers, beefcake, beefcakes, beefeater, beefeaters, beefed, beefer, beefers, beefhead, beefheaded, beefier, beefiest, beefily, beefin, beefiness, beefing, beefish, beefishness, beefless, beeflower, beefs, beefsteak, beefsteaks, beeftongue, beefwood, beefwoods, beefy, beegerite, beehead, beeheaded, beeherd, beehive, beehive's, beehives, beehouse, beeish, beeishness, beek, beekeeper, beekeepers, beekeeping, beekite, beelbow, beele, beelike, beeline, beelines, beelol, beelzebub, beeman, beemaster, beemen, been, beennut, beent, beento, beep, beeped, beeper, beepers, beeping, beeps, beer, beerage, beerbachite, beerbelly, beerbibber, beeregar, beerhouse, beerhouses, beerier, beeriest, beerily, beeriness, beerish, beerishly, beermaker, beermaking, beermonger, beerocracy, beerpull, beers, beery, bees, beest, beesting, beestings, beestride, beeswax, beeswaxes, beeswing, beeswinged, beeswings, beet, beet's, beetewk, beetfly, beeth, beethoven, beetiest, beetle, beetle's, beetled, beetlehead, beetleheaded, beetleheadedness, beetler, beetlers, beetles, beetlestock, beetlestone, beetleweed, beetlike, beetling, beetmister, beetrave, beetroot, beetroots, beetrooty, beets, beety, beeve, beeves, beevish, beeware, beeway, beeweed, beewinged, beewise, beewort, beeyard, beezer, beezers, bef, befall, befallen, befalling, befalls, befame, befamilied, befamine, befan, befancy, befanned, befathered, befavor, befavour, befeather, befell, beferned, befetished, befetter, befezzed, beffroy, befiddle, befilch, befile, befilleted, befilmed, befilth, befinger, befingered, befingering, befingers, befire, befist, befit, befit's, befits, befitted, befitting, befittingly, befittingness, beflag, beflagged, beflagging, beflags, beflannel, beflap, beflatter, beflea, befleaed, befleaing, befleas, befleck, beflecked, beflecking, beflecks, beflounce, beflour, beflout, beflower, beflowered, beflowering, beflowers, beflum, befluster, befoam, befog, befogged, befogging, befogs, befool, befoolable, befooled, befooling, befoolment, befools, befop, before, beforehand, beforehandedness, beforementioned, beforeness, beforesaid, beforested, beforetime, beforetimes, befortune, befoul, befouled, befouler, befoulers, befoulier, befouling, befoulment, befouls, befountained, befraught, befreckle, befreeze, befreight, befret, befrets, befretted, befretting, befriend, befriended, befriender, befriending, befriendment, befriends, befrill, befrilled, befringe, befringed, befringes, befringing, befriz, befrocked, befrogged, befrounce, befrumple, befuddle, befuddled, befuddlement, befuddlements, befuddler, befuddlers, befuddles, befuddling, befume, befur, befurbelowed, befurred, beg, begabled, begad, begall, begalled, begalling, begalls, began, begani, begar, begari, begarie, begarlanded, begarnish, begartered, begary, begash, begass, begat, begats, begattal, begaud, begaudy, begay, begaze, begazed, begazes, begazing, begeck, begem, begemmed, begemming, beget, begets, begettal, begetter, begetters, begetting, beggable, beggar, beggardom, beggared, beggarer, beggaress, beggarhood, beggaries, beggaring, beggarism, beggarlice, beggarlike, beggarliness, beggarly, beggarman, beggars, beggarweed, beggarwise, beggarwoman, beggary, begged, begger, beggiatoaceous, begging, beggingly, beggingwise, beghard, begift, begiggle, begild, begin, beginger, beginner, beginner's, beginners, beginning, beginning's, beginnings, begins, begird, begirded, begirding, begirdle, begirdled, begirdles, begirdling, begirds, begirt, beglad, begladded, begladding, beglads, beglamour, beglare, beglerbeg, beglerbeglic, beglerbeglik, beglerbegluc, beglerbegship, beglerbey, beglew, beglic, beglide, beglitter, beglobed, begloom, beglomed, beglooming, beglooms, begloze, begluc, beglue, begnaw, begnawed, begnawn, bego, begob, begobs, begod, begoggled, begohm, begone, begonia, begoniaceous, begonias, begorah, begorra, begorrah, begorry, begot, begotten, begottenness, begoud, begowk, begowned, begrace, begrain, begrave, begray, begrease, begreen, begrett, begrim, begrime, begrimed, begrimer, begrimes, begriming, begrimmed, begrimming, begrims, begripe, begroan, begroaned, begroaning, begroans, begrown, begrudge, begrudged, begrudger, begrudges, begrudging, begrudgingly, begruntle, begrutch, begrutten, begs, begster, beguard, beguess, beguile, beguiled, beguileful, beguilement, beguilements, beguiler, beguilers, beguiles, beguiling, beguilingly, beguilingness, beguin, beguine, beguines, begulf, begulfed, begulfing, begulfs, begum, begummed, begumming, begums, begun, begunk, begut, behale, behalf, behallow, behalves, behammer, behang, behap, behatted, behav, behave, behaved, behaver, behavers, behaves, behaving, behavior, behavioral, behaviorally, behaviored, behaviorism, behaviorist, behavioristic, behavioristically, behaviorists, behaviors, behaviour, behavioural, behaviourally, behaviourism, behaviourist, behaviours, behead, beheadal, beheaded, beheader, beheading, beheadlined, beheads, behear, behears, behearse, behedge, beheira, beheld, behelp, behemoth, behemothic, behemoths, behen, behenate, behenic, behest, behests, behew, behight, behind, behinder, behindhand, behinds, behindsight, behint, behither, behn, behold, beholdable, beholden, beholder, beholders, beholding, beholdingness, beholds, behoney, behoof, behooped, behoot, behoove, behooved, behooveful, behoovefully, behoovefulness, behooves, behooving, behoovingly, behorn, behorror, behove, behoved, behovely, behoves, behoving, behowl, behowled, behowling, behowls, behung, behusband, behymn, behypocrite, beice, beige, beigel, beiges, beignet, beignets, beigy, beild, bein, being, beingless, beingness, beings, beinked, beinly, beinness, beira, beirut, beisa, beisance, beja, bejabbers, bejabers, bejade, bejan, bejant, bejape, bejaundice, bejazz, bejel, bejeled, bejeling, bejelled, bejelling, bejesuit, bejesus, bejewel, bejeweled, bejeweling, bejewelled, bejewelling, bejewels, bejezebel, bejig, bejuco, bejuggle, bejumble, bejumbled, bejumbles, bejumbling, bekah, bekerchief, bekick, bekilted, beking, bekinkinite, bekiss, bekissed, bekisses, bekissing, bekko, beknave, beknight, beknighted, beknighting, beknights, beknit, beknived, beknot, beknots, beknotted, beknottedly, beknottedness, beknotting, beknow, beknown, bel, bela, belabor, belabored, belaboring, belabors, belabour, belaboured, belabouring, belabours, belace, belaced, beladied, beladies, beladle, belady, beladying, belage, belah, belam, belamour, belamy, belanda, belander, belap, belar, belard, belash, belast, belat, belate, belated, belatedly, belatedness, belating, belatticed, belaud, belauded, belauder, belauding, belauds, belavendered, belay, belayed, belayer, belaying, belays, belch, belched, belcher, belchers, belches, belching, beld, beldam, beldame, beldames, beldams, beldamship, belder, belderroot, belduque, beleaf, beleaguer, beleaguered, beleaguerer, beleaguering, beleaguerment, beleaguers, beleap, beleaped, beleaping, beleaps, beleapt, beleave, belection, belecture, beledgered, belee, beleed, beleft, belemnid, belemnite, belemnitic, belemnoid, beleper, belesprit, beletter, beleve, belfast, belfather, belfried, belfries, belfry, belfry's, belga, belgae, belgard, belgas, belgian, belgian's, belgians, belgium, belgrade, belial, belibel, belibeled, belibeling, belick, belicoseness, belie, belied, belief, belief's, beliefful, belieffulness, beliefless, beliefs, belier, beliers, belies, believability, believable, believableness, believably, believe, believed, believer, believers, believes, believeth, believing, believingly, belight, beliing, belike, beliked, belikely, belime, belimousined, belion, beliquor, beliquored, beliquoring, beliquors, belite, belitter, belittle, belittled, belittlement, belittler, belittlers, belittles, belittling, belive, belk, belknap, bell, bell's, belladonna, bellarmine, bellbind, bellbinder, bellbine, bellbird, bellbirds, bellbottle, bellboy, bellboy's, bellboys, belle, belle's, belled, belledom, belleek, belleeks, bellehood, belleric, bellerophon, belles, belleter, belletrist, belletristic, belletrists, bellevue, bellflower, bellhanger, bellhanging, bellhop, bellhop's, bellhops, bellhouse, belli, bellibone, bellic, bellical, bellicism, bellicist, bellicose, bellicosely, bellicoseness, bellicosities, bellicosity, bellied, bellies, belliferous, belligerence, belligerencies, belligerency, belligerent, belligerent's, belligerently, belligerents, belling, bellipotent, bellite, bellmaker, bellmaking, bellman, bellmanship, bellmaster, bellmen, bellmouth, bellmouthed, bello, bellon, bellona, bellonion, belloot, bellota, bellote, bellow, bellowed, bellower, bellowers, bellowing, bellows, bellowsful, bellowslike, bellowsmaker, bellowsmaking, bellowsman, bellpull, bellpulls, bellrags, bells, belltail, belltopper, belltopperdom, belluine, bellum, bellware, bellwaver, bellweather, bellweed, bellwether, bellwether's, bellwethers, bellwind, bellwine, bellwood, bellwort, bellworts, belly, belly's, bellyache, bellyached, bellyacher, bellyaches, bellyaching, bellyband, bellybutton, bellybuttons, bellyer, bellyfish, bellyflaught, bellyful, bellyfull, bellyfulls, bellyfuls, bellying, bellyland, bellylike, bellyman, bellypiece, bellypinch, beloam, belock, beloeilite, beloid, belomancy, belonephobia, belonesite, belong, belonged, belonger, belonging, belongings, belongs, belonid, belonite, belonoid, belonosphaerite, belook, belord, belorussian, belotte, belouke, belout, belove, beloved, beloveds, below, belowdecks, belowground, belows, belowstairs, belozenged, bels, belshazzar, belsire, belswagger, belt, beltane, beltcourse, belted, belter, beltie, beltine, belting, beltings, beltless, beltline, beltlines, beltmaker, beltmaking, beltman, beltmen, belton, belts, beltway, beltways, beltwise, belue, beluga, belugas, belugite, belute, belve, belvedere, belvedered, belvederes, belvidere, bely, belying, belyingly, belzebub, belzebuth, bema, bemad, bemadam, bemadamed, bemadaming, bemadams, bemadden, bemaddened, bemaddening, bemaddens, bemail, bemaim, bemajesty, beman, bemangle, bemantle, bemar, bemartyr, bemas, bemask, bemaster, bemat, bemata, bemaul, bemazed, beme, bemeal, bemean, bemeaned, bemeaning, bemeans, bemedaled, bemedalled, bemeet, bementite, bemercy, bemete, bemingle, bemingled, bemingles, bemingling, beminstrel, bemire, bemired, bemirement, bemires, bemiring, bemirror, bemirrorment, bemist, bemisted, bemisting, bemistress, bemists, bemitered, bemitred, bemix, bemixed, bemixes, bemixing, bemixt, bemoan, bemoanable, bemoaned, bemoaner, bemoaning, bemoaningly, bemoans, bemoat, bemock, bemocked, bemocking, bemocks, bemoil, bemoisten, bemol, bemole, bemolt, bemonster, bemoon, bemotto, bemoult, bemourn, bemouth, bemuck, bemud, bemuddle, bemuddled, bemuddlement, bemuddles, bemuddling, bemuddy, bemuffle, bemurmur, bemurmure, bemurmured, bemurmuring, bemurmurs, bemuse, bemused, bemusedly, bemusement, bemuses, bemusing, bemusk, bemuslined, bemuzzle, bemuzzled, bemuzzles, bemuzzling, ben, bena, benab, benadryl, bename, benamed, benamee, benames, benami, benamidar, benaming, benasty, benben, bench, benchboard, benched, bencher, benchers, benchership, benches, benchfellow, benchful, benching, benchland, benchless, benchlet, benchman, benchmar, benchmark, benchmark's, benchmarked, benchmarking, benchmarks, benchmen, benchwarmer, benchwork, benchy, bencite, bend, benda, bendability, bendable, benday, bendayed, bendaying, bendays, bended, bendee, bendees, bendel, bendell, bender, benders, bendies, bending, bendingly, bendlet, bends, bendsome, bendways, bendwise, bendy, bendys, bene, beneaped, beneath, beneception, beneceptive, beneceptor, benedicite, benedick, benedicks, benedict, benedictine, benediction, benediction's, benedictional, benedictionale, benedictionary, benedictions, benedictive, benedictively, benedictory, benedicts, benedictus, benedight, benefact, benefaction, benefactions, benefactive, benefactor, benefactor's, benefactors, benefactorship, benefactory, benefactress, benefactresses, benefactrices, benefactrix, benefactrixes, benefic, benefice, beneficed, beneficeless, beneficence, beneficences, beneficency, beneficent, beneficential, beneficently, benefices, beneficiaire, beneficial, beneficially, beneficialness, beneficiaries, beneficiary, beneficiaryship, beneficiate, beneficiated, beneficiating, beneficiation, beneficience, beneficient, beneficing, beneficium, benefit, benefited, benefiter, benefiting, benefits, benefitted, benefitting, benegro, beneighbored, beneme, benempt, benempted, beneplacit, beneplacito, beneplacity, benes, benet, benetted, benetting, benettle, beneurous, benevolence, benevolences, benevolency, benevolent, benevolently, benevolentness, benevolist, beng, bengal, bengali, bengaline, bengals, beni, benic, benight, benighted, benightedly, benightedness, benighten, benighter, benighting, benightmare, benightment, benign, benignancies, benignancy, benignant, benignantly, benignities, benignity, benignly, benignness, benim, benin, beniseed, benison, benisons, benitier, benitoite, benj, benjamin, benjaminite, benjamins, benjoin, benjy, benmost, benn, benne, bennel, bennes, bennet, bennets, bennettitaceous, bennetweed, benni, bennies, bennis, benniseed, benny, beno, benomyl, benomyls, benorth, benote, bens, bensail, bensall, bensel, bensell, bensh, benshea, benshee, benshi, bensil, bent, bentang, bentgrass, benthal, benthamism, benthic, benthon, benthonic, benthopelagic, benthos, benthoscope, benthoses, bentinck, bentiness, benting, bentlet, bentonite, bentonitic, bents, bentstar, bentwood, bentwoods, benty, benumb, benumbed, benumbedness, benumbing, benumbingly, benumbment, benumbs, benvenuto, benward, benweed, benzacridine, benzal, benzalacetone, benzalacetophenone, benzalaniline, benzalazine, benzalcohol, benzalcyanhydrin, benzaldehyde, benzaldiphenyl, benzaldoxime, benzalethylamine, benzalhydrazine, benzalphenylhydrazone, benzalphthalide, benzamide, benzamido, benzamine, benzaminic, benzamino, benzanalgen, benzanilide, benzanthracene, benzanthrone, benzantialdoxime, benzazide, benzazimide, benzazine, benzazole, benzbitriazole, benzdiazine, benzdifuran, benzdioxazine, benzdioxdiazine, benzdioxtriazine, benzedrine, benzein, benzene, benzeneazobenzene, benzenediazonium, benzenes, benzenoid, benzenyl, benzhydrol, benzhydroxamic, benzidin, benzidine, benzidino, benzidins, benzil, benzilic, benzimidazole, benziminazole, benzin, benzinduline, benzine, benzines, benzins, benzo, benzoate, benzoated, benzoates, benzoazurine, benzobis, benzocaine, benzocoumaran, benzodiazine, benzodiazole, benzoflavine, benzofluorene, benzofulvene, benzofuran, benzofuroquinoxaline, benzofuryl, benzoglycolic, benzoglyoxaline, benzohydrol, benzoic, benzoid, benzoin, benzoinated, benzoins, benzoiodohydrin, benzol, benzolate, benzole, benzoles, benzoline, benzolize, benzols, benzomorpholine, benzonaphthol, benzonitrile, benzonitrol, benzoperoxide, benzophenanthrazine, benzophenanthroline, benzophenazine, benzophenol, benzophenone, benzophenothiazine, benzophenoxazine, benzophloroglucinol, benzophosphinic, benzophthalazine, benzopinacone, benzopyran, benzopyranyl, benzopyrazolone, benzopyrene, benzopyrylium, benzoquinoline, benzoquinone, benzoquinoxaline, benzosulfimide, benzosulphimide, benzotetrazine, benzotetrazole, benzothiazine, benzothiazole, benzothiazoline, benzothiodiazole, benzothiofuran, benzothiophene, benzothiopyran, benzotoluide, benzotriazine, benzotriazole, benzotrichloride, benzotrifluoride, benzotrifuran, benzoxate, benzoxy, benzoxyacetic, benzoxycamphor, benzoxyphenanthrene, benzoyl, benzoylate, benzoylated, benzoylating, benzoylation, benzoylformic, benzoylglycine, benzoyls, benzpinacone, benzpyrene, benzthiophen, benztrioxazine, benzyl, benzylamine, benzylic, benzylidene, benzylpenicillin, benzyls, beode, beowulf, bepaid, bepaint, bepainted, bepainting, bepaints, bepale, bepaper, beparch, beparody, beparse, bepart, bepaste, bepastured, bepat, bepatched, bepaw, bepearl, bepelt, bepen, bepepper, beperiwigged, bepester, bepewed, bephilter, bephrase, bepicture, bepiece, bepierce, bepile, bepill, bepillared, bepimple, bepimpled, bepimples, bepimpling, bepinch, bepistoled, bepity, beplague, beplaided, beplaster, beplumed, bepommel, bepowder, bepraise, bepraisement, bepraiser, beprank, bepranked, bepray, bepreach, bepress, bepretty, bepride, beprose, bepuddle, bepuff, bepuffed, bepun, bepurple, bepuzzle, bepuzzlement, bequalm, bequeath, bequeathable, bequeathal, bequeathed, bequeather, bequeathing, bequeathment, bequeaths, bequest, bequest's, bequests, bequirtle, bequote, beqwete, ber, berain, berairou, berakah, berake, beraked, berakes, beraking, berakot, berakoth, berapt, berascal, berascaled, berascaling, berascals, berat, berate, berated, berates, berating, berattle, beraunite, beray, berbamine, berber, berberia, berberid, berberidaceous, berberin, berberine, berberins, berberis, berberry, berbers, berbery, berceau, berceaunette, bercelet, berceuse, berceuses, berdache, berdaches, berdash, bere, bereareft, bereason, bereave, bereaved, bereavement, bereavements, bereaven, bereaver, bereavers, bereaves, bereaving, berede, bereft, berend, berendo, berengelite, berengena, beresite, beret, beret's, berets, beretta, berettas, berewick, berg, bergalith, bergall, bergamasca, bergamasche, bergamask, bergamiol, bergamot, bergamots, bergander, bergaptene, berger, bergere, bergeres, bergeret, bergerette, bergfall, berggylt, bergh, berghaan, berginization, berginize, berglet, bergman, bergmannite, bergomask, bergs, bergschrund, bergut, bergy, bergylt, berhyme, berhymed, berhymes, berhyming, beribanded, beribbon, beribboned, beriber, beriberi, beriberic, beriberis, beribers, beride, berigora, berime, berimed, berimes, beriming, bering, beringed, beringite, beringleted, berinse, berith, berk, berkeleian, berkeley, berkelium, berkovets, berkovtsi, berkowitz, berkshire, berley, berlin, berlina, berline, berliner, berliners, berlines, berlinite, berlins, berloque, berm, berme, bermensch, bermes, berms, bermuda, bermudas, bermudian, bermudians, bermudite, bernacle, bernard, bernardine, berne, bernicle, bernicles, bernoo, berob, berobed, beroe, berogue, beroll, berouged, beround, berreave, berreaved, berreaves, berreaving, berrendo, berret, berretta, berrettas, berrettino, berri, berrichon, berrichonne, berried, berrier, berries, berrigan, berrugate, berry, berry's, berrybush, berrying, berryless, berrylike, berryman, berrypicker, berrypicking, bersagliere, bersaglieri, berseem, berseems, berserk, berserker, berserks, bersim, berskin, berstel, berth, bertha, berthage, berthas, berthed, berther, berthierite, berthing, berths, bertillonage, bertin, bertram, bertrandite, bertrum, beruffed, beruffled, berun, berust, bervie, berwick, berycid, beryciform, berycine, berycoid, berycoidean, beryl, berylate, beryline, beryllate, beryllia, berylline, berylliosis, beryllium, berylloid, beryllonate, beryllonite, beryllosis, beryls, beryx, berzelianite, berzeliite, bes, besa, besagne, besague, besaiel, besaile, besaint, besan, besanctify, besand, besant, besauce, besayle, bescab, bescarf, bescatter, bescent, bescorch, bescorched, bescorches, bescorching, bescorn, bescoundrel, bescour, bescoured, bescourge, bescouring, bescours, bescramble, bescrape, bescratch, bescrawl, bescreen, bescreened, bescreening, bescreens, bescribble, bescribbled, bescribbling, bescurf, bescurvy, bescutcheon, beseam, besee, beseech, beseeched, beseecher, beseechers, beseeches, beseeching, beseechingly, beseechingness, beseechment, beseek, beseem, beseemed, beseeming, beseemingly, beseemingness, beseemliness, beseemly, beseems, beseen, beseige, beset, besetment, besets, besetter, besetters, besetting, besew, beshackle, beshade, beshadow, beshadowed, beshadowing, beshadows, beshag, beshake, beshame, beshamed, beshames, beshaming, beshawled, beshear, beshell, beshield, beshine, beshiver, beshivered, beshivering, beshivers, beshlik, beshod, beshout, beshouted, beshouting, beshouts, beshow, beshower, beshrew, beshrewed, beshrewing, beshrews, beshriek, beshrivel, beshroud, beshrouded, beshrouding, beshrouds, besiclometer, beside, besides, besiege, besieged, besiegement, besieger, besiegers, besieges, besieging, besiegingly, besigh, besilver, besin, besing, besiren, besit, beslab, beslabber, beslap, beslash, beslave, beslaved, beslaver, besleeve, beslime, beslimed, beslimer, beslimes, besliming, beslings, beslipper, beslobber, beslow, beslubber, besluit, beslur, beslushed, besmear, besmeared, besmearer, besmearing, besmears, besmell, besmile, besmiled, besmiles, besmiling, besmirch, besmirched, besmircher, besmirchers, besmirches, besmirching, besmirchment, besmoke, besmoked, besmokes, besmoking, besmooth, besmoothed, besmoothing, besmooths, besmother, besmottered, besmouch, besmudge, besmudged, besmudges, besmudging, besmut, besmutch, besmuts, besmutted, besmutting, besnare, besneer, besnivel, besnow, besnowed, besnowing, besnows, besnuff, besodden, besogne, besognier, besoil, besoin, besom, besomer, besoms, besonio, besonnet, besoot, besoothe, besoothed, besoothement, besoothes, besoothing, besort, besot, besotment, besots, besotted, besottedly, besottedness, besotter, besotting, besottingly, besought, besoul, besour, besouth, bespake, bespangle, bespangled, bespangles, bespangling, bespate, bespatter, bespattered, bespatterer, bespattering, bespatterment, bespatters, bespawl, bespeak, bespeakable, bespeaker, bespeaking, bespeaks, bespecked, bespeckle, bespeckled, bespecklement, bespectacled, besped, bespeech, bespeed, bespell, bespelled, bespend, bespete, bespew, bespice, bespill, bespin, bespirit, bespit, besplash, besplatter, besplit, bespoke, bespoken, bespot, bespotted, bespottedness, bespotting, bespouse, bespoused, bespouses, bespousing, bespout, bespray, bespread, bespreading, bespreads, bespreng, besprent, bespring, besprinkle, besprinkled, besprinkler, besprinkles, besprinkling, besprizorni, bespurred, bespurt, besputter, bespy, besqueeze, besquib, besquirt, besra, bess, bessel, bessemer, bessemerize, bessemerized, bessemerizing, besses, best, bestab, bestad, bestain, bestamp, bestand, bestar, bestare, bestarve, bestatued, bestay, bestayed, bestead, besteaded, besteading, besteads, besteal, bested, besteer, bestench, bester, bestial, bestialise, bestialised, bestialising, bestialism, bestialist, bestialities, bestiality, bestialize, bestialized, bestializes, bestializing, bestially, bestials, bestian, bestiarian, bestiarianism, bestiaries, bestiarist, bestiary, bestick, besticking, bestill, besting, bestink, bestir, bestirred, bestirring, bestirs, bestness, bestock, bestore, bestorm, bestove, bestow, bestowable, bestowage, bestowal, bestowals, bestowed, bestower, bestowing, bestowment, bestows, bestraddle, bestraddled, bestraddling, bestrapped, bestraught, bestraw, bestreak, bestream, bestrew, bestrewed, bestrewing, bestrewment, bestrewn, bestrews, bestrid, bestridden, bestride, bestrided, bestrides, bestriding, bestripe, bestrode, bestrow, bestrowed, bestrowing, bestrown, bestrows, bestrut, bests, bestseller, bestseller's, bestsellerdom, bestsellers, bestselling, bestubble, bestubbled, bestuck, bestud, bestudded, bestudding, bestuds, bestuur, besugar, besugo, besuit, besully, beswarm, beswarmed, beswarming, beswarms, besweatered, besweeten, beswelter, beswim, beswinge, beswink, beswitch, bet, bet's, beta, betacaine, betacism, betacismus, betafite, betag, betail, betailor, betain, betaine, betaines, betainogen, betake, betaken, betakes, betaking, betalk, betallow, betanaphthol, betangle, betanglement, betas, betask, betassel, betatron, betatrons, betatter, betattered, betattering, betatters, betaxed, bete, beteach, betear, beteela, beteem, betel, betelgeuse, betell, betelnut, betelnuts, betels, beterschap, betes, beth, bethabara, bethank, bethanked, bethanking, bethankit, bethanks, bethel, bethels, bethesda, bethesdas, bethflower, bethink, bethinking, bethinks, bethlehem, bethlehemite, bethorn, bethorned, bethorning, bethorns, bethought, bethrall, bethreaten, bethroot, beths, bethumb, bethump, bethumped, bethumping, bethumps, bethunder, bethwack, bethwine, bethylid, betide, betided, betides, betiding, betimber, betime, betimes, betinge, betipple, betire, betis, betise, betises, betitle, betocsin, betoil, betoken, betokened, betokener, betokening, betokenment, betokens, beton, betone, betongue, betonica, betonies, betons, betony, betook, betorcin, betorcinol, betorn, betoss, betowel, betowered, betra'ying, betrace, betrail, betraise, betrample, betrap, betravel, betray, betrayal, betrayals, betrayed, betrayer, betrayers, betraying, betrayment, betrays, betread, betrend, betrim, betrinket, betroth, betrothal, betrothals, betrothed, betrothing, betrothment, betroths, betrough, betrousered, betrumpet, betrunk, betrust, bets, betso, betta, bettas, betted, better, bettered, betterer, bettergates, bettering, betterly, betterment, betterments, bettermost, betterness, betters, betties, betting, bettong, bettonga, bettor, bettors, betty, betuckered, betulaceous, betulin, betulinamaric, betulinic, betulinol, betumbled, beturbaned, betusked, betutor, betutored, betwattled, between, betweenbrain, betweenity, betweenmaid, betweenness, betweens, betweentimes, betweenwhiles, betwine, betwit, betwixen, betwixt, beudanite, beudantite, beulah, beuncled, beuniformed, beurre, bevaring, bevatron, bevatrons, beveil, bevel, beveled, beveler, bevelers, beveling, bevelled, beveller, bevellers, bevelling, bevelment, bevels, bevenom, bever, beverage, beverage's, beverages, beverse, bevesseled, bevesselled, beveto, bevies, bevil, bevillain, bevilled, bevined, bevoiled, bevomit, bevomited, bevomiting, bevomits, bevor, bevors, bevue, bevvy, bevy, bewail, bewailable, bewailed, bewailer, bewailers, bewailing, bewailingly, bewailment, bewails, bewaitered, bewake, bewall, beware, bewared, bewares, bewaring, bewary, bewash, bewaste, bewater, bewearied, bewearies, beweary, bewearying, beweep, beweeper, beweeping, beweeps, bewelcome, bewelter, bewend, bewept, bewest, bewet, bewhig, bewhisker, bewhiskered, bewhisper, bewhistle, bewhite, bewhiten, bewhore, bewidow, bewield, bewig, bewigged, bewigging, bewigs, bewilder, bewildered, bewilderedly, bewilderedness, bewildering, bewilderingly, bewilderment, bewilders, bewimple, bewinged, bewinter, bewired, bewit, bewitch, bewitched, bewitchedness, bewitcher, bewitchery, bewitches, bewitchful, bewitching, bewitchingly, bewitchingness, bewitchment, bewitchments, bewith, bewizard, bewonder, bework, beworm, bewormed, beworming, beworms, beworn, beworried, beworries, beworry, beworrying, beworship, bewpers, bewrap, bewrapped, bewrapping, bewraps, bewrapt, bewrathed, bewray, bewrayed, bewrayer, bewrayers, bewraying, bewrayingly, bewrayment, bewrays, bewreak, bewreath, bewreck, bewrite, bewrought, bewry, bewwept, bey, beydom, beyerite, beylic, beylical, beylics, beylik, beyliks, beyond, beyondness, beyonds, beyrichite, beys, beyship, bezan, bezant, bezante, bezantee, bezants, bezanty, bezazz, bezazzes, bezel, bezels, bezesteen, bezetta, bezette, bezil, bezils, bezique, beziques, bezoar, bezoardic, bezoars, bezonian, bezzant, bezzants, bezzi, bezzle, bezzled, bezzling, bezzo, bf, bg, bhabar, bhagat, bhagavat, bhagavata, bhaiachara, bhaiachari, bhaiyachara, bhajan, bhakta, bhaktas, bhakti, bhaktimarga, bhaktis, bhalu, bhandar, bhandari, bhang, bhangi, bhangs, bhara, bharal, bharti, bhat, bhava, bhavan, bhd, bheestie, bheesties, bheesty, bhikhari, bhikku, bhikshu, bhindi, bhishti, bhisti, bhistie, bhisties, bhokra, bhoosa, bhoot, bhoots, bhoy, bhp, bhumidar, bhunder, bhungi, bhungini, bhut, bhutan, bhutanese, bhutatathata, bhuts, bi, biabo, biacetyl, biacetylene, biacetyls, biacid, biacromial, biacuminate, biacuru, biajaiba, bialate, biali, bialis, biallyl, bialveolar, bialy, bialys, bialystoker, bianchite, bianco, biangular, biangulate, biangulated, biangulous, bianisidine, biannual, biannually, biannulate, biarchy, biarcuate, biarcuated, biarticular, biarticulate, biarticulated, bias, biased, biasedly, biases, biasing, biasness, biasnesses, biassed, biassedly, biasses, biassing, biasteric, biasways, biaswise, biathlon, biathlons, biatomic, biaural, biauricular, biauriculate, biaxal, biaxial, biaxiality, biaxially, biaxillary, bib, bib's, bibacious, bibaciousness, bibacity, bibasic, bibation, bibb, bibbed, bibber, bibberies, bibbers, bibbery, bibbing, bibble, bibbled, bibbler, bibbling, bibbons, bibbs, bibby, bibcock, bibcocks, bibelot, bibelots, bibenzyl, biberon, bibi, bibionid, bibiri, bibiru, bibitory, bibl, bible, bible's, bibles, bibless, biblical, biblically, biblicism, biblicist, biblike, biblioclasm, biblioclast, bibliofilm, bibliog, bibliogenesis, bibliognost, bibliognostic, bibliogony, bibliograph, bibliographer, bibliographers, bibliographic, bibliographical, bibliographically, bibliographies, bibliographize, bibliography, bibliography's, bibliokelpt, biblioklept, bibliokleptomania, bibliokleptomaniac, bibliolater, bibliolatrist, bibliolatrous, bibliolatry, bibliological, bibliologies, bibliologist, bibliology, bibliomancy, bibliomane, bibliomania, bibliomaniac, bibliomaniacal, bibliomanian, bibliomanianism, bibliomanism, bibliomanist, bibliopegic, bibliopegically, bibliopegist, bibliopegistic, bibliopegistical, bibliopegy, bibliophage, bibliophagic, bibliophagist, bibliophagous, bibliophil, bibliophile, bibliophiles, bibliophilic, bibliophilism, bibliophilist, bibliophilistic, bibliophily, bibliophobe, bibliophobia, bibliopolar, bibliopole, bibliopolery, bibliopolic, bibliopolical, bibliopolically, bibliopolism, bibliopolist, bibliopolistic, bibliopoly, bibliosoph, bibliotaph, bibliotaphe, bibliotaphic, bibliothec, bibliotheca, bibliothecae, bibliothecaire, bibliothecal, bibliothecarial, bibliothecarian, bibliothecary, bibliothecas, bibliotheke, bibliotheque, bibliotherapeutic, bibliotherapies, bibliotherapist, bibliotherapy, bibliothetic, bibliothque, bibliotic, bibliotics, bibliotist, biblist, biblists, biblos, biblus, biborate, bibracteate, bibracteolate, bibs, bibulosities, bibulosity, bibulous, bibulously, bibulousness, bicalcarate, bicalvous, bicameral, bicameralism, bicameralist, bicamerist, bicapitate, bicapsular, bicarb, bicarbide, bicarbonate, bicarbonates, bicarbs, bicarbureted, bicarburetted, bicarinate, bicarpellary, bicarpellate, bicaudal, bicaudate, bicched, bice, bicellular, bicentenaries, bicentenarnaries, bicentenary, bicentennial, bicentennially, bicentennials, bicentral, bicentric, bicentrically, bicentricity, bicep, bicep's, bicephalic, bicephalous, biceps, bicepses, bices, bicetyl, bichir, bichloride, bichlorides, bichord, bichos, bichromate, bichromated, bichromatic, bichromatize, bichrome, bichromic, bichy, biciliate, biciliated, bicipital, bicipitous, bicircular, bicirrose, bick, bicker, bickered, bickerer, bickerers, bickering, bickern, bickers, bickiron, biclavate, biclinia, biclinium, bicollateral, bicollaterality, bicolligate, bicolor, bicolored, bicolorous, bicolors, bicolour, bicoloured, bicolourous, bicolours, bicompact, biconcave, biconcavity, biconditional, bicondylar, bicone, biconic, biconical, biconically, biconjugate, biconnected, biconsonantal, biconvex, biconvexity, bicorn, bicornate, bicorne, bicorned, bicornes, bicornous, bicornuate, bicornuous, bicornute, bicorporal, bicorporate, bicorporeal, bicostate, bicrenate, bicrescentic, bicrofarad, bicron, bicrons, bicrural, bicuculline, bicultural, biculturalism, bicursal, bicuspid, bicuspidal, bicuspidate, bicuspids, bicyanide, bicycle, bicycled, bicycler, bicyclers, bicycles, bicyclic, bicyclical, bicycling, bicyclism, bicyclist, bicyclists, bicyclo, bicycloheptane, bicycular, bicylindrical, bid, bid's, bidactyl, bidactyle, bidactylous, bidar, bidarka, bidarkas, bidarkee, bidarkees, bidcock, biddability, biddable, biddableness, biddably, biddance, bidden, bidder, bidder's, bidders, biddery, biddie, biddies, bidding, biddings, biddy, bide, bided, bidene, bident, bidental, bidentalia, bidentate, bidented, bidential, bidenticulate, bider, biders, bidery, bides, bidet, bidets, bidget, bidi, bidiagonal, bidialectal, bidialectalism, bidigitate, bidimensional, biding, bidirectional, bidirectionally, bidiurnal, bidonville, bidree, bidri, bidry, bids, bidstand, biduous, bieberite, bieennia, bielbrief, bielby, bield, bielded, bielding, bields, bieldy, bielectrolysis, bielenite, bien, bienly, biennale, biennales, bienne, bienness, biennia, biennial, biennially, biennials, biennium, bienniums, biens, bienseance, bientt, bienvenu, bienvenue, bier, bierbalk, bierkeller, biers, bierstube, bierstuben, bierstubes, biestings, biethnic, bietle, biface, bifaces, bifacial, bifanged, bifara, bifarious, bifariously, bifer, biferous, biff, biffed, biffies, biffin, biffing, biffins, biffs, biffy, bifid, bifidate, bifidated, bifidities, bifidity, bifidly, bifilar, bifilarly, bifistular, biflabellate, biflagelate, biflagellate, biflecnode, biflected, biflex, biflorate, biflorous, bifluorid, bifluoride, bifocal, bifocals, bifoil, bifold, bifolia, bifoliate, bifoliolate, bifolium, bifollicular, biforate, biforin, biforine, biforked, biforking, biform, biformed, biformity, biforous, bifront, bifrontal, bifronted, bifrost, bifteck, bifunctional, bifurcal, bifurcate, bifurcated, bifurcately, bifurcates, bifurcating, bifurcation, bifurcations, bifurcous, big, biga, bigae, bigam, bigamic, bigamies, bigamist, bigamistic, bigamistically, bigamists, bigamize, bigamized, bigamizing, bigamous, bigamously, bigamy, bigarade, bigarades, bigaroon, bigaroons, bigarreau, bigas, bigate, bigbloom, bigbury, bigemina, bigeminal, bigeminate, bigeminated, bigeminies, bigeminum, bigeminy, bigener, bigeneric, bigential, bigeye, bigeyes, bigfoot, bigg, biggah, bigged, biggen, biggened, biggening, bigger, biggest, biggety, biggie, biggies, biggin, bigging, biggings, biggins, biggish, biggishness, biggity, biggonet, biggy, bigha, bighead, bigheaded, bigheads, bighearted, bigheartedly, bigheartedness, bighorn, bighorns, bight, bight's, bighted, bighting, bights, biglandular, biglenoid, biglot, bigly, bigmitt, bigmouth, bigmouthed, bigmouths, bigness, bignesses, bignonia, bignoniaceous, bignoniad, bignonias, bignou, bigoniac, bigonial, bigot, bigot's, bigoted, bigotedly, bigotedness, bigothero, bigotish, bigotries, bigotry, bigots, bigotty, bigram, bigroot, bigthatch, biguanide, biguttate, biguttulate, bigwig, bigwigged, bigwiggedness, bigwiggery, bigwiggism, bigwigs, bihalve, bihamate, bihari, biharmonic, bihourly, bihydrazine, bija, bijasal, bijection, bijection's, bijections, bijective, bijectively, bijou, bijous, bijouterie, bijoux, bijugate, bijugous, bijugular, bijwoner, bike, bike's, biked, biker, bikers, bikes, bikeway, bikeways, bikh, bikhaconitine, bikie, biking, bikini, bikini's, bikinied, bikinis, bikkurim, bilabe, bilabial, bilabials, bilabiate, bilaciniate, bilalo, bilamellar, bilamellate, bilamellated, bilaminar, bilaminate, bilaminated, biland, bilander, bilanders, bilateral, bilateralism, bilateralistic, bilateralities, bilaterality, bilaterally, bilateralness, bilayer, bilberries, bilberry, bilbi, bilbie, bilbies, bilbo, bilboa, bilboas, bilboes, bilboquet, bilbos, bilby, bilch, bilcock, bildar, bilder, bilders, bile, bilection, bilertinned, biles, bilestone, bileve, bilewhit, bilge, bilge's, bilged, bilges, bilgewater, bilgeway, bilgier, bilgiest, bilging, bilgy, bilharzia, bilharzial, bilharziasis, bilharzic, bilharziosis, bilianic, biliary, biliate, biliation, bilic, bilicyanin, bilifaction, biliferous, bilification, bilifuscin, bilify, bilihumin, bilimbi, bilimbing, bilimbis, biliment, bilinear, bilineate, bilineated, bilingual, bilingualism, bilinguality, bilingually, bilinguar, bilinguist, bilinigrin, bilinite, bilio, bilious, biliously, biliousness, biliprasin, bilipurpurin, bilipyrrhin, bilirubin, bilirubinemia, bilirubinic, bilirubinuria, biliteral, biliteralism, bilith, bilithon, biliverdic, biliverdin, bilixanthin, bilk, bilked, bilker, bilkers, bilking, bilkis, bilks, bill, billa, billable, billabong, billage, billard, billback, billbeetle, billbergia, billboard, billboard's, billboards, billbroking, billbug, billbugs, billed, biller, billers, billet, billete, billeted, billeter, billeters, billethead, billeting, billets, billette, billetty, billetwood, billety, billfish, billfishes, billfold, billfolds, billhead, billheading, billheads, billholder, billhook, billhooks, billian, billiard, billiardist, billiardly, billiards, billie, billies, billikin, billing, billings, billingsgate, billion, billionaire, billionaires, billionism, billions, billionth, billionths, billitonite, billman, billmen, billon, billons, billot, billow, billowed, billowier, billowiest, billowiness, billowing, billows, billowy, billposter, billposting, bills, billsticker, billsticking, billtong, billy, billyboy, billycan, billycans, billycock, billyer, billyhood, billyo, billywix, bilo, bilobate, bilobated, bilobe, bilobed, bilobiate, bilobular, bilocation, bilocellate, bilocular, biloculate, biloculine, bilophodont, biloquist, bilos, bilsh, bilsted, bilsteds, biltong, biltongs, biltongue, bim, bima, bimaculate, bimaculated, bimah, bimahs, bimalar, bimana, bimanal, bimane, bimanous, bimanual, bimanually, bimarginate, bimarine, bimas, bimastic, bimastism, bimastoid, bimasty, bimaxillary, bimbashi, bimbil, bimbo, bimboes, bimbos, bimeby, bimedial, bimensal, bimester, bimesters, bimestrial, bimetal, bimetalic, bimetalism, bimetallic, bimetallism, bimetallist, bimetallistic, bimetallists, bimetals, bimethyl, bimethyls, bimillenary, bimillenial, bimillenium, bimillennia, bimillennium, bimillenniums, bimillionaire, bimilllennia, bimodal, bimodality, bimodule, bimodulus, bimolecular, bimolecularly, bimong, bimonthlies, bimonthly, bimorph, bimorphemic, bimorphs, bimotor, bimotored, bimotors, bimucronate, bimuscular, bin, bin's, binal, binaphthyl, binapthyl, binaries, binarium, binary, binate, binately, bination, binational, binaural, binaurally, binauricular, binbashi, bind, bindable, binder, binderies, binders, bindery, bindheimite, bindi, binding, bindingly, bindingness, bindings, bindis, bindle, bindles, bindlet, bindoree, binds, bindweb, bindweed, bindweeds, bindwith, bindwood, bine, binervate, bines, bineweed, binful, bing, binge, bingee, binges, bingey, bingeys, binghi, bingies, bingle, bingo, bingos, bingy, binh, biniodide, biniou, binit, binits, bink, binman, binmen, binna, binnacle, binnacles, binned, binning, binnite, binnogue, binny, bino, binocle, binocles, binocs, binocular, binocularity, binocularly, binoculars, binoculate, binodal, binode, binodose, binodous, binomen, binomenclature, binomial, binomialism, binomially, binomials, binominal, binominated, binominous, binomy, binormal, binotic, binotonous, binous, binoxalate, binoxide, bins, bint, bintangor, bints, binturong, binuclear, binucleate, binucleated, binucleolate, binukau, bio, bioaccumulation, bioacoustics, bioactivities, bioactivity, bioassay, bioassayed, bioassaying, bioassays, bioastronautical, bioastronautics, bioavailability, biobibliographer, biobibliographic, biobibliographical, biobibliographies, biobibliography, bioblast, bioblastic, biocatalyst, biocatalytic, biocellate, biocenology, biocenosis, biocenotic, biocentric, biochemic, biochemical, biochemically, biochemics, biochemist, biochemistries, biochemistry, biochemists, biochemy, biochore, biochron, biocidal, biocide, biocides, bioclean, bioclimatic, bioclimatician, bioclimatological, bioclimatologically, bioclimatologies, bioclimatologist, bioclimatology, biocoenose, biocoenoses, biocoenosis, biocoenotic, biocontrol, biocycle, biocycles, biod, biodegradability, biodegradable, biodegradation, biodegrade, biodegraded, biodegrading, biodynamic, biodynamical, biodynamics, biodyne, bioecologic, bioecological, bioecologically, bioecologies, bioecologist, bioecology, bioelectric, bioelectrical, bioelectricities, bioelectricity, bioelectrogenesis, bioelectrogenetic, bioelectrogenetically, bioelectronics, bioenergetics, bioengineering, bioenvironmental, bioenvironmentaly, bioethic, bioethics, biofeedback, bioflavinoid, bioflavonoid, biofog, biog, biogas, biogases, biogasses, biogen, biogenase, biogenesis, biogenesist, biogenetic, biogenetical, biogenetically, biogenetics, biogenic, biogenies, biogenous, biogens, biogeny, biogeochemical, biogeochemistry, biogeographer, biogeographers, biogeographic, biogeographical, biogeographically, biogeography, biognosis, biograph, biographee, biographer, biographer's, biographers, biographic, biographical, biographically, biographies, biographist, biographize, biography, biography's, biohazard, bioherm, bioherms, bioinstrument, bioinstrumentation, biokinetics, biol, biolinguistics, biolite, biolith, biologese, biologic, biological, biologically, biologicohumanistic, biologics, biologies, biologism, biologist, biologist's, biologistic, biologists, biologize, biology, bioluminescence, bioluminescent, biolyses, biolysis, biolytic, biomagnetic, biomagnetism, biomass, biomasses, biomaterial, biomathematics, biome, biomechanical, biomechanics, biomedical, biomedicine, biomes, biometeorology, biometer, biometric, biometrical, biometrically, biometrician, biometricist, biometrics, biometries, biometrist, biometry, biomicroscope, biomicroscopies, biomicroscopy, biomorphic, bion, bionditional, bionergy, bionic, bionics, bionomic, bionomical, bionomically, bionomics, bionomies, bionomist, bionomy, biont, biontic, bionts, biophagism, biophagous, biophagy, biophilous, biophor, biophore, biophotometer, biophotophone, biophysic, biophysical, biophysically, biophysicist, biophysicists, biophysicochemical, biophysics, biophysiography, biophysiological, biophysiologist, biophysiology, biophyte, biopic, bioplasm, bioplasmic, bioplasms, bioplast, bioplastic, biopoesis, biopoiesis, biopotential, bioprecipitation, biopsic, biopsies, biopsy, biopsychic, biopsychical, biopsychological, biopsychologies, biopsychologist, biopsychology, bioptic, biopyribole, bioral, biorbital, biordinal, bioreaction, bioresearch, biorgan, biorhythm, biorhythmic, biorhythmicities, biorhythmicity, biorythmic, bios, biosatellite, biosatellites, bioscience, biosciences, bioscientific, bioscientist, bioscope, bioscopes, bioscopic, bioscopies, bioscopy, biose, biosensor, bioseston, biosis, biosocial, biosociological, biosociology, biosome, biospeleology, biosphere, biospheres, biostatic, biostatical, biostatics, biostatistic, biostatistics, biosterin, biosterol, biostratigraphy, biostrome, biosyntheses, biosynthesis, biosynthesize, biosynthetic, biosynthetically, biosystematic, biosystematics, biosystematist, biosystematy, biota, biotas, biotaxy, biotech, biotechnics, biotechnological, biotechnologically, biotechnologicaly, biotechnologies, biotechnology, biotechs, biotelemetric, biotelemetries, biotelemetry, biotherapy, biotic, biotical, biotically, biotics, biotin, biotins, biotite, biotites, biotitic, biotome, biotomy, biotope, biotopes, biotoxin, biotoxins, biotransformation, biotron, biotrons, biotype, biotypes, biotypic, biotypology, biovular, biovulate, bioxalate, bioxide, biozone, bipack, bipacks, bipaleolate, bipalmate, biparasitic, biparental, biparentally, biparietal, biparous, biparted, bipartible, bipartient, bipartile, bipartisan, bipartisanism, bipartisanship, bipartite, bipartitely, bipartition, bipartizan, biparty, bipaschal, bipectinate, bipectinated, biped, bipedal, bipedality, bipedism, bipeds, bipeltate, bipennate, bipennated, bipenniform, biperforate, bipersonal, bipetalous, biphase, biphasic, biphenol, biphenyl, biphenylene, biphenyls, bipinnaria, bipinnariae, bipinnarias, bipinnate, bipinnated, bipinnately, bipinnatifid, bipinnatiparted, bipinnatipartite, bipinnatisect, bipinnatisected, biplace, biplanal, biplanar, biplane, biplane's, biplanes, biplicate, biplicity, biplosion, biplosive, bipod, bipods, bipolar, bipolarity, bipolarization, bipolarize, bipont, biporose, biporous, bipotentialities, bipotentiality, biprism, biprong, bipropellant, bipunctal, bipunctate, bipunctual, bipupillate, bipyramid, bipyramidal, bipyridine, bipyridyl, biquadrantal, biquadrate, biquadratic, biquarterly, biquartz, biquintile, biracial, biracialism, biradial, biradiate, biradiated, biramose, biramous, birational, birch, birchbark, birched, birchen, bircher, birchers, birches, birching, birchism, birchman, birchwood, bird, bird's, birdbander, birdbanding, birdbath, birdbath's, birdbaths, birdberry, birdbrain, birdbrained, birdbrains, birdcage, birdcages, birdcall, birdcalls, birdcatcher, birdcatching, birdclapper, birdcraft, birddom, birde, birded, birdeen, birder, birders, birdeye, birdfarm, birdfarms, birdglue, birdhood, birdhouse, birdhouses, birdie, birdieback, birdied, birdieing, birdies, birdikin, birding, birdland, birdless, birdlet, birdlife, birdlike, birdlime, birdlimed, birdlimes, birdliming, birdling, birdlore, birdman, birdmen, birdmouthed, birdnest, birdnester, birds, birdsall, birdseed, birdseeds, birdseye, birdseyes, birdshot, birdshots, birdsnest, birdsong, birdstone, birdwatch, birdweed, birdwise, birdwitted, birdwoman, birdwomen, birdy, birdyback, birectangular, birefracting, birefraction, birefractive, birefringence, birefringent, bireme, biremes, biretta, birettas, birgand, biri, biriani, biriba, birimose, birk, birken, birkie, birkies, birkremite, birks, birky, birl, birle, birled, birler, birlers, birles, birlie, birlieman, birling, birlings, birlinn, birls, birma, birmingham, birn, birne, birny, birodo, birostrate, birostrated, birota, birotation, birotatory, birr, birred, birretta, birrettas, birri, birring, birrs, birrus, birse, birses, birsit, birsle, birsy, birt, birth, birthbed, birthday, birthday's, birthdays, birthdom, birthed, birthing, birthland, birthless, birthmark, birthmarks, birthmate, birthnight, birthplace, birthplaces, birthrate, birthrates, birthright, birthright's, birthrights, birthroot, births, birthstone, birthstones, birthstool, birthwort, birthy, bis, bisabol, bisaccate, bisacromial, bisagre, bisalt, bisannual, bisantler, bisaxillary, bisayan, bisbeeite, biscacha, biscayan, biscayen, bischofite, biscot, biscotin, biscuit, biscuit's, biscuiting, biscuitlike, biscuitmaker, biscuitmaking, biscuitroot, biscuitry, biscuits, biscutate, bisdiapason, bisdimethylamino, bise, bisect, bisected, bisecting, bisection, bisection's, bisectional, bisectionally, bisections, bisector, bisector's, bisectors, bisectrices, bisectrix, bisects, bisegment, bisellia, bisellium, biseptate, biserial, biserially, biseriate, biseriately, biserrate, bises, biset, bisetose, bisetous, bisexed, bisext, bisexual, bisexualism, bisexuality, bisexually, bisexuals, bisexuous, bisglyoxaline, bish, bishop, bishop's, bishopbird, bishopdom, bishoped, bishopess, bishopful, bishophood, bishoping, bishopless, bishoplet, bishoplike, bishopling, bishopric, bishoprics, bishops, bishopscap, bishopship, bishopstool, bishopweed, bishydroxycoumarin, bisie, bisiliac, bisilicate, bisiliquous, bisimine, bisinuate, bisinuation, bisischiadic, bisischiatic, bisk, biskop, bisks, bislings, bismanol, bismar, bismarck, bismarine, bismark, bisme, bismer, bismerpund, bismethyl, bismillah, bismite, bismuth, bismuthal, bismuthate, bismuthic, bismuthide, bismuthiferous, bismuthine, bismuthinite, bismuthite, bismuthous, bismuths, bismuthyl, bismutite, bismutoplagionite, bismutosmaltite, bismutosphaerite, bisnaga, bisnagas, bisognio, bison, bison's, bisonant, bisons, bisontine, bisphenoid, bispinose, bispinous, bispore, bisporous, bisque, bisques, bisquette, bissabol, bissellia, bissext, bissextile, bissextus, bisso, bisson, bissonata, bist, bistable, bistate, bistephanic, bister, bistered, bisters, bistetrazole, bisti, bistipular, bistipulate, bistipuled, bistort, bistorts, bistouries, bistournage, bistoury, bistratal, bistratose, bistre, bistred, bistres, bistriate, bistriazole, bistro, bistroic, bistros, bisubstituted, bisubstitution, bisulc, bisulcate, bisulcated, bisulfate, bisulfid, bisulfide, bisulfite, bisulphate, bisulphide, bisulphite, bisyllabic, bisyllabism, bisymmetric, bisymmetrical, bisymmetrically, bisymmetry, bisync, bit, bit's, bitable, bitake, bitangent, bitangential, bitanhol, bitartrate, bitbrace, bitch, bitch's, bitched, bitcheries, bitchery, bitches, bitchier, bitchiest, bitchily, bitchiness, bitching, bitchy, bite, biteable, biteche, bited, biteless, bitemporal, bitentaculate, biter, biternate, biternately, biters, bites, bitesheep, bitewing, bitewings, bitheism, biti, biting, bitingly, bitingness, bitless, bitmap, bitmapped, bitnet, bito, bitolyl, bitonal, bitonalities, bitonality, bitore, bitreadle, bitripartite, bitripinnatifid, bitriseptate, bitrochanteric, bits, bitser, bitstalk, bitstock, bitstocks, bitstone, bitsy, bitt, bittacle, bitte, bitted, bitten, bitter, bitterbark, bitterblain, bitterbloom, bitterbrush, bitterbump, bitterbur, bitterbush, bittered, bitterender, bitterer, bitterest, bitterful, bitterhead, bitterhearted, bitterheartedness, bittering, bitterish, bitterishness, bitterless, bitterling, bitterly, bittern, bitterness, bitterns, bitternut, bitterroot, bitters, bittersweet, bittersweetly, bittersweetness, bittersweets, bitterweed, bitterwood, bitterworm, bitterwort, bitthead, bittie, bittier, bittiest, bitting, bittings, bittock, bittocks, bittor, bitts, bitty, bitubercular, bituberculate, bituberculated, bitulithic, bitume, bitumed, bitumen, bitumens, bituminate, bituminiferous, bituminisation, bituminise, bituminised, bituminising, bituminization, bituminize, bituminized, bituminizing, bituminoid, bituminosis, bituminous, bitwise, bityite, bitypic, biune, biunial, biunique, biuniquely, biuniqueness, biunity, biunivocal, biurate, biurea, biuret, bivalence, bivalencies, bivalency, bivalent, bivalents, bivalve, bivalve's, bivalved, bivalves, bivalvian, bivalvous, bivalvular, bivane, bivariant, bivariate, bivascular, bivaulted, bivector, biventer, biventral, biverb, biverbal, bivial, bivinyl, bivinyls, bivious, bivittate, bivium, bivocal, bivocalized, bivoltine, bivoluminous, bivouac, bivouaced, bivouacked, bivouacking, bivouacks, bivouacs, bivvy, biwa, biweeklies, biweekly, biwinter, bixa, bixaceous, bixbyite, bixin, biyearly, biz, bizant, bizardite, bizarre, bizarrely, bizarreness, bizarrerie, bizarres, bizcacha, bize, bizel, bizes, bizet, biznaga, biznagas, bizonal, bizone, bizones, bizygomatic, bizz, bizzarro, bk, bkbndr, bkcy, bkg, bkgd, bklr, bkpr, bkpt, bks, bkt, bl, blaasop, blab, blabbed, blabber, blabbered, blabberer, blabbering, blabbermouth, blabbermouths, blabbers, blabbing, blabby, blabmouth, blabs, blachong, black, blackacre, blackamoor, blackamoors, blackarm, blackback, blackball, blackballed, blackballer, blackballing, blackballs, blackband, blackbeetle, blackbelly, blackberries, blackberry, blackberry's, blackberrylike, blackbine, blackbird, blackbird's, blackbirder, blackbirding, blackbirds, blackboard, blackboard's, blackboards, blackbody, blackboy, blackboys, blackbreast, blackbrush, blackbuck, blackbush, blackbutt, blackcap, blackcaps, blackcoat, blackcock, blackcod, blackcods, blackcurrant, blackdamp, blacked, blacken, blackened, blackener, blackeners, blackening, blackens, blacker, blackest, blacketeer, blackey, blackeye, blackeyes, blackface, blackfeet, blackfellow, blackfellows, blackfigured, blackfin, blackfins, blackfire, blackfish, blackfisher, blackfishes, blackfishing, blackflies, blackfly, blackfoot, blackguard, blackguardism, blackguardize, blackguardly, blackguardry, blackguards, blackgum, blackgums, blackhander, blackhead, blackheads, blackheart, blackhearted, blackheartedly, blackheartedness, blackie, blackies, blacking, blackings, blackish, blackishly, blackishness, blackit, blackjack, blackjack's, blackjacked, blackjacking, blackjacks, blackland, blacklead, blackleg, blacklegged, blackleggery, blacklegging, blacklegism, blacklegs, blacklight, blacklist, blacklisted, blacklister, blacklisting, blacklists, blackly, blackmail, blackmailed, blackmailer, blackmailers, blackmailing, blackmails, blackman, blackneb, blackneck, blackness, blacknob, blackout, blackout's, blackouts, blackpatch, blackplate, blackpoll, blackpot, blackprint, blackrag, blackroot, blacks, blackseed, blackshirt, blackshirted, blacksmith, blacksmithing, blacksmiths, blacksnake, blackstick, blackstrap, blacktail, blackthorn, blackthorns, blacktongue, blacktop, blacktopped, blacktopping, blacktops, blacktree, blackware, blackwash, blackwasher, blackwashing, blackwater, blackweed, blackwood, blackwork, blackwort, blacky, blad, bladder, bladder's, bladderet, bladderless, bladderlike, bladdernose, bladdernut, bladderpod, bladders, bladderseed, bladderweed, bladderwort, bladderwrack, bladdery, blade, blade's, bladebone, bladed, bladeless, bladelet, bladelike, blader, blades, bladesmith, bladewise, blading, bladish, blady, bladygrass, blae, blaeberries, blaeberry, blaeness, blaewort, blaff, blaffert, blaflum, blaggard, blague, blagueur, blah, blahlaut, blahs, blain, blains, blair, blairmorite, blake, blakeberyed, blakeite, blam, blamability, blamable, blamableness, blamably, blame, blameable, blameableness, blameably, blamed, blameful, blamefully, blamefulness, blameless, blamelessly, blamelessness, blamer, blamers, blames, blameworthiness, blameworthy, blaming, blamingly, blams, blan, blanc, blanca, blancard, blanch, blanche, blanched, blancher, blanchers, blanches, blanchi, blanchimeter, blanching, blanchingly, blancmange, blancmanger, blancmanges, blanco, blancs, bland, blanda, blandation, blander, blandest, blandiloquence, blandiloquious, blandiloquous, blandish, blandished, blandisher, blandishers, blandishes, blandishing, blandishingly, blandishment, blandishments, blandly, blandness, blank, blankard, blankbook, blanked, blankeel, blanker, blankest, blanket, blanketed, blanketeer, blanketer, blanketers, blanketflower, blanketing, blanketless, blanketlike, blanketmaker, blanketmaking, blanketry, blankets, blanketweed, blankety, blanking, blankish, blankite, blankly, blankminded, blankmindedness, blankness, blanks, blanky, blanque, blanquette, blanquillo, blanquillos, blaoner, blaoners, blare, blared, blares, blarina, blaring, blarney, blarneyed, blarneyer, blarneying, blarneys, blarnid, blarny, blart, blas, blase, blaseness, blash, blashy, blason, blaspheme, blasphemed, blasphemer, blasphemers, blasphemes, blasphemies, blaspheming, blasphemous, blasphemously, blasphemousness, blasphemy, blast, blastaea, blasted, blastema, blastemal, blastemas, blastemata, blastematic, blastemic, blaster, blasters, blastful, blasthole, blastid, blastide, blastie, blastier, blasties, blastiest, blasting, blastings, blastman, blastment, blastocarpous, blastocele, blastocheme, blastochyle, blastocoel, blastocoele, blastocoelic, blastocolla, blastocyst, blastocyte, blastoderm, blastodermatic, blastodermic, blastodisc, blastodisk, blastoff, blastoffs, blastogenesis, blastogenetic, blastogenic, blastogeny, blastogranitic, blastoid, blastoma, blastomas, blastomata, blastomere, blastomeric, blastomycete, blastomycetic, blastomycetous, blastomycin, blastomycosis, blastomycotic, blastoneuropore, blastophitic, blastophoral, blastophore, blastophoric, blastophthoria, blastophthoric, blastophyllum, blastoporal, blastopore, blastoporic, blastoporphyritic, blastosphere, blastospheric, blastostylar, blastostyle, blastozooid, blastplate, blasts, blastula, blastulae, blastular, blastulas, blastulation, blastule, blasty, blat, blatancies, blatancy, blatant, blatantly, blatch, blatchang, blate, blately, blateness, blateration, blateroon, blather, blathered, blatherer, blathering, blathers, blatherskite, blatherskites, blathery, blatiform, blatjang, blats, blatta, blatted, blatter, blattered, blatterer, blattering, blatters, blatti, blattid, blattiform, blatting, blattoid, blaubok, blauboks, blaunner, blautok, blauwbok, blaver, blaw, blawed, blawing, blawn, blawort, blaws, blay, blayk, blaze, blazed, blazer, blazers, blazes, blazing, blazingly, blazon, blazoned, blazoner, blazoners, blazoning, blazonment, blazonries, blazonry, blazons, blazy, bld, bldg, bldr, blea, bleaberry, bleach, bleachability, bleachable, bleached, bleacher, bleacheries, bleacherite, bleacherman, bleachers, bleachery, bleaches, bleachfield, bleachground, bleachhouse, bleaching, bleachman, bleachs, bleachworks, bleachyard, bleak, bleaker, bleakest, bleakish, bleakly, bleakness, bleaks, bleaky, blear, bleared, blearedness, bleareye, bleareyed, blearier, bleariest, blearily, bleariness, blearing, blearness, blears, bleary, blearyeyedness, bleat, bleated, bleater, bleaters, bleating, bleatingly, bleats, bleaty, bleaunt, bleb, blebby, blebs, blechnoid, bleck, bled, blee, bleed, bleeder, bleeders, bleeding, bleedings, bleeds, bleekbok, bleep, bleeped, bleeping, bleeps, bleery, bleeze, bleezy, bleinerite, blellum, blellums, blemish, blemish's, blemished, blemisher, blemishes, blemishing, blemishment, blemmatrope, blench, blenched, blencher, blenchers, blenches, blenching, blenchingly, blencorn, blend, blendcorn, blende, blended, blender, blenders, blendes, blending, blendor, blends, blendure, blendwater, blenheim, blenk, blennadenitis, blennemesis, blennenteria, blennenteritis, blennies, blenniid, blenniiform, blennioid, blennocele, blennocystitis, blennoemesis, blennogenic, blennogenous, blennoid, blennoma, blennometritis, blennophlogisma, blennophlogosis, blennophobia, blennophthalmia, blennoptysis, blennorhea, blennorrhagia, blennorrhagic, blennorrhea, blennorrheal, blennorrhinia, blennorrhoea, blennosis, blennostasis, blennostatic, blennothorax, blennotorrhea, blennuria, blenny, blennymenitis, blens, blent, bleo, blephara, blepharadenitis, blepharal, blepharanthracosis, blepharedema, blepharelcosis, blepharemphysema, blepharism, blepharitic, blepharitis, blepharoadenitis, blepharoadenoma, blepharoatheroma, blepharoblennorrhea, blepharocarcinoma, blepharochalasis, blepharochromidrosis, blepharoclonus, blepharocoloboma, blepharoconjunctivitis, blepharodiastasis, blepharodyschroia, blepharohematidrosis, blepharolithiasis, blepharomelasma, blepharoncosis, blepharoncus, blepharophimosis, blepharophryplasty, blepharophthalmia, blepharophyma, blepharoplast, blepharoplastic, blepharoplasty, blepharoplegia, blepharoptosis, blepharopyorrhea, blepharorrhaphy, blepharospasm, blepharospath, blepharosphincterectomy, blepharostat, blepharostenosis, blepharosymphysis, blepharosyndesmitis, blepharosynechia, blepharotomy, blepharydatis, blere, blesbok, blesboks, blesbuck, blesbucks, blesmol, bless, blesse, blessed, blesseder, blessedest, blessedly, blessedness, blesser, blessers, blesses, blessing, blessingly, blessings, blest, blet, blethe, blether, bletheration, blethered, blethering, blethers, bletherskate, bletonism, blets, bletted, bletting, bleu, blew, blewits, bleymes, bliaut, blibe, blick, blickey, blickeys, blickie, blickies, blicky, blier, bliest, blight, blightbird, blighted, blighter, blighters, blighties, blighting, blightingly, blights, blighty, blijver, blimbing, blimey, blimp, blimp's, blimpish, blimpishly, blimpishness, blimps, blimy, blin, blind, blindage, blindages, blindball, blindcat, blinded, blindedly, blinder, blinders, blindest, blindeyes, blindfast, blindfish, blindfishes, blindfold, blindfolded, blindfoldedly, blindfoldedness, blindfolder, blindfolding, blindfoldly, blindfolds, blinding, blindingly, blindish, blindism, blindless, blindling, blindly, blindman, blindness, blinds, blindstitch, blindstorey, blindstories, blindstory, blindweed, blindworm, blinger, blini, blinis, blink, blinkard, blinkards, blinked, blinker, blinkered, blinkering, blinkers, blinking, blinkingly, blinks, blinky, blinter, blintz, blintze, blintzes, bliny, blip, blip's, blipped, blippers, blipping, blips, blirt, bliss, blisses, blissful, blissfully, blissfulness, blissless, blissom, blist, blister, blistered, blistering, blisteringly, blisterous, blisters, blisterweed, blisterwort, blistery, blit, blite, blites, blithe, blithebread, blitheful, blithefully, blithehearted, blithelike, blithely, blithemeat, blithen, blitheness, blither, blithered, blithering, blithers, blithesome, blithesomely, blithesomeness, blithest, blitter, blitz, blitz's, blitzbuggy, blitzed, blitzes, blitzing, blitzkrieg, blitzkrieged, blitzkrieging, blitzkriegs, blizz, blizzard, blizzard's, blizzardly, blizzardous, blizzards, blizzardy, blk, blksize, blo, bloat, bloated, bloatedness, bloater, bloaters, bloating, bloats, blob, blob's, blobbed, blobber, blobbier, blobbiest, blobbiness, blobbing, blobby, blobs, bloc, bloc's, blocage, block, block's, blockade, blockaded, blockader, blockaders, blockaderunning, blockades, blockading, blockage, blockage's, blockages, blockboard, blockbuster, blockbusters, blockbusting, blocked, blocker, blockers, blockhead, blockheaded, blockheadedly, blockheadedness, blockheadish, blockheadishness, blockheadism, blockheads, blockhole, blockholer, blockhouse, blockhouses, blockier, blockiest, blockiness, blocking, blockish, blockishly, blockishness, blocklayer, blocklike, blockline, blockmaker, blockmaking, blockman, blockout, blockpate, blocks, blockship, blockwood, blocky, blocs, blodite, bloedite, blok, bloke, bloke's, blokes, blolly, bloman, blomstrandine, blond, blond's, blonde, blonde's, blondeness, blonder, blondes, blondest, blondine, blondish, blondness, blonds, blood, bloodalley, bloodalp, bloodbath, bloodbeat, bloodberry, bloodbird, bloodcurdler, bloodcurdling, bloodcurdlingly, blooddrop, blooddrops, blooded, bloodedness, bloodfin, bloodfins, bloodflower, bloodguilt, bloodguiltiness, bloodguiltless, bloodguilty, bloodhound, bloodhound's, bloodhounds, bloodied, bloodier, bloodies, bloodiest, bloodily, bloodiness, blooding, bloodings, bloodleaf, bloodless, bloodlessly, bloodlessness, bloodletter, bloodletting, bloodlettings, bloodlike, bloodline, bloodlines, bloodlust, bloodlusting, bloodmobile, bloodmobiles, bloodmonger, bloodnoun, bloodred, bloodripe, bloodripeness, bloodroot, bloodroots, bloods, bloodshed, bloodshedder, bloodshedding, bloodshot, bloodshotten, bloodspiller, bloodspilling, bloodstain, bloodstain's, bloodstained, bloodstainedness, bloodstains, bloodstanch, bloodstock, bloodstone, bloodstones, bloodstream, bloodstreams, bloodstroke, bloodsuck, bloodsucker, bloodsuckers, bloodsucking, bloodtest, bloodthirst, bloodthirster, bloodthirstier, bloodthirstiest, bloodthirstily, bloodthirstiness, bloodthirsting, bloodthirsty, bloodweed, bloodwit, bloodwite, bloodwood, bloodworm, bloodwort, bloodworthy, bloody, bloodybones, bloodying, blooey, blooie, bloom, bloomage, bloomed, bloomer, bloomeries, bloomerism, bloomers, bloomery, bloomfell, bloomier, bloomiest, blooming, bloomingly, bloomingness, bloomkin, bloomless, blooms, bloomy, bloop, blooped, blooper, bloopers, blooping, bloops, blooth, blore, blosmy, blossom, blossombill, blossomed, blossomhead, blossoming, blossomless, blossomry, blossoms, blossomtime, blossomy, blot, blot's, blotch, blotched, blotches, blotchier, blotchiest, blotchily, blotchiness, blotching, blotchy, blote, blotless, blotlessness, blots, blotted, blotter, blotters, blottesque, blottesquely, blottier, blottiest, blotting, blottingly, blotto, blottto, blotty, bloubiskop, blouse, blouse's, bloused, blouselike, blouses, blousier, blousiest, blousily, blousing, blouson, blousons, blousy, blout, bloviate, bloviated, bloviates, bloviating, blow, blowback, blowbacks, blowball, blowballs, blowby, blowbys, blowcase, blowcock, blowdown, blowen, blower, blowers, blowess, blowfish, blowfishes, blowflies, blowfly, blowgun, blowguns, blowhard, blowhards, blowhole, blowholes, blowie, blowier, blowiest, blowiness, blowing, blowings, blowiron, blowjob, blowjobs, blowlamp, blowline, blown, blowoff, blowoffs, blowout, blowouts, blowpipe, blowpipes, blowpit, blowpoint, blowproof, blows, blowse, blowsed, blowsier, blowsiest, blowsily, blowspray, blowsy, blowth, blowtorch, blowtorches, blowtube, blowtubes, blowup, blowups, blowy, blowze, blowzed, blowzier, blowziest, blowzily, blowziness, blowzing, blowzy, bls, blub, blubbed, blubber, blubbered, blubberer, blubberers, blubberhead, blubbering, blubberingly, blubberman, blubberous, blubbers, blubbery, blubbing, blucher, bluchers, bludge, bludged, bludgeon, bludgeoned, bludgeoneer, bludgeoner, bludgeoning, bludgeons, bludger, bludging, blue, blueback, blueball, blueballs, bluebead, bluebeard, bluebell, bluebelled, bluebells, blueberries, blueberry, blueberry's, bluebill, bluebills, bluebird, bluebird's, bluebirds, blueblack, blueblaw, blueblood, blueblossom, bluebonnet, bluebonnet's, bluebonnets, bluebook, bluebooks, bluebottle, bluebottles, bluebreast, bluebuck, bluebush, bluebutton, bluecap, bluecaps, bluecoat, bluecoated, bluecoats, bluecup, bluecurls, blued, bluefin, bluefins, bluefish, bluefishes, bluegill, bluegills, bluegown, bluegrass, bluegum, bluegums, bluehead, blueheads, bluehearted, bluehearts, blueing, blueings, blueish, bluejack, bluejacket, bluejackets, bluejacks, bluejay, bluejays, bluejoint, blueleg, bluelegs, blueline, bluelines, bluely, blueness, bluenesses, bluenose, bluenosed, bluenoses, bluepoint, bluepoints, blueprint, blueprint's, blueprinted, blueprinter, blueprinting, blueprints, bluer, blues, bluesides, bluesman, bluesmen, bluest, bluestem, bluestems, bluestocking, bluestockingish, bluestockingism, bluestockings, bluestone, bluestoner, bluesy, bluet, blueth, bluethroat, bluetick, bluetit, bluetongue, bluetop, bluetops, bluets, blueweed, blueweeds, bluewing, bluewood, bluewoods, bluey, blueys, bluff, bluffable, bluffed, bluffer, bluffers, bluffest, bluffing, bluffly, bluffness, bluffs, bluffy, blufter, bluggy, bluing, bluings, bluish, bluishness, bluism, bluisness, blume, blumed, blumes, bluming, blunder, blunderbuss, blunderbusses, blundered, blunderer, blunderers, blunderful, blunderhead, blunderheaded, blunderheadedness, blundering, blunderingly, blunderings, blunders, blundersome, blunge, blunged, blunger, blungers, blunges, blunging, blunk, blunker, blunket, blunks, blunnen, blunt, blunted, blunter, bluntest, blunthead, blunthearted, bluntie, blunting, bluntish, bluntishness, bluntly, bluntness, blunts, blup, blur, blur's, blurb, blurbist, blurbs, blurping, blurred, blurredly, blurredness, blurrer, blurrier, blurriest, blurrily, blurriness, blurring, blurringly, blurry, blurs, blurt, blurted, blurter, blurters, blurting, blurts, blush, blushed, blusher, blushers, blushes, blushet, blushful, blushfully, blushfulness, blushiness, blushing, blushingly, blushless, blusht, blushwort, blushy, bluster, blusteration, blustered, blusterer, blusterers, blustering, blusteringly, blusterous, blusterously, blusters, blustery, blutwurst, blvd, blype, blypes, bm, bn, bnf, bo, bo's'n, boa, boagane, boanergean, boanerges, boanergism, boanthropy, boar, boarcite, board, boardable, boardbill, boarded, boarder, boarders, boarding, boardinghouse, boardinghouse's, boardinghouses, boardings, boardlike, boardly, boardman, boardmanship, boardmen, boardroom, boards, boardsmanship, boardwalk, boardwalks, boardy, boarfish, boarfishes, boarhound, boarish, boarishly, boarishness, boars, boarship, boarskin, boarspear, boarstaff, boart, boarts, boarwood, boas, boast, boasted, boaster, boasters, boastful, boastfully, boastfulness, boasting, boastingly, boastings, boastive, boastless, boasts, boat, boatable, boatage, boatbill, boatbills, boatbuilder, boatbuilding, boated, boatel, boatels, boater, boaters, boatfalls, boatful, boathead, boatheader, boathook, boathouse, boathouse's, boathouses, boatie, boating, boatings, boation, boatkeeper, boatless, boatlike, boatlip, boatload, boatload's, boatloader, boatloading, boatloads, boatly, boatman, boatmanship, boatmaster, boatmen, boatowner, boats, boatsetter, boatshop, boatside, boatsman, boatsmanship, boatsmen, boatsteerer, boatswain, boatswain's, boatswains, boattail, boatward, boatwise, boatwoman, boatwright, boatyard, boatyard's, boatyards, bob, bob's, boba, bobac, bobache, bobachee, bobadil, bobance, bobbed, bobbejaan, bobber, bobberies, bobbers, bobbery, bobbie, bobbies, bobbin, bobbin's, bobbiner, bobbinet, bobbinets, bobbing, bobbins, bobbinwork, bobbish, bobbishly, bobble, bobbled, bobbles, bobbling, bobby, bobbysocks, bobbysoxer, bobbysoxers, bobcat, bobcats, bobcoat, bobeche, bobeches, bobet, bobflies, bobfloat, bobfly, bobierrite, bobization, bobjerom, boblet, bobo, bobol, bobolink, bobolink's, bobolinks, bobooti, bobotee, bobotie, bobowler, bobs, bobsled, bobsledded, bobsledder, bobsledders, bobsledding, bobsleded, bobsleding, bobsleds, bobsleigh, bobstay, bobstays, bobtail, bobtailed, bobtailing, bobtails, bobwhite, bobwhite's, bobwhites, bobwood, boc, boca, bocaccio, bocaccios, bocage, bocal, bocardo, bocasin, bocasine, bocca, boccaccio, boccale, boccarella, boccaro, bocce, bocces, bocci, boccia, boccias, boccie, boccies, boccis, bocconia, boce, bocedization, boche, bocher, boches, bochism, bochur, bock, bockerel, bockeret, bockey, bocking, bocklogged, bocks, bocoy, bocstaff, bod, bodach, bodacious, bodaciously, boddagh, boddhisattva, boddle, bode, boded, bodeful, bodefully, bodefulness, bodega, bodegas, bodegon, bodegones, bodement, bodements, boden, bodenbenderite, boder, bodes, bodewash, bodeword, bodge, bodger, bodgery, bodgie, bodhi, bodhisat, bodhisattva, bodhisattwa, bodice, bodiced, bodicemaker, bodicemaking, bodices, bodied, bodier, bodieron, bodies, bodikin, bodiless, bodilessness, bodiliness, bodilize, bodily, bodiment, boding, bodingly, bodings, bodken, bodkin, bodkins, bodkinwise, bodle, bodleian, bodock, bodoni, bodonid, bodrag, bodrage, bods, bodstick, bodword, body, bodybending, bodybuild, bodybuilder, bodybuilder's, bodybuilders, bodybuilding, bodycheck, bodyguard, bodyguard's, bodyguards, bodyhood, bodying, bodykins, bodyless, bodymaker, bodymaking, bodyplate, bodyshirt, bodysuit, bodysuits, bodysurf, bodysurfed, bodysurfer, bodysurfing, bodysurfs, bodywear, bodyweight, bodywise, bodywood, bodywork, bodyworks, boe, boehmenism, boehmite, boehmites, boeing, boeotarch, boeotia, boeotian, boer, boers, boettner, boff, boffin, boffins, boffo, boffola, boffolas, boffos, boffs, bog, bog's, boga, bogach, bogan, bogans, bogard, bogart, bogatyr, bogbean, bogbeans, bogberries, bogberry, boget, bogey, bogeyed, bogeying, bogeyman, bogeymen, bogeys, bogfern, boggard, boggart, bogged, boggier, boggiest, boggin, bogginess, bogging, boggish, boggishness, boggle, bogglebo, boggled, boggler, bogglers, boggles, boggling, bogglingly, bogglish, boggy, boghole, bogie, bogieman, bogier, bogies, bogland, boglander, bogle, bogled, bogledom, bogles, boglet, bogman, bogmire, bogo, bogong, bogota, bogotana, bogs, bogsucker, bogtrot, bogtrotter, bogtrotting, bogue, bogued, boguing, bogum, bogus, bogusness, bogway, bogwood, bogwoods, bogwort, bogy, bogydom, bogyism, bogyisms, bogyland, bogyman, bogymen, boh, bohawn, bohea, boheas, bohemia, bohemian, bohemianism, bohemians, bohemias, bohemium, bohereen, bohireen, bohmite, boho, bohor, bohora, bohorok, bohunk, bohunks, boid, boiette, boigid, boiguacu, boil, boilable, boildown, boiled, boiler, boilerful, boilerhouse, boilerless, boilermaker, boilermakers, boilermaking, boilerman, boilerplate, boilers, boilersmith, boilerworks, boilery, boiling, boilinglike, boilingly, boiloff, boiloffs, boilover, boils, boily, boing, boise, boiserie, boiseries, boisseau, boisseaux, boist, boisterous, boisterously, boisterousness, boistous, boistously, boistousness, boite, boites, boithrin, bojite, bojo, bokadam, bokard, bokark, boke, bokmakierie, boko, bokom, bokos, bol, bola, bolar, bolas, bolases, bolbanac, bolbonac, bold, boldacious, bolded, bolden, bolder, boldest, boldface, boldfaced, boldfacedly, boldfacedness, boldfaces, boldfacing, boldhearted, boldheartedly, boldheartedness, boldin, boldine, bolding, boldly, boldness, boldnesses, boldo, boldoine, boldos, bole, bolection, bolectioned, boled, boleite, bolelike, bolero, boleros, boles, boletaceous, bolete, boletes, boleti, boletic, boletus, boletuses, boleweed, bolewort, boliche, bolide, bolides, bolimba, bolis, bolita, bolivar, bolivares, bolivarite, bolivars, bolivia, bolivian, boliviano, bolivianos, bolivians, bolivias, bolk, boll, bollandist, bollard, bollards, bolled, bollen, boller, bollies, bolling, bollito, bollix, bollixed, bollixes, bollixing, bollock, bollocks, bollox, bolloxed, bolloxes, bolloxing, bolls, bollworm, bollworms, bolly, bolo, boloball, boloed, bologna, bolognas, bolograph, bolographic, bolographically, bolography, boloing, boloism, boloman, bolomen, bolometer, bolometric, bolometrically, boloney, boloneys, boloroot, bolos, bolshevik, bolshevik's, bolsheviks, bolshevism, bolshevist, bolshevistic, bolshevistically, bolshevists, bolshevize, bolshevized, bolshevizing, bolshie, bolshies, bolshy, bolson, bolsons, bolster, bolstered, bolsterer, bolsterers, bolstering, bolsters, bolsterwork, bolt, boltage, boltant, boltcutter, bolted, boltel, bolter, bolters, bolthead, boltheader, boltheading, boltheads, bolthole, boltholes, bolti, boltin, bolting, boltings, boltless, boltlike, boltmaker, boltmaking, boltonia, boltonias, boltonite, boltrope, boltropes, bolts, boltsmith, boltspreet, boltstrake, boltuprightness, boltwork, bolty, bolus, boluses, bom, boma, bomb, bombable, bombacaceous, bombace, bombard, bombarde, bombarded, bombardelle, bombarder, bombardier, bombardiers, bombarding, bombardman, bombardmen, bombardment, bombardments, bombardo, bombardon, bombards, bombasine, bombast, bombaster, bombastic, bombastical, bombastically, bombasticness, bombastry, bombasts, bombax, bombay, bombazeen, bombazet, bombazette, bombazine, bombe, bombed, bomber, bombernickel, bombers, bombes, bombesin, bombesins, bombic, bombiccite, bombilate, bombilation, bombilla, bombillas, bombinate, bombinating, bombination, bombing, bombings, bomble, bombline, bombload, bombloads, bombo, bombola, bombonne, bombora, bombous, bombproof, bombs, bombshell, bombshells, bombsight, bombsights, bombus, bombycid, bombycids, bombyciform, bombycine, bombycinous, bombylious, bombyx, bombyxes, bomi, bomos, bon, bona, bonace, bonaci, bonacis, bonagh, bonaght, bonailie, bonair, bonaire, bonairly, bonairness, bonally, bonamano, bonang, bonanza, bonanza's, bonanzas, bonapartism, bonapartist, bonassus, bonasus, bonaught, bonav, bonaventure, bonavist, bonbon, bonbonniere, bonbonnieres, bonbons, bonce, bonchief, bond, bondable, bondage, bondager, bondages, bondar, bonded, bonder, bonderize, bonderman, bonders, bondfolk, bondhold, bondholder, bondholders, bondholding, bonding, bondland, bondless, bondmaid, bondmaids, bondman, bondmanship, bondmen, bondminder, bondoc, bondon, bonds, bondservant, bondship, bondslave, bondsman, bondsmen, bondstone, bondswoman, bondswomen, bonduc, bonducnut, bonducs, bondwoman, bondwomen, bone, boneache, bonebinder, boneblack, bonebreaker, boned, bonedog, bonedry, boneen, bonefish, bonefishes, boneflower, bonehead, boneheaded, boneheadedness, boneheads, boneless, bonelessly, bonelessness, bonelet, bonelike, boner, boners, bones, boneset, bonesets, bonesetter, bonesetting, boneshaker, boneshave, boneshaw, bonetail, bonete, bonetta, bonewood, bonework, bonewort, boney, boneyard, boneyards, bonfire, bonfire's, bonfires, bong, bongar, bonged, bonging, bongo, bongoes, bongoist, bongoists, bongos, bongrace, bongs, bonhomie, bonhomies, bonhomme, bonhommie, bonhomous, bonhomously, boniata, bonier, boniest, boniface, bonifaces, bonification, boniform, bonify, bonilass, boniness, boninesses, boning, boninite, bonism, bonita, bonitarian, bonitary, bonitas, bonito, bonitoes, bonitos, bonity, bonjour, bonk, bonked, bonkers, bonking, bonks, bonnaz, bonne, bonnering, bonnes, bonnet, bonneted, bonneter, bonnethead, bonnetiere, bonnetieres, bonneting, bonnetless, bonnetlike, bonnetman, bonnetmen, bonnets, bonnibel, bonnie, bonnier, bonniest, bonnily, bonniness, bonnive, bonnne, bonnnes, bonnock, bonnocks, bonnwis, bonny, bonnyclabber, bonnyish, bonnyvis, bono, bonorum, bonos, bons, bonsai, bonsela, bonser, bonsoir, bonspell, bonspells, bonspiel, bonspiels, bontebok, bonteboks, bontebuck, bontebucks, bontee, bontequagga, bonum, bonus, bonus's, bonuses, bonxie, bony, bonyfish, bonytail, bonze, bonzer, bonzery, bonzes, bonzian, boo, boob, boobery, boobialla, boobies, boobily, boobish, boobishness, booboisie, booboo, boobook, booboos, boobs, booby, boobyalla, boobyish, boobyism, bood, boodh, boodie, boodle, boodled, boodledom, boodleism, boodleize, boodler, boodlers, boodles, boodling, boody, booed, boof, boogaloo, booger, boogerman, boogers, boogeyman, boogeymen, boogie, boogies, boogiewoogie, boogum, boogyman, boogymen, boohoo, boohooed, boohooing, boohoos, booing, boojum, book, bookable, bookbind, bookbinder, bookbinderies, bookbinders, bookbindery, bookbinding, bookboard, bookcase, bookcase's, bookcases, bookcraft, bookdealer, bookdom, booked, bookend, bookends, booker, bookers, bookery, bookfair, bookfold, bookful, bookholder, bookhood, bookie, bookie's, bookies, bookiness, booking, bookings, bookish, bookishly, bookishness, bookism, bookit, bookkeep, bookkeeper, bookkeeper's, bookkeepers, bookkeeping, bookkeeps, bookland, booklear, bookless, booklet, booklet's, booklets, booklice, booklift, booklike, bookling, booklists, booklore, booklores, booklouse, booklover, bookmaker, bookmakers, bookmaking, bookman, bookmark, bookmarker, bookmarks, bookmate, bookmen, bookmobile, bookmobiles, bookmonger, bookplate, bookplates, bookpress, bookrack, bookracks, bookrest, bookrests, bookroom, books, bookseller, bookseller's, booksellerish, booksellerism, booksellers, bookselling, bookshelf, bookshelf's, bookshelves, bookshop, bookshops, bookstack, bookstall, bookstand, bookstore, bookstore's, bookstores, booksy, bookward, bookwards, bookways, bookwise, bookwork, bookworm, bookworms, bookwright, booky, bool, boolean, booleans, booley, booleys, boolies, booly, boolya, boom, boomable, boomage, boomah, boomboat, boombox, boomboxes, boomdas, boomed, boomer, boomerang, boomerang's, boomeranged, boomeranging, boomerangs, boomers, boomier, boomiest, boominess, booming, boomingly, boomkin, boomkins, boomless, boomlet, boomlets, boomorah, booms, boomslang, boomslange, boomster, boomtown, boomtown's, boomtowns, boomy, boon, boondock, boondocker, boondocks, boondoggle, boondoggled, boondoggler, boondogglers, boondoggles, boondoggling, boonfellow, boong, boongary, boonies, boonk, boonless, boons, boopic, boopis, boor, boor's, boordly, boorga, boorish, boorishly, boorishness, boors, boort, boos, boose, boosies, boost, boosted, booster, boosterism, boosters, boosting, boosts, boosy, boot, bootable, bootblack, bootblacks, bootboy, booted, bootee, bootees, booter, booteries, bootery, bootes, bootful, booth, boothage, boothale, bootheel, boother, boothes, boothite, bootholder, boothose, booths, bootie, bootied, booties, bootikin, bootikins, booting, bootjack, bootjacks, bootlace, bootlaces, bootle, bootleg, bootleger, bootlegged, bootlegger, bootlegger's, bootleggers, bootlegging, bootlegs, bootless, bootlessly, bootlessness, bootlick, bootlicked, bootlicker, bootlickers, bootlicking, bootlicks, bootloader, bootmaker, bootmaking, bootman, bootprint, boots, bootstrap, bootstrap's, bootstrapped, bootstrapping, bootstraps, boottop, boottopping, booty, bootyless, booze, boozed, boozehound, boozer, boozers, boozes, boozier, booziest, boozify, boozily, booziness, boozing, boozy, bop, bopeep, bopped, bopper, boppers, bopping, boppist, bops, bopster, bopyrid, bopyridian, bor, bora, borable, boraces, borachio, boracic, boraciferous, boracite, boracites, boracium, boracous, borage, borages, boraginaceous, boragineous, borak, boral, borane, boranes, boras, borasca, borasco, borasque, borasqueborate, borassus, borate, borated, borates, borating, borax, boraxes, borazon, borazons, borborygm, borborygmatic, borborygmi, borborygmic, borborygmies, borborygmus, bord, bordage, bordar, bordarius, bordeaux, bordel, bordelaise, bordello, bordello's, bordellos, bordels, border, bordereau, bordereaux, bordered, borderer, borderers, bordering, borderings, borderism, borderland, borderland's, borderlander, borderlands, borderless, borderlight, borderline, borderlines, bordermark, borders, bordman, bordrag, bordrage, bordroom, bordun, bordure, bordured, bordures, bore, boreable, boread, boreal, borealis, borean, boreas, borecole, borecoles, bored, boredness, boredom, boredoms, boree, boreen, boreens, boregat, borehole, boreholes, boreism, borel, borele, borer, borers, bores, boresight, boresome, boresomely, boresomeness, borg, borgh, borghalpenny, borghi, borh, bori, boric, borickite, borid, boride, borides, borine, boring, boringly, boringness, borings, borish, borism, borith, borities, bority, borize, borlase, borley, born, bornan, bornane, borne, borneo, borneol, borneols, borning, bornite, bornites, bornitic, bornyl, boro, borocalcite, borocarbide, borocitrate, borofluohydric, borofluoric, borofluoride, borofluorin, boroglycerate, boroglyceride, boroglycerine, borohydride, borolanite, boron, boronatrocalcite, boronia, boronic, borons, borophenol, borophenylic, borosalicylate, borosalicylic, borosilicate, borosilicic, borotungstate, borotungstic, borough, boroughlet, boroughmaster, boroughmonger, boroughmongering, boroughmongery, boroughs, boroughship, boroughwide, borowolframic, borracha, borrachio, borrasca, borrel, borrelia, borrow, borrowable, borrowed, borrower, borrowers, borrowing, borrows, bors, borsch, borsches, borscht, borschts, borsholder, borsht, borshts, borstal, borstall, borstals, bort, borts, bortsch, borty, bortz, bortzes, borwort, boryl, borzoi, borzois, bos, bos'n, boscage, boscages, bosch, boschbok, boschboks, boschvark, boschveld, bose, boser, bosey, bosh, boshbok, boshboks, bosher, boshes, boshvark, boshvarks, bosjesman, bosk, boskage, boskages, bosker, bosket, boskets, boskier, boskiest, boskiness, boskopoid, bosks, bosky, bosn, bosom, bosom's, bosomed, bosomer, bosominess, bosoming, bosoms, bosomy, boson, bosonic, bosons, bosporus, bosque, bosques, bosquet, bosquets, boss, bossa, bossage, bossboy, bossdom, bossdoms, bossed, bosselated, bosselation, bosser, bosses, bosset, bosseyed, bossier, bossies, bossiest, bossily, bossiness, bossing, bossism, bossisms, bosslet, bossship, bossy, bostal, bostangi, bostanji, bosthoon, boston, bostonian, bostonian's, bostonians, bostonite, bostons, bostrychid, bostrychoid, bostrychoidal, bostryx, bosun, bosuns, boswell, boswellian, boswellism, boswellize, boswellized, boswellizing, bot, bota, botan, botanic, botanica, botanical, botanically, botanicas, botanics, botanies, botanise, botanised, botaniser, botanises, botanising, botanist, botanist's, botanists, botanize, botanized, botanizer, botanizes, botanizing, botanomancy, botanophile, botanophilist, botany, botargo, botargos, botas, botch, botched, botchedly, botcher, botcheries, botcherly, botchers, botchery, botches, botchier, botchiest, botchily, botchiness, botching, botchka, botchwork, botchy, bote, botel, boteler, botella, botels, boterol, boteroll, botete, botflies, botfly, both, bother, botheration, bothered, botherer, botherheaded, bothering, botherment, bothers, bothersome, bothersomely, bothersomeness, bothie, bothies, bothlike, bothrenchyma, bothria, bothridia, bothridium, bothridiums, bothriolepis, bothrium, bothriums, bothroi, bothropic, bothros, bothsided, bothsidedness, boththridia, bothway, bothy, boti, botling, botone, botonee, botong, botonn, botonnee, botonny, botony, botoyan, botry, botrycymose, botrylle, botryogen, botryoid, botryoidal, botryoidally, botryolite, botryomycoma, botryomycosis, botryomycotic, botryopterid, botryose, botryotherapy, botrytis, botrytises, bots, botswana, bott, botte, bottega, bottegas, botteghe, bottekin, botticelli, bottier, bottine, bottle, bottlebird, bottlebrush, bottled, bottleflower, bottleful, bottlefuls, bottlehead, bottleholder, bottlelike, bottlemaker, bottlemaking, bottleman, bottleneck, bottleneck's, bottlenecks, bottlenest, bottlenose, bottler, bottlers, bottles, bottlesful, bottlestone, bottling, bottom, bottomchrome, bottomed, bottomer, bottomers, bottoming, bottomland, bottomless, bottomlessly, bottomlessness, bottommost, bottomried, bottomries, bottomry, bottomrying, bottoms, bottonhook, botts, bottstick, bottu, botuliform, botulin, botulinal, botulins, botulinum, botulinus, botulinuses, botulism, botulisms, botulismus, boubas, boubou, boubous, boucan, bouch, bouchal, bouchaleen, boucharde, bouche, bouchee, bouchees, boucher, boucherism, boucherize, bouchette, bouchon, bouchons, boucl, boucle, boucles, boud, bouderie, boudeuse, boudin, boudoir, boudoiresque, boudoirs, bouet, bouffage, bouffancy, bouffant, bouffante, bouffants, bouffe, bouffes, bouffon, bougainvillaea, bougainvillaeas, bougainvillea, bougar, bouge, bougee, bougeron, bouget, bough, bough's, boughed, boughless, boughpot, boughpots, boughs, bought, boughten, boughy, bougie, bougies, bouillabaisse, bouilli, bouillon, bouillone, bouillons, bouk, boukit, boul, boulanger, boulangerite, boulder, boulder's, bouldered, boulderhead, bouldering, boulders, bouldery, boule, boules, bouleuteria, bouleuterion, boulevard, boulevard's, boulevardier, boulevardiers, boulevardize, boulevards, bouleverse, bouleversement, boulework, boulimia, boulimy, boulle, boulles, boullework, boult, boultel, boultell, boulter, boulterer, boun, bounce, bounceable, bounceably, bounceback, bounced, bouncer, bouncers, bounces, bouncier, bounciest, bouncily, bounciness, bouncing, bouncingly, bouncy, bound, boundable, boundaries, boundary, boundary's, bounded, boundedly, boundedness, bounden, bounder, bounderish, bounderishly, bounders, bounding, boundingly, boundless, boundlessly, boundlessness, boundly, boundness, bounds, boundure, bounteous, bounteously, bounteousness, bountied, bounties, bountiful, bountifully, bountifulness, bountihead, bountiousness, bountith, bountree, bounty, bounty's, bountyless, bouquet, bouquet's, bouquetiere, bouquetin, bouquets, bouquiniste, bour, bourage, bourasque, bourbon, bourbonism, bourbonize, bourbons, bourd, bourder, bourdis, bourdon, bourdons, bourette, bourg, bourgade, bourgeois, bourgeoise, bourgeoises, bourgeoisie, bourgeoisify, bourgeoisitic, bourgeon, bourgeoned, bourgeoning, bourgeons, bourgs, bourguignonne, bourkha, bourlaw, bourn, bourne, bournes, bournless, bournonite, bournous, bourns, bourock, bourr, bourran, bourrasque, bourre, bourreau, bourree, bourrees, bourrelet, bourride, bourrides, bourse, bourses, bourtree, bourtrees, bouse, boused, bouser, bouses, bousing, bousouki, bousoukia, bousoukis, boussingaultite, boustrophedon, boustrophedonic, bousy, bout, bout's, boutade, boutefeu, boutel, boutell, bouteria, bouteselle, boutique, boutiques, bouto, bouton, boutonniere, boutonnieres, boutons, boutre, bouts, boutylka, bouvardia, bouvier, bouviers, bouw, bouzouki, bouzoukia, bouzoukis, bovarism, bovarist, bovaristic, bovarysm, bovate, bove, bovenland, bovey, bovicide, boviculture, bovid, bovids, boviform, bovine, bovinely, bovines, bovinities, bovinity, bovld, bovoid, bovovaccination, bovovaccine, bovver, bow, bowable, bowback, bowbells, bowbent, bowboy, bowden, bowditch, bowdlerisation, bowdlerise, bowdlerised, bowdlerising, bowdlerism, bowdlerization, bowdlerizations, bowdlerize, bowdlerized, bowdlerizer, bowdlerizes, bowdlerizing, bowdrill, bowe, bowed, bowedness, bowel, bowel's, boweled, boweling, bowelled, bowelless, bowellike, bowelling, bowels, bowenite, bower, bowerbird, bowered, boweries, bowering, bowerlet, bowerlike, bowerly, bowermaiden, bowermay, bowers, bowerwoman, bowery, bowess, bowet, bowfin, bowfins, bowfront, bowge, bowgrace, bowhead, bowheads, bowie, bowieful, bowing, bowingly, bowings, bowk, bowkail, bowker, bowknot, bowknots, bowl, bowla, bowlder, bowlderhead, bowldering, bowlders, bowldery, bowle, bowled, bowleg, bowlegged, bowleggedness, bowlegs, bowler, bowlers, bowles, bowless, bowlful, bowlfuls, bowlike, bowlin, bowline, bowline's, bowlines, bowling, bowlings, bowllike, bowlmaker, bowls, bowly, bowmaker, bowmaking, bowman, bowmen, bown, bowne, bowpin, bowpot, bowpots, bowralite, bows, bowsaw, bowse, bowsed, bowser, bowsery, bowses, bowshot, bowshots, bowsie, bowsing, bowsman, bowsprit, bowsprits, bowssen, bowstaff, bowstave, bowstring, bowstring's, bowstringed, bowstringing, bowstrings, bowstrung, bowtel, bowtell, bowtie, bowwoman, bowwood, bowwort, bowwow, bowwows, bowyang, bowyangs, bowyer, bowyers, box, boxball, boxberries, boxberry, boxboard, boxboards, boxbush, boxcar, boxcar's, boxcars, boxed, boxen, boxer, boxers, boxes, boxfish, boxfishes, boxful, boxfuls, boxhaul, boxhauled, boxhauling, boxhauls, boxhead, boxholder, boxiana, boxier, boxiest, boxiness, boxinesses, boxing, boxings, boxkeeper, boxlike, boxmaker, boxmaking, boxman, boxroom, boxthorn, boxthorns, boxtop, boxtop's, boxtops, boxtree, boxty, boxwallah, boxwood, boxwoods, boxwork, boxy, boy, boy's, boyang, boyar, boyard, boyardism, boyardom, boyards, boyarism, boyarisms, boyars, boyau, boyaus, boyaux, boychick, boychicks, boychik, boychiks, boycott, boycottage, boycotted, boycotter, boycotting, boycottism, boycotts, boydekyn, boydom, boyer, boyfriend, boyfriend's, boyfriends, boyg, boyhood, boyhoods, boyish, boyishly, boyishness, boyism, boyla, boylas, boylike, boylikeness, boyo, boyology, boyos, boys, boysenberries, boysenberry, boyship, boyuna, boza, bozal, bozine, bozo, bozos, bozze, bozzetto, bp, bpi, bps, bpt, br, br'er, bra, bra's, braata, brab, brabagious, brabant, brabble, brabbled, brabblement, brabbler, brabblers, brabbles, brabbling, brabblingly, braca, bracae, braccae, braccate, braccia, bracciale, braccianite, braccio, brace, braced, bracelet, bracelet's, braceleted, bracelets, bracer, bracero, braceros, bracers, bracery, braces, brach, brache, brachelytrous, bracherer, brachering, braches, brachet, brachets, brachia, brachial, brachialgia, brachialis, brachials, brachiate, brachiated, brachiating, brachiation, brachiator, brachiferous, brachigerous, brachiocephalic, brachiocrural, brachiocubital, brachiocyllosis, brachiofacial, brachiofaciolingual, brachioganoid, brachiolaria, brachiolarian, brachiopod, brachiopode, brachiopodist, brachiopodous, brachioradial, brachioradialis, brachiorrhachidian, brachiorrheuma, brachiosaur, brachiosaurus, brachiostrophosis, brachiotomy, brachistocephali, brachistocephalic, brachistocephalous, brachistocephaly, brachistochrone, brachistochronic, brachistochronous, brachium, brachman, brachtmema, brachyaxis, brachycardia, brachycatalectic, brachycephal, brachycephales, brachycephali, brachycephalic, brachycephalies, brachycephalism, brachycephalization, brachycephalize, brachycephalous, brachycephaly, brachyceral, brachyceric, brachycerous, brachychronic, brachycnemic, brachycranial, brachycranic, brachycrany, brachydactyl, brachydactylia, brachydactylic, brachydactylism, brachydactylous, brachydactyly, brachydiagonal, brachydodrome, brachydodromous, brachydomal, brachydomatic, brachydome, brachydont, brachydontism, brachyfacial, brachyglossal, brachygnathia, brachygnathism, brachygnathous, brachygrapher, brachygraphic, brachygraphical, brachygraphy, brachyhieric, brachylogies, brachylogy, brachymetropia, brachymetropic, brachyphalangia, brachypinacoid, brachypinacoidal, brachypleural, brachypnea, brachypodine, brachypodous, brachyprism, brachyprosopic, brachypterous, brachypyramid, brachyrrhinia, brachysclereid, brachyskelic, brachysm, brachystaphylic, brachystochrone, brachystomatous, brachystomous, brachytic, brachytmema, brachytypous, brachyural, brachyuran, brachyuranic, brachyure, brachyurous, bracing, bracingly, bracingness, bracings, braciola, braciolas, braciole, bracioles, brack, brackebuschite, bracked, bracken, brackened, brackens, bracker, bracket, bracketed, bracketing, brackets, bracketted, bracketwise, bracking, brackish, brackishness, brackmard, bracky, braconid, braconids, braconniere, bracozzo, bract, bractea, bracteal, bracteate, bracted, bracteiform, bracteolate, bracteole, bracteose, bractless, bractlet, bractlets, bracts, brad, bradawl, bradawls, bradded, bradding, bradenhead, bradmaker, bradoon, bradoons, brads, bradsot, bradyacousia, bradyauxesis, bradyauxetic, bradyauxetically, bradycardia, bradycardic, bradycauma, bradycinesia, bradycrotic, bradydactylia, bradyesthesia, bradyglossia, bradykinesia, bradykinesis, bradykinetic, bradykinin, bradylalia, bradylexia, bradylogia, bradynosus, bradypepsia, bradypepsy, bradypeptic, bradyphagia, bradyphasia, bradyphemia, bradyphrasia, bradyphrenia, bradypnea, bradypnoea, bradypod, bradypode, bradypodoid, bradyseism, bradyseismal, bradyseismic, bradyseismical, bradyseismism, bradyspermatism, bradysphygmia, bradystalsis, bradyteleocinesia, bradyteleokinesis, bradytelic, bradytely, bradytocia, bradytrophic, bradyuria, brae, brae's, braeface, braehead, braeman, braes, braeside, brag, bragas, brager, braggadocian, braggadocianism, braggadocio, braggadocios, braggardism, braggart, braggartism, braggartly, braggartry, braggarts, braggat, bragged, bragger, braggers, braggery, braggest, bragget, braggier, braggiest, bragging, braggingly, braggish, braggishly, braggite, braggle, braggy, bragi, bragite, bragless, bragly, bragozzo, brags, braguette, bragwort, brahm, brahma, brahmachari, brahman, brahmanism, brahmanist, brahmanists, brahmans, brahmapootra, brahmas, brahmic, brahmin, brahminee, brahminism, brahminist, brahminists, brahmins, brahmism, brahms, braid, braided, braider, braiders, braiding, braidings, braidism, braids, braies, brail, brailed, brailing, braille, brailled, brailler, brailles, braillewriter, brailling, brails, brain, brainache, braincap, braincase, brainchild, brainchild's, brainchildren, braincraft, brained, brainer, brainfag, brainge, brainier, brainiest, brainily, braininess, braining, brainish, brainless, brainlessly, brainlessness, brainlike, brainpan, brainpans, brainpower, brains, brainsick, brainsickly, brainsickness, brainstem, brainstem's, brainstems, brainstone, brainstorm, brainstorm's, brainstormer, brainstorming, brainstorms, brainteaser, brainteasers, brainward, brainwash, brainwashed, brainwasher, brainwashers, brainwashes, brainwashing, brainwashjng, brainwater, brainwave, brainwood, brainwork, brainworker, brainy, braird, brairded, brairding, braireau, brairo, braise, braised, braises, braising, braize, braizes, brake, brakeage, brakeages, braked, brakehand, brakehead, brakeless, brakeload, brakemaker, brakemaking, brakeman, brakemen, braker, brakeroot, brakes, brakesman, brakesmen, brakie, brakier, brakiest, braking, braky, braless, bramah, bramantip, bramble, bramble's, brambleberries, brambleberry, bramblebush, brambled, brambles, bramblier, brambliest, brambling, brambly, brambrack, brame, bran, brancard, brancardier, branch, branchage, branched, branchedness, brancher, branchery, branches, branchful, branchi, branchia, branchiae, branchial, branchiate, branchicolous, branchier, branchiest, branchiferous, branchiform, branchihyal, branchiness, branching, branchings, branchiocardiac, branchiogenous, branchiomere, branchiomeric, branchiomerism, branchiopallial, branchiopneustic, branchiopod, branchiopodan, branchiopodous, branchiopoo, branchiopulmonate, branchiosaur, branchiosaurian, branchiostegal, branchiostegan, branchiostege, branchiostegite, branchiostegous, branchiostomid, branchiostomous, branchireme, branchiurous, branchless, branchlet, branchlike, branchling, branchman, branchstand, branchway, branchy, brand, brandade, branded, brandenburgh, brandenburgs, brander, brandering, branders, brandied, brandies, brandify, branding, brandiron, brandise, brandish, brandished, brandisher, brandishers, brandishes, brandishing, brandisite, brandle, brandless, brandling, brandon, brandreth, brandrith, brands, brandsolder, brandy, brandyball, brandying, brandyman, brandywine, brangle, brangled, branglement, brangler, brangling, branial, brank, brankie, brankier, brankiest, branks, brankursine, branky, branle, branles, branned, branner, brannerite, branners, brannier, branniest, brannigan, branniness, branning, branny, brans, bransle, bransles, bransolder, brant, brantail, brantails, brantcorn, brantle, brantness, brants, branular, braquemard, brarow, bras, brasen, brasero, braseros, brash, brasher, brashes, brashest, brashier, brashiest, brashiness, brashly, brashness, brashy, brasier, brasiers, brasil, brasilein, brasilete, brasiletto, brasilia, brasilin, brasilins, brasils, brasque, brasqued, brasquing, brass, brassage, brassages, brassard, brassards, brassart, brassarts, brassate, brassbound, brassbounder, brasse, brassed, brasser, brasserie, brasseries, brasses, brasset, brassey, brasseys, brassic, brassica, brassicaceous, brassicas, brassidic, brassie, brassier, brassiere, brassieres, brassies, brassiest, brassily, brassiness, brassish, brasslike, brassware, brasswork, brassworker, brassworks, brassy, brassylic, brast, brat, brat's, bratchet, bratina, bratling, brats, bratstva, bratstvo, brattach, brattice, bratticed, bratticer, brattices, bratticing, brattie, brattier, brattiest, brattiness, brattish, brattishing, brattle, brattled, brattles, brattling, bratty, bratwurst, braula, brauna, braunite, braunites, braunschweiger, brava, bravade, bravado, bravadoed, bravadoes, bravadoing, bravadoism, bravados, bravas, brave, braved, bravehearted, bravely, braveness, braver, braveries, bravers, bravery, braves, bravest, bravi, braving, bravish, bravissimo, bravo, bravoed, bravoes, bravoing, bravoite, bravos, bravura, bravuraish, bravuras, bravure, braw, brawer, brawest, brawl, brawled, brawler, brawlers, brawlie, brawlier, brawliest, brawling, brawlingly, brawlis, brawls, brawlsome, brawly, brawlys, brawn, brawned, brawnedness, brawner, brawnier, brawniest, brawnily, brawniness, brawns, brawny, braws, braxies, braxy, bray, braye, brayed, brayer, brayera, brayerin, brayers, brayette, braying, brays, braystone, braza, brazas, braze, brazed, brazee, brazen, brazened, brazenface, brazenfaced, brazenfacedly, brazenfacedness, brazening, brazenly, brazenness, brazens, brazer, brazera, brazers, brazes, brazier, brazier's, braziers, braziery, brazil, brazilein, brazilette, braziletto, brazilian, brazilianite, brazilians, brazilin, brazilins, brazilite, brazils, brazilwood, brazing, breach, breached, breacher, breachers, breaches, breachful, breaching, breachy, bread, breadbasket, breadbaskets, breadberry, breadboard, breadboard's, breadboards, breadbox, breadbox's, breadboxes, breadearner, breadearning, breaded, breaden, breadfruit, breadfruits, breading, breadless, breadlessness, breadline, breadmaker, breadmaking, breadman, breadness, breadnut, breadnuts, breadroot, breads, breadseller, breadstitch, breadstuff, breadstuffs, breadth, breadthen, breadthless, breadthriders, breadths, breadthways, breadthwise, breadwinner, breadwinner's, breadwinners, breadwinning, breaghe, break, breakability, breakable, breakableness, breakables, breakably, breakage, breakages, breakaway, breakax, breakaxe, breakback, breakbone, breakbones, breakdown, breakdown's, breakdowns, breaker, breakerman, breakermen, breakers, breakfast, breakfasted, breakfaster, breakfasters, breakfasting, breakfastless, breakfasts, breakfront, breakfronts, breaking, breakings, breakless, breaklist, breakneck, breakoff, breakout, breakouts, breakover, breakpoint, breakpoint's, breakpoints, breaks, breakshugh, breakstone, breakthrough, breakthrough's, breakthroughes, breakthroughs, breakup, breakups, breakwater, breakwater's, breakwaters, breakweather, breakwind, bream, breamed, breaming, breams, breards, breast, breastband, breastbeam, breastbone, breastbones, breasted, breaster, breastfast, breastfeeding, breastful, breastheight, breasthook, breastie, breasting, breastless, breastmark, breastpiece, breastpin, breastplate, breastplates, breastplough, breastplow, breastrail, breastrope, breasts, breaststroke, breaststroker, breaststrokes, breastsummer, breastweed, breastwise, breastwood, breastwork, breastwork's, breastworks, breath, breathability, breathable, breathableness, breathalyse, breathe, breatheableness, breathed, breather, breathers, breathes, breathful, breathier, breathiest, breathily, breathiness, breathing, breathingly, breathless, breathlessly, breathlessness, breaths, breathseller, breathtaking, breathtakingly, breathy, breba, breccia, breccial, breccias, brecciate, brecciated, brecciating, brecciation, brecham, brechams, brechan, brechans, brecht, brechtian, brecia, breck, brecken, bred, bredbergite, brede, bredes, bredestitch, bredi, bredstitch, bree, breech, breech's, breechblock, breechcloth, breechcloths, breechclout, breeched, breeches, breechesflower, breechesless, breeching, breechless, breechloader, breechloading, breed, breedable, breedbate, breeder, breeders, breediness, breeding, breedings, breedling, breeds, breedy, breek, breekless, breeks, breekums, breenge, breenger, brees, breeze, breeze's, breezed, breezeful, breezeless, breezelike, breezes, breezeway, breezeways, breezier, breeziest, breezily, breeziness, breezing, breezy, bregma, bregmata, bregmate, bregmatic, brehon, brehonia, brehonship, brei, breird, breislakite, breithauptite, brekkle, brekky, brelan, brelaw, breloque, brember, breme, bremely, bremeness, bremsstrahlung, bren, brended, brendice, brennage, brennschluss, brens, brent, brents, brephic, brerd, brere, bressomer, bressummer, brest, bret, bretelle, bretesse, breth, brethel, brethren, brethrenism, breton, bretons, brett, brettice, bretwalda, breunnerite, brev, breva, breve, breves, brevet, brevetcies, brevetcy, brevete, breveted, breveting, brevets, brevetted, brevetting, brevi, breviaries, breviary, breviate, breviature, brevicauda, brevicaudate, brevicipitid, brevicomis, breviconic, brevier, breviers, brevifoliate, breviger, brevilingual, breviloquence, breviloquent, breviped, brevipen, brevipennate, breviradiate, brevirostral, brevirostrate, brevis, brevit, brevities, brevity, brew, brewage, brewages, brewed, brewer, breweries, brewers, brewership, brewery, brewery's, brewhouse, brewhouses, brewing, brewings, brewis, brewises, brewmaster, brews, brewst, brewster, brewsterite, brey, brezhnev, brian, briar, briar's, briarberry, briard, briards, briared, briareus, briarroot, briars, briarwood, briary, bribability, bribable, bribe, bribeability, bribeable, bribed, bribee, bribees, bribegiver, bribegiving, bribeless, bribemonger, briber, briberies, bribers, bribery, bribes, bribetaker, bribetaking, bribeworthy, bribing, brichen, brichette, brick, brickbat, brickbats, brickbatted, brickbatting, brickcroft, bricked, brickel, bricken, bricker, brickfield, brickfielder, brickhood, brickier, brickiest, bricking, brickish, brickkiln, bricklay, bricklayer, bricklayer's, bricklayers, bricklaying, brickle, brickleness, bricklike, brickliner, bricklining, brickly, brickmaker, brickmaking, brickmason, brickred, bricks, brickset, bricksetter, bricktimber, bricktop, brickwall, brickwise, brickwork, bricky, brickyard, bricole, bricoles, brid, bridal, bridale, bridaler, bridally, bridals, bridalty, bride, bride's, bridebed, bridebowl, bridecake, bridechamber, bridecup, bridegod, bridegroom, bridegrooms, bridegroomship, bridehead, bridehood, bridehouse, brideknot, bridelace, brideless, bridelike, bridelope, bridely, bridemaid, bridemaiden, bridemaidship, brideman, brides, brideship, bridesmaid, bridesmaid's, bridesmaiding, bridesmaids, bridesman, bridesmen, bridestake, bridewain, brideweed, bridewell, bridewort, bridge, bridgeable, bridgeboard, bridgebote, bridgebuilder, bridgebuilding, bridged, bridgehead, bridgehead's, bridgeheads, bridgekeeper, bridgeless, bridgelike, bridgemaker, bridgemaking, bridgeman, bridgemaster, bridgemen, bridgeport, bridgepot, bridger, bridges, bridgetin, bridgetree, bridgewall, bridgeward, bridgewards, bridgewater, bridgeway, bridgework, bridgework's, bridging, bridgings, bridie, bridle, bridled, bridleless, bridleman, bridler, bridlers, bridles, bridlewise, bridling, bridoon, bridoons, brie, brief, briefcase, briefcase's, briefcases, briefed, briefer, briefers, briefest, briefing, briefing's, briefings, briefless, brieflessly, brieflessness, briefly, briefness, briefs, brier, brierberry, briered, brierroot, briers, brierwood, briery, bries, brieve, brig, brig's, brigade, brigade's, brigaded, brigades, brigadier, brigadier's, brigadiers, brigadiership, brigading, brigalow, brigand, brigandage, brigander, brigandine, brigandish, brigandishly, brigandism, brigands, brigantine, brigantinebrigantines, brigantines, brigatry, brigbote, brigetty, bright, brighten, brightened, brightener, brighteners, brightening, brightens, brighter, brightest, brighteyes, brightish, brightly, brightness, brights, brightsmith, brightsome, brightsomeness, brightwork, brigous, brigs, brigsail, brigue, brigued, briguer, briguing, brike, brill, brillante, brilliance, brilliancies, brilliancy, brilliandeer, brilliant, brilliantine, brilliantined, brilliantly, brilliantness, brilliants, brilliantwise, brilliolette, brillolette, brills, brim, brimborion, brimborium, brimful, brimfull, brimfullness, brimfully, brimfulness, briming, brimless, brimly, brimmed, brimmer, brimmered, brimmering, brimmers, brimmimg, brimming, brimmingly, brims, brimse, brimstone, brimstonewort, brimstony, brin, brince, brinded, brindisi, brindle, brindled, brindles, brindlish, brine, brined, brinehouse, brineless, brineman, briner, briners, brines, bring, bringal, bringall, bringdown, bringed, bringela, bringer, bringers, bringeth, bringing, brings, bringsel, brinie, brinier, brinies, briniest, brininess, brining, brinish, brinishness, brinjal, brinjaree, brinjarries, brinjarry, brinjaul, brink, brinkless, brinkmanship, brinks, brinksmanship, brinny, brins, brinsell, brinston, briny, brio, brioche, brioches, briolet, briolette, briolettes, brionies, brionine, briony, brios, brique, briquet, briquets, briquette, briquetted, briquettes, briquetting, brisa, brisance, brisances, brisant, brisbane, briscola, brise, briseis, brisement, brises, brisk, brisked, brisken, briskened, briskening, brisker, briskest, brisket, briskets, brisking, briskish, briskly, briskness, brisks, brisky, brisling, brislings, brisque, briss, brisses, brist, bristle, bristlebird, bristlecone, bristled, bristleless, bristlelike, bristlemouth, bristlemouths, bristler, bristles, bristletail, bristlewort, bristlier, bristliest, bristliness, bristling, bristly, bristol, bristols, brisure, brit, britain, britannia, britannic, britannica, britany, britchel, britches, britchka, brite, brith, brither, briticism, british, britisher, britishers, briton, briton's, britons, brits, britska, britskas, britt, britten, brittle, brittlebush, brittled, brittlely, brittleness, brittler, brittles, brittlest, brittlestem, brittlewood, brittlewort, brittling, brittonic, britts, britzka, britzkas, britzska, britzskas, briza, brizz, brl, bro, broach, broached, broacher, broachers, broaches, broaching, broad, broadacre, broadax, broadaxe, broadaxes, broadband, broadbill, broadbrim, broadcast, broadcasted, broadcaster, broadcasters, broadcasting, broadcastings, broadcasts, broadcloth, broaden, broadened, broadener, broadeners, broadening, broadenings, broadens, broader, broadest, broadgage, broadhead, broadhearted, broadhorn, broadish, broadleaf, broadleaves, broadling, broadlings, broadloom, broadlooms, broadly, broadmindedly, broadmouth, broadness, broadpiece, broads, broadshare, broadsheet, broadside, broadsided, broadsider, broadsides, broadsiding, broadspread, broadsword, broadswords, broadtail, broadthroat, broadway, broadways, broadwife, broadwise, broadwives, brob, brobdingnag, brobdingnagian, brocade, brocaded, brocades, brocading, brocage, brocard, brocardic, brocatel, brocatelle, brocatello, brocatels, broccoli, broccolis, broch, brochan, brochant, brochantite, broche, brochette, brochettes, brochidodromous, brocho, brochophony, brocht, brochure, brochure's, brochures, brock, brockage, brockages, brocked, brocket, brockets, brockish, brockle, brocks, brocoli, brocolis, brod, brodder, broddle, brodee, brodeglass, brodekin, brodequin, broderer, broderie, brodie, brodyaga, brodyagi, broeboe, brog, brogan, brogans, brogger, broggerite, broggle, brogh, brogue, brogued, brogueful, brogueneer, broguer, brogueries, broguery, brogues, broguing, broguish, broid, broiden, broider, broidered, broiderer, broideress, broideries, broidering, broiders, broidery, broigne, broil, broiled, broiler, broilers, broilery, broiling, broilingly, broils, brokage, brokages, broke, broken, brokenhearted, brokenheartedly, brokenheartedness, brokenly, brokenness, broker, brokerage, brokerages, brokeress, brokerly, brokers, brokership, brokery, brokes, broking, broletti, broletto, brolga, broll, brollies, brolly, broma, bromacetanilide, bromacetate, bromacetic, bromacetone, bromal, bromalbumin, bromals, bromamide, bromargyrite, bromate, bromated, bromates, bromating, bromatium, bromatology, bromaurate, bromauric, brombenzamide, brombenzene, brombenzyl, bromcamphor, bromcresol, brome, bromegrass, bromeigon, bromeikon, bromeliaceous, bromeliad, bromelin, bromelins, bromellite, bromeosin, bromes, bromethyl, bromethylene, bromgelatin, bromhidrosis, bromhydrate, bromhydric, bromic, bromid, bromide, bromide's, bromides, bromidic, bromidically, bromidrosiphobia, bromidrosis, bromids, bromin, brominate, brominated, brominating, bromination, bromindigo, bromine, bromines, brominism, brominize, bromins, bromiodide, bromisation, bromise, bromised, bromising, bromism, bromisms, bromite, bromization, bromize, bromized, bromizer, bromizes, bromizing, bromlite, bromo, bromoacetone, bromoaurate, bromoaurates, bromoauric, bromobenzene, bromobenzyl, bromocamphor, bromochloromethane, bromochlorophenol, bromocresol, bromocyanid, bromocyanidation, bromocyanide, bromocyanogen, bromodeoxyuridine, bromoethylene, bromoform, bromogelatin, bromohydrate, bromohydrin, bromoil, bromoiodid, bromoiodide, bromoiodism, bromoiodized, bromoketone, bromol, bromomania, bromomenorrhea, bromomethane, bromometric, bromometrical, bromometrically, bromometry, bromonaphthalene, bromophenol, bromopicrin, bromopikrin, bromopnea, bromoprotein, bromos, bromothymol, bromouracil, bromous, bromphenol, brompicrin, bromthymol, bromuret, bromvoel, bromvogel, bromyrite, bronc, bronchadenitis, bronchi, bronchia, bronchial, bronchially, bronchiarctia, bronchiectasis, bronchiectatic, bronchiloquy, bronchiocele, bronchiocrisis, bronchiogenic, bronchiolar, bronchiole, bronchiole's, bronchioles, bronchioli, bronchiolitis, bronchiolus, bronchiospasm, bronchiostenosis, bronchitic, bronchitis, bronchium, broncho, bronchoadenitis, bronchoalveolar, bronchoaspergillosis, bronchoblennorrhea, bronchobuster, bronchocavernous, bronchocele, bronchocephalitis, bronchoconstriction, bronchoconstrictor, bronchodilatation, bronchodilator, bronchoegophony, bronchoesophagoscopy, bronchogenic, bronchographic, bronchography, bronchohemorrhagia, broncholemmitis, broncholith, broncholithiasis, bronchomotor, bronchomucormycosis, bronchomycosis, bronchopathy, bronchophonic, bronchophony, bronchophthisis, bronchoplasty, bronchoplegia, bronchopleurisy, bronchopneumonia, bronchopneumonic, bronchopulmonary, bronchorrhagia, bronchorrhaphy, bronchorrhea, bronchos, bronchoscope, bronchoscopic, bronchoscopically, bronchoscopist, bronchoscopy, bronchospasm, bronchostenosis, bronchostomies, bronchostomy, bronchotetany, bronchotome, bronchotomist, bronchotomy, bronchotracheal, bronchotyphoid, bronchotyphus, bronchovesicular, bronchus, bronco, broncobuster, broncobusters, broncobusting, broncos, broncs, brongniardite, bronk, bronstrops, bronteon, brontephobia, bronteum, brontide, brontides, brontogram, brontograph, brontolite, brontolith, brontology, brontometer, brontophobia, brontops, brontosaur, brontosauri, brontosaurs, brontosaurus, brontosauruses, brontoscopy, brontothere, bronx, bronze, bronzed, bronzelike, bronzen, bronzer, bronzers, bronzes, bronzesmith, bronzewing, bronzier, bronziest, bronzify, bronzine, bronzing, bronzings, bronzite, bronzitite, bronzy, broo, brooch, brooch's, brooched, brooches, brooching, brood, brooded, brooder, brooders, broodier, broodiest, broodily, broodiness, brooding, broodingly, broodless, broodlet, broodling, broodmare, broods, broodsac, broody, brook, brookable, brooked, brookflower, brookie, brookier, brookiest, brooking, brookite, brookites, brookless, brooklet, brooklets, brooklike, brooklime, brooklyn, brooks, brookside, brookweed, brooky, brool, broom, broom's, broomball, broomballer, broombush, broomcorn, broomed, broomer, broomier, broomiest, brooming, broommaker, broommaking, broomrape, broomroot, brooms, broomshank, broomsquire, broomstaff, broomstick, broomstick's, broomsticks, broomstraw, broomtail, broomweed, broomwood, broomwort, broomy, broon, broos, broose, broozled, broquery, broquineer, bros, brose, broses, brosot, brosse, brosy, brot, brotan, brotany, brotchen, brotel, broth, brothe, brothel, brothel's, brotheler, brothellike, brothelry, brothels, brother, brother's, brothered, brotherhood, brothering, brotherless, brotherlike, brotherliness, brotherly, brotherred, brothers, brothership, brotherwort, brothier, brothiest, broths, brothy, brotocrystal, brott, brotula, brotulid, brotuliform, brouette, brough, brougham, broughams, brought, broughta, broughtas, brouhaha, brouhahas, brouille, brouillon, brouze, brow, brow's, browache, browallia, browband, browbands, browbeat, browbeaten, browbeater, browbeating, browbeats, browbound, browd, browden, browed, browet, browis, browless, browman, brown, brownback, browned, browner, brownest, brownian, brownie, brownie's, brownier, brownies, browniest, browniness, browning, brownish, brownishness, brownism, brownly, brownness, brownnose, brownnoser, brownout, brownouts, brownprint, browns, brownshirt, brownstone, brownstones, browntail, browntop, brownweed, brownwort, browny, browpiece, browpost, brows, browsability, browsage, browse, browsed, browser, browsers, browses, browsick, browsing, browst, browzer, brr, brrr, bruang, brubru, brubu, bruce, brucella, brucellae, brucellas, brucellosis, bruchid, bruchus, brucia, brucin, brucina, brucine, brucines, brucins, brucite, bruckle, bruckled, bruckleness, bruet, bruges, brugh, brughs, brugnatellite, bruin, bruins, bruise, bruised, bruiser, bruisers, bruises, bruisewort, bruising, bruisingly, bruit, bruited, bruiter, bruiters, bruiting, bruits, bruja, brujas, brujeria, brujo, brujos, bruke, brule, brulee, brules, brulot, brulots, brulyie, brulyiement, brulyies, brulzie, brulzies, brum, brumaire, brumal, brumbee, brumbie, brumbies, brumby, brume, brumes, brummagem, brummagen, brummer, brummy, brumous, brumstane, brumstone, brunch, brunched, brunches, brunching, brune, brunel, brunelliaceous, brunet, brunetness, brunets, brunette, brunetteness, brunettes, brunhild, brunion, brunissure, brunizem, brunizems, brunneous, brunonian, brunswick, brunt, brunts, bruscha, bruscus, brush, brushability, brushable, brushback, brushball, brushbird, brushbush, brushcut, brushed, brusher, brushers, brushes, brushet, brushfire, brushfire's, brushfires, brushful, brushier, brushiest, brushiness, brushing, brushite, brushland, brushless, brushlessness, brushlet, brushlike, brushmaker, brushmaking, brushman, brushmen, brushoff, brushoffs, brushpopper, brushproof, brushup, brushups, brushwood, brushwork, brushy, brusk, brusker, bruskest, bruskly, bruskness, brusque, brusquely, brusqueness, brusquer, brusquerie, brusquest, brussel, brussels, brustle, brustled, brustling, brusure, brut, brutage, brutal, brutalisation, brutalise, brutalised, brutalising, brutalism, brutalist, brutalitarian, brutalitarianism, brutalities, brutality, brutalization, brutalize, brutalized, brutalizes, brutalizing, brutally, brutalness, brute, brute's, bruted, brutedom, brutelike, brutely, bruteness, brutes, brutification, brutified, brutifies, brutify, brutifying, bruting, brutish, brutishly, brutishness, brutism, brutisms, brutter, brutus, bruxism, bruxisms, bruyere, bruzz, bryaceous, bryan, bryndza, brynhild, brynza, bryogenin, bryological, bryologies, bryologist, bryology, bryon, bryonia, bryonidin, bryonies, bryonin, bryony, bryophyta, bryophyte, bryophytes, bryophytic, bryozoa, bryozoan, bryozoans, bryozoon, bryozoum, brython, brythonic, bs, bsf, bsh, bskt, bt, btise, btl, btry, btu, bu, bual, buat, buaze, bub, buba, bubal, bubale, bubales, bubaline, bubalis, bubalises, bubals, bubas, bubba, bubber, bubbies, bubble, bubblebow, bubbled, bubbleless, bubblelike, bubblement, bubbler, bubblers, bubbles, bubbletop, bubbletops, bubblier, bubblies, bubbliest, bubbliness, bubbling, bubblingly, bubblish, bubbly, bubby, bubbybush, bubinga, bubingas, bubo, buboed, buboes, bubonalgia, bubonic, bubonocele, bubonoceze, bubos, bubs, bubukle, bucare, bucayo, bucca, buccal, buccally, buccan, buccaned, buccaneer, buccaneering, buccaneerish, buccaneers, buccaning, buccanned, buccanning, buccaro, buccate, bucchero, buccheros, buccin, buccina, buccinae, buccinal, buccinator, buccinatory, bucciniform, buccinoid, buccinum, buccobranchial, buccocervical, buccogingival, buccolabial, buccolingual, bucconasal, buccopharyngeal, buccula, bucculae, bucellas, bucentaur, bucentur, bucephalus, buchanan, bucharest, buchite, buchnerite, buchonite, buchu, buck, buckaroo, buckaroos, buckass, buckayro, buckayros, buckbean, buckbeans, buckberry, buckboard, buckboard's, buckboards, buckbrush, buckbush, bucked, buckeen, buckeens, bucker, buckeroo, buckeroos, buckers, bucket, bucket's, bucketed, bucketeer, bucketer, bucketful, bucketfull, bucketfuls, bucketing, bucketmaker, bucketmaking, bucketman, buckets, bucketsful, bucketshop, buckety, buckeye, buckeyed, buckeyes, buckhorn, buckhound, buckhounds, buckie, bucking, buckish, buckishly, buckishness, buckism, buckjump, buckjumper, buckland, bucklandite, buckle, buckled, buckleless, buckler, bucklered, bucklering, bucklers, buckles, buckling, bucklum, bucko, buckoes, buckone, buckplate, buckpot, buckra, buckram, buckramed, buckraming, buckrams, buckras, bucks, bucksaw, bucksaws, buckshee, buckshees, buckshot, buckshots, buckskin, buckskinned, buckskins, buckstall, buckstay, buckstone, bucktail, bucktails, buckteeth, buckthorn, bucktooth, bucktoothed, bucku, buckwagon, buckwash, buckwasher, buckwashing, buckwheat, buckwheater, buckwheatlike, buckwheats, bucky, bucoliast, bucolic, bucolical, bucolically, bucolicism, bucolics, bucrane, bucrania, bucranium, bucrnia, bud, bud's, buda, budapest, budbreak, buddage, buddah, budded, budder, budders, buddha, buddhahood, buddhi, buddhism, buddhist, buddhists, buddie, buddies, budding, buddle, buddled, buddleia, buddleias, buddleman, buddler, buddles, buddling, buddy, buddy's, bude, budge, budged, budger, budgeree, budgereegah, budgerigah, budgerigar, budgerigars, budgero, budgerow, budgers, budgerygah, budges, budget, budgetary, budgeted, budgeteer, budgeter, budgeters, budgetful, budgeting, budgets, budgie, budgies, budging, budgy, budless, budlet, budlike, budling, budmash, buds, budtime, budwood, budworm, budzart, budzat, buenas, bueno, buenos, bufagin, buff, buff's, buffa, buffability, buffable, buffalo, buffaloback, buffaloed, buffaloes, buffalofish, buffalofishes, buffaloing, buffalos, buffball, buffbar, buffcoat, buffe, buffed, buffer, buffer's, buffered, buffering, bufferrer, bufferrer's, bufferrers, buffers, buffet, buffeted, buffeter, buffeters, buffeting, buffetings, buffets, buffi, buffier, buffiest, buffin, buffing, buffle, bufflehead, buffleheaded, bufflehorn, buffo, buffone, buffont, buffoon, buffoon's, buffooneries, buffoonery, buffoonesque, buffoonish, buffoonishness, buffoonism, buffoons, buffos, buffs, buffware, buffy, bufidin, bufo, bufonid, bufonite, bufotalin, bufotenin, bufotenine, bufotoxin, bug, bug's, bugaboo, bugaboos, bugala, bugan, bugara, bugbane, bugbanes, bugbear, bugbeardom, bugbearish, bugbears, bugbite, bugdom, bugeye, bugeyed, bugeyes, bugfish, buggane, bugged, bugger, bugger's, buggered, buggeries, buggering, buggers, buggery, buggess, buggier, buggies, buggiest, bugginess, bugging, buggy, buggy's, buggyman, buggymen, bughead, bughouse, bughouses, bught, bugle, bugled, bugler, buglers, bugles, buglet, bugleweed, buglewort, bugling, bugloss, buglosses, bugologist, bugology, bugong, bugout, bugproof, bugre, bugs, bugseed, bugseeds, bugsha, bugshas, bugweed, bugwort, buhl, buhlbuhl, buhls, buhlwork, buhlworks, buhr, buhrmill, buhrs, buhrstone, buibui, buick, buicks, build, buildable, builded, builder, builders, building, buildingless, buildings, buildress, builds, buildup, buildup's, buildups, built, builtin, buirdly, buisson, buist, bukh, bukshee, bukshi, bul, bulak, bulb, bulb's, bulbaceous, bulbar, bulbed, bulbel, bulbels, bulbier, bulbiest, bulbiferous, bulbiform, bulbil, bulbilla, bulbils, bulbine, bulbless, bulblet, bulblike, bulbocapnin, bulbocapnine, bulbocavernosus, bulbocavernous, bulbomedullary, bulbomembranous, bulbonuclear, bulborectal, bulbose, bulbospinal, bulbotuber, bulbourethral, bulbous, bulbously, bulbs, bulbul, bulbule, bulbuls, bulbus, bulby, bulchin, bulder, bulgar, bulgaria, bulgarian, bulgarians, bulge, bulged, bulger, bulgers, bulges, bulgier, bulgiest, bulginess, bulging, bulgingly, bulgur, bulgurs, bulgy, bulies, bulimia, bulimiac, bulimias, bulimic, bulimiform, bulimoid, bulimus, bulimy, bulk, bulkage, bulkages, bulked, bulker, bulkhead, bulkhead's, bulkheaded, bulkheading, bulkheads, bulkier, bulkiest, bulkily, bulkin, bulkiness, bulking, bulkish, bulks, bulky, bull, bulla, bullace, bullaces, bullae, bullalaria, bullamacow, bullan, bullaria, bullaries, bullarium, bullary, bullate, bullated, bullation, bullback, bullbaiting, bullbat, bullbats, bullbeggar, bullberry, bullbird, bullboat, bullcart, bullcomber, bulldog, bulldog's, bulldogged, bulldoggedness, bulldogger, bulldogging, bulldoggish, bulldoggishly, bulldoggishness, bulldoggy, bulldogism, bulldogs, bulldoze, bulldozed, bulldozer, bulldozers, bulldozes, bulldozing, bulldust, bulled, buller, bullescene, bullet, bullet's, bulleted, bullethead, bulletheaded, bulletheadedness, bulletin, bulletin's, bulletined, bulleting, bulletining, bulletins, bulletless, bulletlike, bulletmaker, bulletmaking, bulletproof, bulletproofed, bulletproofing, bulletproofs, bullets, bulletwood, bullety, bullfeast, bullfice, bullfight, bullfighter, bullfighters, bullfighting, bullfights, bullfinch, bullfinches, bullfist, bullflower, bullfoot, bullfrog, bullfrogs, bullgine, bullhead, bullheaded, bullheadedly, bullheadedness, bullheads, bullhide, bullhoof, bullhorn, bullhorns, bullied, bullier, bullies, bulliest, bulliform, bullimong, bulling, bullion, bullionism, bullionist, bullionless, bullions, bullish, bullishly, bullishness, bullism, bullit, bullition, bulllike, bullneck, bullnecked, bullnecks, bullnose, bullnoses, bullnut, bullock, bullocker, bullockman, bullocks, bullocky, bullose, bullous, bullpates, bullpen, bullpens, bullpoll, bullpout, bullpouts, bullpup, bullragged, bullragging, bullring, bullrings, bullroarer, bullrush, bullrushes, bulls, bullseye, bullshit, bullshits, bullshitted, bullshitting, bullshot, bullshots, bullskin, bullsnake, bullsticker, bullsucker, bullswool, bullterrier, bulltoad, bullule, bullweed, bullweeds, bullwhack, bullwhacker, bullwhip, bullwhipped, bullwhipping, bullwhips, bullwork, bullwort, bully, bullyable, bullyboy, bullyboys, bullydom, bullyhuff, bullying, bullyingly, bullyism, bullyrag, bullyragged, bullyragger, bullyragging, bullyrags, bullyrock, bullyrook, bulnbuln, bulreedy, bulrush, bulrushes, bulrushlike, bulrushy, bulse, bult, bultell, bulten, bulter, bultey, bultong, bultow, bulwand, bulwark, bulwarked, bulwarking, bulwarks, bum, bum's, bumaloe, bumaree, bumbailiff, bumbailiffship, bumbard, bumbarge, bumbass, bumbaste, bumbaze, bumbee, bumbelo, bumbershoot, bumble, bumblebee, bumblebee's, bumblebeefish, bumblebeefishes, bumblebees, bumbleberry, bumblebomb, bumbled, bumbledom, bumblefoot, bumblekite, bumblepuppy, bumbler, bumblers, bumbles, bumbling, bumblingly, bumblingness, bumblings, bumbo, bumboat, bumboatman, bumboatmen, bumboats, bumboatwoman, bumclock, bumf, bumfeg, bumfs, bumfuzzle, bumicky, bumkin, bumkins, bummack, bummalo, bummalos, bummaree, bummed, bummel, bummer, bummerish, bummers, bummery, bummest, bummie, bummil, bumming, bummle, bummler, bummock, bump, bumped, bumpee, bumper, bumpered, bumperette, bumpering, bumpers, bumph, bumpier, bumpiest, bumpily, bumpiness, bumping, bumpingly, bumpity, bumpkin, bumpkinet, bumpkinish, bumpkinly, bumpkins, bumpoff, bumpology, bumps, bumpsy, bumptious, bumptiously, bumptiousness, bumpy, bums, bumsucking, bumtrap, bumwood, bun, bun's, buna, buncal, bunce, bunch, bunchbacked, bunchberries, bunchberry, bunched, buncher, bunches, bunchflower, bunchier, bunchiest, bunchily, bunchiness, bunching, bunchy, bunco, buncoed, buncoing, buncombe, buncombes, buncos, bund, bunder, bundh, bundies, bundist, bundists, bundle, bundled, bundler, bundlerooted, bundlers, bundles, bundlet, bundling, bundlings, bundobust, bundoc, bundocks, bundook, bunds, bundt, bundts, bundu, bundweed, bundy, bunemost, bung, bungaloid, bungalow, bungalow's, bungalows, bungarum, bunged, bungee, bunger, bungerly, bungey, bungfu, bungfull, bunghole, bungholes, bunging, bungle, bungled, bungler, bunglers, bungles, bunglesome, bungling, bunglingly, bunglings, bungmaker, bungo, bungos, bungs, bungstarter, bungtown, bungwall, bungy, bunion, bunion's, bunions, bunjara, bunk, bunked, bunker, bunker's, bunkerage, bunkered, bunkering, bunkerman, bunkermen, bunkers, bunkery, bunkhouse, bunkhouse's, bunkhouses, bunkie, bunking, bunkload, bunkmate, bunkmate's, bunkmates, bunko, bunkoed, bunkoing, bunkos, bunks, bunkum, bunkums, bunn, bunnell, bunnia, bunnies, bunning, bunns, bunny, bunny's, bunnymouth, bunodont, bunolophodont, bunoselenodont, bunraku, bunrakus, buns, bunsen, bunsenite, bunt, buntal, bunted, bunter, bunters, buntine, bunting, buntings, buntline, buntlines, bunton, bunts, bunty, bunuelo, bunya, bunyah, bunyan, bunyas, bunyip, buonamani, buonamano, buoy, buoyage, buoyages, buoyance, buoyances, buoyancies, buoyancy, buoyant, buoyantly, buoyantness, buoyed, buoying, buoys, buphthalmia, buphthalmic, buphthalmos, bupleurol, buplever, buprestid, buprestidan, buprestis, buqsha, buqshas, bur, bura, buran, burans, burao, buras, burbank, burbankian, burbark, burberry, burble, burbled, burbler, burblers, burbles, burblier, burbliest, burbling, burbly, burbolt, burbot, burbots, burbs, burbush, burd, burdalone, burdash, burden, burdenable, burdened, burdener, burdeners, burdening, burdenless, burdenous, burdens, burdensome, burdensomely, burdensomeness, burdie, burdies, burdock, burdocks, burdon, burds, bure, bureau, bureau's, bureaucracies, bureaucracy, bureaucracy's, bureaucrat, bureaucrat's, bureaucratese, bureaucratic, bureaucratical, bureaucratically, bureaucratism, bureaucratist, bureaucratization, bureaucratize, bureaucratized, bureaucratizes, bureaucratizing, bureaucrats, bureaus, bureaux, burel, burelage, burele, burelle, burelly, burely, buret, burets, burette, burettes, burez, burfish, burg, burga, burgage, burgages, burgality, burgall, burgamot, burganet, burgau, burgaudine, burge, burgee, burgees, burgensic, burgeon, burgeoned, burgeoning, burgeons, burger, burgers, burgess, burgess's, burgessdom, burgesses, burggrave, burgh, burghal, burghalpenny, burghbote, burghemot, burgher, burgher's, burgherage, burgherdom, burgheress, burgherhood, burgheristh, burghermaster, burghers, burghership, burghmaster, burghmoot, burghmote, burghs, burglar, burglar's, burglaries, burglarious, burglariously, burglarise, burglarised, burglarising, burglarize, burglarized, burglarizes, burglarizing, burglarproof, burglarproofed, burglarproofing, burglarproofs, burglars, burglary, burglary's, burgle, burgled, burgles, burgling, burgomaster, burgomasters, burgomastership, burgonet, burgonets, burgoo, burgoos, burgout, burgouts, burgoyne, burgrave, burgraves, burgraviate, burgs, burgul, burgullian, burgundian, burgundies, burgundy, burgus, burgware, burgwere, burh, burhead, burhel, burhmoot, buri, buriable, burial, burials, burian, buried, buriels, burier, buriers, buries, burin, burinist, burins, burion, buriti, burk, burka, burke, burked, burkei, burker, burkers, burkes, burkha, burking, burkite, burkites, burkundauze, burkundaz, burl, burlace, burladero, burlap, burlaps, burlecue, burled, burler, burlers, burlesk, burlesks, burlesque, burlesqued, burlesquely, burlesquer, burlesques, burlesquing, burlet, burletta, burley, burleycue, burleys, burlier, burlies, burliest, burlily, burliness, burling, burls, burly, burma, burmanniaceous, burmese, burmite, burn, burnable, burnbeat, burned, burner, burners, burnet, burnetize, burnets, burnettize, burnettized, burnettizing, burnewin, burnfire, burnie, burniebee, burnies, burning, burningly, burnings, burnish, burnishable, burnished, burnisher, burnishers, burnishes, burnishing, burnishment, burnoose, burnoosed, burnooses, burnous, burnoused, burnouses, burnout, burnouts, burnover, burns, burnside, burnsides, burnt, burntly, burntness, burntweed, burnup, burnut, burnweed, burnwood, burny, buro, buroo, burp, burped, burping, burps, burr, burr's, burrah, burratine, burrawang, burrbark, burred, burree, burrel, burrer, burrers, burrfish, burrfishes, burrgrailer, burrhead, burrheaded, burrheadedness, burrhel, burrier, burriest, burring, burrio, burrish, burrito, burritos, burrknot, burro, burro's, burrobrush, burrock, burros, burroughs, burrow, burrowed, burroweed, burrower, burrowers, burrowing, burrows, burrowstown, burrs, burrstone, burry, burs, bursa, bursae, bursal, bursar, bursarial, bursaries, bursars, bursarship, bursary, bursas, bursate, bursati, bursattee, bursautee, bursch, burse, bursectomy, burseed, burseeds, bursera, burseraceous, burses, bursicle, bursiculate, bursiform, bursitis, bursitises, bursitos, burst, bursted, burster, bursters, burstiness, bursting, burstone, burstones, bursts, burstwort, bursty, bursula, burt, burthen, burthened, burthening, burthenman, burthens, burthensome, burton, burtonization, burtonize, burtons, burtree, burucha, burundi, burundians, burweed, burweeds, bury, burying, burys, bus, busbar, busbars, busbies, busboy, busboy's, busboys, busby, buscarl, buscarle, bused, busera, buses, bush, bushbaby, bushbashing, bushbeater, bushbeck, bushbodies, bushbody, bushboy, bushbuck, bushbucks, bushcraft, bushed, bushel, bushel's, bushelage, bushelbasket, busheled, busheler, bushelers, bushelful, bushelfuls, busheling, bushelled, busheller, bushelling, bushelman, bushelmen, bushels, bushelwoman, busher, bushers, bushes, bushet, bushfighter, bushfighting, bushfire, bushfires, bushful, bushgoat, bushgoats, bushgrass, bushhammer, bushi, bushido, bushidos, bushie, bushier, bushiest, bushily, bushiness, bushing, bushings, bushland, bushlands, bushless, bushlet, bushlike, bushmaker, bushmaking, bushman, bushmanship, bushmaster, bushmasters, bushmen, bushment, bushpig, bushranger, bushranging, bushrope, bushtit, bushtits, bushveld, bushwa, bushwack, bushwah, bushwahs, bushwalking, bushwas, bushwhack, bushwhacked, bushwhacker, bushwhackers, bushwhacking, bushwhacks, bushwife, bushwoman, bushwood, bushy, busied, busier, busies, busiest, busily, busine, business, business's, businesses, businessese, businesslike, businesslikeness, businessman, businessmen, businesswoman, businesswomen, busing, busings, busk, busked, busker, buskers, busket, buskin, buskined, busking, buskins, buskle, busks, busky, busload, busman, busmen, buss, bussed, busser, busses, bussing, bussings, bussock, bussu, bussy, bust, bustard, bustard's, bustards, busted, bustee, buster, busters, busthead, busti, bustian, bustic, busticate, bustics, bustier, bustiest, busting, bustle, bustled, bustler, bustlers, bustles, bustling, bustlingly, busto, busts, busty, busulfan, busulfans, busuuti, busway, busy, busybodied, busybodies, busybody, busybodyish, busybodyism, busybodyness, busyhead, busying, busyish, busyness, busynesses, busywork, busyworks, but, butacaine, butadiene, butadiyne, butanal, butane, butanes, butanoic, butanol, butanolid, butanolide, butanols, butanone, butanones, butat, butch, butcha, butcher,

butcher's, butcherbird, butcherbroom, butcherdom, butchered, butcherer, butcheress, butcheries, butchering, butcherless, butcherliness, butcherly, butcherous, butchers, butchery, butches, butein, butene, butenes, butenyl, buteo, buteonine, buteos, butic, butin, butine, butle, butled, butler, butler's, butlerage, butlerdom, butleress, butleries, butlerism, butlerlike, butlers, butlership, butlery, butles, butling, butment, butolism, butomaceous, butoxy, butoxyl, buts, butsudan, butt, butt's, buttal, buttals, butte, butted, butter, butteraceous, butterback, butterball, butterbill, butterbird, butterbough, butterbox, butterbump, butterbur, butterburr, butterbush, buttercup, buttercups, buttered, butterer, butterers, butterfat, butterfingered, butterfingers, butterfish, butterfishes, butterflied, butterflies, butterflower, butterfly, butterfly's, butterflyer, butterflyfish, butterflyfishes, butterflying, butterflylike, butterhead, butterier, butteries, butteriest, butterine, butteriness, buttering, butteris, butterjags, butterless, butterlike, buttermaker, buttermaking, butterman, buttermilk, buttermonger, buttermouth, butternose, butternut, butternuts, butterpaste, butterroot, butters, butterscotch, butterweed, butterwife, butterwoman, butterworker, butterwort, butterwright, buttery, butteryfingered, buttes, buttgenbachite, butties, butting, buttinski, buttinskies, buttinsky, buttle, buttled, buttling, buttock, buttock's, buttocked, buttocker, buttocks, button, buttonball, buttonbur, buttonbush, buttoned, buttoner, buttoners, buttonhold, buttonholder, buttonhole, buttonhole's, buttonholed, buttonholer, buttonholes, buttonholing, buttonhook, buttoning, buttonless, buttonlike, buttonmold, buttonmould, buttons, buttonweed, buttonwood, buttony, buttress, buttressed, buttresses, buttressing, buttressless, buttresslike, butts, buttstock, buttstrap, buttstrapped, buttstrapping, buttwoman, buttwomen, buttwood, butty, buttyman, butut, bututs, butyl, butylamine, butylate, butylated, butylates, butylating, butylation, butylene, butylenes, butylic, butyls, butyne, butyr, butyraceous, butyral, butyraldehyde, butyrals, butyrate, butyrates, butyric, butyrically, butyrin, butyrinase, butyrins, butyrochloral, butyrolactone, butyrometer, butyrometric, butyrone, butyrous, butyrousness, butyryl, butyryls, buvette, buxaceous, buxeous, buxerries, buxerry, buxine, buxom, buxomer, buxomest, buxomly, buxomness, buy, buyable, buyback, buybacks, buyer, buyer's, buyers, buying, buyout, buyouts, buys, buz, buzane, buzuki, buzukia, buzukis, buzylene, buzz, buzzard, buzzard's, buzzardlike, buzzardly, buzzards, buzzbomb, buzzed, buzzer, buzzerphone, buzzers, buzzes, buzzgloak, buzzier, buzzies, buzziest, buzzing, buzzingly, buzzle, buzzsaw, buzzwig, buzzwigs, buzzword, buzzword's, buzzwords, buzzy, bv, bvt, bwana, bwanas, bx, bxs, by, byard, bycoket, bye, byee, byegaein, byelaw, byelaws, byelorussia, byelorussian, byelorussians, byeman, byepath, byerite, byerlite, byes, byestreet, byeworker, byeworkman, bygane, byganging, bygo, bygoing, bygone, bygones, byhand, byland, bylander, bylaw, bylaw's, bylawman, bylaws, bylina, byline, byline's, bylined, byliner, byliners, bylines, bylining, byliny, byname, bynames, bynedestin, bynin, byon, byordinar, byordinary, byous, byously, byp, bypass, bypassed, bypasser, bypasses, bypassing, bypast, bypath, bypaths, byplace, byplay, byplays, byproduct, byproduct's, byproducts, byre, byreman, byres, byrewards, byrewoman, byrl, byrlady, byrlakin, byrlaw, byrlawman, byrlawmen, byrled, byrling, byrls, byrnie, byrnies, byroad, byroads, byron, byronic, byrri, byrrus, byrthynsak, bys, bysen, bysmalith, byspell, byss, byssaceous, byssal, byssi, byssiferous, byssin, byssine, byssinosis, byssogenous, byssoid, byssolite, byssus, byssuses, bystander, bystander's, bystanders, bystreet, bystreets, bytalk, bytalks, byte, byte's, bytes, byth, bytime, bytownite, bytownitite, bywalk, bywalker, bywalking, byward, byway, byways, bywoner, byword, byword's, bywords, bywork, byworks, byzant, byzantian, byzantine, byzantium, byzants, bz, c, c's, c/d, c/f, c/m, c/o, ca, ca', ca'canny, caaba, caam, caama, caaming, caapeba, caatinga, cab, cab's, caba, cabaa, cabaan, caback, cabaho, cabal, cabala, cabalas, cabalassou, cabaletta, cabalic, cabalism, cabalisms, cabalist, cabalistic, cabalistical, cabalistically, cabalists, caball, caballed, caballer, caballeria, caballero, caballeros, caballine, caballing, caballo, caballos, cabals, caban, cabana, cabanas, cabane, cabaret, cabaretier, cabarets, cabas, cabasa, cabasset, cabassou, cabbage, cabbage's, cabbaged, cabbagehead, cabbageheaded, cabbageheadedness, cabbagelike, cabbages, cabbagetown, cabbagewood, cabbageworm, cabbaging, cabbagy, cabbala, cabbalah, cabbalahs, cabbalas, cabbalism, cabbalist, cabbalistic, cabbalistical, cabbalistically, cabbalize, cabbed, cabber, cabbie, cabbies, cabbing, cabble, cabbled, cabbler, cabbling, cabby, cabda, cabdriver, cabdriving, cabecera, cabecudo, cabeliau, cabellerote, caber, cabernet, cabernets, cabers, cabestro, cabestros, cabezon, cabezone, cabezones, cabezons, cabful, cabiai, cabildo, cabildos, cabilliau, cabin, cabin's, cabined, cabinet, cabinet's, cabineted, cabineting, cabinetmake, cabinetmaker, cabinetmakers, cabinetmaking, cabinetry, cabinets, cabinetted, cabinetwork, cabinetworker, cabinetworking, cabining, cabinlike, cabins, cabio, cable, cablecast, cabled, cablegram, cablegrams, cablelaid, cableless, cablelike, cableman, cablemen, cabler, cables, cablese, cablet, cablets, cableway, cableways, cabling, cablish, cabman, cabmen, cabob, cabobs, caboceer, caboche, caboched, cabochon, cabochons, cabocle, caboclo, caboclos, cabomba, cabombas, caboodle, caboodles, cabook, caboose, cabooses, caboshed, cabossed, cabot, cabotage, cabotages, cabotin, cabotinage, cabots, cabouca, cabre, cabree, cabrerite, cabresta, cabrestas, cabresto, cabrestos, cabret, cabretta, cabrettas, cabreuva, cabrie, cabrilla, cabrillas, cabriole, cabrioles, cabriolet, cabriolets, cabrit, cabrito, cabs, cabstand, cabstands, cabuja, cabulla, cabureiba, caburn, cabuya, cabuyas, caca, cacaesthesia, cacafuego, cacafugo, cacam, cacanapa, cacanthrax, cacao, cacaos, cacas, cacaxte, caccagogue, caccia, caccias, cacciatora, cacciatore, cace, cacei, cacemphaton, cacesthesia, cacesthesis, cachaca, cachaemia, cachaemic, cachalot, cachalote, cachalots, cachaza, cache, cache's, cachectic, cachectical, cached, cachemia, cachemic, cachepot, cachepots, caches, cachespell, cachet, cacheted, cachetic, cacheting, cachets, cachexia, cachexias, cachexic, cachexies, cachexy, cachibou, cachila, cachimailla, cachina, cachinate, caching, cachinnate, cachinnated, cachinnating, cachinnation, cachinnator, cachinnatory, cachoeira, cacholong, cachot, cachou, cachous, cachrys, cachua, cachucha, cachuchas, cachucho, cachunde, caci, cacidrosis, cacimbo, cacimbos, caciocavallo, cacique, caciques, caciqueship, caciquism, cack, cacked, cackerel, cacking, cackle, cackled, cackler, cacklers, cackles, cackling, cacks, cacocholia, cacochroia, cacochylia, cacochymia, cacochymic, cacochymical, cacochymy, cacocnemia, cacodaemon, cacodaemoniac, cacodaemonial, cacodaemonic, cacodemon, cacodemonia, cacodemoniac, cacodemonial, cacodemonic, cacodemonize, cacodemonomania, cacodontia, cacodorous, cacodoxian, cacodoxical, cacodoxy, cacodyl, cacodylate, cacodylic, cacodyls, cacoeconomy, cacoenthes, cacoepist, cacoepistic, cacoepy, cacoethes, cacoethic, cacogalactia, cacogastric, cacogenesis, cacogenic, cacogenics, cacogeusia, cacoglossia, cacographer, cacographic, cacographical, cacography, cacolet, cacolike, cacological, cacology, cacomagician, cacomelia, cacomistle, cacomixl, cacomixle, cacomixls, cacomorphia, cacomorphosis, caconychia, caconym, caconymic, cacoon, cacopathy, cacopharyngia, cacophonia, cacophonic, cacophonical, cacophonically, cacophonies, cacophonist, cacophonists, cacophonize, cacophonous, cacophonously, cacophony, cacophthalmia, cacoplasia, cacoplastic, cacoproctia, cacorhythmic, cacorrhachis, cacorrhinia, cacosmia, cacospermia, cacosplanchnia, cacostomia, cacothansia, cacothelin, cacotheline, cacothes, cacothesis, cacothymia, cacotopia, cacotrichia, cacotrophia, cacotrophic, cacotrophy, cacotype, cacoxene, cacoxenite, cacozeal, cacozealous, cacozyme, cacqueteuse, cacqueteuses, cactaceous, cactal, cacti, cactiform, cactoid, cactus, cactuses, cactuslike, cacumen, cacuminal, cacuminate, cacumination, cacuminous, cacur, cad, cadalene, cadamba, cadaster, cadasters, cadastral, cadastrally, cadastration, cadastre, cadastres, cadaver, cadaveric, cadaverin, cadaverine, cadaverize, cadaverous, cadaverously, cadaverousness, cadavers, cadbait, cadbit, cadbote, cadded, caddesse, caddice, caddiced, caddicefly, caddices, caddie, caddied, caddies, caddiing, cadding, caddis, caddised, caddises, caddisflies, caddisfly, caddish, caddishly, caddishness, caddisworm, caddle, caddow, caddy, caddying, cade, cadeau, cadee, cadelle, cadelles, cadence, cadenced, cadences, cadencies, cadencing, cadency, cadenette, cadent, cadential, cadenza, cadenzas, cader, caderas, cadere, cades, cadesse, cadet, cadetcy, cadets, cadetship, cadette, cadettes, cadew, cadge, cadged, cadger, cadgers, cadges, cadgily, cadginess, cadging, cadgy, cadi, cadie, cadilesker, cadillac, cadillacs, cadillo, cadinene, cadis, cadish, cadism, cadiueio, cadjan, cadlock, cadmean, cadmia, cadmic, cadmide, cadmiferous, cadmium, cadmiumize, cadmiums, cadmus, cados, cadouk, cadrans, cadre, cadres, cads, cadua, caduac, caduca, caducary, caducean, caducecaducean, caducecei, caducei, caduceus, caduciaries, caduciary, caducibranch, caducibranchiate, caducicorn, caducities, caducity, caducous, caduke, cadus, cadweed, cadwell, cady, cadying, caeca, caecal, caecally, caecectomy, caecias, caeciform, caecilian, caecitis, caecity, caecocolic, caecostomy, caecotomy, caecum, caelometer, caelum, caenogenesis, caenogenetic, caenogenetically, caenostylic, caenostyly, caenozoic, caeoma, caeomas, caeremoniarius, caesalpiniaceous, caesar, caesarean, caesareans, caesarian, caesarism, caesarists, caesaropapacy, caesaropapism, caesaropapist, caesaropopism, caesious, caesium, caesiums, caespitose, caespitosely, caestus, caestuses, caesura, caesurae, caesural, caesuras, caesuric, caf, cafard, cafardise, cafe, cafe's, cafeneh, cafenet, cafes, cafetal, cafeteria, cafeterias, cafetiere, cafetorium, caff, caffa, caffeate, caffeic, caffein, caffeina, caffeine, caffeines, caffeinic, caffeinism, caffeins, caffeism, caffeol, caffeone, caffetannic, caffetannin, caffiaceous, caffiso, caffle, caffled, caffling, caffoline, caffoy, caffre, cafh, cafila, cafiz, cafoy, caftan, caftaned, caftans, cafuso, cag, cagayan, cagayans, cage, caged, cageful, cagefuls, cageless, cagelike, cageling, cagelings, cageman, cageot, cager, cagers, cages, cagester, cagework, cagey, cageyness, caggy, cagier, cagiest, cagily, caginess, caginesses, caging, cagit, cagmag, cagot, cagoule, cagui, cagy, cahier, cahiers, cahill, cahincic, cahiz, cahoot, cahoots, cahot, cahow, cahows, cahuita, cahuy, cai, caiarara, caic, caickle, caid, caids, cailcedra, caille, cailleach, cailliach, caimacam, caimakam, caiman, caimans, caimitillo, caimito, cain, caingin, cainogenesis, cainozoic, cains, caique, caiquejee, caiques, cair, caird, cairds, cairene, cairn, cairned, cairngorm, cairngorum, cairns, cairny, cairo, caisse, caisson, caissoned, caissons, caitif, caitiff, caitiffs, caitifty, caixinha, cajan, cajang, cajaput, cajaputs, cajava, cajeput, cajeputol, cajeputole, cajeputs, cajeta, cajole, cajoled, cajolement, cajolements, cajoler, cajoleries, cajolers, cajolery, cajoles, cajoling, cajolingly, cajon, cajones, cajou, cajuela, cajun, cajuns, cajuput, cajuputene, cajuputol, cajuputs, cake, cakebox, cakebread, caked, cakehouse, cakemaker, cakemaking, caker, cakes, cakette, cakewalk, cakewalked, cakewalker, cakewalking, cakewalks, cakey, cakier, cakiest, caking, cakra, cakravartin, caky, cal, calaba, calabar, calabash, calabashes, calabaza, calabazilla, calaber, calaboose, calabooses, calabozo, calabrasella, calabrese, calabrian, calabrians, calabur, calade, caladium, caladiums, calahan, calais, calaite, calalu, calamanco, calamancoes, calamancos, calamander, calamansi, calamar, calamariaceous, calamarian, calamaries, calamarioid, calamarmar, calamaroid, calamars, calamary, calambac, calambour, calami, calamiferious, calamiferous, calamiform, calaminaris, calaminary, calamine, calamined, calamines, calamining, calamint, calamints, calamistral, calamistrate, calamistrum, calamite, calamitean, calamites, calamities, calamitoid, calamitous, calamitously, calamitousness, calamity, calamity's, calamondin, calamumi, calamus, calander, calando, calandre, calandria, calangay, calanid, calanque, calantas, calanthe, calapite, calapitte, calascione, calash, calashes, calastic, calathea, calathi, calathian, calathidia, calathidium, calathiform, calathisci, calathiscus, calathos, calaththi, calathus, calavance, calaverite, calbroben, calc, calcaemia, calcaire, calcanea, calcaneal, calcanean, calcanei, calcaneoastragalar, calcaneoastragaloid, calcaneocuboid, calcaneofibular, calcaneonavicular, calcaneoplantar, calcaneoscaphoid, calcaneotibial, calcaneum, calcaneus, calcannea, calcannei, calcar, calcarate, calcarated, calcareoargillaceous, calcareobituminous, calcareocorneous, calcareosiliceous, calcareosulphurous, calcareous, calcareously, calcareousness, calcaria, calcariferous, calcariform, calcarine, calcarium, calcars, calcate, calcavella, calceate, calced, calcedon, calcedony, calceiform, calcemia, calceolaria, calceolate, calceolately, calces, calceus, calchas, calche, calci, calcic, calciclase, calcicole, calcicolous, calcicosis, calciferol, calciferous, calcific, calcification, calcified, calcifies, calciform, calcifugal, calcifuge, calcifugous, calcify, calcifying, calcigenous, calcigerous, calcimeter, calcimine, calcimined, calciminer, calcimines, calcimining, calcinable, calcinate, calcination, calcinator, calcinatory, calcine, calcined, calciner, calcines, calcining, calcinize, calcino, calcinosis, calciobiotite, calciocarnotite, calcioferrite, calcioscheelite, calciovolborthite, calcipexy, calciphile, calciphilia, calciphilic, calciphilous, calciphobe, calciphobic, calciphobous, calciphylactic, calciphylactically, calciphylaxis, calciphyre, calciprivic, calcisponge, calcite, calcites, calcitestaceous, calcitic, calcitonin, calcitrant, calcitrate, calcitration, calcitreation, calcium, calciums, calcivorous, calcographer, calcographic, calcography, calcomp, calcrete, calcsinter, calcspar, calcspars, calctufa, calctufas, calctuff, calctuffs, calculabilities, calculability, calculable, calculableness, calculably, calcular, calculary, calculate, calculated, calculatedly, calculatedness, calculates, calculating, calculatingly, calculation, calculational, calculations, calculative, calculator, calculator's, calculators, calculatory, calculer, calculi, calculiform, calculifrage, calculist, calculous, calculus, calculuses, calcutta, caldadaria, caldaria, caldarium, calden, caldera, calderas, calderium, calderon, caldron, caldrons, calean, calebite, calebites, caleche, caleches, caledonian, caledonite, calef, calefacient, calefaction, calefactive, calefactor, calefactories, calefactory, calefy, calelectric, calelectrical, calelectricity, calembour, calenda, calendal, calendar, calendar's, calendared, calendarer, calendarial, calendarian, calendaric, calendaring, calendarist, calendars, calendas, calender, calendered, calenderer, calendering, calenders, calendric, calendrical, calendry, calends, calendula, calendulas, calendulin, calentural, calenture, calentured, calenturing, calenturish, calenturist, calepin, calesa, calesas, calescence, calescent, calesero, calesin, calf, calfbound, calfdozer, calfhood, calfish, calfkill, calfless, calflike, calfling, calfret, calfs, calfskin, calfskins, calgary, calgon, caliban, caliber, calibered, calibers, calibogus, calibrate, calibrated, calibrater, calibrates, calibrating, calibration, calibrations, calibrator, calibrators, calibre, calibred, calibres, caliburn, calic, calicate, calices, caliche, caliches, caliciform, calicle, calicles, calico, calicoback, calicoed, calicoes, calicos, calicular, caliculate, caliculi, caliculus, calid, calidity, caliduct, calif, califate, califates, california, californian, californiana, californians, californicus, californite, californium, califs, caliga, caligate, caligated, caligation, caliginosity, caliginous, caliginously, caliginousness, caligo, caligrapher, caligraphy, caligulism, calili, calimanco, calimancos, calin, calina, calinda, calindas, caline, calinut, caliological, caliologist, caliology, calipash, calipashes, calipee, calipees, caliper, calipered, caliperer, calipering, calipers, calipeva, caliph, caliphal, caliphate, caliphates, caliphs, caliphship, calippic, calisaya, calisayas, calistheneum, calisthenic, calisthenical, calisthenics, caliver, calix, calixtin, calk, calkage, calked, calker, calkers, calkin, calking, calkins, calks, call, calla, callable, callaesthetic, callainite, callais, callaloo, callaloos, callan, callans, callant, callants, callas, callat, callate, callback, callbacks, callboy, callboys, called, caller, callers, calles, callet, callets, calli, callid, callidity, callidness, calligram, calligraph, calligrapha, calligrapher, calligraphers, calligraphic, calligraphical, calligraphically, calligraphist, calligraphy, calling, callings, calliope, calliopean, calliopes, calliophone, calliopsis, callipash, callipee, callipees, calliper, callipered, calliperer, callipering, callipers, calliphorid, calliphorine, callippic, callipygian, callipygous, callisection, callisteia, callisthenic, callisthenics, callisto, callithrix, callithump, callithumpian, callitrichaceous, callitriche, callitype, callityped, callityping, callo, calloo, callop, callosal, callose, calloses, callosities, callosity, callosomarginal, callosum, callot, callous, calloused, callouses, callousing, callously, callousness, callout, callow, callower, callowest, callowman, callowness, calls, callum, callus, callused, calluses, callusing, calm, calmant, calmative, calmato, calmecac, calmed, calmer, calmest, calmier, calmierer, calmiest, calming, calmingly, calmly, calmness, calmnesses, calms, calmy, calodaemon, calodemon, calodemonial, calogram, calography, calomba, calombigas, calombo, calomel, calomels, calomorphic, calool, calor, caloreceptor, calorescence, calorescent, caloric, calorically, caloricity, calorics, caloriduct, calorie, calorie's, calories, calorifacient, calorific, calorifical, calorifically, calorification, calorifics, calorifier, calorify, calorigenic, calorimeter, calorimeters, calorimetric, calorimetrical, calorimetrically, calorimetry, calorimotor, caloris, calorisator, calorist, calorize, calorized, calorizer, calorizes, calorizing, calory, calosoma, calotermitid, calotin, calotte, calottes, calotype, calotypic, calotypist, caloyer, caloyers, calp, calpac, calpack, calpacked, calpacks, calpacs, calpolli, calpul, calpulli, calque, calqued, calques, calquing, cals, calsouns, caltha, calthrop, calthrops, caltrap, caltraps, caltrop, caltrops, calumba, calumet, calumets, calumnia, calumniate, calumniated, calumniates, calumniating, calumniation, calumniations, calumniative, calumniator, calumniators, calumniatory, calumnies, calumnious, calumniously, calumniousness, calumny, caluptra, calusar, calutron, calutrons, calvados, calvadoses, calvaire, calvaria, calvarial, calvarias, calvaries, calvarium, calvary, calve, calved, calver, calves, calvin, calving, calvinian, calvinism, calvinist, calvinistic, calvinists, calvinize, calvish, calvities, calvity, calvous, calvus, calx, calxes, calybite, calycanth, calycanthaceous, calycanthemous, calycanthemy, calycanthin, calycanthine, calycanthus, calycate, calyceal, calyceraceous, calyces, calyciferous, calycifloral, calyciflorate, calyciflorous, calyciform, calycinal, calycine, calycle, calycled, calycles, calycli, calycoid, calycoideous, calycophoran, calycozoan, calycozoic, calycozoon, calycular, calyculate, calyculated, calycule, calyculi, calyculus, calymma, calyon, calyphyomy, calypsist, calypso, calypsoes, calypsonian, calypsos, calypter, calypters, calyptoblastic, calyptra, calyptras, calyptrate, calyptriform, calyptrimorphous, calyptro, calyptrogen, calyx, calyxes, calzada, calzone, calzoneras, calzones, calzoons, cam, camaca, camacey, camachile, camagon, camaieu, camail, camaile, camailed, camails, camaka, camaldolite, camalig, camalote, caman, camanay, camanchaca, camansi, camara, camarada, camarade, camaraderie, camarasaurus, camarera, camarilla, camarillas, camarin, camarine, camaron, camas, camases, camass, camasses, camata, camatina, camauro, camauros, camay, camb, cambaye, camber, cambered, cambering, cambers, cambia, cambial, cambiata, cambibia, cambiform, cambio, cambiogenetic, cambion, cambism, cambisms, cambist, cambistry, cambists, cambium, cambiums, camblet, cambodia, cambodian, cambodians, camboge, cambogia, cambogias, camboose, cambouis, cambrel, cambresine, cambrian, cambric, cambricleaf, cambrics, cambridge, cambuca, camden, came, cameist, camel, camel's, camelback, cameleer, cameleers, cameleon, camelhair, camelia, camelias, cameline, camelion, camelish, camelishness, camelkeeper, camellia, camellias, camellike, camellin, camelman, cameloid, camelopard, camelopardel, camelopards, camelot, camelry, camels, camembert, camenes, cameo, cameoed, cameograph, cameography, cameoing, cameos, camera, camera's, camerae, cameral, cameralism, cameralist, cameralistic, cameralistics, cameraman, cameramen, cameras, camerate, camerated, cameration, camerawork, camerier, cameriera, camerieri, camerine, camerist, camerlengo, camerlengos, camerlingo, camerlingos, cameronian, cameronians, cameroon, cameroonian, cameroonians, camery, cames, camestres, camias, camiknickers, camilla, camillus, camino, camion, camions, camis, camisa, camisade, camisades, camisado, camisadoes, camisados, camisard, camisas, camiscia, camise, camises, camisia, camisias, camisole, camisoles, camister, camize, camla, camlet, camleted, camleteen, camletine, camleting, camlets, camletted, camletting, cammas, cammed, cammock, cammocky, camoca, camogie, camois, camomile, camomiles, camooch, camoodi, camoodie, camorra, camorras, camorrism, camorrista, camorristi, camote, camoudie, camouflage, camouflageable, camouflaged, camouflager, camouflagers, camouflages, camouflagic, camouflaging, camouflet, camoufleur, camoufleurs, camp, campagi, campagna, campagne, campagnol, campagnols, campagus, campaign, campaigned, campaigner, campaigners, campaigning, campaigns, campal, campana, campane, campanella, campanero, campania, campaniform, campanile, campaniles, campanili, campaniliform, campanilla, campanini, campanist, campanistic, campanologer, campanological, campanologically, campanologist, campanologists, campanology, campanula, campanulaceous, campanular, campanularian, campanulate, campanulated, campanulous, campbell, campbellism, campbellisms, campbellite, campbellites, campcraft, campeche, camped, campement, campephagine, camper, campers, campership, campesino, campesinos, campestral, campestrian, campfight, campfire, campfires, campground, campgrounds, camphane, camphanic, camphanone, camphanyl, camphene, camphenes, camphine, camphines, camphire, camphires, campho, camphocarboxylic, camphoid, camphol, campholic, campholide, camphols, campholytic, camphor, camphoraceous, camphorate, camphorated, camphorates, camphorating, camphoric, camphorize, camphorone, camphoronic, camphoroyl, camphorphorone, camphors, camphorweed, camphorwood, camphory, camphoryl, camphylene, campi, campier, campiest, campilan, campily, campimeter, campimetrical, campimetry, campiness, camping, campings, campion, campions, campit, cample, campman, campmaster, campo, campodean, campodeid, campodeiform, campodeoid, campody, campong, campongs, campoo, campoody, camporee, camporees, campos, campout, camps, campshed, campshedding, campsheeting, campshot, campsite, campsites, campstool, campstools, camptodrome, camptonite, campulitropal, campulitropous, campus, campus's, campuses, campusses, campward, campy, campylite, campylodrome, campylometer, campylospermous, campylotropal, campylotropous, cams, camshach, camshachle, camshaft, camshafts, camstane, camsteary, camsteery, camstone, camstrary, camuning, camus, camuse, camused, camuses, camwood, can, can's, can't, canaan, canaanite, canaanites, canaba, canabae, canacuas, canada, canadian, canadianisms, canadians, canadine, canadite, canadol, canafistola, canafistolo, canafistula, canafistulo, canaglia, canaigre, canaille, canailles, canajong, canakin, canakins, canal, canal's, canalage, canalatura, canalboat, canale, canaled, canaler, canales, canalete, canali, canalicular, canaliculate, canaliculated, canaliculation, canaliculi, canaliculization, canaliculus, canaliferous, canaliform, canaling, canalis, canalisation, canalise, canalised, canalises, canalising, canalization, canalizations, canalize, canalized, canalizes, canalizing, canalla, canalled, canaller, canallers, canalling, canalman, canals, canalside, canamo, canap, canape, canapes, canapina, canard, canards, canari, canaries, canarin, canarine, canary, canary's, canasta, canastas, canaster, canaut, canavalin, canberra, canc, cancan, cancans, canccelli, cancel, cancelability, cancelable, cancelation, canceled, canceleer, canceler, cancelers, cancelier, canceling, cancellability, cancellable, cancellarian, cancellarius, cancellate, cancellated, cancellation, cancellation's, cancellations, cancelled, canceller, cancelli, cancelling, cancellous, cancellus, cancelment, cancels, cancer, cancer's, cancerate, cancerated, cancerating, canceration, cancerdrops, cancered, cancerigenic, cancerin, cancerism, cancerite, cancerization, cancerogenic, cancerophobe, cancerophobia, cancerous, cancerously, cancerousness, cancerphobia, cancerroot, cancers, cancerweed, cancerwort, canch, cancha, canchalagua, canchas, canchito, cancion, cancionero, canciones, cancrid, cancriform, cancrine, cancrinite, cancrisocial, cancrivorous, cancrizans, cancroid, cancroids, cancrophagous, cancrum, cancrums, cand, candareen, candela, candelabra, candelabras, candelabrum, candelabrums, candelas, candelilla, candency, candent, candescence, candescent, candescently, candid, candida, candidacies, candidacy, candidas, candidate, candidate's, candidated, candidates, candidateship, candidating, candidature, candidatures, candide, candider, candidest, candidiasis, candidly, candidness, candidnesses, candids, candied, candiel, candier, candies, candify, candil, candiru, candite, candle, candleball, candlebeam, candleberries, candleberry, candlebomb, candlebox, candled, candlefish, candlefishes, candleholder, candlelight, candlelighted, candlelighter, candlelighting, candlelit, candlemaker, candlemaking, candlemas, candlenut, candlepin, candlepins, candlepower, candler, candlerent, candlers, candles, candleshine, candleshrift, candlesnuffer, candlestand, candlestick, candlestick's, candlesticked, candlesticks, candlestickward, candlewaster, candlewasting, candlewick, candlewicking, candlewicks, candlewood, candlewright, candling, candock, candolleaceous, candor, candors, candour, candours, candroy, candroys, canduc, candy, candyfloss, candyh, candying, candylike, candymaker, candymaking, candys, candystick, candytuft, candyweed, cane, canebrake, canebrakes, caned, canel, canela, canelas, canelike, canell, canella, canellaceous, canellas, canelle, canelo, canelos, caneology, canephor, canephora, canephorae, canephore, canephori, canephoroe, canephoroi, canephoros, canephors, canephorus, canephroi, canepin, caner, caners, canes, canescence, canescene, canescent, caneton, canette, caneva, caneware, canewares, canewise, canework, canezou, canfield, canfieldite, canfields, canful, canfuls, cangan, cangenet, cangia, cangle, cangler, cangue, cangues, cangy, canham, canhoop, canicide, canicola, canicula, canicular, canicule, canid, canids, canikin, canikins, canille, caninal, canine, canines, caning, caniniform, caninities, caninity, caninus, canion, canioned, canions, canistel, canister, canisters, canities, canjac, cank, canker, cankerberry, cankerbird, cankereat, cankered, cankeredly, cankeredness, cankerflower, cankerfret, cankering, cankerous, cankerroot, cankers, cankerweed, cankerworm, cankerworms, cankerwort, cankery, canli, canmaker, canmaking, canman, cann, canna, cannabic, cannabidiol, cannabin, cannabinaceous, cannabine, cannabinol, cannabins, cannabis, cannabises, cannabism, cannaceous, cannach, cannaled, cannalling, cannas, cannat, canned, cannel, cannelated, cannele, cannellate, cannellated, cannelle, cannelloni, cannelon, cannelons, cannels, cannelure, cannelured, cannequin, canner, canner's, canneries, canners, cannery, cannet, cannetille, cannibal, cannibal's, cannibalean, cannibalic, cannibalish, cannibalism, cannibalistic, cannibalistically, cannibality, cannibalization, cannibalize, cannibalized, cannibalizes, cannibalizing, cannibally, cannibals, cannie, cannier, canniest, cannikin, cannikins, cannily, canniness, canning, cannings, cannister, cannister's, cannisters, cannoli, cannon, cannon's, cannonade, cannonaded, cannonades, cannonading, cannonarchy, cannonball, cannonballed, cannonballing, cannonballs, cannoned, cannoneer, cannoneering, cannoneers, cannonier, cannoning, cannonism, cannonproof, cannonries, cannonry, cannons, cannophori, cannot, cannula, cannulae, cannular, cannulas, cannulate, cannulated, cannulating, cannulation, canny, canoe, canoe's, canoed, canoeing, canoeist, canoeists, canoeload, canoeman, canoes, canoewood, canoing, canon, canon's, canoncito, canones, canoness, canonesses, canonic, canonical, canonicalization, canonicalize, canonicalized, canonicalizes, canonicalizing, canonically, canonicalness, canonicals, canonicate, canonici, canonicity, canonics, canonisation, canonise, canonised, canoniser, canonises, canonising, canonist, canonistic, canonistical, canonists, canonizant, canonization, canonizations, canonize, canonized, canonizer, canonizes, canonizing, canonlike, canonries, canonry, canons, canonship, canoodle, canoodled, canoodler, canoodles, canoodling, canopic, canopid, canopied, canopies, canopus, canopy, canopying, canorous, canorously, canorousness, canos, canotier, canreply, canroy, canroyer, cans, cansful, canso, cansos, canst, canstick, cant, cantab, cantabank, cantabile, cantabrigian, cantador, cantala, cantalas, cantalever, cantalite, cantaliver, cantaloup, cantaloupe, cantaloupes, cantando, cantankerous, cantankerously, cantankerousness, cantar, cantara, cantare, cantaro, cantata, cantatas, cantate, cantation, cantative, cantator, cantatory, cantatrice, cantatrices, cantatrici, cantboard, cantdog, cantdogs, canted, canteen, canteens, cantefable, cantel, canter, canterburian, canterburies, canterbury, cantered, canterelle, canterer, cantering, canters, canthal, canthari, cantharic, cantharidal, cantharidate, cantharidated, cantharidating, cantharidean, cantharides, cantharidian, cantharidin, cantharidism, cantharidize, cantharidized, cantharidizing, cantharis, cantharophilous, cantharus, canthathari, canthectomy, canthi, canthitis, cantholysis, canthoplasty, canthorrhaphy, canthotomy, canthus, canthuthi, cantic, canticle, canticles, cantico, cantiga, cantil, cantilated, cantilating, cantilena, cantilene, cantilenes, cantilever, cantilevered, cantilevering, cantilevers, cantillate, cantillated, cantillating, cantillation, cantily, cantina, cantinas, cantiness, canting, cantingly, cantingness, cantinier, cantino, cantion, cantish, cantle, cantles, cantlet, cantline, cantling, canto, canton, canton's, cantonal, cantonalism, cantoned, cantoner, cantonese, cantoning, cantonize, cantonment, cantonments, cantons, cantoon, cantor, cantor's, cantoral, cantoria, cantorial, cantoris, cantorous, cantors, cantorship, cantos, cantraip, cantraips, cantrap, cantraps, cantred, cantref, cantrip, cantrips, cants, cantus, cantut, cantuta, cantwise, canty, canuck, canula, canulae, canular, canulas, canulate, canulated, canulates, canulating, canun, canvas, canvas's, canvasado, canvasback, canvasbacks, canvased, canvaser, canvasers, canvases, canvasing, canvaslike, canvasman, canvass, canvassed, canvasser, canvassers, canvasses, canvassing, canvassy, cany, canyon, canyon's, canyons, canyonside, canzo, canzon, canzona, canzonas, canzone, canzones, canzonet, canzonets, canzonetta, canzoni, canzos, caoba, caoine, caon, caoutchin, caoutchouc, caoutchoucin, cap, cap's, capa, capabilities, capability, capability's, capable, capableness, capabler, capablest, capably, capacify, capacious, capaciously, capaciousness, capacitance, capacitances, capacitate, capacitated, capacitates, capacitating, capacitation, capacitations, capacitative, capacitativly, capacitator, capacities, capacitive, capacitively, capacitor, capacitor's, capacitors, capacity, capanna, capanne, caparison, caparisoned, caparisoning, caparisons, capataces, capataz, capax, capcase, cape, capeador, capeadores, capeadors, caped, capel, capelan, capelans, capelet, capelets, capelin, capeline, capelins, capella, capellane, capellet, capelline, capelocracy, caper, caperbush, capercaillie, capercailye, capercailzie, capercally, capercut, caperdewsie, capered, caperer, caperers, capering, caperingly, capernaite, capernoited, capernoitie, capernoity, capernutie, capers, capersome, capersomeness, caperwort, capes, capeskin, capeskins, capetian, capetown, capette, capeweed, capewise, capework, capeworks, capful, capfuls, caph, caphar, capharnaism, caphite, caphs, capias, capiases, capiatur, capibara, capicha, capilaceous, capillaceous, capillaire, capillament, capillarectasia, capillaries, capillarily, capillarimeter, capillariness, capillariomotor, capillarities, capillaritis, capillarity, capillary, capillation, capillatus, capilli, capilliculture, capilliform, capillitia, capillitial, capillitium, capillose, capillus, capilotade, caping, capistrate, capita, capital, capitaldom, capitaled, capitaling, capitalisable, capitalise, capitalised, capitaliser, capitalising, capitalism, capitalist, capitalist's, capitalistic, capitalistically, capitalists, capitalizable, capitalization, capitalizations, capitalize, capitalized, capitalizer, capitalizers, capitalizes, capitalizing, capitally, capitalness, capitals, capitan, capitana, capitano, capitare, capitasti, capitate, capitated, capitatim, capitation, capitations, capitative, capitatum, capite, capiteaux, capitella, capitellar, capitellate, capitelliform, capitellum, capitle, capitol, capitol's, capitoline, capitols, capitoul, capitoulate, capitula, capitulant, capitular, capitularies, capitularly, capitulars, capitulary, capitulate, capitulated, capitulates, capitulating, capitulation, capitulations, capitulator, capitulatory, capituliform, capitulum, capiturlary, capivi, capkin, caplan, capless, caplet, caplets, caplin, capling, caplins, caplock, capmaker, capmakers, capmaking, capman, capmint, capnomancy, capnomor, capo, capoc, capocchia, capoche, capomo, capon, caponata, caponatas, capone, caponette, caponier, caponiere, caponiers, caponisation, caponise, caponised, caponiser, caponising, caponization, caponize, caponized, caponizer, caponizes, caponizing, caponniere, capons, caporal, caporals, capos, capot, capotasto, capotastos, capote, capotes, capouch, capouches, cappadine, cappadochio, cappae, cappagh, capparid, capparidaceous, capped, cappelenite, cappella, cappelletti, capper, cappers, cappie, cappier, cappiest, capping, cappings, capple, cappuccino, cappy, caprate, caprelline, capreol, capreolar, capreolary, capreolate, capreoline, capreomycin, capretto, capric, capriccetto, capriccettos, capricci, capriccio, capriccios, capriccioso, caprice, caprices, capricious, capriciously, capriciousness, capricorn, capricorns, caprid, caprificate, caprification, caprificator, caprifig, caprifigs, caprifoil, caprifole, caprifoliaceous, caprifolium, capriform, caprigenous, caprimulgine, caprin, caprine, caprinic, capriole, caprioled, caprioles, caprioling, capriped, capripede, capris, caprizant, caproate, caprock, caprocks, caproic, caproin, capron, caprone, capronic, capronyl, caproyl, capryl, caprylate, caprylene, caprylic, caprylin, caprylone, caprylyl, caps, capsa, capsaicin, capsheaf, capshore, capsian, capsicin, capsicins, capsicum, capsicums, capsid, capsidal, capsids, capsizable, capsizal, capsize, capsized, capsizes, capsizing, capsomer, capsomere, capsomers, capstan, capstans, capstone, capstones, capsula, capsulae, capsular, capsulate, capsulated, capsulation, capsule, capsulectomy, capsuled, capsuler, capsules, capsuliferous, capsuliform, capsuligerous, capsuling, capsulitis, capsulize, capsulized, capsulizing, capsulociliary, capsulogenous, capsulolenticular, capsulopupillary, capsulorrhaphy, capsulotome, capsulotomy, capsumin, captacula, captaculum, captain, captaincies, captaincy, captained, captainess, captaining, captainly, captainries, captainry, captains, captainship, captainships, captan, captance, captandum, captans, captate, captation, caption, caption's, captioned, captioning, captionless, captions, captious, captiously, captiousness, captivance, captivate, captivated, captivately, captivates, captivating, captivatingly, captivation, captivative, captivator, captivators, captivatrix, captive, captive's, captived, captives, captiving, captivities, captivity, captor, captor's, captors, captress, capturable, capture, captured, capturer, capturers, captures, capturing, capuche, capuched, capuches, capuchin, capuchins, capucine, capulet, capuli, capulin, caput, caputium, capybara, capybaras, caque, caquet, caqueterie, caqueteuse, caqueteuses, caquetoire, caquetoires, car, car's, carabao, carabaos, carabeen, carabid, carabidan, carabideous, carabidoid, carabids, carabin, carabine, carabineer, carabiner, carabinero, carabineros, carabines, carabinier, carabiniere, carabinieri, carabins, caraboa, caraboid, carabus, caracal, caracals, caracara, caracaras, caracas, carack, caracks, caraco, caracoa, caracol, caracole, caracoled, caracoler, caracoles, caracoli, caracoling, caracolite, caracolled, caracoller, caracolling, caracols, caracora, caracore, caract, caracter, caracul, caraculs, carafe, carafes, carafon, caragana, caraganas, carageen, carageens, caragheen, caraguata, caraibe, caraipe, caraipi, carajo, carajura, caramba, carambola, carambole, caramboled, caramboling, caramel, caramelan, caramelen, caramelin, caramelisation, caramelise, caramelised, caramelising, caramelization, caramelize, caramelized, caramelizes, caramelizing, caramels, caramoussal, carancha, carancho, caranda, caranday, carane, carangid, carangids, carangin, carangoid, caranna, caranx, carap, carapa, carapace, carapaced, carapaces, carapacial, carapacic, carapato, carapax, carapaxes, carapine, carapo, carassow, carassows, carat, caratacus, caratch, carate, carates, carats, carauna, caraunda, caravan, caravan's, caravaned, caravaneer, caravaner, caravaning, caravanist, caravanned, caravanner, caravanning, caravans, caravansaries, caravansary, caravanserai, caravanserial, caravel, caravelle, caravels, caraway, caraways, carbachol, carbacidometer, carbamate, carbamic, carbamide, carbamidine, carbamido, carbamine, carbamino, carbamoyl, carbamyl, carbamyls, carbanil, carbanilic, carbanilid, carbanilide, carbanion, carbarn, carbarns, carbaryl, carbaryls, carbasus, carbazic, carbazide, carbazin, carbazine, carbazole, carbazylic, carbeen, carbene, carberry, carbethoxy, carbethoxyl, carbide, carbides, carbimide, carbin, carbine, carbineer, carbineers, carbines, carbinol, carbinols, carbinyl, carbo, carboazotine, carbocer, carbocinchomeronic, carbocyclic, carbodiimide, carbodynamite, carbogelatin, carbohemoglobin, carbohydrase, carbohydrate, carbohydrates, carbohydraturia, carbohydrazide, carbohydride, carbohydrogen, carbolate, carbolated, carbolating, carbolfuchsin, carbolic, carbolics, carboline, carbolineate, carbolise, carbolised, carbolising, carbolize, carbolized, carbolizes, carbolizing, carboluria, carbolxylol, carbomethene, carbomethoxy, carbomethoxyl, carbomycin, carbon, carbon's, carbona, carbonaceous, carbonade, carbonado, carbonadoed, carbonadoes, carbonadoing, carbonados, carbonari, carbonatation, carbonate, carbonated, carbonates, carbonating, carbonation, carbonatization, carbonator, carbonators, carbondale, carbone, carboned, carbonemia, carbonero, carbones, carbonic, carbonide, carboniferous, carbonification, carbonify, carbonigenous, carbonimeter, carbonimide, carbonisable, carbonisation, carbonise, carbonised, carboniser, carbonising, carbonite, carbonitride, carbonium, carbonizable, carbonization, carbonize, carbonized, carbonizer, carbonizers, carbonizes, carbonizing, carbonless, carbonometer, carbonometry, carbonous, carbons, carbonuria, carbonyl, carbonylate, carbonylated, carbonylating, carbonylation, carbonylene, carbonylic, carbonyls, carbophilous, carbora, carboras, carborundum, carbosilicate, carbostyril, carboxide, carboxy, carboxyhemoglobin, carboxyl, carboxylase, carboxylate, carboxylated, carboxylating, carboxylation, carboxylic, carboxyls, carboxypeptidase, carboy, carboyed, carboys, carbro, carbromal, carbuilder, carbuncle, carbuncled, carbuncles, carbuncular, carbunculation, carbungi, carburan, carburant, carburate, carburated, carburating, carburation, carburator, carbure, carburet, carburetant, carbureted, carbureter, carburetest, carbureting, carburetion, carburetor, carburetors, carburets, carburetted, carburetter, carburetting, carburettor, carburisation, carburise, carburised, carburiser, carburising, carburization, carburize, carburized, carburizer, carburizes, carburizing, carburometer, carby, carbyl, carbylamine, carcajou, carcajous, carcake, carcan, carcanet, carcaneted, carcanets, carcanetted, carcase, carcased, carcases, carcasing, carcass, carcass's, carcassed, carcasses, carcassing, carcassless, carceag, carcel, carcels, carcer, carceral, carcerate, carcerated, carcerating, carceration, carcerist, carchariid, carcharioid, carcharodont, carcinemia, carcinogen, carcinogeneses, carcinogenesis, carcinogenic, carcinogenicity, carcinogens, carcinoid, carcinological, carcinologist, carcinology, carcinolysin, carcinolytic, carcinoma, carcinomas, carcinomata, carcinomatoid, carcinomatosis, carcinomatous, carcinomorphic, carcinophagous, carcinophobia, carcinopolypus, carcinosarcoma, carcinosarcomas, carcinosarcomata, carcinosis, carcinus, carcoon, card, cardaissin, cardamine, cardamom, cardamoms, cardamon, cardamons, cardamum, cardamums, cardanol, cardboard, cardcase, cardcases, cardcastle, cardecu, carded, cardel, carder, carders, cardholder, cardholders, cardhouse, cardia, cardiac, cardiacal, cardiacean, cardiacle, cardiacs, cardiae, cardiagra, cardiagram, cardiagraph, cardiagraphy, cardial, cardialgia, cardialgic, cardialgy, cardiameter, cardiamorphia, cardianesthesia, cardianeuria, cardiant, cardiaplegia, cardiarctia, cardias, cardiasthenia, cardiasthma, cardiataxia, cardiatomy, cardiatrophia, cardiauxe, cardicentesis, cardiectasis, cardiectomize, cardiectomy, cardielcosis, cardiemphraxia, cardiform, cardigan, cardigans, cardin, cardinal, cardinalate, cardinalated, cardinalates, cardinalfish, cardinalfishes, cardinalic, cardinalism, cardinalist, cardinalitial, cardinalitian, cardinalities, cardinality, cardinality's, cardinally, cardinals, cardinalship, cardines, carding, cardings, cardioaccelerator, cardioarterial, cardioblast, cardiocarpum, cardiocele, cardiocentesis, cardiocirrhosis, cardioclasia, cardioclasis, cardiod, cardiodilator, cardiodynamics, cardiodynia, cardiodysesthesia, cardiodysneuria, cardiogenesis, cardiogenic, cardiogram, cardiograms, cardiograph, cardiographer, cardiographic, cardiographies, cardiographs, cardiography, cardiohepatic, cardioid, cardioids, cardiokinetic, cardiolith, cardiologic, cardiological, cardiologies, cardiologist, cardiologists, cardiology, cardiolysis, cardiomalacia, cardiomegalia, cardiomegaly, cardiomelanosis, cardiometer, cardiometric, cardiometry, cardiomotility, cardiomyoliposis, cardiomyomalacia, cardiomyopathy, cardioncus, cardionecrosis, cardionephric, cardioneural, cardioneurosis, cardionosus, cardioparplasis, cardiopath, cardiopathic, cardiopathy, cardiopericarditis, cardiophobe, cardiophobia, cardiophrenia, cardioplasty, cardioplegia, cardiopneumatic, cardiopneumograph, cardioptosis, cardiopulmonary, cardiopuncture, cardiopyloric, cardiorenal, cardiorespiratory, cardiorrhaphy, cardiorrheuma, cardiorrhexis, cardioschisis, cardiosclerosis, cardioscope, cardiospasm, cardiosphygmogram, cardiosphygmograph, cardiosymphysis, cardiotherapies, cardiotherapy, cardiotomy, cardiotonic, cardiotoxic, cardiotrophia, cardiotrophotherapy, cardiovascular, cardiovisceral, cardipaludism, cardipericarditis, cardisophistical, cardita, carditic, carditis, carditises, cardlike, cardmaker, cardmaking, cardo, cardol, cardon, cardona, cardoncillo, cardooer, cardoon, cardoons, cardophagus, cardosanto, cardplayer, cardplaying, cardroom, cards, cardshark, cardsharp, cardsharper, cardsharping, cardsharps, cardstock, carduaceous, cardueline, carduus, care, carecloth, cared, careen, careenage, careened, careener, careeners, careening, careens, career, career's, careered, careerer, careerers, careering, careeringly, careerism, careerist, careeristic, careers, carefox, carefree, carefreeness, careful, carefull, carefuller, carefullest, carefully, carefulness, careless, carelessly, carelessness, careme, carene, carer, carers, cares, caress, caressable, caressant, caressed, caresser, caressers, caresses, caressing, caressingly, caressive, caressively, carest, caret, caretake, caretaken, caretaker, caretakers, caretakes, caretaking, caretook, carets, careworn, carex, carey, careys, carf, carfare, carfares, carfax, carfloat, carfour, carfuffle, carfuffled, carfuffling, carful, carfuls, carga, cargador, cargadores, cargason, cargo, cargoes, cargoose, cargos, cargued, carhop, carhops, carhouse, cariacine, cariama, carib, cariban, caribbean, caribbeans, caribe, caribed, caribes, caribing, caribou, caribous, caricaceous, caricatura, caricaturable, caricatural, caricature, caricatured, caricatures, caricaturing, caricaturist, caricaturists, carices, caricetum, caricographer, caricography, caricologist, caricology, caricous, carid, caridean, carideer, caridoid, caried, carien, caries, cariform, carillon, carilloneur, carillonned, carillonneur, carillonneurs, carillonning, carillons, carina, carinae, carinal, carinaria, carinas, carinate, carinated, carination, caring, cariniform, carinula, carinulate, carinule, carioca, cariocas, cariogenic, cariole, carioles, carioling, cariosity, carious, cariousness, caripeta, carisoprodol, caritas, caritative, carites, caritive, carity, cark, carked, carking, carkingly, carkled, carks, carl, carlage, carle, carles, carless, carlet, carli, carlie, carlin, carlina, carline, carlines, carling, carlings, carlino, carlins, carlish, carlishness, carlism, carlist, carlo, carload, carloading, carloadings, carloads, carlock, carlot, carlovingian, carls, carlylism, carmagnole, carmagnoles, carmaker, carmakers, carmalum, carman, carmel, carmele, carmelite, carmeloite, carmen, carmetta, carminate, carminative, carminatives, carmine, carmines, carminette, carminic, carminite, carminophilous, carmoisin, carmot, carn, carnac, carnage, carnaged, carnages, carnal, carnalism, carnalite, carnalities, carnality, carnalize, carnalized, carnalizing, carnallite, carnally, carnalness, carnaptious, carnary, carnassial, carnate, carnation, carnationed, carnationist, carnations, carnauba, carnaubas, carnaubic, carnaubyl, carne, carneau, carnegie, carnel, carnelian, carnelians, carneol, carneole, carneous, carnet, carnets, carney, carneyed, carneys, carnic, carnie, carnied, carnies, carniferous, carniferrin, carnifex, carnifexes, carnification, carnifices, carnificial, carnified, carnifies, carniform, carnify, carnifying, carnitine, carnival, carnival's, carnivaler, carnivalesque, carnivaller, carnivallike, carnivals, carnivora, carnivoracity, carnivoral, carnivore, carnivores, carnivorism, carnivority, carnivorous, carnivorously, carnivorousness, carnose, carnosin, carnosine, carnosities, carnosity, carnotite, carnous, carns, carny, caroa, caroach, caroaches, carob, caroba, carobs, caroch, caroche, caroches, caroigne, carol, carol's, carole, carolean, caroled, caroler, carolers, caroli, carolin, carolina, carolina's, carolinas, caroline, carolines, caroling, carolingian, carolinian, carolinians, carolitic, carolled, caroller, carollers, carolling, carols, carolus, caroluses, carolyn, carom, carombolette, caromed, caromel, caroming, caroms, carone, caronic, caroome, caroon, carosella, carosse, carot, caroteel, carotene, carotenes, carotenoid, carotic, carotid, carotidal, carotidean, carotids, carotin, carotinaemia, carotinemia, carotinoid, carotins, carotol, carotte, carouba, caroubier, carousal, carousals, carouse, caroused, carousel, carousels, carouser, carousers, carouses, carousing, carousingly, carp, carpaine, carpal, carpale, carpalia, carpals, carpe, carped, carpel, carpellary, carpellate, carpellum, carpels, carpent, carpenter, carpenter's, carpentered, carpentering, carpenters, carpentership, carpenterworm, carpentry, carper, carpers, carpet, carpetbag, carpetbagged, carpetbagger, carpetbaggers, carpetbaggery, carpetbagging, carpetbaggism, carpetbagism, carpetbags, carpetbeater, carpeted, carpeting, carpetlayer, carpetless, carpetmaker, carpetmaking, carpetmonger, carpets, carpetweb, carpetweed, carpetwork, carpetwoven, carpholite, carphology, carphosiderite, carpi, carpid, carpidium, carpincho, carping, carpingly, carpings, carpintero, carpitis, carpium, carpocace, carpocarpal, carpocephala, carpocephalum, carpocerite, carpocervical, carpocratian, carpogam, carpogamy, carpogenic, carpogenous, carpognia, carpogone, carpogonia, carpogonial, carpogonium, carpolite, carpolith, carpological, carpologically, carpologist, carpology, carpomania, carpometacarpal, carpometacarpi, carpometacarpus, carpompi, carpool, carpools, carpopedal, carpophagous, carpophalangeal, carpophore, carpophyl, carpophyll, carpophyte, carpopodite, carpopoditic, carpoptosia, carpoptosis, carport, carports, carpos, carposperm, carposporangia, carposporangial, carposporangium, carpospore, carposporic, carposporous, carpostome, carps, carpsucker, carpus, carpuspi, carquaise, carr, carrack, carracks, carrageen, carrageenan, carrageenin, carragheen, carragheenin, carrat, carraway, carraways, carreau, carree, carrefour, carrel, carrell, carrells, carrels, carreta, carretela, carretera, carreton, carretta, carri, carriable, carriage, carriage's, carriageable, carriageful, carriageless, carriages, carriagesmith, carriageway, carrick, carried, carrier, carriers, carries, carrigeen, carriole, carrioles, carrion, carrions, carritch, carritches, carriwitchet, carrizo, carrocci, carroccio, carroch, carroches, carroll, carrollite, carrom, carromata, carromatas, carromed, carroming, carroms, carronade, carroon, carrosserie, carrot, carrot's, carrotage, carroter, carrotier, carrotiest, carrotin, carrotiness, carroting, carrotins, carrots, carrottop, carrotweed, carrotwood, carroty, carrousel, carrousels, carrow, carrozza, carrs, carrus, carry, carryable, carryall, carryalls, carrycot, carryed, carrying, carryings, carryke, carryon, carryons, carryout, carryouts, carryover, carryovers, carrys, carrytale, cars, carse, carses, carshop, carshops, carsick, carsickness, carsmith, carson, carstone, cart, cartable, cartaceous, cartage, cartages, cartboot, cartbote, carte, carted, cartel, cartelism, cartelist, cartelistic, cartelization, cartelize, cartelized, cartelizing, cartellist, cartels, carter, carterly, carters, cartes, cartesian, cartful, carthame, carthamic, carthamin, carthamus, carthorse, carthusian, cartier, cartiest, cartilage, cartilages, cartilaginean, cartilagineous, cartilaginification, cartilaginoid, cartilaginous, carting, cartisane, cartload, cartloads, cartmaker, cartmaking, cartman, cartobibliography, cartogram, cartograph, cartographer, cartographers, cartographic, cartographical, cartographically, cartographies, cartography, cartomancies, cartomancy, carton, carton's, cartoned, cartoner, cartonful, cartoning, cartonnage, cartonnier, cartonniers, cartons, cartoon, cartoon's, cartooned, cartooning, cartoonist, cartoonists, cartoons, cartop, cartopper, cartouch, cartouche, cartouches, cartridge, cartridge's, cartridges, carts, cartsale, cartularies, cartulary, cartware, cartway, cartwheel, cartwheeler, cartwheels, cartwhip, cartwright, cartwrighting, carty, carua, caruage, carucage, carucal, carucarius, carucate, carucated, caruncle, caruncles, caruncula, carunculae, caruncular, carunculate, carunculated, carunculous, carus, carvacrol, carvacryl, carvage, carval, carve, carved, carvel, carvels, carven, carvene, carver, carvers, carvership, carves, carvestrene, carving, carvings, carvist, carvoeira, carvoepra, carvol, carvomenthene, carvone, carvy, carvyl, carwash, carwashes, carwitchet, caryatic, caryatid, caryatidal, caryatidean, caryatides, caryatidic, caryatids, caryl, caryocaraceous, caryophyllaceous, caryophyllene, caryophylleous, caryophyllin, caryophyllous, caryopilite, caryopses, caryopsides, caryopsis, caryotin, caryotins, carzey, casa, casaba, casabas, casabe, casablanca, casal, casalty, casanova, casanovas, casaque, casaques, casaquin, casas, casate, casaun, casava, casavas, casave, casavi, casbah, casbahs, cascabel, cascabels, cascable, cascables, cascadable, cascade, cascaded, cascades, cascading, cascadite, cascado, cascalho, cascalote, cascan, cascara, cascaras, cascarilla, cascaron, cascavel, caschielawis, caschrom, casco, cascol, cascrom, cascrome, case, casease, caseases, caseate, caseated, caseates, caseating, caseation, casebearer, casebook, casebooks, casebound, casebox, caseconv, cased, casefied, casefies, caseful, casefy, casefying, caseharden, casehardened, casehardening, casehardens, caseic, casein, caseinate, caseine, caseinogen, caseins, casekeeper, caseless, caselessly, caseload, caseloads, caselty, casemaker, casemaking, casemate, casemated, casemates, casement, casement's, casemented, casements, caseolysis, caseose, caseoses, caseous, caser, caserio, caserios, casern, caserne, casernes, caserns, cases, casette, casettes, caseum, caseweed, casewood, casework, caseworker, caseworkers, caseworks, caseworm, caseworms, cash, casha, cashable, cashableness, cashaw, cashaws, cashbook, cashbooks, cashbox, cashboxes, cashboy, cashcuttee, cashdrawer, cashed, casheen, cashel, casher, cashers, cashes, cashew, cashews, cashgirl, cashier, cashier's, cashiered, cashierer, cashiering, cashierment, cashiers, cashing, cashkeeper, cashless, cashment, cashmere, cashmeres, cashmerette, cashoo, cashoos, cashou, casimere, casimeres, casimire, casimires, casina, casinet, casing, casings, casino, casinos, casiri, casita, casitas, cask, cask's, caskanet, casked, casket, casket's, casketed, casketing, casketlike, caskets, casking, casklike, casks, casky, casper, caspian, casque, casqued, casques, casquet, casquetel, casquette, cass, cassaba, cassabanana, cassabas, cassabully, cassada, cassady, cassalty, cassan, cassandra, cassandras, cassapanca, cassare, cassareep, cassata, cassatas, cassate, cassation, cassava, cassavas, casse, casselty, cassena, casserole, casserole's, casseroled, casseroles, casseroling, cassette, cassettes, casshe, cassia, cassias, cassican, cassideous, cassidid, cassidoine, cassidony, cassiduloid, cassie, cassimere, cassina, cassine, cassinette, cassinian, cassino, cassinoid, cassinos, cassioberry, cassiopeia, cassiopeian, cassiopeium, cassique, cassiri, cassis, cassises, cassiterite, cassites, cassius, cassock, cassocked, cassocks, cassolette, casson, cassonade, cassone, cassoni, cassons, cassoon, cassoulet, cassowaries, cassowary, cassumunar, cassumuniar, cassy, cast, cast's, castable, castagnole, castalia, castana, castane, castanean, castaneous, castanet, castanets, castanian, castano, castaway, castaways, caste, casted, casteism, casteisms, casteless, castelet, castellan, castellanies, castellano, castellans, castellanship, castellanus, castellany, castellar, castellate, castellated, castellation, castellatus, castellet, castelli, castellum, casten, caster, casterless, casters, castes, casteth, casthouse, castice, castigable, castigate, castigated, castigates, castigating, castigation, castigations, castigative, castigator, castigatories, castigators, castigatory, castile, castilian, castillo, casting, castings, castle, castled, castlelike, castlery, castles, castlet, castleward, castlewards, castlewise, castling, castock, castoff, castoffs, castor, castoreum, castorial, castorin, castorite, castorized, castors, castory, castra, castral, castrametation, castrate, castrated, castrater, castrates, castrati, castrating, castration, castrations, castrato, castrator, castrators, castratory, castrensial, castrensian, castro, castrum, casts, castuli, casual, casualism, casualist, casuality, casually, casualness, casuals, casualties, casualty, casualty's, casuarina, casuarinaceous, casuary, casuist, casuistess, casuistic, casuistical, casuistically, casuistries, casuistry, casuists, casula, casule, casus, casusistry, caswellite, cat, cat's, catabaptist, catabases, catabasion, catabasis, catabatic, catabibazon, catabiotic, catabolic, catabolically, catabolin, catabolism, catabolite, catabolize, catabolized, catabolizing, catacaustic, catachreses, catachresis, catachresti, catachrestic, catachrestical, catachrestically, catachthonian, catachthonic, cataclasis, cataclasm, cataclasmic, cataclastic, cataclinal, cataclysm, cataclysmal, cataclysmatic, cataclysmatist, cataclysmic, cataclysmically, cataclysmist, cataclysms, catacomb, catacombic, catacombs, catacorner, catacorolla, catacoustics, catacromyodian, catacrotic, catacrotism, catacumba, catacumbal, catadicrotic, catadicrotism, catadioptric, catadioptrical, catadioptrics, catadrome, catadromous, catadupe, catafalco, catafalque, catafalques, catagenesis, catagenetic, catagmatic, catagories, cataian, catakinesis, catakinetic, catakinetomer, catakinomeric, catalan, catalase, catalases, catalatic, catalecta, catalectic, catalecticant, catalects, catalepsies, catalepsis, catalepsy, cataleptic, cataleptically, cataleptics, cataleptiform, cataleptize, cataleptoid, catalexes, catalexis, catalin, catalina, catalineta, catalinite, catallactic, catallactically, catallactics, catallum, catalo, cataloes, catalog, cataloged, cataloger, catalogers, catalogia, catalogic, catalogical, cataloging, catalogist, catalogistic, catalogize, catalogs, catalogue, catalogued, cataloguer, catalogues, cataloguing, cataloguish, cataloguist, cataloguize, cataloon, catalos, catalowne, catalpa, catalpas, catalufa, catalufas, catalyse, catalyses, catalysis, catalyst, catalyst's, catalysts, catalyte, catalytic, catalytical, catalytically, catalyzator, catalyze, catalyzed, catalyzer, catalyzers, catalyzes, catalyzing, catamaran, catamarans, catamenia, catamenial, catamite, catamited, catamites, catamiting, catamneses, catamnesis, catamnestic, catamount, catamountain, catamounts, catan, catanadromous, catapan, catapasm, catapetalous, cataphasia, cataphatic, cataphonic, cataphonics, cataphora, cataphoresis, cataphoretic, cataphoretically, cataphoria, cataphoric, cataphract, cataphracted, cataphractic, cataphrenia, cataphrenic, cataphrygian, cataphrygianism, cataphyll, cataphylla, cataphyllary, cataphyllum, cataphysic, cataphysical, cataplane, cataplasia, cataplasis, cataplasm, cataplastic, catapleiite, cataplexy, catapuce, catapult, catapulted, catapultic, catapultier, catapulting, catapults, cataract, cataractal, cataracted, cataracteg, cataractine, cataractous, cataracts, cataractwise, cataria, catarinite, catarrh, catarrhal, catarrhally, catarrhed, catarrhine, catarrhinian, catarrhous, catarrhs, catasarka, cataspilite, catasta, catastaltic, catastases, catastasis, catastate, catastatic, catasterism, catastrophal, catastrophe, catastrophes, catastrophic, catastrophical, catastrophically, catastrophism, catastrophist, catathymic, catatonia, catatoniac, catatonias, catatonic, catatonics, catatony, catawampous, catawampously, catawamptious, catawamptiously, catawampus, catawba, catawbas, catberry, catbird, catbirds, catboat, catboats, catbrier, catbriers, catcall, catcalled, catcaller, catcalling, catcalls, catch, catchable, catchall, catchalls, catchcry, catched, catcher, catchers, catches, catchflies, catchfly, catchie, catchier, catchiest, catchiness, catching, catchingly, catchingness, catchland, catchlight, catchline, catchment, catchments, catchpennies, catchpenny, catchphrase, catchplate, catchpole, catchpoled, catchpolery, catchpoleship, catchpoling, catchpoll, catchpolled, catchpollery, catchpolling, catchup, catchups, catchwater, catchweed, catchweight, catchword, catchwords, catchwork, catchy, catclaw, catdom, cate, catecheses, catechesis, catechetic, catechetical, catechetically, catechin, catechins, catechisable, catechisation, catechise, catechised, catechiser, catechising, catechism, catechismal, catechisms, catechist, catechistic, catechistical, catechistically, catechists, catechizable, catechization, catechize, catechized, catechizer, catechizes, catechizing, catechol, catecholamine, catecholamines, catechols, catechu, catechumen, catechumenal, catechumenate, catechumenical, catechumenically, catechumenism, catechumens, catechumenship, catechus, catechutannic, categorem, categorematic, categorematical, categorematically, categorial, categoric, categorical, categorically, categoricalness, categories, categorisation, categorise, categorised, categorising, categorist, categorization, categorizations, categorize, categorized, categorizer, categorizers, categorizes, categorizing, category, category's, catel, catelectrode, catelectrotonic, catelectrotonus, catella, catena, catenae, catenane, catenarian, catenaries, catenary, catenas, catenate, catenated, catenates, catenating, catenation, catenative, catenoid, catenoids, catenulate, catepuce, cater, cateran, caterans, caterbrawl, catercap, catercorner, catercornered, catercornerways, catercousin, catered, caterer, caterers, caterership, cateress, cateresses, catering, cateringly, caterpillar, caterpillar's, caterpillared, caterpillarlike, caterpillars, caters, caterva, caterwaul, caterwauled, caterwauler, caterwauling, caterwauls, catery, cates, catesbeiana, cateye, catface, catfaced, catfaces, catfacing, catfall, catfalls, catfight, catfish, catfishes, catfoot, catfooted, catgut, catguts, cath, cathar, catharan, catharine, catharist, catharization, catharize, catharized, catharizing, catharses, catharsis, cathartic, cathartical, cathartically, catharticalness, cathartics, cathartin, cathead, catheads, cathect, cathected, cathectic, cathecting, cathection, cathects, cathedra, cathedrae, cathedral, cathedral's, cathedraled, cathedralesque, cathedralic, cathedrallike, cathedrals, cathedralwise, cathedras, cathedrated, cathedratic, cathedratica, cathedratical, cathedratically, cathedraticum, cathepsin, catheptic, catheretic, catherine, cathern, catheter, catheterisation, catheterise, catheterised, catheterising, catheterism, catheterization, catheterize, catheterized, catheterizes, catheterizing, catheters, catheti, cathetometer, cathetometric, cathetus, cathetusti, cathexes, cathexion, cathexis, cathidine, cathin, cathine, cathinine, cathion, cathisma, cathismata, cathodal, cathode, cathode's, cathodegraph, cathodes, cathodic, cathodical, cathodically, cathodofluorescence, cathodograph, cathodography, cathodoluminescence, cathodoluminescent, cathograph, cathography, cathole, catholic, catholic's, catholical, catholically, catholicalness, catholicate, catholici, catholicisation, catholicise, catholicised, catholiciser, catholicising, catholicism, catholicist, catholicity, catholicization, catholicize, catholicized, catholicizer, catholicizing, catholicly, catholicness, catholicoi, catholicon, catholicos, catholicoses, catholics, catholicus, catholyte, cathood, cathop, cathouse, cathouses, cathro, cathud, cathy, catiline, cating, cation, cationic, cationically, cations, cativo, catjang, catkin, catkinate, catkins, catlap, catlike, catlin, catline, catling, catlings, catlinite, catlins, catmalison, catmint, catmints, catnache, catnap, catnaper, catnapers, catnapped, catnapper, catnapping, catnaps, catnep, catnip, catnips, catoblepas, catocalid, catocarthartic, catocathartic, catochus, catoctin, catodont, catogene, catogenic, catonian, catoptric, catoptrical, catoptrically, catoptrics, catoptrite, catoptromancy, catoptromantic, catostomid, catostomoid, catouse, catpiece, catpipe, catproof, catrigged, cats, catskill, catskin, catskinner, catslide, catso, catsos, catspaw, catspaws, catstane, catstep, catstick, catstitch, catstitcher, catstone, catsup, catsups, cattabu, cattail, cattails, cattalo, cattaloes, cattalos, cattan, catted, catter, catteries, cattery, cattie, cattier, catties, cattiest, cattily, cattimandoo, cattiness, catting, cattish, cattishly, cattishness, cattle, cattlebush, cattlefold, cattlegate, cattlehide, cattleless, cattleman, cattlemen, cattleship, cattleya, cattleyak, cattleyas, catty, cattycorner, cattycornered, cattyman, cattyphoid, catur, catvine, catwalk, catwalks, catwise, catwood, catwort, catydid, catzerie, caubeen, cauboge, caucasian, caucasians, caucasoid, caucasoids, caucasus, cauch, cauchemar, cauchillo, caucho, caucus, caucused, caucuses, caucusing, caucussed, caucusses, caucussing, cauda, caudad, caudae, caudaite, caudal, caudally, caudalward, caudata, caudate, caudated, caudation, caudatolenticular, caudatory, caudatum, caudebeck, caudex, caudexes, caudices, caudicle, caudiform, caudillism, caudillo, caudillos, caudle, caudles, caudocephalad, caudodorsal, caudofemoral, caudolateral, caudotibial, caudotibialis, cauf, caufle, caught, cauk, cauked, cauking, caul, cauld, cauldrife, cauldrifeness, cauldron, cauldrons, caulds, caulerpaceous, caules, caulescent, cauli, caulicle, caulicles, caulicole, caulicolous, caulicule, cauliculi, cauliculus, cauliferous, cauliflorous, cauliflory, cauliflower, cauliflowers, cauliform, cauligenous, caulinar, caulinary, cauline, caulis, caulivorous, caulk, caulked, caulker, caulkers, caulking, caulkings, caulks, caulocarpic, caulocarpous, caulome, caulomer, caulomic, caulophylline, caulopteris, caulosarc, caulotaxis, caulotaxy, caulote, cauls, caum, cauma, caumatic, caunch, caunter, caup, caupo, cauponate, cauponation, caupones, cauponize, caurale, caus, causa, causability, causable, causae, causal, causalgia, causalities, causality, causally, causals, causans, causata, causate, causation, causation's, causational, causationism, causationist, causations, causative, causatively, causativeness, causativity, causator, causatum, cause, caused, causeful, causeless, causelessly, causelessness, causer, causerie, causeries, causers, causes, causeur, causeuse, causeuses, causeway, causeway's, causewayed, causewaying, causewayman, causeways, causey, causeys, causidical, causing, causingness, causon, causse, causson, caustic, caustical, caustically, causticiser, causticism, causticity, causticization, causticize, causticized, causticizer, causticizing, causticly, causticness, caustics, caustification, caustified, caustify, caustifying, cautel, cautela, cautelous, cautelously, cautelousness, cauter, cauterant, cauteries, cauterisation, cauterise, cauterised, cauterising, cauterism, cauterization, cauterize, cauterized, cauterizer, cauterizes, cauterizing, cautery, cautio, caution, cautionaries, cautionary, cautioned, cautioner, cautioners, cautiones, cautioning, cautionings, cautionry, cautions, cautious, cautiously, cautiousness, cautivo, cav, cava, cavae, cavaedia, cavaedium, caval, cavalcade, cavalcaded, cavalcades, cavalcading, cavalero, cavaleros, cavalier, cavaliere, cavaliered, cavalieres, cavalieri, cavaliering, cavalierish, cavalierishness, cavalierism, cavalierly, cavalierness, cavaliero, cavaliers, cavaliership, cavalla, cavallas, cavallies, cavally, cavalries, cavalry, cavalryman, cavalrymen, cavascope, cavate, cavated, cavatina, cavatinas, cavatine, cavayard, cavdia, cave, cavea, caveae, caveat, caveat's, caveated, caveatee, caveating, caveator, caveators, caveats, caved, cavefish, cavefishes, cavekeeper, cavel, cavelet, cavelike, caveman, cavemen, cavendish, caver, cavern, cavern's, cavernal, caverned, cavernicolous, caverning, cavernitis, cavernlike, cavernoma, cavernous, cavernously, caverns, cavernulous, cavers, caves, cavesson, cavetti, cavetto, cavettos, cavey, caviar, caviare, caviares, caviars, cavicorn, cavie, cavies, cavil, caviled, caviler, cavilers, caviling, cavilingly, cavilingness, cavillation, cavillatory, cavilled, caviller, cavillers, cavilling, cavillingly, cavillingness, cavillous, cavils, cavin, caving, cavings, cavish, cavitary, cavitate, cavitated, cavitates, cavitating, cavitation, cavitations, caviteno, cavitied, cavities, cavity, cavity's, caviya, cavort, cavorted, cavorter, cavorters, cavorting, cavorts, cavu, cavum, cavus, cavy, cavyyard, caw, cawed, cawing, cawk, cawker, cawky, cawl, cawney, cawnie, cawny, cawquaw, caws, caxiri, caxon, caxton, cay, cayenne, cayenned, cayennes, cayleyan, cayman, caymans, caynard, cayos, cays, cayuca, cayuco, cayuga, cayugas, cayuse, cayuses, caza, cazibi, cazimi, cazique, caziques, cb, cc, ccesser, cchaddoorck, ccid, ccitt, cckw, ccm, ccw, ccws, cd, cdf, cdg, cdr, ce, ceanothus, cearin, cease, ceased, ceaseless, ceaselessly, ceaselessness, ceases, ceasing, ceasmic, cebell, cebian, cebid, cebids, cebil, cebine, ceboid, ceboids, cebollite, cebur, cebus, ceca, cecal, cecally, cecca, cecchine, cecidiologist, cecidiology, cecidium, cecidogenous, cecidologist, cecidology, cecidomyian, cecidomyiid, cecidomyiidous, cecil, cecilite, cecils, cecitis, cecity, cecograph, cecomorphic, cecopexy, cecostomy, cecotomy, cecropia, cecum, cecums, cecutiency, cedar, cedarbird, cedared, cedarn, cedars, cedarware, cedarwood, cedary, cede, ceded, cedens, cedent, ceder, ceders, cedes, cedi, cedilla, cedillas, ceding, cedis, cedrat, cedrate, cedre, cedrela, cedrene, cedrin, cedrine, cedriret, cedrium, cedrol, cedron, cedry, cedula, cedulas, cedule, ceduous, cee, ceennacuelum, cees, ceiba, ceibas, ceibo, ceibos, ceil, ceile, ceiled, ceiler, ceilers, ceilidh, ceilidhe, ceiling, ceiling's, ceilinged, ceilings, ceilingward, ceilingwards, ceilometer, ceils, ceint, ceinte, ceinture, ceintures, ceja, celadon, celadonite, celadons, celandine, celandines, celarent, celastraceous, celation, celative, celature, cele, celeb, celebe, celebes, celebrant, celebrants, celebrate, celebrated, celebratedly, celebratedness, celebrater, celebrates, celebrating, celebration, celebrationis, celebrations, celebrative, celebrator, celebrators, celebratory, celebre, celebres, celebret, celebrious, celebrities, celebrity, celebrity's, celebs, celemin, celemines, celeomorph, celeomorphic, celeriac, celeriacs, celeries, celerities, celerity, celery, celesta, celestas, celeste, celestes, celestial, celestiality, celestialize, celestialized, celestially, celestialness, celestify, celestina, celestine, celestite, celestitude, celeusma, celiac, celiadelphus, celiagra, celialgia, celibacies, celibacy, celibataire, celibatarian, celibate, celibates, celibatic, celibatist, celibatory, celidographer, celidography, celiectasia, celiectomy, celiemia, celiitis, celiocele, celiocentesis, celiocolpotomy, celiocyesis, celiodynia, celioelytrotomy, celioenterotomy, celiogastrotomy, celiohysterotomy, celiolymph, celiomyalgia, celiomyodynia, celiomyomectomy, celiomyomotomy, celiomyositis, celioncus, celioparacentesis, celiopyosis, celiorrhaphy, celiorrhea, celiosalpingectomy, celiosalpingotomy, celioschisis, celioscope, celioscopy, celiotomies, celiotomy, celite, cell, cella, cellae, cellager, cellar, cellar's, cellarage, cellared, cellarer, cellarers, cellaress, cellaret, cellarets, cellarette, cellaring, cellarless, cellarman, cellarmen, cellarous, cellars, cellarway, cellarwoman, cellated, cellblock, cellblocks, celled, cellepore, celli, celliferous, celliform, cellifugal, celling, cellipetal, cellist, cellist's, cellists, cellmate, cellmates, cello, cellobiose, cellocut, celloid, celloidin, celloist, cellophane, cellos, cellose, cells, cellular, cellularity, cellularly, cellulase, cellulate, cellulated, cellulating, cellulation, cellule, cellules, cellulicidal, celluliferous, cellulifugal, cellulifugally, cellulin, cellulipetal, cellulipetally, cellulitis, cellulocutaneous, cellulofibrous, celluloid, celluloided, cellulolytic, cellulose, cellulosed, celluloses, cellulosic, cellulosing, cellulosities, cellulosity, cellulotoxic, cellulous, celom, celomata, celoms, celoscope, celosia, celosias, celotomies, celotomy, celsian, celsitude, celsius, celt, celtic, celticist, celtiform, celtium, celts, celtuce, celure, cembali, cembalist, cembalo, cembalon, cembalos, cement, cementa, cemental, cementation, cementatory, cemented, cementer, cementers, cementification, cementing, cementite, cementitious, cementless, cementlike, cementmaker, cementmaking, cementoblast, cementoma, cements, cementum, cementwork, cemetaries, cemetary, cemeterial, cemeteries, cemetery, cemetery's, cen, cenacle, cenacles, cenaculum, cenanthous, cenanthy, cenation, cenatory, cencerro, cencerros, cendre, cene, cenesthesia, cenesthesis, cenesthetic, cenizo, cenobe, cenobian, cenobies, cenobite, cenobites, cenobitic, cenobitical, cenobitically, cenobitism, cenobium, cenoby, cenogamy, cenogenesis, cenogenetic, cenogenetically, cenogonous, cenosite, cenosity, cenospecies, cenospecific, cenospecifically, cenotaph, cenotaphic, cenotaphies, cenotaphs, cenotaphy, cenote, cenotes, cenozoic, cenozoology, cense, censed, censer, censerless, censers, censes, censing, censitaire, censive, censor, censorable, censorate, censored, censorial, censorian, censoring, censorious, censoriously, censoriousness, censors, censorship, censual, censurability, censurable, censurableness, censurably, censure, censured, censureless, censurer, censurers, censures, censureship, censuring, census, census's, censused, censuses, censusing, cent, centage, centai, cental, centals, centare, centares, centas, centaur, centaurdom, centaurea, centauress, centauri, centaurial, centaurian, centauric, centauries, centauromachia, centauromachy, centaurs, centaurus, centaury, centavo, centavos, centena, centenar, centenarian, centenarianism, centenarians, centenaries, centenary, centenier, centenionales, centenionalis, centennia, centennial, centennially, centennials, centennium, center, center's, centerable, centerboard, centerboards, centered, centeredly, centeredness, centerer, centerfold, centerfolds, centering, centerless, centerline, centermost, centerpiece, centerpiece's, centerpieces, centerpunch, centers, centervelic, centerward, centerwise, centeses, centesimal, centesimally, centesimate, centesimation, centesimi, centesimo, centesimos, centesis, centesm, centetid, centgener, centgrave, centi, centiar, centiare, centiares, centibar, centiday, centifolious, centigrade, centigrado, centigram, centigramme, centigrams, centile, centiles, centiliter, centiliters, centilitre, centillion, centillions, centillionth, centiloquy, centime, centimes, centimeter, centimeters, centimetre, centimetres, centimo, centimolar, centimos, centinel, centinody, centinormal, centipedal, centipede, centipede's, centipedes, centiplume, centipoise, centistere, centistoke, centner, centners, cento, centon, centones, centonical, centonism, centonization, centos, centra, centrad, central, centrale, centraler, centrales, centralest, centralia, centralisation, centralise, centralised, centraliser, centralising, centralism, centralist, centralistic, centralists, centralities, centrality, centralization, centralize, centralized, centralizer, centralizers, centralizes, centralizing, centrally, centralness, centrals, centranth, centrarchid, centrarchoid, centration, centraxonial, centre, centreboard, centred, centref, centrefold, centreless, centremost, centrepiece, centrer, centres, centrev, centrex, centric, centrical, centricality, centrically, centricalness, centricipital, centriciput, centricity, centriffed, centrifugal, centrifugalisation, centrifugalise, centrifugalization, centrifugalize, centrifugalized, centrifugalizing, centrifugaller, centrifugally, centrifugate, centrifugation, centrifuge, centrifuged, centrifugence, centrifuges, centrifuging, centring, centrings, centriole, centripetal, centripetalism, centripetally, centripetence, centripetency, centriscid, centrisciform, centriscoid, centrism, centrisms, centrist, centrists, centro, centroacinar, centrobaric, centrobarical, centroclinal, centrode, centrodesmose, centrodesmus, centrodorsal, centrodorsally, centroid, centroidal, centroids, centrolecithal, centrolepidaceous, centrolinead, centrolineal, centromere, centromeric, centronote, centronucleus, centroplasm, centrosome, centrosomic, centrosphere, centrosymmetric, centrosymmetrical, centrosymmetry, centrum, centrums, centrutra, centry, cents, centum, centums, centumvir, centumviral, centumvirate, centuple, centupled, centuples, centuplicate, centuplicated, centuplicating, centuplication, centupling, centuply, centure, centuria, centurial, centuriate, centuriation, centuriator, centuried, centuries, centurion, centurions, centurist, century, century's, ceonocyte, ceorl, ceorlish, ceorls, cep, cepa, cepaceous, cepe, cepes, cephadia, cephaeline, cephala, cephalad, cephalagra, cephalalgia, cephalalgic, cephalalgy, cephalanthium, cephalanthous, cephalaspis, cephalate, cephaldemae, cephalemia, cephaletron, cephalexin, cephalhematoma, cephalhydrocele, cephalic, cephalically, cephalin, cephaline, cephalins, cephalism, cephalitis, cephalization, cephaloauricular, cephalob, cephalobranchiate, cephalocathartic, cephalocaudal, cephalocele, cephalocentesis, cephalocercal, cephalochord, cephalochordal, cephalochordate, cephaloclasia, cephaloclast, cephalocone, cephaloconic, cephalocyst, cephalodia, cephalodiscid, cephalodium, cephalodymia, cephalodymus, cephalodynia, cephalofacial, cephalogenesis, cephalogram, cephalograph, cephalohumeral, cephalohumeralis, cephaloid, cephalology, cephalom, cephalomancy, cephalomant, cephalomelus, cephalomenia, cephalomeningitis, cephalomere, cephalometer, cephalometric, cephalometry, cephalomotor, cephalomyitis, cephalon, cephalonasal, cephalopagus, cephalopathy, cephalopharyngeal, cephalophine, cephalophorous, cephalophyma, cephaloplegia, cephaloplegic, cephalopod, cephalopoda, cephalopodan, cephalopodic, cephalopodous, cephalorachidian, cephalorhachidian, cephaloridine, cephalosome, cephalospinal, cephalosporin, cephalostyle, cephalotaceous, cephalotheca, cephalothecal, cephalothoraces, cephalothoracic, cephalothoracopagus, cephalothorax, cephalothoraxes, cephalotome, cephalotomy, cephalotractor, cephalotribe, cephalotripsy, cephalotrocha, cephalous, cepheid, cepheids, cephen, cepheus, cephid, cepous, ceps, cepter, ceptor, cequi, cera, ceraceous, cerago, ceral, ceramal, ceramals, cerambycid, ceramiaceous, ceramic, ceramicist, ceramicists, ceramicite, ceramics, ceramidium, ceramist, ceramists, ceramium, ceramographic, ceramography, cerargyrite, ceras, cerasein, cerasin, cerastes, cerat, cerata, cerate, ceratectomy, cerated, cerates, ceratiasis, ceratiid, ceratin, ceratinous, ceratins, ceratioid, ceration, ceratite, ceratitic, ceratitoid, ceratium, ceratoblast, ceratobranchial, ceratocricoid, ceratocystis, ceratodus, ceratoduses, ceratofibrous, ceratoglossal, ceratoglossus, ceratohyal, ceratohyoid, ceratoid, ceratomandibular, ceratomania, ceratophyllaceous, ceratophyte, ceratopsian, ceratopsid, ceratopteridaceous, ceratorhine, ceratosaurus, ceratospongian, ceratotheca, ceratothecae, ceratothecal, ceraunia, ceraunics, ceraunite, ceraunogram, ceraunograph, ceraunomancy, ceraunophone, ceraunoscope, ceraunoscopy, cerberean, cerberus, cercal, cercaria, cercariae, cercarial, cercarian, cercarias, cercariform, cercelee, cerci, cercis, cercises, cercle, cercomonad, cercopid, cercopithecid, cercopithecoid, cercopithecus, cercopod, cercus, cere, cereal, cereal's, cerealian, cerealin, cerealism, cerealist, cerealose, cereals, cerebbella, cerebella, cerebellar, cerebellifugal, cerebellipetal, cerebellitis, cerebellocortex, cerebellopontile, cerebellopontine, cerebellorubral, cerebellospinal, cerebellum, cerebellums, cerebra, cerebral, cerebralgia, cerebralism, cerebralist, cerebralization, cerebralize, cerebrally, cerebrals, cerebrasthenia, cerebrasthenic, cerebrate, cerebrated, cerebrates, cerebrating, cerebration, cerebrational, cerebrations, cerebri, cerebric, cerebricity, cerebriform, cerebriformly, cerebrifugal, cerebrin, cerebripetal, cerebritis, cerebrize, cerebrocardiac, cerebrogalactose, cerebroganglion, cerebroganglionic, cerebroid, cerebrology, cerebroma, cerebromalacia, cerebromedullary, cerebromeningeal, cerebromeningitis, cerebrometer, cerebron, cerebronic, cerebroparietal, cerebropathy, cerebropedal, cerebrophysiology, cerebropontile, cerebropsychosis, cerebrorachidian, cerebrosclerosis, cerebroscope, cerebroscopy, cerebrose, cerebrosensorial, cerebroside, cerebrosis, cerebrospinal, cerebrospinant, cerebrosuria, cerebrotomy, cerebrotonia, cerebrotonic, cerebrovascular, cerebrovisceral, cerebrum, cerebrums, cerecloth, cerecloths, cered, cereless, cerement, cerements, ceremonial, ceremonialism, ceremonialist, ceremonialists, ceremonialize, ceremonially, ceremonialness, ceremonials, ceremoniary, ceremonies, ceremonious, ceremoniously, ceremoniousness, ceremony, ceremony's, cerenkov, cereous, cerer, cererite, ceres, ceresin, ceresine, cereus, cereuses, cerevis, cerevisial, cereza, cerfoil, ceria, cerianthid, cerianthoid, cerias, ceric, ceride, ceriferous, cerigerous, cerilla, cerillo, ceriman, cerimans, cerin, cerine, cering, cerinthian, ceriops, ceriph, ceriphs, cerise, cerises, cerite, cerites, cerithioid, cerium, ceriums, cermet, cermets, cern, cerned, cerning, cerniture, cernuous, cero, cerograph, cerographer, cerographic, cerographical, cerographies, cerographist, cerography, ceroid, ceroline, cerolite, ceroma, ceromancy, ceromez, ceroon, cerophilous, ceroplast, ceroplastic, ceroplastics, ceroplasty, ceros, cerosin, cerotate, cerote, cerotene, cerotic, cerotin, cerotype, cerotypes, cerous, ceroxyle, cerrero, cerrial, cerris, cert, certain, certainer, certainest, certainly, certainness, certainties, certainty, certes, certie, certif, certifiability, certifiable, certifiableness, certifiably, certificate, certificated, certificates, certificating, certification, certifications, certificative, certificator, certificatory, certified, certifier, certifiers, certifies, certify, certifying, certiorari, certiorate, certiorating, certioration, certis, certitude, certitudes, certosa, certose, certosina, certosino, certy, cerule, cerulean, ceruleans, cerulein, ceruleite, ceruleolactite, ceruleous, cerulescent, ceruleum, cerulific, cerulignol, cerulignone, ceruloplasmin, cerumen, cerumens, ceruminal, ceruminiferous, ceruminous, cerumniparous, ceruse, ceruses, cerusite, cerusites, cerussite, cervalet, cervantes, cervantic, cervantite, cervelas, cervelases, cervelat, cervelats, cerveliere, cervelliere, cervical, cervicaprine, cervicectomy, cervices, cervicicardiac, cervicide, cerviciplex, cervicispinal, cervicitis, cervicoauricular, cervicoaxillary, cervicobasilar, cervicobrachial, cervicobregmatic, cervicobuccal, cervicodorsal, cervicodynia, cervicofacial, cervicohumeral, cervicolabial, cervicolingual, cervicolumbar, cervicomuscular, cerviconasal, cervicorn, cervicoscapular, cervicothoracic, cervicovaginal, cervicovesical, cervid, cervine, cervisia, cervisial, cervix, cervixes, cervoid, cervuline, ceryl, cesar, cesare, cesarean, cesareans, cesarevitch, cesarian, cesarians, cesarolite, cesious, cesium, cesiums, cespititious, cespititous, cespitose, cespitosely, cespitulose, cess, cessant, cessantly, cessation, cessation's, cessations, cessative, cessavit, cessed, cesser, cesses, cessible, cessing, cessio, cession, cessionaire, cessionaries, cessionary, cessionee, cessions, cessment, cessor, cesspipe, cesspit, cesspits, cesspool, cesspools, cest, cesta, cestas, ceste, cesti, cestode, cestodes, cestoi, cestoid, cestoidean, cestoids, ceston, cestos, cestraciont, cestraction, cestrian, cestrum, cestui, cestus, cestuses, cestuy, cesura, cesurae, cesural, cesuras, cesure, cetacea, cetacean, cetaceans, cetaceous, cetaceum, cetane, cetanes, cete, cetene, ceteosaur, cetera, ceterach, cetes, ceti, cetic, ceticide, cetin, cetiosaurian, cetiosaurus, cetological, cetologies, cetologist, cetology, cetomorphic, cetonian, cetorhinid, cetorhinoid, cetotolite, cetraric, cetrarin, cetus, cetyl, cetylene, cetylic, cevadilla, cevadilline, cevadine, cevian, ceviche, ceviches, cevine, cevitamic, ceylanite, ceylon, ceylonese, ceylonite, ceyssatite, cf, cfd, cfh, cfi, cfm, cfs, cg, cgm, cgs, ch, ch'in, cha, chaa, chab, chabasie, chabasite, chabazite, chaber, chablis, chabot, chabouk, chabouks, chabuk, chabuks, chabutra, chacate, chaccon, chace, chachalaca, chachalakas, chack, chacker, chackle, chackled, chackler, chackling, chacma, chacmas, chaco, chacoli, chacona, chaconne, chaconnes, chacra, chacte, chacun, chad, chadacryst, chadar, chadarim, chadars, chadelle, chadless, chadlock, chador, chadors, chadri, chads, chaeta, chaetae, chaetal, chaetiferous, chaetodon, chaetodont, chaetodontid, chaetognath, chaetognathan, chaetognathous, chaetophobia, chaetophoraceous, chaetophorous, chaetopod, chaetopodan, chaetopodous, chaetopterin, chaetosema, chaetotactic, chaetotaxy, chafe, chafed, chafer, chaferies, chafers, chafery, chafes, chafewax, chafeweed, chaff, chaffcutter, chaffed, chaffer, chaffered, chafferer, chafferers, chaffering, chaffers, chaffery, chaffier, chaffiest, chaffinch, chaffinches, chaffiness, chaffing, chaffingly, chaffless, chafflike, chaffman, chaffron, chaffs, chaffseed, chaffwax, chaffweed, chaffy, chafing, chaft, chafted, chagal, chagan, chagigah, chagoma, chagrin, chagrined, chagrining, chagrinned, chagrinning, chagrins, chaguar, chagul, chahar, chahars, chai, chain, chainage, chainbearer, chainbreak, chaine, chained, chainer, chaines, chainette, chaining, chainless, chainlet, chainlike, chainmaker, chainmaking, chainman, chainmen, chainomatic, chainon, chainplate, chains, chainsman, chainsmen, chainsmith, chainstitch, chainwale, chainwork, chair, chairborne, chaired, chairer, chairing, chairladies, chairlady, chairless, chairlift, chairmaker, chairmaking, chairman, chairmaned, chairmaning, chairmanned, chairmanning, chairmans, chairmanship, chairmanships, chairmen, chairmender, chairmending, chairperson, chairperson's, chairpersons, chairs, chairwarmer, chairway, chairwoman, chairwomen, chais, chaise, chaiseless, chaises, chaitra, chaitya, chaityas, chaja, chaka, chakar, chakari, chakazi, chakdar, chakobu, chakra, chakram, chakras, chakravartin, chaksi, chal, chalaco, chalah, chalahs, chalana, chalastic, chalaza, chalazae, chalazal, chalazas, chalaze, chalazia, chalazian, chalaziferous, chalazion, chalazium, chalazogam, chalazogamic, chalazogamy, chalazoidite, chalazoin, chalcanth, chalcanthite, chalcedonian, chalcedonic, chalcedonies, chalcedonous, chalcedony, chalcedonyx, chalchihuitl, chalchuite, chalcid, chalcidian, chalcidica, chalcidicum, chalcidid, chalcidiform, chalcidoid, chalcids, chalcites, chalcocite, chalcogen, chalcogenide, chalcograph, chalcographer, chalcographic, chalcographical, chalcographist, chalcography, chalcolite, chalcolithic, chalcomancy, chalcomenite, chalcon, chalcone, chalcophanite, chalcophile, chalcophyllite, chalcopyrite, chalcosiderite, chalcosine, chalcostibite, chalcotrichite, chalcotript, chalcus, chaldaic, chaldean, chaldee, chalder, chaldese, chaldron, chaldrons, chaleh, chalehs, chalet, chalets, chalice, chalice's, chaliced, chalices, chalicosis, chalicothere, chalicotheriid, chalicotherioid, chalinine, chalk, chalkboard, chalkboards, chalkcutter, chalked, chalker, chalkier, chalkiest, chalkiness, chalking, chalklike, chalkline, chalkography, chalkone, chalkos, chalkosideric, chalkotheke, chalkpit, chalkrail, chalks, chalkstone, chalkstony, chalkworker, chalky, challa, challah, challahs, challas, challengable, challenge, challengeable, challenged, challengee, challengeful, challenger, challengers, challenges, challenging, challengingly, challie, challies, challiho, challihos, challis, challises, challot, challote, challoth, chally, chalmer, chalon, chalone, chalones, chalot, chaloth, chaloupe, chalque, chalta, chaluka, chalumeau, chalumeaux, chalutz, chalutzim, chalybean, chalybeate, chalybeous, chalybite, cham, chama, chamade, chamades, chamaecranial, chamaephyte, chamaeprosopic, chamaerops, chamaerrhine, chamal, chamar, chambellan, chamber, chamberdeacon, chambered, chamberer, chamberfellow, chambering, chamberlain, chamberlain's, chamberlainry, chamberlains, chamberlainship, chamberlet, chamberleted, chamberletted, chambermaid, chambermaids, chambers, chambertin, chamberwoman, chambranle, chambray, chambrays, chambre, chambrel, chambul, chamecephalic, chamecephalous, chamecephalus, chamecephaly, chameleon, chameleonic, chameleonize, chameleonlike, chameleons, chametz, chamfer, chamfered, chamferer, chamfering, chamfers, chamfrain, chamfron, chamfrons, chamisal, chamise, chamises, chamiso, chamisos, chamite, chamlet, chamm, chamma, chammied, chammies, chammy, chammying, chamois, chamoised, chamoises, chamoising, chamoisite, chamoix, chamoline, chamomile, chamosite, chamotte, champ, champac, champaca, champacol, champacs, champagne, champagned, champagneless, champagnes, champagning, champagnize, champagnized, champagnizing, champaign, champain, champak, champaka, champaks, champart, champe, champed, champer, champerator, champers, champert, champerties, champertor, champertous, champerty, champian, champignon, champignons, champine, champing, champion, championed, championess, championing, championize, championless, championlike, champions, championship, championship's, championships, champlev, champleve, champs, champy, chams, chamsin, chan, chance, chanceable, chanceably, chanced, chanceful, chancefully, chancefulness, chancel, chanceled, chanceless, chancelled, chancelleries, chancellery, chancellor, chancellorate, chancelloress, chancellorism, chancellors, chancellorship, chancellorships, chancellory, chancelor, chancelry, chancels, chanceman, chancemen, chancer, chancered, chanceries, chancering, chancery, chances, chancewise, chancey, chanche, chanchito, chancier, chanciest, chancily, chanciness, chancing, chancito, chanco, chancre, chancres, chancriform, chancroid, chancroidal, chancroids, chancrous, chancy, chandala, chandam, chandelier, chandelier's, chandeliers, chandelle, chandelled, chandelles, chandelling, chandi, chandler, chandleress, chandleries, chandlering, chandlerly, chandlers, chandlery, chandoo, chandrakanta, chandrakhi, chandry, chandu, chandui, chandul, chanduy, chaneled, chaneling, chanelled, chanfrin, chanfron, chanfrons, chang, changa, changable, changar, change, changeability, changeable, changeableness, changeably, changeabout, changed, changedale, changedness, changeful, changefully, changefulness, changeless, changelessly, changelessness, changeling, changelings, changemaker, changement, changeover, changeovers, changepocket, changer, changers, changes, changing, changs, chank, chankings, channel, channelbill, channeled, channeler, channeling, channelization, channelize, channelized, channelizes, channelizing, channelled, channeller, channeller's, channellers, channelling, channelly, channels, channelure, channelwards, channer, chanoyu, chanson, chansonette, chansonnette, chansonnier, chansonniers, chansons, chanst, chant, chantable, chantage, chantages, chantant, chantecler, chanted, chantefable, chantepleure, chanter, chanterelle, chanters, chantership, chanteur, chanteuse, chanteuses, chantey, chanteyman, chanteys, chanticleer, chanticleer's, chanticleers, chantier, chanties, chantilly, chanting, chantingly, chantlate, chantment, chantor, chantors, chantress, chantries, chantry, chants, chanty, chanukah, chao, chaogenous, chaology, chaori, chaos, chaoses, chaotic, chaotical, chaotically, chaoticness, chaoua, chaoush, chap, chap's, chapah, chapapote, chaparajos, chaparejos, chaparral, chaparrals, chaparraz, chaparro, chapati, chapaties, chapatis, chapatti, chapatties, chapattis, chapatty, chapbook, chapbooks, chape, chapeau, chapeaus, chapeaux, chaped, chapel, chapel's, chapeled, chapeless, chapelet, chapelgoer, chapelgoing, chapeling, chapelize, chapellage, chapellany, chapelled, chapelling, chapelman, chapelmaster, chapelries, chapelry, chapels, chapelward, chaperno, chaperon, chaperonage, chaperone, chaperoned, chaperoning, chaperonless, chaperons, chapes, chapfallen, chapfallenly, chapin, chapiter, chapiters, chapitle, chapitral, chaplain, chaplain's, chaplaincies, chaplaincy, chaplainry, chaplains, chaplainship, chaplanry, chapless, chaplet, chapleted, chaplets, chaplin, chapman, chapmanship, chapmen, chapon, chapote, chapourn, chapournet, chapournetted, chappal, chappaul, chappe, chapped, chapper, chappie, chappies, chappin, chapping, chappow, chappy, chaprasi, chaprassi, chaps, chapstick, chapt, chaptalization, chaptalize, chaptalized, chaptalizing, chapter, chapter's, chapteral, chaptered, chapterful, chapterhouse, chaptering, chapters, chaptrel, chapwoman, chaqueta, chaquetas, char, chara, charabanc, charabancer, charabancs, charac, characeous, characetum, characid, characids, characin, characine, characinid, characinoid, characins, charact, character, character's, charactered, characterful, characterial, characterical, characteries, charactering, characterisable, characterisation, characterise, characterised, characteriser, characterising, characterism, characterist, characteristic, characteristic's, characteristical, characteristically, characteristicalness, characteristicness, characteristics, characterizable, characterization, characterization's, characterizations, characterize, characterized, characterizer, characterizers, characterizes, characterizing, characterless, characterlessness, characterological, characterologically, characterologist, characterology, characters, characterstring, charactery, charactonym, charade, charades, charadriiform, charadrine, charadrioid, charango, charangos, chararas, charas, charases, charbocle, charbon, charbonnier, charbroil, charbroiled, charbroiling, charbroils, charcia, charco, charcoal, charcoaled, charcoaling, charcoalist, charcoals, charcoaly, charcuterie, charcuteries, charcutier, charcutiers, chard, chardock, chards, chare, chared, charely, charer, chares, charet, chareter, charette, chargable, charge, chargeability, chargeable, chargeableness, chargeably, chargeant, charged, chargedness, chargee, chargeful, chargehouse, chargeless, chargeling, chargeman, charger, chargers, charges, chargeship, chargfaires, charging, charier, chariest, charily, chariness, charing, chariot, chariot's, charioted, chariotee, charioteer, charioteers, charioteership, charioting, chariotlike, chariotman, chariotry, chariots, chariotway, charism, charisma, charismas, charismata, charismatic, charisms, charisticary, charitable, charitableness, charitably, charitative, charities, charity, charity's, charityless, charivan, charivari, charivaried, charivariing, charivaris, chark, charka, charkas, charked, charkha, charkhana, charkhas, charking, charks, charladies, charlady, charlatan, charlatanic, charlatanical, charlatanically, charlatanish, charlatanism, charlatanistic, charlatanries, charlatanry, charlatans, charlatanship, charlemagne, charles, charleston, charlestons, charlesworth, charlet, charley, charleys, charlie, charlies, charlock, charlocks, charlotte, charlottesville, charm, charmed, charmedly, charmel, charmer, charmers, charmeuse, charmful, charmfully, charmfulness, charming, charminger, charmingest, charmingly, charmingness, charmless, charmlessly, charmonium, charms, charmwise, charneco, charnel, charnels, charnockite, charnockites, charnu, charon, charoses, charoset, charoseth, charpai, charpais, charpie, charpit, charpoy, charpoys, charque, charqued, charqui, charquid, charquis, charr, charras, charre, charred, charrette, charrier, charriest, charring, charro, charros, charrs, charry, chars, charshaf, charsingha, chart, charta, chartable, chartaceous, chartae, charted, charter, charterable, charterage, chartered, charterer, charterers, charterhouse, chartering, charterism, charterless, chartermaster, charters, charthouse, charting, chartings, chartism, chartist, chartists, chartless, chartlet, chartographer, chartographic, chartographical, chartographically, chartographist, chartography, chartology, chartometer, chartophylacia, chartophylacium, chartophylax, chartophylaxes, chartreuse, chartreux, chartroom, charts, chartula, chartulae, chartularies, chartulary, chartulas, charuk, charvet, charwoman, charwomen, chary, charybdis, chasable, chase, chaseable, chased, chaser, chasers, chases, chashitsu, chasid, chasing, chasings, chasm, chasm's, chasma, chasmal, chasmed, chasmic, chasmogamic, chasmogamous, chasmogamy, chasmophyte, chasms, chasmy, chass, chasse, chassed, chasseing, chasselas, chassepot, chassepots, chasses, chasseur, chasseurs, chassignite, chassis, chaste, chastelain, chastely, chasten, chastened, chastener, chasteners, chasteness, chastening, chasteningly, chastenment, chastens, chaster, chastest, chasteweed, chastiment, chastisable, chastise, chastised, chastisement, chastiser, chastisers, chastises, chastising, chastities, chastity, chastize, chastizer, chasty, chasuble, chasubled, chasubles, chat, chataka, chatchka, chatchkas, chatchke, chatchkes, chateau, chateau's, chateaubriand, chateaugray, chateaus, chateaux, chatelain, chatelaine, chatelaines, chatelainry, chatelains, chatelet, chatellany, chateus, chathamite, chathamites, chati, chaton, chatons, chatoyance, chatoyancy, chatoyant, chats, chatsome, chatta, chattable, chattack, chattah, chattanooga, chattation, chatted, chattel, chattelhood, chattelism, chattelization, chattelize, chattelized, chattelizing, chattels, chattelship, chatter, chatteration, chatterbag, chatterbox, chatterboxes, chattered, chatterer, chatterers, chattererz, chattering, chatteringly, chattermag, chattermagging, chatters, chattery, chattier, chatties, chattiest, chattily, chattiness, chatting, chattingly, chatty, chatwood, chaucer, chaucerian, chaudfroid, chaudron, chaufer, chaufers, chauffage, chauffer, chauffers, chauffeur, chauffeured, chauffeuring, chauffeurs, chauffeurship, chauffeuse, chauffeuses, chauk, chaukidari, chauldron, chaule, chaulmaugra, chaulmoogra, chaulmoograte, chaulmoogric, chaulmugra, chaum, chaumer, chaumiere, chaumontel, chaunoprockt, chaunt, chaunted, chaunter, chaunters, chaunting, chaunts, chauri, chaus, chausse, chaussee, chausseemeile, chaussees, chausses, chaussure, chaussures, chautauqua, chaute, chauth, chauve, chauvin, chauvinism, chauvinist, chauvinistic, chauvinistically, chauvinists, chave, chavel, chavender, chaver, chavibetol, chavicin, chavicine, chavicol, chavish, chaw, chawan, chawbacon, chawbone, chawbuck, chawdron, chawed, chawer, chawers, chawing, chawk, chawl, chawle, chawn, chaws, chawstick, chay, chaya, chayaroot, chayote, chayotes, chayroot, chays, chazan, chazanim, chazans, chazanut, chazzan, chazzanim, chazzans, chazzanut, chazzen, chazzenim, chazzens, che, cheap, cheapen, cheapened, cheapener, cheapening, cheapens, cheaper, cheapery, cheapest, cheapie, cheapies, cheaping, cheapish, cheapishly, cheapjack, cheaply, cheapness, cheapo, cheapos, cheaps, cheapskate, cheapskates, cheare, cheat, cheatable, cheatableness, cheated, cheatee, cheater, cheateries, cheaters, cheatery, cheating, cheatingly, cheatrie, cheatry, cheats, chebacco, chebec, chebeck, chebecs, chebel, chebog, chebule, chebulic, chebulinic, chechako, chechakos, chechem, chechia, check, checkable, checkage, checkback, checkbird, checkbit, checkbite, checkbits, checkbook, checkbook's, checkbooks, checke, checked, checker, checkerbellies, checkerbelly, checkerberries, checkerberry, checkerbloom, checkerboard, checkerboarded, checkerboarding, checkerboards, checkerbreast, checkered, checkering, checkerist, checkers, checkerspot, checkerwise, checkerwork, checkery, checkhook, checking, checklaton, checkle, checkless, checkline, checklist, checklists, checkman, checkmark, checkmate, checkmated, checkmates, checkmating, checkoff, checkoffs, checkout, checkouts, checkpoint, checkpoint's, checkpointed, checkpointing, checkpoints, checkrack, checkrail, checkrein, checkroll, checkroom, checkrooms, checkrope, checkrow, checkrowed, checkrower, checkrowing, checkrows, checks, checkstone, checkstrap, checkstring, checksum, checksum's, checksummed, checksumming, checksums, checkup, checkups, checkweigher, checkweighman, checkweighmen, checkwork, checkwriter, checky, chedar, cheddar, cheddaring, cheddars, cheddite, cheddites, cheder, cheders, chedite, chedites, chedlock, chedreux, chee, cheecha, cheechaco, cheechako, cheechakos, cheeful, cheefuller, cheefullest, cheek, cheek's, cheekbone, cheekbones, cheeked, cheeker, cheekful, cheekfuls, cheekier, cheekiest, cheekily, cheekiness, cheeking, cheekish, cheekless, cheekpiece, cheeks, cheeky, cheeney, cheep, cheeped, cheeper, cheepers, cheepier, cheepiest, cheepily, cheepiness, cheeping, cheeps, cheepy, cheer, cheered, cheerer, cheerers, cheerful, cheerfulize, cheerfuller, cheerfullest, cheerfully, cheerfulness, cheerfulsome, cheerier, cheeriest, cheerily, cheeriness, cheering, cheeringly, cheerio, cheerios, cheerlead, cheerleader, cheerleaders, cheerleading, cheerled, cheerless, cheerlessly, cheerlessness, cheerly, cheero, cheeros, cheers, cheery, cheese, cheese's, cheeseboard, cheesebox, cheeseburger, cheeseburgers, cheesecake, cheesecakes, cheesecloth, cheesecloths, cheesecurd, cheesecutter, cheesed, cheeseflower, cheeselep, cheeselip, cheesemaker, cheesemaking, cheesemonger, cheesemongering, cheesemongerly, cheesemongery, cheeseparer, cheeseparing, cheeser, cheesery, cheeses, cheesewood, cheesier, cheesiest, cheesily, cheesiness, cheesing, cheesy, cheet, cheetah, cheetahs, cheetal, cheeter, cheetie, cheetul, cheewink, cheezit, chef, chef's, chefdom, chefdoms, chefs, chego, chegoe, chegoes, chegre, cheiceral, cheilion, cheilitis, cheiloplasties, cheiloplasty, cheilostomatous, cheilotomies, cheilotomy, cheimaphobia, cheimatophobia, cheir, cheiragra, cheirognomy, cheirography, cheirolin, cheiroline, cheirology, cheiromancy, cheiromegaly, cheiropatagium, cheiropod, cheiropodist, cheiropody, cheiropompholyx, cheiroptera, cheiropterygium, cheirosophy, cheirospasm, cheirotherium, cheka, chekan, cheke, cheken, chekhov, cheki, chekker, chekmak, chela, chelae, chelas, chelaship, chelatable, chelate, chelated, chelates, chelating, chelation, chelator, chelators, chelem, chelerythrin, chelerythrine, chelicer, chelicera, chelicerae, cheliceral, chelicerate, chelicere, chelide, chelidon, chelidonate, chelidonian, chelidonic, chelidonin, chelidonine, chelifer, cheliferous, cheliform, chelinga, chelingas, chelingo, chelingos, cheliped, chellean, chello, chelodine, cheloid, cheloids, chelone, chelonian, chelonid, cheloniid, chelonin, chelophore, chelp, chelydre, chelydroid, chelys, chem, chemasthenia, chemawinite, chemesthesis, chemiatric, chemiatrist, chemiatry, chemic, chemical, chemicalization, chemicalize, chemically, chemicals, chemick, chemicked, chemicker, chemicking, chemicoastrological, chemicobiologic, chemicobiological, chemicobiology, chemicocautery, chemicodynamic, chemicoengineering, chemicoluminescence, chemicoluminescent, chemicomechanical, chemicomineralogical, chemicopharmaceutical, chemicophysical, chemicophysics, chemicophysiological, chemicovital, chemics, chemiculture, chemigraph, chemigrapher, chemigraphic, chemigraphically, chemigraphy, chemiloon, chemiluminescence, chemiluminescent, chemin, cheminee, chemins, chemiotactic, chemiotaxic, chemiotaxis, chemiotropic, chemiotropism, chemiphotic, chemis, chemise, chemises, chemisette, chemism, chemisms, chemisorb, chemisorption, chemisorptive, chemist, chemist's, chemistries, chemistry, chemists, chemitype, chemitypies, chemitypy, chemizo, chemmy, chemoautotrophic, chemoautotrophically, chemoautotrophy, chemoceptor, chemokinesis, chemokinetic, chemolysis, chemolytic, chemolyze, chemonite, chemopallidectomies, chemopallidectomy, chemopause, chemophysiological, chemophysiology, chemoprophyalctic, chemoprophylactic, chemoprophylaxis, chemoreception, chemoreceptive, chemoreceptivities, chemoreceptivity, chemoreceptor, chemoreflex, chemoresistance, chemosensitive, chemosensitivities, chemosensitivity, chemoserotherapy, chemoses, chemosis, chemosmoic, chemosmoses, chemosmosis, chemosmotic, chemosorb, chemosorption, chemosorptive, chemosphere, chemospheric, chemostat, chemosterilant, chemosterilants, chemosurgery, chemosurgical, chemosynthesis, chemosynthetic, chemosynthetically, chemotactic, chemotactically, chemotaxis, chemotaxonomic, chemotaxonomically, chemotaxonomist, chemotaxonomy, chemotaxy, chemotherapeutic, chemotherapeutical, chemotherapeutically, chemotherapeuticness, chemotherapeutics, chemotherapies, chemotherapist, chemotherapists, chemotherapy, chemotic, chemotroph, chemotrophic, chemotropic, chemotropically, chemotropism, chempaduk, chemurgic, chemurgical, chemurgically, chemurgies, chemurgy, chena, chenar, chende, cheneau, cheneaus, cheneaux, chenet, chenevixite, chenfish, cheng, chengal, chenica, chenier, chenille, cheniller, chenilles, chenopod, chenopodiaceous, chenopods, cheongsam, cheoplastic, chepster, cheque, chequebook, chequeen, chequer, chequerboard, chequered, chequering, chequers, chequerwise, chequerwork, cheques, chequin, chequinn, chequy, cher, cherchez, chercock, chere, cherely, cherem, cherenkov, chergui, cherie, cheries, cherimolla, cherimoya, cherimoyer, cherish, cherishable, cherished, cherisher, cherishers, cherishes, cherishing, cherishingly, cherishment, chermes, cherna, chernites, chernozem, chernozemic, cherogril, cherokee, cherokees, cheroot, cheroots, cherried, cherries, cherry, cherry's, cherryblossom, cherrying, cherrylike, cherrystone, cherrystones, chersonese, chert, cherte, chertier, chertiest, cherts, cherty, cherub, cherub's, cherubfish, cherubfishes, cherubic, cherubical, cherubically, cherubim, cherubimic, cherubimical, cherubin, cherublike, cherubs, cherup, chervil, chervils, chervonei, chervonets, chervonetz, chervontsi, chesapeake, chesboil, chesboll, chese, cheselip, cheshire, chesil, cheskey, cheskeys, cheslep, cheson, chesoun, chess, chessart, chessboard, chessboards, chessdom, chessel, chesser, chesses, chesset, chessist, chessman, chessmen, chessner, chessom, chesstree, chessylite, chest, chested, chesteine, chester, chesterbed, chesterfield, chesterfields, chesterlite, chestful, chestfuls, chestier, chestiest, chestily, chestiness, chestnut, chestnut's, chestnuts, chestnutty, chests, chesty, chetah, chetahs, cheth, cheths, chetif, chetive, chetopod, chetrum, chetrums, chettik, chetty, chetverik, chetvert, cheung, chevachee, chevachie, chevage, cheval, chevalet, chevalets, chevalier, chevaliers, chevaline, chevance, chevaux, cheve, chevee, chevelure, cheven, chevener, cheventayn, cheverel, cheveret, cheveril, cheveron, cheverons, chevesaile, chevesne, chevet, chevetaine, cheveys, chevied, chevies, cheville, chevin, cheviot, cheviots, chevisance, chevise, chevon, chevre, chevres, chevret, chevrette, chevreuil, chevrolet, chevrolets, chevron, chevrone, chevroned, chevronel, chevronelly, chevronny, chevrons, chevronwise, chevrony, chevrotain, chevvy, chevy, chevying, chew, chewable, chewbark, chewed, cheweler, chewer, chewers, chewet, chewie, chewier, chewiest, chewing, chewink, chewinks, chews, chewstick, chewy, cheyenne, cheyennes, cheyney, cheyneys, chez, chg, chhatri, chi, chia, chiack, chian, chianti, chiao, chiarooscurist, chiarooscuro, chiarooscuros, chiaroscurist, chiaroscuro, chiaroscuros, chias, chiasm, chiasma, chiasmal, chiasmas, chiasmata, chiasmatic, chiasmatype, chiasmatypy, chiasmi, chiasmic, chiasmodontid, chiasms, chiasmus, chiastic, chiastolite, chiastoneural, chiastoneurous, chiastoneury, chiaus, chiauses, chiave, chiavetta, chiba, chibcha, chibchan, chibinite, chibol, chibouk, chibouks, chibouque, chibrit, chic, chica, chicadee, chicago, chicagoan, chicagoans, chicalote, chicane, chicaned, chicaner, chicaneries, chicaners, chicanery, chicanes, chicaning, chicano, chicanos, chicaric, chicayote, chiccories, chiccory, chicer, chicest, chich, chicha, chicharra, chichevache, chichi, chichicaste, chichili, chichimecan, chichipate, chichipe, chichis, chichituna, chichling, chick, chickabiddy, chickadee, chickadee's, chickadees, chickaree, chickasaw, chickasaws, chickee, chickees, chickell, chicken, chickenberry, chickenbill, chickenbreasted, chickened, chickenhearted, chickenheartedly, chickenheartedness, chickenhood, chickening, chickenpox, chickens, chickenshit, chickenweed, chickenwort, chicker, chickery, chickhood, chickies, chickling, chickories, chickory, chickpea, chickpeas, chicks, chickstone, chickweed, chickweeds, chickwit, chicky, chicle, chiclero, chicles, chicly, chicness, chicnesses, chico, chicories, chicory, chicos, chicot, chicote, chicqued, chicquer, chicquest, chicquing, chics, chid, chidden, chide, chided, chider, chiders, chides, chiding, chidingly, chidingness, chidra, chief, chiefage, chiefdom, chiefdoms, chiefer, chiefery, chiefess, chiefest, chiefish, chiefless, chiefling, chiefly, chiefry, chiefs, chiefship, chieftain, chieftain's, chieftaincies, chieftaincy, chieftainess, chieftainries, chieftainry, chieftains, chieftainship, chieftainships, chieftess, chiefty, chiel, chield, chields, chiels, chien, chierete, chievance, chieve, chiffchaff, chiffer, chifferobe, chiffon, chiffonade, chiffonier, chiffoniers, chiffonnier, chiffonnieres, chiffonniers, chiffons, chiffony, chifforobe, chifforobes, chiffre, chiffrobe, chigetai, chigetais, chigga, chiggak, chigger, chiggers, chiggerweed, chignon, chignoned, chignons, chigoe, chigoes, chih, chihfu, chihuahua, chihuahuas, chikara, chikee, chil, chilacavote, chilacayote, chilalgia, chilaria, chilarium, chilblain, chilblained, chilblains, child, childage, childbear, childbearing, childbed, childbeds, childbirth, childbirths, childcrowing, childe, childed, childermas, childes, childhood, childhoods, childing, childish, childishly, childishness, childkind, childless, childlessness, childlier, childliest, childlike, childlikeness, childly, childminder, childness, childproof, childre, children, children's, childrenite, childridden, childship, childward, childwife, childwite, chile, chilean, chileans, chilectropion, chilenite, chiles, chili, chiliad, chiliadal, chiliadic, chiliadron, chiliads, chiliaedron, chiliagon, chiliahedron, chiliarch, chiliarchia, chiliarchy, chiliasm, chiliasms, chiliast, chiliastic, chiliasts, chilicote, chilicothe, chilidium, chilidog, chilidogs, chilies, chilindre, chiliomb, chilipepper, chilitis, chill, chilla, chillagite, chilled, chiller, chillers, chillest, chilli, chillier, chillies, chilliest, chillily, chilliness, chilling, chillingly, chillis, chillish, chillness, chillo, chilloes, chillroom, chills, chillsome, chillum, chillumchee, chillums, chilly, chilodon, chilognath, chilognathan, chilognathous, chilogrammo, chiloma, chilomata, chiloncus, chiloplasty, chilopod, chilopodan, chilopodous, chilopods, chilostomatous, chilostome, chilotomies, chilotomy, chilte, chiltern, chilver, chimachima, chimaera, chimaeras, chimaerid, chimaeroid, chimango, chimar, chimars, chimb, chimbe, chimble, chimbley, chimbleys, chimblies, chimbly, chimbs, chime, chime's, chimed, chimer, chimera, chimeral, chimeras, chimere, chimeres, chimeric, chimerical, chimerically, chimericalness, chimerism, chimers, chimes, chimesmaster, chimin, chiminage, chiming, chimla, chimlas, chimley, chimleys, chimney, chimney's, chimneyed, chimneyhead, chimneying, chimneyless, chimneylike, chimneyman, chimneypiece, chimneypot, chimneys, chimopeelagic, chimopelagic, chimp, chimpanzee, chimpanzees, chimps, chin, chin's, china, chinaberries, chinaberry, chinafish, chinafy, chinalike, chinaman, chinamania, chinamaniac, chinamen, chinampa, chinanta, chinaphthol, chinar, chinaroot, chinas, chinatown, chinaware, chinawoman, chinband, chinbeak, chinbone, chinbones, chincapin, chinch, chincha, chinchayote, chinche, chincher, chincherinchee, chincherinchees, chinches, chinchier, chinchiest, chinchilla, chinchillas, chinchillette, chinchiness, chinching, chinchona, chinchy, chincloth, chincof, chincona, chincough, chindee, chindi, chine, chined, chinela, chinenses, chines, chinese, chinfest, ching, chingma, chinik, chiniks, chinin, chining, chiniofon, chink, chinkapin, chinkara, chinked, chinker, chinkerinchee, chinkers, chinkier, chinkiest, chinking, chinkle, chinks, chinky, chinles, chinless, chinnam, chinned, chinner, chinners, chinnier, chinniest, chinning, chinny, chino, chinoa, chinoidin, chinoidine, chinois, chinoiserie, chinol, chinoleine, chinoline, chinologist, chinone, chinones, chinook, chinookan, chinooks, chinos, chinotoxine, chinotti, chinotto, chinovnik, chinpiece, chinquapin, chins, chinse, chinsed, chinsing, chint, chints, chintses, chintz, chintze, chintzes, chintzier, chintziest, chintziness, chintzy, chinwag, chinwood, chiococcine, chiolite, chionablepsia, chionodoxa, chionophobia, chiopin, chiotilla, chip, chip's, chipboard, chipchap, chipchop, chiplet, chipling, chipmuck, chipmucks, chipmunk, chipmunk's, chipmunks, chipolata, chippable, chippage, chipped, chippendale, chipper, chippered, chippering, chippers, chippewa, chippewas, chippie, chippier, chippies, chippiest, chipping, chippings, chipproof, chippy, chips, chipwood, chipyard, chiquero, chiquest, chiragra, chiragrical, chiral, chiralgia, chirality, chirapsia, chirarthritis, chirata, chirayta, chirimen, chirimia, chirimoya, chirimoyer, chirinola, chiripa, chirivita, chirk, chirked, chirker, chirkest, chirking, chirks, chirl, chirm, chirmed, chirming, chirms, chiro, chirocosmetics, chirogale, chirognomic, chirognomically, chirognomist, chirognomy, chirognostic, chirograph, chirographary, chirographer, chirographers, chirographic, chirographical, chirography, chirogymnast, chirolas, chirological, chirologically, chirologies, chirologist, chirology, chiromance, chiromancer, chiromancist, chiromancy, chiromant, chiromantic, chiromantical, chiromegaly, chirometer, chironomic, chironomid, chironomy, chironym, chiropatagium, chiroplasty, chiropod, chiropodial, chiropodic, chiropodical, chiropodist, chiropodistry, chiropodists, chiropodous, chiropody, chiropompholyx, chiropractic, chiropractor, chiropractors, chiropraxis, chiropter, chiropteran, chiropterite, chiropterophilous, chiropterous, chiropterygian, chiropterygious, chiropterygium, chiros, chirosophist, chirospasm, chirotherian, chirothesia, chirotonsor, chirotonsory, chirotony, chirotype, chirp, chirped, chirper, chirpers, chirpier, chirpiest, chirpily, chirpiness, chirping, chirpingly, chirpling, chirps, chirpy, chirr, chirre, chirred, chirres, chirring, chirrs, chirrup, chirruped, chirruper, chirruping, chirrupper, chirrups, chirrupy, chirt, chiru, chirurgeon, chirurgeonly, chirurgery, chirurgic, chirurgical, chirurgy, chis, chisel, chiseled, chiseler, chiselers, chiseling, chiselled, chiseller, chisellers, chisellike, chiselling, chiselly, chiselmouth, chisels, chisled, chistera, chistka, chit, chitak, chital, chitarra, chitarrino, chitarrone, chitarroni, chitchat, chitchats, chitchatted, chitchatting, chitchatty, chithe, chitin, chitinization, chitinized, chitinocalcareous, chitinogenous, chitinoid, chitinous, chitins, chitlin, chitling, chitlings, chitlins, chiton, chitons, chitosamine, chitosan, chitosans, chitose, chitra, chits, chittack, chittak, chittamwood, chitted, chitter, chittered, chittering, chitterling, chitterlings, chitters, chitties, chitting, chitty, chiule, chiurm, chiv, chivachee, chivage, chivalresque, chivalric, chivalries, chivalrous, chivalrously, chivalrousness, chivalry, chivaree, chivareed, chivareeing, chivarees, chivareing, chivari, chivaried, chivariing, chivaring, chivaris, chivarra, chivarras, chivarro, chive, chiver, chiveret, chives, chivey, chiviatite, chivied, chivies, chivvied, chivvies, chivvy, chivvying, chivw, chivy, chivying, chizz, chizzel, chkalik, chkfil, chkfile, chladnite, chlamyd, chlamydate, chlamydeous, chlamydes, chlamydobacteriaceous, chlamydomonas, chlamydophore, chlamydospore, chlamydosporic, chlamydozoan, chlamyphore, chlamys, chlamyses, chloanthite, chloasma, chloasmata, chloe, chlor, chloracetate, chloracne, chloraemia, chloragen, chloragogen, chloragogue, chloral, chloralformamide, chloralide, chloralism, chloralization, chloralize, chloralized, chloralizing, chloralose, chloralosed, chlorals, chloralum, chlorambucil, chloramide, chloramin, chloramine, chloramphenicol, chloranaemia, chloranemia, chloranemic, chloranhydride, chloranil, chloranthaceous, chloranthus, chloranthy, chlorapatite, chlorargyrite, chlorastrolite, chlorate, chlorates, chlorazide, chlorcosane, chlordan, chlordane, chlordans, chlordiazepoxide, chlore, chlored, chlorella, chlorellaceous, chloremia, chloremic, chlorenchyma, chlorguanide, chlorhexidine, chlorhydrate, chlorhydric, chloriamb, chloriambus, chloric, chlorid, chloridate, chloridated, chloridation, chloride, chlorider, chlorides, chloridic, chloridize, chloridized, chloridizing, chlorids, chlorimeter, chlorimetric, chlorimetry, chlorin, chlorinate, chlorinated, chlorinates, chlorinating, chlorination, chlorinator, chlorinators, chlorine, chlorines, chlorinity, chlorinize, chlorinous, chlorins, chloriodide, chlorite, chlorites, chloritic, chloritization, chloritize, chloritoid, chlorize, chlormethane, chlormethylic, chlornal, chloro, chloroacetate, chloroacetic, chloroacetone, chloroacetophenone, chloroamide, chloroamine, chloroanaemia, chloroanemia, chloroaurate, chloroauric, chloroaurite, chlorobenzene, chlorobromide, chlorobromomethane, chlorocalcite, chlorocarbon, chlorocarbonate, chlorochromates, chlorochromic, chlorochrous, chlorocresol, chlorocruorin, chlorodize, chlorodized, chlorodizing, chlorodyne, chloroethene, chloroethylene, chlorofluorocarbon, chlorofluoromethane, chloroform, chloroformate, chloroformed, chloroformic, chloroforming, chloroformism, chloroformist, chloroformization, chloroformize, chloroforms, chlorogenic, chlorogenine, chloroguanide, chlorohydrin, chlorohydrocarbon, chlorohydroquinone, chloroid, chloroiodide, chloroleucite, chloroma, chloromata, chloromelanite, chlorometer, chloromethane, chlorometric, chlorometry, chloromycetin, chloronaphthalene, chloronitrate, chloropal, chloropalladates, chloropalladic, chlorophaeite, chlorophane, chlorophenol, chlorophenothane, chlorophoenicite, chlorophyceous, chlorophyl, chlorophyll, chlorophyllaceous, chlorophyllan, chlorophyllase, chlorophyllian, chlorophyllide, chlorophylliferous, chlorophylligenous, chlorophylligerous, chlorophyllin, chlorophyllite, chlorophylloid, chlorophyllose, chlorophyllous, chloropia, chloropicrin, chloroplast, chloroplast's, chloroplastic, chloroplastid, chloroplasts, chloroplatinate, chloroplatinic, chloroplatinite, chloroplatinous, chloroprene, chloropsia, chloroquine, chlorosilicate, chlorosis, chlorospinel, chlorosulphonic, chlorothiazide, chlorotic, chlorotically, chlorotrifluoroethylene, chlorotrifluoromethane, chlorous, chlorozincate, chlorpheniramine, chlorphenol, chlorpicrin, chlorpikrin, chlorpromazine, chlorpropamide, chlorprophenpyridamine, chlorsalol, chlortetracycline, chloryl, chm, chmn, chn, cho, choachyte, choak, choana, choanate, choanite, choanocytal, choanocyte, choanoflagellate, choanoid, choanophorous, choanosomal, choanosome, choate, choaty, chob, chobdar, chobie, choca, chocalho, chocard, chocho, chochos, chock, chock's, chockablock, chocked, chocker, chockful, chocking, chockler, chockman, chocks, chockstone, choco, chocolate, chocolate's, chocolates, chocolatey, chocolatier, chocolatiere, chocolaty, choctaw, choctaws, choel, choenix, choffer, choga, chogak, chogset, choice, choiceful, choiceless, choicelessness, choicely, choiceness, choicer, choices, choicest, choicier, choiciest, choicy, choil, choile, choiler, choir, choir's, choirboy, choirboys, choired, choirgirl, choiring, choirlike, choirman, choirmaster, choirmasters, choirs, choirwise, choise, chok, chokage, choke, chokeable, chokeberries, chokeberry, chokebore, chokecherries, chokecherry, choked, chokedamp, choker, chokered, chokerman, chokers, chokes, chokestrap, chokeweed, chokey, chokeys, chokidar, chokier, chokies, chokiest, choking, chokingly, choko, chokra, choky, chol, chola, cholaemia, cholagogic, cholagogue, cholalic, cholam, cholane, cholangiographic, cholangiography, cholangioitis, cholangitis, cholanic, cholanthrene, cholate, cholates, chold, choleate, cholecalciferol, cholecyanin, cholecyanine, cholecyst, cholecystalgia, cholecystectasia, cholecystectomies, cholecystectomized, cholecystectomy, cholecystenterorrhaphy, cholecystenterostomy, cholecystgastrostomy, cholecystic, cholecystis, cholecystitis, cholecystnephrostomy, cholecystocolostomy, cholecystocolotomy, cholecystoduodenostomy, cholecystogastrostomy, cholecystogram, cholecystography, cholecystoileostomy, cholecystojejunostomy, cholecystokinin, cholecystolithiasis, cholecystolithotripsy, cholecystonephrostomy, cholecystopexy, cholecystorrhaphy, cholecystostomies, cholecystostomy, cholecystotomies, cholecystotomy, choledoch, choledochal, choledochectomy, choledochitis, choledochoduodenostomy, choledochoenterostomy, choledocholithiasis, choledocholithotomy, choledocholithotripsy, choledochoplasty, choledochorrhaphy, choledochostomies, choledochostomy, choledochotomies, choledochotomy, choledography, cholee, cholehematin, choleic, choleine, choleinic, cholelith, cholelithiasis, cholelithic, cholelithotomy, cholelithotripsy, cholelithotrity, cholemia, cholent, cholents, choleokinase, cholepoietic, choler, cholera, choleraic, choleras, choleric, cholerically, cholericly, cholericness, choleriform, cholerigenous, cholerine, choleroid, choleromania, cholerophobia, cholerrhagia, cholers, cholestane, cholestanol, cholesteatoma, cholesteatomatous, cholestene, cholesterate, cholesteremia, cholesteric, cholesterin, cholesterinemia, cholesterinic, cholesterinuria, cholesterol, cholesterolemia, cholesteroluria, cholesterosis, cholesteryl, choletelin, choletherapy, choleuria, choli, choliamb, choliambic, choliambist, cholic, cholick, choline, cholinergic, cholines, cholinesterase, cholinic, cholinolytic, cholla, chollas, choller, chollers, cholo, cholochrome, cholocyanine, chologenetic, choloid, choloidic, choloidinic, chololith, chololithic, cholophaein, cholophein, cholorrhea, cholos, choloscopy, cholralosed, cholterheaded, choltry, cholum, choluria, chomage, chomer, chomp, chomped, chomper, chompers, chomping, chomps, chon, chonchina, chondral, chondralgia, chondrarsenite, chondre, chondrectomy, chondrenchyma, chondri, chondria, chondric, chondrification, chondrified, chondrify, chondrigen, chondrigenous, chondrin, chondrinous, chondriocont, chondrioma, chondriome, chondriomere, chondriomite, chondriosomal, chondriosome, chondriosomes, chondriosphere, chondrite, chondrites, chondritic, chondritis, chondroadenoma, chondroalbuminoid, chondroangioma, chondroarthritis, chondroblast, chondroblastoma, chondrocarcinoma, chondrocele, chondroclasis, chondroclast, chondrocoracoid, chondrocostal, chondrocranial, chondrocranium, chondrocyte, chondrodite, chondroditic, chondrodynia, chondrodystrophia, chondrodystrophy, chondroendothelioma, chondroepiphysis, chondrofetal, chondrofibroma, chondrofibromatous, chondrogen, chondrogenesis, chondrogenetic, chondrogenous, chondrogeny, chondroglossal, chondroglossus, chondrography, chondroid, chondroitic, chondroitin, chondrolipoma, chondrology, chondroma, chondromalacia, chondromas, chondromata, chondromatous, chondromucoid, chondromyoma, chondromyxoma, chondromyxosarcoma, chondropharyngeal, chondropharyngeus, chondrophore, chondrophyte, chondroplast, chondroplastic, chondroplasty, chondroprotein, chondropterygian, chondropterygious, chondrosamine, chondrosarcoma, chondrosarcomas, chondrosarcomata, chondrosarcomatous, chondroseptum, chondrosin, chondrosis, chondroskeleton, chondrostean, chondrosteoma, chondrosteous, chondrosternal, chondrotome, chondrotomy, chondroxiphoid, chondrule, chondrules, chondrus, chonicrite, chonk, chonolith, chonta, chontawood, choochoo, chook, chookie, chookies, chooky, choom, choop, choora, choosable, choosableness, choose, chooseable, chooser, choosers, chooses, choosey, choosier, choosiest, choosiness, choosing, choosingly, choosy, chop, chopa, chopas, chopboat, chopdar, chopfallen, chophouse, chophouses, chopin, chopine, chopines, chopins, choplogic, choplogical, chopped, chopper, chopper's, choppered, choppers, choppier, choppiest, choppily, choppin, choppiness, chopping, choppy, chops, chopstick, chopsticks, choragi, choragic, choragion, choragium, choragus, choraguses, choragy, choral, choralcelo, chorale, choraleon, chorales, choralist, chorally, chorals, chord, chord's, chorda, chordacentrous, chordacentrum, chordaceous, chordal, chordally, chordamesoderm, chordamesodermal, chordamesodermic, chordata, chordate, chordates, chorded, chordee, chording, chorditis, chordoid, chordomesoderm, chordophone, chordotomy, chordotonal, chords, chore, chorea, choreal, choreas, choreatic, chored, choree, choregi, choregic, choregrapher, choregraphic, choregraphically, choregraphy, choregus, choreguses, choregy, chorei, choreic, choreiform, choreman, choremen, choreodrama, choreograph, choreographed, choreographer, choreographers, choreographic, choreographical, choreographically, choreographing, choreographs, choreography, choreoid, choreomania, chorepiscopal, chorepiscope, chorepiscopus, chores, choreus, choreutic, chorgi, chorial, choriamb, choriambi, choriambic, choriambize, choriambs, choriambus, choriambuses, choribi, choric, chorically, chorine, chorines, choring, chorio, chorioadenoma, chorioallantoic, chorioallantoid, chorioallantois, choriocapillaris, choriocapillary, choriocarcinoma, choriocarcinomas, choriocarcinomata, choriocele, chorioepithelioma, chorioepitheliomas, chorioepitheliomata, chorioid, chorioidal, chorioiditis, chorioidocyclitis, chorioidoiritis, chorioidoretinitis, chorioids, chorioma, choriomas, choriomata, chorion, chorionepithelioma, chorionic, chorions, chorioptic, chorioretinal, chorioretinitis, choripetalous, choriphyllous, chorisepalous, chorisis, chorism, choriso, chorisos, chorist, choristate, chorister, choristers, choristership, choristic, choristoblastoma, choristoma, choristoneura, choristry, chorization, chorizo, chorizont, chorizontal, chorizontes, chorizontic, chorizontist, chorizos, chorobates, chorogi, chorograph, chorographer, chorographic, chorographical, chorographically, chorographies, chorography, choroid, choroidal, choroidea, choroiditis, choroidocyclitis, choroidoiritis, choroidoretinitis, choroids, chorological, chorologist, chorology, choromania, choromanic, chorometry, chorook, chorous, chort, chorten, chortle, chortled, chortler, chortlers, chortles, chortling, chortosterol, chorus, chorused, choruser, choruses, chorusing, choruslike, chorusmaster, chorussed, chorusses, chorussing, choryos, chose, chosen, choses, chosing, chott, chotts, chou, chouan, choucroute, chouette, choufleur, chough, choughs, chouka, choule, choultries, choultry, chounce, choup, choupic, chouquette, chous, chouse, choused, chouser, chousers, chouses, choush, choushes, chousing, chousingha, chout, choux, chow, chowchow, chowchows, chowder, chowdered, chowderhead, chowderheaded, chowderheadedness, chowdering, chowders, chowed, chowhound, chowing, chowk, chowries, chowry, chows, chowse, chowsed, chowses, chowsing, chowtime, chowtimes, choy, choya, choyaroot, choyroot, chrematheism, chrematist, chrematistic, chrematistics, chremsel, chremzel, chremzlach, chreotechnics, chresard, chresards, chresmology, chrestomathic, chrestomathics, chrestomathies, chrestomathy, chria, chrimsel, chrism, chrisma, chrismal, chrismale, chrismary, chrismatine, chrismation, chrismatite, chrismatize, chrismatories, chrismatory, chrismon, chrismons, chrisms, chrisom, chrisomloosing, chrisoms, chrisroot, christ, christcross, christdom, christed, christen, christendom, christened, christener, christeners, christenhead, christening, christens, christhood, christian, christian's, christiania, christianism, christianite, christianity, christianization, christianize, christianized, christianizes, christianizing, christians, christie, christies, christine, christless, christlike, christly, christmas, christmases, christmastide, christological, christology, christophany, christopher, christs, christward, christy, chroatol, chroma, chromaffin, chromaffinic, chromamamin, chromammine, chromaphil, chromaphore, chromas, chromascope, chromate, chromates, chromatic, chromatical, chromatically, chromatician, chromaticism, chromaticity, chromaticness, chromatics, chromatid, chromatin, chromatinic, chromatism, chromatist, chromatize, chromatocyte, chromatodysopia, chromatogenous, chromatogram, chromatograph, chromatographic, chromatographically, chromatography, chromatoid, chromatologies, chromatology, chromatolysis, chromatolytic, chromatometer, chromatone, chromatopathia, chromatopathic, chromatopathy, chromatophil, chromatophile, chromatophilia, chromatophilic, chromatophilous, chromatophobia, chromatophore, chromatophoric, chromatophorous, chromatoplasm, chromatopsia, chromatoptometer, chromatoptometry, chromatoscope, chromatoscopy, chromatosis, chromatosphere, chromatospheric, chromatrope, chromaturia, chromatype, chromazurine, chromdiagnosis, chrome, chromed, chromene, chromeplate, chromeplated, chromeplating, chromes, chromesthesia, chrometophobia, chromhidrosis, chromic, chromicize, chromicizing, chromid, chromide, chromides, chromidial, chromidiogamy, chromidiosome, chromidium, chromidrosis, chromiferous, chrominance, chroming, chromiole, chromism, chromite, chromites, chromitite, chromium, chromiums, chromize, chromized, chromizes, chromizing, chromo, chromoblast, chromocenter, chromocentral, chromochalcographic, chromochalcography, chromocollograph, chromocollographic, chromocollography, chromocollotype, chromocollotypy, chromocratic, chromoctye, chromocyte, chromocytometer, chromodermatosis, chromodiascope, chromogen, chromogene, chromogenesis, chromogenetic, chromogenic, chromogenous, chromogram, chromograph, chromoisomer, chromoisomeric, chromoisomerism, chromoleucite, chromolipoid, chromolith, chromolithic, chromolithograph, chromolithographer, chromolithographic, chromolithography, chromolysis, chromomere, chromomeric, chromometer, chromone, chromonema, chromonemal, chromonemata, chromonematal, chromonematic, chromonemic, chromoparous, chromophage, chromophane, chromophil, chromophile, chromophilia, chromophilic, chromophilous, chromophobe, chromophobia, chromophobic, chromophor, chromophore, chromophoric, chromophorous, chromophotograph, chromophotographic, chromophotography, chromophotolithograph, chromophyl, chromophyll, chromoplasm, chromoplasmic, chromoplast, chromoplastid, chromoprotein, chromopsia, chromoptometer, chromoptometrical, chromos, chromosantonin, chromoscope, chromoscopic, chromoscopy, chromosomal, chromosomally, chromosome, chromosomes, chromosomic, chromosphere, chromospheres, chromospheric, chromotherapist, chromotherapy, chromotrope, chromotropic, chromotropism, chromotropy, chromotype, chromotypic, chromotypographic, chromotypography, chromotypy, chromous, chromoxylograph, chromoxylography, chromule, chromy, chromyl, chron, chronal, chronanagram, chronaxia, chronaxie, chronaxies, chronaxy, chroncmeter, chronic, chronica, chronical, chronically, chronicity, chronicle, chronicled, chronicler, chroniclers, chronicles, chronicling, chronicon, chronics, chronique, chronisotherm, chronist, chronobarometer, chronobiology, chronocarator, chronocinematography, chronocrator, chronocyclegraph, chronodeik, chronogeneous, chronogenesis, chronogenetic, chronogram, chronogrammatic, chronogrammatical, chronogrammatically, chronogrammatist, chronogrammic, chronograph, chronographer, chronographic, chronographical, chronographically, chronographs, chronography, chronoisothermal, chronol, chronologer, chronologic, chronological, chronologically, chronologies, chronologist, chronologists, chronologize, chronologizing, chronology, chronology's, chronomancy, chronomantic, chronomastix, chronometer, chronometers, chronometric, chronometrical, chronometrically, chronometry, chronon, chrononomy, chronons, chronopher, chronophotograph, chronophotographic, chronophotography, chronoscope, chronoscopic, chronoscopically, chronoscopv, chronoscopy, chronosemic, chronostichon, chronothermal, chronothermometer, chronotropic, chronotropism, chroococcaceous, chroococcoid, chrotta, chry, chrysal, chrysalid, chrysalida, chrysalidal, chrysalides, chrysalidian, chrysaline, chrysalis, chrysalises, chrysaloid, chrysamine, chrysammic, chrysamminic, chrysanilin, chrysaniline, chrysanisic, chrysanthemin, chrysanthemum, chrysanthemums, chrysanthous, chrysarobin, chrysatropic, chrysazin, chrysazol, chryseis, chryselectrum, chryselephantine, chrysene, chrysenic, chrysid, chrysidid, chrysin, chrysler, chryslers, chrysoaristocracy, chrysoberyl, chrysobull, chrysocale, chrysocarpous, chrysochlore, chrysochlorous, chrysochrous, chrysocolla, chrysocracy, chrysoeriol, chrysogen, chrysograph, chrysographer, chrysography, chrysohermidin, chrysoidine, chrysolite, chrysolitic, chrysology, chrysome, chrysomelid, chrysomonad, chrysomonadine, chrysopal, chrysopee, chrysophan, chrysophane, chrysophanic, chrysophenin, chrysophenine, chrysophilist, chrysophilite, chrysophyll, chrysophyte, chrysopid, chrysopoeia, chrysopoetic, chrysopoetics, chrysoprase, chrysoprasus, chrysorin, chrysosperm, chrysostomic, chrysotherapy, chrysotile, chrystocrene, chs, chteau, chthonian, chthonic, chthonophagia, chthonophagy, chuana, chub, chubasco, chubascos, chubb, chubbed, chubbedness, chubbier, chubbiest, chubbily, chubbiness, chubby, chubs, chubsucker, chuck, chuck's, chuckawalla, chucked, chucker, chuckfarthing, chuckfull, chuckhole, chuckholes, chuckie, chuckies, chucking, chuckingly, chuckle, chuckled, chucklehead, chuckleheaded, chuckleheadedness, chuckler, chucklers, chuckles, chucklesome, chuckling, chucklingly, chuckram, chuckrum, chucks, chuckstone, chuckwalla, chucky, chuddah, chuddahs, chuddar, chuddars, chudder, chudders, chuet, chufa, chufas, chuff, chuffed, chuffer, chuffest, chuffier, chuffiest, chuffily, chuffiness, chuffing, chuffs, chuffy, chug, chugalug, chugalugged, chugalugging, chugalugs, chugged, chugger, chuggers, chugging, chughole, chugs, chuhra, chukar, chukars, chukka, chukkar, chukkars, chukkas, chukker, chukkers, chukor, chulan, chulha, chullo, chullpa, chulpa, chultun, chum, chumar, chumble, chummage, chummed, chummer, chummery, chummier, chummies, chummiest, chummily, chumminess, chumming, chummy, chump, chumpa, chumpaka, chumped, chumpiness, chumping, chumpish, chumpishness, chumps, chumpy, chums, chumship, chumships, chun, chunam, chunari, chundari, chunder, chunderous, chung, chunga, chungking, chunk, chunk's, chunked, chunkhead, chunkier, chunkiest, chunkily, chunkiness, chunking, chunks, chunky, chunner, chunnia, chunter, chuntered, chuntering, chunters, chupak, chupatti, chupatty, chupon, chuppah, chuppahs, chuppoth, chuprassi, chuprassie, chuprassy, churada, church, churchanity, churchcraft, churchdom, churched, churches, churchful, churchgo, churchgoer, churchgoers, churchgoing, churchgrith, churchianity, churchier, churchiest, churchified, churchill, churchiness, churching, churchish, churchism, churchite, churchless, churchlet, churchlier, churchliest, churchlike, churchliness, churchly, churchman, churchmanly, churchmanship, churchmaster, churchmen, churchreeve, churchscot, churchshot, churchward, churchwarden, churchwardenism, churchwardenize, churchwardens, churchwardenship, churchwards, churchway, churchwise, churchwoman, churchwomen, churchy, churchyard, churchyard's, churchyards, churel, churidars, churinga, churingas, churl, churled, churlhood, churlier, churliest, churlish, churlishly, churlishness, churls, churly, churm, churn, churnability, churnable, churned, churner, churners, churnful, churning, churnings, churnmilk, churns, churnstaff, churr, churrasco, churred, churrigueresco, churrigueresque, churring, churrip, churro, churrs, churruck, churrus, churrworm, chuse, chuser, chusite, chut, chute, chute's, chuted, chuter, chutes, chuting, chutist, chutists, chutnee, chutnees, chutney, chutneys, chuttie, chutzpa, chutzpadik, chutzpah, chutzpahs, chutzpanik, chutzpas, chuumnapm, chuvashes, chuzwi, chwas, chyack, chyak, chyazic, chylaceous, chylangioma, chylaqueous, chyle, chylemia, chyles, chylidrosis, chylifaction, chylifactive, chylifactory, chyliferous, chylific, chylification, chylificatory, chylified, chyliform, chylify, chylifying, chylocaulous, chylocaulously, chylocauly, chylocele, chylocyst, chyloid, chylomicron, chylopericardium, chylophyllous, chylophyllously, chylophylly, chylopoetic, chylopoiesis, chylopoietic, chylosis, chylothorax, chylous, chyluria, chymaqueous, chymase, chyme, chymes, chymia, chymic, chymics, chymiferous, chymification, chymified, chymify, chymifying, chymist, chymistry, chymists, chymosin, chymosinogen, chymosins, chymotrypsin, chymotrypsinogen, chymous, chyometer, chypre, chytra, chytrid, chytridiaceous, chytridial, chytridiose, chytridiosis, cia, ciao, cibaria, cibarial, cibarian, cibaries, cibarious, cibarium, cibation, cibbaria, cibboria, cibol, cibolero, cibols, cibophobia, cibophobiafood, ciboria, ciborium, cibory, ciboule, ciboules, cicad, cicada, cicadae, cicadas, cicadid, cicala, cicalas, cicale, cicatrice, cicatrices, cicatricial, cicatricle, cicatricose, cicatricula, cicatriculae, cicatricule, cicatrisant, cicatrisate, cicatrisation, cicatrise, cicatrised, cicatriser, cicatrising, cicatrisive, cicatrix, cicatrixes, cicatrizant, cicatrizate, cicatrization, cicatrize, cicatrized, cicatrizer, cicatrizing, cicatrose, cicelies, cicely, cicer, cicero, ciceronage, cicerone, cicerones, ciceroni, ciceronian, ciceronianism, ciceronianisms, ciceronianist, ciceronianists, ciceronians, ciceroning, ciceronism, ciceronize, ciceros, cichar, cichlid, cichlidae, cichlids, cichloid, cichoraceous, cichoriaceous, cicindelid, cicindelidae, cicisbei, cicisbeism, cicisbeo, ciclatoun, cicone, ciconian, ciconiform, ciconiid, ciconiiform, ciconine, ciconioid, cicoree, cicorees, cicrumspections, cicurate, cicuta, cicutoxin, cid, cidarid, cidaris, cider, ciderish, ciderist, ciderkin, ciderlike, ciders, cie, cienaga, cienega, cierge, cierzo, cierzos, cif, cig, cigala, cigale, cigar, cigar's, cigaresque, cigaret, cigarets, cigarette, cigarette's, cigarettes, cigarfish, cigarillo, cigarillos, cigarito, cigaritos, cigarless, cigars, cigua, ciguatera, cilantro, cilantros, cilectomy, cilery, cilia, ciliary, ciliata, ciliate, ciliated, ciliately, ciliates, ciliation, cilice, cilices, cilicious, cilicism, ciliectomy, ciliella, ciliferous, ciliform, ciliiferous, ciliiform, ciliium, cilioflagellate, ciliograde, ciliola, ciliolate, ciliolum, cilioretinal, cilioscleral, ciliospinal, ciliotomy, cilium, cill, cillosis, cima, cimaise, cimaroon, cimbal, cimbalom, cimbaloms, cimbia, cimborio, cimcumvention, cimelia, cimeliarch, cimelium, cimeter, cimex, cimices, cimicid, cimicide, cimiciform, cimicifugin, cimicoid, cimier, ciminite, cimline, cimmaron, cimmerian, cimnel, cimolite, cinch, cincha, cinched, cincher, cinches, cinching, cincholoipon, cincholoiponic, cinchomeronic, cinchona, cinchonaceous, cinchonamin, cinchonamine, cinchonas, cinchonate, cinchonia, cinchonic, cinchonicin, cinchonicine, cinchonidia, cinchonidine, cinchonin, cinchonine, cinchoninic, cinchonisation, cinchonise, cinchonised, cinchonising, cinchonism, cinchonization, cinchonize, cinchonized, cinchonizing, cinchonology, cinchophen, cinchotine, cinchotoxine, cincinatti, cincinnal, cincinnati, cincinni, cincinnus, cinclides, cinclis, cinct, cincture, cinctured, cinctures, cincturing, cinder, cinder's, cindered, cinderella, cindering, cinderlike, cinderman, cinderous, cinders, cindery, cine, cineangiocardiographic, cineangiocardiography, cineangiographic, cineangiography, cineast, cineaste, cineastes, cineasts, cinecamera, cinefaction, cinefilm, cinel, cinema, cinemactic, cinemagoer, cinemagoers, cinemas, cinematheque, cinematheques, cinematic, cinematical, cinematically, cinematics, cinematize, cinematized, cinematizing, cinematograph, cinematographer, cinematographers, cinematographic, cinematographical, cinematographically, cinematographies, cinematographist, cinematography, cinemelodrama, cinemese, cinemize, cinemograph, cinenchym, cinenchyma, cinenchymatous, cinene, cinenegative, cineol, cineole, cineoles, cineolic, cineols, cinephone, cinephotomicrography, cineplastics, cineplasty, cineraceous, cineradiography, cinerama, cinerararia, cineraria, cinerarias, cinerarium, cinerary, cineration, cinerator, cinerea, cinereal, cinereous, cinerin, cinerins, cineritious, cinerous, cines, cinevariety, cingalese, cingle, cingula, cingular, cingulate, cingulated, cingulectomies, cingulectomy, cingulum, ciniphes, cinnabar, cinnabaric, cinnabarine, cinnabars, cinnamal, cinnamaldehyde, cinnamate, cinnamein, cinnamene, cinnamenyl, cinnamic, cinnamol, cinnamomic, cinnamon, cinnamoned, cinnamonic, cinnamonlike, cinnamonroot, cinnamons, cinnamonwood, cinnamoyl, cinnamyl, cinnamylidene, cinnamyls, cinnolin, cinnoline, cinnyl, cinofoil, cinquain, cinquains, cinquanter, cinque, cinquecentism, cinquecentist, cinquecento, cinquedea, cinquefoil, cinquefoiled, cinquefoils, cinquepace, cinques, cinter, cintre, cinuran, cinurous, cion, cionectomy, cionitis, cionocranial, cionocranian, cionoptosis, cionorrhaphia, cionotome, cionotomy, cions, cioppino, cioppinos, cipaye, cipher,

cipher's, cipherable, cipherdom, ciphered, cipherer, cipherhood, ciphering, ciphers, ciphertext, ciphertexts, ciphonies, ciphony, cipo, cipolin, cipolins, cipollino, cippi, cippus, cir, circ, circa, circadian, circar, circassian, circe, circensian, circinal, circinate, circinately, circination, circinus, circiter, circle, circled, circler, circlers, circles, circlet, circleting, circlets, circlewise, circline, circling, circocele, circovarian, circs, circue, circuit, circuit's, circuitable, circuital, circuited, circuiteer, circuiter, circuities, circuiting, circuition, circuitman, circuitmen, circuitor, circuitous, circuitously, circuitousness, circuitry, circuits, circuituously, circuity, circulable, circulant, circular, circularisation, circularise, circularised, circulariser, circularising, circularism, circularities, circularity, circularization, circularizations, circularize, circularized, circularizer, circularizers, circularizes, circularizing, circularly, circularness, circulars, circularwise, circulatable, circulate, circulated, circulates, circulating, circulation, circulations, circulative, circulator, circulatories, circulators, circulatory, circule, circulet, circuli, circulin, circulus, circum, circumaction, circumadjacent, circumagitate, circumagitation, circumambages, circumambagious, circumambience, circumambiencies, circumambiency, circumambient, circumambiently, circumambulate, circumambulated, circumambulates, circumambulating, circumambulation, circumambulations, circumambulator, circumambulatory, circumanal, circumantarctic, circumarctic, circumarticular, circumaviate, circumaviation, circumaviator, circumaxial, circumaxile, circumaxillary, circumbasal, circumbendibus, circumbendibuses, circumboreal, circumbuccal, circumbulbar, circumcallosal, circumcellion, circumcenter, circumcentral, circumcinct, circumcincture, circumcircle, circumcise, circumcised, circumciser, circumcises, circumcising, circumcision, circumcisions, circumcission, circumclude, circumclusion, circumcolumnar, circumcone, circumconic, circumcorneal, circumcrescence, circumcrescent, circumdate, circumdenudation, circumdiction, circumduce, circumducing, circumduct, circumducted, circumduction, circumesophagal, circumesophageal, circumfer, circumference, circumferences, circumferent, circumferential, circumferentially, circumferentor, circumflant, circumflect, circumflex, circumflexes, circumflexion, circumfluence, circumfluent, circumfluous, circumforaneous, circumfulgent, circumfuse, circumfused, circumfusile, circumfusing, circumfusion, circumgenital, circumgestation, circumgyrate, circumgyration, circumgyratory, circumhorizontal, circumincession, circuminsession, circuminsular, circumintestinal, circumitineration, circumjacence, circumjacencies, circumjacency, circumjacent, circumjovial, circumlental, circumlitio, circumlittoral, circumlocute, circumlocution, circumlocution's, circumlocutional, circumlocutionary, circumlocutionist, circumlocutions, circumlocutory, circumlunar, circummeridian, circummeridional, circummigrate, circummigration, circummundane, circummure, circummured, circummuring, circumnatant, circumnavigable, circumnavigate, circumnavigated, circumnavigates, circumnavigating, circumnavigation, circumnavigations, circumnavigator, circumnavigatory, circumneutral, circumnuclear, circumnutate, circumnutated, circumnutating, circumnutation, circumnutatory, circumocular, circumoesophagal, circumoral, circumorbital, circumpacific, circumpallial, circumparallelogram, circumpentagon, circumplanetary, circumplect, circumplicate, circumplication, circumpolar, circumpolygon, circumpose, circumposition, circumquaque, circumradii, circumradius, circumradiuses, circumrenal, circumrotate, circumrotated, circumrotating, circumrotation, circumrotatory, circumsail, circumsaturnian, circumsciss, circumscissile, circumscribable, circumscribe, circumscribed, circumscriber, circumscribes, circumscribing, circumscript, circumscription, circumscriptions, circumscriptive, circumscriptively, circumscriptly, circumscrive, circumsession, circumsinous, circumsolar, circumspangle, circumspatial, circumspect, circumspection, circumspective, circumspectively, circumspectly, circumspectness, circumspheral, circumsphere, circumstance, circumstance's, circumstanced, circumstances, circumstancing, circumstant, circumstantiability, circumstantiable, circumstantial, circumstantialities, circumstantiality, circumstantially, circumstantialness, circumstantiate, circumstantiated, circumstantiates, circumstantiating, circumstantiation, circumstantiations, circumstellar, circumtabular, circumterraneous, circumterrestrial, circumtonsillar, circumtropical, circumumbilical, circumundulate, circumundulation, circumvallate, circumvallated, circumvallating, circumvallation, circumvascular, circumvent, circumventable, circumvented, circumventer, circumventing, circumvention, circumventions, circumventive, circumventor, circumvents, circumvest, circumviate, circumvoisin, circumvolant, circumvolute, circumvolution, circumvolutory, circumvolve, circumvolved, circumvolving, circumzenithal, circus, circus's, circuses, circusy, circut, circuted, circuting, circuts, cire, cires, cirl, cirmcumferential, cirque, cirques, cirrate, cirrated, cirrhopod, cirrhose, cirrhosed, cirrhosis, cirrhotic, cirrhous, cirrhus, cirri, cirribranch, cirriferous, cirriform, cirrigerous, cirrigrade, cirriped, cirripede, cirripedial, cirripeds, cirrocumular, cirrocumulative, cirrocumulous, cirrocumulus, cirrolite, cirropodous, cirrose, cirrosely, cirrostome, cirrostrative, cirrostratus, cirrous, cirrus, cirsectomies, cirsectomy, cirsocele, cirsoid, cirsomphalos, cirsophthalmia, cirsotome, cirsotomies, cirsotomy, cirterion, ciruela, cirurgian, ciruses, cis, cisalpine, cisandine, cisatlantic, cisco, ciscoes, ciscos, cise, ciseaux, cisele, ciseleur, ciseleurs, ciselure, ciselures, cisgangetic, cising, cisium, cisjurane, cisleithan, cislunar, cismarine, cismontane, cisoceanic, cispadane, cisplatine, cispontine, cisrhenane, cissies, cissing, cissoid, cissoidal, cissoids, cissy, cist, cista, cistaceous, cistae, cisted, cistercian, cistern, cistern's, cisterna, cisternae, cisternal, cisterns, cistic, cistophori, cistophoric, cistophorus, cistori, cistron, cistronic, cistrons, cists, cistus, cistuses, cistvaen, cit, citable, citadel, citadel's, citadels, cital, citation, citation's, citational, citations, citator, citators, citatory, citatum, cite, citeable, cited, citee, citer, citers, cites, citess, cithara, citharas, citharist, citharista, citharoedi, citharoedic, citharoedus, cither, cithern, citherns, cithers, cithren, cithrens, citicism, citicorp, citied, cities, citification, citified, citifies, citify, citifying, citigrade, citing, citizen, citizen's, citizendom, citizeness, citizenhood, citizenish, citizenism, citizenize, citizenized, citizenizing, citizenly, citizenries, citizenry, citizens, citizenship, citola, citolas, citole, citoler, citolers, citoles, citoyen, citoyenne, citoyens, citraconate, citraconic, citral, citrals, citramide, citramontane, citrange, citrangeade, citrate, citrated, citrates, citrean, citrene, citreous, citric, citriculture, citriculturist, citril, citrin, citrination, citrine, citrines, citrinin, citrinins, citrinous, citrins, citrocola, citrometer, citron, citronade, citronalis, citronella, citronellal, citronelle, citronellic, citronellol, citronin, citronize, citrons, citronwood, citropten, citrous, citrul, citrullin, citrulline, citrus, citruses, citrylidene, cittern, citternhead, citterns, citua, city, city's, citybuster, citycism, citydom, cityfied, cityfolk, cityful, cityish, cityless, citylike, cityness, citynesses, cityscape, cityscapes, cityward, citywards, citywide, ciudad, civ, cive, civet, civetlike, civetone, civets, civic, civical, civically, civicism, civicisms, civics, civie, civies, civil, civile, civiler, civilest, civilian, civilian's, civilianization, civilianize, civilians, civilisable, civilisation, civilisational, civilisations, civilisatory, civilise, civilised, civilisedness, civiliser, civilises, civilising, civilist, civilite, civilities, civility, civilizable, civilizade, civilization, civilization's, civilizational, civilizationally, civilizations, civilizatory, civilize, civilized, civilizedness, civilizee, civilizer, civilizers, civilizes, civilizing, civilly, civilness, civism, civisms, civitas, civite, civory, civvies, civvy, civy, ciwies, cixiid, cizar, cize, ck, ckw, cl, clabber, clabbered, clabbering, clabbers, clabbery, clablaria, clabularia, clabularium, clach, clachan, clachans, clachs, clack, clackdish, clacked, clacker, clackers, clacket, clackety, clacking, clacks, clactonian, clad, cladanthous, cladautoicous, cladding, claddings, clade, cladine, cladistic, cladocarpous, cladoceran, cladocerans, cladocerous, cladode, cladodes, cladodial, cladodium, cladodont, cladodontid, cladogenesis, cladogenetic, cladogenetically, cladogenous, cladoniaceous, cladonioid, cladophora, cladophoraceous, cladophyll, cladophyllum, cladoptosis, cladose, cladoselachian, cladosiphonic, clads, cladus, claes, clag, clagged, clagging, claggum, claggy, clags, claik, claim, claimable, claimant, claimant's, claimants, claimed, claimer, claimers, claiming, claimless, claims, claimsman, claimsmen, clair, clairaudience, clairaudient, clairaudiently, clairce, claire, clairecole, clairecolle, claires, clairschach, clairschacher, clairseach, clairseacher, clairsentience, clairsentient, clairvoyance, clairvoyances, clairvoyancies, clairvoyancy, clairvoyant, clairvoyantly, clairvoyants, claith, claithes, claiver, clake, clam, clam's, clamant, clamantly, clamaroo, clamation, clamative, clamatorial, clamatory, clamb, clambake, clambakes, clamber, clambered, clamberer, clambering, clambers, clamcracker, clame, clamehewit, clamer, clamflat, clamjamfery, clamjamfry, clamjamphrie, clamlike, clammed, clammer, clammersome, clammier, clammiest, clammily, clamminess, clamming, clammish, clammy, clammyweed, clamor, clamored, clamorer, clamorers, clamoring, clamorist, clamorous, clamorously, clamorousness, clamors, clamorsome, clamour, clamoured, clamourer, clamouring, clamourist, clamourous, clamours, clamoursome, clamp, clampdown, clamped, clamper, clampers, clamping, clamps, clams, clamshell, clamshells, clamworm, clamworms, clan, clancular, clancularly, clandestine, clandestinely, clandestineness, clandestinity, clanfellow, clang, clanged, clanger, clangful, clanging, clangingly, clangor, clangored, clangoring, clangorous, clangorously, clangorousness, clangors, clangour, clangoured, clangouring, clangours, clangs, clanjamfray, clanjamfrey, clanjamfrie, clanjamphrey, clank, clanked, clankety, clanking, clankingly, clankingness, clankless, clanks, clankum, clanless, clanned, clanning, clannish, clannishly, clannishness, clans, clansfolk, clanship, clansman, clansmanship, clansmen, clanswoman, clanswomen, clap, clapboard, clapboarding, clapboards, clapbread, clapcake, clapdish, clape, clapholt, clapmatch, clapnest, clapnet, clapotis, clappe, clapped, clapper, clapperboard, clapperclaw, clapperclawer, clapperdudgeon, clappered, clappering, clappermaclaw, clappers, clapping, claps, clapstick, clapt, claptrap, claptraps, clapwort, claque, claquer, claquers, claques, claqueur, claqueurs, clar, clarabella, clarain, clare, clarence, clarences, clarenceux, clarendon, clares, claret, claretian, clarets, claribel, claribella, clarichord, claries, clarifiable, clarifiant, clarificant, clarification, clarifications, clarified, clarifier, clarifiers, clarifies, clarify, clarifying, clarigate, clarigation, clarigold, clarin, clarina, clarine, clarinet, clarinetist, clarinetists, clarinets, clarinettist, clarinettists, clarini, clarino, clarinos, clarion, clarioned, clarionet, clarioning, clarions, clarissimo, clarities, claritude, clarity, clark, clarke, clarkeite, clarkeites, clarkia, clarkias, clarksville, claro, claroes, claros, clarre, clarsach, clarseach, clarsech, clarseth, clarshech, clart, clartier, clartiest, clarts, clarty, clary, clash, clashed, clashee, clasher, clashers, clashes, clashing, clashingly, clashy, clasmatocyte, clasmatocytic, clasmatosis, clasp, clasped, clasper, claspers, clasping, clasps, claspt, class, classable, classbook, classed, classer, classers, classes, classfellow, classic, classical, classicalism, classicalist, classicalities, classicality, classicalize, classically, classicalness, classicise, classicised, classicising, classicism, classicist, classicistic, classicists, classicize, classicized, classicizing, classico, classicolatry, classics, classier, classiest, classifiable, classific, classifically, classification, classificational, classifications, classificator, classificatory, classified, classifier, classifiers, classifies, classify, classifying, classily, classiness, classing, classis, classism, classisms, classist, classists, classless, classlessness, classman, classmanship, classmate, classmate's, classmates, classmen, classroom, classroom's, classrooms, classwise, classwork, classy, clast, clastic, clastics, clasts, clat, clatch, clatchy, clathraceous, clathrarian, clathrate, clathroid, clathrose, clathrulate, clatter, clattered, clatterer, clattering, clatteringly, clatters, clattertrap, clattertraps, clattery, clatty, clauber, claucht, claudent, claudetite, claudetites, claudicant, claudicate, claudication, claudius, claught, claughted, claughting, claughts, claus, clausal, clause, clause's, clauses, clauster, clausthalite, claustra, claustral, claustration, claustrophilia, claustrophobe, claustrophobia, claustrophobiac, claustrophobic, claustrum, clausula, clausulae, clausular, clausule, clausum, clausure, claut, clava, clavacin, clavae, claval, clavariaceous, clavate, clavated, clavately, clavatin, clavation, clave, clavecin, clavecinist, clavel, clavelization, clavelize, clavellate, clavellated, claver, clavered, clavering, clavers, claves, clavi, clavial, claviature, clavicembali, clavicembalist, clavicembalo, clavichord, clavichordist, clavichordists, clavichords, clavicithern, clavicittern, clavicle, clavicles, clavicor, clavicorn, clavicornate, clavicotomy, clavicular, clavicularium, claviculate, claviculus, clavicylinder, clavicymbal, clavicytheria, clavicytherium, clavicythetheria, clavier, clavierist, clavieristic, clavierists, claviers, claviform, claviger, clavigerous, claviharp, clavilux, claviol, claviole, clavipectoral, clavis, clavises, clavodeltoid, clavodeltoideus, clavola, clavolae, clavolet, clavus, clavuvi, clavy, claw, clawback, clawed, clawer, clawers, clawhammer, clawing, clawk, clawker, clawless, clawlike, claws, clawsick, claxon, claxons, clay, clay's, claybank, claybanks, claybrained, claye, clayed, clayen, clayer, clayey, clayier, clayiest, clayiness, claying, clayish, claylike, clayman, claymore, claymores, claypan, claypans, clays, claystone, claytonia, clayware, claywares, clayweed, cleach, clead, cleaded, cleading, cleam, cleamer, clean, cleanable, cleaned, cleaner, cleaner's, cleaners, cleanest, cleanhanded, cleanhandedness, cleanhearted, cleaning, cleanings, cleanish, cleanlier, cleanliest, cleanlily, cleanliness, cleanly, cleanness, cleanout, cleans, cleansable, cleanse, cleansed, cleanser, cleansers, cleanses, cleansing, cleanskin, cleanskins, cleanup, cleanups, clear, clearable, clearage, clearance, clearance's, clearances, clearcole, cleared, clearedness, clearer, clearers, clearest, clearheaded, clearheadedly, clearheadedness, clearhearted, clearing, clearing's, clearinghouse, clearinghouses, clearings, clearish, clearly, clearminded, clearness, clears, clearsighted, clearsightedness, clearskins, clearstarch, clearstarcher, clearstoried, clearstories, clearstory, clearwater, clearway, clearweed, clearwing, cleat, cleated, cleating, cleats, cleavability, cleavable, cleavage, cleavages, cleave, cleaved, cleaveful, cleavelandite, cleaver, cleavers, cleaverwort, cleaves, cleaving, cleavingly, cleche, clechee, clechy, cleck, cled, cledde, cledge, cledgy, cledonism, clee, cleech, cleek, cleeked, cleeking, cleeks, cleeky, clef, clefs, cleft, cleft's, clefted, clefts, cleg, cleidagra, cleidarthritis, cleidocostal, cleidocranial, cleidohyoid, cleidoic, cleidomancy, cleidomastoid, cleidorrhexis, cleidoscapular, cleidosternal, cleidotomy, cleidotripsy, cleistocarp, cleistocarpous, cleistogamic, cleistogamically, cleistogamous, cleistogamously, cleistogamy, cleistogene, cleistogenous, cleistogeny, cleistotcia, cleistothecia, cleistothecium, cleithral, cleithrum, clem, clematis, clematises, clematite, clemence, clemencies, clemency, clement, clementine, clemently, clementness, clements, clemmed, clemming, clench, clenched, clencher, clenchers, clenches, clenching, cleoid, cleome, cleomes, cleopatra, clep, clepe, cleped, clepes, cleping, clepsydra, clepsydrae, clepsydras, clept, cleptobioses, cleptobiosis, cleptobiotic, cleptomania, cleptomaniac, clerestoried, clerestories, clerestory, clerete, clergess, clergies, clergion, clergy, clergyable, clergylike, clergyman, clergymen, clergywoman, clergywomen, cleric, clerical, clericalism, clericalist, clericalists, clericality, clericalize, clerically, clericals, clericate, clericature, clericism, clericity, clerics, clericum, clerid, clerids, clerihew, clerihews, clerisies, clerisy, clerk, clerkage, clerkdom, clerkdoms, clerked, clerkery, clerkess, clerkhood, clerking, clerkish, clerkless, clerklier, clerkliest, clerklike, clerkliness, clerkly, clerks, clerkship, clerkships, clernly, cleromancy, cleronomy, clerstory, cleruch, cleruchial, cleruchic, cleruchies, cleruchy, clerum, cletch, clethra, clethraceous, clethrionomys, cleuch, cleuk, cleuks, cleve, cleveite, cleveites, cleveland, clever, cleverality, cleverer, cleverest, cleverish, cleverishly, cleverly, cleverness, clevis, clevises, clew, clewed, clewgarnet, clewing, clews, cli, cliack, clianthus, clich, cliche, cliche's, cliched, cliches, click, clicked, clicker, clickers, clicket, clicking, clickless, clicks, clicky, cliency, client, client's, clientage, cliental, cliented, clientelage, clientele, clienteles, clientless, clientry, clients, clientship, cliff, cliff's, cliffed, cliffhang, cliffhanger, cliffhangers, cliffhanging, cliffier, cliffiest, cliffing, cliffless, clifflet, clifflike, cliffs, cliffside, cliffsman, cliffweed, cliffy, clift, cliftonite, clifts, clifty, clima, climaciaceous, climacter, climacterial, climacteric, climacterical, climacterically, climacterics, climactery, climactic, climactical, climactically, climacus, climant, climata, climatal, climatarchic, climate, climate's, climates, climath, climatic, climatical, climatically, climatize, climatographical, climatography, climatologic, climatological, climatologically, climatologist, climatologists, climatology, climatometer, climatotherapeutics, climatotherapies, climatotherapy, climature, climax, climaxed, climaxes, climaxing, climb, climbable, climbed, climber, climbers, climbing, climbingfish, climbingfishes, climbs, clime, clime's, climes, climograph, clin, clinah, clinal, clinally, clinamen, clinamina, clinandrdria, clinandria, clinandrium, clinanthia, clinanthium, clinch, clinched, clincher, clinchers, clinches, clinching, clinchingly, clinchingness, clinchpoop, cline, clines, cling, clinged, clinger, clingers, clingfish, clingfishes, clingier, clingiest, clinginess, clinging, clingingly, clingingness, clings, clingstone, clingstones, clingy, clinia, clinic, clinic's, clinical, clinically, clinician, clinicians, clinicist, clinicopathologic, clinicopathological, clinicopathologically, clinics, clinid, clinium, clink, clinkant, clinked, clinker, clinkered, clinkerer, clinkering, clinkers, clinkery, clinking, clinks, clinkstone, clinkum, clinoaxis, clinocephalic, clinocephalism, clinocephalous, clinocephalus, clinocephaly, clinochlore, clinoclase, clinoclasite, clinodiagonal, clinodomatic, clinodome, clinograph, clinographic, clinohedral, clinohedrite, clinohumite, clinoid, clinologic, clinology, clinometer, clinometria, clinometric, clinometrical, clinometry, clinophobia, clinopinacoid, clinopinacoidal, clinoprism, clinopyramid, clinopyroxene, clinorhombic, clinospore, clinostat, clinquant, clint, clinting, clintonia, clintonite, clints, clinty, clio, clip, clip's, clipboard, clipboards, clipei, clipeus, clippable, clipped, clipper, clipper's, clipperman, clippers, clippie, clipping, clipping's, clippingly, clippings, clips, clipse, clipsheet, clipsheets, clipsome, clipt, clique, clique's, cliqued, cliquedom, cliqueier, cliqueiest, cliqueless, cliques, cliquey, cliqueyness, cliquier, cliquiest, cliquing, cliquish, cliquishly, cliquishness, cliquism, cliquy, cliseometer, clisere, clishmaclaver, clistocarp, clistocarpous, clistothcia, clistothecia, clistothecium, clit, clitch, clite, clitella, clitellar, clitelliferous, clitelline, clitellum, clitellus, clites, clithe, clithral, clithridiate, clitia, clitic, clition, clitoral, clitoric, clitoridauxe, clitoridean, clitoridectomies, clitoridectomy, clitoriditis, clitoridotomy, clitoris, clitorises, clitorism, clitoritis, clitoromania, clitoromaniac, clitoromaniacal, clitter, clitterclatter, cliv, clival, clive, cliver, clivers, clivia, clivias, clivis, clivises, clivus, clk, clo, cloaca, cloacae, cloacal, cloacaline, cloacas, cloacean, cloacinal, cloacinean, cloacitis, cloak, cloak's, cloakage, cloaked, cloakedly, cloaking, cloakless, cloaklet, cloakmaker, cloakmaking, cloakroom, cloakrooms, cloaks, cloakwise, cloam, cloamen, cloamer, clobber, clobbered, clobberer, clobbering, clobbers, clochan, clochard, clochards, cloche, clocher, cloches, clochette, clock, clockbird, clockcase, clocked, clocker, clockers, clockface, clockhouse, clocking, clockings, clockkeeper, clockless, clocklike, clockmaker, clockmaking, clockmutch, clockroom, clocks, clocksmith, clockwatcher, clockwise, clockwork, clockworked, clockworks, clod, clod's, clodbreaker, clodded, clodder, cloddier, cloddiest, cloddily, cloddiness, clodding, cloddish, cloddishly, cloddishness, cloddy, clodhead, clodhopper, clodhopperish, clodhoppers, clodhopping, clodknocker, clodlet, clodlike, clodpate, clodpated, clodpates, clodpole, clodpoles, clodpoll, clodpolls, clods, cloes, clof, cloff, clofibrate, clog, clog's, clogdogdo, clogged, clogger, cloggier, cloggiest, cloggily, clogginess, clogging, cloggy, cloghad, cloghaun, cloghead, cloglike, clogmaker, clogmaking, clogs, clogwheel, clogwood, clogwyn, cloine, cloiochoanitic, cloison, cloisonless, cloisonn, cloisonne, cloisonnism, cloister, cloister's, cloisteral, cloistered, cloisterer, cloistering, cloisterless, cloisterlike, cloisterliness, cloisterly, cloisters, cloisterwise, cloistral, cloistress, cloit, cloke, clokies, cloky, clomb, clomben, clomiphene, clomp, clomped, clomping, clomps, clon, clonal, clonally, clone, cloned, cloner, cloners, clones, clong, clonic, clonicity, clonicotonic, cloning, clonism, clonisms, clonk, clonked, clonking, clonks, clonorchiasis, clonos, clons, clonus, clonuses, cloof, cloop, cloot, clootie, cloots, clop, clopped, clopping, clops, cloque, cloques, cloragen, clorargyrite, clorinator, cloriodid, clos, closable, close, closeable, closecross, closed, closedown, closefisted, closefistedly, closefistedness, closefitting, closehanded, closehauled, closehearted, closelipped, closely, closemouth, closemouthed, closen, closeness, closenesses, closeout, closeouts, closer, closers, closes, closest, closestool, closet, closeted, closetful, closeting, closets, closeup, closeups, closewing, closh, closing, closings, closish, closkey, closky, closter, clostridia, clostridial, clostridian, clostridium, closure, closure's, closured, closures, closuring, clot, clotbur, clote, cloth, clothbound, clothe, clothed, clothes, clothesbag, clothesbasket, clothesbrush, clotheshorse, clotheshorses, clothesless, clothesline, clotheslines, clothesman, clothesmen, clothesmonger, clothespin, clothespins, clothespress, clothespresses, clothesyard, clothier, clothiers, clothify, clothing, clothings, clothlike, clothmaker, clothmaking, clotho, cloths, clothworker, clothy, clots, clottage, clotted, clottedness, clotter, clotting, clotty, cloture, clotured, clotures, cloturing, clotweed, clou, cloud, cloudage, cloudberries, cloudberry, cloudburst, cloudbursts, cloudcap, clouded, cloudful, cloudier, cloudiest, cloudily, cloudiness, clouding, cloudland, cloudless, cloudlessly, cloudlessness, cloudlet, cloudlets, cloudlike, cloudling, cloudology, clouds, cloudscape, cloudship, cloudward, cloudwards, cloudy, clouee, clough, cloughs, clour, cloured, clouring, clours, clout, clouted, clouter, clouterly, clouters, clouting, clouts, clouty, clove, cloven, clovene, clover, clovered, cloverlay, cloverleaf, cloverleafs, cloverleaves, cloverley, cloveroot, cloverroot, clovers, clovery, cloves, clovewort, clow, clowder, clowders, clower, clown, clownade, clownage, clowned, clowneries, clownery, clownheal, clowning, clownish, clownishly, clownishness, clowns, clownship, clowre, clowring, cloxacillin, cloy, cloyed, cloyedness, cloyer, cloying, cloyingly, cloyingness, cloyless, cloyment, cloyne, cloys, cloysome, cloze, clr, club, club's, clubability, clubable, clubbability, clubbable, clubbed, clubber, clubbers, clubbier, clubbiest, clubbily, clubbiness, clubbing, clubbish, clubbishness, clubbism, clubbist, clubby, clubdom, clubfeet, clubfellow, clubfist, clubfisted, clubfoot, clubfooted, clubhand, clubhands, clubhaul, clubhauled, clubhauling, clubhauls, clubhouse, clubhouses, clubionid, clubland, clubman, clubmate, clubmen, clubmobile, clubmonger, clubridden, clubroom, clubrooms, clubroot, clubroots, clubs, clubstart, clubster, clubweed, clubwoman, clubwomen, clubwood, cluck, clucked, clucking, clucks, clucky, cludder, clue, clue's, clued, clueing, clueless, clues, cluff, cluing, clum, clumber, clumbers, clump, clumped, clumper, clumpier, clumpiest, clumping, clumpish, clumpishness, clumplike, clumproot, clumps, clumpst, clumpy, clumse, clumsier, clumsiest, clumsily, clumsiness, clumsy, clunch, clung, cluniac, clunk, clunked, clunker, clunkers, clunking, clunks, clunter, clupanodonic, clupeid, clupeids, clupeiform, clupein, clupeine, clupeiod, clupeoid, clupeoids, clupien, cluppe, cluricaune, clusiaceous, cluster, clusterberry, clustered, clusterfist, clustering, clusteringly, clusterings, clusters, clustery, clutch, clutched, clutcher, clutches, clutching, clutchingly, clutchman, clutchy, cluther, clutter, cluttered, clutterer, cluttering, clutterment, clutters, cluttery, cly, clydesdale, clyer, clyers, clyfaker, clyfaking, clype, clypeal, clypeaster, clypeastroid, clypeate, clypeated, clypei, clypeiform, clypeola, clypeolar, clypeolate, clypeole, clypeus, clyses, clysis, clysma, clysmian, clysmic, clyssus, clyster, clysterize, clysters, clytemnestra, cm, cmd, cmdg, cmdr, cml, cnemapophysis, cnemial, cnemic, cnemides, cnemidium, cnemis, cneoraceous, cnibophore, cnicin, cnida, cnidae, cnidarian, cnidoblast, cnidocell, cnidocil, cnidocyst, cnidogenous, cnidophobia, cnidophore, cnidophorous, cnidopod, cnidosac, cnidosis, co, coabode, coabound, coabsume, coacceptor, coacervate, coacervated, coacervating, coacervation, coach, coachability, coachable, coachbuilder, coachbuilding, coached, coachee, coacher, coachers, coaches, coachfellow, coachful, coaching, coachlet, coachmaker, coachmaking, coachman, coachmanship, coachmaster, coachmen, coachs, coachsmith, coachsmithing, coachway, coachwhip, coachwise, coachwoman, coachwood, coachwork, coachwright, coachy, coact, coacted, coacting, coaction, coactions, coactive, coactively, coactivity, coactor, coacts, coadamite, coadapt, coadaptation, coadaptations, coadapted, coadapting, coadequate, coadjacence, coadjacency, coadjacent, coadjacently, coadjudicator, coadjument, coadjust, coadjustment, coadjutant, coadjutator, coadjute, coadjutement, coadjutive, coadjutor, coadjutors, coadjutorship, coadjutress, coadjutrice, coadjutrices, coadjutrix, coadjuvancy, coadjuvant, coadjuvate, coadminister, coadministration, coadministrator, coadministratrix, coadmiration, coadmire, coadmired, coadmires, coadmiring, coadmit, coadmits, coadmitted, coadmitting, coadnate, coadore, coadsorbent, coadunate, coadunated, coadunating, coadunation, coadunative, coadunatively, coadunite, coadventure, coadventured, coadventurer, coadventuress, coadventuring, coadvice, coaeval, coaevals, coaffirmation, coafforest, coaged, coagel, coagencies, coagency, coagent, coagents, coaggregate, coaggregated, coaggregation, coagitate, coagitator, coagment, coagmentation, coagonize, coagriculturist, coagula, coagulability, coagulable, coagulant, coagulants, coagulase, coagulate, coagulated, coagulates, coagulating, coagulation, coagulations, coagulative, coagulator, coagulators, coagulatory, coagule, coagulin, coaguline, coagulometer, coagulose, coagulum, coagulums, coaid, coaita, coak, coakum, coal, coala, coalas, coalbag, coalbagger, coalbin, coalbins, coalbox, coalboxes, coaldealer, coaled, coaler, coalers, coalesce, coalesced, coalescence, coalescency, coalescent, coalesces, coalescing, coalface, coalfield, coalfish, coalfishes, coalfitter, coalheugh, coalhole, coalholes, coalier, coaliest, coalification, coalified, coalifies, coalify, coalifying, coaling, coalite, coalition, coalitional, coalitioner, coalitionist, coalitions, coalize, coalized, coalizer, coalizing, coalless, coalmonger, coalmouse, coalpit, coalpits, coalrake, coals, coalsack, coalsacks, coalshed, coalsheds, coalternate, coalternation, coalternative, coaltitude, coaly, coalyard, coalyards, coambassador, coambulant, coamiable, coaming, coamings, coanimate, coannex, coannexed, coannexes, coannexing, coannihilate, coapostate, coapparition, coappear, coappearance, coappeared, coappearing, coappears, coappellee, coapprehend, coapprentice, coappriser, coapprover, coapt, coaptate, coaptation, coapted, coapting, coapts, coaration, coarb, coarbiter, coarbitrator, coarct, coarctate, coarctation, coarcted, coarcting, coardent, coarrange, coarrangement, coarse, coarsely, coarsen, coarsened, coarseness, coarsening, coarsens, coarser, coarsest, coarsish, coart, coarticulate, coarticulation, coascend, coassert, coasserter, coassession, coassessor, coassignee, coassist, coassistance, coassistant, coassisted, coassisting, coassists, coassume, coassumed, coassumes, coassuming, coast, coastal, coastally, coasted, coaster, coasters, coastguard, coastguardman, coastguardsman, coastguardsmen, coasting, coastings, coastland, coastline, coastlines, coastman, coastmen, coasts, coastside, coastwaiter, coastward, coastwards, coastways, coastwise, coat, coatdress, coated, coatee, coatees, coater, coaters, coathangers, coati, coatie, coatimondie, coatimundi, coating, coatings, coation, coatis, coatless, coatrack, coatracks, coatroom, coatrooms, coats, coattail, coattailed, coattails, coattend, coattended, coattending, coattends, coattest, coattestation, coattestator, coattested, coattesting, coattests, coaudience, coauditor, coaugment, coauthered, coauthor, coauthored, coauthoring, coauthority, coauthors, coauthorship, coawareness, coax, coaxal, coaxation, coaxed, coaxer, coaxers, coaxes, coaxial, coaxially, coaxing, coaxingly, coaxy, coazervate, coazervation, cob, cobaea, cobalamin, cobalamine, cobalt, cobaltamine, cobaltammine, cobaltic, cobalticyanic, cobalticyanides, cobaltiferous, cobaltine, cobaltinitrite, cobaltite, cobaltocyanic, cobaltocyanide, cobaltous, cobalts, cobang, cobb, cobbed, cobber, cobberer, cobbers, cobbier, cobbiest, cobbin, cobbing, cobble, cobbled, cobbler, cobbler's, cobblerfish, cobblerism, cobblerless, cobblers, cobblership, cobblery, cobbles, cobblestone, cobblestoned, cobblestones, cobbling, cobbly, cobbra, cobbs, cobby, cobcab, cobdenism, cobego, cobelief, cobeliever, cobelligerent, cobenignity, coberger, cobewail, cobhead, cobhouse, cobia, cobias, cobiron, cobishop, coble, cobleman, cobles, cobless, cobloaf, cobnut, cobnuts, cobol, cobola, coboss, coboundless, cobourg, cobra, cobras, cobreathe, cobridgehead, cobriform, cobrother, cobs, cobstone, coburg, coburgess, coburgher, coburghership, cobweb, cobweb's, cobwebbed, cobwebbery, cobwebbier, cobwebbiest, cobwebbing, cobwebby, cobwebs, cobwork, coca, cocaceous, cocaigne, cocain, cocaine, cocaines, cocainisation, cocainise, cocainised, cocainising, cocainism, cocainist, cocainization, cocainize, cocainized, cocainizing, cocainomania, cocainomaniac, cocains, cocamine, cocao, cocarboxylase, cocarde, cocas, cocash, cocashweed, cocause, cocautioner, coccaceous, coccagee, coccal, cocceian, coccerin, cocci, coccic, coccid, coccidia, coccidial, coccidian, coccidioidal, coccidioidomycosis, coccidiosis, coccidium, coccidology, coccids, cocciferous, cocciform, coccigenic, coccin, coccinella, coccinellid, coccineous, coccionella, cocco, coccobaccilli, coccobacilli, coccobacillus, coccochromatic, coccogone, coccogonium, coccoid, coccoidal, coccoids, coccolite, coccolith, coccolithophorid, coccosphere, coccostean, coccosteid, coccothraustine, coccous, coccule, cocculiferous, cocculus, coccus, coccydynia, coccygalgia, coccygeal, coccygean, coccygectomy, coccygerector, coccyges, coccygeus, coccygine, coccygodynia, coccygomorph, coccygomorphic, coccygotomy, coccyodynia, coccyx, coccyxes, cocentric, coch, cochair, cochaired, cochairing, cochairman, cochairmanship, cochairmen, cochairs, cochal, cocher, cochero, cochief, cochin, cochineal, cochins, cochlea, cochleae, cochlear, cochleare, cochlearifoliate, cochleariform, cochleary, cochleas, cochleate, cochleated, cochleiform, cochleitis, cochleleae, cochleleas, cochleous, cochlidiid, cochliodont, cochlite, cochlitis, cochlospermaceous, cochon, cochromatography, cochurchwarden, cochylis, cocillana, cocin, cocinera, cocineras, cocinero, cocircular, cocircularity, cocitizen, cocitizenship, cock, cockabondy, cockade, cockaded, cockades, cockadoodledoo, cockaigne, cockal, cockalan, cockaleekie, cockalorum, cockamamie, cockamamy, cockamaroo, cockandy, cockapoo, cockapoos, cockard, cockarouse, cockateel, cockatiel, cockatoo, cockatoos, cockatrice, cockatrices, cockawee, cockbell, cockbill, cockbilled, cockbilling, cockbills, cockbird, cockboat, cockboats, cockbrain, cockchafer, cockcrow, cockcrower, cockcrowing, cockcrows, cocked, cocker, cockered, cockerel, cockerels, cockerie, cockering, cockermeg, cockernonnie, cockernony, cockerouse, cockers, cocket, cocketed, cocketing, cockeye, cockeyed, cockeyedly, cockeyedness, cockeyes, cockfight, cockfighter, cockfighting, cockfights, cockhead, cockhorse, cockhorses, cockie, cockieleekie, cockier, cockies, cockiest, cockily, cockiness, cocking, cockish, cockishly, cockishness, cockle, cockleboat, cocklebur, cockled, cockler, cockles, cockleshell, cockleshells, cocklet, cocklewife, cocklight, cocklike, cockling, cockloche, cockloft, cocklofts, cockly, cockmaster, cockmatch, cockmate, cockneian, cockneity, cockney, cockneybred, cockneydom, cockneyese, cockneyess, cockneyfication, cockneyfied, cockneyfy, cockneyfying, cockneyish, cockneyishly, cockneyism, cockneyize, cockneyland, cockneylike, cockneys, cockneyship, cockpaddle, cockpit, cockpits, cockroach, cockroaches, cocks, cockscomb, cockscombed, cockscombs, cocksfoot, cockshead, cockshies, cockshoot, cockshot, cockshut, cockshuts, cockshy, cockshying, cocksparrow, cockspur, cockspurs, cockstone, cocksure, cocksuredom, cocksureism, cocksurely, cocksureness, cocksurety, cockswain, cocksy, cocktail, cocktail's, cocktailed, cocktailing, cocktails, cockthrowing, cockup, cockups, cockweed, cocky, cockyolly, coclea, coco, cocoa, cocoach, cocoanut, cocoanuts, cocoas, cocoawood, cocobola, cocobolas, cocobolo, cocobolos, cocodette, cocomat, cocomats, cocona, coconnection, coconqueror, coconscious, coconsciously, coconsciousness, coconsecrator, coconspirator, coconstituent, cocontractor, coconut, coconut's, coconuts, cocoon, cocoon's, cocooned, cocooneries, cocoonery, cocooning, cocoons, cocopan, cocopans, cocorico, cocoroot, cocos, cocotte, cocottes, cocovenantor, cocowood, cocowort, cocoyam, cocozelle, cocreate, cocreated, cocreates, cocreating, cocreator, cocreatorship, cocreditor, cocrucify, coct, coctile, coction, coctoantigen, coctoprecipitin, cocuisa, cocuiza, cocullo, cocurator, cocurrent, cocurricular, cocus, cocuswood, cocuyo, cocytus, cod, coda, codable, codal, codamin, codamine, codas, codbank, codded, codder, codders, codding, coddle, coddled, coddler, coddlers, coddles, coddling, coddy, code, codebook, codebooks, codebreak, codebreaker, codebtor, codebtors, codec, codeclination, codecree, codecs, coded, codefendant, codefendants, codeia, codeias, codein, codeina, codeinas, codeine, codeines, codeins, codeless, codelight, codelinquency, codelinquent, coden, codenization, codens, codeposit, coder, coderive, coderived, coderives, coderiving, coders, codes, codescendant, codesign, codesigned, codesigning, codesigns, codespairer, codetermination, codetermine, codetta, codettas, codette, codeword, codeword's, codewords, codex, codfish, codfisher, codfisheries, codfishery, codfishes, codfishing, codger, codgers, codhead, codheaded, codiaceous, codical, codices, codicil, codicilic, codicillary, codicils, codicology, codictatorship, codifiability, codification, codification's, codifications, codified, codifier, codifier's, codifiers, codifies, codify, codifying, codilla, codille, coding, codings, codiniac, codirect, codirected, codirecting, codirectional, codirector, codirectorship, codirects, codiscoverer, codisjunct, codist, codivine, codlin, codline, codling, codlings, codlins, codman, codo, codol, codomain, codomestication, codomant, codon, codons, codpiece, codpieces, codpitchings, cods, codshead, codswallop, codworm, coe, coecal, coecum, coed, coedit, coedited, coediting, coeditor, coeditors, coeditorship, coedits, coeds, coeducate, coeducation, coeducational, coeducationalism, coeducationalize, coeducationally, coef, coeff, coeffect, coeffects, coefficacy, coefficient, coefficient's, coefficiently, coefficients, coeffluent, coeffluential, coehorn, coelacanth, coelacanthid, coelacanthine, coelacanthoid, coelacanthous, coelanaglyphic, coelar, coelarium, coelastraceous, coelder, coeldership, coelect, coelection, coelector, coelectron, coelelminth, coelelminthic, coelentera, coelenterata, coelenterate, coelenterates, coelenteric, coelenteron, coelestial, coelestine, coelevate, coelho, coelia, coeliac, coelialgia, coelian, coeligenous, coelin, coeline, coeliomyalgia, coeliorrhea, coeliorrhoea, coelioscopy, coeliotomy, coeloblastic, coeloblastula, coelodont, coelogastrula, coelom, coeloma, coelomata, coelomate, coelomatic, coelomatous, coelome, coelomes, coelomesoblast, coelomic, coelomopore, coeloms, coelonavigation, coelongated, coeloplanula, coeloscope, coelosperm, coelospermous, coelostat, coelozoic, coeltera, coemanate, coembedded, coembodied, coembodies, coembody, coembodying, coembrace, coeminency, coemperor, coemploy, coemployed, coemployee, coemploying, coemployment, coemploys, coempt, coempted, coempting, coemptio, coemption, coemptional, coemptionator, coemptive, coemptor, coempts, coenacle, coenact, coenacted, coenacting, coenactor, coenacts, coenacula, coenaculous, coenaculum, coenaesthesis, coenamor, coenamored, coenamoring, coenamorment, coenamors, coenamourment, coenanthium, coendear, coendure, coendured, coendures, coenduring, coenenchym, coenenchyma, coenenchymal, coenenchymata, coenenchymatous, coenenchyme, coenesthesia, coenesthesis, coenflame, coengage, coengager, coenjoy, coenla, coeno, coenobe, coenobiar, coenobic, coenobiod, coenobioid, coenobite, coenobitic, coenobitical, coenobitism, coenobium, coenoblast, coenoblastic, coenoby, coenocentrum, coenocyte, coenocytic, coenodioecism, coenoecial, coenoecic, coenoecium, coenogamete, coenogenesis, coenogenetic, coenomonoecism, coenosarc, coenosarcal, coenosarcous, coenosite, coenospecies, coenospecific, coenospecifically, coenosteal, coenosteum, coenotrope, coenotype, coenotypic, coenthrone, coenunuri, coenure, coenures, coenuri, coenurus, coenzymatic, coenzymatically, coenzyme, coenzymes, coequal, coequality, coequalize, coequally, coequalness, coequals, coequate, coequated, coequates, coequating, coequation, coerce, coerceable, coerced, coercement, coercend, coercends, coercer, coercers, coerces, coercibility, coercible, coercibleness, coercibly, coercing, coercion, coercionary, coercionist, coercions, coercitive, coercive, coercively, coerciveness, coercivity, coerect, coerected, coerecting, coerects, coeruleolactite, coes, coesite, coesites, coessential, coessentiality, coessentially, coessentialness, coestablishment, coestate, coetanean, coetaneity, coetaneous, coetaneously, coetaneousness, coeternal, coeternally, coeternity, coetus, coeval, coevality, coevally, coevalneity, coevalness, coevals, coevolution, coevolutionary, coevolve, coevolvedcoevolves, coevolving, coexchangeable, coexclusive, coexecutant, coexecutor, coexecutrices, coexecutrix, coexert, coexerted, coexerting, coexertion, coexerts, coexist, coexisted, coexistence, coexistency, coexistent, coexisting, coexists, coexpand, coexpanded, coexperiencer, coexpire, coexplosion, coextend, coextended, coextending, coextends, coextension, coextensive, coextensively, coextensiveness, coextent, cofactor, cofactors, cofaster, cofather, cofathership, cofeature, cofeatures, cofeoffee, coferment, cofermentation, coff, coffee, coffee's, coffeeberries, coffeeberry, coffeebush, coffeecake, coffeecakes, coffeecup, coffeegrower, coffeegrowing, coffeehouse, coffeehoused, coffeehouses, coffeehousing, coffeeleaf, coffeeman, coffeepot, coffeepots, coffeeroom, coffees, coffeetime, coffeeweed, coffeewood, coffer, coffer's, cofferdam, cofferdams, coffered, cofferer, cofferfish, coffering, cofferlike, coffers, cofferwork, coffin, coffin's, coffined, coffing, coffining, coffinite, coffinless, coffinmaker, coffinmaking, coffins, coffle, coffled, coffles, coffling, coffret, coffrets, coffs, cofighter, cofinal, coforeknown, coformulator, cofound, cofounded, cofounder, cofounding, cofoundress, cofounds, cofreighter, coft, cofunction, cog, cogboat, cogence, cogences, cogencies, cogency, cogener, cogeneration, cogeneric, cogenial, cogent, cogently, cogged, cogger, coggers, coggie, cogging, coggle, coggledy, cogglety, coggly, coghle, cogida, cogie, cogit, cogitability, cogitable, cogitabund, cogitabundity, cogitabundly, cogitabundous, cogitant, cogitantly, cogitate, cogitated, cogitates, cogitating, cogitatingly, cogitation, cogitations, cogitative, cogitatively, cogitativeness, cogitativity, cogitator, cogitators, cogito, cogitos, coglorify, coglorious, cogman, cogmen, cognac, cognacs, cognate, cognately, cognateness, cognates, cognati, cognatic, cognatical, cognation, cognatus, cognisability, cognisable, cognisableness, cognisably, cognisance, cognisant, cognise, cognised, cogniser, cognises, cognising, cognition, cognitional, cognitive, cognitively, cognitives, cognitivity, cognitum, cognizability, cognizable, cognizableness, cognizably, cognizance, cognizant, cognize, cognized, cognizee, cognizer, cognizers, cognizes, cognizing, cognizor, cognomen, cognomens, cognomina, cognominal, cognominally, cognominate, cognominated, cognomination, cognosce, cognoscent, cognoscente, cognoscenti, cognoscibility, cognoscible, cognoscing, cognoscitive, cognoscitively, cognovit, cognovits, cogon, cogonal, cogons, cogovernment, cogovernor, cogracious, cograil, cogrediency, cogredient, cogroad, cogs, coguarantor, coguardian, cogue, cogware, cogway, cogways, cogweel, cogweels, cogwheel, cogwheels, cogwood, cohabit, cohabitancy, cohabitant, cohabitate, cohabitation, cohabitations, cohabited, cohabiter, cohabiting, cohabits, cohanim, cohanims, coharmonious, coharmoniously, coharmonize, cohead, coheaded, coheading, coheads, coheartedness, coheir, coheiress, coheirs, coheirship, cohelper, cohelpership, cohen, cohenite, cohens, coherald, cohere, cohered, coherence, coherency, coherent, coherently, coherer, coherers, coheres, coheretic, cohering, coheritage, coheritor, cohert, cohesibility, cohesible, cohesion, cohesionless, cohesions, cohesive, cohesively, cohesiveness, cohibit, cohibition, cohibitive, cohibitor, cohitre, coho, cohob, cohoba, cohobate, cohobated, cohobates, cohobating, cohobation, cohobator, cohog, cohogs, cohol, coholder, coholders, cohomology, cohorn, cohort, cohortation, cohortative, cohorts, cohos, cohosh, cohoshes, cohost, cohosted, cohosting, cohosts, cohow, cohue, cohune, cohunes, cohusband, coidentity, coif, coifed, coiffe, coiffed, coiffes, coiffeur, coiffeurs, coiffeuse, coiffeuses, coiffing, coiffure, coiffured, coiffures, coiffuring, coifing, coifs, coign, coigne, coigned, coignes, coigning, coigns, coigny, coigue, coil, coilability, coiled, coiler, coilers, coiling, coillen, coils, coilsmith, coilyear, coimmense, coimplicant, coimplicate, coimplore, coin, coinable, coinage, coinages, coincide, coincided, coincidence, coincidence's, coincidences, coincidency, coincident, coincidental, coincidentally, coincidently, coincidents, coincider, coincides, coinciding, coinclination, coincline, coinclude, coincorporate, coindicant, coindicate, coindication, coindwelling, coined, coiner, coiners, coinfeftment, coinfer, coinferred, coinferring, coinfers, coinfinite, coinfinity, coing, coinhabit, coinhabitant, coinhabitor, coinhere, coinhered, coinherence, coinherent, coinheres, coinhering, coinheritance, coinheritor, coining, coinitial, coinmaker, coinmaking, coinmate, coinmates, coinquinate, coins, coinspire, coinstantaneity, coinstantaneous, coinstantaneously, coinstantaneousness, coinsurable, coinsurance, coinsure, coinsured, coinsurer, coinsures, coinsuring, cointense, cointension, cointensity, cointer, cointerest, cointerred, cointerring, cointers, cointersecting, cointise, coinventor, coinvolve, coiny, coir, coirs, coislander, coisns, coistrel, coistrels, coistril, coistrils, coit, coital, coitally, coition, coitional, coitions, coitophobia, coiture, coitus, coituses, cojoin, cojones, cojudge, cojudices, cojuror, cojusticiar, coke, coked, cokelike, cokeman, cokeney, coker, cokernut, cokers, cokery, cokes, cokewold, cokey, cokie, coking, cokneyfy, cokuloris, coky, col, cola, colaborer, colacobioses, colacobiosis, colacobiotic, colage, colalgia, colament, colander, colanders, colane, colaphize, colarin, colas, colascione, colasciones, colascioni, colat, colate, colation, colatitude, colatorium, colature, colauxe, colazione, colback, colberter, colbertine, colcannon, colchicia, colchicin, colchicine, colchicum, colchyte, colcothar, cold, coldblood, coldblooded, coldbloodedness, coldcock, colder, coldest, coldfinch, coldhearted, coldheartedly, coldheartedness, coldish, coldly, coldness, coldnesses, coldong, coldproof, colds, coldslaw, coldturkey, cole, coleader, colecannon, colectomies, colectomy, colegatee, colegislator, colemanite, colemouse, colen, colent, coleochaetaceous, coleopter, coleoptera, coleopteral, coleopteran, coleopterist, coleopteroid, coleopterological, coleopterology, coleopteron, coleopterous, coleoptile, coleoptilum, coleopttera, coleorhiza, coleorhizae, coleplant, colera, coles, coleseed, coleseeds, coleslaw, coleslaws, colessee, colessees, colessor, colessors, colet, coletit, coleur, coleus, coleuses, colewort, coleworts, coley, colfox, coli, coliander, colibacillosis, colibacterin, colibert, colibertus, colibri, colic, colical, colichemarde, colicin, colicine, colicines, colicins, colicker, colicky, colicolitis, colicroot, colics, colicweed, colicwort, colicystitis, colicystopyelitis, colies, coliform, coliforms, colilysin, colima, colin, colinear, colinearity, colinephritis, coling, colins, coliphage, coliplication, colipuncture, colipyelitis, colipyuria, colisepsis, coliseum, coliseums, colistin, colistins, colitic, colitis, colitises, colitoxemia, coliuria, colk, coll, colla, collab, collabent, collaborate, collaborated, collaborates, collaborateur, collaborating, collaboration, collaborationism, collaborationist, collaborationists, collaborations, collaborative, collaboratively, collaborativeness, collaborator, collaborator's, collaborators, collada, colladas, collage, collagen, collagenase, collagenic, collagenous, collagens, collages, collagist, collapsability, collapsable, collapsar, collapse, collapsed, collapses, collapsibility, collapsible, collapsing, collar, collarband, collarbird, collarbone, collarbones, collard, collards, collare, collared, collaret, collarets, collarette, collaring, collarino, collarinos, collarless, collarman, collars, collat, collatable, collate, collated, collatee, collateral, collaterality, collateralize, collateralized, collateralizing, collaterally, collateralness, collaterals, collates, collating, collation, collational, collationer, collations, collatitious, collative, collator, collators, collatress, collaud, collaudation, colleague, colleague's, colleagued, colleagues, colleagueship, colleaguesmanship, colleaguing, collect, collectability, collectable, collectables, collectanea, collectarium, collected, collectedly, collectedness, collectibility, collectible, collectibles, collecting, collection, collection's, collectional, collectioner, collections, collective, collectively, collectiveness, collectives, collectivise, collectivism, collectivist, collectivistic, collectivistically, collectivists, collectivities, collectivity, collectivization, collectivize, collectivized, collectivizes, collectivizing, collectivum, collector, collector's, collectorate, collectors, collectorship, collectress, collects, colleen, colleens, collegatary, college, college's, colleger, collegers, colleges, collegese, collegia, collegial, collegialism, collegiality, collegially, collegian, collegianer, collegians, collegiate, collegiately, collegiateness, collegiation, collegiugia, collegium, collegiums, collembolan, collembole, collembolic, collembolous, collen, collenchyma, collenchymatic, collenchymatous, collenchyme, collencytal, collencyte, collery, collet, colletarium, colleted, colleter, colleterial, colleterium, colletic, colleting, collets, colletside, colley, collibert, collicle, colliculate, colliculus, collide, collided, collides, collidin, collidine, colliding, collie, collied, collielike, collier, collieries, colliers, colliery, collies, collieshangie, colliflower, colliform, colligance, colligate, colligated, colligating, colligation, colligative, colligible, collimate, collimated, collimates, collimating, collimation, collimator, collimators, collin, collinal, colline, collinear, collinearity, collinearly, collineate, collineation, colling, collingly, collingual, collins, collinses, collinsia, collinsite, colliquable, colliquament, colliquate, colliquation, colliquative, colliquativeness, colliquefaction, collis, collision, collision's, collisional, collisions, collisive, colloblast, collobrierite, collocal, collocate, collocated, collocates, collocating, collocation, collocationable, collocational, collocations, collocative, collocatory, collochemistry, collochromate, collock, collocution, collocutor, collocutory, collodiochloride, collodion, collodionization, collodionize, collodiotype, collodium, collogen, collogue, collogued, collogues, colloguing, colloid, colloidal, colloidality, colloidally, colloider, colloidize, colloidochemical, colloids, collomia, collop, colloped, collophane, collophanite, collophore, collops, colloq, colloque, colloquia, colloquial, colloquialism, colloquialisms, colloquialist, colloquiality, colloquialize, colloquializer, colloquially, colloquialness, colloquies, colloquiquia, colloquiquiums, colloquist, colloquium, colloquiums, colloquize, colloquized, colloquizing, colloququia, colloquy, collossians, collothun, collotype, collotyped, collotypic, collotyping, collotypy, collow, colloxylin, colluctation, collude, colluded, colluder, colluders, colludes, colluding, collum, collumelliaceous, collun, collunaria, collunarium, collusion, collusive, collusively, collusiveness, collusory, collut, collution, collutoria, collutories, collutorium, collutory, colluvia, colluvial, colluvies, colluvium, colluviums, colly, collyba, collybist, collying, collylyria, collyr, collyria, collyridian, collyrie, collyrite, collyrium, collyriums, collywest, collyweston, collywobbles, colmar, colmars, colmose, colnaria, colob, colobin, colobium, coloboma, colobus, colocate, colocated, colocates, colocating, colocentesis, colocephalous, coloclysis, colocola, colocolic, colocolo, colocynth, colocynthin, colodyspepsia, coloenteritis, colog, cologarithm, cologne, cologned, colognes, cologs, colola, cololite, colomb, colombia, colombian, colombians, colombier, colombin, colombo, colometric, colometrically, colometry, colon, colon's, colonaded, colonalgia, colonate, colonel, colonel's, colonelcies, colonelcy, colonels, colonelship, colonelships, coloner, colones, colonette, colongitude, coloni, colonial, colonialise, colonialised, colonialising, colonialism, colonialist, colonialistic, colonialists, colonialization, colonialize, colonialized, colonializing, colonially, colonialness, colonials, colonic, colonical, colonies, colonisability, colonisable, colonisation, colonisationist, colonise, colonised, coloniser, colonises, colonising, colonist, colonist's, colonists, colonitis, colonizability, colonizable, colonization, colonizationist, colonizations, colonize, colonized, colonizer, colonizers, colonizes, colonizing, colonnade, colonnaded, colonnades, colonnette, colonopathy, colonopexy, colonoscope, colonoscopy, colons, colonus, colony, colony's, colopexia, colopexotomy, colopexy, colophan, colophane, colophany, colophene, colophenic, colophon, colophonate, colophonic, colophonist, colophonite, colophonium, colophons, colophony, coloplication, coloppe, coloproctitis, coloptosis, colopuncture, coloquies, coloquintid, coloquintida, color, colorability, colorable, colorableness, colorably, coloradan, coloradans, colorado, coloradoite, colorant, colorants, colorate, coloration, colorational, colorationally, colorations, colorative, coloratura, coloraturas, colorature, colorbearer, colorblind, colorblindness, colorbreed, colorcast, colorcasted, colorcaster, colorcasting, colorcasts, colorectitis, colorectostomy, colored, coloreds, colorer, colorers, colorfast, colorfastness, colorful, colorfully, colorfulness, colorific, colorifics, colorimeter, colorimetric, colorimetrical, colorimetrically, colorimetrics, colorimetrist, colorimetry, colorin, coloring, colorings, colorism, colorisms, colorist, coloristic, coloristically, colorists, colorization, colorize, colorless, colorlessly, colorlessness, colormaker, colormaking, colorman, coloroto, colorrhaphy, colors, colortype, colory, coloslossi, coloslossuses, coloss, colossal, colossality, colossally, colossean, colosseum, colossi, colossian, colossians, colosso, colossus, colossuses, colostomies, colostomy, colostral, colostration, colostric, colostrous, colostrum, colotomies, colotomy, colotyphoid, colour, colourability, colourable, colourableness, colourably, colouration, colourational, colourationally, colourative, coloured, colourer, colourers, colourfast, colourful, colourfully, colourfulness, colourific, colourifics, colouring, colourist, colouristic, colourize, colourless, colourlessly, colourlessness, colourman, colours, colourtype, coloury, colove, colp, colpenchyma, colpeo, colpeurynter, colpeurysis, colpheg, colpindach, colpitis, colpitises, colpocele, colpocystocele, colpohyperplasia, colpohysterotomy, colpoperineoplasty, colpoperineorrhaphy, colpoplastic, colpoplasty, colpoptosis, colporrhagia, colporrhaphy, colporrhea, colporrhexis, colport, colportage, colporter, colporteur, colporteurs, colposcope, colposcopy, colpostat, colpotomies, colpotomy, colpus, cols, colstaff, colt, colt's, colter, colters, colthood, coltish, coltishly, coltishness, coltlike, coltoria, coltpixie, coltpixy, colts, coltsfoot, coltsfoots, coltskin, colubaria, coluber, colubrid, colubrids, colubriform, colubrine, colubroid, colugo, colugos, columba, columbaceous, columbaria, columbaries, columbarium, columbary, columbate, columbeia, columbeion, columbia, columbiad, columbian, columbic, columbier, columbiferous, columbin, columbine, columbines, columbite, columbium, columbo, columboid, columbotantalate, columbotitanate, columbous, columbus, columel, columella, columellae, columellar, columellate, columelliform, columels, column, column's, columna, columnal, columnar, columnarian, columnarity, columnarized, columnate, columnated, columnates, columnating, columnation, columnea, columned, columner, columniation, columniferous, columniform, columning, columnist, columnistic, columnists, columnization, columnize, columnized, columnizes, columnizing, columns, columnwise, colunar, colure, colures, colusite, colutea, coly, colyba, colymbiform, colymbion, colyone, colyonic, colytic, colyum, colyumist, colza, colzas, com, coma, comacine, comade, comae, comagistracy, comagmatic, comake, comaker, comakers, comaking, comal, comales, comals, comamie, comanche, comanchean, comanches, comandante, comandantes, comandanti, comanic, comarca, comart, comarum, comas, comate, comates, comatic, comatik, comatiks, comatose, comatosely, comatoseness, comatosity, comatous, comatula, comatulae, comatulid, comb, combaron, combasou, combat, combatable, combatant, combatant's, combatants, combated, combater, combaters, combating, combative, combatively, combativeness, combativity, combats, combattant, combattants, combatted, combatter, combatting, combe, combed, comber, combers, combes, combfish, combfishes, combflower, combinability, combinable, combinableness, combinably, combinant, combinantive, combinate, combination, combination's, combinational, combinations, combinative, combinator, combinator's, combinatorial, combinatorially, combinatoric, combinatorics, combinators, combinatory, combind, combine, combined, combinedly, combinedness, combinement, combiner, combiners, combines, combing, combings, combining, combite, comble, combless, comblessness, comblike, combmaker, combmaking, combo, comboloio, combos, comboy, combre, combretaceous, combs, combure, comburendo, comburent, comburgess, comburimeter, comburimetry, comburivorous, combust, combusted, combustibilities, combustibility, combustible, combustibleness, combustibles, combustibly, combusting, combustion, combustious, combustive, combustively, combustor, combusts, combwise, combwright, comby, comd, comdg, comdia, comdr, comdt, come, comeatable, comeback, comebacker, comebacks, comeddle, comedia, comedial, comedian, comedian's, comedians, comediant, comedic, comedical, comedically, comedienne, comediennes, comedies, comedietta, comediettas, comediette, comedist, comedo, comedones, comedos, comedown, comedowns, comedy, comedy's, comelier, comeliest, comelily, comeliness, comeling, comely, comendite, comenic, comephorous, comer, comers, comes, comessation, comestible, comestibles, comestion, comet, comet's, cometaria, cometarium, cometary, cometh, comether, comethers, cometic, cometical, cometlike, cometographer, cometographical, cometography, cometoid, cometology, comets, cometwise, comeupance, comeuppance, comeuppances, comfier, comfiest, comfily, comfiness, comfit, comfits, comfiture, comfort, comfortabilities, comfortability, comfortable, comfortableness, comfortably, comfortation, comfortative, comforted, comforter, comforters, comfortful, comforting, comfortingly, comfortless, comfortlessly, comfortlessness, comfortress, comfortroot, comforts, comfrey, comfreys, comfy, comic, comic's, comical, comicality, comically, comicalness, comices, comicocratic, comicocynical, comicodidactic, comicography, comicoprosaic, comicotragedy, comicotragic, comicotragical, comicry, comics, comida, comiferous, cominformist, cominformists, coming, comingle, comings, comino, comintern, comique, comism, comitadji, comital, comitant, comitatensian, comitative, comitatus, comite, comites, comitia, comitial, comities, comitiva, comitje, comitragedy, comity, coml, comm, comma, comma's, commaes, commaing, command, command's, commandable, commandant, commandant's, commandants, commandatory, commanded, commandedness, commandeer, commandeered, commandeering, commandeers, commander, commanderies, commanders, commandership, commandery, commanding, commandingly, commandingness, commandite, commandless, commandment, commandment's, commandments, commando, commandoes, commandoman, commandos, commandress, commandrie, commandries, commandry, commands, commark, commas, commassation, commassee, commata, commaterial, commatic, commation, commatism, comme, commeasurable, commeasure, commeasured, commeasuring, commeddle, commelinaceous, commem, commemorable, commemorate, commemorated, commemorates, commemorating, commemoration, commemorational, commemorations, commemorative, commemoratively, commemorativeness, commemorator, commemorators, commemoratory, commemorize, commemorized, commemorizing, commence, commenceable, commenced, commencement, commencement's, commencements, commencer, commences, commencing, commend, commenda, commendable, commendableness, commendably, commendador, commendam, commendatary, commendation, commendation's, commendations, commendator, commendatories, commendatorily, commendatory, commended, commender, commending, commendingly, commendment, commends, commensal, commensalism, commensalist, commensalistic, commensality, commensally, commensals, commensurability, commensurable, commensurableness, commensurably, commensurate, commensurated, commensurately, commensurateness, commensurating, commensuration, commensurations, comment, commentable, commentarial, commentarialism, commentaries, commentary, commentary's, commentate, commentated, commentating, commentation, commentative, commentator, commentator's, commentatorial, commentatorially, commentators, commentatorship, commented, commenter, commenting, commentitious, comments, commerce, commerced, commerceless, commercer, commerces, commercia, commerciable, commercial, commercialisation, commercialise, commercialised, commercialising, commercialism, commercialist, commercialistic, commercialists, commerciality, commercialization, commercializations, commercialize, commercialized, commercializes, commercializing, commercially, commercialness, commercials, commercing, commercium, commerge, commers, commesso, commie, commies, commigration, commilitant, comminate, comminated, comminating, commination, comminative, comminator, comminatory, commingle, commingled, comminglement, commingler, commingles, commingling, comminister, comminuate, comminute, comminuted, comminuting, comminution, comminutor, commis, commisce, commise, commiserable, commiserate, commiserated, commiserates, commiserating, commiseratingly, commiseration, commiserations, commiserative, commiseratively, commiserator, commissar, commissarial, commissariat, commissariats, commissaries, commissars, commissary, commissaryship, commission, commissionaire, commissional, commissionary, commissionate, commissionated, commissionating, commissioned, commissioner, commissioners, commissionership, commissionerships, commissioning, commissions, commissionship, commissive, commissively, commissoria, commissural, commissure, commissurotomies, commissurotomy, commistion, commit, commitment, commitment's, commitments, commits, committable, committal, committals, committed, committedly, committedness, committee, committee's, committeeism, committeeman, committeemen, committees, committeeship, committeewoman, committeewomen, committent, committer, committible, committing, committitur, committment, committor, commix, commixed, commixes, commixing, commixt, commixtion, commixture, commo, commodata, commodatary, commodate, commodation, commodatum, commode, commoderate, commodes, commodious, commodiously, commodiousness, commoditable, commodities, commodity, commodity's, commodore, commodore's, commodores, commoigne, commolition, common, commonable, commonage, commonalities, commonality, commonalties, commonalty, commonance, commoned, commonefaction, commoner, commoner's, commoners, commonership, commonest, commoney, commoning, commonish, commonition, commonize, commonly, commonness, commonplace, commonplaceism, commonplacely, commonplaceness, commonplacer, commonplaces, commons, commonsense, commonsensible, commonsensibly, commonsensical, commonsensically, commonty, commonweal, commonweals, commonwealth, commonwealthism, commonwealths, commorancies, commorancy, commorant, commorient, commorse, commorth, commos, commot, commote, commotion, commotional, commotions, commotive, commove, commoved, commoves, commoving, commulation, commulative, communa, communal, communalisation, communalise, communalised, communaliser, communalising, communalism, communalist, communalistic, communality, communalization, communalize, communalized, communalizer, communalizing, communally, communard, communbus, commune, communed, communer, communes, communicability, communicable, communicableness, communicably, communicant, communicant's, communicants, communicate, communicated, communicatee, communicates, communicating, communication, communicational, communications, communicative, communicatively, communicativeness, communicator, communicator's, communicators, communicatory, communing, communion, communionable, communional, communionist, communions, communiqu, communique, communiques, communis, communisation, communise, communised, communising, communism, communist, communist's, communisteries, communistery, communistic, communistical, communistically, communists, communital, communitarian, communitarianism, communitary, communities, communitive, communitorium, community, community's, communitywide, communization, communize, communized, communizing, commutability, commutable, commutableness, commutant, commutate, commutated, commutating, commutation, commutations, commutative, commutatively, commutativity, commutator, commutators, commute, commuted, commuter, commuters, commutes, commuting, commutual, commutuality, commy, comodato, comodo, comoedia, comoedus, comoid, comolecule, comonomer, comonte, comoquer, comorado, comortgagee, comose, comourn, comourner, comournful, comous, comp, compaa, compact, compactability, compactable, compacted, compactedly, compactedness, compacter, compactest, compactible, compactification, compactify, compactile, compacting, compaction, compactions, compactly, compactness, compactor, compactor's, compactors, compacts, compacture, compadre, compadres, compage, compages, compaginate, compagination, compagnie, compagnies, companable, companage, companator, compander, companero, companeros, compania, companiable, companias, companied, companies, companion, companion's, companionability, companionable, companionableness, companionably, companionage, companionate, companioned, companioning, companionize, companionized, companionizing, companionless, companions, companionship, companionway, companionways, company, company's, companying, companyless, compar, comparability, comparable, comparableness, comparably, comparascope, comparate, comparatist, comparatival, comparative, comparatively, comparativeness, comparatives, comparativist, comparator, comparator's, comparators, comparcioner, compare, compared, comparer, comparers, compares, comparing, comparison, comparison's, comparisons, comparition, comparograph, comparsa, compart, comparted, compartimenti, compartimento, comparting, compartition, compartment, compartmental, compartmentalization, compartmentalize, compartmentalized, compartmentalizes, compartmentalizing, compartmentally, compartmentation, compartmented, compartmentize, compartments, compartner, comparts, compass, compassability, compassable, compassed, compasser, compasses, compassing, compassion, compassionable, compassionate, compassionated, compassionately, compassionateness, compassionating, compassionless, compassive, compassivity, compassless, compassment, compaternity, compathy, compatibilities, compatibility, compatibility's, compatible, compatibleness, compatibles, compatibly, compatience, compatient, compatriot, compatriotic, compatriotism, compatriots, compd, compear, compearance, compearant, comped, compeer, compeered, compeering, compeers, compel, compellability, compellable, compellably, compellation, compellative, compelled, compellent, compeller, compellers, compelling, compellingly, compels, compend, compendency, compendent, compendia, compendiary, compendiate, compendious, compendiously, compendiousness, compendium, compendiums, compends, compenetrate, compenetration, compensability, compensable, compensate, compensated, compensates, compensating, compensatingly, compensation, compensational, compensations, compensative, compensatively, compensativeness, compensator, compensators, compensatory, compense, compenser, compere, compered, comperes, compering, compert, compesce, compester, compete, competed, competence, competencies, competency, competent, competently, competentness, competer, competes, competible, competing, competingly, competition, competition's, competitioner, competitions, competitive, competitively, competitiveness, competitor, competitor's, competitors, competitorship, competitory, competitress, competitrix, compilable, compilation, compilation's, compilations, compilator, compilatory, compile, compileable, compiled, compilement, compiler, compiler's, compilers, compiles, compiling, comping, compinge, compital, compitum, complacence, complacencies, complacency, complacent, complacential, complacentially, complacently, complain, complainable, complainant, complainants, complained, complainer, complainers, complaining, complainingly, complainingness, complains, complaint, complaint's, complaintful, complaintive, complaintiveness, complaints, complaisance, complaisant, complaisantly, complaisantness, complanar, complanate, complanation, complant, compleat, compleated, complect, complected, complecting, complection, complects, complement, complemental, complementally, complementalness, complementaries, complementarily, complementariness, complementarism, complementarity, complementary, complementation, complementative, complemented, complementer, complementers, complementing, complementizer, complementoid, complements, completable, complete, completed, completedness, completely, completement, completeness, completer, completers, completes, completest, completing, completion, completions, completive, completively, completories, completory, complex, complexation, complexed, complexedness, complexer, complexes, complexest, complexification, complexify, complexing, complexion, complexionably, complexional, complexionally, complexionary, complexioned, complexionist, complexionless, complexions, complexities, complexity, complexive, complexively, complexly, complexness, complexometric, complexometry, complexus, compliable, compliableness, compliably, compliance, compliances, compliancies, compliancy, compliant, compliantly, complicacies, complicacy, complicant, complicate, complicated, complicatedly, complicatedness, complicates, complicating, complication, complications, complicative, complicator, complicator's, complicators, complice, complices, complicities, complicitous, complicity, complied, complier, compliers, complies, compliment, complimentable, complimental, complimentally, complimentalness, complimentarily, complimentariness, complimentarity, complimentary, complimentation, complimentative, complimented, complimenter, complimenters, complimenting, complimentingly, compliments, complin, compline, complines, complins, complish, complot, complotment, complots, complotted, complotter, complotting, complutensian, compluvia, compluvium, comply, complying, compo, compoed, compoer, compoing, compole, compone, componed, componency, componendo, component, component's, componental, componented, componential, componentry, components, componentwise, compony, comport, comportable, comportance, comported, comporting, comportment, comports, compos, composable, composal, composant, compose, composed, composedly, composedness, composer, composers, composes, composing, composit, composita, compositae, composite, composited, compositely, compositeness, composites, compositing, composition, compositional, compositionally, compositions, compositive, compositively, compositor, compositorial, compositors, compositous, composture, composograph, compossibility, compossible, compost, composted, composting, composts, composture, composure, compot, compotation, compotationship, compotator, compotatory, compote, compotes, compotier, compotiers, compotor, compound, compoundable, compounded, compoundedness, compounder, compounders, compounding, compoundness, compounds, comprachico, comprachicos, comprador, compradore, comprecation, compreg, compregnate, comprehend, comprehended, comprehender, comprehendible, comprehending, comprehendingly, comprehends, comprehense, comprehensibility, comprehensible, comprehensibleness, comprehensibly, comprehension, comprehensive, comprehensively, comprehensiveness, comprehensives, comprehensor, comprend, compresbyter, compresbyterial, compresence, compresent, compress, compressed, compressedly, compresses, compressibilities, compressibility, compressible, compressibleness, compressibly, compressing, compressingly, compression, compressional, compressions, compressive, compressively, compressometer, compressor, compressors, compressure, comprest, compriest, comprint, comprisable, comprisal, comprise, comprised, comprises, comprising, comprizable, comprizal, comprize, comprized, comprizes, comprizing, comprobate, comprobation, comproduce, compromis, compromisable, compromise, compromised, compromiser, compromisers, compromises, compromising, compromisingly, compromissary, compromission, compromissorial, compromit, compromitment, compromitted, compromitting, comprovincial, comps, compsognathus, compt, compte, compted, compter, comptible, comptie, compting, comptly, comptness, comptoir, comptometer, comptonite, comptrol, comptroller, comptroller's, comptrollers, comptrollership, compts, compulsative, compulsatively, compulsatorily, compulsatory, compulse, compulsed, compulsion, compulsion's, compulsions, compulsitor, compulsive, compulsively, compulsiveness, compulsives, compulsivity, compulsorily, compulsoriness, compulsory, compunct, compunction, compunctionary, compunctionless, compunctions, compunctious, compunctiously, compunctive, compupil, compurgation, compurgator, compurgatorial, compurgatory, compursion, computability, computable, computably, computate, computation, computation's, computational, computationally, computations, computative, computatively, computativeness, compute, computed, computer, computer's, computerese, computerise, computerite, computerizable, computerization, computerize, computerized, computerizes, computerizing, computerlike, computernik, computers, computes, computing, computist, computus, comr, comrade, comradeliness, comradely, comradery, comrades, comradeship, comrado, comrogue, coms, comsat, comstock, comstockeries, comstockery, comte, comtes, comtesse, comtesses, comtian, comunidad, comurmurer, comus, comvia, con, conable, conacaste, conacre, conal, conalbumin, conamarin, conamed, conand, conarial, conarium, conation, conational, conationalistic, conations, conative, conatural, conatus, conaxial, conbinas, conc, concactenated, concamerate, concamerated, concameration, concanavalin, concaptive, concarnation, concassation, concatenary, concatenate, concatenated, concatenates, concatenating, concatenation, concatenations, concatenator, concatervate, concaulescence, concausal, concause, concavation, concave, concaved, concavely, concaveness, concaver, concaves, concaving, concavities, concavity, concavo, conceal, concealable, concealed, concealedly, concealedness, concealer, concealers, concealing, concealingly, concealment, conceals, concede, conceded, concededly, conceder, conceders, concedes, conceding, conceit, conceited, conceitedly, conceitedness, conceiting, conceitless, conceits, conceity, conceivability, conceivable, conceivableness, conceivably, conceive, conceived, conceiver, conceivers, conceives, conceiving, concelebrate, concelebrated, concelebrates, concelebrating, concelebration, concelebrations, concent, concenter, concentered, concentering, concentive, concento, concentralization, concentralize, concentrate, concentrated, concentrates, concentrating, concentration, concentrations, concentrative, concentrativeness, concentrator, concentrators, concentre, concentred, concentric, concentrical, concentrically, concentricate, concentricity, concentring, concents, concentual, concentus, concept, concept's, conceptacle, conceptacular, conceptaculum, conceptible, conception, conception's, conceptional, conceptionist, conceptions, conceptism, conceptive, conceptiveness, concepts, conceptual, conceptualisation, conceptualise, conceptualised, conceptualising, conceptualism, conceptualist, conceptualistic, conceptualistically, conceptualists, conceptuality, conceptualization, conceptualization's, conceptualizations, conceptualize, conceptualized, conceptualizer, conceptualizes, conceptualizing, conceptually, conceptus, concern, concernancy, concerned, concernedly, concernedness, concerning, concerningly, concerningness, concernment, concerns, concert, concertante, concertantes, concertanti, concertanto, concertati, concertation, concertato, concertatos, concerted, concertedly, concertedness, concertgoer, concerti, concertina, concertinas, concerting, concertini, concertinist, concertino, concertinos, concertion, concertise, concertised, concertiser, concertising, concertist, concertize, concertized, concertizer, concertizes, concertizing, concertmaster, concertmasters, concertmeister, concertment, concerto, concertos, concerts, concertstck, concertstuck, concessible, concession, concession's, concessionaire, concessionaires, concessional, concessionaries, concessionary, concessioner, concessionist, concessions, concessit, concessive, concessively, concessiveness, concessor, concessory, concetti, concettism, concettist, concetto, conch, concha, conchae, conchal, conchate, conche, conched, concher, conches, conchfish, conchfishes, conchie, conchies, conchiferous, conchiform, conchinin, conchinine, conchiolin, conchite, conchitic, conchitis, concho, conchoid, conchoidal, conchoidally, conchoids, conchol, conchological, conchologically, conchologist, conchologize, conchology, conchometer, conchometry, conchospiral, conchotome, conchs, conchuela, conchy, conchyle, conchylia, conchyliated, conchyliferous, conchylium, conciator, concierge, concierges, concile, conciliable, conciliabule, conciliabulum, conciliar, conciliarism, conciliarly, conciliate, conciliated, conciliates, conciliating, conciliatingly, conciliation, conciliationist, conciliations, conciliative, conciliator, conciliatorily, conciliatoriness, conciliators, conciliatory, concilium, concinnate, concinnated, concinnating, concinnities, concinnity, concinnous, concinnously, concio, concion, concional, concionary, concionate, concionator, concionatory, conciousness, concipiency, concipient, concise, concisely, conciseness, conciser, concisest, concision, concitation, concite, concitizen, conclamant, conclamation, conclave, conclaves, conclavist, concludable, conclude, concluded, concludence, concludency, concludendi, concludent, concludently, concluder, concluders, concludes, concludible, concluding, concludingly, conclusible, conclusion, conclusion's, conclusional, conclusionally, conclusions, conclusive, conclusively, conclusiveness, conclusory, conclusum, concn, concoagulate, concoagulation, concoct, concocted, concocter, concocting, concoction, concoctions, concoctive, concoctor, concocts, concolor, concolorous, concolour, concomitance, concomitancy, concomitant, concomitantly, concomitate, concommitant, concommitantly, conconscious, concord, concordable, concordably, concordal, concordance, concordancer, concordances, concordancy, concordant, concordantial, concordantly, concordat, concordatory, concordats, concordatum, concorder, concordial, concordist, concordity, concordly, concords, concorporate, concorporated, concorporating, concorporation, concours, concourse, concourses, concreate, concredit, concremation, concrement, concresce, concrescence, concrescences, concrescent, concrescible, concrescive, concrete, concreted, concretely, concreteness, concreter, concretes, concreting, concretion, concretional, concretionary, concretions, concretism, concretist, concretive, concretively, concretization, concretize, concretized, concretizing, concretor, concrew, concrfsce, concubinage, concubinal, concubinarian, concubinaries, concubinary, concubinate, concubine, concubinehood, concubines, concubitancy, concubitant, concubitous, concubitus, conculcate, conculcation, concumbency, concupiscence, concupiscent, concupiscible, concupiscibleness, concupy, concur, concurbit, concurred, concurrence, concurrences, concurrencies, concurrency, concurrent, concurrently, concurrentness, concurring, concurringly, concurs, concursion, concurso, concursus, concuss, concussant, concussation, concussed, concusses, concussing, concussion, concussional, concussions, concussive, concussively, concutient, concyclic, concyclically, cond, condecent, condemn, condemnable, condemnably, condemnate, condemnation, condemnations, condemnatory, condemned, condemner, condemners, condemning, condemningly, condemnor, condemns, condensability, condensable, condensance, condensaries, condensary, condensate, condensates, condensation, condensational, condensations, condensative, condensator, condense, condensed, condensedly, condensedness, condenser, condenseries, condensers, condensery, condenses, condensible, condensing, condensity, conder, condescend, condescended, condescendence, condescendent, condescender, condescending, condescendingly, condescendingness, condescends, condescension, condescensions, condescensive, condescensively, condescensiveness, condescent, condiction, condictious, condiddle, condiddled, condiddlement, condiddling, condign, condigness, condignity, condignly, condignness, condiment, condimental, condimentary, condiments, condisciple, condistillation, condite, condition, conditionable, conditional, conditionalism, conditionalist, conditionalities, conditionality, conditionalize, conditionally, conditionals, conditionate, conditione, conditioned, conditioner, conditioners, conditioning, conditions, condititivia, conditivia, conditivium, conditoria, conditorium, conditory, conditotoria, condivision, condo, condog, condolatory, condole, condoled, condolement, condolence, condolences, condolent, condoler, condolers, condoles, condoling, condolingly, condom, condominate, condominial, condominiia, condominiiums, condominium, condominiums, condoms, condonable, condonance, condonation, condonations, condonative, condone, condoned, condonement, condoner, condoners, condones, condoning, condor, condores, condors, condos, condottiere, condottieri, conduce, conduceability, conduced, conducement, conducent, conducer, conducers, conduces, conducible, conducibleness, conducibly, conducing, conducingly, conducive, conduciveness, conduct, conducta, conductance, conductances, conducted, conductibility, conductible, conductility, conductimeter, conductimetric, conducting, conductio, conduction, conductional, conductitious, conductive, conductively, conductivities, conductivity, conductometer, conductometric, conductor, conductor's, conductorial, conductorless, conductors, conductorship, conductory, conductress, conducts, conductus, condue, conduit, conduits, conduplicate, conduplicated, conduplication, condurangin, condurango, condurrite, condylar, condylarth, condylarthrosis, condylarthrous, condyle, condylectomy, condyles, condylion, condyloid, condyloma, condylomas, condylomata, condylomatous, condylome, condylopod, condylopodous, condylos, condylotomy, condylura, condylure, cone, cone's, coned, coneen, coneflower, conehead, coneighboring, coneine, conelet, conelike, conelrad, conelrads, conemaker, conemaking, conenchyma, conenose, conenoses, conepate, conepates, conepatl, conepatls, coner, cones, conessine, conestoga, coney, coneys, conf, confab, confabbed, confabbing, confabs, confabular, confabulate, confabulated, confabulates, confabulating, confabulation, confabulations, confabulator, confabulatory, confact, confarreate, confarreated, confarreation, confated, confect, confected, confecting, confection, confectionaries, confectionary, confectioner, confectioneries, confectioners, confectionery, confectiones, confections, confectory, confects, confecture, confeder, confederacies, confederacy, confederal, confederalist, confederate, confederated, confederater, confederates, confederating, confederatio, confederation, confederationism, confederationist, confederations, confederatism, confederative, confederatize, confederator, confelicity, confer, conferee, conferees, conference, conference's, conferences, conferencing, conferential, conferment, conferrable, conferral, conferred, conferree, conferrence, conferrer, conferrer's, conferrers, conferring, conferruminate, confers, conferted, conferva, confervaceous, confervae, conferval, confervalike, confervas, confervoid, confervous, confess, confessable, confessant, confessarius, confessary, confessed, confessedly, confesser, confesses, confessing, confessingly, confession, confession's, confessional, confessionalian, confessionalism, confessionalist, confessionally, confessionals, confessionaries, confessionary, confessionist, confessions, confessor, confessor's, confessors, confessorship, confessory, confest, confetti, confetto, conficient, confidant, confidant's, confidante, confidantes, confidants, confide, confided, confidence, confidences, confidency, confident, confidente, confidential, confidentiality, confidentially, confidentialness, confidentiary, confidently, confidentness, confider, confiders, confides, confiding, confidingly, confidingness, configurable, configural, configurate, configurated, configurating, configuration, configuration's, configurational, configurationally, configurationism, configurationist, configurations, configurative, configure, configured, configures, configuring, confinable, confine, confineable, confined, confinedly, confinedness, confineless, confinement, confinement's, confinements, confiner, confiners, confines, confining, confinity, confirm, confirmability, confirmable, confirmand, confirmation, confirmation's, confirmational, confirmations, confirmative, confirmatively, confirmatorily, confirmatory, confirmed, confirmedly, confirmedness, confirmee, confirmer, confirming, confirmingly, confirmity, confirmment, confirmor, confirms, confiscable, confiscatable, confiscate, confiscated, confiscates, confiscating, confiscation, confiscations, confiscator, confiscators, confiscatory, confiserie, confisk, confisticating, confit, confitent, confiteor, confiture, confix, confixed, confixing, conflab, conflagrant, conflagrate, conflagrated, conflagrating, conflagration, conflagrations, conflagrative, conflagrator, conflagratory, conflate, conflated, conflates, conflating, conflation, conflexure, conflict, conflicted, conflictful, conflicting, conflictingly, confliction, conflictive, conflictless, conflictory, conflicts, conflictual, conflow, confluence, confluences, confluent, confluently, conflux, confluxes, confluxibility, confluxible, confluxibleness, confocal, confocally, conforbably, conform, conformability, conformable, conformableness, conformably, conformal, conformance, conformant, conformate, conformation, conformational, conformationally, conformations, conformator, conformed, conformer, conformers, conforming, conformingly, conformism, conformist, conformists, conformities, conformity, conforms, confort, confound, confoundable, confounded, confoundedly, confoundedness, confounder, confounders, confounding, confoundingly, confoundment, confounds, confr, confract, confraction, confragose, confrater, confraternal, confraternities, confraternity, confraternization, confrere, confreres, confrerie, confriar, confricamenta, confricamentum, confrication, confront, confrontal, confrontation, confrontation's, confrontational, confrontationism, confrontationist, confrontations, confronte, confronted, confronter, confronters, confronting, confrontment, confronts, confucian, confucianism, confucians, confucius, confusability, confusable, confusably, confuse, confused, confusedly, confusedness, confuser, confusers, confuses, confusing, confusingly, confusion, confusional, confusions, confusive, confusticate, confustication, confutability, confutable, confutation, confutations, confutative, confutator, confute, confuted, confuter, confuters, confutes, confuting, cong, conga, congaed, congaing, congas, conge, congeable, congeal, congealability, congealable congealableness, congealed, congealedness, congealer, congealing, congealment, congeals, conged, congee, congeed, congeeing, congees, congeing, congelation, congelative, congelifract, congelifraction, congeliturbate, congeliturbation, congenator, congener, congeneracy, congeneric, congenerical, congenerous, congenerousness, congeners, congenetic, congenial, congeniality, congenialize, congenially, congenialness, congenital, congenitally, congenitalness, congenite, congeon, conger, congeree, congerie, congeries, congers, congery, conges, congession, congest, congested, congestedness, congestible, congesting, congestion, congestions, congestive, congests, congestus, congiaries, congiary, congii, congius, conglaciate, conglobate, conglobated, conglobately, conglobating, conglobation, conglobe, conglobed, conglobes, conglobing, conglobulate, conglomerate, conglomerated, conglomerates, conglomeratic, conglomerating, conglomeration, conglomerations, conglomerative, conglomerator, conglomeritic, conglutin, conglutinant, conglutinate, conglutinated, conglutinating, conglutination, conglutinative, conglution, congo, congoes, congolese, congoni, congos, congou, congous, congrats, congratulable, congratulant, congratulate, congratulated, congratulates, congratulating, congratulation, congratulational, congratulations, congratulator, congratulatory, congredient, congree, congreet, congregable, congreganist, congregant, congregants, congregate, congregated, congregates, congregating, congregation, congregational, congregationalism, congregationalist, congregationalists, congregationalize, congregationally, congregationist, congregations, congregative, congregativeness, congregator, congress, congress's, congressed, congresser, congresses, congressing, congressional, congressionalist, congressionally, congressionist, congressist, congressive, congressman, congressmen, congresswoman, congresswomen, congreve, congrid, congrio, congroid, congrue, congruence, congruences, congruencies, congruency, congruent, congruential, congruently, congruism, congruist, congruistic, congruities, congruity, congruous, congruously, congruousness, congustable, conhydrin, conhydrine, coni, conia, conic, conical, conicality, conically, conicalness, conicein, coniceine, conichalcite, conicine, conicities, conicity, conicle, conicoid, conicopoly, conics, conidia, conidial, conidian, conidiiferous, conidioid, conidiophore, conidiophorous, conidiospore, conidium, conies, conifer, coniferin, coniferophyte, coniferous, conifers, conification, coniform, coniine, coniines, conima, conimene, conin, conine, conines, coning, coninidia, conins, coniology, coniomycetes, coniosis, coniospermous, coniroster, conirostral, conisance, conite, conium, coniums, conj, conject, conjective, conjecturable, conjecturableness, conjecturably, conjectural, conjecturalist, conjecturality, conjecturally, conjecture, conjectured, conjecturer, conjectures, conjecturing, conjee, conjegates, conjobble, conjoin, conjoined, conjoinedly, conjoiner, conjoining, conjoins, conjoint, conjointly, conjointment, conjointness, conjoints, conjon, conjubilant, conjuctiva, conjugable, conjugably, conjugacy, conjugal, conjugality, conjugally, conjugant, conjugata, conjugate, conjugated, conjugately, conjugateness, conjugates, conjugating, conjugation, conjugational, conjugationally, conjugations, conjugative, conjugator, conjugators, conjugial, conjugium, conjunct, conjuncted, conjunction, conjunction's, conjunctional, conjunctionally, conjunctions, conjunctiva, conjunctivae, conjunctival, conjunctivas, conjunctive, conjunctively, conjunctiveness, conjunctives, conjunctivitis, conjunctly, conjuncts, conjunctur, conjunctural, conjuncture, conjunctures, conjuration, conjurations, conjurator, conjure, conjured, conjurement, conjurer, conjurers, conjurership, conjures, conjuring, conjurison, conjuror, conjurors, conjury, conk, conkanee, conked, conker, conkers, conking, conks, conky, conli, conn, connach, connaisseur, connaraceous, connarite, connascency, connascent, connatal, connate, connately, connateness, connation, connatural, connaturality, connaturalize, connaturally, connaturalness, connature, connaught, connect, connectable, connectant, connected, connectedly, connectedness, connecter, connecters, connectibility, connectible, connectibly, connecticut, connecting, connection, connection's, connectional, connectionism, connectionless, connections, connectival, connective, connective's, connectively, connectives, connectivity, connector, connector's, connectors, connects, conned, connellite, conner, conners, connex, connexes, connexion, connexional, connexionalism, connexities, connexity, connexiva, connexive, connexivum, connexure, connexus, connie, connies, conning, conniption, conniptions, connivance, connivances, connivancy, connivant, connivantly, connive, connived, connivence, connivent, connivently, conniver, connivers, connivery, connives, conniving, connivingly, connixation, connoissance, connoisseur, connoisseur's, connoisseurs, connoisseurship, connotate, connotation, connotational, connotations, connotative, connotatively, connote, connoted, connotes, connoting, connotive, connotively, conns, connu, connubial, connubialism, connubiality, connubially, connubiate, connubium, connumerate, connumeration, connusable, conny, conocarp, conoclinium, conocuneus, conodont, conodonts, conoid, conoidal, conoidally, conoidic, conoidical, conoidically, conoids, conominee, cononintelligent, conopid, conoplain, conopodium, conormal, conoscente, conoscenti, conoscope, conoscopic, conourish, conphaseolin, conplane, conquassate, conquedle, conquer, conquerable, conquerableness, conquered, conquerer, conquerers, conqueress, conquering, conqueringly, conquerment, conqueror, conqueror's, conquerors, conquers, conquest, conquest's, conquests, conquian, conquians, conquinamine, conquinine, conquisition, conquistador, conquistadores, conquistadors, conrail, conrector, conrectorship, conred, conrey, cons, consacre, consanguine, consanguineal, consanguinean, consanguineous, consanguineously, consanguinities, consanguinity, consarcinate, consarn, consarned, conscience, conscience's, conscienceless, consciencelessly, consciencelessness, consciences, consciencewise, conscient, conscientious, conscientiously, conscientiousness, conscionable, conscionableness, conscionably, conscious, consciously, consciousness, conscive, conscribe, conscribed, conscribing, conscript, conscripted, conscripting, conscription, conscriptional, conscriptionist, conscriptions, conscriptive, conscripts, conscripttion, consderations, consecrate, consecrated, consecratedness, consecrater, consecrates, consecrating, consecration, consecrations, consecrative, consecrator, consecratory, consectary, consecute, consecution, consecutive, consecutively, consecutiveness, consecutives, consence, consenescence, consenescency, consension, consensual, consensually, consensus, consensuses, consent, consentable, consentaneity, consentaneous, consentaneously, consentaneousness, consentant, consented, consenter, consenters, consentful, consentfully, consentience, consentient, consentiently, consenting, consentingly, consentingness, consentive, consentively, consentment, consents, consequence, consequence's, consequences, consequency, consequent, consequential, consequentialities, consequentiality, consequentially, consequentialness, consequently, consequents, consertal, consertion, conservable, conservacy, conservancies, conservancy, conservant, conservate, conservation, conservation's, conservational, conservationism, conservationist, conservationist's, conservationists, conservations, conservatism, conservatist, conservative, conservatively, conservativeness, conservatives, conservatize, conservatoire, conservatoires, conservator, conservatorial, conservatories, conservatorio, conservatorium, conservators, conservatorship, conservatory, conservatrix, conserve, conserved, conserver, conservers, conserves, conserving, consider, considerability, considerable, considerableness, considerably, considerance, considerate, considerately, considerateness, consideration, considerations, considerative, consideratively, considerativeness, considerator, considered, considerer, considering, consideringly, considers, consign, consignable, consignataries, consignatary, consignation, consignatory, consigne, consigned, consignee, consignees, consigneeship, consigner, consignificant, consignificate, consignification, consignificative, consignificator, consignified, consignify, consignifying, consigning, consignment, consignments, consignor, consignors, consigns, consiliary, consilience, consilient, consimilar, consimilarity, consimilate, consimilated, consimilating, consimile, consisently, consist, consisted, consistence, consistences, consistencies, consistency, consistent, consistently, consistible, consisting, consistorial, consistorian, consistories, consistory, consists, consition, consitutional, consociate, consociated, consociating, consociation, consociational, consociationism, consociative, consocies, consol, consolable, consolableness, consolably, consolan, consolate, consolation, consolation's, consolations, consolator, consolatorily, consolatoriness, consolatory, consolatrix, console, consoled, consolement, consoler, consolers, consoles, consolette, consolidant, consolidate, consolidated, consolidates, consolidating, consolidation, consolidationist, consolidations, consolidative, consolidator, consolidators, consoling, consolingly, consolitorily, consolitoriness, consols, consolute, consomm, consomme, consommes, consonance, consonances, consonancy, consonant, consonant's, consonantal, consonantalize, consonantalized, consonantalizing, consonantally, consonantic, consonantise, consonantised, consonantising, consonantism, consonantize, consonantized, consonantizing, consonantly, consonantness, consonants, consonate, consonous, consopite, consort, consortable, consorted, consorter, consortia, consortial, consorting, consortion, consortism, consortitia, consortium, consortiums, consorts, consortship, consoude, consound, conspecies, conspecific, conspecifics, conspect, conspection, conspectuity, conspectus, conspectuses, consperg, consperse, conspersion, conspicuity, conspicuous, conspicuously, conspicuousness, conspiracies, conspiracy, conspiracy's, conspirant, conspiration, conspirational, conspirative, conspirator, conspirator's, conspiratorial, conspiratorially, conspirators, conspiratory, conspiratress, conspire, conspired, conspirer, conspirers, conspires, conspiring, conspiringly, conspissate, conspue, conspurcate, const, constable, constable's, constablery, constables, constableship, constabless, constablewick, constabular, constabularies, constabulary, constance, constances, constancy, constant, constantan, constantinian, constantinople, constantinopolitan, constantly, constantness, constants, constat, constatation, constatations, constate, constative, constatory, constellate, constellated, constellating, constellation, constellation's, constellations, constellatory, conster, consternate, consternated, consternating, consternation, constipate, constipated, constipates, constipating, constipation, constituencies, constituency, constituency's, constituent, constituent's, constituently, constituents, constitute, constituted, constituter, constitutes, constituting, constitution, constitutional, constitutionalism, constitutionalist, constitutionality, constitutionalization, constitutionalize, constitutionally, constitutionals, constitutionary, constitutioner, constitutionist, constitutionless, constitutions, constitutive, constitutively, constitutiveness, constitutor, constr, constrain, constrainable, constrained, constrainedly, constrainedness, constrainer, constrainers, constraining, constrainingly, constrainment, constrains, constraint, constraint's, constraints, constrict, constricted, constricting, constriction, constrictions, constrictive, constrictor, constrictors, constricts, constringe, constringed, constringency, constringent, constringing, construability, construable, construal, construct, constructable, constructed, constructer, constructibility, constructible, constructing, construction, construction's, constructional, constructionally, constructionism, constructionist, constructionists, constructions, constructive, constructively, constructiveness, constructivism, constructivist, constructor, constructor's, constructors, constructorship, constructs, constructure, construe, construed, construer, construers, construes, construing, constuctor, constuprate, constupration, consubsist, consubsistency, consubstantial, consubstantialism, consubstantialist, consubstantiality, consubstantially, consubstantiate, consubstantiated, consubstantiating, consubstantiation, consubstantiationist, consubstantive, consuete, consuetitude, consuetude, consuetudinal, consuetudinary, consul, consul's, consulage, consular, consularity, consulary, consulate, consulate's, consulated, consulates, consulating, consuls, consulship, consulships, consult, consulta, consultable, consultancy, consultant, consultant's, consultants, consultantship, consultary, consultation, consultation's, consultations, consultative, consultatively, consultatory, consulted, consultee, consulter, consulting, consultive, consultively, consulto, consultor, consultory, consults, consumable, consumables, consumate, consumated, consumating, consumation, consume, consumed, consumedly, consumeless, consumer, consumer's, consumerism, consumerist, consumers, consumership, consumes, consuming, consumingly, consumingness, consummate, consummated, consummately, consummates, consummating, consummation, consummations, consummative, consummatively, consummativeness, consummator, consummatory, consumo, consumpt, consumpted, consumptible, consumption, consumption's, consumptional, consumptions, consumptive, consumptively, consumptiveness, consumptives, consumptivity, consute, consy, cont, contabescence, contabescent, contact, contactant, contacted, contactile, contacting, contaction, contactor, contacts, contactual, contactually, contadino, contaggia, contagia, contagion, contagioned, contagionist, contagions, contagiosity, contagious, contagiously, contagiousness, contagium, contain, containable, contained, containedly, container, containerboard, containerization, containerize, containerized, containerizes, containerizing, containerport, containers, containership, containerships, containing, containment, containment's, containments, contains, contakia, contakion, contakionkia, contam, contaminable, contaminant, contaminants, contaminate, contaminated, contaminates, contaminating, contamination, contaminations, contaminative, contaminator, contaminous, contangential, contango, contangoes, contangos, contchar, contd, conte, conteck, contect, contection, contek, conteke, contemn, contemned, contemner, contemnible, contemnibly, contemning, contemningly, contemnor, contemns, contemp, contemper, contemperate, contemperature, contemplable, contemplamen, contemplance, contemplant, contemplate, contemplated, contemplatedly, contemplates, contemplating, contemplatingly, contemplation, contemplations, contemplatist, contemplative, contemplatively, contemplativeness, contemplator, contemplators, contemplature, contemple, contemporanean, contemporaneity, contemporaneous, contemporaneously, contemporaneousness, contemporaries, contemporarily, contemporariness, contemporary, contemporise, contemporised, contemporising, contemporize, contemporized, contemporizing, contempt, contemptful, contemptibility, contemptible, contemptibleness, contemptibly, contempts, contemptuous, contemptuously, contemptuousness, contend, contended, contendent, contender, contendere, contenders, contending, contendingly, contendress, contends, contenement, content, contentable, contentation, contented, contentedly, contentedness, contentful, contenting, contention, contention's, contentional, contentions, contentious, contentiously, contentiousness, contentless, contently, contentment, contentness, contents, contenu, conter, conterminable, conterminal, conterminant, conterminate, contermine, conterminous, conterminously, conterminousness, conterraneous, contes, contessa, contesseration, contest, contestability, contestable, contestableness, contestably, contestant, contestants, contestate, contestation, contested, contestee, contester, contesters, contesting, contestingly, contestless, contests, conteur, contex, context, context's, contextive, contexts, contextual, contextualize, contextually, contextural, contexture, contextured, contg, conticent, contignate, contignation, contiguate, contiguities, contiguity, contiguous, contiguously, contiguousness, contin, continence, continency, continent, continent's, continental, continentalism, continentalist, continentality, continentally, continentals, continently, continents, contineu, contingence, contingencies, contingency, contingency's, contingent, contingent's, contingential, contingentialness, contingentiam, contingently, contingentness, contingents, continua, continuable, continual, continuality, continually, continualness, continuance, continuance's, continuances, continuancy, continuando, continuant, continuantly, continuate, continuately, continuateness, continuation, continuation's, continuations, continuative, continuatively, continuativeness, continuator, continue, continued, continuedly, continuedness, continuer, continuers, continues, continuing, continuingly, continuist, continuities, continuity, continuo, continuos, continuous, continuously, continuousness, continuua, continuum, continuums, contise, contline, conto, contoid, contoise, contorniate, contorniates, contorno, contorsion, contorsive, contort, contorta, contorted, contortedly, contortedness, contorting, contortion, contortional, contortionate, contortioned, contortionist, contortionistic, contortionists, contortions, contortive, contortively, contorts, contortuplicate, contos, contour, contour's, contoured, contouring, contourne, contours, contr, contra, contraband, contrabandage, contrabandery, contrabandism, contrabandist, contrabandista, contrabass, contrabassist, contrabasso, contrabassoon, contrabassoonist, contracapitalist, contraception, contraceptionist, contraceptive, contraceptives, contracivil, contraclockwise, contract, contractable, contractant, contractation, contracted, contractedly, contractedness, contractee, contracter, contractibility, contractible, contractibleness, contractibly, contractile, contractility, contracting, contraction, contraction's, contractional, contractionist, contractions, contractive, contractively, contractiveness, contractly, contractor, contractor's, contractors, contracts, contractu, contractual, contractually, contracture, contractured, contractus, contracyclical, contrada, contradance, contrade, contradebt, contradict, contradictable, contradicted, contradictedness, contradicter, contradicting, contradiction, contradiction's, contradictional, contradictions, contradictious, contradictiously, contradictiousness, contradictive, contradictively, contradictiveness, contradictor, contradictories, contradictorily, contradictoriness, contradictory, contradicts, contradiscriminate, contradistinct, contradistinction, contradistinctions, contradistinctive, contradistinctively, contradistinctly, contradistinguish, contradivide, contrafacture, contrafagotto, contrafissura, contrafissure, contraflexure, contraflow, contrafocal, contragredience, contragredient, contrahent, contrail, contrails, contraindicant, contraindicate, contraindicated, contraindicates, contraindicating, contraindication, contraindications, contraindicative, contrair, contraire, contralateral, contralti, contralto, contraltos, contramarque, contramure, contranatural, contrantiscion, contraoctave, contraorbital, contraorbitally, contraparallelogram, contrapletal, contraplete, contraplex, contrapolarization, contrapone, contraponend, contrapose, contraposed, contraposing, contraposit, contraposita, contraposition, contrapositive, contrapositives, contrapposto, contrappostos, contraprogressist, contraprop, contraproposal, contraprops, contraprovectant, contraption, contraption's, contraptions, contraptious, contrapuntal, contrapuntalist, contrapuntally, contrapuntist, contrapunto, contrarational, contraregular, contraregularity, contraremonstrance, contraremonstrant, contrarevolutionary, contrariant, contrariantly, contraries, contrarieties, contrariety, contrarily, contrariness, contrarious, contrariously, contrariousness, contrariwise, contrarotation, contrary, contrascriptural, contrast, contrastable, contrastably, contraste, contrasted, contrastedly, contraster, contrasters, contrastimulant, contrastimulation, contrastimulus, contrasting, contrastingly, contrastive, contrastively, contrastiveness, contrastment, contrasts, contrasty, contrasuggestible, contratabular, contrate, contratempo, contratenor, contratulations, contravalence, contravallation, contravariant, contravene, contravened, contravener, contravenes, contravening, contravention, contraversion, contravindicate, contravindication, contrawise, contrayerva, contrecoup, contrectation, contredanse, contredanses, contreface, contrefort, contrepartie, contretemps, contrib, contributable, contributary, contribute, contributed, contributes, contributing, contribution, contributional, contributions, contributive, contributively, contributiveness, contributor, contributor's, contributorial, contributories, contributorily, contributors, contributorship, contributory, contrist, contrite, contritely, contriteness, contrition, contriturate, contrivable, contrivance, contrivance's, contrivances, contrivancy, contrive, contrived, contrivedly, contrivement, contriver, contrivers, contrives, contriving, control, control's, controled, controling, controllability, controllable, controllableness, controllably, controlled, controller, controller's, controllers, controllership, controlless, controlling, controllingly, controlment, controls, controversal, controverse, controversed, controversial, controversialism, controversialist, controversialists, controversialize, controversially, controversies, controversion, controversional, controversionalism, controversionalist, controversy, controversy's, controvert, controverted, controverter, controvertibility, controvertible, controvertibly, controverting, controvertist, controverts, contrude, conttinua, contubernal, contubernial, contubernium, contumacies, contumacious, contumaciously, contumaciousness, contumacities, contumacity, contumacy, contumax, contumelies, contumelious, contumeliously, contumeliousness, contumely, contund, contune, conturb, conturbation, contuse, contused, contuses, contusing, contusion, contusioned, contusions, contusive, conubium, conule, conumerary, conumerous, conundrum, conundrum's, conundrumize, conundrums, conurbation, conurbations, conure, conus, conusable, conusance, conusant, conusee, conuses, conusor, conutrition, conuzee, conuzor, conv, convalesce, convalesced, convalescence, convalescency, convalescent, convalescently, convalescents, convalesces, convalescing, convallamarin, convallariaceous, convallarin, convally, convect, convected, convecting, convection, convectional, convective, convectively, convector, convects, convell, convenable, convenably, convenance, convenances, convene, convened, convenee, convener, conveneries, conveners, convenership, convenery, convenes, convenience, convenience's, convenienced, conveniences, conveniencies, conveniency, conveniens, convenient, conveniently, convenientness, convening, convent, convent's, convented, conventical, conventically, conventicle, conventicler, conventicles, conventicular, conventing, convention, convention's, conventional, conventionalisation, conventionalise, conventionalised, conventionalising, conventionalism, conventionalist, conventionalities, conventionality, conventionalization, conventionalize, conventionalized, conventionalizes, conventionalizing, conventionally, conventionary, conventioneer, conventioneers, conventioner, conventionism, conventionist, conventionize, conventions, convento, convents, conventual, conventually, converge, converged, convergement, convergence, convergences, convergency, convergent, convergently, converges, convergescence, converginerved, converging, conversable, conversableness, conversably, conversance, conversancy, conversant, conversantly, conversation, conversation's, conversationable, conversational, conversationalism, conversationalist, conversationalists, conversationally, conversationism, conversationist, conversationize, conversations, conversative, conversazione, conversaziones, conversazioni, converse, conversed, conversely, converser, converses, conversi, conversibility, conversible, conversing, conversion, conversional, conversionary, conversionism, conversionist, conversions, conversive, converso, conversus, conversusi, convert, convertable, convertaplane, converted, convertend, converter, converters, convertibility, convertible, convertibleness, convertibles, convertibly, convertingness, convertiplane, convertise, convertism, convertite, convertive, convertoplane, convertor, convertors, converts, conveth, convex, convexed, convexedly, convexedness, convexes, convexities, convexity, convexly, convexness, convexo, convexoconcave, convey, conveyability, conveyable, conveyal, conveyance, conveyance's, conveyancer, conveyances, conveyancing, conveyed, conveyer, conveyers, conveying, conveyor, conveyorization, conveyorize, conveyorized, conveyorizer, conveyorizing, conveyors, conveys, conviciate, convicinity, convict, convictable, convicted, convictfish, convictfishes, convictible, convicting, conviction, conviction's, convictional, convictions, convictism, convictive, convictively, convictiveness, convictment, convictor, convicts, convince, convinced, convincedly, convincedness, convincement, convincer, convincers, convinces, convincibility, convincible, convincing, convincingly, convincingness, convite, convito, convival, convive, convives, convivial, convivialist, conviviality, convivialize, convivially, convivio, convocant, convocate, convocated, convocating, convocation, convocational, convocationally, convocationist, convocations, convocative, convocator, convoke, convoked, convoker, convokers, convokes, convoking, convolute, convoluted, convolutedly, convolutedness, convolutely, convoluting, convolution, convolutional, convolutionary, convolutions, convolutive, convolve, convolved, convolvement, convolves, convolving, convolvulaceous, convolvulad, convolvuli, convolvulic, convolvulin, convolvulinic, convolvulinolic, convolvulus, convolvuluses, convoy, convoyed, convoying, convoys, convulsant, convulse, convulsed, convulsedly, convulses, convulsibility, convulsible, convulsing, convulsion, convulsion's, convulsional, convulsionaries, convulsionary, convulsionism, convulsionist, convulsions, convulsive, convulsively, convulsiveness, cony, conycatcher, conyger, conylene, conynge, conyrin, conyrine, conyza, coo, cooba, coobah, cooboo, cooboos, cooch, cooches, coodle, cooed, cooee, cooeed, cooeeing, cooees, cooer, cooers, cooey, cooeyed, cooeying, cooeys, coof, coofs, cooghneiorvlt, cooing, cooingly, cooja, cook, cookable, cookbook, cookbooks, cookdom, cooked, cookee, cookeite, cooker, cookeries, cookers, cookery, cookey, cookeys, cookhouse, cookhouses, cookie, cookie's, cookies, cooking, cookings, cookish, cookishly, cookless, cookmaid, cookout, cookouts, cookroom, cooks, cookshack, cookshop, cookshops, cookstove, cookware, cookwares, cooky, cool, coolabah, coolaman, coolamon, coolant, coolants, cooled, coolen, cooler, cooler's, coolerman, coolers, coolest, cooley, coolheaded, coolheadedly, coolheadedness, coolhouse, coolibah, coolidge, coolie, coolie's, coolies, cooliman, cooling, coolingly, coolingness, coolish, coolly, coolness, coolnesses, cools, coolth, coolung, coolweed, coolwort, cooly, coom, coomb, coombe, coombes, coombs, coomy, coon, coon's, cooncan, cooncans, cooner, coonhound, coonhounds, coonier, cooniest, coonily, cooniness, coonjine, coonroot, coons, coonskin, coonskins, coontah, coontail, coontie, coonties, coony, coop, cooped, coopee, cooper, cooperage, cooperancy, cooperant, cooperate, cooperated, cooperates, cooperating, cooperatingly, cooperation, cooperationist, cooperations, cooperative, cooperatively, cooperativeness, cooperatives, cooperator, cooperator's, cooperators, coopered, cooperies, coopering, cooperite, coopers, coopery, cooping, coops, coopt, cooptate, cooptation, cooptative, coopted, coopting, cooption, cooptions, cooptive, coopts, coordain, coordinal, coordinate, coordinated, coordinately, coordinateness, coordinates, coordinating, coordination, coordinations, coordinative, coordinator, coordinator's, coordinators, coordinatory, cooree, coorie, cooried, coorieing, coories, cooruptibly, coos, cooser, coosers, coosify, coost, coot, cootch, cooter, cootfoot, cooth, coothay, cootie, cooties, coots, cooty, cop, cop's, copa, copable, copacetic, copaene, copaiba, copaibas, copaibic, copain, copaiva, copaivic, copaiye, copal, copalche, copalchi, copalcocote, copaliferous, copaline, copalite, copaljocote, copalm, copalms, copals, coparallel, coparcenar, coparcenary, coparcener, coparceny, coparenary, coparent, coparents, copart, copartaker, copartiment, copartner, copartners, copartnership, copartnery, coparty, copasetic, copassionate, copastor, copastorate, copastors, copatain, copataine, copatentee, copatriot, copatron, copatroness, copatrons, cope, copeck, copecks, coped, copei, copeia, copelate, copelidine, copellidine, copeman, copemate, copemates, copen, copending, copenetrate, copenhagen, copens, copepod, copepodan, copepodous, copepods, coper, coperception, coperiodic, copernican, copernicans, copernicus, coperose, copers, coperta, copes, copesetic, copesettic, copesman, copesmate, copestone, copetitioner, cophasal, cophosis, cophouse, copia, copiability, copiable, copiapite, copied, copier, copiers, copies, copihue, copihues, copilot, copilots, coping, copings, copingstone, copintank, copiopia, copiopsia, copiosity, copious, copiously, copiousness, copis, copist, copita, coplaintiff, coplanar, coplanarities, coplanarity, coplanation, copleased, coplot, coplots, coplotted, coplotter, coplotting, coploughing, coplowing, copolar, copolymer, copolymeric, copolymerism, copolymerization, copolymerizations, copolymerize, copolymerized, copolymerizing, copolymerous, copolymers, copopoda, copopsia, coportion, copout, copouts, coppa, coppaelite, coppas, copped, copper, copper's, copperah, copperahs, copperas, copperases, copperbottom, coppered, copperer, copperhead, copperheadism, copperheads, coppering, copperish, copperization, copperize, copperleaf, coppernose, coppernosed, copperplate, copperplated, copperproof, coppers, coppersidesman, copperskin, coppersmith, coppersmithing, copperware, copperwing, copperworks, coppery, copperytailed, coppet, coppice, coppiced, coppices, coppicing, coppin, copping, copple, copplecrown, coppled, coppling, coppra, coppras, copps, coppy, copr, copra, copraemia, copraemic, coprah, coprahs, copras, coprecipitate, coprecipitated, coprecipitating, coprecipitation, copremia, copremias, copremic, copresbyter, copresence, copresent, coprincipal, coprincipate, coprinus, coprisoner, coprocessing, coprocessor, coprocessors, coprodaeum, coproduce, coproducer, coproduct, coproduction, coproite, coprojector, coprolagnia, coprolagnist, coprolalia, coprolaliac, coprolite, coprolith, coprolitic, coprology, copromisor, copromoter, coprophagan, coprophagia, coprophagist, coprophagous, coprophagy, coprophilia, coprophiliac, coprophilic, coprophilism, coprophilous, coprophobia, coprophobic, coprophyte, coproprietor, coproprietorship, coprose, coprosma, coprostanol, coprostasia, coprostasis, coprostasophobia, coprosterol, coprozoic, cops, copse, copses, copsewood, copsewooded, copsing, copsole, copsy, copt, copter, copters, coptic, coptine, copula, copulable, copulae, copular, copularium, copulas, copulate, copulated, copulates, copulating, copulation, copulations, copulative, copulatively, copulatory, copunctal, copurchaser, copus, copy, copybook, copybooks, copyboy, copyboys, copycat, copycats, copycatted, copycatting, copycutter, copydesk, copydesks, copyfitter, copyfitting, copygraph, copygraphed, copyhold, copyholder, copyholders, copyholding, copyholds, copying, copyism, copyist, copyists, copyman, copyread, copyreader, copyreaders, copyreading, copyright, copyright's, copyrightable, copyrighted, copyrighter, copyrighting, copyrights, copywise, copywriter, copywriters, copywriting, coque, coquecigrue, coquelicot, coqueluche, coquet, coquetoon, coquetries, coquetry, coquets, coquette, coquetted, coquettes, coquetting, coquettish, coquettishly, coquettishness, coquicken, coquilla, coquillage, coquille, coquilles, coquimbite, coquin, coquina, coquinas, coquita, coquito, coquitos, cor, cora, corach, coracial, coraciiform, coracine, coracle, coracler, coracles, coracoacromial, coracobrachial, coracobrachialis, coracoclavicular, coracocostal, coracohumeral, coracohyoid, coracoid, coracoidal, coracoids, coracomandibular, coracomorph, coracomorphic, coracopectoral, coracoprocoracoid, coracoradialis, coracoscapular, coracosteon, coracovertebral, coradical, coradicate, corage, coraggio, coragio, corah, coraise, coraji, coral, coralbells, coralberries, coralberry, coralbush, coraled, coralene, coralflower, coralist, coralita, coralla, corallet, corallic, corallidomous, coralliferous, coralliform, coralligenous, coralligerous, corallike, corallin, corallinaceous, coralline, corallita, corallite, coralloid, coralloidal, corallum, coralroot, corals, coralwort, coram, coran, corance, coranoch, coranto, corantoes, corantos, coraveca, corban, corbans, corbe, corbeau, corbed, corbeil, corbeille, corbeilles, corbeils, corbel, corbeled, corbeling, corbelled, corbelling, corbels, corbet, corbicula, corbiculae, corbiculate, corbiculum, corbie, corbies, corbiestep, corbina, corbinas, corbleu, corblimey, corblimy, corbovinum, corbula, corby, corcass, corchat, corchorus, corcir, corcle, corcopali, cord, cordage, cordages, cordaitaceous, cordaitalean, cordaitean, cordal, cordant, cordate, cordately, cordax, corded, cordel, cordelier, cordeliere, cordelle, cordelled, cordelling, corder, corders, cordewane, cordia, cordial, cordialities, cordiality, cordialize, cordially, cordialness, cordials, cordiceps, cordicole, cordierite, cordies, cordiform, cordigeri, cordillera, cordilleran, cordilleras, cordinar, cordiner, cording, cordis, cordite, cordites, corditis, cordleaf, cordless, cordlessly, cordlike, cordmaker, cordoba, cordoban, cordobas, cordon, cordonazo, cordonazos, cordoned, cordoning, cordonnet, cordons, cordovan, cordovans, cords, corduroy, corduroyed, corduroying, corduroys, cordwain, cordwainer, cordwainery, cordwains, cordwood, cordwoods, cordy, cordycepin, cordyl, cordyline, core, corebel, corebox, coreceiver, corecipient, coreciprocal, corectome, corectomy, corector, cored, coredeem, coredeemed, coredeemer, coredeeming, coredeems, coredemptress, coreductase, coreflexed, coregence, coregency, coregent, coregnancy, coregnant, coregonid, coregonine, coregonoid, coreid, coreign, coreigner, coreigns, corejoice, corelate, corelated, corelates, corelating, corelation, corelational, corelative, corelatively, coreless, coreligionist, corella, corelysis, coremaker, coremaking, coremia, coremium, coremiumia, coremorphosis, corenounce, coreometer, coreopsis, coreplastic, coreplasty, corepressor, corequisite, corer, corers, cores, coresidence, coresidual, coresign, coresonant, coresort, corespect, corespondency, corespondent, corespondents, coretomy, coreveler, coreveller, corevolve, corf, corge, corgi, corgis, coria, coriaceous, corial, coriamyrtin, coriander, corianders, coriandrol, coriariaceous, coriaus, coriin, corindon, coring, corinne, corinth, corinthes, corinthiac, corinthian, corinthians, coriparian, corita, corium, cork, corkage, corkages, corkboard, corke, corked, corker, corkers, corkier, corkiest, corkiness, corking, corkir, corkish, corkite, corklike, corkline, corkmaker, corkmaking, corks, corkscrew, corkscrewed, corkscrewing, corkscrews, corkscrewy, corkwing, corkwood, corkwoods, corky, corm, cormel, cormels, cormidium, cormlike, cormogen, cormoid, cormophyte, cormophytic, cormorant, cormorants, cormous, corms, cormus, corn, cornaceous, cornada, cornage, cornamute, cornball, cornballs, cornbell, cornberry, cornbin, cornbind, cornbinks, cornbird, cornbole, cornbottle, cornbrash, cornbread, corncake, corncakes, corncob, corncobs, corncockle, corncracker, corncrake, corncrib, corncribs, corncrusher, corncutter, corncutting, corndodger, cornea, corneagen, corneal, corneas, corned, cornein, corneine, corneitis, cornel, cornelian, cornell, cornels, cornemuse, corneocalcareous, corneosclerotic, corneosiliceous, corneous, corner, cornerback, cornerbind, cornercap, cornered, cornerer, cornering, cornerman, cornerpiece, corners, cornerstone, cornerstone's, cornerstones, cornerways, cornerwise, cornet, cornetcies, cornetcy, corneter, cornetfish, cornetfishes, cornetist, cornetists, cornets, cornett, cornette, cornetter, cornetti, cornettino, cornettist, cornetto, corneule, corneum, cornfactor, cornfed, cornfield, cornfield's, cornfields, cornflag, cornflakes, cornfloor, cornflour, cornflower, cornflowers, corngrower, cornhole, cornhouse, cornhusk, cornhusker, cornhusking, cornhusks, cornic, cornice, corniced, cornices, corniche, corniches, cornichon, cornicing, cornicle, cornicles, cornicular, corniculate, corniculer, corniculum, cornier, corniest, corniferous, cornific, cornification, cornified, corniform, cornify, cornigeous, cornigerous, cornily, cornin, corniness, corning, corniplume, cornish, cornishman, cornix, cornland, cornless, cornloft, cornmaster, cornmeal, cornmeals, cornmonger, cornmuse, corno, cornopean, cornpipe, cornrick, cornroot, cornrow, cornrows, corns, cornsack, cornstalk, cornstalks, cornstarch, cornstone, cornstook, cornu, cornua, cornual, cornuate, cornuated, cornubianite, cornucopia, cornucopian, cornucopias, cornucopiate, cornule, cornulite, cornupete, cornus, cornuses, cornute, cornuted, cornutin, cornutine, cornuting, cornuto, cornutos, cornutus, cornwall, cornwallis, cornwallises, cornwallite, corny, coroa, corocleisis, corodiary, corodiastasis, corodiastole, corodies, corody, corojo, corol, corolitic, coroll, corolla, corollaceous, corollarial, corollarially, corollaries, corollary, corollary's, corollas, corollate, corollated, corollet, corolliferous, corollifloral, corolliform, corollike, corolline, corollitic, coromandel, coromell, corometer, corona, coronach, coronachs, coronad, coronadite, coronado, coronados, coronae, coronagraph, coronagraphic, coronal, coronale, coronaled, coronalled, coronally, coronals, coronamen, coronaries, coronary, coronas, coronate, coronated, coronation, coronations, coronatorial, coronavirus, corone, coronel, coronels, coronene, coroner, coroners, coronership, coronet, coronet's, coroneted, coronetlike, coronets, coronetted, coronettee, coronetty, coroniform, coronillin, coronillo, coronion, coronis, coronitis, coronium, coronize, coronobasilar, coronofacial, coronofrontal, coronograph, coronographic, coronoid, coronule, coroparelcysis, coroplast, coroplasta, coroplastae, coroplastic, coroplasty, coroscopy, corosif, corotate, corotated, corotates, corotating, corotation, corotomy, coroun, coroutine, coroutine's, coroutines, corozo, corozos, corp, corpl, corpn, corpora, corporacies, corporacy, corporal, corporal's, corporalcy, corporale, corporales, corporalism, corporalities, corporality, corporally, corporals, corporalship, corporas, corporate, corporately, corporateness, corporation, corporation's, corporational, corporationer, corporationism, corporations, corporatism, corporatist, corporative, corporatively, corporativism, corporator, corporature, corpore, corporeal, corporealist, corporeality, corporealization, corporealize, corporeally, corporealness, corporeals, corporeity, corporeous, corporification, corporify, corporosity, corposant, corps, corpsbruder, corpse, corpse's, corpselike, corpselikeness, corpses, corpsman, corpsmen, corpsy, corpulence, corpulences, corpulencies, corpulency, corpulent, corpulently, corpulentness, corpus, corpuscle, corpuscles, corpuscular, corpuscularian, corpuscularity, corpusculated, corpuscule, corpusculous, corpusculum, corr, corrade, corraded, corrades, corradial, corradiate, corradiated, corradiating, corradiation, corrading, corral, corralled, corralling, corrals, corrasion, corrasive, correal, correality, correct, correctable, correctant, corrected, correctedness, correcter, correctest, correctible, correctify, correcting, correctingly, correction, correctional, correctionalist, correctioner, corrections, correctitude, corrective, correctively, correctiveness, correctives, correctly, correctness, corrector, correctorship, correctory, correctress, correctrice, corrects, corregidor, corregidores, corregidors, corregimiento, corregimientos, correl, correlatable, correlate, correlated, correlates, correlating, correlation, correlational, correlations, correlative, correlatively, correlativeness, correlatives, correlativism, correlativity, correligionist, correllated, correllation, correllations, corrente, correo, correption, corresol, corresp, correspond, corresponded, correspondence, correspondence's, correspondences, correspondencies, correspondency, correspondent, correspondent's, correspondential, correspondentially, correspondently, correspondents, correspondentship, corresponder, corresponding, correspondingly, corresponds, corresponsion, corresponsive, corresponsively, corrida, corridas, corrido, corridor, corridor's, corridored, corridors, corrie, corriedale, corries, corrige, corrigenda, corrigendum, corrigent, corrigibility, corrigible, corrigibleness, corrigibly, corrival, corrivality, corrivalry, corrivals, corrivalship, corrivate, corrivation, corrive, corrobboree, corrober, corroborant, corroborate, corroborated, corroborates, corroborating, corroboration, corroborations, corroborative, corroboratively, corroborator, corroboratorily, corroborators, corroboratory, corroboree, corroboreed, corroboreeing, corroborees, corrobori, corrodant, corrode, corroded, corrodent, corroder, corroders, corrodes, corrodiary, corrodibility, corrodible, corrodier, corrodies, corroding, corrodingly, corrody, corrosibility, corrosible, corrosibleness, corrosion, corrosional, corrosionproof, corrosive, corrosived, corrosively, corrosiveness, corrosives, corrosiving, corrosivity, corrugant, corrugate, corrugated, corrugates, corrugating, corrugation, corrugations, corrugator, corrugators, corrugent, corrump, corrumpable, corrup, corrupable, corrupt, corrupted, corruptedly, corruptedness, corrupter, corruptest, corruptful, corruptibilities, corruptibility, corruptible, corruptibleness, corruptibly, corrupting, corruptingly, corruption, corruptionist, corruptions, corruptious, corruptive, corruptively, corruptless, corruptly, corruptness, corruptor, corruptress, corrupts, corsac, corsacs, corsage, corsages, corsaint, corsair, corsairs, corsak, corse, corselet, corseleted, corseleting, corselets, corselette, corsepresent, corseque, corser, corses, corsesque, corset, corseted, corsetier, corsetiere, corseting, corsetless, corsetry, corsets, corsie, corsite, corslet, corslets, corsned, corso, corsos, corsy, cort, corta, cortaro, cortege, corteges, corteise, cortes, cortex, cortexes, cortez, cortian, cortical, cortically, corticate, corticated, corticating, cortication, cortices, corticiferous, corticiform, corticifugal, corticifugally, corticin, corticine, corticipetal, corticipetally, corticoafferent, corticoefferent, corticoid, corticole, corticoline, corticolous, corticopeduncular, corticose, corticospinal, corticosteroid, corticosteroids, corticosterone, corticostriate, corticotrophin, corticotropin, corticous, cortile, cortin, cortina, cortinae, cortinarious, cortinate, cortine, cortins, cortisol, cortisols, cortisone, cortlandtite, coruco, coruler, corundophilite, corundum, corundums, corupay, coruscant, coruscate, coruscated, coruscates, coruscating, coruscation, coruscations, coruscative, corv, corve, corved, corvee, corvees, corven, corver, corves, corvet, corvets, corvette, corvettes, corvetto, corviform, corvillosum, corvina, corvinas, corvine, corviser, corvisor, corvktte, corvo, corvoid, corvorant, corvus, corybant, corybantiasm, corybantic, corybantish, corybulbin, corybulbine, corycavamine, corycavidin, corycavidine, corycavine, corydalin, corydaline, corydalis, corydine, corydon, corydora, coryl, corylaceous, corylet, corylin, corymb, corymbed, corymbiate, corymbiated, corymbiferous, corymbiform, corymblike, corymbose, corymbosely, corymbous, corymbs, corynebacteria, corynebacterial, corynebacterium, coryneform, corynid, corynine, corynite, corynocarpaceous, corynteria, coryph, coryphaei, coryphaenid, coryphaenoid, coryphaeus, coryphee, coryphees, coryphene, coryphodon, coryphodont, coryphylly, corypphaei, corystoid, corytuberine, coryza, coryzal, coryzas, cos, cosalite, cosaque, cosavior, coscet, coscinomancy, coscoroba, cose, coseasonal, coseat, cosec, cosecant, cosecants, cosech, cosecs, cosectarian, cosectional, cosed, cosegment, coseier, coseiest, coseism, coseismal, coseismic, cosen, cosenator, cosentiency, cosentient, coservant, coses, cosession, coset, cosets, cosettler, cosey, coseys, cosh, cosharer, cosheath, coshed, cosher, coshered, cosherer, cosheries, coshering, coshers, coshery, coshes, coshing, cosie, cosier, cosies, cosiest, cosign, cosignatories, cosignatory, cosigned, cosigner, cosigners, cosignificative, cosigning, cosignitary, cosigns, cosily, cosin, cosinage, cosine, cosines, cosiness, cosinesses, cosing, cosingular, cosins, cosinusoid, cosmecology, cosmesis, cosmete, cosmetic, cosmetical, cosmetically, cosmetician, cosmeticize, cosmetics, cosmetiste, cosmetological, cosmetologist, cosmetologists, cosmetology, cosmic, cosmical, cosmicality, cosmically, cosmine, cosmism, cosmisms, cosmist, cosmists, cosmo, cosmochemical, cosmochemistry, cosmocracy, cosmocrat, cosmocratic, cosmodrome, cosmogenesis, cosmogenetic, cosmogenic, cosmogeny, cosmognosis, cosmogonal, cosmogoner, cosmogonic, cosmogonical, cosmogonies, cosmogonist, cosmogonists, cosmogonize, cosmogony, cosmographer, cosmographic, cosmographical, cosmographically, cosmographies, cosmographist, cosmography, cosmoid, cosmolabe, cosmolatry, cosmoline, cosmolined, cosmolining, cosmologic, cosmological, cosmologically, cosmologies, cosmologist, cosmologists, cosmology, cosmologygy, cosmometry, cosmonaut, cosmonautic, cosmonautical, cosmonautically, cosmonautics, cosmonauts, cosmopathic, cosmoplastic, cosmopoietic, cosmopolicy, cosmopolis, cosmopolises, cosmopolitan, cosmopolitanisation, cosmopolitanise, cosmopolitanised, cosmopolitanising, cosmopolitanism, cosmopolitanization, cosmopolitanize, cosmopolitanized, cosmopolitanizing, cosmopolitanly, cosmopolitans, cosmopolite, cosmopolitic, cosmopolitical, cosmopolitics, cosmopolitism, cosmorama, cosmoramic, cosmorganic, cosmos, cosmoscope, cosmoses, cosmosophy, cosmosphere, cosmotellurian, cosmotheism, cosmotheist, cosmotheistic, cosmothetic, cosmotron, cosmozoan, cosmozoans, cosmozoic, cosmozoism, cosonant, cosounding, cosovereign, cosovereignty, cospecies, cospecific, cosphered, cosplendor, cosplendour, cosponsor, cosponsored, cosponsoring, cosponsors, cosponsorship, cosponsorships, coss, cossack, cossacks, cossas, cosse, cosset, cosseted, cosseting, cossets, cossette, cossetted, cossetting, cosshen, cossic, cossid, cossie, cossnent, cossyrite, cost, costa, costae, costage, costal, costalgia, costally, costander, costar, costard, costards, costarred, costarring, costars, costate, costated, costean, costeaning, costectomies, costectomy, costed, costeen, costellate, coster, costerdom, costermonger, costers, costful, costicartilage, costicartilaginous, costicervical, costiferous, costiform, costing, costious, costipulator, costispinal, costive, costively, costiveness, costless, costlessly, costlessness, costlew, costlier, costliest, costliness, costly, costmaries, costmary, costoabdominal, costoapical, costocentral, costochondral, costoclavicular, costocolic, costocoracoid, costodiaphragmatic, costogenic, costoinferior, costophrenic, costopleural, costopneumopexy, costopulmonary, costoscapular, costosternal, costosuperior, costothoracic, costotome, costotomies, costotomy, costotrachelian, costotransversal, costotransverse, costovertebral, costoxiphoid, costraight, costrel, costrels, costs, costula, costulation, costume, costumed, costumer, costumers, costumery, costumes, costumey, costumic, costumier, costumiere, costumiers, costuming, costumire, costumist, costusroot, cosubject, cosubordinate, cosuffer, cosufferer, cosuggestion, cosuitor, cosurety, cosuretyship, cosustain, coswearer, cosy, cosymmedian, cot, cot's, cotabulate, cotan, cotangent, cotangential, cotangents, cotans, cotarius, cotarnin, cotarnine, cotbetty, cotch, cote, coteau, coteaux, coted, coteen, coteful, cotehardie, cotele, coteline, coteller, cotemporane, cotemporanean, cotemporaneous, cotemporaneously, cotemporaries, cotemporarily, cotemporary, cotenancy, cotenant, cotenants, cotenure, coterell, coterie, coteries, coterminal, coterminous, coterminously, coterminousness, cotery, cotes, cotesian, coth, cotham, cothamore, cothe, cotheorist, cothish, cothon, cothouse, cothurn, cothurnal, cothurnate, cothurned, cothurni, cothurnian, cothurnni, cothurns, cothurnus, cothy, cotice, coticed, coticing, coticular, cotidal, cotillage, cotillion, cotillions, cotillon, cotillons, coting, cotinga, cotingid, cotingoid, cotise, cotised, cotising, cotitular, cotland, cotman, coto, cotoin, cotoneaster, cotonia, cotonier, cotorment, cotoro, cotoros, cotorture, cotquean, cotqueans, cotraitor, cotransduction, cotransfuse, cotranslator, cotranspire, cotransubstantiate, cotrespasser, cotrine, cotripper, cotrustee, cots, cotset, cotsetla, cotsetland, cotsetle, cotswold, cott, cotta, cottabus, cottae, cottage, cottaged, cottager, cottagers, cottages, cottagey, cottar, cottars, cottas, cotte, cotted, cotter, cottered, cotterel, cottering, cotterite, cotters, cotterway, cottid, cottier, cottierism, cottiers, cottiest, cottiform, cottise, cottoid, cotton, cottonade, cottonbush, cottoned, cottonee, cottoneer, cottoner, cottoning, cottonization, cottonize, cottonless, cottonmouth, cottonmouths, cottonocracy, cottonopolis, cottonpickin', cottonpicking, cottons, cottonseed, cottonseeds, cottontail, cottontails, cottontop, cottonweed, cottonwick, cottonwood, cottonwoods, cottony, cottrel, cotty, cotuit, cotula, cotunnite, cotutor, cotwal, cotwin, cotwinned, cotwist, cotyla, cotylar, cotyle, cotyledon, cotyledon's, cotyledonal, cotyledonar, cotyledonary, cotyledonoid, cotyledonous, cotyledons, cotyliform, cotyligerous, cotyliscus, cotyloid, cotyloidal, cotylophorous, cotylopubic, cotylosacral, cotylosaur, cotylosaurian, cotype, cotypes, couac, coucal, couch, couchancy, couchant, couchantly, couche, couched, couchee, coucher, couchers, couches, couchette, couching, couchings, couchmaker, couchmaking, couchmate, couchy, coud, coude, coudee, coue, coueism, cougar, cougars, cough, coughed, cougher, coughers, coughing, coughroot, coughs, coughweed, coughwort, cougnar, couhage, coul, coulage, could, couldest, couldn, couldn't, couldna, couldnt, couldron, couldst, coulee, coulees, couleur, coulibiaca, coulie, coulier, coulis, coulisse, coulisses, couloir, couloirs, coulomb, coulombic, coulombmeter, coulombs, coulometer, coulometric, coulometrically, coulometry, coulter, coulterneb, coulters, coulthard, coulure, couma, coumalic, coumalin, coumaphos, coumara, coumaran, coumarane, coumarate, coumaric, coumarilic, coumarin, coumarinic, coumarins, coumarone, coumarou, coumarous, coumbite, council, council's, councilist, councillary, councillor, councillor's, councillors, councillorship, councilman, councilmanic, councilmen, councilor, councilors, councilorship, councils, councilwoman, councilwomen, counderstand, counite, couniversal, counsel, counselable, counseled, counselee, counselful, counseling, counsellable, counselled, counselling, counsellor, counsellor's, counsellors, counsellorship, counselor, counselor's, counselors, counselorship, counsels, counsinhood, count, countability, countable, countableness, countably, countdom, countdown, countdowns, counted, countenance, countenanced, countenancer, countenances, countenancing, counter, counterabut, counteraccusation, counteracquittance, counteract, counteractant, counteracted, counteracter, counteracting, counteractingly, counteraction, counteractions, counteractive, counteractively, counteractivity, counteractor, counteracts, counteraddress, counteradvance, counteradvantage, counteradvice, counteradvise, counteraffirm, counteraffirmation, counteragency, counteragent, counteragitate, counteragitation, counteralliance, counterambush, counterannouncement, counteranswer, counterappeal, counterappellant, counterapproach, counterapse, counterarch, counterargue, counterargument, counterartillery, counterassertion, counterassociation, counterassurance, counterattack, counterattacked, counterattacker, counterattacking, counterattacks, counterattestation, counterattired, counterattraction, counterattractive, counterattractively, counteraverment, counteravouch, counteravouchment, counterbalance, counterbalanced, counterbalances, counterbalancing, counterband, counterbarrage, counterbase, counterbattery, counterbeating, counterbend, counterbewitch, counterbid, counterblast, counterblow, counterbond, counterborder, counterbore, counterbored, counterborer, counterboring, counterboulle, counterboycott, counterbrace, counterbracing, counterbranch, counterbrand, counterbreastwork, counterbuff, counterbuilding, countercampaign, countercarte, countercathexis, countercause, counterchange, counterchanged, counterchanging, countercharge, countercharged, countercharging, countercharm, countercheck, countercheer, counterclaim, counterclaimant, counterclaimed, counterclaiming, counterclaims, counterclassification, counterclassifications, counterclockwise, countercolored, countercommand, countercompany, countercompetition, countercomplaint, countercompony, countercondemnation, counterconditioning, counterconquest, counterconversion, countercouchant, countercoup, countercoupe, countercourant, countercraft, countercriticism, countercross, countercry, countercultural, counterculture, countercultures, counterculturist, countercurrent, countercurrently, countercurrentwise, counterdance, counterdash, counterdecision, counterdeclaration, counterdecree, counterdefender, counterdemand, counterdemonstrate, counterdemonstration, counterdemonstrator, counterdeputation, counterdesire, counterdevelopment, counterdifficulty, counterdigged, counterdike, counterdiscipline, counterdisengage, counterdisengagement, counterdistinct, counterdistinction, counterdistinguish, counterdoctrine, counterdogmatism, counterdraft, counterdrain, counterdrive, counterearth, countered, counterefficiency, countereffort, counterembattled, counterembowed, counterenamel, counterend, counterenergy, counterengagement, counterengine, counterenthusiasm, counterentry, counterequivalent, counterermine, counterespionage, counterestablishment, counterevidence, counterexaggeration, counterexample, counterexamples, counterexcitement, counterexcommunication, counterexercise, counterexplanation, counterexposition, counterexpostulation, counterextend, counterextension, counterfact, counterfactual, counterfactually, counterfallacy, counterfaller, counterfeisance, counterfeit, counterfeited, counterfeiter, counterfeiters, counterfeiting, counterfeitly, counterfeitment, counterfeitness, counterfeits, counterferment, counterfessed, counterfire, counterfix, counterflange, counterflashing, counterfleury, counterflight, counterflory, counterflow, counterflux, counterfoil, counterforce, counterformula, counterfort, counterfugue, countergabble, countergabion, countergage, countergager, countergambit, countergarrison, countergauge, countergauger, countergift, countergirded, counterglow, counterguard, counterguerilla, counterguerrilla, counterhaft, counterhammering, counterhypothesis, counteridea, counterideal, counterimagination, counterimitate, counterimitation, counterimpulse, counterindentation, counterindented, counterindicate, counterindication, counterindoctrinate, counterindoctrination, counterinfluence, countering, counterinsult, counterinsurgencies, counterinsurgency, counterinsurgent, counterinsurgents, counterintelligence, counterinterest, counterinterpretation, counterintrigue, counterintuitive, counterinvective, counterinvestment, counterion, counterirritant, counterirritate, counterirritation, counterjudging, counterjumper, counterlath, counterlathed, counterlathing, counterlatration, counterlaw, counterleague, counterlegislation, counterlife, counterlight, counterlighted, counterlighting, counterlilit, counterlit, counterlocking, counterlode, counterlove, counterly, countermachination, countermaid, counterman, countermand, countermandable, countermanded, countermanding, countermands, countermaneuver, countermanifesto, countermanifestoes, countermarch, countermarching, countermark, countermarriage, countermeasure, countermeasure's, countermeasures, countermeet, countermen, countermessage, countermigration, countermine, countermined, countermining, countermissile, countermission, countermotion, countermount, countermove, countermoved, countermovement, countermoving, countermure, countermutiny, counternaiant, counternarrative, counternatural, counternecromancy, counternoise, counternotice, counterobjection, counterobligation, counteroffensive, counteroffensives, counteroffer, counteropening, counteropponent, counteropposite, counterorator, counterorder, counterorganization, counterpace, counterpaled, counterpaly, counterpane, counterpaned, counterpanes, counterparadox, counterparallel, counterparole, counterparry, counterpart, counterpart's, counterparts, counterpassant, counterpassion, counterpenalty, counterpendent, counterpetition, counterphobic, counterpicture, counterpillar, counterplan, counterplay, counterplayer, counterplea, counterplead, counterpleading, counterplease, counterplot, counterplotted, counterplotter, counterplotting, counterpoint, counterpointe, counterpointed, counterpointing, counterpoints, counterpoise, counterpoised, counterpoises, counterpoising, counterpoison, counterpole, counterpoles, counterponderate, counterpose, counterposition, counterposting, counterpotence, counterpotency, counterpotent, counterpractice, counterpray, counterpreach, counterpreparation, counterpressure, counterprick, counterprinciple, counterprocess, counterproductive, counterproductively, counterproductiveness, counterproductivity, counterprogramming, counterproject, counterpronunciamento, counterproof, counterpropaganda, counterpropagandize, counterprophet, counterproposal, counterproposition, counterprotection, counterprotest, counterprove, counterpull, counterpunch, counterpuncher, counterpuncture, counterpush, counterquartered, counterquarterly, counterquery, counterquestion, counterquip, counterradiation, counterraid, counterraising, counterrampant, counterrate, counterreaction, counterreason, counterreckoning, counterrecoil, counterreconnaissance, counterrefer, counterreflected, counterreform, counterreformation, counterreligion, counterremonstrant, counterreplied, counterreplies, counterreply, counterreplying, counterreprisal, counterresolution, counterrestoration, counterretreat, counterrevolution, counterrevolutionaries, counterrevolutionary, counterrevolutionist, counterrevolutionize, counterrevolutions, counterriposte, counterroll, counterrotating, counterround, counterruin, counters, countersale, countersalient, countersank, counterscale, counterscalloped, counterscarp, counterscoff, countersconce, counterscrutiny, countersea, counterseal, countersecure, countersecurity, counterselection, countersense, counterservice, countershade, countershading, countershaft, countershafting, countershear, countershine, countershock, countershout, counterside, countersiege, countersign, countersignal, countersignature, countersignatures, countersigned, countersigning, countersigns, countersink, countersinking, countersinks, countersleight, counterslope, countersmile, countersnarl, counterspies, counterspy, counterspying, counterstain, counterstamp, counterstand, counterstatant, counterstatement, counterstatute, counterstep, counterstimulate, counterstimulation, counterstimulus, counterstock, counterstratagem, counterstream, counterstrike, counterstroke, counterstruggle, countersubject, countersuggestion, countersuit, countersun, countersunk, countersunken, countersurprise, countersway, counterswing, countersworn, countersympathy, countersynod, countertack, countertail, countertally, countertaste, countertechnicality, countertendencies, countertendency, countertenor, countertenors, counterterm, counterterror, counterterrorism, counterterrorist, countertheme, countertheory, counterthought, counterthreat, counterthrust, counterthwarting, countertierce, countertime, countertouch, countertraction, countertrades, countertransference, countertranslation, countertraverse, countertreason, countertree, countertrench, countertrend, countertrespass, countertrippant, countertripping, countertruth, countertug, counterturn, counterturned, countertype, countervail, countervailed, countervailing, countervails, countervair, countervairy, countervallation, countervalue, countervaunt, countervene, countervengeance, countervenom, countervibration, counterview, countervindication, countervolition, countervolley, countervote, counterwager, counterwall, counterwarmth, counterwave, counterweigh, counterweighed, counterweighing, counterweight, counterweighted, counterweights, counterwheel, counterwill, counterwilling, counterwind, counterwitness, counterword, counterwork, counterworker, counterworking, counterwrite, countess, countesses, countfish, countian, countians, counties, counting, countinghouse, countless, countlessly, countlessness, countor, countour, countree, countreeman, countrie, countrieman, countries, countrification, countrified, countrifiedness, countrify, country, country's, countryfied, countryfiedness, countryfolk, countryish, countryman, countrymen, countrypeople, countryseat, countryside, countryward, countrywide, countrywoman, countrywomen, counts, countship, county, county's, countys, countywide, coup, coupage, coupe, couped, coupee, coupelet, couper, coupes, couping, couple, coupled, couplement, coupler, coupleress, couplers, couples, couplet, coupleteer, couplets, coupling, couplings, coupon, coupon's, couponed, couponless, coupons, coups, coupstick, coupure, courage, courageous, courageously, courageousness, courager, courages, courant, courante, courantes, couranto, courantoes, courantos, courants, courap, couratari, courb, courbache, courbaril, courbash, courbe, courbette, courbettes, courche, courge, courgette, courida, courie, courier, courier's, couriers, couril, courlan, courlans, couronne, course, coursed, courser, coursers, courses, coursey, coursing, coursings, coursy, court, courtage, courtal, courtbred, courtby, courtcraft, courted, courteous, courteously, courteousness, courtepy, courter, courters, courtesan, courtesanry, courtesans, courtesanship, courtesied, courtesies, courtesy, courtesy's, courtesying, courtezan, courtezanry, courtezanship, courthouse, courthouse's, courthouses, courtier, courtier's, courtierism, courtierly, courtiers, courtiership, courtiery, courtin, courting, courtless, courtlet, courtlier, courtliest, courtlike, courtliness, courtling, courtly, courtman, courtnoll, courtroll, courtroom, courtroom's, courtrooms, courts, courtship, courtships, courtside, courty, courtyard, courtyard's, courtyards, courtzilite, couscous, couscouses, couscousou, couseranite, cousin, cousin's, cousinage, cousiness, cousinhood, cousinly, cousinries, cousinry, cousins, cousinship, cousiny, coussinet, coustumier, couteau, couteaux, coutel, coutelle, couter, couters, couth, couthe, couther, couthest, couthie, couthier, couthiest, couthily, couthiness, couthless, couthly, couths, couthy, coutil, coutille, coutumier, couture, coutures, couturier, couturiere, couturieres, couturiers, couturire, couvade, couvades, couve, couvert, couverte, couveuse, couxia, couxio, covado, covalence, covalences, covalency, covalent, covalently, covariable, covariables, covariance, covariant, covariate, covariates, covariation, covary, covassal, cove, coved, covelline, covellite, coven, covenable, covenably, covenance, covenant, covenant's, covenantal, covenantally, covenanted, covenantee, covenanter, covenanting, covenantor, covenants, covens, covent, coventrate, coventries, coventrize, coventry, cover, coverable, coverage, coverages, coverall, coveralled, coveralls, coverchief, covercle, covered, coverer, coverers, covering, coverings, coverless, coverlet, coverlet's, coverlets, coverlid, coverlids, covers, coversed, coverside, coversine, coverslip, coverslut, covert, covertical, covertly, covertness, coverts, coverture, coverup, coverups, coves, covet, covetable, coveted, coveter, coveters, coveting, covetingly, covetise, covetiveness, covetous, covetously, covetousness, covets, covey, coveys, covibrate, covibration, covid, covido, covillager, covin, covine, coving, covings, covinous, covinously, covisit, covisitor, covite, covolume, covotary, cow, cowage, cowages, cowal, cowan, coward, cowardice, cowardish, cowardliness, cowardly, cowardness, cowards, cowardy, cowbane, cowbanes, cowbarn, cowbell, cowbells, cowberries, cowberry, cowbind, cowbinds, cowbird, cowbirds, cowboy, cowboy's, cowboys, cowbrute, cowbyre, cowcatcher, cowcatchers, cowdie, cowed, cowedly, coween, cower, cowered, cowerer, cowerers, cowering, coweringly, cowers, cowfish, cowfishes, cowgate, cowgirl, cowgirls, cowgram, cowgrass, cowhage, cowhages, cowhand, cowhands, cowheart, cowhearted, cowheel, cowherb, cowherbs, cowherd, cowherds, cowhide, cowhided, cowhides, cowhiding, cowhorn, cowhouse, cowier, cowiest, cowing, cowinner, cowinners, cowish, cowishness, cowitch, cowk, cowkeeper, cowkine, cowl, cowle, cowled, cowleech, cowleeching, cowlick, cowlicks, cowlike, cowling, cowlings, cowls, cowlstaff, cowman, cowmen, coworker, coworkers, coworking, cowpat, cowpath, cowpats, cowpea, cowpeas, cowpen, cowper, cowperian, cowperitis, cowpock, cowpoke, cowpokes, cowpony, cowpox, cowpoxes, cowpunch, cowpuncher, cowpunchers, cowquake, cowrie, cowries, cowroid, cowry, cows, cowshard, cowsharn, cowshed, cowsheds, cowshot, cowshut, cowskin, cowskins, cowslip, cowslip'd, cowslip's, cowslipped, cowslips, cowson, cowsucker, cowtail, cowthwort, cowtongue, cowtown, cowweed, cowwheat, cowy, cowyard, cox, coxa, coxae, coxal, coxalgia, coxalgias, coxalgic, coxalgies, coxalgy, coxankylometer, coxarthritis, coxarthrocace, coxarthropathy, coxbones, coxcomb, coxcombess, coxcombhood, coxcombic, coxcombical, coxcombicality, coxcombically, coxcombity, coxcombries, coxcombry, coxcombs, coxcomby, coxcomical, coxcomically, coxed, coxendix, coxes, coxier, coxiest, coxing, coxite, coxitis, coxocerite, coxoceritic, coxodynia, coxofemoral, coxopodite, coxswain, coxswained, coxswaining, coxswains, coxwain, coxwaining, coxwains, coxy, coy, coyan, coydog, coyed, coyer, coyest, coying, coyish, coyishness, coyly, coyn, coyness, coynesses, coynye, coyo, coyol, coyos, coyote, coyote's, coyotes, coyotillo, coyotillos, coyoting, coypou, coypous, coypu, coypus, coys, coystrel, coyure, coz, coze, cozed, cozeier, cozeiest, cozen, cozenage, cozenages, cozened, cozener, cozeners, cozening, cozeningly, cozens, cozes, cozey, cozeys, cozie, cozier, cozies, coziest, cozily, coziness, cozinesses, cozing, cozy, cozzes, cp, cpd, cpi, cpl, cpm, cpo, cps, cpt, cpu, cpus, cputime, cq, cr, craal, craaled, craaling, craals, crab, crab's, crabapple, crabbed, crabbedly, crabbedness, crabber, crabbers, crabbery, crabbier, crabbiest, crabbily, crabbiness, crabbing, crabbish, crabbit, crabby, crabcatcher, crabeater, crabeating, craber, crabfish, crabgrass, crabhole, crabier, crabit, crablet, crablike, crabman, crabmeat, crabmill, crabs, crabsidle, crabstick, crabut, crabweed, crabwise, crabwood, craccus, crachoir, crack, crackability, crackable, crackableness, crackajack, crackback, crackbrain, crackbrained, crackbrainedness, crackdown, crackdowns, cracked, crackedness, cracker, crackerberries, crackerberry, crackerjack, crackerjacks, crackers, cracket, crackhemp, crackiness, cracking, crackings, crackjaw, crackle, crackled, crackles, crackless, crackleware, cracklier, crackliest, crackling, cracklings, crackly, crackmans, cracknel, cracknels, crackpot, crackpotism, crackpots, crackpottedness, crackrope, cracks, crackskull, cracksman, cracksmen, crackup, crackups, cracky, cracovienne, cracowe, craddy, cradge, cradle, cradleboard, cradlechild, cradled, cradlefellow, cradleland, cradlelike, cradlemaker, cradlemaking, cradleman, cradlemate, cradlemen, cradler, cradlers, cradles, cradleside, cradlesong, cradlesongs, cradletime, cradling, craft, crafted, crafter, craftier, craftiest, craftily, craftiness, crafting, craftless, craftly, craftmanship, crafts, craftsman, craftsmanlike, craftsmanly, craftsmanship, craftsmaster, craftsmen, craftspeople, craftsperson, craftswoman, craftwork, craftworker, crafty, crag, crag's, craggan, cragged, craggedly, craggedness, craggier, craggiest, craggily, cragginess, craggy, craglike, crags, cragsman, cragsmen, cragwork, craichy, craie, craig, craighle, craigmontite, craik, crain, craisey, craizey, crajuru, crake, craked, crakefeet, craker, crakes, craking, crakow, cram, cramasie, crambambulee, crambambuli, crambe, cramberry, crambes, crambid, cramble, crambly, crambo, cramboes, crambos, cramel, crammed, crammel, crammer, crammers, cramming, crammingly, cramoisie, cramoisies, cramoisy, cramp, cramp's, crampbit, cramped, crampedness, cramper, crampet, crampette, crampfish, crampfishes, cramping, crampingly, crampish, crampit, crampits, crampon, cramponnee, crampons, crampoon, crampoons, cramps, crampy, crams, cran, cranage, cranberries, cranberry,

cranberry's, crance, crancelin, cranch, cranched, cranches, cranching, crandall, crandallite, crane, crane's, cranebill, craned, cranelike, cranely, craneman, cranemanship, cranemen, craner, cranes, cranesbill, cranesman, cranet, craneway, craney, crang, crania, craniacromial, craniad, cranial, cranially, cranian, craniata, craniate, craniates, cranic, craniectomy, craning, craninia, craniniums, craniocele, craniocerebral, cranioclasis, cranioclasm, cranioclast, cranioclasty, craniodidymus, craniofacial, craniognomic, craniognomy, craniognosy, craniograph, craniographer, craniography, cranioid, craniol, craniological, craniologically, craniologist, craniology, craniom, craniomalacia, craniomaxillary, craniometer, craniometric, craniometrical, craniometrically, craniometrist, craniometry, craniopagus, craniopathic, craniopathy, craniopharyngeal, craniopharyngioma, craniophore, cranioplasty, craniopuncture, craniorhachischisis, craniosacral, cranioschisis, cranioscopical, cranioscopist, cranioscopy, craniospinal, craniostenosis, craniostosis, craniota, craniotabes, craniotome, craniotomies, craniotomy, craniotopography, craniotympanic, craniovertebral, cranium, craniums, crank, crankbird, crankcase, crankcases, crankdisk, cranked, cranker, crankery, crankest, crankier, crankiest, crankily, crankiness, cranking, crankish, crankism, crankle, crankled, crankles, crankless, crankling, crankly, crankman, crankness, crankous, crankpin, crankpins, crankplate, cranks, crankshaft, crankshafts, crankum, cranky, crannage, crannel, crannequin, crannia, crannied, crannies, crannock, crannog, crannoge, crannoger, crannoges, crannogs, cranny, crannying, cranreuch, cransier, crantara, crants, crany, crap, crapaud, crapaudine, crape, craped, crapefish, crapehanger, crapelike, crapes, crapette, craping, crapon, crapped, crapper, crappers, crappie, crappier, crappies, crappiest, crappin, crappiness, crapping, crapple, crappo, crappy, craps, crapshooter, crapshooters, crapshooting, crapula, crapulate, crapulence, crapulency, crapulent, crapulous, crapulously, crapulousness, crapwa, crapy, craquelure, craquelures, crare, crases, crash, crashed, crasher, crashers, crashes, crashing, crashingly, crashproof, crashworthiness, crashworthy, crasis, craspedal, craspedodromous, craspedon, craspedotal, craspedote, craspedum, crass, crassament, crassamentum, crasser, crassest, crassier, crassilingual, crassis, crassities, crassitude, crassly, crassness, crassula, crassulaceous, cratch, cratchens, cratches, cratchins, crate, crated, crateful, cratemaker, cratemaking, crateman, cratemen, crater, crateral, cratered, crateriform, cratering, crateris, craterkin, craterless, craterlet, craterlike, craterous, craters, crates, craticular, crating, cratometer, cratometric, cratometry, craton, cratonic, cratons, cratsmanship, craunch, craunched, craunches, craunching, craunchingly, cravat, cravat's, cravats, cravatted, cravatting, crave, craved, craven, cravened, cravenette, cravenhearted, cravening, cravenly, cravenness, cravens, craver, cravers, craves, craving, cravingly, cravingness, cravings, cravo, craw, crawberry, crawdad, crawdads, crawfish, crawfished, crawfishes, crawfishing, crawfoot, crawfoots, crawful, crawl, crawled, crawler, crawlerize, crawlers, crawley, crawleyroot, crawlie, crawlier, crawliest, crawling, crawlingly, crawls, crawlsome, crawlspace, crawlway, crawlways, crawly, crawm, craws, crawtae, cray, craye, crayer, crayfish, crayfishes, crayfishing, craylet, crayon, crayoned, crayoning, crayonist, crayonists, crayons, crayonstone, craythur, craze, crazed, crazedly, crazedness, crazes, crazier, crazies, craziest, crazily, craziness, crazing, crazingmill, crazy, crazycat, crazyweed, crc, crcao, crche, cre, crea, creach, creachy, cread, creagh, creaght, creak, creaked, creaker, creakier, creakiest, creakily, creakiness, creaking, creakingly, creaks, creaky, cream, creambush, creamcake, creamcup, creamcups, creamed, creamer, creameries, creamers, creamery, creameryman, creamerymen, creamfruit, creamier, creamiest, creamily, creaminess, creaming, creamlaid, creamless, creamlike, creammaker, creammaking, creamometer, creams, creamsacs, creamware, creamy, creance, creancer, creant, crease, creased, creaseless, creaser, creasers, creases, creashaks, creasier, creasiest, creasing, creasol, creasot, creasy, creat, creatable, create, created, createdness, creates, creatic, creatin, creatine, creatinephosphoric, creatines, creating, creatinin, creatinine, creatininemia, creatins, creatinuria, creation, creational, creationary, creationism, creationist, creationistic, creations, creative, creatively, creativeness, creativity, creatophagous, creator, creator's, creatorhood, creatorrhea, creators, creatorship, creatotoxism, creatress, creatrix, creatural, creature, creature's, creaturehood, creatureless, creatureliness, creatureling, creaturely, creatures, creatureship, creaturize, creaze, crebricostate, crebrisulcate, crebrity, crebrous, creche, creches, creda, credal, creddock, credence, credences, credencive, credenciveness, credenda, credendum, credens, credensive, credensiveness, credent, credential, credentialed, credentialism, credentials, credently, credenza, credenzas, credere, credibilities, credibility, credible, credibleness, credibly, credit, creditabilities, creditability, creditable, creditableness, creditably, credited, crediting, creditive, creditless, creditor, creditor's, creditors, creditorship, creditress, creditrix, credits, crednerite, credo, credos, credulities, credulity, credulous, credulously, credulousness, cree, creed, creed's, creedal, creedalism, creedalist, creedbound, creeded, creedist, creedite, creedless, creedlessness, creedmore, creeds, creedsman, creek, creek's, creeker, creekfish, creekfishes, creeks, creekside, creekstuff, creeky, creel, creeled, creeler, creeling, creels, creem, creen, creep, creepage, creepages, creeper, creepered, creeperless, creepers, creephole, creepie, creepier, creepies, creepiest, creepily, creepiness, creeping, creepingly, creepmouse, creepmousy, creeps, creepy, crees, creese, creeses, creesh, creeshed, creeshes, creeshie, creeshing, creeshy, creirgist, cremaillere, cremains, cremant, cremaster, cremasterial, cremasteric, cremate, cremated, cremates, cremating, cremation, cremationism, cremationist, cremations, cremator, crematoria, crematorial, crematories, crematoriria, crematoririums, crematorium, crematoriums, cremators, crematory, crembalum, creme, cremerie, cremes, cremnophobia, cremocarp, cremometer, cremona, cremone, cremor, cremorne, cremosin, cremule, crena, crenae, crenallation, crenate, crenated, crenately, crenation, crenature, crenel, crenelate, crenelated, crenelates, crenelating, crenelation, crenelations, crenele, creneled, crenelee, crenelet, creneling, crenellate, crenellated, crenellating, crenellation, crenelle, crenelled, crenelles, crenelling, crenels, crengle, crenic, crenitic, crenology, crenotherapy, crenula, crenulate, crenulated, crenulation, creodont, creodonts, creole, creoleize, creoles, creolian, creolism, creolite, creolization, creolize, creolized, creolizing, creophagia, creophagism, creophagist, creophagous, creophagy, creosol, creosols, creosote, creosoted, creosoter, creosotes, creosotic, creosoting, crepance, crepe, creped, crepehanger, crepeier, crepeiest, crepes, crepey, crepidoma, crepidomata, crepier, crepiest, crepine, crepiness, creping, crepis, crepitacula, crepitaculum, crepitant, crepitate, crepitated, crepitating, crepitation, crepitous, crepitus, creply, crepon, crept, crepuscle, crepuscular, crepuscule, crepusculine, crepusculum, crepy, cres, cresamine, cresc, crescence, crescendi, crescendo, crescendoed, crescendoing, crescendos, crescent, crescent's, crescentade, crescentader, crescented, crescentic, crescentiform, crescenting, crescentlike, crescentoid, crescents, crescentwise, crescive, crescively, crescograph, crescographic, cresegol, cresive, cresol, cresolin, cresoline, cresols, cresorcin, cresorcinol, cresotate, cresotic, cresotinate, cresotinic, cresoxid, cresoxide, cresoxy, cresphontes, cress, cressed, cresselle, cresses, cresset, cressets, cressida, cressier, cressiest, cresson, cressweed, cresswort, cressy, crest, crestal, crested, crestfallen, crestfallenly, crestfallenness, crestfish, cresting, crestings, crestless, crestline, crestmoreite, crests, cresyl, cresylate, cresylene, cresylic, cresylite, cresyls, creta, cretaceous, cretaceously, crete, cretefaction, cretic, creticism, cretics, cretification, cretify, cretin, cretinic, cretinism, cretinistic, cretinization, cretinize, cretinized, cretinizing, cretinoid, cretinous, cretins, cretion, cretionary, cretize, cretonne, cretonnes, cretoria, creutzer, crevalle, crevalles, crevass, crevasse, crevassed, crevasses, crevassing, crevet, crevette, crevice, crevice's, creviced, crevices, crevis, crew, crewcut, crewe, crewed, crewel, crewelist, crewellery, crewels, crewelwork, crewer, crewet, crewing, crewless, crewman, crewmanship, crewmen, crewneck, crews, criance, criant, crib, crib's, cribbage, cribbages, cribbed, cribber, cribbers, cribbing, cribbings, cribbiter, cribbiting, cribble, cribbled, cribbling, cribella, cribellum, crible, cribo, cribose, cribral, cribrate, cribrately, cribration, cribriform, cribriformity, cribrose, cribrosity, cribrous, cribs, cribwork, cribworks, cric, cricetid, cricetids, cricetine, crick, cricke, cricked, cricket, cricket's, cricketed, cricketer, cricketers, cricketing, cricketings, cricketlike, crickets, crickety, crickey, cricking, crickle, cricks, cricoarytenoid, cricoid, cricoidectomy, cricoids, cricopharyngeal, cricothyreoid, cricothyreotomy, cricothyroid, cricothyroidean, cricotomy, cricotracheotomy, criddle, cried, crier, criers, cries, criey, crig, crikey, crile, crim, crimble, crime, crime's, crimea, crimean, crimeful, crimeless, crimelessness, crimeproof, crimes, criminal, criminaldom, criminalese, criminalism, criminalist, criminalistic, criminalistician, criminalistics, criminalities, criminality, criminally, criminalness, criminaloid, criminals, criminate, criminated, criminating, crimination, criminative, criminator, criminatory, crimine, crimini, criminis, criminogenesis, criminogenic, criminol, criminologic, criminological, criminologically, criminologies, criminologist, criminologists, criminology, criminosis, criminous, criminously, criminousness, crimison, crimmer, crimmers, crimmy, crimogenic, crimp, crimpage, crimped, crimper, crimpers, crimpier, crimpiest, crimpiness, crimping, crimple, crimpled, crimples, crimpling, crimpness, crimps, crimpy, crimson, crimsoned, crimsoning, crimsonly, crimsonness, crimsons, crimsony, crin, crinal, crinanite, crinate, crinated, crinatory, crinch, crine, crined, crinel, crinet, cringe, cringed, cringeling, cringer, cringers, cringes, cringing, cringingly, cringingness, cringle, cringles, crinicultural, criniculture, crinid, criniere, criniferous, crinigerous, crinion, criniparous, crinital, crinite, crinites, crinitory, crinivorous, crink, crinkle, crinkled, crinkleroot, crinkles, crinklier, crinkliest, crinkliness, crinkling, crinkly, crinkum, crinogenic, crinoid, crinoidal, crinoidean, crinoids, crinolette, crinoline, crinolines, crinose, crinosity, crinula, crinum, crinums, criobolium, crioboly, criocephalus, crioceratite, crioceratitic, criolla, criollas, criollo, criollos, criophore, criosphinges, criosphinx, criosphinxes, crip, cripes, crippied, crippingly, cripple, crippled, crippledom, crippleness, crippler, cripplers, cripples, crippling, cripplingly, cripply, crips, cris, crises, crisic, crisis, crisle, crisp, crispate, crispated, crispation, crispature, crispbread, crisped, crispen, crispened, crispening, crispens, crisper, crispers, crispest, crispier, crispiest, crispily, crispin, crispine, crispiness, crisping, crispins, crisply, crispness, crisps, crispy, criss, crissa, crissal, crisscross, crisscrossed, crisscrosses, crisscrossing, crisset, crissum, crista, cristae, cristate, cristated, cristiform, cristobalite, cristy, crit, critch, critchfield, criteria, criteriia, criteriions, criteriology, criterion, criterional, criterions, criterium, crith, crithmene, crithomancy, critic, critic's, critical, criticality, critically, criticalness, criticaster, criticasterism, criticastry, criticisable, criticise, criticised, criticiser, criticises, criticising, criticisingly, criticism, criticism's, criticisms, criticist, criticizable, criticize, criticized, criticizer, criticizers, criticizes, criticizing, criticizingly, critickin, critics, criticship, criticsm, criticule, critique, critiqued, critiques, critiquing, critism, critize, critling, critter, critteria, critters, crittur, critturs, crivetz, crizzel, crizzle, crizzled, crizzling, crl, cro, croak, croaked, croaker, croakers, croakier, croakiest, croakily, croakiness, croaking, croaks, croaky, croape, croat, croatian, croc, crocard, croceic, crocein, croceine, croceines, croceins, croceous, crocetin, croceus, croche, crochet, crocheted, crocheter, crocheters, crocheteur, crocheting, crochets, croci, crociary, crociate, crocidolite, crocin, crocine, crock, crockard, crocked, crocker, crockeries, crockery, crockeryware, crocket, crocketed, crocketing, crockets, crocking, crocko, crocks, crocky, crocodile, crocodilean, crocodiles, crocodilian, crocodiline, crocodilite, crocodility, crocodiloid, crocoisite, crocoite, crocoites, croconate, croconic, crocus, crocused, crocuses, crocuta, croft, crofter, crofterization, crofterize, crofters, crofting, croftland, crofts, croh, croighle, croiik, crois, croisad, croisade, croisard, croise, croisee, croises, croisette, croissant, croissante, croissants, crojack, crojik, crojiks, croker, cromaltite, crombec, crome, cromfordite, cromlech, cromlechs, cromme, crommel, cromorna, cromorne, cromster, cromwell, cromwellian, crone, croneberry, cronel, crones, cronet, cronian, cronie, cronied, cronies, cronish, cronk, cronkness, cronstedtite, cronus, crony, cronying, cronyism, cronyisms, crooch, crood, croodle, crooisite, crook, crookback, crookbacked, crookbill, crookbilled, crooked, crookedbacked, crookeder, crookedest, crookedly, crookedness, crooken, crookeries, crookery, crookesite, crookfingered, crookheaded, crooking, crookkneed, crookle, crooklegged, crookneck, crooknecked, crooknecks, crooknosed, crooks, crookshouldered, crooksided, crooksterned, crooktoothed, crool, croon, crooned, crooner, crooners, crooning, crooningly, croons, croose, crop, crop's, crophead, cropland, croplands, cropless, cropman, croppa, cropped, cropper, cropper's, croppers, croppie, croppies, cropping, cropplecrown, croppy, crops, cropshin, cropsick, cropsickness, cropweed, croquet, croqueted, croqueting, croquets, croquette, croquettes, croquignole, croquis, crore, crores, crosa, crosby, crose, croset, crosette, croshabell, crosier, crosiered, crosiers, croslet, crosne, crosnes, cross, crossability, crossable, crossarm, crossarms, crossband, crossbanded, crossbanding, crossbar, crossbar's, crossbarred, crossbarring, crossbars, crossbbred, crossbeak, crossbeam, crossbeams, crossbearer, crossbelt, crossbench, crossbencher, crossbill, crossbirth, crossbite, crossbolt, crossbolted, crossbones, crossbow, crossbowman, crossbowmen, crossbows, crossbred, crossbreds, crossbreed, crossbreeding, crossbreeds, crosscheck, crosscourt, crosscrosslet, crosscurrent, crosscurrented, crosscurrents, crosscut, crosscuts, crosscutter, crosscutting, crosse, crossed, crosser, crossers, crosses, crossest, crossette, crossfall, crossfertilizable, crossfire, crossfired, crossfiring, crossfish, crossflow, crossflower, crossfoot, crossgrainedness, crosshackle, crosshair, crosshairs, crosshand, crosshatch, crosshatched, crosshatcher, crosshatches, crosshatching, crosshaul, crosshauling, crosshead, crossing, crossings, crossite, crossjack, crosslap, crosslegs, crosslet, crossleted, crosslets, crossley, crosslight, crosslighted, crosslike, crossline, crosslink, crossly, crossness, crossopodia, crossopt, crossopterygian, crossosomataceous, crossover, crossover's, crossovers, crosspatch, crosspatches, crosspath, crosspiece, crosspieces, crosspoint, crosspoints, crosspost, crossrail, crossroad, crossroading, crossroads, crossrow, crossruff, crosstail, crosstalk, crosstie, crosstied, crossties, crosstoes, crosstown, crosstrack, crosstree, crosstrees, crosswalk, crosswalks, crossway, crossways, crossweb, crossweed, crosswind, crosswise, crosswiseness, crossword, crossword's, crossworder, crosswords, crosswort, crost, crostarie, crotal, crotalaria, crotalic, crotalid, crotaliform, crotalin, crotaline, crotalism, crotalo, crotaloid, crotalum, crotalus, crotaphic, crotaphion, crotaphite, crotaphitic, crotch, crotched, crotches, crotchet, crotcheted, crotcheteer, crotchetiness, crotcheting, crotchets, crotchety, crotching, crotchwood, crotchy, crotesco, crotin, croton, crotonaldehyde, crotonate, crotonbug, crotonic, crotonization, crotons, crotonyl, crotonylene, crottal, crottels, crottle, crotyl, crouch, crouchant, crouchback, crouche, crouched, croucher, crouches, crouchie, crouching, crouchingly, crouchmas, crouke, crounotherapy, croup, croupade, croupal, croupe, crouperbush, croupes, croupier, croupiers, croupiest, croupily, croupiness, croupon, croupous, croups, croupy, crouse, crousely, croustade, crout, croute, crouth, crouton, croutons, crow, crowbait, crowbar, crowbars, crowbell, crowberries, crowberry, crowbill, crowboot, crowd, crowded, crowdedly, crowdedness, crowder, crowders, crowdie, crowdies, crowding, crowdle, crowds, crowdweed, crowdy, crowed, crower, crowers, crowfeet, crowflower, crowfoot, crowfooted, crowfoots, crowhop, crowhopper, crowing, crowingly, crowkeeper, crowl, crown, crownal, crownation, crownband, crownbeard, crowncapping, crowned, crowner, crowners, crownet, crownets, crowning, crownland, crownless, crownlet, crownlike, crownling, crownmaker, crownment, crownpiece, crowns, crownwork, crownwort, crows, crowshay, crowstep, crowstepped, crowsteps, crowstick, crowstone, crowtoe, croy, croyden, croydon, croyl, croze, crozed, crozer, crozers, crozes, crozier, croziers, crozing, crozle, crozzle, crozzly, crpe, crs, crts, cru, crub, crubeen, cruce, cruces, crucethouse, cruche, crucial, cruciality, crucially, crucialness, crucian, crucians, cruciate, cruciated, cruciately, cruciating, cruciation, crucible, crucibles, crucifer, cruciferous, crucifers, crucificial, crucified, crucifier, crucifies, crucifige, crucifix, crucifixes, crucifixion, crucifixions, cruciform, cruciformity, cruciformly, crucify, crucifyfied, crucifyfying, crucifying, crucigerous, crucilly, crucily, crucis, cruck, crud, crudded, crudding, cruddle, cruddy, crude, crudelity, crudely, crudeness, cruder, crudes, crudest, crudites, crudities, crudity, crudle, cruds, crudwort, crudy, cruel, crueler, cruelest, cruelhearted, cruelize, crueller, cruellest, cruelly, cruelness, cruels, cruelties, cruelty, cruent, cruentate, cruentation, cruentous, cruet, cruets, cruety, cruise, cruised, cruiser, cruisers, cruiserweight, cruises, cruiseway, cruising, cruisingly, cruiskeen, cruisken, cruive, crull, cruller, crullers, crum, crumb, crumbable, crumbcloth, crumbed, crumber, crumbers, crumbier, crumbiest, crumbing, crumble, crumbled, crumblement, crumbles, crumblet, crumblier, crumbliest, crumbliness, crumbling, crumblingness, crumblings, crumbly, crumbs, crumbum, crumby, crumen, crumena, crumenal, crumhorn, crumlet, crummable, crummed, crummer, crummie, crummier, crummies, crummiest, crumminess, crumming, crummock, crummy, crump, crumped, crumper, crumpet, crumpets, crumping, crumple, crumpled, crumpler, crumples, crumpling, crumply, crumps, crumpy, crumster, crunch, crunchable, crunched, cruncher, crunchers, crunches, crunchier, crunchiest, crunchily, crunchiness, crunching, crunchingly, crunchingness, crunchweed, crunchy, crunk, crunkle, crunodal, crunode, crunodes, crunt, cruor, cruorin, cruors, crup, cruppen, crupper, cruppered, cruppering, cruppers, crura, crural, crureus, crurogenital, cruroinguinal, crurotarsal, crus, crusade, crusaded, crusader, crusaders, crusades, crusading, crusado, crusadoes, crusados, cruse, cruses, cruset, crusets, crush, crushability, crushable, crushableness, crushed, crusher, crushers, crushes, crushing, crushingly, crushproof, crusie, crusile, crusilee, crusily, crust, crust's, crusta, crustacea, crustaceal, crustacean, crustacean's, crustaceans, crustaceological, crustaceologist, crustaceology, crustaceorubrin, crustaceous, crustade, crustal, crustalogical, crustalogist, crustalogy, crustate, crustated, crustation, crusted, crustedly, cruster, crustier, crustiest, crustific, crustification, crustily, crustiness, crusting, crustless, crustose, crustosis, crusts, crusty, crut, crutch, crutch's, crutched, crutcher, crutches, crutching, crutchlike, cruth, crutter, crux, crux's, cruxes, cruzado, cruzadoes, cruzados, cruzeiro, cruzeiros, cruziero, cruzieros, crwd, crwth, crwths, cry, cryable, cryaesthesia, cryal, cryalgesia, cryanesthesia, crybabies, crybaby, cryesthesia, crying, cryingly, crymoanesthesia, crymodynia, crymotherapy, cryobiological, cryobiologically, cryobiologist, cryobiology, cryocautery, cryochore, cryochoric, cryoconite, cryogen, cryogenic, cryogenically, cryogenics, cryogenies, cryogens, cryogeny, cryohydrate, cryohydric, cryolite, cryolites, cryological, cryology, cryometer, cryometry, cryonic, cryonics, cryopathy, cryophile, cryophilic, cryophoric, cryophorus, cryophyllite, cryophyte, cryoplankton, cryoprobe, cryoprotective, cryoscope, cryoscopic, cryoscopies, cryoscopy, cryosel, cryosphere, cryospheric, cryostase, cryostat, cryostats, cryosurgeon, cryosurgery, cryosurgical, cryotherapies, cryotherapy, cryotron, cryotrons, crypt, crypta, cryptaesthesia, cryptal, cryptamnesia, cryptamnesic, cryptanalysis, cryptanalyst, cryptanalytic, cryptanalytical, cryptanalytically, cryptanalytics, cryptanalyze, cryptanalyzed, cryptanalyzing, cryptarch, cryptarchy, crypted, cryptesthesia, cryptesthetic, cryptic, cryptical, cryptically, crypticness, crypto, cryptoagnostic, cryptoanalysis, cryptoanalyst, cryptoanalytic, cryptoanalytically, cryptoanalytics, cryptobatholithic, cryptobranch, cryptobranchiate, cryptocarp, cryptocarpic, cryptocarpous, cryptocephalous, cryptocerous, cryptoclastic, cryptoclimate, cryptoclimatology, cryptococcal, cryptococci, cryptococcic, cryptococcosis, cryptococcus, cryptocommercial, cryptocrystalline, cryptocrystallization, cryptodeist, cryptodiran, cryptodire, cryptodirous, cryptodouble, cryptodynamic, cryptogam, cryptogame, cryptogamia, cryptogamian, cryptogamic, cryptogamical, cryptogamist, cryptogamous, cryptogamy, cryptogenetic, cryptogenic, cryptogenous, cryptoglioma, cryptogram, cryptogrammatic, cryptogrammatical, cryptogrammatist, cryptogrammic, cryptograms, cryptograph, cryptographal, cryptographer, cryptographers, cryptographic, cryptographical, cryptographically, cryptographist, cryptography, cryptoheresy, cryptoheretic, cryptoinflationist, cryptolite, cryptolith, cryptologic, cryptological, cryptologist, cryptology, cryptolunatic, cryptomere, cryptomeria, cryptomerous, cryptometer, cryptomnesia, cryptomnesic, cryptomonad, cryptonema, cryptoneurous, cryptonym, cryptonymic, cryptonymous, cryptopapist, cryptoperthite, cryptophthalmos, cryptophyte, cryptophytic, cryptopin, cryptopine, cryptoporticus, cryptoproselyte, cryptoproselytism, cryptopyic, cryptopyrrole, cryptorchid, cryptorchidism, cryptorchis, cryptorchism, cryptorrhesis, cryptorrhetic, cryptos, cryptoscope, cryptoscopy, cryptosplenetic, cryptostoma, cryptostomate, cryptostome, cryptous, cryptovalence, cryptovalency, cryptovolcanic, cryptovolcanism, cryptoxanthin, cryptozoic, cryptozoite, cryptozonate, cryptozygosity, cryptozygous, cryptozygy, crypts, cryst, crystal, crystal's, crystaled, crystaling, crystalitic, crystalize, crystall, crystalled, crystallic, crystalliferous, crystalliform, crystalligerous, crystallike, crystallin, crystalline, crystalling, crystallinity, crystallisability, crystallisable, crystallisation, crystallise, crystallised, crystallising, crystallite, crystallites, crystallitic, crystallitis, crystallizability, crystallizable, crystallization, crystallize, crystallized, crystallizer, crystallizes, crystallizing, crystalloblastic, crystallochemical, crystallochemistry, crystallod, crystallogenesis, crystallogenetic, crystallogenic, crystallogenical, crystallogeny, crystallogram, crystallograph, crystallographer, crystallographers, crystallographic, crystallographical, crystallographically, crystallography, crystallogy, crystalloid, crystalloidal, crystallology, crystalloluminescence, crystallomagnetic, crystallomancy, crystallometric, crystallometry, crystallophobia, crystallophyllian, crystallose, crystallurgy, crystals, crystalwort, cryste, crystic, crystograph, crystoleum, crystosphene, crzette, cs, csardas, csc, csch, csect, csects, csi, csk, csmp, csnet, csp, cst, csw, ct, cte, ctelette, ctene, ctenidia, ctenidial, ctenidium, cteniform, ctenii, cteninidia, ctenizid, ctenocyst, ctenodactyl, ctenodont, ctenoid, ctenoidean, ctenoidian, ctenolium, ctenophora, ctenophoral, ctenophoran, ctenophore, ctenophoric, ctenophorous, ctenostomatous, ctenostome, ctetology, ctf, ctg, ctge, ctimo, ctn, cto, ctr, ctrl, cts, cu, cuadra, cuadrilla, cuadrillas, cuadrillero, cuamuchil, cuapinole, cuarenta, cuarta, cuartel, cuarteron, cuartilla, cuartillo, cuartino, cuarto, cub, cub's, cuba, cubage, cubages, cubalaya, cuban, cubane, cubangle, cubanite, cubans, cubas, cubation, cubatory, cubature, cubatures, cubbies, cubbing, cubbish, cubbishly, cubbishness, cubby, cubbyhole, cubbyholes, cubbyhouse, cubbyu, cubbyyew, cubdom, cube, cubeb, cubebs, cubed, cubehead, cubelet, cuber, cubera, cubers, cubes, cubhood, cubi, cubic, cubica, cubical, cubically, cubicalness, cubicities, cubicity, cubicle, cubicles, cubicly, cubicone, cubicontravariant, cubicovariant, cubics, cubicula, cubicular, cubiculary, cubiculo, cubiculum, cubiform, cubing, cubism, cubisms, cubist, cubistic, cubistically, cubists, cubit, cubital, cubitale, cubitalia, cubited, cubiti, cubitiere, cubito, cubitocarpal, cubitocutaneous, cubitodigital, cubitometacarpal, cubitopalmar, cubitoplantar, cubitoradial, cubits, cubitus, cubla, cubmaster, cubocalcaneal, cuboctahedron, cubocube, cubocuneiform, cubododecahedral, cuboid, cuboidal, cuboides, cuboids, cubomancy, cubomedusan, cubometatarsal, cubonavicular, cubs, cubti, cuca, cucaracha, cuchia, cuck, cuckhold, cucking, cuckold, cuckolded, cuckolding, cuckoldize, cuckoldly, cuckoldom, cuckoldry, cuckolds, cuckoldy, cuckoo, cuckoo's, cuckooed, cuckooflower, cuckooing, cuckoomaid, cuckoomaiden, cuckoomate, cuckoopint, cuckoopintle, cuckoos, cuckquean, cuckstool, cucoline, cucularis, cucule, cuculiform, cuculine, cuculla, cucullaris, cucullate, cucullated, cucullately, cuculle, cuculliform, cucullus, cuculoid, cucumber, cucumber's, cucumbers, cucumiform, cucupha, cucurb, cucurbit, cucurbitaceous, cucurbital, cucurbite, cucurbitine, cucurbits, cucuy, cucuyo, cud, cuda, cudava, cudbear, cudbears, cudden, cuddie, cuddies, cuddle, cuddleable, cuddled, cuddles, cuddlesome, cuddlier, cuddliest, cuddling, cuddly, cuddy, cuddyhole, cudeigh, cudgel, cudgel's, cudgeled, cudgeler, cudgelers, cudgeling, cudgelled, cudgeller, cudgelling, cudgels, cudgerie, cuds, cudweed, cudweeds, cudwort, cue, cueball, cueca, cuecas, cued, cueing, cueist, cueman, cuemanship, cuemen, cuerda, cuerpo, cues, cuesta, cuestas, cuff, cuff's, cuffed, cuffer, cuffin, cuffing, cuffle, cuffless, cufflink, cufflinks, cuffs, cuffy, cuffyism, cufic, cuggermugger, cuichunchulli, cuidado, cuiejo, cuiejos, cuif, cuifs, cuinage, cuinfo, cuing, cuir, cuirass, cuirassed, cuirasses, cuirassier, cuirassing, cuirie, cuish, cuishes, cuisinary, cuisine, cuisines, cuisinier, cuissard, cuissart, cuisse, cuissen, cuisses, cuisten, cuit, cuitle, cuitled, cuitling, cuittikin, cuittle, cuittled, cuittles, cuittling, cuj, cuke, cukes, cul, culation, culbert, culbut, culbute, culbuter, culch, culches, culdee, culebra, culerage, culet, culets, culett, culeus, culex, culgee, culices, culicid, culicidal, culicide, culicids, culiciform, culicifugal, culicifuge, culicine, culicines, culilawan, culinarian, culinarily, culinary, cull, culla, cullage, cullas, cullay, cullays, culled, cullender, culler, cullers, cullet, cullets, cullibility, cullible, cullied, cullies, culling, cullion, cullionly, cullionry, cullions, cullis, cullisance, cullises, culls, cully, cullying, culm, culmed, culmen, culmicolous, culmiferous, culmigenous, culminal, culminant, culminate, culminated, culminates, culminating, culmination, culminations, culminative, culming, culms, culmy, culot, culotte, culottes, culottic, culottism, culp, culpa, culpabilis, culpability, culpable, culpableness, culpably, culpae, culpas, culpate, culpatory, culpeo, culpon, culpose, culprit, culprit's, culprits, culrage, culsdesac, cult, cult's, cultch, cultches, cultellation, cultelli, cultellus, culter, culteranismo, culti, cultic, cultigen, cultigens, cultirostral, cultish, cultism, cultismo, cultisms, cultist, cultistic, cultists, cultivability, cultivable, cultivably, cultivar, cultivars, cultivatability, cultivatable, cultivate, cultivated, cultivates, cultivating, cultivation, cultivations, cultivative, cultivator, cultivator's, cultivators, cultive, cultrate, cultrated, cultriform, cultrirostral, cults, culttelli, cultual, culturable, cultural, culturalist, culturally, culture, cultured, cultureless, cultures, culturine, culturing, culturist, culturization, culturize, culturological, culturologically, culturologist, culturology, cultus, cultuses, culver, culverfoot, culverhouse, culverin, culverineer, culveriner, culverins, culverkey, culverkeys, culvers, culvert, culvertage, culverts, culverwort, cum, cumacean, cumaceous, cumal, cumaldehyde, cumaphyte, cumaphytic, cumaphytism, cumara, cumarin, cumarins, cumarone, cumaru, cumay, cumbent, cumber, cumbered, cumberer, cumberers, cumbering, cumberland, cumberlandite, cumberless, cumberment, cumbers, cumbersome, cumbersomely, cumbersomeness, cumberworld, cumbha, cumble, cumbly, cumbraite, cumbrance, cumbre, cumbrous, cumbrously, cumbrousness, cumbu, cumene, cumengite, cumenyl, cumflutter, cumhal, cumic, cumidin, cumidine, cumin, cuminal, cuminic, cuminoin, cuminol, cuminole, cumins, cuminseed, cuminyl, cumly, cummer, cummerbund, cummerbunds, cummers, cummin, cummingtonite, cummins, cummock, cumol, cump, cumquat, cumquats, cumsha, cumshaw, cumshaws, cumulant, cumular, cumulate, cumulated, cumulately, cumulates, cumulating, cumulation, cumulatist, cumulative, cumulatively, cumulativeness, cumulene, cumulet, cumuli, cumuliform, cumulite, cumulocirrus, cumulonimbus, cumulophyric, cumulose, cumulostratus, cumulous, cumulus, cumyl, cun, cunabula, cunabular, cunctation, cunctatious, cunctative, cunctator, cunctatorship, cunctatory, cunctatury, cunctipotent, cund, cundeamor, cundite, cundum, cundums, cundurango, cundy, cunea, cuneal, cuneate, cuneated, cuneately, cuneatic, cuneator, cunei, cuneiform, cuneiformist, cunenei, cuneocuboid, cuneonavicular, cuneoscaphoid, cunette, cuneus, cungeboi, cungevoi, cunicular, cuniculi, cuniculus, cuniform, cuniforms, cunila, cunili, cunit, cunjah, cunjer, cunjevoi, cunner, cunners, cunni, cunnilinctus, cunnilinguism, cunnilingus, cunning, cunningaire, cunninger, cunningest, cunningly, cunningness, cunnings, cunny, cunoniaceous, cunt, cunts, cunye, cunyie, cunzie, cuorin, cup, cup's, cupay, cupbearer, cupbearers, cupboard, cupboard's, cupboards, cupcake, cupcakes, cupel, cupeled, cupeler, cupelers, cupeling, cupellation, cupelled, cupeller, cupellers, cupelling, cupels, cupflower, cupful, cupfulfuls, cupfuls, cuphead, cupholder, cupid, cupidinous, cupidities, cupidity, cupidon, cupidone, cupids, cupiuba, cupless, cuplike, cupmaker, cupmaking, cupman, cupmate, cupola, cupolaed, cupolaing, cupolaman, cupolar, cupolas, cupolated, cuppa, cuppas, cupped, cuppen, cupper, cuppers, cuppier, cuppiest, cuppin, cupping, cuppings, cuppy, cuprammonia, cuprammonium, cuprate, cuprein, cupreine, cuprene, cupreous, cupressineous, cupric, cupride, cupriferous, cuprite, cuprites, cuproammonium, cuprobismutite, cuprocyanide, cuprodescloizite, cuproid, cuproiodargyrite, cupromanganese, cupronickel, cuproplumbite, cuproscheelite, cuprose, cuprosilicon, cuprotungstite, cuprous, cuprum, cuprums, cups, cupseed, cupsful, cupstone, cupula, cupulae, cupular, cupulate, cupule, cupules, cupuliferous, cupuliform, cur, cura, curability, curable, curableness, curably, curacao, curacaos, curace, curacies, curacoa, curacoas, curacy, curage, curagh, curaghs, curara, curaras, curare, curares, curari, curarine, curarines, curaris, curarization, curarize, curarized, curarizes, curarizing, curassow, curassows, curat, curatage, curate, curatel, curates, curateship, curatess, curatial, curatic, curatical, curation, curative, curatively, curativeness, curatives, curatize, curatolatry, curator, curatorial, curatorium, curators, curatorship, curatory, curatrices, curatrix, curb, curbable, curbash, curbed, curber, curbers, curbing, curbings, curbless, curblike, curbline, curbs, curbside, curbstone, curbstoner, curbstones, curby, curcas, curch, curchef, curches, curchy, curcuddoch, curculio, curculionid, curculionist, curculios, curcuma, curcumas, curcumin, curd, curded, curdier, curdiest, curdiness, curding, curdle, curdled, curdler, curdlers, curdles, curdling, curdly, curdoo, curds, curdwort, curdy, cure, cured, cureless, curelessly, curelessness, curemaster, curer, curers, cures, curet, curets, curettage, curette, curetted, curettement, curettes, curetting, curf, curfew, curfew's, curfewed, curfewing, curfews, curfs, curia, curiae, curiage, curial, curialism, curialist, curialistic, curialities, curiality, curiam, curiara, curiate, curiboca, curie, curiegram, curies, curiescopy, curiet, curietherapy, curin, curine, curing, curio, curiolofic, curiologic, curiological, curiologically, curiologics, curiology, curiomaniac, curios, curiosa, curiosi, curiosities, curiosity, curiosity's, curioso, curiosos, curious, curiouser, curiousest, curiously, curiousness, curiousnesses, curite, curites, curium, curiums, curl, curled, curledly, curledness, curler, curlers, curlew, curlewberry, curlews, curlicue, curlicued, curlicues, curlicuing, curlier, curliest, curliewurlie, curliewurly, curlike, curlily, curliness, curling, curlingly, curlings, curlpaper, curls, curly, curlycue, curlycues, curlyhead, curlyheads, curlylocks, curmudgeon, curmudgeonery, curmudgeonish, curmudgeonly, curmudgeons, curmurging, curmurring, curn, curney, curneys, curnie, curnies, curnock, curns, curpel, curpin, curple, curr, currach, currachs, currack, curragh, curraghs, currajong, curran, currance, currane, currans, currant, currant's, currants, currantworm, curratow, currawang, currawong, curred, currencies, currency, currency's, current, currently, currentness, currents, currentwise, curricla, curricle, curricled, curricles, curricling, curricula, curricular, curricularization, curricularize, curriculum, curriculum's, curriculums, currie, curried, currier, currieries, curriers, curriery, curries, curriing, currijong, curring, currish, currishly, currishness, currock, currs, curry, currycomb, currycombed, currycombing, currycombs, curryfavel, curryfavour, currying, curs, cursal, cursaro, curse, cursed, curseder, cursedest, cursedly, cursedness, cursement, cursen, curser, cursers, curses, curship, cursillo, cursing, cursitate, cursitor, cursive, cursively, cursiveness, cursives, cursor, cursor's, cursorary, cursores, cursorial, cursorily, cursoriness, cursorious, cursors, cursory, curst, curstful, curstfully, curstly, curstness, cursus, curt, curtail, curtailed, curtailedly, curtailer, curtailing, curtailment, curtailments, curtails, curtain, curtained, curtaining, curtainless, curtains, curtainwise, curtal, curtalax, curtalaxes, curtals, curtana, curtate, curtation, curtaxe, curtays, curted, curtein, curtelace, curteous, curter, curtesies, curtest, curtesy, curtilage, curtlax, curtly, curtness, curtnesses, curtsey, curtseyed, curtseying, curtseys, curtsied, curtsies, curtsy, curtsy's, curtsying, curua, curuba, curucucu, curucui, curule, curupay, curupays, curupey, cururo, cururos, curvaceous, curvaceously, curvaceousness, curvacious, curval, curvant, curvate, curvated, curvation, curvative, curvature, curvatures, curve, curveball, curved, curvedly, curvedness, curver, curves, curvesome, curvesomeness, curvet, curveted, curveting, curvets, curvette, curvetted, curvetting, curvey, curvicaudate, curvicostate, curvidentate, curvier, curviest, curvifoliate, curviform, curvilinead, curvilineal, curvilinear, curvilinearity, curvilinearly, curvimeter, curvinervate, curvinerved, curviness, curving, curvirostral, curviserial, curvital, curvities, curvity, curvle, curvograph, curvometer, curvous, curvulate, curvy, curwhibble, curwillet, cury, curying, cuscohygrin, cuscohygrine, cusconin, cusconine, cuscus, cuscuses, cuscutaceous, cusec, cusecs, cuselite, cush, cushag, cushat, cushats, cushaw, cushaws, cushewbird, cushie, cushier, cushiest, cushily, cushiness, cushing, cushion, cushioncraft, cushioned, cushionet, cushionflower, cushioniness, cushioning, cushionless, cushionlike, cushions, cushiony, cushitic, cushlamochree, cushy, cusie, cusinero, cusk, cusks, cusp, cusp's, cuspal, cusparia, cusparidine, cusparine, cuspate, cuspated, cusped, cuspid, cuspidal, cuspidate, cuspidated, cuspidation, cuspides, cuspidine, cuspidor, cuspidors, cuspids, cusping, cuspis, cusps, cuspule, cuss, cussed, cussedly, cussedness, cusser, cussers, cusses, cussing, cusso, cussos, cussword, cusswords, cust, custard, custards, custerite, custode, custodee, custodes, custodia, custodial, custodiam, custodian, custodian's, custodians, custodianship, custodier, custodies, custody, custom, customable, customableness, customably, customance, customaries, customarily, customariness, customary, customed, customer, customers, customhouse, customhouses, customing, customizable, customization, customization's, customizations, customize, customized, customizer, customizers, customizes, customizing, customly, customs, customshouse, custos, custrel, custron, custroun, custumal, custumals, cut, cut's, cutability, cutaneal, cutaneous, cutaneously, cutaway, cutaways, cutback, cutbacks, cutbank, cutch, cutcha, cutcher, cutcheries, cutcherries, cutcherry, cutchery, cutches, cutdown, cutdowns, cute, cutely, cuteness, cutenesses, cuter, cutes, cutesier, cutesiest, cutest, cutesy, cutey, cuteys, cutgrass, cutgrasses, cutheal, cuticle, cuticles, cuticolor, cuticula, cuticulae, cuticular, cuticularization, cuticularize, cuticulate, cutidure, cutiduris, cutie, cuties, cutification, cutify, cutigeral, cutikin, cutin, cutinisation, cutinise, cutinised, cutinises, cutinising, cutinization, cutinize, cutinized, cutinizes, cutinizing, cutins, cutireaction, cutis, cutisector, cutises, cutitis, cutization, cutlas, cutlases, cutlash, cutlass, cutlasses, cutlassfish, cutlassfishes, cutler, cutleress, cutleriaceous, cutleries, cutlers, cutlery, cutlet, cutlets, cutline, cutlines, cutling, cutlings, cutlips, cutocellulose, cutoff, cutoffs, cutose, cutout, cutouts, cutover, cutpurse, cutpurses, cuts, cutset, cuttable, cuttage, cuttages, cuttail, cuttanee, cutted, cutter, cutter's, cutterhead, cutterman, cutters, cutthroat, cutthroats, cutties, cuttikin, cutting, cuttingly, cuttingness, cuttings, cuttle, cuttlebone, cuttlebones, cuttled, cuttlefish, cuttlefishes, cuttler, cuttles, cuttling, cuttoe, cuttoo, cuttoos, cutty, cuttyhunk, cutup, cutups, cutwal, cutwater, cutwaters, cutweed, cutwork, cutworks, cutworm, cutworms, cuvage, cuve, cuvee, cuvette, cuvettes, cuvies, cuvy, cuya, cuyas, cuzceno, cv, cwierc, cwm, cwms, cwo, cwrite, cwt, cy, cyaathia, cyamelid, cyamelide, cyamid, cyamoid, cyan, cyanacetic, cyanamid, cyanamide, cyanamids, cyananthrol, cyanate, cyanates, cyanaurate, cyanauric, cyanbenzyl, cyancarbonic, cyanea, cyanean, cyanemia, cyaneous, cyanephidrosis, cyanformate, cyanformic, cyanhidrosis, cyanhydrate, cyanhydric, cyanhydrin, cyanic, cyanicide, cyanid, cyanidation, cyanide, cyanided, cyanides, cyanidin, cyanidine, cyaniding, cyanidrosis, cyanids, cyanimide, cyanin, cyanine, cyanines, cyanins, cyanite, cyanites, cyanitic, cyanize, cyanized, cyanizing, cyanmethemoglobin, cyano, cyanoacetate, cyanoacetic, cyanoacrylate, cyanoaurate, cyanoauric, cyanobenzene, cyanocarbonic, cyanochlorous, cyanochroia, cyanochroic, cyanocobalamin, cyanocobalamine, cyanocrystallin, cyanoderma, cyanoethylate, cyanoethylation, cyanogen, cyanogenamide, cyanogenesis, cyanogenetic, cyanogenic, cyanogens, cyanoguanidine, cyanohermidin, cyanohydrin, cyanol, cyanole, cyanomaclurin, cyanometer, cyanomethaemoglobin, cyanomethemoglobin, cyanometric, cyanometries, cyanometry, cyanopathic, cyanopathy, cyanophil, cyanophile, cyanophilous, cyanophoric, cyanophose, cyanophycean, cyanophyceous, cyanophycin, cyanopia, cyanoplastid, cyanoplatinite, cyanoplatinous, cyanopsia, cyanose, cyanosed, cyanoses, cyanosis, cyanosite, cyanotic, cyanotrichite, cyanotype, cyans, cyanuramide, cyanurate, cyanuret, cyanuric, cyanurin, cyanurine, cyanus, cyaphenine, cyath, cyatheaceous, cyathi, cyathia, cyathiform, cyathium, cyathoid, cyatholith, cyathophylline, cyathophylloid, cyathos, cyathozooid, cyathus, cybele, cybercultural, cyberculture, cybernate, cybernated, cybernating, cybernation, cybernetic, cybernetical, cybernetically, cybernetician, cyberneticist, cyberneticists, cybernetics, cybernion, cyborg, cyborgs, cyc, cycad, cycadaceous, cycadean, cycadeoid, cycadeous, cycadiform, cycadite, cycadlike, cycadofilicale, cycadofilicales, cycadofilicinean, cycadophyte, cycads, cycas, cycases, cycasin, cycasins, cycl, cyclades, cyclamate, cyclamates, cyclamen, cyclamens, cyclamin, cyclamine, cyclammonium, cyclane, cyclanthaceous, cyclar, cyclarthrodial, cyclarthrosis, cyclarthrsis, cyclas, cyclase, cyclases, cyclazocine, cycle, cyclecar, cyclecars, cycled, cycledom, cyclene, cycler, cyclers, cycles, cyclesmith, cyclian, cyclic, cyclical, cyclicality, cyclically, cyclicalness, cyclicism, cyclicity, cyclicly, cyclide, cyclindroid, cycling, cyclings, cyclism, cyclist, cyclistic, cyclists, cyclitic, cyclitis, cyclitol, cyclitols, cyclization, cyclize, cyclized, cyclizes, cyclizing, cyclo, cycloacetylene, cycloaddition, cycloaliphatic, cycloalkane, cyclobutane, cyclocephaly, cyclocoelic, cyclocoelous, cyclode, cyclodiene, cyclodiolefin, cyclodiolefine, cycloganoid, cyclogenesis, cyclogram, cyclograph, cyclographer, cycloheptane, cycloheptanone, cyclohexadienyl, cyclohexane, cyclohexanol, cyclohexanone, cyclohexatriene, cyclohexene, cycloheximide, cyclohexyl, cyclohexylamine, cycloid, cycloid's, cycloidal, cycloidally, cycloidean, cycloidian, cycloidotrope, cycloids, cyclolith, cyclolysis, cyclomania, cyclometer, cyclometers, cyclometric, cyclometrical, cyclometries, cyclometry, cyclomyarian, cyclonal, cyclone, cyclone's, cyclones, cyclonic, cyclonical, cyclonically, cyclonist, cyclonite, cyclonologist, cyclonology, cyclonometer, cyclonoscope, cycloolefin, cycloolefine, cycloolefinic, cyclop, cyclopaedia, cyclopaedias, cyclopaedic, cyclopaedically, cyclopaedist, cycloparaffin, cyclope, cyclopean, cyclopedia, cyclopedias, cyclopedic, cyclopedical, cyclopedically, cyclopedist, cyclopentadiene, cyclopentane, cyclopentanone, cyclopentene, cyclopes, cyclophoria, cyclophoric, cyclophosphamide, cyclophrenia, cyclopia, cyclopic, cyclopism, cyclopite, cycloplegia, cycloplegic, cyclopoid, cyclopropane, cyclops, cyclopteroid, cyclopterous, cyclopy, cyclorama, cycloramas, cycloramic, cyclorrhaphous, cyclos, cycloscope, cyclose, cycloserine, cycloses, cyclosilicate, cyclosis, cyclospermous, cyclospondylic, cyclospondylous, cyclosporous, cyclostomate, cyclostomatous, cyclostome, cyclostomous, cyclostrophic, cyclostylar, cyclostyle, cyclothem, cyclothure, cyclothurine, cyclothyme, cyclothymia, cyclothymiac, cyclothymic, cyclotome, cyclotomic, cyclotomies, cyclotomy, cyclotrimethylenetrinitramine, cyclotron, cyclotrons, cyclovertebral, cyclus, cyder, cyders, cydippe, cydippian, cydippid, cydon, cydonium, cyeses, cyesiology, cyesis, cyetic, cygneous, cygnet, cygnets, cygnine, cygnus, cyke, cyl, cylices, cylinder, cylinder's, cylindered, cylinderer, cylindering, cylinderlike, cylinders, cylindraceous, cylindrarthrosis, cylindrelloid, cylindrenchema, cylindrenchyma, cylindric, cylindrical, cylindricality, cylindrically, cylindricalness, cylindricity, cylindricule, cylindriform, cylindrite, cylindrocellular, cylindrocephalic, cylindroconical, cylindroconoidal, cylindrocylindric, cylindrodendrite, cylindrograph, cylindroid, cylindroidal, cylindroma, cylindromata, cylindromatous, cylindrometric, cylindroogival, cylindruria, cylix, cylloses, cyllosis, cyma, cymae, cymagraph, cymaise, cymaphen, cymaphyte, cymaphytic, cymaphytism, cymar, cymarin, cymarose, cymars, cymas, cymatia, cymation, cymatium, cymba, cymbaeform, cymbal, cymbal's, cymbaled, cymbaleer, cymbaler, cymbalers, cymbaline, cymbalist, cymbalists, cymballed, cymballike, cymballing, cymbalo, cymbalom, cymbalon, cymbals, cymbate, cymbel, cymbid, cymbidium, cymbiform, cymblin, cymbling, cymblings, cymbocephalic, cymbocephalous, cymbocephaly, cyme, cymelet, cymene, cymenes, cymes, cymiferous, cymlin, cymling, cymlings, cymlins, cymobotryose, cymogene, cymogenes, cymograph, cymographic, cymoid, cymol, cymols, cymometer, cymophane, cymophanous, cymophenol, cymophobia, cymoscope, cymose, cymosely, cymotrichous, cymotrichy, cymous, cymric, cymrite, cymry, cymtia, cymule, cymulose, cynanche, cynanthropy, cynaraceous, cynarctomachy, cynareous, cynaroid, cynebot, cynegetic, cynegetics, cynegild, cynghanedd, cynhyena, cyniatria, cyniatrics, cynic, cynical, cynically, cynicalness, cynicism, cynicisms, cynicist, cynics, cynipid, cynipidous, cynipoid, cynips, cynism, cynocephalic, cynocephalous, cynocephalus, cynoclept, cynocrambaceous, cynodictis, cynodon, cynodont, cynogenealogist, cynogenealogy, cynography, cynoid, cynology, cynomolgus, cynomoriaceous, cynomorphic, cynomorphous, cynophile, cynophilic, cynophilist, cynophobe, cynophobia, cynopithecoid, cynopodous, cynorrhoda, cynorrhodon, cynosural, cynosure, cynosures, cynotherapy, cynthia, cyp, cyperaceous, cyperus, cyphella, cyphellae, cyphellate, cypher, cyphered, cyphering, cyphers, cyphonautes, cyphonism, cyphosis, cypraea, cypraeid, cypraeiform, cypraeoid, cypre, cypres, cypreses, cypress, cypressed, cypresses, cypressroot, cyprian, cyprians, cyprid, cypridinoid, cyprine, cyprinid, cyprinids, cypriniform, cyprinin, cyprinine, cyprinodont, cyprinodontoid, cyprinoid, cyprinoidean, cypriot, cypriote, cypriotes, cypriots, cypripedin, cypripedium, cypris, cyproheptadine, cyproterone, cyprus, cypruses, cypsela, cypselae, cypseliform, cypseline, cypseloid, cypselomorph, cypselomorphic, cypselous, cyptozoic, cyrenaic, cyrillaceous, cyrillic, cyriologic, cyriological, cyrtoceracone, cyrtoceratite, cyrtoceratitic, cyrtograph, cyrtolite, cyrtometer, cyrtopia, cyrtosis, cyrtostyle, cyrus, cyst, cystadenoma, cystadenosarcoma, cystal, cystalgia, cystamine, cystaster, cystathionine, cystatrophia, cystatrophy, cysteamine, cystectasia, cystectasy, cystectomies, cystectomy, cysted, cystein, cysteine, cysteines, cysteinic, cysteins, cystelcosis, cystenchyma, cystenchymatous, cystenchyme, cystencyte, cysterethism, cystic, cysticarpic, cysticarpium, cysticercerci, cysticerci, cysticercoid, cysticercoidal, cysticercosis, cysticercus, cysticerus, cysticle, cysticolous, cystid, cystidean, cystidia, cystidicolous, cystidium, cystidiums, cystiferous, cystiform, cystigerous, cystignathine, cystin, cystine, cystines, cystinosis, cystinuria, cystirrhea, cystis, cystitides, cystitis, cystitome, cystoadenoma, cystocarcinoma, cystocarp, cystocarpic, cystocele, cystocolostomy, cystocyte, cystodynia, cystoelytroplasty, cystoenterocele, cystoepiplocele, cystoepithelioma, cystofibroma, cystoflagellate, cystogenesis, cystogenous, cystogram, cystoid, cystoidean, cystoids, cystolith, cystolithectomy, cystolithiasis, cystolithic, cystoma, cystomas, cystomata, cystomatous, cystometer, cystomorphous, cystomyoma, cystomyxoma, cystonectous, cystonephrosis, cystoneuralgia, cystoparalysis, cystophore, cystophotography, cystophthisis, cystoplasty, cystoplegia, cystoproctostomy, cystoptosis, cystopyelitis, cystopyelography, cystopyelonephritis, cystoradiography, cystorrhagia, cystorrhaphy, cystorrhea, cystosarcoma, cystoschisis, cystoscope, cystoscopic, cystoscopies, cystoscopy, cystose, cystospasm, cystospastic, cystospore, cystostomies, cystostomy, cystosyrinx, cystotome, cystotomies, cystotomy, cystotrachelotomy, cystoureteritis, cystourethritis, cystourethrography, cystous, cysts, cytase, cytasic, cytaster, cytasters, cythera, cytherea, cytherean, cytidine, cytidines, cytinaceous, cytioderm, cytioderma, cytisine, cytisus, cytitis, cytoanalyzer, cytoarchitectural, cytoarchitecturally, cytoarchitecture, cytoblast, cytoblastema, cytoblastemal, cytoblastematous, cytoblastemic, cytoblastemous, cytocentrum, cytochalasin, cytochemical, cytochemistry, cytochrome, cytochylema, cytocide, cytoclasis, cytoclastic, cytococci, cytococcus, cytocyst, cytode, cytodendrite, cytoderm, cytodiagnosis, cytodieresis, cytodieretic, cytodifferentiation, cytoecology, cytogamy, cytogene, cytogenesis, cytogenetic, cytogenetical, cytogenetically, cytogeneticist, cytogenetics, cytogenic, cytogenies, cytogenous, cytogeny, cytoglobin, cytoglobulin, cytohyaloplasm, cytoid, cytokinesis, cytokinetic, cytokinin, cytol, cytolist, cytologic, cytological, cytologically, cytologies, cytologist, cytologists, cytology, cytolymph, cytolysin, cytolysis, cytolytic, cytoma, cytome, cytomegalic, cytomegalovirus, cytomere, cytometer, cytomicrosome, cytomitome, cytomorphological, cytomorphology, cytomorphosis, cyton, cytone, cytons, cytopahgous, cytoparaplastin, cytopathic, cytopathogenic, cytopathogenicity, cytopathologic, cytopathological, cytopathologically, cytopathology, cytopenia, cytophagic, cytophagous, cytophagy, cytopharynges, cytopharynx, cytopharynxes, cytophil, cytophilic, cytophysics, cytophysiology, cytoplasm, cytoplasmic, cytoplasmically, cytoplast, cytoplastic, cytoproct, cytopyge, cytoreticulum, cytoryctes, cytosin, cytosine, cytosines, cytosome, cytospectrophotometry, cytost, cytostatic, cytostatically, cytostomal, cytostome, cytostroma, cytostromatic, cytotactic, cytotaxis, cytotaxonomic, cytotaxonomically, cytotaxonomy, cytotechnologist, cytotechnology, cytotoxic, cytotoxicity, cytotoxin, cytotrophoblast, cytotrophoblastic, cytotrophy, cytotropic, cytotropism, cytovirin, cytozoa, cytozoic, cytozoon, cytozymase, cytozyme, cytozzoa, cytula, cytulae, cyul, cywydd, cyzicene, czar, czardas, czardases, czardom, czardoms, czarevitch, czarevna, czarevnas, czarian, czaric, czarina, czarinas, czarinian, czarish, czarism, czarisms, czarist, czaristic, czarists, czaritza, czaritzas, czarowitch, czarowitz, czars, czarship, czech, czechoslovak, czechoslovakia, czechoslovakian, czechoslovakians, czechoslovaks, czechs, czigany, d, d', d'accord, d'art, d'etat, d'oeuvre, d's, da, daalder, dab, dabb, dabba, dabbed, dabber, dabbers, dabbing, dabble, dabbled, dabbler, dabblers, dabbles, dabbling, dabblingly, dabblingness, dabblings, dabby, dabchick, dabchicks, dablet, daboia, daboya, dabs, dabster, dabsters, dabuh, dace, dacelonine, daces, dacha, dachas, dachs, dachshound, dachshund, dachshunde, dachshunds, dacite, dacitic, dacker, dackered, dackering, dackers, dacoit, dacoitage, dacoited, dacoities, dacoiting, dacoits, dacoity, dacron, dacrya, dacryadenalgia, dacryadenitis, dacryagogue, dacrycystalgia, dacryd, dacryelcosis, dacryoadenalgia, dacryoadenitis, dacryoblenorrhea, dacryocele, dacryocyst, dacryocystalgia, dacryocystitis, dacryocystoblennorrhea, dacryocystocele, dacryocystoptosis, dacryocystorhinostomy, dacryocystosyringotomy, dacryocystotome, dacryocystotomy, dacryohelcosis, dacryohemorrhea, dacryolin, dacryolite, dacryolith, dacryolithiasis, dacryoma, dacryon, dacryops, dacryopyorrhea, dacryopyosis, dacryorrhea, dacryosolenitis, dacryostenosis, dacryosyrinx, dacryuria, dactyl, dactylar, dactylate, dactyli, dactylic, dactylically, dactylics, dactylioglyph, dactylioglyphic, dactylioglyphist, dactylioglyphtic, dactylioglyphy, dactyliographer, dactyliographic, dactyliography, dactyliology, dactyliomancy, dactylion, dactyliotheca, dactylist, dactylitic, dactylitis, dactylogram, dactylograph, dactylographer, dactylographic, dactylography, dactyloid, dactylologies, dactylology, dactylomegaly, dactylonomy, dactylopatagium, dactylopodite, dactylopore, dactylorhiza, dactyloscopic, dactyloscopy, dactylose, dactylosternal, dactylosymphysis, dactylotheca, dactylous, dactylozooid, dactyls, dactylus, dacyorrhea, dad, dad's, dada, dadaism, dadaisms, dadaist, dadaistic, dadaistically, dadaists, dadap, dadas, dadburned, dadder, daddies, dadding, daddle, daddled, daddles, daddling, daddock, daddocky, daddums, daddy, daddynut, dade, dadenhudd, dading, dado, dadoed, dadoes, dadoing, dados, dadouchos, dads, daduchus, dae, daedal, daedaleous, daedalian, daedalist, daedaloid, daedalous, daedalus, daekon, daemon, daemon's, daemones, daemonian, daemonic, daemonies, daemonistic, daemonology, daemons, daemonurgist, daemonurgy, daemony, daer, daeva, daff, daffadillies, daffadilly, daffadowndillies, daffadowndilly, daffed, daffery, daffier, daffiest, daffiness, daffing, daffish, daffle, daffled, daffling, daffodil, daffodil's, daffodillies, daffodilly, daffodils, daffodowndillies, daffodowndilly, daffs, daffy, daffydowndilly, daft, daftar, daftardar, daftberry, dafter, daftest, daftlike, daftly, daftness, daftnesses, dag, dagaba, dagame, dagassa, dagesh, dagga, daggar, dagged, dagger, daggerboard, daggerbush, daggered, daggering, daggerlike, daggerproof, daggers, dagging, daggle, daggled, daggles, daggletail, daggletailed, daggling, daggly, daggy, daghesh, daglock, daglocks, dago, dagoba, dagobas, dagoes, dagon, dagos, dags, dagswain, daguerreotype, daguerreotyped, daguerreotyper, daguerreotypes, daguerreotypic, daguerreotyping, daguerreotypist, daguerreotypy, daguilla, dah, dahabeah, dahabeahs, dahabeeyah, dahabiah, dahabiahs, dahabieh, dahabiehs, dahabiya, dahabiyas, dahabiyeh, dahlia, dahlias, dahlin, dahlsten, dahms, dahomey, dahoon, dahoons, dahs, daidle, daidled, daidlie, daidling, daidly, daiker, daikered, daikering, daikers, daikon, dailies, dailiness, daily, daimen, daimiate, daimiel, daimio, daimioate, daimios, daimiote, daimon, daimones, daimonic, daimonion, daimonistic, daimonology, daimons, daimyo, daimyos, dain, daincha, dainchas, dainful, daint, dainteous, dainteth, daintier, dainties, daintiest, daintified, daintify, daintifying, daintihood, daintily, daintiness, daintith, daintrel, dainty, daiquiri, daiquiris, daira, dairi, dairies, dairous, dairt, dairy, dairying, dairyings, dairymaid, dairymaids, dairyman, dairymen, dairywoman, dairywomen, dais, daised, daisee, daises, daishiki, daishikis, daisied, daisies, daising, daisy, daisy's, daisybush, daisycutter, daitya, daiva, dak, daker, dakerhen, dakerhens, dakhma, dakir, dakoit, dakoities, dakoits, dakoity, dakota, dakotan, dakotans, dakotas, daks, daktylon, daktylos, dal, dalaga, dalai, dalan, dalapon, dalapons, dalar, dalasi, dalasis, dale, dale's, daledh, daleman, daler, dales, dalesfolk, dalesman, dalesmen, dalespeople, daleswoman, daleth, daleths, dalf, dali, daliance, dalis, dalk, dallack, dallan, dallas, dalle, dalles, dalliance, dalliances, dallied, dallier, dalliers, dallies, dallis, dallop, dally, dallying, dallyingly, dallyman, dalmatian, dalmatians, dalmatic, dalmatics, dalt, dalteen, dalton, daltonian, daltonic, daltonism, dam, dam's, dama, damage, damageability, damageable, damageableness, damageably, damaged, damagement, damageous, damager, damagers, damages, damaging, damagingly, damalic, daman, damans, damar, damars, damas, damascene, damascened, damascener, damascenes, damascenine, damascening, damascus, damask, damasked, damaskeen, damaskeening, damaskin, damaskine, damasking, damasks, damasse, damassin, damboard, dambonite, dambonitol, dambose, dambrod, dame, damenization, dames, damewort, dameworts, damfool, damfoolish, damiana, damie, damier, damine, damkjernite, damlike, dammar, dammara, dammaret, dammars, damme, dammed, dammer, dammers, damming, dammish, dammit, damn, damnabilities, damnability, damnable, damnableness, damnably, damnation, damnatory, damndest, damndests, damned, damneder, damnedest, damner, damners, damnification, damnificatus, damnified, damnifies, damnify, damnifying, damning, damningly, damningness, damnit, damnonians, damnosa, damnous, damnously, damns, damnum, damnyankee, damocles, damoiseau, damoisel, damoiselle, damolic, damon, damonico, damosel, damosels, damourite, damozel, damozels, damp, dampang, dampcourse, damped, dampen, dampened, dampener, dampeners, dampening, dampens, damper, dampers, dampest, damping, dampish, dampishly, dampishness, damply, dampne, dampness, dampnesses, dampproof, dampproofer, dampproofing, damps, dampy, dams, damsel, damsel's, damselfish, damselfishes, damselflies, damselfly, damselhood, damsels, damsite, damson, damsons, damyankee, dan, dana, danae, danaid, danaide, danaine, danaite, danalite, danaro, danburite, dancalite, dance, danceability, danceable, danced, dancer, danceress, dancers, dancery, dances, dancette, dancettee, dancetty, dancing, dancingly, dancy, dand, danda, dandelion, dandelion's, dandelions, dander, dandered, dandering, danders, dandiacal, dandiacally, dandically, dandie, dandier, dandies, dandiest, dandification, dandified, dandifies, dandify, dandifying, dandilly, dandily, dandiprat, dandis, dandisette, dandizette, dandle, dandled, dandler, dandlers, dandles, dandling, dandlingly, dandriff, dandriffs, dandriffy, dandruff, dandruffs, dandruffy, dandy, dandydom, dandyish, dandyishly, dandyishy, dandyism, dandyisms, dandyize, dandyling, dandyprat, dane, danebrog, danegeld, danegelds, danegelt, danelaw, danes, daneweed, daneweeds, danewort, daneworts, dang, danged, danger, danger's, dangered, dangerful, dangerfully, dangering, dangerless, dangerous, dangerously, dangerousness, dangers, dangersome, danging, dangle, dangleberries, dangleberry, dangled, danglement, dangler, danglers, dangles, danglin, dangling, danglingly, dangs, danic, danicism, daniel, danio, danios, danish, danism, dank, danke, danker, dankest, dankish, dankishness, dankly, dankness, danknesses, danli, dannebrog, dannemorite, danner, dannock, danny, danoranja, dansant, dansants, danseur, danseurs, danseuse, danseuses, danseusse, dansk, dansker, dansy, danta, dante, dantean, dantesque, danton, danube, danzon, dao, daoine, dap, daphnad, daphne, daphnes, daphnetin, daphni, daphnia, daphnias, daphnid, daphnin, daphnioid, daphnis, daphnite, daphnoid, dapicho, dapico, dapifer, dapped, dapper, dapperer, dapperest, dapperling, dapperly, dapperness, dapping, dapple, dappled, dappledness, dappleness, dapples, dappling, daps, dapson, dar, darabukka, darac, daraf, darapti, darat, darb, darbha, darbies, darbs, darbukka, darby, darbyism, darcy, dard, dardan, dardanarius, dardanium, dardaol, dare, dareall, dared, daredevil, daredevilism, daredevilry, daredevils, daredeviltry, dareful, daren't, darer, darers, dares, daresay, darg, dargah, darger, dargsman, dargue, dari, daribah, daric, darics, darii, daring, daringly, daringness, darings, dariole, darioles, darjeeling, dark, darked, darken, darkened, darkener, darkeners, darkening, darkens, darker, darkest, darkey, darkeys, darkful, darkhaired, darkhearted, darkheartedness, darkie, darkies, darking, darkish, darkishness, darkle, darkled, darkles, darklier, darkliest, darkling, darklings, darkly, darkmans, darkness, darknesses, darkroom, darkrooms, darks, darkskin, darksome, darksomeness, darksum, darktown, darky, darling, darling's, darlingly, darlingness, darlings, darn, darnation, darndest, darndests, darned, darneder, darnedest, darnel, darnels, darner, darners, darnex, darning, darnings, darnix, darns, daroga, darogah, darogha, daroo, darr, darraign, darrein, darshan, darshana, darst, dart, dartars, dartboard, darted, darter, darters, darting, dartingly, dartingness, dartle, dartled, dartles, dartlike, dartling, dartman, dartoic, dartoid, dartos, dartre, dartrose, dartrous, darts, dartsman, darvon, darwan, darwesh, darwin, darwinian, darwinians, darwinism, darwinist, darwinistic, darwinists, darwinite, darya, darzee, das, dase, dasein, dasewe, dash, dashboard, dashboards, dashed, dashedly, dashee, dasheen, dasheens, dashel, dasher, dashers, dashes, dashier, dashiest, dashiki, dashikis, dashing, dashingly, dashmaker, dashplate, dashpot, dashpots, dasht, dashwheel, dashy, dasi, dasn't, dasnt, dassent, dassie, dassies, dassn't, dassy, dastard, dastardize, dastardliness, dastardly, dastards, dastardy, dastur, dasturi, daswen, dascycladaceous, dasymeter, dasypaedal, dasypaedes, dasypaedic, dasyphyllous, dasypod, dasypodoid, dasyprocta, dasyproctine, dasypygal, dasyure, dasyures, dasyurid, dasyurine, dasyuroid, dat, data, database, database's, databases, datable, datableness, datably, datacell, datafile, dataflow, datagram, datagrams, datakit, datamation, datana, datapac, datapunch, dataria, dataries, datary, dataset, datasetname, datasets, datatype, datatypes, datch, datcha, datchas, date, dateable, dateableness, datebook, dated, datedly, datedness, dateless, datelessness, dateline, datelined, datelines, datelining, datemark, dater, daterman, daters, dates, datil, dating, dation, datisca, datiscaceous, datiscetin, datiscin, datiscosid, datiscoside, datisi, datival, dative, datively, datives, dativogerundial, dato, datolite, datolitic, datos, datsun, datsuns, datsw, datto, dattock, dattos, datum, datums, datura, daturas, daturic, daturism, dau, daub, daube, daubed, dauber, dauberies, daubers, daubery, daubes, daubier, daubiest, daubing, daubingly, daubreeite, daubreelite, daubreite, daubries, daubry, daubs, daubster, dauby, daud, dauded, dauding, daudit, dauerlauf, dauerschlaf, daughter, daughterhood, daughterkin, daughterless, daughterlike, daughterliness, daughterling, daughterly, daughters, daughtership, dauk, dauke, daukin, dault, daun, daunch, dauncy, daunder, daundered, daundering, daunders, dauner, daunomycin, daunt, daunted, daunter, daunters, daunting, dauntingly, dauntingness, dauntless, dauntlessly, dauntlessness, daunton, daunts, dauphin, dauphine, dauphines, dauphiness, dauphins, daurna, daut, dauted, dautie, dauties, dauting, dauts, dauw, davach, davainea, dave, daven, davened, davening, davenport, davenports, davens, daver, daverdy, david, davidist, davidsonite, daviely, davies, daviesite, davis, davit, davits, davoch, davy, davyne, davyum, daw, dawcock, dawdle, dawdled, dawdler, dawdlers, dawdles, dawdling, dawdlingly, dawdy, dawe, dawed, dawen, dawing, dawish, dawk, dawkin, dawks, dawn, dawned, dawning, dawnlight, dawnlike, dawns, dawnstreak, dawnward, dawny, dawpate, daws, dawsoniaceous, dawsonite, dawt, dawted, dawtet, dawtie, dawties, dawting, dawtit, dawts, dawut, day, day's, dayabhaga, dayak, dayal, dayan, dayanim, daybeacon, daybeam, daybed, daybeds, dayberry, daybill, dayblush, daybook, daybooks, dayboy, daybreak, daybreaks, daydawn, daydream, daydreamed, daydreamer, daydreamers, daydreaming, daydreamlike, daydreams, daydreamt, daydreamy, daydrudge, dayflies, dayflower, dayflowers, dayfly, dayglow, dayglows, daygoing, daying, dayless, daylight, daylight's, daylighted, daylighting, daylights, daylilies, daylily, daylit, daylong, dayman, daymare, daymares, daymark, daymen, dayment, daynet, daypeep, dayroom, dayrooms, days, dayshine, dayside, daysides, daysman, daysmen, dayspring, daystar, daystars, daystreak, daytale, daytide, daytime, daytimes, dayton, dayward, daywork, dayworker, daywrit, daze, dazed, dazedly, dazedness, dazement, dazes, dazing, dazingly, dazy, dazzle, dazzled, dazzlement, dazzler, dazzlers, dazzles, dazzling, dazzlingly, dazzlingness, db, dbl, dbms, dbridement, dbrn, dc, dca, dcb, dcbname, dclass, dcollet, dcolletage, dcor, dd, ddname, ddt, de, dea, deaccession, deaccessioned, deaccessioning, deaccessions, deacetylate, deacetylated, deacetylating, deacetylation, deacidification, deacidified, deacidify, deacidifying, deacon, deacon's, deaconal, deaconate, deaconed, deaconess, deaconesses, deaconhood, deaconing, deaconize, deaconries, deaconry, deacons, deaconship, deactivate, deactivated, deactivates, deactivating, deactivation, deactivations, deactivator, deactivators, dead, deadbeat, deadbeats, deadborn, deadcenter, deaden, deadened, deadener, deadeners, deadening, deadeningly, deadens, deader, deadest, deadeye, deadeyes, deadfall, deadfalls, deadflat, deadhand, deadhead, deadheaded, deadheading, deadheadism, deadheads, deadhearted, deadheartedly, deadheartedness, deadhouse, deading, deadish, deadishly, deadishness, deadlatch, deadlier, deadliest, deadlight, deadlihead, deadlily, deadline, deadline's, deadlines, deadliness, deadlock, deadlocked, deadlocking, deadlocks, deadly, deadman, deadmelt, deadmen, deadness, deadnesses, deadpan, deadpanned, deadpanner, deadpanning, deadpans, deadpay, deadrise, deadrize, deads, deadtongue, deadweight, deadwood, deadwoods, deadwork, deadworks, deadwort, deady, deaerate, deaerated, deaerates, deaerating, deaeration, deaerator, deaf, deafen, deafened, deafening, deafeningly, deafens, deafer, deafest, deafforest, deafforestation, deafish, deafly, deafmuteness, deafness, deafnesses, deair, deaired, deairing, deairs, deal, dealable, dealate, dealated, dealates, dealation, dealbate, dealbation, dealbuminize, dealcoholist, dealcoholization, dealcoholize, dealer, dealerdom, dealers, dealership, dealerships, dealfish, dealfishes, dealing, dealings, dealkalize, dealkylate, dealkylation, deallocate, deallocated, deallocates, deallocating, deallocation, deallocations, deals, dealt, deambulate, deambulation, deambulatories, deambulatory, deamidase, deamidate, deamidation, deamidization, deamidize, deaminase, deaminate, deaminated, deaminating, deamination, deaminization, deaminize, deaminized, deaminizing, deammonation, dean, dean's, deanathematize, deaned, deaner, deaneries, deanery, deaness, deanimalize, deaning, deans, deanship, deanships, deanthropomorphic, deanthropomorphism, deanthropomorphization, deanthropomorphize, deappetizing, deaquation, dear, dearborn, deare, dearer, dearest, dearie, dearies, dearling, dearly, dearn, dearness, dearnesses, dearomatize, dears, dearsenicate, dearsenicator, dearsenicize, dearth, dearthfu, dearths, dearticulation, dearworth, dearworthily, dearworthiness, deary, deas, deash, deashed, deashes, deashing, deasil, deaspirate, deaspiration, deassimilation, death, deathbed, deathbeds, deathblow, deathblows, deathcup, deathcups, deathday, deathful, deathfully, deathfulness, deathify, deathin, deathiness, deathless, deathlessly, deathlessness, deathlike, deathlikeness, deathliness, deathling, deathly, deathrate, deathrate's, deathrates, deathroot, deaths, deathshot, deathsman, deathsmen, deathtime, deathtrap, deathtraps, deathward, deathwards, deathwatch, deathwatches, deathweed, deathworm, deathy, deaurate, deave, deaved, deavely, deaves, deaving, deb, debacchate, debacle, debacles, debadge, debag, debagged, debagging, debamboozle, debar, debarbarization, debarbarize, debark, debarkation, debarkations, debarked, debarking, debarkment, debarks, debarment, debarrance, debarrass, debarration, debarred, debarring, debars, debase, debased, debasedness, debasement, debaser, debasers, debases, debasing, debasingly, debat, debatable, debatably, debate, debateable, debated, debateful, debatefully, debatement, debater, debaters, debates, debating, debatingly, debatter, debauch, debauched, debauchedly, debauchedness, debauchee, debauchees, debaucher, debaucheries, debauchery, debauches, debauching, debauchment, debbie, debbies, debby, debcle, debe, debeak, debeaker, debeige, debel, debell, debellate, debellation, debellator, deben, debenture, debentured, debentureholder, debentures, debenzolize, debile, debilissima, debilitant, debilitate, debilitated, debilitates, debilitating, debilitation, debilitations, debilitative, debilities, debility, debind, debit, debitable, debite, debited, debiteuse, debiting, debitor, debitrix, debits, debitum, debitumenize, debituminization, debituminize, deblai, deblaterate, deblateration, deblock, deblocked, deblocking, deboise, deboist, deboistly, deboistness, deboite, deboites, debonair, debonaire, debonairity, debonairly, debonairness, debonairty, debone, deboned, deboner, deboners, debones, deboning, debonnaire, deborah, debord, debordment, debosh, deboshed, deboshment, deboss, debouch, debouche, debouched, debouches, debouching, debouchment, debouchure, debout, debowel, debride, debrided, debridement, debriding, debrief, debriefed, debriefing, debriefings, debriefs, debris, debrominate, debromination, debruise, debruised, debruises, debruising, debs, debt, debt's, debted, debtee, debtful, debtless, debtor, debtors, debtorship, debts, debug, debugged, debugger, debugger's, debuggers, debugging, debugs, debullition, debunk, debunked, debunker, debunkers, debunking, debunkment, debunks, deburr, deburse, debus, debused, debusing, debussed, debussing, debussy, debut, debutant, debutante, debutantes, debutants, debuted, debuting, debuts, debye, debyes, dec, decachord, decad, decadactylous, decadal, decadally, decadarch, decadarchy, decadary, decadation, decade, decade's, decadence, decadency, decadent, decadentism, decadently, decadents, decadenza, decades, decadescent, decadi, decadianome, decadic, decadist, decadrachm, decadrachma, decadrachmae, decaedron, decaesarize, decaffeinate, decaffeinated, decaffeinates, decaffeinating, decaffeinize, decafid, decagon, decagonal, decagonally, decagons, decagram, decagramme, decagrams, decagynous, decahedra, decahedral, decahedrodra, decahedron, decahedrons, decahydrate, decahydrated, decahydronaphthalene, decal, decalage, decalcification, decalcified, decalcifier, decalcifies, decalcify, decalcifying, decalcomania, decalcomaniac, decalcomanias, decalescence, decalescent, decaliter, decaliters, decalitre, decalobate, decalog, decalogue, decalomania, decals, decalvant, decalvation, decameral, decameron, decamerous, decameter, decameters, decamethonium, decametre, decametric, decamp, decamped, decamping, decampment, decamps, decan, decanal, decanally, decanate, decancellate, decancellated, decancellating, decancellation, decandently, decandria, decandrous, decane, decanery, decanes, decangular, decani, decanically, decannulation, decanol, decanonization, decanonize, decanormal, decanoyl, decant, decantate, decantation, decanted, decanter, decanters, decantherous, decanting, decantist, decants, decap, decapetalous, decaphyllous, decapitable, decapitalization, decapitalize, decapitate, decapitated, decapitates, decapitating, decapitation, decapitations, decapitator, decapod, decapoda, decapodal, decapodan, decapodiform, decapodous, decapods, decapper, decapsulate, decapsulation, decarbonate, decarbonated, decarbonating, decarbonation, decarbonator, decarbonisation, decarbonise, decarbonised, decarboniser, decarbonising, decarbonization, decarbonize, decarbonized, decarbonizer, decarbonizing, decarbonylate, decarbonylated, decarbonylating, decarbonylation, decarboxylase, decarboxylate, decarboxylated, decarboxylating, decarboxylation, decarboxylization, decarboxylize, decarburation, decarburisation, decarburise, decarburised, decarburising, decarburization, decarburize, decarburized, decarburizing, decarch, decarchies, decarchy, decard, decardinalize, decare, decares, decarhinus, decarnate, decarnated, decart, decartelization, decartelize, decartelized, decartelizing, decasemic, decasepalous, decaspermal, decaspermous, decast, decastellate, decastere, decastich, decastylar, decastyle, decastylos, decasualisation, decasualise, decasualised, decasualising, decasualization, decasualize, decasualized, decasualizing, decasyllabic, decasyllable, decasyllables, decasyllabon, decate, decathlon, decathlons, decatholicize, decating, decatize, decatizer, decatizing, decatoic, decator, decatyl, decaudate, decaudation, decay, decayable, decayed, decayedness, decayer, decayers, decaying, decayless, decays, deccennia, decciare, decciares, decd, decease, deceased, deceases, deceasing, decede, decedent, decedents, deceit, deceitful, deceitfully, deceitfulness, deceits, deceivability, deceivable, deceivableness, deceivably, deceivance, deceive, deceived, deceiver, deceivers, deceives, deceiving, deceivingly, decelerate, decelerated, decelerates, decelerating, deceleration, decelerations, decelerator, decelerators, decelerometer, deceleron, decem, december, decembrist, decemcostate, decemdentate, decemfid, decemflorous, decemfoliate, decemfoliolate, decemjugate, decemlocular, decempartite, decempeda, decempedal, decempedate, decempennate, decemplex, decemplicate, decempunctate, decemstriate, decemuiri, decemvii, decemvir, decemviral, decemvirate, decemviri, decemvirs, decemvirship, decenaries, decenary, decence, decencies, decency, decency's, decene, decener, decennal, decennaries, decennary, decennia, decenniad, decennial, decennially, decennials, decennium, decenniums, decennoval, decent, decenter, decentered, decentering, decenters, decentest, decently, decentness, decentralisation, decentralise, decentralised, decentralising, decentralism, decentralist, decentralization, decentralizationist, decentralizations, decentralize, decentralized, decentralizes, decentralizing, decentration, decentre, decentred, decentres, decentring, decenyl, decephalization, decephalize, deceptibility, deceptible, deception, deception's, deceptional, deceptions, deceptious, deceptiously, deceptitious, deceptive, deceptively, deceptiveness, deceptivity, deceptory, decerebrate, decerebrated, decerebrating, decerebration, decerebrize, decern, decerned, decerning, decerniture, decernment, decerns, decerp, decertation, decertification, decertificaton, decertified, decertify, decertifying, decess, decession, decessit, decessor, decharm, dechemicalization, dechemicalize, dechenite, dechlore, dechloridation, dechloridize, dechloridized, dechloridizing, dechlorinate, dechlorinated, dechlorinating, dechlorination, dechoralize, dechristianization, dechristianize, deciare, deciares, deciatine, decibar, decibel, decibels, deciceronize, decidability, decidable, decide, decided, decidedly, decidedness, decidement, decidence, decidendi, decident, decider, deciders, decides, deciding, decidingly, decidua, deciduae, decidual, deciduary, deciduas, deciduata, deciduate, deciduitis, deciduity, deciduoma, deciduous, deciduously, deciduousness, decigram, decigramme, decigrams, decil, decile, deciles, deciliter, deciliters, decilitre, decillion, decillionth, decima, decimal, decimalisation, decimalise, decimalised, decimalising, decimalism, decimalist, decimalization, decimalize, decimalized, decimalizes, decimalizing, decimally, decimals, decimate, decimated, decimates, decimating, decimation, decimator, decime, decimestrial, decimeter, decimeters, decimetre, decimetres, decimolar, decimole, decimosexto, decimus, decine, decinormal, decipher, decipherability, decipherable, decipherably, deciphered, decipherer, deciphering, decipherment, deciphers, decipium, decipolar, decise, decision, decision's, decisional, decisionmake, decisions, decisis, decisive, decisively, decisiveness, decistere, decisteres, decitizenize, decivilization, decivilize, deck, decke, decked, deckedout, deckel, deckels, decken, decker, deckers, deckhand, deckhands, deckhead, deckhouse, deckhouses, deckie, decking, deckings, deckle, deckles, deckload, deckman, deckpipe, decks, deckswabber, decl, declaim, declaimant, declaimed, declaimer, declaimers, declaiming, declaims, declamando, declamation, declamations, declamator, declamatoriness, declamatory, declarable, declarant, declaration, declaration's, declarations, declarative, declaratively, declaratives, declarator, declaratorily, declarators, declaratory, declare, declared, declaredly, declaredness, declarer, declarers, declares, declaring, declass, declasse, declassed, declassee, declasses, declassicize, declassification, declassifications, declassified, declassifies, declassify, declassifying, declassing, declension, declensional, declensionally, declensions, declericalize, declimatize, declinable, declinal, declinate, declination, declination's, declinational, declinations, declinator, declinatory, declinature, decline, declined, declinedness, decliner, decliners, declines, declining, declinograph, declinometer, declivate, declive, declivent, declivities, declivitous, declivitously, declivity, declivous, declutch, decnet, deco, decoagulate, decoagulated, decoagulation, decoat, decocainize, decoct, decocted, decoctible, decocting, decoction, decoctive, decocts, decoctum, decodable, decode, decoded, decoder, decoders, decodes, decoding, decodings, decohere, decoherence, decoherer, decohesion, decoic, decoke, decoll, decollate, decollated, decollating, decollation, decollator, decolletage, decollete, decollimate, decolonisation, decolonise, decolonised, decolonising, decolonization, decolonize, decolonized, decolonizes, decolonizing, decolor, decolorant, decolorate, decoloration, decolored, decolorimeter, decoloring, decolorisation, decolorise, decolorised, decoloriser, decolorising, decolorization, decolorize, decolorized, decolorizer, decolorizing, decolors, decolour, decolouration, decoloured, decolouring, decolourisation, decolourise, decolourised, decolouriser, decolourising, decolourization, decolourize, decolourized, decolourizer, decolourizing, decolours, decommission, decommissioned, decommissioning, decommissions, decompensate, decompensated, decompensates, decompensating, decompensation, decompensations, decompensatory, decompile, decompiler, decomplex, decomponent, decomponible, decomposability, decomposable, decompose, decomposed, decomposer, decomposers, decomposes, decomposing, decomposite, decomposition, decomposition's, decompositional, decompositions, decomposure, decompound, decompoundable, decompoundly, decompress, decompressed, decompresses, decompressing, decompression, decompressions, decompressive, deconcatenate, deconcentrate, deconcentrated, deconcentrating, deconcentration, deconcentrator, decondition, decongest, decongestant, decongestants, decongested, decongesting, decongestion, decongestive, decongests, deconsecrate, deconsecrated, deconsecrating, deconsecration, deconsider, deconsideration, decontaminate, decontaminated, decontaminates, decontaminating, decontamination, decontaminations, decontaminative, decontaminator, decontaminators, decontrol, decontrolled, decontrolling, decontrols, deconventionalize, deconvolution, deconvolve, decopperization, decopperize, decor, decorability, decorable, decorably, decorament, decorate, decorated, decorates, decorating, decoration, decorationist, decorations, decorative, decoratively, decorativeness, decorator, decorators, decoratory, decore, decorement, decorist, decorous, decorously, decorousness, decorrugative, decors, decorticate, decorticated, decorticating, decortication, decorticator, decorticosis, decortization, decorum, decorums, decostate, decoupage, decouple, decoupled, decouples, decoupling, decourse, decourt, decousu, decoy, decoy's, decoyed, decoyer, decoyers, decoying, decoyman, decoymen, decoys, decrassified, decrassify, decream, decrease, decreased, decreaseless, decreases, decreasing, decreasingly, decreation, decreative, decree, decreeable, decreed, decreeing, decreement, decreer, decreers, decrees, decreet, decreing, decrement, decremental, decremented, decrementing, decrementless, decrements, decremeter, decrepid, decrepit, decrepitate, decrepitated, decrepitating, decrepitation, decrepitly, decrepitness, decrepitude, decrepity, decreptitude, decresc, decrescence, decrescendo, decrescendos, decrescent, decretal, decretalist, decretals, decrete, decretion, decretist, decretive, decretively, decretorial, decretorian, decretorily, decretory, decretum, decrew, decrial, decrials, decried, decrier, decriers, decries, decriminalization, decriminalize, decriminalized, decriminalizes, decriminalizing, decrown, decrowned, decrowning, decrowns, decrudescence, decrustation, decry, decrying, decrypt, decrypted, decrypting, decryption, decryptions, decryptograph, decrypts, decrystallization, decubation, decubital, decubiti, decubitus, decultivate, deculturate, decuman, decumana, decumani, decumanus, decumary, decumbence, decumbency, decumbent, decumbently, decumbiture, decuple, decupled, decuples, decuplet, decupling, decuria, decuries, decurion, decurionate, decurions, decurrence, decurrences, decurrencies, decurrency, decurrent, decurrently, decurring, decursion, decursive, decursively, decurt, decurtate, decurvation, decurvature, decurve, decurved, decurves, decurving, decury, decus, decuss, decussate, decussated, decussately, decussating, decussation, decussatively, decussion, decussis, decussoria, decussorium, decwriter, decyl, decylene, decylenic, decylic, decyne, deda, dedal, dedans, dedd, deddy, dedecorate, dedecoration, dedecorous, dedenda, dedendum, dedentition, dedicant, dedicate, dedicated, dedicatedly, dedicatee, dedicates, dedicating, dedication, dedicational, dedications, dedicative, dedicator, dedicatorial, dedicatorily, dedicators, dedicatory, dedicature, dedifferentiate, dedifferentiated, dedifferentiating, dedifferentiation, dedignation, dedimus, dedit, deditician, dediticiancy, dedition, dedo, dedoggerelize, dedogmatize, dedolation, dedolence, dedolency, dedolent, dedolomitization, dedolomitize, dedolomitized, dedolomitizing, deduce, deduced, deducement, deducer, deduces, deducibility, deducible, deducibleness, deducibly, deducing, deducive, deduct, deducted, deductibility, deductible, deductibles, deductile, deducting, deductio, deduction, deduction's, deductions, deductive, deductively, deductory, deducts, deduit, deduplication, dee, deecodder, deed, deedbote, deedbox, deeded, deedeed, deedful, deedfully, deedholder, deedier, deediest, deedily, deediness, deeding, deedless, deeds, deedy, deejay, deejays, deek, deem, deemed, deemer, deemie, deeming, deemphasis, deemphasize, deemphasized, deemphasizes, deemphasizing, deems, deemster, deemsters, deemstership, deener, deeny, deep, deepen, deepened, deepener, deepeners, deepening, deepeningly, deepens, deeper, deepest, deepfreeze, deepfreezed, deepfreezing, deepfroze, deepfrozen, deepgoing, deeping, deepish, deeplier, deeply, deepmost, deepmouthed, deepness, deepnesses, deeps, deepsome, deepwater, deepwaterman, deepwatermen, deer, deerberry, deerdog, deerdrive, deerflies, deerfly, deerflys, deerfood, deergrass, deerhair, deerherd, deerhorn, deerhound, deerkill, deerlet, deerlike, deermeat, deers, deerskin, deerskins, deerstalker, deerstalkers, deerstalking, deerstand, deerstealer, deertongue, deervetch, deerweed, deerweeds, deerwood, deeryard, deeryards, dees, deescalate, deescalated, deescalates, deescalating, deescalation, deescalations, deeses, deesis, deess, deevey, deevilick, deewan, deewans, def, deface, defaceable, defaced, defacement, defacements, defacer, defacers, defaces, defacing, defacingly, defacto, defade, defaecate, defail, defailance, defaillance, defailment, defaisance, defaitisme, defaitiste, defalcate, defalcated, defalcates, defalcating, defalcation, defalcations, defalcator, defalk, defamation, defamations, defamatory, defame, defamed, defamer, defamers, defames, defaming, defamingly, defamous, defamy, defang, defassa, defat, defatigable, defatigate, defatigated, defatigation, defats, defatted, defatting, default, defaultant, defaulted, defaulter, defaulters, defaulting, defaultless, defaults, defaulture, defeasance, defeasanced, defease, defeasibility, defeasible, defeasibleness, defeasive, defeat, defeated, defeatee, defeater, defeaters, defeating, defeatism, defeatist, defeatists, defeatment, defeats, defeature, defecant, defecate, defecated, defecates, defecating, defecation, defecator, defect, defected, defecter, defecters, defectibility, defectible, defecting, defection, defection's, defectionist, defections, defectious, defective, defectively, defectiveness, defectless, defectlessness, defectology, defector, defectors, defectoscope, defects, defectum, defectuous, defedation, defeise, defeit, defeminisation, defeminise, defeminised, defeminising, defeminization, defeminize, defeminized, defeminizing, defence, defenceable, defenceless, defencelessly, defencelessness, defences, defencive, defend, defendable, defendant, defendant's, defendants, defended, defender, defenders, defending, defendress, defends, defenestrate, defenestrated, defenestrates, defenestrating, defenestration, defensative, defense, defensed, defenseless, defenselessly, defenselessness, defenseman, defensemen, defenser, defenses, defensibility, defensible, defensibleness, defensibly, defensing, defension, defensive, defensively, defensiveness, defensor, defensorship, defensory, defer, deferable, deference, deferens, deferent, deferentectomy, deferential, deferentiality, deferentially, deferentitis, deferents, deferment, deferment's, deferments, deferrable, deferral, deferrals, deferred, deferrer, deferrer's, deferrers, deferring, deferrization, deferrize, deferrized, deferrizing, defers, defervesce, defervesced, defervescence, defervescent, defervescing, defet, defeudalize, defi, defiable, defial, defiance, defiances, defiant, defiantly, defiantness, defiatory, defiber, defibrillate, defibrillated, defibrillating, defibrillation, defibrillative, defibrillator, defibrillatory, defibrinate, defibrination, defibrinize, deficience, deficiencies, deficiency, deficient, deficiently, deficit, deficit's, deficits, defied, defier, defiers, defies, defiguration, defigure, defilable, defilade, defiladed, defilades, defilading, defile, defiled, defiledness, defilement, defilements, defiler, defilers, defiles, defiliation, defiling, defilingly, definability, definable, definably, define, defined, definedly, definement, definer, definers, defines, definienda, definiendum, definiens, definientia, defining, definish, definite, definitely, definiteness, definition, definition's, definitional, definitiones, definitions, definitise, definitised, definitising, definitive, definitively, definitiveness, definitization, definitize, definitized, definitizing, definitor, definitude, defis, defix, deflagrability, deflagrable, deflagrate, deflagrated, deflagrates, deflagrating, deflagration, deflagrations, deflagrator, deflate, deflated, deflater, deflates, deflating, deflation, deflationary, deflationist, deflations, deflator, deflators, deflea, defleaed, defleaing, defleas, deflect, deflectable, deflected, deflecting, deflection, deflectional, deflectionization, deflectionize, deflections, deflective, deflectometer, deflector, deflectors, deflects, deflesh, deflex, deflexed, deflexibility, deflexible, deflexing, deflexion, deflexionize, deflexure, deflocculant, deflocculate, deflocculated, deflocculating, deflocculation, deflocculator, deflocculent, deflorate, defloration, deflorations, deflore, deflorescence, deflourish, deflow, deflower, deflowered, deflowerer, deflowering, deflowerment, deflowers, defluent, defluous, defluvium, deflux, defluxion, defoam, defoamed, defoamer, defoamers, defoaming, defoams, defocus, defocusses, defoedation, defog, defogged, defogger, defoggers, defogging, defogs, defoil, defoliage, defoliant, defoliants, defoliate, defoliated, defoliates, defoliating, defoliation, defoliations, defoliator, defoliators, deforce, deforced, deforcement, deforceor, deforcer, deforces, deforciant, deforcing, deforest, deforestation, deforested, deforester, deforesting, deforests, deform, deformability, deformable, deformalize, deformation, deformation's, deformational, deformations, deformative, deformed, deformedly, deformedness, deformer, deformers, deformeter, deforming, deformism, deformities, deformity, deformity's, deforms, deforse, defortify, defossion, defoul, defraud, defraudation, defrauded, defrauder, defrauders, defrauding, defraudment, defrauds, defray, defrayable, defrayal, defrayals, defrayed, defrayer, defrayers, defraying, defrayment, defrays, defreeze, defrication, defrock, defrocked, defrocking, defrocks, defrost, defrosted, defroster, defrosters, defrosting, defrosts, defs, deft, defter, defterdar, deftest, deftly, deftness, deftnesses, defunct, defunction, defunctionalization, defunctionalize, defunctive, defunctness, defuse, defused, defuses, defusing, defusion, defuze, defuzed, defuzes, defuzing, defy, defying, defyingly, deg, degage, degame, degames, degami, degamis, deganglionate, degarnish, degas, degases, degasification, degasifier, degasify, degass, degassed, degasser, degassers, degasses, degassing, degauss, degaussed, degausser, degausses, degaussing, degelatinize, degelation, degender, degener, degeneracies, degeneracy, degeneralize, degenerate, degenerated, degenerately, degenerateness, degenerates, degenerating, degeneration, degenerationist, degenerations, degenerative, degeneratively, degenerescence, degenerescent, degeneroos, degentilize, degerm, degermed, degerminate, degerminator, degerming, degerms, degged, degger, degging, deglaciation, deglamorization, deglamorize, deglamorized, deglamorizing, deglaze, deglazed, deglazes, deglazing, deglory, deglut, deglute, deglutinate, deglutinated, deglutinating, deglutination, deglutition, deglutitious, deglutitive, deglutitory, deglycerin, deglycerine, degold, degomme, degorder, degorge, degradability, degradable, degradand, degradation, degradation's, degradational, degradations, degradative, degrade, degraded, degradedly, degradedness, degradement, degrader, degraders, degrades, degrading, degradingly, degradingness, degraduate, degraduation, degrain, degranulation, degras, degratia, degravate, degrease, degreased, degreaser, degreases, degreasing, degree, degree's, degreed, degreeing, degreeless, degrees, degreewise, degression, degressive, degressively, degringolade, degu, deguelin, degum, degummed, degummer, degumming, degums, degust, degustate, degustation, degusted, degusting, degusts, dehache, dehair, dehairer, deheathenize, dehematize, dehepatize, dehisce, dehisced, dehiscence, dehiscent, dehisces, dehiscing, dehistoricize, dehnstufe, dehonestate, dehonestation, dehorn, dehorned, dehorner, dehorners, dehorning, dehorns, dehors, dehort, dehortation, dehortative, dehortatory, dehorted, dehorter, dehorting, dehorts, dehull, dehumanisation, dehumanise, dehumanised, dehumanising, dehumanization, dehumanize, dehumanized, dehumanizes, dehumanizing, dehumidification, dehumidified, dehumidifier, dehumidifiers, dehumidifies, dehumidify, dehumidifying, dehusk, dehydrant, dehydrase, dehydratase, dehydrate, dehydrated, dehydrates, dehydrating, dehydration, dehydrator, dehydrators, dehydroascorbic, dehydrochlorinase, dehydrochlorinate, dehydrochlorination, dehydrocorticosterone, dehydrocorydaline, dehydroffroze, dehydroffrozen, dehydrofreeze, dehydrofreezing, dehydrofroze, dehydrofrozen, dehydrogenase, dehydrogenate, dehydrogenated, dehydrogenates, dehydrogenating, dehydrogenation, dehydrogenisation, dehydrogenise, dehydrogenised, dehydrogeniser, dehydrogenising, dehydrogenization, dehydrogenize, dehydrogenized, dehydrogenizer, dehydromucic, dehydroretinol, dehydrosparteine, dehydrotestosterone, dehypnotize, dehypnotized, dehypnotizing, dei, deia, deicate, deice, deiced, deicer, deicers, deices, deicidal, deicide, deicides, deicing, deictic, deictical, deictically, deidealize, deific, deifical, deification, deifications, deificatory, deified, deifier, deifiers, deifies, deiform, deiformity, deify, deifying, deign, deigned, deigning, deignous, deigns, deil, deils, deincrustant, deindividualization, deindividualize, deindividuate, deindustrialization, deindustrialize, deink, deinos, deinosaur, deinstitutionalization, deinsularize, deintellectualization, deintellectualize, deionization, deionizations, deionize, deionized, deionizer, deionizes, deionizing, deipara, deiparous, deipnodiplomatic, deipnophobia, deipnosophism, deipnosophist, deipnosophistic, deipotent, deirid, deis, deiseal, deisidaimonia, deisin, deism, deisms, deist, deistic, deistical, deistically, deisticalness, deists, deitate, deities, deity, deity's, deityship, deixis, deja, deject, dejecta, dejected, dejectedly, dejectedness, dejectile, dejecting, dejection, dejections, dejectly, dejectory, dejects, dejecture, dejerate, dejeration, dejerator, dejeune, dejeuner, dejeuners, dejunkerize, dekadarchy, dekadrachm, dekagram, dekagramme, dekagrams, dekaliter, dekaliters, dekalitre, dekameter, dekameters, dekametre, dekaparsec, dekapode, dekarch, dekare, dekares, dekastere, deke, deked, dekes, deking, dekko, dekkos, dekle, deknight, del, delabialization, delabialize, delabialized, delabializing, delace, delacerate, delacrimation, delactation, delaine, delaines, delaminate, delaminated, delaminating, delamination, delapse, delapsion, delassation, delassement, delate, delated, delater, delates, delating, delatinization, delatinize, delation, delations, delative, delator, delatorian, delators, delaw, delaware, delawarean, delawn, delay, delayable, delayage, delayed, delayer, delayers, delayful, delaying, delayingly, delays, dele, delead, deleaded, deleading, deleads, deleatur, deleble, delectability, delectable, delectableness, delectably, delectate, delectated, delectating, delectation, delectations, delectible, delectus, deled, deleerit, delegable, delegacies, delegacy, delegalize, delegalized, delegalizing, delegant, delegare, delegate, delegated, delegatee, delegates, delegateship, delegati, delegating, delegation, delegations, delegative, delegator, delegatory, delegatus, deleing, delenda, deleniate, deles, delesseriaceous, delete, deleted, deleter, deleterious, deleteriously, deleteriousness, deletery, deletes, deleting, deletion, deletions, deletive, deletory, delf, delfs, delft, delfts, delftware, delhi, deli, delian, delibate, deliber, deliberalization, deliberalize, deliberandum, deliberant, deliberate, deliberated, deliberately, deliberateness, deliberates, deliberating, deliberation, deliberations, deliberative, deliberatively, deliberativeness, deliberator, deliberator's, deliberators, delible, delicacies, delicacy, delicacy's, delicat, delicate, delicately, delicateness, delicates, delicatesse, delicatessen, delicatessens, delice, delicense, deliciae, deliciate, delicioso, delicious, deliciouses, deliciously, deliciousness, delict, delicti, delicto, delicts, delictual, delictum, delictus, delieret, delies, deligated, deligation, delight, delightable, delighted, delightedly, delightedness, delighter, delightful, delightfully, delightfulness, delighting, delightingly, delightless, delights, delightsome, delightsomely, delightsomeness, delignate, delignated, delignification, delilah, deliliria, delim, delime, delimed, delimer, delimes, deliming, delimit, delimitate, delimitated, delimitating, delimitation, delimitations, delimitative, delimited, delimiter, delimiters, delimiting, delimitize, delimitized, delimitizing, delimits, deline, delineable, delineament, delineate, delineated, delineates, delineating, delineation, delineations, delineative, delineator, delineatory, delineature, delineavit, delinition, delinquence, delinquencies, delinquency, delinquent, delinquently, delinquents, delint, delinter, deliquate, deliquesce, deliquesced, deliquescence, deliquescent, deliquesces, deliquescing, deliquiate, deliquiesce, deliquium, deliracy, delirament, delirant, delirate, deliration, delire, deliria, deliriant, deliriate, delirifacient, delirious, deliriously, deliriousness, delirium, deliriums, delirous, delis, delisk, delist, delisted, delisting, delists, delit, delitescence, delitescency, delitescent, delitous, deliver, deliverability, deliverable, deliverables, deliverance, delivered, deliverer, deliverers, deliveress, deliveries, delivering, deliverly, deliveror, delivers, delivery, delivery's, deliveryman, deliverymen, dell, dell', dell's, della, dellaring, dellenite, dellies, dells, delly, delocalisation, delocalise, delocalised, delocalising, delocalization, delocalize, delocalized, delocalizing, delomorphic, delomorphous, deloo, deloul, delouse, deloused, delouses, delousing, delph, delphacid, delphian, delphically, delphin, delphine, delphinia, delphinic, delphinin, delphinine, delphinite, delphinium, delphiniums, delphinoid, delphinoidine, delphinus, delphocurarine, dels, delta, delta's, deltafication, deltahedra, deltahedron, deltaic, deltaite, deltal, deltalike, deltarium, deltas, deltation, delthyria, delthyrial, delthyrium, deltic, deltidia, deltidial, deltidium, deltiology, deltohedra, deltohedron, deltoid, deltoidal, deltoidei, deltoideus, deltoids, delubra, delubrubra, delubrum, deluce, deludable, delude, deluded, deluder, deluders, deludes, deludher, deluding, deludingly, deluge, deluged, deluges, deluging, delumbate, deluminize, delundung, delusion, delusion's, delusional, delusionary, delusionist, delusions, delusive, delusively, delusiveness, delusory, deluster, delusterant, delustered, delustering, delusters, delustrant, deluxe, delve, delved, delver, delvers, delves, delving, dely, dem, demagnetisable, demagnetisation, demagnetise, demagnetised, demagnetiser, demagnetising, demagnetizable, demagnetization, demagnetize, demagnetized, demagnetizer, demagnetizes, demagnetizing, demagnification, demagnify, demagog, demagogic, demagogical, demagogically, demagogies, demagogism, demagogs, demagogue, demagoguery, demagogues, demagoguism, demagogy, demain, demal, demand, demandable, demandant, demandative, demanded, demander, demanders, demanding, demandingly, demandingness, demands, demanganization, demanganize, demantoid, demarcate, demarcated, demarcates, demarcating, demarcation, demarcations, demarcator, demarcatordemarcators, demarcators, demarcature, demarch, demarche, demarches, demarchy, demaree, demargarinate, demark, demarkation, demarked, demarking, demarks, demasculinisation, demasculinise, demasculinised, demasculinising, demasculinization, demasculinize, demasculinized, demasculinizing, demast, demasted, demasting, demasts, dematerialisation, dematerialise, dematerialised, dematerialising, dematerialization, dematerialize, dematerialized, dematerializing, dematiaceous, deme, demean, demeaned, demeaning, demeanor, demeanored, demeanors, demeanour, demeans, demegoric, demele, demembration, demembre, demency, dement, dementate, dementation, demented, dementedly, dementedness, dementholize, dementi, dementia, demential, dementias, dementie, dementing, dementis, dements, demeore, demephitize, demerara, demerge, demerit, demerited, demeriting, demeritorious, demeritoriously, demerits, demerol, demersal, demerse, demersed, demersion, demes, demesgne, demesgnes, demesman, demesmerize, demesne, demesnes, demesnial, demetallize, demeter, demethylate, demethylation, demethylchlortetracycline, demetricize, demi, demiadult, demiangel, demiassignation, demiatheism, demiatheist, demibarrel, demibastion, demibastioned, demibath, demibeast, demibelt, demibob, demibombard, demibrassart, demibrigade, demibrute, demibuckram, demicadence, demicannon, demicanon, demicanton, demicaponier, demichamfron, demicircle, demicircular, demicivilized, demicolumn, demicoronal, demicritic, demicuirass, demiculverin, demicylinder, demicylindrical, demidandiprat, demideify, demideity, demidevil, demidigested, demidistance, demiditone, demidoctor, demidog, demidolmen, demidome, demieagle, demies, demifarthing, demifigure, demiflouncing, demifusion, demigardebras, demigauntlet, demigentleman, demiglace, demiglobe, demigod, demigoddess, demigoddessship, demigods, demigorge, demigrate, demigriffin, demigroat, demihag, demihagbut, demihague, demihake, demihaque, demihearse, demiheavenly, demihigh, demihogshead, demihorse, demihuman, demijambe, demijohn, demijohns, demikindred, demiking, demilance, demilancer, demilawyer, demilegato, demilion, demilitarisation, demilitarise, demilitarised, demilitarising, demilitarization, demilitarize, demilitarized, demilitarizes, demilitarizing, demiliterate, demilune, demilunes, demiluster, demilustre, demiman, demimark, demimentoniere, demimetope, demimillionaire, demimondain, demimondaine, demimondaines, demimonde, demimonk, deminatured, demineralization, demineralize, demineralized, demineralizer, demineralizes, demineralizing, deminude, deminudity, demioctagonal, demioctangular, demiofficial, demiorbit, demiourgoi, demiowl, demiox, demipagan, demiparadise, demiparallel, demipauldron, demipectinate, demipesade, demipike, demipillar, demipique, demiplacate, demiplate, demipomada, demipremise, demipremiss, demipriest, demipronation, demipuppet, demiquaver, demiracle, demiram, demirelief, demirep, demireps, demirevetment, demirhumb, demirilievo, demirobe, demisability, demisable, demisacrilege, demisang, demisangue, demisavage, demiscible, demise, demiseason, demisecond, demised, demisemiquaver, demisemitone, demises, demisheath, demishirt, demising, demisolde, demisovereign, demisphere, demiss, demission, demissionary, demissive, demissly, demissness, demissory, demist, demisuit, demit, demitasse, demitasses, demitint, demitoilet, demitone, demitrain, demitranslucence, demits, demitted, demitting, demitube, demiturned, demiurge, demiurgeous, demiurges, demiurgic, demiurgical, demiurgically, demiurgism, demiurgos, demiurgus, demivambrace, demivierge, demivirgin, demivoice, demivol, demivolt, demivolte, demivolts, demivotary, demiwivern, demiwolf, demiworld, demnition, demo, demob, demobbed, demobbing, demobilisation, demobilise, demobilised, demobilising, demobilization, demobilizations, demobilize, demobilized, demobilizes, demobilizing, demobs, democracies, democracy, democracy's, democrat, democrat's, democratian, democratic, democratical, democratically, democratifiable, democratisation, democratise, democratised, democratising, democratism, democratist, democratization, democratize, democratized, democratizer, democratizes, democratizing, democrats, democraw, democritean, demode, demodectic, demoded, demodex, demodulate, demodulated, demodulates, demodulating, demodulation, demodulations, demodulator, demogenic, demogorgon, demographer, demographers, demographic, demographical, demographically, demographics, demographies, demographist, demography, demoid, demoiselle, demoiselles, demolish, demolished, demolisher, demolishes, demolishing, demolishment, demolition, demolitionary, demolitionist, demolitions, demological, demology, demon, demon's, demonastery, demoness, demonesses, demonetisation, demonetise, demonetised, demonetising, demonetization, demonetize, demonetized, demonetizes, demonetizing, demoniac, demoniacal, demoniacally, demoniacism, demoniacs, demonial, demonian, demonianism, demoniast, demonic, demonical, demonically, demonifuge, demonio, demonise, demonised, demonises, demonish, demonishness, demonising, demonism, demonisms, demonist, demonists, demonization, demonize, demonized, demonizes, demonizing, demonkind, demonland, demonlike, demonocracy, demonograph, demonographer, demonographies, demonography, demonolater, demonolatrous, demonolatrously, demonolatry, demonologer, demonologic, demonological, demonologically, demonologies, demonologist, demonology, demonomancy, demonomanie, demonomist, demonomy, demonophobia, demonopolize, demonry, demons, demonship, demonstrability, demonstrable, demonstrableness, demonstrably, demonstrance, demonstrandum, demonstrant, demonstratability, demonstratable, demonstrate, demonstrated, demonstratedly, demonstrater, demonstrates, demonstrating, demonstration, demonstrational, demonstrationist, demonstrationists, demonstrations, demonstrative, demonstratively, demonstrativeness, demonstrator, demonstrator's, demonstrators, demonstratorship, demonstratory, demophil, demophile, demophilism, demophobe, demophobia, demorage, demoralisation, demoralise, demoralised, demoraliser, demoralising, demoralization, demoralize, demoralized, demoralizer, demoralizers, demoralizes, demoralizing, demoralizingly, demorphinization, demorphism, demos, demoses, demosthenic, demot, demote, demoted, demotes, demothball, demotic, demotics, demoting, demotion, demotions, demotist, demotists, demount, demountability, demountable, demounted, demounting, demounts, demove, dempne, dempster, dempsters, demulce, demulceate, demulcent, demulcents, demulsibility, demulsification, demulsified, demulsifier, demulsify, demulsifying, demulsion, demultiplex, demultiplexed, demultiplexer, demultiplexers, demultiplexes, demultiplexing, demur, demure, demurely, demureness, demurer, demurest, demurity, demurrable, demurrage, demurrages, demurral, demurrals, demurrant, demurred, demurrer, demurrers, demurring, demurringly, demurs, demutization, demy, demyelinate, demyelination, demyship, demystification, demystify, demythify, demythologisation, demythologise, demythologised, demythologising, demythologization, demythologizations, demythologize, demythologized, demythologizer, demythologizes, demythologizing, den, den's, dename, denar, denarcotization, denarcotize, denari, denaries, denarii, denarinarii, denarius, denaro, denary, denasalize, denasalized, denasalizing, denat, denationalisation, denationalise, denationalised, denationalising, denationalization, denationalize, denationalized, denationalizing, denaturalisation, denaturalise, denaturalised, denaturalising, denaturalization, denaturalize, denaturalized, denaturalizing, denaturant, denaturants, denaturate, denaturation, denaturational, denature, denatured, denatures, denaturing, denaturisation, denaturise, denaturised, denaturiser, denaturising, denaturization, denaturize, denaturized, denaturizer, denaturizing, denay, denazification, denazified, denazifies, denazify, denazifying, denda, dendra, dendrachate, dendral, dendraxon, dendric, dendriform, dendrite, dendrites, dendritic, dendritical, dendritically, dendritiform, dendrobe, dendroceratine, dendrochronological, dendrochronologically, dendrochronologist, dendrochronology, dendroclastic, dendrocoelan, dendrocoele, dendrocoelous, dendrocolaptine, dendroctonus, dendrodic, dendrodont, dendrodra, dendrograph, dendrography, dendroid, dendroidal, dendrolater, dendrolatry, dendrolite, dendrologic, dendrological, dendrologist, dendrologists, dendrologous, dendrology, dendrometer, dendron, dendrons, dendrophagous, dendrophil, dendrophile, dendrophilous, dene, deneb, denegate, denegation, denehole, denervate, denervation, denes, deneutralization, dengue, dengues, deniability, deniable, deniably, denial, denial's, denials, denicotine, denicotinize, denicotinized, denicotinizes, denicotinizing, denied, denier, denierage, denierer, deniers, denies, denigrate, denigrated, denigrates, denigrating, denigration, denigrations, denigrative, denigrator, denigrators, denigratory, denim, denims, denitrate, denitrated, denitrating, denitration, denitrator, denitrificant, denitrification, denitrificator, denitrified, denitrifier, denitrify, denitrifying, denitrize, denizate, denization, denize, denizen, denizenation, denizened, denizening, denizenize, denizens, denizenship, denmark, denned, dennet, denning, dennis, denom, denominable, denominant, denominate, denominated, denominates, denominating, denomination, denomination's, denominational, denominationalism, denominationalist, denominationalize, denominationally, denominations, denominative, denominatively, denominator, denominator's, denominators, denormalized, denotable, denotate, denotation, denotation's, denotational, denotationally, denotations, denotative, denotatively, denotativeness, denotatum, denote, denoted, denotement, denotes, denoting, denotive, denouement, denouements, denounce, denounced, denouncement, denouncements, denouncer, denouncers, denounces, denouncing, dens, densate, densation, dense, densely, densen, denseness, denser, densest, denshare, densher, denshire, densification, densified, densifier, densifies, densify, densifying, densimeter, densimetric, densimetrically, densimetry, densities, densitometer, densitometers, densitometric, densitometry, density, density's, densus, dent, dentagra, dental, dentale, dentalgia, dentalia, dentalisation, dentalise, dentalised, dentalising, dentalism, dentality, dentalium, dentaliums, dentalization, dentalize, dentalized, dentalizing, dentallia, dentally, dentalman, dentalmen, dentals, dentaphone, dentaries, dentary, dentata, dentate, dentated, dentately, dentation, dentatoangulate, dentatocillitate, dentatocostate, dentatocrenate, dentatoserrate, dentatosetaceous, dentatosinuate, dented, dentel, dentelated, dentellated, dentelle, dentelliere, dentello, dentelure, denter, dentes, dentex, dentical, denticate, denticete, denticle, denticles, denticular, denticulate, denticulated, denticulately, denticulation, denticule, dentiferous, dentification, dentiform, dentifrice, dentifrices, dentigerous, dentil, dentilabial, dentilated, dentilation, dentile, dentiled, dentilingual, dentiloguy, dentiloquist, dentiloquy, dentils, dentimeter, dentin, dentinal, dentinalgia, dentinasal, dentine, dentines, denting, dentinitis, dentinoblast, dentinocemental, dentinoid, dentinoma, dentins, dentiparous, dentiphone, dentiroster, dentirostral, dentirostrate, dentiscalp, dentist, dentist's, dentistic, dentistical, dentistries, dentistry, dentists, dentition, dentoid, dentolabial, dentolingual, dentololabial, dentonasal, dentosurgical, dents, dentulous, dentural, denture, dentures, denty, denuclearization, denuclearize, denuclearized, denuclearizes, denuclearizing, denucleate, denudant, denudate, denudated, denudates, denudating, denudation, denudational, denudations, denudative, denudatory, denude, denuded, denudement, denuder, denuders, denudes, denuding, denumberment, denumerability, denumerable, denumerably, denumeral, denumerant, denumerantive, denumeration, denumerative, denunciable, denunciant, denunciate, denunciated, denunciating, denunciation, denunciations, denunciative, denunciatively, denunciator, denunciatory, denutrition, denver, deny, denyer, denying, denyingly, deobstruct, deobstruent, deoccidentalize, deoculate, deodand, deodands, deodar, deodara, deodaras, deodars, deodate, deodorant, deodorants, deodorisation, deodorise, deodorised, deodoriser, deodorising, deodorization, deodorize, deodorized, deodorizer, deodorizers, deodorizes, deodorizing, deonerate, deontic, deontological, deontologist, deontology, deoperculate, deoppilant, deoppilate, deoppilation, deoppilative, deordination, deorganization, deorganize, deorientalize, deorsum, deorsumvergence, deorsumversion, deorusumduction, deosculate, deossification, deossify, deota, deoxidant, deoxidate, deoxidation, deoxidative, deoxidator, deoxidisation, deoxidise, deoxidised, deoxidiser, deoxidising, deoxidization, deoxidize, deoxidized, deoxidizer, deoxidizers, deoxidizes, deoxidizing, deoxycorticosterone, deoxygenate, deoxygenated, deoxygenating, deoxygenation, deoxygenization, deoxygenize, deoxygenized, deoxygenizing, deoxyribonuclease, deoxyribonucleic, deoxyribonucleoprotein, deoxyribonucleotide, deoxyribose, deozonization, deozonize, deozonizer, dep, depa, depaganize, depaint, depainted, depainting, depaints, depair, depancreatization, depancreatize, depardieu, depark, deparliament, depart, departed, departement, departements, departer, departing, departisanize, departition, department, department's, departmental, departmentalisation, departmentalise, departmentalised, departmentalising, departmentalism, departmentalization, departmentalize, departmentalized, departmentalizes, departmentalizing, departmentally, departmentization, departmentize, departments, departs, departure, departure's, departures, depas, depascent, depass, depasturable, depasturage, depasturation, depasture, depastured, depasturing, depatriate, depauperate, depauperation, depauperization, depauperize, depauperized, depayse, depaysee, depe, depeach, depeche, depectible, depeculate, depeinct, depel, depencil, depend, dependabilities, dependability, dependable, dependableness, dependably, dependance, dependancy, dependant, dependantly, dependants, depended, dependence, dependencies, dependency, dependent, dependently, dependents, depender, depending, dependingly, depends, depeople, depeopled, depeopling, deperdit, deperdite, deperditely, deperdition, deperition, deperm, depermed, deperming, deperms, depersonalise, depersonalised, depersonalising, depersonalization, depersonalize, depersonalized, depersonalizes, depersonalizing, depersonize, depertible, depetalize, depeter, depetticoat, dephase, dephased, dephasing, dephilosophize, dephlegm, dephlegmate, dephlegmated, dephlegmation, dephlegmatize, dephlegmator, dephlegmatory, dephlegmedness, dephlogisticate, dephlogisticated, dephlogistication, dephosphorization, dephosphorize, dephycercal, dephysicalization, dephysicalize, depickle, depict, depicted, depicter, depicters, depicting, depiction, depictions, depictive, depictment, depictor, depictors, depicts, depicture, depictured, depicturing, depiedmontize, depigment, depigmentate, depigmentation, depigmentize, depilate, depilated, depilates, depilating, depilation, depilator, depilatories, depilatory, depilitant, depilous, depit, deplace, deplaceable, deplane, deplaned, deplanes, deplaning, deplant, deplantation, deplasmolysis, deplaster, deplenish, depletable, deplete, depleteable, depleted, depletes, deplethoric, depleting, depletion, depletions, depletive, depletory, deploitation, deplorabilia, deplorability, deplorable, deplorableness, deplorably, deplorate, deploration, deplore, deplored, deploredly, deploredness, deplorer, deplorers, deplores, deploring, deploringly, deploy, deployable, deployed, deploying, deployment, deployment's, deployments, deploys, deplumate, deplumated, deplumation, deplume, deplumed, deplumes, depluming, deplump, depoetize, depoh, depolarisation, depolarise, depolarised, depolariser, depolarising, depolarization, depolarize, depolarized, depolarizer, depolarizers, depolarizes, depolarizing, depolish, depolished, depolishes, depolishing, depoliticize, depoliticized, depoliticizes, depoliticizing, depolymerization, depolymerize, depolymerized, depolymerizing, depone, deponed, deponent, deponents, deponer, depones, deponing, depopularize, depopulate, depopulated, depopulates, depopulating, depopulation, depopulations, depopulative, depopulator, depopulators, deport, deportability, deportable, deportation, deportations, deporte, deported, deportee, deportees, deporter, deporting, deportment, deports, deporture, deposable, deposal, deposals, depose, deposed, deposer, deposers, deposes, deposing, deposit, deposita, depositaries, depositary, deposition, deposited, depositee, depositing, deposition, deposition's, depositional, depositions, depositive, deposito, depositor, depositor's, depositories, depositors, depository, deposits, depositum, depositure, deposure, depot, depot's, depotentiate, depotentiation, depots, depr, depravate, depravation, deprave, depraved, depravedly, depravedness, depravement, depraver, depravers, depraves, depraving, depravingly, depravities, depravity, deprecable, deprecate, deprecated, deprecates, deprecating, deprecatingly, deprecation, deprecations, deprecative, deprecatively, deprecator, deprecatorily, deprecatoriness, deprecators, deprecatory, depreciable, depreciant, depreciate, depreciated, depreciates, depreciating, depreciatingly, depreciation, depreciations, depreciative, depreciatively, depreciator, depreciatoriness, depreciators, depreciatory, depredable, depredate, depredated, depredating, depredation, depredationist, depredations, depredator, depredatory, depredicate, deprehend, deprehensible, deprehension, depress, depressant, depressanth, depressants, depressed, depresses, depressibilities, depressibility, depressible, depressing, depressingly, depressingness, depression, depression's, depressional, depressionary, depressions, depressive, depressively, depressiveness, depressives, depressomotor, depressor, depressors, depressure, depressurize, deprest, depreter, deprevation, depriment, deprint, depriorize, deprisure, deprivable, deprival, deprivals, deprivate, deprivation, deprivation's, deprivations, deprivative, deprive, deprived, deprivement, depriver, deprivers, deprives, depriving, deprocedured, deproceduring, deprogram, deprogrammed, deprogrammer, deprogrammers, deprogramming, deprogrammings, deprograms, deprome, deprostrate, deprotestantize, deprovincialize, depsid, depside, depsides, dept, depth, depthen, depthing, depthless, depthlessness, depthometer, depths, depthways, depthwise, depucel, depudorate, depullulation, depulse, depurant, depurate, depurated, depurates, depurating, depuration, depurative, depurator, depuratory, depure, depurge, depurged, depurging, depurition, depursement, deputable, deputation, deputational, deputationist, deputationize, deputations, deputative, deputatively, deputator, depute, deputed, deputes, deputies, deputing, deputise, deputised, deputising, deputization, deputize, deputized, deputizes, deputizing, deputy, deputy's, deputyship, dequantitate, dequeen, dequeue, dequeued, dequeues, dequeuing, der, derabbinize, deracialize, deracinate, deracinated, deracinating, deracination, deracine, deradelphus, deradenitis, deradenoncus, derah, deraign, deraigned, deraigning, deraignment, deraigns, derail, derailed, derailer, derailing, derailleur, derailleurs, derailment, derailments, derails, derange, derangeable, deranged, derangement, derangements, deranger, deranges, deranging, derat, derate, derated, derater, derating, deration, derationalization, derationalize, deratization, deratize, deratized, deratizing, derats, deratted, deratting, deray, derays, derbies, derbukka, derby, derbylite, derbyshire, dere, derealization, derecho, dereference, dereferenced, dereferences, dereferencing, deregister, deregulate, deregulated, deregulates, deregulating, deregulation, deregulationize, deregulations, deregulatory, dereign, dereism, dereistic, dereistically, derelict, derelicta, dereliction, derelictions, derelictly, derelictness, derelicts, dereligion, dereligionize, dereling, derelinquendi, derelinquish, derencephalocele, derencephalus, derepress, derepression, derequisition, derere, deresinate, deresinize, derestrict, derf, derfly, derfness, derham, deric, deride, derided, derider, deriders, derides, deriding, deridingly, deringer, deringers, derisible, derision, derisions, derisive, derisively, derisiveness, derisory, deriv, derivability, derivable, derivably, derival, derivant, derivate, derivately, derivates, derivation, derivation's, derivational, derivationally, derivationist, derivations, derivatist, derivative, derivative's, derivatively, derivativeness, derivatives, derive, derived, derivedly, derivedness, deriver, derivers, derives, deriving, derk, derm, derma, dermabrasion, dermad, dermahemia, dermal, dermalgia, dermalith, dermamycosis, dermamyiasis, dermanaplasty, dermapostasis, dermaptera, dermapteran, dermapterous, dermas, dermaskeleton, dermasurgery, dermatagra, dermatalgia, dermataneuria, dermatatrophia, dermatauxe, dermathemia, dermatherm, dermatic, dermatine, dermatitis, dermatitises, dermatocele, dermatocellulitis, dermatoconiosis, dermatocoptic, dermatocyst, dermatodynia, dermatogen, dermatoglyphic, dermatoglyphics, dermatograph, dermatographia, dermatographic, dermatographism, dermatography, dermatoheteroplasty, dermatoid, dermatologic, dermatological, dermatologies, dermatologist, dermatologists, dermatology, dermatolysis, dermatoma, dermatome, dermatomere, dermatomic, dermatomuscular, dermatomyces, dermatomycosis, dermatomyoma, dermatoneural, dermatoneurology, dermatoneurosis, dermatonosus, dermatopathia, dermatopathic, dermatopathology, dermatopathophobia, dermatophobia, dermatophone, dermatophony, dermatophyte, dermatophytic, dermatophytosis, dermatoplasm, dermatoplast, dermatoplastic, dermatoplasty, dermatopnagic, dermatopsy, dermatoptic, dermatorrhagia, dermatorrhea, dermatorrhoea, dermatosclerosis, dermatoscopy, dermatoses, dermatosiophobia, dermatosis, dermatoskeleton, dermatotherapy, dermatotome, dermatotomy, dermatotropic, dermatoxerasia, dermatozoon, dermatozoonosis, dermatozzoa, dermatrophia, dermatrophy, dermatropic, dermenchysis, dermestes, dermestid, dermestoid, dermic, dermis, dermises, dermitis, dermititis, dermoblast, dermobranchiata, dermobranchiate, dermochrome, dermococcus, dermogastric, dermographia, dermographic, dermographism, dermography, dermohemal, dermohemia, dermohumeral, dermoid, dermoidal, dermoidectomy, dermol, dermolysis, dermomuscular, dermomycosis, dermonecrotic, dermoneural, dermoneurosis, dermonosology, dermoosseous, dermoossification, dermopathic, dermopathy, dermophlebitis, dermophobe, dermophyte, dermophytic, dermoplasty, dermopteran, dermopterous, dermoreaction, dermorhynchous, dermosclerite, dermoskeletal, dermoskeleton, dermostenosis, dermostosis, dermosynovitis, dermotherm, dermotropic, dermovaccine, derms, dermutation, dern, derned, derner, dernful, dernier, derning, dernly, dero, derobe, derodidymus, derog, derogate, derogated, derogately, derogates, derogating, derogation, derogations, derogative, derogatively, derogator, derogatorily, derogatoriness, derogatory, deromanticize, derotremate, derotrematous, derotreme, derout, derri, derrick, derricking, derrickman, derrickmen, derricks, derrid, derride, derriere, derrieres, derries, derringer, derringers, derrire, derris, derrises, derry, derth, dertra, dertrotheca, dertrum, deruinate, deruralize, derust, derv, derve, dervish, dervishes, dervishhood, dervishism, dervishlike, des, desaccharification, desacralization, desacralize, desagrement, desalinate, desalinated, desalinates, desalinating, desalination, desalinator, desalinization, desalinize, desalinized, desalinizes, desalinizing, desalt, desalted, desalter, desalters, desalting, desalts, desamidase, desamidization, desaminase, desand, desanded, desanding, desands, desaturate, desaturation, desaurin, desaurine, desc, descale, descaled, descaling, descamisado, descamisados, descant, descanted, descanter, descanting, descantist, descants, descartes, descend, descendability, descendable, descendance, descendant, descendant's, descendants, descended, descendence, descendent, descendental, descendentalism, descendentalist, descendentalistic, descendents, descender, descenders, descendibility, descendible, descending, descendingly, descends, descension, descensional, descensionist, descensive, descensories, descensory, descent, descent's, descents, deschool, descloizite, descort, descrial, describability, describable, describably, describe, described, describent, describer, describers, describes, describing, descried, descrier, descriers, descries, descript, description, description's, descriptionist, descriptionless, descriptions, descriptive, descriptively, descriptiveness, descriptives, descriptivism, descriptor, descriptor's, descriptors, descriptory, descrive, descry, descrying, descure, desdemona, deseam, deseasonalize, desecate, desecrate, desecrated, desecrater, desecrates, desecrating, desecration, desecrations, desecrator, desectionalize, deseed, desegmentation, desegmented, desegregate, desegregated, desegregates, desegregating, desegregation, deselect, deselected, deselecting, deselects, desemer, desensitization, desensitizations, desensitize, desensitized, desensitizer, desensitizers, desensitizes, desensitizing, desentimentalize, deseret, desert, deserted, desertedly, desertedness, deserter, deserters, desertful, desertfully, desertic, deserticolous, desertification, deserting, desertion, desertions, desertism, desertless, desertlessly, desertlike, desertness, desertress, desertrice, deserts, desertward, deserve, deserved, deservedly, deservedness, deserveless, deserver, deservers, deserves, deserving, deservingly, deservingness, deservings, deseperance, desex, desexed, desexes, desexing, desexualization, desexualize, desexualized, desexualizing, deshabille, desi, desiatin, desicate, desiccant, desiccants, desiccate, desiccated, desiccates, desiccating, desiccation, desiccations, desiccative, desiccator, desiccators, desiccatory, desiderable, desiderant, desiderata, desiderate, desiderated, desiderating, desideration, desiderative, desideratum, desiderium, desiderta, desidiose, desidious, desight, desightment, design, designable, designado, designate, designated, designates, designating, designation, designations, designative, designator, designator's, designators, designatory, designatum, designed, designedly, designedness, designee, designees, designer, designer's, designers, designful, designfully, designfulness, designing, designingly, designless, designlessly, designlessness, designment, designs, desilicate, desilicated, desilicating, desilicification, desilicified, desilicify, desiliconization, desiliconize, desilt, desilver, desilvered, desilvering, desilverization, desilverize, desilverized, desilverizer, desilverizing, desilvers, desinence, desinent, desinential, desiodothyroxine, desipience, desipiency, desipient, desipramine, desirability, desirable, desirableness, desirably, desire, desireable, desired, desiredly, desiredness, desireful, desirefulness, desireless, desirelessness, desirer, desirers, desires, desiring, desiringly, desirous, desirously, desirousness, desist, desistance, desisted, desistence, desisting, desistive, desists, desition, desitive, desize, desk, desk's, deskbound, deskill, desklike, deskman, deskmen, desks, desktop, deslime, desma, desmachymatous, desmachyme, desmacyte, desman, desmans, desmarestiaceous, desmectasia, desmepithelium, desmic, desmid, desmidiaceous, desmidian, desmidiologist, desmidiology, desmids, desmine, desmitis, desmocyte, desmocytoma, desmodont, desmodynia, desmogen, desmogenous, desmognathism, desmognathous, desmography, desmohemoblast, desmoid, desmoids, desmolase, desmology, desmoma, desmon, desmoneme, desmoneoplasm, desmonosology, desmopathologist, desmopathology, desmopathy, desmopelmous, desmopexia, desmopyknosis, desmorrhexis, desmose, desmosis, desmosite, desmosome, desmotomy, desmotrope, desmotropic, desmotropism, desmotropy, desobligeant, desocialization, desocialize, desoeuvre, desolate, desolated, desolately, desolateness, desolater, desolates, desolating, desolatingly, desolation, desolations, desolative, desolator, desole, desonation, desophisticate, desophistication, desorb, desorbed, desorbing, desorbs, desorption, desoxalate, desoxalic, desoxyanisoin, desoxybenzoin, desoxycinchonine, desoxycorticosterone, desoxyephedrine, desoxymorphine, desoxyribonuclease, desoxyribonucleic, desoxyribonucleoprotein, desoxyribose, despair, despaired, despairer, despairful, despairfully, despairfulness, despairing, despairingly, despairingness, despairs, desparple, despatch, despatched, despatcher, despatchers, despatches, despatching, despeche, despecialization, despecialize, despecificate, despecification, despect, despectant, despeed, despend, desperacy, desperado, desperadoes, desperadoism, desperados, desperance, desperate, desperately, desperateness, desperation, despert, despicability, despicable, despicableness, despicably, despiciency, despin, despiritualization, despiritualize, despisable, despisableness, despisal, despise, despised, despisedness, despisement, despiser, despisers, despises, despising, despisingly, despite, despited, despiteful, despitefully, despitefulness, despiteous, despiteously, despites, despiting, despitous, despoil, despoiled, despoiler, despoilers, despoiling, despoilment, despoilments, despoils, despoliation, despoliations, despond, desponded, despondence, despondencies, despondency, despondent, despondently, despondentness, desponder, desponding, despondingly, desponds, desponsage, desponsate, desponsories, despose, despot, despot's, despotat, despotic, despotical, despotically, despoticalness, despoticly, despotism, despotisms, despotist, despotize, despots, despouse, despraise, despumate, despumated, despumating, despumation, despume, desquamate, desquamated, desquamating, desquamation, desquamative, desquamatory, desray, dess, dessa, dessert, dessert's, desserts, dessertspoon, dessertspoonful, dessertspoonfuls, dessiatine, dessicate, dessil, dessous, dessus, destabilization, destabilize, destabilized, destabilizing, destain, destained, destaining, destains, destalinization, destalinize, destandardize, destemper, desterilization, desterilize, desterilized, desterilizing, destigmatization, destigmatize, destigmatizing, destin, destinal, destinate, destination, destination's, destinations, destine, destined, destines, destinezite, destinies, destining, destinism, destinist, destiny, destiny's, destituent, destitute, destituted, destitutely, destituteness, destituting, destitution, desto, destool, destoolment, destour, destrer, destress, destressed, destrier, destriers, destroy, destroyable, destroyed, destroyer, destroyer's, destroyers, destroying, destroyingly, destroys, destruct, destructed, destructibility, destructible, destructibleness, destructing, destruction, destruction's, destructional, destructionism, destructionist, destructions, destructive, destructively, destructiveness, destructivism, destructivity, destructor, destructors, destructory, destructs, destructuralize, destrudo, destry, destuff, destuffing, destuffs, desubstantialize, desubstantiate, desucration, desudation, desuete, desuetude, desuetudes, desugar, desugared, desugaring, desugarize, desugars, desulfur, desulfurate, desulfurated, desulfurating, desulfuration, desulfured, desulfuring, desulfurisation, desulfurise, desulfurised, desulfuriser, desulfurising, desulfurization, desulfurize, desulfurized, desulfurizer, desulfurizing, desulfurs, desulphur, desulphurate, desulphurated, desulphurating, desulphuration, desulphuret, desulphurise, desulphurised, desulphurising, desulphurization, desulphurize, desulphurized, desulphurizer, desulphurizing, desultor, desultorily, desultoriness, desultorious, desultory, desume, desuperheater, desuvre, desyatin, desyl, desynapsis, desynaptic, desynchronize, desynchronizing, desynonymization, desynonymize, det, detach, detachability, detachable, detachableness, detachably, detache, detached, detachedly, detachedness, detacher, detachers, detaches, detaching, detachment, detachment's, detachments, detachs, detacwable, detail, detailed, detailedly, detailedness, detailer, detailers, detailing, detailism, detailist, details, detain, detainable, detainal, detained, detainee, detainees, detainer, detainers, detaining, detainingly, detainment, detains, detant, detar, detassel, detat, detax, detd, detect, detectability, detectable, detectably, detectaphone, detected, detecter, detecters, detectible, detecting, detection, detection's, detections, detective, detectives, detectivism, detector, detector's, detectors, detects, detenant, detenebrate, detent, detente, detentes, detention, detentive, detents, detenu, detenue, detenues, detenus, deter, deterge, deterged, detergence, detergency, detergent, detergents, deterger, detergers, deterges, detergible, deterging, detering, deteriorate, deteriorated, deteriorates, deteriorating, deterioration, deteriorationist, deteriorations, deteriorative, deteriorator, deteriorism, deteriority, determ, determa, determent, determents, determinability, determinable, determinableness, determinably, determinacy, determinant, determinant's, determinantal, determinants, determinate, determinated, determinately, determinateness, determinating, determination, determinations, determinative, determinatively, determinativeness, determinator, determine, determined, determinedly, determinedness, determiner, determiners, determines, determining, determinism, determinist, deterministic, deterministically, determinists, determinoid, deterrability, deterrable, deterration, deterred, deterrence, deterrent, deterrently, deterrents, deterrer, deterrers, deterring, deters, detersion, detersive, detersively, detersiveness, detest, detestability, detestable, detestableness, detestably, detestation, detestations, detested, detester, detesters, detesting, detests, dethronable, dethrone, dethroned, dethronement, dethronements, dethroner, dethrones, dethroning, dethyroidism, deti, detick, deticked, deticker, detickers, deticking, deticks, detin, detinet, detinue, detinues, detinuit, detn, detonability, detonable, detonatability, detonatable, detonate, detonated, detonates, detonating, detonation, detonational, detonations, detonative, detonator, detonators, detonize, detorsion, detort, detour, detoured, detouring, detournement, detours, detoxicant, detoxicate, detoxicated, detoxicating, detoxication, detoxicator, detoxification, detoxified, detoxifier, detoxifies, detoxify, detoxifying, detract, detracted, detracter, detracting, detractingly, detraction, detractions, detractive, detractively, detractiveness, detractor, detractor's, detractors, detractory, detractress, detracts, detrain, detrained, detraining, detrainment, detrains, detraque, detray, detrect, detrench, detribalization, detribalize, detribalized, detribalizing, detriment, detrimental, detrimentality, detrimentally, detrimentalness, detriments, detrital, detrited, detrition, detritivorous, detritus, detrivorous, detroit, detruck, detrude, detruded, detrudes, detruding, detruncate, detruncated, detruncating, detruncation, detrusion, detrusive, detrusor, detruss, dette, detubation, detumescence, detumescent, detune, detuned, detuning, detur, deturb, deturn, deturpate, deucalion, deuce, deuced, deucedly, deuces, deucing, deul, deunam, deuniting, deurbanize, deurwaarder, deus, deusan, deutencephalic, deutencephalon, deuteragonist, deuteranomal, deuteranomalous, deuteranomaly, deuteranope, deuteranopia, deuteranopic, deuterate, deuteration, deuteric, deuteride, deuterium, deuteroalbumose, deuterocanonical, deuterocasease, deuterocone, deuteroconid, deuterodome, deuteroelastose, deuterofibrinose, deuterogamist, deuterogamy, deuterogelatose, deuterogenesis, deuterogenic, deuteroglobulose, deuteromorphic, deuteromyosinose, deuteron, deuteronomic, deuteronomist, deuteronomy, deuterons, deuteropathic, deuteropathy, deuteroplasm, deuteroprism, deuteroproteose, deuteroscopic, deuteroscopy, deuterostoma, deuterostomatous, deuterostome, deuterosy, deuterotokous, deuterotoky, deuterotype, deuterovitellose, deuterozooid, deutobromide, deutocarbonate, deutochloride, deutomala, deutomalal, deutomalar, deutomerite, deuton, deutonephron, deutonymph, deutonymphal, deutoplasm, deutoplasmic, deutoplastic, deutoscolex, deutovum, deutoxide, deutsche, deutschemark, deutschland, deutzia, deutzias, deux, deuzan, dev, deva, devachan, devadasi, deval, devall, devaloka, devalorize, devaluate, devaluated, devaluates, devaluating, devaluation, devaluations, devalue, devalued, devalues, devaluing, devanagari, devance, devant, devaporate, devaporation, devaraja, devarshi, devas, devast, devastate, devastated, devastates, devastating, devastatingly, devastation, devastations, devastative, devastator, devastators, devastavit, devaster, devata, devaul, devaunt, devchar, deve, devein, deveined, deveining, deveins, devel, develed, develin, develing, develop, developability, developable, develope, developed, developedness, developement, developer, developers, developes, developing, developist, development, development's, developmental, developmentalist, developmentally, developmentarian, developmentary, developmentist, developments, developoid, developpe, developpes, develops, devels, devenustate, deverbative, devertebrated, devest, devested, devesting, devests, devex, devexity, devi, deviability, deviable, deviance, deviances, deviancies, deviancy, deviant, deviant's, deviants, deviascope, deviate, deviated, deviately, deviates, deviating, deviation, deviational, deviationism, deviationist, deviations, deviative, deviator, deviators, deviatory, device, device's, deviceful, devicefully, devicefulness, devices, devide, devil, devil's, devilbird, devildom, deviled, deviler, deviless, devilet, devilfish, devilfishes, devilhood, deviling, devilish, devilishly, devilishness, devilism, devility, devilize, devilized, devilizing, devilkin, devilkins, devilled, devillike, devilling, devilman, devilment, devilments, devilmonger, devilries, devilry, devils, devilship, deviltries, deviltry, devilward, devilwise, devilwood, devily, devinct, devious, deviously, deviousness, devirginate, devirgination, devirginator, devirilize, devisability, devisable, devisal, devisals, deviscerate, devisceration, devise, devised, devisee, devisees, deviser, devisers, devises, devising, devisings, devisor, devisors, devitalisation, devitalise, devitalised, devitalising, devitalization, devitalize, devitalized, devitalizes, devitalizing, devitaminize, devitation, devitrifiable, devitrification, devitrified, devitrify, devitrifying, devocalisation, devocalise, devocalised, devocalising, devocalization, devocalize, devocalized, devocalizing, devocate, devocation, devoice, devoiced, devoices, devoicing, devoid, devoir, devoirs, devolatilisation, devolatilise, devolatilised, devolatilising, devolatilization, devolatilize, devolatilized, devolatilizing, devolute, devolution, devolutionary, devolutionist, devolutive, devolve, devolved, devolvement, devolvements, devolves, devolving, devon, devonian, devonite, devonport, devons, devonshire, devoration, devorative, devot, devota, devotary, devote, devoted, devotedly, devotedness, devotee, devotee's, devoteeism, devotees, devotement, devoter, devotes, devoting, devotion, devotional, devotionalism, devotionalist, devotionality, devotionally, devotionalness, devotionary, devotionate, devotionist, devotions, devoto, devour, devourable, devoured, devourer, devourers, devouress, devouring, devouringly, devouringness, devourment, devours, devout, devoutful, devoutless, devoutlessly, devoutlessness, devoutly, devoutness, devove, devow, devs, devulcanization, devulcanize, devulgarize, devvel, devwsor, dew, dewal, dewan, dewanee, dewani, dewanny, dewans, dewanship, dewar, dewata, dewater, dewatered, dewaterer, dewatering, dewaters, dewax, dewaxed, dewaxes, dewaxing, dewbeam, dewberries, dewberry, dewcap, dewclaw, dewclawed, dewclaws, dewcup, dewdamp, dewdrop, dewdrop's, dewdropper, dewdrops, dewed, dewer, deweylite, dewfall, dewfalls, dewflower, dewier, dewiest, dewily, dewiness, dewinesses, dewing, dewitt, dewlap, dewlapped, dewlaps, dewless, dewlight, dewlike, dewool, dewooled, dewooling, dewools, deworm, dewormed, deworming, deworms, dewret, dewrot, dews, dewtry, dewworm, dewy, dex, dexamethasone, dexes, dexies, dexiocardia, dexiotrope, dexiotropic, dexiotropism, dexiotropous, dexter, dexterical, dexterity, dexterous, dexterously, dexterousness, dextorsal, dextrad, dextral, dextrality, dextrally, dextran, dextranase, dextrane, dextrans, dextraural, dextrer, dextrin, dextrinase, dextrinate, dextrine, dextrines, dextrinize, dextrinous, dextrins, dextro, dextroamphetamine, dextroaural, dextrocardia, dextrocardial, dextrocerebral, dextrocular, dextrocularity, dextroduction, dextroglucose, dextrogyrate, dextrogyration, dextrogyratory, dextrogyre, dextrogyrous, dextrolactic, dextrolimonene, dextromanual, dextropedal, dextropinene, dextrorotary, dextrorotatary, dextrorotation, dextrorotatory, dextrorsal, dextrorse, dextrorsely, dextrosazone, dextrose, dextroses, dextrosinistral, dextrosinistrally, dextrosuria, dextrotartaric, dextrotropic, dextrotropous, dextrous, dextrously, dextrousness, dextroversion, dey, deyhouse, deynt, deys, deyship, deywoman, dezinc, dezincation, dezinced, dezincification, dezincified, dezincify, dezincifying, dezincing, dezincked, dezincking, dezincs, dezinkify, dezymotize, dfault, dft, dg, dgag, dghaisa, dha, dhabb, dhai, dhak, dhaks, dhal, dhaman, dhamma, dhamnoo, dhan, dhangar, dhanuk, dhanush, dharana, dharani, dharma, dharmakaya, dharmas, dharmashastra, dharmasmriti, dharmasutra, dharmic, dharmsala, dharna, dharnas, dhaura, dhauri, dhava, dhaw, dheri, dhikr, dhikrs, dhobee, dhobey, dhobi, dhobie, dhobies, dhobis, dhoby, dhole, dholes, dhoney, dhoni, dhooley, dhoolies, dhooly, dhoon, dhoora, dhooras, dhooti, dhootie, dhooties, dhootis, dhotee, dhoti, dhotis, dhoty, dhoul, dhourra, dhourras, dhow, dhows, dhu, dhunchee, dhunchi, dhurna, dhurnas, dhurra, dhurrie, dhurry, dhuti, dhutis, dhyal, dhyana, di, dia, diabantite, diabase, diabases, diabasic, diabaterial, diabetes, diabetic, diabetical, diabetics, diabetogenic, diabetogenous, diabetometer, diabetophobia, diable, diablene, diablerie, diableries, diablery, diablo, diablotin, diabolarch, diabolarchy, diabolatry, diabolepsy, diaboleptic, diabolic, diabolical, diabolically, diabolicalness, diabolification, diabolifuge, diabolify, diabolisation, diabolise, diabolised, diabolising, diabolism, diabolist, diabolization, diabolize, diabolized, diabolizing, diabolo, diabological, diabology, diabolology, diabolonian, diabolos, diabolus, diabrosis, diabrotic, diacanthous, diacatholicon, diacaustic, diacetamide, diacetate, diacetic, diacetin, diacetine, diacetonuria, diaceturia, diacetyl, diacetylene, diacetylmorphine, diacetyls, diachaenium, diachoresis, diachoretic, diachronic, diachronically, diachronicness, diachrony, diachylon, diachylum, diachyma, diacid, diacidic, diacids, diacipiperazine, diaclase, diaclasis, diaclasite, diaclastic, diacle, diaclinal, diacoca, diacodion, diacodium, diacoele, diacoelia, diacoelosis, diaconal, diaconate, diaconia, diaconica, diaconicon, diaconicum, diaconus, diacope, diacoustics, diacranterian, diacranteric, diacrisis, diacritic, diacritical, diacritically, diacritics, diacromyodian, diact, diactin, diactinal, diactine, diactinic, diactinism, diaculum, diadelphia, diadelphian, diadelphic, diadelphous, diadem, diademed, diademing, diadems, diaderm, diadermic, diadic, diadkokinesia, diadoche, diadochian, diadochic, diadochite, diadochokinesia, diadochokinesis, diadochokinetic, diadochy, diadokokinesis, diadoumenos, diadrom, diadrome, diadromous, diadumenus, diaene, diaereses, diaeresis, diaeretic, diaetetae, diag, diagenesis, diagenetic, diagenetically, diageotropic, diageotropism, diageotropy, diaglyph, diaglyphic, diaglyptic, diagnosable, diagnose, diagnoseable, diagnosed, diagnoses, diagnosing, diagnosis, diagnostic, diagnostic's, diagnostical, diagnostically, diagnosticate, diagnosticated, diagnosticating, diagnostication, diagnostician, diagnosticians, diagnostics, diagometer, diagonal, diagonality, diagonalizable, diagonalization, diagonalize, diagonally, diagonals, diagonalwise, diagonial, diagonic, diagram, diagram's, diagramed, diagraming, diagrammable, diagrammatic, diagrammatical, diagrammatically, diagrammatician, diagrammatize, diagrammed, diagrammer, diagrammer's, diagrammers, diagrammeter, diagramming, diagrammitically, diagrams, diagraph, diagraphic, diagraphical, diagraphics, diagraphs, diagredium, diagrydium, diaheliotropic, diaheliotropically, diaheliotropism, diaka, diakineses, diakinesis, diakinetic, diakonika, diakonikon, dial, dialcohol, dialdehyde, dialect, dialect's, dialectal, dialectalize, dialectally, dialectic, dialectical, dialectically, dialectician, dialecticism, dialecticize, dialectics, dialectologer, dialectologic, dialectological, dialectologically, dialectologies, dialectologist, dialectology, dialector, dialects, dialed, dialer, dialers, dialin, dialiness, dialing, dialings, dialist, dialists, dialkyl, dialkylamine, dialkylic, diallage, diallages, diallagic, diallagite, diallagoid, dialled, diallel, diallela, dialleli, diallelon, diallelus, dialler, diallers, dialling, diallings, diallist, diallists, diallyl, dialog, dialog's, dialoger, dialogers, dialogged, dialogging, dialogic, dialogical, dialogically, dialogised, dialogising, dialogism, dialogist, dialogistic, dialogistical, dialogistically, dialogite, dialogize, dialogized, dialogizing, dialogs, dialogue, dialogue's, dialogued, dialoguer, dialogues, dialoguing, dials, dialup, dialuric, dialycarpous, dialypetalous, dialyphyllous, dialysability, dialysable, dialysate, dialysation, dialyse, dialysed, dialysepalous, dialyser, dialysers, dialyses, dialysing, dialysis, dialystaminous, dialystelic, dialystely, dialytic, dialytically, dialyzability, dialyzable, dialyzate, dialyzation, dialyzator, dialyze, dialyzed, dialyzer, dialyzers, dialyzes, dialyzing, diam, diamagnet, diamagnetic, diamagnetically, diamagnetism, diamagnetize, diamagnetometer, diamant, diamante, diamantiferous, diamantine, diamantoid, diamat, diamb, diamber, diambic, diamegnetism, diamesogamous, diameter, diameter's, diameters, diametral, diametrally, diametric, diametrical, diametrically, diamicton, diamide, diamides, diamido, diamidogen, diamin, diamine, diamines, diaminogen, diaminogene, diamins, diammine, diamminobromide, diamminonitrate, diammonium, diamond, diamond's, diamondback, diamondbacked, diamondbacks, diamonded, diamondiferous, diamonding, diamondize, diamondized, diamondizing, diamondlike, diamonds, diamondwise, diamondwork, diamorphine, diamorphosis, diamyl, diamylene, diamylose, dian, diana, diander, diandria, diandrian, diandrous, diane, dianetics, dianilid, dianilide, dianisidin, dianisidine, dianite, dianodal, dianoetic, dianoetical, dianoetically, dianoia, dianoialogy, dianthus, dianthuses, diantre, diapalma, diapase, diapasm, diapason, diapasonal, diapasons, diapause, diapaused, diapauses, diapausing, diapedeses, diapedesis, diapedetic, diapensiaceous, diapente, diaper, diaper's, diapered, diapering, diapers, diapery, diaphane, diaphaneity, diaphanie, diaphanometer, diaphanometric, diaphanometry, diaphanoscope, diaphanoscopy, diaphanotype, diaphanous, diaphanously, diaphanousness, diaphany, diaphemetric, diaphone, diaphones, diaphonia, diaphonic, diaphonical, diaphonies, diaphony, diaphorase, diaphoreses, diaphoresis, diaphoretic, diaphoretical, diaphoretics, diaphorite, diaphote, diaphototropic, diaphototropism, diaphragm, diaphragm's, diaphragmal, diaphragmatic, diaphragmatically, diaphragmed, diaphragming, diaphragms, diaphtherin, diaphyseal, diaphyses, diaphysial, diaphysis, diapir, diapiric, diapirs, diaplases, diaplasis, diaplasma, diaplex, diaplexal, diaplexus, diapnoe, diapnoic, diapnotic, diapophyses, diapophysial, diapophysis, diaporesis, diapositive, diapsid, diapsidan, diapyesis, diapyetic, diarch, diarchial, diarchic, diarchies, diarchy, diarhemia, diarial, diarian, diaries, diarist, diaristic, diarists, diarize, diarrhea, diarrheal, diarrheas, diarrheic, diarrhetic, diarrhoea, diarrhoeal, diarrhoeic, diarrhoetic, diarsenide, diarthric, diarthrodial, diarthroses, diarthrosis, diarticular, diary, diary's, dias, diaschisis, diaschisma, diaschistic, diascope, diascopy, diascord, diascordium, diasene, diaskeuasis, diaskeuast, diasper, diaspidine, diaspine, diaspirin, diaspora, diasporas, diaspore, diaspores, diastalses, diastalsis, diastaltic, diastase, diastases, diastasic, diastasimetry, diastasis, diastataxic, diastataxy, diastatic, diastatically, diastem, diastema, diastemata, diastematic, diastematomyelia, diaster, diastereoisomer, diastereoisomeric, diastereoisomerism, diastereomer, diasters, diastimeter, diastole, diastoles, diastolic, diastomatic, diastral, diastrophe, diastrophic, diastrophically, diastrophism, diastrophy, diastyle, diasynthesis, diasyrm, diasystem, diatessaron, diatesseron, diathermacy, diathermal, diathermance, diathermancy, diathermaneity, diathermanous, diathermia, diathermic, diathermies, diathermize, diathermometer, diathermotherapy, diathermous, diathermy, diatheses, diathesic, diathesis, diathetic, diatom, diatomacean, diatomaceoid, diatomaceous, diatomean, diatomic, diatomicity, diatomiferous, diatomin, diatomine, diatomist, diatomite, diatomous, diatoms, diatonic, diatonical, diatonically, diatonicism, diatonous, diatoric, diatreme, diatribe, diatribe's, diatribes, diatribist, diatropic, diatropism, diatryma, diauli, diaulic, diaulos, diavolo, diaxial, diaxon, diaxone, diaxonic, diazenithal, diazepam, diazepams, diazeuctic, diazeutic, diazeuxis, diazid, diazide, diazin, diazine, diazines, diazins, diazo, diazoalkane, diazoamin, diazoamine, diazoamino, diazoaminobenzene, diazoanhydride, diazoate, diazobenzene, diazohydroxide, diazoic, diazoimide, diazoimido, diazole, diazoles, diazoma, diazomethane, diazonium, diazotate, diazotic, diazotizability, diazotizable, diazotization, diazotize, diazotized, diazotizing, diazotype, dib, dibase, dibasic, dibasicity, dibatag, dibbed, dibber, dibbers, dibbing, dibble, dibbled, dibbler, dibblers, dibbles, dibbling, dibbuk, dibbukim, dibbuks, dibenzophenazine, dibenzopyrrole, dibenzoyl, dibenzyl, dibhole, diblastula, diborate, dibrach, dibranch, dibranchiate, dibranchious, dibrom, dibromid, dibromide, dibromoacetaldehyde, dibromobenzene, dibs, dibstone, dibstones, dibucaine, dibutyl, dibutyrate, dibutyrin, dicacity, dicacodyl, dicaeology, dicalcic, dicalcium, dicarbonate, dicarbonic, dicarboxylate, dicarboxylic, dicarpellary, dicaryon, dicaryophase, dicaryophyte, dicaryotic, dicast, dicasteries, dicastery, dicastic, dicasts, dicatalectic, dicatalexis, dice, diceboard, dicebox, dicecup, diced, dicellate, diceman, dicentra, dicentras, dicentrin, dicentrine, dicephalism, dicephalous, dicephalus, diceplay, dicer, dicerion, dicerous, dicers, dices, dicetyl, dicey, dich, dichas, dichasia, dichasial, dichasium, dichastasis, dichastic, dichlamydeous, dichlone, dichloramin, dichloramine, dichlorhydrin, dichloride, dichloroacetic, dichlorobenzene, dichlorodifluoromethane, dichlorodiphenyltrichloroethane, dichlorohydrin, dichloromethane, dichlorvos, dichocarpism, dichocarpous, dichogamic, dichogamous, dichogamy, dichondra, dichopodial, dichoptic, dichord, dichoree, dichotic, dichotically, dichotomal, dichotomic, dichotomically, dichotomies, dichotomisation, dichotomise, dichotomised, dichotomising, dichotomist, dichotomistic, dichotomization, dichotomize, dichotomized, dichotomizing, dichotomous, dichotomously, dichotomousness, dichotomy, dichotriaene, dichroic, dichroiscope, dichroiscopic, dichroism, dichroite, dichroitic, dichromasia, dichromasy, dichromat, dichromate, dichromatic, dichromaticism, dichromatism, dichromatopsia, dichromic, dichromism, dichronous, dichrooscope, dichrooscopic, dichroous, dichroscope, dichroscopic, dicht, dicier, diciest, dicing, dick, dickcissel, dickens, dickenses, dickensian, dicker, dickered, dickering, dickers, dickey, dickeybird, dickeys, dickie, dickies, dickinsonite, dickite, dicks, dickty, dicky, dickybird, diclesium, diclinic, diclinies, diclinism, diclinous, dicliny, dicoccous, dicodeine, dicoelious, dicoelous, dicolic, dicolon, dicondylian, dicophane, dicot, dicots, dicotyl, dicotyledon, dicotyledonary, dicotyledonous, dicotyledons, dicotylous, dicotyls, dicoumarin, dicoumarol, dicranaceous, dicranoid, dicranterian, dicrostonyx, dicrotal, dicrotic, dicrotism, dicrotous, dict, dicta, dictagraph, dictamen, dictamina, dictaphone, dictaphones, dictate, dictated, dictates, dictating, dictatingly, dictation, dictational, dictations, dictative, dictator, dictator's, dictatorial, dictatorialism, dictatorially, dictatorialness, dictators, dictatorship, dictatorships, dictatory, dictatress, dictatrix, dictature, dictery, dictic, diction, dictional, dictionally, dictionarian, dictionaries, dictionary, dictionary's, dictions, dictograph, dictronics, dictum, dictum's, dictums, dicty, dictynid, dictyoceratine, dictyodromous, dictyogen, dictyogenous, dictyoid, dictyonine, dictyopteran, dictyosiphonaceous, dictyosome, dictyostele, dictyostelic, dictyotaceous, dictyotic, dicyan, dicyandiamide, dicyanid, dicyanide, dicyanin, dicyanine, dicyanodiamide, dicyanogen, dicycle, dicyclic, dicyclies, dicyclist, dicyclopentadienyliron, dicycly, dicyemid, dicynodont, did, didache, didact, didactic, didactical, didacticality, didactically, didactician, didacticism, didacticity, didactics, didactive, didacts, didactyl, didactylism, didactylous, didal, didapper, didappers, didascalar, didascaliae, didascalic, didascalos, didascaly, didder, diddered, diddering, diddest, diddies, diddikai, diddle, diddled, diddler, diddlers, diddles, diddling, diddy, didelph, didelphian, didelphic, didelphid, didelphine, didelphoid, didelphous, didepsid, didepside, didest, didgeridoo, didicoy, didie, didies, didine, didle, didler, didn, didn't, didna, didnt, dido, didodecahedral, didodecahedron, didoes, didonia, didos, didrachm, didrachma, didrachmal, didrachmas, didric, didromies, didromy, didst, diduce, diduced, diducing, diduction, diductively, diductor, didy, didym, didymate, didymia, didymis, didymitis, didymium, didymiums, didymoid, didymolite, didymous, didymus, didynamia, didynamian, didynamic, didynamies, didynamous, didynamy, die, dieb, dieback, diebacks, diecase, diecious, dieciously, diectasis, died, diedral, diedric, diegesis, diego, diehard, diehards, dieing, diel, dieldrin, dieldrins, dielec, dielectric, dielectric's, dielectrical, dielectrically, dielectrics, dielike, diem, diemaker, diemakers, diemaking, diencephala, diencephalic, diencephalon, diencephalons, diene, diener, dienes, dier, diereses, dieresis, dieretic, dies, diesel, dieselization, dieselize, dieselized, dieselizing, diesels, dieses, diesinker, diesinking, diesis, diester, diesters, diestock, diestocks, diestrous, diestrual, diestrum, diestrums, diestrus, diestruses, diet, dietal, dietarian, dietaries, dietarily, dietary, dieted, dieter, dieters, dietetic, dietetical, dietetically, dietetics, dietetist, diethanolamine, diether, diethyl, diethylacetal, diethylamide, diethylamine, diethylaminoethanol, diethylenediamine, diethylethanolamine, diethylmalonylurea, diethylstilbestrol, diethylstilboestrol, diethyltryptamine, dietic, dietical, dietician, dieticians, dietics, dieties, dietine, dieting, dietist, dietitian, dietitian's, dietitians, dietotherapeutics, dietotherapy, dietotoxic, dietotoxicity, dietrichite, diets, dietted, diety, dietzeite, dieugard, diewise, diezeugmenon, dif, diferrion, diff, diffame, diffareation, diffarreation, diffeomorphic, diffeomorphism, differ, differed, differen, difference, difference's, differenced, differences, differencing, differencingly, differency, different, differentia, differentiability, differentiable, differentiae, differential, differential's, differentialize, differentially, differentials, differentiant, differentiate, differentiated, differentiates, differentiating, differentiation, differentiations, differentiative, differentiator, differentiators, differently, differentness, differer, differers, differing, differingly, differs, difficile, difficileness, difficilitate, difficult, difficulties, difficultly, difficultness, difficulty, difficulty's, diffidation, diffide, diffided, diffidence, diffident, diffidently, diffidentness, diffiding, diffinity, difflation, diffluence, diffluent, difform, difforme, difformed, difformity, diffract, diffracted, diffracting, diffraction, diffractional, diffractions, diffractive, diffractively, diffractiveness, diffractometer, diffracts, diffranchise, diffrangibility, diffrangible, diffugient, diffund, diffusate, diffuse, diffused, diffusedly, diffusedness, diffusely, diffuseness, diffuser, diffusers, diffuses, diffusibility, diffusible, diffusibleness, diffusibly, diffusimeter, diffusing, diffusiometer, diffusion, diffusional, diffusionism, diffusionist, diffusions, diffusive, diffusively, diffusiveness, diffusivity, diffusor, diffusors, difluence, difluoride, diformin, difunctional, dig, digallate, digallic, digametic, digamies, digamist, digamists, digamma, digammas, digammate, digammated, digammic, digamous, digamy, digastric, digeneous, digenesis, digenetic, digenic, digenite, digenous, digeny, digerent, digest, digestant, digested, digestedly, digestedness, digester, digesters, digestibility, digestible, digestibleness, digestibly, digestif, digesting, digestion, digestional, digestive, digestively, digestiveness, digestment, digestor, digestors, digestory, digests, digesture, diggable, digged, digger, digger's, diggers, digging, diggings, dight, dighted, dighter, dighting, dights, digit, digit's, digital, digitalein, digitalic, digitaliform, digitalin, digitalis, digitalism, digitalization, digitalize, digitalized, digitalizing, digitally, digitals, digitate, digitated, digitately, digitation, digitiform, digitigrade, digitigradism, digitinervate, digitinerved, digitipinnate, digitisation, digitise, digitised, digitising, digitization, digitize, digitized, digitizer, digitizes, digitizing, digitogenin, digitonin, digitoplantar, digitorium, digitoxigenin, digitoxin, digitoxose, digitron, digits, digitule, digitus, digladiate, digladiated, digladiating, digladiation, digladiator, diglossia, diglot, diglots, diglottic, diglottism, diglottist, diglucoside, diglyceride, diglyph, diglyphic, digmeat, dignation, digne, dignification, dignified, dignifiedly, dignifiedness, dignifies, dignify, dignifying, dignitarial, dignitarian, dignitaries, dignitary, dignitas, dignities, dignity, dignosce, dignosle, dignotion, digonal, digoneutic, digoneutism, digonoporous, digonous, digoxin, digoxins, digram, digraph, digraphic, digraphically, digraphs, digredience, digrediency, digredient, digress, digressed, digresser, digresses, digressing, digressingly, digression, digression's, digressional, digressionary, digressions, digressive, digressively, digressiveness, digressory, digs, diguanide, digue, digynia, digynian, digynous, dihalid, dihalide, dihalo, dihalogen, dihdroxycholecalciferol, dihedral, dihedrals, dihedron, dihedrons, dihelios, dihelium, dihely, dihexagonal, dihexahedral, dihexahedron, dihybrid, dihybridism, dihybrids, dihydrate, dihydrated, dihydrazone, dihydric, dihydride, dihydrite, dihydrochloride, dihydrocupreine, dihydrocuprin, dihydroergotamine, dihydrogen, dihydrol, dihydromorphinone, dihydronaphthalene, dihydronicotine, dihydrosphingosine, dihydrostreptomycin, dihydrotachysterol, dihydroxy, dihydroxyacetone, dihydroxysuccinic, dihydroxytoluene, dihysteria, diiamb, diiambus, diiodid, diiodide, diiodo, diiodoform, diiodotyrosine, diipenates, diisatogen, dijudicant, dijudicate, dijudicated, dijudicating, dijudication, dika, dikage, dikamali, dikamalli, dikaryon, dikaryophase, dikaryophasic, dikaryophyte, dikaryophytic, dikaryotic, dikast, dikdik, dikdiks, dike, dike's, diked, dikegrave, dikelet, dikelocephalid, dikephobia, diker, dikereeve, dikeria, dikerion, dikers, dikes, dikeside, diketene, diketo, diketone, diking, dikkop, diksha, diktat, diktats, diktyonite, dil, dilacerate, dilacerated, dilacerating, dilaceration, dilactic, dilactone, dilambdodont, dilamination, dilaniate, dilantin, dilapidate, dilapidated, dilapidating, dilapidation, dilapidator, dilatability, dilatable, dilatableness, dilatably, dilatancy, dilatant, dilatants, dilatate, dilatation, dilatational, dilatations, dilatative, dilatator, dilatatory, dilate, dilated, dilatedly, dilatedness, dilatement, dilater, dilaters, dilates, dilating, dilatingly, dilation, dilations, dilative, dilatometer, dilatometric, dilatometrically, dilatometry, dilator, dilatorily, dilatoriness, dilators, dilatory, dildo, dildoe, dildoes, dildos, dilection, dilemma, dilemma's, dilemmas, dilemmatic, dilemmatical, dilemmatically, dilemmic, diletant, dilettanist, dilettant, dilettante, dilettanteish, dilettanteism, dilettantes, dilettanteship, dilettanti, dilettantish, dilettantism, dilettantist, dilettantship, diligence, diligences, diligency, diligent, diligentia, diligently, diligentness, dilis, dilker, dill, dillenia, dilleniaceous, dilleniad, dillesk, dilli, dillier, dillies, dilligrout, dilling, dillis, dillisk, dills, dillseed, dillue, dilluer, dillweed, dilly, dillydallied, dillydallier, dillydallies, dillydally, dillydallying, dillyman, dillymen, dilo, dilogarithm, dilogical, dilogy, dilos, dilucid, dilucidate, diluendo, diluent, diluents, dilutant, dilute, diluted, dilutedly, dilutedness, dilutee, dilutely, diluteness, dilutent, diluter, diluters, dilutes, diluting, dilution, dilutions, dilutive, dilutor, dilutors, diluvia, diluvial, diluvialist, diluvian, diluvianism, diluviate, diluvion, diluvions, diluvium, diluviums, diluvy, dim, dimagnesic, dimane, dimanganion, dimanganous, dimaris, dimastigate, dimber, dimberdamber, dimble, dime, dime's, dimedon, dimedone, dimenhydrinate, dimensible, dimension, dimensional, dimensionality, dimensionally, dimensioned, dimensioning, dimensionless, dimensions, dimensive, dimensum, dimensuration, dimer, dimeran, dimercaprol, dimercuric, dimercurion, dimercury, dimeric, dimeride, dimerism, dimerisms, dimerization, dimerize, dimerized, dimerizes, dimerizing, dimerlie, dimerous, dimers, dimes, dimetallic, dimeter, dimeters, dimethoate, dimethoxy, dimethoxymethane, dimethyl, dimethylamine, dimethylamino, dimethylaniline, dimethylanthranilate, dimethylbenzene, dimethylcarbinol, dimethyldiketone, dimethylhydrazine, dimethylketol, dimethylketone, dimethylmethane, dimethylnitrosamine, dimethyls, dimethylsulfoxide, dimethylsulphoxide, dimethyltryptamine, dimetient, dimetria, dimetric, dimetrodon, dimication, dimidiate, dimidiated, dimidiating, dimidiation, dimin, diminish, diminishable, diminishableness, diminished, diminisher, diminishes, diminishing, diminishingly, diminishingturns, diminishment, diminishments, diminue, diminuendo, diminuendoed, diminuendoes, diminuendos, diminuent, diminutal, diminute, diminuted, diminutely, diminuting, diminution, diminutional, diminutions, diminutival, diminutive, diminutively, diminutiveness, diminutivize, dimiss, dimissaries, dimission, dimissorial, dimissory, dimit, dimities, dimitted, dimitting, dimity, dimly, dimmable, dimmed, dimmedness, dimmer, dimmer's, dimmers, dimmest, dimmet, dimming, dimmish, dimmit, dimmock, dimmy, dimness, dimnesses, dimolecular, dimoric, dimorph, dimorphic, dimorphism, dimorphisms, dimorphite, dimorphotheca, dimorphous, dimorphs, dimout, dimouts, dimple, dimpled, dimplement, dimples, dimplier, dimpliest, dimpling, dimply, dimps, dimpsy, dims, dimuence, dimwit, dimwits, dimwitted, dimwittedly, dimwittedness, dimyarian, dimyaric, dimyary, din, dinamode, dinanderie, dinaphthyl, dinar, dinarchies, dinarchy, dinars, dinder, dindle, dindled, dindles, dindling, dindon, dine, dined, diner, dinergate, dineric, dinero, dineros, diners, dines, dinetic, dinette, dinettes, dineuric, dineutron, ding, dingar, dingbat, dingbats, dingdong, dingdonged, dingdonging, dingdongs, dinge, dinged, dingee, dingeing, dinger, dingey, dingeys, dinghee, dinghies, dinghy, dingier, dingies, dingiest, dingily, dinginess, dinging, dingle, dingleberry, dinglebird, dingled, dingledangle, dingles, dingling, dingly, dingman, dingmaul, dingo, dingoes, dings, dingthrift, dingus, dinguses, dingwall, dingy, dinheiro, dinic, dinical, dinichthyid, dining, dinitrate, dinitril, dinitrile, dinitro, dinitrobenzene, dinitrocellulose, dinitrophenol, dinitrophenylhydrazine, dinitrotoluene, dink, dinked, dinkey, dinkeys, dinkier, dinkies, dinkiest, dinking, dinkly, dinks, dinkum, dinky, dinman, dinmont, dinned, dinner, dinner's, dinnerless, dinnerly, dinners, dinnertime, dinnerware, dinnery, dinning, dinoceras, dinoceratan, dinoceratid, dinoflagellate, dinomic, dinornis, dinornithic, dinornithid, dinornithine, dinornithoid, dinos, dinosaur, dinosaurian, dinosauric, dinosaurs, dinothere, dinotherian, dins, dinsome, dint, dinted, dinting, dintless, dints, dinucleotide, dinumeration, dinus, diobely, diobol, diobolon, diobolons, diobols, dioc, diocesan, diocesans, diocese, dioceses, diocesian, diocoel, dioctahedral, diode, diode's, diodes, diodon, diodont, dioecia, dioecian, dioeciodimorphous, dioeciopolygamous, dioecious, dioeciously, dioeciousness, dioecism, dioecisms, dioecy, dioestrous, dioestrum, dioestrus, diogenes, diogenite, dioicous, dioicously, dioicousness, diol, diolefin, diolefine, diolefinic, diolefins, diols, diomate, diomedes, dionaea, dionise, dionize, dionym, dionymal, dionysia, dionysiac, dionysian, dionysus, diophantine, diophysite, diopside, diopsides, diopsidic, diopsimeter, dioptase, dioptases, diopter, diopters, dioptograph, dioptometer, dioptometry, dioptomiter, dioptoscopy, dioptra, dioptral, dioptrate, dioptre, dioptres, dioptric, dioptrical, dioptrically, dioptrics, dioptrometer, dioptrometry, dioptroscopy, dioptry, diorama, dioramas, dioramic, diordinal, diorism, diorite, diorites, dioritic, diorthoses, diorthosis, diorthotic, dioscoreaceous, dioscorein, dioscorine, dioscuri, diose, diosgenin, diosmin, diosmose, diosmosed, diosmosing, diosmosis, diosmotic, diosphenol, diospyraceous, diota, diothelism, dioti, diotic, diotrephes, diovular, dioxan, dioxane, dioxanes, dioxid, dioxide, dioxides, dioxids, dioxime, dioxin, dioxindole, dioxy, dip, diparentum, dipartite, dipartition, dipaschal, dipchick, dipcoat, dipentene, dipentine, dipeptid, dipeptidase, dipeptide, dipetalous, dipetto, diphase, diphaser, diphasic, diphead, diphenan, diphenhydramine, diphenol, diphenoxylate, diphenyl, diphenylacetylene, diphenylamine, diphenylaminechlorarsine, diphenylchloroarsine, diphenylene, diphenylenimide, diphenylenimine, diphenylguanidine, diphenylhydantoin, diphenylmethane, diphenylquinomethane, diphenyls, diphenylthiourea, diphonia, diphosgene, diphosphate, diphosphid, diphosphide, diphosphoric, diphosphothiamine, diphrelatic, diphtheria, diphtherial, diphtherian, diphtheriaphor, diphtheric, diphtheritic, diphtheritically, diphtheritis, diphtheroid, diphtheroidal, diphtherotoxin, diphthong, diphthongal, diphthongalize, diphthongally, diphthongation, diphthonged, diphthongia, diphthongic, diphthonging, diphthongisation, diphthongise, diphthongised, diphthongising, diphthongization, diphthongize, diphthongized, diphthongizing, diphthongous, diphthongs, diphycercal, diphycercy, diphyesis, diphygenic, diphyletic, diphyllous, diphyodont, diphyozooid, diphysite, diphyzooid, dipicrate, dipicrylamin, dipicrylamine, dipl, diplacuses, diplacusis, diplanar, diplanetic, diplanetism, diplantidian, diplarthrism, diplarthrous, diplasiasmus, diplasic, diplasion, diple, diplegia, diplegias, diplegic, dipleidoscope, dipleiodoscope, dipleura, dipleural, dipleuric, dipleurobranchiate, dipleurogenesis, dipleurogenetic, dipleurula, dipleurulas, dipleurule, diplex, diplexer, diplobacillus, diplobacterium, diploblastic, diplocardia, diplocardiac, diplocaulescent, diplocephalous, diplocephalus, diplocephaly, diplochlamydeous, diplococcal, diplococcemia, diplococci, diplococcic, diplococcoci, diplococcoid, diplococcus, diploconical, diplocoria, diplodocus, diplodocuses, diploe, diploes, diploetic, diplogangliate, diplogenesis, diplogenetic, diplogenic, diploglossate, diplograph, diplographic, diplographical, diplography, diplohedral, diplohedron, diploic, diploid, diploidic, diploidies, diploidion, diploidize, diploids, diploidy, diplois, diplokaryon, diploma, diploma's, diplomacies, diplomacy, diplomaed, diplomaing, diplomas, diplomat, diplomat's, diplomata, diplomate, diplomates, diplomatic, diplomatical, diplomatically, diplomatics, diplomatique, diplomatism, diplomatist, diplomatists, diplomatize, diplomatized, diplomatology, diplomats, diplomyelia, diplonema, diplonephridia, diploneural, diplont, diplontic, diplonts, diploperistomic, diplophase, diplophonia, diplophonic, diplophyte, diplopia, diplopiaphobia, diplopias, diplopic, diploplacula, diploplacular, diploplaculate, diplopod, diplopodic, diplopodous, diplopods, diplopterous, diplopy, diploses, diplosis, diplosome, diplosphenal, diplosphene, diplospondylic, diplospondylism, diplostemonous, diplostemony, diplostichous, diplotegia, diplotene, diplozoon, diplumbic, dipmeter, dipneedle, dipneumonous, dipneust, dipneustal, dipnoan, dipnoans, dipnoid, dipnoous, dipode, dipodic, dipodid, dipodies, dipody, dipolar, dipolarization, dipolarize, dipole, dipoles, dipolsphene, diporpa, dipotassic, dipotassium, dippable, dipped, dipper, dipper's, dipperful, dippers, dippier, dippiest, dipping, dippings, dipppier, dipppiest, dipppy, dippy, diprimary, diprismatic, dipropargyl, dipropellant, dipropyl, diprotic, diprotodan, diprotodont, dips, dipsacaceous, dipsaceous, dipsades, dipsadine, dipsas, dipsetic, dipsey, dipsie, dipso, dipsomania, dipsomaniac, dipsomaniacal, dipsomaniacs, dipsopathy, dipsos, dipsosis, dipstick, dipsticks, dipsy, dipt, dipter, diptera, dipteraceous, dipterad, dipteral, dipteran, dipterans, dipterist, dipterocarp, dipterocarpaceous, dipterocarpous, dipterocecidium, dipteroi, dipterological, dipterologist, dipterology, dipteron, dipteros, dipterous, dipterus, dipterygian, diptote, diptyca, diptycas, diptych, diptychon, diptychs, dipus, dipware, dipygi, dipygus, dipylon, dipyramid, dipyramidal, dipyre, dipyrenous, dipyridyl, diquat, diquats, dir, diradiation, dircaean, dird, dirdum, dirdums, dire, direcly, direct, directable, directcarving, directdiscourse, directed, directer, directest, directeur, directexamination, directing, direction, direction's, directional, directionality, directionalize, directionally, directionize, directionless, directions, directitude, directive, directive's, directively, directiveness, directives, directivity, directly, directness, directoire, director, director's, directoral, directorate, directorates, directorial, directorially, directories, directors, directorship, directorships, directory, directory's, directress, directrices, directrix, directrixes, directs, direful, direfully, direfulness, direly, dirempt, diremption, direness, direnesses, direption, direr, direst, direx, direxit, dirge, dirge's, dirged, dirgeful, dirgelike, dirgeman, dirges, dirgie, dirging, dirgler, dirgy, dirham, dirhams, dirhem, dirhinous, dirige, dirigent, dirigibility, dirigible, dirigibles, dirigo, dirigomotor, diriment, dirity, dirk, dirked, dirking, dirks, dirl, dirled, dirling, dirls, dirndl, dirndls, dirt, dirtbird, dirtboard, dirten, dirtfarmer, dirtied, dirtier, dirties, dirtiest, dirtily, dirtiness, dirtplate, dirts, dirty, dirtying, diruption, dis, disabilities, disability, disability's, disable, disabled, disablement, disableness, disabler, disablers, disables, disabling, disabusal, disabuse, disabused, disabuses, disabusing, disacceptance, disaccharid, disaccharidase, disaccharide, disaccharides, disaccharose, disaccommodate, disaccommodation, disaccomodate, disaccord, disaccordance, disaccordant, disaccredit, disaccustom, disaccustomed, disaccustomedness, disacidified, disacidify, disacknowledge, disacknowledgement, disacknowledgements, disacquaint, disacquaintance, disacryl, disadjust, disadorn, disadvance, disadvanced, disadvancing, disadvantage, disadvantage's, disadvantaged, disadvantagedness, disadvantageous, disadvantageously, disadvantageousness, disadvantages, disadvantaging, disadventure, disadventurous, disadvise, disadvised, disadvising, disaffect, disaffectation, disaffected, disaffectedly, disaffectedness, disaffecting, disaffection, disaffectionate, disaffections, disaffects, disaffiliate, disaffiliated, disaffiliates, disaffiliating, disaffiliation, disaffiliations, disaffinity, disaffirm, disaffirmance, disaffirmation, disaffirmative, disaffirming, disafforest, disafforestation, disafforestment, disagglomeration, disaggregate, disaggregated, disaggregation, disaggregative, disagio, disagree, disagreeability, disagreeable, disagreeableness, disagreeables, disagreeably, disagreeance, disagreed, disagreeing, disagreement, disagreement's, disagreements, disagreer, disagrees, disagreing, disalicylide, disalign, disaligned, disaligning, disalignment, disalike, disalliege, disallow, disallowable, disallowableness, disallowance, disallowances, disallowed, disallowing, disallows, disally, disaltern, disambiguate, disambiguated, disambiguates, disambiguating, disambiguation, disambiguations, disamenity, disamis, disanagrammatize, disanalogous, disanalogy, disanchor, disangelical, disangularize, disanimal, disanimate, disanimated, disanimating, disanimation, disannex, disannexation, disanney, disannul, disannulled, disannuller, disannulling, disannulment, disannuls, disanoint, disanswerable, disapostle, disapparel, disappear, disappearance, disappearance's, disappearances, disappeared, disappearer, disappearing, disappears, disappendancy, disappendant, disappoint, disappointed, disappointedly, disappointer, disappointing, disappointingly, disappointingness, disappointment, disappointment's, disappointments, disappoints, disappreciate, disappreciation, disapprobation, disapprobations, disapprobative, disapprobatory, disappropriate, disappropriation, disapprovable, disapproval, disapprovals, disapprove, disapproved, disapprover, disapproves, disapproving, disapprovingly, disaproned, disarchbishop, disard, disarm, disarmament, disarmature, disarmed, disarmer, disarmers, disarming, disarmingly, disarms, disarrange, disarranged, disarrangement, disarrangements, disarranger, disarranges, disarranging, disarray, disarrayed, disarraying, disarrays, disarrest, disarticulate, disarticulated, disarticulating, disarticulation, disarticulator, disasinate, disasinize, disassemble, disassembled, disassembler, disassembles, disassembling, disassembly, disassent, disassiduity, disassimilate, disassimilated, disassimilating, disassimilation, disassimilative, disassociable, disassociate, disassociated, disassociates, disassociating, disassociation, disaster, disaster's, disasterly, disasters, disastimeter, disastrous, disastrously, disastrousness, disattaint, disattire, disattune, disaugment, disauthentic, disauthenticate, disauthorize, disavail, disavaunce, disavouch, disavow, disavowable, disavowal, disavowals, disavowance, disavowed, disavowedly, disavower, disavowing, disavowment, disavows, disawa, disazo, disbalance, disbalancement, disband, disbanded, disbanding, disbandment, disbandments, disbands, disbar, disbark, disbarment, disbarments, disbarred, disbarring, disbars, disbase, disbecome, disbelief, disbeliefs, disbelieve, disbelieved, disbeliever, disbelievers, disbelieves, disbelieving, disbelievingly, disbench, disbenched, disbenching, disbenchment, disbend, disbind, disblame, disbloom, disboard, disbodied, disbody, disbogue, disboscation, disbosom, disbosomed, disbosoming, disbosoms, disbound, disbowel, disboweled, disboweling, disbowelled, disbowelling, disbowels, disbrain, disbranch, disbranched, disbranching, disbud, disbudded, disbudder, disbudding, disbuds, disburden, disburdened, disburdening, disburdenment, disburdens, disburgeon, disbursable, disbursal, disbursals, disburse, disbursed, disbursement, disbursement's, disbursements, disburser, disburses, disbursing, disburthen, disbury, disbutton, disc, disc's, discabinet, discage, discal, discalceate, discalced, discamp, discandy, discanonization, discanonize, discanonized, discant, discanted, discanter, discanting, discants, discantus, discapacitate, discard, discardable, discarded, discarder, discarding, discardment, discards, discarnate, discarnation, discase, discased, discases, discasing, discastle, discatter, disced, discede, discept, disceptation, disceptator, discepted, discepting, discepts, discern, discernable, discernableness, discernably, discerned, discerner, discerners, discernibility, discernible, discernibleness, discernibly, discerning, discerningly, discernment, discerns, discerp, discerped, discerpibility, discerpible, discerpibleness, discerping, discerptibility, discerptible, discerptibleness, discerption, discerptive, discession, discharacter, discharge, dischargeable, discharged, dischargee, discharger, dischargers, discharges, discharging, discharity, discharm, dischase, dischevel, dischurch, disci, discide, disciferous, discifloral, disciflorous, disciform, discigerous, discinct, discind, discing, discinoid, disciple, disciple's, discipled, disciplelike, disciples, discipleship, disciplinability, disciplinable, disciplinableness, disciplinal, disciplinant, disciplinarian, disciplinarianism, disciplinarians, disciplinarily, disciplinarity, disciplinary, disciplinate, disciplinative, disciplinatory, discipline, disciplined, discipliner, discipliners, disciplines, discipling, disciplining, discipular, discircumspection, discission, discitis, disclaim, disclaimant, disclaimed, disclaimer, disclaimers, disclaiming, disclaims, disclamation, disclamatory, disclander, disclass, disclassify, disclike, disclimax, discloak, discloister, disclosable, disclose, disclosed, discloser, discloses, disclosing, disclosive, disclosure, disclosure's, disclosures, discloud, disclout, disclusion, disco, discoach, discoactine, discoast, discoblastic, discoblastula, discoboli, discobolos, discobolus, discocarp, discocarpium, discocarpous, discocephalous, discodactyl, discodactylous, discogastrula, discoglossid, discoglossoid, discographer, discographic, discographical, discographically, discographies, discography, discoherent, discohexaster, discoid, discoidal, discoids, discolichen, discolith, discolor, discolorate, discolorated, discoloration, discolorations, discolored, discoloredness, discoloring, discolorization, discolorment, discolors, discolour, discoloured, discolouring, discolourization, discombobulate, discombobulated, discombobulates, discombobulating, discombobulation, discomedusan, discomedusoid, discomfit, discomfited, discomfiter, discomfiting, discomfits, discomfiture, discomfort, discomfortable, discomfortableness, discomfortably, discomforted, discomforter, discomforting, discomfortingly, discomforts, discommend, discommendable, discommendableness, discommendably, discommendation, discommender, discommission, discommodate, discommode, discommoded, discommodes, discommoding, discommodious, discommodiously, discommodiousness, discommodities, discommodity, discommon, discommoned, discommoning, discommons, discommune, discommunity, discomorula, discompanied, discomplexion, discompliance, discompose, discomposed, discomposedly, discomposedness, discomposes, discomposing, discomposingly, discomposure, discompt, discomycete, discomycetous, disconanthous, disconcert, disconcerted, disconcertedly, disconcertedness, disconcerting, disconcertingly, disconcertingness, disconcertion, disconcertment, disconcerts, disconcord, disconduce, disconducive, disconfirm, disconfirmation, disconfirmed, disconform, disconformable, disconformably, disconformities, disconformity, discongruity, disconjure, disconnect, disconnected, disconnectedly, disconnectedness, disconnecter, disconnecting, disconnection, disconnections, disconnective, disconnectiveness, disconnector, disconnects, disconsent, disconsider, disconsideration, disconsolacy, disconsolance, disconsolate, disconsolately, disconsolateness, disconsolation, disconsonancy, disconsonant, discontent, discontented, discontentedly, discontentedness, discontentful, discontenting, discontentive, discontentment, discontentments, discontents, discontiguity, discontiguous, discontiguousness, discontinuable, discontinual, discontinuance, discontinuances, discontinuation, discontinuations, discontinue, discontinued, discontinuee, discontinuer, discontinues, discontinuing, discontinuities, discontinuity, discontinuity's, discontinuor, discontinuous, discontinuously, discontinuousness, disconula, disconvenience, disconvenient, disconventicle, discophile, discophoran, discophore, discophorous, discoplacenta, discoplacental, discoplacentalian, discoplasm, discopodous, discord, discordable, discordance, discordancies, discordancy, discordant, discordantly, discordantness, discorded, discorder, discordful, discording, discordous, discords, discorporate, discorrespondency, discorrespondent, discos, discost, discostate, discostomatous, discotheque, discotheques, discothque, discounsel, discount, discountable, discounted, discountenance, discountenanced, discountenancer, discountenances, discountenancing, discounter, discounters, discounting, discountinuous, discounts, discouple, discour, discourage, discourageable, discouraged, discouragedly, discouragement, discouragements, discourager, discourages, discouraging, discouragingly, discouragingness, discourse, discourse's, discoursed, discourseless, discourser, discoursers, discourses, discoursing, discoursive, discoursively, discoursiveness, discourt, discourteous, discourteously, discourteousness, discourtesies, discourtesy, discourtship, discous, discovenant, discover, discoverability, discoverable, discoverably, discovered, discoverer, discoverers, discoveries, discovering, discovers, discovert, discoverture, discovery, discovery's, discradle, discreate, discreated, discreating, discreation, discredence, discredit, discreditability, discreditable, discreditableness, discreditably, discredited, discrediting, discredits, discreet, discreeter, discreetest, discreetly, discreetness, discrepance, discrepancies, discrepancries, discrepancy, discrepancy's, discrepant, discrepantly, discrepate, discrepated, discrepating, discrepation, discrepencies, discrested, discrete, discretely, discreteness, discretion, discretional, discretionally, discretionarily, discretionary, discretive, discretively, discretiveness, discriminability, discriminable, discriminably, discriminal, discriminant, discriminantal, discriminate, discriminated, discriminately, discriminateness, discriminates, discriminating, discriminatingly, discriminatingness, discrimination, discriminational, discriminations, discriminative, discriminatively, discriminativeness, discriminator, discriminatorily, discriminators, discriminatory, discriminoid, discriminous, discrive, discrown, discrowned, discrowning, discrownment, discrowns, discruciate, discs, discubation, discubitory, disculpate, disculpation, disculpatory, discumb, discumber, discure, discuren, discurre, discurrent, discursative, discursativeness, discursify, discursion, discursive, discursively, discursiveness, discursory, discursus, discurtain, discus, discuses, discuss, discussable, discussant, discussants, discussed, discusser, discusses, discussible, discussing, discussion, discussion's, discussional, discussionis, discussionism, discussionist, discussions, discussive, discussment, discustom, discutable, discute, discutient, disdain, disdainable, disdained, disdainer, disdainful, disdainfully, disdainfulness, disdaining, disdainly, disdainous, disdains, disdar, disdeceive, disdeify, disdein, disdenominationalize, disdiaclasis, disdiaclast, disdiaclastic, disdiapason, disdiazo, disdiplomatize, disdodecahedroid, disdub, disease, diseased, diseasedly, diseasedness, diseaseful, diseasefulness, diseases, diseasing, diseasy, disecondary, diseconomy, disedge, disedification, disedify, diseducate, disegno, diselder, diselectrification, diselectrify, diselenid, diselenide, disematism, disembalm, disembargo, disembargoed, disembargoing, disembark, disembarkation, disembarkations, disembarked, disembarking, disembarkment, disembarks, disembarrass, disembarrassed, disembarrassment, disembattle, disembay, disembed, disembellish, disembitter, disembocation, disembodied, disembodies, disembodiment, disembodiments, disembody, disembodying, disembogue, disembogued, disemboguement, disemboguing, disembosom, disembowel, disemboweled, disemboweling, disembowelled, disembowelling, disembowelment, disembowelments, disembowels, disembower, disembrace, disembrangle, disembroil, disembroilment, disemburden, diseme, disemic, disemplane, disemplaned, disemploy, disemployed, disemploying, disemployment, disemploys, disempower, disemprison, disenable, disenabled, disenablement, disenabling, disenact, disenactment, disenamor, disenamour, disenchain, disenchant, disenchanted, disenchanter, disenchanting, disenchantingly, disenchantment, disenchantments, disenchantress, disenchants, disencharm, disenclose, disencourage, disencrease, disencumber, disencumbered, disencumbering, disencumberment, disencumbers, disencumbrance, disendow, disendowed, disendower, disendowing, disendowment, disendows, disenfranchise, disenfranchised, disenfranchisement, disenfranchisements, disenfranchises, disenfranchising, disengage, disengaged, disengagedness, disengagement, disengagements, disengages, disengaging, disengirdle, disenjoy, disenjoyment, disenmesh, disennoble, disennui, disenorm, disenrol, disenroll, disensanity, disenshroud, disenslave, disensoul, disensure, disentail, disentailment, disentangle, disentangled, disentanglement, disentanglements, disentangler, disentangles, disentangling, disenter, disenthral, disenthrall, disenthralled, disenthralling, disenthrallment, disenthralls, disenthralment, disenthrone, disenthroned, disenthronement, disenthroning, disentitle, disentitled, disentitlement, disentitling, disentomb, disentombment, disentraced, disentrail, disentrain, disentrainment, disentrammel, disentrance, disentranced, disentrancement, disentrancing, disentwine, disentwined, disentwining, disenvelop, disepalous, disequality, disequalization, disequalize, disequalizer, disequilibrate, disequilibration, disequilibria, disequilibrium, disequilibriums, disert, disespouse, disestablish, disestablished, disestablisher, disestablishes, disestablishing, disestablishment, disestablishmentarian, disestablishmentarianism, disestablismentarian, disestablismentarianism, disesteem, disesteemed, disesteemer, disesteeming, disestimation, diseur, diseurs, diseuse, diseuses, disexcommunicate, disexercise, disfaith, disfame, disfashion, disfavor, disfavored, disfavorer, disfavoring, disfavors, disfavour, disfavourable, disfavoured, disfavourer, disfavouring, disfeature, disfeatured, disfeaturement, disfeaturing, disfellowship, disfen, disfiguration, disfigurative, disfigure, disfigured, disfigurement, disfigurements, disfigurer, disfigures, disfiguring, disfiguringly, disflesh, disfoliage, disfoliaged, disforest, disforestation, disform, disformity, disfortune, disframe, disfranchise, disfranchised, disfranchisement, disfranchisements, disfranchiser, disfranchisers, disfranchises, disfranchising, disfrancnise, disfrequent, disfriar, disfrock, disfrocked, disfrocking, disfrocks, disfunction, disfunctions, disfurnish, disfurnished, disfurnishment, disfurniture, disgage, disgallant, disgarland, disgarnish, disgarrison, disgavel, disgaveled, disgaveling, disgavelled, disgavelling, disgeneric, disgenic, disgenius, disgig, disglorify, disglory, disglut, disgood, disgorge, disgorged, disgorgement, disgorger, disgorges, disgorging, disgospel, disgospelize, disgout, disgown, disgrace, disgraced, disgraceful, disgracefully, disgracefulness, disgracement, disgracer, disgracers, disgraces, disgracia, disgracing, disgracious, disgracive, disgradation, disgrade, disgraded, disgrading, disgradulate, disgregate, disgregated, disgregating, disgregation, disgress, disgross, disgruntle, disgruntled, disgruntlement, disgruntles, disgruntling, disguisable, disguisal, disguisay, disguise, disguised, disguisedly, disguisedness, disguiseless, disguisement, disguisements, disguiser, disguises, disguising, disgulf, disgust, disgusted, disgustedly, disgustedness, disguster, disgustful, disgustfully, disgustfulness, disgusting, disgustingly, disgustingness, disgusts, dish, dishabilitate, dishabilitation, dishabille, dishabit, dishabited, dishabituate, dishabituated, dishabituating, dishable, dishallow, dishallucination, disharmonic, disharmonical, disharmonies, disharmonious, disharmonise, disharmonised, disharmonising, disharmonism, disharmonize, disharmonized, disharmonizing, disharmony, dishaunt, dishboard, dishcloth, dishcloths, dishclout, dishcross, disheart, dishearten, disheartened, disheartenedly, disheartener, disheartening, dishearteningly, disheartenment, disheartens, disheathing, disheaven, dished, disheir, dishellenize, dishelm, dishelmed, dishelming, dishelms, disher, disherent, disherison, disherit, disherited, disheriting, disheritment, disheritor, disherits, dishes, dishevel, disheveled, disheveling, dishevelled, dishevelling, dishevelment, dishevelments, dishevels, dishevely, dishexecontahedroid, dishful, dishfuls, dishier, dishiest, dishing, dishlike, dishling, dishmaker, dishmaking, dishmonger, dishmop, dishome, dishonest, dishonesties, dishonestly, dishonesty, dishonor, dishonorable, dishonorableness, dishonorably, dishonorary, dishonored, dishonorer, dishonoring, dishonors, dishonour, dishonourable, dishonourableness, dishonourably, dishonourary, dishonoured, dishonourer, dishonouring, dishorn, dishorner, dishorse, dishouse, dishpan, dishpanful, dishpans, dishrag, dishrags, dishtowel, dishtowels, dishumanize, dishumor, dishumour, dishware, dishwares, dishwash, dishwasher, dishwashers, dishwashing, dishwashings, dishwater, dishwatery, dishwiper, dishwiping, dishy, disidentify, disilane, disilicane, disilicate, disilicic, disilicid, disilicide, disillude, disilluded, disilluminate, disillusion, disillusionary, disillusioned, disillusioning, disillusionise, disillusionised, disillusioniser, disillusionising, disillusionist, disillusionize, disillusionized, disillusionizer, disillusionizing, disillusionment, disillusionment's, disillusionments, disillusions, disillusive, disimagine, disimbitter, disimitate, disimitation, disimmure, disimpark, disimpassioned, disimprison, disimprisonment, disimprove, disimprovement, disincarcerate, disincarceration, disincarnate, disincarnation, disincentive, disinclination, disinclinations, disincline, disinclined, disinclines, disinclining, disinclose, disincorporate, disincorporated, disincorporating, disincorporation, disincrease, disincrust, disincrustant, disincrustion, disindividualize, disinfect, disinfectant, disinfectants, disinfected, disinfecter, disinfecting, disinfection, disinfections, disinfective, disinfector, disinfects, disinfest, disinfestant, disinfestation, disinfeudation, disinflame, disinflate, disinflated, disinflating, disinflation, disinflationary, disinformation, disingenious, disingenuity, disingenuous, disingenuously, disingenuousness, disinhabit, disinherison, disinherit, disinheritable, disinheritance, disinheritances, disinherited, disinheriting, disinherits, disinhibition, disinhume, disinhumed, disinhuming, disinsection, disinsectization, disinsulation, disinsure, disintegrable, disintegrant, disintegrate, disintegrated, disintegrates, disintegrating, disintegration, disintegrationist, disintegrations, disintegrative, disintegrator, disintegrators, disintegratory, disintegrity, disintegrous, disintensify, disinter, disinteress, disinterest, disinterested, disinterestedly, disinterestedness, disinteresting, disintermediation, disinterment, disinterred, disinterring, disinters, disintertwine, disinthrall, disintoxicate, disintoxication, disintrench, disintricate, disinure, disinvagination, disinvest, disinvestiture, disinvestment, disinvigorate, disinvite, disinvolve, disinvolvement, disjasked, disjasket, disjaskit, disject, disjected, disjecting, disjection, disjects, disjeune, disjoin, disjoinable, disjoined, disjoining, disjoins, disjoint, disjointed, disjointedly, disjointedness, disjointing, disjointly, disjointness, disjoints, disjointure, disjudication, disjunct, disjunction, disjunctions, disjunctive, disjunctively, disjunctor, disjuncts, disjuncture, disjune, disk, disk's, disked, diskelion, disker, diskery, diskette, diskettes, diskindness, disking, diskless, disklike, disknow, diskography, diskophile, diskos, disks, dislade, dislady, dislaurel, disleaf, disleafed, disleafing, disleal, disleave, disleaved, disleaving, dislegitimate, dislevelment, disli, dislicense, dislikable, dislike, dislikeable, disliked, dislikeful, dislikelihood, disliken, dislikeness, disliker, dislikers, dislikes, disliking, dislimb, dislimn, dislimned, dislimning, dislimns, dislink, dislip, dislive, dislluminate, disload, dislocability, dislocable, dislocate, dislocated, dislocatedly, dislocatedness, dislocates, dislocating, dislocation, dislocations, dislocator, dislocatory, dislock, dislodge, dislodgeable, dislodged, dislodgement, dislodges, dislodging, dislodgment, disloign, dislove, disloyal, disloyalist, disloyally, disloyalties, disloyalty, disluster, dislustered, dislustering, dislustre, dislustred, dislustring, dismail, dismain, dismal, dismaler, dismalest, dismalities, dismality, dismalize, dismally, dismalness, dismals, disman, dismantle, dismantled, dismantlement, dismantler, dismantles, dismantling, dismarble, dismarch, dismark, dismarket, dismarketed, dismarketing, dismarry, dismarshall, dismask, dismast, dismasted, dismasting, dismastment, dismasts, dismaw, dismay, dismayable, dismayed, dismayedness, dismayful, dismayfully, dismaying, dismayingly, dismayingness, dismays, disme, dismeasurable, dismeasured, dismember, dismembered, dismemberer, dismembering, dismemberment, dismemberments, dismembers, dismembrate, dismembrated, dismembrator, dismerit, dismes, dismettled, disminion, disminister, dismiss, dismissable, dismissal, dismissal's, dismissals, dismissed, dismisser, dismissers, dismisses, dismissible, dismissing, dismissingly, dismission, dismissive, dismissory, dismit, dismoded, dismortgage, dismortgaged, dismortgaging, dismount, dismountable, dismounted, dismounting, dismounts, dismutation, disna, disnatural, disnaturalization, disnaturalize, disnature, disnatured, disnaturing, disnest, disnew, disney, disneyland, disniche, disnosed, disnumber, disobedience, disobedient, disobediently, disobey, disobeyal, disobeyed, disobeyer, disobeyers, disobeying, disobeys, disobligation, disobligatory, disoblige, disobliged, disobliger, disobliges, disobliging, disobligingly, disobligingness, disobstruct, disoccident, disocclude, disoccluded, disoccluding, disoccupation, disoccupied, disoccupy, disoccupying, disodic, disodium, disomatic, disomatous, disomaty, disomic, disomus, disoperation, disoperculate, disopinion, disoppilate, disorb, disorchard, disordain, disordained, disordeine, disorder, disordered, disorderedly, disorderedness, disorderer, disordering, disorderliness, disorderly, disorders, disordinance, disordinate, disordinated, disordination, disorganic, disorganise, disorganised, disorganiser, disorganising, disorganization, disorganize, disorganized, disorganizer, disorganizers, disorganizes, disorganizing, disorient, disorientate, disorientated, disorientates, disorientating, disorientation, disoriented, disorienting, disorients, disour, disown, disownable, disowned, disowning, disownment, disowns, disoxidate, disoxygenate, disoxygenation, disozonize, disp, dispace, dispaint, dispair, dispand, dispansive, dispapalize, dispar, disparadise, disparage, disparageable, disparaged, disparagement, disparagements, disparager, disparages, disparaging, disparagingly, disparate, disparately, disparateness, disparation, disparatum, disparish, disparison, disparities, disparition, disparity, disparity's, dispark, disparkle, disparple, disparpled, disparpling, dispart, disparted, disparting, dispartment, disparts, dispassion, dispassionate, dispassionately, dispassionateness, dispassioned, dispatch, dispatched, dispatcher, dispatchers, dispatches, dispatchful, dispatching, dispathy, dispatriated, dispauper, dispauperize, dispeace, dispeaceful, dispeed, dispel, dispell, dispellable, dispelled, dispeller, dispelling, dispells, dispels, dispence, dispend, dispended, dispender, dispending, dispendious, dispendiously, dispenditure, dispends, dispensability, dispensable, dispensableness, dispensaries, dispensary, dispensate, dispensated, dispensating, dispensation, dispensational, dispensationalism, dispensations, dispensative, dispensatively, dispensator, dispensatories, dispensatorily, dispensatory, dispensatress, dispensatrix, dispense, dispensed, dispenser, dispensers, dispenses, dispensible, dispensing, dispensingly, dispensive, dispeople, dispeopled, dispeoplement, dispeopler, dispeopling, disperato, dispergate, dispergated, dispergating, dispergation, dispergator, disperge, dispericraniate, disperiwig, dispermic, dispermous, dispermy, disperple, dispersal, dispersals, dispersant, disperse, dispersed, dispersedelement, dispersedly, dispersedness, dispersedye, dispersement, disperser, dispersers, disperses, dispersibility, dispersible, dispersing, dispersion, dispersions, dispersity, dispersive, dispersively, dispersiveness, dispersoid, dispersoidological, dispersoidology, dispersonalize, dispersonate, dispersonification, dispersonify, dispetal, disphenoid, dispicion, dispiece, dispirem, dispireme, dispirit, dispirited, dispiritedly, dispiritedness, dispiriting, dispiritingly, dispiritment, dispirits, dispiteous, dispiteously, dispiteousness, displace, displaceability, displaceable, displaced, displacement, displacement's, displacements, displacency, displacer, displaces, displacing, displant, displanted, displanting, displants, displat, display, displayable, displayed, displayer, displaying, displays, disple, displeasance, displeasant, displease, displeased, displeasedly, displeaser, displeases, displeasing, displeasingly, displeasingness, displeasurable, displeasurably, displeasure, displeasureable, displeasureably, displeasured, displeasurement, displeasures, displeasuring, displenish, displicence, displicency, displode, disploded, displodes, disploding, displosion, displume, displumed, displumes, displuming, displuviate, dispoint, dispond, dispondaic, dispondee, dispone, disponed, disponee, disponent, disponer, disponge, disponing, dispope, dispopularize, disporous, disport, disported, disporting, disportive, disportment, disports, disposability, disposable, disposableness, disposal, disposal's, disposals, dispose, disposed, disposedly, disposedness, disposement, disposer, disposers, disposes, disposing, disposingly, disposit, disposition, disposition's, dispositional, dispositionally, dispositioned, dispositions, dispositive, dispositively, dispositor, dispossed, dispossess, dispossessed, dispossesses, dispossessing, dispossession, dispossessor, dispossessory, dispost, disposure, dispowder, dispractice, dispraise, dispraised, dispraiser, dispraising, dispraisingly, dispread, dispreader, dispreading, dispreads, disprejudice, disprepare, dispress, disprince, disprison, disprivacied, disprivilege, disprize, disprized, disprizes, disprizing, disprobabilization, disprobabilize, disprobative, disprofess, disprofit, disprofitable, dispromise, disproof, disproofs, disproperty, disproportion, disproportionable, disproportionableness, disproportionably, disproportional, disproportionality, disproportionally, disproportionalness, disproportionate, disproportionately, disproportionateness, disproportionates, disproportionation, disproportions, dispropriate, disprovable, disproval, disprove, disproved, disprovement, disproven, disprover, disproves, disprovide, disproving, dispulp, dispunct, dispunge, dispunishable, dispunitive, dispurpose, dispurse, dispurvey, disputability, disputable, disputableness, disputably, disputacity, disputant, disputants, disputation, disputations, disputatious, disputatiously, disputatiousness, disputative, disputatively, disputativeness, disputator, dispute, disputed, disputeful, disputeless, disputer, disputers, disputes, disputing, disputisoun, disqualifiable, disqualification, disqualifications, disqualified, disqualifies, disqualify, disqualifying, disquantity, disquarter, disquiet, disquieted, disquietedly, disquietedness, disquieten, disquieter, disquieting, disquietingly, disquietingness, disquietly, disquietness, disquiets, disquietude, disquietudes, disquiparancy, disquiparant, disquiparation, disquisit, disquisite, disquisited, disquisiting, disquisition, disquisitional, disquisitionary, disquisitions, disquisitive, disquisitively, disquisitor, disquisitorial, disquisitory, disquixote, disraeli, disrange, disrank, disrate, disrated, disrates, disrating, disray, disrealize, disreason, disrecommendation, disregard, disregardable, disregardance, disregardant, disregarded, disregarder, disregardful, disregardfully, disregardfulness, disregarding, disregards, disregular, disrelate, disrelated, disrelation, disrelish, disrelishable, disremember, disrepair, disreport, disreputability, disreputable, disreputableness, disreputably, disreputation, disrepute, disreputed, disrespect, disrespectability, disrespectable, disrespecter, disrespectful, disrespectfully, disrespectfulness, disrespective, disrespondency, disrest, disrestore, disreverence, disring, disrobe, disrobed, disrobement, disrober, disrobers, disrobes, disrobing, disroof, disroost, disroot, disrooted, disrooting, disroots, disrout, disrudder, disruddered, disruly, disrump, disrupt, disruptability, disruptable, disrupted, disrupter, disrupting, disruption, disruption's, disruptionist, disruptions, disruptive, disruptively, disruptiveness, disruptment, disruptor, disrupts, disrupture, diss, dissait, dissatisfaction, dissatisfaction's, dissatisfactions, dissatisfactorily, dissatisfactoriness, dissatisfactory, dissatisfied, dissatisfiedly, dissatisfiedness, dissatisfies, dissatisfy, dissatisfying, dissatisfyingly, dissaturate, dissava, dissavage, dissave, dissaved, dissaves, dissaving, dissavs, disscepter, dissceptered, dissceptre, dissceptred, dissceptring, disscussive, disseason, disseat, disseated, disseating, disseats, dissect, dissected, dissectible, dissecting, dissection, dissectional, dissections, dissective, dissector, dissectors, dissects, disseise, disseised, disseisee, disseises, disseisor, disseisoress, disseize, disseized, disseizee, disseizes, disseizor, disseizoress, disseizure, disselboom, dissemblance, dissemble, dissembled, dissembler, dissemblers, dissembles, dissemblies, dissembling, dissemblingly, dissembly, dissemilative, disseminate, disseminated, disseminates, disseminating, dissemination, disseminations, disseminative, disseminator, disseminule, dissension, dissension's, dissensions, dissensious, dissensualize, dissent, dissentaneous, dissentaneousness, dissentation, dissented, dissenter, dissenterism, dissenters, dissentiate, dissentience, dissentiency, dissentient, dissentiently, dissentients, dissenting, dissentingly, dissention, dissentious, dissentiously, dissentism, dissentive, dissentment, dissents, dissepiment, dissepimental, dissert, dissertate, dissertated, dissertating, dissertation, dissertation's, dissertational, dissertationist, dissertations, dissertative, dissertator, disserted, disserting, disserts, disserve, disserved, disserves, disservice, disserviceable, disserviceableness, disserviceably, disservices, disserving, dissettle, dissettlement, dissever, disseverance, disseveration, dissevered, dissevering, disseverment, dissevers, disshadow, disssheathe, disssheathed, disship, disshiver, disshroud, dissidence, dissident, dissident's, dissidently, dissidents, dissight, dissightly, dissilience, dissiliency, dissilient, dissilition, dissimilar, dissimilarities, dissimilarity, dissimilarity's, dissimilarly, dissimilars, dissimilate, dissimilated, dissimilating, dissimilation, dissimilative, dissimilatory, dissimile, dissimilitude, dissimulate, dissimulated, dissimulates, dissimulating, dissimulation, dissimulations, dissimulative, dissimulator, dissimulators, dissimule, dissimuler, dissinew, dissipable, dissipate, dissipated, dissipatedly, dissipatedness, dissipater, dissipaters, dissipates, dissipating, dissipation, dissipations, dissipative, dissipativity, dissipator, dissipators, dissite, disslander, dissociability, dissociable, dissociableness, dissociably, dissocial, dissociality, dissocialize, dissociant, dissociate, dissociated, dissociates, dissociating, dissociation, dissociations, dissociative, dissoconch, dissogeny, dissogony, dissolubility, dissoluble, dissolubleness, dissolute, dissolutely, dissoluteness, dissolution, dissolution's, dissolutional, dissolutionism, dissolutionist, dissolutions, dissolutive, dissolvability, dissolvable, dissolvableness, dissolvative, dissolve, dissolveability, dissolved, dissolvent, dissolver, dissolves, dissolving, dissolvingly, dissonance, dissonances, dissonancies, dissonancy, dissonant, dissonantly, dissonate, dissonous, dissoul, dissour, disspirit, disspread, disspreading, disstate, dissuadable, dissuade, dissuaded, dissuader, dissuades, dissuading, dissuasion, dissuasions, dissuasive, dissuasively, dissuasiveness, dissuasory, dissue, dissuit, dissuitable, dissuited, dissunder, dissweeten, dissyllabic, dissyllabification, dissyllabify, dissyllabise, dissyllabised, dissyllabising, dissyllabism, dissyllabize, dissyllabized, dissyllabizing, dissyllable, dissymmetric, dissymmetrical, dissymmetrically, dissymmetry, dissymmettric, dissympathize, dissympathy, dist, distad, distaff, distaffs, distain, distained, distaining, distains, distal, distale, distalia, distally, distalwards, distance, distanced, distanceless, distances, distancing, distancy, distannic, distant, distantly, distantness, distaste, distasted, distasteful, distastefully, distastefulness, distastes, distasting, distater, distaves, distelfink, distemonous, distemper, distemperance, distemperate, distemperature, distempered, distemperedly, distemperedness, distemperer, distempering, distemperment, distemperoid, distemperure, distenant, distend, distended, distendedly, distendedness, distender, distending, distends, distensibilities, distensibility, distensible, distensile, distension, distensions, distensive, distent, distention, distentions, dister, disterminate, disterr, disthene, disthrall, disthrone, disthroned, disthroning, distich, distichal, distichiasis, distichous, distichously, distichs, distil, distileries, distilery, distill, distillable, distillage, distilland, distillate, distillates, distillation, distillations, distillator, distillatory, distilled, distiller, distilleries, distillers, distillery, distilling, distillment, distillmint, distills, distilment, distils, distinct, distincter, distinctest, distinctify, distinctio, distinction, distinction's, distinctional, distinctionless, distinctions, distinctity, distinctive, distinctively, distinctiveness, distinctly, distinctness, distinctor, distingu, distingue, distinguee, distinguish, distinguishability, distinguishable, distinguishableness, distinguishably, distinguished, distinguishedly, distinguisher, distinguishes, distinguishing, distinguishingly, distinguishment, distintion, distitle, distn, distoclusion, distoma, distomatosis, distomatous, distome, distomes, distomian, distomiasis, distort, distortable, distorted, distortedly, distortedness, distorter, distorters, distorting, distortion, distortion's, distortional, distortionist, distortionless, distortions, distortive, distorts, distr, distract, distracted, distractedly, distractedness, distracter, distractibility, distractible, distractile, distracting, distractingly, distraction, distraction's, distractions, distractive, distractively, distracts, distrail, distrain, distrainable, distrained, distrainee, distrainer, distraining, distrainment, distrainor, distrains, distraint, distrait, distraite, distraught, distraughted, distraughtly, distream, distress, distressed, distressedly, distressedness, distresses, distressful, distressfully, distressfulness, distressing, distressingly, distrest, distributable, distributaries, distributary, distribute, distributed, distributedly, distributee, distributer, distributes, distributing, distribution, distribution's, distributional, distributionist, distributions, distributival, distributive, distributively, distributiveness, distributivity, distributor, distributor's, distributors, distributorship, distributress, distributution, district, district's, districted, districting, distriction, districtly, districts, distringas, distritbute, distritbuted, distritbutes, distritbuting, distrito, distritos, distrix, distrouble, distrouser, distruss, distrust, distrusted, distruster, distrustful, distrustfully, distrustfulness, distrusting, distrustingly, distrusts, distune, disturb, disturbance, disturbance's, disturbances, disturbant, disturbation, disturbative, disturbed, disturbedly, disturber, disturbers, disturbing, disturbingly, disturbor, disturbs, disturn, disturnpike, disty, distylar, distyle, disubstituted, disubstitution, disulfate, disulfid, disulfide, disulfids, disulfiram, disulfonic, disulfoton, disulfoxid, disulfoxide, disulfuret, disulfuric, disulphate, disulphid, disulphide, disulphonate, disulphone, disulphonic, disulphoxid, disulphoxide, disulphuret, disulphuric, disunified, disuniform, disuniformity, disunify, disunifying, disunion, disunionism, disunionist, disunions, disunite, disunited, disuniter, disuniters, disunites, disunities, disuniting, disunity, disusage, disusance, disuse, disused, disuses, disusing, disutility, disutilize, disvaluation, disvalue, disvalued, disvalues, disvaluing, disvantage, disvelop, disventure, disvertebrate, disvisage, disvisor, disvoice, disvouch, disvulnerability, diswarn, diswarren, diswarrened, diswarrening, diswashing, disweapon, diswench, diswere, diswit, diswont, diswood, disworkmanship, disworship, disworth, disyllabic, disyllabism, disyllabize, disyllabized, disyllabizing, disyllable, disyntheme, disyoke, disyoked, disyokes, disyoking, dit, dita, dital, ditali, ditalini, ditas, ditation, ditch, ditch's, ditchbank, ditchbur, ditchdigger, ditchdigging, ditchdown, ditched, ditcher, ditchers, ditches, ditching, ditchless, ditchside, ditchwater, dite, diter, diterpene, ditertiary, dites, ditetragonal, ditetrahedral, dithalous, dithecal, dithecous, ditheism, ditheisms, ditheist, ditheistic, ditheistical, ditheists, dithematic, dither, dithered, ditherer, dithering, dithers, dithery, dithiobenzoic, dithioglycol, dithioic, dithiol, dithion, dithionate, dithionic, dithionite, dithionous, dithymol, dithyramb, dithyrambic, dithyrambically, dithyrambs, diting, dition, ditokous, ditolyl, ditone, ditrematous, ditremid, ditrichotomous, ditriglyph, ditriglyphic, ditrigonal, ditrigonally, ditrochean, ditrochee, ditrochous, ditroite, dits, ditt, dittamy, dittander, dittanies, dittany, dittay, ditted, dittied, ditties, ditting, ditto, dittoed, dittoes, dittogram, dittograph, dittographic, dittography, dittoing, dittologies, dittology, ditton, dittos, ditty, dittying, diumvirate, diuranate, diureide, diureses, diuresis, diuretic, diuretical, diuretically, diureticalness, diuretics, diurn, diurnal, diurnally, diurnalness, diurnals, diurnation, diurne, diurnule, diuron, diurons, diuturnal, diuturnity, div, diva, divagate, divagated, divagates, divagating, divagation, divagational, divagationally, divagations, divagatory, divalence, divalent, divan, divan's, divans, divaporation, divariant, divaricate, divaricated, divaricately, divaricating, divaricatingly, divarication, divaricator, divas, divast, divata, dive, divebomb, dived, divekeeper, divel, divell, divelled, divellent, divellicate, divelling, diver, diverb, diverberate, diverge, diverged, divergement, divergence, divergence's, divergences, divergencies, divergency, divergenge, divergent, divergently, diverges, diverging, divergingly, divers, diverse, diversely, diverseness, diversicolored, diversifiability, diversifiable, diversification, diversifications, diversified, diversifier, diversifies, diversiflorate, diversiflorous, diversifoliate, diversifolious, diversiform, diversify, diversifying, diversion, diversional, diversionary, diversionist, diversions, diversipedate, diversisporous, diversities, diversity, diversly, diversory, divert, diverted, divertedly, diverter, diverters, divertibility, divertible, diverticle, diverticula, diverticular, diverticulate, diverticulitis, diverticulosis, diverticulum, divertila, divertimenti, divertimento, divertimentos, diverting, divertingly, divertingness, divertise, divertisement, divertissant, divertissement, divertissements, divertive, divertor, diverts, dives, divest, divested, divestible, divesting, divestitive, divestiture, divestitures, divestment, divests, divesture, divet, divi, divia, divid, dividable, dividableness, dividant, divide, divided, dividedly, dividedness, dividend, dividend's, dividends, dividendus, divident, divider, dividers, divides, dividing, dividingly, dividivis, dividual, dividualism, dividually, dividuity, dividuous, divinability, divinable, divinail, divination, divinations, divinator, divinatory, divine, divined, divinely, divineness, diviner, divineress, diviners, divines, divinesse, divinest, diving, divinified, divinify, divinifying, divining, diviningly, divinisation, divinise, divinised, divinises, divinising, divinister, divinistre, divinities, divinity, divinity's, divinityship, divinization, divinize, divinized, divinizes, divinizing, divinyl, divisa, divise, divisi, divisibilities, divisibility, divisible, divisibleness, divisibly, division, division's, divisional, divisionally, divisionary, divisionism, divisionist, divisionistic, divisions, divisive, divisively, divisiveness, divisor, divisor's, divisorial, divisors, divisory, divisural, divorce, divorceable, divorced, divorcee, divorcees, divorcement, divorcements, divorcer, divorcers, divorces, divorceuse, divorcible, divorcing, divorcive, divort, divot, divoto, divots, divulgate, divulgated, divulgater, divulgating, divulgation, divulgator, divulgatory, divulge, divulged, divulgement, divulgence, divulgences, divulger, divulgers, divulges, divulging, divulse, divulsed, divulsing, divulsion, divulsive, divulsor, divus, divvied, divvies, divvy, divvying, diwan, diwani, diwans, diwata, dix, dixain, dixenite, dixie, dixiecrat, dixieland, dixies, dixit, dixits, dixy, dizain, dizaine, dizdar, dizen, dizened, dizening, dizenment, dizens, dizoic, dizygotic, dizygous, dizz, dizzard, dizzardly, dizzen, dizzied, dizzier, dizzies, dizziest, dizzily, dizziness, dizzy, dizzying, dizzyingly, dj, djagoong, djakarta, djalmaite, djasakid, djave, djebel, djebels, djehad, djelab, djelfa, djellab, djellaba, djellabah, djellabas, djerib, djersa, djibbah, djibouti, djin, djinn, djinni, djinns, djinny, djins, dk, dkg, dkl, dkm, dks, dl, dlr, dlvy, dm, dmarche, dmod, dn, dnieper, do, do's, doa, doab, doability, doable, doand, doarium, doat, doated, doater, doating, doatish, doats, doaty, dob, dobbed, dobber, dobbers, dobbie, dobbies, dobbin, dobbing, dobbins, dobby, dobchick, dobe, doberman, dobermans, dobie, dobies, dobl, dobla, doblas, doblon, doblones, doblons, dobos, dobra, dobrao, dobras, dobroes, dobson, dobsonflies, dobsonfly, dobsons, dobule, doby, dobzhansky, doc, docent, docents, docentship, docetae, docetic, docetism, dochmiac, dochmiacal, dochmiasis, dochmii, dochmius, dochter, docibility, docible, docibleness, docile, docilely, docilities, docility, docimasia, docimasies, docimastic, docimastical, docimasy, docimology, docious, docity, dock, dockage, dockages, docked, docken, docker, dockers, docket, docketed, docketing, dockets, dockhand, dockhands, dockhead, dockhouse, docking, dockization, dockize, dockland, docklands, dockmackie, dockman, dockmaster, docks, dockside, docksides, dockworker, dockyard, dockyardman, dockyards, docmac, docoglossan, docoglossate, docosane, docosanoic, docquet, docs, doctor, doctoral, doctorally, doctorate, doctorate's, doctorates, doctorbird, doctordom, doctored, doctoress, doctorfish, doctorfishes, doctorhood, doctorial, doctorially, doctoring, doctorization, doctorize, doctorless, doctorlike, doctorly, doctors, doctors'commons, doctorship, doctress, doctrinable, doctrinaire, doctrinairism, doctrinal, doctrinalism, doctrinalist, doctrinality, doctrinally, doctrinarian, doctrinarianism, doctrinarily, doctrinarity, doctrinary, doctrinate, doctrine, doctrine's, doctrines, doctrinism, doctrinist, doctrinization, doctrinize, doctrinized, doctrinizing, doctrix, doctus, docudrama, docudramas, document, documentable, documental, documentalist, documentarian, documentaries, documentarily, documentarist, documentary, documentary's, documentation, documentation's, documentational, documentations, documented, documenter, documenters, documenting, documentize, documentor, documents, dod, dodd, doddard, doddart, dodded, dodder, doddered, dodderer, dodderers, doddering, dodders, doddery, doddie, doddies, dodding, doddle, doddy, doddypoll, dodecade, dodecadrachm, dodecafid, dodecagon, dodecagonal, dodecaheddra, dodecahedra, dodecahedral, dodecahedric, dodecahedron, dodecahedrons, dodecahydrate, dodecahydrated, dodecamerous, dodecanal, dodecane, dodecanoic, dodecant, dodecapartite, dodecapetalous, dodecaphonic, dodecaphonically, dodecaphonism, dodecaphonist, dodecaphony, dodecarch, dodecarchy, dodecasemic, dodecastylar, dodecastyle, dodecastylos, dodecasyllabic, dodecasyllable, dodecatemory, dodecatoic, dodecatyl, dodecatylic, dodecuplet, dodecyl, dodecylene, dodecylic, dodecylphenol, dodgasted, dodge, dodged, dodgeful, dodger, dodgeries, dodgers, dodgery, dodges, dodgier, dodgiest, dodgily, dodginess, dodging, dodgy, dodipole, dodkin, dodlet, dodman, dodo, dodoes, dodoism, dodoisms, dodoma, dodonaena, dodos, dodrans, dodrantal, dods, dodunk, doe, doebird, doeglic, doegling, doek, doeling, doer, doers, does, doeskin, doeskins, doesn, doesn't, doesnt, doest, doeth, doeuvre, doff, doffed, doffer, doffers, doffing, doffs, doftberry, dofunny, dog, dog's, dogal, dogana, dogaressa, dogate, dogbane, dogbanes, dogberries, dogberry, dogbite, dogblow, dogboat, dogbodies, dogbody, dogbolt, dogbush, dogcart, dogcarts, dogcatcher, dogcatchers, dogdom, dogdoms, doge, dogear, dogeared, dogears, dogedom, dogedoms, dogeless, doges, dogeship, dogeships, dogey, dogeys, dogface, dogfaces, dogfall, dogfennel, dogfight, dogfighting, dogfights, dogfish, dogfishes, dogfoot, dogfought, dogged, doggedly, doggedness, dogger, doggerel, doggereled, doggereler, doggerelism, doggerelist, doggerelize, doggerelizer, doggerelizing, doggerelled, doggerelling, doggerels, doggeries, doggers, doggery, doggess, dogget, doggie, doggier, doggies, doggiest, dogging, doggish, doggishly, doggishness, doggle, doggo, doggone, doggoned, doggoneder, doggonedest, doggoner, doggones, doggonest, doggoning, doggrel, doggrelize, doggrels, doggy, doghead, doghearted, doghole, doghood, doghouse, doghouses, dogie, dogies, dogleg, doglegged, doglegging, doglegs, dogless, doglike, dogly, dogma, dogma's, dogman, dogmas, dogmata, dogmatic, dogmatical, dogmatically, dogmaticalness, dogmatician, dogmatics, dogmatisation, dogmatise, dogmatised, dogmatiser, dogmatising, dogmatism, dogmatist, dogmatists, dogmatization, dogmatize, dogmatized, dogmatizer, dogmatizing, dogmeat, dogmen, dogmouth, dognap, dognaped, dognaper, dognapers, dognaping, dognapped, dognapper, dognapping, dognaps, dogplate, dogproof, dogs, dogsbodies, dogsbody, dogship, dogshore, dogskin, dogsled, dogsleds, dogsleep, dogstail, dogstone, dogstones, dogtail, dogteeth, dogtie, dogtooth, dogtoothing, dogtrick, dogtrot, dogtrots, dogtrotted, dogtrotting, dogvane, dogvanes, dogwatch, dogwatches, dogwinkle, dogwood, dogwoods, dogy, doh, dohickey, dohter, doigt, doigte, doiled, doilies, doily, doina, doing, doings, doit, doited, doitkin, doitrified, doits, dojigger, dojiggy, dojo, dojos, doke, dokhma, dokimastic, dol, dola, dolabra, dolabrate, dolabre, dolabriform, dolcan, dolce, dolcemente, dolci, dolcian, dolciano, dolcinist, dolcino, dolcissimo, doldrum, doldrums, dole, doleance, doled, dolefish, doleful, dolefuller, dolefullest, dolefully, dolefulness, dolefuls, dolent, dolente, dolentissimo, dolently, dolerin, dolerite, dolerites, doleritic, dolerophanite, doles, dolesman, dolesome, dolesomely, dolesomeness, doless, doley, dolf, doli, dolia, dolichoblond, dolichocephal, dolichocephali, dolichocephalic, dolichocephalism, dolichocephalize, dolichocephalous, dolichocephaly, dolichocercic, dolichocnemic, dolichocranial, dolichocranic, dolichocrany, dolichofacial, dolichohieric, dolichopellic, dolichopodous, dolichoprosopic, dolichos, dolichosaur, dolichosaurus, dolichostylous, dolichotmema, dolichuric, dolichurus, dolina, doline, doling, dolioform, dolisie, dolite, dolittle, dolium, doll, doll's, dollar, dollarbird, dollardee, dollardom, dollarfish, dollarfishes, dollarleaf, dollars, dollarwise, dollbeer, dolldom, dolled, dolley, dollface, dollfaced, dollfish, dollhood, dollhouse, dollhouses, dollia, dollie, dollied, dollier, dollies, dollin, dolliness, dolling, dollish, dollishly, dollishness, dollmaker, dollmaking, dollop, dollops, dolls, dollship, dolly, dolly's, dollying, dollyman, dollymen, dollyway, dolman, dolmans, dolmas, dolmen, dolmenic, dolmens, dolomite, dolomites, dolomitic, dolomitise, dolomitised, dolomitising, dolomitization, dolomitize, dolomitized, dolomitizing, dolomization, dolomize, dolor, dolores, doloriferous, dolorific, dolorifuge, dolorimeter, dolorimetric, dolorimetrically, dolorimetry, dolorogenic, doloroso, dolorous, dolorously, dolorousness, dolors, dolos, dolose, dolour, dolours, dolous, dolphin, dolphin's, dolphinfish, dolphinfishes, dolphinlike, dolphins, dols, dolt, dolthead, doltish, doltishly, doltishness, dolts, dolus, dolven, dom, domable, domage, domain, domain's, domainal, domains, domajig, domajigger, domal, domanial, domatium, domatophobia, domba, domboc, domdaniel, dome, domed, domelike, doment, domer, domes, domesday, domesdays, domestic, domesticability, domesticable, domesticality, domestically, domesticate, domesticated, domesticates, domesticating, domestication, domestications, domesticative, domesticator, domesticities, domesticity, domesticize, domesticized, domestics, domett, domeykite, domic, domical, domically, domicil, domicile, domiciled, domicilement, domiciles, domiciliar, domiciliary, domiciliate, domiciliated, domiciliating, domiciliation, domicilii, domiciling, domicils, domiculture, domification, domify, domina, dominae, dominance, dominancy, dominant, dominantly, dominants, dominate, dominated, dominates, dominating, dominatingly, domination, dominations, dominative, dominator, dominators, domine, dominee, domineer, domineered, domineerer, domineering, domineeringly, domineeringness, domineers, domines, doming, domini, dominial, dominica, dominical, dominicale, dominican, dominicans, dominick, dominicker, dominicks, dominie, dominies, dominion, dominionism, dominionist, dominions, dominique, dominium, dominiums, domino, dominoes, dominos, dominule, dominus, domitable, domite, domitic, domn, domnei, domoid, dompt, dompteuse, doms, domus, domy, don, don't, don'ts, dona, donable, donaciform, donack, donald, donar, donaries, donary, donas, donat, donataries, donatary, donate, donated, donatee, donates, donating, donatio, donation, donationes, donations, donatism, donatist, donative, donatively, donatives, donator, donatories, donators, donatory, donatress, donax, doncella, doncy, dondaine, dondine, done, donec, donee, donees, doneness, donenesses, donet, doney, dong, donga, donging, dongola, dongolas, dongon, dongs, doni, donicker, donis, donjon, donjons, donk, donkey, donkey's, donkeyback, donkeyish, donkeyism, donkeyman, donkeymen, donkeys, donkeywork, donna, donnard, donnas, donne, donned, donnee, donnees, donnerd, donnered, donnert, donnick, donning, donnish, donnishly, donnishness, donnism, donnock, donnot, donny, donnybrook, donnybrooks, donor, donors, donorship, donought, donovan, dons, donship, donsie, donsky, donsy, dont, donum, donut, donuts, donzel, donzella, donzels, doo, doob, doocot, doodab, doodad, doodads, doodah, doodle, doodlebug, doodled, doodler, doodlers, doodles, doodlesack, doodling, doodskop, doohickey, doohickeys, doohickus, doohinkey, doohinkus, dooja, dook, dooket, dookit, dool, doolee, doolees, dooley, doolfu, dooli, doolie, doolies, dooly, doom, doomage, doombook, doomed, doomer, doomful, doomfully, doomfulness, dooming, doomlike, dooms, doomsayer, doomsday, doomsdays, doomsman, doomstead, doomster, doomsters, doomwatcher, doon, dooputty, door, door's, doorba, doorbell, doorbells, doorboy, doorbrand, doorcase, doorcheek, doored, doorframe, doorhawk, doorhead, dooring, doorjamb, doorjambs, doorkeep, doorkeeper, doorknob, doorknobs, doorless, doorlike, doormaid, doormaker, doormaking, doorman, doormat, doormats, doormen, doornail, doornails, doornboom, doorpiece, doorplate, doorplates, doorpost, doorposts, doors, doorsill, doorsills, doorstead, doorstep, doorstep's, doorsteps, doorstone, doorstop, doorstops, doorward, doorway, doorway's, doorways, doorweed, doorwise, dooryard, dooryards, doover, dooxidize, doozer, doozers, doozies, doozy, dop, dopa, dopamelanin, dopamine, dopaminergic, dopamines, dopant, dopants, dopaoxidase, dopas, dopatta, dopchick, dope, dopebook, doped, dopehead, doper, dopers, dopes, dopesheet, dopester, dopesters, dopey, dopier, dopiest, dopiness, dopinesses, doping, dopped, doppelganger, doppelkummel, dopper, dopperbird, doppia, dopping, doppio, doppler, dopplerite, dopster, dopy, dor, dora, dorab, dorad, doradilla, dorado, dorados, doralium, doraphobia, doray, dorbeetle, dorbel, dorbie, dorbug, dorbugs, dorcas, dorcastry, doree, dorestane, dorey, dorhawk, dorhawks, doria, dorian, doric, dories, dorippid, doris, dorism, dorize, dorje, dorking, dorlach, dorlot, dorm, dormancies, dormancy, dormant, dormantly, dormer, dormered, dormers, dormette, dormeuse, dormice, dormie, dormient, dormilona, dormin, dormins, dormitary, dormition, dormitive, dormitories, dormitory, dormitory's, dormmice, dormouse, dorms, dormy, dorn, dorneck, dornecks, dornic, dornick, dornicks, dornock, dornocks, doronicum, dorosacral, doroscentral, dorosternal, dorothy, dorp, dorper, dorpers, dorps, dorr, dorrbeetle, dorrs, dors, dorsa, dorsabdominal, dorsabdominally, dorsad, dorsal, dorsale, dorsales, dorsalgia, dorsalis, dorsally, dorsalmost, dorsals, dorsalward, dorsalwards, dorse, dorsel, dorser, dorsers, dorsi, dorsibranch, dorsibranchiate, dorsicollar, dorsicolumn, dorsicommissure, dorsicornu, dorsiduct, dorsiferous, dorsifixed, dorsiflex, dorsiflexion, dorsiflexor, dorsigerous, dorsigrade, dorsilateral, dorsilumbar, dorsimedian, dorsimesal, dorsimeson, dorsiparous, dorsipinal, dorsispinal, dorsiventral, dorsiventrality, dorsiventrally, dorsoabdominal, dorsoanterior, dorsoapical, dorsocaudad, dorsocaudal, dorsocentral, dorsocephalad, dorsocephalic, dorsocervical, dorsocervically, dorsodynia, dorsoepitrochlear, dorsointercostal, dorsointestinal, dorsolateral, dorsolum, dorsolumbar, dorsomedial, dorsomedian, dorsomesal, dorsonasal, dorsonuchal, dorsopleural, dorsoposteriad, dorsoposterior, dorsoradial, dorsosacral, dorsoscapular, dorsosternal, dorsothoracic, dorsoventrad, dorsoventral, dorsoventrality, dorsoventrally, dorsula, dorsulum, dorsum, dorsumbonal, dort, dorter, dortiness, dortiship, dortour, dorts, dorty, doruck, dory, doryline, doryman, dorymen, doryphoros, doryphorus, dos, dosa, dosadh, dosage, dosages, dosain, dose, dosed, doser, dosers, doses, dosimeter, dosimeters, dosimetric, dosimetrician, dosimetries, dosimetrist, dosimetry, dosing, dosiology, dosis, dosology, doss, dossal, dossals, dossed, dossel, dossels, dossennus, dosser, dosseret, dosserets, dossers, dosses, dossety, dosshouse, dossier, dossiere, dossiers, dossil, dossils, dossing, dossman, dossmen, dossy, dost, dostoevsky, dot, dot's, dotage, dotages, dotal, dotant, dotard, dotardism, dotardly, dotards, dotardy, dotarie, dotate, dotation, dotations, dotchin, dote, doted, doter, doters, dotes, doth, dother, dothideaceous, dothienenteritis, dotier, dotiest, dotiness, doting, dotingly, dotingness, dotish, dotishness, dotkin, dotless, dotlet, dotlike, dotriacontane, dots, dottard, dotted, dottedness, dottel, dottels, dotter, dotterel, dotterels, dotters, dottier, dottiest, dottily, dottiness, dotting, dottle, dottled, dottler, dottles, dottling, dottrel, dottrels, dotty, doty, douane, douanes, douanier, douar, doub, double, doubled, doubledamn, doubleganger, doublegear, doublehanded, doublehandedly, doublehandedness, doublehatching, doubleheader, doubleheaders, doublehearted, doubleheartedness, doublehorned, doublehung, doubleleaf, doublelunged, doubleness, doubleprecision, doubler, doublers, doubles, doublespeak, doublet, doublet's, doubleted, doublethink, doublethinking, doublethought, doubleton, doubletone, doubletree, doublets, doublette, doublewidth, doubleword, doublewords, doubleyou, doubling, doubloon, doubloons, doublure, doublures, doubly, doubt, doubtable, doubtably, doubtance, doubted, doubtedly, doubter, doubters, doubtful, doubtfully, doubtfulness, doubting, doubtingly, doubtingness, doubtless, doubtlessly, doubtlessness, doubtmonger, doubtous, doubts, doubtsome, doubty, douc, douce, doucely, douceness, doucepere, doucet, douceur, douceurs, douche, douched, douches, douching, doucin, doucine, doucker, doudle, dough, doughbellies, doughbelly, doughbird, doughboy, doughboys, doughface, doughfaceism, doughfeet, doughfoot, doughfoots, doughhead, doughier, doughiest, doughiness, doughlike, doughmaker, doughmaking, doughman, doughmen, doughnut, doughnut's, doughnuts, doughs, dought, doughtier, doughtiest, doughtily, doughtiness, doughty, doughy, dougl, douglas, doukhobor, doulce, doulocracy, doum, douma, doumaist, doumas, doundake, doup, douper, douping, doupion, doupioni, douppioni, dour, doura, dourade, dourah, dourahs, douras, dourer, dourest, douricouli, dourine, dourines, dourly, dourness, dournesses, douroucouli, douse, doused, douser, dousers, douses, dousing, dout, douter, doutous, douvecot, doux, douzaine, douzaines, douzainier, douzeper, douzepers, douzieme, douziemes, dove, dovecot, dovecote, dovecotes, dovecots, doveflower, dovefoot, dovehouse, dovekey, dovekeys, dovekie, dovekies, dovelet, dovelike, dovelikeness, doveling, doven, dovened, dovening, dovens, dover, doves, dovetail, dovetailed, dovetailer, dovetailing, dovetails, dovetailwise, doveweed, dovewood, dovey, dovish, dovishness, dow, dowable, dowage, dowager, dowagerism, dowagers, dowcet, dowcote, dowd, dowdier, dowdies, dowdiest, dowdily, dowdiness, dowdy, dowdyish, dowdyism, dowed, dowel, doweled, doweling, dowelled, dowelling, dowels, dower, doweral, dowered, doweress, doweries, dowering, dowerless, dowers, dowery, dowf, dowfart, dowhacky, dowie, dowily, dowiness, dowing, dowitch, dowitcher, dowitchers, dowl, dowlas, dowless, dowly, dowment, down, downbear, downbeard, downbeat, downbeats, downbend, downbent, downby, downbye, downcast, downcastly, downcastness, downcasts, downcome, downcomer, downcomes, downcoming, downcourt, downcried, downcry, downcrying, downcurve, downcurved, downcut, downdale, downdraft, downdraught, downed, downer, downers, downface, downfall, downfallen, downfalling, downfalls, downfeed, downfield, downflow, downfold, downfolded, downgate, downgoing, downgone, downgrade, downgraded, downgrades, downgrading, downgrowth, downgyved, downhanging, downhaul, downhauls, downheaded, downhearted, downheartedly, downheartedness, downhill, downhills, downier, downiest, downily, downiness, downing, downland, downless, downlie, downlier, downligging, downlike, downline, downlink, downlinked, downlinking, downlinks, download, downloadable, downloaded, downloading, downloads, downlooked, downlooker, downlying, downmost, downness, downpipe, downplay, downplayed, downplaying, downplays, downpour, downpouring, downpours, downrange, downright, downrightly, downrightness, downriver, downrush, downrushing, downs, downset, downshare, downshift, downshifted, downshifting, downshifts, downshore, downside, downsinking, downsitting, downsize, downsized, downsizes, downsizing, downslide, downsliding, downslip, downslope, downsman, downsome, downspout, downstage, downstair, downstairs, downstate, downstater, downsteepy, downstream, downstreet, downstroke, downstrokes, downswing, downswings, downtake, downthrow, downthrown, downthrust, downtime, downtimes, downtown, downtowner, downtowns, downtrampling, downtreading, downtrend, downtrends, downtrod, downtrodden, downtroddenness, downturn, downturned, downturns, downward, downwardly, downwardness, downwards, downwarp, downwash, downway, downweed, downweigh, downweight, downweighted, downwind, downwith, downy, dowp, dowress, dowries, dowry, dows, dowsabel, dowsabels, dowse, dowsed, dowser, dowsers, dowses, dowset, dowsets, dowsing, dowve, dowy, doxa, doxastic, doxasticon, doxie, doxies, doxographer, doxographical, doxography, doxological, doxologically, doxologies, doxologize, doxologized, doxologizing, doxology, doxy, doxycycline, doyen, doyenne, doyennes, doyens, doyley, doyleys, doylies, doylt, doyly, doyst, doz, doze, dozed, dozen, dozened, dozener, dozening, dozens, dozent, dozenth, dozenths, dozer, dozers, dozes, dozier, doziest, dozily, doziness, dozinesses, dozing, dozy, dozzle, dozzled, dp, dpt, dr, drab, drabant, drabbed, drabber, drabbest, drabbet, drabbets, drabbing, drabbish, drabble, drabbled, drabbler, drabbles, drabbletail, drabbletailed, drabbling, drabby, drabler, drably, drabness, drabnesses, drabs, dracaena, dracaenas, drachen, drachm, drachma, drachmae, drachmai, drachmal, drachmas, drachms, dracin, dracma, draco, dracone, draconian, draconic, draconically, draconin, draconites, draconitic, dracontian, dracontiasis, dracontic, dracontine, dracontites, dracunculus, drad, dradge, draegerman, draegermen, draff, draffier, draffiest, draffish, draffman, draffs, draffsack, draffy, draft, draftable, draftage, drafted, draftee, draftees, drafter, drafters, draftier, draftiest, draftily, draftiness, drafting, draftings, draftman, draftmanship, draftproof, drafts, draftsman, draftsmanship, draftsmen, draftsperson, draftswoman, draftswomanship, draftwoman, drafty, drag, dragade, dragaded, dragading, dragbar, dragboat, dragbolt, dragee, dragees, drageoir, dragged, dragger, draggers, draggier, draggiest, draggily, dragginess, dragging, draggingly, draggle, draggled, draggles, draggletail, draggletailed, draggletailedly, draggletailedness, draggling, draggly, draggy, draghound, dragline, draglines, dragman, dragnet, dragnets, drago, dragoman, dragomanate, dragomanic, dragomanish, dragomans, dragomen, dragon, dragon's, dragonade, dragonesque, dragoness, dragonet, dragonets, dragonfish, dragonfishes, dragonflies, dragonfly, dragonhead, dragonhood, dragonish, dragonism, dragonize, dragonkind, dragonlike, dragonnade, dragonne, dragonroot, dragons, dragontail, dragonwort, dragoon, dragoonable, dragoonade, dragoonage, dragooned, dragooner, dragooning, dragoons, dragrope, dragropes, drags, dragsaw, dragsawing, dragshoe, dragsman, dragsmen, dragstaff, dragster, dragsters, drahthaar, drail, drailed, drailing, drails, drain, drainable, drainage, drainages, drainageway, drainboard, draine, drained, drainer, drainerman, drainermen, drainers, drainfield, draining, drainless, drainman, drainpipe, drainpipes, drains, drainspout, draintile, drainway, draisene, draisine, drake, drakefly, drakelet, drakes, drakestone, drakonite, dram, drama, drama's, dramalogue, dramamine, dramas, dramatic, dramatical, dramatically, dramaticism, dramaticle, dramatics, dramaticule, dramatis, dramatisable, dramatise, dramatised, dramatiser, dramatising, dramatism, dramatist, dramatist's, dramatists, dramatizable, dramatization, dramatizations, dramatize, dramatized, dramatizer, dramatizes, dramatizing, dramaturge, dramaturgic, dramaturgical, dramaturgically, dramaturgist, dramaturgy, drame, dramm, drammach, drammage, dramme, drammed, drammer, dramming, drammock, drammocks, drams, dramseller, dramshop, dramshops, drang, drank, drant, drapability, drapable, drape, drapeability, drapeable, draped, draper, draperess, draperied, draperies, drapers, drapery, drapery's, drapes, drapet, drapetomania, draping, drapping, drassid, drastic, drastically, drat, dratchell, drate, drats, dratted, dratting, draught, draught's, draughtboard, draughted, draughter, draughthouse, draughtier, draughtiest, draughtily, draughtiness, draughting, draughtman, draughtmanship, draughts, draughtsboard, draughtsman, draughtsmanship, draughtsmen, draughtswoman, draughtswomanship, draughty, drave, dravidian, dravite, dravya, draw, drawability, drawable, drawarm, drawback, drawback's, drawbacks, drawbar, drawbars, drawbeam, drawbench, drawboard, drawbolt, drawbore, drawbored, drawbores, drawboring, drawboy, drawbridge, drawbridge's, drawbridges, drawcansir, drawcard, drawcut, drawdown, drawdowns, drawee, drawees, drawer, drawerful, drawers, drawfile, drawfiling, drawgate, drawgear, drawglove, drawhead, drawhorse, drawing, drawings, drawk, drawknife, drawknives, drawknot, drawl, drawlatch, drawled, drawler, drawlers, drawlier, drawliest, drawling, drawlingly, drawlingness, drawlink, drawloom, drawls, drawly, drawn, drawnet, drawnly, drawnness, drawnwork, drawoff, drawout, drawplate, drawpoint, drawrod, draws, drawshave, drawsheet, drawspan, drawspring, drawstop, drawstring, drawstrings, drawtongs, drawtube, drawtubes, dray, drayage, drayages, drayed, drayhorse, draying, drayman, draymen, drays, drazel, drch, dread, dreadable, dreaded, dreader, dreadful, dreadfully, dreadfulness, dreadfuls, dreading, dreadingly, dreadless, dreadlessly, dreadlessness, dreadlocks, dreadly, dreadnaught, dreadness, dreadnought, dreadnoughts, dreads, dream, dreamage, dreamboat, dreamed, dreamer, dreamers, dreamery, dreamful, dreamfully, dreamfulness, dreamhole, dreamier, dreamiest, dreamily, dreaminess, dreaming, dreamingful, dreamingly, dreamish, dreamland, dreamless, dreamlessly, dreamlessness, dreamlet, dreamlike, dreamlikeness, dreamlit, dreamlore, dreams, dreamscape, dreamsily, dreamsiness, dreamsy, dreamt, dreamtide, dreamtime, dreamwhile, dreamwise, dreamworld, dreamy, drear, drearfully, drearier, drearies, dreariest, drearihead, drearily, dreariment, dreariness, drearing, drearisome, drearisomely, drearisomeness, drearly, drearness, dreary, dreche, dreck, drecks, dredge, dredged, dredgeful, dredger, dredgers, dredges, dredging, dredgings, dree, dreed, dreegh, dreeing, dreep, dreepiness, dreepy, drees, dreg, dreggier, dreggiest, dreggily, dregginess, dreggish, dreggy, dregless, dregs, dreich, dreidel, dreidels, dreidl, dreidls, dreigh, dreikanter, dreikanters, dreiling, dreint, dreissiger, drek, dreks, drench, drenched, drencher, drenchers, drenches, drenching, drenchingly, dreng, drengage, drengh, drent, drepane, drepania, drepanid, drepaniform, drepanium, drepanoid, dresden, dress, dressage, dressages, dressed, dresser, dressers, dressership, dresses, dressier, dressiest, dressily, dressiness, dressing, dressings, dressline, dressmake, dressmaker, dressmaker's, dressmakers, dressmakership, dressmakery, dressmaking, dressoir, dressoirs, dressy, drest, dretch, drevel, drew, drewite, drey, dreynt, drias, drib, dribbed, dribber, dribbet, dribbing, dribble, dribbled, dribblement, dribbler, dribblers, dribbles, dribblet, dribblets, dribbling, driblet, driblets, dribs, dridder, driddle, drie, driech, dried, driegh, drier, drier's, drierman, driers, dries, driest, drift, driftage, driftages, driftbolt, drifted, drifter, drifters, driftfish, driftfishes, driftier, driftiest, drifting, driftingly, driftland, driftless, driftlessness, driftlet, driftman, driftpiece, driftpin, driftpins, drifts, driftway, driftweed, driftwind, driftwood, drifty, drighten, drightin, drill, drillability, drillable, drillbit, drilled, driller, drillers, drillet, drilling, drillings, drillman, drillmaster, drillmasters, drills, drillstock, drilvis, drily, dringle, drink, drinkability, drinkable, drinkableness, drinkables, drinkably, drinker, drinkers, drinkery, drinking, drinkless, drinkproof, drinks, drinky, drinn, drip, drip's, dripless, dripolator, drippage, dripped, dripper, drippers, drippier, drippiest, dripping, drippings, dripple, dripproof, drippy, drips, dripstick, dripstone, dript, drisheen, drisk, drissel, drivable, drivage, drive, driveable, driveaway, driveboat, drivebolt, drivecap, drivehead, drivel, driveled, driveler, drivelers, driveline, driveling, drivelingly, drivelled, driveller, drivellers, drivelling, drivellingly, drivels, driven, drivenness, drivepipe, driver, driverless, drivers, drivership, drives, drivescrew, driveway, driveway's, driveways, drivewell, driving, drivingly, drizzle, drizzled, drizzles, drizzlier, drizzliest, drizzling, drizzlingly, drizzly, drochuil, droddum, drof, drofland, droger, drogerman, drogermen, drogh, drogher, drogherman, droghlin, drogoman, drogue, drogues, droguet, droh, droich, droil, droit, droits, droitsman, droitural, droiture, droiturel, drolerie, droll, drolled, droller, drolleries, drollery, drollest, drolling, drollingly, drollish, drollishness, drollist, drollness, drolls, drolly, drolushness, dromaeognathism, dromaeognathous, drome, dromed, dromedarian, dromedaries, dromedarist, dromedary, drometer, dromic, dromical, dromioid, dromograph, dromoi, dromomania, dromometer, dromon, dromond, dromonds, dromons, dromophobia, dromornis, dromos, dromotropic, drona, dronage, drone, drone's, droned, dronel, dronepipe, droner, droners, drones, dronet, drongo, drongos, droning, droningly, dronish, dronishly, dronishness, dronkelew, dronkgrass, dronte, drony, droob, drool, drooled, droolier, drooliest, drooling, drools, drooly, droop, drooped, drooper, droopier, droopiest, droopily, droopiness, drooping, droopingly, droopingness, droops, droopt, droopy, drop, drop's, dropax, dropberry, dropcloth, dropflower, dropforge, dropforged, dropforger, dropforging, drophead, dropheads, dropkick, dropkicker, dropkicks, droplet, droplets, droplight, droplike, dropline, dropling, dropman, dropmeal, dropout, dropouts, droppage, dropped, dropper, dropper's, dropperful, droppers, dropping, dropping's, droppingly, droppings, droppy, drops, dropseed, dropshot, dropshots, dropsical, dropsically, dropsicalness, dropsied, dropsies, dropsonde, dropsy, dropsywort, dropt, dropvie, dropwise, dropworm, dropwort, dropworts, drosera, droseraceous, droseras, droshkies, droshky, droskies, drosky, drosograph, drosometer, drosophila, drosophilae, drosophilas, dross, drossed, drossel, drosser, drosses, drossier, drossiest, drossiness, drossing, drossless, drossy, drostden, drostdy, drou, droud, droughermen, drought, drought's, droughtier, droughtiest, droughtiness, droughts, droughty, drouk, droukan, drouked, drouket, drouking, droukit, drouks, droumy, drouth, drouthier, drouthiest, drouthiness, drouths, drouthy, drove, droved, drover, drovers, droves, droving, drovy, drow, drown, drownd, drownded, drownding, drownds, drowned, drowner, drowners, drowning, drowningly, drownings, drownproofing, drowns, drowse, drowsed, drowses, drowsier, drowsiest, drowsihead, drowsihood, drowsily, drowsiness, drowsing, drowsy, drowte, droyl, drub, drubbed, drubber, drubbers, drubbing, drubbings, drubble, drubbly, drubly, drubs, drucken, drudge, drudged, drudger, drudgeries, drudgers, drudgery, drudges, drudging, drudgingly, drudgism, druery, druffen, drug, drug's, drugeteria, drugge, drugged, drugger, druggeries, druggery, drugget, druggeting, druggets, druggier, druggiest, drugging, druggist, druggist's, druggister, druggists, druggy, drugless, drugmaker, drugman, drugs, drugshop, drugstore, drugstores, druid, druidess, druidesses, druidic, druidical, druidism, druidisms, druidology, druidry, druids, druith, drum, drum's, drumbeat, drumbeater, drumbeating, drumbeats, drumble, drumbled, drumbledore, drumbler, drumbles, drumbling, drumfire, drumfires, drumfish, drumfishes, drumhead, drumheads, drumler, drumlier, drumliest, drumlike, drumlin, drumline, drumlinoid, drumlins, drumloid, drumloidal, drumly, drummed, drummer, drummer's, drummers, drumming, drummock, drummy, drumread, drumreads, drumroll, drumrolls, drums, drumskin, drumslade, drumsler, drumstick, drumsticks, drumwood, drung, drungar, drunk, drunkard, drunkard's, drunkards, drunkelew, drunken, drunkeness, drunkenly, drunkenness, drunkensome, drunkenwise, drunker, drunkeries, drunkery, drunkest, drunkly, drunkometer, drunks, drunt, drupaceous, drupal, drupe, drupel, drupelet, drupelets, drupeole, drupes, drupetum, drupiferous, drupose, drury, druse, drused, druses, drusy, druther, druthers, druttle, druxey, druxiness, druxy, druze, dry, dryable, dryad, dryades, dryadetum, dryadic, dryads, dryas, dryasdust, drybeard, drybrained, drybrush, drycoal, drydenian, dryer, dryerman, dryermen, dryers, dryest, dryfarm, dryfarmer, dryfat, dryfist, dryfoot, drygoodsman, dryhouse, drying, dryinid, dryish, drylot, drylots, dryly, dryness, drynesses, dryopithecid, dryopithecine, dryopteroid, drypoint, drypoints, dryrot, drys, drysalter, drysalteries, drysaltery, drysne, dryster, dryth, drywall, drywalls, dryworker, ds, dsect, dsects, dsname, dsnames, dsp, dsr, dsri, dt, dt's, dtd, dtente, dtset, du, duad, duadic, duads, dual, duali, dualin, dualism, dualisms, dualist, dualistic, dualistically, dualists, dualities, duality, duality's, dualization, dualize, dualized, dualizes, dualizing, dually, dualogue, duals, duan, duant, duarch, duarchies, duarchy, dub, dubash, dubb, dubba, dubbah, dubbed, dubbeh, dubbeltje, dubber, dubbers, dubbin, dubbing, dubbings, dubbins, dubby, dubieties, dubiety, dubio, dubiocrystalline, dubiosities, dubiosity, dubious, dubiously, dubiousness, dubitable, dubitably, dubitancy, dubitant, dubitante, dubitate, dubitatingly, dubitation, dubitative, dubitatively, dublin, duboisin, duboisine, dubonnet, dubonnets, dubs, duc, ducal, ducally, ducamara, ducape, ducat, ducato, ducaton, ducatoon, ducats, ducatus, ducdame, duce, duces, duchan, duchery, duchess, duchess's, duchesse, duchesses, duchesslike, duchies, duchy, duci, duck, duckbill, duckbills, duckblind, duckboard, duckboards, duckboat, ducked, ducker, duckeries, duckers, duckery, duckfoot, duckfooted, duckhearted, duckhood, duckhouse, duckhunting, duckie, duckier, duckies, duckiest, ducking, duckish, ducklar, ducklet, duckling, ducklings, ducklingship, duckmeat, duckmole, duckpin, duckpins, duckpond, ducks, duckstone, ducktail, ducktails, duckweed, duckweeds, duckwheat, duckwife, duckwing, ducky, ducs, duct, ductal, ducted, ductibility, ductible, ductile, ductilely, ductileness, ductilimeter, ductility, ductilize, ductilized, ductilizing, ducting, ductings, duction, ductless, ductor, ducts, ductule, ductules, ducture, ductus, ductwork, dud, dudaim, dudder, duddery, duddie, duddies, duddle, duddy, dude, dudeen, dudeens, dudelsack, dudes, dudgen, dudgeon, dudgeons, dudine, dudish, dudishly, dudishness, dudism, dudler, dudley, dudleyite, dudman, duds, due, duecentist, duecento, duecentos, dueful, duel, dueled, dueler, duelers, dueling, duelist, duelistic, duelists, duelled, dueller, duellers, duelli, duelling, duellist, duellistic, duellists, duellize, duello, duellos, duels, duenas, duende, duendes, dueness, duenesses, duenna, duennadom, duennas, duennaship, duer, dues, duet, duets, duetted, duetting, duettino, duettist, duettists, duetto, duff, duffadar, duffed, duffel, duffels, duffer, dufferdom, duffers, duffies, duffing, duffle, duffles, duffs, duffy, dufoil, dufrenite, dufrenoysite, dufter, dufterdar, duftery, duftite, duftry, dug, dugal, dugdug, dugento, duggler, dugong, dugongs, dugout, dugouts, dugs, dugway, duhat, dui, duiker, duikerbok, duikerboks, duikerbuck, duikers, duim, duinhewassel, duit, duits, dujan, duka, duke, duke's, dukedom, dukedoms, dukeling, dukely, dukery, dukes, dukeship, dukhn, dukhobor, dukker, dukkeripen, dukkha, dukuma, dulbert, dulc, dulcamara, dulcarnon, dulce, dulcely, dulceness, dulcet, dulcetly, dulcetness, dulcets, dulcian, dulciana, dulcianas, dulcid, dulcification, dulcified, dulcifies, dulcifluous, dulcify, dulcifying, dulcigenic, dulciloquent, dulciloquy, dulcimer, dulcimers, dulcimore, dulcinea, dulcineas, dulcite, dulcitol, dulcitude, dulcity, dulcor, dulcorate, dulcose, duledge, duler, dulia, dulias, dull, dullard, dullardism, dullardness, dullards, dullbrained, dulled, duller, dullery, dullest, dullhead, dullhearted, dullification, dullify, dulling, dullish, dullishly, dullity, dullness, dullnesses, dullpate, dulls, dullsome, dullsville, dully, dulness, dulnesses, dulocracy, dulosis, dulotic, dulse, dulseman, dulses, dult, dultie, duluth, dulwilly, duly, dum, duma, dumaist, dumas, dumb, dumba, dumbbell, dumbbell's, dumbbeller, dumbbells, dumbcow, dumbed, dumber, dumbest, dumbfish, dumbfound, dumbfounded, dumbfounder, dumbfounderment, dumbfounding, dumbfoundment, dumbhead, dumbheaded, dumbing, dumble, dumbledore, dumbly, dumbness, dumbnesses, dumbs, dumbstricken, dumbstruck, dumbwaiter, dumbwaiters, dumby, dumdum, dumdums, dumetose, dumfound, dumfounded, dumfounder, dumfounderment, dumfounding, dumfounds, dumka, dumky, dummel, dummered, dummerer, dummied, dummies, dumminess, dummkopf, dummkopfs, dummy, dummy's, dummying, dummyism, dummyweed, dumontite, dumortierite, dumose, dumosity, dumous, dump, dumpage, dumpcart, dumpcarts, dumped, dumper, dumpers, dumpfile, dumpier, dumpies, dumpiest, dumpily, dumpiness, dumping, dumpings, dumpish, dumpishly, dumpishness, dumple, dumpled, dumpler, dumpling, dumplings, dumpoke, dumps, dumpty, dumpy, dumsola, dun, dunair, dunal, dunamis, dunbird, dunce, dunce's, duncedom, duncehood, duncery, dunces, dunch, dunches, dunciad, duncical, duncify, duncifying, duncish, duncishly, duncishness, dundasite, dundavoe, dundee, dundee's, dundees, dunder, dunderbolt, dunderfunk, dunderhead, dunderheaded, dunderheadedness, dunderheads, dunderpate, dunderpates, dundrearies, dundreary, dune, dune's, duneland, dunelands, dunelike, dunes, dunfish, dung, dungannonite, dungaree, dungarees, dungari, dungas, dungbeck, dungbird, dungbred, dunged, dungeon, dungeon's, dungeoner, dungeonlike, dungeons, dunger, dunghill, dunghills, dunghilly, dungier, dungiest, dunging, dungol, dungon, dungs, dungy, dungyard, duniewassal, dunite, dunites, dunitic, duniwassal, dunk, dunkadoo, dunked, dunker, dunkers, dunking, dunkirk, dunkle, dunkled, dunkling, dunks, dunlin, dunlins, dunnage, dunnaged, dunnages, dunnaging, dunnakin, dunne, dunned, dunner, dunness, dunnesses, dunnest, dunniewassel, dunning, dunnish, dunnite, dunnites, dunno, dunnock, dunny, dunpickle, duns, dunst, dunstable, dunster, dunstone, dunt, dunted, dunter, dunting, duntle, dunts, duny, dunziekte, duo, duocosane, duodecagon, duodecahedral, duodecahedron, duodecane, duodecastyle, duodecennial, duodecillion, duodecillions, duodecillionth, duodecimal, duodecimality, duodecimally, duodecimals, duodecimfid, duodecimo, duodecimole, duodecimomos, duodecimos, duodecuple, duodedena, duodedenums, duodena, duodenal, duodenary, duodenas, duodenate, duodenation, duodene, duodenectomy, duodenitis, duodenocholangitis, duodenocholecystostomy, duodenocholedochotomy, duodenocystostomy, duodenoenterostomy, duodenogram, duodenojejunal, duodenojejunostomies, duodenojejunostomy, duodenopancreatectomy, duodenoscopy, duodenostomy, duodenotomy, duodenum, duodenums, duodial, duodiode, duodiodepentode, duodrama, duodynatron, duograph, duogravure, duole, duoliteral, duolog, duologs, duologue, duologues, duomachy, duomi, duomo, duomos, duopod, duopolies, duopolist, duopolistic, duopoly, duopsonies, duopsonistic, duopsony, duos, duosecant, duotone, duotoned, duotones, duotriacontane, duotriode, duotype, duoviri, dup, dupability, dupable, dupatta, dupe, duped, dupedom, duper, duperies, dupers, dupery, dupes, duping, dupion, dupioni, dupla, duplation, duple, duplet, duplex, duplexed, duplexer, duplexers, duplexes, duplexing, duplexity, duplexs, duplicability, duplicable, duplicand, duplicando, duplicate, duplicated, duplicately, duplicates, duplicating, duplication, duplications, duplicative, duplicator, duplicator's, duplicators, duplicature, duplicatus, duplicia, duplicident, duplicidentate, duplicious, duplicipennate, duplicitas, duplicities, duplicitous, duplicitously, duplicity, duplification, duplified, duplify, duplifying, duplon, duplone, duply, dupondidii, dupondii, dupondius, duppa, dupped, dupper, duppies, dupping, duppy, dups, dur, dura, durabilities, durability, durable, durableness, durables, durably, duracine, durain, dural, duralumin, duramater, duramatral, duramen, duramens, durance, durances, durangite, durant, durante, duraplasty, duraquara, duras, duraspinalis, duration, duration's, durational, durationless, durations, durative, duratives, durax, durbachite, durbar, durbars, durdenite, durdum, dure, dured, duree, dureful, durene, durenol, dureresque, dures, duress, duresses, duressor, duret, duretto, durezza, durgah, durgan, durgen, durham, durian, durians, duricrust, duridine, during, duringly, durion, durions, durity, durmast, durmasts, durn, durndest, durned, durneder, durnedest, durning, durns, duro, duroc, durocs, durometer, duroquinone, duros, durous, duroy, durr, durra, durras, durrie, durries, durrin, durrs, durry, durst, durukuli, durum, durums, durwan, durwaun, duryl, durzee, durzi, dusack, duscle, dusenwind, dush, dusio, dusk, dusked, dusken, duskier, duskiest, duskily, duskiness, dusking, duskingtide, duskish, duskishly, duskishness, duskly, duskness, dusks, dusky, dusserah, dust, dustband, dustbin, dustbins, dustblu, dustbox, dustcart, dustcloth, dustcloths, dustcoat, dustcover, dusted, dustee, duster, dusterman, dustermen, dusters, dustfall, dustheap, dustheaps, dustier, dustiest, dustily, dustiness, dusting, dustless, dustlessness, dustlike, dustman, dustmen, dustoor, dustoori, dustour, dustpan, dustpans, dustpoint, dustproof, dustrag, dustrags, dusts, dustsheet, duststorm, dusttight, dustuck, dustuk, dustup, dustups, dustwoman, dusty, dustyfoot, dutch, dutched, dutchess, dutchify, dutching, dutchman, dutchmen, duteous, duteously, duteousness, dutiability, dutiable, dutied, duties, dutiful, dutifully, dutifulness, dutra, dutuburi, duty, duty's, dutymonger, duumvir, duumviral, duumvirate, duumviri, duumvirs, duvet, duvetine, duvetines, duvetyn, duvetyne, duvetynes, duvetyns, dux, duxelles, duxes, duyker, dvaita, dvandva, dvigu, dvorak, dvornik, dwaible, dwaibly, dwale, dwalm, dwang, dwarf, dwarfed, dwarfer, dwarfest, dwarfing, dwarfish, dwarfishly, dwarfishness, dwarfism, dwarfisms, dwarflike, dwarfling, dwarfness, dwarfs, dwarfy, dwarves, dwayberry, dweeble, dwell, dwelled, dweller, dwellers, dwelling, dwellings, dwells, dwelt, dwight, dwindle, dwindled, dwindlement, dwindles, dwindling, dwine, dwined, dwines, dwining, dwt, dx, dy, dyable, dyad, dyadic, dyadically, dyadics, dyads, dyak, dyakisdodecahedron, dyarchic, dyarchical, dyarchies, dyarchy, dyas, dyaster, dybbuk, dybbukim, dybbuks, dyce, dye, dyeability, dyeable, dyebeck, dyed, dyehouse, dyeing, dyeings, dyeleaves, dyeline, dyemaker, dyemaking, dyer, dyers, dyes, dyester, dyestuff, dyestuffs, dyeware, dyeweed, dyeweeds, dyewood, dyewoods, dygogram, dying, dyingly, dyingness, dyings, dykage, dyke, dyked, dykehopper, dyker, dykereeve, dykes, dyking, dyn, dynactinometer, dynagraph, dynam, dynameter, dynametric, dynametrical, dynamic, dynamical, dynamically, dynamicity, dynamics, dynamis, dynamism, dynamisms, dynamist, dynamistic, dynamists, dynamitard, dynamite, dynamited, dynamiter, dynamiters, dynamites, dynamitic, dynamitical, dynamitically, dynamiting, dynamitish, dynamitism, dynamitist, dynamization, dynamize, dynamo, dynamoelectric, dynamoelectrical, dynamogeneses, dynamogenesis, dynamogenic, dynamogenous, dynamogenously, dynamogeny, dynamograph, dynamometamorphic, dynamometamorphism, dynamometamorphosed, dynamometer, dynamometers, dynamometric, dynamometrical, dynamometry, dynamomorphic, dynamoneure, dynamophone, dynamos, dynamoscope, dynamostatic, dynamotor, dynapolis, dynast, dynastic, dynastical, dynastically, dynasticism, dynastid, dynastidan, dynasties, dynasts, dynasty, dynasty's, dynatron, dynatrons, dyne, dynel, dynes, dynode, dynodes, dyophone, dyophysite, dyostyle, dyotheism, dyothelete, dyphone, dypnone, dys, dysacousia, dysacousis, dysacousma, dysacusia, dysadaptation, dysaesthesia, dysaesthetic, dysanagnosia, dysanalyte, dysaphia, dysaptation, dysarthria, dysarthric, dysarthrosis, dysautonomia, dysbarism, dysbulia, dysbulic, dyschiria, dyschroa, dyschroia, dyschromatopsia, dyschromatoptic, dyschronous, dyscrase, dyscrased, dyscrasia, dyscrasial, dyscrasic, dyscrasing, dyscrasite, dyscrasy, dyscratic, dyscrinism, dyscrystalline, dysenteric, dysenterical, dysenteries, dysentery, dysepulotic, dysepulotical, dyserethisia, dysergasia, dysergia, dysesthesia, dysesthetic, dysfunction, dysfunctional, dysfunctioning, dysfunctions, dysgenesic, dysgenesis, dysgenetic, dysgenic, dysgenical, dysgenics, dysgeogenous, dysgnosia, dysgonic, dysgraphia, dysidrosis, dyskeratosis, dyskinesia, dyskinetic, dyslalia, dyslectic, dyslexia, dyslexias, dyslexic, dyslexics, dyslogia, dyslogistic, dyslogistically, dyslogy, dysluite, dyslysin, dysmenorrhagia, dysmenorrhea, dysmenorrheal, dysmenorrheic, dysmenorrhoea, dysmenorrhoeal, dysmerism, dysmeristic, dysmerogenesis, dysmerogenetic, dysmeromorph, dysmeromorphic, dysmetria, dysmnesia, dysmorphism, dysmorphophobia, dysneuria, dysnomy, dysodile, dysodontiasis, dysodyle, dysorexia, dysorexy, dysoxidation, dysoxidizable, dysoxidize, dyspareunia, dyspathetic, dyspathy, dyspepsia, dyspepsies, dyspepsy, dyspeptic, dyspeptical, dyspeptically, dyspeptics, dysphagia, dysphagic, dysphasia, dysphasic, dysphemia, dysphemism, dysphemistic, dysphemize, dysphemized, dysphonia, dysphonic, dysphoria, dysphoric, dysphotic, dysphrasia, dysphrenia, dyspituitarism, dysplasia, dysplastic, dyspnea, dyspneal, dyspneas, dyspneic, dyspnoea, dyspnoeal, dyspnoeas, dyspnoeic, dyspnoi, dyspnoic, dysporomorph, dyspraxia, dysprosia, dysprosium, dysraphia, dysrhythmia, dyssnite, dysspermatism, dyssynergia, dyssynergy, dyssystole, dystaxia, dystaxias, dystectic, dysteleological, dysteleologically, dysteleologist, dysteleology, dysthymia, dysthymic, dysthyroidism, dystocia, dystocial, dystocias, dystome, dystomic, dystomous, dystonia, dystonias, dystonic, dystopia, dystopian, dystopias, dystrophia, dystrophic, dystrophies, dystrophy, dysuria, dysurias, dysuric, dysury, dysyntribite, dytiscid, dyvour, dyvours, dz, dzeren, dzerin, dzeron, dziggetai, dzo, e, e'en, e'er, e's, ea, eably, eaceworm, each, eachwhere, ead, eadi, eadios, eadish, eager, eagerer, eagerest, eagerly, eagerness, eagers, eagle, eagle's, eagled, eaglehawk, eaglelike, eagles, eagless, eaglestone, eaglet, eaglets, eaglewood, eagling, eagrass, eagre, eagres, ealderman, ealdorman, ealdormen, eam, ean, eaning, eanling, eanlings, ear, earable, earache, earaches, earbash, earbob, earcap, earclip, earcockle, eardrop, eardropper, eardrops, eardrum, eardrums, eared, earflap, earflaps, earflower, earful, earfuls, earhead, earhole, earing, earings, earjewel, earl, earl's, earlap, earlaps, earldom, earldoms, earlduck, earless, earlesss, earlet, earlier, earliest, earlike, earliness, earlish, earlobe, earlobes, earlock, earlocks, earls, earlship, earlships, early, earlyish, earlywood, earmark, earmarked, earmarking, earmarkings, earmarks, earmindedness, earmuff, earmuffs, earn, earnable, earned, earner, earner's, earners, earnest, earnestful, earnestly, earnestness, earnests, earnful, earning, earnings, earns, earock, earphone, earphones, earpick, earpiece, earpieces, earplug, earplugs, earreach, earring, earring's, earringed, earrings, ears, earscrew, earsh, earshell, earshot, earshots, earsore, earsplitting, earspool, earstone, earstones, eartab, eartag, eartagged, earth, earthboard, earthborn, earthbound, earthbred, earthdrake, earthed, earthen, earthenhearted, earthenware, earthfall, earthfast, earthgall, earthgrubber, earthian, earthier, earthiest, earthily, earthiness, earthing, earthkin, earthless, earthlier, earthliest, earthlight, earthlike, earthliness, earthling, earthlings, earthly, earthmaker, earthmaking, earthman, earthmen, earthmove, earthmover, earthmoving, earthnut, earthnuts, earthpea, earthpeas, earthquake, earthquake's, earthquaked, earthquaken, earthquakes, earthquaking, earthquave, earthrise, earths, earthset, earthsets, earthshaker, earthshaking, earthshakingly, earthshattering, earthshine, earthshock, earthslide, earthsmoke, earthstar, earthtongue, earthwall, earthward, earthwards, earthwork, earthworks, earthworm, earthworm's, earthworms, earthy, earwax, earwaxes, earwig, earwigged, earwigginess, earwigging, earwiggy, earwigs, earwitness, earworm, earworms, earwort, ease, eased, easeful, easefully, easefulness, easel, easeled, easeless, easels, easement, easement's, easements, easer, easers, eases, easier, easies, easiest, easily, easiness, easinesses, easing, eassel, east, eastabout, eastbound, easted, easter, eastering, easterlies, easterliness, easterling, easterly, eastermost, eastern, easterner, easterners, easternize, easternized, easternizing, easternly, easternmost, easters, eastertide, easting, eastings, eastland, eastlander, eastlin, eastling, eastlings, eastlins, eastman, eastmost, eastness, easts, eastward, eastwardly, eastwards, easy, easygoing, easygoingly, easygoingness, easylike, eat, eatability, eatable, eatableness, eatables, eatage, eatberry, eatche, eaten, eater, eateries, eaters, eatery, eath, eathly, eating, eatings, eats, eau, eaux, eave, eaved, eavedrop, eavedropper, eavedropping, eaver, eaves, eavesdrip, eavesdrop, eavesdropped, eavesdropper, eavesdropper's, eavesdroppers, eavesdropping, eavesdrops, eavesing, ebauche, ebauchoir, ebb, ebbed, ebbet, ebbets, ebbing, ebbman, ebbs, ebcasc, ebcd, ebcdic, ebdomade, ebenaceous, ebeneous, ebenezer, ebionite, eblis, eboe, ebon, ebonies, ebonige, ebonise, ebonised, ebonises, ebonising, ebonist, ebonite, ebonites, ebonize, ebonized, ebonizes, ebonizing, ebons, ebony, eboulement, ebracteate, ebracteolate, ebraick, ebriate, ebriated, ebricty, ebriety, ebrillade, ebriose, ebriosity, ebrious, ebriously, ebullate, ebulliate, ebullience, ebulliency, ebullient, ebulliently, ebulliometer, ebulliometry, ebullioscope, ebullioscopic, ebullioscopy, ebullition, ebullitions, ebullitive, ebulus, eburated, eburin, eburine, eburnated, eburnation, eburnean, eburneoid, eburneous, eburnian, eburnification, ec, ecad, ecalcarate, ecalcavate, ecanda, ecardinal, ecardine, ecarinate, ecart, ecarte, ecartes, ecaudate, ecb, ecbasis, ecbatic, ecblastesis, ecblastpsis, ecbole, ecbolic, ecbolics, eccaleobion, ecce, eccentrate, eccentric, eccentric's, eccentrical, eccentrically, eccentricities, eccentricity, eccentrics, eccentring, eccentrometer, ecch, ecchondroma, ecchondrosis, ecchondrotome, ecchymoma, ecchymose, ecchymosed, ecchymoses, ecchymosis, ecchymotic, eccl, eccles, ecclesia, ecclesiae, ecclesial, ecclesiarch, ecclesiarchy, ecclesiast, ecclesiastes, ecclesiastic, ecclesiastical, ecclesiasticalism, ecclesiastically, ecclesiasticalness, ecclesiasticism, ecclesiasticize, ecclesiastics, ecclesiastry, ecclesioclastic, ecclesiography, ecclesiolater, ecclesiolatry, ecclesiologic, ecclesiological, ecclesiologically, ecclesiologist, ecclesiology, ecclesiophobia, eccoprotic, eccoproticophoric, eccrine, eccrinology, eccrisis, eccritic, eccyclema, eccyesis, ecdemic, ecdemite, ecderon, ecderonic, ecdyses, ecdysial, ecdysiast, ecdysis, ecdyson, ecdysone, ecdysones, ecdysons, ecesic, ecesis, ecesises, ecgonin, ecgonine, echafaudage, echappe, echappee, echar, echard, echards, eche, echea, eched, echelette, echelle, echelon, echeloned, echeloning, echelonment, echelons, echeneid, echeneidid, echeneidoid, echeneis, eches, echevaria, echeveria, echevin, echidna, echidnae, echidnas, echinacea, echinal, echinate, echinated, eching, echini, echinid, echinidan, echiniform, echinital, echinite, echinochrome, echinococcosis, echinococcus, echinoderm, echinodermal, echinodermata, echinodermatous, echinodermic, echinoid, echinoids, echinologist, echinology, echinopsine, echinostome, echinostomiasis, echinulate, echinulated, echinulation, echinuliform, echinus, echitamine, echites, echiurid, echiuroid, echnida, echo, echocardiogram, echoed, echoencephalography, echoer, echoers, echoes, echoey, echogram, echograph, echoic, echoing, echoingly, echoism, echoisms, echoist, echoize, echoized, echoizing, echolalia, echolalic, echoless, echolocate, echolocation, echometer, echopractic, echopraxia, echos, echovirus, echowise, echt, eciliate, ecize, ecklein, eclair, eclaircise, eclaircissement, eclairissement, eclairs, eclampsia, eclamptic, eclat, eclated, eclating, eclats, eclectic, eclectical, eclectically, eclecticism, eclecticist, eclecticize, eclectics, eclectism, eclectist, eclegm, eclegma, eclegme, eclipsable, eclipsareon, eclipsation, eclipse, eclipsed, eclipser, eclipses, eclipsing, eclipsis, eclipsises, ecliptic, ecliptical, ecliptically, ecliptics, eclogic, eclogite, eclogites, eclogue, eclogues, eclosion, eclosions, ecmnesia, eco, ecocidal, ecocide, ecoclimate, ecod, ecodeme, ecoid, ecol, ecole, ecoles, ecologic, ecological, ecologically, ecologies, ecologist, ecologists, ecology, ecomomist, econ, economese, econometer, econometric, econometrical, econometrically, econometrician, econometrics, econometrist, economic, economical, economically, economicalness, economics, economies, economise, economised, economiser, economising, economism, economist, economist's, economists, economization, economize, economized, economizer, economizers, economizes, economizing, economy, economy's, ecophene, ecophobia, ecophysiological, ecophysiology, ecorch, ecorche, ecorticate, ecospecies, ecospecific, ecospecifically, ecosphere, ecossaise, ecostate, ecosystem, ecosystems, ecotipically, ecotonal, ecotone, ecotones, ecotopic, ecotype, ecotypes, ecotypic, ecotypically, ecoute, ecphasis, ecphonema, ecphonesis, ecphorable, ecphore, ecphoria, ecphoriae, ecphorias, ecphorization, ecphorize, ecphory, ecphova, ecphractic, ecphrasis, ecrase, ecraseur, ecraseurs, ecrasite, ecrevisse, ecroulement, ecru, ecrus, ecrustaceous, ecstasies, ecstasis, ecstasize, ecstasy, ecstatic, ecstatica, ecstatical, ecstatically, ecstaticize, ecstatics, ecstrophy, ectad, ectadenia, ectal, ectally, ectases, ectasia, ectasis, ectatic, ectene, ectental, ectepicondylar, ecteron, ectethmoid, ectethmoidal, ecthetically, ecthlipses, ecthlipsis, ecthyma, ecthymata, ecthymatous, ectiris, ectobatic, ectoblast, ectoblastic, ectobronchium, ectocardia, ectocarpaceous, ectocarpic, ectocarpous, ectocelic, ectochondral, ectocinerea, ectocinereal, ectocoelic, ectocommensal, ectocondylar, ectocondyle, ectocondyloid, ectocornea, ectocranial, ectocrine, ectocuneiform, ectocuniform, ectocyst, ectodactylism, ectoderm, ectodermal, ectodermic, ectodermoidal, ectodermosis, ectoderms, ectodynamomorphic, ectoentad, ectoenzym, ectoenzyme, ectoethmoid, ectogeneous, ectogenesis, ectogenetic, ectogenic, ectogenous, ectoglia, ectolecithal, ectoloph, ectomere, ectomeres, ectomeric, ectomesoblast, ectomorph, ectomorphic, ectomorphism, ectomorphy, ectonephridium, ectoparasite, ectoparasitic, ectopatagia, ectopatagium, ectophloic, ectophyte, ectophytic, ectopia, ectopias, ectopic, ectoplacenta, ectoplasm, ectoplasmatic, ectoplasmic, ectoplastic, ectoplasy, ectoproct, ectoproctan, ectoproctous, ectopterygoid, ectopy, ectoretina, ectorganism, ectorhinal, ectosarc, ectosarcous, ectosarcs, ectoskeleton, ectosomal, ectosome, ectosphenoid, ectosphenotic, ectosphere, ectosteal, ectosteally, ectostosis, ectotheca, ectotherm, ectothermic, ectotoxin, ectotrophic, ectotropic, ectozoa, ectozoan, ectozoans, ectozoic, ectozoon, ectrodactylia, ectrodactylism, ectrodactylous, ectrodactyly, ectrogenic, ectrogeny, ectromelia, ectromelian, ectromelic, ectromelus, ectropion, ectropionization, ectropionize, ectropionized, ectropionizing, ectropium, ectropometer, ectrosyndactyly, ectrotic, ecttypal, ectypal, ectype, ectypes, ectypography, ecu, ecuador, ecuelle, ecuelling, ecumenacy, ecumene, ecumenic, ecumenical, ecumenicalism, ecumenicality, ecumenically, ecumenicism, ecumenicist, ecumenicity, ecumenicize, ecumenics, ecumenism, ecumenist, ecumenistic, ecumenopolis, ecurie, ecus, ecyphellate, eczema, eczemas, eczematization, eczematoid, eczematosis, eczematous, ed, edacious, edaciously, edaciousness, edacities, edacity, edam, edaphic, edaphically, edaphodont, edaphology, edaphon, edaphosaurid, edda, edder, eddic, eddied, eddies, eddish, eddo, eddoes, eddy, eddy's, eddying, eddyroot, edea, edeagra, edeitis, edelweiss, edelweisses, edema, edemas, edemata, edematose, edematous, edemic, eden, edenite, edental, edentalous, edentata, edentate, edentates, edentulate, edentulous, edeodynia, edeology, edeomania, edeoscopy, edeotomy, edestan, edestin, edgar, edge, edgebone, edgeboned, edged, edgeless, edgeling, edgemaker, edgemaking, edgeman, edger, edgerman, edgers, edges, edgeshot, edgestone, edgeway, edgeways, edgeweed, edgewise, edgier, edgiest, edgily, edginess, edginesses, edging, edgingly, edgings, edgrew, edgrow, edgy, edh, edhs, edibile, edibility, edible, edibleness, edibles, edict, edict's, edictal, edictally, edicts, edictum, edicule, ediface, edificable, edificant, edificate, edification, edificative, edificator, edificatory, edifice, edifice's, edificed, edifices, edificial, edificing, edified, edifier, edifiers, edifies, edify, edifying, edifyingly, edifyingness, edile, ediles, edility, edinburgh, edingtonite, edison, edit, editable, edital, editchar, edited, edith, editing, edition, edition's, editions, editor, editor's, editorial, editorialist, editorialization, editorializations, editorialize, editorialized, editorializer, editorializers, editorializes, editorializing, editorially, editorials, editors, editorship, editorships, editress, editresses, edits, edituate, edomite, edomitish, edp, edplot, edriophthalmatous, edriophthalmian, edriophthalmic, edriophthalmous, eds, educ, educabilian, educability, educable, educables, educand, educatability, educatable, educate, educated, educatedly, educatedness, educatee, educates, educating, education, educationable, educational, educationalism, educationalist, educationally, educationary, educationese, educationist, educations, educative, educator, educator's, educators, educatory, educatress, educe, educed, educement, educes, educible, educing, educive, educt, eduction, eductions, eductive, eductor, eductors, educts, edulcorate, edulcorated, edulcorating, edulcoration, edulcorative, edulcorator, edward, edwardian, edwards, ee, eebree, eegrass, eel, eel's, eelback, eelblennies, eelblenny, eelboat, eelbob, eelbobber, eelcake, eelcatcher, eeler, eelery, eelfare, eelfish, eelgrass, eelgrasses, eelier, eeliest, eeling, eellike, eelpot, eelpout, eelpouts, eels, eelshop, eelskin, eelspear, eelware, eelworm, eelworms, eely, eemis, een, eequinoctium, eer, eerie, eerier, eeriest, eerily, eeriness, eerinesses, eerisome, eerock, eery, eesome, eeten, eeyuch, eeyuck, ef, efecks, eff, effable, efface, effaceable, effaced, effacement, effacer, effacers, effaces, effacing, effare, effascinate, effate, effatum, effect, effected, effecter, effecters, effectful, effectible, effecting, effective, effectively, effectiveness, effectivity, effectless, effector, effector's, effectors, effectress, effects, effectual, effectuality, effectualize, effectually, effectualness, effectuate, effectuated, effectuates, effectuating, effectuation, effectuous, effeir, effeminacy, effeminate, effeminated, effeminately, effeminateness, effeminating, effemination, effeminatize, effeminisation, effeminise, effeminised, effeminising, effeminization, effeminize, effeminized, effeminizing, effendi, effendis, efference, efferent, efferently, efferents, efferous, effervesce, effervesced, effervescence, effervescency, effervescent, effervescently, effervesces, effervescible, effervescing, effervescingly, effervescive, effet, effete, effetely, effeteness, effetman, effetmen, efficace, efficacies, efficacious, efficaciously, efficaciousness, efficacity, efficacy, efficience, efficiencies, efficiency, efficient, efficiently, effierce, effigial, effigiate, effigiated, effigiating, effigiation, effigies, effigurate, effiguration, effigy, efflagitate, efflate, efflation, effleurage, effloresce, effloresced, efflorescence, efflorescency, efflorescent, effloresces, efflorescing, efflower, effluence, effluences, effluency, effluent, effluents, effluve, effluvia, effluviable, effluvial, effluvias, effluviate, effluviography, effluvious, effluvium, effluviums, effluvivia, effluviviums, efflux, effluxes, effluxion, effodient, effoliate, efforce, efford, efform, efformation, efformative, effort, effort's, effortful, effortfully, effortfulness, effortless, effortlessly, effortlessness, efforts, effossion, effraction, effractor, effranchise, effranchisement, effray, effrenate, effront, effronted, effronteries, effrontery, effs, effude, effulge, effulged, effulgence, effulgences, effulgent, effulgently, effulges, effulging, effumability, effume, effund, effuse, effused, effusely, effuses, effusing, effusiometer, effusion, effusions, effusive, effusively, effusiveness, effuso, effuviate, efl, eflagelliferous, efoliolate, efoliose, efoveolate, efph, efractory, efreet, efs, eft, eftest, efts, eftsoon, eftsoons, eg, egad, egads, egal, egalitarian, egalitarianism, egalitarians, egalite, egalites, egality, egall, egally, egards, egence, egency, eger, egeran, egeria, egers, egest, egesta, egested, egesting, egestion, egestions, egestive, egests, egg, eggar, eggars, eggbeater, eggbeaters, eggberries, eggberry, eggcrate, eggcup, eggcupful, eggcups, eggeater, egged, egger, eggers, eggfish, eggfruit, egghead, eggheaded, eggheadedness, eggheads, egghot, egging, eggler, eggless, egglike, eggment, eggnog, eggnogs, eggplant, eggplants, eggroll, eggrolls, eggs, eggshell, eggshells, eggwhisk, eggy, egilops, egipto, egis, egises, eglandular, eglandulose, eglandulous, eglantine, eglantines, eglatere, eglateres, eglestonite, egling, eglogue, eglomerate, eglomise, egma, ego, egocentric, egocentrically, egocentricities, egocentricity, egocentrism, egocentristic, egohood, egoism, egoisms, egoist, egoistic, egoistical, egoistically, egoisticalness, egoistry, egoists, egoity, egoize, egoizer, egol, egolatrous, egomania, egomaniac, egomaniacal, egomaniacally, egomanias, egomism, egophonic, egophony, egos, egosyntonic, egotheism, egotism, egotisms, egotist, egotistic, egotistical, egotistically, egotisticalness, egotists, egotize, egotized, egotizing, egracias, egranulose, egre, egregious, egregiously, egregiousness, egremoigne, egress, egressed, egresses, egressing, egression, egressive, egressor, egret, egrets, egrid, egrimonle, egrimony, egriot, egritude, egromancy, egualmente, egueiite, egurgitate, egurgitated, egurgitating, eguttulate, egypt, egyptian, egyptians, egyptologist, egyptology, eh, eheu, ehlite, ehrman, ehrwaldite, ehtanethial, ehuawa, eichbergite, eichwaldite, eicosane, eide, eident, eidently, eider, eiderdown, eiders, eidetic, eidetically, eidograph, eidola, eidolic, eidolism, eidology, eidolology, eidolon, eidolons, eidoptometry, eidos, eidouranion, eiffel, eigenfrequency, eigenfunction, eigenspace, eigenstate, eigenvalue, eigenvalue's, eigenvalues, eigenvector, eigenvectors, eigh, eight, eightball, eightballs, eighteen, eighteenfold, eighteenmo, eighteenmos, eighteens, eighteenth, eighteenthly, eighteenths, eightfoil, eightfold, eighth, eighth's, eighthes, eighthly, eighths, eighties, eightieth, eightieths, eightling, eightpenny, eights, eightscore, eightsman, eightsmen, eightsome, eightvo, eightvos, eighty, eightyfold, eigne, eikon, eikones, eikonology, eikons, eila, eild, eimer, eimeria, einkanter, einkorn, einkorns, einstein, einsteinian, einsteinium, eir, eirack, eire, eirenarch, eirenic, eirenicon, eiresione, eiry, eisegeses, eisegesis, eisegetic, eisegetical, eisell, eisenberg, eisenhower, eisodic, eisoptrophobia, eisteddfod, eisteddfodau, eisteddfodic, eisteddfodism, eisteddfods, either, ejacula, ejaculate, ejaculated, ejaculates, ejaculating, ejaculation, ejaculations, ejaculative, ejaculator, ejaculators, ejaculatory, ejaculum, eject, ejecta, ejectable, ejectamenta, ejected, ejectee, ejecting, ejection, ejections, ejective, ejectively, ejectives, ejectivity, ejectment, ejector, ejectors, ejects, ejectum, ejicient, ejidal, ejido, ejidos, ejoo, ejulate, ejulation, ejurate, ejuration, ejusd, ejusdem, ekaboron, ekacaesium, ekaha, ekamanganese, ekasilicon, ekatantalum, eke, ekebergite, eked, ekename, eker, ekerite, ekes, ekhimi, eking, ekistic, ekistics, ekka, ekphore, ekphoria, ekphorias, ekphorize, ekphory, ektene, ektenes, ektexine, ektexines, ektodynamorphic, el, ela, elabor, elaborate, elaborated, elaborately, elaborateness, elaborates, elaborating, elaboration, elaborations, elaborative, elaboratively, elaborator, elaborators, elaboratory, elabrate, elachistaceous, elacolite, elaeagnaceous, elaenia, elaeoblast, elaeoblastic, elaeocarpaceous, elaeodochon, elaeomargaric, elaeometer, elaeopten, elaeoptene, elaeosaccharum, elaeosia, elaeothesia, elaeothesium, elaic, elaidate, elaidic, elaidin, elaidinic, elain, elaine, elains, elaioleucite, elaioplast, elaiosome, elamite, elamp, elan, elance, eland, elands, elanet, elans, elaphine, elaphure, elaphurine, elapid, elapids, elapine, elapoid, elaps, elapse, elapsed, elapses, elapsing, elargement, elasmobranch, elasmobranchian, elasmobranchiate, elasmosaur, elasmosaurus, elasmothere, elastance, elastase, elastases, elastic, elastica, elastically, elasticate, elastician, elasticin, elasticities, elasticity, elasticize, elasticized, elasticizer, elasticizes, elasticizing, elasticness, elastics, elasticum, elastin, elastins, elastivity, elastomer, elastomeric, elastomers, elastometer, elastometry, elastose, elatcha, elate, elated, elatedly, elatedness, elater, elaterid, elaterids, elaterin, elaterins, elaterist, elaterite, elaterium, elateroid, elaterometer, elaters, elatery, elates, elatinaceous, elating, elation, elations, elative, elatives, elator, elatrometer, elayl, elb, elboic, elbow, elbowboard, elbowbush, elbowchair, elbowed, elbower, elbowing, elbowpiece, elbowroom, elbows, elbowy, elbuck, elcaja, elchee, eld, elder, elderberries, elderberry, elderbrotherhood, elderbrotherish, elderbrotherly, elderbush, elderhood, elderlies, elderliness, elderling, elderly, elderman, eldermen, eldern, elders, eldership, eldersisterly, elderwoman, elderwomen, elderwood, elderwort, eldest, eldfather, eldin, elding, eldmother, eldorado, eldress, eldrich, eldritch, elds, eleanor, eleatic, elec, elecampane, elechi, elecive, elecives, elect, electability, electable, electant, electary, elected, electee, electees, electic, electicism, electing, election, election's, electionary, electioneer, electioneered, electioneerer, electioneering, electioneers, elections, elective, electively, electiveness, electives, electivism, electivity, electly, electo, elector, elector's, electoral, electorally, electorate, electorates, electorial, electors, electorship, electra, electragist, electragy, electral, electralize, electre, electrepeter, electress, electret, electrets, electric, electrical, electricalize, electrically, electricalness, electrican, electricans, electrician, electricians, electricity, electricize, electrics, electriferous, electrifiable, electrification, electrified, electrifier, electrifiers, electrifies, electrify, electrifying, electrine, electrion, electrionic, electrizable, electrization, electrize, electrized, electrizer, electrizing, electro, electroacoustic, electroacoustical, electroacoustically, electroacoustics, electroaffinity, electroamalgamation, electroanalysis, electroanalytic, electroanalytical, electroanesthesia, electroballistic, electroballistically, electroballistician, electroballistics, electrobath, electrobiological, electrobiologically, electrobiologist, electrobiology, electrobioscopy, electroblasting, electrobrasser, electrobus, electrocapillarity, electrocapillary, electrocardiogram, electrocardiograms, electrocardiograph, electrocardiographic, electrocardiographically, electrocardiographs, electrocardiography, electrocatalysis, electrocatalytic, electrocataphoresis, electrocataphoretic, electrocauteries, electrocauterization, electrocautery, electroceramic, electrochemical, electrochemically, electrochemist, electrochemistry, electrochronograph, electrochronographic, electrochronometer, electrochronometric, electrocoagulation, electrocoating, electrocolloidal, electrocontractility, electroconvulsive, electrocorticogram, electrocratic, electroculture, electrocute, electrocuted, electrocutes, electrocuting, electrocution, electrocutional, electrocutioner, electrocutions, electrocystoscope, electrode, electrode's, electrodeless, electrodentistry, electrodeposit, electrodepositable, electrodeposition, electrodepositor, electrodes, electrodesiccate, electrodesiccation, electrodiagnoses, electrodiagnosis, electrodiagnostic, electrodiagnostically, electrodialitic, electrodialitically, electrodialyses, electrodialysis, electrodialytic, electrodialyze, electrodialyzer, electrodiplomatic, electrodispersive, electrodissolution, electrodynamic, electrodynamical, electrodynamics, electrodynamism, electrodynamometer, electroed, electroencephalogram, electroencephalograms, electroencephalograph, electroencephalographic, electroencephalographical, electroencephalographically, electroencephalographs, electroencephalography, electroendosmose, electroendosmosis, electroendosmotic, electroengrave, electroengraving, electroergometer, electroetching, electroethereal, electroextraction, electrofishing, electroform, electroforming, electrofuse, electrofused, electrofusion, electrogalvanic, electrogalvanization, electrogalvanize, electrogasdynamics, electrogenesis, electrogenetic, electrogenic, electrogild, electrogilding, electrogilt, electrogram, electrograph, electrographic, electrographite, electrography, electrograving, electroharmonic, electrohemostasis, electrohomeopathy, electrohorticulture, electrohydraulic, electrohydraulically, electroimpulse, electroindustrial, electroing, electroionic, electroirrigation, electrojet, electrokinematics, electrokinetic, electrokinetics, electroless, electrolier, electrolithotrity, electrologic, electrological, electrologist, electrologists, electrology, electroluminescence, electroluminescent, electrolysation, electrolyse, electrolysed, electrolyser, electrolyses, electrolysing, electrolysis, electrolyte, electrolyte's, electrolytes, electrolytic, electrolytical, electrolytically, electrolyzability, electrolyzable, electrolyzation, electrolyze, electrolyzed, electrolyzer, electrolyzing, electromagnet, electromagnetic, electromagnetical, electromagnetically, electromagnetics, electromagnetism, electromagnetist, electromagnetize, electromagnets, electromassage, electromechanical, electromechanically, electromechanics, electromedical, electromer, electromeric, electromerism, electrometallurgical, electrometallurgist, electrometallurgy, electrometeor, electrometer, electrometric, electrometrical, electrometrically, electrometry, electromobile, electromobilism, electromotion, electromotiv, electromotive, electromotivity, electromotograph, electromotor, electromuscular, electromyogram, electromyograph, electromyographic, electromyographical, electromyographically, electromyography, electron, electron's, electronarcosis, electronegative, electronegativity, electronervous, electroneutral, electroneutrality, electronic, electronically, electronics, electronographic, electronography, electrons, electronvolt, electrooculogram, electrooptic, electrooptical, electrooptically, electrooptics, electroori, electroosmosis, electroosmotic, electroosmotically, electrootiatrics, electropathic, electropathology, electropathy, electropercussive, electrophilic, electrophilically, electrophobia, electrophone, electrophonic, electrophonically, electrophore, electrophorese, electrophoresed, electrophoreses, electrophoresing, electrophoresis, electrophoretic, electrophoretically, electrophoretogram, electrophori, electrophoric, electrophorus, electrophotographic, electrophotography, electrophotometer, electrophotometry, electrophotomicrography, electrophototherapy, electrophrenic, electrophysicist, electrophysics, electrophysiologic, electrophysiological, electrophysiologically, electrophysiologist, electrophysiology, electropism, electroplaque, electroplate, electroplated, electroplater, electroplates, electroplating, electroplax, electropneumatic, electropneumatically, electropoion, electropolar, electropolish, electropositive, electropotential, electropower, electropsychrometer, electropult, electropuncturation, electropuncture, electropuncturing, electropyrometer, electroreceptive, electroreduction, electrorefine, electrorefining, electroresection, electroretinogram, electroretinograph, electroretinographic, electroretinography, electros, electroscission, electroscope, electroscopes, electroscopic, electrosensitive, electrosherardizing, electroshock, electroshocks, electrosmosis, electrostatic, electrostatical, electrostatically, electrostatics, electrosteel, electrostenolysis, electrostenolytic, electrostereotype, electrostriction, electrostrictive, electrosurgeries, electrosurgery, electrosurgical, electrosurgically, electrosynthesis, electrosynthetic, electrosynthetically, electrotactic, electrotautomerism, electrotaxis, electrotechnic, electrotechnical, electrotechnician, electrotechnics, electrotechnologist, electrotechnology, electrotelegraphic, electrotelegraphy, electrotelethermometer, electrotellurograph, electrotest, electrothanasia, electrothanatosis, electrotherapeutic, electrotherapeutical, electrotherapeutics, electrotherapeutist, electrotherapies, electrotherapist, electrotheraputic, electrotheraputical, electrotheraputically, electrotheraputics, electrotherapy, electrothermal, electrothermally, electrothermancy, electrothermic, electrothermics, electrothermometer, electrothermostat, electrothermostatic, electrothermotic, electrotitration, electrotonic, electrotonicity, electrotonize, electrotonus, electrotrephine, electrotropic, electrotropism, electrotype, electrotyped, electrotyper, electrotypes, electrotypic, electrotyping, electrotypist, electrotypy, electrovalence, electrovalency, electrovalent, electrovalently, electrovection, electroviscous, electrovital, electrowin, electrowinning, electrum, electrums, elects, electuaries, electuary, eledoisin, eledone, eleemosinar, eleemosynar, eleemosynarily, eleemosynariness, eleemosynary, elegance, elegances, elegancies, elegancy, elegant, elegante, eleganter, elegantly, elegiac, elegiacal, elegiacally, elegiacs, elegiambic, elegiambus, elegiast, elegibility, elegies, elegious, elegise, elegised, elegises, elegising, elegist, elegists, elegit, elegits, elegize, elegized, elegizes, elegizing, elegy, eleidin, elektra, elelments, elem, eleme, element, element's, elemental, elementalism, elementalist, elementalistic, elementalistically, elementality, elementalize, elementally, elementaloid, elementals, elementarily, elementariness, elementarism, elementarist, elementarity, elementary, elementate, elementish, elementoid, elements, elemi, elemicin, elemin, elemis, elemol, elemong, elench, elenchi, elenchic, elenchical, elenchically, elenchize, elenchtic, elenchtical, elenchus, elenctic, elenctical, elenge, elengely, elengeness, eleoblast, eleolite, eleomargaric, eleometer, eleonorite, eleoplast, eleoptene, eleostearate, eleostearic, eleotrid, elepaio, elephancy, elephant, elephant's, elephanta, elephantiac, elephantiases, elephantiasic, elephantiasis, elephantic, elephanticide, elephantine, elephantlike, elephantoid, elephantoidal, elephantous, elephantry, elephants, eleuin, eleusinian, eleutherarch, eleutherian, eleutherism, eleutherodactyl, eleutheromania, eleutheromaniac, eleutheromorph, eleutheropetalous, eleutherophobia, eleutherophyllous, eleutherosepalous, eleutherozoan, elev, elevable, elevate, elevated, elevatedly, elevatedness, elevates, elevating, elevatingly, elevation, elevational, elevations, elevato, elevator, elevator's, elevators, elevatory, eleve, eleven, elevener, elevenfold, elevens, elevenses, eleventeenth, eleventh, eleventhly, elevenths, elevon, elevons, elf, elfdom, elfenfolk, elfhood, elfic, elfin, elfins, elfinwood, elfish, elfishly, elfishness, elfkin, elfland, elflike, elflock, elflocks, elfship, elfwife, elfwort, elhi, eli, eliasite, elicit, elicitable, elicitate, elicitation, elicited, eliciting, elicitor, elicitors, elicitory, elicits, elide, elided, elides, elidible, eliding, eligenda, eligent, eligibilities, eligibility, eligible, eligibleness, eligibles, eligibly, elijah, eliminability, eliminable, eliminand, eliminant, eliminate, eliminated, eliminates, eliminating, elimination, eliminations, eliminative, eliminator, eliminators, eliminatory, elinguate, elinguated, elinguating, elinguation, elingued, elinvar, eliquate, eliquated, eliquating, eliquation, eliquidate, elisha, elision, elisions, elisor, elite, elites, elitism, elitisms, elitist, elitists, elix, elixate, elixation, elixed, elixir, elixirs, elixiviate, elizabeth, elizabethan, elizabethans, elk, elk's, elkhorn, elkhound, elkhounds, elks, elkslip, elkwood, ell, ellachick, ellagate, ellagic, ellagitannin, ellan, elle, ellebore, elleck, ellen, ellenyard, ellfish, elling, ellinge, ellipse, ellipse's, ellipses, ellipsis, ellipsograph, ellipsoid, ellipsoid's, ellipsoidal, ellipsoids, ellipsometer, ellipsometry, ellipsone, ellipsonic, elliptic, elliptical, elliptically, ellipticalness, ellipticity, elliptograph, elliptoid, ellops, ells, ellwand, elm, elmer, elmier, elmiest, elms, elmwood, elmy, elne, elocation, elocular, elocute, elocution, elocutionary, elocutioner, elocutionist, elocutionists, elocutionize, elocutive, elod, elodea, elodeas, eloge, elogium, elogy, elohim, elohist, eloign, eloigned, eloigner, eloigners, eloigning, eloignment, eloigns, eloin, eloine, eloined, eloiner, eloiners, eloining, eloinment, eloins, elong, elongate, elongated, elongates, elongating, elongation, elongations, elongative, elope, eloped, elopement, elopements, eloper, elopers, elopes, eloping, elops, eloquence, eloquent, eloquential, eloquently, eloquentness, elotillo, elpasolite, elpidite, elrage, elritch, elroquite, els, else, elsehow, elses, elsewards, elseways, elsewhat, elsewhen, elsewhere, elsewheres, elsewhither, elsewise, elshin, elsin, elt, eltime, eltrot, eluant, eluants, eluate, eluated, eluates, eluating, elucid, elucidate, elucidated, elucidates, elucidating, elucidation, elucidations, elucidative, elucidator, elucidators, elucidatory, eluctate, eluctation, elucubrate, elucubration, elude, eluded, eluder, eluders, eludes, eludible, eluding, eluent, eluents, elul, elumbated, elusion, elusions, elusive, elusively, elusiveness, elusoriness, elusory, elute, eluted, elutes, eluting, elution, elutions, elutor, elutriate, elutriated, elutriating, elutriation, elutriator, eluvia, eluvial, eluviate, eluviated, eluviates, eluviating, eluviation, eluvies, eluvium, eluviums, eluvivia, eluxate, elvan, elvanite, elvanitic, elve, elver, elvers, elves, elvet, elvis, elvish, elvishly, elychnious, elydoric, elysia, elysian, elysium, elytra, elytral, elytriferous, elytriform, elytrigerous, elytrin, elytrocele, elytroclasia, elytroid, elytron, elytroplastic, elytropolypus, elytroposis, elytroptosis, elytrorhagia, elytrorrhagia, elytrorrhaphy, elytrostenosis, elytrotomy, elytrous, elytrtra, elytrum, elzevir, em, emacerate, emacerated, emaceration, emaciate, emaciated, emaciates, emaciating, emaciation, emaculate, emagram, email, emailed, emajagua, emamelware, emanant, emanate, emanated, emanates, emanating, emanation, emanational, emanationism, emanationist, emanations, emanatism, emanatist, emanatistic, emanativ, emanative, emanatively, emanator, emanators, emanatory, emancipate, emancipated, emancipates, emancipating, emancipation, emancipationist, emancipations, emancipatist, emancipative, emancipator, emancipators, emancipatory, emancipatress, emancipist, emandibulate, emane, emanent, emanium, emarcid, emarginate, emarginated, emarginately, emarginating, emargination, emasculate, emasculated, emasculates, emasculating, emasculation, emasculations, emasculative, emasculator, emasculators, emasculatory, embace, embacle, embain, embale, emball, emballonurid, emballonurine, embalm, embalmed, embalmer, embalmers, embalming, embalmment, embalms, embank, embanked, embanking, embankment, embankments, embanks, embannered, embaphium, embar, embarcadero, embarcation, embarge, embargo, embargoed, embargoes, embargoing, embargoist, embargos, embark, embarkation, embarkations, embarked, embarking, embarkment, embarks, embarment, embarque, embarras, embarrased, embarrass, embarrassed, embarrassedly, embarrasses, embarrassing, embarrassingly, embarrassment, embarrassments, embarred, embarrel, embarren, embarricado, embarring, embars, embase, embassade, embassador, embassadress, embassage, embassiate, embassies, embassy, embassy's, embastardize, embastioned, embathe, embatholithic, embattle, embattled, embattlement, embattles, embattling, embay, embayed, embaying, embayment, embays, embden, embeam, embed, embeddable, embedded, embedder, embedding, embedment, embeds, embeggar, embelic, embelif, embelin, embellish, embellished, embellisher, embellishers, embellishes, embellishing, embellishment, embellishment's, embellishments, ember, embergeese, embergoose, emberizidae, emberizine, embers, embetter, embezzle, embezzled, embezzlement, embezzlements, embezzler, embezzlers, embezzles, embezzling, embiid, embillow, embind, embiotocid, embiotocoid, embira, embitter, embittered, embitterer, embittering, embitterment, embitterments, embitters, embladder, emblanch, emblaze, emblazed, emblazer, emblazers, emblazes, emblazing, emblazon, emblazoned, emblazoner, emblazoning, emblazonment, emblazonments, emblazonry, emblazons, emblem, emblema, emblematic, emblematical, emblematically, emblematicalness, emblematicize, emblematise, emblematised, emblematising, emblematist, emblematize, emblematized, emblematizing, emblematology, emblemed, emblement, emblements, embleming, emblemish, emblemist, emblemize, emblemized, emblemizing, emblemology, emblems, emblic, embliss, embloom, emblossom, embodied, embodier, embodiers, embodies, embodiment, embodiment's, embodiments, embody, embodying, embog, embogue, emboil, emboite, emboitement, emboites, embolden, emboldened, emboldener, emboldening, emboldens, embole, embolectomies, embolectomy, embolemia, emboli, embolic, embolies, emboliform, embolimeal, embolism, embolismic, embolisms, embolismus, embolite, embolium, embolization, embolize, embolo, embololalia, embolomalerism, embolomerism, embolomerous, embolomycotic, embolon, emboltement, embolum, embolus, emboly, embonpoint, emborder, embordered, embordering, emborders, emboscata, embosk, embosked, embosking, embosks, embosom, embosomed, embosoming, embosoms, emboss, embossable, embossage, embossed, embosser, embossers, embosses, embossing, embossman, embossmen, embossment, embossments, embost, embosture, embottle, embouchement, embouchment, embouchure, embouchures, embound, embourgeoisement, embow, embowed, embowel, emboweled, emboweler, emboweling, embowelled, emboweller, embowelling, embowelment, embowels, embower, embowered, embowering, embowerment, embowers, embowing, embowl, embowment, embows, embox, embrace, embraceable, embraceably, embraced, embracement, embraceor, embraceorr, embracer, embraceries, embracers, embracery, embraces, embracing, embracingly, embracingness, embracive, embraciveg, embraid, embrail, embrake, embranchment, embrangle, embrangled, embranglement, embrangling, embrase, embrasure, embrasured, embrasures, embrasuring, embrave, embrawn, embreach, embread, embreastment, embreathe, embreathement, embrectomy, embrew, embright, embrighten, embrittle, embrittled, embrittlement, embrittling, embroaden, embrocado, embrocate, embrocated, embrocates, embrocating, embrocation, embrocations, embroche, embroglio, embroglios, embroider, embroidered, embroiderer, embroiderers, embroideress, embroideries, embroidering, embroiders, embroidery, embroil, embroiled, embroiler, embroiling, embroilment, embroilments, embroils, embronze, embroscopic, embrothelled, embrowd, embrown, embrowned, embrowning, embrowns, embrue, embrued, embrues, embruing, embrute, embruted, embrutes, embruting, embryectomies, embryectomy, embryo, embryo's, embryocardia, embryoctonic, embryoctony, embryoferous, embryogenesis, embryogenetic, embryogenic, embryogeny, embryogony, embryographer, embryographic, embryography, embryoid, embryoism, embryol, embryologic, embryological, embryologically, embryologies, embryologist, embryologists, embryology, embryoma, embryomas, embryomata, embryon, embryonal, embryonally, embryonary, embryonate, embryonated, embryonic, embryonically, embryoniferous, embryoniform, embryons, embryony, embryopathology, embryophagous, embryophore, embryophyte, embryoplastic, embryos, embryoscope, embryoscopic, embryotega, embryotegae, embryotic, embryotome, embryotomies, embryotomy, embryotroph, embryotrophe, embryotrophic, embryotrophy, embryous, embryulci, embryulcia, embryulculci, embryulcus, embryulcuses, embubble, embue, embuia, embulk, embull, embus, embush, embusk, embuskin, embusqu, embusque, embussed, embussing, embusy, emcee, emceed, emceeing, emcees, emceing, emcumbering, emda, emden, eme, emeer, emeerate, emeerates, emeers, emeership, emend, emendable, emendandum, emendate, emendated, emendately, emendates, emendating, emendation, emendations, emendator, emendatory, emended, emender, emenders, emendicate, emending, emends, emer, emerald, emerald's, emeraldine, emeralds, emerant, emeras, emeraude, emerge, emerged, emergence, emergences, emergencies, emergency, emergency's, emergent, emergently, emergentness, emergents, emergers, emerges, emerging, emerick, emeried, emeries, emeril, emerit, emerita, emerited, emeriti, emeritus, emerituti, emerize, emerized, emerizing, emerod, emerods, emeroid, emeroids, emerse, emersed, emersion, emersions, emerson, emery, emerying, emes, emeses, emesis, emetatrophia, emetia, emetic, emetical, emetically, emetics, emetin, emetine, emetines, emetins, emetocathartic, emetology, emetomorphine, emetophobia, emeu, emeus, emeute, emeutes, emf, emforth, emgalla, emhpasizing, emic, emicant, emicate, emication, emiction, emictory, emigate, emigated, emigates, emigating, emigr, emigrant, emigrant's, emigrants, emigrate, emigrated, emigrates, emigrating, emigration, emigrational, emigrationist, emigrations, emigrative, emigrator, emigratory, emigre, emigree, emigres, emily, eminence, eminences, eminencies, eminency, eminent, eminently, emir, emirate, emirates, emirs, emirship, emissaria, emissaries, emissarium, emissary, emissaryship, emissi, emissile, emission, emissions, emissitious, emissive, emissivity, emissory, emit, emits, emittance, emitted, emittent, emitter, emitters, emitting, emlen, emma, emmantle, emmarble, emmarbled, emmarbling, emmarvel, emmeleia, emmenagogic, emmenagogue, emmenia, emmenic, emmeniopathy, emmenology, emmensite, emmer, emmergoose, emmers, emmet, emmetrope, emmetropia, emmetropic, emmetropism, emmetropy, emmets, emmew, emmies, emmove, emmy, emodin, emodins, emollescence, emolliate, emollience, emollient, emollients, emollition, emoloa, emolument, emolumental, emolumentary, emoluments, emong, emony, emory, emote, emoted, emoter, emoters, emotes, emoting, emotiometabolic, emotiomotor, emotiomuscular, emotion, emotion's, emotionable, emotional, emotionalise, emotionalised, emotionalising, emotionalism, emotionalist, emotionalistic, emotionality, emotionalization, emotionalize, emotionalized, emotionalizing, emotionally, emotioned, emotionist, emotionize, emotionless, emotionlessly, emotionlessness, emotions, emotiovascular, emotive, emotively, emotiveness, emotivism, emotivity, emove, emp, empacket, empaestic, empair, empaistic, empale, empaled, empalement, empaler, empalers, empales, empaling, empall, empanada, empanel, empaneled, empaneling, empanelled, empanelling, empanelment, empanels, empannel, empanoply, empaper, emparadise, emparchment, empark, emparl, empasm, empasma, empassion, empathetic, empathetically, empathic, empathically, empathies, empathize, empathized, empathizes, empathizing, empathy, empatron, empearl, empeine, empeirema, empemata, empennage, empennages, empeople, empeopled, empeoplement, emperess, emperies, emperil, emperish, emperize, emperor, emperor's, emperors, emperorship, empery, empest, empestic, empetraceous, empetrous, empexa, emphase, emphases, emphasis, emphasise, emphasised, emphasising, emphasize, emphasized, emphasizes, emphasizing, emphatic, emphatical, emphatically, emphaticalness, emphemeralness, emphlysis, emphractic, emphraxis, emphrensy, emphysema, emphysematous, emphyteusis, emphyteuta, emphyteutic, empicture, empiecement, empierce, empiercement, empight, empire, empire's, empirema, empires, empiric, empirical, empirically, empiricalness, empiricism, empiricist, empiricist's, empiricists, empirics, empiriocritcism, empiriocritical, empiriological, empirism, empiristic, empiry, emplace, emplaced, emplacement, emplacements, emplaces, emplacing, emplane, emplaned, emplanement, emplanes, emplaning, emplaster, emplastic, emplastra, emplastration, emplastrum, emplead, emplectic, emplection, emplectite, emplecton, empleomania, emplore, employ, employability, employable, employe, employed, employee, employee's, employees, employer, employer's, employers, employes, employing, employless, employment, employment's, employments, employs, emplume, emplunge, empocket, empodia, empodium, empoison, empoisoned, empoisoner, empoisoning, empoisonment, empoisons, empolder, emporetic, emporeutic, emporia, emporial, emporiria, empoririums, emporium, emporiums, emporte, emportment, empory, empover, empoverish, empower, empowered, empowering, empowerment, empowers, emprent, empresa, empresario, empress, empresse, empressement, empressements, empresses, empressment, emprime, emprint, emprise, emprises, emprison, emprize, emprizes, emprosthotonic, emprosthotonos, emprosthotonus, empt, emptiable, emptied, emptier, emptiers, empties, emptiest, emptily, emptiness, emptings, emptins, emptio, emption, emptional, emptive, emptor, emptores, emptory, empty, emptyhearted, emptying, emptysis, empurple, empurpled, empurples, empurpling, empusa, empuzzle, empyema, empyemas, empyemata, empyemic, empyesis, empyocele, empyreal, empyrean, empyreans, empyreum, empyreuma, empyreumata, empyreumatic, empyreumatical, empyreumatize, empyrical, empyromancy, empyrosis, emraud, emrode, ems, emu, emulable, emulant, emulate, emulated, emulates, emulating, emulation, emulations, emulative, emulatively, emulator, emulator's, emulators, emulatory, emulatress, emule, emulge, emulgence, emulgens, emulgent, emulous, emulously, emulousness, emuls, emulsibility, emulsible, emulsic, emulsifiability, emulsifiable, emulsification, emulsifications, emulsified, emulsifier, emulsifiers, emulsifies, emulsify, emulsifying, emulsin, emulsion, emulsionize, emulsions, emulsive, emulsoid, emulsoidal, emulsoids, emulsor, emunct, emunctories, emunctory, emundation, emunge, emus, emuscation, emusified, emusifies, emusify, emusifying, emusive, emyd, emyde, emydes, emydian, emydosaurian, emyds, en, enable, enabled, enablement, enabler, enablers, enables, enabling, enact, enactable, enacted, enacting, enaction, enactive, enactment, enactments, enactor, enactors, enactory, enacts, enacture, enaena, enage, enalid, enaliosaur, enaliosaurian, enalite, enallachrome, enallage, enaluron, enalyron, enam, enamber, enambush, enamdar, enamel, enameled, enameler, enamelers, enameling, enamelist, enamellar, enamelled, enameller, enamellers, enamelless, enamelling, enamellist, enameloma, enamels, enamelware, enamelwork, enami, enamine, enamines, enamor, enamorado, enamorate, enamorato, enamored, enamoredness, enamoring, enamorment, enamors, enamour, enamoured, enamouredness, enamouring, enamourment, enamours, enanguish, enanthem, enanthema, enanthematous, enanthesis, enantiobiosis, enantioblastic, enantioblastous, enantiomer, enantiomeric, enantiomeride, enantiomorph, enantiomorphic, enantiomorphism, enantiomorphous, enantiomorphously, enantiomorphy, enantiopathia, enantiopathic, enantiopathy, enantioses, enantiosis, enantiotropic, enantiotropy, enantobiosis, enapt, enarbor, enarbour, enarch, enarched, enargite, enarm, enarme, enarration, enarthrodia, enarthrodial, enarthroses, enarthrosis, enascent, enatant, enate, enates, enatic, enation, enations, enaunter, enbaissing, enbibe, enbloc, enbranglement, enbrave, enbusshe, enc, encadre, encaenia, encage, encaged, encages, encaging, encake, encalendar, encallow, encamp, encamped, encamping, encampment, encampments, encamps, encanker, encanthis, encapsulate, encapsulated, encapsulates, encapsulating, encapsulation, encapsulations, encapsule, encapsuled, encapsules, encapsuling, encaptivate, encaptive, encardion, encarditis, encarnadine, encarnalise, encarnalised, encarnalising, encarnalize, encarnalized, encarnalizing, encarpa, encarpi, encarpium, encarpus, encarpuspi, encase, encased, encasement, encases, encash, encashable, encashed, encashes, encashing, encashment, encasing, encasserole, encastage, encastered, encastre, encastrement, encatarrhaphy, encauma, encaustes, encaustic, encaustically, encave, encefalon, enceint, enceinte, enceintes, encell, encense, encenter, encephala, encephalalgia, encephalasthenia, encephalic, encephalin, encephalitic, encephalitis, encephalitogenic, encephalocele, encephalocoele, encephalodialysis, encephalogram, encephalograph, encephalographic, encephalographically, encephalography, encephaloid, encephalola, encephalolith, encephalology, encephaloma, encephalomalacia, encephalomalacosis, encephalomalaxis, encephalomas, encephalomata, encephalomeningitis, encephalomeningocele, encephalomere, encephalomeric, encephalometer, encephalometric, encephalomyelitic, encephalomyelitis, encephalomyelopathy, encephalomyocarditis, encephalon, encephalonarcosis, encephalopathia, encephalopathic, encephalopathy, encephalophyma, encephalopsychesis, encephalopyosis, encephalorrhagia, encephalos, encephalosclerosis, encephaloscope, encephaloscopy, encephalosepsis, encephalosis, encephalospinal, encephalothlipsis, encephalotome, encephalotomies, encephalotomy, encephalous, enchafe, enchain, enchained, enchainement, enchainements, enchaining, enchainment, enchainments, enchains, enchair, enchalice, enchancement, enchannel, enchant, enchanted, enchanter, enchanters, enchantery, enchanting, enchantingly, enchantingness, enchantment, enchantments, enchantress, enchantresses, enchants, encharge, encharged, encharging, encharm, encharnel, enchase, enchased, enchaser, enchasers, enchases, enchasing, enchasten, encheason, encheat, encheck, encheer, encheiria, enchequer, encheson, enchesoun, enchest, enchilada, enchiladas, enchiridia, enchiridion, enchiridions, enchiriridia, enchisel, enchodontid, enchodontoid, enchondroma, enchondromas, enchondromata, enchondromatous, enchondrosis, enchorial, enchoric, enchronicle, enchurch, enchylema, enchylematous, enchyma, enchymatous, enchytrae, enchytraeid, encia, enciente, encina, encinal, encinas, encincture, encinctured, encincturing, encinder, encinillo, encipher, enciphered, encipherer, enciphering, encipherment, encipherments, enciphers, encircle, encircled, encirclement, encirclements, encircler, encircles, encircling, encist, encitadel, encl, enclaret, enclasp, enclasped, enclasping, enclasps, enclave, enclaved, enclavement, enclaves, enclaving, enclear, enclisis, enclitic, enclitical, enclitically, enclitics, encloak, enclog, encloister, enclosable, enclose, enclosed, encloser, enclosers, encloses, enclosing, enclosure, enclosure's, enclosures, enclothe, encloud, encoach, encode, encoded, encodement, encoder, encoders, encodes, encoding, encodings, encoffin, encoffinment, encoignure, encoignures, encoil, encolden, encollar, encolor, encolour, encolpia, encolpion, encolumn, encolure, encomendero, encomia, encomiast, encomiastic, encomiastical, encomiastically, encomic, encomienda, encomiendas, encomimia, encomimiums, encomiologic, encomium, encomiumia, encomiums, encommon, encompany, encompass, encompassed, encompasser, encompasses, encompassing, encompassment, encomy, encoop, encopreses, encopresis, encorbellment, encorbelment, encore, encored, encores, encoring, encoronal, encoronate, encoronet, encorpore, encounter, encounterable, encountered, encounterer, encounterers, encountering, encounters, encourage, encouraged, encouragement, encouragements, encourager, encouragers, encourages, encouraging, encouragingly, encover, encowl, encraal, encradle, encranial, encratic, encratism, encratite, encraty, encrease, encreel, encrimson, encrinal, encrinic, encrinidae, encrinital, encrinite, encrinitic, encrinitical, encrinoid, encrinus, encrisp, encroach, encroached, encroacher, encroaches, encroaching, encroachingly, encroachment, encroachments, encrotchet, encrown, encrownment, encrust, encrustant, encrustation, encrusted, encrusting, encrustment, encrusts, encrypt, encrypted, encrypting, encryption, encryptions, encrypts, encuirassed, enculturate, enculturated, enculturating, enculturation, enculturative, encumber, encumbered, encumberer, encumbering, encumberingly, encumberment, encumbers, encumbrance, encumbrancer, encumbrances, encumbrous, encup, encurl, encurtain, encushion, ency, encyc, encycl, encyclic, encyclical, encyclicals, encyclics, encyclopaedia, encyclopaediac, encyclopaedial, encyclopaedian, encyclopaedias, encyclopaedic, encyclopaedical, encyclopaedically, encyclopaedism, encyclopaedist, encyclopaedize, encyclopedia, encyclopedia's, encyclopediac, encyclopediacal, encyclopedial, encyclopedian, encyclopedias, encyclopediast, encyclopedic, encyclopedical, encyclopedically, encyclopedism, encyclopedist, encyclopedize, encydlopaedic, encyrtid, encyst, encystation, encysted, encysting, encystment, encystments, encysts, end, endable, endamage, endamageable, endamaged, endamagement, endamages, endamaging, endamask, endameba, endamebae, endamebas, endamebiasis, endamebic, endamnify, endamoeba, endamoebae, endamoebas, endamoebiasis, endamoebic, endangeitis, endanger, endangered, endangerer, endangering, endangerment, endangerments, endangers, endangiitis, endangitis, endangium, endaortic, endaortitis, endarch, endarchies, endarchy, endark, endarterectomy, endarteria, endarterial, endarteritis, endarterium, endarteteria, endaseh, endaspidean, endaze, endball, endboard, endbrain, endbrains, enddamage, enddamaged, enddamaging, ende, endear, endearance, endeared, endearedly, endearedness, endearing, endearingly, endearingness, endearment, endearments, endears, endeavor, endeavored, endeavorer, endeavoring, endeavors, endeavour, endeavoured, endeavourer, endeavouring, endebt, endecha, ended, endeictic, endeign, endellionite, endemial, endemic, endemical, endemically, endemicity, endemics, endemiological, endemiology, endemism, endemisms, endenization, endenize, endenizen, endent, ender, endere, endergonic, endermatic, endermic, endermically, enderon, enderonic, enders, endevil, endew, endexine, endexines, endfile, endgame, endgate, endhand, endia, endiablee, endiadem, endiaper, endict, endimanche, ending, endings, endite, endited, endites, enditing, endive, endives, endjunk, endleaf, endleaves, endless, endlessly, endlessness, endlichite, endlong, endmatcher, endmost, endnote, endnotes, endoabdominal, endoangiitis, endoaortitis, endoappendicitis, endoarteritis, endoauscultation, endobatholithic, endobiotic, endoblast, endoblastic, endobronchial, endobronchially, endobronchitis, endocannibalism, endocardia, endocardiac, endocardial, endocarditic, endocarditis, endocardium, endocarp, endocarpal, endocarpic, endocarpoid, endocarps, endocellular, endocentric, endoceratite, endoceratitic, endocervical, endocervicitis, endochondral, endochorion, endochorionic, endochrome, endochylous, endoclinal, endocline, endocoelar, endocoele, endocoeliac, endocolitis, endocolpitis, endocondensation, endocone, endoconidia, endoconidium, endocorpuscular, endocortex, endocrania, endocranial, endocranium, endocrin, endocrinal, endocrine, endocrines, endocrinic, endocrinism, endocrinologic, endocrinological, endocrinologies, endocrinologist, endocrinologists, endocrinology, endocrinopath, endocrinopathic, endocrinopathy, endocrinotherapy, endocrinous, endocritic, endocycle, endocyclic, endocyemate, endocyst, endocystitis, endocytic, endocytosis, endocytotic, endoderm, endodermal, endodermic, endodermis, endoderms, endodontia, endodontic, endodontically, endodontics, endodontist, endodontium, endodontologist, endodontology, endodynamomorphic, endoenteritis, endoenzyme, endoergic, endoerythrocytic, endoesophagitis, endofaradism, endogalvanism, endogamic, endogamies, endogamous, endogamy, endogastric, endogastrically, endogastritis, endogen, endogenesis, endogenetic, endogenic, endogenicity, endogenies, endogenous, endogenously, endogens, endogeny, endoglobular, endognath, endognathal, endognathion, endogonidium, endointoxication, endokaryogamy, endolabyrinthitis, endolaryngeal, endolemma, endolithic, endolumbar, endolymph, endolymphangial, endolymphatic, endolymphic, endolysin, endomastoiditis, endome, endomesoderm, endometria, endometrial, endometriosis, endometritis, endometrium, endometry, endomictic, endomitosis, endomitotic, endomixis, endomorph, endomorphic, endomorphism, endomorphy, endomysial, endomysium, endoneurial, endoneurium, endonuclear, endonuclease, endonucleolus, endoparasite, endoparasitic, endoparasitism, endopathic, endopelvic, endopeptidase, endopericarditis, endoperidial, endoperidium, endoperitonitis, endophagous, endophagy, endophasia, endophasic, endophlebitis, endophragm, endophragmal, endophyllous, endophytal, endophyte, endophytic, endophytically, endophytous, endoplasm, endoplasma, endoplasmic, endoplast, endoplastron, endoplastular, endoplastule, endopleura, endopleural, endopleurite, endopleuritic, endopod, endopodite, endopoditic, endopods, endopolyploid, endopolyploidy, endoproct, endoproctous, endopsychic, endopterygote, endopterygotic, endopterygotism, endopterygotous, endorachis, endoradiosonde, endoral, endore, endorhinitis, endorphin, endorsable, endorsation, endorse, endorsed, endorsee, endorsees, endorsement, endorsements, endorser, endorsers, endorses, endorsing, endorsingly, endorsor, endorsors, endosalpingitis, endosarc, endosarcode, endosarcous, endosarcs, endosclerite, endoscope, endoscopes, endoscopic, endoscopically, endoscopies, endoscopist, endoscopy, endosecretory, endosepsis, endosiphon, endosiphonal, endosiphonate, endosiphuncle, endoskeletal, endoskeleton, endoskeletons, endosmic, endosmometer, endosmometric, endosmos, endosmose, endosmoses, endosmosic, endosmosis, endosmotic, endosmotically, endosome, endosomes, endosperm, endospermic, endospermous, endospore, endosporia, endosporic, endosporium, endosporous, endosporously, endoss, endostea, endosteal, endosteally, endosteitis, endosteoma, endosteomas, endosteomata, endosternite, endosternum, endosteum, endostitis, endostoma, endostomata, endostome, endostosis, endostraca, endostracal, endostracum, endostylar, endostyle, endostylic, endosulfan, endosymbiosis, endotheca, endothecal, endothecate, endothecia, endothecial, endothecium, endothelia, endothelial, endothelioblastoma, endotheliocyte, endothelioid, endotheliolysin, endotheliolytic, endothelioma, endotheliomas, endotheliomata, endotheliomyoma, endotheliomyxoma, endotheliotoxin, endotheliulia, endothelium, endotheloid, endotherm, endothermal, endothermic, endothermically, endothermism, endothermous, endothermy, endothoracic, endothorax, endothys, endotoxic, endotoxin, endotoxoid, endotracheal, endotracheitis, endotrachelitis, endotrophic, endotropic, endotys, endoubt, endoute, endovaccination, endovasculitis, endovenous, endover, endow, endowed, endower, endowers, endowing, endowment, endowment's, endowments, endows, endozoa, endozoic, endpaper, endpapers, endpiece, endplate, endplates, endplay, endpleasure, endpoint, endpoints, endrin, endrins, endrudge, endrumpf, ends, endseal, endshake, endsheet, endship, endsweep, endue, endued, enduement, endues, enduing, endungeon, endura, endurability, endurable, endurableness, endurably, endurance, endurant, endure, endured, endurer, endures, enduring, enduringly, enduringness, enduro, enduros, endways, endwise, endyma, endymal, endymion, endysis, enecate, eneclann, ened, eneid, enema, enema's, enemas, enemata, enemied, enemies, enemy, enemy's, enemying, enemylike, enemyship, enent, enepidermic, energeia, energesis, energetic, energetical, energetically, energeticalness, energeticist, energeticness, energetics, energetistic, energiatye, energic, energical, energico, energid, energids, energies, energise, energised, energiser, energises, energising, energism, energist, energistic, energize, energized, energizer, energizers, energizes, energizing, energumen, energumenon, energy, enervate, enervated, enervates, enervating, enervation, enervative, enervator, enervators, enerve, enervous, enetophobia, eneuch, eneugh, enew, enface, enfaced, enfacement, enfaces, enfacing, enfamish, enfamous, enfant, enfants, enfarce, enfasten, enfatico, enfavor, enfeature, enfect, enfeeble, enfeebled, enfeeblement, enfeeblements, enfeebler, enfeebles, enfeebling, enfeeblish, enfelon, enfeoff, enfeoffed, enfeoffing, enfeoffment, enfeoffs, enfester, enfetter, enfettered, enfettering, enfetters, enfever, enfevered, enfevering, enfevers, enfief, enfield, enfierce, enfigure, enfilade, enfiladed, enfilades, enfilading, enfile, enfiled, enfin, enfire, enfirm, enflagellate, enflagellation, enflame, enflamed, enflames, enflaming, enflesh, enfleurage, enflower, enflowered, enflowering, enfoeffment, enfoil, enfold, enfolded, enfolden, enfolder, enfolders, enfolding, enfoldings, enfoldment, enfolds, enfollow, enfonce, enfonced, enfoncee, enforce, enforceability, enforceable, enforced, enforcedly, enforcement, enforcer, enforcers, enforces, enforcibility, enforcible, enforcing, enforcingly, enforcive, enforcively, enforest, enfork, enform, enfort, enforth, enfortune, enfoul, enfoulder, enfrai, enframe, enframed, enframement, enframes, enframing, enfranch, enfranchisable, enfranchise, enfranchised, enfranchisement, enfranchisements, enfranchiser, enfranchises, enfranchising, enfree, enfrenzy, enfroward, enfuddle, enfume, enfurrow, eng, engage, engaged, engagedly, engagedness, engagee, engagement, engagement's, engagements, engager, engagers, engages, engaging, engagingly, engagingness, engallant, engaol, engarb, engarble, engarde, engarland, engarment, engarrison, engastrimyth, engastrimythic, engaud, engaze, engelmann, engelmanni, engem, engender, engendered, engenderer, engendering, engenderment, engenders, engendrure, engendure, engerminate, enghle, enghosted, engild, engilded, engilding, engilds, engin, engine, engine's, engined, engineer, engineer's, engineered, engineering, engineeringly, engineers, engineership, engineery, enginehouse, engineless, enginelike, engineman, enginemen, engineries, enginery, engines, engining, enginous, engird, engirded, engirding, engirdle, engirdled, engirdles, engirdling, engirds, engirt, engiscope, engjateigur, engl, englacial, englacially, englad, engladden, england, englander, englanders, englante, engle, engleim, english, englished, englisher, englishes, englishing, englishism, englishly, englishman, englishmen, englishry, englishwoman, englishwomen, englobe, englobed, englobement, englobing, engloom, englory, englue, englut, englute, engluts, englutted, englutting, englyn, englyns, engnessang, engobe, engold, engolden, engore, engorge, engorged, engorgement, engorges, engorging, engoue, engouee, engouement, engouled, engoument, engr, engrace, engraced, engracing, engraff, engraffed, engraffing, engraft, engraftation, engrafted, engrafter, engrafting, engraftment, engrafts, engrail, engrailed, engrailing, engrailment, engrails, engrain, engrained, engrainedly, engrainer, engraining, engrains, engram, engramma, engrammatic, engramme, engrammes, engrammic, engrams, engrandize, engrandizement, engraphia, engraphic, engraphically, engraphy, engrapple, engrasp, engrave, engraved, engravement, engraven, engraver, engravers, engraves, engraving, engravings, engreaten, engreen, engrege, engregge, engrid, engrieve, engroove, engross, engrossed, engrossedly, engrosser, engrossers, engrosses, engrossing, engrossingly, engrossingness, engrossment, engs, enguard, engulf, engulfed, engulfing, engulfment, engulfs, engyscope, engysseismology, enhaemospore, enhallow, enhalo, enhaloed, enhaloes, enhaloing, enhalos, enhamper, enhance, enhanced, enhancement, enhancement's, enhancements, enhancer, enhancers, enhances, enhancing, enhancive, enhappy, enharbor, enharbour, enharden, enhardy, enharmonic, enharmonical, enharmonically, enhat, enhaulse, enhaunt, enhazard, enhearse, enheart, enhearten, enheaven, enhedge, enhelm, enhemospore, enherit, enheritage, enheritance, enhorror, enhort, enhuile, enhunger, enhungered, enhusk, enhydrite, enhydritic, enhydros, enhydrous, enhypostasia, enhypostasis, enhypostatic, enhypostatize, eniac, enigma, enigmas, enigmata, enigmatic, enigmatical, enigmatically, enigmaticalness, enigmatist, enigmatization, enigmatize, enigmatized, enigmatizing, enigmatographer, enigmatography, enigmatology, enigua, enisle, enisled, enisles, enisling, enjail, enjamb, enjambed, enjambement, enjambements, enjambment, enjambments, enjelly, enjeopard, enjeopardy, enjewel, enjoin, enjoinder, enjoinders, enjoined, enjoiner, enjoiners, enjoining, enjoinment, enjoins, enjoy, enjoyable, enjoyableness, enjoyably, enjoyed, enjoyer, enjoyers, enjoying, enjoyingly, enjoyment, enjoyments, enjoys, enkennel, enkerchief, enkernel, enkindle, enkindled, enkindler, enkindles, enkindling, enkolpia, enkolpion, enkraal, enl, enlace, enlaced, enlacement, enlaces, enlacing, enlard, enlarge, enlargeable, enlargeableness, enlarged, enlargedly, enlargedness, enlargement, enlargement's, enlargements, enlarger, enlargers, enlarges, enlarging, enlargingly, enlaurel, enlay, enleaf, enleague, enleagued, enleen, enlength, enlevement, enlief, enlife, enlight, enlighten, enlightened, enlightenedly, enlightenedness, enlightener, enlighteners, enlightening, enlighteningly, enlightenment, enlightenments, enlightens, enlimn, enlink, enlinked, enlinking, enlinkment, enlist, enlisted, enlistee, enlistees, enlister, enlisters, enlisting, enlistment, enlistments, enlists, enlive, enliven, enlivened, enlivener, enlivening, enliveningly, enlivenment, enlivenments, enlivens, enlock, enlodge, enlodgement, enlumine, enlure, enlute, enmagazine, enmanche, enmarble, enmarbled, enmarbling, enmask, enmass, enmesh, enmeshed, enmeshes, enmeshing, enmeshment, enmeshments, enmew, enmist, enmities, enmity, enmoss, enmove, enmuffle, ennage, enneacontahedral, enneacontahedron, ennead, enneadianome, enneadic, enneads, enneaeteric, enneagon, enneagonal, enneagons, enneagynous, enneahedra, enneahedral, enneahedria, enneahedron, enneahedrons, enneandrian, enneandrous, enneapetalous, enneaphyllous, enneasemic, enneasepalous, enneaspermous, enneastylar, enneastyle, enneastylos, enneasyllabic, enneateric, enneatic, enneatical, ennedra, ennerve, ennew, ennia, enniche, ennoble, ennobled, ennoblement, ennoblements, ennobler, ennoblers, ennobles, ennobling, ennoblingly, ennoblment, ennoic, ennomic, ennoy, ennui, ennuied, ennuis, ennuyant, ennuyante, ennuye, ennuyee, ennuying, enoch, enocyte, enodal, enodally, enodate, enodation, enode, enoil, enoint, enol, enolase, enolases, enolate, enolic, enolizable, enolization, enolize, enolized, enolizing, enological, enologies, enologist, enology, enols, enomania, enomaniac, enomotarch, enomoty, enophthalmos, enophthalmus, enoplan, enoplion, enoptromancy, enorganic, enorm, enormious, enormities, enormity, enormous, enormously, enormousness, enorn, enorthotrope, enosis, enosises, enosist, enostosis, enough, enoughs, enounce, enounced, enouncement, enounces, enouncing, enow, enows, enphytotic, enpia, enplane, enplaned, enplanement, enplanes, enplaning, enquarter, enquere, enqueue, enqueued, enqueues, enquicken, enquire, enquired, enquirer, enquires, enquiries, enquiring, enquiry, enrace, enrage, enraged, enragedly, enragedness, enragement, enrages, enraging, enrail, enramada, enrange, enrank, enrapt, enrapted, enrapting, enrapts, enrapture, enraptured, enrapturedly, enrapturer, enraptures, enrapturing, enravish, enravished, enravishes, enravishing, enravishingly, enravishment, enray, enregiment, enregister, enregistered, enregistering, enregistration, enregistry, enrheum, enrib, enrich, enriched, enrichener, enricher, enrichers, enriches, enriching, enrichingly, enrichment, enrichments, enridged, enright, enring, enringed, enringing, enripen, enrive, enrobe, enrobed, enrobement, enrober, enrobers, enrobes, enrobing, enrockment, enrol, enroll, enrolle, enrolled, enrollee, enrollees, enroller, enrollers, enrolles, enrolling, enrollment, enrollment's, enrollments, enrolls, enrolment, enrols, enroot, enrooted, enrooting, enroots, enrough, enround, enruin, enrut, ens, ensafe, ensaffron, ensaint, ensalada, ensample, ensampler, ensamples, ensand, ensandal, ensanguine, ensanguined, ensanguining, ensate, enscale, enscene, enschedule, ensconce, ensconced, ensconces, ensconcing, enscroll, enscrolled, enscrolling, enscrolls, ensculpture, ense, enseal, ensealed, ensealing, enseam, ensear, ensearch, ensearcher, enseat, enseated, enseating, enseel, enseem, ensellure, ensemble, ensemble's, ensembles, ensepulcher, ensepulchered, ensepulchering, ensepulchre, enseraph, enserf, enserfed, enserfing, enserfment, enserfs, ensete, enshade, enshadow, enshawl, ensheath, ensheathe, ensheathed, ensheathes, ensheathing, ensheaths, enshell, enshelter, enshield, enshielded, enshielding, enshrine, enshrined, enshrinement, enshrinements, enshrines, enshrining, enshroud, enshrouded, enshrouding, enshrouds, ensient, ensiform, ensign, ensign's, ensigncies, ensigncy, ensigned, ensignhood, ensigning, ensignment, ensignry, ensigns, ensignship, ensilability, ensilage, ensilaged, ensilages, ensilaging, ensilate, ensilation, ensile, ensiled, ensiles, ensiling, ensilist, ensilver, ensindon, ensisternal, ensisternum, enskied, enskies, ensky, enskyed, enskying, enslave, enslaved, enslavedness, enslavement, enslavements, enslaver, enslavers, enslaves, enslaving, enslumber, ensmall, ensnare, ensnared, ensnarement, ensnarements, ensnarer, ensnarers, ensnares, ensnaring, ensnaringly, ensnarl, ensnarled, ensnarling, ensnarls, ensnow, ensober, ensophic, ensorcel, ensorceled, ensorceling, ensorcelize, ensorcell, ensorcellment, ensorcels, ensorcerize, ensorrow, ensoul, ensouled, ensouling, ensouls, enspangle, enspell, ensphere, ensphered, enspheres, ensphering, enspirit, ensporia, enstamp, enstar, enstate, enstatite, enstatitic, enstatitite, enstatolite, ensteel, ensteep, enstool, enstore, enstranged, enstrengthen, enstyle, ensuable, ensuance, ensuant, ensue, ensued, ensuer, ensues, ensuing, ensuingly, ensuite, ensulphur, ensurance, ensure, ensured, ensurer, ensurers, ensures, ensuring, enswathe, enswathed, enswathement, enswathes, enswathing, ensweep, ensweeten, ensynopticity, entablature, entablatured, entablement, entablements, entach, entackle, entad, entail, entailable, entailed, entailer, entailers, entailing, entailment, entailments, entails, ental, entalent, entally, entame, entameba, entamebae, entamebas, entamebic, entamoeba, entamoebiasis, entamoebic, entangle, entangleable, entangled, entangledly, entangledness, entanglement, entanglements, entangler, entanglers, entangles, entangling, entanglingly, entapophysial, entapophysis, entarthrotic, entases, entasia, entasias, entasis, entassment, entastic, entea, entelam, entelechial, entelechies, entelechy, entellus, entelluses, entelodont, entempest, entemple, entender, entendre, entendres, entente, ententes, entepicondylar, enter, entera, enterable, enteraden, enteradenographic, enteradenography, enteradenological, enteradenology, enteral, enteralgia, enterally, enterate, enterauxe, enterclose, enterectomies, enterectomy, entered, enterer, enterers, enterfeat, entergogenic, enteria, enteric, entericoid, entering, enteritidis, enteritis, entermete, entermise, enteroanastomosis, enterobacterial, enterobacterium, enterobiasis, enterobiliary, enterocele, enterocentesis, enteroceptor, enterochirurgia, enterochlorophyll, enterocholecystostomy, enterochromaffin, enterocinesia, enterocinetic, enterocleisis, enteroclisis, enteroclysis, enterococcal, enterococci, enterococcus, enterocoel, enterocoele, enterocoelic, enterocoelous, enterocolitis, enterocolostomy, enterocrinin, enterocyst, enterocystoma, enterodelous, enterodynia, enteroepiplocele, enterogastritis, enterogastrone, enterogenous, enterogram, enterograph, enterography, enterohelcosis, enterohemorrhage, enterohepatitis, enterohydrocele, enteroid, enterointestinal, enteroischiocele, enterokinase, enterokinesia, enterokinetic, enterolith, enterolithiasis, enterologic, enterological, enterology, enterolysis, enteromegalia, enteromegaly, enteromere, enteromesenteric, enteromycosis, enteromyiasis, enteron, enteroneuritis, enterons, enteroparalysis, enteroparesis, enteropathogenic, enteropathy, enteropexia, enteropexy, enterophthisis, enteroplasty, enteroplegia, enteropneust, enteropneustal, enteropneustan, enteroptosis, enteroptotic, enterorrhagia, enterorrhaphy, enterorrhea, enterorrhexis, enteroscope, enteroscopy, enterosepsis, enterospasm, enterostasis, enterostenosis, enterostomies, enterostomy, enterosyphilis, enterotome, enterotomy, enterotoxemia, enterotoxication, enterotoxin, enteroviral, enterovirus, enterozoa, enterozoan, enterozoic, enterozoon, enterparlance, enterpillar, enterprise, enterprised, enterpriseless, enterpriser, enterprises, enterprising, enterprisingly, enterprisingness, enterprize, enterritoriality, enterrologist, enters, entertain, entertainable, entertained, entertainer, entertainers, entertaining, entertainingly, entertainingness, entertainment, entertainment's, entertainments, entertains, entertake, entertissue, entete, entfaoilff, enthalpies, enthalpy, entheal, enthean, entheasm, entheate, enthelmintha, enthelminthes, enthelminthic, entheos, enthetic, enthral, enthraldom, enthrall, enthralldom, enthralled, enthraller, enthralling, enthrallingly, enthrallment, enthrallments, enthralls, enthralment, enthrals, enthrill, enthrone, enthroned, enthronement, enthronements, enthrones, enthrong, enthroning, enthronise, enthronised, enthronising, enthronization, enthronize, enthronized, enthronizing, enthuse, enthused, enthuses, enthusiasm, enthusiasms, enthusiast, enthusiast's, enthusiastic, enthusiastical, enthusiastically, enthusiasticalness, enthusiastly, enthusiasts, enthusing, enthymematic, enthymematical, enthymeme, entia, entice, enticeable, enticed, enticeful, enticement, enticements, enticer, enticers, entices, enticing, enticingly, enticingness, entier, enties, entifical, entification, entify, entincture, entire, entirely, entireness, entires, entireties, entirety, entiris, entirities, entitative, entitatively, entities, entitle, entitled, entitledness, entitlement, entitles, entitling, entitule, entity, entity's, entoblast, entoblastic, entobranchiate, entobronchium, entocalcaneal, entocarotid, entocele, entocnemial, entocoel, entocoele, entocoelic, entocondylar, entocondyle, entocondyloid, entocone, entoconid, entocornea, entocranial, entocuneiform, entocuniform, entocyemate, entocyst, entoderm, entodermal, entodermic, entoderms, entogastric, entogenous, entoglossal, entohyal, entoil, entoiled, entoiling, entoilment, entoils, entoire, entom, entomb, entombed, entombing, entombment, entombments, entombs, entomere, entomeric, entomic, entomical, entomion, entomofauna, entomogenous, entomoid, entomol, entomolegist, entomolite, entomologic, entomological, entomologically, entomologies, entomologise, entomologised, entomologising, entomologist, entomologists, entomologize, entomologized, entomologizing, entomology, entomophagan, entomophagous, entomophilous, entomophily, entomophobia, entomophthoraceous, entomophthorous, entomophytous, entomostracan, entomostracous, entomotaxy, entomotomist, entomotomy, entone, entonement, entonic, entoolitic, entoparasite, entoparasitic, entoperipheral, entophytal, entophyte, entophytic, entophytically, entophytous, entopic, entopical, entoplasm, entoplastic, entoplastral, entoplastron, entopopliteal, entoproct, entoproctous, entopterygoid, entoptic, entoptical, entoptically, entoptics, entoptoscope, entoptoscopic, entoptoscopy, entoretina, entorganism, entortill, entosarc, entosclerite, entosphenal, entosphenoid, entosphere, entosterna, entosternal, entosternite, entosternum, entosthoblast, entothorax, entotic, entotympanic, entour, entourage, entourages, entozoa, entozoal, entozoan, entozoans, entozoarian, entozoic, entozoological, entozoologically, entozoologist, entozoology, entozoon, entr, entr'acte, entr'actes, entracte, entrada, entradas, entrail, entrails, entrain, entrained, entrainer, entraining, entrainment, entrains, entrammel, entrance, entranced, entrancedly, entrancement, entrancements, entrancer, entrances, entranceway, entrancing, entrancingly, entrant, entrants, entrap, entrapment, entrapments, entrapped, entrapper, entrapping, entrappingly, entraps, entre, entreasure, entreasured, entreasuring, entreat, entreatable, entreated, entreater, entreatful, entreaties, entreating, entreatingly, entreatment, entreats, entreaty, entrec, entrechat, entrechats, entrecote, entrecotes, entredeux, entree, entrees, entrefer, entrelac, entremess, entremets, entrench, entrenched, entrenches, entrenching, entrenchment, entrenchments, entrep, entrepas, entrepeneur, entrepeneurs, entrepot, entrepots, entreprenant, entrepreneur, entrepreneur's, entrepreneurial, entrepreneurs, entrepreneurship, entrepreneuse, entrepreneuses, entrept, entrer, entresalle, entresol, entresols, entresse, entrez, entria, entries, entrike, entrochite, entrochus, entropies, entropion, entropionize, entropium, entropy, entrough, entrust, entrusted, entrusting, entrustment, entrusts, entry, entry's, entryman, entrymen, entryway, entryways, entte, entune, enturret, entwine, entwined, entwinement, entwines, entwining, entwist, entwisted, entwisting, entwists, entwite, entypies, enucleate, enucleated, enucleating, enucleation, enucleator, enumerability, enumerable, enumerably, enumerate, enumerated, enumerates, enumerating, enumeration, enumerations, enumerative, enumerator, enumerators, enunciability, enunciable, enunciate, enunciated, enunciates, enunciating, enunciation, enunciations, enunciative, enunciatively, enunciator, enunciators, enunciatory, enure, enured, enures, enureses, enuresis, enuresises, enuretic, enuring, enurny, env, envapor, envapour, envassal, envassalage, envault, envaye, enveigle, enveil, envelop, envelope, enveloped, enveloper, envelopers, envelopes, enveloping, envelopment, envelopments, envelops, envenom, envenomation, envenomed, envenoming, envenomization, envenomous, envenoms, enventual, enverdure, envergure, envermeil, enviable, enviableness, enviably, envied, envier, enviers, envies, envigor, envine, envined, envineyard, envious, enviously, enviousness, envire, enviroment, environ, environage, environal, environed, environic, environing, environment, environment's, environmental, environmentalism, environmentalist, environmentalists, environmentally, environments, environs, envisage, envisaged, envisagement, envisages, envisaging, envision, envisioned, envisioning, envisionment, envisions, envoi, envois, envolume, envolupen, envoy, envoy's, envoys, envoyship, envy, envying, envyingly, enwall, enwallow, enweave, enweaved, enweaving, enweb, enwheel, enwheeled, enwheeling, enwheels, enwiden, enwind, enwinding, enwinds, enwing, enwingly, enwisen, enwoman, enwomb, enwombed, enwombing, enwombs, enwood, enworthed, enworthy, enwound, enwove, enwoven, enwrap, enwrapment, enwrapped, enwrapping, enwraps, enwrapt, enwreath, enwreathe, enwreathed, enwreathing, enwrite, enwrought, enwwove, enwwoven, enzone, enzootic, enzootically, enzootics, enzooty, enzygotic, enzym, enzymatic, enzymatically, enzyme, enzymes, enzymic, enzymically, enzymologies, enzymologist, enzymology, enzymolysis, enzymolytic, enzymosis, enzymotic, enzyms, eo, eoan, eobiont, eobionts, eocene, eodiscid, eof, eohippus, eohippuses, eoith, eoiths, eolation, eole, eolian, eolienne, eolipile, eolipiles, eolith, eolithic, eoliths, eolopile, eolopiles, eolotropic, eom, eon, eonian, eonism, eonisms, eons, eophyte, eophytic, eophyton, eorhyolite, eos, eosate, eoside, eosin, eosinate, eosine, eosines, eosinic, eosinlike, eosinoblast, eosinophil, eosinophile, eosinophilia, eosinophilic, eosinophilous, eosins, eosophobia, eosphorite, eozoic, eozoon, eozoonal, ep, epa, epacmaic, epacme, epacrid, epacridaceous, epact, epactal, epacts, epaenetic, epagoge, epagogic, epagomenae, epagomenal, epagomenic, epagomenous, epaleaceous, epalpate, epalpebrate, epanadiplosis, epanalepsis, epanaleptic, epanaphora, epanaphoral, epanastrophe, epanisognathism, epanisognathous, epanodos, epanody, epanorthoses, epanorthosis, epanorthotic, epanthous, epapillate, epapophysial, epapophysis, epappose, eparch, eparchate, eparchial, eparchies, eparchs, eparchy, eparcuale, eparterial, epaule, epaulement, epaulet, epaulet's, epauleted, epaulets, epaulette, epauletted, epauliere, epaxial, epaxially, epedaphic, epee, epeeist, epeeists, epees, epeidia, epeiric, epeirid, epeirogenesis, epeirogenetic, epeirogenic, epeirogenically, epeirogeny, epeisodia, epeisodion, epembryonic, epencephal, epencephala, epencephalic, epencephalon, epencephalons, ependyma, ependymal, ependymary, ependyme, ependymitis, ependymoma, ependytes, epenetic, epenla, epentheses, epenthesis, epenthesize, epenthetic, epephragmal, epepophysial, epepophysis, epergne, epergnes, eperlan, eperotesis, eperva, epeus, epexegeses, epexegesis, epexegetic, epexegetical, epexegetically, epha, ephah, ephahs, ephapse, epharmonic, epharmony, ephas, ephebe, ephebea, ephebeia, ephebeibeia, ephebeion, ephebes, ephebeubea, ephebeum, ephebi, ephebic, epheboi, ephebos, ephebus, ephectic, ephedra, ephedras, ephedrin, ephedrine, ephedrins, ephelcystic, ephelis, ephemera, ephemerae, ephemeral, ephemeralities, ephemerality, ephemerally, ephemeralness, ephemeran, ephemeras, ephemeric, ephemerid, ephemerides, ephemeris, ephemerist, ephemeromorph, ephemeromorphic, ephemeron, ephemerons, ephemerous, ephererist, ephesian, ephesians, ephesine, ephestia, ephestian, ephetae, ephete, ephetic, ephialtes, ephidrosis, ephippia, ephippial, ephippium, ephod, ephods, ephoi, ephor, ephoral, ephoralty, ephorate, ephorates, ephori, ephoric, ephors, ephorship, ephorus, ephphatha, ephraim, ephthianure, ephydriad, ephydrid, ephymnium, ephyra, ephyrae, ephyrula, epi, epibasal, epibatholithic, epibatus, epibenthic, epibenthos, epibiotic, epiblast, epiblastema, epiblastic, epiblasts, epiblema, epiblemata, epibole, epibolic, epibolies, epibolism, epiboly, epiboulangerite, epibranchial, epic, epic's, epical, epically, epicalyces, epicalyx, epicalyxes, epicanthi, epicanthic, epicanthus, epicardia, epicardiac, epicardial, epicardium, epicarid, epicaridan, epicarp, epicarpal, epicarps, epicede, epicedia, epicedial, epicedian, epicedium, epicele, epicene, epicenes, epicenism, epicenity, epicenter, epicenters, epicentra, epicentral, epicentre, epicentrum, epicentrums, epicerastic, epicerebral, epicheirema, epicheiremata, epichil, epichile, epichilia, epichilium, epichindrotic, epichirema, epichlorohydrin, epichondrosis, epichondrotic, epichordal, epichorial, epichoric, epichorion, epichoristic, epichristian, epicier, epicism, epicist, epiclastic, epicleidian, epicleidium, epicleses, epiclesis, epiclidal, epiclike, epiclinal, epicly, epicnemial, epicoelar, epicoele, epicoelia, epicoeliac, epicoelian, epicoeloma, epicoelous, epicolic, epicondylar, epicondyle, epicondylian, epicondylic, epicondylitis, epicontinental, epicoracohumeral, epicoracoid, epicoracoidal, epicormic, epicorolline, epicortical, epicostal, epicotyl, epicotyleal, epicotyledonary, epicotyls, epicranial, epicranium, epicranius, epicrasis, epicrises, epicrisis, epicritic, epicrystalline, epics, epicure, epicurean, epicureanism, epicureans, epicures, epicurish, epicurishly, epicurism, epicurize, epicuticle, epicuticular, epicycle, epicycles, epicyclic, epicyclical, epicycloid, epicycloidal, epicyemate, epicyesis, epicystotomy, epicyte, epideictic, epideictical, epideistic, epidemial, epidemic, epidemic's, epidemical, epidemically, epidemicalness, epidemicity, epidemics, epidemiographist, epidemiography, epidemiologic, epidemiological, epidemiologically, epidemiologies, epidemiologist, epidemiology, epidemy, epidendral, epidendric, epidendron, epidendrum, epiderm, epiderma, epidermal, epidermatic, epidermatoid, epidermatous, epidermic, epidermical, epidermically, epidermidalization, epidermis, epidermization, epidermoid, epidermoidal, epidermolysis, epidermomycosis, epidermophytosis, epidermose, epidermous, epiderms, epidesmine, epidia, epidialogue, epidiascope, epidiascopic, epidictic, epidictical, epididymal, epididymectomy, epididymides, epididymis, epididymite, epididymitis, epididymodeferentectomy, epididymodeferential, epididymovasostomy, epidiorite, epidiorthosis, epidiplosis, epidosite, epidote, epidotes, epidotic, epidotiferous, epidotization, epidural, epidymides, epifascial, epifauna, epifaunae, epifaunal, epifaunas, epifocal, epifolliculitis, epigaeous, epigamic, epigaster, epigastraeum, epigastral, epigastria, epigastrial, epigastric, epigastrical, epigastriocele, epigastrium, epigastrocele, epigeal, epigean, epigee, epigeic, epigene, epigenesis, epigenesist, epigenetic, epigenetically, epigenic, epigenist, epigenous, epigeous, epigeum, epiglot, epiglottal, epiglottic, epiglottidean, epiglottides, epiglottiditis, epiglottis, epiglottises, epiglottitis, epignathous, epigne, epigon, epigonal, epigonation, epigone, epigoneion, epigones, epigoni, epigonic, epigonism, epigonium, epigonos, epigonous, epigonousepigons, epigonus, epigram, epigrammatarian, epigrammatic, epigrammatical, epigrammatically, epigrammatise, epigrammatised, epigrammatising, epigrammatism, epigrammatist, epigrammatize, epigrammatized, epigrammatizer, epigrammatizing, epigramme, epigrams, epigraph, epigrapher, epigraphic, epigraphical, epigraphically, epigraphist, epigraphs, epigraphy, epiguanine, epigyne, epigynies, epigynous, epigynum, epigyny, epihyal, epihydric, epihydrinic, epikeia, epikia, epikleses, epiklesis, epiky, epil, epilabra, epilabrum, epilamellar, epilaryngeal, epilate, epilated, epilating, epilation, epilator, epilatory, epilegomenon, epilemma, epilemmal, epileny, epilepsia, epilepsies, epilepsy, epileptic, epileptical, epileptically, epileptics, epileptiform, epileptogenic, epileptogenous, epileptoid, epileptologist, epileptology, epilimnetic, epilimnia, epilimnial, epilimnion, epilimnionia, epilithic, epilobe, epilog, epilogate, epilogation, epilogic, epilogical, epilogism, epilogist, epilogistic, epilogize, epilogized, epilogizing, epilogs, epilogue, epilogued, epilogues, epiloguing, epiloguize, epiloia, epimacus, epimandibular, epimanikia, epimanikion, epimer, epimeral, epimerase, epimere, epimeres, epimeric, epimeride, epimerise, epimerised, epimerising, epimerism, epimerite, epimeritic, epimerize, epimerized, epimerizing, epimeron, epimers, epimerum, epimorpha, epimorphic, epimorphism, epimorphosis, epimyocardial, epimyocardium, epimysia, epimysium, epimyth, epinaoi, epinaos, epinard, epinastic, epinastically, epinasties, epinasty, epineolithic, epinephrin, epinephrine, epinette, epineuneuria, epineural, epineuria, epineurial, epineurium, epingle, epinglette, epinicia, epinicial, epinician, epinicion, epinikia, epinikian, epinikion, epinine, epinyctis, epionychia, epionychium, epionynychia, epiopticon, epiotic, epipaleolithic, epipanies, epipany, epiparasite, epiparodos, epipastic, epipedometry, epipelagic, epiperipheral, epipetalous, epiphanic, epiphanies, epiphanise, epiphanised, epiphanising, epiphanize, epiphanized, epiphanizing, epiphanous, epiphany, epipharyngeal, epipharynx, epiphenomena, epiphenomenal, epiphenomenalism, epiphenomenalist, epiphenomenally, epiphenomenon, epiphloedal, epiphloedic, epiphloeum, epiphonema, epiphonemae, epiphonemas, epiphora, epiphragm, epiphragmal, epiphylaxis, epiphyll, epiphylline, epiphyllospermous, epiphyllous, epiphysary, epiphyseal, epiphyseolysis, epiphyses, epiphysial, epiphysis, epiphysitis, epiphytal, epiphyte, epiphytes, epiphytic, epiphytical, epiphytically, epiphytism, epiphytology, epiphytotic, epiphytous, epipial, epiplankton, epiplanktonic, epiplasm, epiplasmic, epiplastral, epiplastron, epiplectic, epipleura, epipleurae, epipleural, epiplexis, epiploce, epiplocele, epiploic, epiploitis, epiploon, epiplopexy, epipodia, epipodial, epipodiale, epipodialia, epipodite, epipoditic, epipodium, epipolic, epipolism, epipolize, epiprecoracoid, epiproct, epipteric, epipterous, epipterygoid, epipubes, epipubic, epipubis, epirhizous, epirogenetic, epirogenic, epirogeny, epirot, epirotulian, epirrhema, epirrhematic, epirrheme, episarcine, episarkine, episcenia, episcenium, episcia, episcias, episclera, episcleral, episcleritis, episcopable, episcopacies, episcopacy, episcopal, episcopalian, episcopalianism, episcopalians, episcopalism, episcopality, episcopally, episcopant, episcoparian, episcopate, episcopates, episcopation, episcopature, episcope, episcopes, episcopicide, episcopise, episcopised, episcopising, episcopization, episcopize, episcopized, episcopizing, episcopolatry, episcopy, episcotister, episedia, episematic, episememe, episepalous, episiocele, episiohematoma, episioplasty, episiorrhagia, episiorrhaphy, episiostenosis, episiotomies, episiotomy, episkeletal, episkotister, episodal, episode, episode's, episodes, episodial, episodic, episodical, episodically, episomal, episomally, episome, episomes, epispadia, epispadiac, epispadias, epispastic, episperm, epispermic, epispinal, episplenitis, episporangium, epispore, episporium, epist, epistapedial, epistases, epistasies, epistasis, epistasy, epistatic, epistaxis, episteme, epistemic, epistemically, epistemolog, epistemological, epistemologically, epistemologist, epistemology, epistemonic, epistemonical, epistemophilia, epistemophiliac, epistemophilic, epistena, episterna, episternal, episternalia, episternite, episternum, episthotonos, epistilbite, epistlar, epistle, epistle's, epistler, epistlers, epistles, epistolar, epistolarian, epistolarily, epistolary, epistolatory, epistolean, epistoler, epistolet, epistolic, epistolical, epistolise, epistolised, epistolising, epistolist, epistolizable, epistolization, epistolize, epistolized, epistolizer, epistolizing, epistolographer, epistolographic, epistolographist, epistolography, epistoma, epistomal, epistomata, epistome, epistomian, epistroma, epistrophe, epistropheal, epistropheus, epistrophic, epistrophy, epistylar, epistyle, epistyles, episyllogism, episynaloephe, episynthetic, episyntheton, epit, epitactic, epitaph, epitapher, epitaphial, epitaphian, epitaphic, epitaphical, epitaphist, epitaphize, epitaphless, epitaphs, epitases, epitasis, epitaxial, epitaxially, epitaxic, epitaxies, epitaxis, epitaxy, epitela, epitendineum, epitenon, epithalami, epithalamia, epithalamial, epithalamiast, epithalamic, epithalamion, epithalamium, epithalamiumia, epithalamiums, epithalamize, epithalamus, epithalamy, epithalline, epithamia, epitheca, epithecal, epithecate, epithecia, epithecial, epithecicia, epithecium, epithelia, epithelial, epithelialize, epithelilia, epitheliliums, epithelioblastoma, epithelioceptor, epitheliogenetic, epithelioglandular, epithelioid, epitheliolysin, epitheliolysis, epitheliolytic, epithelioma, epitheliomas, epitheliomata, epitheliomatous, epitheliomuscular, epitheliosis, epitheliotoxin, epitheliulia, epithelium, epitheliums, epithelization, epithelize, epitheloid, epithem, epitheme, epithermal, epithermally, epithesis, epithet, epithet's, epithetic, epithetical, epithetically, epithetician, epithetize, epitheton, epithets, epithi, epithumetic, epithyme, epithymetic, epithymetical, epitimesis, epitoke, epitomate, epitomator, epitomatory, epitome, epitomes, epitomic, epitomical, epitomically, epitomisation, epitomise, epitomised, epitomiser, epitomising, epitomist, epitomization, epitomize, epitomized, epitomizer, epitomizes, epitomizing, epitonic, epitonion, epitoxoid, epitra, epitrachelia, epitrachelion, epitrchelia, epitria, epitrichial, epitrichium, epitrite, epitritic, epitrochlea, epitrochlear, epitrochoid, epitrochoidal, epitrope, epitrophic, epitrophy, epituberculosis, epituberculous, epitympa, epitympanic, epitympanum, epityphlitis, epityphlon, epiural, epivalve, epixylous, epizeuxis, epizoa, epizoal, epizoan, epizoarian, epizoic, epizoicide, epizoism, epizoisms, epizoite, epizoites, epizoology, epizoon, epizootic, epizootically, epizooties, epizootiologic, epizootiological, epizootiologically, epizootiology, epizootology, epizooty, epizzoa, eplot, epoch, epocha, epochal, epochally, epoche, epochism, epochist, epochs, epode, epodes, epodic, epoist, epollicate, eponge, eponychium, eponym, eponymic, eponymies, eponymism, eponymist, eponymize, eponymous, eponyms, eponymus, eponymy, epoophoron, epop, epopee, epopees, epopoean, epopoeia, epopoeias, epopoeist, epopt, epoptes, epoptic, epoptist, epornitic, epornitically, epos, eposes, epotation, epoxide, epoxides, epoxidize, epoxied, epoxies, epoxy, epoxyed, epoxying, eppes, epris, eprise, eprosy, eprouvette, epruinose, epsilon, epsilons, epsom, epsomite, epulary, epulation, epulis, epulo, epuloid, epulones, epulosis, epulotic, epupillate, epural, epurate, epuration, epyllia, epyllion, eq, eqpt, equability, equable, equableness, equably, equaeval, equal, equalable, equaled, equaling, equalisation, equalise, equalised, equalises, equalising, equalist, equalitarian, equalitarianism, equalities, equality, equality's, equalization, equalize, equalized, equalizer, equalizers, equalizes, equalizing, equalled, equaller, equalling, equally, equalness, equals, equangular, equanimity, equanimous, equanimously, equanimousness, equant, equatability, equatable, equate, equated, equates, equating, equation, equational, equationally, equationism, equationist, equations, equative, equator, equator's, equatoreal, equatorial, equatorially, equators, equatorward, equatorwards, equerries, equerry, equerryship, eques, equestrial, equestrian, equestrianism, equestrianize, equestrians, equestrianship, equestrienne, equestriennes, equianchorate, equiangle, equiangular, equiangularity, equianharmonic, equiarticulate, equiatomic, equiaxe, equiaxed, equiaxial, equibalance, equibalanced, equibiradiate, equicaloric, equicellular, equichangeable, equicohesive, equicontinuous, equiconvex, equicostate, equicrural, equicurve, equid, equidense, equidensity, equidiagonal, equidifferent, equidimensional, equidist, equidistance, equidistant, equidistantial, equidistantly, equidistribution, equidiurnal, equidivision, equidominant, equidurable, equielliptical, equiexcellency, equiform, equiformal, equiformity, equiglacial, equigranular, equijacent, equilater, equilateral, equilaterally, equilibrant, equilibrate, equilibrated, equilibrates, equilibrating, equilibration, equilibrations, equilibrative, equilibrator, equilibratory, equilibria, equilibrial, equilibriate, equilibrio, equilibrious, equilibriria, equilibrist, equilibristat, equilibristic, equilibrity, equilibrium, equilibriums, equilibrize, equilin, equiliria, equilobate, equilobed, equilocation, equilucent, equimodal, equimolal, equimolar, equimolecular, equimomental, equimultiple, equinal, equinate, equine, equinecessary, equinely, equines, equinia, equinities, equinity, equinoctial, equinoctially, equinovarus, equinox, equinoxes, equinumerally, equinus, equiomnipotent, equip, equipaga, equipage, equipages, equiparable, equiparant, equiparate, equiparation, equipartile, equipartisan, equipartition, equiped, equipedal, equipede, equipendent, equiperiodic, equipluve, equipment, equipments, equipoise, equipoised, equipoises, equipoising, equipollence, equipollency, equipollent, equipollently, equipollentness, equiponderance, equiponderancy, equiponderant, equiponderate, equiponderated, equiponderating, equiponderation, equiponderous, equipondious, equipostile, equipotent, equipotential, equipotentiality, equipped, equipper, equippers, equipping, equiprobabilism, equiprobabilist, equiprobability, equiprobable, equiprobably, equiproducing, equiproportional, equiproportionality, equips, equipt, equiradial, equiradiate, equiradical, equirotal, equisegmented, equiseta, equisetaceous, equisetic, equisetum, equisetums, equisided, equisignal, equisized, equison, equisonance, equisonant, equispaced, equispatial, equisufficiency, equisurface, equitability, equitable, equitableness, equitably, equitangential, equitant, equitation, equitative, equitemporal, equitemporaneous, equites, equities, equitist, equitriangular, equity, equiv, equivale, equivalence, equivalenced, equivalences, equivalencies, equivalencing, equivalency, equivalent, equivalently, equivalents, equivaliant, equivalue, equivaluer, equivalve, equivalved, equivalvular, equivelocity, equivocacies, equivocacy, equivocal, equivocalities, equivocality, equivocally, equivocalness, equivocate, equivocated, equivocates, equivocating, equivocatingly, equivocation, equivocations, equivocator, equivocators, equivocatory, equivoke, equivokes, equivoluminal, equivoque, equivorous, equivote, equoid, equoidean, equulei, equuleus, equvalent, er, era, era's, erade, eradiate, eradiated, eradiates, eradiating, eradiation, eradicable, eradicably, eradicant, eradicate, eradicated, eradicates, eradicating, eradication, eradications, eradicative, eradicator, eradicators, eradicatory, eradiculose, eral, eranist, eras, erasability, erasable, erase, erased, erasement, eraser, erasers, erases, erasing, erasion, erasions, erasmian, erasmus, erastian, erasure, erasures, erat, erato, erbia, erbium, erbiums, erd, erdvark, ere, erebus, erect, erectable, erected, erecter, erecters, erectile, erectilities, erectility, erecting, erection, erection's, erections, erective, erectly, erectness, erectopatent, erector, erector's, erectors, erects, erelong, eremacausis, eremic, eremital, eremite, eremites, eremiteship, eremitic, eremitical, eremitish, eremitism, eremochaetous, eremology, eremophilous, eremophyte, eremuri, eremurus, erenach, erenow, erepsin, erepsins, erept, ereptase, ereptic, ereption, erer, erethic, erethisia, erethism, erethismic, erethisms, erethistic, erethitic, erewhile, erewhiles, erf, erg, ergal, ergamine, ergasia, ergasterion, ergastic, ergastoplasm, ergastoplasmic, ergastulum, ergatandromorph, ergatandromorphic, ergatandrous, ergatandry, ergate, ergates, ergative, ergatocracy, ergatocrat, ergatogyne, ergatogynous, ergatogyny, ergatoid, ergatomorph, ergatomorphic, ergatomorphism, ergmeter, ergo, ergocalciferol, ergodic, ergodicity, ergogram, ergograph, ergographic, ergoism, ergology, ergomaniac, ergometer, ergometric, ergometrine, ergon, ergonomic, ergonomically, ergonomics, ergonomist, ergonovine, ergophile, ergophobia, ergophobiac, ergophobic, ergoplasm, ergostat, ergosterin, ergosterol, ergot, ergotamine, ergotaminine, ergoted, ergothioneine, ergotic, ergotin, ergotine, ergotinine, ergotism, ergotisms, ergotist, ergotization, ergotize, ergotized, ergotizing, ergotoxin, ergotoxine, ergots, ergs, ergusia, eria, eric, erica, ericaceous, ericad, erical, ericas, ericetal, ericeticolous, ericetum, erichthoid, erichthus, erichtoid, ericineous, ericius, ericoid, ericolin, ericophyte, erie, erigeron, erigerons, erigible, eriglossate, erika, erikite, erin, erinaceous, erineum, eringo, eringoes, eringos, erinite, erinnic, erinose, erinys, eriocaulaceous, erioglaucine, eriometer, erionite, eriophorum, eriophyid, eriophyllous, eris, eristic, eristical, eristically, eristics, erizo, erk, erke, erliche, erlking, erlkings, erme, ermelin, ermiline, ermine, ermine's, ermined, erminee, ermines, erminette, ermining, erminites, erminois, ermit, ermitophobia, ern, erne, ernes, ernesse, ernest, erns, erodability, erodable, erode, eroded, erodent, erodes, erodibility, erodible, eroding, erodium, erogate, erogeneity, erogenesis, erogenetic, erogenic, erogenous, erogeny, eromania, eros, erose, erosely, eroses, erosible, erosion, erosional, erosionally, erosionist, erosions, erosive, erosiveness, erosivity, erostrate, erotema, eroteme, erotesis, erotetic, erotic, erotica, erotical, erotically, eroticism, eroticist, eroticization, eroticize, eroticizing, eroticomania, eroticomaniac, eroticomaniacal, erotics, erotism, erotisms, erotization, erotize, erotized, erotizing, erotogeneses, erotogenesis, erotogenetic, erotogenic, erotogenicity, erotographomania, erotology, erotomania, erotomaniac, erotomaniacal, erotopath, erotopathic, erotopathy, erotophobia, erotylid, erpetologist, erpetology, err, errability, errable, errableness, errabund, errancies, errancy, errand, errands, errant, errantly, errantness, errantries, errantry, errants, errata, erratas, erratic, erratical, erratically, erraticalness, erraticism, erraticness, erratics, erratum, erratums, erratuta, erred, errhine, errhines, erring, erringly, errite, erron, erroneous, erroneously, erroneousness, error, error's, errordump, errorful, errorist, errorless, errors, errs, errsyn, ers, ersatz, ersatzes, erse, erses, ersh, erst, erstwhile, erstwhiles, erth, erthen, erthling, erthly, erubescence, erubescent, erubescite, eruc, eruca, erucic, eruciform, erucin, erucivorous, eruct, eructance, eructate, eructated, eructates, eructating, eructation, eructative, eructed, eructing, eruction, eructs, erudit, erudite, eruditely, eruditeness, eruditical, erudition, eruditional, eruditionist, erugate, erugation, erugatory, eruginous, erugo, erugos, erump, erumpent, erupt, erupted, eruptible, erupting, eruption, eruptional, eruptions, eruptive, eruptively, eruptiveness, eruptives, eruptivity, erupts, erupturient, ervenholder, ervil, ervils, eryhtrism, eryngo, eryngoes, eryngos, eryopid, eryopsid, erysipelas, erysipelatoid, erysipelatous, erysipeloid, erysipelothrix, erysipelous, erythema, erythemal, erythemas, erythematic, erythematous, erythemic, erythorbate, erythraean, erythraemia, erythrasma, erythrean, erythremia, erythremomelalgia, erythrene, erythric, erythrin, erythrina, erythrine, erythrism, erythrismal, erythristic, erythrite, erythritic, erythritol, erythroblast, erythroblastic, erythroblastosis, erythroblastotic, erythrocarpous, erythrocatalysis, erythrochroic, erythrochroism, erythroclasis, erythroclastic, erythrocyte, erythrocytes, erythrocytic, erythrocytoblast, erythrocytolysin, erythrocytolysis, erythrocytolytic, erythrocytometer, erythrocytometry, erythrocytorrhexis, erythrocytoschisis, erythrocytosis, erythrodegenerative, erythroderma, erythrodermia, erythrodextrin, erythrogen, erythrogenesis, erythrogenic, erythroglucin, erythrogonium, erythroid, erythrol, erythrolein, erythrolitmin, erythrolysin, erythrolysis, erythrolytic, erythromania, erythromelalgia, erythromycin, erythron, erythroneocytosis, erythronium, erythrons, erythropenia, erythrophage, erythrophagous, erythrophilous, erythrophleine, erythrophobia, erythrophore, erythrophyll, erythrophyllin, erythropia, erythroplastid, erythropoiesis, erythropoietic, erythropoietin, erythropsia, erythropsin, erythrorrhexis, erythroscope, erythrose, erythrosiderite, erythrosin, erythrosine, erythrosinophile, erythrosis, erythroxylaceous, erythroxyline, erythrozincite, erythrozyme, erythrulose, erzahler, es, esau, esbatement, esbay, esc, esca, escadrille, escadrilles, escalade, escaladed, escalader, escalades, escalading, escalado, escalan, escalate, escalated, escalates, escalating, escalation, escalations, escalator, escalators, escalatory, escalier, escalin, escallonia, escalloniaceous, escallop, escalloped, escalloping, escallops, escalop, escalope, escaloped, escaloping, escalops, escambio, escambron, escamotage, escamoteur, escandalize, escapable, escapade, escapade's, escapades, escapado, escapage, escape, escaped, escapee, escapee's, escapees, escapeful, escapeless, escapement, escapements, escaper, escapers, escapes, escapeway, escaping, escapingly, escapism, escapisms, escapist, escapists, escapologist, escapology, escar, escarbuncle, escargatoire, escargot, escargotieres, escargots, escarmouche, escarole, escaroles, escarp, escarped, escarping, escarpment, escarpments, escarps, escars, escarteled, escartelly, eschalot, eschalots, eschar, eschara, escharine, escharoid, escharotic, eschars, eschatocol, eschatological, eschatologically, eschatologist, eschatology, eschaufe, eschaunge, escheat, escheatable, escheatage, escheated, escheating, escheatment, escheator, escheatorship, escheats, eschel, eschele, escheve, eschevin, eschew, eschewal, eschewals, eschewance, eschewed, eschewer, eschewers, eschewing, eschews, eschoppe, eschrufe, eschscholtzia, eschynite, esclandre, esclavage, escoba, escobadura, escobedo, escobilla, escobita, escocheon, escolar, escolars, esconson, escopet, escopeta, escopette, escort, escortage, escorted, escortee, escorting, escortment, escorts, escot, escoted, escoting, escots, escout, escribano, escribe, escribed, escribiente, escribientes, escribing, escrime, escript, escritoire, escritoires, escritorial, escrod, escrol, escroll, escropulo, escrow, escrowed, escrowee, escrowing, escrows, escruage, escry, escuage, escuages, escudero, escudo, escudos, escuela, esculapian, esculent, esculents, esculetin, esculic, esculin, escurialize, escutcheon, escutcheoned, escutcheons, escutellate, esd, esdragol, ese, esemplastic, esemplasy, eseptate, esere, eserin, eserine, eserines, eses, esexual, esguard, eshin, esiphonal, eskar, eskars, esker, eskers, eskimo, eskimoes, eskimos, eslabon, eslisor, esloign, esmayle, esmeralda, esmeraldite, esne, esnecy, esoanhydride, esocataphoria, esociform, esocyclic, esodic, esoenteritis, esoethmoiditis, esogastritis, esonarthex, esoneural, esopgi, esophagal, esophagalgia, esophageal, esophagean, esophagectasia, esophagectomy, esophagi, esophagism, esophagismus, esophagitis, esophago, esophagocele, esophagodynia, esophagogastroscopy, esophagogastrostomy, esophagomalacia, esophagometer, esophagomycosis, esophagopathy, esophagoplasty, esophagoplegia, esophagoplication, esophagoptosis, esophagorrhagia, esophagoscope, esophagoscopy, esophagospasm, esophagostenosis, esophagostomy, esophagotome, esophagotomy, esophagus, esophoria, esophoric, esoteric, esoterica, esoterical, esoterically, esotericism, esotericist, esoterics, esoterism, esoterist, esoterize, esotery, esothyropexy, esotrope, esotropia, esotropic, esox, esp, espace, espacement, espada, espadon, espadrille, espadrilles, espagnole, espagnolette, espalier, espaliered, espaliering, espaliers, espanol, espanoles, espantoon, esparcet, esparsette, esparto, espartos, espathate, espave, espavel, espec, espece, especial, especially, especialness, espeire, esperance, esperanto, esphresis, espial, espials, espichellite, espied, espiegle, espieglerie, espiegleries, espier, espies, espigle, espiglerie, espinal, espinel, espinette, espingole, espinillo, espino, espinos, espionage, espiritual, esplanade, esplanades, esplees, esponton, espontoon, espousage, espousal, espousals, espouse, espoused, espousement, espouser, espousers, espouses, espousing, espressivo, espresso, espressos, espringal, esprise, esprit, esprits, esprove, espundia, espy, espying, esq, esquamate, esquamulose, esquimau, esquire, esquirearchy, esquired, esquiredom, esquires, esquireship, esquiring, esquisse, esrog, esrogim, esrogs, ess, essancia, essancias, essang, essart, essay, essayed, essayer, essayers, essayette, essayical, essaying, essayish, essayism, essayist, essayistic, essayistical, essayists, essaylet, essays, esse, essed, esseda, essede, essee, essence, essence's, essenced, essences, essencing, essency, essene, essenhout, essentia, essential, essentialism, essentialist, essentialities, essentiality, essentialization, essentialize, essentialized, essentializing, essentially, essentialness, essentials, essentiate, essenwood, essera, esses, essexite, essive, essling, essoign, essoin, essoined, essoinee, essoiner, essoining, essoinment, essoins, essonite, essonites, essorant, est, estab, estable, establish, establishable, established, establisher, establishes, establishing, establishment, establishment's, establishmentarian, establishmentarianism, establishmentism, establishments, establismentarian, establismentarianism, estacade, estadal, estadel, estadio, estado, estafa, estafet, estafette, estafetted, estall, estamene, estamin, estaminet, estaminets, estamp, estampage, estampede, estampedero, estampie, estancia, estancias, estanciero, estancieros, estang, estantion, estate, estate's, estated, estately, estates, estatesman, estatesmen, estating, estats, esteem, esteemable, esteemed, esteemer, esteeming, esteems, estensible, ester, esterase, esterases, esterellite, esteriferous, esterifiable, esterification, esterified, esterifies, esterify, esterifying, esterization, esterize, esterizing, esterling, esteros, esters, estevin, esthematology, esther, estherian, estheses, esthesia, esthesias, esthesio, esthesioblast, esthesiogen, esthesiogenic, esthesiogeny, esthesiography, esthesiology, esthesiometer, esthesiometric, esthesiometry, esthesioneurosis, esthesiophysiology, esthesis, esthesises, esthete, esthetes, esthetic, esthetical, esthetically, esthetician, estheticism, esthetics, esthetology, esthetophore, esthiomene, esthiomenus, estimable, estimableness, estimably, estimate, estimated, estimates, estimating, estimatingly, estimation, estimations, estimative, estimator, estimators, estipulate, estivage, estival, estivate, estivated, estivates, estivating, estivation, estivator, estive, estmark, estoc, estocada, estocs, estoil, estoile, estolide, estonia, estonian, estonians, estop, estoppage, estoppal, estopped, estoppel, estoppels, estopping, estops, estoque, estovers, estrada, estradas, estrade, estradiol, estradiot, estrado, estragol, estragole, estragon, estragons, estral, estramazone, estrange, estranged, estrangedness, estrangelo, estrangement, estrangements, estranger, estranges, estranging, estrangle, estrapade, estray, estrayed, estraying, estrays, estre, estreat, estreated, estreating, estreats, estrepe, estrepement, estriate, estrich, estriche, estrif, estrildine, estrin, estrins, estriol, estriols, estrogen, estrogenic, estrogenically, estrogenicity, estrogens, estrone, estrones, estrous, estrual, estruate, estruation, estrum, estrums, estrus, estruses, estuant, estuarial, estuarian, estuaries, estuarine, estuary, estuate, estudy, estufa, estuosity, estuous, esture, estus, esu, esugarization, esurience, esuriency, esurient, esuriently, esurine, et, eta, etaballi, etabelli, etacism, etacist, etaerio, etagere, etageres, etagre, etalage, etalon, etamin, etamine, etamines, etamins, etang, etape, etapes, etas, etatism, etatisme, etatisms, etatist, etc, etcetera, etceteras, etch, etchant, etched, etcher, etchers, etches, etching, etchings, eten, eteocles, eteostic, eterminable, eternal, eternalise, eternalised, eternalising, eternalism, eternalist, eternality, eternalization, eternalize, eternalized, eternalizing, eternally, eternalness, eternals, eterne, eternisation, eternise, eternised, eternises, eternish, eternising, eternities, eternity, eternization, eternize, eternized, eternizes, eternizing, etesian, etesians, eth, ethal, ethaldehyde, ethambutol, ethanal, ethanamide, ethane, ethanedial, ethanediol, ethanedithiol, ethanes, ethanethial, ethanethiol, ethanim, ethanol, ethanolamine, ethanols, ethanolysis, ethanoyl, ethchlorvynol, ethel, etheling, ethene, ethenes, ethenic, ethenoid, ethenoidal, ethenol, ethenyl, etheostomoid, ether, ether's, etherate, ethereal, etherealisation, etherealise, etherealised, etherealising, etherealism, ethereality, etherealization, etherealize, etherealized, etherealizing, ethereally, etherealness, etherean, ethered, etherene, ethereous, etherial, etherialisation, etherialise, etherialised, etherialising, etherialism, etherialization, etherialize, etherialized, etherializing, etherially, etheric, etherical, etherification, etherified, etherifies, etheriform, etherify, etherifying, etherin, etherion, etherish, etherism, etherization, etherize, etherized, etherizer, etherizes, etherizing, etherlike, ethernet, ethernets, etherol, etherolate, etherous, ethers, ethic, ethical, ethicalism, ethicalities, ethicality, ethically, ethicalness, ethicals, ethician, ethicians, ethicism, ethicist, ethicists, ethicize, ethicized, ethicizes, ethicizing, ethicoaesthetic, ethicophysical, ethicopolitical, ethicoreligious, ethicosocial, ethics, ethid, ethide, ethidene, ethinamate, ethine, ethinyl, ethinyls, ethiodide, ethion, ethionamide, ethionic, ethionine, ethions, ethiop, ethiopia, ethiopian, ethiopians, ethiopic, ethiops, ethize, ethmofrontal, ethmoid, ethmoidal, ethmoiditis, ethmoids, ethmolachrymal, ethmolith, ethmomaxillary, ethmonasal, ethmopalatal, ethmopalatine, ethmophysal, ethmopresphenoidal, ethmose, ethmosphenoid, ethmosphenoidal, ethmoturbinal, ethmoturbinate, ethmovomer, ethmovomerine, ethmyphitis, ethnal, ethnarch, ethnarchies, ethnarchs, ethnarchy, ethnic, ethnical, ethnically, ethnicism, ethnicist, ethnicity, ethnicize, ethnicon, ethnics, ethnish, ethnize, ethnobiological, ethnobiology, ethnobotanic, ethnobotanical, ethnobotanist, ethnobotany, ethnocentric, ethnocentrically, ethnocentricity, ethnocentrism, ethnocracy, ethnodicy, ethnoflora, ethnog, ethnogenic, ethnogenies, ethnogenist, ethnogeny, ethnogeographer, ethnogeographic, ethnogeographical, ethnogeographically, ethnogeography, ethnographer, ethnographic, ethnographical, ethnographically, ethnographies, ethnographist, ethnography, ethnohistorian, ethnohistoric, ethnohistorical, ethnohistorically, ethnohistory, ethnol, ethnolinguist, ethnolinguistic, ethnolinguistics, ethnologer, ethnologic, ethnological, ethnologically, ethnologist, ethnologists, ethnology, ethnomaniac, ethnomanic, ethnomusicological, ethnomusicologically, ethnomusicologist, ethnomusicology, ethnopsychic, ethnopsychological, ethnopsychology, ethnos, ethnoses, ethnotechnics, ethnotechnography, ethnozoological, ethnozoology, ethography, etholide, ethologic, ethological, ethologically, ethologies, ethologist, ethologists, ethology, ethonomic, ethonomics, ethonone, ethopoeia, ethopoetic, ethos, ethoses, ethoxide, ethoxy, ethoxycaffeine, ethoxyethane, ethoxyl, ethoxyls, ethrog, ethrogim, ethrogs, eths, ethyl, ethylamide, ethylamime, ethylamin, ethylamine, ethylate, ethylated, ethylates, ethylating, ethylation, ethylbenzene, ethyldichloroarsine, ethylenation, ethylene, ethylenediamine, ethylenes, ethylenic, ethylenically, ethylenimine, ethylenoid, ethylhydrocupreine, ethylic, ethylidene, ethylidyne, ethylin, ethylmorphine, ethyls, ethylsulphuric, ethylthioethane, ethylthioether, ethyne, ethynes, ethynyl, ethynylation, ethynyls, ethysulphuric, etiam, etiogenic, etiolate, etiolated, etiolates, etiolating, etiolation, etiolin, etiolize, etiologic, etiological, etiologically, etiologies, etiologist, etiologue, etiology, etiophyllin, etioporphyrin, etiotropic, etiotropically, etiquet, etiquette, etiquettes, etiquettical, etna, etnas, etoffe, etoile, etoiles, eton, etonian, etouffe, etourderie, etrenne, etrier, etrog, etrogim, etrogs, etruria, etrurian, etruscan, etruscans, ettercap, ettirone, ettle, ettled, ettling, etua, etude, etudes, etui, etuis, etuve, etuvee, etwas, etwee, etwees, etwite, ety, etym, etyma, etymic, etymography, etymol, etymologer, etymologic, etymological, etymologically, etymologicon, etymologies, etymologisable, etymologise, etymologised, etymologising, etymologist, etymologists, etymologizable, etymologization, etymologize, etymologized, etymologizing, etymology, etymon, etymonic, etymons, etypic, etypical, etypically, eu, euangiotic, euaster, eubacteria, eubacterium, euboic, eubteria, eucaine, eucaines, eucairite, eucalyn, eucalypt, eucalypteol, eucalypti, eucalyptian, eucalyptic, eucalyptography, eucalyptol, eucalyptole, eucalypts, eucalyptus, eucalyptuses, eucarpic, eucarpous, eucaryote, eucaryotic, eucatropine, eucephalous, eucgia, eucharis, eucharises, eucharist, eucharistial, eucharistic, eucharistical, eucharistically, eucharistize, eucharistized, eucharistizing, eucharists, euchite, euchlorhydria, euchloric, euchlorine, euchlorite, euchologia, euchological, euchologies, euchologion, euchology, euchre, euchred, euchres, euchring, euchroic, euchroite, euchromatic, euchromatin, euchrome, euchromosome, euchrone, euchymous, euchysiderite, euciliate, euclase, euclases, eucleid, euclid, euclidean, euclidian, eucolite, eucone, euconic, eucosmid, eucrasia, eucrasite, eucrasy, eucre, eucrite, eucrites, eucritic, eucryphiaceous, eucryptite, eucrystalline, eucti, euctical, eucyclic, euda, eudaemon, eudaemonia, eudaemonic, eudaemonical, eudaemonics, eudaemonism, eudaemonist, eudaemonistic, eudaemonistical, eudaemonistically, eudaemonize, eudaemons, eudaemony, eudaimonia, eudaimonism, eudaimonist, eudalene, eudemon, eudemonia, eudemonic, eudemonics, eudemonism, eudemonist, eudemonistic, eudemonistical, eudemonistically, eudemons, eudemony, eudesmol, eudiagnostic, eudialyte, eudiaphoresis, eudidymite, eudiometer, eudiometric, eudiometrical, eudiometrically, eudiometry, eudipleural, euectic, euemerism, euflavine, euge, eugene, eugenesic, eugenesis, eugenetic, eugenia, eugenic, eugenical, eugenically, eugenicist, eugenicists, eugenics, eugenism, eugenist, eugenists, eugenol, eugenolate, eugenols, eugeny, eugeosynclinal, eugeosyncline, euglena, euglenas, euglenoid, euglobulin, eugonic, eugranitic, euhages, euharmonic, euhedral, euhemerise, euhemerised, euhemerising, euhemerism, euhemerist, euhemeristic, euhemeristically, euhemerize, euhemerized, euhemerizing, euhyostylic, euhyostyly, eukairite, eukaryote, euktolite, eulachan, eulachans, eulachon, eulachons, eulalia, eulamellibranch, eulamellibranchiate, euler, eulerian, eulogia, eulogiae, eulogias, eulogic, eulogical, eulogically, eulogies, eulogious, eulogisation, eulogise, eulogised, eulogiser, eulogises, eulogising, eulogism, eulogist, eulogistic, eulogistical, eulogistically, eulogists, eulogium, eulogiums, eulogization, eulogize, eulogized, eulogizer, eulogizers, eulogizes, eulogizing, eulogy, eulophid, eulysite, eulytin, eulytine, eulytite, eumelanin, eumemorrhea, eumenid, eumenides, eumenorrhea, eumerism, eumeristic, eumerogenesis, eumerogenetic, eumeromorph, eumeromorphic, eumitosis, eumitotic, eumoiriety, eumoirous, eumolpique, eumorphic, eumorphous, eumycete, eumycetic, eundem, eunicid, eunomy, eunuch, eunuchal, eunuchise, eunuchised, eunuchising, eunuchism, eunuchize, eunuchized, eunuchizing, eunuchoid, eunuchoidism, eunuchry, eunuchs, euodic, euomphalid, euonym, euonymin, euonymous, euonymus, euonymuses, euonymy, euornithic, euosmite, euouae, eupad, eupathy, eupatoriaceous, eupatorin, eupatorine, eupatorium, eupatory, eupatrid, eupatridae, eupatrids, eupepsia, eupepsias, eupepsies, eupepsy, eupeptic, eupeptically, eupepticism, eupepticity, euphausid, euphausiid, euphemian, euphemious, euphemiously, euphemisation, euphemise, euphemised, euphemiser, euphemising, euphemism, euphemism's, euphemisms, euphemist, euphemistic, euphemistical, euphemistically, euphemization, euphemize, euphemized, euphemizer, euphemizing, euphemous, euphemy, euphenic, euphenics, euphon, euphone, euphonetic, euphonetics, euphonia, euphoniad, euphonic, euphonical, euphonically, euphonicalness, euphonies, euphonious, euphoniously, euphoniousness, euphonise, euphonised, euphonising, euphonism, euphonium, euphonize, euphonized, euphonizing, euphonon, euphonous, euphony, euphonym, euphorbia, euphorbiaceous, euphorbial, euphorbine, euphorbium, euphoria, euphoriant, euphorias, euphoric, euphorically, euphory, euphotic, euphotide, euphrasia, euphrasies, euphrasy, euphrates, euphroe, euphroes, euphrosyne, euphues, euphuism, euphuisms, euphuist, euphuistic, euphuistical, euphuistically, euphuists, euphuize, euphuized, euphuizing, euphyllite, eupion, eupione, eupittone, eupittonic, euplastic, euploid, euploidies, euploids, euploidy, euplotid, eupnea, eupneas, eupneic, eupnoea, eupnoeas, eupnoeic, eupolyzoan, eupotamic, eupractic, eupraxia, eupsychics, eupyrchroite, eupyrene, eupyrion, euraquilo, eurasia, eurasian, eurasians, eure, eureka, eurhodine, eurhodol, eurhythmic, eurhythmical, eurhythmics, eurhythmy, euripi, euripidean, euripides, euripos, euripupi, euripus, eurite, eurithermophile, eurithermophilic, euro, eurobin, eurocentric, euroclydon, eurodollar, eurodollars, europa, europe, european, europeanism, europeanize, europeans, europhium, europium, europiums, euros, eurous, eurus, euryalean, euryalidan, eurybathic, eurybenthic, eurycephalic, eurycephalous, eurycerous, eurychoric, eurydice, eurygnathic, eurygnathism, eurygnathous, euryhaline, eurylaimoid, euryon, euryphage, euryphagous, euryprognathous, euryprosopic, eurypterid, eurypteroid, eurypylous, euryscope, eurystomatous, euryte, eurytherm, eurythermal, eurythermic, eurythermous, eurythmic, eurythmical, eurythmics, eurythmies, eurythmy, eurytomid, eurytopic, eurytopicity, eurytropic, euryzygous, eusebian, euskarian, eusol, eusporangiate, eustachian, eustachium, eustacies, eustacy, eustatic, eustatically, eustele, eusteles, eustomatous, eustyle, eusuchian, eusynchite, eutannin, eutaxic, eutaxie, eutaxies, eutaxite, eutaxitic, eutaxy, eutechnic, eutechnics, eutectic, eutectics, eutectoid, eutelegenic, euterpe, eutexia, euthanasia, euthanasic, euthanasy, euthanatize, euthenasia, euthenic, euthenics, euthenist, eutherian, euthermic, euthycomic, euthymy, euthyneural, euthyneurous, euthyroid, euthytatic, euthytropic, eutocia, eutomous, eutony, eutopia, eutrophic, eutrophication, eutrophies, eutrophy, eutropic, eutropous, eutychian, euvrou, euxanthate, euxanthic, euxanthin, euxanthone, euxenite, euxenites, evacuant, evacuants, evacuate, evacuated, evacuates, evacuating, evacuation, evacuations, evacuative, evacuator, evacuators, evacue, evacuee, evacuees, evadable, evade, evaded, evader, evaders, evades, evadible, evading, evadingly, evagation, evaginable, evaginate, evaginated, evaginating, evagination, eval, evaluable, evaluate, evaluated, evaluates, evaluating, evaluation, evaluations, evaluative, evaluator, evaluator's, evaluators, evalue, evanesce, evanesced, evanescence, evanescency, evanescenrly, evanescent, evanescently, evanesces, evanescible, evanescing, evang, evangel, evangelary, evangelian, evangeliaries, evangeliarium, evangeliary, evangelic, evangelical, evangelicalism, evangelicality, evangelically, evangelicalness, evangelicals, evangelican, evangelicism, evangelicity, evangelion, evangelisation, evangelise, evangelised, evangeliser, evangelising, evangelism, evangelist, evangelistaries, evangelistarion, evangelistarium, evangelistary, evangelistic, evangelistically, evangelistics, evangelists, evangelistship, evangelium, evangelization, evangelize, evangelized, evangelizer, evangelizes, evangelizing, evangels, evangely, evanid, evanish, evanished, evanishes, evanishing, evanishment, evanition, evans, evansite, evap, evaporability, evaporable, evaporate, evaporated, evaporates, evaporating, evaporation, evaporations, evaporative, evaporatively, evaporativity, evaporator, evaporators, evaporimeter, evaporite, evaporitic, evaporize, evaporometer, evapotranspiration, evase, evasible, evasion, evasional, evasions, evasive, evasively, evasiveness, eve, evechurr, eveck, evectant, evected, evectic, evection, evectional, evections, evector, evejar, evelight, evelong, even, evenblush, evendown, evene, evened, evener, eveners, evenest, evenfall, evenfalls, evenforth, evenglome, evenglow, evenhand, evenhanded, evenhandedly, evenhandedness, evenhead, evening, evening's, evenings, evenlight, evenlong, evenly, evenmete, evenminded, evenmindedness, evenness, evennesses, evenoo, evens, evensong, evensongs, event, event's, eventail, eventerate, eventful, eventfully, eventfulness, eventide, eventides, eventilate, eventime, eventless, eventlessly, eventlessness, eventognath, eventognathous, eventration, events, eventual, eventualities, eventuality, eventualize, eventually, eventuate, eventuated, eventuates, eventuating, eventuation, eventuations, evenwise, evenworthy, eveque, ever, everbearer, everbearing, everbloomer, everblooming, everduring, everest, everglade, everglades, evergreen, evergreenery, evergreenite, evergreens, everich, everlasting, everlastingly, everlastingness, everliving, everly, evermo, evermore, everness, evernioid, everse, eversible, eversion, eversions, eversive, eversporting, evert, evertebral, evertebrate, everted, evertile, everting, evertor, evertors, everts, everwhich, everwho, every, everybody, everyday, everydayness, everydeal, everyhow, everylike, everyman, everymen, everyness, everyone, everyone's, everyplace, everything, everyway, everywhen, everywhence, everywhere, everywhereness, everywheres, everywhither, everywoman, eves, evese, evestar, evetide, eveweed, evg, evibrate, evicke, evict, evicted, evictee, evictees, evicting, eviction, eviction's, evictions, evictor, evictors, evicts, evidence, evidenced, evidences, evidencing, evidencive, evident, evidential, evidentially, evidentiary, evidently, evidentness, evigilation, evil, evildoer, evildoers, evildoing, eviler, evilest, evilhearted, eviller, evillest, evilly, evilmouthed, evilness, evilnesses, evilproof, evils, evilsayer, evilspeaker, evilspeaking, evilwishing, evince, evinced, evincement, evinces, evincible, evincibly, evincing, evincingly, evincive, evirate, eviration, evirato, evirtuate, eviscerate, eviscerated, eviscerates, eviscerating, evisceration, eviscerations, eviscerator, evisite, evitable, evitate, evitation, evite, evited, eviternal, evites, eviting, evittate, evocable, evocate, evocated, evocating, evocation, evocations, evocative, evocatively, evocativeness, evocator, evocators, evocatory, evocatrix, evoe, evoke, evoked, evoker, evokers, evokes, evoking, evolate, evolute, evolute's, evolutes, evolutility, evolution, evolution's, evolutional, evolutionally, evolutionarily, evolutionary, evolutionism, evolutionist, evolutionistic, evolutionistically, evolutionists, evolutionize, evolutions, evolutive, evolutoid, evolvable, evolve, evolved, evolvement, evolvements, evolvent, evolver, evolvers, evolves, evolving, evolvulus, evomit, evonymus, evonymuses, evovae, evulgate, evulgation, evulge, evulse, evulsion, evulsions, evviva, evzone, evzones, ew, ewder, ewe, ewe's, ewelease, ewer, ewerer, eweries, ewers, ewery, ewes, ewest, ewhow, ewing, ewound, ewry, ewte, ex, exacerbate, exacerbated, exacerbates, exacerbating, exacerbatingly, exacerbation, exacerbations, exacerbescence, exacerbescent, exacervation, exacinate, exact, exacta, exactable, exactas, exacted, exacter, exacters, exactest, exacting, exactingly, exactingness, exaction, exaction's, exactions, exactitude, exactive, exactiveness, exactly, exactment, exactness, exactor, exactors, exactress, exacts, exactus, exacuate, exacum, exadverso, exadversum, exaestuate, exaggerate, exaggerated, exaggeratedly, exaggeratedness, exaggerates, exaggerating, exaggeratingly, exaggeration, exaggerations, exaggerative, exaggeratively, exaggerativeness, exaggerator, exaggerators, exaggeratory, exagitate, exagitation, exairesis, exalate, exalbuminose, exalbuminous, exallotriote, exalt, exaltate, exaltation, exaltations, exaltative, exalte, exalted, exaltedly, exaltedness, exaltee, exalter, exalters, exalting, exaltment, exalts, exam, exam's, examen, examens, exameter, examinability, examinable, examinant, examinate, examination, examination's, examinational, examinationism, examinationist, examinations, examinative, examinator, examinatorial, examinatory, examine, examined, examinee, examinees, examiner, examiners, examinership, examines, examining, examiningly, examplar, example, example's, exampled, exampleless, examples, exampleship, exampless, exampling, exams, exanguin, exanimate, exanimation, exannulate, exanthalose, exanthem, exanthema, exanthemas, exanthemata, exanthematic, exanthematous, exanthems, exanthine, exantlate, exantlation, exappendiculate, exarate, exaration, exarch, exarchal, exarchate, exarchateship, exarchies, exarchist, exarchs, exarchy, exareolate, exarillate, exaristate, exarteritis, exarticulate, exarticulation, exasper, exasperate, exasperated, exasperatedly, exasperater, exasperates, exasperating, exasperatingly, exasperation, exasperative, exaspidean, exauctorate, exaugurate, exauguration, exaun, exauthorate, exauthorize, exauthorizeexc, excalate, excalation, excalcarate, excalceate, excalceation, excalfaction, excalibur, excamb, excamber, excambion, excandescence, excandescency, excandescent, excantation, excardination, excarnate, excarnation, excarnificate, excathedral, excaudate, excavate, excavated, excavates, excavating, excavation, excavational, excavationist, excavations, excavator, excavatorial, excavators, excavatory, excave, excecate, excecation, excedent, exceed, exceedable, exceeded, exceeder, exceeders, exceeding, exceedingly, exceedingness, exceeds, excel, excelente, excelled, excellence, excellences, excellencies, excellency, excellent, excellently, excelling, excels, excelse, excelsin, excelsior, excelsitude, excentral, excentric, excentrical, excentricity, excepable, except, exceptant, excepted, excepter, excepting, exceptio, exception, exception's, exceptionability, exceptionable, exceptionableness, exceptionably, exceptional, exceptionality, exceptionally, exceptionalness, exceptionary, exceptioner, exceptionless, exceptions, exceptious, exceptiousness, exceptive, exceptively, exceptiveness, exceptless, exceptor, excepts, excercise, excerebrate, excerebration, excern, excerp, excerpt, excerpta, excerpted, excerpter, excerptible, excerpting, excerption, excerptive, excerptor, excerpts, excess, excesses, excessive, excessively, excessiveness, excessman, excessmen, exch, exchange, exchangeability, exchangeable, exchangeably, exchanged, exchangee, exchanger, exchanges, exchanging, excheat, exchequer, exchequer's, exchequers, excide, excided, excides, exciding, excipient, exciple, exciples, excipula, excipular, excipule, excipuliform, excipulum, excircle, excisable, excise, excised, exciseman, excisemanship, excisemen, excises, excising, excision, excisions, excisor, excitabilities, excitability, excitable, excitableness, excitably, excitancy, excitant, excitants, excitate, excitation, excitation's, excitations, excitative, excitator, excitatory, excite, excited, excitedly, excitedness, excitement, excitements, exciter, exciters, excites, exciting, excitingly, excitive, excitoglandular, excitometabolic, excitomotion, excitomotor, excitomotory, excitomuscular, exciton, excitonic, excitons, excitonutrient, excitor, excitors, excitory, excitosecretory, excitovascular, excitron, excl, exclaim, exclaimed, exclaimer, exclaimers, exclaiming, exclaimingly, exclaims, exclam, exclamation, exclamation's, exclamational, exclamations, exclamative, exclamatively, exclamatorily, exclamatory, exclaustration, exclave, exclaves, exclosure, excludability, excludable, exclude, excluded, excluder, excluders, excludes, excludible, excluding, excludingly, exclusion, exclusionary, exclusioner, exclusionism, exclusionist, exclusions, exclusive, exclusively, exclusiveness, exclusivism, exclusivist, exclusivistic, exclusivity, exclusory, excoct, excoction, excogitable, excogitate, excogitated, excogitates, excogitating, excogitation, excogitative, excogitator, excommenge, excommune, excommunicable, excommunicant, excommunicate, excommunicated, excommunicates, excommunicating, excommunication, excommunications, excommunicative, excommunicator, excommunicators, excommunicatory, excommunion, exconjugant, excoriable, excoriate, excoriated, excoriates, excoriating, excoriation, excoriations, excoriator, excorticate, excorticated, excorticating, excortication, excreation, excrement, excremental, excrementally, excrementary, excrementitial, excrementitious, excrementitiously, excrementitiousness, excrementive, excrementize, excrementous, excrements, excresce, excrescence, excrescences, excrescencies, excrescency, excrescent, excrescential, excrescently, excresence, excression, excreta, excretal, excrete, excreted, excreter, excreters, excretes, excreting, excretion, excretionary, excretions, excretitious, excretive, excretolic, excretory, excriminate, excruciable, excruciate, excruciated, excruciating, excruciatingly, excruciatingness, excruciation, excruciator, excubant, excubitoria, excubitorium, excubittoria, excud, excudate, excuderunt, excudit, exculpable, exculpate, exculpated, exculpates, exculpating, exculpation, exculpations, exculpative, exculpatorily, exculpatory, excur, excurrent, excurse, excursed, excursing, excursion, excursion's, excursional, excursionary, excursioner, excursionism, excursionist, excursionists, excursionize, excursions, excursive, excursively, excursiveness, excursory, excursus, excursuses, excurvate, excurvated, excurvation, excurvature, excurved, excusability, excusable, excusableness, excusably, excusal, excusation, excusative, excusator, excusatory, excuse, excused, excuseful, excusefully, excuseless, excuser, excusers, excuses, excusing, excusingly, excusive, excusively, excuss, excussed, excussing, excussio, excussion, excyst, excystation, excysted, excystment, exdelicto, exdie, exdividend, exeat, exec, execeptional, execrable, execrableness, execrably, execrate, execrated, execrates, execrating, execration, execrations, execrative, execratively, execrator, execrators, execratory, execs, exect, executable, executancy, executant, execute, executed, executer, executers, executes, executing, execution, executional, executioneering, executioner, executioneress, executioners, executionist, executions, executive, executive's, executively, executiveness, executives, executiveship, executonis, executor, executor's, executorial, executors, executorship, executory, executress, executrices, executrix, executrixes, executrixship, executry, exede, exedent, exedra, exedrae, exedral, exegeses, exegesis, exegesist, exegete, exegetes, exegetic, exegetical, exegetically, exegetics, exegetist, exembryonate, exempla, exemplar, exemplaric, exemplarily, exemplariness, exemplarism, exemplarity, exemplars, exemplary, exempli, exemplifiable, exemplification, exemplificational, exemplifications, exemplificative, exemplificator, exemplified, exemplifier, exemplifiers, exemplifies, exemplify, exemplifying, exemplum, exemplupla, exempt, exempted, exemptible, exemptile, exempting, exemption, exemptionist, exemptions, exemptive, exempts, exencephalia, exencephalic, exencephalous, exencephalus, exendospermic, exendospermous, exenterate, exenterated, exenterating, exenteration, exenteritis, exequatur, exequial, exequies, exequy, exerce, exercent, exercisable, exercise, exercised, exerciser, exercisers, exercises, exercising, exercitant, exercitation, exercite, exercitor, exercitorial, exercitorian, exeresis, exergonic, exergual, exergue, exergues, exert, exerted, exerting, exertion, exertion's, exertionless, exertions, exertive, exerts, exes, exesion, exestuate, exeunt, exfetation, exfiguration, exfigure, exfiltrate, exfiltration, exflagellate, exflagellation, exflect, exfodiate, exfodiation, exfoliate, exfoliated, exfoliating, exfoliation, exfoliative, exfoliatory, exgorgitation, exhalable, exhalant, exhalants, exhalate, exhalation, exhalations, exhalatory, exhale, exhaled, exhalent, exhalents, exhales, exhaling, exhance, exhaust, exhaustable, exhausted, exhaustedly, exhaustedness, exhauster, exhaustibility, exhaustible, exhausting, exhaustingly, exhaustion, exhaustive, exhaustively, exhaustiveness, exhaustivity, exhaustless, exhaustlessly, exhaustlessness, exhausts, exhbn, exhedra, exhedrae, exheredate, exheredation, exhibit, exhibitable, exhibitant, exhibited, exhibiter, exhibiters, exhibiting, exhibition, exhibition's, exhibitional, exhibitioner, exhibitionism, exhibitionist, exhibitionistic, exhibitionists, exhibitionize, exhibitions, exhibitive, exhibitively, exhibitor, exhibitor's, exhibitorial, exhibitors, exhibitorship, exhibitory, exhibits, exhilarant, exhilarate, exhilarated, exhilarates, exhilarating, exhilaratingly, exhilaration, exhilarative, exhilarator, exhilaratory, exhort, exhortation, exhortation's, exhortations, exhortative, exhortatively, exhortator, exhortatory, exhorted, exhorter, exhorters, exhorting, exhortingly, exhorts, exhumate, exhumated, exhumating, exhumation, exhumations, exhumator, exhumatory, exhume, exhumed, exhumer, exhumers, exhumes, exhuming, exhusband, exibilate, exies, exigeant, exigeante, exigence, exigences, exigencies, exigency, exigent, exigenter, exigently, exigible, exiguities, exiguity, exiguous, exiguously, exiguousness, exilable, exilarch, exilarchate, exile, exiled, exiledom, exilement, exiler, exiles, exilian, exilic, exiling, exilition, exility, eximidus, eximious, eximiously, eximiousness, exinanite, exinanition, exindusiate, exine, exines, exing, exinguinal, exinite, exintine, exion, exist, existability, existant, existed, existence, existences, existent, existential, existentialism, existentialist, existentialist's, existentialistic, existentialistically, existentialists, existentialize, existentially, existently, existents, exister, existibility, existible, existimation, existing, existless, existlessness, exists, exit, exitance, exite, exited, exitial, exiting, exition, exitious, exits, exiture, exitus, exla, exlex, exmeridian, exmoor, exoarteritis, exoascaceous, exobiological, exobiologist, exobiologists, exobiology, exocannibalism, exocardia, exocardiac, exocardial, exocarp, exocarps, exocataphoria, exoccipital, exocentric, exochorion, exoclinal, exocline, exocoelar, exocoele, exocoelic, exocoelom, exocoelum, exocolitis, exocone, exocrine, exocrines, exocrinologies, exocrinology, exoculate, exoculated, exoculating, exoculation, exocyclic, exocytosis, exode, exoderm, exodermal, exodermis, exoderms, exodic, exodist, exodium, exodoi, exodontia, exodontic, exodontics, exodontist, exodos, exodromic, exodromy, exodus, exoduses, exody, exoenzyme, exoenzymic, exoergic, exoerythrocytic, exogamic, exogamies, exogamous, exogamy, exogastric, exogastrically, exogastritis, exogen, exogenetic, exogenic, exogenism, exogenous, exogenously, exogens, exogeny, exognathion, exognathite, exograph, exolemma, exolete, exolution, exolve, exometritis, exomion, exomis, exomologesis, exomorphic, exomorphism, exomphalos, exomphalous, exomphalus, exon, exonarthex, exoner, exonerate, exonerated, exonerates, exonerating, exoneration, exonerations, exonerative, exonerator, exonerators, exoneretur, exoneural, exonship, exonuclease, exonym, exopathic, exopeptidase, exoperidium, exophagous, exophagy, exophasia, exophasic, exophoria, exophoric, exophthalmia, exophthalmic, exophthalmos, exophthalmus, exoplasm, exopod, exopodite, exopoditic, exopt, exopterygote, exopterygotic, exopterygotism, exopterygotous, exor, exorability, exorable, exorableness, exorate, exorbital, exorbitance, exorbitancy, exorbitant, exorbitantly, exorbitate, exorbitation, exorcisation, exorcise, exorcised, exorcisement, exorciser, exorcisers, exorcises, exorcising, exorcism, exorcismal, exorcisms, exorcisory, exorcist, exorcista, exorcistic, exorcistical, exorcists, exorcization, exorcize, exorcized, exorcizement, exorcizer, exorcizes, exorcizing, exordia, exordial, exordium, exordiums, exordize, exorganic, exorhason, exormia, exornate, exornation, exortion, exosculation, exosepsis, exoskeletal, exoskeleton, exosmic, exosmose, exosmoses, exosmosis, exosmotic, exosperm, exosphere, exospheres, exospheric, exospherical, exosporal, exospore, exospores, exosporium, exosporous, exossate, exosseous, exostome, exostosed, exostoses, exostosis, exostotic, exostra, exostracism, exostracize, exostrae, exoteric, exoterica, exoterical, exoterically, exotericism, exoterics, exotery, exotheca, exothecal, exothecate, exothecium, exothermal, exothermally, exothermic, exothermically, exothermicity, exothermous, exotic, exotica, exotically, exoticalness, exoticism, exoticist, exoticity, exoticness, exotics, exotism, exotisms, exotospore, exotoxic, exotoxin, exotoxins, exotropia, exotropic, exotropism, exp, expalpate, expand, expandability, expandable, expanded, expandedly, expandedness, expander, expander's, expanders, expandibility, expandible, expanding, expandingly, expands, expanse, expanses, expansibility, expansible, expansibleness, expansibly, expansile, expansion, expansional, expansionary, expansionism, expansionist, expansionistic, expansionists, expansions, expansive, expansively, expansiveness, expansivity, expansometer, expansum, expansure, expatiate, expatiated, expatiater, expatiates, expatiating, expatiatingly, expatiation, expatiations, expatiative, expatiator, expatiators, expatiatory, expatriate, expatriated, expatriates, expatriating, expatriation, expatriations, expatriatism, expdt, expect, expectable, expectably, expectance, expectancies, expectancy, expectant, expectantly, expectation, expectation's, expectations, expectative, expected, expectedly, expectedness, expecter, expecters, expecting, expectingly, expection, expective, expectorant, expectorants, expectorate, expectorated, expectorates, expectorating, expectoration, expectorations, expectorative, expectorator, expectorators, expects, expede, expeded, expediate, expedience, expediences, expediencies, expediency, expedient, expediente, expediential, expedientially, expedientist, expediently, expedients, expediment, expeding, expeditate, expeditated, expeditating, expeditation, expedite, expedited, expeditely, expediteness, expediter, expediters, expedites, expediting, expedition, expedition's, expeditionary, expeditionist, expeditions, expeditious, expeditiously, expeditiousness, expeditive, expeditor, expel, expellable, expellant, expelled, expellee, expellees, expellent, expeller, expellers, expelling, expels, expend, expendability, expendable, expendables, expended, expender, expenders, expendible, expending, expenditor, expenditrix, expenditure, expenditure's, expenditures, expends, expense, expensed, expenseful, expensefully, expensefulness, expenseless, expenselessness, expenses, expensilation, expensing, expensive, expensively, expensiveness, expenthesis, expergefacient, expergefaction, experience, experienceable, experienced, experienceless, experiencer, experiences, experiencible, experiencing, experient, experiential, experientialism, experientialist, experientialistic, experientially, experiment, experimental, experimentalism, experimentalist, experimentalists, experimentalize, experimentally, experimentarian, experimentation, experimentation's, experimentations, experimentative, experimentator, experimented, experimentee, experimenter, experimenters, experimenting, experimentist, experimentize, experimently, experimentor, experiments, expermentized, experrection, expert, experted, experting, expertise, expertised, expertising, expertism, expertize, expertized, expertizing, expertly, expertness, experts, expertship, expetible, expiable, expiate, expiated, expiates, expiating, expiation, expiational, expiations, expiatist, expiative, expiator, expiatoriness, expiators, expiatory, expilate, expilation, expilator, expirable, expirant, expirate, expiration, expiration's, expirations, expirator, expiratory, expire, expired, expiree, expirer, expirers, expires, expiries, expiring, expiringly, expiry, expiscate, expiscated, expiscating, expiscation, expiscator, expiscatory, explain, explainability, explainable, explainableness, explained, explainer, explainers, explaining, explainingly, explains, explait, explanate, explanation, explanation's, explanations, explanative, explanatively, explanator, explanatorily, explanatoriness, explanatory, explanitory, explant, explantation, explanted, explanting, explants, explat, explees, explement, explemental, explementary, explete, expletive, expletively, expletiveness, expletives, expletory, explicability, explicable, explicableness, explicably, explicanda, explicandum, explicans, explicantia, explicate, explicated, explicates, explicating, explication, explications, explicative, explicatively, explicator, explicators, explicatory, explicit, explicitly, explicitness, explicits, explida, explodable, explode, exploded, explodent, exploder, exploders, explodes, exploding, exploit, exploitable, exploitage, exploitation, exploitation's, exploitationist, exploitations, exploitative, exploitatively, exploitatory, exploited, exploitee, exploiter, exploiters, exploiting, exploitive, exploits, exploiture, explorable, explorate, exploration, exploration's, explorational, explorations, explorative, exploratively, explorativeness, explorator, exploratory, explore, explored, explorement, explorer, explorers, explores, exploring, exploringly, explosibility, explosible, explosimeter, explosion, explosion's, explosionist, explosions, explosive, explosively, explosiveness, explosives, expo, expoliate, expolish, expone, exponence, exponency, exponent, exponent's, exponential, exponentially, exponentials, exponentiate, exponentiated, exponentiates, exponentiating, exponentiation, exponentiation's, exponentiations, exponention, exponents, exponible, export, exportability, exportable, exportation, exportations, exported, exporter, exporters, exporting, exports, expos, exposable, exposal, exposals, expose, exposed, exposedness, exposer, exposers, exposes, exposing, exposit, exposited, expositing, exposition, exposition's, expositional, expositionary, expositions, expositive, expositively, expositor, expositorial, expositorially, expositorily, expositoriness, expositors, expository, expositress, exposits, expostulate, expostulated, expostulates, expostulating, expostulatingly, expostulation, expostulations, expostulative, expostulatively, expostulator, expostulatory, exposture, exposure, exposure's, exposures, expound, expoundable, expounded, expounder, expounders, expounding, expounds, expreme, express, expressable, expressage, expressed, expresser, expresses, expressibility, expressible, expressibly, expressing, expressio, expression, expression's, expressionable, expressional, expressionful, expressionism, expressionist, expressionistic, expressionistically, expressionists, expressionless, expressionlessly, expressionlessness, expressions, expressive, expressively, expressiveness, expressivism, expressivity, expressless, expressly, expressman, expressmen, expressness, expresso, expressor, expressure, expressway, expressways, exprimable, exprobate, exprobrate, exprobration, exprobratory, expromission, expromissor, expropriable, expropriate, expropriated, expropriates, expropriating, expropriation, expropriations, expropriator, expropriatory, expt, exptl, expugn, expugnable, expuition, expulsatory, expulse, expulsed, expulser, expulses, expulsing, expulsion, expulsionist, expulsions, expulsive, expulsory, expunction, expunge, expungeable, expunged, expungement, expunger, expungers, expunges, expunging, expurgate, expurgated, expurgates, expurgating, expurgation, expurgational, expurgations, expurgative, expurgator, expurgatorial, expurgators, expurgatory, expurge, expwy, expy, exquire, exquisite, exquisitely, exquisiteness, exquisitism, exquisitive, exquisitively, exquisitiveness, exr, exradio, exradius, exrupeal, exrx, exsanguinate, exsanguinated, exsanguinating, exsanguination, exsanguine, exsanguineous, exsanguinity, exsanguinous, exsanguious, exscind, exscinded, exscinding, exscinds, exscissor, exscribe, exscript, exscriptural, exsculp, exsculptate, exscutellate, exsec, exsecant, exsecants, exsect, exsected, exsectile, exsecting, exsection, exsector, exsects, exsequatur, exsert, exserted, exsertile, exserting, exsertion, exserts, exsheath, exship, exsibilate, exsibilation, exsiccant, exsiccatae, exsiccate, exsiccated, exsiccating, exsiccation, exsiccative, exsiccator, exsiliency, exsolution, exsolve, exsolved, exsolving, exsomatic, exspoliation, exspuition, exsputory, exstemporal, exstemporaneous, exstill, exstimulate, exstipulate, exstrophy, exstruct, exsuccous, exsuction, exsudate, exsufflate, exsufflation, exsufflicate, exsuperance, exsuperate, exsurge, exsurgent, exsuscitate, ext, exta, extacie, extance, extancy, extant, extatic, extbook, extemporal, extemporally, extemporalness, extemporaneity, extemporaneous, extemporaneously, extemporaneousness, extemporarily, extemporariness, extemporary, extempore, extemporisation, extemporise, extemporised, extemporiser, extemporising, extemporization, extemporize, extemporized, extemporizer, extemporizes, extemporizing, extempory, extend, extendability, extendable, extended, extendedly, extendedness, extender, extenders, extendibility, extendible, extending, extendlessness, extends, extense, extensibility, extensible, extensibleness, extensile, extensimeter, extension, extension's, extensional, extensionalism, extensionality, extensionally, extensionist, extensionless, extensions, extensity, extensive, extensively, extensiveness, extensivity, extensometer, extensor, extensors, extensory, extensum, extensure, extent, extent's, extentions, extents, extenuate, extenuated, extenuates, extenuating, extenuatingly, extenuation, extenuations, extenuative, extenuator, extenuatory, exter, exterior, exterior's, exteriorate, exterioration, exteriorisation, exteriorise, exteriorised, exteriorising, exteriority, exteriorization, exteriorize, exteriorized, exteriorizing, exteriorly, exteriorness, exteriors, exterminable, exterminate, exterminated, exterminates, exterminating, extermination, exterminations, exterminative, exterminator, exterminators, exterminatory, exterminatress, exterminatrix, extermine, extermined, extermining, exterminist, extern, externa, external, externalisation, externalise, externalised, externalising, externalism, externalist, externalistic, externalities, externality, externalization, externalize, externalized, externalizes, externalizing, externally, externalness, externals, externat, externate, externation, externe, externes, externity, externization, externize, externomedian, externs, externship, externum, exteroceptist, exteroceptive, exteroceptor, exterous, exterraneous, exterrestrial, exterritorial, exterritoriality, exterritorialize, exterritorially, extersive, extg, extill, extima, extime, extimulate, extinct, extincted, extincteur, extincting, extinction, extinctionist, extinctions, extinctive, extinctor, extincts, extine, extinguised, extinguish, extinguishable, extinguishant, extinguished, extinguisher, extinguishers, extinguishes, extinguishing, extinguishment, extipulate, extirp, extirpate, extirpated, extirpateo, extirpates, extirpating, extirpation, extirpationist, extirpations, extirpative, extirpator, extirpatory, extispex, extispices, extispicious, extispicy, extogenous, extol, extoled, extoling, extoll, extollation, extolled, extoller, extollers, extolling, extollingly, extollment, extolls, extolment, extols, extoolitic, extorsion, extorsive, extorsively, extort, extorted, extorter, extorters, extorting, extortion, extortionary, extortionate, extortionately, extortionateness, extortioner, extortioners, extortionist, extortionists, extortions, extortive, extorts, extra, extrabold, extraboldface, extrabranchial, extrabronchial, extrabuccal, extrabulbar, extrabureau, extraburghal, extracalendar, extracalicular, extracanonical, extracapsular, extracardial, extracarpal, extracathedral, extracellular, extracellularly, extracerebral, extrachromosomal, extracivic, extracivically, extraclassroom, extraclaustral, extracloacal, extracollegiate, extracolumella, extracondensed, extraconscious, extraconstellated, extraconstitutional, extracorporeal, extracorporeally, extracorpuscular, extracosmic, extracosmical, extracostal, extracranial, extract, extractability, extractable, extractant, extracted, extractibility, extractible, extractiform, extracting, extraction, extraction's, extractions, extractive, extractively, extractor, extractor's, extractors, extractorship, extracts, extracultural, extracurial, extracurricular, extracurriculum, extracutaneous, extracystic, extradecretal, extradialectal, extradict, extradictable, extradicted, extradicting, extradictionary, extraditable, extradite, extradited, extradites, extraditing, extradition, extraditions, extradomestic, extrados, extradosed, extradoses, extradotal, extraduction, extradural, extraembryonal, extraembryonic, extraenteric, extraepiphyseal, extraequilibrium, extraessential, extraessentially, extrafascicular, extrafine, extrafloral, extrafocal, extrafoliaceous, extraforaneous, extraformal, extragalactic, extragastric, extrahazardous, extrahepatic, extrait, extrajudicial, extrajudicially, extralateral, extralegal, extralegally, extraliminal, extralimital, extralinguistic, extralinguistically, extralite, extrality, extramarginal, extramarital, extramatrical, extramedullary, extramental, extrameridian, extrameridional, extrametaphysical, extrametrical, extrametropolitan, extramission, extramodal, extramolecular, extramorainal, extramorainic, extramoral, extramoralist, extramundane, extramural, extramurally, extramusical, extranational, extranatural, extranean, extraneity, extraneous, extraneously, extraneousness, extranidal, extranormal, extranuclear, extraocular, extraofficial, extraoral, extraorbital, extraorbitally, extraordinaries, extraordinarily, extraordinariness, extraordinary, extraorganismal, extraovate, extraovular, extraparenchymal, extraparental, extraparietal, extraparliamentary, extraparochial, extraparochially, extrapatriarchal, extrapelvic, extraperineal, extraperiodic, extraperiosteal, extraperitoneal, extraphenomenal, extraphysical, extraphysiological, extrapituitary, extraplacental, extraplanetary, extrapleural, extrapoetical, extrapolar, extrapolate, extrapolated, extrapolates, extrapolating, extrapolation, extrapolations, extrapolative, extrapolator, extrapolatory, extrapopular, extraposition, extraprofessional, extraprostatic, extraprovincial, extrapulmonary, extrapunitive, extrapyramidal, extraquiz, extrared, extraregarding, extraregular, extraregularly, extrarenal, extraretinal, extrarhythmical, extras, extrasacerdotal, extrascholastic, extraschool, extrascientific, extrascriptural, extrascripturality, extrasensible, extrasensorial, extrasensory, extrasensuous, extraserous, extrasocial, extrasolar, extrasomatic, extraspectral, extraspherical, extraspinal, extrastapedial, extrastate, extrasterile, extrastomachal, extrasyllabic, extrasyllogistic, extrasyphilitic, extrasystole, extrasystolic, extratabular, extratarsal, extratellurian, extratelluric, extratemporal, extratension, extratensive, extraterrene, extraterrestrial, extraterrestrially, extraterrestrials, extraterritorial, extraterritoriality, extraterritorially, extraterritorials, extrathecal, extratheistic, extrathermodynamic, extrathoracic, extratorrid, extratracheal, extratribal, extratropical, extratubal, extratympanic, extraught, extrauterine, extravagance, extravagances, extravagancies, extravagancy, extravagant, extravagantly, extravagantness, extravaganza, extravaganzas, extravagate, extravagated, extravagating, extravagation, extravagence, extravaginal, extravasate, extravasated, extravasating, extravasation, extravascular, extravehicular, extravenate, extraventricular, extraversion, extraversive, extraversively, extravert, extraverted, extravertish, extravertive, extravertively, extravillar, extraviolet, extravisceral, extrazodiacal, extreat, extrema, extremal, extreme, extremeless, extremely, extremeness, extremer, extremes, extremest, extremis, extremism, extremist, extremist's, extremistic, extremists, extremital, extremities, extremity, extremity's, extremum, extremuma, extricable, extricably, extricate, extricated, extricates, extricating, extrication, extrications, extrinsic, extrinsical, extrinsicality, extrinsically, extrinsicalness, extrinsicate, extrinsication, extroitive, extromit, extropical, extrorsal, extrorse, extrorsely, extrospect, extrospection, extrospective, extroversion, extroversive, extroversively, extrovert, extroverted, extrovertedness, extrovertish, extrovertive, extrovertively, extroverts, extruct, extrudability, extrudable, extrude, extruded, extruder, extruders, extrudes, extruding, extrusible, extrusile, extrusion, extrusions, extrusive, extrusory, extubate, extubation, extuberance, extuberant, extuberate, extumescence, extund, exturb, extusion, extypal, exuberance, exuberancy, exuberant, exuberantly, exuberantness, exuberate, exuberated, exuberating, exuberation, exuccous, exucontian, exudate, exudates, exudation, exudations, exudative, exudatory, exude, exuded, exudence, exudes, exuding, exul, exulate, exulcerate, exulcerated, exulcerating, exulceration, exulcerative, exulceratory, exulding, exult, exultance, exultancy, exultant, exultantly, exultation, exulted, exultet, exulting, exultingly, exults, exululate, exumbral, exumbrella, exumbrellar, exundance, exundancy, exundate, exundation, exungulate, exuperable, exurb, exurban, exurbanite, exurbanites, exurbia, exurbias, exurbs, exurge, exuscitate, exust, exuvia, exuviability, exuviable, exuviae, exuvial, exuviate, exuviated, exuviates, exuviating, exuviation, exuvium, exxon, exzodiacal, ey, eyah, eyalet, eyas, eyases, eyass, eydent, eye, eyeable, eyeball, eyeballed, eyeballing, eyeballs, eyebalm, eyebar, eyebath, eyebeam, eyebeams, eyeberry, eyeblack, eyeblink, eyebolt, eyebolts, eyebree, eyebridled, eyebright, eyebrow, eyebrow's, eyebrows, eyecup, eyecups, eyed, eyedness, eyednesses, eyedot, eyedrop, eyedropper, eyedropperful, eyedroppers, eyeflap, eyeful, eyefuls, eyeglance, eyeglass, eyeglasses, eyeground, eyehole, eyeholes, eyehook, eyehooks, eyeing, eyelash, eyelashes, eyelast, eyeless, eyelessness, eyelet, eyeleted, eyeleteer, eyeleting, eyelets, eyeletted, eyeletter, eyeletting, eyelid, eyelid's, eyelids, eyelight, eyelike, eyeline, eyeliner, eyeliners, eyemark, eyen, eyeopener, eyepiece, eyepiece's, eyepieces, eyepit, eyepoint, eyepoints, eyepopper, eyer, eyereach, eyeroot, eyers, eyes, eyesalve, eyeseed, eyeservant, eyeserver, eyeservice, eyeshade, eyeshades, eyeshield, eyeshine, eyeshot, eyeshots, eyesight, eyesights, eyesome, eyesore, eyesores, eyespot, eyespots, eyess, eyestalk, eyestalks, eyestone, eyestones, eyestrain, eyestring, eyestrings, eyeteeth, eyetooth, eyewaiter, eyewash, eyewashes, eyewater, eyewaters, eyewear, eyewink, eyewinker, eyewinks, eyewitness, eyewitness's, eyewitnesses, eyewort, eyey, eyght, eying, eyl, eyliad, eyn, eyne, eyot, eyoty, eyr, eyra, eyrant, eyrar, eyras, eyre, eyren, eyrer, eyres, eyrie, eyries, eyrir, eyry, eysoge, ezan, ezba, ezekiel, ezod, ezra, f, f's, fa, faade, faailk, fab, fabaceous, fabella, fabes, fabian, fabiform, fable, fabled, fabledom, fableist, fableland, fablemaker, fablemonger, fablemongering, fabler, fablers, fables, fabliau, fabliaux, fabling, fabric, fabric's, fabricable, fabricant, fabricate, fabricated, fabricates, fabricating, fabrication, fabricational, fabrications, fabricative, fabricator, fabricators, fabricatress, fabricature, fabrics, fabrikoid, fabrile, fabrique, fabula, fabular, fabulate, fabulist, fabulists, fabulize, fabulosity, fabulous, fabulously, fabulousness, faburden, fac, facadal, facade, facaded, facades, face, faceable, facebar, facebow, facebread, facecloth, faced, facedown, faceharden, faceless, facelessness, facelift, facelifts, facellite, facemaker, facemaking, faceman, facemark, faceoff, facepiece, faceplate, facer, facers, faces, facesaving, facet, facete, faceted, facetely, faceteness, facetiae, facetiation, faceting, facetious, facetiously, facetiousness, facets, facette, facetted, facetting, faceup, facewise, facework, facia, facial, facially, facials, facias, faciata, faciation, facie, faciend, faciends, faciendum, facient, facier, facies, faciest, facile, facilely, facileness, facilitate, facilitated, facilitates, facilitating, facilitation, facilitations, facilitative, facilitator, facilities, facility, facility's, facily, facing, facingly, facings, facinorous, facinorousness, faciobrachial, faciocervical, faciolingual, facioplegia, facioscapulohumeral, facit, fack, fackeltanz, fackings, fackins, facks, faconde, faconne, facsim, facsimile, facsimile's, facsimiled, facsimileing, facsimiles, facsimiling, facsimilist, facsimilize, fact, fact's, factable, factabling, factfinder, factful, factice, facticide, facticity, faction, faction's, factional, factionalism, factionalist, factionally, factionaries, factionary, factionate, factioneer, factionism, factionist, factionistism, factions, factious, factiously, factiousness, factish, factitial, factitious, factitiously, factitiousness, factitive, factitively, factitude, factive, facto, factor, factorability, factorable, factorage, factordom, factored, factoress, factorial, factorially, factorials, factories, factoring, factorist, factorization, factorization's, factorizations, factorize, factorized, factorizing, factors, factorship, factory, factory's, factorylike, factoryship, factotum, factotums, factrix, facts, factual, factualism, factualist, factualistic, factuality, factually, factualness, factum, facture, factures, facty, facula, faculae, facular, faculative, faculous, facultate, facultative, facultatively, facultied, faculties, facultize, faculty, faculty's, facund, facundity, facy, fad, fadable, fadaise, faddier, faddiest, faddiness, fadding, faddish, faddishly, faddishness, faddism, faddisms, faddist, faddists, faddle, faddy, fade, fadeaway, fadeaways, faded, fadedly, fadedness, fadednyess, fadeless, fadelessly, faden, fadeout, fader, faders, fades, fadge, fadged, fadges, fadging, fading, fadingly, fadingness, fadings, fadlike, fadme, fadmonger, fadmongering, fadmongery, fado, fados, fadridden, fads, fady, fae, faecal, faecalith, faeces, faecula, faeculence, faena, faenas, faence, faenus, faerie, faeries, faeroese, faery, faeryland, fafaronade, faff, faffle, faffy, fafnir, fag, fagaceous, fagald, fagara, fage, fager, fagged, fagger, faggery, fagging, faggingly, faggot, faggoted, faggoting, faggotry, faggots, faggoty, faggy, fagin, fagine, fagins, fagopyrism, fagopyrismus, fagot, fagoted, fagoter, fagoters, fagoting, fagotings, fagots, fagott, fagotte, fagottino, fagottist, fagotto, fagottone, fagoty, fags, faham, fahlband, fahlbands, fahlerz, fahlore, fahlunite, fahlunitte, fahrenheit, fahrenhett, faience, faiences, faikes, fail, failance, failed, failing, failingly, failingness, failings, faille, failles, fails, failsafe, failsoft, failure, failure's, failures, fain, fainaigue, fainaigued, fainaiguer, fainaiguing, fainant, faineance, faineancy, faineant, faineantise, faineantism, faineants, fainer, fainest, fainly, fainness, fains, faint, fainted, fainter, fainters, faintest, faintful, faintheart, fainthearted, faintheartedly, faintheartedness, fainting, faintingly, faintise, faintish, faintishness, faintling, faintly, faintness, faints, fainty, faipule, fair, fairbanks, faire, faired, fairer, fairest, fairfieldite, fairgoer, fairgoing, fairgrass, fairground, fairgrounds, fairhead, fairies, fairily, fairing, fairings, fairish, fairishly, fairishness, fairkeeper, fairlead, fairleader, fairleads, fairlike, fairling, fairly, fairm, fairness, fairnesses, fairs, fairship, fairsome, fairstead, fairtime, fairwater, fairway, fairways, fairy, fairy's, fairydom, fairyfloss, fairyfolk, fairyhood, fairyish, fairyism, fairyisms, fairyland, fairylands, fairylike, fairyologist, fairyology, fairyship, faisan, faisceau, fait, faitery, faith, faithbreach, faithbreaker, faithed, faithful, faithfully, faithfulness, faithfuls, faithing, faithless, faithlessly, faithlessness, faiths, faithwise, faithworthiness, faithworthy, faitor, faitour, faitours, faits, fake, faked, fakeer, fakeers, fakement, faker, fakeries, fakers, fakery, fakes, faki, fakiness, faking, fakir, fakirism, fakirs, faky, fala, falafel, falanaka, falangist, falbala, falbalas, falbelo, falcade, falcate, falcated, falcation, falcer, falces, falchion, falchions, falcial, falcidian, falciform, falciparum, falcon, falconbill, falconelle, falconer, falconers, falconet, falconets, falconiform, falconine, falconlike, falconnoid, falconoid, falconries, falconry, falcons, falcopern, falcula, falcular, falculate, falda, faldage, falderal, falderals, falderol, falderols, faldetta, faldfee, falding, faldistory, faldstool, faldworth, falern, falernian, falk, fall, falla, fallace, fallacia, fallacies, fallacious, fallaciously, fallaciousness, fallacy, fallacy's, fallage, fallal, fallalery, fallalishly, fallals, fallation, fallaway, fallback, fallbacks, fallectomy, fallen, fallency, fallenness, faller, fallers, fallfish, fallfishes, fallibilism, fallibilist, fallibility, fallible, fallibleness, fallibly, falling, fallings, falloff, falloffs, fallopian, fallostomy, fallotomy, fallout, fallouts, fallow, fallowed, fallowing, fallowist, fallowness, fallows, falls, falltime, fallway, fally, falsary, false, falsedad, falseface, falsehearted, falseheartedly, falseheartedness, falsehood, falsehood's, falsehoods, falsely, falsen, falseness, falser, falsest, falsettist, falsetto, falsettos, falsework, falsidical, falsie, falsies, falsifiability, falsifiable, falsificate, falsification, falsifications, falsificator, falsified, falsifier, falsifiers, falsifies, falsify, falsifying, falsism, falsiteit, falsities, falsity, falstaffian, falsum, faltboat, faltboats, faltche, falter, faltere, faltered, falterer, falterers, faltering, falteringly, falters, falun, falus, falutin, falx, fam, famacide, famatinite, famble, fame, famed, fameflower, fameful, fameless, famelessly, famelessness, famelic, fames, fameworthy, familarity, familia, familial, familiar, familiarisation, familiarise, familiarised, familiariser, familiarising, familiarisingly, familiarism, familiarities, familiarity, familiarization, familiarizations, familiarize, familiarized, familiarizer, familiarizes, familiarizing, familiarizingly, familiarly, familiarness, familiars, familiary, familic, families, familism, familist, familistere, familistery, familistic, familistical, famille, family, family's, familyish, famine, famine's, famines, faming, famish, famished, famishes, famishing, famishment, famose, famous, famously, famousness, famp, famular, famulary, famulative, famuli, famulli, famulus, fan, fan's, fana, fanakalo, fanal, fanaloka, fanam, fanatic, fanatic's, fanatical, fanatically, fanaticalness, fanaticise, fanaticised, fanaticising, fanaticism, fanaticize, fanaticized, fanaticizing, fanatico, fanatics, fanatism, fanback, fanbearer, fanciable, fancical, fancied, fancier, fancier's, fanciers, fancies, fanciest, fanciful, fancifully, fancifulness, fancify, fanciless, fancily, fanciness, fancy, fancying, fancymonger, fancysick, fancywork, fand, fandangle, fandango, fandangos, fandom, fandoms, fane, fanega, fanegada, fanegadas, fanegas, fanes, fanfarade, fanfare, fanfares, fanfaron, fanfaronade, fanfaronading, fanfarons, fanfish, fanfishes, fanflower, fanfold, fanfolds, fanfoot, fang, fang's, fanga, fangas, fanged, fanger, fanging, fangle, fangled, fanglement, fangless, fanglet, fanglike, fanglomerate, fango, fangot, fangotherapy, fangs, fangy, fanhouse, faniente, fanion, fanioned, fanions, fanit, fanjet, fanjets, fankle, fanleaf, fanlight, fanlights, fanlike, fanmaker, fanmaking, fanman, fanned, fannel, fanneling, fannell, fanner, fanners, fannier, fannies, fanning, fannings, fannon, fanny, fano, fanon, fanons, fanos, fanout, fans, fant, fantad, fantaddish, fantail, fantailed, fantails, fantaisie, fantaseid, fantasia, fantasias, fantasie, fantasied, fantasies, fantasist, fantasists, fantasize, fantasized, fantasizes, fantasizing, fantasm, fantasmagoria, fantasmagoric, fantasmagorically, fantasmal, fantasms, fantasque, fantassin, fantast, fantastic, fantastical, fantasticality, fantastically, fantasticalness, fantasticate, fantastication, fantasticism, fantasticly, fantasticness, fantastico, fantastry, fantasts, fantasy, fantasy's, fantasying, fanteague, fantee, fanteeg, fanterie, fantigue, fantoccini, fantocine, fantod, fantoddish, fantods, fantom, fantoms, fanum, fanums, fanweed, fanwise, fanwork, fanwort, fanworts, fanwright, fanzine, fanzines, faon, fapesmo, faq, faqir, faqirs, faquir, faquirs, far, farad, faradaic, faraday, faradays, faradic, faradisation, faradise, faradised, faradiser, faradises, faradising, faradism, faradisms, faradization, faradize, faradized, faradizer, faradizes, faradizing, faradmeter, faradocontractility, faradomuscular, faradonervous, faradopalpation, farads, farand, farandine, farandman, farandmen, farandola, farandole, farandoles, faraon, farasula, faraway, farawayness, farce, farce's, farced, farcelike, farcemeat, farcer, farcers, farces, farcetta, farceur, farceurs, farceuse, farceuses, farci, farcial, farcialize, farcical, farcicality, farcically, farcicalness, farcie, farcied, farcies, farcify, farcilite, farcin, farcing, farcinoma, farcist, farctate, farcy, fard, fardage, farde, farded, fardel, fardelet, fardels, fardh, farding, fardo, fards, fare, fared, farenheit, farer, farers, fares, faretta, farewell, farewelled, farewelling, farewells, farfal, farfara, farfel, farfels, farfet, farfetch, farfetched, farfetchedness, farforthly, fargite, fargoing, fargood, farhand, farhands, farina, farinaceous, farinaceously, farinacious, farinas, farine, faring, farinha, farinhas, farinometer, farinose, farinosel, farinosely, farinulent, fario, farish, farkleberries, farkleberry, farl, farle, farles, farleu, farley, farls, farm, farmable, farmage, farmed, farmer, farmeress, farmerette, farmeries, farmerish, farmerlike, farmerly, farmers, farmership, farmery, farmhand, farmhands, farmhold, farmhouse, farmhouse's, farmhouses, farmhousey, farming, farmings, farmland, farmlands, farmost, farmout, farmplace, farms, farmscape, farmstead, farmsteading, farmsteads, farmtown, farmwife, farmy, farmyard, farmyard's, farmyards, farmyardy, farnesol, farnesols, farness, farnesses, faro, faroeish, faroelite, faroese, faroff, farolito, faros, farouche, farrage, farraginous, farrago, farragoes, farragos, farrand, farrandly, farrant, farrantly, farreachingly, farreate, farreation, farrel, farrier, farrieries, farrierlike, farriers, farriery, farris, farrisite, farrow, farrowed, farrowing, farrows, farruca, farsakh, farsalah, farsang, farse, farseeing, farseeingness, farseer, farset, farsight, farsighted, farsightedly, farsightedness, farstepped, fart, farted, farth, farther, fartherance, fartherer, farthermore, farthermost, farthest, farthing, farthingale, farthingales, farthingdeal, farthingless, farthings, farting, fartlek, farts, farweltered, fas, fasc, fasces, fascet, fascia, fasciae, fascial, fascias, fasciate, fasciated, fasciately, fasciation, fascicle, fascicled, fascicles, fascicular, fascicularly, fasciculate, fasciculated, fasciculately, fasciculation, fascicule, fasciculi, fasciculite, fasciculus, fascili, fascinate, fascinated, fascinatedly, fascinates, fascinating, fascinatingly, fascination, fascinations, fascinative, fascinator, fascinatress, fascine, fascinery, fascines, fascintatingly, fasciodesis, fasciola, fasciolae, fasciolar, fasciole, fasciolet, fascioliasis, fascioloid, fascioplasty, fasciotomy, fascis, fascism, fascisms, fascist, fascista, fascistic, fascistically, fascisticization, fascisticize, fascistization, fascistize, fascists, fasels, fash, fashed, fasher, fasherie, fashery, fashes, fashing, fashion, fashionability, fashionable, fashionableness, fashionably, fashional, fashionative, fashioned, fashioner, fashioners, fashioning, fashionist, fashionize, fashionless, fashionmonger, fashionmonging, fashions, fashious, fashiousness, fasibitikite, fasinite, fasnacht, fasola, fass, fassaite, fassalite, fast, fastback, fastbacks, fastball, fastballs, fasted, fasten, fastened, fastener, fasteners, fastening, fastenings, fastens, faster, fastest, fastgoing, fasthold, fasti, fastidiosity, fastidious, fastidiously, fastidiousness, fastidium, fastigate, fastigated, fastigia, fastigiate, fastigiated, fastigiately, fastigious, fastigium, fastigiums, fastiia, fasting, fastingly, fastings, fastish, fastland, fastly, fastnacht, fastness, fastnesses, fasts, fastuous, fastuously, fastuousness, fastus, fastwalk, fat, fatal, fatale, fatales, fatalism, fatalisms, fatalist, fatalistic, fatalistically, fatalists, fatalities, fatality, fatality's, fatalize, fatally, fatalness, fatals, fatback, fatbacks, fatbird, fatbirds, fatbrained, fatcake, fate, fated, fateful, fatefully, fatefulness, fatelike, fates, fath, fathead, fatheaded, fatheadedly, fatheadedness, fatheads, fathearted, father, father's, fathercraft, fathered, fatherhood, fathering, fatherkin, fatherland, fatherlandish, fatherlands, fatherless, fatherlessness, fatherlike, fatherliness, fatherling, fatherly, fathers, fathership, fathmur, fathogram, fathom, fathomable, fathomableness, fathomage, fathomed, fathomer, fathometer, fathoming, fathomless, fathomlessly, fathomlessness, fathoms, faticableness, fatidic, fatidical, fatidically, fatiferous, fatigability, fatigable, fatigableness, fatigate, fatigated, fatigating, fatigation, fatiguabilities, fatiguability, fatiguable, fatigue, fatigued, fatigueless, fatigues, fatiguesome, fatiguing, fatiguingly, fatiha, fatihah, fatil, fatiloquent, fating, fatiscence, fatiscent, fatless, fatlike, fatling, fatlings, fatly, fatness, fatnesses, fator, fats, fatshedera, fatsia, fatso, fatsoes, fatsos, fatstock, fatstocks, fattable, fatted, fatten, fattenable, fattened, fattener, fatteners, fattening, fattens, fatter, fattest, fattier, fatties, fattiest, fattily, fattiness, fatting, fattish, fattishness, fattrels, fatty, fatuate, fatuism, fatuities, fatuitous, fatuitousness, fatuity, fatuoid, fatuous, fatuously, fatuousness, fatuus, fatwa, fatwood, faubourg, faubourgs, faucal, faucalize, faucals, fauces, faucet, faucets, fauchard, fauchards, faucial, faucitis, fauconnier, faucre, faufel, faugh, faujasite, faujdar, fauld, faulds, faulkner, fault, faultage, faulted, faulter, faultfind, faultfinder, faultfinders, faultfinding, faultful, faultfully, faultier, faultiest, faultily, faultiness, faulting, faultless, faultlessly, faultlessness, faults, faultsman, faulty, faulx, faun, fauna, faunae, faunal, faunally, faunas, faunated, faunch, faunish, faunist, faunistic, faunistical, faunistically, faunlike, faunological, faunology, fauns, fauntleroy, faunula, faunule, faunus, faurd, faured, fausant, fause, fausen, faussebraie, faussebraye, faussebrayed, faust, fauster, faustian, faut, faute, fauterer, fauteuil, fauteuils, fautor, fautorship, fauve, fauves, fauvette, fauvism, fauvisms, fauvist, fauvists, faux, fauxbourdon, favaginous, favel, favela, favelas, favelidium, favella, favellae, favellidia, favellidium, favellilidia, favelloid, faveolate, faveoli, faveoluli, faveolus, faverel, faverole, favi, faviform, favilla, favillae, favillous, favism, favissa, favissae, favn, favonian, favor, favorability, favorable, favorableness, favorably, favored, favoredly, favoredness, favorer, favorers, favoress, favoring, favoringly, favorite, favorites, favoritism, favorless, favors, favose, favosely, favosite, favosites, favositoid, favour, favourable, favourableness, favourably, favoured, favouredly, favouredness, favourer, favourers, favouress, favouring, favouringly, favourite, favouritism, favourless, favours, favous, favus, favuses, fawe, fawkener, fawn, fawned, fawner, fawners, fawnery, fawnier, fawniest, fawning, fawningly, fawningness, fawnlike, fawns, fawnskin, fawny, fax, faxed, faxes, faxing, fay, fayalite, fayalites, fayed, fayence, faying, fayles, fays, faze, fazed, fazenda, fazendas, fazendeiro, fazes, fazing, fb, fbi, fc, fchar, fcomp, fconv, fconvert, fcp, fcs, fcy, fdname, fdnames, fdtype, fdub, fdubs, fe, feaberry, feague, feak, feaked, feaking, feal, fealties, fealty, fear, fearable, fearbabe, feared, fearedly, fearedness, fearer, fearers, fearful, fearfuller, fearfullest, fearfully, fearfulness, fearing, fearingly, fearless, fearlessly, fearlessness, fearnaught, fearnought, fears, fearsome, fearsomely, fearsomeness, feasance, feasances, feasant, fease, feased, feases, feasibilities, feasibility, feasible, feasibleness, feasibly, feasing, feasor, feast, feasted, feasten, feaster, feasters, feastful, feastfully, feasting, feastless, feastly, feastraw, feasts, feat, feat's, feateous, feater, featest, feather, featherback, featherbed, featherbedded, featherbedding, featherbird, featherbone, featherbrain, featherbrained, feathercut, featherdom, feathered, featheredge, featheredged, featheredges, featherer, featherers, featherfew, featherfoil, featherhead, featherheaded, featherier, featheriest, featheriness, feathering, featherleaf, featherless, featherlessness, featherlet, featherlight, featherlike, featherman, feathermonger, featherpate, featherpated, feathers, featherstitch, featherstitching, feathertop, featherway, featherweed, featherweight, featherweights, featherwing, featherwise, featherwood, featherwork, featherworker, feathery, featish, featishly, featishness, featless, featlier, featliest, featliness, featly, featness, featous, feats, featural, featurally, feature, featured, featureful, featureless, featurelessness, featureliness, featurely, features, featurette, featuring, featurish, featy, feaze, feazed, feazes, feazing, feazings, febres, febricant, febricide, febricitant, febricitation, febricity, febricula, febrifacient, febriferous, febrific, febrifugal, febrifuge, febrifuges, febrile, febrility, febriphobia, febris, febronian, februaries, february, february's, februation, fec, fecal, fecalith, fecaloid, fecche, feceris, feces, fecial, fecials, fecifork, fecit, feck, fecket, feckful, feckfully, feckless, fecklessly, fecklessness, feckly, fecks, feckulence, fecula, feculae, feculence, feculency, feculent, fecund, fecundate, fecundated, fecundates, fecundating, fecundation, fecundations, fecundative, fecundator, fecundatory, fecundify, fecundities, fecundity, fecundize, fed, fedarie, fedayee, fedayeen, feddan, feddans, fedelini, fedellini, federacies, federacy, federal, federalese, federalisation, federalise, federalised, federalising, federalism, federalist, federalistic, federalists, federalization, federalizations, federalize, federalized, federalizes, federalizing, federally, federalness, federals, federarie, federary, federate, federated, federates, federating, federation, federational, federationist, federations, federatist, federative, federatively, federator, fedifragous, fedity, fedn, fedora, fedoras, feds, fee, feeable, feeb, feeble, feeblebrained, feeblehearted, feebleheartedly, feebleheartedness, feebleminded, feeblemindedly, feeblemindedness, feebleness, feebler, feebless, feeblest, feebling, feeblish, feebly, feed, feedable, feedback, feedbacks, feedbag, feedbags, feedbin, feedboard, feedbox, feedboxes, feeded, feeder, feeders, feedhead, feeding, feedings, feedingstuff, feedlot, feedlots, feedman, feeds, feedsman, feedstock, feedstuff, feedstuffs, feedwater, feedway, feedy, feeing, feel, feelable, feeler, feelers, feeless, feelies, feeling, feelingful, feelingless, feelinglessly, feelingly, feelingness, feelings, feels, feely, feer, feere, feerie, feering, fees, feest, feet, feetage, feetfirst, feetless, feeze, feezed, feezes, feezing, feff, fefnicute, fegary, fegs, feh, fei, feif, feigher, feign, feigned, feignedly, feignedness, feigner, feigners, feigning, feigningly, feigns, feijoa, feil, feinschmecker, feinschmeckers, feint, feinted, feinter, feinting, feints, feirie, feis, feiseanna, feist, feistier, feistiest, feists, feisty, felafel, felaheen, felahin, felanders, felapton, feldsher, feldspar, feldsparphyre, feldspars, feldspath, feldspathic, feldspathization, feldspathoid, feldspathoidal, feldspathose, fele, felicide, felicific, felicify, felicitate, felicitated, felicitates, felicitating, felicitation, felicitations, felicitator, felicitators, felicities, felicitous, felicitously, felicitousness, felicity, felid, felids, feliform, feline, felinely, felineness, felines, felinities, felinity, felinophile, felinophobe, felis, felix, fell, fella, fellable, fellage, fellagha, fellah, fellaheen, fellahin, fellahs, fellas, fellata, fellate, fellated, fellatee, fellating, fellatio, fellation, fellations, fellatios, fellator, fellatory, fellatrice, fellatrices, fellatrix, fellatrixes, felled, fellen, feller, fellers, fellest, fellfare, fellic, felliducous, fellies, fellifluous, felling, fellingbird, fellinic, fellmonger, fellmongered, fellmongering, fellmongery, fellness, fellnesses, felloe, felloes, fellon, fellow, fellow's, fellowcraft, fellowed, fellowess, fellowheirship, fellowing, fellowless, fellowlike, fellowly, fellowman, fellowmen, fellowred, fellows, fellowship, fellowship's, fellowshiped, fellowshiping, fellowshipped, fellowshipping, fellowships, fells, fellside, fellsman, felly, feloid, felon, felones, feloness, felonies, felonious, feloniously, feloniousness, felonous, felonries, felonry, felons, felonsetter, felonsetting, felonweed, felonwood, felonwort, felony, fels, felsic, felsite, felsites, felsitic, felsobanyite, felsophyre, felsophyric, felsosphaerite, felspar, felspars, felspath, felspathic, felspathose, felstone, felstones, felt, felted, felter, felting, feltings, feltlike, feltmaker, feltmaking, feltman, feltmonger, feltness, felts, feltwork, feltwort, felty, feltyfare, feltyflier, felucca, feluccas, felwort, felworts, fem, female, female's, femalely, femaleness, females, femalist, femality, femalize, femcee, feme, femereil, femerell, femes, femic, femicide, feminacies, feminacy, feminal, feminality, feminate, femineity, feminie, feminility, feminin, feminine, femininely, feminineness, feminines, femininism, femininity, feminisation, feminise, feminised, feminises, feminising, feminism, feminisms, feminist, feministic, feministics, feminists, feminities, feminity, feminization, feminize, feminized, feminizes, feminizing, feminologist, feminology, feminophobe, femme, femmes, femora, femoral, femorocaudal, femorocele, femorococcygeal, femorofibular, femoropopliteal, femororotulian, femorotibial, fempty, femur, femur's, femurs, fen, fenagle, fenagled, fenagler, fenagles, fenagling, fenbank, fenberry, fence, fenced, fenceful, fenceless, fencelessness, fencelet, fencelike, fenceplay, fencepost, fencer, fenceress, fencers, fences, fenchene, fenchol, fenchone, fenchyl, fencible, fencibles, fencing, fencings, fend, fendable, fended, fender, fendered, fendering, fenderless, fenders, fendillate, fendillation, fending, fends, fendy, fenerate, feneration, fenestella, fenestellae, fenestellid, fenester, fenestra, fenestrae, fenestral, fenestrate, fenestrated, fenestration, fenestrato, fenestrone, fenestrule, fenetre, fengite, fenian, fenite, fenks, fenland, fenlander, fenman, fenmen, fennec, fennecs, fennel, fennelflower, fennels, fenner, fennici, fennig, fennish, fenny, fenouillet, fenouillette, fens, fensive, fenster, fent, fentanyl, fenter, fenugreek, feod, feodal, feodality, feodaries, feodary, feodatory, feods, feodum, feoff, feoffed, feoffee, feoffees, feoffeeship, feoffer, feoffers, feoffing, feoffment, feoffor, feoffors, feoffs, feower, fer, feracious, feracities, feracity, feral, feralin, ferally, ferash, ferbam, ferbams, ferberite, ferd, ferdwit, fere, feres, feretories, feretory, feretra, feretrum, ferfathmur, ferfel, ferfet, ferforth, ferganite, fergusite, fergusonite, feria, feriae, ferial, ferias, feriation, feridgi, feridjee, feridji, ferie, ferigee, ferijee, ferine, ferinely, ferineness, feringhee, ferio, ferison, ferities, ferity, ferk, ferkin, ferlie, ferlied, ferlies, ferling, ferly, ferlying, fermacy, fermage, fermail, fermal, fermata, fermatas, fermate, ferme, ferment, fermentability, fermentable, fermental, fermentarian, fermentate, fermentation, fermentation's, fermentations, fermentative, fermentatively, fermentativeness, fermentatory, fermented, fermenter, fermentescible, fermenting, fermentitious, fermentive, fermentology, fermentor, ferments, fermentum, fermerer, fermery, fermi, fermila, fermillet, fermion, fermions, fermis, fermium, fermiums, fermorite, fern, fern's, fernambuck, fernandinite, fernbird, fernbrake, ferned, ferneries, fernery, ferngale, ferngrower, fernier, ferniest, ferninst, fernland, fernleaf, fernless, fernlike, ferns, fernseed, fernshaw, fernsick, ferntickle, ferntickled, fernticle, fernwort, ferny, fernyear, feroce, ferocious, ferociously, ferociousness, ferocities, ferocity, feroher, ferous, ferox, ferr, ferrado, ferrament, ferrandin, ferrara, ferrary, ferrash, ferrate, ferrated, ferrateen, ferrates, ferratin, ferrean, ferredoxin, ferreiro, ferrel, ferreled, ferreling, ferrelled, ferrelling, ferrels, ferren, ferreous, ferrer, ferret, ferreted, ferreter, ferreters, ferreting, ferrets, ferretto, ferrety, ferri, ferriage, ferriages, ferric, ferrichloride, ferricyanate, ferricyanhydric, ferricyanic, ferricyanide, ferricyanogen, ferried, ferrier, ferries, ferriferous, ferrihemoglobin, ferrihydrocyanic, ferrimagnet, ferrimagnetic, ferrimagnetically, ferrimagnetism, ferring, ferriprussiate, ferriprussic, ferris, ferrite, ferrites, ferritic, ferritin, ferritins, ferritization, ferritungstite, ferrivorous, ferroalloy, ferroaluminum, ferroboron, ferrocalcite, ferrocene, ferrocerium, ferrochrome, ferrochromium, ferroconcrete, ferroconcretor, ferrocyanate, ferrocyanhydric, ferrocyanic, ferrocyanide, ferrocyanogen, ferroelectric, ferroelectrically, ferroelectricity, ferroglass, ferrogoslarite, ferrohydrocyanic, ferroinclave, ferromagnesian, ferromagnet, ferromagnetic, ferromagneticism, ferromagnetism, ferromanganese, ferrometer, ferromolybdenum, ferronatrite, ferronickel, ferrophosphorus, ferroprint, ferroprussiate, ferroprussic, ferrosilicon, ferrotitanium, ferrotungsten, ferrotype, ferrotyped, ferrotyper, ferrotypes, ferrotyping, ferrous, ferrovanadium, ferrozirconium, ferruginate, ferruginated, ferruginating, ferrugination, ferruginean, ferrugineous, ferruginous, ferrugo, ferrule, ferruled, ferruler, ferrules, ferruling, ferrum, ferruminate, ferruminated, ferruminating, ferrumination, ferrums, ferry, ferryage, ferryboat, ferryboats, ferryhouse, ferrying, ferryman, ferrymen, ferryway, fers, fersmite, ferter, ferth, ferther, ferthumlungur, fertile, fertilely, fertileness, fertilisability, fertilisable, fertilisation, fertilisational, fertilise, fertilised, fertiliser, fertilising, fertilitate, fertilities, fertility, fertilizability, fertilizable, fertilization, fertilizational, fertilizations, fertilize, fertilized, fertilizer, fertilizers, fertilizes, fertilizing, feru, ferula, ferulaceous, ferulae, ferulaic, ferular, ferulas, ferule, feruled, ferules, ferulic, feruling, ferv, fervanite, fervence, fervencies, fervency, fervent, fervently, ferventness, fervescence, fervescent, fervid, fervidity, fervidly, fervidness, fervor, fervor's, fervorless, fervorlessness, fervorous, fervors, fervour, fervours, fesapo, fescennine, fescenninity, fescue, fescues, fesels, fess, fesse, fessed, fessely, fesses, fessewise, fessing, fessways, fesswise, fest, festa, festae, festal, festally, festellae, fester, festered, festering, festerment, festers, festilogies, festilogy, festin, festinance, festinate, festinated, festinately, festinating, festination, festine, festing, festino, festival, festival's, festivalgoer, festivally, festivals, festive, festively, festiveness, festivities, festivity, festivous, festology, feston, festoon, festooned, festooneries, festoonery, festooning, festoons, festoony, festschrift, festschriften, festschrifts, festshrifts, festuca, festucine, festucous, festy, fet, feta, fetal, fetalism, fetalization, fetas, fetation, fetations, fetch, fetched, fetcher, fetchers, fetches, fetching, fetchingly, fete, feted, feteless, feterita, feteritas, fetes, fetial, fetiales, fetialis, fetials, fetich, fetiches, fetichic, fetichism, fetichist, fetichistic, fetichize, fetichlike, fetichmonger, fetichry, feticidal, feticide, feticides, fetid, fetidity, fetidly, fetidness, fetiferous, feting, fetiparous, fetis, fetise, fetish, fetisheer, fetisher, fetishes, fetishic, fetishism, fetishist, fetishistic, fetishists, fetishization, fetishize, fetishlike, fetishmonger, fetishry, fetlock, fetlocked, fetlocks, fetlow, fetography, fetologies, fetologist, fetology, fetometry, fetoplacental, fetor, fetors, fets, fetted, fetter, fetterbush, fettered, fetterer, fetterers, fettering, fetterless, fetterlock, fetters, fetticus, fetting, fettle, fettled, fettler, fettles, fettling, fettlings, fettstein, fettuccine, fettucine, fettucini, feture, fetus, fetuses, fetwa, feu, feuage, feuar, feuars, feucht, feud, feud's, feudal, feudalisation, feudalise, feudalised, feudalising, feudalism, feudalist, feudalistic, feudalists, feudalities, feudality, feudalizable, feudalization, feudalize, feudalized, feudalizing, feudally, feudaries, feudary, feudatary, feudatorial, feudatories, feudatory, feuded, feudee, feuder, feuding, feudist, feudists, feudovassalism, feuds, feudum, feued, feuillage, feuille, feuillemorte, feuillet, feuilleton, feuilletonism, feuilletonist, feuilletonistic, feuilletons, feuing, feulamort, feus, feute, feuter, feuterer, fever, feverberries, feverberry, feverbush, fevercup, fevered, feveret, feverfew, feverfews, fevergum, fevering, feverish, feverishly, feverishness, feverless, feverlike, feverous, feverously, feverroot, fevers, fevertrap, fevertwig, fevertwitch, feverweed, feverwort, fevery, few, fewer, fewest, fewmand, fewmets, fewnes, fewneses, fewness, fewnesses, fewsome, fewter, fewterer, fewtrils, fey, feyer, feyest, feyness, feynesses, fez, fezes, fezzed, fezzes, fezzy, ff, ffa, fg, fgn, fgrid, fhrer, fi, fiacre, fiacres, fiador, fiancailles, fiance, fianced, fiancee, fiancees, fiances, fianchetti, fianchetto, fiancing, fiant, fiants, fiar, fiard, fiaroblast, fiars, fiaschi, fiasco, fiascoes, fiascos, fiat, fiatconfirmatio, fiats, fiaunt, fib, fibbed, fibber, fibbers, fibbery, fibbing, fibdom, fiber, fiber's, fiberboard, fibered, fiberfill, fiberglass, fiberization, fiberize, fiberized, fiberizer, fiberizes, fiberizing, fiberless, fiberous, fibers, fiberscope, fiberware, fibra, fibration, fibratus, fibre, fibreboard, fibred, fibrefill, fibreglass, fibreless, fibres, fibreware, fibriform, fibril, fibrilated, fibrilation, fibrilations, fibrilla, fibrillae, fibrillar, fibrillary, fibrillate, fibrillated, fibrillating, fibrillation, fibrillations, fibrilled, fibrilliferous, fibrilliform, fibrillose, fibrillous, fibrils, fibrin, fibrinate, fibrination, fibrine, fibrinemia, fibrinoalbuminous, fibrinocellular, fibrinogen, fibrinogenetic, fibrinogenic, fibrinogenically, fibrinogenous, fibrinoid, fibrinokinase, fibrinolyses, fibrinolysin, fibrinolysis, fibrinolytic, fibrinoplastic, fibrinoplastin, fibrinopurulent, fibrinose, fibrinosis, fibrinous, fibrins, fibrinuria, fibro, fibroadenia, fibroadenoma, fibroadipose, fibroangioma, fibroareolar, fibroblast, fibroblastic, fibrobronchitis, fibrocalcareous, fibrocarcinoma, fibrocartilage, fibrocartilaginous, fibrocaseose, fibrocaseous, fibrocellular, fibrocement, fibrochondritis, fibrochondroma, fibrochondrosteal, fibrocrystalline, fibrocyst, fibrocystic, fibrocystoma, fibrocyte, fibrocytic, fibroelastic, fibroenchondroma, fibrofatty, fibroferrite, fibroglia, fibroglioma, fibrohemorrhagic, fibroid, fibroids, fibroin, fibroins, fibrointestinal, fibroligamentous, fibrolipoma, fibrolipomatous, fibrolite, fibrolitic, fibroma, fibromas, fibromata, fibromatoid, fibromatosis, fibromatous, fibromembrane, fibromembranous, fibromucous, fibromuscular, fibromyectomy, fibromyitis, fibromyoma, fibromyomatous, fibromyomectomy, fibromyositis, fibromyotomy, fibromyxoma, fibromyxosarcoma, fibroneuroma, fibronuclear, fibronucleated, fibropapilloma, fibropericarditis, fibroplasia, fibroplastic, fibropolypus, fibropsammoma, fibropurulent, fibroreticulate, fibrosarcoma, fibrose, fibroserous, fibroses, fibrosis, fibrosities, fibrositis, fibrosity, fibrotic, fibrotuberculosis, fibrous, fibrously, fibrousness, fibrovasal, fibrovascular, fibry, fibs, fibster, fibula, fibulae, fibular, fibulare, fibularia, fibulas, fibulocalcaneal, fica, ficaries, ficary, ficche, fice, ficelle, fices, fichat, fiche, fiches, fichtelite, fichu, fichus, ficiform, ficin, ficins, fickle, ficklehearted, fickleness, fickler, ficklest, ficklety, ficklewise, fickly, fico, ficoes, ficoid, ficoidal, ficoides, fict, fictation, fictil, fictile, fictileness, fictility, fiction, fiction's, fictional, fictionalization, fictionalize, fictionalized, fictionalizes, fictionalizing, fictionally, fictionary, fictioneer, fictioneering, fictioner, fictionisation, fictionise, fictionised, fictionising, fictionist, fictionistic, fictionization, fictionize, fictionized, fictionizing, fictionmonger, fictions, fictious, fictitious, fictitiously, fictitiousness, fictive, fictively, fictor, ficus, fid, fidalgo, fidate, fidation, fidawi, fidded, fidding, fiddle, fiddleback, fiddlebow, fiddlebrained, fiddlecome, fiddled, fiddlededee, fiddledeedee, fiddlefaced, fiddlehead, fiddleheaded, fiddleneck, fiddler, fiddlerfish, fiddlerfishes, fiddlers, fiddlery, fiddles, fiddlestick, fiddlesticks, fiddlestring, fiddlewood, fiddley, fiddleys, fiddlies, fiddling, fiddly, fide, fideicommiss, fideicommissa, fideicommissaries, fideicommissary, fideicommission, fideicommissioner, fideicommissor, fideicommissum, fideicommissumissa, fideism, fideisms, fideist, fideistic, fideists, fidejussion, fidejussionary, fidejussor, fidejussory, fidel, fideles, fidelis, fidelities, fidelity, fideos, fidepromission, fidepromissor, fides, fidfad, fidge, fidged, fidges, fidget, fidgetation, fidgeted, fidgeter, fidgeters, fidgetily, fidgetiness, fidgeting, fidgetingly, fidgets, fidgety, fidging, fidibus, fidicinal, fidicinales, fidicula, fidiculae, fidley, fidleys, fido, fidos, fids, fiducia, fiducial, fiducially, fiduciaries, fiduciarily, fiduciary, fiducinales, fie, fied, fiedlerite, fief, fiefdom, fiefdoms, fiefs, fiel, field, fieldball, fieldbird, fielded, fielden, fielder, fielders, fieldfare, fieldfight, fieldie, fielding, fieldish, fieldleft, fieldman, fieldmen, fieldmice, fieldmouse, fieldpiece, fieldpieces, fields, fieldsman, fieldsmen, fieldstone, fieldstrip, fieldward, fieldwards, fieldwork, fieldworker, fieldwort, fieldy, fiend, fiendful, fiendfully, fiendhead, fiendish, fiendishly, fiendishness, fiendism, fiendlier, fiendliest, fiendlike, fiendliness, fiendly, fiends, fiendship, fient, fierasferid, fierasferoid, fierce, fiercehearted, fiercely, fiercen, fiercened, fierceness, fiercening, fiercer, fiercest, fiercly, fierding, fieri, fierier, fieriest, fierily, fieriness, fierte, fiery, fiesta, fiestas, fieulamort, fife, fifed, fifer, fifers, fifes, fifie, fifing, fifish, fifo, fifteen, fifteener, fifteenfold, fifteens, fifteenth, fifteenthly, fifteenths, fifth, fifthly, fifths, fifties, fiftieth, fiftieths, fifty, fiftyfold, fiftypenny, fig, fig's, figaro, figary, figbird, figboy, figeater, figeaters, figent, figeter, figged, figgery, figgier, figgiest, figging, figgle, figgum, figgy, fight, fightable, fighter, fighteress, fighters, fighting, fightingly, fightings, fights, fightwite, figless, figlike, figment, figmental, figments, figo, figpecker, figs, figshell, figulate, figulated, figuline, figulines, figura, figurability, figurable, figurae, figural, figurally, figurant, figurante, figurants, figurate, figurately, figuration, figurational, figurations, figurative, figuratively, figurativeness, figurato, figure, figured, figuredly, figurehead, figureheadless, figureheads, figureheadship, figureless, figurer, figurers, figures, figuresome, figurette, figurial, figurine, figurines, figuring, figurings, figurism, figurist, figuriste, figurize, figury, figworm, figwort, figworts, fiji, fijian, fike, fiked, fikery, fikey, fikh, fikie, fiking, fil, fila, filace, filaceous, filacer, filagree, filagreed, filagreeing, filagrees, filagreing, filament, filament's, filamentar, filamentary, filamented, filamentiferous, filamentoid, filamentose, filamentous, filaments, filamentule, filander, filanders, filao, filar, filaree, filarees, filaria, filariae, filarial, filarian, filariasis, filaricidal, filariform, filariid, filariids, filarious, filasse, filate, filator, filatory, filature, filatures, filaze, filazer, filbert, filberts, filch, filched, filcher, filchers, filchery, filches, filching, filchingly, file, file's, filea, fileable, filecard, filechar, filed, filefish, filefishes, filelike, filemaker, filemaking, filemark, filemarks, filemot, filename, filename's, filenames, filer, filers, files, filesave, filesmith, filesniff, filespec, filestatus, filet, fileted, fileting, filets, fili, filial, filiality, filially, filialness, filiate, filiated, filiates, filiating, filiation, filibeg, filibegs, filibranch, filibranchiate, filibuster, filibustered, filibusterer, filibusterers, filibustering, filibusterism, filibusterous, filibusters, filibustrous, filical, filicauline, filicic, filicidal, filicide, filicides, filiciform, filicin, filicinean, filicinian, filicite, filicoid, filicoids, filicologist, filicology, filiety, filiferous, filiform, filiformed, filigerous, filigrain, filigrained, filigrane, filigraned, filigree, filigreed, filigreeing, filigrees, filigreing, filii, filing, filings, filionymic, filiopietistic, filioque, filipendula, filipendulous, filipino, filipinos, filippi, filippic, filippo, filipuncture, filister, filisters, filite, filius, fill, filla, fillable, fillagree, fillagreed, fillagreing, fille, fillebeg, filled, fillemot, filler, fillercap, fillers, filles, fillet, filleted, filleter, filleting, filletlike, fillets, filletster, filleul, fillies, filling, fillingly, fillingness, fillings, fillip, filliped, fillipeen, filliping, fillips, fillister, fillmass, fillmore, fillock, fillowite, fills, filly, film, filmable, filmcard, filmcards, filmdom, filmdoms, filmed, filmer, filmet, filmgoer, filmgoers, filmgoing, filmic, filmically, filmier, filmiest, filmiform, filmily, filminess, filming, filmish, filmist, filmize, filmized, filmizing, filmland, filmlands, filmlike, filmmake, filmmaker, filmmaking, filmogen, filmographies, filmography, films, filmset, filmsets, filmsetter, filmsetting, filmslide, filmstrip, filmstrips, filmy, filo, filoplumaceous, filoplume, filopodia, filopodium, filose, filoselle, filosofe, filosus, fils, filt, filter, filter's, filterability, filterable, filterableness, filtered, filterer, filterers, filtering, filterman, filtermen, filters, filth, filthier, filthiest, filthified, filthify, filthifying, filthily, filthiness, filthless, filths, filthy, filtrability, filtrable, filtratable, filtrate, filtrated, filtrates, filtrating, filtration, filtre, filum, fimble, fimbles, fimbria, fimbriae, fimbrial, fimbriate, fimbriated, fimbriating, fimbriation, fimbriatum, fimbricate, fimbricated, fimbrilla, fimbrillae, fimbrillate, fimbrilliferous, fimbrillose, fimbriodentate, fimetarious, fimetic, fimicolous, fin, fin's, finable, finableness, finagle, finagled, finagler, finaglers, finagles, finagling, final, finale, finales, finalis, finalism, finalisms, finalist, finalists, finalities, finality, finalization, finalizations, finalize, finalized, finalizes, finalizing, finally, finals, finance, financed, financer, finances, financial, financialist, financially, financier, financier's, financiere, financiered, financiering, financiers, financiery, financing, financist, finary, finback, finbacks, finbone, finca, fincas, finch, finchbacked, finched, finchery, finches, find, findability, findable, findal, finder, finders, findfault, findhorn, finding, findings, findjan, findon, finds, findy, fine, fineable, fineableness, finebent, finecomb, fined, finedraw, finedrawing, fineer, fineish, fineleaf, fineless, finely, finement, fineness, finenesses, finer, fineries, finery, fines, finespun, finesse, finessed, finesser, finesses, finessing, finest, finestill, finestiller, finestra, finetop, finew, finewed, finfish, finfishes, finfoot, finfoots, fingan, fingent, finger, fingerable, fingerberry, fingerboard, fingerboards, fingerbreadth, fingered, fingerer, fingerers, fingerfish, fingerfishes, fingerflower, fingerhold, fingerhook, fingering, fingerings, fingerleaf, fingerless, fingerlet, fingerlike, fingerling, fingerlings, fingermark, fingernail, fingernails, fingerparted, fingerpost, fingerprint, fingerprinted, fingerprinting, fingerprints, fingerroot, fingers, fingersmith, fingerspin, fingerstall, fingerstone, fingertip, fingertips, fingerwise, fingerwork, fingery, fingian, fingram, fingrigo, fini, finial, finialed, finials, finical, finicality, finically, finicalness, finicism, finick, finickier, finickiest, finickily, finickin, finickiness, finicking, finickingly, finickingness, finicky, finific, finify, finikin, finiking, fining, finings, finis, finises, finish, finishable, finished, finisher, finishers, finishes, finishing, finitary, finite, finitely, finiteness, finites, finitesimal, finitism, finitive, finitude, finitudes, finity, finjan, fink, finked, finkel, finking, finks, finland, finlandization, finless, finlet, finlike, finmark, finmarks, finn, finnac, finnack, finnan, finned, finner, finnesko, finnic, finnick, finnickier, finnickiest, finnicking, finnicky, finnier, finniest, finning, finnip, finnish, finnmark, finnmarks, finnoc, finnochio, finns, finny, fino, finochio, finochios, fins, finspot, fintadores, fiord, fiorded, fiords, fiorin, fiorite, fioritura, fioriture, fip, fipenny, fippence, fipple, fipples, fiqh, fique, fiques, fir, firca, fire, fireable, firearm, firearm's, firearmed, firearms, fireback, fireball, fireballs, firebase, firebases, firebed, firebird, firebirds, fireblende, fireboard, fireboat, fireboats, firebolt, firebolted, firebomb, firebombed, firebombing, firebombs, fireboot, firebote, firebox, fireboxes, fireboy, firebrand, firebrands, firebrat, firebrats, firebreak, firebreaks, firebrick, firebricks, firebug, firebugs, fireburn, fireclay, fireclays, firecoat, firecracker, firecrackers, firecrest, fired, firedamp, firedamps, firedog, firedogs, firedragon, firedrake, firefall, firefang, firefanged, firefanging, firefangs, firefight, firefighter, firefighters, firefighting, fireflaught, fireflies, fireflirt, fireflower, firefly, firefly's, fireguard, firehall, firehalls, firehouse, firehouses, fireless, firelight, firelike, fireling, firelit, firelock, firelocks, fireman, firemanship, firemaster, firemen, firepan, firepans, firepink, firepinks, fireplace, fireplace's, fireplaces, fireplough, fireplow, fireplug, fireplugs, firepot, firepower, fireproof, fireproofed, fireproofing, fireproofness, firer, fireroom, firerooms, firers, fires, firesafe, firesafeness, firesafety, fireshaft, fireshine, fireside, firesider, firesides, firesideship, firespout, firestone, firestop, firestopping, firestorm, firetail, firethorn, firetop, firetower, firetrap, firetraps, firewall, fireward, firewarden, firewater, fireweed, fireweeds, firewood, firewoods, firework, fireworkless, fireworks, fireworky, fireworm, fireworms, firiness, firing, firings, firk, firked, firker, firkin, firking, firkins, firlot, firm, firma, firmament, firmamental, firmaments, firman, firmance, firmans, firmarii, firmarius, firmation, firmed, firmer, firmers, firmest, firmhearted, firming, firmisternal, firmisternial, firmisternous, firmitude, firmity, firmland, firmless, firmly, firmness, firmnesses, firms, firmware, firn, firnification, firns, firring, firry, firs, first, firstborn, firstcomer, firster, firstfruits, firsthand, firstling, firstlings, firstly, firstness, firsts, firstship, firth, firths, firy, fisc, fiscal, fiscalify, fiscalism, fiscality, fiscalization, fiscalize, fiscalized, fiscalizing, fiscally, fiscals, fischerite, fiscs, fiscus, fise, fisetin, fish, fishability, fishable, fishback, fishbed, fishberries, fishberry, fishboat, fishboats, fishbolt, fishbolts, fishbone, fishbones, fishbowl, fishbowls, fisheater, fished, fisher, fisherboat, fisherboy, fisheress, fisherfolk, fishergirl, fisheries, fisherman, fishermen, fisherpeople, fishers, fisherwoman, fishery, fishes, fishet, fisheye, fisheyes, fishfall, fishfinger, fishful, fishgarth, fishgig, fishgigs, fishgrass, fishhold, fishhood, fishhook, fishhooks, fishhouse, fishier, fishiest, fishified, fishify, fishifying, fishily, fishiness, fishing, fishingly, fishings, fishless, fishlet, fishlike, fishline, fishlines, fishling, fishman, fishmeal, fishmeals, fishmen, fishmonger, fishmouth, fishnet, fishnets, fishplate, fishpole, fishpoles, fishpond, fishponds, fishpool, fishpot, fishpotter, fishpound, fishskin, fishspear, fishtail, fishtailed, fishtailing, fishtails, fishway, fishways, fishweed, fishweir, fishwife, fishwives, fishwoman, fishwood, fishworker, fishworks, fishworm, fishy, fishyard, fishyback, fishybacking, fisk, fisnoga, fissate, fissicostate, fissidactyl, fissidentaceous, fissile, fissileness, fissilingual, fissility, fission, fissionability, fissionable, fissional, fissioned, fissioning, fissions, fissipalmate, fissipalmation, fissiparation, fissiparism, fissiparity, fissiparous, fissiparously, fissiparousness, fissiped, fissipedal, fissipedate, fissipedial, fissipeds, fissirostral, fissirostrate, fissive, fissle, fissura, fissural, fissuration, fissure, fissured, fissureless, fissures, fissuriform, fissuring, fissury, fist, fisted, fister, fistfight, fistful, fistfuls, fistiana, fistic, fistical, fisticuff, fisticuffer, fisticuffery, fisticuffing, fisticuffs, fistify, fistiness, fisting, fistinut, fistle, fistlike, fistmele, fistnote, fistnotes, fists, fistuca, fistula, fistulae, fistular, fistularioid, fistulas, fistulate, fistulated, fistulatome, fistulatous, fistule, fistuliform, fistulization, fistulize, fistulized, fistulizing, fistulose, fistulous, fistwise, fisty, fit, fitch, fitche, fitched, fitchee, fitcher, fitchered, fitchering, fitchery, fitches, fitchet, fitchets, fitchew, fitchews, fitchy, fitful, fitfully, fitfulness, fitified, fitly, fitment, fitments, fitness, fitnesses, fitout, fitroot, fits, fittable, fittage, fitted, fittedness, fitten, fitter, fitter's, fitters, fittest, fittier, fittiest, fittily, fittiness, fitting, fittingly, fittingness, fittings, fittit, fitty, fittyfied, fittyways, fittywise, fitweed, fitz, fiumara, five, fivebar, fivefold, fivefoldness, fiveling, fivepence, fivepenny, fivepins, fiver, fivers, fives, fivescore, fivesome, fivestones, fivish, fix, fixable, fixage, fixate, fixated, fixates, fixatif, fixatifs, fixating, fixation, fixations, fixative, fixatives, fixator, fixature, fixe, fixed, fixedly, fixedness, fixer, fixers, fixes, fixgig, fixidity, fixin's, fixing, fixings, fixion, fixities, fixity, fixive, fixt, fixture, fixture's, fixtureless, fixtures, fixup, fixups, fixure, fixures, fiz, fizelyite, fizgig, fizgigs, fizz, fizzed, fizzer, fizzers, fizzes, fizzier, fizziest, fizzing, fizzle, fizzled, fizzles, fizzling, fizzwater, fizzy, fjarding, fjeld, fjelds, fjerding, fjord, fjorded, fjords, fl, flab, flabella, flabbergast, flabbergastation, flabbergasted, flabbergasting, flabbergastingly, flabbergasts, flabbier, flabbiest, flabbily, flabbiness, flabby, flabel, flabella, flabellarium, flabellate, flabellation, flabellifoliate, flabelliform, flabellinerved, flabellum, flabile, flabra, flabrum, flabs, flaccid, flaccidities, flaccidity, flaccidly, flaccidness, flacherie, flachery, flacian, flack, flacked, flacker, flackery, flacket, flacks, flacon, flacons, flacourtiaceous, flaff, flaffer, flag, flag's, flagarie, flagboat, flagella, flagellant, flagellantism, flagellants, flagellar, flagellariaceous, flagellate, flagellated, flagellates, flagellating, flagellation, flagellations, flagellative, flagellator, flagellators, flagellatory, flagelliferous, flagelliform, flagellist, flagellosis, flagellula, flagellulae, flagellum, flagellums, flageolet, flageolets, flagfall, flagfish, flagfishes, flagged, flaggelate, flaggelated, flaggelating, flaggelation, flaggella, flagger, flaggers, flaggery, flaggier, flaggiest, flaggily, flagginess, flagging, flaggingly, flaggings, flaggish, flaggy, flagilate, flagitate, flagitation, flagitious, flagitiously, flagitiousness, flagleaf, flagless, flaglet, flaglike, flagmaker, flagmaking, flagman, flagmen, flagon, flagonet, flagonless, flagons, flagpole, flagpoles, flagrance, flagrancy, flagrant, flagrante, flagrantly, flagrantness, flagrate, flagroot, flags, flagship, flagships, flagstaff, flagstaffs, flagstaves, flagstick, flagstone, flagstones, flagworm, flail, flailed, flailing, flaillike, flails, flain, flair, flairs, flaite, flaith, flaithship, flajolotite, flak, flakage, flake, flakeboard, flaked, flakeless, flakelet, flaker, flakers, flakes, flakier, flakiest, flakily, flakiness, flaking, flaky, flam, flamant, flamb, flambage, flambant, flambe, flambeau, flambeaus, flambeaux, flambee, flambeed, flambeing, flamberg, flamberge, flambes, flamboyance, flamboyancy, flamboyant, flamboyantism, flamboyantize, flamboyantly, flamboyer, flame, flamed, flamefish, flamefishes, flameflower, flameholder, flameless, flamelet, flamelike, flamen, flamenco, flamencos, flamens, flamenship, flameout, flameouts, flameproof, flameproofer, flamer, flamers, flames, flamethrower, flamethrowers, flamfew, flamier, flamiest, flamineous, flamines, flaming, flamingly, flamingo, flamingoes, flamingos, flaminica, flaminical, flamless, flammability, flammable, flammably, flammant, flammation, flammed, flammeous, flammiferous, flammigerous, flamming, flammivomous, flammulated, flammulation, flammule, flams, flamy, flan, flancard, flancards, flanch, flanchard, flanche, flanched, flanconade, flanconnade, flandan, flanderkin, flanders, flandowser, flane, flanerie, flaneries, flanes, flaneur, flaneurs, flang, flange, flanged, flangeless, flanger, flangers, flanges, flangeway, flanging, flank, flankard, flanked, flanken, flanker, flankers, flanking, flanks, flankwise, flanky, flanned, flannel, flannel's, flannelboard, flannelbush, flanneled, flannelet, flannelette, flannelflower, flanneling, flannelleaf, flannelleaves, flannelled, flannelling, flannelly, flannelmouth, flannelmouthed, flannelmouths, flannels, flanning, flanque, flans, flap, flap's, flapcake, flapdock, flapdoodle, flapdragon, flaperon, flapjack, flapjacks, flapless, flapmouthed, flappable, flapped, flapper, flapperdom, flappered, flapperhood, flappering, flapperish, flapperism, flappers, flappet, flappier, flappiest, flapping, flappy, flaps, flare, flareback, flareboard, flared, flareless, flarer, flares, flarfish, flarfishes, flaring, flaringly, flary, flaser, flash, flashback, flashbacks, flashboard, flashbulb, flashbulbs, flashcube, flashcubes, flashed, flasher, flashers, flashes, flashet, flashflood, flashforward, flashforwards, flashgun, flashguns, flashier, flashiest, flashily, flashiness, flashing, flashingly, flashings, flashlamp, flashlamps, flashlight, flashlight's, flashlights, flashlike, flashly, flashness, flashover, flashpan, flashproof, flashtester, flashtube, flashtubes, flashy, flask, flasker, flasket, flaskets, flaskful, flasklet, flasks, flasque, flat, flatbed, flatbeds, flatboat, flatboats, flatbottom, flatbread, flatbrod, flatcap, flatcaps, flatcar, flatcars, flatdom, flated, flateria, flatette, flatfeet, flatfish, flatfishes, flatfoot, flatfooted, flatfootedly, flatfootedness, flatfooting, flatfoots, flathat, flathe, flathead, flatheads, flatiron, flatirons, flative, flatland, flatlander, flatlanders, flatlands, flatlet, flatlets, flatling, flatlings, flatlong, flatly, flatman, flatmate, flatmen, flatness, flatnesses, flatnose, flats, flatted, flatten, flattened, flattener, flatteners, flattening, flattens, flatter, flatterable, flattercap, flatterdock, flattered, flatterer, flatterers, flatteress, flatteries, flattering, flatteringly, flatteringness, flatterous, flatters, flattery, flattest, flatteur, flattie, flatting, flattish, flattop, flattops, flatulence, flatulences, flatulencies, flatulency, flatulent, flatulently, flatulentness, flatuosity, flatuous, flatus, flatuses, flatware, flatwares, flatwash, flatwashes, flatway, flatways, flatweed, flatwise, flatwoods, flatwork, flatworks, flatworm, flatworms, flaubert, flaucht, flaught, flaughtbred, flaughter, flaughts, flaunch, flaunche, flaunched, flaunching, flaunt, flaunted, flaunter, flaunters, flauntier, flauntiest, flauntily, flauntiness, flaunting, flauntingly, flaunts, flaunty, flautino, flautist, flautists, flauto, flav, flavanilin, flavaniline, flavanone, flavanthrene, flavanthrone, flavedo, flavedos, flavescence, flavescent, flavic, flavicant, flavid, flavin, flavine, flavines, flavins, flavo, flavobacteria, flavobacterium, flavone, flavones, flavonoid, flavonol, flavonols, flavoprotein, flavopurpurin, flavor, flavored, flavorer, flavorers, flavorful, flavorfully, flavorfulness, flavoriness, flavoring, flavorings, flavorless, flavorlessness, flavorous, flavorousness, flavors, flavorsome, flavorsomeness, flavory, flavour, flavoured, flavourer, flavourful, flavourfully, flavouring, flavourless, flavourous, flavours, flavoursome, flavoury, flavous, flaw, flawed, flawedness, flawflower, flawful, flawier, flawiest, flawing, flawless, flawlessly, flawlessness, flawn, flaws, flawy, flax, flaxbird, flaxboard, flaxbush, flaxdrop, flaxen, flaxes, flaxier, flaxiest, flaxlike, flaxman, flaxseed, flaxseeds, flaxtail, flaxweed, flaxwench, flaxwife, flaxwoman, flaxwort, flaxy, flay, flayed, flayer, flayers, flayflint, flaying, flays, flb, flche, flchette, fld, fldxt, flea, flea's, fleabag, fleabags, fleabane, fleabanes, fleabite, fleabites, fleabiting, fleabitten, fleabug, fleabugs, fleadock, fleahopper, fleak, fleam, fleams, fleamy, fleapit, flear, fleas, fleaseed, fleaweed, fleawood, fleawort, fleaworts, fleay, flebile, flebotomy, fleche, fleches, flechette, flechettes, fleck, flecked, flecken, flecker, fleckered, fleckering, fleckier, fleckiest, fleckiness, flecking, fleckled, fleckless, flecklessly, flecks, flecky, flecnodal, flecnode, flect, flection, flectional, flectionless, flections, flector, fled, fledge, fledged, fledgeless, fledgeling, fledges, fledgier, fledgiest, fledging, fledgling,

fledgling's, fledglings, fledgy, flee, fleece, fleece's, fleeceable, fleeced, fleeceflower, fleeceless, fleecelike, fleecer, fleecers, fleeces, fleech, fleeched, fleeches, fleeching, fleechment, fleecier, fleeciest, fleecily, fleeciness, fleecing, fleecy, fleeing, fleer, fleered, fleerer, fleering, fleeringly, fleerish, fleers, flees, fleet, fleeted, fleeten, fleeter, fleetest, fleetful, fleeting, fleetingly, fleetingness, fleetings, fleetly, fleetness, fleets, fleetwing, flegm, fleing, fleishig, fleme, flemer, fleming, flemings, flemish, flemished, flemishes, flemishing, flench, flenched, flenches, flenching, flense, flensed, flenser, flensers, flenses, flensing, flentes, flerried, flerry, flerrying, flesh, fleshbrush, fleshed, fleshen, flesher, fleshers, fleshes, fleshful, fleshhood, fleshhook, fleshier, fleshiest, fleshiness, fleshing, fleshings, fleshless, fleshlessness, fleshlier, fleshliest, fleshlike, fleshlily, fleshliness, fleshling, fleshly, fleshment, fleshmonger, fleshpot, fleshpots, fleshquake, fleshy, flet, fletch, fletched, fletcher, fletcherism, fletchers, fletches, fletching, fletchings, flether, fletton, fleur, fleuret, fleurette, fleurettee, fleuretty, fleuron, fleuronee, fleuronne, fleuronnee, fleury, flew, flewed, flewit, flews, flex, flexanimous, flexed, flexes, flexibilities, flexibility, flexibilty, flexible, flexibleness, flexibly, flexile, flexility, flexing, flexion, flexional, flexionless, flexions, flexitime, flexity, flexive, flexo, flexographic, flexographically, flexography, flexor, flexors, flexuose, flexuosely, flexuoseness, flexuosities, flexuosity, flexuous, flexuously, flexuousness, flexura, flexural, flexure, flexured, flexures, fley, fleyed, fleyedly, fleyedness, fleying, fleyland, fleys, fleysome, flibbertigibbet, flibbertigibbets, flibbertigibbety, flibustier, flic, flicflac, flichter, flichtered, flichtering, flichters, flick, flicked, flicker, flickered, flickering, flickeringly, flickermouse, flickerproof, flickers, flickertail, flickery, flicking, flicks, flicky, flics, flidder, flidge, flied, flier, fliers, flies, fliest, fliffus, fligged, fligger, flight, flight's, flighted, flighter, flightful, flighthead, flightier, flightiest, flightily, flightiness, flighting, flightless, flights, flightshot, flightworthy, flighty, flimflam, flimflammed, flimflammer, flimflammery, flimflamming, flimflams, flimmer, flimp, flimsier, flimsies, flimsiest, flimsily, flimsilyst, flimsiness, flimsy, flinch, flinched, flincher, flinchers, flinches, flinching, flinchingly, flinder, flinders, flindosa, flindosy, fling, fling's, flingdust, flinger, flingers, flinging, flings, flingy, flinkite, flint, flinted, flinter, flinthead, flinthearted, flintier, flintiest, flintified, flintify, flintifying, flintily, flintiness, flinting, flintless, flintlike, flintlock, flintlocks, flints, flintstone, flintwood, flintwork, flintworker, flinty, flioma, flip, flipe, fliped, flipflop, fliping, flipjack, flippance, flippancies, flippancy, flippant, flippantly, flippantness, flipped, flipper, flipperling, flippers, flippery, flippest, flipping, flips, flirt, flirtable, flirtation, flirtational, flirtationless, flirtations, flirtatious, flirtatiously, flirtatiousness, flirted, flirter, flirters, flirtier, flirtiest, flirtigig, flirting, flirtingly, flirtish, flirtishness, flirtling, flirts, flirty, flisk, flisked, fliskier, fliskiest, flisky, flit, flitch, flitched, flitchen, flitches, flitching, flitchplate, flite, flited, flites, flitfold, fliting, flits, flitted, flitter, flitterbat, flittered, flittering, flittermice, flittermmice, flittermouse, flittern, flitters, flittiness, flitting, flittingly, flitty, flitwite, flivver, flivvers, flix, flixweed, fll, flnerie, flneur, flneuse, flo, fload, float, floatability, floatable, floatage, floatages, floatation, floatative, floatboard, floated, floater, floaters, floatier, floatiest, floatiness, floating, floatingly, floative, floatless, floatmaker, floatman, floatmen, floatplane, floats, floatsman, floatsmen, floatstone, floaty, flob, flobby, floc, flocced, flocci, floccilation, floccillation, floccing, floccipend, floccose, floccosely, flocculable, flocculant, floccular, flocculate, flocculated, flocculating, flocculation, flocculator, floccule, flocculence, flocculency, flocculent, flocculently, floccules, flocculi, flocculose, flocculous, flocculus, floccus, flock, flockbed, flocked, flocker, flockier, flockiest, flocking, flockings, flockless, flocklike, flockling, flockman, flockmaster, flockowner, flocks, flockwise, flocky, flocoon, flocs, flodge, floe, floeberg, floes, floey, flog, floggable, flogged, flogger, floggers, flogging, floggingly, floggings, flogmaster, flogs, flogster, floit, flokite, flon, flong, flongs, flood, floodable, floodage, floodboard, floodcock, flooded, flooder, flooders, floodgate, floodgates, flooding, floodless, floodlet, floodlight, floodlighted, floodlighting, floodlights, floodlike, floodlilit, floodlit, floodmark, floodometer, floodplain, floodproof, floods, floodtime, floodwall, floodwater, floodway, floodways, floodwood, floody, flooey, flook, flookan, floor, floorage, floorages, floorboard, floorboards, floorcloth, floorcloths, floored, floorer, floorers, floorhead, flooring, floorings, floorless, floorman, floormen, floors, floorshift, floorshifts, floorshow, floorthrough, floorwalker, floorwalkers, floorward, floorway, floorwise, floosies, floosy, floozie, floozies, floozy, flop, flop's, floperoo, flophouse, flophouses, flopover, flopovers, flopped, flopper, floppers, floppier, floppies, floppiest, floppily, floppiness, flopping, floppy, flops, flopwing, flor, flora, florae, floral, floralize, florally, floramor, floramour, floran, floras, florate, floreal, floreat, floreate, floreated, floreating, florence, florences, florent, florentine, florentines, florentium, flores, florescence, florescent, floressence, floret, floreta, floreted, florets, florette, floretty, floretum, floriage, floriate, floriated, floriation, floribunda, florican, floricin, floricomous, floricultural, floriculturally, floriculture, floriculturist, florid, florida, floridan, floridans, floridean, florideous, floridian, floridians, floridities, floridity, floridly, floridness, floriferous, floriferously, floriferousness, florification, floriform, florigen, florigenic, florigens, florigraphy, florikan, floriken, florilage, florilege, florilegia, florilegium, florimania, florimanist, florin, florins, floriparous, floripondio, floriscope, florist, floristic, floristically, floristics, floristry, florists, florisugent, florivorous, florizine, floroon, floroscope, floroun, floruit, floruits, florula, florulae, florulas, florulent, flory, floscular, floscularian, floscule, flosculet, flosculose, flosculous, flosh, floss, flossa, flossed, flosser, flosses, flossflower, flossie, flossier, flossies, flossiest, flossification, flossiness, flossing, flossy, flot, flota, flotage, flotages, flotant, flotas, flotation, flotations, flotative, flote, floter, flotilla, flotillas, flotorial, flots, flotsam, flotsams, flotsan, flotsen, flotson, flotten, flotter, flounce, flounced, flounces, flouncey, flouncier, flounciest, flouncing, flouncy, flounder, floundered, floundering, flounderingly, flounders, flour, floured, flourescent, flouriness, flouring, flourish, flourishable, flourished, flourisher, flourishes, flourishing, flourishingly, flourishment, flourishy, flourless, flourlike, flours, floury, flouse, floush, flout, flouted, flouter, flouters, flouting, floutingly, flouts, flow, flowable, flowage, flowages, flowchart, flowcharted, flowcharting, flowcharts, flowcontrol, flowe, flowed, flower, flowerage, flowerbed, flowered, flowerer, flowerers, floweret, flowerets, flowerfence, flowerfly, flowerful, flowerier, floweriest, flowerily, floweriness, flowering, flowerist, flowerless, flowerlessness, flowerlet, flowerlike, flowerpecker, flowerpot, flowerpots, flowers, flowerwork, flowery, flowing, flowingly, flowingness, flowk, flowmanostat, flowmeter, flown, flowoff, flows, flowstone, floyt, flrie, flu, fluate, fluavil, fluavile, flub, flubbed, flubbing, flubdub, flubdubberies, flubdubbery, flubdubs, flubs, flucan, fluctiferous, fluctigerous, fluctisonant, fluctisonous, fluctuability, fluctuable, fluctuant, fluctuate, fluctuated, fluctuates, fluctuating, fluctuation, fluctuational, fluctuations, fluctuosity, fluctuous, flue, flued, fluegelhorn, flueless, fluellen, fluellin, fluellite, flueman, fluemen, fluence, fluencies, fluency, fluent, fluently, fluentness, fluer, flueric, fluerics, flues, fluework, fluey, fluff, fluffed, fluffer, fluffier, fluffiest, fluffily, fluffiness, fluffing, fluffs, fluffy, flugel, flugelhorn, flugelman, flugelmen, fluible, fluid, fluidacetextract, fluidal, fluidally, fluidextract, fluidglycerate, fluidible, fluidic, fluidics, fluidification, fluidified, fluidifier, fluidify, fluidifying, fluidimeter, fluidisation, fluidise, fluidised, fluidiser, fluidises, fluidising, fluidism, fluidist, fluidities, fluidity, fluidization, fluidize, fluidized, fluidizer, fluidizes, fluidizing, fluidly, fluidmeter, fluidness, fluidounce, fluidrachm, fluidram, fluidrams, fluids, fluigram, fluigramme, fluing, fluitant, fluke, fluked, flukeless, flukes, flukeworm, flukewort, flukey, flukier, flukiest, flukily, flukiness, fluking, fluky, flumadiddle, flumdiddle, flume, flumed, flumerin, flumes, fluming, fluminose, fluminous, flummadiddle, flummer, flummeries, flummery, flummox, flummoxed, flummoxes, flummoxing, flummydiddle, flump, flumped, flumping, flumps, flung, flunk, flunked, flunker, flunkers, flunkey, flunkeydom, flunkeyhood, flunkeyish, flunkeyism, flunkeyistic, flunkeyite, flunkeyize, flunkeys, flunkies, flunking, flunks, flunky, flunkydom, flunkyhood, flunkyish, flunkyism, flunkyistic, flunkyite, flunkyize, fluoaluminate, fluoaluminic, fluoarsenate, fluoborate, fluoboric, fluoborid, fluoboride, fluoborite, fluobromide, fluocarbonate, fluocerine, fluocerite, fluochloride, fluohydric, fluophosphate, fluor, fluoran, fluorane, fluoranthene, fluorapatite, fluorate, fluorated, fluorbenzene, fluorboric, fluorene, fluorenes, fluorenyl, fluoresage, fluoresce, fluoresced, fluorescein, fluoresceine, fluorescence, fluorescent, fluorescer, fluoresces, fluorescigenic, fluorescigenous, fluorescing, fluorhydric, fluoric, fluorid, fluoridate, fluoridated, fluoridates, fluoridating, fluoridation, fluoridations, fluoride, fluorides, fluoridisation, fluoridise, fluoridised, fluoridising, fluoridization, fluoridize, fluoridized, fluoridizing, fluorids, fluorimeter, fluorimetric, fluorimetry, fluorin, fluorinate, fluorinated, fluorinates, fluorinating, fluorination, fluorinations, fluorindin, fluorindine, fluorine, fluorines, fluorins, fluorite, fluorites, fluormeter, fluorobenzene, fluoroborate, fluorocarbon, fluorocarbons, fluorochrome, fluoroform, fluoroformol, fluorogen, fluorogenic, fluorographic, fluorography, fluoroid, fluorometer, fluorometric, fluorometry, fluorophosphate, fluoroscope, fluoroscoped, fluoroscopes, fluoroscopic, fluoroscopically, fluoroscopies, fluoroscoping, fluoroscopist, fluoroscopists, fluoroscopy, fluorosis, fluorotic, fluorotype, fluorouracil, fluors, fluorspar, fluoryl, fluosilicate, fluosilicic, fluotantalate, fluotantalic, fluotitanate, fluotitanic, fluozirconic, fluphenazine, flurn, flurr, flurried, flurriedly, flurries, flurriment, flurry, flurrying, flurt, flus, flush, flushable, flushboard, flushed, flusher, flusherman, flushermen, flushers, flushes, flushest, flushgate, flushing, flushingly, flushness, flushy, flusk, flusker, fluster, flusterate, flusterated, flusterating, flusteration, flustered, flusterer, flustering, flusterment, flusters, flustery, flustrate, flustrated, flustrating, flustration, flustrine, flustroid, flustrum, flute, flutebird, fluted, flutelike, flutemouth, fluter, fluters, flutes, flutework, flutey, fluther, flutier, flutiest, flutina, fluting, flutings, flutist, flutists, flutter, flutterable, flutteration, flutterboard, fluttered, flutterer, flutterers, flutteriness, fluttering, flutteringly, flutterless, flutterment, flutters, fluttersome, fluttery, fluty, fluvanna, fluvial, fluvialist, fluviatic, fluviatile, fluviation, fluvicoline, fluvio, fluvioglacial, fluviograph, fluviolacustrine, fluviology, fluviomarine, fluviometer, fluviose, fluvioterrestrial, fluvious, fluviovolcanic, flux, fluxation, fluxed, fluxer, fluxes, fluxgraph, fluxibility, fluxible, fluxibleness, fluxibly, fluxile, fluxility, fluxing, fluxion, fluxional, fluxionally, fluxionary, fluxionist, fluxions, fluxive, fluxmeter, fluxroot, fluxure, fluxweed, fluyt, fluyts, fly, flyability, flyable, flyaway, flyaways, flyback, flyball, flybane, flybelt, flybelts, flyblew, flyblow, flyblowing, flyblown, flyblows, flyboat, flyboats, flybook, flyboy, flybrush, flyby, flybys, flycaster, flycatcher, flycatchers, flyeater, flyer, flyer's, flyers, flyflap, flyflapper, flyflower, flying, flyingly, flyings, flyleaf, flyleaves, flyless, flyman, flymen, flyness, flyoff, flyover, flyovers, flypaper, flypapers, flypast, flypasts, flype, flyproof, flysch, flysches, flyspeck, flyspecked, flyspecking, flyspecks, flyswat, flyswatter, flytail, flyte, flyted, flytes, flytier, flytiers, flytime, flyting, flytings, flytrap, flytraps, flyway, flyways, flyweight, flyweights, flywheel, flywheels, flywinch, flywire, flywort, fm, fmt, fn, fname, fnese, fo, fo'c's'le, fo'c'sle, foal, foaled, foalfoot, foalfoots, foalhood, foaling, foals, foaly, foam, foambow, foamed, foamer, foamers, foamflower, foamier, foamiest, foamily, foaminess, foaming, foamingly, foamless, foamlike, foams, foamy, fob, fobbed, fobbing, fobs, focal, focalisation, focalise, focalised, focalises, focalising, focalization, focalize, focalized, focalizes, focalizing, focally, focaloid, foci, focimeter, focimetry, fockle, focoids, focometer, focometry, focsle, focus, focusable, focused, focuser, focusers, focuses, focusing, focusless, focussed, focusses, focussing, fod, fodda, fodder, foddered, fodderer, foddering, fodderless, fodders, foder, fodge, fodgel, fodient, foe, foe's, foederal, foederati, foederatus, foederis, foeffment, foehn, foehnlike, foehns, foeish, foeless, foelike, foeman, foemanship, foemen, foenngreek, foes, foeship, foetal, foetalism, foetalization, foetation, foeti, foeticidal, foeticide, foetid, foetiferous, foetiparous, foetor, foetors, foeture, foetus, foetuses, fofarraw, fog, fog's, fogas, fogbank, fogbound, fogbow, fogbows, fogdog, fogdogs, fogdom, foge, fogeater, fogey, fogeys, fogfruit, fogfruits, foggage, foggages, foggara, fogged, fogger, foggers, foggier, foggiest, foggily, fogginess, fogging, foggish, foggy, foghorn, foghorns, fogie, fogies, fogle, fogless, foglietto, fogman, fogmen, fogo, fogon, fogou, fogproof, fogram, fogramite, fogramity, fogrum, fogs, fogscoffer, fogus, fogy, fogydom, fogyish, fogyishness, fogyism, fogyisms, foh, fohat, fohn, fohns, foible, foibles, foiblesse, foil, foilable, foiled, foiler, foiling, foils, foilsman, foilsmen, foin, foined, foining, foiningly, foins, foison, foisonless, foisons, foist, foisted, foister, foistiness, foisting, foists, foisty, foiter, fokker, fol, folacin, folacins, folate, folates, folcgemot, fold, foldable, foldage, foldaway, foldboat, foldboater, foldboating, foldboats, foldcourse, folded, foldedly, folden, folder, folderol, folderols, folders, folding, foldless, foldout, foldouts, folds, foldskirt, foldstool, foldure, foldwards, foldy, fole, foleye, folgerite, folia, foliaceous, foliaceousness, foliage, foliaged, foliageous, foliages, foliaging, folial, foliar, foliary, foliate, foliated, foliates, foliating, foliation, foliator, foliature, folic, folie, folies, foliicolous, foliiferous, foliiform, folily, folio, foliobranch, foliobranchiate, foliocellosis, folioed, folioing, foliolate, foliole, folioliferous, foliolose, folios, foliose, foliosity, foliot, folious, foliously, folium, foliums, folk, folk's, folkboat, folkcraft, folkfree, folkish, folkishness, folkland, folklike, folklore, folklores, folkloric, folklorish, folklorism, folklorist, folkloristic, folklorists, folkmoot, folkmooter, folkmoots, folkmot, folkmote, folkmoter, folkmotes, folkmots, folkright, folks, folksay, folksey, folksier, folksiest, folksily, folksiness, folksinger, folksinging, folksong, folksongs, folksy, folktale, folktales, folkway, folkways, folky, foll, foller, folles, folletage, folletti, folletto, follicle, follicles, follicular, folliculate, folliculated, follicule, folliculin, folliculitis, folliculose, folliculosis, folliculous, follied, follies, folliful, follily, follis, follow, followable, followed, follower, followers, followership, followeth, following, followingly, followings, follows, followup, folly, follyer, follying, follyproof, folsom, fomalhaut, foment, fomentation, fomentations, fomented, fomenter, fomenters, fomenting, fomento, foments, fomes, fomites, fon, fonctionnaire, fond, fondaco, fondak, fondant, fondants, fondateur, fonded, fonder, fondest, fonding, fondish, fondle, fondled, fondler, fondlers, fondles, fondlesome, fondlike, fondling, fondlingly, fondlings, fondly, fondness, fondnesses, fondon, fondouk, fonds, fondu, fondue, fondues, fonduk, fondus, fone, fonly, fonnish, fono, fons, font, font's, fontal, fontally, fontanel, fontanelle, fontanels, fontange, fontanges, fonted, fontes, fontful, fonticulus, fontina, fontinal, fontinalaceous, fontinas, fontlet, fonts, foo, foobar, food, food's, fooder, foodful, foodless, foodlessness, foods, foodservices, foodstuff, foodstuff's, foodstuffs, foody, foofaraw, foofaraws, fool, foolable, fooldom, fooled, fooler, fooleries, foolery, fooless, foolfish, foolfishes, foolhardier, foolhardiest, foolhardihood, foolhardily, foolhardiness, foolhardiship, foolhardy, foolhead, foolheaded, foolheadedness, foolify, fooling, foolish, foolisher, foolishest, foolishly, foolishness, foollike, foolmonger, foolocracy, foolproof, foolproofness, fools, foolscap, foolscaps, foolship, fooner, fooster, foosterer, foot, footage, footages, footback, football, football's, footballer, footballist, footballs, footband, footbath, footbaths, footbeat, footblower, footboard, footboards, footboy, footboys, footbreadth, footbridge, footbridges, footcandle, footcandles, footcloth, footcloths, footed, footeite, footer, footers, footfall, footfalls, footfarer, footfault, footfeed, footfolk, footful, footganger, footgear, footgears, footgeld, footglove, footgrip, foothalt, foothil, foothill, foothills, foothils, foothold, footholds, foothook, foothot, footie, footier, footiest, footing, footingly, footings, footle, footled, footler, footlers, footles, footless, footlessly, footlessness, footlicker, footlicking, footlight, footlights, footlike, footling, footlining, footlock, footlocker, footlockers, footlog, footloose, footmaker, footman, footmanhood, footmanry, footmanship, footmark, footmarks, footmen, footmenfootpad, footnote, footnote's, footnoted, footnotes, footnoting, footpace, footpaces, footpad, footpaddery, footpads, footpath, footpaths, footpick, footplate, footpound, footpounds, footprint, footprint's, footprints, footrace, footraces, footrail, footrest, footrests, footrill, footroom, footrope, footropes, foots, footscald, footscraper, footsie, footsies, footslog, footslogged, footslogger, footslogging, footslogs, footsoldier, footsoldiers, footsore, footsoreness, footsores, footstalk, footstall, footstep, footsteps, footstick, footstock, footstone, footstool, footstools, footsy, footwalk, footwall, footwalls, footwarmer, footwarmers, footway, footways, footwear, footwears, footweary, footwork, footworks, footworn, footy, fooyoung, fooyung, foozle, foozled, foozler, foozlers, foozles, foozling, fop, fopdoodle, fopling, fopped, fopperies, fopperly, foppery, fopping, foppish, foppishly, foppishness, foppy, fops, fopship, for, fora, forage, foraged, foragement, forager, foragers, forages, foraging, foralite, foram, foramen, foramens, foramina, foraminal, foraminate, foraminated, foramination, foraminifer, foraminifera, foraminiferal, foraminiferan, foraminiferous, foraminose, foraminous, foraminulate, foraminule, foraminulose, foraminulous, forams, forane, foraneen, foraneous, foraramens, foraramina, forasmuch, forastero, foray, foray's, forayed, forayer, forayers, foraying, forays, forb, forbad, forbade, forbar, forbare, forbarred, forbathe, forbbore, forbborne, forbear, forbear's, forbearable, forbearance, forbearances, forbearant, forbearantly, forbearer, forbearers, forbearing, forbearingly, forbearingness, forbears, forbecause, forbesite, forbid, forbidal, forbidals, forbiddable, forbiddal, forbiddance, forbidden, forbiddenly, forbiddenness, forbidder, forbidding, forbiddingly, forbiddingness, forbids, forbit, forbite, forblack, forbled, forblow, forbode, forboded, forbodes, forboding, forbore, forborn, forborne, forbow, forbreak, forbruise, forbs, forby, forbye, forbysen, forbysening, forcaria, forcarve, forcat, force, force's, forceable, forced, forcedly, forcedness, forceful, forcefully, forcefulness, forceless, forcelessness, forcelet, forcemeat, forcement, forcene, forceps, forcepses, forcepslike, forceput, forcer, forcers, forces, forcet, forchase, forche, forches, forcibility, forcible, forcibleness, forcibly, forcing, forcingly, forcipal, forcipate, forcipated, forcipation, forcipes, forcipial, forcipiform, forcipressure, forcipulate, forcite, forcive, forcleave, forclose, forconceit, forcut, forcy, ford, fordable, fordableness, fordam, fordays, fordeal, forded, fordid, fording, fordless, fordo, fordoes, fordoing, fordone, fordrive, fords, fordull, fordwine, fordy, fore, foreaccounting, foreaccustom, foreacquaint, foreact, foreadapt, foreadmonish, foreadvertise, foreadvice, foreadvise, foreallege, foreallot, foreannounce, foreannouncement, foreanswer, foreappoint, foreappointment, forearm, forearm's, forearmed, forearming, forearms, foreassign, foreassurance, forebackwardly, forebar, forebay, forebays, forebear, forebearing, forebears, forebemoan, forebemoaned, forebespeak, forebitt, forebitten, forebitter, forebless, foreboard, forebode, foreboded, forebodement, foreboder, forebodes, forebodies, foreboding, forebodingly, forebodingness, forebodings, forebody, foreboom, forebooms, foreboot, forebow, forebowels, forebowline, forebows, forebrace, forebrain, forebreast, forebridge, forebroads, foreburton, forebush, foreby, forebye, forecabin, forecaddie, forecar, forecarriage, forecast, forecasted, forecaster, forecasters, forecasting, forecastingly, forecastle, forecastlehead, forecastleman, forecastlemen, forecastles, forecastors, forecasts, forecatching, forecatharping, forechamber, forechase, forechoice, forechoir, forechoose, forechurch, forecited, foreclaw, foreclosable, foreclose, foreclosed, forecloses, foreclosing, foreclosure, foreclosures, forecome, forecomingness, forecommend, foreconceive, foreconclude, forecondemn, foreconscious, foreconsent, foreconsider, forecontrive, forecool, forecooler, forecounsel, forecount, forecourse, forecourt, forecourts, forecover, forecovert, foredate, foredated, foredates, foredating, foredawn, foreday, foredays, foredeck, foredecks, foredeclare, foredecree, foredeem, foredeep, foredefeated, foredefine, foredenounce, foredescribe, foredeserved, foredesign, foredesignment, foredesk, foredestine, foredestined, foredestining, foredestiny, foredetermination, foredetermine, foredevised, foredevote, foredid, forediscern, foredispose, foredivine, foredo, foredoes, foredoing, foredone, foredoom, foredoomed, foredoomer, foredooming, foredooms, foredoor, foredune, foreface, forefaces, forefather, forefather's, forefatherly, forefathers, forefault, forefeel, forefeeling, forefeelingly, forefeels, forefeet, forefelt, forefence, forefend, forefended, forefending, forefends, foreffelt, forefield, forefigure, forefin, forefinger, forefinger's, forefingers, forefit, foreflank, foreflap, foreflipper, forefoot, forefront, forefronts, foregahger, foregallery, foregame, foreganger, foregate, foregather, foregift, foregirth, foreglance, foregleam, foreglimpse, foreglimpsed, foreglow, forego, foregoer, foregoers, foregoes, foregoing, foregone, foregoneness, foreground, foregrounds, foreguess, foreguidance, foregut, foreguts, forehalf, forehall, forehammer, forehand, forehanded, forehandedly, forehandedness, forehands, forehandsel, forehard, forehatch, forehatchway, forehead, forehead's, foreheaded, foreheads, forehear, forehearth, foreheater, forehent, forehew, forehill, forehinting, forehock, forehold, forehood, forehoof, forehoofs, forehook, forehooves, forehorse, foreign, foreigneering, foreigner, foreigners, foreignership, foreignism, foreignization, foreignize, foreignly, foreignness, foreigns, foreimagination, foreimagine, foreimpressed, foreimpression, foreinclined, foreinstruct, foreintend, foreiron, forejudge, forejudged, forejudger, forejudging, forejudgment, forekeel, foreking, foreknee, foreknew, foreknow, foreknowable, foreknowableness, foreknower, foreknowing, foreknowingly, foreknowledge, foreknown, foreknows, forel, foreladies, forelady, forelaid, foreland, forelands, forelay, forelaying, foreleader, foreleech, foreleg, forelegs, forelimb, forelimbs, forelive, forellenstein, forelock, forelocks, forelook, foreloop, forelooper, foreloper, forelouper, foremade, foreman, foremanship, foremarch, foremark, foremartyr, foremast, foremasthand, foremastman, foremastmen, foremasts, foremean, foremeant, foremelt, foremen, foremention, forementioned, foremessenger, foremilk, foremilks, foremind, foremisgiving, foremistress, foremost, foremostly, foremother, forename, forenamed, forenames, forenent, forenews, forenight, forenoon, forenoons, forenote, forenoted, forenotice, forenotion, forensal, forensic, forensical, forensicality, forensically, forensics, foreordain, foreordained, foreordaining, foreordainment, foreordainments, foreordains, foreorder, foreordinate, foreordinated, foreordinating, foreordination, foreorlop, forepad, forepale, forepaled, forepaling, foreparent, foreparents, forepart, foreparts, forepass, forepassed, forepast, forepaw, forepaws, forepayment, forepeak, forepeaks, foreperiod, forepiece, foreplace, foreplan, foreplanting, foreplay, foreplays, forepleasure, foreplot, forepoint, forepointer, forepole, forepoled, forepoling, foreporch, forepossessed, forepost, forepredicament, forepreparation, foreprepare, forepretended, foreprise, foreprize, foreproduct, foreproffer, forepromise, forepromised, foreprovided, foreprovision, forepurpose, forequarter, forequarters, forequoted, forerake, foreran, forerank, foreranks, forereach, forereaching, foreread, forereading, forerecited, forereckon, forerehearsed, foreremembered, forereport, forerequest, forerevelation, forerib, foreribs, forerigging, foreright, foreroom, foreroyal, forerun, forerunner, forerunners, forerunnership, forerunning, forerunnings, foreruns, fores, foresaddle, foresaid, foresail, foresails, foresaw, foresay, foresaying, foresays, forescene, forescent, foreschool, foreschooling, forescript, foreseason, foreseat, foresee, foreseeability, foreseeable, foreseeing, foreseeingly, foreseen, foreseer, foreseers, foresees, foreseing, foreseize, foresend, foresense, foresentence, foreset, foresettle, foresettled, foresey, foreshadow, foreshadowed, foreshadower, foreshadowing, foreshadows, foreshaft, foreshank, foreshape, foresheet, foresheets, foreshift, foreship, foreshock, foreshoe, foreshop, foreshore, foreshorten, foreshortened, foreshortening, foreshortens, foreshot, foreshots, foreshoulder, foreshow, foreshowed, foreshower, foreshowing, foreshown, foreshows, foreshroud, foreside, foresides, foresight, foresighted, foresightedly, foresightedness, foresightful, foresightless, foresights, foresign, foresignify, foresin, foresing, foresinger, foreskin, foreskins, foreskirt, foreslack, foresleeve, foreslow, foresound, forespake, forespeak, forespeaker, forespeaking, forespecified, forespeech, forespeed, forespencer, forespent, forespoke, forespoken, forest, forestaff, forestaffs, forestage, forestair, forestal, forestall, forestalled, forestaller, forestalling, forestallment, forestalls, forestalment, forestarling, forestate, forestation, forestaves, forestay, forestays, forestaysail, forestcraft, forested, foresteep, forestem, forestep, forester, foresters, forestership, forestery, forestful, forestial, forestick, forestine, foresting, forestish, forestland, forestless, forestlike, forestology, forestral, forestress, forestries, forestry, forests, forestside, forestudy, forestwards, foresty, foresummer, foresummon, foreswear, foreswearing, foresweat, foreswore, foresworn, foret, foretack, foretackle, foretake, foretalk, foretalking, foretaste, foretasted, foretaster, foretastes, foretasting, foreteach, foreteeth, foretell, foretellable, foretellableness, foreteller, foretellers, foretelling, foretells, forethink, forethinker, forethinking, forethough, forethought, forethoughted, forethoughtful, forethoughtfully, forethoughtfulness, forethoughtless, forethrift, foretime, foretimed, foretimes, foretoken, foretokened, foretokening, foretokens, foretold, foretooth, foretop, foretopman, foretopmast, foretopmen, foretops, foretopsail, foretrace, foretriangle, foretrysail, foreturn, foretype, foretypified, foreuse, foreutter, forevalue, forever, forevermore, foreverness, forevers, foreview, forevision, forevouch, forevouched, forevow, foreward, forewarm, forewarmer, forewarn, forewarned, forewarner, forewarning, forewarningly, forewarnings, forewarns, forewaters, foreween, foreweep, foreweigh, forewent, forewind, forewing, forewings, forewinning, forewisdom, forewish, forewit, forewoman, forewomen, forewonted, foreword, forewords, foreworld, foreworn, forewritten, forewrought, forex, foreyard, foreyards, foreyear, forfairn, forfalt, forfar, forfare, forfars, forfault, forfaulture, forfear, forfeit, forfeitable, forfeitableness, forfeited, forfeiter, forfeiting, forfeits, forfeiture, forfeitures, forfend, forfended, forfending, forfends, forfex, forficate, forficated, forfication, forficiform, forficulate, forfit, forfouchten, forfoughen, forfoughten, forgab, forgainst, forgat, forgather, forgathered, forgathering, forgathers, forgave, forge, forgeability, forgeable, forged, forgedly, forgeful, forgeman, forgemen, forger, forgeries, forgers, forgery, forgery's, forges, forget, forgetable, forgetful, forgetfully, forgetfulness, forgetive, forgetness, forgets, forgett, forgettable, forgettably, forgette, forgetter, forgetters, forgettery, forgetting, forgettingly, forgie, forgift, forging, forgings, forgivable, forgivableness, forgivably, forgive, forgiveable, forgiveably, forgiveless, forgiven, forgiveness, forgivenesses, forgiver, forgivers, forgives, forgiving, forgivingly, forgivingness, forgo, forgoer, forgoers, forgoes, forgoing, forgone, forgot, forgotten, forgottenness, forgrow, forgrown, forhaile, forhale, forheed, forhoo, forhooie, forhooy, forhow, forinsec, forinsecal, forint, forints, forisfamiliate, forisfamiliation, forjaskit, forjesket, forjudge, forjudged, forjudger, forjudges, forjudging, forjudgment, fork, forkable, forkbeard, forked, forkedly, forkedness, forker, forkers, forkful, forkfuls, forkhead, forkier, forkiest, forkiness, forking, forkless, forklift, forklifts, forklike, forkman, forkmen, forks, forksful, forksmith, forktail, forkwise, forky, forlain, forlana, forlanas, forlane, forlay, forleave, forleaving, forleft, forleit, forlese, forlet, forletting, forlie, forlive, forloin, forlore, forlorn, forlorner, forlornest, forlornity, forlornly, forlornness, form, forma, formability, formable, formably, formagen, formagenic, formal, formalazine, formaldehyd, formaldehyde, formaldehydesulphoxylate, formaldehydesulphoxylic, formaldoxime, formalesque, formalin, formalins, formalisation, formalise, formalised, formaliser, formalising, formalism, formalism's, formalisms, formalist, formalistic, formalistically, formaliter, formalith, formalities, formality, formalizable, formalization, formalization's, formalizations, formalize, formalized, formalizer, formalizes, formalizing, formally, formalness, formals, formamide, formamidine, formamido, formamidoxime, formanilide, formant, formants, format, formate, formated, formates, formating, formation, formation's, formational, formations, formative, formatively, formativeness, formats, formatted, formatter, formatter's, formatters, formatting, formature, formazan, formazyl, formboard, formby, forme, formed, formedon, formee, formel, formelt, formene, formenic, formentation, former, formeret, formerly, formerness, formers, formes, formfeed, formfeeds, formfitting, formful, formiate, formic, formica, formican, formicaria, formicarian, formicaries, formicarioid, formicarium, formicaroid, formicary, formicate, formicated, formicating, formication, formicative, formicicide, formicid, formicide, formicine, formicivorous, formidability, formidable, formidableness, formidably, formidolous, formin, forminate, forming, formism, formity, formless, formlessly, formlessness, formly, formnail, formol, formolit, formolite, formols, formonitrile, formose, formosity, formous, formoxime, forms, formula, formula's, formulable, formulae, formulaic, formulaically, formular, formularies, formularisation, formularise, formularised, formulariser, formularising, formularism, formularist, formularistic, formularization, formularize, formularized, formularizer, formularizing, formulary, formulas, formulate, formulated, formulates, formulating, formulation, formulations, formulator, formulator's, formulators, formulatory, formule, formulisation, formulise, formulised, formuliser, formulising, formulism, formulist, formulistic, formulization, formulize, formulized, formulizer, formulizing, formwork, formy, formyl, formylal, formylate, formylated, formylating, formylation, formyls, fornacic, fornaxid, forncast, fornenst, fornent, fornical, fornicate, fornicated, fornicates, fornicating, fornication, fornications, fornicator, fornicators, fornicatory, fornicatress, fornicatrices, fornicatrix, fornices, forniciform, forninst, fornix, forold, forpass, forpet, forpine, forpined, forpining, forpit, forprise, forra, forrad, forrader, forrard, forrarder, forrel, forride, forril, forrit, forritsome, forrue, forsado, forsake, forsaken, forsakenly, forsakenness, forsaker, forsakers, forsakes, forsaking, forsar, forsay, forsee, forseeable, forseek, forseen, forset, forshape, forslack, forslake, forsloth, forslow, forsook, forsooth, forspeak, forspeaking, forspend, forspent, forspoke, forspoken, forspread, forstall, forstand, forsteal, forsterite, forstraught, forsung, forswat, forswear, forswearer, forswearing, forswears, forswore, forsworn, forswornness, forsythia, forsythias, fort, fort's, fortake, fortalice, fortaxed, forte, fortemente, fortepiano, fortes, fortescue, fortescure, forth, forthbring, forthbringer, forthbringing, forthbrought, forthby, forthcall, forthcame, forthcome, forthcomer, forthcoming, forthcomingness, forthcut, forthfare, forthfigured, forthgaze, forthgo, forthgoing, forthink, forthinking, forthon, forthought, forthputting, forthright, forthrightly, forthrightness, forthrights, forthset, forthtell, forthteller, forthward, forthwith, forthy, fortier, forties, fortieth, fortieths, fortifiable, fortification, fortifications, fortified, fortifier, fortifiers, fortifies, fortify, fortifying, fortifyingly, fortifys, fortilage, fortin, fortiori, fortis, fortissimi, fortissimo, fortissimos, fortitude, fortitudes, fortitudinous, fortlet, fortnight, fortnightlies, fortnightly, fortnights, fortran, fortranh, fortravail, fortread, fortress, fortress's, fortressed, fortresses, fortressing, forts, fortuities, fortuitism, fortuitist, fortuitous, fortuitously, fortuitousness, fortuitus, fortuity, fortunate, fortunately, fortunateness, fortunation, fortune, fortune's, fortuned, fortunel, fortuneless, fortunes, fortunetell, fortuneteller, fortunetellers, fortunetelling, fortuning, fortunite, fortunize, fortunous, fortuuned, forty, fortyfive, fortyfives, fortyfold, fortyish, fortypenny, forum, forum's, forumize, forums, forvay, forwake, forwaked, forwalk, forwander, forward, forwardal, forwardation, forwarded, forwarder, forwarders, forwardest, forwarding, forwardly, forwardness, forwards, forwardsearch, forwarn, forwaste, forwean, forwear, forwearied, forweary, forwearying, forweend, forweep, forwelk, forwent, forwhy, forwoden, forworden, forwore, forwork, forworn, forwrap, foryield, forz, forzando, forzandos, forzato, fosh, fosie, foss, fossa, fossae, fossage, fossane, fossarian, fossate, fosse, fossed, fosses, fosset, fossette, fossettes, fossick, fossicked, fossicker, fossicking, fossicks, fossified, fossiform, fossil, fossilage, fossilated, fossilation, fossildom, fossiled, fossiliferous, fossilification, fossilify, fossilisable, fossilisation, fossilise, fossilised, fossilising, fossilism, fossilist, fossilizable, fossilization, fossilize, fossilized, fossilizes, fossilizing, fossillike, fossilogist, fossilogy, fossilological, fossilologist, fossilology, fossils, fosslfying, fosslify, fosslology, fossor, fossores, fossorial, fossorious, fossors, fossula, fossulae, fossulate, fossule, fossulet, fostell, foster, fosterable, fosterage, fostered, fosterer, fosterers, fosterhood, fostering, fosteringly, fosterite, fosterland, fosterling, fosterlings, fosters, fostership, fostress, fot, fotch, fotched, fother, fothering, fotive, fotmal, fotui, fou, foud, foudroyant, fouett, fouette, fouettee, fouettes, fougade, fougasse, fought, foughten, foughty, fougue, foujdar, foujdarry, foujdary, foul, foulage, foulard, foulards, foulbrood, foulder, fouldre, fouled, fouler, foulest, fouling, foulings, foulish, foully, foulmart, foulminded, foulmouth foulmouthed, foulmouthedly, foulmouthedness, foulness, foulnesses, fouls, foulsome, foumart, foun, founce, found, foundation, foundation's, foundational, foundationally, foundationary, foundationed, foundationer, foundationless, foundationlessness, foundations, founded, founder, foundered, foundering, founderous, founders, foundership, foundery, founding, foundling, foundlings, foundress, foundries, foundrous, foundry, foundry's, foundryman, foundrymen, founds, fount, fount's, fountain, fountain's, fountained, fountaineer, fountainhead, fountainheads, fountaining, fountainless, fountainlet, fountainlike, fountainous, fountainously, fountains, fountainwise, founte, fountful, founts, fouquieriaceous, four, fourb, fourbagger, fourball, fourberie, fourble, fourche, fourchee, fourcher, fourchet, fourchette, fourchite, fourdrinier, fourer, fourfiusher, fourflusher, fourflushers, fourfold, fourgon, fourgons, fourhanded, fourier, fourierism, fourling, fourneau, fourness, fourniture, fourpence, fourpenny, fourposter, fourposters, fourpounder, fourquine, fourrag, fourragere, fourrageres, fourre, fourrier, fours, fourscore, fourscorth, foursome, foursomes, foursquare, foursquarely, foursquareness, fourstrand, fourteen, fourteener, fourteenfold, fourteens, fourteenth, fourteenthly, fourteenths, fourth, fourther, fourthly, fourths, foussa, foute, fouter, fouth, foutra, foutre, fouty, fovea, foveae, foveal, foveate, foveated, foveation, foveiform, fovent, foveola, foveolae, foveolar, foveolarious, foveolas, foveolate, foveolated, foveole, foveoles, foveolet, foveolets, fovilla, fow, fowage, fowells, fowent, fowk, fowl, fowled, fowler, fowlerite, fowlers, fowlery, fowlfoot, fowling, fowlings, fowlpox, fowlpoxes, fowls, fox, fox's, foxbane, foxberries, foxberry, foxchop, foxed, foxer, foxery, foxes, foxfeet, foxfinger, foxfire, foxfires, foxfish, foxfishes, foxglove, foxgloves, foxhole, foxholes, foxhound, foxhounds, foxie, foxier, foxiest, foxily, foxiness, foxinesses, foxing, foxings, foxish, foxite, foxlike, foxly, foxproof, foxship, foxskin, foxskins, foxtail, foxtailed, foxtails, foxtongue, foxtrot, foxwood, foxy, foy, foyaite, foyaitic, foyboat, foyer, foyers, foys, foysen, fozier, foziest, foziness, fozinesses, fozy, fp, fplot, fpm, fps, fpsps, fr, fra, frab, frabbit, frabjous, frabjously, frabous, fracas, fracases, fracedinous, frache, fracid, frack, fract, fractable, fractabling, fractal, fractals, fracted, fractile, fraction, fraction's, fractional, fractionalism, fractionalization, fractionalize, fractionalized, fractionalizing, fractionally, fractionary, fractionate, fractionated, fractionating, fractionation, fractionator, fractioned, fractioning, fractionisation, fractionise, fractionised, fractionising, fractionization, fractionize, fractionized, fractionizing, fractionlet, fractions, fractious, fractiously, fractiousness, fractocumulus, fractonimbus, fractostratus, fractuosity, fractur, fracturable, fracturableness, fractural, fracture, fractured, fractureproof, fractures, fracturing, fracturs, fractus, fradicin, frae, fraela, fraena, fraenula, fraenular, fraenulum, fraenum, fraenums, frag, fragged, fragging, fraggings, fraghan, fragile, fragilely, fragileness, fragilities, fragility, fragment, fragmental, fragmentalize, fragmentally, fragmentarily, fragmentariness, fragmentary, fragmentate, fragmentation, fragmented, fragmenting, fragmentisation, fragmentise, fragmentised, fragmentising, fragmentist, fragmentitious, fragmentization, fragmentize, fragmentized, fragmentizer, fragmentizing, fragments, fragor, fragrance, fragrance's, fragrances, fragrancies, fragrancy, fragrant, fragrantly, fragrantness, frags, fraicheur, fraid, fraidycat, fraik, frail, fraile, frailejon, frailer, frailero, fraileros, frailes, frailest, frailish, frailly, frailness, frails, frailties, frailty, fraischeur, fraise, fraised, fraiser, fraises, fraising, fraist, fraken, frakfurt, fraktur, frakturs, framable, framableness, frambesia, framboesia, framboise, frame, framea, frameable, frameableness, frameae, framed, frameless, framer, framers, frames, frameshift, framesmith, framework, framework's, frameworks, framing, frammit, frampler, frampold, franc, franca, francas, france, france's, frances, franchisal, franchise, franchise's, franchised, franchisee, franchisees, franchisement, franchiser, franchisers, franchises, franchising, franchisor, francia, francic, francis, francisc, francisca, franciscan, franciscans, francisco, francium, franciums, francize, franco, francolin, francolite, francophil, francophile, francophone, francs, frangent, franger, frangibility, frangible, frangibleness, frangipane, frangipani, frangipanis, frangipanni, frangula, frangulic, frangulin, frangulinic, franion, frank, frankability, frankable, frankalmoign, frankalmoigne, frankalmoin, franked, frankeniaceous, frankenstein, frankensteins, franker, frankers, frankest, frankfold, frankfort, frankforter, frankfurt, frankfurter, frankfurters, frankhearted, frankheartedly, frankheartedness, frankheartness, frankincense, frankincensed, franking, frankish, franklandite, franklin, franklinian, franklinite, franklins, frankly, frankmarriage, frankness, frankpledge, franks, franseria, frantic, frantically, franticly, franticness, franz, franzy, frap, frape, fraple, frapler, frapp, frappe, frapped, frappeed, frappeing, frappes, frapping, fraps, frary, frasco, frase, fraser, frasier, frass, frasse, frat, fratch, fratched, fratcheous, fratcher, fratchety, fratching, fratchy, frate, frater, frateries, fraternal, fraternalism, fraternalist, fraternality, fraternally, fraternate, fraternation, fraternisation, fraternise, fraternised, fraterniser, fraternising, fraternism, fraternities, fraternity, fraternity's, fraternization, fraternize, fraternized, fraternizer, fraternizes, fraternizing, fraters, fratery, fratority, fratriage, fratricidal, fratricide, fratricides, fratries, fratry, frats, frau, fraud, fraud's, frauder, fraudful, fraudfully, fraudless, fraudlessly, fraudlessness, fraudproof, frauds, fraudulence, fraudulency, fraudulent, fraudulently, fraudulentness, frauen, fraughan, fraught, fraughtage, fraughted, fraughting, fraughts, fraulein, frauleins, fraunch, fraus, fravashi, frawn, fraxetin, fraxin, fraxinella, fray, frayed, frayedly, frayedness, fraying, frayings, frayn, frayne, frayproof, frays, fraze, frazed, frazer, frazil, frazing, frazzle, frazzled, frazzles, frazzling, frden, freak, freak's, freakdom, freaked, freakery, freakful, freakier, freakiest, freakily, freakiness, freaking, freakish, freakishly, freakishness, freakout, freakouts, freakpot, freaks, freaky, fream, freath, freck, frecked, frecken, freckened, frecket, freckle, freckled, freckledness, freckleproof, freckles, frecklier, freckliest, freckliness, freckling, frecklish, freckly, fred, fredaine, freddo, frederick, frederik, fredricite, free, freebee, freebees, freebie, freebies, freeboard, freeboot, freebooted, freebooter, freebooters, freebootery, freebooting, freeboots, freebooty, freeborn, freeby, freed, freedman, freedmen, freedom, freedom's, freedoms, freedoot, freedstool, freedwoman, freedwomen, freefd, freeform, freehand, freehanded, freehandedly, freehandedness, freehearted, freeheartedly, freeheartedness, freehold, freeholder, freeholders, freeholdership, freeholding, freeholds, freeing, freeings, freeish, freelage, freelance, freelanced, freelancer, freelances, freelancing, freeload, freeloaded, freeloader, freeloaders, freeloading, freeloads, freeloving, freelovism, freely, freeman, freemanship, freemartin, freemason, freemasonic, freemasonical, freemasonism, freemasonry, freemasons, freemen, freen, freend, freeness, freenesses, freeport, freer, freers, frees, freesheet, freesia, freesias, freesilverism, freesilverite, freesp, freespac, freespace, freest, freestanding, freestone, freestones, freestyle, freestyler, freet, freethink, freethinker, freethinkers, freethinking, freetrader, freety, freeward, freeway, freeways, freewheel, freewheeler, freewheelers, freewheeling, freewheelingness, freewill, freewoman, freewomen, freezable, freeze, freezed, freezer, freezers, freezes, freezing, freezingly, freezy, fregit, freibergite, freieslebenite, freiezlebenhe, freight, freightage, freighted, freighter, freighters, freighting, freightless, freightliner, freightment, freights, freightyard, freijo, freinage, freir, freit, freith, freity, fremd, fremdly, fremdness, fremescence, fremescent, fremitus, fremituses, fremt, fren, frena, frenal, frenate, french, frenched, frenchen, frenches, frenchification, frenchify, frenching, frenchism, frenchman, frenchmen, frenchwoman, frenchwomen, frenetic, frenetical, frenetically, frenetics, frenne, frenula, frenular, frenulum, frenum, frenums, frenuna, frenzelite, frenzic, frenzied, frenziedly, frenziedness, frenzies, frenzily, frenzy, frenzying, freon, freq, frequence, frequencies, frequency, frequent, frequentable, frequentage, frequentation, frequentative, frequented, frequenter, frequenters, frequentest, frequenting, frequently, frequentness, frequents, frere, freres, frescade, fresco, frescoed, frescoer, frescoers, frescoes, frescoing, frescoist, frescoists, frescos, fresh, freshed, freshen, freshened, freshener, fresheners, freshening, freshens, fresher, freshes, freshest, freshet, freshets, freshhearted, freshing, freshish, freshly, freshman, freshmanhood, freshmanic, freshmanship, freshmen, freshment, freshness, freshwater, freshwoman, fresison, fresne, fresnel, fresnels, fresno, fress, fresser, fret, fretful, fretfully, fretfulness, fretish, fretize, fretless, frets, fretsaw, fretsaws, fretsome, frett, frettage, frettation, frette, fretted, fretten, fretter, fretters, frettier, frettiest, fretting, frettingly, fretty, fretum, fretways, fretwise, fretwork, fretworked, fretworks, freud, freudian, freudianism, freudians, frey, freya, freyalite, friability, friable, friableness, friand, friandise, friar, friar's, friarbird, friarhood, friaries, friarling, friarly, friars, friary, friation, frib, fribble, fribbled, fribbleism, fribbler, fribblers, fribblery, fribbles, fribbling, fribblish, fribby, friborg, friborgh, fribourg, fricace, fricandeau, fricandeaus, fricandeaux, fricandel, fricandelle, fricando, fricandoes, fricassee, fricasseed, fricasseeing, fricassees, fricasseing, frication, fricative, fricatives, fricatrice, frickle, fricti, friction, friction's, frictionable, frictional, frictionally, frictionize, frictionized, frictionizing, frictionless, frictionlessly, frictionlessness, frictionproof, frictions, friday, friday's, fridays, fridge, fridges, fridstool, fried, friedcake, friedelite, friedman, friedrichsdor, friend, friend's, friended, friending, friendless, friendlessness, friendlier, friendlies, friendliest, friendlike, friendlily, friendliness, friendliwise, friendly, friends, friendship, friendship's, friendships, frier, friers, fries, friese, frieseite, friesian, frieze, frieze's, friezed, friezer, friezes, friezing, friezy, frig, frigage, frigate, frigate's, frigates, frigatoon, frigefact, frigga, frigged, frigger, frigging, friggle, fright, frightable, frighted, frighten, frightenable, frightened, frightenedly, frightenedness, frightener, frightening, frighteningly, frighteningness, frightens, frighter, frightful, frightfully, frightfulness, frighting, frightless, frightment, frights, frightsome, frighty, frigid, frigidaire, frigidaria, frigidarium, frigiddaria, frigidities, frigidity, frigidly, frigidness, frigidoreceptor, frigiferous, frigolabile, frigor, frigoric, frigorific, frigorifical, frigorifico, frigorify, frigorimeter, frigostable, frigotherapy, frigs, frijol, frijole, frijoles, frijolillo, frijolito, frike, frilal, frill, frill's, frillback, frilled, friller, frillers, frillery, frillier, frillies, frilliest, frillily, frilliness, frilling, frillings, frills, frilly, frim, frimaire, frimitts, fringe, fringed, fringeflower, fringefoot, fringehead, fringeless, fringelet, fringelike, fringent, fringepod, fringes, fringier, fringiest, fringillaceous, fringillid, fringilliform, fringilline, fringilloid, fringiness, fringing, fringy, friponerie, fripper, fripperer, fripperies, frippery, frippet, fris, frisado, frisbee, frisbees, frisca, friscal, frisch, frisco, frise, frises, frisette, frisettes, friseur, friseurs, frisian, frisk, frisked, frisker, friskers, friskest, frisket, friskets, friskful, friskier, friskiest, friskily, friskin, friskiness, frisking,

215

friskingly, friskle, frisks, frisky, frislet, frisolee, frison, friss, frisson, frissons, frist, frisure, friszka, frit, frith, frithborgh, frithborh, frithbot, frithles, friths, frithsoken, frithstool, frithwork, frithy, fritillaria, fritillaries, fritillary, fritniency, frits, fritt, frittata, fritted, fritter, frittered, fritterer, fritterers, frittering, fritters, fritting, fritts, fritz, frivol, frivoled, frivoler, frivolers, frivoling, frivolism, frivolist, frivolities, frivolity, frivolize, frivolized, frivolizing, frivolled, frivoller, frivolling, frivolous, frivolously, frivolousness, frivols, frixion, friz, frizado, frize, frized, frizel, frizer, frizers, frizes, frizette, frizettes, frizing, frizz, frizzante, frizzed, frizzen, frizzer, frizzers, frizzes, frizzier, frizziest, frizzily, frizziness, frizzing, frizzle, frizzled, frizzler, frizzlers, frizzles, frizzlier, frizzliest, frizzling, frizzly, frizzy, fro, frock, frock's, frocked, frocking, frockless, frocklike, frockmaker, frocks, froe, froeman, froes, frog, frog's, frogbit, frogeater, frogeye, frogeyed, frogeyes, frogface, frogfish, frogfishes, frogflower, frogfoot, frogged, frogger, froggery, froggier, froggies, froggiest, frogginess, frogging, froggish, froggy, froghood, froghopper, frogland, frogleaf, frogleg, froglet, froglets, froglike, frogling, frogman, frogmarch, frogmen, frogmouth, frogmouths, frognose, frogs, frogskin, frogskins, frogspawn, frogstool, frogtongue, frogwort, frohlich, froideur, froise, froisse, frokin, frolic, frolicful, frolicked, frolicker, frolickers, frolicking, frolickly, frolicks, frolicky, frolicly, frolicness, frolics, frolicsome, frolicsomely, frolicsomeness, from, fromage, fromages, fromenties, fromenty, fromfile, fromward, fromwards, frond, frondage, frondation, fronde, fronded, frondent, frondesce, frondesced, frondescence, frondescent, frondescing, frondeur, frondeurs, frondiferous, frondiform, frondigerous, frondivorous, frondless, frondlet, frondose, frondosely, frondous, fronds, frons, front, frontad, frontage, frontager, frontages, frontal, frontalis, frontality, frontally, frontals, frontate, frontbencher, frontcourt, fronted, frontenis, fronter, frontes, frontier, frontier's, frontierless, frontierlike, frontierman, frontiers, frontiersman, frontiersmen, frontignac, frontignan, fronting, frontingly, frontis, frontispiece, frontispieced, frontispieces, frontispiecing, frontlash, frontless, frontlessly, frontlessness, frontlet, frontlets, frontoauricular, frontoethmoid, frontogenesis, frontolysis, frontomalar, frontomallar, frontomaxillary, frontomental, fronton, frontonasal, frontons, frontooccipital, frontoorbital, frontoparietal, frontopontine, frontosphenoidal, frontosquamosal, frontotemporal, frontozygomatic, frontpiece, frontrunner, fronts, frontsman, frontspiece, frontspieces, frontstall, fronture, frontward, frontwards, frontways, frontwise, froom, froppish, frore, froren, frory, frosh, frosk, frost, frostation, frostbird, frostbit, frostbite, frostbiter, frostbites, frostbiting, frostbitten, frostbound, frostbow, frosted, frosteds, froster, frostfish, frostfishes, frostflower, frostier, frostiest, frostily, frostiness, frosting, frostings, frostless, frostlike, frostnipped, frostproof, frostproofing, frostroot, frosts, frostweed, frostwork, frostwort, frosty, frot, froth, frothed, frother, frothier, frothiest, frothily, frothiness, frothing, frothless, froths, frothsome, frothy, frottage, frottages, frotted, frotteur, frotteurs, frotting, frottola, frottole, frotton, froufrou, froufrous, frough, froughy, frounce, frounced, frounceless, frounces, frouncing, frousier, frousiest, froust, frousty, frousy, frouze, frouzier, frouziest, frouzy, frow, froward, frowardly, frowardness, frower, frowl, frown, frowned, frowner, frowners, frownful, frowning, frowningly, frownless, frowns, frowny, frows, frowsier, frowsiest, frowsily, frowsiness, frowst, frowstier, frowstiest, frowstily, frowstiness, frowsty, frowsy, frowy, frowze, frowzier, frowziest, frowzily, frowziness, frowzled, frowzly, frowzy, froze, frozen, frozenhearted, frozenly, frozenness, frs, frsiket, frsikets, frt, frubbish, fruchtschiefer, fructed, fructescence, fructescent, fructiculose, fructicultural, fructiculture, fructidor, fructiferous, fructiferously, fructiferousness, fructification, fructificative, fructified, fructifier, fructifies, fructiform, fructify, fructifying, fructiparous, fructivorous, fructokinase, fructosan, fructose, fructoses, fructoside, fructuarius, fructuary, fructuate, fructuose, fructuosity, fructuous, fructuously, fructuousness, fructure, fructus, frug, frugal, frugalism, frugalist, frugalities, frugality, frugally, frugalness, fruggan, frugged, fruggin, frugging, frugiferous, frugiferousness, frugivorous, frugs, fruit, fruit's, fruitade, fruitage, fruitages, fruitarian, fruitarianism, fruitbearing, fruitcake, fruitcakes, fruitcakey, fruited, fruiter, fruiterer, fruiterers, fruiteress, fruiteries, fruiters, fruitery, fruitester, fruitful, fruitfuller, fruitfullest, fruitfullness, fruitfully, fruitfulness, fruitgrower, fruitgrowing, fruitier, fruitiest, fruitiness, fruiting, fruition, fruitions, fruitist, fruitive, fruitless, fruitlessly, fruitlessness, fruitlet, fruitlets, fruitlike, fruitling, fruits, fruitstalk, fruittime, fruitwise, fruitwoman, fruitwomen, fruitwood, fruitworm, fruity, frumaryl, frument, frumentaceous, frumentarious, frumentation, frumenties, frumentum, frumenty, frumety, frump, frumperies, frumpery, frumpier, frumpiest, frumpily, frumpiness, frumpish, frumpishly, frumpishness, frumple, frumpled, frumpling, frumps, frumpy, frundel, frush, frusla, frust, frusta, frustrable, frustraneous, frustrate, frustrated, frustrately, frustrater, frustrates, frustrating, frustratingly, frustration, frustrations, frustrative, frustratory, frustula, frustule, frustulent, frustules, frustulose, frustulum, frustum, frustums, frutage, frutescence, frutescent, frutex, fruticant, fruticeous, frutices, fruticeta, fruticetum, fruticose, fruticous, fruticulose, fruticulture, frutify, frutilla, fruz, frwy, fry, fryer, fryers, frying, frypan, frypans, fs, fsiest, fstore, ft, fth, fthm, ftncmd, ftnerr, fu, fuage, fub, fubbed, fubbery, fubbing, fubby, fubs, fubsier, fubsiest, fubsy, fucaceous, fucate, fucation, fucatious, fuchi, fuchsia, fuchsias, fuchsin, fuchsine, fuchsines, fuchsinophil, fuchsinophilous, fuchsins, fuchsite, fuchsone, fuci, fucinita, fuciphagous, fucivorous, fuck, fucked, fucker, fucking, fucks, fuckwit, fucoid, fucoidal, fucoidin, fucoids, fucosan, fucose, fucoses, fucous, fucoxanthin, fucoxanthine, fucus, fucused, fucuses, fud, fudder, fuddle, fuddlebrained, fuddled, fuddledness, fuddlement, fuddler, fuddles, fuddling, fuder, fudge, fudged, fudger, fudges, fudging, fudgy, fuds, fuegian, fuehrer, fuehrers, fuel, fueled, fueler, fuelers, fueling, fuelizer, fuelled, fueller, fuellers, fuelling, fuels, fuerte, fuff, fuffit, fuffle, fuffy, fug, fugacious, fugaciously, fugaciousness, fugacities, fugacity, fugacy, fugal, fugally, fugara, fugard, fugate, fugato, fugatos, fugged, fuggier, fuggiest, fugging, fuggy, fughetta, fughettas, fughette, fugie, fugient, fugio, fugios, fugit, fugitate, fugitated, fugitating, fugitation, fugitive, fugitive's, fugitively, fugitiveness, fugitives, fugitivism, fugitivity, fugle, fugled, fugleman, fuglemanship, fuglemen, fugler, fugles, fugling, fugs, fugu, fugue, fugued, fuguelike, fugues, fuguing, fuguist, fuguists, fuhrer, fuhrers, fuidhir, fuirdays, fuji, fujis, fula, fulani, fulciform, fulciment, fulcra, fulcraceous, fulcral, fulcrate, fulcrum, fulcrumage, fulcrumed, fulcruming, fulcrums, fulfil, fulfill, fulfilled, fulfiller, fulfillers, fulfilling, fulfillment, fulfillments, fulfills, fulfilment, fulfils, fulful, fulfullment, fulgence, fulgency, fulgent, fulgently, fulgentness, fulgid, fulgide, fulgidity, fulgor, fulgorid, fulgorous, fulgour, fulgourous, fulgural, fulgurant, fulgurantly, fulgurata, fulgurate, fulgurated, fulgurating, fulguration, fulgurator, fulgurite, fulgurous, fulham, fulhams, fulicine, fuliginosity, fuliginous, fuliginously, fuliginousness, fuligo, fuliguline, fulimart, fulk, full, fullage, fullam, fullams, fullback, fullbacks, fullbodied, fulldo, fulled, fuller, fullerboard, fullered, fulleries, fullering, fullers, fullery, fullest, fullface, fullfaces, fullfil, fullgrownness, fullhearted, fulling, fullish, fullmouth, fullmouthed, fullmouthedly, fullness, fullnesses, fullom, fulls, fullterm, fulltime, fullword, fullwords, fully, fullymart, fulmar, fulmars, fulmen, fulmicotton, fulmina, fulminancy, fulminant, fulminate, fulminated, fulminates, fulminating, fulmination, fulminations, fulminator, fulminatory, fulmine, fulmined, fulmineous, fulmines, fulminic, fulmining, fulminous, fulminurate, fulminuric, fulness, fulnesses, fulsamic, fulsome, fulsomely, fulsomeness, fulth, fultz, fulvene, fulvescent, fulvid, fulvidness, fulvous, fulwa, fulyie, fulzie, fum, fumacious, fumade, fumado, fumados, fumage, fumagine, fumant, fumarase, fumarases, fumarate, fumarates, fumaria, fumariaceous, fumaric, fumarin, fumarine, fumarium, fumaroid, fumaroidal, fumarole, fumaroles, fumarolic, fumaryl, fumatoria, fumatories, fumatorium, fumatoriums, fumatory, fumattoria, fumble, fumbled, fumbler, fumblers, fumbles, fumbling, fumblingly, fumblingness, fumbulator, fume, fumed, fumeless, fumelike, fumer, fumerel, fumeroot, fumers, fumes, fumet, fumets, fumette, fumettes, fumeuse, fumeuses, fumewort, fumid, fumidity, fumiduct, fumier, fumiest, fumiferana, fumiferous, fumify, fumigant, fumigants, fumigate, fumigated, fumigates, fumigating, fumigation, fumigations, fumigator, fumigatories, fumigatorium, fumigators, fumigatory, fumily, fuminess, fuming, fumingly, fumish, fumishing, fumishly, fumishness, fumistery, fumitories, fumitory, fummel, fummle, fumose, fumosity, fumous, fumously, fumuli, fumulus, fumy, fun, funambulant, funambulate, funambulated, funambulating, funambulation, funambulator, funambulatory, funambule, funambulic, funambulism, funambulist, funambulo, funambuloes, funariaceous, funbre, function, function's, functional, functionalism, functionalist, functionalistic, functionalities, functionality, functionalize, functionalized, functionalizing, functionally, functionals, functionaries, functionarism, functionary, functionate, functionated, functionating, functionation, functioned, functioning, functionize, functionless, functionlessness, functionnaire, functions, functor, functor's, functorial, functors, functus, fund, fundable, fundal, fundament, fundamental, fundamentalism, fundamentalist, fundamentalistic, fundamentalists, fundamentality, fundamentally, fundamentalness, fundamentals, fundatorial, fundatrices, fundatrix, funded, funder, funders, fundholder, fundi, fundic, fundiform, funding, funditor, funditores, fundless, fundmonger, fundmongering, fundraise, fundraising, funds, funduck, funduline, fundungi, fundus, funebre, funebrial, funebrious, funebrous, funeral, funeral's, funeralize, funerally, funerals, funerary, funerate, funeration, funereal, funereality, funereally, funerealness, funest, funestal, funfair, funfairs, funfest, fungaceous, fungal, fungals, fungate, fungated, fungating, fungation, funge, fungi, fungian, fungibility, fungible, fungibles, fungic, fungicidal, fungicidally, fungicide, fungicides, fungicolous, fungid, fungiferous, fungiform, fungify, fungilliform, fungillus, fungin, fungistat, fungistatic, fungistatically, fungite, fungitoxic, fungitoxicity, fungivorous, fungo, fungoes, fungoid, fungoidal, fungoids, fungological, fungologist, fungology, fungose, fungosities, fungosity, fungous, fungus, fungused, funguses, funguslike, fungusy, funic, funicle, funicles, funicular, funiculars, funiculate, funicule, funiculi, funiculitis, funiculus, funiform, funiliform, funipendulous, funis, funk, funked, funker, funkers, funkia, funkias, funkier, funkiest, funkiness, funking, funks, funky, funli, funmaker, funmaking, funned, funnel, funneled, funnelform, funneling, funnelled, funnellike, funnelling, funnels, funnelwise, funnier, funnies, funniest, funnily, funniment, funniness, funning, funny, funnyman, funnymen, funori, funorin, funs, funster, funt, fur, fur's, furacana, furacious, furaciousness, furacity, fural, furaldehyde, furan, furandi, furane, furanes, furanoid, furanose, furanoses, furanoside, furans, furazan, furazane, furazolidone, furbearer, furbelow, furbelowed, furbelowing, furbelows, furbish, furbishable, furbished, furbisher, furbishes, furbishing, furbishment, furca, furcae, furcal, furcate, furcated, furcately, furcates, furcating, furcation, furcellate, furciferine, furciferous, furciform, furcilia, furcraea, furcraeas, furcula, furculae, furcular, furcule, furculum, furdel, furdle, furfur, furfuraceous, furfuraceously, furfural, furfuralcohol, furfuraldehyde, furfurals, furfuramid, furfuramide, furfuran, furfurans, furfuration, furfures, furfurine, furfuroid, furfurol, furfurole, furfurous, furfuryl, furfurylidene, furial, furiant, furibund, furicane, furied, furies, furify, furil, furile, furilic, furiosa, furiosity, furioso, furious, furiouser, furiousity, furiously, furiousness, furison, furivae, furl, furlable, furlana, furlanas, furlane, furled, furler, furlers, furless, furling, furlong, furlongs, furlough, furloughed, furloughing, furloughs, furls, furmente, furmenties, furmenty, furmeties, furmety, furmint, furmities, furmity, furnace, furnace's, furnaced, furnacelike, furnaceman, furnacemen, furnacer, furnaces, furnacing, furnacite, furnage, furner, furniment, furnish, furnishable, furnished, furnisher, furnishes, furnishing, furnishings, furnishment, furnishness, furnit, furniture, furnitureless, furnitures, furoate, furodiazole, furoic, furoid, furoin, furole, furomethyl, furomonazole, furor, furore, furores, furors, furosemide, furphy, furred, furrier, furriered, furrieries, furriers, furriery, furriest, furrily, furriner, furriners, furriness, furring, furrings, furrow, furrowed, furrower, furrowers, furrowing, furrowless, furrowlike, furrows, furrowy, furrure, furry, furs, fursemide, furstone, further, furtherance, furtherances, furthered, furtherer, furtherest, furthering, furtherly, furthermore, furthermost, furthers, furthersome, furthest, furthy, furtive, furtively, furtiveness, furtum, furuncle, furuncles, furuncular, furunculoid, furunculosis, furunculous, furunculus, fury, fury's, furyl, furze, furzechat, furzed, furzeling, furzery, furzes, furzetop, furzier, furziest, furzy, fusain, fusains, fusarial, fusariose, fusariosis, fusarole, fusate, fusc, fuscescent, fuscin, fuscohyaline, fuscous, fuse, fuseau, fuseboard, fused, fusee, fusees, fusel, fuselage, fuselages, fuseless, fuselike, fusels, fuseplug, fuses, fusetron, fusht, fusibility, fusible, fusibleness, fusibly, fusiform, fusil, fusilade, fusiladed, fusilades, fusilading, fusile, fusileer, fusileers, fusilier, fusiliers, fusillade, fusilladed, fusillades, fusillading, fusilly, fusils, fusing, fusinist, fusinite, fusion, fusional, fusionism, fusionist, fusionless, fusions, fusk, fusobacteria, fusobacterium, fusobteria, fusoid, fuss, fussbudget, fussbudgets, fussbudgety, fussed, fusser, fussers, fusses, fussier, fussiest, fussification, fussify, fussily, fussiness, fussing, fussle, fussock, fusspot, fusspots, fussy, fust, fustanella, fustanelle, fustee, fuster, fusteric, fustet, fustian, fustianish, fustianist, fustianize, fustians, fustic, fustics, fustie, fustier, fustiest, fustigate, fustigated, fustigating, fustigation, fustigator, fustigatory, fustilarian, fustilugs, fustily, fustin, fustinella, fustiness, fustle, fustoc, fusty, fusula, fusulae, fusulas, fusuma, fusure, fut, futchel, futchell, fute, futharc, futharcs, futhark, futharks, futhermore, futhorc, futhorcs, futhork, futhorks, futile, futilely, futileness, futiley, futilitarian, futilitarianism, futilities, futility, futilize, futilous, futtah, futter, futteret, futtermassel, futtock, futtocks, futurable, futural, futurama, futuramic, future, future's, futureless, futurely, futureness, futures, futuric, futurism, futurisms, futurist, futuristic, futuristically, futurists, futurities, futurition, futurity, futurize, futuro, futurologist, futurologists, futurology, futwa, fuye, fuze, fuzed, fuzee, fuzees, fuzes, fuzil, fuzils, fuzing, fuzz, fuzzball, fuzzed, fuzzes, fuzzier, fuzziest, fuzzily, fuzzines, fuzziness, fuzzing, fuzzle, fuzztail, fuzzy, fv, fw, fwd, fwelling, fy, fyce, fyces, fyke, fykes, fylfot, fylfots, fylgja, fylgjur, fylker, fyrd, fyrdung, fytte, fyttes, fz, g, g's, ga, gaatch, gab, gabardine, gabardines, gabari, gabarit, gabback, gabbai, gabbais, gabbard, gabbards, gabbart, gabbarts, gabbed, gabber, gabbers, gabbier, gabbiest, gabbiness, gabbing, gabble, gabbled, gabblement, gabbler, gabblers, gabbles, gabbling, gabbro, gabbroic, gabbroid, gabbroitic, gabbros, gabby, gabeler, gabelle, gabelled, gabelleman, gabeller, gabelles, gabendum, gaberdine, gaberdines, gaberloonie, gaberlunzie, gabert, gabfest, gabfests, gabgab, gabi, gabies, gabion, gabionade, gabionage, gabioned, gabions, gablatores, gable, gableboard, gabled, gableended, gablelike, gabler, gables, gablet, gablewindowed, gablewise, gabling, gablock, gabon, gaboon, gaboons, gabriel, gabs, gaby, gachupin, gad, gadabout, gadabouts, gadaea, gadarene, gadbee, gadbush, gadded, gadder, gadders, gaddi, gadding, gaddingly, gaddis, gaddish, gaddishness, gade, gadean, gader, gades, gadflies, gadfly, gadge, gadger, gadget, gadget's, gadgeteer, gadgeteers, gadgetries, gadgetry, gadgets, gadgety, gadhelic, gadi, gadid, gadids, gadinic, gadinine, gadis, gaditan, gadite, gadling, gadman, gadoid, gadoids, gadolinia, gadolinic, gadolinite, gadolinium, gadroon, gadroonage, gadrooned, gadrooning, gadroons, gads, gadsman, gadso, gaduin, gadwall, gadwalls, gadwell, gadzooks, gae, gaea, gaed, gaedelian, gaedown, gael, gaelic, gaels, gaen, gaes, gaet, gaff, gaffe, gaffed, gaffer, gaffers, gaffes, gaffing, gaffle, gaffs, gaffsail, gaffsman, gag, gaga, gagaku, gagate, gage, gageable, gaged, gagee, gageite, gagelike, gager, gagers, gagership, gages, gagged, gagger, gaggers, gaggery, gagging, gaggle, gaggled, gaggler, gaggles, gaggling, gaging, gagman, gagmen, gagor, gagroot, gags, gagster, gagsters, gagtooth, gagwriter, gahnite, gahnites, gaiassa, gaieties, gaiety, gail, gaillard, gaillardia, gaily, gain, gainable, gainage, gainbirth, gaincall, gaincome, gaincope, gaine, gained, gainer, gainers, gainful, gainfully, gainfulness, gaingiving, gaining, gainings, gainless, gainlessness, gainlier, gainliest, gainliness, gainly, gainor, gainpain, gains, gainsaid, gainsay, gainsayer, gainsayers, gainsaying, gainsays, gainset, gainsome, gainspeaker, gainspeaking, gainst, gainstand, gainstrive, gainturn, gaintwist, gainward, gainyield, gair, gairfish, gairfowl, gaisling, gaist, gait, gaited, gaiter, gaiterless, gaiters, gaiting, gaits, gaitt, gaius, gaize, gaj, gal, gala, galabeah, galabia, galabieh, galabiya, galactagog, galactagogue, galactagoguic, galactan, galactase, galactemia, galacthidrosis, galactic, galactically, galactidrosis, galactin, galactite, galactocele, galactodendron, galactodensimeter, galactogenetic, galactogogue, galactohemia, galactoid, galactolipide, galactolipin, galactolysis, galactolytic, galactoma, galactometer, galactometry, galactonic, galactopathy, galactophagist, galactophagous, galactophlebitis, galactophlysis, galactophore, galactophoritis, galactophorous, galactophthysis, galactophygous, galactopoiesis, galactopoietic, galactopyra, galactorrhea, galactorrhoea, galactosamine, galactosan, galactoscope, galactose, galactosemia, galactosemic, galactosidase, galactoside, galactosis, galactostasis, galactosuria, galactosyl, galactotherapy, galactotrophy, galacturia, galagala, galago, galagos, galah, galahad, galahads, galahs, galanas, galanga, galangal, galangals, galangin, galant, galante, galantine, galantuomo, galany, galapago, galapee, galas, galatea, galateas, galatians, galatine, galatotrophic, galavant, galavanted, galavanting, galavants, galax, galaxes, galaxian, galaxies, galaxy, galaxy's, galban, galbanum, galbanums, galbe, galbraithian, galbulus, gale, galea, galeae, galeage, galeas, galeass, galeate, galeated, galeche, galee, galeenies, galeeny, galegine, galeid, galeiform, galempong, galempung, galen, galena, galenas, galenic, galenical, galenism, galenist, galenite, galenites, galenobismutite, galenoid, galeod, galeoid, galeopithecus, galeproof, galera, galere, galeres, galericulate, galerie, galerite, galerum, galerus, gales, galesaur, galet, galette, galewort, galey, galgal, gali, galianes, galilean, galilee, galilees, galilei, galileo, galimatias, galinaceous, galingale, galiongee, galionji, galiot, galiots, galipidine, galipine, galipoidin, galipoidine, galipoipin, galipot, galipots, galium, galivant, galivanted, galivanting, galivants, galjoen, gall, galla, gallacetophenone, gallach, gallah, gallamine, gallanilide, gallant, gallanted, gallanting, gallantize, gallantly, gallantness, gallantries, gallantry, gallants, gallate, gallates, gallature, gallberries, gallberry, gallbladder, gallbladders, gallbush, galleass, galleasses, galled, gallein, galleine, galleins, galleon, galleons, galler, gallera, gallerian, galleried, galleries, galleriies, gallery, gallerygoer, gallerying, galleryite, gallerylike, gallet, galleta, galletas, galleting, galley, galley's, galleylike, galleyman, galleypot, galleys, galleyworm, gallflies, gallflower, gallfly, galliambic, galliambus, gallian, galliard, galliardise, galliardize, galliardly, galliardness, galliards, galliass, galliasses, gallic, gallican, gallicanism, gallicism, gallicisms, gallicization, gallicize, gallicizer, gallicola, gallicole, gallicolous, gallied, gallies, galliferous, gallification, galliform, galligaskin, galligaskins, gallimatia, gallimaufries, gallimaufry, gallinacean, gallinaceous, gallinaginous, gallinazo, galline, galliney, galling, gallingly, gallingness, gallinipper, gallinule, gallinulelike, gallinules, gallinuline, galliot, galliots, gallipot, gallipots, gallish, gallisin, gallium, galliums, gallivant, gallivanted, gallivanter, gallivanters, gallivanting, gallivants, gallivat, gallivorous, galliwasp, gallize, gallnut, gallnuts, gallocyanin, gallocyanine, galloflavin, galloflavine, galloglass, gallon, gallon's, gallonage, galloner, gallons, galloon, gallooned, galloons, galloot, galloots, gallop, gallopade, galloped, galloper, gallopers, gallophile, galloping, gallops, galloptious, gallotannate, gallotannic, gallotannin, gallous, gallow, galloway, gallowglass, gallows, gallowses, gallowsmaker, gallowsness, gallowsward, galls, gallstone, gallstones, galluot, gallup, galluptious, gallus, gallused, galluses, gallweed, gallwort, gally, gallybagger, gallybeggar, gallycrow, gallygaskins, gallying, gallywasp, galoch, galoot, galoots, galop, galopade, galopades, galoped, galopin, galoping, galops, galore, galores, galosh, galoshe, galoshed, galoshes, galoubet, galp, galravage, galravitch, gals, galt, galtrap, galuchat, galumph, galumphed, galumphing, galumphs, galumptious, galut, galuth, galv, galvanic, galvanical, galvanically, galvanisation, galvanise, galvanised, galvaniser, galvanising, galvanism, galvanist, galvanization, galvanizations, galvanize, galvanized, galvanizer, galvanizers, galvanizes, galvanizing, galvanocauteries, galvanocauterization, galvanocautery, galvanocontractility, galvanofaradization, galvanoglyph, galvanoglyphy, galvanograph, galvanographic, galvanography, galvanologist, galvanology, galvanolysis, galvanomagnet, galvanomagnetic, galvanomagnetism, galvanometer, galvanometers, galvanometric, galvanometrical, galvanometrically, galvanometry, galvanoplastic, galvanoplastical, galvanoplastically, galvanoplastics, galvanoplasty, galvanopsychic, galvanopuncture, galvanoscope, galvanoscopic, galvanoscopy, galvanosurgery, galvanotactic, galvanotaxis, galvanotherapy, galvanothermometer, galvanothermy, galvanotonic, galvanotropic, galvanotropism, galvayne, galvayned, galvayning, galvo, galvvanoscopy, galways, galwegian, galyac, galyacs, galyak, galyaks, galziekte, gam, gamahe, gamari, gamash, gamashes, gamasid, gamb, gamba, gambade, gambades, gambado, gambadoes, gambados, gambang, gambas, gambe, gambeer, gambeered, gambeering, gambelli, gambes, gambeson, gambesons, gambet, gambetta, gambette, gambia, gambiae, gambian, gambians, gambias, gambier, gambiers, gambir, gambirs, gambist, gambit, gambits, gamble, gambled, gambler, gamblers, gambles, gamblesome, gamblesomeness, gambling, gambodic, gamboge, gamboges, gambogian, gambogic, gamboised, gambol, gamboled, gamboler, gamboling, gambolled, gamboller, gambolling, gambols, gambone, gambrel, gambreled, gambrelled, gambrels, gambroon, gambs, gambusia, gambusias, gamdeboo, gamdia, game, gamebag, gameball, gamecock, gamecocks, gamecraft, gamed, gameful, gamekeeper, gamekeepers, gamekeeping, gamelan, gamelang, gamelans, gameless, gamelike, gamelin, gamelote, gamelotte, gamely, gamene, gameness, gamenesses, gamer, games, gamesman, gamesmanship, gamesome, gamesomely, gamesomeness, gamest, gamester, gamesters, gamestress, gametal, gametange, gametangia, gametangium, gamete, gametes, gametic, gametically, gametocyst, gametocyte, gametogenesis, gametogenic, gametogenous, gametogeny, gametogonium, gametogony, gametoid, gametophagia, gametophobia, gametophore, gametophoric, gametophyll, gametophyte, gametophytic, gamey, gamgee, gamgia, gamic, gamier, gamiest, gamily, gamin, gamine, gamines, gaminesque, gaminess, gaminesses, gaming, gamings, gaminish, gamins, gamma, gammacism, gammacismus, gammadia, gammadion, gammarid, gammarine, gammaroid, gammas, gammation, gammed, gammelost, gammer, gammerel, gammers, gammerstang, gammexane, gammick, gamming, gammock, gammon, gammoned, gammoner, gammoners, gammoning, gammons, gammy, gamobium, gamodeme, gamodemes, gamodesmic, gamodesmy, gamogamy, gamogenesis, gamogenetic, gamogenetical, gamogenetically, gamogeny, gamogony, gamomania, gamond, gamone, gamont, gamopetalous, gamophagia, gamophagy, gamophyllous, gamori, gamosepalous, gamostele, gamostelic, gamostely, gamotropic, gamotropism, gamp, gamphrel, gamps, gams, gamut, gamuts, gamy, gan, ganam, ganancial, gananciales, ganancias, ganch, ganched, ganching, ganda, gander, gandered, ganderess, gandergoose, gandering, gandermooner, ganders, ganderteeth, gandertmeeth, gandhi, gandhian, gandoura, gandul, gandum, gandurah, gane, ganef, ganefs, ganev, ganevs, gang, gang's, ganga, gangan, gangava, gangbang, gangboard, gangbuster, gangdom, gange, ganged, ganger, gangerel, gangers, ganges, gangetic, gangflower, ganggang, ganging, gangion, gangism, gangland, ganglander, ganglands, ganglia, gangliac, ganglial, gangliar, gangliasthenia, gangliate, gangliated, gangliectomy, ganglier, gangliest, gangliform, gangliglia, gangliglions, gangliitis, gangling, ganglioblast, gangliocyte, ganglioform, ganglioid, ganglioma, gangliomas, gangliomata, ganglion, ganglionary, ganglionate, ganglionated, ganglionectomies, ganglionectomy, ganglioneural, ganglioneure, ganglioneuroma, ganglioneuron, ganglionic, ganglionitis, ganglionless, ganglions, ganglioplexus, ganglioside, gangly, gangman, gangmaster, gangplank, gangplanks, gangplow, gangplows, gangrel, gangrels, gangrenate, gangrene, gangrened, gangrenes, gangrenescent, gangrening, gangrenous, gangs, gangsa, gangshag, gangsman, gangster, gangster's, gangsterism, gangsters, gangtide, gangue, gangues, gangwa, gangway, gangwayed, gangwayman, gangwaymen, gangways, ganister, ganisters, ganja, ganjas, ganner, gannet, gannetry, gannets, gannister, ganoblast, ganocephalan, ganocephalous, ganodont, ganof, ganofs, ganoid, ganoidal, ganoidean, ganoidian, ganoids, ganoin, ganoine, ganomalite, ganophyllite, ganoses, ganosis, gansa, gansel, ganser, gansey, gansy, gant, ganta, gantang, gantangs, gantelope, gantlet, gantleted, gantleting, gantlets, gantline, gantlines, gantlope, gantlopes, ganton, gantries, gantry, gantryman, gantsl, ganyie, ganymede, ganymedes, ganza, ganzie, gaol, gaolage, gaolbird, gaoled, gaoler, gaolering, gaolerness, gaolers, gaoling, gaoloring, gaols, gap, gap's, gapa, gape, gaped, gaper, gapers, gapes, gapeseed, gapeseeds, gapeworm, gapeworms, gaping, gapingly, gapingstock, gapless, gaplessness, gapo, gaposis, gaposises, gapped, gapper, gapperi, gappier, gappiest, gapping, gappy, gaps, gapy, gar, gara, garabato, garad, garage, garaged, garageman, garages, garaging, garance, garancin, garancine, garapata, garapato, garau, garava, garavance, garawi, garb, garbage, garbage's, garbages, garbanzo, garbanzos, garbardine, garbed, garbel, garbell, garbill, garbing, garble, garbleable, garbled, garbler, garblers, garbles, garbless, garbline, garbling, garblings, garbo, garboard, garboards, garboil, garboils, garbologist, garbs, garbure, garce, garcon, garcons, gard, gardant, gardbrace, garde, gardebras, gardeen, garden, gardenable, gardencraft, gardened, gardener, gardeners, gardenership, gardenesque, gardenful, gardenhood, gardenia, gardenias, gardening, gardenize, gardenless, gardenlike, gardenly, gardenmaker, gardenmaking, gardens, gardenwards, gardenwise, gardeny, garderobe, gardeviance, gardevin, gardevisure, gardinol, gardnap, gardon, gardy, gardyloo, gare, garefowl, garefowls, gareh, gareth, garetta, garewaite, garfield, garfish, garfishes, garg, gargalize, garganey, garganeys, gargantua, gargantuan, gargarism, gargarize, garget, gargets, gargety, gargil, gargle, gargled, gargler, garglers, gargles, gargling, gargol, gargoyle, gargoyled, gargoyles, gargoyley, gargoylish, gargoylishly, gargoylism, garial, gariba, garibaldi, garigue, garish, garishly, garishness, garland, garlandage, garlanded, garlanding, garlandless, garlandlike, garlandry, garlands, garlandwise, garle, garlic, garlicky, garliclike, garlicmonger, garlics, garlicwort, garlion, garlopa, garment, garment's, garmented, garmenting, garmentless, garmentmaker, garments, garmenture, garmentworker, garn, garnel, garner, garnerage, garnered, garnering, garners, garnet, garnetberry, garneter, garnetiferous, garnetlike, garnets, garnett, garnetter, garnetwork, garnetz, garni, garnice, garniec, garnierite, garnish, garnishable, garnished, garnishee, garnisheed, garnisheeing, garnisheement, garnishees, garnisheing, garnisher, garnishes, garnishing, garnishment, garnishments, garnishry, garnison, garniture, garnitures, garon, garoo, garookuh, garote, garoted, garoter, garotes, garoting, garotte, garotted, garotter, garotters, garottes, garotting, garous, garpike, garpikes, garrafa, garran, garrat, garred, garret, garreted, garreteer, garretmaster, garrets, garrick, garridge, garrigue, garring, garrison, garrisoned, garrisoning, garrisons, garrnishable, garron, garrons, garroo, garrooka, garrot, garrote, garroted, garroter, garroters, garrotes, garroting, garrotte, garrotted, garrotter, garrottes, garrotting, garruline, garrulity, garrulous, garrulously, garrulousness, garrupa, garrya, gars, garse, garsil, garston, garten, garter, garter's, gartered, gartering, garterless, garters, garth, garthman, garths, garua, garum, garvance, garvanzo, garvey, garveys, garvie, garvock, gary, gas, gas's, gasalier, gasaliers, gasbag, gasbags, gasboat, gascheck, gascoign, gascoigny, gascon, gasconade, gasconaded, gasconader, gasconading, gasconism, gascons, gascoyne, gascromh, gaseity, gaselier, gaseliers, gaseosity, gaseous, gaseously, gaseousness, gases, gasfiring, gash, gash's, gashed, gasher, gashes, gashest, gashful, gashing, gashliness, gashly, gasholder, gashouse, gashouses, gashy, gasifiable, gasification, gasified, gasifier, gasifiers, gasifies, gasiform, gasify, gasifying, gasket, gaskets, gaskin, gasking, gaskings, gaskins, gasless, gaslight, gaslighted, gaslighting, gaslightness, gaslights, gaslike, gaslit, gaslock, gasmaker, gasman, gasmen, gasmetophytic, gasogen, gasogene, gasogenes, gasogenic, gasohol, gasolene, gasolenes, gasolier, gasoliers, gasoliery, gasoline, gasolineless, gasoliner, gasolines, gasolinic, gasometer, gasometric, gasometrical, gasometrically, gasometry, gasoscope, gasp, gasparillo, gasped, gasper, gaspereau, gaspereaus, gaspergou, gaspergous, gaspers, gaspiness, gasping, gaspingly, gasproof, gasps, gaspy, gassed, gassendist, gasser, gasserian, gassers, gasses, gassier, gassiest, gassiness, gassing, gassings, gassit, gassy, gast, gastaldite, gastaldo, gasted, gaster, gasteralgia, gasteria, gasteromycete, gasteromycetous, gasteropod, gasteropoda, gasterosteid, gasterosteiform, gasterosteoid, gasterotheca, gasterothecal, gasterotrichan, gasterozooid, gastful, gasthaus, gasthauser, gasthauses, gastight, gastightness, gasting, gastly, gastness, gastnesses, gastradenitis, gastraea, gastraead, gastraeal, gastraeas, gastraeum, gastral, gastralgia, gastralgic, gastralgy, gastraneuria, gastrasthenia, gastratrophia, gastrea, gastreas, gastrectasia, gastrectasis, gastrectomies, gastrectomy, gastrelcosis, gastric, gastricism, gastrilegous, gastriloquial, gastriloquism, gastriloquist, gastriloquous, gastriloquy, gastrimargy, gastrin, gastrins, gastritic, gastritis, gastroadenitis, gastroadynamic, gastroalbuminorrhea, gastroanastomosis, gastroarthritis, gastroatonia, gastroatrophia, gastroblennorrhea, gastrocatarrhal, gastrocele, gastrocentrous, gastrocnemial, gastrocnemian, gastrocnemii, gastrocnemius, gastrocoel, gastrocoele, gastrocolic, gastrocoloptosis, gastrocolostomy, gastrocolotomy, gastrocolpotomy, gastrocystic, gastrocystis, gastrodermal, gastrodermis, gastrodialysis, gastrodiaphanoscopy, gastrodidymus, gastrodisc, gastrodisk, gastroduodenal, gastroduodenitis, gastroduodenoscopy, gastroduodenostomies, gastroduodenostomy, gastroduodenotomy, gastrodynia, gastroelytrotomy, gastroenteralgia, gastroenteric, gastroenteritic, gastroenteritis, gastroenteroanastomosis, gastroenterocolitis, gastroenterocolostomy, gastroenterologic, gastroenterological, gastroenterologically, gastroenterologist, gastroenterologists, gastroenterology, gastroenteroptosis, gastroenterostomies, gastroenterostomy, gastroenterotomy, gastroepiploic, gastroesophageal, gastroesophagostomy, gastrogastrotomy, gastrogenic, gastrogenital, gastrogenous, gastrograph, gastrohelcosis, gastrohepatic, gastrohepatitis, gastrohydrorrhea, gastrohyperneuria, gastrohypertonic, gastrohysterectomy, gastrohysteropexy, gastrohysterorrhaphy, gastrohysterotomy, gastroid, gastrointestinal, gastrojejunal, gastrojejunostomies, gastrojejunostomy, gastrolater, gastrolatrous, gastrolavage, gastrolienal, gastrolith, gastrologer, gastrological, gastrologically, gastrologist, gastrologists, gastrology, gastrolysis, gastrolytic, gastromalacia, gastromancy, gastromelus, gastromenia, gastromyces, gastromycosis, gastromyxorrhea, gastronephritis, gastronome, gastronomer, gastronomes, gastronomic, gastronomical, gastronomically, gastronomics, gastronomist, gastronomy, gastronosus, gastropancreatic, gastropancreatitis, gastroparalysis, gastroparesis, gastroparietal, gastropathic, gastropathy, gastroperiodynia, gastropexy, gastrophile, gastrophilism, gastrophilist, gastrophilite, gastrophrenic, gastrophthisis, gastroplasty, gastroplenic, gastropleuritis, gastroplication, gastropneumatic, gastropneumonic, gastropod, gastropodan, gastropodous, gastropods, gastropore, gastroptosia, gastroptosis, gastropulmonary, gastropulmonic, gastropyloric, gastrorrhagia, gastrorrhaphy, gastrorrhea, gastroschisis, gastroscope, gastroscopic, gastroscopies, gastroscopist, gastroscopy, gastrosoph, gastrosopher, gastrosophy, gastrospasm, gastrosplenic, gastrostaxis, gastrostegal, gastrostege, gastrostenosis, gastrostomies, gastrostomize, gastrostomy, gastrosuccorrhea, gastrotaxis, gastrotheca, gastrothecal, gastrotome, gastrotomic, gastrotomies, gastrotomy, gastrotrich, gastrotrichan, gastrotubotomy, gastrotympanites, gastrovascular, gastroxynsis, gastrozooid, gastrula, gastrulae, gastrular, gastrulas, gastrulate, gastrulated, gastrulating, gastrulation, gastruran, gasts, gasworker, gasworks, gat, gata, gatch, gatchwork, gate, gateado, gateage, gateau, gateaux, gatecrasher, gatecrashers, gated, gatefold, gatefolds, gatehouse, gatehouses, gatekeep, gatekeeper, gatekeepers, gateless, gatelike, gatemaker, gateman, gatemen, gatepost, gateposts, gater, gates, gatetender, gateward, gatewards, gateway, gateway's, gatewaying, gatewayman, gatewaymen, gateways, gatewise, gatewoman, gateworks, gatewright, gather, gatherable, gathered, gatherer, gatherers, gathering, gatherings, gathers, gatherum, gating, gatling, gator, gats, gatsby, gatten, gatter, gatteridge, gattine, gau, gaub, gauby, gauche, gauchely, gaucheness, gaucher, gaucherie, gaucheries, gauchest, gaucho, gauchos, gaucie, gaucy, gaud, gaudeamus, gaudeamuses, gauderies, gaudery, gaudful, gaudier, gaudies, gaudiest, gaudily, gaudiness, gaudish, gaudless, gauds, gaudsman, gaudy, gaufer, gauffer, gauffered, gaufferer, gauffering, gauffers, gauffre, gauffred, gaufre, gaufrette, gaufrettes, gauge, gaugeable, gaugeably, gauged, gauger, gaugers, gaugership, gauges, gauging, gauily, gauk, gaul, gaulding, gauleiter, gaulin, gaulish, gaullism, gauloiserie, gauls, gaulsh, gault, gaulter, gaultherase, gaultheria, gaultherin, gaultherine, gaults, gaum, gaumed, gauming, gaumish, gaumless, gaumlike, gaums, gaumy, gaun, gaunch, gaunt, gaunted, gaunter, gauntest, gauntlet, gauntleted, gauntleting, gauntlets, gauntly, gauntness, gauntree, gauntries, gauntry, gaunty, gaup, gauping, gaupus, gaur, gaure, gauric, gaurie, gaurs, gaus, gauss, gaussage, gaussbergite, gausses, gaussmeter, gauster, gausterer, gaut, gauteite, gauze, gauzelike, gauzes, gauzewing, gauzier, gauziest, gauzily, gauziness, gauzy, gavage, gavages, gavall, gave, gavel, gavelage, gaveled, gaveler, gavelet, gaveling, gavelkind, gavelkinder, gavelled, gaveller, gavelling, gavelman, gavelmen, gavelock, gavelocks, gavels, gaverick, gavial, gavialoid, gavials, gavot, gavots, gavotte, gavotted, gavottes, gavotting, gavyuti, gaw, gawain, gawby, gawcey, gawcie, gawgaw, gawish, gawk, gawked, gawker, gawkers, gawkhammer, gawkier, gawkies, gawkiest, gawkihood, gawkily, gawkiness, gawking, gawkish, gawkishly, gawkishness, gawks, gawky, gawm, gawn, gawney, gawp, gawsie, gawsy, gay, gayal, gayals, gayatri, gaybine, gaycat, gaydiang, gayer, gayest, gayeties, gayety, gayish, gaylies, gaylussite, gayly, gayment, gayness, gaynesses, gays, gaysome, gayway, gaywing, gaywings, gayyou, gaz, gazabo, gazaboes, gazabos, gazangabin, gaze, gazebo, gazeboes, gazebos, gazed, gazee, gazeful, gazehound, gazel, gazeless, gazelle, gazellelike, gazelles, gazelline, gazement, gazer, gazers, gazes, gazet, gazettal, gazette, gazetted, gazetteer, gazetteerage, gazetteerish, gazetteers, gazetteership, gazettes, gazetting, gazi, gazing, gazingly, gazingstock, gazogene, gazogenes, gazolyte, gazometer, gazon, gazook, gazophylacium, gazoz, gazpacho, gazpachos, gazump, gazy, gazzetta, gcd, gconv, gconvert, gd, gdinfo, gds, ge, geadephagous, geal, gean, geanticlinal, geanticline, gear, gearbox, gearboxes, gearcase, gearcases, geared, gearing, gearings, gearksutite, gearless, gearman, gears, gearset, gearshift, gearshifts, gearwheel, gearwheels, gease, geason, geast, geat, geb, gebang, gebanga, gebbie, gebur, gecarcinian, geck, gecked, gecking, gecko, geckoes, geckoid, geckos, geckotian, geckotid, geckotoid, gecks, ged, gedackt, gedact, gedanite, gedanken, gedd, gedder, gedds, gedeckt, gedecktwork, gedrite, geds, gedunk, gee, geebong, geebung, geed, geegaw, geegaws, geeing, geejee, geek, geeks, geelbec, geelbeck, geelbek, geeldikkop, geelhout, geepound, geepounds, geer, geerah, gees, geese, geest, geests, geet, geez, geezer, geezers, gefilte, gefulltefish, gegenion, gegenschein, gegg, geggee, gegger, geggery, gehenna, gehey, gehlenite, geic, geiger, geikielite, gein, geir, geira, geisa, geisha, geishas, geison, geisotherm, geisothermal, geissospermin, geissospermine, geist, geistlich, geitjie, geitonogamous, geitonogamy, gekkonid, gekkonoid, gel, gel's, gelable, gelada, geladas, gelandejump, gelandelaufer, gelandesprung, gelant, gelants, gelastic, gelate, gelated, gelates, gelatia, gelatification, gelatigenous, gelatin, gelatinate, gelatinated, gelatinating, gelatination, gelatine, gelatined, gelatines, gelating, gelatiniferous, gelatiniform, gelatinify, gelatinigerous, gelatinisation, gelatinise, gelatinised, gelatiniser, gelatinising, gelatinity, gelatinizability, gelatinizable, gelatinization, gelatinize, gelatinized, gelatinizer, gelatinizing, gelatinobromide, gelatinochloride, gelatinoid, gelatinotype, gelatinous, gelatinously, gelatinousness, gelatins, gelation, gelations, gelatose, geld, geldability, geldable, geldant, gelded, gelder, gelders, geldesprung, gelding, geldings, gelds, gelechiid, gelee, geleem, gelees, gelid, gelidities, gelidity, gelidly, gelidness, gelignite, gelilah, gelinotte, gell, gellant, gellants, gelled, gelling, gelly, gelndesprung, gelofer, gelofre, gelogenic, gelong, geloscopy, gelose, gelosie, gelosin, gelosine, gelotherapy, gelotometer, gelotoscopy, gelototherapy, gels, gelsemia, gelsemic, gelsemin, gelsemine, gelseminic, gelseminine, gelsemium, gelsemiumia, gelsemiums, gelt, gelts, gem, gem's, gemara, gematria, gematrical, gematriot, gemauve, gemeinde, gemeinschaft, gemeinschaften, gemel, gemeled, gemelled, gemellion, gemellione, gemellus, gemels, geminal, geminally, geminate, geminated, geminately, geminates, geminating, gemination, geminations, geminative, gemini, geminiflorous, geminiform, geminis, geminorum, geminous, gemitorial, gemless, gemlich, gemlike, gemma, gemmaceous, gemmae, gemman, gemmary, gemmate, gemmated, gemmates, gemmating, gemmation, gemmative, gemmed, gemmel, gemmeous, gemmer, gemmery, gemmier, gemmiest, gemmiferous, gemmiferousness, gemmification, gemmiform, gemmily, gemminess, gemming, gemmipara, gemmipares, gemmiparity, gemmiparous, gemmiparously, gemmoid, gemmological, gemmologist, gemmologists, gemmology, gemmula, gemmulation, gemmule, gemmules, gemmuliferous, gemmy, gemological, gemologies, gemologist, gemologists, gemology, gemonies, gemot, gemote, gemotes, gemots, gempylid, gems, gemsbok, gemsboks, gemsbuck, gemsbucks, gemse, gemses, gemshorn, gemstone, gemstones, gemuetlich, gemul, gemuti, gemutlich, gemutlichkeit, gemwork, gen, gena, genae, genal, genapp, genappe, genapped, genapper, genapping, genarch, genarcha, genarchaship, genarchship, gendarme, gendarmerie, gendarmery, gendarmes, gender, gender's, gendered, genderer, gendering, genderless, genders, gene, gene's, geneal, genealogic, genealogical, genealogically, genealogies, genealogist, genealogists, genealogize, genealogizer, genealogy, genear, genearch, geneat, genecologic, genecological, genecologically, genecologist, genecology, genecor, geneki, genep, genepi, genera, generability, generable, generableness, general, generalate, generalcies, generalcy, generale, generalia, generalific, generalisable, generalisation, generalise, generalised, generaliser, generalising, generalism, generalissima, generalissimo, generalissimos, generalist, generalist's, generalistic, generalists, generaliter, generalities, generality, generalizable, generalization, generalization's, generalizations, generalize, generalizeable, generalized, generalizer, generalizers, generalizes, generalizing, generall, generally, generalness, generals, generalship, generalships, generalty, generant, generate, generated, generater, generates, generating, generation, generational, generationism, generations, generative, generatively, generativeness, generator, generator's, generators, generatrices, generatrix, generic, generical, generically, genericalness, genericness, generics, generification, generis, generosities, generosity, generosity's, generous, generously, generousness, genes, geneserin, geneserine, geneses, genesial, genesic, genesiology, genesis, genesiurgic, genet, genethliac, genethliacal, genethliacally, genethliacism, genethliacon, genethliacs, genethlialogic, genethlialogical, genethlialogy, genethliatic, genethlic, genetic, genetical, genetically, geneticism, geneticist, geneticists, genetics, genetika, genetmoil, genetoid, genetor, genetous, genetrix, genets, genette, genettes, geneva, genevan, genevas, genevese, genevoise, genghis, genial, geniality, genialize, genially, genialness, genian, genic, genically, genicular, geniculate, geniculated, geniculately, geniculation, geniculum, genie, genies, genii, genin, genio, genioglossal, genioglossi, genioglossus, geniohyoglossal, geniohyoglossus, geniohyoid, geniolatry, genion, genioplasty, genip, genipa, genipap, genipapada, genipaps, genips, genisaro, genista, genistein, genistin, genit, genital, genitalia, genitalial, genitalic, genitally, genitals, geniting, genitival, genitivally, genitive, genitives, genitocrural, genitofemoral, genitor, genitorial, genitors, genitory, genitourinary, geniture, genitures, genius, genius's, geniuses, genizah, genizero, genl, genoa, genoas, genoblast, genoblastic, genocidal, genocide, genocides, genoese, genoise, genom, genome, genomes, genomic, genoms, genonema, genophobia, genos, genospecies, genotype, genotypes, genotypic, genotypical, genotypically, genotypicity, genouillere, genovino, genre, genre's, genres, genro, genros, gens, genseng, gensengs, genson, gent, gentamicin, genteel, genteeler, genteelest, genteelish, genteelism, genteelize, genteelly, genteelness, gentes, genthite, gentian, gentianaceous, gentianal, gentianella, gentianic, gentianin, gentianose, gentians, gentianwort, gentiin, gentil, gentile, gentiledom, gentiles, gentilesse, gentilhomme, gentilic, gentilish, gentilism, gentilitial, gentilitian, gentilities, gentilitious, gentility, gentilization, gentilize, gentiobiose, gentiopicrin, gentisate, gentisein, gentisic, gentisin, gentium, gentle, gentled, gentlefolk, gentlefolks, gentlehearted, gentleheartedly, gentleheartedness, gentlehood, gentleman, gentlemanhood, gentlemanism, gentlemanize, gentlemanlike, gentlemanlikeness, gentlemanliness, gentlemanly, gentlemanship, gentlemen, gentlemens, gentlemouthed, gentleness, gentlepeople, gentler, gentles, gentleship, gentlest, gentlewoman, gentlewomanhood, gentlewomanish, gentlewomanlike, gentlewomanliness, gentlewomanly, gentlewomen, gentling, gently, gentman, gentoo, gentrice, gentrices, gentries, gentrification, gentry, gents, genty, genu, genua, genual, genuclast, genuflect, genuflected, genuflecting, genuflection, genuflections, genuflector, genuflectory, genuflects, genuflex, genuflexion, genuflexuous, genuine, genuinely, genuineness, genupectoral, genus, genuses, genyantrum, genyoplasty, genyplasty, genys, geo, geoaesthesia, geoagronomic, geobiologic, geobiology, geobiont, geobios, geoblast, geobotanic, geobotanical, geobotanically, geobotanist, geobotany, geocarpic, geocentric, geocentrical, geocentrically, geocentricism, geocerite, geochemical, geochemically, geochemist, geochemistry, geochemists, geochronic, geochronologic, geochronological, geochronologically, geochronologist, geochronology, geochronometric, geochronometry, geochrony, geocline, geocoronium, geocratic, geocronite, geocyclic, geod, geodaesia, geodal, geode, geodes, geodesia, geodesic, geodesical, geodesics, geodesies, geodesist, geodesists, geodesy, geodete, geodetic, geodetical, geodetically, geodetician, geodetics, geodiatropism, geodic, geodiferous, geodist, geoduck, geoducks, geodynamic, geodynamical, geodynamicist, geodynamics, geoemtry, geoethnic, geoffroyin, geoffroyine, geoform, geog, geogen, geogenesis, geogenetic, geogenic, geogenous, geogeny, geoglyphic, geognosies, geognosis, geognosist, geognost, geognostic, geognostical, geognostically, geognosy, geogonic, geogonical, geogony, geographer, geographers, geographic, geographical, geographically, geographics, geographies, geographism, geographize, geographized, geography, geohydrologic, geohydrologist, geohydrology, geoid, geoidal, geoids, geoisotherm, geol, geolatry, geolinguistics, geologer, geologers, geologian, geologic, geological, geologically, geologician, geologies, geologise, geologised, geologising, geologist, geologist's, geologists, geologize, geologized, geologizing, geology, geom, geomagnetic, geomagnetically, geomagnetician, geomagnetics, geomagnetism, geomagnetist, geomalic, geomalism, geomaly, geomance, geomancer, geomancies, geomancy, geomant, geomantic, geomantical, geomantically, geomechanics, geomedical, geomedicine, geometdecrne, geometer, geometers, geometric, geometrical, geometrically, geometrician, geometricians, geometricism, geometricist, geometricize, geometrid, geometries, geometriform, geometrine, geometrise, geometrised, geometrising, geometrize, geometrized, geometrizing, geometroid, geometry, geomoroi, geomorphic, geomorphist, geomorphogenic, geomorphogenist, geomorphogeny, geomorphologic, geomorphological, geomorphologically, geomorphologist, geomorphology, geomorphy, geomyid, geonavigation, geonegative, geonoma, geonyctinastic, geonyctitropic, geoparallelotropic, geophagia, geophagies, geophagism, geophagist, geophagous, geophagy, geophilid, geophilous, geophone, geophones, geophysical, geophysically, geophysicist, geophysicists, geophysics, geophyte, geophytes, geophytic, geoplagiotropism, geopolar, geopolitic, geopolitical, geopolitically, geopolitician, geopolitics, geopolitist, geoponic, geoponical, geoponics, geopony, geopositive, geopotential, georama, geordie, george, georgette, georgia, georgiadesite, georgian, georgians, georgic, georgical, georgics, georgium, geoscience, geoscientist, geoscientists, geoscopic, geoscopy, geoselenic, geosid, geoside, geosphere, geostatic, geostatics, geostationary, geostrategic, geostrategist, geostrategy, geostrophic, geostrophically, geosynchronous, geosynclinal, geosyncline, geosynclines, geotactic, geotactically, geotaxes, geotaxis, geotaxy, geotechnic, geotechnics, geotectology, geotectonic, geotectonically, geotectonics, geotherm, geothermal, geothermally, geothermic, geothermometer, geotic, geotical, geotilla, geotonic, geotonus, geotropic, geotropically, geotropism, geotropy, geoty, gephyrean, gephyrocercal, gephyrocercy, gephyrophobia, gepoun, ger, geraera, gerah, gerahs, gerald, geraniaceous, geranial, geranials, geranic, geranin, geraniol, geraniols, geranium, geraniums, geranomorph, geranomorphic, geranyl, gerara, gerardia, gerardias, gerastian, gerate, gerated, gerately, geratic, geratologic, geratologous, geratology, geraty, gerb, gerbe, gerbera, gerberas, gerbil, gerbille, gerbilles, gerbils, gerbo, gercrow, gere, gereagle, gerefa, gerenda, gerendum, gerent, gerents, gerenuk, gerenuks, gerfalcon, gerful, gerhardtite, geriatric, geriatrician, geriatrics, geriatrist, gerim, gerip, gerkin, gerland, germ, germ's, germain, germal, german, german's, germander, germane, germanely, germaneness, germanic, germanies, germanious, germanism, germanist, germanite, germanity, germanium, germaniums, germanization, germanize, germanized, germanous, germans, germantown, germany, germanyl, germarium, germen, germens, germfree, germicidal, germicide, germicides, germiculture, germier, germiest, germifuge, germigene, germigenous, germin, germina, germinability, germinable, germinal, germinally, germinance, germinancy, germinant, germinate, germinated, germinates, germinating, germination, germinational, germinations, germinative, germinatively, germinator, germing, germiniparous, germinogony, germiparity, germiparous, germless, germlike, germling, germon, germproof, germs, germule, germy, gernative, gernitz, gerocomia, gerocomical, gerocomy, geroderma, gerodermia, gerodontia, gerodontic, gerodontics, gerodontology, geromorphism, geronomite, geront, gerontal, gerontes, gerontic, gerontine, gerontism, geronto, gerontocracies, gerontocracy, gerontocrat, gerontocratic, gerontogeous, gerontologic, gerontological, gerontologies, gerontologist, gerontologists, gerontology, gerontomorphosis, gerontophilia, gerontotherapies, gerontotherapy, gerontoxon, geropiga, gerousia, gerrhosaurid, gerrymander, gerrymandered, gerrymanderer, gerrymandering, gerrymanders, gers, gersdorffite, gersum, gertrude, gerund, gerundial, gerundially, gerundival, gerundive, gerundively, gerunds, gerusia, gervais, gervao, gery, gerygone, geryon, geryonid, gesellschaft, gesellschaften, gesith, gesithcund, gesithcundman, gesling, gesneraceous, gesnerad, gesneria, gesneriaceous, gesning, gess, gessamine, gesseron, gesso, gessoes, gest, gestae, gestalt, gestalten, gestalter, gestaltist, gestalts, gestant, gestapo, gestapos, gestate, gestated, gestates, gestating, gestation, gestational, gestations, gestative, gestatorial, gestatorium, gestatory, geste, gested, gesten, gestening, gester, gestes, gestic, gestical, gesticulacious, gesticulant, gesticular, gesticularious, gesticulate, gesticulated, gesticulates, gesticulating, gesticulation, gesticulations, gesticulative, gesticulatively, gesticulator, gesticulatory, gestio, gestion, gestning, gestonie, gestor, gests, gestura, gestural, gesture, gestured, gestureless, gesturer, gesturers, gestures, gesturing, gesturist, gesundheit, geswarp, get, geta, getable, getah, getas, getatability, getatable, getatableness, getaway, getaways, getfd, gether, gethsemane, gethsemanic, getid, getling, getmesost, getmjlkost, getpenny, gets, getspa, getspace, gettable, gettableness, getter, getter's, gettered, gettering, getters, getting, gettings, gettysburg, getup, getups, geulah, geum, geumatophobia, geums, gewgaw, gewgawed, gewgawish, gewgawry, gewgaws, gewgawy, gey, geyan, geyerite, geylies, geyser, geyseral, geyseric, geyserine, geyserish, geyserite, geysers, gez, gezerah, ggr, ghaffir, ghafir, ghain, ghaist, ghalva, ghana, ghanaian, ghanaians, ghanian, gharial, gharnao, gharri, gharries, gharris, gharry, ghast, ghastful, ghastfully, ghastfulness, ghastily, ghastlier, ghastliest, ghastlily, ghastliness, ghastly, ghat, ghats, ghatti, ghatwal, ghatwazi, ghaut, ghauts, ghawazee, ghawazi, ghazal, ghazel, ghazi, ghazies, ghazis, ghazism, ghbor, gheber, ghebeta, ghee, ghees, gheleem, ghenting, gherao, gheraoed, gheraoes, gheraoing, gherkin, gherkins, ghess, ghetchoo, ghetti, ghetto, ghettoed, ghettoes, ghettoing, ghettoization, ghettoize, ghettoized, ghettoizes, ghettoizing, ghettos, ghi, ghibelline, ghibellinism, ghibli, ghiblis, ghillie, ghillies, ghis, ghizite, ghole, ghoom, ghorkhar, ghost, ghostcraft, ghostdom, ghosted, ghoster, ghostess, ghostfish, ghostfishes, ghostflower, ghosthood, ghostier, ghostiest, ghostified, ghostily, ghosting, ghostish, ghostism, ghostland, ghostless, ghostlet, ghostlier, ghostliest, ghostlify, ghostlike, ghostlikeness, ghostlily, ghostliness, ghostly, ghostmonger, ghostology, ghosts, ghostship, ghostweed, ghostwrite, ghostwriter, ghostwriters, ghostwrites, ghostwriting, ghostwritten, ghostwrote, ghosty, ghoul, ghoulery, ghoulie, ghoulish, ghoulishly, ghoulishness, ghouls, ghrush, ghurry, ghyll, ghylls, gi, giallolino, giambeux, giansar, giant, giant's, giantesque, giantess, giantesses, gianthood, giantish, giantism, giantisms, giantize, giantkind, giantlike, giantlikeness, giantly, giantry, giants, giantship, giantsize, giaour, giaours, giardia, giardiasis, giarra, giarre, gib, gibaro, gibbals, gibbar, gibbartas, gibbed, gibber, gibbered, gibberellin, gibbergunyah, gibbering, gibberish, gibberose, gibberosity, gibbers, gibbert, gibbet, gibbeted, gibbeting, gibbets, gibbetted, gibbetting, gibbetwise, gibbier, gibbing, gibbled, gibblegabble, gibblegabbler, gibblegable, gibbles, gibbol, gibbon, gibbons, gibbose, gibbosely, gibboseness, gibbosities, gibbosity, gibbous, gibbously, gibbousness, gibbsite, gibbsites, gibbus, gibby, gibe, gibed, gibel, gibelite, gibeonite, giber, gibers, gibes, gibetting, gibier, gibing, gibingly, gibleh, giblet, giblets, gibli, giboia, gibraltar, gibs, gibson, gibsons, gibstaff, gibus, gibuses, gid, giddap, giddea, giddied, giddier, giddies, giddiest, giddify, giddily, giddiness, giddy, giddyberry, giddybrain, giddyhead, giddying, giddyish, giddypate, gideon, gidgea, gidgee, gidjee, gids, gidyea, gie, gieaway, gieaways, gied, gieing, gien, gierfalcon, gies, gieseckite, giesel, gif, gifblaar, giffgaff, gift, giftbook, gifted, giftedly, giftedness, giftie, gifting, giftless, giftlike, giftling, gifts, gifture, giftware, giftwrap, giftwrapping, gig, giga, gigabit, gigabits, gigabyte, gigabytes, gigacycle, gigadoid, gigahertz, gigahertzes, gigaherz, gigamaree, gigameter, gigant, gigantal, gigantean, gigantesque, gigantic, gigantical, gigantically, giganticidal, giganticide, giganticness, gigantine, gigantism, gigantize, gigantoblast, gigantocyte, gigantolite, gigantological, gigantology, gigantomachia, gigantomachy, gigantostracan, gigantostracous, gigartinaceous, gigas, gigasecond, gigaton, gigatons, gigavolt, gigawatt, gigawatts, gigback, gigelira, gigeria, gigerium, gigful, gigge, gigged, gigger, gigget, gigging, giggish, giggit, giggle, giggled, giggledom, gigglement, giggler, gigglers, giggles, gigglesome, gigglier, giggliest, giggling, gigglingly, gigglish, giggly, gighe, giglet, giglets, gigliato, giglio, giglot, giglots, gigman, gigmaness, gigmanhood, gigmania, gigmanic, gigmanically, gigmanism, gigmanity, gignate, gignitive, gigolo, gigolos, gigot, gigots, gigs, gigsman, gigsmen, gigster, gigtree, gigue, gigues, gigunu, giher, giinwale, gila, gilbert, gilbertage, gilbertian, gilbertine, gilbertite, gilberts, gild, gildable, gilded, gildedness, gilden, gilder, gilders, gildhall, gildhalls, gilding, gildings, gilds, gildship, gildsman, gildsmen, gile, gilenyer, gilenyie, giles, gilet, gilgai, gilgames, gilgamesh, gilgie, gilgul, gilgulim, gilguy, gilia, giliak, gilim, gill, gill's, gillar, gillaroo, gillbird, gilled, giller, gillers, gillflirt, gillhooter, gillian, gillie, gillied, gillies, gilliflirt, gilliflower, gilling, gillion, gilliver, gillnet, gillnets, gillnetted, gillnetting, gillot, gillotage, gillotype, gills, gillstoup, gilly, gillyflower, gillygaupus, gillying, gilo, gilour, gilpey, gilpy, gilravage, gilravager, gils, gilse, gilsonite, gilt, giltcup, gilten, gilthead, giltheads, gilts, gilttail, gilty, gilver, gim, gimbal, gimbaled, gimbaling, gimbaljawed, gimballed, gimballing, gimbals, gimbawawed, gimberjawed, gimble, gimblet, gimbri, gimcrack, gimcrackery, gimcrackiness, gimcracks, gimcracky, gimel, gimels, gimlet, gimleted, gimleteyed, gimleting, gimlets, gimlety, gimmal, gimmaled, gimmals, gimme, gimmer, gimmeringly, gimmerpet, gimmick, gimmick's, gimmicked, gimmickery, gimmicking, gimmickry, gimmicks, gimmicky, gimmor, gimp, gimped, gimper, gimpier, gimpiest, gimping, gimps, gimpy, gin, gin's, ginep, ginete, ging, gingal, gingall, gingalls, gingals, gingeley, gingeleys, gingeli, gingelies, gingelis, gingellies, gingelly, gingely, ginger, gingerade, gingerberry, gingerbread, gingerbready, gingered, gingering, gingerleaf, gingerline, gingerliness, gingerly, gingerness, gingernut, gingerol, gingerous, gingerroot, gingers, gingersnap, gingersnaps, gingerspice, gingerwork, gingerwort, gingery, gingham, ginghamed, ginghams, gingili, gingilis, gingiva, gingivae, gingival, gingivalgia, gingivectomy, gingivitis, gingivoglossitis, gingivolabial, gingko, gingkoes, gingle, gingles, ginglmi, ginglyform, ginglymi, ginglymoarthrodia, ginglymoarthrodial, ginglymodian, ginglymoid, ginglymoidal, ginglymostomoid, ginglymus, ginglyni, gingras, ginhound, ginhouse, gink, ginkgo, ginkgoaceous, ginkgoes, ginks, ginmill, ginn, ginned, ginnel, ginner, ginneries, ginners, ginnery, ginnet, ginney, ginnier, ginniest, ginning, ginnings, ginnle, ginny, ginorite, gins, ginseng, ginsengs, ginward, ginzo, ginzoes, gio, giobertite, giocoso, giojoso, giornata, giornatate, giottesque, gip, gipon, gipons, gipped, gipper, gippers, gipping, gippo, gippy, gips, gipseian, gipser, gipsied, gipsies, gipsiologist, gipsire, gipsology, gipsy, gipsy's, gipsydom, gipsyesque, gipsyfy, gipsyhead, gipsyhood, gipsying, gipsyish, gipsyism, gipsylike, gipsyry, gipsyweed, gipsywort, giraffe, giraffe's, giraffes, giraffesque, giraffine, giraffish, giraffoid, girandola, girandole, girasol, girasole, girasoles, girasols, girba, gird, girded, girder, girder's, girderage, girdering, girderless, girders, girding, girdingly, girdle, girdlecake, girdled, girdlelike, girdler, girdlers, girdles, girdlestead, girdling, girdlingly, girds, gire, girja, girkin, girl, girl's, girland, girlchild, girleen, girlery, girlfriend, girlfriends, girlfully, girlhood, girlhoods, girlie, girlies, girliness, girling, girlish, girlishly, girlishness, girlism, girllike, girllikeness, girls, girly, girn, girnal, girned, girnel, girnie, girning, girns, girny, giro, giroflore, giron, gironde, girondist, gironny, girons, giros, girosol, girosols, girouette, girouettes, girouettism, girr, girrit, girrock, girse, girsh, girshes, girsle, girt, girted, girth, girthed, girthing, girthline, girths, girting, girtline, girtonian, girts, gis, gisant, gisants, gisarme, gisarmes, gise, gisel, gisement, gish, gisla, gisler, gismo, gismondine, gismondite, gismos, gispin, gist, gists, git, gitaligenin, gitalin, gitana, gitanemuk, gitano, gitanos, gite, giterne, gith, gitim, gitonin, gitoxigenin, gitoxin, gitter, gittern, gitterns, gittith, giulio, giunta, giuseppe, giust, giustamente, giustina, giusto, give, giveable, giveaway, giveaways, given, givenness, givens, giver, givers, gives, giveth, givey, givin, giving, givingness, gizmo, gizmos, gizz, gizzard, gizzards, gizzen, gizzened, gizzern, gjedost, gjetost, gjetosts, gl, glabbella, glabella, glabellae, glabellar, glabellous, glabellum, glabrate, glabreity, glabrescent, glabriety, glabrous, glabrousness, glace, glaceed, glaceing, glaces, glaciable, glacial, glacialism, glacialist, glacialize, glacially, glaciaria, glaciarium, glaciate, glaciated, glaciates, glaciating, glaciation, glacier, glacier's, glaciered, glacieret, glacierist, glaciers, glacification, glacify, glacioaqueous, glaciolacustrine, glaciologic, glaciological, glaciologist, glaciologists, glaciology, glaciomarine, glaciometer, glacionatant, glacious, glacis, glacises, glack, glacon, glad, gladatorial, gladded, gladden, gladdened, gladdener, gladdening, gladdens, gladder, gladdest, gladding, gladdon, gladdy, glade, gladelike, gladen, glades, gladeye, gladful, gladfully, gladfulness, gladhearted, gladiate, gladiator, gladiatorial, gladiatorism, gladiators, gladiatorship, gladiatory, gladiatrix, gladier, gladiest, gladify, gladii, gladiola, gladiolar, gladiolas, gladiole, gladioli, gladiolus, gladioluses, gladite, gladius, gladkaite, gladless, gladlier, gladliest, gladly, gladness, gladnesses, gladrags, glads, gladship, gladsome, gladsomely, gladsomeness, gladsomer, gladsomest, gladstone, gladstonian, gladwin, glady, glaga, glagah, glaieul, glaik, glaiket, glaiketness, glaikit, glaikitness, glaiks, glair, glaire, glaired, glaireous, glaires, glairier, glairiest, glairin, glairiness, glairing, glairs, glairy, glaister, glaistig, glaive, glaived, glaives, glaizie, glaked, glaky, glali, glam, glamberry, glamor, glamorization, glamorizations, glamorize, glamorized, glamorizer, glamorizes, glamorizing, glamorous, glamorously, glamorousness, glamors, glamour, glamoured, glamourie, glamouring, glamourization, glamourize, glamourizer, glamourless, glamourous, glamourously, glamourousness, glamours, glamoury, glance, glanced, glancer, glances, glancing, glancingly, gland, gland's, glandaceous, glandarious, glander, glandered, glanderous, glanders, glandes, glandiferous, glandiform, glanditerous, glandless, glandlike, glands, glandula, glandular, glandularly, glandulation, glandule, glandules, glanduliferous, glanduliform, glanduligerous, glandulose, glandulosity, glandulous, glandulousness, glanis, glans, glar, glare, glared, glareless, glareole, glareous, glareproof, glares, glareworm, glarier, glariest, glarily, glariness, glaring, glaringly, glaringness, glarry, glary, glaserite, glasgow, glashan, glass, glassblower, glassblowers, glassblowing, glassed, glassen, glasser, glasses, glasseye, glassfish, glassful, glassfuls, glasshouse, glasshouses, glassie, glassier, glassies, glassiest, glassily, glassin, glassine, glassines, glassiness, glassing, glassite, glassless, glasslike, glasslikeness, glassmaker, glassmaking, glassman, glassmen, glassophone, glassrope, glasssteel, glassware, glassweed, glasswork, glassworker, glassworkers, glassworking, glassworks, glassworm, glasswort, glassy, glastonbury, glauber, glauberite, glaucescence, glaucescent, glaucic, glaucin, glaucine, glaucochroite, glaucodot, glaucodote, glaucolite, glaucoma, glaucomas, glaucomatous, glauconiferous, glauconite, glauconitic, glauconitization, glaucophane, glaucophanite, glaucophanization, glaucophanize, glaucophyllous, glaucosis, glaucosuria, glaucous, glaucously, glaucousness, glaucus, glaum, glaumrie, glaur, glaury, glave, glaver, glavered, glavering, glaymore, glaze, glazed, glazement, glazen, glazer, glazers, glazes, glazework, glazier, glazieries, glaziers, glaziery, glaziest, glazily, glaziness, glazing, glazings, glazy, glb, gld, glead, gleam, gleamed, gleamier, gleamiest, gleamily, gleaminess, gleaming, gleamingly, gleamless, gleams, gleamy, glean, gleanable, gleaned, gleaner, gleaners, gleaning, gleanings, gleans, gleary, gleave, gleba, glebae, glebal, glebe, glebeless, glebes, glebous, gleby, gled, glede, gledes, gledge, gleds, gledy, glee, gleed, gleeds, gleeful, gleefully, gleefulness, gleeishly, gleek, gleeked, gleeking, gleeks, gleemaiden, gleeman, gleemen, gleen, glees, gleesome, gleesomely, gleesomeness, gleet, gleeted, gleetier, gleetiest, gleeting, gleets, gleety, gleewoman, gleg, glegly, glegness, glegnesses, gleir, gleit, gleization, glen, glen's, glendale, glendover, glene, glengarries, glengarry, glenlike, glenlivet, glenohumeral, glenoid, glenoidal, glens, glent, glenwood, glessite, gletscher, gletty, glew, gley, gleyde, gleys, glia, gliadin, gliadine, gliadines, gliadins, glial, glib, glibber, glibbery, glibbest, glibly, glibness, glibnesses, glick, glidder, gliddery, glide, glided, glideless, glideness, glider, gliderport, gliders, glides, glidewort, gliding, glidingly, gliff, gliffing, gliffs, gliffy, glike, glim, glime, glimed, glimes, gliming, glimmer, glimmered, glimmering, glimmeringly, glimmerings, glimmerite, glimmerous, glimmers, glimmery, glimpse, glimpsed, glimpser, glimpsers, glimpses, glimpsing, glims, glink, glinse, glint, glinted, glinting, glints, gliocyte, glioma, gliomas, gliomata, gliomatous, gliosa, gliosis, gliriform, glirine, glisk, glisky, gliss, glissade, glissaded, glissader, glissades, glissading, glissandi, glissando, glissandos, glissette, glist, glisten, glistened, glistening, glisteningly, glistens, glister, glistered, glistering, glisteringly, glisters, glitch, glitches, glitter, glitterance, glittered, glittering, glitteringly, glitters, glittersome, glittery, glitzy, gloam, gloaming, gloamings, gloams, gloat, gloated, gloater, gloaters, gloating, gloatingly, gloats, glob, global, globalism, globalist, globalists, globality, globalization, globalize, globalized, globalizing, globally, globate, globated, globe, globe's, globed, globefish, globefishes, globeflower, globeholder, globelet, globelike, globes, globetrotter, globetrotters, globetrotting, globical, globiferous, globigerina, globigerinae, globigerinas, globigerine, globin, globing, globins, globoid, globoids, globose, globosely, globoseness, globosite, globosities, globosity, globosphaerite, globous, globously, globousness, globs, globular, globulariaceous, globularity, globularly, globularness, globule, globules, globulet, globulicidal, globulicide, globuliferous, globuliform, globulimeter, globulin, globulins, globulinuria, globulite, globulitic, globuloid, globulolysis, globulose, globulous, globulousness, globulysis, globus, globy, glochchidia, glochid, glochideous, glochidia, glochidial, glochidian, glochidiate, glochidium, glochids, glochines, glochis, glockenspiel, glockenspiels, glod, gloea, gloeal, gloeocapsoid, gloeosporiose, glogg, gloggs, glom, glome, glomeli, glomera, glomerate, glomeration, glomeroporphyritic, glomerular, glomerulate, glomerule, glomeruli, glomerulitis, glomerulonephritis, glomerulose, glomerulus, glomi, glommed, glomming, glommox, gloms, glomus, glonoin, glonoine, glood, gloom, gloomed, gloomful, gloomfully, gloomier, gloomiest, gloomily, gloominess, glooming, gloomingly, gloomings, gloomless, glooms, gloomth, gloomy, glop, glopnen, gloppen, gloppy, glops, glor, glore, gloria, gloriam, glorias, gloriation, gloried, glories, gloriette, glorifiable, glorification, glorifications, glorified, glorifier, glorifiers, glorifies, glorify, glorifying, gloriole, glorioles, gloriosity, glorioso, glorious, gloriously, gloriousness, glory, gloryful, glorying, gloryingly, gloryless, glos, gloss, glossa, glossae, glossagra, glossal, glossalgia, glossalgy, glossanthrax, glossarial, glossarially, glossarian, glossaries, glossarist, glossarize, glossary, glossary's, glossas, glossate, glossator, glossatorial, glossectomies, glossectomy, glossed, glossem, glossematic, glossematics, glosseme, glossemes, glossemic, glosser, glossers, glosses, glossic, glossier, glossies, glossiest, glossily, glossina, glossinas, glossiness, glossing, glossingly, glossist, glossitic, glossitis, glossless, glossmeter, glossocarcinoma, glossocele, glossocoma, glossocomium, glossocomon, glossodynamometer, glossodynia, glossoepiglottic, glossoepiglottidean, glossograph, glossographer, glossographical, glossography, glossohyal, glossoid, glossokinesthetic, glossolabial, glossolabiolaryngeal, glossolabiopharyngeal, glossolalia, glossolalist, glossolaly, glossolaryngeal, glossological, glossologies, glossologist, glossology, glossolysis, glossoncus, glossopalatine, glossopalatinus, glossopathy, glossopetra, glossophagine, glossopharyngeal, glossopharyngeus, glossophobia, glossophorous, glossophytia, glossoplasty, glossoplegia, glossopode, glossopodium, glossoptosis, glossopyrosis, glossorrhaphy, glossoscopia, glossoscopy, glossospasm, glossosteresis, glossotomies, glossotomy, glossotype, glossy, glost, glosts, glottal, glottalite, glottalization, glottalize, glottalized, glottalizing, glottic, glottid, glottidean, glottides, glottis, glottiscope, glottises, glottitis, glottochronological, glottochronology, glottogonic, glottogonist, glottogony, glottologic, glottological, glottologies, glottologist, glottology, glotum, gloucester, glout, glouted, glouting, glouts, glove, gloved, gloveless, glovelike, glovemaker, glovemaking, gloveman, glovemen, glover, gloveress, glovers, gloves, glovey, gloving, glow, glowbard, glowbird, glowed, glower, glowered, glowerer, glowering, gloweringly, glowers, glowflies, glowfly, glowing, glowingly, glows, glowworm, glowworms, gloxinia, gloxinias, gloy, gloze, glozed, glozer, glozes, glozing, glozingly, glt, glub, glucaemia, glucagon, glucagons, glucase, glucate, glucemia, glucic, glucid, glucide, glucidic, glucina, glucine, glucinic, glucinium, glucinum, glucinums, gluck, glucke, glucocorticoid, glucocorticord, glucofrangulin, glucogene, glucogenesis, glucogenic, glucokinase, glucokinin, glucolipid, glucolipide, glucolipin, glucolipine, glucolysis, gluconate, gluconeogenesis, gluconeogenetic, gluconeogenic, gluconokinase, glucoprotein, glucosaemia, glucosamine, glucosan, glucosane, glucosazone, glucose, glucosemia, glucoses, glucosic, glucosid, glucosidal, glucosidase, glucoside, glucosidic, glucosidically, glucosin, glucosine, glucosone, glucosulfone, glucosuria, glucosuric, glucuronic, glucuronidase, glucuronide, glue, glued, glueing, gluelike, gluelikeness, gluemaker, gluemaking, glueman, gluepot, gluer, gluers, glues, gluey, glueyness, glug, glugglug, gluhwein, gluier, gluiest, gluily, gluiness, gluing, gluish, gluishness, glum, gluma, glumaceous, glumal, glume, glumelike, glumella, glumes, glumiferous, glumly, glummer, glummest, glummy, glumness, glumnesses, glumose, glumosity, glumous, glump, glumpier, glumpiest, glumpily, glumpiness, glumpish, glumpy, glunch, glunched, glunches, glunching, glunimie, gluon, glusid, gluside, glut, glutael, glutaeous, glutamate, glutamates, glutamic, glutaminase, glutamine, glutaminic, glutaraldehyde, glutaric, glutathione, glutch, gluteal, glutei, glutelin, glutelins, gluten, glutenin, glutenous, glutens, gluteofemoral, gluteoinguinal, gluteoperineal, glutetei, glutethimide, gluteus, glutimate, glutin, glutinant, glutinate, glutination, glutinative, glutinize, glutinose, glutinosity, glutinous, glutinously, glutinousness, glutition, glutoid, glutose, gluts, glutted, gluttei, glutter, gluttery, glutting, gluttingly, glutton, gluttoness, gluttonies, gluttonise, gluttonised, gluttonish, gluttonising, gluttonism, gluttonize, gluttonized, gluttonizing, gluttonous, gluttonously, gluttonousness, gluttons, gluttony, glyc, glycaemia, glycaemic, glycan, glycans, glycemia, glycemic, glyceral, glyceraldehyde, glycerate, glyceric, glyceride, glyceridic, glycerin, glycerinate, glycerinated, glycerinating, glycerination, glycerine, glycerinize, glycerins, glycerite, glycerize, glycerizin, glycerizine, glycerogel, glycerogelatin, glycerol, glycerolate, glycerole, glycerolize, glycerols, glycerolyses, glycerolysis, glycerophosphate, glycerophosphoric, glycerose, glyceroxide, glyceryl, glyceryls, glycic, glycid, glycide, glycidic, glycidol, glycin, glycine, glycines, glycinin, glycins, glycocholate, glycocholic, glycocin, glycocoll, glycogelatin, glycogen, glycogenase, glycogenesis, glycogenetic, glycogenic, glycogenize, glycogenolysis, glycogenolytic, glycogenosis, glycogenous, glycogens, glycogeny, glycohaemia, glycohemia, glycol, glycolaldehyde, glycolate, glycolic, glycolide, glycolipid, glycolipide, glycolipin, glycolipine, glycollate, glycollic, glycollide, glycols, glycoluric, glycoluril, glycolyl, glycolylurea, glycolysis, glycolytic, glycolytically, glyconean, glyconeogenesis, glyconeogenetic, glyconic, glyconics, glyconin, glycopeptide, glycopexia, glycopexis, glycoproteid, glycoprotein, glycosaemia, glycose, glycosemia, glycosidase, glycoside, glycosides, glycosidic, glycosidically, glycosin, glycosine, glycosuria, glycosuric, glycosyl, glycosyls, glycuresis, glycuronic, glycuronid, glycuronide, glycyl, glycyls, glycyphyllin, glycyrize, glycyrrhizin, glykopectic, glykopexic, glyn, glyoxal, glyoxalase, glyoxalic, glyoxalin, glyoxaline, glyoxilin, glyoxim, glyoxime, glyoxyl, glyoxylic, glyph, glyphic, glyphograph, glyphographer, glyphographic, glyphography, glyphs, glyptal, glyptic, glyptical, glyptician, glyptics, glyptodon, glyptodont, glyptodontoid, glyptograph, glyptographer, glyptographic, glyptography, glyptolith, glyptological, glyptologist, glyptology, glyptotheca, glyster, gm, gmelinite, gn, gnabble, gnamma, gnaphalioid, gnapweed, gnar, gnarl, gnarled, gnarlier, gnarliest, gnarliness, gnarling, gnarls, gnarly, gnarr, gnarred, gnarring, gnarrs, gnars, gnash, gnashed, gnashes, gnashing, gnashingly, gnast, gnat, gnat's, gnatcatcher, gnateater, gnatflower, gnathal, gnathalgia, gnathic, gnathidium, gnathion, gnathions, gnathism, gnathite, gnathites, gnathitis, gnatho, gnathobase, gnathobasic, gnathometer, gnathonic, gnathonical, gnathonically, gnathonism, gnathonize, gnathophorous, gnathoplasty, gnathopod, gnathopodite, gnathopodous, gnathostegite, gnathostomatous, gnathostome, gnathostomous, gnathotheca, gnatlike, gnatling, gnatoo, gnatproof, gnats, gnatsnap, gnatsnapper, gnatter, gnattier, gnattiest, gnatty, gnatworm, gnaw, gnawable, gnawed, gnawer, gnawers, gnawing, gnawingly, gnawings, gnawn, gnaws, gneiss, gneisses, gneissic, gneissitic, gneissoid, gneissose, gneissy, gnessic, gnetaceous, gnetums, gneu, gnide, gnocchetti, gnocchi, gnoff, gnome, gnomed, gnomelike, gnomes, gnomesque, gnomic, gnomical, gnomically, gnomide, gnomish, gnomist, gnomists, gnomologic, gnomological, gnomologist, gnomology, gnomon, gnomonic, gnomonical, gnomonics, gnomonological, gnomonologically, gnomonology, gnomons, gnoses, gnosiological, gnosiology, gnosis, gnostic, gnostical, gnostically, gnosticism, gnosticity, gnosticize, gnosticizer, gnostology, gnotobiologies, gnotobiology, gnotobiosis, gnotobiote, gnotobiotic, gnotobiotically, gnotobiotics, gnow, gns, gnu, gnus, go, goa, goad, goaded, goading, goadlike, goads, goadsman, goadster, goaf, goal, goal's, goalage, goaled, goalee, goaler, goalers, goalie, goalies, goaling, goalkeeper, goalkeepers, goalkeeping, goalless, goalmouth, goalpost, goalposts, goals, goaltender, goaltenders, goaltending, goanna, goar, goas, goat, goat's, goatbeard, goatbrush, goatbush, goatee, goatee's, goateed, goatees, goatfish, goatfishes, goatherd, goatherdess, goatherds, goatish, goatishly, goatishness, goatland, goatlike, goatling, goatly, goatpox, goatroot, goats, goatsbane, goatsbeard, goatsfoot, goatskin, goatskins, goatstone, goatsucker, goatweed, goaty, goave, goaves, gob, goback, goban, gobang, gobangs, gobans, gobbe, gobbed, gobber, gobbet, gobbets, gobbin, gobbing, gobble, gobbled, gobbledegook, gobbledygook, gobbler, gobblers, gobbles, gobbling, gobby, gobelin, gobemouche, gobernadora, gobet, gobi, gobies, gobiesocid, gobiesociform, gobiid, gobiiform, gobioid, gobioids, goblet, goblet's, gobleted, gobletful, goblets, goblin, goblin's, gobline, goblinesque, goblinish, goblinism, goblinize, goblinry, goblins, gobmouthed, gobo, goboes, gobonated, gobonee, gobony, gobos, gobs, gobstick, gobstopper, goburra, goby, gobylike, gocart, goclenian, god, god's, godawful, godchild, godchildren, goddam, goddammed, goddamming, goddammit, goddamn, goddamndest, goddamned, goddamnedest, goddamning, goddamnit, goddamns, goddams, goddard, goddaughter, goddaughters, godded, goddess, goddess's, goddesses, goddesshood, goddessship, goddikin, godding, goddize, gode, godelich, godendag, godet, godetia, godfather, godfatherhood, godfathers, godfathership, godforsaken, godhead, godheads, godhood, godhoods, godiva, godkin, godless, godlessly, godlessness, godlet, godlier, godliest, godlike, godlikeness, godlily, godliness, godling, godlings, godly, godmaker, godmaking, godmamma, godmother, godmother's, godmotherhood, godmothers, godmothership, godown, godowns, godpapa, godparent, godparents, godroon, godroons, gods, godsend, godsends, godsent, godship, godships, godsib, godson, godsons, godsonship, godspeed, godward, godwit, godwits, goebbels, goeduck, goel, goelism, goen, goer, goers, goes, goethe, goethian, goethite, goethites, goetia, goetic, goetical, goety, gofer, gofers, goff, goffer, goffered, gofferer, goffering, goffers, goffle, gog, gogetting, gogga, goggan, goggle, gogglebox, goggled, goggler, gogglers, goggles, gogglier, goggliest, goggling, goggly, goglet, goglets, gogmagog, gogo, gogos, goi, goiabada, goidel, goidelic, going, goings, gois, goitcho, goiter, goitered, goiterogenic, goiters, goitral, goitre, goitres, goitrogen, goitrogenic, goitrogenicity, goitrous, gol, gola, golach, goladar, golandaas, golandause, golconda, golcondas, gold, goldang, goldanged, goldarn, goldarned, goldarnedest, goldarns, goldbeater, goldbeating, goldbrick, goldbricker, goldbrickers, goldbricks, goldbug, goldbugs, goldcrest, goldcup, golden, goldenback, goldener, goldenest, goldeney, goldeneye, goldeneyes, goldenfleece, goldenhair, goldenknop, goldenlocks, goldenly, goldenmouthed, goldenness, goldenpert, goldenrod, goldenrods, goldenseal, goldentop, goldenwing, golder, goldest, goldeye, goldeyes, goldfield, goldfielder, goldfields, goldfinch, goldfinches, goldfinnies, goldfinny, goldfish, goldfishes, goldflower, goldhammer, goldhead, goldie, goldilocks, goldin, golding, goldish, goldless, goldlike, goldminer, goldmist, goldney, golds, goldseed, goldsinny, goldsmith, goldsmithery, goldsmithing, goldsmithry, goldsmiths, goldspink, goldstone, goldtail, goldthread, goldtit, goldurn, goldurned, goldurnedest, goldurns, goldwater, goldweed, goldwork, goldworker, goldy, goldylocks, golee, golem, golems, goles, golet, golf, golfdom, golfed, golfer, golfers, golfing, golfings, golfs, golgotha, golgothas, goli, goliad, goliard, goliardery, goliardeys, goliardic, goliards, goliath, goliathize, goliaths, golilla, golkakra, goll, golland, gollar, goller, golliwog, golliwogg, golliwogs, gollop, golly, gollywobbler, gollywog, goloch, goloe, goloka, golosh, goloshes, golp, golpe, golundauze, goluptious, gomari, gomarist, gomart, gomashta, gomasta, gomavel, gombay, gombeen, gombeenism, gombo, gombos, gombroon, gombroons, gome, gomer, gomeral, gomerals, gomerec, gomerel, gomerels, gomeril, gomerils, gomlah, gommelin, gommier, gomorrah, gomorrean, gomphiasis, gomphodont, gomphoses, gomphosis, gomukhi, gomuti, gomutis, gon, gonad, gonadal, gonadectomies, gonadectomized, gonadectomizing, gonadectomy, gonadial, gonadic, gonadotrope, gonadotrophic, gonadotrophin, gonadotropic, gonadotropin, gonads, gonaduct, gonagia, gonagra, gonake, gonakie, gonal, gonalgia, gonangia, gonangial, gonangium, gonangiums, gonapod, gonapophysal, gonapophysial, gonapophysis, gonarthritis, goncalo, gond, gondang, gondi, gondite, gondola, gondolas, gondolet, gondoletta, gondolier, gondoliere, gondoliers, gone, goneness, gonenesses, goneoclinic, gonepoiesis, gonepoietic, goner, goners, gonesome, goney, gonfalcon, gonfalon, gonfalonier, gonfalonierate, gonfaloniership, gonfalons, gonfanon, gonfanons, gong, gong's, gonged, gonging, gonglike, gongman, gongorism, gongoristic, gongs, gonia, goniac, gonial, goniale, goniatite, goniatitic, goniatitid, goniatitoid, gonid, gonidangium, gonidia, gonidial, gonidic, gonidiferous, gonidiogenous, gonidioid, gonidiophore, gonidiose, gonidiospore, gonidium, gonif, gonifs, gonimic, gonimium, gonimoblast, gonimolobe, gonimous, goninidia, goniocraniometry, goniometer, goniometric, goniometrical, goniometrically, goniometry, gonion, gonionia, goniostat, goniotheca, goniotropous, gonitis, gonium, goniums, goniunia, gonk, gonna, gonnardite, gonne, gonoblast, gonoblastic, gonoblastidial, gonoblastidium, gonocalycine, gonocalyx, gonocheme, gonochorism, gonochorismal, gonochorismus, gonochoristic, gonococcal, gonococci, gonococcic, gonococcocci, gonococcoid, gonococcus, gonocoel, gonocoele, gonocyte, gonocytes, gonoecium, gonof, gonofs, gonogenesis, gonomere, gonomery, gonoph, gonophore, gonophoric, gonophorous, gonophs, gonoplasm, gonopod, gonopodia, gonopodial, gonopodium, gonopodpodia, gonopoietic, gonopore, gonopores, gonorrhea, gonorrheal, gonorrheic, gonorrhoea, gonorrhoeal, gonorrhoeic, gonosomal, gonosome, gonosphere, gonostyle, gonotheca, gonothecae, gonothecal, gonotocont, gonotokont, gonotome, gonotyl, gonotype, gonozooid, gony, gonyalgia, gonyaulax, gonycampsis, gonydeal, gonydial, gonyocele, gonyoncus, gonys, gonystylaceous, gonytheca, gonzalo, gonzo, goo, goober, goobers, good, goodby, goodbye, goodbyes, goodbys, goodeniaceous, gooder, gooders, goodhap, goodhearted, goodheartedly, goodheartedness, goodhumoredness, goodie, goodies, gooding, goodish, goodishness, goodless, goodlier, goodliest, goodlihead, goodlike, goodliness, goodly, goodman, goodmanship, goodmen, goodnaturedness, goodness, goodnesses, goodnight, goodrich, goods, goodship, goodsire, goodsome, goodtemperedness, goodwife, goodwilies, goodwill, goodwilled, goodwillie, goodwillies, goodwillit, goodwills, goodwilly, goodwily, goodwives, goody, goody's, goodyear, goodyish, goodyism, goodyness, goodyship, gooey, goof, goofah, goofball, goofballs, goofed, goofer, goofier, goofiest, goofily, goofiness, goofing, goofs, goofy, goog, googlies, googly, googol, googolplex, googols, googul, gooier, gooiest, gook, gooks, gooky, gool, goolah, goolde, gools, gooma, goombay, goon, goonch, goonda, goondie, gooney, gooneys, goonie, goonies, goons, goony, goop, goops, goopy, gooral, goorals, gooranut, gooroo, goos, goosander, goose, goosebeak, gooseberries, gooseberry, goosebill, goosebird, goosebone, gooseboy, goosecap, goosed, goosefish, goosefishes, gooseflesh, gooseflower, goosefoot, goosefoots, goosegirl, goosegog, goosegrass, gooseherd, goosehouse, gooselike, gooseliver, goosemouth, gooseneck, goosenecked, goosepimply, gooseries, gooserumped, goosery, gooses, gooseskin, goosetongue, gooseweed, goosewing, goosewinged, goosey, goosier, goosiest, goosing, goosish, goosishly, goosishness, goosy, gootee, goozle, gopak, gopher, gopherberries, gopherberry, gopherman, gopherroot, gophers, gopherwood, gopura, gor, gora, goracco, goral, goralog, gorals, goran, gorb, gorbal, gorbellied, gorbellies, gorbelly, gorbet, gorbit, gorble, gorblimey, gorblimy, gorblin, gorce, gorcock, gorcocks, gorcrow, gordiacean, gordiaceous, gordian, gordiid, gordioid, gordolobo, gordunite, gore, gorebill, gored, gorefish, gorer, gores, gorevan, gorfly, gorge, gorgeable, gorged, gorgedly, gorgelet, gorgeous, gorgeously, gorgeousness, gorger, gorgeret, gorgerin, gorgerins, gorgers, gorges, gorget, gorgeted, gorgets, gorgia, gorging, gorgio, gorglin, gorgon, gorgonacean, gorgonaceous, gorgoneia, gorgoneion, gorgoneioneia, gorgonesque, gorgoneum, gorgonia, gorgoniacean, gorgoniaceous, gorgonian, gorgonin, gorgonise, gorgonised, gorgonising, gorgonize, gorgonized, gorgonizing, gorgonlike, gorgons, gorgonzola, gorgosaurus, gorhen, gorhens, goric, gorier, goriest, gorilla, gorilla's, gorillalike, gorillas, gorillaship, gorillian, gorilline, gorilloid, gorily, goriness, gorinesses, goring, gorki, gorkun, gorlin, gorling, gorlois, gorman, gormand, gormandise, gormandised, gormandiser, gormandising, gormandism, gormandize, gormandized, gormandizer, gormandizers, gormandizes, gormandizing, gormands, gormaw, gormed, gormless, gorra, gorraf, gorrel, gorry, gorse, gorsebird, gorsechat, gorsedd, gorsehatch, gorses, gorsier, gorsiest, gorst, gorsy, gory, gos, gosain, goschen, goschens, gosh, goshawful, goshawk, goshawks, goshdarn, goshen, goshenite, goslarite, goslet, gosling, goslings, gosmore, gospel, gospeler, gospelers, gospelist, gospelize, gospeller, gospellike, gospelly, gospelmonger, gospels, gospelwards, gospoda, gospodar, gospodin, gospodipoda, gosport, gosports, goss, gossamer, gossamered, gossameriness, gossamers, gossamery, gossampine, gossan, gossaniferous, gossans, gossard, gossep, gossip, gossipdom, gossiped, gossipee, gossiper, gossipers, gossiphood, gossipiness, gossiping, gossipingly, gossipmonger, gossipmongering, gossipped, gossipper, gossipping, gossipred, gossipries, gossipry, gossips, gossipy, gossoon, gossoons, gossy, gossypin, gossypine, gossypol, gossypols, gossypose, goster, gosther, got, gotch, gotched, gotchy, gote, goter, goth, gotha, gotham, gothic, gothically, gothicism, gothicist, gothicize, gothics, gothish, gothite, gothites, goths, goto, gotos, gotra, gotraja, gotta, gotten, gou, gouache, gouaches, gouaree, gouda, gouge, gouged, gouger, gougers, gouges, gouging, gougingly, goujat, goujay, goujon, goujons, goulan, goularo, goulash, goulashes, gouldian, goumi, goumier, gounau, goundou, goup, goupen, goupin, gour, goura, gourami, gouramis, gourd, gourde, gourded, gourdes, gourdful, gourdhead, gourdiness, gourding, gourdlike, gourds, gourdworm, gourdy, gourmand, gourmander, gourmanderie, gourmandise, gourmandism, gourmandize, gourmandizer, gourmands, gourmet, gourmetism, gourmets, gournard, gourounut, goury, goustie, goustrous, gousty, gout, gouter, goutier, goutiest, goutify, goutily, goutiness, goutish, gouts, goutte, goutweed, goutwort, gouty, gouvernante, gouvernantes, gov, gove, govern, governability, governable, governableness, governably, governail, governance, governante, governed, governeress, governess, governessdom, governesses, governesshood, governessy, governing, governingly, governless, government, government's, governmental, governmentalism, governmentalist, governmentalize, governmentally, governmentish, governments, governor, governor's, governorate, governors, governorship, governorships, governs, govt, gowan, gowaned, gowans, gowany, gowd, gowdie, gowdnie, gowdnook, gowds, gowdy, gowf, gowfer, gowiddie, gowk, gowked, gowkedly, gowkedness, gowkit, gowks, gowl, gowlan, gowland, gown, gowned, gowning, gownlet, gowns, gownsman, gownsmen, gowpen, gowpin, gox, goxes, goy, goyazite, goyim, goyin, goyish, goyle, goys, gozell, gozill, gozzan, gozzard, gp, gpad, gpcd, gpd, gph, gpm, gps, gpss, gr, gra, graafian, graal, graals, grab, grabbable, grabbed, grabber, grabber's, grabbers, grabbier, grabbiest, grabbing, grabbings, grabble, grabbled, grabbler, grabblers, grabbles, grabbling, grabbots, grabby, graben, grabens, grabhook, grabman, grabouche, grabs, grace, graced, graceful, gracefuller, gracefullest, gracefully, gracefulness, graceless, gracelessly, gracelessness, gracelike, gracer, graces, gracias, gracilariid, gracile, gracileness, graciles, gracilescent, gracilis, gracility, gracing, graciosity, gracioso, graciosos, gracious, graciously, graciousness, grackle, grackles, gracy, grad, gradable, gradal, gradate, gradated, gradates, gradatim, gradating, gradation, gradation's, gradational, gradationally, gradationately, gradations, gradative, gradatively, gradatory, graddan, grade, graded, gradefinder, gradeless, gradely, grademark, grader, graders, grades, gradgrind, gradient, gradient's, gradienter, gradients, gradin, gradine, gradines, grading, gradings, gradino, gradins, gradiometer, gradiometric, gradometer, grads, gradual, graduale, gradualism, gradualist, gradualistic, graduality, gradually, gradualness, graduals, graduand, graduands, graduate, graduated, graduates, graduateship, graduatical, graduating, graduation, graduations, graduator, graduators, gradus, graduses, graeae, graecian, graecism, graecize, graecized, graecizes, graecizing, graecomania, graecophil, graf, graff, graffage, graffer, graffiti, graffito, grafship, graft, graftage, graftages, graftdom, grafted, grafter, grafters, grafting, graftonite, graftproof, grafts, grager, gragers, graham, graham's, grahamism, grahamite, grahams, grail, grailer, grailing, graille, grails, grain, grainage, graine, grained, grainedness, grainer, grainering, grainers, grainery, grainfield, grainier, grainiest, graininess, graining, grainland, grainless, grainman, grains, grainsick, grainsickness, grainsman, grainsmen, grainways, grainy, graip, graisse, graith, graithly, grakle, grallatorial, grallatory, grallic, gralline, gralloch, gram, grama, gramaphone, gramaries, gramary, gramarye, gramaryes, gramas, gramash, gramashes, grame, gramenite, gramercies, gramercy, gramicidin, graminaceous, gramineal, gramineous, gramineousness, graminicolous, graminiferous, graminifolious, graminiform, graminin, graminivore, graminivorous, graminological, graminology, graminous, gramma, grammalogue, grammar, grammar's, grammarian, grammarianism, grammarians, grammarless, grammars, grammates, grammatic, grammatical, grammaticality, grammatically, grammaticalness, grammaticaster, grammatication, grammaticism, grammaticize, grammatics, grammatist, grammatistical, grammatite, grammatolator, grammatolatry, grammatology, gramme, grammel, grammes, grammies, grammy, gramoches, gramophone, gramophones, gramophonic, gramophonical, gramophonically, gramophonist, gramp, grampa, gramper, gramps, grampus, grampuses, grams, gramy, grana, granada, granadilla, granadillo, granado, granage, granam, granaries, granary, granary's, granat, granate, granatite, granatum, granch, grand, grandad, grandada, grandaddy, grandads, grandam, grandame, grandames, grandams, grandaunt, grandaunts, grandbaby, grandchild, grandchildren, granddad, granddada, granddaddies, granddaddy, granddads, granddam, granddaughter, granddaughterly, granddaughters, grande, grandee, grandeeism, grandees, grandeeship, grander, grandesque, grandest, grandeur, grandeurs, grandeval, grandevity, grandevous, grandeza, grandezza, grandfather, grandfather's, grandfatherhood, grandfatherish, grandfatherless, grandfatherly, grandfathers, grandfathership, grandfer, grandfilial, grandgore, grandiflora, grandiloquence, grandiloquent, grandiloquently, grandiloquous, grandiose, grandiosely, grandioseness, grandiosity, grandioso, grandisonant, grandisonian, grandisonous, grandity, grandly, grandma, grandmama, grandmamma, grandmammy, grandmas, grandmaster, grandmaternal, grandmother, grandmother's, grandmotherhood, grandmotherism, grandmotherliness, grandmotherly, grandmothers, grandnephew, grandnephews, grandness, grandniece, grandnieces, grando, grandpa, grandpap, grandpapa, grandpappy, grandparent, grandparentage, grandparental, grandparenthood, grandparents, grandpas, grandpaternal, grandrelle, grands, grandsir, grandsire, grandsirs, grandson, grandson's, grandsons, grandsonship, grandstand, grandstanded, grandstander, grandstanding, grandstands, grandtotal, granduncle, granduncles, grane, granes, granet, grange, granger, grangerisation, grangerise, grangerised, grangeriser, grangerising, grangerism, grangerite, grangerization, grangerize, grangerized, grangerizer, grangerizing, grangers, granges, graniferous, graniform, granilla, granita, granite, granitelike, granites, graniteware, granitic, granitical, graniticoline, granitiferous, granitification, granitiform, granitite, granitization, granitize, granitized, granitizing, granitoid, granitoidal, granivore, granivorous, granjeno, grank, granma, grannam, grannie, grannies, grannom, granny, grannybush, grannyknot, grano, granoblastic, granodiorite, granodioritic, granogabbro, granola, granolite, granolith, granolithic, granomerite, granophyre, granophyric, granose, granospherite, grant, grantable, granted, grantedly, grantee, grantees, granter, granters, granthi, granting, grantor, grantors, grants, grantsman, grantsmanship, grantsmen, granula, granular, granularity, granularly, granulary, granulate, granulated, granulater, granulates, granulating, granulation, granulations, granulative, granulator, granulators, granule, granules, granulet, granuliferous, granuliform, granulite, granulitic, granulitis, granulitization, granulitize, granulization, granulize, granuloadipose, granuloblast, granuloblastic, granulocyte, granulocytic, granulocytopoiesis, granuloma, granulomas, granulomata, granulomatosis, granulomatous, granulometric, granulosa, granulose, granulosis, granulous, granum, granza, granzita, grape, grape's, graped, grapeflower, grapefruit, grapefruits, grapeful, grapeless, grapelet, grapelike, grapeline, grapenuts, graperies, graperoot, grapery, grapes, grapeshot, grapeskin, grapestalk, grapestone, grapevine, grapevines, grapewise, grapewort, grapey, grapeys, graph, graph's, graphalloy, graphanalysis, graphed, grapheme, graphemes, graphemic, graphemically, graphemics, graphic, graphical, graphically, graphicalness, graphicly, graphicness, graphics, graphing, graphiological, graphiologist, graphiology, graphite, graphiter, graphites, graphitic, graphitizable, graphitization, graphitize, graphitized, graphitizing, graphitoid, graphitoidal, graphoanalytical, grapholite, graphologic, graphological, graphologies, graphologist, graphologists, graphology, graphomania, graphomaniac, graphomaniacal, graphometer, graphometric, graphometrical, graphometrist, graphometry, graphomotor, graphonomy, graphophobia, graphophone, graphophonic, graphorrhea, graphoscope, graphospasm, graphostatic, graphostatical, graphostatics, graphotype, graphotypic, graphs, graphy, grapier, grapiest, graping, graplin, grapline, graplines, graplins, grapnel, grapnels, grappa, grappas, grapple, grappled, grapplement, grappler, grapplers, grapples, grappling, grapsoid, graptolite, graptolitic, graptomancy, grapy, gras, grasni, grasp, graspable, grasped, grasper, graspers, grasping, graspingly, graspingness, graspless, grasps, grass, grassant, grassation, grassbird, grasschat, grasscut, grasscutter, grassed, grasser, grasserie, grassers, grasses, grasset, grasseye, grassfinch, grassfire, grassflat, grassflower, grasshook, grasshop, grasshopper, grasshopperdom, grasshopperish, grasshoppers, grasshouse, grassie, grassier, grassiest, grassily, grassiness, grassing, grassland, grasslands, grassless, grasslike, grassman, grassmen, grassnut, grassplat, grassplot, grassquit, grassroots, grasswards, grassweed, grasswidow, grasswidowhood, grasswork, grassworm, grassy, grat, grata, gratae, grate, grated, grateful, gratefuller, gratefullest, gratefully, gratefulness, grateless, gratelike, grateman, grater, graters, grates, gratewise, grather, gratia, gratias, graticulate, graticulation, graticule, gratifiable, gratification, gratifications, gratified, gratifiedly, gratifier, gratifies, gratify, gratifying, gratifyingly, gratility, gratillity, gratin, gratinate, gratinated, gratinating, grating, gratingly, gratings, gratins, gratiola, gratiolin, gratiosolin, gratis, gratitude, grattage, gratten, gratters, grattoir, grattoirs, gratton, gratuitant, gratuities, gratuito, gratuitous, gratuitously, gratuitousness, gratuity, gratuity's, gratulant, gratulate, gratulated, gratulating, gratulation, gratulatorily, gratulatory, graunt, graupel, graupels, graustark, grauwacke, grav, gravamem, gravamen, gravamens, gravamina, gravaminous, gravat, gravata, grave, graveclod, gravecloth, graveclothes, graved, gravedigger, gravediggers, gravedo, gravegarth, gravel, graveldiver, graveled, graveless, gravelike, graveling, gravelish, gravelled, gravelliness, gravelling, gravelly, gravelous, gravelroot, gravels, gravelstone, gravelweed, gravely, gravemaker, gravemaking, graveman, gravemaster, graven, graveness, graveolence, graveolency, graveolent, graver, graverobber, graverobbing, gravers, gravery, graves, graveship, graveside, gravest, gravestead, gravestone, gravestones, gravette, graveward, gravewards, graveyard, graveyards, gravic, gravicembali, gravicembalo, gravicembalos, gravid, gravida, gravidae, gravidas, gravidate, gravidation, gravidity, gravidly, gravidness, graviers, gravies, gravific, gravigrade, gravilea, gravimeter, gravimeters, gravimetric, gravimetrical, gravimetrically, gravimetry, graving, gravipause, gravisphere, gravispheric, gravitate, gravitated, gravitater, gravitates, gravitating, gravitation, gravitational, gravitationally, gravitations, gravitative, gravitic, gravities, gravitometer, graviton, gravitons, gravity, gravure, gravures, gravy, grawls, gray, grayback, graybacks, graybeard, graybearded, graybeards, graycoat, grayed, grayer, grayest, grayfish, grayfishes, grayfly, grayhair, grayhead, grayhound, graying, grayish, grayishness, graylag, graylags, grayling, graylings, grayly, graymalkin, graymill, grayness, graynesses, grayout, grayouts, graypate, grays, graysbies, graysby, graywacke, graywall, grayware, graywether, grazable, graze, grazeable, grazed, grazer, grazers, grazes, grazie, grazier, grazierdom, graziers, graziery, grazing, grazingly, grazings, grazioso, gre, greable, greably, grease, greaseball, greasebush, greased, greasehorn, greaseless, greaselessness, greasepaint, greaseproof, greaseproofness, greaser, greasers, greases, greasewood, greasier, greasiest, greasily, greasiness, greasing, greasy, great, greatcoat, greatcoated, greatcoats, greaten, greatened, greatening, greatens, greater, greatest, greathead, greatheart, greathearted, greatheartedly, greatheartedness, greatish, greatly, greatmouthed, greatness, greats, greave, greaved, greaves, grebe, grebes, grecale, grece, grecian, grecianize, grecians, grecing, grecism, grecize, grecized, grecizes, grecizing, greco, grecoue, grecque, gree, greece, greed, greedier, greediest, greedily, greediness, greedless, greeds, greedsome, greedy, greedygut, greedyguts, greegree, greegrees, greeing, greek, greek's, greekish, greekize, greekling, greeks, green, greenable, greenage, greenalite, greenback, greenbacker, greenbackism, greenbacks, greenbark, greenbelt, greenboard, greenbone, greenbottle, greenbrier, greenbug, greenbugs, greenbul, greencoat, greened, greener, greeneries, greenery, greenest, greeney, greenfinch, greenfish, greenfishes, greenflies, greenfly, greengage, greengill, greengrocer, greengroceries, greengrocers, greengrocery, greenhead, greenheaded, greenheart, greenhearted, greenhew, greenhide, greenhood, greenhorn, greenhornism, greenhorns, greenhouse, greenhouse's, greenhouses, greenier, greeniest, greening, greenings, greenish, greenishness, greenkeeper, greenkeeping, greenland, greenlandite, greenleaf, greenleek, greenless, greenlet, greenlets, greenling, greenly, greenness, greenockite, greenovite, greenroom, greenrooms, greens, greensand, greensauce, greenshank, greensick, greensickness, greenside, greenskeeper, greenslade, greenstick, greenstone, greenstuff, greensward, greenswarded, greentail, greenth, greenths, greenthumbed, greenuk, greenware, greenwax, greenweed, greenwich, greenwing, greenwithe, greenwood, greenwoods, greenwort, greeny, greenyard, grees, greesagh, greese, greeshoch, greet, greeted, greeter, greeters, greeting, greetingless, greetingly, greetings, greets, greeve, greffe, greffier, greffotome, gregal, gregale, gregaloid, gregarian, gregarianism, gregarine, gregarinian, gregarinidal, gregariniform, gregarinosis, gregarinous, gregarious, gregariously, gregariousness, gregaritic, gregatim, gregau, grege, greggle, greggriffin, grego, gregor, gregorian, gregorianist, gregory, gregos, greige, greiges, greillade, grein, greing, greisen, greisens, greit, greith, greking, grelot, gremial, gremiale, gremials, gremio, gremlin, gremlins, gremmie, gremmies, gremmy, grenada, grenade, grenade's, grenades, grenadier, grenadierial, grenadierly, grenadiers, grenadiership, grenadilla, grenadin, grenadine, grenadines, grenado, grenat, grenatite, grene, grenier, gres, gresil, gressible, gressorial, gressorious, gret, greta, grete, greund, grew, grewhound, grewsome, grewsomely, grewsomeness, grewsomer, grewsomest, grewt, grex, grey, greyback, greybeard, greycoat, greyed, greyer, greyest, greyfish, greyflies, greyfly, greyhen, greyhens, greyhound, greyhounds, greying, greyish, greylag, greylags, greyling, greyly, greyness, greynesses, greypate, greys, greyskin, greystone, greywacke, greyware, greywether, grf, gribane, gribble, gribbles, grice, grid, grid's, gridded, gridder, gridding, griddle, griddlecake, griddlecakes, griddled, griddler, griddles, griddling, gride, grided, gridelin, grides, griding, gridiron, gridirons, gridlock, grids, grieben, griece, grieced, griecep, grief, grief's, griefful, grieffully, griefless, grieflessness, griefs, griege, grieko, grieshoch, grieshuckle, grievable, grievance, grievance's, grievances, grievant, grievants, grieve, grieved, grievedly, griever, grievers, grieves, grieveship, grieving, grievingly, grievous, grievously, grievousness, griff, griffade, griffado, griffaun, griffe, griffes, griffin, griffinage, griffinesque, griffinhood, griffinish, griffinism, griffins, griffithite, griffon, griffonage, griffonne, griffons, griffs, grift, grifted, grifter, grifters, grifting, grifts, grig, griggles, grignet, grigri, grigris, grigs, grihastha, grihyasutra, grike, grill, grillade, grilladed, grillades, grillading, grillage, grillages, grille, grilled, grillee, griller, grillers, grilles, grillework, grilling, grillroom, grills, grillwork, grilly, grilse, grilses, grim, grimace, grimaced, grimacer, grimacers, grimaces, grimacier, grimacing, grimacingly, grimalkin, grime, grimed, grimes, grimful, grimgribber, grimier, grimiest, grimily, grimines, griminess, griming, grimliness, grimly, grimm, grimme, grimmer, grimmest, grimmiaceous, grimmish, grimness, grimnesses, grimoire, grimp, grimsir, grimsire, grimy, grin, grinagog, grinch, grincome, grind, grindable, grindal, grinded, grindelia, grinder, grinderies, grinderman, grinders, grindery, grinding, grindingly, grindings, grindle, grinds, grindstone, grindstone's, grindstones, gringo, gringole, gringolee, gringophobia, gringos, grinned, grinner, grinners, grinnie, grinning, grinningly, grinny, grins, grint, grinter, grintern, griot, griots, griotte, grip, gripe, griped, gripeful, griper, gripers, gripes, gripey, gripgrass, griph, griphe, griphite, griphus, gripier, gripiest, griping, gripingly, gripless, gripman, gripmen, gripment, grippal, grippe, gripped, grippelike, gripper, grippers, grippes, grippier, grippiest, grippiness, gripping, grippingly, grippingness, grippit, gripple, grippleness, grippotoxin, grippy, grips, gripsack, gripsacks, gript, gripy, griquaite, gris, grisaille, grisailles, grisard, grisbet, grise, griselda, griseofulvin, griseous, grisette, grisettes, grisettish, grisgris, griskin, griskins, grisled, grislier, grisliest, grisliness, grisly, grison, grisons, grisounite, grisoutine, grisping, grissen, grissens, grisset, grissons, grist, gristbite, grister, gristle, gristles, gristlier, gristliest, gristliness, gristly, gristmill, gristmiller, gristmilling, grists, gristy, grit, grit's, grith, grithbreach, grithman, griths, gritless, gritrock, grits, gritstone, gritted, gritten, gritter, grittie, grittier, grittiest, grittily, grittiness, gritting, grittle, gritty, grivation, grivet, grivets, grivna, grivois, grivoise, grizard, grizel, grizelin, grizzle, grizzled, grizzler, grizzlers, grizzles, grizzlier, grizzlies, grizzliest, grizzliness, grizzling, grizzly, grizzlyman, gro, groan, groaned, groaner, groaners, groanful, groaning, groaningly, groans, groat, groats, groatsworth, grobian, grobianism, grocer, grocer's, grocerdom, groceress, groceries, grocerly, grocers, grocerwise, grocery, groceryman, grocerymen, groceteria, grockle, groenlandicus, groff, grog, grogged, grogger, groggeries, groggery, groggier, groggiest, groggily, grogginess, grogging, groggy, grognard, grogram, grograms, grogs, grogshop, grogshops, groin, groined, groinery, groining, groins, groma, gromatic, gromatical, gromatics, gromet, gromil, grommet, grommets, gromwell, gromwells, gromyl, grond, grondwet, gront, groof, groom, groomed, groomer, groomers, grooming, groomish, groomishly, groomlet, groomling, grooms, groomsman, groomsmen, groomy, groop, grooper, groose, groot, grooty, groove, grooved, grooveless, groovelike, groover, grooverhead, groovers, grooves, groovier, grooviest, grooviness, grooving, groovy, groow, grope, groped, groper, gropers, gropes, groping, gropingly, gropple, groroilite, grorudite, gros, grosbeak, grosbeaks, groschen, groser, groset, grosgrain, grosgrained, grosgrains, gross, grossart, grosse, grossed, grossen, grosser, grossers, grosses, grossest, grosshead, grossierete, grossification, grossify, grossing, grossirete, grossly, grossness, grosso, grossulaceous, grossular, grossularia, grossulariaceous, grossularious, grossularite, grosz, groszy, grot, grote, groten, grotesco, grotesque, grotesquely, grotesqueness, grotesquerie, grotesqueries, grotesquery, grotesques, grothine, grothite, grots, grottesco, grotto, grotto's, grottoed, grottoes, grottolike, grottos, grottowork, grotty, grotzen, grouch, grouched, grouches, grouchier, grouchiest, grouchily, grouchiness, grouching, grouchingly, groucho, grouchy, grouf, grough, ground, groundable, groundably, groundage, groundberry, groundbird, groundbreaker, grounded, groundedly, groundedness, grounden, groundenell, grounder, grounders, groundflower, groundhog, grounding, groundkeeper, groundless, groundlessly, groundlessness, groundline, groundliness, groundling, groundlings, groundly, groundman, groundmass, groundneedle, groundnut, groundout, groundplot, grounds, groundsel, groundsheet, groundsill, groundskeep, groundskeeping, groundsman, groundspeed, groundswell, groundswells, groundwall, groundward, groundwards, groundwater, groundwave, groundway, groundwood, groundwork, groundy, group, groupable, groupage, groupageness, grouped, grouper, groupers, groupie, groupies, grouping, groupings, groupist, grouplet, groupment, groupoid, groupoids, groups, groupthink, groupwise, grouse, grouseberry, groused, grouseless, grouselike, grouser, grousers, grouses, grouseward, grousewards, grousing, grousy, grout, grouted, grouter, grouters, grouthead, groutier, groutiest, grouting, groutite, groutnoll, grouts, grouty, grouze, grove, groved, grovel, groveled, groveler, grovelers, groveless, groveling, grovelingly, grovelings, grovelled, groveller, grovelling, grovellingly, grovellings, grovels, grover, grovers, groves, grovet, grovy, grow, growable, growan, growed, grower, growers, growing, growingly, growingupness, growl, growled, growler, growleries, growlers, growlery, growlier, growliest, growliness, growling, growlingly, growls, growly, grown, grownup, grownup's, grownups, grows, growse, growsome, growth, growthful, growthiness, growthless, growths, growthy, growze, groyne, groynes, grozart, grozer, grozet, grr, grs, grub, grub's, grubbed, grubber, grubberies, grubbers, grubbery, grubbier, grubbies, grubbiest, grubbily, grubbiness, grubbing, grubble, grubby, grubhood, grubless, grubroot, grubs, grubstake, grubstaked, grubstaker, grubstakes, grubstaking, grubstreet, grubworm, grubworms, grucche, grudge, grudge's, grudged, grudgeful, grudgefully, grudgefulness, grudgekin, grudgeless, grudgeons, grudger, grudgers, grudgery, grudges, grudging, grudgingly, grudgingness, grudgment, grue, gruel, grueled, grueler, gruelers, grueling, gruelingly, gruelings, gruelled, grueller, gruellers, gruelling, gruellings, gruelly, gruels, gruesome, gruesomely, gruesomeness, gruesomer, gruesomest, gruf, gruff, gruffed, gruffer, gruffest, gruffier, gruffiest, gruffily, gruffiness, gruffing, gruffish, gruffly, gruffness, gruffs, gruffy, gruft, grufted, grugous, grugru, grugrus, gruiform, gruine, grulla, grum, grumble, grumbled, grumbler, grumblers, grumbles, grumblesome, grumbletonian, grumbling, grumblingly, grumbly, grume, grumes, grumly, grummel, grummels, grummer, grummest, grummet, grummeter, grummets, grumness, grumose, grumous, grumousness, grump, grumped, grumph, grumphie, grumphies, grumphy, grumpier, grumpiest, grumpily, grumpiness, grumping, grumpish, grumpishness, grumps, grumpy, grun, grunch, grundel, grundsil, grundy, grunerite, gruneritization, grungier, grungiest, grungy, grunion, grunions, grunswel, grunt, grunted, grunter, grunters, grunting, gruntingly, gruntle, gruntled, gruntles, gruntling, grunts, grunzie, gruppetto, gruppo, grush, grushie, gruss, grutch, grutched, grutches, grutching, grutten, gruyere, gruys, grx, gry, gryde, grylle, grylli, gryllid, gryllos, gryllotalpa, gryllus, grypanian, grype, gryph, gryphite, gryphon, gryphons, gryposis, grysbok, gs, gt, gtc, gtd, gte, gteau, gthite, gtt, gu, guaba, guacacoa, guacamole, guachamaca, guacharo, guacharoes, guacharos, guachipilin, guacho, guacimo, guacin, guaco, guaconize, guacos, guadalcazarite, guadua, guageable, guaguanche, guahivo, guaiac, guaiacol, guaiacolize, guaiacols, guaiaconic, guaiacs, guaiacum, guaiacums, guaiaretic, guaiasanol, guaican, guaiocum, guaiocums, guaiol, guajillo, guajira, guajiras, guaka, guam, guama, guamachil, guamuchil, guan, guana, guanabana, guanabano, guanaco, guanacos, guanajuatite, guanamine, guanare, guanase, guanases, guanay, guanayes, guanays, guaneide, guanethidine, guango, guanidin, guanidine, guanidins, guanidopropionic, guaniferous, guanin, guanine, guanines, guanins, guanize, guano, guanophore, guanos, guanosine, guans, guanyl, guanylic, guao, guapena, guapilla, guapinol, guar, guara, guarabu, guaracha, guarachas, guarache, guaraguao, guarana, guarand, guarani, guaranies, guaranin, guaranine, guaranis, guarantee, guaranteed, guaranteeing, guaranteer, guaranteers, guarantees, guaranteeship, guaranteing, guarantied, guaranties, guarantine, guarantor, guarantors, guarantorship, guaranty, guarantying, guarapo, guarapucu, guard, guardable, guardage, guardant, guardants, guarded, guardedly, guardedness, guardee, guardeen, guarder, guarders, guardfish, guardful, guardfully, guardhouse, guardhouses, guardian, guardian's, guardiancy, guardianess, guardianless, guardianly, guardians, guardianship, guardianships, guarding, guardingly, guardless, guardlike, guardo, guardrail, guardrails, guardroom, guards, guardship, guardsman, guardsmen, guardstone, guariba, guarico, guarinite, guarish, guarneri, guarnerius, guarri, guars, guary, guasa, guatambu, guatemala, guatemalan, guatemalans, guatibero, guativere, guava, guavaberry, guavas, guavina, guaxima, guayaba, guayabera, guayaberas, guayabi, guayabo, guayacan, guayroto, guayule, guayules, guaza, guazuti, guazzo, gubat, gubbertush, gubbin, gubbings, gubbins, gubbo, guberla, gubernacula, gubernacular, gubernaculum, gubernance, gubernation, gubernative, gubernator, gubernatorial, gubernatrix, gubernia, guberniya, guck, gucked, gucki, gucks, gud, gudame, guddle, guddled, guddler, guddling, gude, gudebrother, gudefather, gudemother, gudes, gudesake, gudesakes, gudesire, gudewife, gudge, gudgeon, gudgeoned, gudgeoning, gudgeons, gudget, gudok, gudrun, gue, guebre, guebucu, guejarite, guelf, guelph, guelphic, guemal, guemul, guenepe, guenon, guenons, guepard, gueparde, guerdon, guerdonable, guerdoned, guerdoner, guerdoning, guerdonless, guerdons, guereba, guereza, guergal, gueridon, gueridons, guerilla, guerillaism, guerillas, guerison, guerite, guerites, guernsey, guernseyed, guernseys, guerre, guerrila, guerrilla, guerrilla's, guerrillaism, guerrillas, guerrillaship, guess, guessable, guessed, guesser, guessers, guesses, guessing, guessingly, guessive, guesstimate, guesstimated, guesstimates, guesstimating, guesswork, guessworker, guest, guest's, guestchamber, guested, guesten, guester, guesthouse, guesthouses, guestimate, guestimated, guestimating, guesting, guestive, guestless, guestling, guestmaster, guests, guestship, guestwise, guetre, gufa, guff, guffaw, guffawed, guffawing, guffaws, guffer, guffin, guffs, guffy, gufought, gugal, guggle, guggled, guggles, gugglet, guggling, guglet, guglets, guglia, guglio, gugu, guhr, guiac, guiana, guib, guiba, guichet, guid, guidable, guidage, guidance, guidances, guide, guideboard, guidebook, guidebook's, guidebookish, guidebooks, guidebooky, guidecraft, guided, guideless, guideline, guideline's, guidelines, guidepost, guideposts, guider, guideress, guiders, guidership, guides, guideship, guideway, guiding, guidingly, guidman, guidon, guidonian, guidons, guids, guidsire, guidwife, guidwillie, guidwilly, guige, guigne, guignol, guijo, guild, guilder, guilders, guildhall, guildic, guildite, guildry, guilds, guildship, guildsman, guildsmen, guile, guiled, guileful, guilefully, guilefulness, guileless, guilelessly, guilelessness, guiler, guilery, guiles, guilfat, guiling, guillem, guillemet, guillemot, guillevat, guilloche, guillochee, guillotinade, guillotine, guillotined, guillotinement, guillotiner, guillotines, guillotining, guillotinism, guillotinist, guilt, guiltful, guiltier, guiltiest, guiltily, guiltiness, guiltless, guiltlessly, guiltlessness, guilts, guiltsick, guilty, guily, guimbard, guimpe, guimpes, guinde, guinea, guinean, guineapig, guineas, guinevere, guinfo, guinness, guipure, guipures, guirlande, guiro, guisard, guisards, guisarme, guise, guise's, guised, guiser, guises, guisian, guising, guitar, guitar's, guitarfish, guitarfishes, guitarist, guitarists, guitarlike, guitars, guitermanite, guitguit, gujarati, gujerat, gul, gula, gulae, gulaman, gulancha, guland, gular, gularis, gulas, gulash, gulch, gulch's, gulches, guld, gulden, guldengroschen, guldens, gule, gules, gulf, gulf's, gulfed, gulfier, gulfiest, gulfing, gulflike, gulfs, gulfside, gulfwards, gulfweed, gulfweeds, gulfy, gulgul, gulinula, gulinulae, gulinular, gulist, gulix, gull, gullability, gullable, gullably, gullage, gullah, gulled, guller, gulleries, gullery, gullet, gulleting, gullets, gulley, gulleys, gullibility, gullible, gullibly, gullied, gullies, gulling, gullion, gullish, gullishly, gullishness, gulliver, gulllike, gulls, gully, gully's, gullygut, gullyhole, gullying, gulmohar, gulo, gulonic, gulose, gulosities, gulosity, gulp, gulped, gulper, gulpers, gulph, gulpier, gulpiest, gulpin, gulping, gulpingly, gulps, gulpy, gulravage, guls, gulsach, gult, guly, gum, gum's, gumbo, gumboil, gumboils, gumbolike, gumboots, gumbos, gumbotil, gumbotils, gumby, gumchewer, gumdigger, gumdigging, gumdrop, gumdrops, gumfield, gumflower, gumhar, gumi, gumihan, gumlah, gumless, gumlike, gumlikeness, gumly, gumma, gummage, gummaker, gummaking, gummas, gummata, gummatous, gummed, gummer, gummers, gummic, gummier, gummiest, gummiferous, gumminess, gumming, gummite, gummites, gummose, gummoses, gummosis, gummosity, gummous, gummy, gump, gumpheon, gumphion, gumption, gumptionless, gumptions, gumptious, gumpus, gums, gumshield, gumshoe, gumshoed, gumshoeing, gumshoes, gumshoing, gumtree, gumtrees, gumweed, gumweeds, gumwood, gumwoods, gun, gun's, guna, gunarchy, gunate, gunated, gunating, gunation, gunbarrel, gunbearer, gunboat, gunboats, gunbright, gunbuilder, guncotton, gunda, gundalow, gundeck, gundelet, gundelow, gundi, gundie, gundog, gundogs, gundy, gundygut, gunebo, gunfight, gunfighter, gunfighters, gunfighting, gunfights, gunfire, gunfires, gunflint, gunflints, gunfought, gung, gunge, gunhouse, gunite, guniter, gunj, gunja, gunjah, gunk, gunkhole, gunkholed, gunkholing, gunks, gunky, gunl, gunlayer, gunlaying, gunless, gunline, gunlock, gunlocks, gunmaker, gunmaking, gunman, gunmanship, gunmen, gunmetal, gunmetals, gunnage, gunne, gunned, gunnel, gunnels, gunnen, gunner, gunner's, gunneress, gunneries, gunners, gunnership, gunnery, gunnies, gunning, gunnings, gunnung, gunny, gunnysack, gunnysacks, gunocracy, gunong, gunpaper, gunpapers, gunplay, gunplays, gunpoint, gunpoints, gunport, gunpowder, gunpowderous, gunpowdery, gunpower, gunrack, gunreach, gunroom, gunrooms, gunrunner, gunrunning, guns, gunsel, gunsels, gunship, gunships, gunshop, gunshot, gunshots, gunsling, gunslinger, gunslingers, gunslinging, gunsman, gunsmith, gunsmithery, gunsmithing, gunsmiths, gunster, gunstick, gunstock, gunstocker, gunstocking, gunstocks, gunstone, gunter, gunther, guntub, gunung, gunwale, gunwales, gunwhale, gunyah, gunyang, gunyeh, gup, guppies, guppy, guptavidya, gur, gurdfish, gurdle, gurdwara, gurdy, gurge, gurged, gurgeon, gurgeons, gurges, gurging, gurgitation, gurgle, gurgled, gurgles, gurglet, gurglets, gurgling, gurglingly, gurgly, gurgoyl, gurgoyle, gurgulation, gurgulio, gurjan, gurjun, gurk, gurkha, gurl, gurle, gurlet, gurly, gurnard, gurnards, gurnet, gurnets, gurnetty, gurney, gurneys, gurniad, gurr, gurrah, gurries, gurry, gursh, gurshes, gurt, gurts, guru, gurus, guruship, guruships, gusain, guser, guserid, gush, gushed, gusher, gushers, gushes, gushet, gushier, gushiest, gushily, gushiness, gushing, gushingly, gushingness, gushy, gusla, gusle, guslee, guss, gusset, gusseted, gusseting, gussets, gussie, gussied, gussies, gussy, gussying, gust, gust's, gustable, gustables, gustard, gustation, gustative, gustativeness, gustatorial, gustatorially, gustatorily, gustatory, gusted, gustful, gustfully, gustfulness, gustier, gustiest, gustily, gustiness, gusting, gustless, gusto, gustoes, gustoish, gustoso, gusts, gusty, gut, gutbucket, gutierrez, gutless, gutlessness, gutlike, gutling, guts, gutser, gutsier, gutsiest, gutsily, gutsiness, gutsy, gutt, gutta, guttable, guttae, guttar, guttate, guttated, guttatim, guttation, gutte, gutted, guttee, gutter, gutteral, gutterblood, guttered, guttering, gutterize, gutterlike, gutterling, gutterman, gutters, guttersnipe, guttersnipes, guttersnipish, gutterspout, gutterwise, guttery, gutti, guttide, guttie, guttier, guttiest, guttifer, guttiferal, guttiferous, guttiform, guttiness, gutting, guttle, guttled, guttler, guttlers, guttles, guttling, guttula, guttulae, guttular, guttulate, guttule, guttulous, guttur, guttural, gutturalisation, gutturalise, gutturalised, gutturalising, gutturalism, gutturality, gutturalization, gutturalize, gutturalized, gutturalizing, gutturally, gutturalness, gutturals, gutturine, gutturize, gutturonasal, gutturopalatal, gutturopalatine, gutturotetany, guttus, gutty, gutweed, gutwise, gutwort, guv, guvacine, guvacoline, guy, guyana, guydom, guyed, guyer, guyers, guying, guyline, guyot, guyots, guys, guytrash, guywire, guz, guze, guzerat, guzmania, guzzle, guzzled, guzzledom, guzzler, guzzlers, guzzles, guzzling, gv, gwag, gwantus, gweduc, gweduck, gweducks, gweducs, gweed, gweeon, gwely, gwerziou, gwine, gwiniad, gwyniad, gyal, gyascutus, gyassa, gybe, gybed, gybes, gybing, gye, gyle, gym, gymel, gymkhana, gymkhanas, gymmal, gymnanthous, gymnasia, gymnasial, gymnasiarch, gymnasiarchy, gymnasiast, gymnasic, gymnasisia, gymnasisiums, gymnasium, gymnasium's, gymnasiums, gymnast, gymnast's, gymnastic, gymnastical, gymnastically, gymnastics, gymnasts, gymnemic, gymnetrous, gymnic, gymnical, gymnics, gymnite, gymnoblastic, gymnocarpic, gymnocarpous, gymnoceratous, gymnocidium, gymnodiniaceous, gymnodont, gymnogen, gymnogene, gymnogenous, gymnoglossate, gymnogynous, gymnolaematous, gymnopaedic, gymnophiona, gymnophobia, gymnoplast, gymnorhinal, gymnosoph, gymnosophical, gymnosophist, gymnosophy, gymnosperm, gymnospermal, gymnospermic, gymnospermism, gymnospermous, gymnosperms, gymnospermy, gymnospore, gymnosporous, gymnostomous, gymnotid, gymnotokous, gymnotus, gymnure, gymnurine, gympie, gyms, gymsia, gymslip, gyn, gynaecea, gynaeceum, gynaecia, gynaecian, gynaecic, gynaecium, gynaecocoenic, gynaecocracies, gynaecocracy, gynaecocrat, gynaecocratic, gynaecoid, gynaecol, gynaecologic, gynaecological, gynaecologist, gynaecology, gynaecomastia, gynaecomasty, gynaecomorphous, gynaeconitis, gynaeocracy, gynaeolater, gynaeolatry, gynander, gynandrarchic, gynandrarchy, gynandria, gynandrian, gynandries, gynandrism, gynandroid, gynandromorph, gynandromorphic, gynandromorphism, gynandromorphous, gynandromorphy, gynandrophore, gynandrosporous, gynandrous, gynandry, gynantherous, gynarchic, gynarchies, gynarchy, gyne, gyneccia, gynecia, gynecic, gynecicgynecidal, gynecidal, gynecide, gynecium, gynecocentric, gynecocracies, gynecocracy, gynecocrat, gynecocratic, gynecocratical, gynecoid, gynecol, gynecolatry, gynecologic, gynecological, gynecologies, gynecologist, gynecologists, gynecology, gynecomania, gynecomaniac, gynecomaniacal, gynecomastia, gynecomastism, gynecomasty, gynecomazia, gynecomorphous, gyneconitis, gynecopathic, gynecopathy, gynecophore, gynecophoric, gynecophorous, gynecotelic, gynecratic, gyneocracy, gyneolater, gyneolatry, gynephobia, gynethusia, gynetype, gyniatrics, gyniatries, gyniatry, gynic, gynics, gyniolatry, gynobase, gynobaseous, gynobasic, gynocardia, gynocardic, gynocracy, gynocratic, gynodioecious, gynodioeciously, gynodioecism, gynoecia, gynoecium, gynoeciumcia, gynogenesis, gynogenetic, gynomonecious, gynomonoecious, gynomonoeciously, gynomonoecism, gynopara, gynophagite, gynophore, gynophoric, gynosporangium, gynospore, gynostegia, gynostegigia, gynostegium, gynostemia, gynostemium, gynostemiumia, gyokuro, gyp, gype, gypped, gypper, gyppers, gyppery, gypping, gyps, gypseian, gypseous, gypsied, gypsies, gypsiferous, gypsine, gypsiologist, gypsite, gypsography, gypsologist, gypsology, gypsophila, gypsophilous, gypsophily, gypsoplast, gypsous, gypster, gypsum, gypsumed, gypsuming, gypsums, gypsy, gypsy's, gypsydom, gypsydoms, gypsyesque, gypsyfy, gypsyhead, gypsyhood, gypsying, gypsyish, gypsyism, gypsyisms, gypsylike, gypsyry, gypsyweed, gypsywise, gypsywort, gyral, gyrally, gyrant, gyrate, gyrated, gyrates, gyrating, gyration, gyrational, gyrations, gyrator, gyrators, gyratory, gyre, gyrectomies, gyrectomy, gyred, gyrencephalate, gyrencephalic, gyrencephalous, gyrene, gyrenes, gyres, gyrfalcon, gyrfalcons, gyri, gyric, gyring, gyrinid, gyro, gyrocar, gyroceracone, gyroceran, gyrochrome, gyrocompass, gyrocompasses, gyrodyne, gyrofrequencies, gyrofrequency, gyrogonite, gyrograph, gyrohorizon, gyroidal, gyroidally, gyrolite, gyrolith, gyroma, gyromagnetic, gyromancy, gyromele, gyrometer, gyron, gyronny, gyrons, gyrophoric, gyropigeon, gyropilot, gyroplane, gyros, gyroscope, gyroscope's, gyroscopes, gyroscopic, gyroscopically, gyroscopics, gyrose, gyrostabilized, gyrostabilizer, gyrostat, gyrostatic, gyrostatically, gyrostatics, gyrostats, gyrosyn, gyrous, gyrovagi, gyrovague, gyrovagues, gyrowheel, gyrus, gyse, gyte, gytling, gytrash, gyttja, gyve, gyved, gyves, gyving, h, h'm, h's, ha, ha', ha'nt, ha'p'orth, ha'pennies, ha'penny, haab, haaf, haafs, haak, haar, haars, hab, habaera, habakkuk, habanera, habaneras, habble, habbub, habdalah, habdalahs, habeas, habena, habenal, habenar, habendum, habenula, habenulae, habenular, haberdash, haberdasher, haberdasheress, haberdasheries, haberdashers, haberdashery, haberdine, habere, habergeon, habet, habilable, habilant, habilatory, habile, habilement, habiliment, habilimental, habilimentary, habilimentation, habilimented, habiliments, habilitate, habilitated, habilitating, habilitation, habilitator, hability, habille, habit, habit's, habitability, habitable, habitableness, habitably, habitacle, habitacule, habitally, habitan, habitance, habitancies, habitancy, habitans, habitant, habitants, habitat, habitat's, habitatal, habitate, habitatio, habitation, habitation's, habitational, habitations, habitative, habitator, habitats, habited, habiting, habits, habitual, habituality, habitualize, habitually, habitualness, habituate, habituated, habituates, habituating, habituation, habituations, habitude, habitudes, habitudinal, habitue, habitues, habiture, habitus, hable, habnab, haboob, haboub, habronemiasis, habronemic, habrowne, habsburg, habu, habub, habuka, habus, habutae, habutai, habutaye, haccucal, hacek, haceks, hacendado, hache, hachis, hachment, hacht, hachure, hachured, hachures, hachuring, hacienda, haciendado, haciendas, hack, hackamatak, hackamore, hackbarrow, hackberries, hackberry, hackbolt, hackbush, hackbut, hackbuteer, hackbuts, hackbutter, hackdriver, hacked, hackee, hackeem, hackees, hacker, hackeries, hackers, hackery, hackeymal, hackia, hackie, hackies, hackin, hacking, hackingly, hackle, hackleback, hackled, hackler, hacklers, hackles, hacklet, hacklier, hackliest, hackling, hacklog, hackly, hackmack, hackmall, hackman, hackmatack, hackmen, hackney, hackneyed, hackneyedly, hackneyedness, hackneyer, hackneying, hackneyism, hackneyman, hackneys, hacks, hacksaw, hacksaws, hacksilber, hackster, hackthorn, hacktree, hackwood, hackwork, hackworks, hacky, hacqueton, had, hadada, hadal, hadarim, hadaway, hadbot, hadbote, hadden, hadder, haddest, haddie, haddin, haddo, haddock, haddocker, haddocks, hade, haded, hadentomoid, hadephobia, hades, hading, hadit, hadith, hadiths, hadj, hadjee, hadjees, hadjes, hadji, hadjis, hadland, hadn't, hadnt, hadrom, hadrome, hadromycosis, hadron, hadronic, hadrons, hadrosaur, hadrosaurus, hadst, hae, haec, haecceities, haecceity, haed, haeing, haem, haemachrome, haemacytometer, haemad, haemagglutinate, haemagglutinated, haemagglutinating, haemagglutination, haemagglutinative, haemagglutinin, haemagogue, haemal, haemangioma, haemangiomas, haemangiomata, haemangiomatosis, haemapophysis, haemaspectroscope, haematal, haematein, haematemesis, haematherm, haemathermal, haemathermous, haematic, haematics, haematid, haematin, haematinic, haematinon, haematins, haematinum, haematite, haematitic, haematoblast, haematobranchiate, haematocele, haematocrit, haematocryal, haematocyst, haematocystis, haematocyte, haematogenesis, haematogenous, haematoid, haematoidin, haematoin, haematologic, haematological, haematologist, haematology, haematolysis, haematoma, haematomas, haematomata, haematometer, haematophiline, haematophyte, haematopoiesis, haematopoietic, haematorrhachis, haematosepsis, haematosin, haematosis, haematothermal, haematoxylic, haematoxylin, haematoxylon, haematozoa, haematozoal, haematozoic, haematozoon, haematozzoa, haematuria, haemic, haemin, haemins, haemoblast, haemochrome, haemocoel, haemoconcentration, haemocyanin, haemocyte, haemocytoblast, haemocytoblastic, haemocytometer, haemodialysis, haemodilution, haemodoraceous, haemodynamic, haemodynamics, haemoflagellate, haemoglobic, haemoglobin, haemoglobinous, haemoglobinuria, haemogram, haemoid, haemolysin, haemolysis, haemolytic, haemometer, haemonchiasis, haemonchosis, haemony, haemophil, haemophile, haemophilia, haemophiliac, haemophilic, haemopod, haemopoiesis, haemoptysis, haemorrhage, haemorrhaged, haemorrhagia, haemorrhagic, haemorrhaging, haemorrhagy, haemorrhoid, haemorrhoidal, haemorrhoidectomy, haemorrhoids, haemosporid, haemosporidian, haemostasia, haemostasis, haemostat, haemostatic, haemothorax, haemotoxic, haemotoxin, haems, haemuloid, haen, haeredes, haeremai, haeres, haes, haet, haets, haf, haff, haffat, haffet, haffets, haffit, haffits, haffkinize, haffle, hafflins, hafis, hafiz, haflin, hafnia, hafnium, hafniums, hafnyl, haft, haftarah, haftarahs, haftarot, haftaroth, hafted, hafter, hafters, hafting, haftorah, haftorahs, haftorot, haftoroth, hafts, hag, hagada, hagadic, hagadist, hagadists, hagar, hagarene, hagberries, hagberry, hagboat, hagbolt, hagborn, hagbush, hagbushes, hagbut, hagbuts, hagden, hagdin, hagdon, hagdons, hagdown, hageen, hagein, hagfish, hagfishes, haggada, haggadah, haggadal, haggaday, haggadic, haggadical, haggadist, haggadistic, haggai, haggard, haggardly, haggardness, haggards, hagged, haggeis, hagger, hagging, haggiographal, haggis, haggises, haggish, haggishly, haggishness, haggister, haggle, haggled, haggler, hagglers, haggles, haggling, haggly, haggy, hagi, hagia, hagiarchies, hagiarchy, hagigah, hagiocracies, hagiocracy, hagiographa, hagiographal, hagiographer, hagiographers, hagiographic, hagiographical, hagiographies, hagiographist, hagiography, hagiolater, hagiolatrous, hagiolatry, hagiolith, hagiologic, hagiological, hagiologically, hagiologies, hagiologist, hagiology, hagiophobia, hagioscope, hagioscopic, haglet, haglike, haglin, hagmall, hagmane, hagmena, hagmenay, hagrid, hagridden, hagride, hagrider, hagrides, hagriding, hagrode, hagrope, hags, hagseed, hagship, hagstone, hagtaper, hague, hagueton, hagweed, hagworm, hah, haha, hahnium, hahs, haiari, haick, haidingerite, haiduck, haik, haika, haikai, haikal, haiks, haiku, haikun, haikwan, hail, hailed, hailer, hailers, hailes, hailing, hailproof, hails, hailse, hailshot, hailstone, hailstoned, hailstones, hailstorm, hailstorms, hailweed, haily, haimsucken, hain, hain""t, hain't, hainberry, hainch, haine, hained, hair, hair's, hairball, hairballs, hairband, hairbands, hairbeard, hairbell, hairbird, hairbrain, hairbrained, hairbreadth, hairbreadths, hairbrush, hairbrushes, haircap, haircaps, haircloth, haircloths, haircut, haircut's, haircuts, haircutter, haircutting, hairdo, hairdodos, hairdos, hairdress, hairdresser, hairdressers, hairdressing, hairdryer, hairdryer's, hairdryers, haire, haired, hairen, hairgrass, hairgrip, hairhoof, hairhound, hairier, hairiest, hairif, hairiness, hairlace, hairless, hairlessness, hairlet, hairlike, hairline, hairlines, hairlock, hairlocks, hairmeal, hairmoneering, hairmonger, hairnet, hairof, hairpiece, hairpieces, hairpin, hairpins, hairs, hairsbreadth, hairsbreadths, hairse, hairsplitter, hairsplitters, hairsplitting, hairspray, hairsprays, hairspring, hairsprings, hairst, hairstane, hairstone, hairstreak, hairstyle, hairstyles, hairstyling, hairstylist, hairstylists, hairtail, hairup, hairweave, hairweaver, hairweavers, hairweaving, hairweed, hairwood, hairwork, hairworks, hairworm, hairworms, hairy, hairychested, hait, haiti, haitian, haitians, haitsai, haiver, haj, haje, hajes, haji, hajib, hajilij, hajis, hajj, hajjes, hajji, hajjis, hak, hakafoth, hakam, hakamim, hakdar, hake, hakea, hakeem, hakeems, hakenkreuz, hakes, hakim, hakims, hako, haku, hala, halacha, halachah, halachist, halaka, halakah, halakahs, halakhist, halakic, halakist, halakistic, halakists, halakoth, halal, halala, halalah, halalahs, halalas, halalcor, halapepe, halas, halation, halations, halavah, halavahs, halazone, halberd, halberdier, halberdman, halberds, halberdsman, halbert, halberts, halch, halcyon, halcyonian, halcyonic, halcyonine, halcyons, haldu, hale, halebi, halecret, haled, haleday, halely, haleness, halenesses, haler, halers, haleru, halerz, hales, halesia, halesome, halest, haleweed, half, halfa, halfback, halfbacks, halfbeak, halfbeaks, halfblood, halfcock, halfcocked, halfen, halfendeal, halfer, halfheaded, halfhearted, halfheartedly, halfheartedness, halfhourly, halflang, halflife, halflin, halfling, halflings, halflives, halfly, halfman, halfmoon, halfness, halfnesses, halfpace, halfpaced, halfpence, halfpennies, halfpenny, halfpennyworth, halftime, halftimes, halftone, halftones, halftrack, halfungs, halfway, halfwise, halfwit, halfword, halfwords, halfy, halibios, halibiotic, halibiu, halibut, halibuter, halibuts, halichondrine, halichondroid, halicore, halicot, halid, halide, halides, halidom, halidome, halidomes, halidoms, halids, halieutic, halieutical, halieutically, halieutics, halifax, halimot, halimous, haling, halinous, haliographer, haliography, haliotis, haliotoid, haliplankton, haliplid, halisteresis, halisteretic, halite, halites, halitoses, halitosis, halituosity, halituous, halitus, halituses, halkahs, halke, hall, hall's, hallabaloo, hallage, hallah, hallahs, hallalcor, hallali, hallan, hallanshaker, hallboy, hallcist, hallebardier, hallecret, halleflinta, halleflintoid, hallel, hallels, halleluiah, hallelujah, hallelujahs, hallelujatic, hallex, halliard, halliards, halliblash, hallicet, hallidome, hallier, halling, hallion, hallman, hallmark, hallmark's, hallmarked, hallmarker, hallmarking, hallmarks, hallmoot, hallmote, hallo, halloa, halloaed, halloaing, halloas, hallock, halloed, halloes, halloing, halloo, hallooed, hallooing, halloos, hallopodous, hallos, hallot, halloth, hallow, hallowd, hallowed, hallowedly, hallowedness, halloween, halloweens, hallower, hallowers, hallowing, hallowmas, hallows, halloysite, hallroom, halls, hallstatt, hallucal, halluces, hallucinate, hallucinated, hallucinates, hallucinating, hallucination, hallucinational, hallucinations, hallucinative, hallucinator, hallucinatory, hallucined, hallucinogen, hallucinogenic, hallucinogens, hallucinoses, hallucinosis, hallux, hallway, hallway's, hallways, halm, halma, halmalille, halmawise, halms, halo, halobiont, halobios, halobiotic, halocaine, halocarbon, halochromism, halochromy, halocline, haloed, haloes, haloesque, halogen, halogenate, halogenated, halogenating, halogenation, halogenoid, halogenous, halogens, halogeton, halohydrin, haloid, haloids, haloing, halolike, halolimnic, halomancy, halometer, halomorphic, halomorphism, haloperidol, halophile, halophilic, halophilism, halophilous, halophyte, halophytic, halophytism, haloragidaceous, halos, haloscope, halosere, halothane, halotrichite, haloxene, haloxylin, halp, halpace, halper, hals, halse, halsen, halser, halsfang, halt, halte, halted, halter, halterbreak, haltere, haltered, halteres, haltering, halterlike, halterproof, halters, halting, haltingly, haltingness, haltless, halts, halucket, halukkah, halurgist, halurgy, halutz, halutzim, halva, halvah, halvahs, halvaner, halvans, halvas, halve, halved, halvelings, halver, halvers, halves, halving, halwe, halyard, halyards, ham, ham's, hamacratic, hamada, hamadryad, hamadryades, hamadryads, hamadryas, hamal, hamald, hamals, hamamelidaceous, hamamelidin, hamamelin, haman, hamantasch, hamantaschen, hamantash, hamantashen, hamartia, hamartias, hamartiologist, hamartiology, hamartite, hamartophobia, hamata, hamate, hamated, hamates, hamatum, hamaul, hamauls, hamber, hambergite, hamble, hambone, hambro, hambroline, hamburg, hamburger, hamburger's, hamburgers, hamburgs, hamdmaid, hame, hameil, hamel, hamelt, hames, hamesoken, hamesucken, hametugs, hametz, hamewith, hamfare, hamfat, hamfatter, hamhung, hami, hamiform, hamilt, hamilton, hamiltonian, hamiltonianism, hamingja, haminoea, hamirostrate, hamite, hamitic, hamlah, hamlet, hamlet's, hamleted, hamleteer, hamletization, hamletize, hamlets, hamli, hamline, hamlinite, hammada, hammaid, hammal, hammals, hammam, hammed, hammer, hammerable, hammerbird, hammercloth, hammercloths, hammerdress, hammered, hammerer, hammerers, hammerfish, hammerhead, hammerheaded, hammerheads, hammering, hammeringly, hammerkop, hammerless, hammerlike, hammerlock, hammerlocks, hammerman, hammers, hammersmith, hammerstone, hammertoe, hammertoes, hammerwise, hammerwork, hammerwort, hammier, hammiest, hammily, hamminess, hamming, hammochrysos, hammock, hammock's, hammocklike, hammocks, hammy, hamose, hamotzi, hamous, hamper, hampered, hamperedly, hamperedness, hamperer, hamperers, hampering, hamperman, hampers, hampshire, hampshireman, hampshiremen, hampshirite, hampshirites, hamrongite, hams, hamsa, hamshackle, hamster, hamsters, hamstring, hamstringed, hamstringing, hamstrings, hamstrung, hamular, hamulate, hamule, hamuli, hamulose, hamulous, hamulus, hamus, hamza, hamzah, hamzahs, hamzas, han, han't, hanahill, hanap, hanaper, hanapers, hanaster, hanbury, hance, hanced, hances, hanch, hancockite, hand, handarm, handbag, handbag's, handbags, handball, handballer, handballs, handbank, handbanker, handbarrow, handbarrows, handbell, handbells, handbill, handbills, handblow, handbolt, handbook, handbook's, handbooks, handbound, handbow, handbrake, handbreadth, handbreed, handcar, handcars, handcart, handcarts, handclap, handclapping, handclasp, handclasps, handcloth, handcraft, handcrafted, handcrafting, handcraftman, handcrafts, handcraftsman, handcuff, handcuffed, handcuffing, handcuffs, handed, handedly, handedness, handel, hander, handersome, handfast, handfasted, handfasting, handfastly, handfastness, handfasts, handfeed, handfish, handflag, handflower, handful, handfuls, handgallop, handgrasp, handgravure, handgrip, handgriping, handgrips, handgun, handguns, handhaving, handhold, handholds, handhole, handicap, handicap's, handicapped, handicapper, handicappers, handicapping, handicaps, handicraft, handicrafter, handicrafts, handicraftship, handicraftsman, handicraftsmanship, handicraftsmen, handicraftswoman, handicuff, handier, handiest, handily, handiness, handing, handiron, handistroke, handiwork, handjar, handkercher, handkerchief, handkerchief's, handkerchiefful, handkerchiefs, handkerchieves, handlaid, handle, handleable, handlebar, handlebars, handled, handleless, handler, handlers, handles, handless, handlike, handline, handling, handlings, handlist, handlists, handload, handloader, handloading, handlock, handloom, handloomed, handlooms, handmade, handmaid, handmaiden, handmaidenly, handmaidens, handmaids, handoff, handoffs, handout, handouts, handpick, handpicked, handpicking, handpicks, handpiece, handpost, handpress, handprint, handrail, handrailing, handrails, handreader, handreading, handrest, hands, handsale, handsaw, handsawfish, handsawfishes, handsaws, handsbreadth, handscrape, handsel, handseled, handseling, handselled, handseller, handselling, handsels, handset, handsets, handsetting, handsew, handsewed, handsewing, handsewn, handsful, handshake, handshaker, handshakes, handshaking, handsled, handsmooth, handsome, handsomeish, handsomely, handsomeness, handsomer, handsomest, handspade, handspan, handspec, handspike, handspoke, handspring, handsprings, handstaff, handstand, handstands, handstone, handstroke, handtrap, handwaled, handwaving, handwear, handweaving, handwheel, handwhile, handwork, handworked, handworker, handworkman, handworks, handworm, handwoven, handwrist, handwrit, handwrite, handwrites, handwriting, handwritings, handwritten, handwrote, handwrought, handy, handybillies, handybilly, handyblow, handybook, handycuff, handyfight, handyframe, handygrip, handygripe, handyman, handymen, hanefiyeh, hang, hangability, hangable, hangalai, hangar, hangar's, hangared, hangaring, hangars, hangbird, hangbirds, hangby, hangdog, hangdogs, hange, hanged, hangee, hanger, hangers, hangfire, hangfires, hangie, hanging, hangingly, hangings, hangkang, hangle, hangman, hangmanship, hangmen, hangment, hangnail, hangnails, hangnest, hangnests, hangout, hangouts, hangover, hangover's, hangovers, hangs, hangtag, hangtags, hangul, hangup, hangups, hangwoman, hangworm, hangworthy, hanif, hanifism, hanifite, hanifiya, hank, hanked, hanker, hankered, hankerer, hankerers, hankering, hankeringly, hankerings, hankers, hankie, hankies, hanking, hankle, hanks, hanksite, hankt, hankul, hanky, hanna, hannayite, hanoi, hanologate, hanover, hanoverian, hans, hansa, hansard, hanse, hanseatic, hansel, hanseled, hanseling, hanselled, hanselling, hansels, hansenosis, hanses, hansgrave, hansom, hansomcab, hansoms, hant, hanted, hanting, hantle, hantles, hants, hanukkah, hanuman, hanumans, hao, haole, haoles, haoma, haori, haoris, hap, hapalote, hapax, hapaxanthous, hapaxes, hapchance, haphazard, haphazardly, haphazardness, haphazardry, haphophobia, haphtarah, hapiton, hapless, haplessly, haplessness, haplite, haplites, haplitic, haplobiont, haplobiontic, haplocaulescent, haplochlamydeous, haplodont, haplodonty, haplography, haploid, haploidic, haploidies, haploids, haploidy, haplolaly, haplologic, haplology, haploma, haplome, haplomid, haplomitosis, haplomous, haplont, haplontic, haplonts, haploperistomic, haploperistomous, haplopetalous, haplophase, haplophyte, haplopia, haplopias, haploscope, haploscopic, haploses, haplosis, haplostemonous, haplotype, haply, happed, happen, happenchance, happened, happening, happenings, happens, happenstance, happer, happier, happiest, happify, happiless, happily, happiness, happing, happy, haps, hapsburg, hapten, haptene, haptenes, haptenic, haptens, haptera, haptere, hapteron, haptic, haptical, haptics, haptoglobin, haptometer, haptophobia, haptophor, haptophoric, haptophorous, haptor, haptotropic, haptotropically, haptotropism, hapu, hapuku, haquebut, haqueton, harace, harakeke, harakiri, haram, harambee, harang, harangue, harangued, harangueful, haranguer, haranguers, harangues, haranguing, haras, harass, harassable, harassed, harassedly, harasser, harassers, harasses, harassing, harassingly, harassment, harassments, harast, haratch, harateen, haraucana, harbergage, harbi, harbinge, harbinger, harbingers, harbingership, harbingery, harbor, harborage, harbored, harborer, harborers, harborful, harboring, harborless, harbormaster, harborough, harborous, harbors, harborside, harborward, harbour, harbourage, harboured, harbourer, harbouring, harbourless, harbourous, harbours, harbourside, harbourward, harbrough, hard, hardanger, hardback, hardbacks, hardbake, hardball, hardballs, hardbeam, hardberry, hardboard, hardboiled, hardboot, hardboots, hardbought, hardbound, hardcase, hardcopy, hardcore, hardcover, hardcovered, hardcovers, harden, hardenability, hardenable, hardened, hardenedness, hardener, hardeners, hardening, hardenite, hardens, harder, harderian, hardest, hardfern, hardfist, hardfisted, hardfistedness, hardhack, hardhacks, hardhanded, hardhandedness, hardhat, hardhats, hardhead, hardheaded, hardheadedly, hardheadedness, hardheads, hardhearted, hardheartedly, hardheartedness, hardhewer, hardie, hardier, hardies, hardiesse, hardiest, hardihead, hardihood, hardily, hardim, hardiment, hardiness, harding, hardish, hardishrew, hardly, hardmouth, hardmouthed, hardness, hardnesses, hardnose, hardock, hardpan, hardpans, hards, hardsalt, hardscrabble, hardset, hardshell, hardship, hardship's, hardships, hardstand, hardstanding, hardstands, hardtack, hardtacks, hardtail, hardtails, hardtop, hardtops, hardwall, hardware, hardwareman, hardwares, hardway, hardweed, hardwired, hardwood, hardwoods, hardworking, hardy, hardyhead, hardystonite, hare, hare's, harebell, harebells, harebottle, harebrain, harebrained, harebrainedly, harebrainedness, harebur, hared, hareem, hareems, harefoot, harefooted, harehearted, harehound, hareld, harelike, harelip, harelipped, harelips, harem, haremism, haremlik, harems, harengiform, harenut, hares, harewood, harfang, hariana, harianas, harico, haricot, haricots, harier, hariffe, harigalds, harijan, harijans, harikari, harim, haring, hariolate, hariolation, hariolize, harish, hark, harka, harked, harkee, harken, harkened, harkener, harkeners, harkening, harkens, harking, harks, harl, harle, harled, harleian, harlem, harlequin, harlequina, harlequinade, harlequinery, harlequinesque, harlequinic, harlequinism, harlequinize, harlequins, harling, harlock, harlot, harlot's, harlotries, harlotry, harlots, harls, harm, harmal, harmala, harmalin, harmaline, harman, harmattan, harmed, harmel, harmer, harmers, harmful, harmfully, harmfulness, harmin, harmine, harmines, harming, harminic, harmins, harmless, harmlessly, harmlessness, harmonia, harmoniacal, harmonial, harmonic, harmonica, harmonical, harmonically, harmonicalness, harmonicas, harmonichord, harmonici, harmonicism, harmonicon, harmonics, harmonies, harmonious, harmoniously, harmoniousness, harmoniphon, harmoniphone, harmonisable, harmonisation, harmonise, harmonised, harmoniser, harmonising, harmonist, harmonistic, harmonistically, harmonium, harmoniums, harmonizable, harmonization, harmonizations, harmonize, harmonized, harmonizer, harmonizers, harmonizes, harmonizing, harmonogram, harmonograph, harmonometer, harmony, harmoot, harmost, harmotome, harmotomic, harmout, harmproof, harms, harn, harness, harnessed, harnesser, harnessers, harnesses, harnessing, harnessless, harnesslike, harnessry, harnpan, harns, harold, haroset, haroseth, harp, harpago, harpagon, harpaxophobia, harped, harper, harperess, harpers, harpier, harpies, harpin, harping, harpingly, harpings, harpins, harpist, harpists, harpless, harplike, harpoon, harpooned, harpooneer, harpooner, harpooners, harpooning, harpoonlike, harpoons, harpress, harps, harpsical, harpsichon, harpsichord, harpsichordist, harpsichords, harpula, harpwaytuning, harpwise, harpy, harpylike, harquebus, harquebusade, harquebuse, harquebuses, harquebusier, harquebuss, harr, harrage, harrateen, harre, harrid, harridan, harridans, harried, harrier, harriers, harries, harriet, harris, harrisite, harrison, harrovian, harrow, harrowed, harrower, harrowers, harrowing, harrowingly, harrowingness, harrowment, harrows, harrowtry, harrumph, harrumphed, harrumphing, harrumphs, harry, harrycane, harrying, harsh, harshen, harshened, harshening, harshens, harsher, harshest, harshish, harshlet, harshlets, harshly, harshness, harshweed, harslet, harslets, harst, harstigite, harstrang, harstrong, hart, hartail, hartake, hartal, hartall, hartals, hartberry, hartebeest, hartebeests, harten, hartford, hartin, hartite, hartleian, hartly, harts, hartshorn, hartstongue, harttite, hartwort, haruspex, haruspical, haruspicate, haruspication, haruspice, haruspices, haruspicy, harvard, harvest, harvestable, harvestbug, harvested, harvester, harvesters, harvestfish, harvestfishes, harvesting, harvestless, harvestman, harvestmen, harvestry, harvests, harvesttime, harvey, harynges, harzburgite, has, hasan, hasard, hasenpfeffer, hash, hashab, hashabi, hashed, hasheesh, hasheeshes, hasher, hashery, hashes, hashhead, hashheads, hashimite, hashing, hashish, hashishes, hasht, hashy, hasid, hasidic, hasidim, hasidism, hask, haskard, haskness, haskwort, hasky, haslet, haslets, haslock, hasmonaeans, hasn, hasn't, hasnt, hasp, hasped, haspicol, hasping, haspling, hasps, haspspecs, hassar, hassel, hassels, hassenpfeffer, hassing, hassle, hassled, hassles, hasslet, hassling, hassock, hassocks, hassocky, hast, hasta, hastate, hastated, hastately, hastati, hastatolanceolate, hastatosagittate, haste, hasted, hasteful, hastefully, hasteless, hastelessness, hasten, hastened, hastener, hasteners, hastening, hastens, hasteproof, haster, hastes, hastier, hastiest, hastif, hastifly, hastifness, hastifoliate, hastiform, hastile, hastilude, hastily, hastiness, hasting, hastings, hastingsite, hastish, hastive, hastler, hastula, hasty, hat, hat's, hatable, hatband, hatbands, hatbox, hatboxes, hatbrim, hatbrush, hatch, hatchability, hatchable, hatchback, hatchbacks, hatcheck, hatched, hatchel, hatcheled, hatcheler, hatcheling, hatchelled, hatcheller, hatchelling, hatchels, hatcher, hatcheries, hatchers, hatchery, hatcheryman, hatches, hatchet, hatchet's, hatchetback, hatchetfaced, hatchetfish, hatchetfishes, hatchetlike, hatchetman, hatchets, hatchettin, hatchettine, hatchettite, hatchettolite, hatchety, hatchgate, hatching, hatchings, hatchite, hatchling, hatchman, hatchment, hatchminder, hatchway, hatchwayman, hatchways, hate, hateable, hated, hateful, hatefully, hatefulness, hatel, hateless, hatelessness, hatemonger, hatemongering, hater, haters, hates, hatful, hatfuls, hath, hatherlite, hathi, hathpace, hating, hatless, hatlessness, hatlike, hatmaker, hatmakers, hatmaking, hatpin, hatpins, hatrack, hatracks, hatrail, hatred, hatreds, hatress, hats, hatsful, hatstand, hatt, hatte, hatted, hatter, hatteria, hatterias, hatters, hattery, hatti, hatting, hattock, hatty, hau, haubergeon, hauberget, hauberk, hauberks, hauberticum, haubois, hauchecornite, hauerite, hauflin, haugh, haughland, haughs, haught, haughtier, haughtiest, haughtily, haughtiness, haughtly, haughtness, haughtonite, haughty, haul, haulabout, haulage, haulages, haulageway, haulaway, haulback, hauld, hauled, hauler, haulers, haulier, hauliers, hauling, haulm, haulmier, haulmiest, haulms, haulmy, hauls, haulse, haulster, hault, haulyard, haulyards, haum, haunce, haunch, haunch's, haunched, hauncher, haunches, haunching, haunchless, haunchy, haunt, haunted, haunter, haunters, haunting, hauntingly, haunts, haunty, haupia, hauriant, haurient, hausa, hause, hausen, hausens, hausfrau, hausfrauen, hausfraus, hausmannite, hausse, haussmannize, haust, haustella, haustellate, haustellated, haustellous, haustellum, haustement, haustoria, haustorial, haustorium, haustral, haustrum, haustus, haut, hautain, hautbois, hautboy, hautboyist, hautboys, haute, hautein, hautesse, hauteur, hauteurs, hauyne, hauynite, hauynophyre, hav, havage, havana, havance, havdalah, havdalahs, have, haveable, haveage, havel, haveless, havelock, havelocks, haven, haven's, haven't, havenage, havened, havener, havenership, havenet, havenful, havening, havenless, havens, havent, havenward, haver, haveral, havercake, havered, haverel, haverels, haverer, havergrass, havering, havermeal, havers, haversack, haversacks, haversian, haversine, haves, havier, havildar, having, havingness, havings, havior, haviored, haviors, haviour, havioured, haviours, havlagah, havoc, havocked, havocker, havockers, havocking, havocs, haw, hawaii, hawaiian, hawaiians, hawaiite, hawbuck, hawcuaite, hawcubite, hawebake, hawed, hawer, hawfinch, hawfinches, hawing, hawk, hawkbill, hawkbills, hawkbit, hawked, hawker, hawkers, hawkery, hawkey, hawkeye, hawkeys, hawkie, hawkies, hawking, hawkings, hawkins, hawkish, hawkishly, hawkishness, hawklike, hawkmoth, hawkmoths, hawknose, hawknosed, hawknoses, hawknut, hawks, hawksbeak, hawksbill, hawkshaw, hawkshaws, hawkweed, hawkweeds, hawkwise, hawky, hawm, hawok, haws, hawse, hawsed, hawsehole, hawseman, hawsepiece, hawsepipe, hawser, hawsers, hawserwise, hawses, hawsing, hawthorn, hawthorne, hawthorned, hawthorns, hawthorny, hay, haya, hayband, haybird, haybote, haybox, hayburner, haycap, haycart, haycock, haycocks, haydenite, haydn, haye, hayed, hayer, hayers, hayes, hayey, hayfield, hayfields, hayfork, hayforks, haygrower, haying, hayings, haylage, haylages, haylift, hayloft, haylofts, haymaker, haymakers, haymaking, haymarket, haymish, haymow, haymows, hayne, hayrack, hayracks, hayrake, hayraker, hayrick, hayricks, hayride, hayrides, hays, hayseed, hayseeds, haysel, hayshock, haystack, haystacks, haysuck, haythorn, haytime, haywagon, hayward, haywards, hayweed, haywire, haywires, hayz, hazan, hazanim, hazans, hazanut, hazard, hazard's, hazardable, hazarded, hazarder, hazardful, hazarding, hazardize, hazardless, hazardous, hazardously, hazardousness, hazardry, hazards, haze, haze's, hazed, hazel, hazeled, hazeless, hazelhen, hazeline, hazelly, hazelnut, hazelnuts, hazels, hazelwood, hazelwort, hazemeter, hazen, hazer, hazers, hazes, hazier, haziest, hazily, haziness, hazinesses, hazing, hazings, hazle, haznadar, hazy, hazzan, hazzanim, hazzans, hazzanut, hb, hcb, hcf, hcl, hconvert, hd, hdbk, hdkf, hdlc, hdqrs, hdwe, he, he""ll, he'd, he'll, he's, head, headache, headache's, headaches, headachier, headachiest, headachy, headband, headbander, headbands, headboard, headboards, headborough, headbox, headcap, headchair, headcheese, headchute, headcloth, headclothes, headcloths, headdress, headdresses, headed, headend, headender, headends, header, headers, headfast, headfirst, headfish, headfishes, headforemost, headframe, headful, headgate, headgates, headgear, headgears, headhunt, headhunted, headhunter, headhunters, headhunting, headhunts, headier, headiest, headily, headiness, heading, heading's, headings, headkerchief, headlamp, headlamps, headland, headland's, headlands, headle, headledge, headless, headlessness, headlight, headlighting, headlights, headlike, headliked, headline, headlined, headliner, headliners, headlines, headling, headlining, headload, headlock, headlocks, headlong, headlongly, headlongness, headlongs, headlongwise, headly, headman, headmark, headmaster, headmasterly, headmasters, headmastership, headmen, headmistress, headmistresses, headmistressship, headmold, headmost, headmould, headnote, headnotes, headpenny, headphone, headphones, headpiece, headpieces, headpin, headpins, headplate, headpost, headquarter, headquartered, headquartering, headquarters, headrace, headraces, headrail, headreach, headrent, headrest, headrests, headrig, headright, headring, headroom, headrooms, headrope, heads, headsail, headsails, headsaw, headscarf, headset, headsets, headshake, headshaker, headsheet, headsheets, headship, headships, headshrinker, headsill, headskin, headsman, headsmen, headspace, headspring, headsquare, headstall, headstalls, headstand, headstands, headstay, headstays, headstick, headstock, headstone, headstones, headstream, headstrong, headstrongly, headstrongness, headtire, headwaiter, headwaiters, headwall, headward, headwards, headwark, headwater, headwaters, headway, headways, headwear, headwind, headwinds, headword, headwords, headwork, headworker, headworking, headworks, heady, heaf, heal, healable, heald, healder, healed, healer, healers, healful, healing, healingly, healless, heals, healsome, healsomeness, health, healthcare, healthcraft, healthful, healthfully, healthfulness, healthguard, healthier, healthiest, healthily, healthiness, healthless, healthlessness, healths, healthsome, healthsomely, healthsomeness, healthward, healthy, heap, heaped, heaper, heaping, heaps, heapstead, heapy, hear, hearable, heard, hearer, hearers, hearing, hearingless, hearings, hearken, hearkened, hearkener, hearkening, hearkens, hears, hearsay, hearsays, hearse, hearsecloth, hearsed, hearselike, hearses, hearsing, hearst, heart, heartache, heartaches, heartaching, heartbeat, heartbeats, heartbird, heartblock, heartblood, heartbreak, heartbreaker, heartbreaking, heartbreakingly, heartbreaks, heartbroke, heartbroken, heartbrokenly, heartbrokenness, heartburn, heartburning, heartburns, heartdeep, heartease, hearted, heartedly, heartedness, hearten, heartened, heartener, heartening, hearteningly, heartens, heartfelt, heartful, heartfully, heartfulness, heartgrief, hearth, hearthless, hearthman, hearthpenny, hearthrug, hearths, hearthside, hearthsides, hearthstead, hearthstone, hearthstones, hearthward, hearthwarming, heartier, hearties, heartiest, heartikin, heartily, heartiness, hearting, heartland, heartlands, heartleaf, heartless, heartlessly, heartlessness, heartlet, heartlike, heartling, heartly, heartnut, heartpea, heartquake, heartrending, heartrendingly, heartroot, heartrot, hearts, heartscald, heartsease, heartseed, heartsette, heartshake, heartsick, heartsickening, heartsickness, heartsmitten, heartsome, heartsomely, heartsomeness, heartsore, heartsoreness, heartstring, heartstrings, heartthrob, heartthrobs, heartward, heartwarming, heartwater, heartweed, heartwise, heartwood, heartworm, heartwort, heartwounding, hearty, heat, heatable, heatdrop, heatdrops, heated, heatedly, heatedness, heaten, heater, heaterman, heaters, heatful, heath, heathberries, heathberry, heathbird, heathbrd, heathen, heathendom, heatheness, heathenesse, heathenhood, heathenise, heathenised, heathenish, heathenishly, heathenishness, heathenising, heathenism, heathenist, heathenize, heathenized, heathenizing, heathenly, heathenness, heathenry, heathens, heathenship, heather, heathered, heatheriness, heathers, heathery, heathfowl, heathier, heathiest, heathless, heathlike, heathrman, heaths, heathwort, heathy, heating, heatingly, heatless, heatlike, heatmaker, heatmaking, heatproof, heatronic, heats, heatsman, heatstroke, heatstrokes, heaume, heaumer, heaumes, heautarit, heautomorphism, heautophany, heave, heaved, heaveless, heaven, heavenful, heavenhood, heavenish, heavenishly, heavenize, heavenless, heavenlier, heavenliest, heavenlike, heavenliness, heavenly, heavens, heavenward, heavenwardly, heavenwardness, heavenwards, heaver, heavers, heaves, heavier, heavies, heaviest, heavily, heaviness, heaving, heavinsogme, heavisome, heavity, heavy, heavyback, heavyhanded, heavyhandedness, heavyheaded, heavyhearted, heavyheartedly, heavyheartedness, heavyset, heavyweight, heavyweights, heazy, hebamic, hebdomad, hebdomadal, hebdomadally, hebdomadaries, hebdomadary, hebdomader, hebdomads, hebdomarian, hebdomary, hebdomcad, hebe, hebeanthous, hebecarpous, hebecladous, hebegynous, heben, hebenon, hebeosteotomy, hebepetalous, hebephrenia, hebephreniac, hebephrenic, hebetate, hebetated, hebetates, hebetating, hebetation, hebetative, hebete, hebetic, hebetomy, hebetude, hebetudes, hebetudinous, hebotomy, hebraean, hebraic, hebraism, hebraist, hebraistic, hebraists, hebraization, hebraize, hebraized, hebraizes, hebraizing, hebrew, hebrews, hebrician, hebridean, hebronite, hecastotheism, hecate, hecatomb, hecatombed, hecatombs, hecatomped, hecatompedon, hecatonstylon, hecatontarchy, hecatontome, hecatophyllous, hecchsmhaer, hecco, hecctkaerre, hech, hechsher, hechsherim, hechshers, hecht, heck, heckelphone, heckimal, heckle, heckled, heckler, hecklers, heckles, heckling, hecks, hectar, hectare, hectares, hecte, hectic, hectical, hectically, hecticly, hecticness, hective, hectocotyl, hectocotyle, hectocotyli, hectocotyliferous, hectocotylization, hectocotylize, hectocotylus, hectogram, hectogramme, hectograms, hectograph, hectographic, hectography, hectoliter, hectoliters, hectolitre, hectometer, hectometers, hector, hectored, hectorer, hectoring, hectoringly, hectorism, hectorly, hectors, hectorship, hectostere, hectowatt, hectyli, hecuba, hed, heddle, heddlemaker, heddler, heddles, hede, hedebo, hedenbergite, heder, hederaceous, hederaceously, hederal, hederated, hederic, hederiferous, hederiform, hederigerent, hederin, hederose, heders, hedge, hedgebe, hedgeberry, hedgeborn, hedgebote, hedgebreaker, hedged, hedgehog, hedgehog's, hedgehoggy, hedgehogs, hedgehop, hedgehoppe, hedgehopped, hedgehopper, hedgehopping, hedgehops, hedgeless, hedgemaker, hedgemaking, hedgepig, hedgepigs, hedger, hedgerow, hedgerows, hedgers, hedges, hedgesmith, hedgetaper, hedgeweed, hedgewise, hedgewood, hedgier, hedgiest, hedging, hedgingly, hedgy, hedonic, hedonical, hedonically, hedonics, hedonism, hedonisms, hedonist, hedonistic, hedonistically, hedonists, hedonology, hedonophobia, hedriophthalmous, hedrocele, hedrumite, hedyphane, hee, heed, heeded, heeder, heeders, heedful, heedfully, heedfulness, heedily, heediness, heeding, heedless, heedlessly, heedlessness, heeds, heedy, heehaw, heehawed, heehawing, heehaws, heel, heelball, heelballs, heelband, heelcap, heeled, heeler, heelers, heelgrip, heeling, heelings, heelless, heelmaker, heelmaking, heelpath, heelpiece, heelplate, heelpost, heelposts, heelprint, heels, heelstrap, heeltap, heeltaps, heeltree, heelwork, heemraad, heemraat, heep, heer, heeze, heezed, heezes, heezie, heezing, heezy, heft, hefted, hefter, hefters, heftier, heftiest, heftily, heftiness, hefting, hefts, hefty, hegari, hegaris, hegelian, hegelianism, hegemon, hegemonic, hegemonical, hegemonies, hegemonist, hegemonistic, hegemonizer, hegemony, hegira, hegiras, hegumen, hegumene, hegumenes, hegumeness, hegumenies, hegumenos, hegumens, hegumeny, heh, hei, heiau, heifer, heiferhood, heifers, heigh, heighday, height, heighted, heighten, heightened, heightener, heightening, heightens, heighth, heighths, heights, heii, heil, heild, heiled, heiling, heils, heily, heimdal, heimin, heimish, heinie, heinies, heinous, heinously, heinousness, heintzite, heir, heir's, heirdom, heirdoms, heired, heiress, heiress's, heiressdom, heiresses, heiresshood, heiring, heirless, heirlo, heirloom, heirlooms, heirs, heirship, heirships, heirskip, heist, heisted, heister, heisters, heisting, heists, heitiki, heize, heized, heizing, hejira, hejiras, hekhsher, hekhsherim, hekhshers, hektare, hektares, hekteus, hektogram, hektograph, hektoliter, hektometer, hektostere, hel, helas, helbeh, helco, helcoid, helcology, helcoplasty, helcosis, helcotic, held, heldentenor, heldentenore, heldentenors, helder, hele, helen, helena, helenin, helenioid, helenn, helepole, helewou, heliac, heliacal, heliacally, heliaea, heliaean, helianthaceous, helianthic, helianthin, helianthus, helianthuses, heliast, heliastic, heliasts, heliazophyte, helibus, helical, helically, heliced, helices, helichryse, helichrysum, heliciform, helicin, helicine, helicitic, helicities, helicity, helicline, helicograph, helicogyrate, helicogyre, helicoid, helicoidal, helicoidally, helicoids, helicometry, helicon, heliconian, heliconist, helicons, helicoprotein, helicopt, helicopted, helicopter, helicopters, helicopting, helicopts, helicorubin, helicotrema, helictite, helide, helidrome, heling, helio, heliocentric, heliocentrical, heliocentrically, heliocentricism, heliocentricity, heliochrome, heliochromic, heliochromoscope, heliochromotype, heliochromy, helioculture, heliodon, heliodor, helioelectric, helioengraving, heliofugal, heliogram, heliograph, heliographer, heliographic, heliographical, heliographically, heliographs, heliography, heliogravure, helioid, heliolater, heliolator, heliolatrous, heliolatry, heliolite, heliolithic, heliological, heliologist, heliology, heliometer, heliometric, heliometrical, heliometrically, heliometry, heliomicrometer, heliophilia, heliophiliac, heliophilous, heliophobe, heliophobia, heliophobic, heliophobous, heliophotography, heliophyllite, heliophyte, heliopore, heliopticon, helios, helioscope, helioscopic, helioscopy, heliosis, heliostat, heliostatic, heliotactic, heliotaxis, heliotherapies, heliotherapy, heliothermometer, heliotrope, heliotroper, heliotropes, heliotropian, heliotropic, heliotropical, heliotropically, heliotropin, heliotropine, heliotropism, heliotropy, heliotype, heliotyped, heliotypic, heliotypically, heliotyping, heliotypography, heliotypy, heliozoan, heliozoic, helipad, helipads, heliport, heliports, helispheric, helispherical, helistop, helistops, helium, heliums, helix, helixes, helixin, helizitic, hell, hell's, hellandite, hellanodic, hellbender, hellbent, hellbore, hellborn, hellbox, hellboxes, hellbred, hellbroth, hellcat, hellcats, helldiver, helldog, helleboraceous, helleboraster, hellebore, helleborein, hellebores, helleboric, helleborin, helleborine, helleborism, helled, hellene, hellenes, hellenian, hellenic, hellenism, hellenist, hellenistic, hellenists, hellenization, hellenize, heller, helleri, helleries, hellers, hellery, hellespont, hellfire, hellfires, hellgrammite, hellgrammites, hellhag, hellhole, hellholes, hellhound, hellicat, hellicate, hellier, hellim, helling, hellion, hellions, hellish, hellishly, hellishness, hellkite, hellkites, hellman, hellness, hello, helloed, helloes, helloing, hellos, hellroot, hells, hellship, helluo, helluva, hellvine, hellward, hellweed, helly, helm, helmage, helmed, helmet, helmet's, helmeted, helmetflower, helmeting, helmetlike, helmetmaker, helmetmaking, helmetpod, helmets, helming, helminth, helminthagogic, helminthagogue, helminthiasis, helminthic, helminthism, helminthite, helminthoid, helminthologic, helminthological, helminthologist, helminthology, helminthophobia, helminthosporiose, helminthosporoid, helminthous, helminths, helmless, helms, helmsman, helmsmanship, helmsmen, helobious, heloderm, helodermatoid, helodermatous, helodes, heloe, heloma, helonin, helosis, helot, helotage, helotages, helotism, helotisms, helotize, helotomy, helotries, helotry, helots, help, helpable, helped, helper, helpers, helpful, helpfully, helpfulness, helping, helpingly, helpings, helpless, helplessly, helplessness, helply, helpmate, helpmates, helpmeet, helpmeets, helps, helpsome, helpworthy, helsingkite, helsinki, helterskelteriness, helve, helved, helvell, helvellaceous, helvellic, helver, helves, helvetian, helvetic, helvetii, helvin, helvine, helving, helvite, helzel, hem, hem's, hemabarometer, hemachate, hemachrome, hemachrosis, hemacite, hemacytometer, hemad, hemadrometer, hemadrometry, hemadromograph, hemadromometer, hemadynameter, hemadynamic, hemadynamics, hemadynamometer, hemafibrite, hemagglutinate, hemagglutinated, hemagglutinating, hemagglutination, hemagglutinative, hemagglutinin, hemagog, hemagogic, hemagogs, hemagogue, hemal, hemalbumen, hemameba, hemamoeba, heman, hemanalysis, hemangioma, hemangiomas, hemangiomata, hemangiomatosis, hemangiosarcoma, hemaphein, hemaphobia, hemapod, hemapodous, hemapoiesis, hemapoietic, hemapophyseal, hemapophysial, hemapophysis, hemarthrosis, hemase, hemaspectroscope, hemastatics, hematachometer, hematachometry, hematal, hematein, hemateins, hematemesis, hematemetic, hematencephalon, hematherapy, hematherm, hemathermal, hemathermous, hemathidrosis, hematic, hematics, hematid, hematidrosis, hematimeter, hematin, hematine, hematines, hematinic, hematinometer, hematinometric, hematins, hematinuria, hematite, hematites, hematitic, hematobic, hematobious, hematobium, hematoblast, hematoblastic, hematobranchiate, hematocatharsis, hematocathartic, hematocele, hematochezia, hematochrome, hematochyluria, hematoclasia, hematoclasis, hematocolpus, hematocrit, hematocryal, hematocrystallin, hematocyanin, hematocyst, hematocystis, hematocyte, hematocytoblast, hematocytogenesis, hematocytometer, hematocytotripsis, hematocytozoon, hematocyturia, hematodynamics, hematodynamometer, hematodystrophy, hematogen, hematogenesis, hematogenetic, hematogenic, hematogenous, hematoglobulin, hematography, hematohidrosis, hematoid, hematoidin, hematoids, hematolin, hematolite, hematologic, hematological, hematologies, hematologist, hematologists, hematology, hematolymphangioma, hematolysis, hematolytic, hematoma, hematomancy, hematomas, hematomata, hematometer, hematometra, hematometry, hematomphalocele, hematomyelia, hematomyelitis, hematonephrosis, hematonic, hematopathology, hematopericardium, hematopexis, hematophagous, hematophobia, hematophyte, hematoplast, hematoplastic, hematopoiesis, hematopoietic, hematopoietically, hematoporphyria, hematoporphyrin, hematoporphyrinuria, hematorrhachis, hematorrhea, hematosalpinx, hematoscope, hematoscopy, hematose, hematosepsis, hematosin, hematosis, hematospectrophotometer, hematospectroscope, hematospermatocele, hematospermia, hematostibiite, hematotherapy, hematothermal, hematothorax, hematoxic, hematoxylic, hematoxylin, hematozoa, hematozoal, hematozoan, hematozoic, hematozoon, hematozymosis, hematozymotic, hematozzoa, hematuresis, hematuria, hematuric, hemautogram, hemautograph, hemautographic, hemautography, heme, hemellitene, hemellitic, hemelytra, hemelytral, hemelytron, hemelytrum, hemelyttra, hemen, hemera, hemeralope, hemeralopia, hemeralopic, hemerobian, hemerocallis, hemerologium, hemerology, hemerythrin, hemes, hemiablepsia, hemiacetal, hemiachromatopsia, hemiageusia, hemiageustia, hemialbumin, hemialbumose, hemialbumosuria, hemialgia, hemiamaurosis, hemiamb, hemiamblyopia, hemiamyosthenia, hemianacusia, hemianalgesia, hemianatropous, hemianesthesia, hemianopia, hemianopic, hemianopsia, hemianoptic, hemianosmia, hemiapraxia, hemiasynergia, hemiataxia, hemiataxy, hemiathetosis, hemiatrophy, hemiauxin, hemiazygous, hemibasidium, hemibathybian, hemibenthic, hemibenthonic, hemibranch, hemibranchiate, hemic, hemicanities, hemicardia, hemicardiac, hemicarp, hemicatalepsy, hemicataleptic, hemicellulose, hemicentrum, hemicephalous, hemicerebrum, hemicholinium, hemichordate, hemichorea, hemichromatopsia, hemicircle, hemicircular, hemiclastic, hemicollin, hemicrane, hemicrania, hemicranic, hemicrany, hemicrystalline, hemicycle, hemicyclic, hemicyclium, hemicylindrical, hemidactyl, hemidactylous, hemidemisemiquaver, hemidiapente, hemidiaphoresis, hemiditone, hemidomatic, hemidome, hemidrachm, hemidysergia, hemidysesthesia, hemidystrophy, hemiekton, hemielliptic, hemielytra, hemielytral, hemielytron, hemiepes, hemiepilepsy, hemifacial, hemiform, hemigastrectomy, hemigeusia, hemiglobin, hemiglossal, hemiglossitis, hemiglyph, hemignathous, hemihdry, hemihedral, hemihedrally, hemihedric, hemihedrism, hemihedron, hemiholohedral, hemihydrate, hemihydrated, hemihydrosis, hemihypalgesia, hemihyperesthesia, hemihyperidrosis, hemihypertonia, hemihypertrophy, hemihypesthesia, hemihypoesthesia, hemihypotonia, hemikaryon, hemikaryotic, hemilaminectomy, hemilaryngectomy, hemilethargy, hemiligulate, hemilingual, hemimellitene, hemimellitic, hemimelus, hemimetabola, hemimetabole, hemimetabolic, hemimetabolism, hemimetabolous, hemimetaboly, hemimetamorphic, hemimetamorphosis, hemimetamorphous, hemimorph, hemimorphic, hemimorphism, hemimorphite, hemimorphy, hemin, hemina, hemine, heminee, hemineurasthenia, hemingway, hemins, hemiobol, hemiola, hemiolas, hemiolia, hemiolic, hemionus, hemiope, hemiopia, hemiopic, hemiopsia, hemiorthotype, hemiparalysis, hemiparanesthesia, hemiparaplegia, hemiparasite, hemiparasitic, hemiparasitism, hemiparesis, hemiparesthesia, hemiparetic, hemipenis, hemipeptone, hemiphrase, hemipic, hemipinnate, hemiplane, hemiplankton, hemiplegia, hemiplegic, hemiplegy, hemipod, hemipodan, hemipode, hemippe, hemiprism, hemiprismatic, hemiprotein, hemipter, hemiptera, hemipteral, hemipteran, hemipteroid, hemipterological, hemipterology, hemipteron, hemipterous, hemipters, hemipyramid, hemiquinonoid, hemiramph, hemiramphine, hemisaprophyte, hemisaprophytic, hemiscotosis, hemisect, hemisection, hemispasm, hemispheral, hemisphere, hemisphere's, hemisphered, hemispheres, hemispheric, hemispherical, hemispherically, hemispheroid, hemispheroidal, hemispherule, hemistater, hemistich, hemistichal, hemistichs, hemistrumectomy, hemisymmetrical, hemisymmetry, hemisystematic, hemisystole, hemiterata, hemiteratic, hemiteratics, hemiteria, hemiterpene, hemitery, hemithyroidectomy, hemitone, hemitremor, hemitrichous, hemitriglyph, hemitropal, hemitrope, hemitropic, hemitropism, hemitropous, hemitropy, hemitype, hemitypic, hemivagotony, hemizygote, hemizygous, heml, hemline, hemlines, hemlock, hemlock's, hemlocks, hemmed, hemmel, hemmer, hemmers, hemming, hemoalkalimeter, hemoblast, hemochromatosis, hemochromatotic, hemochrome, hemochromogen, hemochromometer, hemochromometry, hemoclasia, hemoclasis, hemoclastic, hemocoel, hemocoele, hemocoelic, hemocoelom, hemocoels, hemoconcentration, hemoconia, hemoconiosis, hemocry, hemocrystallin, hemoculture, hemocyanin, hemocyte, hemocytes, hemocytoblast, hemocytoblastic, hemocytogenesis, hemocytolysis, hemocytometer, hemocytotripsis, hemocytozoon, hemocyturia, hemodia, hemodiagnosis, hemodialyses, hemodialysis, hemodialyzer, hemodilution, hemodrometer, hemodrometry, hemodromograph, hemodromometer, hemodynameter, hemodynamic, hemodynamically, hemodynamics, hemodystrophy, hemoerythrin, hemoflagellate, hemofuscin, hemogastric, hemogenesis, hemogenetic, hemogenia, hemogenic, hemogenous, hemoglobic, hemoglobin, hemoglobinemia, hemoglobinic, hemoglobiniferous, hemoglobinocholia, hemoglobinometer, hemoglobinopathy, hemoglobinophilic, hemoglobinous, hemoglobinuria, hemoglobinuric, hemoglobulin, hemogram, hemogregarine, hemoid, hemokonia, hemokoniosis, hemol, hemoleucocyte, hemoleucocytic, hemologist, hemology, hemolymph, hemolymphatic, hemolysate, hemolysin, hemolysis, hemolytic, hemolyze, hemolyzed, hemolyzes, hemolyzing, hemomanometer, hemometer, hemometry, hemonephrosis, hemopathology, hemopathy, hemopericardium, hemoperitoneum, hemopexis, hemophage, hemophagia, hemophagocyte, hemophagocytosis, hemophagous, hemophagy, hemophile, hemophilia, hemophiliac, hemophiliacs, hemophilic, hemophilioid, hemophobia, hemophthalmia, hemophthisis, hemopiezometer, hemoplasmodium, hemoplastic, hemopneumothorax, hemopod, hemopoiesis, hemopoietic, hemoproctia, hemoprotein, hemoptoe, hemoptysis, hemopyrrole, hemorrhage, hemorrhaged, hemorrhages, hemorrhagic, hemorrhaging, hemorrhea, hemorrhodin, hemorrhoid, hemorrhoidal, hemorrhoidectomies, hemorrhoidectomy, hemorrhoids, hemosalpinx, hemoscope, hemoscopy, hemosiderin, hemosiderosis, hemosiderotic, hemospasia, hemospastic, hemospermia, hemosporid, hemosporidian, hemostasia, hemostasis, hemostat, hemostatic, hemostats, hemotachometer, hemotherapeutics, hemotherapy, hemothorax, hemotoxic, hemotoxin, hemotrophe, hemotrophic, hemotropic, hemozoon, hemp, hempbush, hempen, hempherds, hempie, hempier, hempiest, hemplike, hemps, hempseed, hempseeds, hempstring, hempweed, hempweeds, hempwort, hempy, hems, hemself, hemstitch, hemstitched, hemstitcher, hemstitches, hemstitching, hemule, hen, hen's, henad, henbane, henbanes, henbill, henbit, henbits, hence, henceforth, henceforward, henceforwards, henchboy, henchman, henchmanship, henchmen, hencoop, hencoops, hencote, hend, hendecacolic, hendecagon, hendecagonal, hendecahedra, hendecahedral, hendecahedron, hendecahedrons, hendecane, hendecasemic, hendecasyllabic, hendecasyllable, hendecatoic, hendecoic, hendecyl, hendedra, hendiadys, hendly, hendness, hendy, heneicosane, henen, henequen, henequens, henequin, henequins, henfish, heng, henge, hengest, henhawk, henhearted, henheartedness, henhouse, henhouses, henhussies, henhussy, heniquen, heniquens, henism, henlike, henmoldy, henna, hennaed, hennaing, hennas, henneries, hennery, hennes, hennin, hennish, henny, henogeny, henotheism, henotheist, henotheistic, henotic, henpeck, henpecked, henpecking, henpecks, henpen, henries, henroost, henry, henrys, hens, hent, hented, henter, henting, hentriacontane, hents, henware, henwife, henwile, henwise, henwoodite, henyard, heo, heortological, heortologion, heortology, hep, hepar, heparin, heparinization, heparinize, heparinized, heparinizing, heparinoid, heparins, hepatalgia, hepatatrophia, hepatatrophy, hepatauxe, hepatectomies, hepatectomize, hepatectomized, hepatectomizing, hepatectomy, hepatic, hepatica, hepaticae, hepatical, hepaticas, hepaticoduodenostomy, hepaticoenterostomies, hepaticoenterostomy, hepaticogastrostomy, hepaticologist, hepaticology, hepaticopulmonary, hepaticostomy, hepaticotomy, hepatics, hepatisation, hepatise, hepatised, hepatising, hepatite, hepatitis, hepatization, hepatize, hepatized, hepatizes, hepatizing, hepatocele, hepatocellular, hepatocirrhosis, hepatocolic, hepatocystic, hepatocyte, hepatoduodenal, hepatoduodenostomy, hepatodynia, hepatodysentery, hepatoenteric, hepatoflavin, hepatogastric, hepatogenic, hepatogenous, hepatography, hepatoid, hepatolenticular, hepatolith, hepatolithiasis, hepatolithic, hepatological, hepatologist, hepatology, hepatolysis, hepatolytic, hepatoma, hepatomalacia, hepatomas, hepatomata, hepatomegalia, hepatomegaly, hepatomelanosis, hepatonephric, hepatopancreas, hepatopathy, hepatoperitonitis, hepatopexia, hepatopexy, hepatophlebitis, hepatophlebotomy, hepatophyma, hepatopneumonic, hepatoportal, hepatoptosia, hepatoptosis, hepatopulmonary, hepatorenal, hepatorrhagia, hepatorrhaphy, hepatorrhea, hepatorrhexis, hepatorrhoea, hepatoscopies, hepatoscopy, hepatostomy, hepatotherapy, hepatotomy, hepatotoxemia, hepatotoxic, hepatotoxicity, hepatotoxin, hepatoumbilical, hepburn, hepcat, hepcats, hephaestus, hephthemimer, hephthemimeral, hepialid, heppen, hepper, hepplewhite, heptacapsular, heptace, heptachlor, heptachord, heptachronous, heptacolic, heptacosane, heptad, heptadecane, heptadecyl, heptadic, heptads, heptaglot, heptagon, heptagonal, heptagons, heptagrid, heptagynia, heptagynous, heptahedra, heptahedral, heptahedrdra, heptahedrical, heptahedron, heptahedrons, heptahexahedral, heptahydrate, heptahydrated, heptahydric, heptahydroxy, heptal, heptameride, heptamerous, heptameter, heptameters, heptamethylene, heptametrical, heptanaphthene, heptandria, heptandrous, heptane, heptanes, heptangular, heptanoic, heptanone, heptapetalous, heptaphyllous, heptaploid, heptaploidy, heptapodic, heptapody, heptarch, heptarchal, heptarchic, heptarchical, heptarchies, heptarchist, heptarchs, heptarchy, heptasemic, heptasepalous, heptaspermous, heptastich, heptastrophic, heptastylar, heptastyle, heptastylos, heptasulphide, heptasyllabic, heptasyllable, heptateuch, heptatomic, heptatonic, heptavalent, heptene, hepteris, heptine, heptite, heptitol, heptode, heptoic, heptorite, heptose, heptoses, heptoxide, heptyl, heptylene, heptylic, heptyne, her, her'n, hera, heraclean, heracleid, heracleonite, heraclitean, herakles, herald, heralded, heraldess, heraldic, heraldical, heraldically, heralding, heraldist, heraldists, heraldize, heraldress, heraldries, heraldry, heralds, heraldship, herapathite, heraud, heraus, herb, herb's, herba, herbaceous, herbaceously, herbage, herbaged, herbager, herbages, herbagious, herbal, herbalism, herbalist, herbalists, herbalize, herbals, herbane, herbar, herbarbaria, herbaria, herbarial, herbarian, herbariia, herbariiums, herbarism, herbarist, herbarium, herbariums, herbarize, herbarized, herbarizing, herbary, herbbane, herber, herbergage, herberger, herbert, herbescent, herbicidal, herbicidally, herbicide, herbicides, herbicolous, herbid, herbier, herbiest, herbiferous, herbish, herbist, herbivora, herbivore, herbivores, herbivorism, herbivority, herbivorous, herbivorously, herbivorousness, herbless, herblet, herblike, herbman, herborist, herborization, herborize, herborized, herborizer, herborizing, herbose, herbosity, herbous, herbrough, herbs, herbwife, herbwoman, herby, hercogamous, hercogamy, herculanean, herculean, hercules, herculeses, hercynian, hercynite, herd, herdbook, herdboy, herded, herder, herderite, herders, herdess, herdic, herdics, herding, herdlike, herdman, herdmen, herds, herdship, herdsman, herdsmen, herdswoman, herdswomen, herdwick, here, here's, hereabout, hereabouts, hereadays, hereafter, hereafterward, hereagain, hereagainst, hereamong, hereanent, hereat, hereaway, hereaways, herebefore, hereby, heredes, heredia, heredipetous, heredipety, hereditability, hereditable, hereditably, heredital, hereditament, hereditaments, hereditarian, hereditarianism, hereditarily, hereditariness, hereditarist, hereditary, hereditas, hereditation, hereditative, heredities, hereditism, hereditist, hereditivity, heredity, heredium, heredofamilial, heredolues, heredoluetic, heredosyphilis, heredosyphilitic, heredosyphilogy, heredotuberculosis, hereford, herefords, herefore, herefrom, heregeld, heregild, herehence, herein, hereinabove, hereinafter, hereinbefore, hereinbelow, hereinto, herem, heremeit, herenach, hereness, hereniging, hereof, hereon, hereout, hereright, herero, heres, heresiarch, heresies, heresimach, heresiographer, heresiographies, heresiography, heresiologer, heresiologies, heresiologist, heresiology, heresy, heresyphobia, heresyproof, heretic, heretic's, heretical, heretically, hereticalness, hereticate, hereticated, heretication, hereticator, hereticide, hereticize, heretics, hereto, heretoch, heretofore, heretoforetime, heretoga, heretrices, heretrix, heretrixes, hereunder, hereunto, hereupon, hereupto, hereward, herewith, herewithal, herezeld, herigaut, herile, heriot, heriotable, heriots, herisson, heritabilities, heritability, heritable, heritably, heritage, heritages, heritance, heritor, heritors, heritress, heritrices, heritrix, heritrixes, herl, herling, herls, herm, herma, hermae, hermaean, hermai, hermaic, herman, hermandad, hermaphrodeity, hermaphrodism, hermaphrodite, hermaphrodites, hermaphroditic, hermaphroditical, hermaphroditically, hermaphroditish, hermaphroditism, hermaphroditize, hermaphroditus, hermatypic, hermele, hermeneut, hermeneutic, hermeneutical, hermeneutically, hermeneutics, hermeneutist, hermes, hermetic, hermetical, hermetically, hermeticism, hermetics, hermetism, hermetist, hermi, hermidin, hermit, hermit's, hermitage, hermitages, hermitary, hermitess, hermitian, hermitic, hermitical, hermitically, hermitish, hermitism, hermitize, hermitlike, hermitries, hermitry, hermits, hermitship, hermodact, hermodactyl, hermogenian, hermogeniarnun, hermoglyphic, hermoglyphist, hermokopid, herms, hern, hernandiaceous, hernanesell, hernani, hernant, herne, hernia, herniae, hernial, herniarin, herniary, hernias, herniate, herniated, herniates, herniating, herniation, herniations, hernioenterotomy, hernioid, herniology, hernioplasties, hernioplasty, herniopuncture, herniorrhaphies, herniorrhaphy, herniotome, herniotomies, herniotomist, herniotomy, herns, hernsew, hernshaw, hero, heroarchy, herodian, herodionine, heroes, heroess, herohead, herohood, heroic, heroical, heroically, heroicalness, heroicity, heroicly, heroicness, heroicomic, heroicomical, heroics, heroid, heroify, heroin, heroine, heroine's, heroines, heroineship, heroinism, heroinize, heroins, heroism, heroisms, heroistic, heroization, heroize, heroized, heroizes, heroizing, herola, herolike, heromonger, heron, heron's, heronbill, heroner, heronite, heronries, heronry, herons, heronsew, heroogony, heroologist, heroology, heros, heroship, herotheism, heroworshipper, herp, herpangina, herpes, herpeses, herpestine, herpesvirus, herpet, herpetic, herpetiform, herpetism, herpetography, herpetoid, herpetologic, herpetological, herpetologically, herpetologist, herpetologists, herpetology, herpetomonad, herpetophobia, herpetotomist, herpetotomy, herpolhode, herquein, herr, herrengrundite, herrenvolk, herrgrdsost, herried, herries, herring, herring's, herringbone, herringbones, herringer, herringlike, herrings, herrnhuter, herry, herrying, herryment, hers, hersall, herschel, herschelian, herschelite, herse, hersed, herself, hershey, hership, hersir, hert, hertfordshire, hertz, hertzes, hertzian, hery, hes, heshvan, hesitance, hesitancies, hesitancy, hesitant, hesitantly, hesitate, hesitated, hesitater, hesitaters, hesitates, hesitating, hesitatingly, hesitatingness, hesitation, hesitations, hesitative, hesitatively, hesitator, hesitatory, hesped, hespel, hespeperidia, hesper, hesperian, hesperid, hesperidate, hesperidene, hesperideous, hesperides, hesperidia, hesperidin, hesperidium, hesperiid, hesperinon, hesperinos, hesperitin, hesperornis, hesperornithid, hesperornithoid, hesperus, hessian, hessians, hessite, hessites, hessonite, hest, hestern, hesternal, hesthogenous, hestia, hests, hesychast, hesychastic, het, hetaera, hetaerae, hetaeras, hetaeria, hetaeric, hetaerio, hetaerism, hetaerist, hetaeristic, hetaerocracy, hetaerolite, hetaery, hetaira, hetairai, hetairas, hetairia, hetairic, hetairism, hetairist, hetairistic, hetairy, hetchel, hete, heteradenia, heteradenic, heterakid, heterandrous, heterandry, heteratomic, heterauxesis, heteraxial, heterecious, heteric, heterically, hetericism, hetericist, heterism, heterization, heterize, hetero, heteroagglutinin, heteroalbumose, heteroaromatic, heteroatom, heteroatomic, heteroautotrophic, heteroauxin, heteroblastic, heteroblastically, heteroblasty, heterocarpism, heterocarpous, heterocaryon, heterocaryosis, heterocaryotic, heterocaseose, heterocellular, heterocentric, heterocephalous, heterocerc, heterocercal, heterocercality, heterocercy, heterocerous, heterochiral, heterochlamydeous, heterochromatic, heterochromatin, heterochromatism, heterochromatization, heterochromatized, heterochrome, heterochromia, heterochromic, heterochromosome, heterochromous, heterochromy, heterochronic, heterochronism, heterochronistic, heterochronous, heterochrony, heterochrosis, heterochthon, heterochthonous, heterocline, heteroclinous, heteroclital, heteroclite, heteroclitic, heteroclitica, heteroclitical, heteroclitous, heterocoelous, heterocrine, heterocycle, heterocyclic, heterocyst, heterocystous, heterodactyl, heterodactylous, heterodont, heterodontism, heterodontoid, heterodox, heterodoxal, heterodoxical, heterodoxies, heterodoxly, heterodoxness, heterodoxy, heterodromous, heterodromy, heterodyne, heterodyned, heterodyning, heteroecious, heteroeciously, heteroeciousness, heteroecism, heteroecismal, heteroecy, heteroepic, heteroepy, heteroerotic, heteroerotism, heterofermentative, heterofertilization, heterogalactic, heterogamete, heterogametic, heterogametism, heterogamety, heterogamic, heterogamous, heterogamy, heterogangliate, heterogen, heterogene, heterogeneal, heterogenean, heterogeneities, heterogeneity, heterogeneous, heterogeneously, heterogeneousness, heterogenesis, heterogenetic, heterogenetically, heterogenic, heterogenicity, heterogenisis, heterogenist, heterogenous, heterogeny, heteroglobulose, heterognath, heterogone, heterogonic, heterogonism, heterogonous, heterogonously, heterogony, heterograft, heterographic, heterographical, heterographies, heterography, heterogynal, heterogynous, heteroicous, heteroimmune, heteroinfection, heteroinoculable, heteroinoculation, heterointoxication, heterokaryon, heterokaryosis, heterokaryotic, heterokinesia, heterokinesis, heterokinetic, heterokontan, heterolalia, heterolateral, heterolecithal, heterolith, heterolobous, heterologic, heterological, heterologically, heterologies, heterologous, heterologously, heterology, heterolysin, heterolysis, heterolytic, heteromallous, heteromastigate, heteromastigote, heteromeral, heteromeran, heteromeric, heteromerous, heteromesotrophic, heterometabole, heterometabolic, heterometabolism, heterometabolous, heterometaboly, heterometatrophic, heterometric, heteromorphic, heteromorphism, heteromorphite, heteromorphosis, heteromorphous, heteromorphy, heteromyarian, heteronereid, heteronereis, heteronomic, heteronomous, heteronomously, heteronomy, heteronuclear, heteronym, heteronymic, heteronymous, heteronymously, heteronymy, heteroousia, heteroousian, heteroousious, heteropathic, heteropathy, heteropelmous, heteropetalous, heterophagous, heterophasia, heterophemism, heterophemist, heterophemistic, heterophemize, heterophemy, heterophil, heterophile, heterophilic, heterophobia, heterophonic, heterophony, heterophoria, heterophoric, heterophylesis, heterophyletic, heterophyllous, heterophylly, heterophyly, heterophyte, heterophytic, heteroplasia, heteroplasm, heteroplastic, heteroplasties, heteroplasty, heteroploid, heteroploidy, heteropod, heteropoda, heteropodal, heteropodous, heteropolar, heteropolarity, heteropoly, heteropolysaccharide, heteroproteide, heteroproteose, heteropter, heteroptera, heteropterous, heteroptics, heteropycnosis, heteros, heteroscedasticity, heteroscian, heteroscope, heteroscopy, heteroses, heterosex, heterosexual, heterosexuality, heterosexually, heterosexuals, heteroside, heterosis, heterosomatous, heterosome, heterosomous, heterosphere, heterosporic, heterosporous, heterospory, heterostatic, heterostemonous, heterostracan, heterostrophic, heterostrophous, heterostrophy, heterostructure, heterostyled, heterostylism, heterostylous, heterostyly, heterosuggestion, heterosyllabic, heterotactic, heterotactous, heterotaxia, heterotaxic, heterotaxis, heterotaxy, heterotelic, heterotelism, heterothallic, heterothallism, heterothermal, heterothermic, heterotic, heterotopia, heterotopic, heterotopism, heterotopous, heterotopy, heterotransplant, heterotransplantation, heterotrich, heterotrichosis, heterotrichous, heterotropal, heterotroph, heterotrophic, heterotrophically, heterotrophy, heterotropia, heterotropic, heterotropous, heterotype, heterotypic, heterotypical, heteroxanthine, heteroxenous, heterozetesis, heterozygosis, heterozygosity, heterozygote, heterozygotes, heterozygotic, heterozygous, heterozygousness, heth, hethen, hething, heths, hetman, hetmanate, hetmans, hetmanship, hetter, hetterly, heuau, heuch, heuchs, heugh, heughs, heuk, heulandite, heumite, heureka, heuretic, heuristic, heuristic's, heuristically, heuristics, heuvel, hevea, heved, hevi, hew, hewable, hewe, hewed, hewel, hewer, hewers, hewettite, hewgag, hewgh, hewhall, hewhole, hewing, hewn, hews, hewt, hex, hexa, hexabasic, hexabiose, hexabromid, hexabromide, hexacanth, hexacanthous, hexacapsular, hexacarbon, hexace, hexachloraphene, hexachlorethane, hexachloride, hexachlorocyclohexane, hexachloroethane, hexachlorophene, hexachord, hexachronous, hexacid, hexacolic, hexacorallan, hexacosane, hexacosihedroid, hexact, hexactinal, hexactine, hexactinellid, hexactinellidan, hexactinelline, hexactinian, hexacyclic, hexad, hexadactyle, hexadactylic, hexadactylism, hexadactylous, hexadactyly, hexadd, hexade, hexadecahedroid, hexadecane, hexadecanoic, hexadecene, hexadecimal, hexadecyl, hexades, hexadic, hexadiene, hexadiine, hexadiyne, hexads, hexaemeric, hexaemeron, hexafluoride, hexafoil, hexaglot, hexagon, hexagonal, hexagonally, hexagonial, hexagonical, hexagonous, hexagons, hexagram, hexagrammoid, hexagrams, hexagyn, hexagynia, hexagynian, hexagynous, hexahedra, hexahedral, hexahedron, hexahedrons, hexahemeric, hexahemeron, hexahydrate, hexahydrated, hexahydric, hexahydride, hexahydrite, hexahydrobenzene, hexahydrothymol, hexahydroxy, hexahydroxycyclohexane, hexakisoctahedron, hexakistetrahedron, hexamer, hexameral, hexameric, hexamerism, hexameron, hexamerous, hexameter, hexameters, hexamethonium, hexamethylenamine, hexamethylene, hexamethylenetetramine, hexametral, hexametric, hexametrical, hexametrist, hexametrize, hexametrographer, hexamine, hexamines, hexamitiasis, hexammin, hexammine, hexammino, hexanal, hexanaphthene, hexandria, hexandric, hexandrous, hexandry, hexane, hexanedione, hexanes, hexangle, hexangular, hexangularly, hexanitrate, hexanitrodiphenylamine, hexapartite, hexaped, hexapetaloid, hexapetaloideous, hexapetalous, hexaphyllous, hexapla, hexaplar, hexaplarian, hexaplaric, hexaplas, hexaploid, hexaploidy, hexapod, hexapodal, hexapodan, hexapodic, hexapodies, hexapodous, hexapods, hexapody, hexapterous, hexaradial, hexarch, hexarchies, hexarchy, hexascha, hexaseme, hexasemic, hexasepalous, hexaspermous, hexastemonous, hexaster, hexastich, hexasticha, hexastichic, hexastichon, hexastichous, hexastichy, hexastigm, hexastylar, hexastyle, hexastylos, hexasulphide, hexasyllabic, hexasyllable, hexatetrahedron, hexateuch, hexathlon, hexatomic, hexatriacontane, hexatriose, hexavalent, hexaxon, hexdra, hexecontane, hexed, hexenbesen, hexene, hexer, hexerei, hexereis, hexeris, hexers, hexes, hexestrol, hexicological, hexicology, hexine, hexing, hexiological, hexiology, hexis, hexitol, hexobarbital, hexobiose, hexoctahedral, hexoctahedron, hexode, hexoestrol, hexogen, hexoic, hexokinase, hexone, hexones, hexonic, hexosamine, hexosaminic, hexosan, hexosans, hexose, hexosediphosphoric, hexosemonophosphoric, hexosephosphatase, hexosephosphoric, hexoses, hexoylene, hexpartite, hexs, hexsub, hexyl, hexylene, hexylic, hexylresorcinol, hexyls, hexyne, hey, heyday, heydays, heydeguy, heydey, heydeys, heyduck, heygh, heynne, heypen, heyrat, hezekiah, hf, hg, hgrnotine, hgt, hgwy, hhd, hi, hia, hiant, hiatal, hiate, hiation, hiatus, hiatuses, hiawatha, hibachi, hibachis, hibbin, hibernacle, hibernacula, hibernacular, hibernaculum, hibernal, hibernate, hibernated, hibernates, hibernating, hibernation, hibernator, hibernators, hibernian, hibernicism, hibiscus, hibiscuses, hibla, hic, hicaco, hicatee, hiccough, hiccoughed, hiccoughing, hiccoughs, hiccup, hiccuped, hiccuping, hiccupped, hiccupping, hiccups, hicht, hichu, hick, hicket, hickey, hickeyes, hickeys, hickified, hickish, hickishness, hickories, hickory, hicks, hickscorner, hicksite, hickwall, hickway, hicky, hid, hidable, hidage, hidalgism, hidalgo, hidalgoism, hidalgos, hidated, hidation, hiddels, hidden, hiddenite, hiddenly, hiddenmost, hiddenness, hide, hideaway, hideaways, hidebind, hidebound, hideboundness, hided, hidegeld, hidel, hideland, hideless, hideling, hideosity, hideous, hideously, hideousness, hideout, hideout's, hideouts, hider, hiders, hides, hiding, hidings, hidling, hidlings, hidlins, hidradenitis, hidrocystoma, hidromancy, hidropoiesis, hidropoietic, hidroses, hidrosis, hidrotic, hie, hied, hieder, hieing, hielaman, hielamen, hielamon, hieland, hield, hielmite, hiemal, hiemate, hiemation, hiems, hiera, hieracite, hieracium, hieracosphinges, hieracosphinx, hieracosphinxes, hierapicra, hierarch, hierarchal, hierarchial, hierarchic, hierarchical, hierarchically, hierarchies, hierarchise, hierarchised, hierarchising, hierarchism, hierarchist, hierarchize, hierarchized, hierarchizing, hierarchs, hierarchy, hierarchy's, hieratic, hieratica, hieratical, hieratically, hieraticism, hieratite, hierocracies, hierocracy, hierocratic, hierocratical, hierodeacon, hierodule, hierodulic, hierogamy, hieroglyph, hieroglypher, hieroglyphic, hieroglyphical, hieroglyphically, hieroglyphics, hieroglyphist, hieroglyphize, hieroglyphologist, hieroglyphology, hieroglyphy, hierogram, hierogrammat, hierogrammate, hierogrammateus, hierogrammatic, hierogrammatical, hierogrammatist, hierograph, hierographer, hierographic, hierographical, hierography, hierolatry, hierologic, hierological, hierologist, hierology, hieromachy, hieromancy, hieromartyr, hieromnemon, hieromonach, hieromonk, hieron, hieronymian, hieronymite, hieropathic, hierophancy, hierophant, hierophantes, hierophantic, hierophantically, hierophanticly, hierophants, hierophobia, hieros, hieroscopy, hierosolymitan, hierurgical, hierurgies, hierurgy, hies, hifalutin, hifalutin', higdon, higgaion, higginsite, higgle, higgled, higglehaggle, higgler, higglers, higglery, higgles, higgling, high, highball, highballed, highballing, highballs, highbelia, highbinder, highbinding, highboard, highborn, highboy, highboys, highbred, highbrow, highbrowed, highbrowism, highbrows, highbush, highchair, highchairs, highdaddies, highdaddy, higher, highermost, highest, highfalutin, highfalutin', highfaluting, highfalutinism, highflier, highflyer, highflying, highhanded, highhandedly, highhandedness, highhat, highhatting, highhearted, highheartedly, highheartedness, highholder, highhole, highish, highjack, highjacked, highjacker, highjacking, highjacks, highland, highlander, highlanders, highlandish, highlands, highlife, highlight, highlighted, highlighting, highlights, highline, highliving, highlow, highly, highman, highmoor, highmost, highness, highness's, highnesses, highpockets, highroad, highroads, highs, highschool, hight, hightail, hightailed, hightailing, hightails, highted, highth, highths, highting, hightoby, hightop, hights, highveld, highway, highway's, highwayman, highwaymen, highways, higra, higuero, hijack, hijacked, hijacker, hijackers, hijacking, hijackings, hijacks, hijinks, hijra, hike, hiked, hiker, hikers, hikes, hiking, hikuli, hila, hilar, hilarious, hilariously, hilariousness, hilarities, hilarity, hilary, hilasmic, hilborn, hilch, hildebrandic, hilding, hildings, hile, hili, hiliferous, hill, hill's, hillberry, hillbillies, hillbilly, hillbird, hillcrest, hillculture, hillebrandite, hilled, hiller, hillers, hillet, hillfort, hillier, hilliest, hilliness, hilling, hillman, hillmen, hillo, hilloa, hilloaed, hilloaing, hilloas, hillock, hillocked, hillocks, hillocky, hilloed, hilloing, hillos, hills, hillsale, hillsalesman, hillside, hillsides, hillsite, hillsman, hilltop, hilltop's, hilltopped, hilltopper, hilltopping, hilltops, hilltrot, hillward, hillwoman, hillwort, hilly, hilsa, hilsah, hilt, hilt's, hilted, hilting, hiltless, hilts, hilum, hilus, him, himalayan, himalayas, himamatia, himantopus, himati, himatia, himation, himations, himene, himming, himne, himp, himple, himself, himward, himwards, himyarite, himyaritic, hin, hinau, hinayana, hinch, hind, hindberry, hindbrain, hindcast, hinddeck, hinder, hinderance, hindered, hinderer, hinderers, hinderest, hinderful, hinderfully, hindering, hinderingly, hinderlands, hinderlings, hinderlins, hinderly, hinderment, hindermost, hinders, hindersome, hindgut, hindguts, hindhand, hindhead, hindi, hindmost, hindoo, hindquarter, hindquarters, hindrance, hindrances, hinds, hindsaddle, hindsight, hindu, hinduism, hindus, hindustan, hindustani, hindward, hindwards, hine, hiney, hing, hinge, hingecorner, hinged, hingeflower, hingeless, hingelike, hinger, hingers, hinges, hingeways, hinging, hingle, hinner, hinney, hinnible, hinnied, hinnies, hinny, hinnying, hinoid, hinoideous, hinoki, hins, hinsdalite, hint, hinted, hintedly, hinter, hinterland, hinterlander, hinterlands, hinters, hinting, hintingly, hintproof, hints, hintzeite, hiodont, hiortdahlite, hip, hip's, hipberry, hipbone, hipbones, hipe, hiper, hipflask, hiphalt, hiphape, hiphuggers, hiplength, hipless, hiplike, hipline, hipmi, hipmold, hipness, hipnesses, hippalectryon, hipparch, hipparchs, hipparion, hippeastrum, hipped, hippen, hipper, hippest, hippi, hippian, hippiater, hippiatric, hippiatrical, hippiatrics, hippiatrist, hippiatry, hippic, hippie, hippiedom, hippiehood, hippier, hippies, hippiest, hipping, hippish, hipple, hippo, hipposcid, hippocamp, hippocampal, hippocampi, hippocampine, hippocampus, hippocastanaceous, hippocaust, hippocentaur, hippocentauric, hippocerf, hippocoprosterol, hippocras, hippocrateaceous, hippocrates, hippocratic, hippocratism, hippocrene, hippocrepian, hippocrepiform, hippodame, hippodamous, hippodrome, hippodromes, hippodromic, hippodromist, hippogastronomy, hippogriff, hippogriffin, hippogryph, hippoid, hippolite, hippolith, hippological, hippologist, hippology, hippolytus, hippomachy, hippomancy, hippomanes, hippomelanin, hippomenes, hippometer, hippometric, hippometry, hipponosological, hipponosology, hipponous, hippopathological, hippopathology, hippophagi, hippophagism, hippophagist, hippophagistical, hippophagous, hippophagy, hippophile, hippophobia, hippopod, hippopotami, hippopotamian, hippopotamic, hippopotamine, hippopotamoid, hippopotamus, hippopotamuses, hippos, hippotigrine, hippotomical, hippotomist, hippotomy, hippotragine, hippurate, hippuria, hippuric, hippurid, hippurite, hippuritic, hippuritoid, hippus, hippy, hips, hipshot, hipster, hipsterism, hipsters, hipwort, hir, hirable, hiragana, hiraganas, hircarra, hircic, hircin, hircine, hircinous, hircocerf, hircocervus, hircosity, hircus, hire, hireable, hired, hireless, hireling, hirelings, hireman, hiren, hirer, hirers, hires, hiring, hirings, hirling, hirmologion, hirmos, hiro, hirondelle, hiroshima, hirple, hirpled, hirples, hirpling, hirrient, hirse, hirsel, hirseled, hirseling, hirselled, hirselling, hirsels, hirsle, hirsled, hirsles, hirsling, hirst, hirstie, hirsute, hirsuteness, hirsuties, hirsutism, hirsutulous, hirtch, hirtellous, hirudin, hirudinal, hirudine, hirudinean, hirudiniculture, hirudinize, hirudinoid, hirudins, hirundine, hirundinous, his, his'n, hish, hisingerite, hisis, hislopite, hisn, hispanic, hispanics, hispanidad, hispaniola, hispaniolate, hispanism, hispano, hispid, hispidity, hispidulate, hispidulous, hiss, hissed, hissel, hisself, hisser, hissers, hisses, hissing, hissingly, hissings, hissproof, hissy, hist, histamin, histaminase, histamine, histaminergic, histamines, histaminic, histamins, histed, hister, histidin, histidine, histidins, histie, histing, histiocyte, histiocytic, histioid, histiology, histoblast, histochemic, histochemical, histochemically, histochemistry, histoclastic, histocompatibility, histocyte, histodiagnosis, histodialysis, histodialytic, histogen, histogenesis, histogenetic, histogenetically, histogenic, histogenous, histogens, histogeny, histogram, histogram's, histograms, histographer, histographic, histographical, histographically, histographies, histography, histoid, histologic, histological, histologically, histologies, histologist, histologists, histology, histolysis, histolytic, histometabasis, histomorphological, histomorphologically, histomorphology, histon, histonal, histone, histones, histonomy, histopathologic, histopathological, histopathologically, histopathologist, histopathology, histophyly, histophysiologic, histophysiological, histophysiology, histoplasmin, histoplasmosis, historial, historian, historian's, historians, historiated, historic, historical, historically, historicalness, historician, historicism, historicist, historicity, historicize, historicocabbalistical, historicocritical, historicocultural, historicodogmatic, historicogeographical, historicophilosophica, historicophysical, historicopolitical, historicoprophetic, historicoreligious, historics, historicus, historied, historier, histories, historiette, historify, historiograph, historiographer, historiographers, historiographership, historiographic, historiographical, historiographically, historiographies, historiography, historiological, historiology, historiometric, historiometry, historionomer, historious, historism, historize, history, history's, histotherapist, histotherapy, histothrombin, histotome, histotomies, histotomy, histotrophic, histotrophy, histotropic, histozoic, histozyme, histrio, histrion, histrionic, histrionical, histrionically, histrionicism, histrionics, histrionism, histrionize, hists, hit, hit's, hitch, hitched, hitchel, hitcher, hitchers, hitches, hitchhike, hitchhiked, hitchhiker, hitchhikers, hitchhikes, hitchhiking, hitchier, hitchiest, hitchily, hitchiness, hitching, hitchproof, hitchy, hithe, hither, hithermost, hithertills, hitherto, hithertoward, hitherunto, hitherward, hitherwards, hitler, hitlerian, hitlerism, hitless, hits, hittable, hitter, hitter's, hitters, hitting, hittite, hive, hived, hiveless, hivelike, hiver, hives, hiveward, hiving, hiyakkin, hizz, hizzie, hl, hld, hlqn, hm, hny, ho, hoactzin, hoactzines, hoactzins, hoagie, hoagies, hoagy, hoaming, hoar, hoard, hoarded, hoarder, hoarders, hoarding, hoardings, hoards, hoardward, hoared, hoarfrost, hoarfrosts, hoarhead, hoarheaded, hoarhound, hoarier, hoariest, hoarily, hoariness, hoarish, hoarness, hoars, hoarse, hoarsely, hoarsen, hoarsened, hoarseness, hoarsening, hoarsens, hoarser, hoarsest, hoarstone, hoarwort, hoary, hoaryheaded, hoast, hoastman, hoatching, hoatzin, hoatzines, hoatzins, hoax, hoaxability, hoaxable, hoaxed, hoaxee, hoaxer, hoaxers, hoaxes, hoaxing, hoaxproof, hoazin, hob, hobbed, hobber, hobbesian, hobbet, hobbies, hobbil, hobbing, hobbinoll, hobbism, hobbit, hobble, hobblebush, hobbled, hobbledehoy, hobbledehoydom, hobbledehoyhood, hobbledehoyish, hobbledehoyishness, hobbledehoyism, hobbledehoys, hobbledygee, hobbler, hobblers, hobbles, hobbling, hobblingly, hobbly, hobby, hobby's, hobbyhorse, hobbyhorses, hobbyhorsical, hobbyhorsically, hobbyism, hobbyist, hobbyist's, hobbyists, hobbyless, hobgoblin, hobgoblins, hobhouchin, hobiler, hobits, hoblike, hoblob, hobnail, hobnailed, hobnailer, hobnails, hobnob, hobnobbed, hobnobber, hobnobbing, hobnobs, hobo, hoboe, hoboed, hoboes, hoboing, hoboism, hoboisms, hobos, hobs, hobthrush, hoc, hocco, hoch, hochheimer, hochhuth, hock, hockamore, hocked, hockelty, hocker, hockers, hocket, hockey, hockeys, hocking, hockle, hockled, hockling, hockmoney, hocks, hockshin, hockshop, hockshops, hocktide, hocky, hocus, hocused, hocuses, hocusing, hocussed, hocusses, hocussing, hod, hodad, hodaddies, hodaddy, hodads, hodden, hoddens, hodder, hoddin, hoddins, hoddle, hoddy, hoddypeak, hodening, hodful, hodge, hodgepodge, hodgepodges, hodgkinsonite, hodiernal, hodman, hodmandod, hodmen, hodograph, hodometer, hodometrical, hodophobia, hodoscope, hods, hodure, hoe, hoe's, hoecake, hoecakes, hoed, hoedown, hoedowns, hoeful, hoeing, hoelike, hoer, hoernesite, hoers, hoes, hoeshin, hoey, hog, hog's, hoga, hogan, hogans, hogarthian, hogback, hogbacks, hogbush, hogchoker, hogcote, hogen, hogfish, hogfishes, hogframe, hogg, hoggaster, hogged, hoggee, hogger, hoggerel, hoggeries, hoggers, hoggery, hogget, hoggie, hoggin, hogging, hoggins, hoggish, hoggishly, hoggishness, hoggism, hoggler, hoggs, hoggy, hoghead, hogherd, hoghide, hoghood, hoglike, hogling, hogmace, hogmanay, hogmanays, hogmane, hogmanes, hogmenay, hogmenays, hogmollies, hogmolly, hognose, hognoses, hognut, hognuts, hogo, hogpen, hogreeve, hogrophyte, hogs, hogshead, hogsheads, hogship, hogshouther, hogskin, hogsteer, hogsty, hogsucker, hogtie, hogtied, hogtieing, hogties, hogtiing, hogton, hogtying, hogward, hogwash, hogwashes, hogweed, hogweeds, hogwort, hogyard, hohenstaufen, hohenzollern, hoho, hoi, hoick, hoicked, hoicking, hoicks, hoiden, hoidened, hoidening, hoidenish, hoidens, hoihere, hoin, hoise, hoised, hoises, hoising, hoist, hoistaway, hoisted, hoister, hoisters, hoisting, hoistman, hoists, hoistway, hoit, hoju, hoke, hoked, hoker, hokerer, hokerly, hokes, hokey, hokeyness, hokeypokey, hokier, hokiest, hoking, hokku, hokum, hokums, hokypokies, hokypoky, hol, hola, holagogue, holandric, holandry, holarctic, holard, holards, holarthritic, holarthritis, holaspidean, holcad, holcodont, hold, holdable, holdall, holdalls, holdback, holdbacks, holden, holdenite, holder, holders, holdership, holdfast, holdfastness, holdfasts, holding, holdingly, holdings, holdman, holdout, holdouts, holdover, holdovers, holds, holdsman, holdup, holdups, hole, holeable, holectypoid, holed, holeless, holeman, holeproof, holer, holes, holethnic, holethnos, holewort, holey, holgate, holi, holia, holibut, holibuts, holidam, holiday, holiday's, holidayed, holidayer, holidaying, holidayism, holidaymaker, holidaymaking, holidays, holier, holies, holiest, holily, holiness, holinesses, holing, holinight, holishkes, holism, holisms, holist, holistic, holistically, holists, holk, holked, holking, holks, holl, holla, hollaed, hollaing, hollaite, holland, hollandaise, hollander, hollanders, hollandite, hollands, hollantide, hollas, holleke, holler, hollered, hollering, hollers, hollies, hollin, holliper, hollo, holloa, holloaed, holloaing, holloas, hollock, holloed, holloes, holloing, hollong, holloo, hollooed, hollooing, holloos, hollos, hollow, holloware, hollowed, hollower, hollowest, hollowfaced, hollowfoot, hollowhearted, hollowheartedness, hollowing, hollowly, hollowness, hollowroot, hollows, hollowware, holluschick, holluschickie, holly, hollyhock, hollyhocks, hollyleaf, hollywood, holm, holmberry, holmes, holmgang, holmia, holmic, holmium, holmiums, holmos, holms, holobaptist, holobenthic, holoblastic, holoblastically, holobranch, holocaine, holocarpic, holocarpous, holocaust, holocaustal, holocaustic, holocausts, holocene, holocentrid, holocentroid, holocephalan, holocephalian, holocephalous, holochoanitic, holochoanoid, holochoanoidal, holochordate, holochroal, holoclastic, holocrine, holocryptic, holocrystalline, holodactylic, holodedron, holoenzyme, holofernes, hologamous, hologamy, hologastrula, hologastrular, holognathous, hologonidia, hologonidium, hologoninidia, hologram, hologram's, holograms, holograph, holographic, holographical, holographically, holographies, holographs, holography, hologynic, hologynies, hologyny, holohedral, holohedric, holohedrism, holohedron, holohedry, holohemihedral, holohyaline, holoku, hololith, holomastigote, holometabola, holometabole, holometabolian, holometabolic, holometabolism, holometabolous, holometaboly, holometer, holomorph, holomorphic, holomorphism, holomorphosis, holomorphy, holomyarian, holoparasite, holoparasitic, holophane, holophotal, holophote, holophotometer, holophrase, holophrases, holophrasis, holophrasm, holophrastic, holophyte, holophytic, holoplankton, holoplanktonic, holoplexia, holopneustic, holoproteide, holoptic, holoptychian, holoptychiid, holoquinoid, holoquinoidal, holoquinonic, holoquinonoid, holorhinal, holosaprophyte, holosaprophytic, holoscope, holosericeous, holoside, holosiderite, holosiphonate, holosomatous, holospondaic, holostean, holosteous, holosteric, holostomate, holostomatous, holostome, holostomous, holostylic, holosymmetric, holosymmetrical, holosymmetry, holosystematic, holosystolic, holothecal, holothoracic, holothurian, holothurioid, holotonia, holotonic, holotony, holotrich, holotrichal, holotrichous, holotype, holotypes, holotypic, holour, holozoic, holp, holpen, hols, holsom, holstein, holsteins, holster, holstered, holsters, holt, holts, holw, holy, holyday, holydays, holyokeite, holystone, holystoned, holystones, holystoning, holytide, holytides, hom, homacanth, homage, homageable, homaged, homager, homagers, homages, homaging, homagium, homalogonatous, homalographic, homaloid, homaloidal, homalosternal, homard, homarine, homaroid, homatomic, homaxial, homaxonial, homaxonic, hombre, hombres, homburg, homburgs, home, homebodies, homebody, homeborn, homebound, homebred, homebreds, homebrew, homebrewed, homebuild, homebuilder, homebuilders, homebuilding, homecome, homecomer, homecoming, homecomings, homecraft, homecroft, homecrofter, homecrofting, homed, homefarer, homefarm, homefelt, homefolk, homefolks, homegoer, homeground, homegrown, homekeeper, homekeeping, homeland, homelander, homelands, homeless, homelessly, homelessness, homelet, homelier, homeliest, homelife, homelike, homelikeness, homelily, homeliness, homeling, homelovingness, homely, homelyn, homemade, homemake, homemaker, homemaker's, homemakers, homemaking, homeoblastic, homeochromatic, homeochromatism, homeochronous, homeocrystalline, homeogenic, homeogenous, homeoid, homeoidal, homeoidality, homeokinesis, homeokinetic, homeomerous, homeomorph, homeomorphic, homeomorphism, homeomorphism's, homeomorphisms, homeomorphous, homeomorphy, homeopath, homeopathic, homeopathically, homeopathician, homeopathicity, homeopathies, homeopathist, homeopathy, homeophony, homeoplasia, homeoplastic, homeoplasy, homeopolar, homeosis, homeostases, homeostasis, homeostatic, homeostatically, homeostatis, homeotherapy, homeotherm, homeothermal, homeothermic, homeothermism, homeothermous, homeothermy, homeotic, homeotransplant, homeotransplantation, homeotype, homeotypic, homeotypical, homeown, homeowner, homeowners, homeozoic, homeplace, homer, homered, homeric, homerid, homering, homerite, homerology, homeroom, homerooms, homers, homes, homeseeker, homesick, homesickly, homesickness, homesite, homesites, homesome, homespun, homespuns, homestall, homestead, homesteader, homesteaders, homesteads, homester, homestretch, homestretches, hometown, hometowns, homeward, homewardly, homewards, homework, homeworker, homeworks, homewort, homey, homeyness, homichlophobia, homicidal, homicidally, homicide, homicides, homicidious, homicidium, homiculture, homier, homiest, homiform, homilete, homiletic, homiletical, homiletically, homiletics, homiliaries, homiliarium, homiliary, homilies, homilist, homilists, homilite, homilize, homily, hominal, hominem, hominess, hominesses, homing, hominian, hominians, hominid, hominidae, hominids, hominies, hominiform, hominify, hominine, hominisection, hominivorous, hominization, hominized, hominoid, hominoids, hominy, homish, homishness, hommack, hommage, homme, hommock, hommocks, homo, homoanisaldehyde, homoanisic, homoarecoline, homobaric, homoblastic, homoblasty, homobront, homocarpous, homocategoric, homocentric, homocentrical, homocentrically, homocerc, homocercal, homocercality, homocercy, homocerebrin, homochiral, homochlamydeous, homochromatic, homochromatism, homochrome, homochromic, homochromosome, homochromous, homochromy, homochronous, homoclinal, homocline, homocoelous, homocreosol, homocycle, homocyclic, homodermic, homodermy, homodont, homodontism, homodox, homodoxian, homodromal, homodrome, homodromous, homodromy, homodynamic, homodynamous, homodynamy, homodyne, homoecious, homoeoarchy, homoeoblastic, homoeochromatic, homoeochronous, homoeocrystalline, homoeogenic, homoeogenous, homoeography, homoeoid, homoeokinesis, homoeomerae, homoeomeral, homoeomeria, homoeomerian, homoeomerianism, homoeomeric, homoeomerical, homoeomerous, homoeomery, homoeomorph, homoeomorphic, homoeomorphism, homoeomorphous, homoeomorphy, homoeopath, homoeopathic, homoeopathically, homoeopathician, homoeopathicity, homoeopathist, homoeopathy, homoeophony, homoeophyllous, homoeoplasia, homoeoplastic, homoeoplasy, homoeopolar, homoeosis, homoeotel, homoeoteleutic, homoeoteleuton, homoeotic, homoeotopy, homoeotype, homoeotypic, homoeotypical, homoeozoic, homoerotic, homoeroticism, homoerotism, homofermentative, homogametic, homogamic, homogamies, homogamous, homogamy, homogangliate, homogen, homogenate, homogene, homogeneal, homogenealness, homogeneate, homogeneities, homogeneity, homogeneity's, homogeneization, homogeneize, homogeneous, homogeneously, homogeneousness, homogenesis, homogenetic, homogenetical, homogenetically, homogenic, homogenies, homogenization, homogenize, homogenized, homogenizer, homogenizers, homogenizes, homogenizing, homogenous, homogentisic, homogeny, homoglot, homogone, homogonies, homogonous, homogonously, homogony, homograft, homograph, homographic, homographs, homography, homohedral, homoiotherm, homoiothermal, homoiothermic, homoiothermism, homoiothermous, homoiothermy, homoiousia, homoiousian, homoiousianism, homoiousious, homolateral, homolecithal, homolegalis, homolog, homologal, homologate, homologated, homologating, homologation, homologic, homological, homologically, homologies, homologise, homologised, homologiser, homologising, homologist, homologize, homologized, homologizer, homologizing, homologon, homologoumena, homologous, homolographic, homolography, homologs, homologue, homologumena, homology, homolosine, homolysin, homolysis, homolytic, homomallous, homomeral, homomerous, homometrical, homometrically, homomorph, homomorphic, homomorphism, homomorphism's, homomorphisms, homomorphosis, homomorphous, homomorphy, homonid, homonomous, homonomy, homonuclear, homonym, homonymic, homonymies, homonymity, homonymous, homonymously, homonyms, homonymy, homoousia, homoousian, homoousianism, homoousious, homopathy, homopause, homoperiodic, homopetalous, homophene, homophenous, homophile, homophiles, homophobia, homophobic, homophone, homophones, homophonic, homophonically, homophonous, homophony, homophthalic, homophylic, homophyllous, homophyly, homopiperonyl, homoplasis, homoplasmic, homoplasmy, homoplassy, homoplast, homoplastic, homoplastically, homoplasy, homopolar, homopolarity, homopolic, homopolymer, homopolymerization, homopolymerize, homopter, homoptera, homopteran, homopteron, homopterous, homorganic, homos, homoscedastic, homoscedasticity, homoseismal, homosexual, homosexualism, homosexualist, homosexuality, homosexually, homosexuals, homosphere, homosporous, homospory, homostyled, homostylic, homostylism, homostylous, homostyly, homosystemic, homotactic, homotatic, homotaxeous, homotaxia, homotaxial, homotaxially, homotaxic, homotaxis, homotaxy, homothallic, homothallism, homotherm, homothermal, homothermic, homothermism, homothermous, homothermy, homothetic, homothety, homotonic, homotonous, homotonously, homotony, homotopic, homotopy, homotransplant, homotransplantation, homotropal, homotropous, homotypal, homotype, homotypic, homotypical, homotypy, homousian, homovanillic, homovanillin, homoveratric, homoveratrole, homozygosis, homozygosity, homozygote, homozygotes, homozygotic, homozygous, homozygously, homozygousness, homrai, homuncio, homuncle, homuncular, homuncule, homunculi, homunculus, homy, hon, honan, honans, honcho, honchos, hond, honda, hondas, hondo, honduran, hondurans, honduras, hone, honed, honer, honers, hones, honest, honester, honestest, honestete, honesties, honestly, honestness, honestone, honesty, honewort, honeworts, honey, honeyballs, honeybee, honeybees, honeyberry, honeybind, honeyblob, honeybloom, honeybun, honeybunch, honeybuns, honeycomb, honeycombed, honeycombing, honeycombs, honeycreeper, honeycup, honeydew, honeydewed, honeydews, honeydrop, honeyed, honeyedly, honeyedness, honeyfall, honeyflower, honeyfogle, honeyfugle, honeyful, honeyhearted, honeying, honeyless, honeylike, honeylipped, honeymonth, honeymoon, honeymooned, honeymooner, honeymooners, honeymooning, honeymoonlight, honeymoons, honeymoonshine, honeymoonstruck, honeymoony, honeymouthed, honeypod, honeypot, honeys, honeystone, honeystucker, honeysuck, honeysucker, honeysuckle, honeysuckled, honeysuckles, honeysweet, honeyware, honeywood, honeywort, hong, hongkong, hongs, honied, honily, honing, honiton, honk, honked, honker, honkers, honkey, honkeys, honkie, honkies, honking, honks, honky, honkytonks, honolulu, honor, honorability, honorable, honorableness, honorables, honorableship, honorably, honorance, honorand, honorands, honorararia, honoraria, honoraries, honorarily, honorarium, honorariums, honorary, honored, honoree, honorees, honorer, honorers, honoress, honorific, honorifical, honorifically, honorifics, honoring, honorless, honorous, honors, honorsman, honorworthy, honour, honourable, honourableness, honourably, honoured, honourer, honourers, honouring, honourless, honours, hont, hontish, hontous, hoo, hooch, hooches, hoochinoo, hood, hoodcap, hooded, hoodedness, hoodful, hoodie, hoodies, hooding, hoodle, hoodless, hoodlike, hoodlum, hoodlumish, hoodlumism, hoodlumize, hoodlums, hoodman, hoodmen, hoodmold, hoodoes, hoodoo, hoodooed, hoodooing, hoodooism, hoodoos, hoods, hoodsheaf, hoodshy, hoodshyness, hoodwink, hoodwinkable, hoodwinked, hoodwinker, hoodwinking, hoodwinks, hoodwise, hoodwort, hoody, hooey, hooeys, hoof, hoof's, hoofbeat, hoofbeats, hoofbound, hoofed, hoofer, hoofers, hoofiness, hoofing, hoofish, hoofless, hooflet, hooflike, hoofmark, hoofmarks, hoofprint, hoofrot, hoofs, hoofworm, hoofy, hoogaars, hook, hooka, hookah, hookahs, hookaroon, hookas, hookcheck, hooked, hookedness, hookedwise, hooker, hookerman, hookers, hookey, hookeys, hookheal, hookier, hookies, hookiest, hooking, hookish, hookland, hookless, hooklet, hooklets, hooklike, hookmaker, hookmaking, hookman, hooknose, hooknoses, hooks, hookshop, hooksmith, hookswinging, hooktip, hookum, hookup, hookups, hookupu, hookweed, hookwise, hookworm, hookwormer, hookworms, hookwormy, hooky, hool, hoolakin, hoolaulea, hoolee, hooley, hoolie, hooligan, hooliganish, hooliganism, hooliganize, hooligans, hoolihan, hoolock, hooly, hoom, hoon, hoondee, hoondi, hoonoomaun, hoop, hooped, hooper, hooperman, hoopers, hooping, hoopla, hooplas, hoople, hoopless, hooplike, hoopmaker, hoopman, hoopmen, hoopoe, hoopoes, hoopoo, hoopoos, hoops, hoopskirt, hoopster, hoopsters, hoopstick, hoopwood, hoorah, hoorahed, hoorahing, hoorahs, hooray, hoorayed, hooraying, hoorays, hooroo, hooroosh, hoose, hoosegow, hoosegows, hoosgow, hoosgows, hoosh, hoosier, hoosiers, hoot, hootay, hootch, hootches, hooted, hootenannies, hootenanny, hooter, hooters, hooting, hootingly, hootmalalie, hoots, hoove, hooved, hooven, hoover, hooves, hoovey, hooye, hop, hopak, hopbind, hopbine, hopbush, hopcalite, hopcrease, hope, hoped, hopeful, hopefully, hopefulness, hopefuls, hopeite, hopeless, hopelessly, hopelessness, hoper, hopers, hopes, hophead, hopheads, hopi, hoping, hopingly, hopis, hoplite, hoplites, hoplitic, hoplitodromos, hoplology, hoplomachic, hoplomachist, hoplomachos, hoplomachy, hoplonemertean, hoplonemertine, hoplophoneus, hopoff, hopped, hopper, hopper's, hopperburn, hoppercar, hopperdozer, hopperette, hoppergrass, hopperings, hopperman, hoppers, hoppestere, hoppet, hopping, hoppingly, hoppity, hopple, hoppled, hopples, hoppling, hoppo, hoppy, hoppytoad, hops, hopsack, hopsacking, hopsacks, hopsage, hopscotch, hopscotcher, hopthumb, hoptoad, hoptoads, hoptree, hopvine, hopyard, hor, hora, horace, horae, horah, horahs, horal, horary, horas, horatian, horation, horatius, horatiye, horatory, horbachite, hordarian, hordary, horde, horde's, hordeaceous, hordeate, horded, hordeiform, hordein, hordeins, hordenine, hordeola, hordeolum, hordes, hording, hordock, hore, horehoond, horehound, horehounds, horismology, horizometer, horizon, horizon's, horizonal, horizonless, horizons, horizontal, horizontalism, horizontality, horizontalization, horizontalize, horizontally, horizontalness, horizontic, horizontical, horizontically, horizonward, horkey, horla, horme, hormephobia, hormetic, hormic, hormigo, hormion, hormism, hormist, hormogon, hormogonium, hormogonous, hormonal, hormonally, hormone, hormone's, hormonelike, hormones, hormonic, hormonize, hormonogenesis, hormonogenic, hormonoid, hormonology, hormonopoiesis, hormonopoietic, hormos, horn, hornada, hornbeak, hornbeam, hornbeams, hornbill, hornbills, hornblende, hornblendic, hornblendite, hornblendophyre, hornblower, hornbook, hornbooks, horned, hornedness, horner, hornerah, hornero, hornet, hornet's, hornets, hornety, hornfair, hornfels, hornfish, hornful, horngeld, hornier, horniest, hornification, hornified, hornify, hornily, horniness, horning, hornish, hornist, hornito, hornitos, hornkeck, hornless, hornlessness, hornlet, hornlike, hornmouth, hornotine, hornpipe, hornpipes, hornplant, hornpout, hornpouts, horns, hornslate, hornsman, hornstay, hornstone, hornswaggle, hornswoggle, hornswoggled, hornswoggling, horntail, horntails, hornthumb, horntip, hornweed, hornwood, hornwork, hornworm, hornworms, hornwort, hornworts, hornwrack, horny, hornyhanded, hornyhead, horograph, horographer, horography, horokaka, horol, horologe, horologer, horologes, horologia, horologic, horological, horologically, horologies, horologigia, horologiography, horologist, horologists, horologium, horologue, horology, horometer, horometrical, horometry, horopito, horopter, horopteric, horoptery, horoscopal, horoscope, horoscoper, horoscopes, horoscopic, horoscopical, horoscopist, horoscopy, horotelic, horotely, horrah, horral, horray, horrendous, horrendously, horrent, horrescent, horreum, horribility, horrible, horribleness, horribles, horribly, horrid, horridity, horridly, horridness, horrific, horrifically, horrification, horrified, horrifiedly, horrifies, horrify, horrifying, horrifyingly, horripilant, horripilate, horripilated, horripilating, horripilation, horrisonant, horror, horror's, horrorful, horrorish, horrorist, horrorize, horrormonger, horrormongering, horrorous, horrors, horrorsome, horry, hors, horse, horseback, horsebacker, horsebane, horsebean, horsebox, horseboy, horsebreaker, horsebush, horsecar, horsecars, horsecart, horsecloth, horsecloths, horsecraft, horsed, horsedom, horsedrawing, horseess, horsefair, horsefeathers, horsefettler, horsefight, horsefish, horsefishes, horseflesh, horseflies, horseflower, horsefly, horsefoot, horsegate, horsehair, horsehaired, horsehead, horseheads, horseheal, horseheel, horseherd, horsehide, horsehides, horsehood, horsehoof, horseier, horseiest, horsejockey, horsekeeper, horsekeeping, horselaugh, horselaugher, horselaughs, horselaughter, horseleach, horseleech, horseless, horselike, horseload, horselock, horsely, horseman, horsemanship, horsemastership, horsemen, horsemint, horsemonger, horsenail, horsepipe, horseplay, horseplayer, horseplayers, horseplayful, horsepond, horsepower, horsepowers, horsepox, horser, horseradish, horseradishes, horses, horseshit, horseshoe, horseshoed, horseshoeing, horseshoer, horseshoers, horseshoes, horseshoing, horsetail, horsetails, horsetongue, horsetree, horseway, horseweed, horsewhip, horsewhipped, horsewhipper, horsewhipping, horsewhips, horsewoman, horsewomanship, horsewomen, horsewood, horsey, horsfordite, horsier, horsiest, horsify, horsily, horsiness, horsing, horst, horste, horstes, horsts, horsy, horsyism, hort, hortation, hortative, hortatively, hortator, hortatorily, hortatory, hortensia, hortensial, hortensian, hortesian, horticultor, horticultural, horticulturalist, horticulturally, horticulture, horticulturist, horticulturists, hortite, hortonolite, hortorium, hortulan, hortyard, hory, hosanna, hosannaed, hosannaing, hosannas, hose, hose's, hosea, hosebird, hosecock, hosed, hosel, hoseless, hoselike, hosels, hoseman, hosen, hosepipe, hoses, hosier, hosieries, hosiers, hosiery, hosing, hosiomartyr, hosp, hospice, hospices, hospita, hospitable, hospitableness, hospitably, hospitage, hospital, hospital's, hospitalary, hospitaler, hospitalism, hospitalities, hospitality, hospitalization, hospitalizations, hospitalize, hospitalized, hospitalizes, hospitalizing, hospitaller, hospitalman, hospitalmen, hospitals, hospitant, hospitate, hospitation, hospitator, hospitia, hospitious, hospitium, hospitize, hospodar, hospodariat, hospodariate, hospodars, hoss, host, hosta, hostage, hostage's, hostaged, hostager, hostages, hostageship, hostaging, hostal, hosted, hostel, hosteled, hosteler, hostelers, hosteling, hosteller, hostelling, hostelries, hostelry, hostels, hoster, hostess, hostess's, hostessed, hostesses, hostessing, hostie, hostile, hostilely, hostileness, hostiles, hostiley, hostilities, hostility, hostilize, hosting, hostle, hostler, hostlers, hostlership, hostlerwife, hostless, hostly, hostry, hosts, hostship, hot, hotbed, hotbeds, hotblood, hotblooded, hotbloods, hotbox, hotboxes, hotbrained, hotcake, hotcakes, hotch, hotcha, hotched, hotches, hotching, hotchkiss, hotchpot, hotchpotch, hotchpotchly, hotchpots, hotdog, hotdogged, hotdogger, hotdogging, hotdogs, hote, hotel, hotel's, hoteldom, hotelhood, hotelier, hoteliers, hotelization, hotelize, hotelkeeper, hotelless, hotelman, hotelmen, hotels, hotelward, hotfoot, hotfooted, hotfooting, hotfoots, hothead, hotheaded, hotheadedly, hotheadedness, hotheads, hothearted, hotheartedly, hotheartedness, hothouse, hothouses, hoti, hotkey, hotline, hotly, hotmelt, hotmouthed, hotness, hotnesses, hotplate, hotpot, hotpress, hotpressed, hotpresses, hotpressing, hotrod, hotrods, hots, hotshot, hotshots, hotsprings, hotspur, hotspurred, hotspurs, hotted, hottentot, hotter, hottery, hottest, hottie, hotting, hottish, hottle, hotzone, houbara, houdah, houdahs, houdan, hough, houghband, hougher, houghite, houghmagandy, houghsinew, houhere, houlet, hoult, houmous, hounce, hound, hounded, hounder, hounders, houndfish, houndfishes, hounding, houndish, houndlike, houndman, hounds, houndsbane, houndsberry, houndsfoot, houndshark, houndy, hounskull, houpelande, houppelande, hour, hourful, hourglass, hourglasses, houri, houris, hourless, hourlong, hourly, hours, housage, housal, house, houseball, houseboat, houseboating, houseboats, housebote, housebound, houseboy, houseboys, housebreak, housebreaker, housebreakers, housebreaking, housebroke, housebroken, housebrokenness, housebug, housebuilder, housebuilding, housecarl, houseclean, housecleaned, housecleaner, housecleaning, housecleans, housecoat, housecoats, housecraft, housed, housedress, housefast, housefather, houseflies, housefly, housefly's, housefront, houseful, housefuls, housefurnishings, houseguest, household, householder, householders, householdership, householding, householdry, households, househusband, househusbands, housekeep, housekeeper, housekeeper's, housekeeperlike, housekeeperly, housekeepers, housekeeping, housekept, housekkept, housel, houseled, houseleek, houseless, houselessness, houselet, houselights, houseline, houseling, houselled, houselling, housels, housemaid, housemaidenly, housemaiding, housemaids, housemaidy, houseman, housemaster, housemastership, housemate, housemating, housemen, houseminder, housemistress, housemother, housemotherly, housemothers, houseowner, housepaint, houseparent, housephone, houseplant, houser, houseridden, houseroom, housers, houses, housesat, housesit, housesits, housesitting, housesmith, housetop, housetop's, housetops, houseward, housewares, housewarm, housewarmer, housewarming, housewarmings, housewear, housewife, housewifeliness, housewifely, housewifery, housewifeship, housewifish, housewive, housewives, housework, houseworker, houseworkers, housewrecker, housewright, housing, housings, housling, houss, houston, houstonia, housty, housy, hout, houting, houtou, houvari, houve, houyhnhnm, hove, hovedance, hovel, hovel's, hoveled, hoveler, hoveling, hovelled, hoveller, hovelling, hovels, hoven, hover, hovercar, hovercraft, hovercrafts, hovered, hoverer, hoverers, hovering, hoveringly, hoverly, hoverport, hovers, hovertrain, how, howadji, howardite, howbeit, howdah, howdahs, howder, howdie, howdies, howdy, howe, howe'er, howel, howes, however, howf, howff, howffs, howfing, howfs, howgates, howish, howitz, howitzer, howitzers, howk, howked, howker, howking, howkit, howks, howl, howled, howler, howlers, howlet, howlets, howling, howlingly, howlite, howls, hows, howsabout, howso, howsoever, howsomever, howsour, howtowdie, hox, hoy, hoya, hoyden, hoydened, hoydenhood, hoydening, hoydenish, hoydenishness, hoydenism, hoydens, hoyle, hoyles, hoyman, hoys, hp, hpital, hq, hr, hrdwre, hrs, hrzn, hs, hsien, ht, htel, hts, huaca, huaco, huajillo, huamuchil, huanaco, huantajayite, huapango, huapangos, huarache, huaraches, huaracho, huarachos, huarizo, hub, hub's, hubb, hubba, hubbaboo, hubbed, hubber, hubbies, hubbing, hubble, hubbly, hubbob, hubbub, hubbuboo, hubbubs, hubby, hubcap, hubcaps, hubmaker, hubmaking, hubnerite, hubris, hubrises, hubristic, hubristically, hubs, hubshi, huccatoon, huchen, hucho, huck, huckaback, huckle, huckleback, hucklebacked, huckleberries, huckleberry, hucklebone, huckles, huckmuck, hucks, huckster, hucksterage, huckstered, hucksterer, hucksteress, huckstering, hucksterism, hucksterize, hucksters, huckstery, huckstress, hud, hudderon, huddle, huddled, huddledom, huddlement, huddler, huddlers, huddles, huddling, huddlingly, huddock, huddroun, huddup, hudibrastic, hudson, hudsonia, hudsonite, hue, hue's, hued, hueful, huehuetl, hueless, huelessness, huemul, huer, huerta, hues, huff, huffaker, huffcap, huffed, huffer, huffier, huffiest, huffily, huffiness, huffing, huffingly, huffish, huffishly, huffishness, huffle, huffler, huffs, huffy, hug, huge, hugelite, hugely, hugeness, hugenesses, hugeous, hugeously, hugeousness, huger, hugest, huggable, hugged, hugger, huggermugger, huggermuggery, huggers, huggery, hugging, huggingly, huggle, hugh, hugmatee, hugo, hugonis, hugs, hugsome, huguenot, huguenots, hugy, huh, huia, huic, huile, huipil, huipilla, huisache, huiscoyol, huisher, huisquil, huissier, huitain, huitre, huke, hula, hulas, hulch, hulchy, huldee, hulk, hulkage, hulked, hulkier, hulkiest, hulkily, hulkiness, hulking, hulkingly, hulkingness, hulks, hulky, hull, hull's, hullaballoo, hullaballoos, hullabaloo, hullabaloos, hulled, huller, hullers, hulling, hullo, hulloa, hulloaed, hulloaing, hulloas, hullock, hulloed, hulloes, hulloing, hulloo, hullooed, hullooing, hulloos, hullos, hulls, huloist, hulotheism, hulsite, hulster, hulu, hulver, hulverhead, hulverheaded, hulwort, huly, hum, human, humanate, humane, humanely, humaneness, humaner, humanest, humanhood, humanics, humanification, humaniform, humaniformian, humanify, humanisation, humanise, humanised, humaniser, humanises, humanish, humanising, humanism, humanisms, humanist, humanistic, humanistical, humanistically, humanists, humanitarian, humanitarianism, humanitarianist, humanitarianize, humanitarians, humanitary, humanitian, humanities, humanity, humanity's, humanitymonger, humanization, humanize, humanized, humanizer, humanizers, humanizes, humanizing, humankind, humanlike, humanly, humanness, humanoid, humanoids, humans, humate, humates, humation, humbird, humble, humblebee, humbled, humblehearted, humblemouthed, humbleness, humbler, humblers, humbles, humblesse, humblesso, humblest, humblie, humbling, humblingly, humbly, humbo, humboldtilite, humboldtine, humboldtite, humbug, humbugability, humbugable, humbugged, humbugger, humbuggers, humbuggery, humbugging, humbuggism, humbugs, humbuzz, humdinger, humdingers, humdrum, humdrumminess, humdrummish, humdrummishness, humdrumness, humdrums, humdudgeon, humect, humectant, humectate, humectation, humective, humeral, humerals, humeri, humermeri, humeroabdominal, humerocubital, humerodigital, humerodorsal, humerometacarpal, humeroradial, humeroscapular, humeroulnar, humerus, humet, humettee, humetty, humhum, humic, humicubation, humid, humidate, humidfied, humidfies, humidification, humidified, humidifier, humidifiers, humidifies, humidify, humidifying, humidistat, humidities, humidity, humidityproof, humidly, humidness, humidor, humidors, humific, humification, humified, humifuse, humify, humilation, humiliant, humiliate, humiliated, humiliates, humiliating, humiliatingly, humiliation, humiliations, humiliative, humiliator, humiliatory, humilific, humilis, humilities, humilitude, humility, humin, humistratous, humit, humite, humiture, humlie, hummable, hummaul, hummed, hummel, hummeler, hummer, hummeri, hummers, hummie, humming, hummingbird, hummingbirds, hummingly, hummock, hummocks, hummocky, hummum, hummus, humongous, humor, humoral, humoralism, humoralist, humoralistic, humored, humorer, humorers, humoresque, humoresquely, humorful, humorific, humoring, humorism, humorist, humoristic, humoristical, humorists, humorize, humorless, humorlessly, humorlessness, humorology, humorous, humorously, humorousness, humorproof, humors, humorsome, humorsomely, humorsomeness, humour, humoural, humoured, humourful, humouring, humourist, humourize, humourless, humourlessness, humours, humoursome, humous, hump, humpback, humpbacked, humpbacks, humped, humph, humphed, humphing, humphs, humpier, humpies, humpiest, humpiness, humping, humpless, humps, humpty, humpy, hums, humstrum, humuhumunukunukuapuaa, humulene, humulon, humulone, humus, humuses, humuslike, hun, hunch, hunchback, hunchbacked, hunchbacks, hunched, hunches, hunchet, hunching, hunchy, hund, hunder, hundi, hundred, hundredal, hundredary, hundreder, hundredfold, hundredman, hundredpenny, hundreds, hundredth, hundredths, hundredweight, hundredweights, hundredwork, hunfysh, hung, hungar, hungarian, hungarians, hungaric, hungarite, hungary, hunger, hungered, hungerer, hungering, hungeringly, hungerless, hungerly, hungerproof, hungerroot, hungers, hungerweed, hungrier, hungriest, hungrify, hungrily, hungriness, hungry, hunh, hunk, hunk's, hunker, hunkered, hunkering, hunkerous, hunkerousness, hunkers, hunkies, hunks, hunky, hunner, hunnish, hunnishness, huns, hunt, huntable, huntaway, hunted, huntedly, hunter, hunterian, hunterlike, hunters, huntilite, hunting, huntings, huntley, huntress, huntresses, hunts, huntsman, huntsmanship, huntsmen, huntswoman, hup, hupaithric, huppah, huppahs, huppot, huppoth, hura, hurcheon, hurden, hurdies, hurdis, hurdle, hurdled, hurdleman, hurdler, hurdlers, hurdles, hurdlewise, hurdling, hurds, hure, hureaulite, hureek, hurgila, hurkaru, hurkle, hurl, hurlbarrow, hurlbat, hurled, hurlement, hurler, hurlers, hurley, hurleyhacket, hurleyhouse, hurleys, hurlies, hurling, hurlings, hurlock, hurlpit, hurls, hurlwind, hurly, huron, huronian, hurr, hurrah, hurrahed, hurrahing, hurrahs, hurray, hurrayed, hurraying, hurrays, hurrer, hurricane, hurricane's, hurricanes, hurricanize, hurricano, hurridly, hurried, hurriedly, hurriedness, hurrier, hurriers, hurries, hurrisome, hurrock, hurroo, hurroosh, hurry, hurrygraph, hurrying, hurryingly, hurryproof, hursinghar, hurst, hurt, hurtable, hurted, hurter, hurters, hurtful, hurtfully, hurtfulness, hurting, hurtingest, hurtle, hurtleberries, hurtleberry, hurtled, hurtles, hurtless, hurtlessly, hurtlessness, hurtling, hurtlingly, hurts, hurtsome, hurty, husband, husband's, husbandable, husbandage, husbanded, husbander, husbandfield, husbandhood, husbanding, husbandland, husbandless, husbandlike, husbandliness, husbandly, husbandman, husbandmen, husbandress, husbandry, husbands, husbandship, huscarl, huse, hush, hushable, hushaby, hushcloth, hushed, hushedly, husheen, hushel, husher, hushes, hushful, hushfully, hushing, hushingly, hushion, hushllsost, husho, hushpuppies, hushpuppy, husht, husk, huskanaw, husked, huskened, husker, huskers, huskershredder, huskier, huskies, huskiest, huskily, huskiness, husking, huskings, husklike, huskroot, husks, huskwort, husky, huso, huspel, huspil, huss, hussar, hussars, hussies, hussite, hussitism, hussy, hussydom, hussyness, hust, husting, hustings, hustle, hustlecap, hustled, hustlement, hustler, hustlers, hustles, hustling, huswife, huswifes, huswives, hut, hut's, hutch, hutched, hutcher, hutches, hutchet, hutchie, hutching, hutchinsonian, hutchinsonite, huthold, hutholder, hutia, hutkeeper, hutlet, hutlike, hutment, hutments, hutre, huts, hutted, hutting, huttonian, huttoning, huttonweed, hutukhtu, hutuktu, hutung, hutzpa, hutzpah, hutzpahs, hutzpas, huurder, huvelyk, huxter, huyghenian, huzoor, huzz, huzza, huzzaed, huzzah, huzzahed, huzzahing, huzzahs, huzzaing, huzzard, huzzas, huzzy, hv, hvy, hw, hwan, hwt, hwy, hwyl, hy, hyacine, hyacinth, hyacinthian, hyacinthin, hyacinthine, hyacinths, hyacinthus, hyades, hyaena, hyaenas, hyaenic, hyaenid, hyaenodon, hyaenodont, hyaenodontoid, hyahya, hyalescence, hyalescent, hyalin, hyaline, hyalines, hyalinization, hyalinize, hyalinized, hyalinizing, hyalinocrystalline, hyalinosis, hyalins, hyalite, hyalites, hyalithe, hyalitis, hyaloandesite, hyalobasalt, hyalocrystalline, hyalodacite, hyalogen, hyalogens, hyalograph, hyalographer, hyalography, hyaloid, hyaloiditis, hyaloids, hyaloliparite, hyalolith, hyalomelan, hyalomere, hyalomucoid, hyalonema, hyalophagia, hyalophane, hyalophyre, hyalopilitic, hyaloplasm, hyaloplasma, hyaloplasmic, hyalopsite, hyalopterous, hyalosiderite, hyalotekite, hyalotype, hyalts, hyaluronic, hyaluronidase, hyblaean, hybodont, hybosis, hybrid, hybrida, hybridae, hybridal, hybridation, hybridisable, hybridise, hybridised, hybridiser, hybridising, hybridism, hybridist, hybridity, hybridizable, hybridization, hybridizations, hybridize, hybridized, hybridizer, hybridizers, hybridizes, hybridizing, hybridous, hybrids, hybris, hybrises, hybristic, hyd, hydage, hydantoate, hydantoic, hydantoin, hydathode, hydatic, hydatid, hydatidiform, hydatidinous, hydatidocele, hydatids, hydatiform, hydatigenous, hydatogenesis, hydatogenic, hydatogenous, hydatoid, hydatomorphic, hydatomorphism, hydatopneumatic, hydatopneumatolytic, hydatopyrogenic, hydatoscopy, hyde, hydnaceous, hydnocarpate, hydnocarpic, hydnoid, hydnoraceous, hydra, hydracetin, hydrachnid, hydracid, hydracids, hydracoral, hydracrylate, hydracrylic, hydractinian, hydradephagan, hydradephagous, hydrae, hydraemia, hydraemic, hydragog, hydragogs, hydragogue, hydragogy, hydralazine, hydramide, hydramine, hydramnion, hydramnios, hydrangea, hydrangeaceous, hydrangeas, hydrant, hydranth, hydranths, hydrants, hydrarch, hydrargillite, hydrargyrate, hydrargyria, hydrargyriasis, hydrargyric, hydrargyrism, hydrargyrosis, hydrargyrum, hydrarthrosis, hydrarthrus, hydras, hydrase, hydrases, hydrastine, hydrastinine, hydrastis, hydrate, hydrated, hydrates, hydrating, hydration, hydrations, hydrator, hydrators, hydratropic, hydraucone, hydraul, hydrauli, hydraulic, hydraulically, hydraulician, hydraulicity, hydraulicked, hydraulicking, hydraulicon, hydraulics, hydraulis, hydraulist, hydraulus, hydrauluses, hydrazide, hydrazidine, hydrazimethylene, hydrazin, hydrazine, hydrazino, hydrazo, hydrazoate, hydrazobenzene, hydrazoic, hydrazone, hydrazyl, hydremia, hydremic, hydrencephalocele, hydrencephaloid, hydrencephalus, hydria, hydriad, hydriae, hydriatric, hydriatrist, hydriatry, hydric, hydrically, hydrid, hydride, hydrides, hydrids, hydriform, hydrindene, hydriodate, hydriodic, hydriodide, hydrion, hydriotaphia, hydro, hydroa, hydroacoustic, hydroadipsia, hydroaeric, hydroairplane, hydroalcoholic, hydroaromatic, hydroatmospheric, hydroaviation, hydrobarometer, hydrobenzoin, hydrobilirubin, hydrobiological, hydrobiologist, hydrobiology, hydrobiosis, hydrobiplane, hydrobomb, hydroboracite,

256

hydroborofluoric, hydrobranchiate, hydrobromate, hydrobromic, hydrobromid, hydrobromide, hydrocarbide, hydrocarbon, hydrocarbonaceous, hydrocarbonate, hydrocarbonic, hydrocarbonous, hydrocarbons, hydrocarbostyril, hydrocarburet, hydrocardia, hydrocaryaceous, hydrocatalysis, hydrocauline, hydrocaulus, hydrocele, hydrocellulose, hydrocephali, hydrocephalic, hydrocephalies, hydrocephalocele, hydrocephaloid, hydrocephalous, hydrocephalus, hydrocephaly, hydroceramic, hydrocerussite, hydrocharidaceous, hydrocharitaceous, hydrochemical, hydrochemistry, hydrochlorate, hydrochlorauric, hydrochloric, hydrochlorid, hydrochloride, hydrochlorothiazide, hydrochlorplatinic, hydrochlorplatinous, hydrocholecystis, hydrocinchonine, hydrocinnamaldehyde, hydrocinnamic, hydrocinnamoyl, hydrocinnamyl, hydrocirsocele, hydrocladium, hydroclastic, hydroclimate, hydrocobalticyanic, hydrocoele, hydrocollidine, hydrocolloid, hydrocolloidal, hydroconion, hydrocoral, hydrocoralline, hydrocorisan, hydrocortisone, hydrocotarnine, hydrocoumaric, hydrocrack, hydrocracking, hydrocupreine, hydrocyanate, hydrocyanic, hydrocyanide, hydrocycle, hydrocyclic, hydrocyclist, hydrocyst, hydrocystic, hydrodesulfurization, hydrodesulphurization, hydrodrome, hydrodromican, hydrodynamic, hydrodynamical, hydrodynamically, hydrodynamicist, hydrodynamics, hydrodynamometer, hydroeconomics, hydroelectric, hydroelectrically, hydroelectricity, hydroelectrization, hydroergotinine, hydroextract, hydroextractor, hydroferricyanic, hydroferrocyanate, hydroferrocyanic, hydrofluate, hydrofluoboric, hydrofluoric, hydrofluorid, hydrofluoride, hydrofluosilicate, hydrofluosilicic, hydrofluozirconic, hydrofoil, hydrofoils, hydroformer, hydroforming, hydroformylation, hydrofranklinite, hydrofuge, hydrogalvanic, hydrogasification, hydrogel, hydrogels, hydrogen, hydrogen's, hydrogenase, hydrogenate, hydrogenated, hydrogenates, hydrogenating, hydrogenation, hydrogenations, hydrogenator, hydrogenic, hydrogenide, hydrogenisation, hydrogenise, hydrogenised, hydrogenising, hydrogenium, hydrogenization, hydrogenize, hydrogenized, hydrogenizing, hydrogenolyses, hydrogenolysis, hydrogenous, hydrogens, hydrogeologic, hydrogeological, hydrogeologist, hydrogeology, hydroglider, hydrognosy, hydrogode, hydrograph, hydrographer, hydrographers, hydrographic, hydrographical, hydrographically, hydrography, hydroguret, hydrogymnastics, hydrohalide, hydrohematite, hydrohemothorax, hydroid, hydroidean, hydroids, hydroiodic, hydrokineter, hydrokinetic, hydrokinetical, hydrokinetics, hydrol, hydrolant, hydrolase, hydrolatry, hydrolize, hydrologic, hydrological, hydrologically, hydrologist, hydrologists, hydrology, hydrolysable, hydrolysate, hydrolysation, hydrolyse, hydrolysed, hydrolyser, hydrolyses, hydrolysing, hydrolysis, hydrolyst, hydrolyte, hydrolytic, hydrolytically, hydrolyzable, hydrolyzate, hydrolyzation, hydrolyze, hydrolyzed, hydrolyzer, hydrolyzing, hydromagnesite, hydromagnetic, hydromagnetics, hydromancer, hydromancy, hydromania, hydromaniac, hydromantic, hydromantical, hydromantically, hydromassage, hydrome, hydromechanic, hydromechanical, hydromechanics, hydromedusa, hydromedusae, hydromedusan, hydromedusoid, hydromel, hydromels, hydromeningitis, hydromeningocele, hydrometallurgical, hydrometallurgically, hydrometallurgy, hydrometamorphism, hydrometeor, hydrometeorologic, hydrometeorological, hydrometeorologist, hydrometeorology, hydrometer, hydrometers, hydrometra, hydrometric, hydrometrical, hydrometrid, hydrometry, hydromica, hydromicaceous, hydromonoplane, hydromorph, hydromorphic, hydromorphous, hydromorphy, hydromotor, hydromyelia, hydromyelocele, hydromyoma, hydronaut, hydrone, hydronegative, hydronephelite, hydronephrosis, hydronephrotic, hydronic, hydronically, hydronitric, hydronitrogen, hydronitroprussic, hydronitrous, hydronium, hydropac, hydroparacoumaric, hydropath, hydropathic, hydropathical, hydropathically, hydropathist, hydropathy, hydropericarditis, hydropericardium, hydroperiod, hydroperitoneum, hydroperitonitis, hydroperoxide, hydrophane, hydrophanous, hydrophid, hydrophil, hydrophile, hydrophilic, hydrophilicity, hydrophilid, hydrophilism, hydrophilite, hydrophiloid, hydrophilous, hydrophily, hydrophobe, hydrophobia, hydrophobic, hydrophobical, hydrophobicity, hydrophobist, hydrophobophobia, hydrophobous, hydrophoby, hydrophoid, hydrophone, hydrophones, hydrophoran, hydrophore, hydrophoria, hydrophorous, hydrophthalmia, hydrophthalmos, hydrophthalmus, hydrophylacium, hydrophyll, hydrophyllaceous, hydrophylliaceous, hydrophyllium, hydrophysometra, hydrophyte, hydrophytic, hydrophytism, hydrophyton, hydrophytous, hydropic, hydropical, hydropically, hydropigenous, hydroplane, hydroplaned, hydroplaner, hydroplanes, hydroplaning, hydroplanula, hydroplatinocyanic, hydroplutonic, hydropneumatic, hydropneumatization, hydropneumatosis, hydropneumopericardium, hydropneumothorax, hydropolyp, hydroponic, hydroponically, hydroponicist, hydroponics, hydroponist, hydropositive, hydropot, hydropower, hydropropulsion, hydrops, hydropses, hydropsies, hydropsy, hydroptic, hydropult, hydropultic, hydroquinine, hydroquinol, hydroquinoline, hydroquinone, hydrorachis, hydrorhiza, hydrorhizae, hydrorhizal, hydrorrhachis, hydrorrhachitis, hydrorrhea, hydrorrhoea, hydrorubber, hydros, hydrosalpinx, hydrosalt, hydrosarcocele, hydroscope, hydroscopic, hydroscopical, hydroscopicity, hydroscopist, hydroselenic, hydroselenide, hydroselenuret, hydroseparation, hydrosere, hydrosilicate, hydrosilicon, hydroski, hydrosol, hydrosole, hydrosolic, hydrosols, hydrosoma, hydrosomal, hydrosomata, hydrosomatous, hydrosome, hydrosorbic, hydrospace, hydrosphere, hydrospheres, hydrospheric, hydrospire, hydrospiric, hydrostat, hydrostatic, hydrostatical, hydrostatically, hydrostatician, hydrostatics, hydrostome, hydrosulfate, hydrosulfide, hydrosulfite, hydrosulfurous, hydrosulphate, hydrosulphide, hydrosulphite, hydrosulphocyanic, hydrosulphurated, hydrosulphuret, hydrosulphureted, hydrosulphuric, hydrosulphurous, hydrosulphuryl, hydrotachymeter, hydrotactic, hydrotalcite, hydrotasimeter, hydrotaxis, hydrotechnic, hydrotechnical, hydrotechnologist, hydrotechny, hydroterpene, hydrotheca, hydrothecae, hydrothecal, hydrotherapeutic, hydrotherapeutical, hydrotherapeutically, hydrotherapeutician, hydrotherapeuticians, hydrotherapeutics, hydrotherapies, hydrotherapist, hydrotherapy, hydrothermal, hydrothermally, hydrothoracic, hydrothorax, hydrotic, hydrotical, hydrotimeter, hydrotimetric, hydrotimetry, hydrotomy, hydrotropic, hydrotropically, hydrotropism, hydroturbine, hydrotype, hydrous, hydrovane, hydroxamic, hydroxamino, hydroxide, hydroxides, hydroximic, hydroxy, hydroxyacetic, hydroxyanthraquinone, hydroxyapatite, hydroxyazobenzene, hydroxybenzene, hydroxybutyricacid, hydroxycorticosterone, hydroxydehydrocorticosterone, hydroxydesoxycorticosterone, hydroxyketone, hydroxyl, hydroxylactone, hydroxylamine, hydroxylase, hydroxylate, hydroxylation, hydroxylic, hydroxylization, hydroxylize, hydroxyls, hydroxyproline, hydroxytryptamine, hydroxyurea, hydroxyzine, hydrozincite, hydrozoa, hydrozoal, hydrozoan, hydrozoic, hydrozoon, hydrula, hydruret, hydrus, hydurilate, hydurilic, hye, hyemal, hyena, hyenadog, hyenanchin, hyenas, hyenia, hyenic, hyeniform, hyenine, hyenoid, hyetal, hyetograph, hyetographic, hyetographical, hyetographically, hyetography, hyetological, hyetologist, hyetology, hyetometer, hyetometric, hyetometrograph, hyetometrographic, hygeen, hygeia, hygeian, hygeiolatry, hygeist, hygeistic, hygeists, hygenics, hygeology, hygiantic, hygiantics, hygiastic, hygiastics, hygieist, hygieists, hygienal, hygiene, hygienes, hygienic, hygienical, hygienically, hygienics, hygienist, hygienists, hygienization, hygienize, hygiologist, hygiology, hygric, hygrin, hygrine, hygristor, hygroblepharic, hygrodeik, hygroexpansivity, hygrogram, hygrograph, hygrology, hygroma, hygromatous, hygrometer, hygrometers, hygrometric, hygrometrical, hygrometrically, hygrometries, hygrometry, hygrophaneity, hygrophanous, hygrophilous, hygrophobia, hygrophthalmic, hygrophyte, hygrophytic, hygroplasm, hygroplasma, hygroscope, hygroscopic, hygroscopical, hygroscopically, hygroscopicity, hygroscopy, hygrostat, hygrostatics, hygrostomia, hygrothermal, hygrothermograph, hying, hyingly, hyke, hyla, hylactic, hylactism, hylaeosaurus, hylarchic, hylarchical, hylas, hylasmus, hyle, hylean, hyleg, hylegiacal, hyli, hylic, hylicism, hylicist, hylidae, hylids, hylism, hylist, hylobatian, hylobatic, hylobatine, hylodes, hylogenesis, hylogeny, hyloid, hyloist, hylology, hylomorphic, hylomorphical, hylomorphism, hylomorphist, hylomorphous, hylopathism, hylopathist, hylopathy, hylophagous, hylotheism, hylotheist, hylotheistic, hylotheistical, hylotomous, hylotropic, hylozoic, hylozoism, hylozoist, hylozoistic, hylozoistically, hymen, hymenaic, hymenal, hymeneal, hymeneally, hymeneals, hymenean, hymenia, hymenial, hymenic, hymenicolar, hymeniferous, hymeniophore, hymenium, hymeniumnia, hymeniums, hymenogeny, hymenoid, hymenomycetal, hymenomycete, hymenomycetoid, hymenomycetous, hymenophore, hymenophorum, hymenophyllaceous, hymenopter, hymenoptera, hymenopteran, hymenopterist, hymenopterological, hymenopterologist, hymenopterology, hymenopteron, hymenopterous, hymenopttera, hymenotome, hymenotomies, hymenotomy, hymens, hymn, hymn's, hymnal, hymnals, hymnaria, hymnaries, hymnarium, hymnariunaria, hymnary, hymnbook, hymnbooks, hymned, hymner, hymnic, hymning, hymnist, hymnists, hymnless, hymnlike, hymnode, hymnodical, hymnodies, hymnodist, hymnody, hymnograher, hymnographer, hymnography, hymnologic, hymnological, hymnologically, hymnologist, hymnology, hymns, hymnwise, hynd, hynde, hynder, hyne, hyobranchial, hyocholalic, hyocholic, hyoepiglottic, hyoepiglottidean, hyoglossal, hyoglossi, hyoglossus, hyoglycocholic, hyoid, hyoidal, hyoidan, hyoideal, hyoidean, hyoides, hyoids, hyolithid, hyolithoid, hyomandibula, hyomandibular, hyomental, hyoplastral, hyoplastron, hyoscapular, hyoscine, hyoscines, hyoscyamine, hyoscyamus, hyosternal, hyosternum, hyostylic, hyostyly, hyothere, hyothyreoid, hyothyroid, hyp, hypabyssal, hypabyssally, hypacusia, hypacusis, hypaesthesia, hypaesthesic, hypaethral, hypaethron, hypaethros, hypaethrum, hypalgesia, hypalgesic, hypalgia, hypalgic, hypallactic, hypallage, hypanthia, hypanthial, hypanthium, hypantrum, hypapophysial, hypapophysis, hyparterial, hypaspist, hypate, hypaton, hypautomorphic, hypaxial, hype, hyped, hypegiaphobia, hyper, hyperabelian, hyperabsorption, hyperaccuracy, hyperaccurate, hyperaccurately, hyperaccurateness, hyperacid, hyperacidaminuria, hyperacidity, hyperacousia, hyperacoustics, hyperaction, hyperactive, hyperactively, hyperactivities, hyperactivity, hyperacuity, hyperacuness, hyperacusia, hyperacusis, hyperacute, hyperacuteness, hyperadenosis, hyperadipose, hyperadiposis, hyperadiposity, hyperadrenalemia, hyperadrenalism, hyperadrenia, hyperaemia, hyperaemic, hyperaeolism, hyperaesthesia, hyperaesthete, hyperaesthetic, hyperalbuminosis, hyperaldosteronism, hyperalgebra, hyperalgesia, hyperalgesic, hyperalgesis, hyperalgetic, hyperalgia, hyperalimentation, hyperalkalinity, hyperaltruism, hyperaltruist, hyperaltruistic, hyperaminoacidemia, hyperanabolic, hyperanabolism, hyperanacinesia, hyperanakinesia, hyperanakinesis, hyperanarchic, hyperanarchy, hyperangelic, hyperangelical, hyperangelically, hyperaphia, hyperaphic, hyperapophyseal, hyperapophysial, hyperapophysis, hyperarchaeological, hyperarchepiscopal, hyperaspist, hyperazotemia, hyperazoturia, hyperbarbarism, hyperbarbarous, hyperbarbarously, hyperbarbarousness, hyperbaric, hyperbarically, hyperbarism, hyperbata, hyperbatbata, hyperbatic, hyperbatically, hyperbaton, hyperbatons, hyperbola, hyperbolae, hyperbolaeon, hyperbolas, hyperbole, hyperboles, hyperbolic, hyperbolical, hyperbolically, hyperbolicly, hyperbolism, hyperbolist, hyperbolize, hyperbolized, hyperbolizing, hyperboloid, hyperboloidal, hyperboreal, hyperborean, hyperbrachycephal, hyperbrachycephalic, hyperbrachycephaly, hyperbrachycranial, hyperbrachyskelic, hyperbranchia, hyperbranchial, hyperbrutal, hyperbrutally, hyperbulia, hypercalcaemia, hypercalcemia, hypercalcemic, hypercalcinaemia, hypercalcinemia, hypercalcinuria, hypercalciuria, hypercalcuria, hypercapnia, hypercapnic, hypercarbamidemia, hypercarbia, hypercarbureted, hypercarburetted, hypercarnal, hypercarnally, hypercatabolism, hypercatalectic, hypercatalexis, hypercatharsis, hypercathartic, hypercathexis, hypercenosis, hyperchamaerrhine, hypercharge, hyperchloraemia, hyperchloremia, hyperchlorhydria, hyperchloric, hyperchlorination, hypercholesteremia, hypercholesteremic, hypercholesterinemia, hypercholesterolemia, hypercholesterolemic, hypercholesterolia, hypercholia, hypercivilization, hypercivilized, hyperclassical, hyperclassicality, hyperclimax, hypercoagulability, hypercoagulable, hypercomplex, hypercomposite, hyperconcentration, hypercone, hyperconfidence, hyperconfident, hyperconfidently, hyperconformist, hyperconformity, hyperconscientious, hyperconscientiously, hyperconscientiousness, hyperconscious, hyperconsciousness, hyperconservatism, hyperconservative, hyperconservatively, hyperconservativeness, hyperconstitutional, hyperconstitutionalism, hyperconstitutionally, hypercoracoid, hypercorrect, hypercorrection, hypercorrectness, hypercorticoidism, hypercosmic, hypercreaturely, hypercrinemia, hypercrinia, hypercrinism, hypercrisia, hypercritic, hypercritical, hypercritically, hypercriticalness, hypercriticism, hypercriticize, hypercryaesthesia, hypercryalgesia, hypercryesthesia, hypercube, hypercyanosis, hypercyanotic, hypercycle, hypercylinder, hypercythemia, hypercytosis, hyperdactyl, hyperdactylia, hyperdactylism, hyperdactyly, hyperdeification, hyperdeified, hyperdeify, hyperdeifying, hyperdelicacy, hyperdelicate, hyperdelicately, hyperdelicateness, hyperdelicious, hyperdeliciously, hyperdeliciousness, hyperdelness, hyperdemocracy, hyperdemocratic, hyperdeterminant, hyperdiabolical, hyperdiabolically, hyperdiabolicalness, hyperdialectism, hyperdiapason, hyperdiapente, hyperdiastole, hyperdiastolic, hyperdiatessaron, hyperdiazeuxis, hyperdicrotic, hyperdicrotism, hyperdicrotous, hyperdimensional, hyperdimensionality, hyperdiploid, hyperdissyllable, hyperdistention, hyperditone, hyperdivision, hyperdolichocephal, hyperdolichocephalic, hyperdolichocephaly, hyperdolichocranial, hyperdoricism, hyperdulia, hyperdulic, hyperdulical, hyperelegance, hyperelegancy, hyperelegant, hyperelegantly, hyperelliptic, hyperemesis, hyperemetic, hyperemia, hyperemic, hyperemization, hyperemotional, hyperemotionally, hyperemotive, hyperemotively, hyperemotiveness, hyperemotivity, hyperemphasize, hyperemphasized, hyperemphasizing, hyperendocrinia, hyperendocrinism, hyperendocrisia, hyperenergetic, hyperenthusiasm, hyperenthusiastic, hyperenthusiastically, hypereosinophilia, hyperephidrosis, hyperepinephria, hyperepinephrinemia, hyperepinephry, hyperequatorial, hypererethism, hyperessence, hyperesthesia, hyperesthete, hyperesthetic, hyperethical, hyperethically, hyperethicalness, hypereuryprosopic, hypereutectic, hypereutectoid, hyperexaltation, hyperexcitability, hyperexcitable, hyperexcitableness, hyperexcitably, hyperexcitement, hyperexcursive, hyperexcursively, hyperexcursiveness, hyperexophoria, hyperextend, hyperextension, hyperfastidious, hyperfastidiously, hyperfastidiousness, hyperfederalist, hyperfine, hyperflexibility, hyperflexible, hyperflexibleness, hyperflexibly, hyperflexion, hyperfocal, hyperform, hyperfunction, hyperfunctional, hyperfunctionally, hyperfunctioning, hypergalactia, hypergalactosia, hypergalactosis, hypergamous, hypergamy, hypergenesis, hypergenetic, hypergenetical, hypergenetically, hypergeneticalness, hypergeometric, hypergeometrical, hypergeometry, hypergeusesthesia, hypergeusia, hypergeustia, hyperglobulia, hyperglobulism, hyperglycaemia, hyperglycaemic, hyperglycemia, hyperglycemic, hyperglycistia, hyperglycorrhachia, hyperglycosuria, hypergoddess, hypergol, hypergolic, hypergolically, hypergols, hypergrammatical, hypergrammatically, hypergrammaticalness, hyperhedonia, hyperhemoglobinemia, hyperhepatia, hyperhidrosis, hyperhidrotic, hyperhilarious, hyperhilariously, hyperhilariousness, hyperhypocrisy, hypericaceous, hypericin, hypericism, hypericum, hyperidealistic, hyperidealistically, hyperideation, hyperidrosis, hyperimmune, hyperimmunity, hyperimmunization, hyperimmunize, hyperimmunized, hyperimmunizing, hyperin, hyperinflation, hyperingenuity, hyperinosis, hyperinotic, hyperinsulinism, hyperinsulinization, hyperinsulinize, hyperintellectual, hyperintellectually, hyperintellectualness, hyperintelligence, hyperintelligent, hyperintelligently, hyperinvolution, hyperion, hyperirritability, hyperirritable, hyperisotonic, hyperite, hyperkalemia, hyperkalemic, hyperkaliemia, hyperkatabolism, hyperkeratoses, hyperkeratosis, hyperkeratotic, hyperkinesia, hyperkinesis, hyperkinetic, hyperlactation, hyperleptoprosopic, hyperlethal, hyperlethargy, hyperleucocytosis, hyperleucocytotic, hyperleukocytosis, hyperlexis, hyperlipaemia, hyperlipaemic, hyperlipemia, hyperlipemic, hyperlipidemia, hyperlipoidemia, hyperlithuria, hyperlogical, hyperlogicality, hyperlogically, hyperlogicalness, hyperlustrous, hyperlustrously, hyperlustrousness, hypermagical, hypermagically, hypermakroskelic, hypermarket, hypermedication, hypermegasoma, hypermenorrhea, hypermetabolism, hypermetamorphic, hypermetamorphism, hypermetamorphoses, hypermetamorphosis, hypermetamorphotic, hypermetaphoric, hypermetaphorical, hypermetaphysical, hypermetaplasia, hypermeter, hypermetric, hypermetrical, hypermetron, hypermetrope, hypermetropia, hypermetropic, hypermetropical, hypermetropy, hypermicrosoma, hypermiraculous, hypermiraculously, hypermiraculousness, hypermixolydian, hypermnesia, hypermnesic, hypermnesis, hypermnestic, hypermodest, hypermodestly, hypermodestness, hypermonosyllable, hypermoral, hypermorally, hypermorph, hypermorphic, hypermorphism, hypermorphosis, hypermotile, hypermotility, hypermyotonia, hypermyotrophy, hypermyriorama, hypermystical, hypermystically, hypermysticalness, hypernatremia, hypernatronemia, hypernatural, hypernaturally, hypernaturalness, hypernephroma, hyperneuria, hyperneurotic, hypernic, hypernik, hypernitrogenous, hypernomian, hypernomic, hypernormal, hypernormality, hypernormally, hypernormalness, hypernote, hypernotion, hypernotions, hypernutrition, hypernutritive, hyperoartian, hyperobtrusive, hyperobtrusively, hyperobtrusiveness, hyperodontogeny, hyperon, hyperons, hyperoodon, hyperoon, hyperope, hyperopes, hyperopia, hyperopic, hyperorganic, hyperorganically, hyperorthodox, hyperorthodoxy, hyperorthognathic, hyperorthognathous, hyperorthognathy, hyperosmia, hyperosmic, hyperosteogeny, hyperostoses, hyperostosis, hyperostotic, hyperothodox, hyperothodoxy, hyperotretan, hyperotretous, hyperovaria, hyperovarianism, hyperovarism, hyperoxemia, hyperoxidation, hyperoxide, hyperoxygenate, hyperoxygenating, hyperoxygenation, hyperoxygenize, hyperoxygenized, hyperoxygenizing, hyperoxymuriate, hyperoxymuriatic, hyperpanegyric, hyperparasite, hyperparasitic, hyperparasitism, hyperparasitize, hyperparathyroidism, hyperparoxysm, hyperpathetic, hyperpathetical, hyperpathetically, hyperpathia, hyperpathic, hyperpatriotic, hyperpatriotically, hyperpatriotism, hyperpencil, hyperpepsinia, hyperper, hyperperfection, hyperperistalsis, hyperperistaltic, hyperpersonal, hyperpersonally, hyperphagia, hyperphagic, hyperphalangeal, hyperphalangism, hyperpharyngeal, hyperphenomena, hyperphoria, hyperphoric, hyperphosphatemia, hyperphospheremia, hyperphosphorescence, hyperphysical, hyperphysically, hyperphysics, hyperpiesia, hyperpiesis, hyperpietic, hyperpietist, hyperpigmentation, hyperpigmented, hyperpinealism, hyperpituitarism, hyperpituitary, hyperplagiarism, hyperplane, hyperplasia, hyperplasic, hyperplastic, hyperplatyrrhine, hyperploid, hyperploidy, hyperpnea, hyperpneic, hyperpnoea, hyperpolarization, hyperpolarize, hyperpolysyllabic, hyperpolysyllabically, hyperpotassemia, hyperpotassemic, hyperpredator, hyperprism, hyperproduction, hyperprognathous, hyperprophetic, hyperprophetical, hyperprophetically, hyperprosexia, hyperpulmonary, hyperpure, hyperpurist, hyperpyramid, hyperpyretic, hyperpyrexia, hyperpyrexial, hyperquadric, hyperrational, hyperrationally, hyperreactive, hyperrealize, hyperrealized, hyperrealizing, hyperresonance, hyperresonant, hyperreverential, hyperrhythmical, hyperridiculous, hyperridiculously, hyperridiculousness, hyperritualism, hyperritualistic, hyperromantic, hyperromantically, hyperromanticism, hypersacerdotal, hypersaintly, hypersalivation, hypersceptical, hyperscholastic, hyperscholastically, hyperscrupulosity, hyperscrupulous, hypersecretion, hypersensibility, hypersensitisation, hypersensitise, hypersensitised, hypersensitising, hypersensitive, hypersensitiveness, hypersensitivities, hypersensitivity, hypersensitization, hypersensitize, hypersensitized, hypersensitizing, hypersensual, hypersensualism, hypersensually, hypersensualness, hypersensuous, hypersensuously, hypersensuousness, hypersentimental, hypersentimentally, hypersexual, hypersexualities, hypersexuality, hypersolid, hypersomnia, hypersonic, hypersonically, hypersonics, hypersophisticated, hypersophistication, hyperspace, hyperspatial, hyperspeculative, hyperspeculatively, hyperspeculativeness, hypersphere, hyperspherical, hyperspiritualizing, hypersplenia, hypersplenism, hyperstatic, hypersthene, hypersthenia, hypersthenic, hypersthenite, hyperstoic, hyperstoical, hyperstrophic, hypersubtle, hypersubtlety, hypersuggestibility, hypersuggestible, hypersuggestibleness, hypersuggestibly, hypersuperlative, hypersurface, hypersusceptibility, hypersusceptible, hypersystole, hypersystolic, hypertechnical, hypertechnically, hypertechnicalness, hypertelic, hypertely, hypertense, hypertensely, hypertenseness, hypertensin, hypertensinase, hypertensinogen, hypertension, hypertensive, hyperterrestrial, hypertetrahedron, hyperthermal, hyperthermalgesia, hyperthermally, hyperthermesthesia, hyperthermia, hyperthermic, hyperthermy, hyperthesis, hyperthetic, hyperthetical, hyperthrombinemia, hyperthymia, hyperthyreosis, hyperthyroid, hyperthyroidism, hyperthyroidization, hyperthyroidize, hyperthyroids, hypertocicity, hypertonia, hypertonic, hypertonicity, hypertonus, hypertorrid, hypertoxic, hypertoxicity, hypertragic, hypertragical, hypertragically, hypertranscendent, hypertrichosis, hypertrichy, hypertridimensional, hypertrophic, hypertrophied, hypertrophies, hypertrophous, hypertrophy, hypertrophying, hypertrophyphied, hypertropia, hypertropical, hypertype, hypertypic, hypertypical, hyperurbanism, hyperuresis, hyperuricemia, hypervascular, hypervascularity, hypervelocity, hypervenosity, hyperventilate, hyperventilation, hypervigilant, hypervigilantly, hypervigilantness, hyperviscosity, hyperviscous, hypervitalization, hypervitalize, hypervitalized, hypervitalizing, hypervitaminosis, hypervolume, hypervoluminous, hyperwrought, hypes, hypesthesia, hypesthesic, hypethral, hypha, hyphae, hyphaeresis, hyphal, hyphantria, hyphedonia, hyphema, hyphemia, hyphemias, hyphen, hyphen's, hyphenate, hyphenated, hyphenates, hyphenating, hyphenation, hyphenations, hyphened, hyphenic, hyphening, hyphenisation, hyphenise, hyphenised, hyphenising, hyphenism, hyphenization, hyphenize, hyphenized, hyphenizing, hyphenless, hyphens, hypho, hyphodrome, hyphomycete, hyphomycetic, hyphomycetous, hyphomycosis, hyphopdia, hyphopodia, hyphopodium, hypidiomorphic, hypidiomorphically, hyping, hypinosis, hypinotic, hypnaceous, hypnagogic, hypnale, hypnesthesis, hypnesthetic, hypnic, hypnoanalyses, hypnoanalysis, hypnoanalytic, hypnobate, hypnocyst, hypnody, hypnoetic, hypnogenesis, hypnogenetic, hypnogenetically, hypnogia, hypnogogic, hypnograph, hypnoid, hypnoidal, hypnoidization, hypnoidize, hypnologic, hypnological, hypnologist, hypnology, hypnone, hypnopaedia, hypnophobia, hypnophobias, hypnophobic, hypnophoby, hypnopompic, hypnoses, hypnosis, hypnosperm, hypnosporangia, hypnosporangium, hypnospore, hypnosporic, hypnotherapist, hypnotherapy, hypnotic, hypnotically, hypnotics, hypnotisability, hypnotisable, hypnotisation, hypnotise, hypnotised, hypnotiser, hypnotising, hypnotism, hypnotist, hypnotistic, hypnotists, hypnotizability, hypnotizable, hypnotization, hypnotize, hypnotized, hypnotizer, hypnotizes, hypnotizing, hypnotoid, hypnotoxin, hypnum, hypo, hypoacid, hypoacidity, hypoactive, hypoactivity, hypoacusia, hypoacussis, hypoadenia, hypoadrenia, hypoaeolian, hypoalbuminemia, hypoalimentation, hypoalkaline, hypoalkalinity, hypoalonemia, hypoaminoacidemia, hypoantimonate, hypoazoturia, hypobaric, hypobarism, hypobaropathy, hypobasal, hypobases, hypobasis, hypobatholithic, hypobenthonic, hypobenthos, hypoblast, hypoblastic, hypobole, hypobranchial, hypobranchiate, hypobromite, hypobromites, hypobromous, hypobulia, hypobulic, hypocalcemia, hypocalcemic, hypocarp, hypocarpium, hypocarpogean, hypocatharsis, hypocathartic, hypocathexis, hypocaust, hypocenter, hypocenters, hypocentral, hypocentre, hypocentrum, hypocephalus, hypochchilia, hypochdria, hypochil, hypochilia, hypochilium, hypochloremia, hypochloremic, hypochlorhydria, hypochlorhydric, hypochloric, hypochloridemia, hypochlorite, hypochlorous, hypochloruria, hypochnose, hypocholesteremia, hypocholesterinemia, hypocholesterolemia, hypochonder, hypochondria, hypochondriac, hypochondriacal, hypochondriacally, hypochondriacism, hypochondriacs, hypochondrial, hypochondriasis, hypochondriast, hypochondric, hypochondrium, hypochondry, hypochordal, hypochromia, hypochromic, hypochrosis, hypochylia, hypocist, hypocistis, hypocleidian, hypocleidium, hypocoelom, hypocondylar, hypocone, hypoconid, hypoconule, hypoconulid, hypocopy, hypocoracoid, hypocorism, hypocoristic, hypocoristical, hypocoristically, hypocotyl, hypocotyleal, hypocotyledonary, hypocotyledonous, hypocotylous, hypocrater, hypocrateriform, hypocraterimorphous, hypocreaceous, hypocrinia, hypocrinism, hypocrisies, hypocrisis, hypocrisy, hypocrital, hypocrite, hypocrite's, hypocrites, hypocritic, hypocritical, hypocritically, hypocriticalness, hypocrize, hypocrystalline, hypocycloid, hypocycloidal, hypocystotomy, hypocytosis, hypodactylum, hypoderm, hypoderma, hypodermal, hypodermatic, hypodermatically, hypodermatoclysis, hypodermatomy, hypodermic, hypodermically, hypodermics, hypodermis, hypodermoclysis, hypodermosis, hypodermous, hypoderms, hypodiapason, hypodiapente, hypodiastole, hypodiatessaron, hypodiazeuxis, hypodicrotic, hypodicrotous, hypodiploid, hypodiploidy, hypoditone, hypodorian, hypodynamia, hypodynamic, hypoed, hypoeliminator, hypoendocrinia, hypoendocrinism, hypoendocrisia, hypoeosinophilia, hypoergic, hypoeutectic, hypoeutectoid, hypofunction, hypogaeic, hypogamy, hypogastria, hypogastric, hypogastrium, hypogastrocele, hypogea, hypogeal, hypogeally, hypogean, hypogee, hypogeic, hypogeiody, hypogene, hypogenesis, hypogenetic, hypogenic, hypogenous, hypogeocarpous, hypogeous, hypogeugea, hypogeum, hypogeusia, hypoglobulia, hypoglossal, hypoglossis, hypoglossitis, hypoglossus, hypoglottis, hypoglycaemia, hypoglycemia, hypoglycemic, hypognathism, hypognathous, hypogonadia, hypogonadism, hypogonation, hypogyn, hypogynic, hypogynies, hypogynium, hypogynous, hypogyny, hypohalous, hypohemia, hypohepatia, hypohidrosis, hypohyal, hypohyaline, hypohydrochloria, hypohypophysism, hypoid, hypoidrosis, hypoing, hypoinosemia, hypoiodite, hypoiodous, hypoionian, hypoischium, hypoisotonic, hypokalemia, hypokalemic, hypokaliemia, hypokeimenometry, hypokinemia, hypokinesia, hypokinesis, hypokinetic, hypokoristikon, hypolemniscus, hypoleptically, hypoleucocytosis, hypolimnetic, hypolimnia, hypolimnial, hypolimnion, hypolimnionia, hypolithic, hypolocrian, hypolydian, hypomania, hypomanic, hypomelancholia, hypomeral, hypomere, hypomeron, hypometropia, hypomixolydian, hypomnematic, hypomnesia, hypomnesis, hypomochlion, hypomorph, hypomorphic, hypomotility, hypomyotonia, hyponastic, hyponastically, hyponasty, hyponatremia, hyponea, hyponeas, hyponeuria, hyponitric, hyponitrite, hyponitrous, hyponoetic, hyponoia, hyponoias, hyponome, hyponomic, hyponychial, hyponychium, hyponym, hyponymic, hyponymous, hypoparathyroidism, hypopepsia, hypopepsinia, hypopepsy, hypopetalous, hypopetaly, hypophalangism, hypophamin, hypophamine, hypophare, hypopharyngeal, hypopharynges, hypopharyngoscope, hypopharyngoscopy, hypopharynx, hypopharynxes, hypophloeodal, hypophloeodic, hypophloeous, hypophonesis, hypophonia, hypophonic, hypophonous, hypophora, hypophoria, hypophosphate, hypophosphite, hypophosphoric, hypophosphorous, hypophrenia, hypophrenic, hypophrenosis, hypophrygian, hypophyge, hypophyll, hypophyllium, hypophyllous, hypophyllum, hypophypophysism, hypophyse, hypophyseal, hypophysectomies, hypophysectomize, hypophysectomized, hypophysectomizing, hypophysectomy, hypophyseoprivic, hypophyseoprivous, hypophyses, hypophysial, hypophysical, hypophysics, hypophysis, hypophysitis, hypopial, hypopiesia, hypopiesis, hypopinealism, hypopituitarism, hypopituitary, hypoplankton, hypoplanktonic, hypoplasia, hypoplastic, hypoplastral, hypoplastron, hypoplasty, hypoplasy, hypoploid, hypoploidy, hypopnea, hypopneas, hypopnoea, hypopoddia, hypopodia, hypopodium, hypopotassemia, hypopotassemic, hypopraxia, hypoprosexia, hypoproteinemia, hypoproteinosis, hypopselaphesia, hypopsychosis, hypopteral, hypopteron, hypoptilar, hypoptilum, hypoptosis, hypoptyalism, hypopus, hypopygial, hypopygidium, hypopygium, hypopyon, hypopyons, hyporadial, hyporadiolus, hyporadius, hyporchema, hyporchemata, hyporchematic, hyporcheme, hyporchesis, hyporhachidian, hyporhachis, hyporhined, hyporight, hyporit, hyporrhythmic, hypos, hyposalemia, hyposarca, hyposcenium, hyposcleral, hyposcope, hyposecretion, hyposensitive, hyposensitivity, hyposensitization, hyposensitize, hyposensitized, hyposensitizing, hyposkeletal, hyposmia, hypospadiac, hypospadias, hyposphene, hyposphresia, hypospray, hypostase, hypostases, hypostasis, hypostasise, hypostasised, hypostasising, hypostasization, hypostasize, hypostasized, hypostasizing, hypostasy, hypostatic, hypostatical, hypostatically, hypostatisation, hypostatise, hypostatised, hypostatising, hypostatization, hypostatize, hypostatized, hypostatizing, hyposternal, hyposternum, hyposthenia, hyposthenic, hyposthenuria, hypostigma, hypostilbite, hypostoma, hypostomatic, hypostomatous, hypostome, hypostomial, hypostomous, hypostrophe, hypostyle, hypostypsis, hypostyptic, hyposulfite, hyposulfurous, hyposulphate, hyposulphite, hyposulphuric, hyposulphurous, hyposuprarenalism, hyposyllogistic, hyposynaphe, hyposynergia, hyposystole, hypotactic, hypotarsal, hypotarsus, hypotaxia, hypotaxic, hypotaxis, hypotension, hypotensive, hypotensor, hypotenusal, hypotenuse, hypotenuses, hypoth, hypothalami, hypothalamic, hypothalamus, hypothalli, hypothalline, hypothallus, hypothami, hypothec, hypotheca, hypothecal, hypothecary, hypothecate, hypothecated, hypothecater, hypothecates, hypothecating, hypothecation, hypothecative, hypothecator, hypothecatory, hypothecia, hypothecial, hypothecium, hypothecs, hypothenal, hypothenar, hypothenic, hypothenusal, hypothenuse, hypothermal, hypothermia, hypothermic, hypothermy, hypotheses, hypothesi, hypothesis, hypothesise, hypothesised, hypothesiser, hypothesising, hypothesist, hypothesists, hypothesize, hypothesized, hypothesizer, hypothesizers, hypothesizes, hypothesizing, hypothetic, hypothetical, hypothetically, hypotheticalness, hypothetics, hypothetist, hypothetize, hypothetizer, hypothyreosis, hypothyroid, hypothyroidism, hypothyroids, hypotonia, hypotonic, hypotonically, hypotonicity, hypotonus, hypotony, hypotoxic, hypotoxicity, hypotrachelia, hypotrachelium, hypotralia, hypotrich, hypotrichosis, hypotrichous, hypotrochanteric, hypotrochoid, hypotrochoidal, hypotrophic, hypotrophies, hypotrophy, hypotthalli, hypotympanic, hypotype, hypotypic, hypotypical, hypotyposis, hypovalve, hypovanadate, hypovanadic, hypovanadious, hypovanadous, hypovitaminosis, hypoxanthic, hypoxanthine, hypoxemia, hypoxemic, hypoxia, hypoxias, hypoxic, hypozeugma, hypozeuxis, hypozoan, hypozoic, hypped, hyppish, hyps, hypsibrachycephalic, hypsibrachycephalism, hypsibrachycephaly, hypsicephalic, hypsicephalous, hypsicephaly, hypsidolichocephalic, hypsidolichocephalism, hypsidolichocephaly, hypsiliform, hypsiloid, hypsilophodont, hypsilophodontid, hypsilophodontoid, hypsipyle, hypsistarian, hypsistenocephalic, hypsistenocephalism, hypsistenocephaly, hypsobathymetric, hypsocephalous, hypsochrome, hypsochromic, hypsochromy, hypsodont, hypsodontism, hypsodonty, hypsographic, hypsographical, hypsography, hypsoisotherm, hypsometer, hypsometric, hypsometrical, hypsometrically, hypsometrist, hypsometry, hypsophobia, hypsophoeia, hypsophonous, hypsophyll, hypsophyllar, hypsophyllary, hypsophyllous, hypsophyllum, hypsothermometer, hypt, hypural, hyraces, hyraceum, hyracid, hyraciform, hyracodont, hyracodontid, hyracodontoid, hyracoid, hyracoidean, hyracoidian, hyracoids, hyracothere, hyracotherian, hyrate, hyrax, hyraxes, hyrse, hyrst, hyson, hysons, hyssop, hyssops, hystazarin, hysteralgia, hysteralgic, hysteranthous, hysterectomies, hysterectomize, hysterectomized, hysterectomizes, hysterectomizing, hysterectomy, hysterelcosis, hysteresial, hysteresis, hysteretic, hysteretically, hysteria, hysteriac, hysterias, hysteric, hysterical, hysterically, hystericky, hysterics, hystericus, hysteriform, hysterioid, hysterocatalepsy, hysterocele, hysterocleisis, hysterocrystalline, hysterocystic, hysterodynia, hysterogen, hysterogenetic, hysterogenic, hysterogenous, hysterogeny, hysteroid, hysteroidal, hysterolaparotomy, hysterolith, hysterolithiasis, hysterology, hysterolysis, hysteromania, hysteromaniac, hysteromaniacal, hysterometer, hysterometry, hysteromorphous, hysteromyoma, hysteromyomectomy, hysteron, hysteroneurasthenia, hysteropathy, hysteropexia, hysteropexy, hysterophore, hysterophytal, hysterophyte, hysteroproterize, hysteroptosia, hysteroptosis, hysterorrhaphy, hysterorrhexis, hysteroscope, hysterosis, hysterotely, hysterotome, hysterotomies, hysterotomy, hysterotraumatism, hystriciasis, hystricid, hystricine, hystricism, hystricismus, hystricoid, hystricomorph, hystricomorphic, hystricomorphous, hyte, hythergraph, hyzone, i, i', i'd, i'faith, i'll, i'm, i's, i've, i/c, ia, iago, iamatology, iamb, iambelegus, iambi, iambic, iambical, iambically, iambics, iambist, iambize, iambographer, iambs, iambus, iambuses, ianthine, ianthinite, iao, iare, iarovization, iarovize, iarovized, iarovizing, iatraliptic, iatraliptics, iatric, iatrical, iatrochemic, iatrochemical, iatrochemically, iatrochemist, iatrochemistry, iatrogenic, iatrogenically, iatrogenicity, iatrological, iatrology, iatromathematical, iatromathematician, iatromathematics, iatromechanical, iatromechanist, iatrophysical, iatrophysicist, iatrophysics, iatrotechnics, ib, iba, iberia, iberian, iberians, iberite, ibex, ibexes, ibices, ibid, ibidem, ibidine, ibis, ibisbill, ibises, ibm, ibolium, ibota, ibsenism, ibuprofen, ic, icacinaceous, icaco, icarian, icarus, icasm, icbm, ice, iceberg, iceberg's, icebergs, iceblink, iceblinks, iceboat, iceboater, iceboating, iceboats, icebone, icebound, icebox, iceboxes, icebreaker, icebreakers, icecap, icecaps, icecraft, iced, icefall, icefalls, icefish, icefishes, icehouse, icehouses, icekhana, icekhanas, iceland, icelander, icelanders, icelandic, iceleaf, iceless, icelike, iceman, icemen, iceni, icepick, icequake, iceroot, ices, iceskate, iceskated, iceskating, icespar, icework, ich, ichebu, ichibu, ichneumon, ichneumoned, ichneumonid, ichneumonidan, ichneumoniform, ichneumonized, ichneumonoid, ichneumonology, ichneumous, ichneutic, ichnite, ichnites, ichnographic, ichnographical, ichnographically, ichnographies, ichnography, ichnolite, ichnolithology, ichnolitic, ichnological, ichnology, ichnomancy, icho, ichoglan, ichor, ichorous, ichorrhaemia, ichorrhea, ichorrhemia, ichorrhoea, ichors, ichs, ichth, ichthammol, ichthulin, ichthulinic, ichthus, ichthyal, ichthyian, ichthyic, ichthyician, ichthyism, ichthyisms, ichthyismus, ichthyization, ichthyized, ichthyobatrachian, ichthyocephalous, ichthyocol, ichthyocolla, ichthyocoprolite, ichthyodian, ichthyodont, ichthyodorulite, ichthyodorylite, ichthyofauna, ichthyofaunal, ichthyoform, ichthyographer, ichthyographia, ichthyographic, ichthyographies, ichthyography, ichthyoid, ichthyoidal, ichthyol, ichthyolatrous, ichthyolatry, ichthyolite, ichthyolitic, ichthyologic, ichthyological, ichthyologically, ichthyologist, ichthyologists, ichthyology, ichthyomancy, ichthyomania, ichthyomantic, ichthyomorphic, ichthyomorphous, ichthyonomy, ichthyopaleontology, ichthyophagan, ichthyophagi, ichthyophagian, ichthyophagist, ichthyophagize, ichthyophagous, ichthyophagy, ichthyophile, ichthyophobia, ichthyophthalmite, ichthyophthiriasis, ichthyophthirius, ichthyopolism, ichthyopolist, ichthyopsid, ichthyopsida, ichthyopsidan, ichthyopterygian, ichthyopterygium, ichthyornis, ichthyornithic, ichthyornithoid, ichthyosaur, ichthyosaurian, ichthyosaurid, ichthyosauroid, ichthyosaurus, ichthyosauruses, ichthyosiform, ichthyosis, ichthyosism, ichthyotic, ichthyotomist, ichthyotomous, ichthyotomy, ichthyotoxin, ichthyotoxism, ichthys, ichthytaxidermy, ichu, ichulle, icica, icicle, icicled, icicles, icier, iciest, icily, iciness, icinesses, icing, icings, icker, ickers, ickier, ickiest, ickle, icky, icod, icon, icones, iconic, iconical, iconically, iconicity, iconism, iconize, iconoclasm, iconoclast, iconoclastic, iconoclastically, iconoclasticism, iconoclasts, iconodule, iconodulic, iconodulist, iconoduly, iconograph, iconographer, iconographic, iconographical, iconographically, iconographies, iconographist, iconography, iconolagny, iconolater, iconolatrous, iconolatry, iconological, iconologist, iconology, iconomachal, iconomachist, iconomachy, iconomania, iconomatic, iconomatically, iconomaticism, iconomatography, iconometer, iconometric, iconometrical, iconometrically, iconometry, iconophile, iconophilism, iconophilist, iconophily, iconoplast, iconoscope, iconostas, iconostases, iconostasion, iconostasis, iconotype, icons, iconv, iconvert, icosaheddra, icosahedra, icosahedral, icosahedron, icosahedrons, icosandria, icosasemic, icosian, icositedra, icositetrahedra, icositetrahedron, icositetrahedrons, icosteid, icosteine, icotype, icteric, icterical, icterics, icterine, icteritious, icteritous, icterode, icterogenetic, icterogenic, icterogenous, icterohematuria, icteroid, icterous, icterus, icteruses, ictic, ictuate, ictus, ictuses, icy, id, idaein, idaho, idahoan, idahoans, idalia, idant, idcue, iddat, iddhi, ide, idea, idea'd, idea's, ideaed, ideaful, ideagenous, ideaistic, ideal, idealess, idealisation, idealise, idealised, idealiser, idealises, idealising, idealism, idealisms, idealist, idealistic, idealistical, idealistically, idealists, idealities, ideality, idealization, idealization's, idealizations, idealize, idealized, idealizer, idealizes, idealizing, idealless, ideally, idealness, idealogical, idealogies, idealogue, idealogy, ideals, idealy, ideamonger, ideas, ideata, ideate, ideated, ideates, ideating, ideation, ideational, ideationally, ideations, ideative, ideatum, idee, ideefixe, ideist, idem, idemfactor, idempotency, idempotent, idence, idenitifiers, ident, identic, identical, identicalism, identically, identicalness, identies, identifer, identifers, identifiability, identifiable, identifiableness, identifiably, identific, identification, identificational, identifications, identified, identifier, identifiers, identifies, identify, identifying, identism, identities, identity, identity's, ideo, ideogenetic, ideogenical, ideogenous, ideogeny, ideoglyph, ideogram, ideogramic, ideogrammatic, ideogrammic, ideograms, ideograph, ideographic, ideographical, ideographically, ideographs, ideography, ideokinetic, ideolatry, ideolect, ideologic, ideological, ideologically, ideologies, ideologise, ideologised, ideologising, ideologist, ideologize, ideologized, ideologizing, ideologue, ideology, ideomania, ideomotion, ideomotor, ideoogist, ideophobia, ideophone, ideophonetics, ideophonous, ideoplastia, ideoplastic, ideoplastics, ideoplasty, ideopraxist, ideotype, ides, idesia, idest, ideta, idgah, idiasm, idic, idigbo, idiobiology, idioblast, idioblastic, idiochromatic, idiochromatin, idiochromosome, idiocies, idiocrasies, idiocrasis, idiocrasy, idiocratic, idiocratical, idiocratically, idiocy, idiocyclophanous, idiodynamic, idiodynamics, idioelectric, idioelectrical, idiogenesis, idiogenetic, idiogenous, idioglossia, idioglottic, idiogram, idiograph, idiographic, idiographical, idiohypnotism, idiolalia, idiolatry, idiolect, idiolectal, idiolects, idiologism, idiolysin, idiom, idiomatic, idiomatical, idiomatically, idiomaticalness, idiomaticity, idiomaticness, idiomelon, idiometer, idiomography, idiomology, idiomorphic, idiomorphically, idiomorphism, idiomorphous, idioms, idiomuscular, idion, idiopathetic, idiopathic, idiopathical, idiopathically, idiopathies, idiopathy, idiophanism, idiophanous, idiophone, idiophonic, idioplasm, idioplasmatic, idioplasmic, idiopsychological, idiopsychology, idioreflex, idiorepulsive, idioretinal, idiorrhythmic, idiorrhythmism, idiorrhythmy, idiosome, idiospasm, idiospastic, idiostatic, idiosyncracies, idiosyncracy, idiosyncrasies, idiosyncrasy, idiosyncrasy's, idiosyncratic, idiosyncratical, idiosyncratically, idiot, idiot's, idiotcies, idiotcy, idiothalamous, idiothermic, idiothermous, idiothermy, idiotic, idiotical, idiotically, idioticalness, idioticon, idiotise, idiotised, idiotish, idiotising, idiotism, idiotisms, idiotize, idiotized, idiotizing, idiotropian, idiotropic, idiotry, idiots, idiotype, idiotypic, idiozome, idite, iditol, idle, idleby, idled, idleful, idleheaded, idlehood, idleman, idlemen, idlement, idleness, idlenesses, idler, idlers, idles, idleset, idleship, idlesse, idlesses, idlest, idlety, idling, idlish, idly, ido, idocrase, idocrases, idol, idol's, idola, idolaster, idolastre, idolater, idolaters, idolatress, idolatric, idolatrical, idolatries, idolatrise, idolatrised, idolatriser, idolatrising, idolatrize, idolatrized, idolatrizer, idolatrizing, idolatrous, idolatrously, idolatrousness, idolatry, idolet, idolify, idolisation, idolise, idolised, idoliser, idolisers, idolises, idolish, idolising, idolism, idolisms, idolist, idolistic, idolization, idolize, idolized, idolizer, idolizers, idolizes, idolizing, idoloclast, idoloclastic, idolodulia, idolographical, idololater, idololatrical, idololatry, idolomancy, idolomania, idolon, idolothyte, idolothytic, idolous, idols, idolum, idoneal, idoneities, idoneity, idoneous, idoneousness, idorgan, idosaccharic, idose, idrialin, idrialine, idrialite, idrosis, idryl, ids, idyl, idyler, idylian, idylism, idylist, idylists, idylize, idyll, idyller, idyllia, idyllian, idyllic, idyllical, idyllically, idyllicism, idyllion, idyllist, idyllists, idyllium, idylls, idyls, ie, ieee, if, ife, ifecks, iff, iffier, iffiest, iffiness, iffinesses, iffy, ifint, ifreal, ifree, ifrit, ifs, igad, igarape, igasuric, igdrasil, igelstromite, ighly, igitur, iglesia, igloo, igloos, iglu, iglus, ign, igname, ignaro, ignatia, ignatian, ignatias, ignavia, ignaw, igneoaqueous, igneous, ignescence, ignescent, ignicolist, igniferous, igniferousness, ignified, ignifies, ignifluous, igniform, ignifuge, ignify, ignifying, ignigenous, ignipotent, ignipuncture, ignis, ignitability, ignitable, ignite, ignited, igniter, igniters, ignites, ignitibility, ignitible, igniting, ignition, ignitions, ignitive, ignitor, ignitors, ignitron, ignitrons, ignivomous, ignivomousness, ignobility, ignoble, ignobleness, ignoblesse, ignobly, ignominies, ignominious, ignominiously, ignominiousness, ignominy, ignomious, ignorable, ignoramus, ignoramuses, ignorance, ignorant, ignorantia, ignorantine, ignorantism, ignorantist, ignorantly, ignorantness, ignoration, ignore, ignored, ignorement, ignorer, ignorers, ignores, ignoring, ignote, ignotus, igorot, igraine, iguana, iguanas, iguanian, iguanians, iguanid, iguaniform, iguanodon, iguanodont, iguanodontoid, iguanoid, ihi, ihleite, ihp, ihram, ihrams, ihs, ii, iiasa, iii, iiwi, ijithad, ijma, ijmaa, ijolite, ijussite, ik, ikan, ikary, ikat, ike, ikebana, ikebanas, ikey, ikeyness, ikon, ikona, ikons, ikra, il, ilama, ile, ilea, ileac, ileal, ileectomy, ileitides, ileitis, ileocaecal, ileocaecum, ileocecal, ileocolic, ileocolitis, ileocolostomy, ileocolotomy, ileon, ileosigmoidostomy, ileostomies, ileostomy, ileotomy, ilesite, ileum, ileus, ileuses, ilex, ilexes, ilia, iliac, iliacus, iliad, iliads, iliahi, ilial, iliau, ilicaceous, ilicic, ilicin, ilima, iliocaudal, iliocaudalis, iliococcygeal, iliococcygeus, iliococcygian, iliocostal, iliocostales, iliocostalis, iliodorsal, iliofemoral, iliohypogastric, ilioinguinal, ilioischiac, ilioischiatic, iliolumbar, ilion, iliopectineal, iliopelvic, ilioperoneal, iliopsoas, iliopsoatic, iliopubic, iliosacral, iliosciatic, ilioscrotal, iliospinal, iliotibial, iliotrochanteric, ilium, ilixanthin, ilk, ilka, ilkane, ilks, ill, illabile, illaborate, illachrymable, illachrymableness, illamon, illapsable, illapse, illapsed, illapsing, illapsive, illaqueable, illaqueate, illaqueation, illation, illations, illative, illatively, illatives, illaudable, illaudably, illaudation, illaudatory, illbred, illdisposedness, illecebration, illecebrous, illeck, illect, illegal, illegalisation, illegalise, illegalised, illegalising, illegalities, illegality, illegalization, illegalize, illegalized, illegalizing, illegally, illegalness, illegibility, illegible, illegibleness, illegibly, illegitimacies, illegitimacy, illegitimate, illegitimated, illegitimately, illegitimateness, illegitimating, illegitimation, illegitimatise, illegitimatised, illegitimatising, illegitimatize, illegitimatized, illegitimatizing, illeism, illeist, iller, illess, illest, illeviable, illfare, illguide, illguided, illguiding, illhumor, illhumored, illiberal, illiberalise, illiberalism, illiberality, illiberalize, illiberalized, illiberalizing, illiberally, illiberalness, illicit, illicitly, illicitness, illicium, illigation, illighten, illimitability, illimitable, illimitableness, illimitably, illimitate, illimitation, illimited, illimitedly, illimitedness, illing, illinition, illinium, illiniums, illinois, illinoisan, illipene, illiquation, illiquid, illiquidity, illiquidly, illish, illision, illite, illiteracies, illiteracy, illiteral, illiterate, illiterately, illiterateness, illiterates, illiterati, illiterature, illites, illitic, illium, illmanneredness, illnature, illness, illness's, illnesses, illocal, illocality, illocally, illocution, illogic, illogical, illogicalities, illogicality, illogically, illogicalness, illogician, illogicity, illogics, illoricate, illoricated, illoyal, illoyalty, ills, illtempered, illth, illtreatment, illucidate, illucidation, illucidative, illude, illuded, illudedly, illuder, illuding, illume, illumed, illumer, illumes, illuminability, illuminable, illuminance, illuminant, illuminate, illuminated, illuminates, illuminati, illuminating, illuminatingly, illumination, illuminational, illuminations, illuminatism, illuminatist, illuminative, illuminato, illuminator, illuminators, illuminatory, illuminatus, illumine, illumined, illuminee, illuminer, illumines, illuming, illumining, illuminism, illuminist, illuminize, illuminometer, illuminous, illumonate, illupi, illure, illurement, illus, illusible, illusion, illusion's, illusionable, illusional, illusionary, illusioned, illusionism, illusionist, illusionistic, illusionists, illusions, illusive, illusively, illusiveness, illusor, illusorily, illusoriness, illusory, illust, illustrable, illustratable, illustrate, illustrated, illustrates, illustrating, illustration, illustrational, illustrations, illustrative, illustratively, illustrator, illustrator's, illustrators, illustratory, illustratress, illustre, illustricity, illustrious, illustriously, illustriousness, illustrissimo, illustrous, illutate, illutation, illuvia, illuvial, illuviate, illuviated, illuviating, illuviation, illuvium, illuviums, illuvivia, illy, illyrian, ilmenite, ilmenites, ilmenitite, ilmenorutile, ilocano, ilot, ilth, ilvaite, ilysioid, im, image, imageable, imaged, imageless, imagen, imager, imagerial, imagerially, imageries, imagery, images, imagilet, imaginability, imaginable, imaginableness, imaginably, imaginal, imaginant, imaginaries, imaginarily, imaginariness, imaginary, imaginate, imaginated, imaginating, imagination, imagination's, imaginational, imaginationalism, imaginations, imaginative, imaginatively, imaginativeness, imaginator, imagine, imagined, imaginer, imaginers, imagines, imaging, imagining, imaginings, imaginist, imaginous, imagism, imagisms, imagist, imagistic, imagistically, imagists, imagnableness, imago, imagoes, imam, imamah, imamate, imamates, imambara, imambarah, imambarra, imamic, imams, imamship, iman, imanlaut, imaret, imarets, imaum, imaumbarah, imaums, imbalance, imbalances, imbalm, imbalmed, imbalmer, imbalmers, imbalming, imbalmment, imbalms, imban, imband, imbannered, imbarge, imbark, imbarkation, imbarked, imbarking, imbarkment, imbarks, imbarn, imbase, imbased, imbastardize, imbat, imbathe, imbauba, imbe, imbecile, imbecilely, imbeciles, imbecilic, imbecilitate, imbecilitated, imbecilities, imbecility, imbed, imbedded, imbedding, imbeds, imbellic, imbellious, imber, imberbe, imbesel, imbibe, imbibed, imbiber, imbibers, imbibes, imbibing, imbibition, imbibitional, imbibitions, imbibitory, imbirussu, imbitter, imbittered, imbitterer, imbittering, imbitterment, imbitters, imblaze, imblazed, imblazes, imblazing, imbodied, imbodies, imbodiment, imbody, imbodying, imbolden, imboldened, imboldening, imboldens, imbolish, imbondo, imbonity, imborder, imbordure, imborsation, imboscata, imbosk, imbosom, imbosomed, imbosoming, imbosoms, imbower, imbowered, imbowering, imbowers, imbraceries, imbracery, imbranch, imbrangle, imbrangled, imbrangling, imbreathe, imbred, imbreviate, imbreviated, imbreviating, imbrex, imbricate, imbricated, imbricately, imbricating, imbrication, imbrications, imbricative, imbrices, imbrier, imbrium, imbrocado, imbroccata, imbroglio, imbroglios, imbroin, imbrown, imbrowned, imbrowning, imbrowns, imbrue, imbrued, imbruement, imbrues, imbruing, imbrute, imbruted, imbrutement, imbrutes, imbruting, imbu, imbue, imbued, imbuement, imbues, imbuia, imbuing, imburse, imbursed, imbursement, imbursing, imbute, imcnt, imdtly, imelle, imi, imid, imidazol, imidazole, imidazolyl, imide, imides, imidic, imido, imidogen, imids, iminazole, imine, imines, imino, iminohydrin, iminourea, imipramine, imit, imitability, imitable, imitableness, imitancy, imitant, imitate, imitated, imitatee, imitates, imitating, imitation, imitational, imitationist, imitations, imitative, imitatively, imitativeness, imitator, imitators, imitatorship, imitatress, imitatrix, immaculacy, immaculance, immaculate, immaculately, immaculateness, immailed, immalleable, immanacle, immanacled, immanacling, immanation, immane, immanely, immanence, immanency, immaneness, immanent, immanental, immanentism, immanentist, immanentistic, immanently, immanifest, immanifestness, immanity, immantle, immantled, immantling, immarble, immarcescible, immarcescibly, immarcibleness, immarginate, immartial, immask, immatchable, immatchless, immatereality, immaterial, immaterialise, immaterialised, immaterialising, immaterialism, immaterialist, immaterialistic, immaterialities, immateriality, immaterialization, immaterialize, immaterialized, immaterializing, immaterially, immaterialness, immaterials, immateriate, immatriculate, immatriculation, immature, immatured, immaturely, immatureness, immatures, immaturities, immaturity, immeability, immeasurability, immeasurable, immeasurableness, immeasurably, immeasured, immechanical, immechanically, immediacies, immediacy, immedial, immediate, immediately, immediateness, immediatism, immediatist, immediatly, immedicable, immedicableness, immedicably, immelmann, immelodious, immember, immemorable, immemorial, immemorially, immense, immensely, immenseness, immenser, immensest, immensible, immensities, immensittye, immensity, immensive, immensurability, immensurable, immensurableness, immensurate, immerd, immerge, immerged, immergence, immergent, immerges, immerging, immerit, immerited, immeritorious, immeritoriously, immeritous, immerse, immersed, immersement, immerses, immersible, immersing, immersion, immersionism, immersionist, immersions, immersive, immesh, immeshed, immeshes, immeshing, immethodic, immethodical, immethodically, immethodicalness, immethodize, immetrical, immetrically, immetricalness, immeubles, immew, immi, immies, immigrant, immigrant's, immigrants, immigrate, immigrated, immigrates, immigrating, immigration, immigrational, immigrations, immigrator, immigratory, immind, imminence, imminency, imminent, imminently, imminentness, immingle, immingled, immingles, immingling, imminute, imminution, immis, immiscibility, immiscible, immiscibly, immiss, immission, immit, immitigability, immitigable, immitigableness, immitigably, immittance, immitted, immix, immixable, immixed, immixes, immixing, immixt, immixting, immixture, immobile, immobiles, immobilia, immobilisation, immobilise, immobilised, immobilising, immobilism, immobilities, immobility, immobilization, immobilize, immobilized, immobilizer, immobilizes, immobilizing, immoderacy, immoderate, immoderately, immoderateness, immoderation, immodest, immodestly, immodesty, immodish, immodulated, immolate, immolated, immolates, immolating, immolation, immolations, immolator, immoment, immomentous, immonastered, immoral, immoralise, immoralised, immoralising, immoralism, immoralist, immoralities, immorality, immoralize, immoralized, immoralizing, immorally, immorigerous, immorigerousness, immortability, immortable, immortal, immortalisable, immortalisation, immortalise, immortalised, immortaliser, immortalising, immortalism, immortalist, immortalities, immortality, immortalizable, immortalization, immortalize, immortalized, immortalizer, immortalizes, immortalizing, immortally, immortalness, immortals, immortalship, immortelle, immortification, immortified, immote, immotile, immotility, immotioned, immotive, immound, immov, immovability, immovable, immovableness, immovables, immovably, immoveability, immoveable, immoveableness, immoveables, immoveably, immoved, immun, immund, immundicity, immundity, immune, immunes, immunisation, immunise, immunised, immuniser, immunises, immunising, immunist, immunities, immunity, immunity's, immunization, immunizations, immunize, immunized, immunizer, immunizes, immunizing, immunoassay, immunochemical, immunochemically, immunochemistry, immunodiffusion, immunoelectrophoresis, immunoelectrophoretic, immunoelectrophoretically, immunofluorescence, immunofluorescent, immunogen, immunogenesis, immunogenetic, immunogenetical, immunogenetically, immunogenetics, immunogenic, immunogenically, immunogenicity, immunoglobulin, immunohematologic, immunohematological, immunohematology, immunol, immunologic, immunological, immunologically, immunologies, immunologist, immunologists, immunology, immunopathologic, immunopathological, immunopathologist, immunopathology, immunoreaction, immunoreactive, immunoreactivity, immunosuppressant, immunosuppressants, immunosuppression, immunosuppressive, immunotherapies, immunotherapy, immunotoxin, immuration, immure, immured, immurement, immures, immuring, immusical, immusically, immutability, immutable, immutableness, immutably, immutate, immutation, immute, immutilate, immutual, immy, imonium, imp, impacability, impacable, impack, impackment, impact, impacted, impacter, impacters, impactful, impacting, impaction, impactionize, impactite, impactive, impactment, impactor, impactor's, impactors, impacts, impactual, impages, impaint, impainted, impainting, impaints, impair, impairable, impaired, impairer, impairers, impairing, impairment, impairments, impairs, impala, impalace, impalas, impalatable, impale, impaled, impalement, impalements, impaler, impalers, impales, impaling, impall, impallid, impalm, impalmed, impalpability, impalpable, impalpably, impalsy, impaludism, impanate, impanated, impanation, impanator, impane, impanel, impaneled, impaneling, impanelled, impanelling, impanelment, impanels, impapase, impapyrate, impapyrated, impar, imparadise, imparadised, imparadising, imparalleled, imparasitic, impardonable, impardonably, imparidigitate, imparipinnate, imparisyllabic, imparities, imparity, impark, imparkation, imparked, imparking, imparks, imparl, imparlance, imparled, imparling, imparsonee, impart, impartability, impartable, impartance, impartation, imparted, imparter, imparters, impartial, impartialism, impartialist, impartiality, impartially, impartialness, impartibilibly, impartibility, impartible, impartibly, imparticipable, imparting, impartite, impartive, impartivity, impartment, imparts, impassability, impassable, impassableness, impassably, impasse, impasses, impassibilibly, impassibility, impassible, impassibleness, impassibly, impassion, impassionable, impassionate, impassionately, impassioned, impassionedly, impassionedness, impassioning, impassionment, impassive, impassively, impassiveness, impassivity, impastation, impaste, impasted, impastes, impasting, impasto, impastoed, impastos, impasture, impaternate, impatible, impatience, impatiency, impatiens, impatient, impatientaceous, impatiently, impatientness, impatronize, impave, impavid, impavidity, impavidly, impawn, impawned, impawning, impawns, impayable, impeach, impeachability, impeachable, impeachableness, impeached, impeacher, impeachers, impeaches, impeaching, impeachment, impeachments, impearl, impearled, impearling, impearls, impeccability, impeccable, impeccableness, impeccably, impeccance, impeccancy, impeccant, impeccunious, impectinate, impecuniary, impecuniosity, impecunious, impecuniously, impecuniousness, imped, impedance, impedance's, impedances, impede, impeded, impeder, impeders, impedes, impedibility, impedible, impedient, impediment, impediment's, impedimenta, impedimental, impedimentary, impediments, impeding, impedingly, impedit, impedite, impedition, impeditive, impedometer, impedor, impeevish, impel, impelled, impellent, impeller, impellers, impelling, impellor, impellors, impels, impen, impend, impended, impendence, impendency, impendent, impending, impendingly, impends, impenetrability, impenetrable, impenetrableness, impenetrably, impenetrate, impenetration, impenetrative, impenitence, impenitency, impenitent, impenitently, impenitentness, impenitible, impenitibleness, impennate, impennous, impent, impeople, imper, imperance, imperant, imperate, imperation, imperatival, imperativally, imperative, imperatively, imperativeness, imperatives, imperator, imperatorial, imperatorially, imperatorian, imperatorin, imperatorious, imperatorship, imperatory, imperatrice, imperatrix, imperceivable, imperceivableness, imperceivably, imperceived, imperceiverant, imperceptibility, imperceptible, imperceptibleness, imperceptibly, imperception, imperceptive, imperceptiveness, imperceptivity, impercipience, impercipient, imperdible, imperence, imperent, imperf, imperfect, imperfectability, imperfected, imperfectibility, imperfectible, imperfection, imperfection's, imperfections, imperfectious, imperfective, imperfectly, imperfectness, imperfects, imperforable, imperforate, imperforated, imperforates, imperforation, imperformable, imperia, imperial, imperialin, imperialine, imperialisation, imperialise, imperialised, imperialising, imperialism, imperialist, imperialist's, imperialistic, imperialistically, imperialists, imperialities, imperiality, imperialization, imperialize, imperialized, imperializing, imperially, imperialness, imperials, imperialty, imperii, imperil, imperiled, imperiling, imperilled, imperilling, imperilment, imperilments, imperils, imperious, imperiously, imperiousness, imperish, imperishability, imperishable, imperishableness, imperishably, imperite, imperium, imperiums, impermanence, impermanency, impermanent, impermanently, impermeabilities, impermeability, impermeabilization, impermeabilize, impermeable, impermeableness, impermeably, impermeated, impermeator, impermissibility, impermissible, impermissibly, impermixt, impermutable, imperperia, impers, imperscriptible, imperscrutable, imperseverant, impersonable, impersonal, impersonalisation, impersonalise, impersonalised, impersonalising, impersonalism, impersonalities, impersonality, impersonalization, impersonalize, impersonalized, impersonalizing, impersonally, impersonate, impersonated, impersonates, impersonating, impersonation, impersonations, impersonative, impersonator, impersonators, impersonatress, impersonatrix, impersonification, impersonify, impersonization, impersonize, imperspicable, imperspicuity, imperspicuous, imperspirability, imperspirable, impersuadability, impersuadable, impersuadableness, impersuasibility, impersuasible, impersuasibleness, impersuasibly, impertinacy, impertinence, impertinences, impertinencies, impertinency, impertinent, impertinently, impertinentness, impertransible, imperturbability, imperturbable, imperturbableness, imperturbably, imperturbation, imperturbed, imperverse, impervertible, impervestigable, imperviability, imperviable, imperviableness, impervial, impervious, imperviously, imperviousness, impery, impest, impestation, impester, impeticos, impetiginous, impetigo, impetigos, impetition, impetrable, impetrate, impetrated, impetrating, impetration, impetrative, impetrator, impetratory, impetre, impetulant, impetulantly, impetuosities, impetuosity, impetuoso, impetuous, impetuously, impetuousness, impeturbability, impetus, impetuses, impeyan, impf, imphee, imphees, impi, impicture, impierce, impierceable, impies, impieties, impiety, impignorate, impignorated, impignorating, impignoration, imping, impinge, impinged, impingement, impingements, impingence, impingent, impinger, impingers, impinges, impinging, impings, impinguate, impious, impiously, impiousness, impis, impish, impishly, impishness, impiteous, impitiably, implacability, implacable, implacableness, implacably, implacement, implacental, implacentalia, implacentate, implant, implantable, implantation, implanted, implanter, implanting, implants, implastic, implasticity, implate, implausibilities, implausibility, implausible, implausibleness, implausibly, impleach, implead, impleadable, impleaded, impleader, impleading, impleads, impleasing, impledge, impledged, impledges, impledging, implement, implementable, implemental, implementation, implementation's, implementational, implementations, implemented, implementer, implementers, implementiferous, implementing, implementor, implementor's, implementors, implements, implete, impletion, impletive, implex, impliability, impliable, impliably, implial, implicant, implicant's, implicants, implicate, implicated, implicately, implicateness, implicates, implicating, implication, implicational, implications, implicative, implicatively, implicativeness, implicatory, implicit, implicitly, implicitness, implicity, implied, impliedly, impliedness, implies, impling, implode, imploded, implodent, implodes, imploding, implorable, imploration, implorations, implorator, imploratory, implore, implored, implorer, implorers, implores, imploring, imploringly, imploringness, implosion, implosions, implosive, implosively, implume, implumed, implunge, impluvia, impluvium, imply, implying, impocket, impofo, impoison, impoisoner, impolarily, impolarizable, impolder, impolicies, impolicy, impolished, impolite, impolitely, impoliteness, impolitic, impolitical, impolitically, impoliticalness, impoliticly, impoliticness, impollute, imponderabilia, imponderability, imponderable, imponderableness, imponderables, imponderably, imponderous, impone, imponed, imponent, impones, imponing, impoor, impopular, impopularly, imporosity, imporous, import, importability, importable, importableness, importably, importance, importancy, important, importantly, importation, importations, imported, importee, importer, importers, importing, importless, importment, importraiture, importray, imports, importunable, importunacy, importunance, importunate, importunately, importunateness, importunator, importune, importuned, importunely, importunement, importuner, importunes, importuning, importunite, importunities, importunity, imposable, imposableness, imposal, impose, imposed, imposement, imposer, imposers, imposes, imposing, imposingly, imposingness, imposition, imposition's, impositional, impositions, impositive, impossibilia, impossibilification, impossibilism, impossibilist, impossibilitate, impossibilities, impossibility, impossible, impossibleness, impossibly, impost, imposted, imposter, imposterous, imposters, imposthumate, imposthume, imposting, impostor, impostor's, impostorism, impostors, impostorship, impostress, impostrix, impostrous, imposts, impostumate, impostumation, impostume, imposture, impostures, imposturism, imposturous, impostury, imposure, impot, impotable, impotence, impotences, impotencies, impotency, impotent, impotently, impotentness, impotents, impotionate, impound, impoundable, impoundage, impounded, impounder, impounding, impoundment, impoundments, impounds, impoverish, impoverished, impoverisher, impoverishes, impoverishing, impoverishment, impower, impowered, impowering, impowers, impracticability, impracticable, impracticableness, impracticably, impractical, impracticalities, impracticality, impractically, impracticalness, imprasa, imprecant, imprecate, imprecated, imprecates, imprecating, imprecation, imprecations, imprecator, imprecatorily, imprecators, imprecatory, imprecise, imprecisely, impreciseness, imprecision, imprecisions, impredicability, impredicable, impreg, impregn, impregnability, impregnable, impregnableness, impregnably, impregnant, impregnate, impregnated, impregnates, impregnating, impregnation, impregnations, impregnative, impregnator, impregnatory, impregned, impregning, impregns, imprejudicate, imprejudice, impremeditate, imprenable, impreparation, impresa, impresari, impresario, impresarios, impresas, imprescience, imprescribable, imprescriptibility, imprescriptible, imprescriptibly, imprese, impreses, impress, impressa, impressable, impressari, impressario, impressed, impressedly, impresser, impressers, impresses, impressibility, impressible, impressibleness, impressibly, impressing, impression, impression's, impressionability, impressionable, impressionableness, impressionably, impressional, impressionalist, impressionality, impressionally, impressionary, impressionis, impressionism, impressionist, impressionistic, impressionistically, impressionists, impressionless, impressions, impressive, impressively, impressiveness, impressment, impressments, impressor, impressure, imprest, imprestable, imprested, impresting, imprests, imprevalency, impreventability, impreventable, imprevisibility, imprevisible, imprevision, imprevu, imprimatur, imprimatura, imprimaturs, imprime, impriment, imprimery, imprimis, imprimitive, imprimitivity, imprint, imprinted, imprinter, imprinters, imprinting, imprints, imprison, imprisonable, imprisoned, imprisoner, imprisoning, imprisonment, imprisonment's, imprisonments, imprisons, improbabilities, improbability, improbabilize, improbable, improbableness, improbably, improbate, improbation, improbative, improbatory, improbity, improcreant, improcurability, improcurable, improducible, improduction, improficience, improficiency, improfitable, improgressive, improgressively, improgressiveness, improlific, improlificate, improlificical, imprompt, impromptitude, impromptu, impromptuary, impromptuist, improof, improper, improperation, improperly, improperness, impropitious, improportion, impropriate, impropriated, impropriating, impropriation, impropriator, impropriatrice, impropriatrix, improprieties, impropriety, improprium, impropry, improsperity, improsperous, improvability, improvable, improvableness, improvably, improve, improved, improvement, improvements, improver, improvers, improvership, improves, improvided, improvidence, improvident, improvidentially, improvidently, improving, improvingly, improvisate, improvisation, improvisation's, improvisational, improvisations, improvisatize, improvisator, improvisatore, improvisatorial, improvisatorially, improvisatorize, improvisatory, improvisatrice, improvise, improvised, improvisedly, improviser, improvisers, improvises, improvising, improvision, improviso, improvisor, improvisors, improvvisatore, improvvisatori, imprudence, imprudency, imprudent, imprudential, imprudently, imprudentness, imps, impship, impsonite, impuberal, impuberate, impuberty, impubic, impudence, impudencies, impudency, impudent, impudently, impudentness, impudicity, impugn, impugnability, impugnable, impugnation, impugned, impugner, impugners, impugning, impugnment, impugns, impuissance, impuissant, impulse, impulsed, impulses, impulsing, impulsion, impulsions, impulsive, impulsively, impulsiveness, impulsivity, impulsor, impulsory, impunctate, impunctual, impunctuality, impune, impunely, impunible, impunibly, impunities, impunitive, impunity, impuration, impure, impurely, impureness, impurify, impuritan, impuritanism, impurities, impurity, impurity's, impurple, imput, imputability, imputable, imputableness, imputably, imputation, imputations, imputative, imputatively, imputativeness, impute, imputed, imputedly, imputer, imputers, imputes, imputing, imputrescence, imputrescibility, imputrescible, imputrid, imputting, impv, impy, imshi, imsonic, imu, imvia, in, in't, inabilities, inability, inable, inabordable, inabstinence, inabstracted, inabusively, inaccentuated, inaccentuation, inacceptable, inaccessibility, inaccessible, inaccessibleness, inaccessibly, inaccordance, inaccordancy, inaccordant, inaccordantly, inaccuracies, inaccuracy, inaccurate, inaccurately, inaccurateness, inachid, inachoid, inacquaintance, inacquiescent, inact, inactinic, inaction, inactionist, inactions, inactivate, inactivated, inactivates, inactivating, inactivation, inactivations, inactive, inactively, inactiveness, inactivities, inactivity, inactuate, inactuation, inadaptability, inadaptable, inadaptation, inadaptive, inadept, inadeptly, inadeptness, inadequacies, inadequacy, inadequate, inadequately, inadequateness, inadequation, inadequative, inadequatively, inadherent, inadhesion, inadhesive, inadjustability, inadjustable, inadmissability, inadmissable, inadmissibility, inadmissible, inadmissibly, inadulterate, inadventurous, inadvertant, inadvertantly, inadvertence, inadvertences, inadvertencies, inadvertency, inadvertent, inadvertently, inadvertisement, inadvisability, inadvisable, inadvisableness, inadvisably, inadvisedly, inaesthetic, inaffability, inaffable, inaffably, inaffectation, inaffected, inagglutinability, inagglutinable, inaggressive, inagile, inaidable, inaidible, inaja, inalacrity, inalienability, inalienable, inalienableness, inalienably, inalimental, inalterability, inalterable, inalterableness, inalterably, inamia, inamissibility, inamissible, inamissibleness, inamorata, inamoratas, inamorate, inamoration, inamorato, inamoratos, inamour, inamovability, inamovable, inane, inanely, inaneness, inaner, inaners, inanes, inanest, inanga, inangular, inangulate, inanimadvertence, inanimate, inanimated, inanimately, inanimateness, inanimation, inanities, inanition, inanity, inantherate, inapathy, inapostate, inapparent, inapparently, inappealable, inappeasable, inappellability, inappellable, inappendiculate, inapperceptible, inappertinent, inappetence, inappetency, inappetent, inappetible, inapplicability, inapplicable, inapplicableness, inapplicably, inapplication, inapposite, inappositely, inappositeness, inappreciability, inappreciable, inappreciably, inappreciation, inappreciative, inappreciatively, inappreciativeness, inapprehensibility, inapprehensible, inapprehensibly, inapprehension, inapprehensive, inapprehensively, inapprehensiveness, inapproachability, inapproachable, inapproachably, inappropriable, inappropriableness, inappropriate, inappropriately, inappropriateness, inapropos, inapt, inaptitude, inaptly, inaptness, inaquate, inaqueous, inarable, inarch, inarched, inarches, inarching, inarculum, inarguable, inarguably, inark, inarm, inarmed, inarming, inarms, inarticulacy, inarticulate, inarticulated, inarticulately, inarticulateness, inarticulation, inartificial, inartificiality, inartificially, inartificialness, inartistic, inartistical, inartisticality, inartistically, inasmuch, inassimilable, inassimilation, inassuageable, inattackable, inattention, inattentive, inattentively, inattentiveness, inaudibility, inaudible, inaudibleness, inaudibly, inaugur, inaugural, inaugurals, inaugurate, inaugurated, inaugurates, inaugurating, inauguration, inaugurations, inaugurative, inaugurator, inauguratory, inaugurer, inaunter, inaurate, inauration, inauspicate, inauspicious, inauspiciously, inauspiciousness, inauthentic, inauthenticity, inauthoritative, inauthoritativeness, inaxon, inbardge, inbassat, inbbred, inbd, inbe, inbeaming, inbearing, inbeing, inbeings, inbending, inbent, inbetweener, inbirth, inbits, inblow, inblowing, inblown, inboard, inboards, inbody, inbond, inborn, inbound, inbounds, inbow, inbowed, inbread, inbreak, inbreaking, inbreath, inbreathe, inbreathed, inbreather, inbreathing, inbred, inbreed, inbreeder, inbreeding, inbreeds, inbring, inbringer, inbringing, inbrought, inbuilt, inburning, inburnt, inburst, inbursts, inbush, inby, inbye, inc, inca, incage, incaged, incages, incaging, incalculability, incalculable, incalculableness, incalculably, incalendared, incalescence, incalescency, incalescent, incaliculate, incalver, incalving, incameration, incamp, incan, incandent, incandesce, incandesced, incandescence, incandescency, incandescent, incandescently, incandescing, incanescent, incanous, incant, incantation, incantational, incantations, incantator, incantatory, incanton, incapabilities, incapability, incapable, incapableness, incapably, incapacious, incapaciousness, incapacitant, incapacitate, incapacitated, incapacitates, incapacitating, incapacitation, incapacitator, incapacities, incapacity, incapsulate, incapsulated, incapsulating, incapsulation, incaptivate, incarcerate, incarcerated, incarcerates, incarcerating, incarceration, incarcerations, incarcerative, incarcerator, incarcerators, incardinate, incardinated, incardinating, incardination, incarmined, incarn, incarnadine, incarnadined, incarnadines, incarnadining, incarnalise, incarnalised, incarnalising, incarnalize, incarnalized, incarnalizing, incarnant, incarnate, incarnated, incarnates, incarnating, incarnation, incarnation's, incarnational, incarnationist, incarnations, incarnative, incarve, incas, incase, incased, incasement, incases, incasing, incask, incast, incastellate, incastellated, incatenate, incatenation, incautelous, incaution, incautious, incautiously, incautiousness, incavate, incavated, incavation, incave, incavern, incavo, incede, incedingly, incelebrity, incend, incendiaries, incendiarism, incendiarist, incendiarize, incendiarized, incendiary, incendious, incendium, incendivity, incensation, incense, incensed, incenseless, incensement, incenser, incenses, incensing, incension, incensive, incensor, incensories, incensory, incensurable, incensurably, incenter, incentive, incentive's, incentively, incentives, incentor, incentre, incept, incepted, incepting, inception, inceptions, inceptive, inceptively, inceptor, inceptors, incepts, incerate, inceration, incertain, incertainty, incertitude, incessable, incessably, incessancy, incessant, incessantly, incessantness, incession, incest, incests, incestuous, incestuously, incestuousness, incgrporate, inch, inchain, inchamber, inchangeable, inchant, incharitable, incharity, inchase, inchastity, inched, incher, inches, inchest, inching, inchling, inchmeal, inchoacy, inchoant, inchoate, inchoated, inchoately, inchoateness, inchoating, inchoation, inchoative, inchoatively, inchpin, inchurch, inchworm, inchworms, incicurable, incide, incidence, incidency, incident, incident's, incidental, incidentalist, incidentally, incidentalness, incidentals, incidentless, incidently, incidents, incienso, incinerable, incinerate, incinerated, incinerates, incinerating, incineration, incinerations, incinerator, incinerators, incipience, incipiencies, incipiency, incipient, incipiently, incipit, incipits, incipitur, incircle, incirclet, incircumscriptible, incircumscription, incircumspect, incircumspection, incircumspectly, incircumspectness, incisal, incise, incised, incisely, incises, incisiform, incising, incision, incisions, incisive, incisively, incisiveness, incisor, incisorial, incisors, incisory, incisura, incisural, incisure, incisures, incitability, incitable, incitamentum, incitant, incitants, incitate, incitation, incitations, incitative, incite, incited, incitement, incitements, inciter, inciters, incites, inciting, incitingly, incitive, incitory, incitress, incivic, incivil, incivilities, incivility, incivilization, incivilly, incivism, incl, inclamation, inclasp, inclasped, inclasping, inclasps, inclaudent, inclavate, inclave, incle, inclemencies, inclemency, inclement, inclemently, inclementness, inclinable, inclinableness, inclination, inclination's, inclinational, inclinations, inclinator, inclinatorily, inclinatorium, inclinatory, incline, inclined, incliner, incliners, inclines, inclining, inclinograph, inclinometer, inclip, inclipped, inclipping, inclips, incloister, inclose, inclosed, incloser, inclosers, incloses, inclosing, inclosure, incloude, includable, include, included, includedness, includer, includes, includible, including, inclusa, incluse, inclusion, inclusion's, inclusionist, inclusions, inclusive, inclusively, inclusiveness, inclusory, inclusus, incoached, incoacted, incoagulable, incoalescence, incocted, incoercible, incoexistence, incoffin, incog, incogent, incogitability, incogitable, incogitance, incogitancy, incogitant, incogitantly, incogitative, incognita, incognite, incognitive, incognito, incognitos, incognizability, incognizable, incognizance, incognizant, incognoscent, incognoscibility, incognoscible, incogs, incoherence, incoherences, incoherencies, incoherency, incoherent, incoherentific, incoherently, incoherentness, incohering, incohesion, incohesive, incoincidence, incoincident, incolant, incolumity, incomber, incombining, incombustibility, incombustible, incombustibleness, incombustibly, incombustion, income, incomeless, incomer, incomers, incomes, incoming, incomings, incommend, incommensurability, incommensurable, incommensurableness, incommensurably, incommensurate, incommensurately, incommensurateness, incommiscibility, incommiscible, incommixed, incommodate, incommodation, incommode, incommoded, incommodement, incommodes, incommoding, incommodious, incommodiously, incommodiousness, incommodities, incommodity, incommunicability, incommunicable, incommunicableness, incommunicably, incommunicado, incommunicated, incommunicative, incommunicatively, incommunicativeness, incommutability, incommutable, incommutableness, incommutably, incompact, incompacted, incompactly, incompactness, incomparability, incomparable, incomparableness, incomparably, incompared, incompassion, incompassionate, incompassionately, incompassionateness, incompatibilities, incompatibility, incompatibility's, incompatible, incompatibleness, incompatibles, incompatibly, incompendious, incompensated, incompensation, incompetence, incompetence, incompetencies, incompetency, incompetent, incompetent's, incompetently, incompetentness, incompetents, incompetible, incompletability, incompletable, incompletableness, incomplete, incompleted, incompletely, incompleteness, incompletion, incomplex, incompliable, incompliance, incompliancies, incompliancy, incompliant, incompliantly, incomplicate, incomplying, incomportable, incomposed, incomposedly, incomposedness, incomposite, incompossibility, incompossible, incomposure, incomprehended, incomprehending, incomprehendingly, incomprehense, incomprehensibility, incomprehensible, incomprehensibleness, incomprehensiblies, incomprehensibly, incomprehension, incomprehensive, incomprehensively, incomprehensiveness, incompressable, incompressibility, incompressible, incompressibleness, incompressibly, incompt, incomputable, incomputably, inconcealable, inconceivabilities, inconceivability, inconceivable, inconceivableness, inconceivably, inconceptible, inconcernino, inconcievable, inconciliable, inconcinn, inconcinnate, inconcinnately, inconcinnity, inconcinnous, inconcludent, inconcluding, inconclusible, inconclusion, inconclusive, inconclusively, inconclusiveness, inconcoct, inconcocted, inconcoction, inconcrete, inconcurrent, inconcurring, inconcussible, incondensability, incondensable, incondensibility, incondensible, incondite, inconditional, inconditionate, inconditioned, inconducive, inconel, inconfirm, inconfirmed, inconform, inconformable, inconformably, inconformity, inconfused, inconfusedly, inconfusion, inconfutable, inconfutably, incongealable, incongealableness, incongenerous, incongenial, incongeniality, inconglomerate, incongruence, incongruent, incongruently, incongruities, incongruity, incongruous, incongruously, incongruousness, inconjoinable, inconjunct, inconnected, inconnectedness, inconnection, inconnexion, inconnu, inconnus, inconquerable, inconscience, inconscient, inconsciently, inconscionable, inconscious, inconsciously, inconsecutive, inconsecutively, inconsecutiveness, inconsequence, inconsequent, inconsequentia, inconsequential, inconsequentiality, inconsequentially, inconsequently, inconsequentness, inconsiderable, inconsiderableness, inconsiderably, inconsideracy, inconsiderate, inconsiderately, inconsiderateness, inconsideration, inconsidered, inconsistable, inconsistence, inconsistences, inconsistencies, inconsistency, inconsistency's, inconsistent, inconsistently, inconsistentness, inconsolability, inconsolable, inconsolableness, inconsolably, inconsolate, inconsolately, inconsonance, inconsonant, inconsonantly, inconspicuous, inconspicuously, inconspicuousness, inconstance, inconstancy, inconstant, inconstantly, inconstantness, inconstruable, inconsultable, inconsumable, inconsumably, inconsumed, inconsummate, inconsumptible, incontaminable, incontaminate, incontaminateness, incontemptible, incontestabilities, incontestability, incontestable, incontestableness, incontestably, incontested, incontiguous, incontinence, incontinencies, incontinency, incontinent, incontinently, incontinuity, incontinuous, incontracted, incontractile, incontraction, incontrollable, incontrollably, incontrolled, incontrovertibility, incontrovertible, incontrovertibleness, incontrovertibly, inconvenience, inconvenienced, inconveniences, inconveniencies, inconveniencing, inconveniency, inconvenient, inconvenienti, inconveniently, inconvenientness, inconversable, inconversant, inconversibility, inconverted, inconvertibilities, inconvertibility, inconvertible, inconvertibleness, inconvertibly, inconvinced, inconvincedly, inconvincibility, inconvincible, inconvincibly, incony, incoordinate, incoordinated, incoordination, incopresentability, incopresentable, incor, incord, incornished, incoronate, incoronated, incoronation, incorp, incorporable, incorporal, incorporality, incorporally, incorporalness, incorporate, incorporated, incorporatedness, incorporates, incorporating, incorporation, incorporations, incorporative, incorporator, incorporators, incorporatorship, incorporeal, incorporealism, incorporealist, incorporeality, incorporealize, incorporeally, incorporealness, incorporeities, incorporeity, incorporeous, incorpse, incorpsed, incorpses, incorpsing, incorr, incorrect, incorrection, incorrectly, incorrectness, incorrespondence, incorrespondency, incorrespondent, incorresponding, incorrigibility, incorrigible, incorrigibleness, incorrigibly, incorrodable, incorrodible, incorrosive, incorrupt, incorrupted, incorruptibilities, incorruptibility, incorruptible, incorruptibleness, incorruptibly, incorruption, incorruptive, incorruptly, incorruptness, incoup, incourse, incourteous, incourteously, incr, incra, incrash, incrassate, incrassated, incrassating, incrassation, incrassative, increasable, increasableness, increase, increased, increasedly, increaseful, increasement, increaser, increasers, increases, increasing, increasingly, increate, increately, increative, incredibilities, incredibility, incredible, incredibleness, incredibly, increditability, increditable, incredited, incredulity, incredulous, incredulously, incredulousness, increep, increeping, incremable, incremate, incremated, incremating, incremation, increment, incremental, incrementalism, incrementalist, incrementally, incrementation, incremented, incrementer, incrementing, increments, increpate, increpation, incrept, increscence, increscent, increst, incretion, incretionary, incretory, incriminate, incriminated, incriminates, incriminating, incrimination, incriminator, incriminatory, incross, incrossbred, incrosses, incrossing, incrotchet, incroyable, incruent, incruental, incruentous, incrust, incrustant, incrustate, incrustated, incrustating, incrustation, incrustations, incrustator, incrusted, incrusting, incrustive, incrustment, incrusts, incrystal, incrystallizable, inctirate, inctri, incubate, incubated, incubates, incubating, incubation, incubational, incubations, incubative, incubator, incubator's, incubatorium, incubators, incubatory, incube, incubee, incubi, incubiture, incubous, incubus, incubuses, incudal, incudate, incudectomy, incudes, incudomalleal, incudostapedial, inculcate, inculcated, inculcates, inculcating, inculcation, inculcative, inculcator, inculcatory, inculk, inculp, inculpability, inculpable, inculpableness, inculpably, inculpate, inculpated, inculpates, inculpating, inculpation, inculpative, inculpatory, incult, incultivated, incultivation, inculture, incumbant, incumbence, incumbencies, incumbency, incumbent, incumbentess, incumbently, incumbents, incumber, incumbered, incumbering, incumberment, incumbers, incumbition, incumbrance, incumbrancer, incumbrances, incunable, incunabula, incunabular, incunabulist, incunabulum, incunabuulum, incuneation, incur, incurability, incurable, incurableness, incurably, incuriosity, incurious, incuriously, incuriousness, incurment, incurrable, incurred, incurrence, incurrent, incurrer, incurring, incurs, incurse, incursion, incursionary, incursionist, incursions, incursive, incurtain, incurvate, incurvated, incurvating, incurvation, incurvature, incurve, incurved, incurves, incurving, incurvity, incurvous, incus, incuse, incused, incuses, incusing, incuss, incut, incute, incutting, incysted, ind, indaba, indabas, indaconitin, indaconitine, indagate, indagated, indagates, indagating, indagation, indagative, indagator, indagatory, indamage, indamin, indamine, indamines, indamins, indan, indane, indanthrene, indart, indazin, indazine, indazol, indazole, inde, indear, indebitatus, indebt, indebted, indebtedness, indebting, indebtment, indecence, indecencies, indecency, indecent, indecenter, indecentest, indecently, indecentness, indeciduate, indeciduous, indecimable, indecipherability, indecipherable, indecipherableness, indecipherably, indecision, indecisive, indecisively, indecisiveness, indecl, indeclinable, indeclinableness, indeclinably, indecomponible, indecomposable, indecomposableness, indecorous, indecorously, indecorousness, indecorum, indeed, indeedy, indef, indefaceable, indefatigability, indefatigable, indefatigableness, indefatigably, indefeasibility, indefeasible, indefeasibleness, indefeasibly, indefeatable, indefectibility, indefectible, indefectibly, indefective, indefensibility, indefensible, indefensibleness, indefensibly, indefensive, indeficiency, indeficient, indeficiently, indefinability, indefinable, indefinableness, indefinably, indefinite, indefinitely, indefiniteness, indefinitive, indefinitively, indefinitiveness, indefinitude, indefinity, indeflectible, indefluent, indeformable, indehiscence, indehiscent, indelectable, indelegability, indelegable, indeliberate, indeliberately, indeliberateness, indeliberation, indelibility, indelible, indelibleness, indelibly, indelicacies, indelicacy, indelicate, indelicately, indelicateness, indemnification, indemnifications, indemnificator, indemnificatory, indemnified, indemnifier, indemnifies, indemnify, indemnifying, indemnitee, indemnities, indemnitor, indemnity, indemnization, indemoniate, indemonstrability, indemonstrable, indemonstrableness, indemonstrably, indene, indenes, indenize, indent, indentation, indentation's, indentations, indented, indentedly, indentee, indenter, indenters, indentifiers, indenting, indention, indentions, indentment, indentor, indentors, indents, indenture, indentured, indentures, indentureship, indenturing, indentwise, independable, independence, independencies, independency, independent, independentism, independently, independents, independing, indeposable, indepravate, indeprehensible, indeprivability, indeprivable, inderite, inderivative, indescribabilities, indescribability, indescribable, indescribableness, indescribably, indescript, indescriptive, indesert, indesignate, indesinent, indesirable, indestructibility, indestructible, indestructibleness, indestructibly, indetectable, indeterminable, indeterminableness, indeterminably, indeterminacies, indeterminacy, indeterminacy's, indeterminancy, indeterminate, indeterminately, indeterminateness, indetermination, indeterminative, indetermined, indeterminism, indeterminist, indeterministic, indevirginate, indevote, indevoted, indevotion, indevotional, indevout, indevoutly, indevoutness, indew, index, indexable, indexation, indexed, indexer, indexers, indexes, indexical, indexically, indexing, indexless, indexlessness, indexterity, india, indiadem, indiademed, indiaman, indian, indian's, indiana, indianaite, indianan, indianans, indianapolis, indianian, indianians, indianist, indianite, indianization, indianize, indians, indiary, indic, indicable, indical, indican, indicans, indicant, indicants, indicanuria, indicatable, indicate, indicated, indicates, indicating, indication, indicational, indications, indicative, indicatively, indicativeness, indicatives, indicator, indicator's, indicators, indicatory, indicatrix, indicavit, indice, indices, indicia, indicial, indicially, indicias, indicible, indicium, indiciums, indico, indicolite, indict, indictability, indictable, indictableness, indictably, indicted, indictee, indictees, indicter, indicters, indicting, indiction, indictional, indictive, indictment, indictment's, indictments, indictor, indictors, indicts, indidicia, indienne, indies, indiferous, indifference, indifferencies, indifferency, indifferent, indifferential, indifferentiated, indifferentism, indifferentist, indifferentistic, indifferently, indifferentness, indifulvin, indifuscin, indigen, indigena, indigenae, indigenal, indigenate, indigence, indigency, indigene, indigeneity, indigenes, indigenist, indigenity, indigenous, indigenously, indigenousness, indigens, indigent, indigently, indigents, indiges, indigest, indigested, indigestedness, indigestibility, indigestibilty, indigestible, indigestibleness, indigestibly, indigestion, indigestive, indigitamenta, indigitate, indigitation, indigites, indiglucin, indign, indignance, indignancy, indignant, indignantly, indignation, indignatory, indignified, indignify, indignifying, indignities, indignity, indignly, indigo, indigoberry, indigoes, indigoferous, indigogen, indigoid, indigoids, indigometer, indigos, indigotate, indigotic, indigotin, indigotindisulphonic, indigotine, indiguria, indihumin, indii, indijbiously, indilatory, indiligence, indimensible, indimensional, indiminishable, indimple, indin, indirect, indirected, indirecting, indirection, indirections, indirectly, indirectness, indirects, indirubin, indirubine, indiscernibility, indiscernible, indiscernibleness, indiscernibly, indiscerpible, indiscerptibility, indiscerptible, indiscerptibleness, indiscerptibly, indisciplinable, indiscipline, indisciplined, indiscoverable, indiscoverably, indiscovered, indiscovery, indiscreet, indiscreetly, indiscreetness, indiscrete, indiscretely, indiscretion, indiscretionary, indiscretions, indiscrimanently, indiscriminantly, indiscriminate, indiscriminated, indiscriminately, indiscriminateness, indiscriminating, indiscriminatingly, indiscrimination, indiscriminative, indiscriminatively, indiscriminatory, indiscussable, indiscussed, indiscussible, indish, indispellable, indispensabilities, indispensability, indispensable, indispensableness, indispensably, indispensible, indispersed, indispose, indisposed, indisposedness, indisposing, indisposition, indispositions, indisputability, indisputable, indisputableness, indisputably, indisputed, indissipable, indissociable, indissociably, indissolubility, indissoluble, indissolubleness, indissolubly, indissolute, indissolvability, indissolvable, indissolvableness, indissolvably, indissuadable, indissuadably, indistance, indistant, indistinct, indistinctible, indistinction, indistinctive, indistinctively, indistinctiveness, indistinctly, indistinctness, indistinguishability, indistinguishable, indistinguishableness, indistinguishably, indistinguished, indistinguishing, indistortable, indistributable, indisturbable, indisturbance, indisturbed, inditch, indite, indited, inditement, inditer, inditers, indites, inditing, indium, indiums, indiv, indivertible, indivertibly, individ, individable, individed, individua, individual, individual's, individualisation, individualise, individualised, individualiser, individualising, individualism, individualist, individualistic, individualistically, individualists, individualities, individuality, individualization, individualize, individualized, individualizer, individualizes, individualizing, individualizingly, individually, individuals, individuate, individuated, individuates, individuating, individuation, individuative, individuator, individuity, individuous, individuum, individuums, indivinable, indivinity, indivisibility, indivisible, indivisibleness, indivisibly, indivisim, indivision, indn, indochina, indochinese, indocibility, indocible, indocibleness, indocile, indocilely, indocility, indoctrinate, indoctrinated, indoctrinates, indoctrinating, indoctrination, indoctrinations, indoctrinator, indoctrine, indoctrinization, indoctrinize, indoctrinized, indoctrinizing, indogen, indogenide, indoin, indol, indole, indolence, indolent, indolently, indoles, indolin, indoline, indologenous, indoloid, indols, indolyl, indomable, indomethacin, indomitability, indomitable, indomitableness, indomitably, indone, indonesia, indonesian, indonesians, indoor, indoors, indophenin, indophenol, indorsable, indorsation, indorse, indorsed, indorsee, indorsees, indorsement, indorser, indorsers, indorses, indorsing, indorsor, indorsors, indow, indowed, indowing, indows, indoxyl, indoxylic, indoxyls, indoxylsulphuric, indraft, indrafts, indrape, indraught, indrawal, indrawing, indrawn, indrench, indri, indris, indubious, indubiously, indubitability, indubitable, indubitableness, indubitably, indubitate, indubitatively, induc, induce, induceable, induced, inducedly, inducement, inducement's, inducements, inducer, inducers, induces, induciae, inducibility, inducible, inducing, inducive, induct, inductance, inductances, inducted, inductee, inductees, inducteous, inductile, inductility, inducting, induction, induction's, inductional, inductionally, inductionless, inductions, inductive, inductively, inductiveness, inductivity, inductometer, inductophone, inductor, inductor's, inductorium, inductors, inductory, inductoscope, inductothermy, inductril, inducts, indue, indued, induement, indues, induing, induism, indulge, indulgeable, indulged, indulgement, indulgence, indulgence's, indulgenced, indulgences, indulgencies, indulgencing, indulgency, indulgent, indulgential, indulgentially, indulgently, indulgentness, indulger, indulgers, indulges, indulgiate, indulging, indulgingly, indulin, induline, indulines, indulins, indult, indulto, indults, indument, indumenta, indumentum, indumentums, induna, induplicate, induplication, induplicative, indurable, indurance, indurate, indurated, indurates, indurating, induration, indurations, indurative, indure, indurite, indus, indusia, indusial, indusiate, indusiated, indusiform, indusioid, indusium, industrial, industrialisation, industrialise, industrialised, industrialising, industrialism, industrialist, industrialist's, industrialists, industrialization, industrialize, industrialized, industrializes, industrializing, industrially, industrialness, industrials, industries, industrious, industriously, industriousness, industrochemical, industry, industry's, industrys, indutive, induviae, induvial, induviate, indwell, indweller, indwelling, indwellingness, indwells, indwelt, indy, indyl, indylic, inearth, inearthed, inearthing, inearths, inebriacy, inebriant, inebriate, inebriated, inebriates, inebriating, inebriation, inebriative, inebriety, inebrious, ineconomic, ineconomy, inedibility, inedible, inedita, inedited, ineducabilian, ineducability, ineducable, ineducation, ineffability, ineffable, ineffableness, ineffably, ineffaceability, ineffaceable, ineffaceably, ineffectible, ineffectibly, ineffective, ineffectively, ineffectiveness, ineffectual, ineffectuality, ineffectually, ineffectualness, ineffervescence, ineffervescent, ineffervescibility, ineffervescible, inefficacious, inefficaciously, inefficaciousness, inefficacity, inefficacy, inefficience, inefficiencies, inefficiency, inefficient, inefficiently, ineffulgent, inegalitarian, inelaborate, inelaborated, inelaborately, inelastic, inelastically, inelasticate, inelasticity, inelegance, inelegances, inelegancies, inelegancy, inelegant, inelegantly, ineligibility, ineligible, ineligibleness, ineligibles, ineligibly, ineliminable, ineloquence, ineloquent, ineloquently, ineluctability, ineluctable, ineluctably, ineludible, ineludibly, inembryonate, inemendable, inemotivity, inemulous, inenarrability, inenarrable, inenarrably, inenergetic, inenubilable, inenucleable, inept, ineptitude, ineptly, ineptness, inequable, inequal, inequalitarian, inequalities, inequality, inequally, inequalness, inequation, inequiaxial, inequicostate, inequidistant, inequigranular, inequilateral, inequilaterally, inequilibrium, inequilobate, inequilobed, inequipotential, inequipotentiality, inequitable, inequitableness, inequitably, inequitate, inequities, inequity, inequivalent, inequivalve, inequivalved, inequivalvular, ineradicability, ineradicable, ineradicableness, ineradicably, inerasable, inerasableness, inerasably, inerasible, inergetic, inerm, inermous, inerrability, inerrable, inerrableness, inerrably, inerrancy, inerrant, inerrantly, inerratic, inerring, inerringly, inerroneous, inert, inertance, inertia, inertiae, inertial, inertially, inertias, inertion, inertly, inertness, inerts, inerubescent, inerudite, ineruditely, inerudition, inescapable, inescapableness, inescapably, inescate, inescation, inesculent, inescutcheon, inesite, inessential, inessentiality, inessive, inesthetic, inestimability, inestimable, inestimableness, inestimably, inestivation, inethical, ineunt, ineuphonious, inevadible, inevadibly, inevaporable, inevasible, inevasibleness, inevasibly, inevidence, inevident, inevitabilities, inevitability, inevitable, inevitableness, inevitably, inexact, inexacting, inexactitude, inexactly, inexactness, inexcellence, inexcitability, inexcitable, inexcitableness, inexcitably, inexclusive, inexclusively, inexcommunicable, inexcusability, inexcusable, inexcusableness, inexcusably, inexecrable, inexecutable, inexecution, inexertion, inexhalable, inexhaust, inexhausted, inexhaustedly, inexhaustibility, inexhaustible, inexhaustibleness, inexhaustibly, inexhaustive, inexhaustively, inexhaustless, inexigible, inexist, inexistence, inexistency, inexistent, inexorability, inexorable, inexorableness, inexorably, inexpansible, inexpansive, inexpectable, inexpectance, inexpectancy, inexpectant, inexpectation, inexpected, inexpectedly, inexpectedness, inexpedience, inexpediency, inexpedient, inexpediently, inexpensive, inexpensively, inexpensiveness, inexperience, inexperienced, inexpert, inexpertly, inexpertness, inexperts, inexpiable, inexpiableness, inexpiably, inexpiate, inexplainable, inexpleble, inexplicability, inexplicable, inexplicableness, inexplicables, inexplicably, inexplicit, inexplicitly, inexplicitness, inexplorable, inexplosive, inexportable, inexposable, inexposure, inexpress, inexpressibilities, inexpressibility, inexpressible, inexpressibleness, inexpressibles, inexpressibly, inexpressive, inexpressively, inexpressiveness, inexpugnability, inexpugnable, inexpugnableness, inexpugnably, inexpungeable, inexpungibility, inexpungible, inexsuperable, inextant, inextended, inextensibility, inextensible, inextensile, inextension, inextensional, inextensive, inexterminable, inextinct, inextinguible, inextinguishability, inextinguishable, inextinguishables, inextinguishably, inextinguished, inextirpable, inextirpableness, inextricability, inextricable, inextricableness, inextricably, ineye, inf, inface, infair, infall, infallibilism, infallibilist, infallibility, infallible, infallibleness, infallibly, infallid, infalling, infalsificable, infamation, infamatory, infame, infamed, infamia, infamies, infamiliar, infamiliarity, infamize, infamized, infamizing, infamonize, infamous, infamously, infamousness, infamy, infancies, infancy, infand, infandous, infang, infanglement, infangthef, infangthief, infans, infant, infant's, infanta, infantado, infantas, infante, infantes, infanthood, infanticidal, infanticide, infanticides, infantile, infantilism, infantility, infantilize, infantine, infantive, infantlike, infantly, infantries, infantry, infantryman, infantrymen, infants, infarce, infarct, infarctate, infarcted, infarction, infarctions, infarcts, infare, infares, infashionable, infatigable, infatuate, infatuated, infatuatedly, infatuatedness, infatuates, infatuating, infatuation, infatuations, infatuator, infauna, infaunae, infaunal, infaunas, infaust, infausting, infeasibility, infeasible, infeasibleness, infect, infectant, infected, infectedness, infecter, infecters, infectible, infecting, infection, infection's, infectionist, infections, infectious, infectiously, infectiousness, infective, infectiveness, infectivity, infector, infectors, infectress, infects, infectum, infectuous, infecund, infecundity, infeeble, infeed, infeft, infefting, infeftment, infeijdation, infelicific, infelicities, infelicitous, infelicitously, infelicitousness, infelicity, infelonious, infelt, infeminine, infenible, infeodation, infeof, infeoff, infeoffed, infeoffing, infeoffment, infeoffs, infer, inferable, inferably, inference, inference's, inferences, inferent, inferential, inferentialism, inferentialist, inferentially, inferial, inferible, inferior, inferior's, inferiorism, inferiorities, inferiority, inferiorize, inferiorly, inferiorness, inferiors, infern, infernal, infernalism, infernality, infernalize, infernally, infernalry, infernalship, inferno, inferno's, infernos, inferoanterior, inferobranch, inferobranchiate, inferofrontal, inferolateral, inferomedian, inferoposterior, inferred, inferrer, inferrers, inferribility, inferrible, inferring, inferringly, infers, infertile, infertilely, infertileness, infertility, infest, infestant, infestation, infestations, infested, infester, infesters, infesting, infestious, infestive, infestivity, infestment, infests, infeudate, infeudation, infibulate, infibulation, inficete, infidel, infidel's, infidelic, infidelical, infidelism, infidelistic, infidelities, infidelity, infidelize, infidelly, infidels, infield, infielder, infielders, infields, infieldsman, infight, infighter, infighters, infighting, infigured, infile, infill, infilling, infilm, infilter, infiltered, infiltering, infiltrate, infiltrated, infiltrates, infiltrating, infiltration, infiltrations, infiltrative, infiltrator, infiltrators, infima, infimum, infin, infinitant, infinitarily, infinitary, infinitate, infinitated, infinitating, infinitation, infinite, infinitely, infiniteness, infinites, infinitesimal, infinitesimalism, infinitesimality, infinitesimally, infinitesimalness, infinitesimals, infiniteth, infinities, infinitieth, infinitival, infinitivally, infinitive, infinitive's, infinitively, infinitives, infinitize, infinitized, infinitizing, infinitude, infinitum, infinituple, infinity, infirm, infirmable, infirmarer, infirmaress, infirmarian, infirmaries, infirmary, infirmate, infirmation, infirmative, infirmatory, infirmed, infirming, infirmities, infirmity, infirmly, infirmness, infirms, infissile, infit, infitter, infix, infixal, infixation, infixed, infixes, infixing, infixion, infixions, infl, inflamable, inflame, inflamed, inflamedly, inflamedness, inflamer, inflamers, inflames, inflaming, inflamingly, inflammabilities, inflammability, inflammable, inflammableness, inflammably, inflammation, inflammations, inflammative, inflammatorily, inflammatory, inflatable, inflate, inflated, inflatedly, inflatedness, inflater, inflaters, inflates, inflatile, inflating, inflatingly, inflation, inflationary, inflationism, inflationist, inflationists, inflations, inflative, inflator, inflators, inflatus, inflect, inflected, inflectedness, inflecting, inflection, inflectional, inflectionally, inflectionless, inflections, inflective, inflector, inflects, inflesh, inflex, inflexed, inflexibility, inflexible, inflexibleness, inflexibly, inflexion, inflexional, inflexionally, inflexionless, inflexive, inflexure, inflict, inflictable, inflicted, inflicter, inflicting, infliction, inflictions, inflictive, inflictor, inflicts, inflight, inflood, inflooding, inflorescence, inflorescent, inflow, inflowering, inflowing, inflows, influe, influencability, influencable, influence, influenceabilities, influenceability, influenceable, influenced, influencer, influences, influencing, influencive, influent, influential, influentiality, influentially, influentialness, influents, influenza, influenzal, influenzalike, influenzas, influenzic, influx, influxable, influxes, influxible, influxibly, influxion, influxionism, influxious, influxive, info, infold, infolded, infolder, infolders, infolding, infoldment, infolds, infoliate, inforgiveable, inform, informable, informal, informalism, informalist, informalities, informality, informalize, informally, informalness, informant, informant's, informants, informatics, information, informational, informative, informatively, informativeness, informatory, informatus, informed, informedly, informer, informers, informidable, informing, informingly, informity, informous, informs, infortiate, infortitude, infortunate, infortunately, infortunateness, infortune, infortunity, infos, infound, infra, infrabasal, infrabestial, infrabranchial, infrabuccal, infracanthal, infracaudal, infracelestial, infracentral, infracephalic, infraclavicle, infraclavicular, infraclusion, infraconscious, infracortical, infracostal, infracostalis, infracotyloid, infract, infracted, infractible, infracting, infraction, infractions, infractor, infracts, infradentary, infradiaphragmatic, infragenual, infraglacial, infraglenoid, infraglottic, infragrant, infragular, infrahuman, infrahyoid, infralabial, infralapsarian, infralapsarianism, infralinear, infralittoral, inframammary, inframammillary, inframandibular, inframarginal, inframaxillary, inframedian, inframercurial, inframercurian, inframolecular, inframontane, inframundane, infranatural, infranaturalism, infranchise, infrangibility, infrangible, infrangibleness, infrangibly, infranodal, infranuclear, infraoccipital, infraocclusion, infraocular, infraoral, infraorbital, infraordinary, infrapapillary, infrapatellar, infraperipherial, infrapose, infraposed, infraposing, infraposition, infraprotein, infrapubian, infraradular, infrared, infrareds, infrarenal, infrarenally, infrarimal, infrascapular, infrascapularis, infrascientific, infrasonic, infrasonics, infraspecific, infraspinal, infraspinate, infraspinatus, infraspinous, infrastapedial, infrasternal, infrastigmatal, infrastipular, infrastructure, infrastructures, infrasutral, infratemporal, infraterrene, infraterritorial, infrathoracic, infratonsillar, infratracheal, infratrochanteric, infratrochlear, infratubal, infraturbinal, infravaginal, infraventral, infree, infrequence, infrequency, infrequent, infrequentcy, infrequently, infrigidate, infrigidation, infrigidative, infringe, infringed, infringement, infringement's, infringements, infringer, infringers, infringes, infringible, infringing, infructiferous, infructuose, infructuosity, infructuous, infructuously, infrugal, infrunite, infrustrable, infrustrably, infula, infulae, infumate, infumated, infumation, infume, infund, infundibula, infundibular, infundibulate, infundibuliform, infundibulum, infuneral, infuriate, infuriated, infuriatedly, infuriately, infuriates, infuriating, infuriatingly, infuriation, infuscate, infuscated, infuscation, infuse, infused, infusedly, infuser, infusers, infuses, infusibility, infusible, infusibleness, infusile, infusing, infusion, infusionism, infusionist, infusions, infusive, infusoria, infusorial, infusorian, infusories, infusoriform, infusorioid, infusorium, infusory, ing, ingallantry, ingan, ingang, ingangs, ingannation, ingate, ingates, ingather, ingathered, ingatherer, ingathering, ingathers, ingeldable, ingem, ingeminate, ingeminated, ingeminating, ingemination, ingender, ingene, ingenerability, ingenerable, ingenerably, ingenerate, ingenerated, ingenerately, ingenerating, ingeneration, ingenerative, ingeniary, ingeniate, ingenie, ingenier, ingenio, ingeniosity, ingenious, ingeniously, ingeniousness, ingenit, ingenital, ingenite, ingent, ingenu, ingenue, ingenues, ingenuities, ingenuity, ingenuous, ingenuously, ingenuousness, ingeny, ingerminate, ingest, ingesta, ingestant, ingested, ingester, ingestible, ingesting, ingestion, ingestive, ingests, inghamite, ingine, ingirt, ingiver, ingiving, ingle, inglenook, ingles, inglesa, ingleside, inglobate, inglobe, inglobed, inglobing, inglorious, ingloriously, ingloriousness, inglu, inglut, inglutition, ingluvial, ingluvies, ingluviitis, ingluvious, ingnue, ingoing, ingoingness, ingorge, ingot, ingoted, ingoting, ingotman, ingotmen, ingots, ingracious, ingraft, ingraftation, ingrafted, ingrafter, ingrafting, ingraftment, ingrafts, ingrain, ingrained, ingrainedly, ingrainedness, ingraining, ingrains, ingrammaticism, ingramness, ingrandize, ingrapple, ingrate, ingrateful, ingratefully, ingratefulness, ingrately, ingrates, ingratiate, ingratiated, ingratiates, ingratiating, ingratiatingly, ingratiation, ingratiatory, ingratitude, ingrave, ingravescence, ingravescent, ingravidate, ingravidation, ingreat, ingredience, ingredient, ingredient's, ingredients, ingress, ingresses, ingression, ingressive, ingressiveness, ingreve, ingross, ingrossing, ingroup, ingroups, ingrow, ingrowing, ingrown, ingrownness, ingrowth, ingrowths, ingruent, inguen, inguilty, inguinal, inguinoabdominal, inguinocrural, inguinocutaneous, inguinodynia, inguinolabial, inguinoscrotal, ingulf, ingulfed, ingulfing, ingulfment, ingulfs, ingurgitate, ingurgitated, ingurgitating, ingurgitation, ingustable, inhabile, inhabit, inhabitability, inhabitable, inhabitance, inhabitancies, inhabitancy, inhabitant, inhabitant's, inhabitants, inhabitate, inhabitation, inhabitative, inhabitativeness, inhabited, inhabitedness, inhabiter, inhabiting, inhabitiveness, inhabitress, inhabits, inhalant, inhalants, inhalation, inhalational, inhalations, inhalator, inhalators, inhale, inhaled, inhalement, inhalent, inhaler, inhalers, inhales, inhaling, inhame, inhance, inharmonic, inharmonical, inharmonious, inharmoniously, inharmoniousness, inharmony, inhaul, inhauler, inhaulers, inhauls, inhaust, inhaustion, inhearse, inheaven, inhelde, inhell, inhere, inhered, inherence, inherencies, inherency, inherent, inherently, inheres, inhering, inherit, inheritabilities, inheritability, inheritable, inheritableness, inheritably, inheritage, inheritance, inheritance's, inheritances, inherited, inheriting, inheritor, inheritor's, inheritors, inheritress, inheritress's, inheritresses, inheritrice, inheritrices, inheritrix, inherits, inherle, inhesion, inhesions, inhesive, inhiate, inhibit, inhibitable, inhibited, inhibiter, inhibiting, inhibition, inhibition's, inhibitionist, inhibitions, inhibitive, inhibitor, inhibitors, inhibitory, inhibits, inhive, inhold, inholder, inholding, inhomogeneities, inhomogeneity, inhomogeneous, inhomogeneously, inhonest, inhoop, inhospitable, inhospitableness, inhospitably, inhospitality, inhuman, inhumane, inhumanely, inhumaneness, inhumanism, inhumanities, inhumanity, inhumanize, inhumanly, inhumanness, inhumate, inhumation, inhumationist, inhume, inhumed, inhumer, inhumers, inhumes, inhuming, inhumorous, inhumorously, inia, inial, inidoneity, inidoneous, inimaginable, inimicability, inimicable, inimical, inimicality, inimically, inimicalness, inimicitious, inimicous, inimitability, inimitable, inimitableness, inimitably, inimitative, iniome, iniomous, inion, inique, iniquitable, iniquitably, iniquities, iniquitous, iniquitously, iniquitousness, iniquity, iniquity's, iniquous, inirritability, inirritable, inirritably, inirritant, inirritative, inisle, inissuable, init, inital, initial, initialed, initialer, initialing, initialisation, initialise, initialised, initialism, initialist, initialization, initialization's, initializations, initialize, initialized, initializer, initializers, initializes, initializing, initialled, initialler, initialling, initially, initialness, initials, initiant, initiary, initiate, initiated, initiates, initiating, initiation, initiations, initiative, initiative's, initiatively, initiatives, initiator, initiator's, initiatorily, initiators, initiatory, initiatress, initiatrices, initiatrix, initiatrixes, initio, inition, initis, initive, inject, injectable, injectant, injected, injecting, injection, injection's, injections, injective, injector, injectors, injects, injelly, injoin, injoint, injucundity, injudicial, injudicially, injudicious, injudiciously, injudiciousness, injunct, injunction, injunction's, injunctions, injunctive, injunctively, injurable, injure, injured, injuredly, injuredness, injurer, injurers, injures, injuria, injuries, injuring, injurious, injuriously, injuriousness, injury, injury's, injust, injustice, injustice's, injustices, injustifiable, injustly, ink, inkberries, inkberry, inkblot, inkblots, inkbush, inked, inken, inker, inkers, inket, inkfish, inkholder, inkhorn, inkhornism, inkhornist, inkhornize, inkhornizer, inkhorns, inkie, inkier, inkies, inkiest, inkindle, inkiness, inkinesses, inking, inkings, inkish, inkle, inkles, inkless, inklike, inkling, inkling's, inklings, inkmaker, inkmaking, inkman, inknit, inknot, inkos, inkosi, inkpot, inkpots, inkroot, inks, inkshed, inkslinger, inkslinging, inkstain, inkstand, inkstandish, inkstands, inkster, inkstone, inkweed, inkwell, inkwells, inkwood, inkwoods, inkwriter, inky, inlace, inlaced, inlaces, inlacing, inlagary, inlagation, inlaid, inlaik, inlake, inland, inlander, inlanders, inlandish, inlands, inlapidate, inlapidatee, inlard, inlaut, inlaw, inlawry, inlay, inlayed, inlayer, inlayers, inlaying, inlays, inleague, inleagued, inleaguer, inleaguing, inleak, inleakage, inless, inlet, inlet's, inlets, inletting, inlier, inliers, inlighten, inlike, inline, inlook, inlooker, inlooking, inly, inlying, inmate, inmate's, inmates, inmeat, inmeats, inmesh, inmeshed, inmeshes, inmeshing, inmew, inmigrant, inmixture, inmore, inmost, inmprovidence, inn, innage, innards, innascibility, innascible, innate, innately, innateness, innatism, innative, innatural, innaturality, innaturally, innavigable, inne, inned, inneity, inner, innerly, innermore, innermost, innermostly, innerness, inners, innersole, innerspring, innervate, innervated, innervates, innervating, innervation, innervational, innervations, innerve, innerved, innerves, innerving, inness, innest, innet, innholder, inning, innings, inninmorite, innitency, innkeeper, innkeepers, innless, innobedient, innocence, innocencies, innocency, innocent, innocenter, innocentest, innocently, innocentness, innocents, innocuity, innoculate, innoculated, innoculating, innoculation, innocuous, innocuously, innocuousness, innodate, innominability, innominable, innominables, innominata, innominate, innominatum, innomine, innovant, innovate, innovated, innovates, innovating, innovation, innovation's, innovational, innovationist, innovations, innovative, innovatively, innovativeness, innovator, innovators, innovatory, innoxious, innoxiously, innoxiousness, inns, innuate, innubilous, innuendo, innuendoed, innuendoes, innuendoing, innuendos, innumerability, innumerable, innumerableness, innumerably, innumerate, innumerous, innutrient, innutrition, innutritious, innutritiousness, innutritive, innyard, inobedience, inobedient, inobediently, inoblast, inobnoxious, inobscurable, inobservable, inobservance, inobservancy, inobservant, inobservantly, inobservantness, inobservation, inobtainable, inobtrusive, inobtrusively, inobtrusiveness, inobvious, inocarpin, inoccupation, inochondritis, inochondroma, inocula, inoculability, inoculable, inoculant, inocular, inoculate, inoculated, inoculates, inoculating, inoculation, inoculations, inoculative, inoculativity, inoculator, inoculum, inoculums, inocystoma, inocyte, inodiate, inodorate, inodorous, inodorously, inodorousness, inoepithelioma, inoffending, inoffensive, inoffensively, inoffensiveness, inofficial, inofficially, inofficiosity, inofficious, inofficiously, inofficiousness, inogen, inogenesis, inogenic, inogenous, inoglia, inohymenitic, inolith, inoma, inominous, inomyoma, inomyositis, inomyxoma, inone, inoneuroma, inoperability, inoperable, inoperation, inoperational, inoperative, inoperativeness, inopercular, inoperculate, inopinable, inopinate, inopinately, inopine, inopportune, inopportunely, inopportuneness, inopportunism, inopportunist, inopportunity, inoppressive, inoppugnable, inopulent, inorb, inorderly, inordinacy, inordinance, inordinancy, inordinary, inordinate, inordinately, inordinateness, inordination, inorg, inorganic, inorganical, inorganically, inorganity, inorganizable, inorganization, inorganized, inoriginate, inornate, inornateness, inorthography, inosclerosis, inoscopy, inosculate, inosculated, inosculating, inosculation, inosic, inosilicate, inosin, inosine, inosinic, inosite, inosites, inositol, inositols, inostensible, inostensibly, inotropic, inower, inoxidability, inoxidable, inoxidizable, inoxidize, inoxidized, inoxidizing, inparabola, inpardonable, inparfit, inpatient, inpatients, inpayment, inpensioner, inphase, inphases, inpolygon, inpolyhedron, inponderable, inport, inpour, inpoured, inpouring, inpours, inpush, input, input's, input/output, inputfile, inputs, inputted, inputting, inqilab, inquaintance, inquartation, inquest, inquests, inquestual, inquiet, inquietation, inquieted, inquieting, inquietly, inquietness, inquiets, inquietude, inquietudes, inquiline, inquilinism, inquilinity, inquilinous, inquinate, inquinated, inquinating, inquination, inquirable, inquirance, inquirant, inquiration, inquire, inquired, inquirendo, inquirent, inquirer, inquirers, inquires, inquiries, inquiring, inquiringly, inquiry, inquiry's, inquisible, inquisit, inquisite, inquisition, inquisition's, inquisitional, inquisitionist, inquisitions, inquisitive, inquisitively, inquisitiveness, inquisitor, inquisitorial, inquisitorially, inquisitorialness, inquisitorious, inquisitors, inquisitorship, inquisitory, inquisitress, inquisitrix, inquisiturient, inracinate, inradii, inradius, inradiuses, inrail, inreality, inregister, inrigged, inrigger, inrighted, inring, inro, inroad, inroader, inroads, inrol, inroll, inrolling, inrooted, inrub, inrun, inrunning, inruption, inrush, inrushes, inrushing, ins, insabbatist, insack, insafety, insagacity, insalivate, insalivated, insalivating, insalivation, insalubrious, insalubriously, insalubriousness, insalubrities, insalubrity, insalutary, insalvability, insalvable, insame, insanable, insane, insanely, insaneness, insaner, insanest, insaniate, insanie, insanify, insanitariness, insanitary, insanitation, insanities, insanity, insapiency, insapient, insapory, insatiability, insatiable, insatiableness, insatiably, insatiate, insatiated, insatiately, insatiateness, insatiety, insatisfaction, insatisfactorily, insaturable, inscape, inscenation, inscibile, inscience, inscient, inscious, insconce, inscribable, inscribableness, inscribe, inscribed, inscriber, inscribers, inscribes, inscribing, inscript, inscriptible, inscription, inscription's, inscriptional, inscriptioned, inscriptionist, inscriptionless, inscriptions, inscriptive, inscriptively, inscriptured, inscroll, inscrolled, inscrolling, inscrolls, inscrutability, inscrutable, inscrutableness, inscrutables, inscrutably, insculp, insculped, insculping, insculps, insculpture, insculptured, inscutcheon, insea, inseam, inseamer, inseams, insearch, insecable, insect, insect's, insecta, insectan, insectaria, insectaries, insectarium, insectariums, insectary, insectation, insectean, insected, insecticidal, insecticidally, insecticide, insecticides, insectiferous, insectiform, insectifuge, insectile, insectine, insection, insectival, insectivora, insectivore, insectivorous, insectivory, insectlike, insectmonger, insectologer, insectologist, insectology, insectproof, insects, insecure, insecurely, insecureness, insecurities, insecurity, insecution, insee, inseeing, inseer, inselberg, inselberge, inseminate, inseminated, inseminates, inseminating, insemination, inseminations, inseminator, inseminators, insenescible, insensate, insensately, insensateness, insense, insensed, insensibilities, insensibility, insensibilization, insensibilize, insensibilizer, insensible, insensibleness, insensibly, insensing, insensitive, insensitively, insensitiveness, insensitivities, insensitivity, insensuous, insentience, insentiency, insentient, insep, inseparability, inseparable, inseparableness, inseparables, inseparably, inseparate, inseparately, insequent, insert, insertable, inserted, inserter, inserters, inserting, insertion, insertion's, insertional, insertions, insertive, inserts, inserve, inserviceable, inservient, insession, insessor, insessores, insessorial, inset, insets, insetted, insetter, insetters, insetting, inseverable, inseverably, inshade, inshave, insheath, insheathe, insheathed, insheathing, insheaths, inshell, inshining, inship, inshoe, inshoot, inshore, inshrine, inshrined, inshrines, inshrining, inside, insident, insider, insiders, insides, insidiate, insidiation, insidiator, insidiosity, insidious, insidiously, insidiousness, insight, insight's, insighted, insightful, insightfully, insights, insigne, insignes, insignia, insignias, insignificance, insignificancies, insignificancy, insignificant, insignificantly, insignificative, insignisigne, insignment, insimplicity, insimulate, insincere, insincerely, insincerities, insincerity, insinew, insinking, insinuant, insinuate, insinuated, insinuates, insinuating, insinuatingly, insinuation, insinuations, insinuative, insinuatively, insinuativeness, insinuator, insinuators, insinuatory, insinuendo, insipid, insipidities, insipidity, insipidly, insipidness, insipience, insipient, insipiently, insist, insisted, insistence, insistencies, insistency, insistent, insistently, insister, insisters, insisting, insistingly, insistive, insists, insisture, insistuvree, insite, insitiency, insition, insititious, insnare, insnared, insnarement, insnarer, insnarers, insnares, insnaring, insobriety, insociability, insociable, insociableness, insociably, insocial, insocially, insociate, insofar, insol, insolate, insolated, insolates, insolating, insolation, insole, insolence, insolency, insolent, insolently, insolentness, insolents, insoles, insolid, insolidity, insolite, insolubilities, insolubility, insolubilization, insolubilize, insolubilized, insolubilizing, insoluble, insolubleness, insolubly, insolvability, insolvable, insolvably, insolvence, insolvencies, insolvency, insolvent, insomnia, insomniac, insomniacs, insomnias, insomnious, insomnolence, insomnolency, insomnolent, insomnolently, insomuch, insonorous, insooth, insorb, insorbent, insordid, insouciance, insouciant, insouciantly, insoul, insouled, insouling, insouls, insp, inspake, inspan, inspanned, inspanning, inspans, inspeak, inspeaking, inspect, inspectability, inspectable, inspected, inspecting, inspectingly, inspection, inspection's, inspectional, inspectioneer, inspections, inspective, inspector, inspector's, inspectoral, inspectorate, inspectorial, inspectors, inspectorship, inspectress, inspectrix, inspects, insperge, insperse, inspeximus, inspheration, insphere, insphered, inspheres, insphering, inspinne, inspirability, inspirable, inspirant, inspirate, inspiration, inspiration's, inspirational, inspirationalism, inspirationally, inspirationist, inspirations, inspirative, inspirator, inspiratory, inspiratrix, inspire, inspired, inspiredly, inspirer, inspirers, inspires, inspiring, inspiringly, inspirit, inspirited, inspiriter, inspiriting, inspiritingly, inspiritment, inspirits, inspirometer, inspissant, inspissate, inspissated, inspissating, inspissation, inspissator, inspissosis, inspoke, inspoken, inspreith, inst, instabilities, instability, instable, instal, install, installant, installation, installation's, installations, installed, installer, installers, installing, installment, installment's, installments, installs, instalment, instals, instamp, instance, instanced, instances, instancies, instancing, instancy, instanding, instant, instantaneity, instantaneous, instantaneously, instantaneousness, instanter, instantial, instantiate, instantiated, instantiates, instantiating, instantiation, instantiation's, instantiations, instantly, instantness, instants, instar, instarred, instarring, instars, instate, instated, instatement, instates, instating, instaurate, instauration, instaurator, instead, instealing, insteam, insteep, instellatinn, instellation, instep, insteps, instigant, instigate, instigated, instigates, instigating, instigatingly, instigation, instigative, instigator, instigator's, instigators, instigatrix, instil, instill, instillation, instillator, instillatory, instilled, instiller, instillers, instilling, instillment, instills, instilment, instils, instimulate, instinct, instinct's, instinction, instinctive, instinctively, instinctiveness, instinctivist, instinctivity, instincts, instinctual, instinctually, instipulate, institor, institorial, institorian, institory, institue, institute, instituted, instituter, instituters, institutes, instituting, institution, institutional, institutionalisation, institutionalise, institutionalised, institutionalising, institutionalism, institutionalist, institutionalists, institutionality, institutionalization, institutionalize, institutionalized, institutionalizes, institutionalizing, institutionally, institutionary, institutionize, institutions, institutive, institutively, institutor, institutors, institutress, institutrix, instonement, instop, instore, instr, instratified, instreaming, instrengthen, instressed, instroke, instrokes, instruct, instructable, instructed, instructedly, instructedness, instructer, instructible, instructing, instruction, instruction's, instructional, instructionary, instructions, instructive, instructively, instructiveness, instructor, instructor's, instructorial, instructorless, instructors, instructorship, instructorships, instructress, instructs, instrument, instrumental, instrumentalism, instrumentalist, instrumentalist's, instrumentalists, instrumentalities, instrumentality, instrumentalize, instrumentally, instrumentals, instrumentary, instrumentate, instrumentation, instrumentations, instrumentative, instrumented, instrumenting, instrumentist, instrumentman, instruments, instyle, insuavity, insubduable, insubjection, insubmergible, insubmersible, insubmission, insubmissive, insubordinate, insubordinately, insubordinateness, insubordination, insubstantial, insubstantiality, insubstantialize, insubstantially, insubstantiate, insubstantiation, insubvertible, insuccate, insuccation, insuccess, insuccessful, insucken, insue, insuetude, insufferable, insufferableness, insufferably, insufficience, insufficiencies, insufficiency, insufficient, insufficiently, insufficientness, insufflate, insufflated, insufflating, insufflation, insufflator, insuitable, insula, insulae, insulance, insulant, insulants, insular, insularism, insularity, insularize, insularized, insularizing, insularly, insulars, insulary, insulate, insulated, insulates, insulating, insulation, insulations, insulator, insulator's, insulators, insulin, insulinase, insulination, insulinize, insulinized, insulinizing, insulins, insulize, insulphured, insulse, insulsity, insult, insultable, insultant, insultation, insulted, insulter, insulters, insulting, insultingly, insultment, insultproof, insults, insume, insunk, insuper, insuperability, insuperable, insuperableness, insuperably, insupportable, insupportableness, insupportably, insupposable, insuppressibility, insuppressible, insuppressibly, insuppressive, insurability, insurable, insurance, insurant, insurants, insure, insured, insureds, insuree, insurer, insurers, insures, insurge, insurgence, insurgences, insurgencies, insurgency, insurgent, insurgent's, insurgentism, insurgently, insurgents, insurgescence, insuring, insurmountability, insurmountable, insurmountableness, insurmountably, insurpassable, insurrect, insurrection, insurrection's, insurrectional, insurrectionally, insurrectionaries, insurrectionary, insurrectionise, insurrectionised, insurrectionising, insurrectionism, insurrectionist, insurrectionists, insurrectionize, insurrectionized, insurrectionizing, insurrections, insurrecto, insurrectory, insusceptibilities, insusceptibility, insusceptible, insusceptibly, insusceptive, insuspect, insusurration, inswamp, inswarming, inswathe, inswathed, inswathement, inswathes, inswathing, insweeping, inswell, inswept, inswing, inswinger, int, inta, intablature, intabulate, intact, intactible, intactile, intactly, intactness, intagli, intagliated, intagliation, intaglio, intaglioed, intaglioing, intaglios, intagliotype, intail, intake, intaker, intakes, intaminated, intangibilities, intangibility, intangible, intangible's, intangibleness, intangibles, intangibly, intangle, intaria, intarissable, intarsa, intarsas, intarsia, intarsias, intarsiate, intarsist, intastable, intaxable, intebred, intebreeding, intechnicality, integer, integer's, integers, integrability, integrable, integral, integral's, integrality, integralization, integralize, integrally, integrals, integrand, integrant, integraph, integrate, integrated, integrates, integrating, integration, integrationist, integrations, integrative, integrator, integrifolious, integrious, integriously, integripallial, integripalliate, integrities, integrity, integrodifferential, integropallial, integropalliate, integumation, integument, integumental, integumentary, integumentation, integuments, inteind, intel, intellect, intellect's, intellectation, intellected, intellectible, intellection, intellective, intellectively, intellects, intellectual, intellectualisation, intellectualise, intellectualised, intellectualiser, intellectualising, intellectualism, intellectualist, intellectualistic, intellectualistically, intellectualities, intellectuality, intellectualization, intellectualizations, intellectualize, intellectualized, intellectualizer, intellectualizes, intellectualizing, intellectually, intellectualness, intellectuals, intelligence, intelligenced, intelligencer, intelligences, intelligencing, intelligency, intelligent, intelligential, intelligentiary, intelligently, intelligentsia, intelligibilities, intelligibility, intelligible, intelligibleness, intelligibly, intelligize, intelsat, intemerate, intemerately, intemerateness, intemeration, intemperable, intemperably, intemperament, intemperance, intemperances, intemperancy, intemperant, intemperate, intemperately, intemperateness, intemperature, intemperies, intempestive, intempestively, intempestivity, intemporal, intemporally, intenability, intenable, intenancy, intend, intendance, intendancies, intendancy, intendant, intendantism, intendantship, intended, intendedly, intendedness, intendeds, intendence, intendencia, intendencies, intendency, intendente, intender, intenders, intendible, intendiment, intending, intendingly, intendit, intendment, intends, intenerate, intenerated, intenerating, inteneration, intenible, intens, intensate, intensation, intensative, intense, intensely, intenseness, intenser, intensest, intensification, intensifications, intensified, intensifier, intensifiers, intensifies, intensify, intensifying, intension, intensional, intensionally, intensities, intensitive, intensitometer, intensity, intensive, intensively, intensiveness, intensivenyess, intensives, intent, intentation, intented, intention, intentional, intentionalism, intentionality, intentionally, intentioned, intentionless, intentions, intentive, intentively, intentiveness, intently, intentness, intents, inter, interabang, interabsorption, interacademic, interacademically, interaccessory, interaccuse, interaccused, interaccusing, interacinar, interacinous, interacra, interact, interactant, interacted, interacting, interaction, interaction's, interactional, interactionism, interactionist, interactions, interactive, interactively, interactivity, interacts, interadaptation, interadaption, interadditive, interadventual, interaffiliate, interaffiliated, interaffiliation, interagencies, interagency, interagent, interagglutinate, interagglutinated, interagglutinating, interagglutination, interagree, interagreed, interagreeing, interagreement, interalar, interall, interalliance, interallied, interally, interalveolar, interambulacra, interambulacral, interambulacrum, interamnian, interangular, interanimate, interanimated, interanimating, interannular, interantagonism, interantennal, interantennary, interapophysal, interapophyseal, interapplication, interarboration, interarch, interarcualis, interarmy, interarrival, interarticular, interartistic, interarytenoid, interassociate, interassociated, interassociation, interassure, interassured, interassuring, interasteroidal, interastral, interatomic, interatrial, interattrition, interaulic, interaural, interauricular, interavailability, interavailable, interaxal, interaxes, interaxial, interaxillary, interaxis, interbalance, interbalanced, interbalancing, interbanded, interbank, interbanking, interbastate, interbbred, interbed, interbedded, interbelligerent, interblend, interblended, interblending, interblent, interblock, interbody, interbonding, interborough, interbourse, interbrachial, interbrain, interbranch, interbranchial, interbreath, interbred, interbreed, interbreeding, interbreeds, interbrigade, interbring, interbronchial, interbrood, intercadence, intercadent, intercalar, intercalare, intercalarily, intercalarium, intercalary, intercalate, intercalated, intercalates, intercalating, intercalation, intercalations, intercalative, intercalatory, intercale, intercalm, intercanal, intercanalicular, intercapillary, intercardinal, intercarotid, intercarpal, intercarpellary, intercarrier, intercartilaginous, intercaste, intercatenated, intercausative, intercavernous, intercede, interceded, intercedent, interceder, intercedes, interceding, intercellular, intercellularly, intercensal, intercentra, intercentral, intercentrum, intercept, interceptable, intercepted, intercepter, intercepting, interception, interceptions, interceptive, interceptor, interceptors, interceptress, intercepts, intercerebral, intercess, intercession, intercessional, intercessionary, intercessionate, intercessionment, intercessions, intercessive, intercessor, intercessorial, intercessors, intercessory, interchaff, interchain, interchange, interchangeability, interchangeable, interchangeableness, interchangeably, interchanged, interchangement, interchanger, interchanges, interchanging, interchangings, interchannel, interchapter, intercharge, intercharged, intercharging, interchase, interchased, interchasing, intercheck, interchoke, interchoked, interchoking, interchondral, interchurch, intercident, interciliary, intercilium, intercipient, intercircle, intercircled, intercircling, intercirculate, intercirculated, intercirculating, intercirculation, intercision, intercitizenship, intercity, intercivic, intercivilization, interclash, interclasp, interclass, interclavicle, interclavicular, interclerical, interclose, intercloud, interclub, interclude, interclusion, intercoastal, intercoccygeal, intercoccygean, intercohesion, intercollege, intercollegian, intercollegiate, intercolline, intercolonial, intercolonially, intercolonization, intercolonize, intercolonized, intercolonizing, intercolumn, intercolumnal, intercolumnar, intercolumnation, intercolumniation, intercom, intercombat, intercombination, intercombine, intercombined, intercombining, intercome, intercommission, intercommissural, intercommon, intercommonable, intercommonage, intercommoned, intercommoner, intercommoning, intercommunal, intercommune, intercommuned, intercommuner, intercommunicability, intercommunicable, intercommunicate, intercommunicated, intercommunicates, intercommunicating, intercommunication, intercommunicational, intercommunications, intercommunicative, intercommunicator, intercommuning, intercommunion, intercommunional, intercommunities, intercommunity, intercompany, intercomparable, intercompare, intercompared, intercomparing, intercomparison, intercomplexity, intercomplimentary, intercoms, interconal, interconciliary, intercondenser, intercondylar, intercondylic, intercondyloid, interconfessional, interconfound, interconnect, interconnected, interconnectedness, interconnecting, interconnection, interconnection's, interconnections, interconnects, interconnexion, interconsonantal, intercontinental, intercontorted, intercontradiction, intercontradictory, interconversion, interconvert, interconvertibility, interconvertible, interconvertibly, intercooler, intercooling, intercoracoid, intercorporate, intercorpuscular, intercorrelate, intercorrelated, intercorrelating, intercorrelation, intercorrelations, intercortical, intercosmic, intercosmically, intercostal, intercostally, intercostobrachial, intercostohumeral, intercotylar, intercounty, intercouple, intercoupled, intercoupling, intercourse, intercoxal, intercranial, intercreate, intercreated, intercreating, intercreedal, intercrescence, intercrinal, intercrop, intercropped, intercropping, intercross, intercrossed, intercrossing, intercrural, intercrust, intercrystalline, intercrystallization, intercrystallize, intercultural, interculturally, interculture, intercupola, intercur, intercurl, intercurrence, intercurrent, intercurrently, intercursation, intercuspidal, intercut, intercutaneous, intercuts, intercutting, intercystic, interdash, interdata, interdeal, interdealer, interdebate, interdebated, interdebating, interdenominational, interdenominationalism, interdental, interdentally, interdentil, interdepartmental, interdepartmentally, interdepend, interdependability, interdependable, interdependence, interdependencies, interdependency, interdependent, interdependently, interderivative, interdespise, interdestructive, interdestructively, interdestructiveness, interdetermination, interdetermine, interdetermined, interdetermining, interdevour, interdict, interdicted, interdicting, interdiction, interdictions, interdictive, interdictor, interdictory, interdicts, interdictum, interdifferentiate, interdifferentiated, interdifferentiating, interdifferentiation, interdiffuse, interdiffused, interdiffusiness, interdiffusing, interdiffusion, interdiffusive, interdiffusiveness, interdigital, interdigitally, interdigitate, interdigitated, interdigitating, interdigitation, interdine, interdiscal, interdisciplinary, interdispensation, interdistinguish, interdistrict, interdivision, interdome, interdorsal, interdrink, intereat, interelectrode, interelectrodic, interembrace, interembraced, interembracing, interempire, interemption, interenjoy, interentangle, interentangled, interentanglement, interentangling, interepidemic, interepimeral, interepithelial, interequinoctial, interess, interesse, interessee, interessor, interest, interested, interestedly, interestedness, interester, interesterification, interesting, interestingly, interestingness, interestless, interests, interestuarine, interexchange, interface, interfaced, interfacer, interfaces, interfacial, interfacing, interfactional, interfaith, interfamily, interfascicular, interfault, interfector, interfederation, interfemoral, interfenestral, interfenestration, interferant, interfere, interfered, interference, interferences, interferent, interferential, interferer, interferers, interferes, interfering, interferingly, interferingness, interferogram, interferometer, interferometers, interferometric, interferometrically, interferometries, interferometry, interferon, interferric, interfertile, interfertility, interfibrillar, interfibrillary, interfibrous, interfilamentar, interfilamentary, interfilamentous, interfilar, interfile, interfiled, interfiles, interfiling, interfilling, interfiltrate, interfiltrated, interfiltrating, interfiltration, interfinger, interfirm, interflange, interflashing, interflow, interfluence, interfluent, interfluminal, interfluous, interfluve, interfluvial, interflux, interfold, interfoliaceous, interfoliar, interfoliate, interfollicular, interforce, interframe, interfraternal, interfraternally, interfraternity, interfret, interfretted, interfriction, interfrontal, interfruitful, interfulgent, interfuse, interfused, interfusing, interfusion, intergalactic, interganglionic, intergatory, intergenerant, intergenerating, intergeneration, intergenerational, intergenerative, intergeneric, intergential, intergesture, intergilt, interglacial, interglandular, interglobular, interglyph, intergonial, intergossip, intergossiped, intergossiping, intergossipped, intergossipping, intergovernmental, intergradation, intergradational, intergrade, intergraded, intergradient, intergrading, intergraft, intergranular, intergrapple, intergrappled, intergrappling, intergrave, intergroup, intergroupal, intergrow, intergrown, intergrowth, intergular, intergyral, interhabitation, interhaemal, interhemal, interhemispheric, interhostile, interhuman, interhyal, interhybridize, interhybridized, interhybridizing, interieur, interim, interimist, interimistic, interimistical, interimistically, interimperial, interims, interincorporation, interindependence, interindicate, interindicated, interindicating, interindividual, interinfluence, interinfluenced, interinfluencing, interinhibition, interinhibitive, interinsert, interinsular, interinsurance, interinsurer, interinvolve, interinvolved, interinvolving, interionic, interior, interior's, interiorism, interiorist, interiority, interiorization, interiorize, interiorized, interiorizes, interiorizing, interiorly, interiorness, interiors, interirrigation, interisland, interj, interjacence, interjacency, interjacent, interjaculate, interjaculateded, interjaculating, interjaculatory, interjangle, interjealousy, interject, interjected, interjecting, interjection, interjectional, interjectionalise, interjectionalised, interjectionalising, interjectionalize, interjectionalized, interjectionalizing, interjectionally, interjectionary, interjectionize, interjections, interjectiveness, interjector, interjectorily, interjectors, interjectory, interjects, interjectural, interjoin, interjoinder, interjoist, interjudgment, interjugal, interjugular, interjunction, interkinesis, interkinetic, interknit, interknitted, interknitting, interknot, interknotted, interknotting, interknow, interknowledge, interlabial, interlaboratory, interlace, interlaced, interlacedly, interlacement, interlacer, interlacery, interlaces, interlacing, interlacustrine, interlaid, interlain, interlake, interlamellar, interlamellation, interlaminar, interlaminate, interlaminated, interlaminating, interlamination, interlanguage, interlap, interlapped, interlapping, interlaps, interlapse, interlard, interlardation, interlarded, interlarding, interlardment, interlards, interlatitudinal, interlaudation, interlay, interlayer, interlayering, interlaying, interlays, interleaf, interleague, interleave, interleaved, interleaver, interleaves, interleaving, interlibel, interlibeled, interlibelling, interlibrary, interlie, interligamentary, interligamentous, interlight, interlimitation, interline, interlineal, interlineally, interlinear, interlinearily, interlinearly, interlineary, interlineate, interlineated, interlineating, interlineation, interlineations, interlined, interlinement, interliner, interlines, interlingua, interlingual, interlinguist, interlinguistic, interlining, interlink, interlinkage, interlinked, interlinking, interlinks, interlisp, interloan, interlobar, interlobate, interlobular, interlocally, interlocate, interlocated, interlocating, interlocation, interlock, interlocked, interlocker, interlocking, interlocks, interlocular, interloculli, interloculus, interlocus, interlocution, interlocutive, interlocutor, interlocutorily, interlocutors, interlocutory, interlocutress, interlocutresses, interlocutrice, interlocutrices, interlocutrix, interloli, interloop, interlope, interloped, interloper, interlopers, interlopes, interloping, interlot, interlotted, interlotting, interlucate, interlucation, interlucent, interlude, interluder, interludes, interludial, interluency, interlunar, interlunary, interlunation, interlying, intermachine, intermalar, intermalleolar, intermammary, intermammillary, intermandibular, intermanorial, intermarginal, intermarine, intermarriage, intermarriageable, intermarriages, intermarried, intermarries, intermarry, intermarrying, intermason, intermastoid, intermat, intermatch, intermatted, intermatting, intermaxilla, intermaxillar, intermaxillary, intermaze, intermazed, intermazing, intermean, intermeasurable, intermeasure, intermeasured, intermeasuring, intermeddle, intermeddled, intermeddlement, intermeddler, intermeddlesome, intermeddlesomeness, intermeddling, intermeddlingly, intermede, intermedia, intermediacy, intermediae, intermedial, intermediaries, intermediary, intermediate, intermediate's, intermediated, intermediately, intermediateness, intermediates, intermediating, intermediation, intermediator, intermediatory, intermedin, intermedious, intermedium, intermedius, intermeet, intermeeting, intermell, intermelt, intermembral, intermembranous, intermeningeal, intermenstrual, intermenstruum, interment, intermental, intermention, interments, intermercurial, intermesenterial, intermesenteric, intermesh, intermeshed, intermeshes, intermeshing, intermessage, intermessenger, intermet, intermetacarpal, intermetallic, intermetameric, intermetatarsal, intermew, intermewed, intermewer, intermezzi, intermezzo, intermezzos, intermiddle, intermigrate, intermigrated, intermigrating, intermigration, interminability, interminable, interminableness, interminably, interminant, interminate, interminated, intermination, intermine, intermined, intermingle, intermingled, intermingledom, interminglement, intermingles, intermingling, intermining, interminister, interministerial, interministerium, intermise, intermission, intermissions, intermissive, intermit, intermits, intermitted, intermittedly, intermittence, intermittencies, intermittency, intermittent, intermittently, intermitter, intermitting, intermittingly, intermittor, intermix, intermixable, intermixed, intermixedly, intermixes, intermixing, intermixt, intermixtly, intermixture, intermixtures, intermmet, intermobility, intermodification, intermodillion, intermodulation, intermodule, intermolar, intermolecular, intermolecularly, intermomentary, intermontane, intermorainic, intermotion, intermountain, intermundane, intermundial, intermundian, intermundium, intermunicipal, intermunicipality, intermural, intermure, intermuscular, intermuscularity, intermuscularly, intermutation, intermutual, intermutually, intermutule, intern, internal, internalities, internality, internalization, internalize, internalized, internalizes, internalizing, internally, internalness, internals, internarial, internasal, internat, internation, international, internationale, internationalisation, internationalise, internationalised, internationalising, internationalism, internationalist, internationalists, internationality, internationalization, internationalizations, internationalize, internationalized, internationalizes, internationalizing, internationally, internationals, internatl, interne, interneciary, internecinal, internecine, internecion, internecive, internect, internection, interned, internee, internees, internegative, internes, internescine, interneship, internet, internetted, internetwork, internetworking, internetworks, interneural, interneuron, interneuronal, interneuronic, internidal, interning, internist, internists, internity, internment, internments, internobasal, internodal, internode, internodes, internodia, internodial, internodian, internodium, internodular, interns, internship, internships, internuclear, internunce, internuncial, internuncially, internunciary, internunciatory, internunciess, internuncio, internuncios, internuncioship, internuncius, internuptial, internuptials, interobjective, interoceanic, interoceptive, interoceptor, interocular, interoffice, interolivary, interopercle, interopercular, interoperculum, interoptic, interorbital, interorbitally, interoscillate, interoscillated, interoscillating, interosculant, interosculate, interosculated, interosculating, interosculation, interosseal, interossei, interosseous, interosseus, interownership, interpage, interpalatine, interpale, interpalpebral, interpapillary, interparenchymal, interparental, interparenthetic, interparenthetical, interparenthetically, interparietal, interparietale, interparliament, interparliamentary, interparoxysmal, interparty, interpass, interpause, interpave, interpaved, interpaving, interpeal, interpectoral, interpeduncular, interpel, interpellant, interpellate, interpellated, interpellating, interpellation, interpellator, interpelled, interpelling, interpendent, interpenetrable, interpenetrant, interpenetrate, interpenetrated, interpenetrating, interpenetration, interpenetrative, interpenetratively, interpermeate, interpermeated, interpermeating, interpersonal, interpersonally, interpervade, interpervaded, interpervading, interpervasive, interpervasively, interpervasiveness, interpetaloid, interpetalous, interpetiolar, interpetiolary, interphalangeal, interphase, interphone, interphones, interpiece, interpilaster, interpilastering, interplace, interplacental, interplait, interplanetary, interplant, interplanting, interplay, interplaying, interplays, interplea, interplead, interpleaded, interpleader, interpleading, interpleads, interpled, interpledge, interpledged, interpledging, interpleural, interplical, interplicate, interplication, interplight, interpoint, interpol, interpolable, interpolant, interpolar, interpolary, interpolate, interpolated, interpolater, interpolates, interpolating, interpolation, interpolations, interpolative, interpolatively, interpolator, interpolators, interpolatory, interpole, interpolish, interpolitical, interpolity, interpollinate, interpollinated, interpollinating, interpolymer, interpone, interportal, interposable, interposal, interpose, interposed, interposer, interposers, interposes, interposing, interposingly, interposition, interpositions, interposure, interpour, interppled, interppoliesh, interprater, interpressure, interpret, interpretability, interpretable, interpretableness, interpretably, interpretament, interpretate, interpretation, interpretation's, interpretational, interpretations, interpretative, interpretatively, interpreted, interpreter, interpreters, interpretership, interpreting, interpretive, interpretively, interpretorial, interpretress, interprets, interprismatic, interprocess, interproduce, interproduced, interproducing, interprofessional, interprofessionally, interproglottidal, interproportional, interprotoplasmic, interprovincial, interproximal, interproximate, interpterygoid, interpubic, interpulmonary, interpunct, interpunction, interpunctuate, interpunctuation, interpupillary, interquarrel, interquarreled, interquarreling, interquarter, interrace, interracial, interracialism, interradial, interradially, interradiate, interradiated, interradiating, interradiation, interradii, interradium, interradius, interrailway, interramal, interramicorn, interramification, interran, interreact, interreceive, interreceived, interreceiving, interrecord, interred, interreflect, interreflection, interregal, interregency, interregent, interreges, interregimental, interregional, interregionally, interregna, interregnal, interregnum, interregnums, interreign, interrelate, interrelated, interrelatedly, interrelatedness, interrelates, interrelating, interrelation, interrelations, interrelationship, interrelationship's, interrelationships, interreligious, interreligiously, interrena, interrenal, interrenalism, interrepellent, interrepulsion, interrer, interresist, interresistance, interresistibility, interresponsibility, interresponsible, interresponsive, interreticular, interreticulation, interrex, interrhyme, interrhymed, interrhyming, interright, interring, interriven, interroad, interrobang, interrog, interrogability, interrogable, interrogant, interrogate, interrogated, interrogatedness, interrogatee, interrogates, interrogating, interrogatingly, interrogation, interrogational, interrogations, interrogative, interrogatively, interrogator, interrogatories, interrogatorily, interrogators, interrogatory, interrogatrix, interrogee, interroom, interrule, interruled, interruling, interrun, interrunning, interrupt, interruptable, interrupted, interruptedly, interruptedness, interrupter, interrupters, interruptible, interrupting, interruptingly, interruption, interruption's, interruptions, interruptive, interruptively, interruptor, interruptory, interrupts, inters, intersale, intersalute, intersaluted, intersaluting, interscapilium, interscapular, interscapulum, interscendent, interscene, interscholastic, interschool, interscience, interscribe, interscribed, interscribing, interscription, interseaboard, interseam, interseamed, intersecant, intersect, intersectant, intersected, intersecting, intersection, intersection's, intersectional, intersections, intersector, intersects, intersegmental, interseminal, interseminate, interseminated, interseminating, intersentimental, interseptal, interseptum, intersert, intersertal, interservice, intersesamoid, intersession, intersessional, intersessions, interset, intersetting, intersex, intersexes, intersexual, intersexualism, intersexualities, intersexuality, intersexually, intershade, intershaded, intershading, intershifting, intershock, intershoot, intershooting, intershop, intershot, intersidereal, intersituate, intersituated, intersituating, intersocial, intersocietal, intersociety, intersoil, intersole, intersoled, intersoling, intersolubility, intersoluble, intersomnial, intersomnious, intersonant, intersow, interspace, interspaced, interspacing, interspatial, interspatially, interspeaker, interspecial, interspecies, interspecific, interspeech, interspersal, intersperse, interspersed, interspersedly, intersperses, interspersing, interspersion, interspersions, interspheral, intersphere, interspicular, interspinal, interspinalis, interspinous, interspiral, interspiration, interspire, intersporal, intersprinkle, intersprinkled, intersprinkling, intersqueeze, intersqueezed, intersqueezing, intersshot, interstade, interstadial, interstage, interstaminal, interstapedial, interstate, interstates, interstation, interstellar, interstellary, intersterile, intersterility, intersternal, interstice, intersticed, interstices, intersticial, interstimulate, interstimulated, interstimulating, interstimulation, interstinctive, interstitial, interstitially, interstition, interstitious, interstitium, interstratification, interstratified, interstratify, interstratifying, interstreak, interstream, interstreet, interstrial, interstriation, interstrive, interstriven, interstriving, interstrove, interstructure, intersubjective, intersubjectively, intersubjectivity, intersubsistence, intersubstitution, intersuperciliary, intersusception, intersystem, intersystematic, intersystematical, intersystematically, intertalk, intertangle, intertangled, intertanglement, intertangles, intertangling, intertarsal, intertask, interteam, intertear, intertentacular, intertergal, interterminal, interterritorial, intertessellation, intertestamental, intertex, intertexture, interthing, interthread, interthreaded, interthreading, interthronging, intertidal, intertidally, intertie, intertied, intertieing, interties, intertill, intertillage, intertinge, intertinged, intertinging, intertissue, intertissued, intertoll, intertone, intertongue, intertonic, intertouch, intertown, intertrabecular, intertrace, intertraced, intertracing, intertrade, intertraded, intertrading, intertraffic, intertrafficked, intertrafficking, intertragian, intertransformability, intertransformable, intertransmissible, intertransmission, intertranspicuous, intertransversal, intertransversalis, intertransversary, intertransverse, intertrappean, intertree, intertribal, intertriginous, intertriglyph, intertrigo, intertrinitarian, intertrochanteric, intertrochlear, intertropic, intertropical, intertropics, intertrude, intertuberal, intertubercular, intertubular, intertwin, intertwine, intertwined, intertwinement, intertwinements, intertwines, intertwining, intertwiningly, intertwist, intertwisted, intertwisting, intertwistingly, interungular, interungulate, interunion, interuniversity, interurban, interureteric, intervaginal, interval, interval's, intervale, intervaled, intervalic, intervaling, intervalled, intervalley, intervallic, intervalling, intervallum, intervalometer, intervals, intervalvular, intervariation, intervaried, intervarietal, intervarsity, intervary, intervarying, intervascular, intervein, interveinal, interveined, interveining, interveinous, intervenant, intervene, intervened, intervener, interveners, intervenes, intervenience, interveniency, intervenient, intervening, intervenium, intervenor, intervent, intervention, intervention's, interventional, interventionism, interventionist, interventionists, interventions, interventive, interventor, interventral, interventralia, interventricular, intervenue, intervenular, interverbal, interversion, intervert, intervertebra, intervertebral, intervertebrally, interverting, intervesicular, interview, interviewable, interviewed, interviewee, interviewees, interviewer, interviewers, interviewing, interviews, intervillous, intervisibility, intervisible, intervisit, intervisitation, intervital, intervocal, intervocalic, intervocalically, intervolute, intervolution, intervolve, intervolved, intervolving, interwar, interwarred, interwarring, interweave, interweaved, interweavement, interweaver, interweaves, interweaving, interweavingly, interwed, interweld, interwhiff, interwhile, interwhistle, interwhistled, interwhistling, interwind, interwinded, interwinding, interwish, interword, interwork, interworked, interworking, interworks, interworld, interworry, interwound, interwove, interwoven, interwovenly, interwrap, interwrapped, interwrapping, interwreathe, interwreathed, interwreathing, interwrought, interwwrought, interxylary, interzonal, interzone, interzooecial, interzygapophysial, intestable, intestacies, intestacy, intestate, intestation, intestinal, intestinally, intestine, intestine's, intestineness, intestines, intestiniform, intestinovesical, intexine, intext, intextine, intexture, inthral, inthrall, inthralled, inthralling, inthrallment, inthralls, inthralment, inthrals, inthrone, inthroned, inthrones, inthrong, inthroning, inthronistic, inthronizate, inthronization, inthronize, inthrow, inthrust, intially, intice, intil, intill, intima, intimacies, intimacy, intimado, intimados, intimae, intimal, intimas, intimate, intimated, intimately, intimateness, intimater, intimaters, intimates, intimating, intimation, intimations, intime, intimidate, intimidated, intimidates, intimidating, intimidation, intimidations, intimidator, intimidatory, intimidity, intimism, intimist, intimiste, intimity, intimous, intinct, intinction, intinctivity, intine, intines, intire, intisy, intitle, intitled, intitles, intitling, intitulation, intitule, intituled, intitules, intituling, intl, intnl, into, intoed, intolerability, intolerable, intolerableness, intolerably, intolerance, intolerancy, intolerant, intolerantly, intolerantness, intolerated, intolerating, intoleration, intollerably, intomb, intombed, intombing, intombment, intombs, intonable, intonaci, intonaco, intonacos, intonate, intonated, intonates, intonating, intonation, intonation's, intonational, intonations, intonator, intone, intoned, intonement, intoner, intoners, intones, intoning, intoothed, intorsion, intort, intorted, intortillage, intorting, intortion, intorts, intortus, intourist, intower, intown, intoxation, intoxicable, intoxicant, intoxicantly, intoxicants, intoxicate, intoxicated, intoxicatedly, intoxicatedness, intoxicates, intoxicating, intoxicatingly, intoxication, intoxications, intoxicative, intoxicatively, intoxicator, intoxicators, intr, intra, intraabdominal, intraarterial, intraarterially, intrabiontic, intrabranchial, intrabred, intrabronchial, intrabuccal, intracalicular, intracanalicular, intracanonical, intracapsular, intracardiac, intracardial, intracardially, intracarpal, intracarpellary, intracartilaginous, intracellular, intracellularly, intracephalic, intracerebellar, intracerebral, intracerebrally, intracervical, intrachordal, intracistern, intracity, intraclitelline, intracloacal, intracoastal, intracoelomic, intracolic, intracollegiate, intracommunication, intracompany, intracontinental, intracorporeal, intracorpuscular, intracortical, intracosmic, intracosmical, intracosmically, intracostal, intracranial, intracranially, intractability, intractable, intractableness, intractably, intractile, intracutaneous, intracutaneously, intracystic, intrada, intradepartment, intradepartmental, intradermal, intradermally, intradermic, intradermically, intradermo, intradistrict, intradivisional, intrado, intrados, intradoses, intradoss, intraduodenal, intradural, intraecclesiastical, intraepiphyseal, intraepithelial, intrafactory, intrafascicular, intrafissural, intrafistular, intrafoliaceous, intraformational, intrafusal, intragalactic, intragantes, intragastric, intragemmal, intraglacial, intraglandular, intraglobular, intragroup, intragroupal, intragyral, intrahepatic, intrahyoid, intrail, intraimperial, intrait, intrajugular, intralamellar, intralaryngeal, intralaryngeally, intraleukocytic, intraligamentary, intraligamentous, intraliminal, intraline, intralingual, intralobar, intralobular, intralocular, intralogical, intralumbar, intramachine, intramammary, intramarginal, intramastoid, intramatrical, intramatrically, intramedullary, intramembranous, intrameningeal, intramental, intrametropolitan, intramolecular, intramolecularly, intramontane, intramorainic, intramundane, intramural, intramuralism, intramurally, intramuscular, intramuscularly, intramyocardial, intranarial, intranasal, intranatal, intranational, intraneous, intranet, intranetwork, intraneural, intranidal, intranquil, intranquillity, intrans, intranscalency, intranscalent, intransferable, intransferrable, intransformable, intransfusible, intransgressible, intransient, intransigeance, intransigeancy, intransigeant, intransigeantly, intransigence, intransigency, intransigent, intransigentism, intransigentist, intransigently, intransigents, intransitable, intransitive, intransitively, intransitiveness, intransitives, intransitivity, intransitu, intranslatable, intransmissible, intransmutability, intransmutable, intransparency, intransparent, intrant, intrants, intranuclear, intraoctave, intraocular, intraoffice, intraoral, intraorbital, intraorganization, intraossal, intraosseous, intraosteal, intraovarian, intrap, intrapair, intraparenchymatous, intraparietal, intraparochial, intraparty, intrapelvic, intrapericardiac, intrapericardial, intraperineal, intraperiosteal, intraperitoneal, intraperitoneally, intrapersonal, intrapetiolar, intraphilosophic, intrapial, intraplacental, intraplant, intrapleural, intrapolar, intrapontine, intrapopulation, intraprocess, intraprocessor, intraprostatic, intraprotoplasmic, intrapsychic, intrapsychical, intrapsychically, intrapulmonary, intrapyretic, intrarachidian, intrarectal, intrarelation, intrarenal, intraretinal, intrarhachidian, intraschool, intrascrotal, intrasegmental, intraselection, intrasellar, intraseminal, intraseptal, intraserous, intrashop, intraspecies, intraspecific, intraspecifically, intraspinal, intraspinally, intrastate, intrastromal, intrasusception, intrasynovial, intratarsal, intrate, intratelluric, intraterritorial, intratesticular, intrathecal, intrathoracic, intrathyroid, intratomic, intratonsillar, intratrabecular, intratracheal, intratracheally, intratropical, intratubal, intratubular, intratympanic, intrauterine, intravaginal, intravalvular, intravasation, intravascular, intravascularly, intravenous, intravenously, intraventricular, intraverbal, intraversable, intravertebral, intravertebrally, intravesical, intravital, intravitally, intravitam, intravitelline, intravitreous, intraxylary, intrazonal, intreasure, intreat, intreatable, intreated, intreating, intreats, intrench, intrenchant, intrenched, intrencher, intrenches, intrenching, intrenchment, intrepid, intrepidity, intrepidly, intrepidness, intricable, intricacies, intricacy, intricate, intricately, intricateness, intrication, intrigant, intrigante, intrigantes, intrigants, intrigaunt, intrigo, intriguant, intriguante, intrigue, intrigued, intrigueproof, intriguer, intriguers, intriguery, intrigues, intriguess, intriguing, intriguingly, intrince, intrine, intrinse, intrinsic, intrinsical, intrinsicality, intrinsically, intrinsicalness, intrinsicate, intro, introactive, introceptive, introconversion, introconvertibility, introconvertible, introd, introdden, introduce, introduced, introducee, introducement, introducer, introducers, introduces, introducible, introducing, introduct, introduction, introduction's, introductions, introductive, introductively, introductor, introductorily, introductoriness, introductory, introductress, introfaction, introfied, introfier, introfies, introflex, introflexion, introfy, introfying, introgressant, introgression, introgressive, introinflection, introit, introits, introitus, introject, introjection, introjective, intromissibility, intromissible, intromission, intromissive, intromit, intromits, intromitted, intromittence, intromittent, intromitter, intromitting, intropression, intropulsive, intropunitive, introreception, introrsal, introrse, introrsely, intros, introscope, introsensible, introsentient, introspect, introspectable, introspected, introspectible, introspecting, introspection, introspectional, introspectionism, introspectionist, introspectionistic, introspections, introspective, introspectively, introspectiveness, introspectivism, introspectivist, introspector, introsuction, introsume, introsuscept, introsusception, introthoracic, introtraction, introvenient, introverse, introversibility, introversible, introversion, introversions, introversive, introversively, introvert, introverted, introvertedness, introverting, introvertive, introverts, introvision, introvolution, intrudance, intrude, intruded, intruder, intruder's, intruders, intrudes, intruding, intrudingly, intrudress, intrunk, intrus, intruse, intrusion, intrusion's, intrusional, intrusionism, intrusionist, intrusions, intrusive, intrusively, intrusiveness, intruso, intrust, intrusted, intrusting, intrusts, intsv, intubate, intubated, intubates, intubating, intubation, intubationist, intubator, intubatting, intube, intue, intuent, intuicity, intuit, intuitable, intuited, intuiting, intuition, intuition's, intuitional, intuitionalism, intuitionalist, intuitionally, intuitionism, intuitionist, intuitionistic, intuitionless, intuitions, intuitive, intuitively, intuitiveness, intuitivism, intuitivist, intuito, intuits, intumesce, intumesced, intumescence, intumescent, intumescing, intumulate, intune, inturbidate, inturgescence, inturn, inturned, inturning, inturns, intuse, intussuscept, intussusception, intussusceptive, intwine, intwined, intwinement, intwines, intwining, intwist, intwisted, intwisting, intwists, inukshuk, inula, inulaceous, inulase, inulases, inulin, inulins, inuloid, inumbrate, inumbration, inunct, inunction, inunctum, inunctuosity, inunctuous, inundable, inundant, inundate, inundated, inundates, inundating, inundation, inundations, inundator, inundatory, inunderstandable, inunderstanding, inurbane, inurbanely, inurbaneness, inurbanity, inure, inured, inuredness, inurement, inurements, inures, inuring, inurn, inurned, inurning, inurnment, inurns, inusitate, inusitateness, inusitation, inust, inustion, inutile, inutilely, inutilities, inutility, inutilized, inutterable, inv, invaccinate, invaccination, invadable, invade, invaded, invader, invaders, invades, invading, invaginable, invaginate, invaginated, invaginating, invagination, invalescence, invaletudinary, invalid, invalidate, invalidated, invalidates, invalidating, invalidation, invalidations, invalidator, invalidcy, invalided, invalidhood, invaliding, invalidish, invalidism, invalidities, invalidity, invalidly, invalidness, invalids, invalidship, invalorous, invaluable, invaluableness, invaluably, invalued, invar, invariability, invariable, invariableness, invariably, invariance, invariancy, invariant, invariantive, invariantively, invariantly, invariants, invaried, invars, invasion, invasion's, invasionary, invasionist, invasions, invasive, invasiveness, invecked, invect, invected, invection, invective, invectively, invectiveness, invectives, invectivist, invector, inveigh, inveighed, inveigher, inveighing, inveighs, inveigle, inveigled, inveiglement, inveigler, inveiglers, inveigles, inveigling, inveil, invein, invendibility, invendible, invendibleness, inveneme, invenient, invenit, invent, inventable, inventary, invented, inventer, inventers, inventful, inventibility, inventible, inventibleness, inventing, invention, invention's, inventional, inventionless, inventions, inventive, inventively, inventiveness, inventor, inventor's, inventoriable, inventorial, inventorially, inventoried, inventories, inventors, inventory, inventory's, inventorying, inventress, inventresses, invents, inventurous, inveracious, inveracities, inveracity, inverebrate, inverisimilitude, inverities, inverity, inverminate, invermination, invernacular, inverness, invernesses, inversable, inversatile, inverse, inversed, inversedly, inversely, inverses, inversing, inversion, inversionist, inversions, inversive, inversor, invert, invertant, invertase, invertebracy, invertebral, invertebrata, invertebrate, invertebrate's, invertebrated, invertebrateness, invertebrates, inverted, invertedly, invertend, inverter, inverters, invertibility, invertible, invertile, inverting, invertive, invertor, invertors, inverts, invest, investable, invested, investible, investient, investigable, investigatable, investigate, investigated, investigates, investigating, investigatingly, investigation, investigational, investigations, investigative, investigator, investigator's, investigatorial, investigators, investigatory, investing, investion, investitive, investitor, investiture, investitures, investment, investment's, investments, investor, investor's, investors, invests, investure, inveteracy, inveterate, inveterately, inveterateness, inveteration, inviabilities, inviability, inviable, inviably, invict, invicted, invictive, invidia, invidious, invidiously, invidiousness, invigilance, invigilancy, invigilate, invigilated, invigilating, invigilation, invigilator, invigor, invigorant, invigorate, invigorated, invigorates, invigorating, invigoratingly, invigoratingness, invigoration, invigorations, invigorative, invigoratively, invigorator, invigour, invile, invillage, invinate, invination, invincibility, invincible, invincibleness, invincibly, inviolability, inviolable, inviolableness, inviolably, inviolacy, inviolate, inviolated, inviolately, inviolateness, invious, inviousness, invirile, invirility, invirtuate, inviscate, inviscation, inviscerate, inviscid, inviscidity, invised, invisibility, invisible, invisibleness, invisibly, invision, invitable, invital, invitant, invitation, invitation's, invitational, invitations, invitatory, invite, invited, invitee, invitees, invitement, inviter, inviters, invites, invitiate, inviting, invitingly, invitingness, invitress, invitrifiable, invivid, invocable, invocant, invocate, invocated, invocates, invocating, invocation, invocation's, invocational, invocations, invocative, invocator, invocatory, invoice, invoiced, invoices, invoicing, invoke, invoked, invoker, invokers, invokes, invoking, involatile, involatility, involucel, involucelate, involucelated, involucellate, involucellated, involucra, involucral, involucrate, involucre, involucred, involucres, involucriform, involucrum, involuntarily, involuntariness, involuntary, involute, involuted, involutedly, involutely, involutes, involuting, involution, involutional, involutionary, involutions, involutorial, involutory, involve, involved, involvedly, involvedness, involvement, involvement's, involvements, involvent, involver, involvers, involves, involving, invoy, invt, invulgar, invulnerability, invulnerable, invulnerableness, invulnerably, invulnerate, invultuation, invultvation, inwale, inwall, inwalled, inwalling, inwalls, inwandering, inward, inwardly, inwardness, inwards, inweave, inweaved, inweaves, inweaving, inwedged, inweed, inweight, inwheel, inwick, inwind, inwinding, inwinds, inwit, inwith, inwood, inwork, inworks, inworn, inwound, inwove, inwoven, inwrap, inwrapment, inwrapped, inwrapping, inwraps, inwrapt, inwreathe, inwreathed, inwreathing, inwrit, inwritten, inwrought, inyala, inyoite, inyoke, io, iocs, iodal, iodate, iodated, iodates, iodating, iodation, iodations, iode, iodhydrate, iodhydric, iodhydrin, iodic, iodid, iodide, iodides, iodids, iodiferous, iodimetric, iodimetry, iodin, iodinate, iodinated, iodinates, iodinating, iodination, iodine, iodines, iodinium, iodinophil, iodinophile, iodinophilic, iodinophilous, iodins, iodisation, iodism, iodisms, iodite, iodization, iodize, iodized, iodizer, iodizers, iodizes, iodizing, iodo, iodobehenate, iodobenzene, iodobromite, iodocasein, iodochlorid, iodochloride, iodochromate, iodocresol, iododerma, iodoethane, iodoform, iodoforms, iodogallicin, iodohydrate, iodohydric, iodohydrin, iodol, iodols, iodomercurate, iodomercuriate, iodomethane, iodometric, iodometrical, iodometrically, iodometry, iodonium, iodophor, iodophors, iodoprotein, iodopsin, iodopsins, iodoso, iodosobenzene, iodospongin, iodotannic, iodotherapy, iodothyrin, iodous, iodoxy, iodoxybenzene, iodyrite, iof, iolite, iolites, ion, ionian, ionic, ionical, ionicities, ionicity, ionics, ionisable, ionisation, ionise, ionised, ioniser, ionises, ionising, ionium, ioniums, ionizable, ionization, ionizations, ionize, ionized, ionizer, ionizers, ionizes, ionizing, ionogen, ionogenic, ionomer, ionomers, ionone, ionones, ionopause, ionophore, ionosphere, ionospheres, ionospheric, ionospherically, ions, iontophoresis, ioparameters, iortn, ios, iota, iotacism, iotacisms, iotacismus, iotacist, iotas, iotization, iotize, iotized, iotizing, iou, iowa, iowan, iowans, iowt, ipecac, ipecacs, ipecacuanha, ipecacuanhic, iph, iphigenia, ipid, ipil, ipilipil, ipl, ipm, ipocras, ipomea, ipomoea, ipomoeas, ipomoein, ipr, iproniazid, ips, ipse, ipseand, ipsedixitish, ipsedixitism, ipsedixitist, ipseity, ipsilateral, ipsilaterally, ipso, iq, iqs, ir, ira, iracund, iracundity, iracundulous, irade, irades, iran, iranian, iranians, iraq, iraqi, iraqis, irascent, irascibility, irascible, irascibleness, irascibly, irate, irately, irateness, irater, iratest, irbis, irchin, ire, ire's, ired, ireful, irefully, irefulness, ireland, ireland's, ireless, irenarch, irene, irenic, irenica, irenical, irenically, irenicism, irenicist, irenicon, irenics, irenicum, ireos, ires, irian, iricism, irid, iridaceous, iridadenosis, iridal, iridalgia, iridate, iridauxesis, iridectome, iridectomies, iridectomise, iridectomised, iridectomising, iridectomize, iridectomized, iridectomizing, iridectomy, iridectropium, iridemia, iridencleisis, iridentropium, irideous, irideremia, irides, iridesce, iridescence, iridescences, iridescency, iridescent, iridescently, iridial, iridian, iridiate, iridic, iridical, iridin, iridine, iridiocyte, iridiophore, iridioplatinum, iridious, iridite, iridium, iridiums, iridization, iridize, iridized, iridizing, irido, iridoavulsion, iridocapsulitis, iridocele, iridoceratitic, iridochoroiditis, iridocoloboma, iridoconstrictor, iridocyclitis, iridocyte, iridodesis, iridodiagnosis, iridodialysis, iridodonesis, iridokinesia, iridoline, iridomalacia, iridomotor, iridoncus, iridoparalysis, iridophore, iridoplegia, iridoptosis, iridopupillary, iridorhexis, iridosclerotomy, iridosmine, iridosmium, iridotasis, iridotome, iridotomies, iridotomy, iridous, iring, iris, irisate, irisated, irisation, iriscope, irised, irises, irish, irishism, irishman, irishmen, irishry, irishwoman, irishwomen, irisin, irising, irislike, irisroot, iritic, iritis, iritises, irk, irked, irking, irks, irksome, irksomely, irksomeness, irok, iroko, iron, ironback, ironbark, ironbarks, ironbound, ironbush, ironclad, ironclads, irone, ironed, ironer, ironers, irones, ironfisted, ironflower, ironhanded, ironhandedly, ironhandedness, ironhard, ironhead, ironheaded, ironheads, ironhearted, ironheartedly, ironheartedness, ironic, ironical, ironically, ironicalness, ironice, ironies, ironing, ironings, ironiously, ironish, ironism, ironist, ironists, ironize, ironless, ironlike, ironly, ironmaker, ironmaking, ironman, ironmaster, ironmen, ironmonger, ironmongeries, ironmongering, ironmongery, ironness, ironnesses, irons, ironshod, ironshot, ironside, ironsided, ironsides, ironsmith, ironstone, ironstones, ironware, ironwares, ironweed, ironweeds, ironwood, ironwoods, ironwork, ironworked, ironworker, ironworkers, ironworking, ironworks, ironwort, irony, iroquoian, iroquoians, iroquois, irous, irpe, irradiance, irradiancy, irradiant, irradiate, irradiated, irradiates, irradiating, irradiatingly, irradiation, irradiations, irradiative, irradiator, irradicable, irradicably, irradicate, irradicated, irrarefiable, irrate, irrationability, irrationable, irrationably, irrational, irrationalise, irrationalised, irrationalising, irrationalism, irrationalist, irrationalistic, irrationalities, irrationality, irrationalize, irrationalized, irrationalizing, irrationally, irrationalness, irrationals, irreal, irreality, irrealizable, irrebuttable, irreceptive, irreceptivity, irreciprocal, irreciprocity, irreclaimability, irreclaimable, irreclaimableness, irreclaimably, irreclaimed, irrecognition, irrecognizability, irrecognizable, irrecognizably, irrecognizant, irrecollection, irreconcilability, irreconcilable, irreconcilableness, irreconcilably, irreconcile, irreconciled, irreconcilement, irreconciliability, irreconciliable, irreconciliableness, irreconciliably, irreconciliation, irrecordable, irrecoverable, irrecoverableness, irrecoverably, irrecuperable, irrecurable, irrecusable, irrecusably, irred, irredeemability, irredeemable, irredeemableness, irredeemably, irredeemed, irredenta, irredential, irredentism, irredentist, irredentists, irredressibility, irredressible, irredressibly, irreducibilities, irreducibility, irreducible, irreducibleness, irreducibly, irreductibility, irreductible, irreduction, irreferable, irreflection, irreflective, irreflectively, irreflectiveness, irreflexive, irreformability, irreformable, irrefragability, irrefragable, irrefragableness, irrefragably, irrefrangibility, irrefrangible, irrefrangibleness, irrefrangibly, irrefusable, irrefutability, irrefutable, irrefutableness, irrefutably, irreg, irregardless, irregeneracy, irregenerate, irregeneration, irregular, irregularism, irregularist, irregularities, irregularity, irregularize, irregularly, irregularness, irregulars, irregulate, irregulated, irregulation, irregulous, irrejectable, irrelate, irrelated, irrelation, irrelative, irrelatively, irrelativeness, irrelevance, irrelevances, irrelevancies, irrelevancy, irrelevant, irrelevantly, irreliability, irrelievable, irreligion, irreligionism, irreligionist, irreligionize, irreligiosity, irreligious, irreligiously, irreligiousness, irreluctant, irremeable, irremeably, irremediable, irremediableness, irremediably, irremediless, irrememberable, irremissibility, irremissible, irremissibleness, irremissibly, irremission, irremissive, irremittable, irremovability, irremovable, irremovableness, irremovably, irremunerable, irrenderable, irrenewable, irrenowned, irrenunciable, irrepair, irrepairable, irreparability, irreparable, irreparableness, irreparably, irrepassable, irrepatriable, irrepealability, irrepealable, irrepealableness, irrepealably, irrepentance, irrepentant, irrepentantly, irrepetant, irreplacable, irreplacably, irreplaceability, irreplaceable, irreplaceableness, irreplaceably, irrepleviable, irreplevisable, irreportable, irreprehensibility, irreprehensible, irreprehensibleness, irreprehensibly, irrepresentable, irrepresentableness, irrepressibility, irrepressible, irrepressibleness, irrepressibly, irrepressive, irreproachability, irreproachable, irreproachableness, irreproachably, irreproducibility, irreproducible, irreproductive, irreprovable, irreprovableness, irreprovably, irreption, irreptitious, irrepublican, irreputable, irresilience, irresiliency, irresilient, irresistable, irresistably, irresistance, irresistibility, irresistible, irresistibleness, irresistibly, irresistless, irresolubility, irresoluble, irresolubleness, irresolute, irresolutely, irresoluteness, irresolution, irresolvability, irresolvable, irresolvableness, irresolved, irresolvedly, irresonance, irresonant, irrespectability, irrespectable, irrespectful, irrespective, irrespectively, irrespirable, irrespondence, irresponsibilities, irresponsibility, irresponsible, irresponsibleness, irresponsibly, irresponsive, irresponsiveness, irrestrainable, irrestrainably, irrestrictive, irresultive, irresuscitable, irresuscitably, irretention, irretentive, irretentiveness, irreticence, irreticent, irretraceable, irretraceably, irretractable, irretractile, irretrievability, irretrievable, irretrievableness, irretrievably, irreturnable, irrevealable, irrevealably, irreverence, irreverences, irreverend, irreverendly, irreverent, irreverential, irreverentialism, irreverentially, irreverently, irreversibility, irreversible, irreversibleness, irreversibly, irrevertible, irreviewable, irrevisable, irrevocability, irrevocable, irrevocableness, irrevocably, irrevoluble, irrhation, irride, irridenta, irrigable, irrigably, irrigant, irrigate, irrigated, irrigates, irrigating, irrigation, irrigational, irrigationist, irrigations, irrigative, irrigator, irrigatorial, irrigators, irrigatory, irriguous, irriguousness, irrisible, irrision, irrisor, irrisory, irritabilities, irritability, irritable, irritableness, irritably, irritament, irritancies, irritancy, irritant, irritants, irritate, irritated, irritatedly, irritates, irritating, irritatingly, irritation, irritations, irritative, irritativeness, irritator, irritatory, irrite, irritomotile, irritomotility, irrogate, irrorate, irrorated, irroration, irrotational, irrotationally, irrubrical, irrugate, irrumation, irrupt, irrupted, irruptible, irrupting, irruption, irruptions, irruptive, irruptively, irrupts, irs, irvingite, is, isaac, isabel, isabelina, isabelita, isabelite, isabella, isabelline, isabnormal, isaconitine, isacoustic, isadelphous, isadnormal, isagoge, isagoges, isagogic, isagogical, isagogically, isagogics, isagon, isaiah, isallobar, isallobaric, isallotherm, isamin, isamine, isandrous, isanemone, isangoma, isanomal, isanomalous, isanthous, isapostolic, isarioid, isarithm, isarithms, isatate, isatic, isatid, isatide, isatin, isatine, isatines, isatinic, isatins, isatis, isatogen, isatogenic, isauxesis, isauxetic, isazoxy, isba, isbas, iscariot, ischaemia, ischaemic, ischar, ischchia, ischemia, ischemias, ischemic, ischia, ischiac, ischiadic, ischiadicus, ischial, ischialgia, ischialgic, ischiatic, ischidrosis, ischioanal, ischiobulbar, ischiocapsular, ischiocaudal, ischiocavernosus, ischiocavernous, ischiocele, ischiocerite, ischiococcygeal, ischiofemoral, ischiofibular, ischioiliac, ischioneuralgia, ischioperineal, ischiopodite, ischiopubic, ischiopubis, ischiorectal, ischiorrhogic, ischiosacral, ischiotibial, ischiovaginal, ischiovertebral, ischium, ischocholia, ischuretic, ischuria, ischury, iscose, isdn, ise, ised, isenergic, isenthalpic, isentrope, isentropic, isentropically, isepiptesial, isepiptesis, iserine, iserite, isethionate, isethionic, iseult, ish, ishime, ishmael, ishmaelite, ishpingo, ishshakku, isiac, isicle, isidia, isidiiferous, isidioid, isidiophorous, isidiose, isidium, isidoid, isidorian, isindazole, ising, isinglass, isis, isize, isl, islam, islamic, island, islanded, islander, islanders, islandhood, islandic, islanding, islandish, islandless, islandlike, islandman, islandmen, islandologist, islandology, islandress, islandry, islands, islandy, islay, isle, isle's, isled, isleless, isleman, isles, islesman, islesmen, islet, islet's, isleted, islets, isleward, isling, islot, isls, ism, ismaelian, ismaelite, ismal, ismatic, ismatical, ismaticalness, ismdom, isms, ismy, isn, isn't, isnad, isnt, iso, isoabnormal, isoagglutination, isoagglutinative, isoagglutinin, isoagglutinogen, isoalantolactone, isoalloxazine, isoallyl, isoamarine, isoamid, isoamide, isoamyl, isoamylamine, isoamylene, isoamylethyl, isoamylidene, isoantibody, isoantigen, isoantigenic, isoantigenicity, isoapiole, isoasparagine, isoaurore, isobar, isobarbaloin, isobarbituric, isobare, isobares, isobaric, isobarism, isobarometric, isobars, isobase, isobath, isobathic, isobaths, isobathytherm, isobathythermal, isobathythermic, isobenzofuran, isobilateral, isobilianic, isobiogenetic, isoborneol, isobornyl, isobront, isobronton, isobutane, isobutene, isobutyl, isobutylene, isobutyraldehyde, isobutyrate, isobutyric, isobutyryl, isocamphor, isocamphoric, isocaproic, isocarbostyril, isocarpic, isocarpous, isocellular, isocephalic, isocephalism, isocephalous, isocephaly, isoceraunic, isocercal, isocercy, isochasm, isochasmic, isocheim, isocheimal, isocheimenal, isocheimic, isocheimonal, isocheims, isochela, isochimal, isochime, isochimenal, isochimes, isochlor, isochlorophyll, isochlorophyllin, isocholanic, isocholesterin, isocholesterol, isochor, isochore, isochores, isochoric, isochors, isochromatic, isochron, isochronal, isochronally, isochrone, isochronic, isochronical, isochronism, isochronize, isochronized, isochronizing, isochronon, isochronous, isochronously, isochrons, isochrony, isochroous, isocinchomeronic, isocinchonine, isocitric, isoclasite, isoclimatic, isoclinal, isoclinally, isocline, isoclines, isoclinic, isoclinically, isocodeine, isocola, isocolic, isocolon, isocoria, isocorybulbin, isocorybulbine, isocorydine, isocoumarin, isocracies, isocracy, isocrat, isocratic, isocreosol, isocrotonic, isocrymal, isocryme, isocrymic, isocyanate, isocyanic, isocyanid, isocyanide, isocyanin, isocyanine, isocyano, isocyanogen, isocyanurate, isocyanuric, isocyclic, isocymene, isocytic, isodactylism, isodactylous, isodef, isodiabatic, isodialuric, isodiametric, isodiametrical, isodiaphere, isodiazo, isodiazotate, isodimorphic, isodimorphism, isodimorphous, isodomic, isodomon, isodomous, isodomum, isodont, isodontous, isodose, isodrin, isodrome, isodrosotherm, isodulcite, isodurene, isodynamia, isodynamic, isodynamical, isodynamous, isoelastic, isoelectric, isoelectrically, isoelectronic, isoelectronically, isoelemicin, isoemodin, isoenergetic, isoenzymatic, isoenzyme, isoenzymic, isoerucic, isoeugenol, isoflavone, isoflor, isogam, isogamete, isogametic, isogametism, isogamic, isogamies, isogamous, isogamy, isogen, isogeneic, isogenesis, isogenetic, isogenic, isogenies, isogenotype, isogenotypic, isogenous, isogeny, isogeotherm, isogeothermal, isogeothermic, isogloss, isoglossal, isoglosses, isognathism, isognathous, isogon, isogonal, isogonality, isogonally, isogonals, isogone, isogones, isogonic, isogonics, isogonies, isogoniostat, isogonism, isogons, isogony, isogradient, isograft, isogram, isograms, isograph, isographic, isographical, isographically, isographs, isography, isogriv, isogrivs, isogynous, isogyre, isohaline, isohalsine, isohel, isohels, isohemolysis, isohemopyrrole, isoheptane, isohesperidin, isohexyl, isohume, isohydric, isohydrocyanic, isohydrosorbic, isohyet, isohyetal, isohyets, isoimmune, isoimmunity, isoimmunization, isoimmunize, isoindazole, isoindigotin, isoindole, isoionone, isokeraunic, isokeraunographic, isokeraunophonic, isokontan, isokurtic, isolability, isolable, isolapachol, isolatable, isolate, isolated, isolatedly, isolates, isolating, isolation, isolationalism, isolationalist, isolationalists, isolationism, isolationist, isolationists, isolations, isolative, isolator, isolators, isolde, isolead, isoleads, isolecithal, isolette, isoleucine, isolex, isolichenin, isoline, isolines, isolinolenic, isoln, isolog, isologous, isologs, isologue, isologues, isology, isolysin, isolysis, isomagnetic, isomaltose, isomastigate, isomelamine, isomenthone, isomer, isomerase, isomere, isomeric, isomerical, isomerically, isomeride, isomerism, isomerization, isomerize, isomerized, isomerizing, isomeromorphism, isomerous, isomers, isomery, isometric, isometrical, isometrically, isometrics, isometries, isometrograph, isometropia, isometry, isomorph, isomorphic, isomorphically, isomorphism, isomorphism's, isomorphisms, isomorphous, isomorphs, isomyarian, isoneph, isonephelic, isonergic, isoniazid, isonicotinic, isonitramine, isonitril, isonitrile, isonitro, isonitroso, isonomic, isonomies, isonomous, isonomy, isonuclear, isonym, isonymic, isonymy, isooctane, isooleic, isoosmosis, isopach, isopachous, isopag, isoparaffin, isopathy, isopectic, isopedin, isopedine, isopelletierin, isopelletierine, isopentane, isopentyl, isoperimeter, isoperimetric, isoperimetrical, isoperimetry, isopetalous, isophanal, isophane, isophasal, isophene, isophenomenal, isophone, isophoria, isophorone, isophotal, isophote, isophotes, isophthalic, isophthalyl, isophyllous, isophylly, isopicramic, isopiestic, isopiestically, isopilocarpine, isoplere, isopleth, isoplethic, isopleths, isopleural, isopleuran, isopleure, isopleurous, isopod, isopodan, isopodans, isopodiform, isopodimorphous, isopodous, isopods, isopogonous, isopolite, isopolitical, isopolity, isopoly, isopor, isoporic, isoprenaline, isoprene, isoprenes, isoprenoid, isopropanol, isopropenyl, isopropyl, isopropylacetic, isopropylamine, isopropylideneacetone, isoproterenol, isopsephic, isopsephism, isopterous, isoptic, isopulegone, isopurpurin, isopycnal, isopycnic, isopyre, isopyromucic, isopyrrole, isoquercitrin, isoquinine, isoquinoline, isorcinol, isorhamnose, isorhodeose, isorhythm, isorhythmic, isorhythmically, isorithm, isorosindone, isorrhythmic, isorropic, isort, isosaccharic, isosaccharin, isoscele, isosceles, isoscope, isoseismal, isoseismic, isoseismical, isoseist, isoserine, isosmotic, isosmotically, isospin, isospins, isospondylous, isospore, isosporic, isospories, isosporous, isospory, isostacy, isostasies, isostasist, isostasy, isostatic, isostatical, isostatically, isostemonous, isostemony, isoster, isostere, isosteric, isosterism, isostructural, isostrychnine, isosuccinic, isosulphide, isosulphocyanate, isosulphocyanic, isosultam, isotac, isotach, isotachs, isotactic, isoteles, isotely, isoteniscope, isotere, isoteric, isotheral, isothere, isotheres, isotherm, isothermal, isothermally, isothermic, isothermical, isothermobath, isothermobathic, isothermobaths, isothermous, isotherms, isotherombrose, isothiocyanates, isothiocyanic, isothiocyano, isothujone, isotimal, isotimic, isotome, isotomous, isotone, isotones, isotonia, isotonic, isotonically, isotonicity, isotony, isotope, isotope's, isotopes, isotopic, isotopically, isotopies, isotopism, isotopy, isotrehalose, isotrimorphic, isotrimorphism, isotrimorphous, isotron, isotronic, isotrope, isotropic, isotropies, isotropil, isotropism, isotropous, isotropy, isotype, isotypes, isotypic, isotypical, isovalerate, isovalerianate, isovalerianic, isovaleric, isovalerone, isovaline, isovanillic, isovoluminal, isoxanthine, isoxazine, isoxazole, isoxime, isoxylene, isoyohimbine, isozooid, isozyme, isozymes, isozymic, ispaghul, ispravnik, ispraynik, israel, israeli, israelis, israelite, israelites, issachar, issanguila, issei, isseis, issite, issuable, issuably, issuance, issuances, issuant, issue, issued, issueless, issuer, issuers, issues, issuing, ist, istana, istanbul, isth, isthm, isthmal, isthmectomies, isthmectomy, isthmi, isthmial, isthmian, isthmians, isthmiate, isthmic, isthmics, isthmist, isthmistic, isthmistical, isthmistics, isthmoid, isthmus, isthmuses, istiophorid, istle, istles, istoke, isuret, isuretine, isuroid, isz, it, it""ll, it'd, it'll, it's, ita, itabirite, itacism, itacist, itacistic, itacolumite, itaconate, itaconic, itai, ital, italian, italian's, italianate, italianiron, italianism, italianization, italianize, italians, italic, italicism, italicization, italicize, italicized, italicizes, italicizing, italics, italiot, italite, italy, itamalate, itamalic, itatartaric, itatartrate, itauba, itch, itched, itcheoglan, itches, itchier, itchiest, itchiness, itching, itchingly, itchings, itchless, itchproof, itchreed, itchweed, itchwood, itchy, itcze, itd, itel, item, item's, itemed, iteming, itemise, itemization, itemization's, itemizations, itemize, itemized, itemizer, itemizers, itemizes, itemizing, items, itemy, iter, iterable, iterance, iterances, iterancy, iterant, iterate, iterated, iterately, iterates, iterating, iteration, iterations, iterative, iteratively, iterativeness, iterator, iterator's, iterators, iteroparity, iteroparous, iters, iterum, ithagine, ithand, ither, itherness, ithomiid, ithyphallic, ithyphyllous, itineracy, itinerancy, itinerant, itinerantly, itinerants, itineraria, itinerarian, itineraries, itinerarium, itinerariums, itinerary, itinerate, itinerated, itinerating, itineration, itinereraria, itinerite, itinerition, itineritious, itineritis, itineritive, itinerous, itll, itmo, itonidid, itoubou, its, itself, itsy, ittria, iturite, itzebu, iud, iuds, iulidan, iulus, iurant, iuus, iv, iva, ive, ivied, ivies, ivin, ivoried, ivories, ivorine, ivoriness, ivorist, ivory, ivorybill, ivorylike, ivorytype, ivorywood, ivray, ivresse, ivy, ivy's, ivybells, ivyberries, ivyberry, ivyflower, ivylike, ivyweed, ivywood, ivywort, iw, iwa, iwaiwa, iwbells, iwberry, iwearth, iwflower, iwis, iworth, iwound, iwurche, iwurthen, iwwood, iwwort, ix, ixia, ixias, ixion, ixodian, ixodic, ixodid, ixodids, ixtle, ixtles, iyar, iyo, izafat, izar, izard, izars, izba, izing, izle, izote, iztle, izvozchik, izzard, izzards, izzat, j, j'adoube, j'ouvert, j's, ja, jaap, jab, jab's, jabalina, jabbed, jabber, jabbered, jabberer, jabberers, jabbering, jabberingly, jabberment, jabbernowl, jabbers, jabberwockian, jabberwocky, jabbing, jabbingly, jabble, jabers, jabia, jabiru, jabirus, jaborandi, jaborandis, jaborin, jaborine, jabot, jaboticaba, jabots, jabs, jabul, jabules, jaburan, jacal, jacales, jacals, jacamar, jacamars, jacameropine, jacami, jacamin, jacana, jacanas, jacaranda, jacarandas, jacarandi, jacare, jacate, jacatoo, jacchus, jacconet, jacconot, jacens, jacent, jacht, jacinth, jacinthe, jacinthes, jacinths, jacitara, jack, jackal, jackals, jackanapes, jackanapeses, jackanapish, jackaroo, jackarooed, jackarooing, jackaroos, jackash, jackass, jackassery, jackasses, jackassification, jackassism, jackassness, jackbird, jackboot, jackbooted, jackboots, jackbox, jackboy, jackdaw, jackdaws, jacked, jackeen, jacker, jackeroo, jackerooed, jackerooing, jackeroos, jackers, jacket, jacketed, jacketing, jacketless, jacketlike, jackets, jacketwise, jackety, jackey, jackfish, jackfishes, jackfruit, jackhammer, jackhammers, jackhead, jackie, jackies, jacking, jackknife, jackknifed, jackknifes, jackknifing, jackknives, jackleg, jacklegs, jacklight, jacklighter, jackman, jackmen, jacknifed, jacknifing, jacknives, jacko, jackpile, jackpiling, jackplane, jackpot, jackpots, jackpudding, jackpuddinghood, jackrabbit, jackrod, jackroll, jackrolled, jackrolling, jackrolls, jacks, jacksaw, jackscrew, jackscrews, jackshaft, jackshay, jackshea, jackslave, jacksmelt, jacksmelts, jacksmith, jacksnipe, jacksnipes, jackson, jacksonian, jacksonville, jackstay, jackstays, jackstock, jackstone, jackstones, jackstraw, jackstraws, jacktan, jacktar, jackweed, jackwood, jacky, jackyard, jackyarder, jacob, jacobaea, jacobaean, jacobean, jacobian, jacobin, jacobinism, jacobinize, jacobins, jacobite, jacobitism, jacobsite, jacobus, jacobuses, jacoby, jacolatt, jaconace, jaconet, jaconets, jacounce, jacquard, jacquards, jacqueline, jacquemart, jacquerie, jactance, jactancy, jactant, jactation, jacteleg, jactitate, jactitated, jactitating, jactitation, jactivus, jactura, jacture, jactus, jacu, jacuaru, jaculate, jaculated, jaculates, jaculating, jaculation, jaculative, jaculator, jaculatorial, jaculatory, jaculiferous, jacutinga, jad, jadded, jadder, jadding, jade, jaded, jadedly, jadedness, jadeite, jadeites, jadelike, jadery, jades, jadesheen, jadeship, jadestone, jading, jadish, jadishly, jadishness, jaditic, jady, jaegars, jaeger, jaegers, jag, jaga, jagamohan, jagannath, jagat, jageer, jager, jagers, jagg, jaggar, jaggaries, jaggary, jagged, jaggeder, jaggedest, jaggedly, jaggedness, jagger, jaggeries, jaggers, jaggery, jaggheries, jagghery, jaggier, jaggiest, jagging, jaggs, jaggy, jagheer, jagheerdar, jaghir, jaghirdar, jaghire, jaghiredar, jagir, jagirdar, jagla, jagless, jagong, jagra, jagras, jagrata, jags, jagua, jaguar, jaguarete, jaguarondi, jaguars, jaguarundi, jaguarundis, jaguey, jah, jahannan, jahveh, jahvism, jai, jail, jailage, jailbait, jailbird, jailbirds, jailbreak, jailbreaker, jailbreaks, jaildom, jailed, jailer, jaileress, jailering, jailers, jailership, jailhouse, jailhouses, jailing, jailish, jailkeeper, jailless, jaillike, jailmate, jailor, jailoring, jailors, jails, jailward, jailyard, jain, jainism, jajman, jak, jakarta, jake, jakes, jakey, jakfruit, jako, jakos, jalap, jalapa, jalapeno, jalapenos, jalapic, jalapin, jalapins, jalaps, jalee, jalet, jalkar, jalloped, jalop, jalopies, jaloppies, jaloppy, jalops, jalopy, jalor, jalouse, jaloused, jalousie, jalousied, jalousies, jalousing, jalpaite, jalur, jam, jama, jamadar, jamaica, jamaican, jamaicans, jaman, jamb, jambalaya, jambart, jambarts, jambe, jambeau, jambeaux, jambed, jambee, jamber, jambes, jambing, jambiya, jambo, jambolan, jambolana, jambon, jambone, jambonneau, jambool, jamboree, jamborees, jambos, jambosa, jamboy, jambs, jambstone, jambul, jamdanee, jamdani, james, jamesian, jameson, jamesonite, jamestown, jami, jamlike, jammed, jammedness, jammer, jammers, jamming, jammy, jamnut, jamoke, jampacked, jampan, jampanee, jampani, jamrosade, jams, jamshid, jamtland, jamwood, janapa, janapan, janapum, janders, jane, janeiro, janes, janet, jangada, jangar, jangkar, jangle, jangled, jangler, janglers, janglery, jangles, jangling, jangly, janiceps, janiform, janisaries, janisary, janissary, janitor, janitor's, janitorial, janitors, janitorship, janitress, janitresses, janitrix, janizaries, janizary, jank, janker, jankers, jann, janner, jannock, jansenism, jansenist, jant, jantee, jantu, janty, janua, januaries, january, january's, janus, jaob, jap, japaconin, japaconine, japaconitin, japaconitine, japan, japanese, japanesery, japanization, japanize, japanized, japanizes, japanizing, japanned, japanner, japanners, japannery, japanning, japans, jape, japed, japer, japeries, japers, japery, japes, japheth, japhetic, japing, japingly, japish, japishly, japishness, japonaiserie, japonic, japonica, japonicas, japygid, japygoid, jaquette, jaquima, jar, jar's, jara, jarabe, jaragua, jarana, jararaca, jararacussu, jarbird, jarble, jarbot, jarde, jardin, jardini, jardiniere, jardinieres, jardon, jareed, jarfly, jarful, jarfuls, jarg, jargle, jargogle, jargon, jargonal, jargoned, jargoneer, jargonel, jargonelle, jargonels, jargoner, jargonesque, jargonic, jargoning, jargonisation, jargonise, jargonised, jargonish, jargonising, jargonist, jargonistic, jargonium, jargonization, jargonize, jargonized, jargonizer, jargonizing, jargonnelle, jargons, jargoon, jargoons, jarhead, jarina, jarinas, jark, jarkman, jarl, jarldom, jarldoms, jarless, jarlite, jarls, jarlship, jarnut, jarool, jarosite, jarosites, jarovization, jarovize, jarovized, jarovizes, jarovizing, jarp, jarra, jarrah, jarrahs, jarred, jarret, jarring, jarringly, jarringness, jarry, jars, jarsful, jarvey, jarveys, jarvie, jarvies, jarvy, jasey, jaseyed, jaseys, jasies, jasmin, jasmine, jasmined, jasminelike, jasmines, jasminewood, jasmins, jasmone, jason, jasp, jaspachate, jaspagate, jaspe, jasper, jasperated, jaspered, jasperite, jasperize, jasperized, jasperizing, jasperoid, jaspers, jasperware, jaspery, jaspidean, jaspideous, jaspilite, jaspilyte, jaspis, jaspoid, jasponyx, jaspopal, jass, jassid, jassids, jassoid, jasy, jasz, jat, jataco, jataka, jatamansi, jateorhizin, jateorhizine, jatha, jati, jato, jatoba, jatos, jatrophic, jatrorrhizine, jaudie, jauk, jauked, jauking, jauks, jaun, jaunce, jaunced, jaunces, jauncing, jaunder, jaunders, jaundice, jaundiced, jaundiceroot, jaundices, jaundicing, jauner, jaunt, jaunt's, jaunted, jauntie, jauntier, jauntiest, jauntily, jauntiness, jaunting, jauntingly, jaunts, jaunty, jaup, jauped, jauping, jaups, java, javali, javan, javanese, javanine, javas, javel, javelin, javelin's, javelina, javelinas, javeline, javelined, javelineer, javelining, javelins, javelot, javer, jaw, jaw's, jawab, jawan, jawans, jawbation, jawbone, jawboned, jawbones, jawboning, jawbreak, jawbreaker, jawbreakers, jawbreaking, jawbreakingly, jawcrusher, jawed, jawfall, jawfallen, jawfeet, jawfish, jawfishes, jawfoot, jawfooted, jawhole, jawing, jawless, jawlike, jawline, jawlines, jawn, jawp, jawrope, jaws, jawsmith, jawtwister, jawy, jay, jaybird, jaybirds, jaycee, jaycees, jaygee, jaygees, jayhawk, jayhawker, jaypie, jaypiet, jays, jayvee, jayvees, jaywalk, jaywalked, jaywalker, jaywalkers, jaywalking, jaywalks, jazeran, jazerant, jazey, jazeys, jazies, jazy, jazz, jazzbow, jazzed, jazzer, jazzers, jazzes, jazzier, jazziest, jazzily, jazziness, jazzing, jazzist, jazzlike, jazzman, jazzmen, jazzy, jcl, jct, jctn, jealous, jealouse, jealousies, jealously, jealousness, jealousy, jeames, jean, jean's, jeanne, jeannette, jeans, jear, jebat, jebel, jebels, jebusite, jecoral, jecorin, jecorize, jed, jedburgh, jedcock, jedding, jeddock, jee, jeed, jeeing, jeel, jeep, jeep's, jeepers, jeepney, jeepneys, jeeps, jeer, jeer's, jeered, jeerer, jeerers, jeering, jeeringly, jeerproof, jeers, jeery, jees, jeetee, jeewhillijers, jeewhillikens, jeez, jefe, jefes, jeff, jefferisite, jefferson, jeffersonian, jeffersonians, jeffersonite, jeg, jehad, jehads, jehoshaphat, jehovah, jehovist, jehu, jehup, jehus, jejuna, jejunal, jejunator, jejune, jejunectomies, jejunectomy, jejunely, jejuneness, jejunities, jejunitis, jejunity, jejunoduodenal, jejunoileitis, jejunostomies, jejunostomy, jejunotomy, jejunum, jejunums, jekyll, jelab, jelerang, jelib, jelick, jell, jellab, jellaba, jellabas, jelled, jellib, jellica, jellico, jellied, jelliedness, jellies, jellification, jellified, jellifies, jellify, jellifying, jellily, jelling, jello, jelloid, jells, jelly, jelly's, jellybean, jellybeans, jellydom, jellyfish, jellyfishes, jellying, jellyleaf, jellylike, jellylikeness, jellyroll, jelotong, jelutong, jelutongs, jemadar, jemadars, jembe, jemble, jemidar, jemidars, jemima, jemmied, jemmies, jemmily, jemminess, jemmy, jemmying, jen, jenequen, jenkin, jenna, jennerization, jennerize, jennet, jenneting, jennets, jennie, jennier, jennies, jenny, jenoar, jentacular, jeofail, jeon, jeopard, jeoparded, jeoparder, jeopardied, jeopardies, jeoparding, jeopardious, jeopardise, jeopardised, jeopardising, jeopardize, jeopardized, jeopardizes, jeopardizing, jeopardous, jeopardously, jeopardousness, jeopards, jeopardy, jeopardying, jequerity, jequirities, jequirity, jer, jerbil, jerboa, jerboas, jere, jereed, jereeds, jeremejevite, jeremiad, jeremiads, jeremiah, jeremy, jerez, jerfalcon, jerib, jerican, jericho, jerid, jerids, jerk, jerked, jerker, jerkers, jerkier, jerkies, jerkiest, jerkily, jerkin, jerkined, jerkiness, jerking, jerkingly, jerkings, jerkinhead, jerkins, jerkish, jerks, jerksome, jerkwater, jerky, jerl, jerm, jermonal, jermoonal, jernie, jeroboam, jeroboams, jeronymite, jeropiga, jerque, jerqued, jerquer, jerquing, jerreed, jerreeds, jerrican, jerricans, jerrid, jerrids, jerries, jerry, jerrybuild, jerrybuilding, jerrybuilt, jerrycan, jerrycans, jerryism, jersey, jersey's, jerseyed, jerseyite, jerseyites, jerseys, jert, jerusalem, jervia, jervin, jervina, jervine, jess, jessakeed, jessamies, jessamine, jessamy, jessant, jesse, jessed, jesses, jessing, jessur, jest, jestbook, jested, jestee, jester, jesters, jestful, jesting, jestingly, jestings, jestingstock, jestmonger, jestproof, jests, jestwise, jestword, jesuist, jesuit, jesuited, jesuitess, jesuitic, jesuitical, jesuitically, jesuitism, jesuitize, jesuitries, jesuitry, jesuits, jesus, jet, jet's, jetavator, jetbead, jetbeads, jete, jetes, jetliner, jetliners, jeton, jetons, jetport, jetports, jets, jetsam, jetsams, jetsom, jetsoms, jetstream, jettage, jettatore, jettatura, jetteau, jetted, jetter, jettied, jetties, jettiness, jetting, jettingly, jettison, jettisonable, jettisoned, jettisoning, jettisons, jetton, jettons, jettru, jetty, jettyhead, jettying, jettywise, jetware, jeu, jeunesse, jeux, jew, jewbird, jewbush, jewed, jewel, jeweled, jeweler, jewelers, jewelfish, jewelfishes, jewelhouse, jeweling, jewelled, jeweller, jewellers, jewellery, jewelless, jewellike, jewelling, jewelly, jewelries, jewelry, jewels, jewelsmith, jewelweed, jewelweeds, jewely, jewess, jewfish, jewfishes, jewing, jewis, jewish, jewishness, jewism, jewry, jews, jews'harp, jezail, jezails, jezebel, jezebels, jezekite, jeziah, jg, jger, jharal, jheel, jhool, jhow, jhvh, jiao, jib, jibb, jibba, jibbah, jibbed, jibbeh, jibber, jibbers, jibbing, jibbings, jibbons, jibboom, jibbooms, jibbs, jibby, jibe, jibed, jiber, jibers, jibes, jibhead, jibi, jibing, jibingly, jibman, jibmen, jiboa, jiboya, jibs, jibstay, jicama, jicamas, jicara, jiff, jiffies, jiffle, jiffs, jiffy, jig, jig's, jigaboo, jigaboos, jigamaree, jigged, jigger, jiggered, jiggerer, jiggerman, jiggermast, jiggers, jigget, jiggety, jigginess, jigging, jiggish, jiggit, jiggle, jiggled, jiggler, jiggles, jigglier, jiggliest, jiggling, jiggly, jiggumbob, jiggy, jiglike, jigman, jigmen, jigote, jigs, jigsaw, jigsawed, jigsawing, jigsawn, jigsaws, jihad, jihads, jikungu, jill, jillaroo, jillet, jillflirt, jilling, jillion, jillions, jills, jilt, jilted, jiltee, jilter, jilters, jilting, jiltish, jilts, jim, jimbang, jimberjaw, jimberjawed, jimbo, jimcrack, jimigaki, jiminy, jimjam, jimjams, jimjums, jimmer, jimmied, jimmies, jimminy, jimmy, jimmying, jimmyweed, jimp, jimper, jimpest, jimply, jimpness, jimpricute, jimpy, jimsedge, jimson, jimsonweed, jin, jina, jincamas, jinete, jing, jingal, jingall, jingalls, jingals, jingbang, jingko, jingkoes, jingle, jinglebob, jingled, jinglejangle, jingler, jinglers, jingles, jinglet, jinglier, jingliest, jingling, jinglingly, jingly, jingo, jingodom, jingoed, jingoes, jingoing, jingoish, jingoism, jingoisms, jingoist, jingoistic, jingoistically, jingoists, jingu, jinja, jinjili, jink, jinked, jinker, jinkers, jinket, jinking, jinkle, jinks, jinn, jinnee, jinnestan, jinni, jinnies, jinniwink, jinniyeh, jinns, jinny, jinnywink, jinricksha, jinrickshaw, jinriki, jinrikiman, jinrikimen, jinrikisha, jinrikishas, jinriksha, jins, jinsha, jinshang, jinsing, jinx, jinxed, jinxes, jinxing, jipijapa, jipijapas, jipper, jiqui, jirble, jirga, jirgah, jirkinet, jism, jisms, jissom, jiti, jitneur, jitneuse, jitney, jitneyed, jitneying, jitneyman, jitneys, jitro, jitter, jitterbug, jitterbugged, jitterbugger, jitterbugging, jitterbugs, jittered, jitteriness, jittering, jitters, jittery, jiujitsu, jiujitsus, jiujutsu, jiujutsus, jiva, jivatma, jive, jiveass, jived, jives, jiving, jixie, jizya, jizyah, jizzen, jms, jnana, jnanamarga, jnanas, jnanashakti, jnanayoga, jnanendriya, jnd, jnt, jo, joan, joannes, joaquinite, job, job's, jobade, jobarbe, jobation, jobbed, jobber, jobberies, jobbernowl, jobbernowlism, jobbers, jobbery, jobbet, jobbing, jobbish, jobble, jobe, jobholder, jobholders, jobless, joblessness, joblots, jobman, jobmaster, jobmen, jobmistress, jobmonger, jobname, jobnames, jobo, jobs, jobsite, jobsmith, jobson, jocant, jocasta, jocatory, joch, jock, jocker, jockette, jockettes, jockey, jockeydom, jockeyed, jockeying, jockeyish, jockeyism, jockeylike, jockeys, jockeyship, jocko, jockos, jocks, jockstrap, jockstraps, jockteleg, jocooserie, jocoque, jocoqui, jocose, jocosely, jocoseness, jocoseriosity, jocoserious, jocosities, jocosity, jocote, jocteleg, jocu, jocular, jocularities, jocularity, jocularly, jocularness, joculator, joculatory, jocum, jocuma, jocund, jocundities, jocundity, jocundly, jocundness, jocundry, jocuno, jocunoity, jodel, jodelr, jodhpur, jodhpurs, joe, joebush, joel, joes, joewood, joey, joeyes, joeys, jog, jogged, jogger, joggers, jogging, joggle, joggled, joggler, jogglers, joggles, jogglety, jogglework, joggling, joggly, jogjakarta, jogs, jogtrot, jogtrottism, johannean, johannes, johannesburg, johannine, johannisberger, johannite, john, johnboat, johnboats, johnian, johnin, johnnie, johnnies, johnny, johnnycake, johnnydom, johns, johnson, johnsonese, johnsonian, johnstrupite, joie, join, joinable, joinant, joinder, joinders, joined, joiner, joinered, joineries, joinering, joiners, joinery, joinhand, joining, joiningly, joinings, joins, joint, joint's, jointage, jointed, jointedly, jointedness, jointer, jointers, jointing, jointist, jointless, jointlessness, jointly, jointress, joints, jointure, jointured, jointureless, jointures, jointuress, jointuring, jointweed, jointwood, jointworm, jointy, joist, joisted, joisting, joistless, joists, jojoba, jojobas, joke, jokebook, joked, jokeless, jokelet, jokeproof, joker, jokers, jokes, jokesmith, jokesome, jokesomeness, jokester, jokesters, jokey, jokier, jokiest, joking, jokingly, jokish, jokist, joktaleg, jokul, joky, jole, joles, joll, jolleyman, jollied, jollier, jollies, jolliest, jollification, jollifications, jollified, jollifies, jollify, jollifying, jollily, jolliment, jolliness, jollities, jollitry, jollity, jollop, jolloped, jolly, jollyer, jollyhead, jollying, jollytail, jolt, jolted, jolter, jolterhead, jolterheaded, jolterheadedness, jolters, jolthead, joltheaded, joltier, joltiest, joltily, joltiness, jolting, joltingly, joltless, joltproof, jolts, jolty, jomon, jonah, jonahs, jonathan, jondla, jones, joneses, jonglem, jonglery, jongleur, jongleurs, jonnick, jonnock, jonque, jonquil, jonquille, jonquils, jonsonian, jonvalization, jonvalize, jook, jookerie, joola, joom, joram, jorams, jordan, jordanian, jordanians, jordanite, jordanon, jordans, jorden, joree, jornada, jornadas, joropo, joropos, jorram, jorum, jorums, jose, josefite, joseite, joseph, josephine, josephinite, josephs, josey, josh, joshed, josher, joshers, joshes, joshi, joshing, joshua, josie, joskin, joss, jossakeed, josser, josses, jostle, jostled, jostlement, jostler, jostlers, jostles, jostling, jot, jota, jotas, jotation, jotisaru, jotisi, jots, jotted, jotter, jotters, jotting, jottings, jotty, jotunn, jotunnheim, joual, jouals, joubarb, joug, jough, jougs, jouisance, jouissance, jouk, jouked, joukery, joukerypawkery, jouking, jouks, joul, joule, joulean, joulemeter, joules, jounce, jounced, jounces, jouncier, jounciest, jouncing, jouncy, jour, journ, journal, journal's, journalary, journaled, journalese, journaling, journalise, journalised, journalish, journalising, journalism, journalist, journalist's, journalistic, journalistically, journalists, journalization, journalize, journalized, journalizer, journalizes, journalizing, journalled, journalling, journals, journey, journeycake, journeyed, journeyer, journeyers, journeying, journeyings, journeyman, journeymen, journeys, journeywoman, journeywomen, journeywork, journeyworker, journo, jours, joust, jousted, jouster, jousters, jousting, jousts, joutes, jove, jovial, jovialist, jovialistic, joviality, jovialize, jovialized, jovializing, jovially, jovialness, jovialties, jovialty, jovian, jovicentric, jovilabe, jovinianist, jovy, jow, jowar, jowari, jowars, jowed, jowel, jower, jowery, jowing, jowl, jowled, jowler, jowlier, jowliest, jowlish, jowlop, jowls, jowly, jowpy, jows, jowser, jowter, joy, joy's, joyance, joyances, joyancy, joyant, joyce, joycean, joyed, joyful, joyfuller, joyfullest, joyfully, joyfulness, joyhop, joyhouse, joying, joyleaf, joyless, joylessly, joylessness, joylet, joyous, joyously, joyousness, joypop, joypopped, joypopper, joypopping, joypops, joyproof, joyridden, joyride, joyrider, joyriders, joyrides, joyriding, joyrode, joys, joysome, joystick, joysticks, joyweed, jr, js, jt, juamave, juan, juans, juba, jubarb, jubardy, jubartas, jubartes, jubas, jubate, jubbah, jubbahs, jubbe, jube, juberous, jubes, jubhah, jubhahs, jubilance, jubilancy, jubilant, jubilantly, jubilar, jubilarian, jubilate, jubilated, jubilates, jubilating, jubilatio, jubilation, jubilations, jubilatory, jubile, jubileal, jubilean, jubilee, jubilees, jubiles, jubili, jubilist, jubilization, jubilize, jubilus, jubus, juchart, juck, juckies, jucundity, jud, judah, judaic, judaica, judaical, judaiser, judaism, judaist, judaistic, judaization, judaize, judaizer, judas, judases, judcock, judder, juddered, juddering, judders, juddock, jude, judex, judge, judgeable, judged, judgeless, judgelike, judgement, judgemental, judgements, judger, judgers, judges, judgeship, judgeships, judging, judgingly, judgmatic, judgmatical, judgmatically, judgment, judgment's, judgmental, judgments, judgmetic, judgship, judicable, judical, judicata, judicate, judicatio, judication, judicative, judicator, judicatorial, judicatories, judicatory, judicature, judicatures, judice, judices, judicia, judiciable, judicial, judicialis, judiciality, judicialize, judicialized, judicializing, judicially, judicialness, judiciaries, judiciarily, judiciary, judicious, judiciously, judiciousness, judicium, judith, judo, judogi, judoist, judoists, judoka, judokas, judophobia, judos, judy, jueces, juffer, jufti, jufts, jug, jug's, juga, jugal, jugale, jugate, jugated, jugation, juger, jugerum, jugful, jugfuls, jugged, jugger, juggernaut, juggernauts, jugging, juggins, jugginses, juggle, juggled, jugglement, juggler, juggleries, jugglers, jugglery, juggles, juggling, jugglingly, jugglings, jughead, jugheads, juglandaceous, juglandin, juglar, juglone, jugoslav, jugs, jugsful, jugula, jugular, jugulars, jugulary, jugulate, jugulated, jugulates, jugulating, jugulation, jugulum, jugum, jugums, juice, juice's, juiced, juiceful, juicehead, juiceless, juicelessness, juicer, juicers, juices, juicier, juiciest, juicily, juiciness, juicing, juicy, juise, jujitsu, jujitsus, juju, jujube, jujubes, jujuism, jujuisms, jujuist, jujuists, jujus, jujutsu, jujutsus, juke, jukebox, jukeboxes, juked, jukes, juking, julaceous, julep, juleps, julian, julid, julidan, julienite, julienne, juliennes, julies, juliet, juliett, julio, juliott, julius, juloid, juloidian, julole, julolidin, julolidine, julolin, juloline, july, july's, julyflower, jumada, jumart, jumba, jumbal, jumbals, jumbie, jumble, jumbled, jumblement, jumbler, jumblers, jumbles, jumbling, jumblingly, jumbly, jumbo, jumboesque, jumboism, jumbos, jumbuck, jumbucks, jumby, jumelle, jument, jumentous, jumfru, jumillite, jumma, jump, jumpable, jumped, jumper, jumperism, jumpers, jumpier, jumpiest, jumpily, jumpiness, jumping, jumpingly, jumpmaster, jumpness, jumpoff, jumpoffs, jumprock, jumprocks, jumps, jumpscrape, jumpseed, jumpsome, jumpsuit, jumpsuits, jumpy, jun, junc, juncaceous, juncaginaceous, juncagineous, juncat, junciform, juncite, junco, juncoes, juncos, juncous, junction, junction's, junctional, junctions, junctive, junctly, junctor, junctural, juncture, juncture's, junctures, juncus, jundie, jundied, jundies, jundy, jundying, june, juneating, juneau, juneberry, junectomy, junefish, jungermanniaceous, jungian, jungle, jungle's, jungled, junglegym, jungles, jungleside, junglewards, junglewood, jungli, junglier, jungliest, jungly, juniata, junior, junior's, juniorate, juniority, juniors, juniorship, juniper, junipers, junk, junkboard, junkdealer, junked, junker, junkerdom, junkerish, junkerism, junkers, junket, junketed, junketeer, junketeers, junketer, junketers, junketing, junkets, junketter, junkie, junkier, junkies, junkiest, junking, junkman, junkmen, junks, junky, junkyard, junkyards, juno, junoesque, junt, junta, juntas, junto, juntos, jupard, jupati, jupe, jupes, jupiter, jupon, jupons, jura, jural, jurally, jurament, juramenta, juramentado, juramentados, juramental, juramentally, juramentum, jurant, jurants, jurara, jurare, jurassic, jurat, jurata, juration, jurative, jurator, juratorial, juratory, jurats, jure, jurel, jurels, juridic, juridical, juridically, juridicial, juridicus, juries, juring, juris, jurisconsult, jurisdiction, jurisdiction's, jurisdictional, jurisdictionalism, jurisdictionally, jurisdictions, jurisdictive, jurisp, jurisprude, jurisprudence, jurisprudent, jurisprudential, jurisprudentialist, jurisprudentially, jurist, juristic, juristical, juristically, jurists, juror, juror's, jurors, jurupaite, jury, jury's, juryless, juryman, jurymen, juryrigged, jurywoman, jurywomen, jus, juslik, juslted, jusquaboutisme, jusquaboutist, jussal, jussel, jusshell, jussion, jussive, jussives, jussory, just, justaucorps, justed, justen, juster, justers, justest, justice, justice's, justiced, justicehood, justiceless, justicelike, justicer, justices, justiceship, justiceweed, justicia, justiciability, justiciable, justicial, justiciar, justiciaries, justiciarship, justiciary, justiciaryship, justiciatus, justicier, justicies, justicing, justico, justicoat, justifably, justifiability, justifiable, justifiableness, justifiably, justification, justifications, justificative, justificator, justificatory, justified, justifiedly, justifier, justifier's, justifiers, justifies, justify, justifying, justifyingly, justing, justinian, justinianeus, justitia, justle, justled, justler, justles, justling, justly, justment, justments, justness, justnesses, justo, justs, jut, jute, jutelike, jutes, jutka, juts, jutted, juttied, jutties, jutting, juttingly, jutty, juttying, juv, juvenal, juvenals, juvenate, juvenescence, juvenescent, juvenile, juvenile's, juvenilely, juvenileness, juveniles, juvenilia, juvenilify, juvenilism, juvenilities, juvenility, juvenilize, juvenocracy, juvenolatry, juvent, juventude, juvia, juvite, juwise, juxta, juxtalittoral, juxtamarine, juxtapose, juxtaposed, juxtaposes, juxtaposing, juxtaposit, juxtaposition, juxtapositional, juxtapositions, juxtapositive, juxtapyloric, juxtaspinal, juxtaterrestrial, juxtatropical, jymold, jyngine, jynx, k, k's, ka, kaaba, kaama, kaas, kaataplectic, kab, kabab, kababs, kabaka, kabakas, kabala, kabalas, kabar, kabaragoya, kabars, kabassou, kabaya, kabayas, kabbala, kabbalah, kabbalahs, kabbalas, kabel, kabeljou, kabeljous, kaberu, kabiet, kabiki, kabikis, kabob, kabobs, kabs, kabuki, kabukis, kabuzuchi, kabyle, kacha, kachcha, kachin, kachina, kachinas, kadaya, kadder, kaddish, kaddishes, kaddishim, kadein, kadi, kadikane, kadine, kadis, kadischi, kadish, kadishim, kados, kadsura, kae, kaempferol, kaes, kaf, kaferita, kaffeeklatsch, kaffir, kaffirs, kaffiyeh, kaffiyehs, kafila, kafir, kafiri, kafirin, kafirs, kafiz, kafka, kafta, kaftan, kaftans, kago, kagos, kagu, kagura, kagus, kaha, kahala, kahar, kahau, kahawai, kahikatea, kahili, kahu, kahuna, kahunas, kai, kaiak, kaiaks, kaid, kaif, kaifs, kaik, kaikara, kaikawaka, kail, kails, kailyard, kailyarder, kailyardism, kailyards, kaimakam, kaiman, kain, kainga, kaingin, kainit, kainite, kainites, kainits, kainogenesis, kainozoic, kains, kainsi, kainyn, kairin, kairine, kairolin, kairoline, kairos, kairotic, kaiser, kaiserdom, kaiserin, kaiserins, kaiserism, kaisers, kaisership, kaitaka, kaivalya, kaiwhiria, kaiwi, kajawah, kajeput, kajeputs, kajugaru, kaka, kakapo, kakapos, kakar, kakarali, kakaralli, kakariki, kakas, kakawahie, kakemono, kakemonos, kaki, kakidrosis, kakis, kakistocracies, kakistocracy, kakistocratical, kakkak, kakke, kakogenic, kakorraphiaphobia, kakortokite, kakotopia, kal, kala, kalaazar, kalach, kaladana, kalam, kalamalo, kalamansanai, kalamkari, kalams, kalan, kalanchoe, kalasie, kalathoi, kalathos, kale, kaleege, kaleidescope, kaleidophon, kaleidophone, kaleidoscope, kaleidoscopes, kaleidoscopic, kaleidoscopical, kaleidoscopically, kalema, kalend, kalendar, kalendarial, kalends, kales, kalewife, kalewives, kaleyard, kaleyards, kali, kalian, kalians, kaliborite, kalidium, kalif, kalifate, kalifates, kaliform, kalifs, kaligenous, kalimba, kalimbas, kalinite, kaliophilite, kalipaya, kaliph, kaliphs, kalis, kalium, kaliums, kalkvis, kallah, kallege, kallidin, kallidins, kallilite, kallitype, kalmia, kalmias, kalmuck, kalmuk, kalo, kalogeros, kalokagathia, kalon, kalong, kalongs, kalpa, kalpak, kalpaks, kalpas, kalpis, kalsomine, kalsomined, kalsominer, kalsomining, kaltemail, kalumpang, kalumpit, kalunti, kalymmaukion, kalymmocyte, kalyptra, kalyptras, kalysis, kam, kama, kamaaina, kamaainas, kamachi, kamachile, kamacite, kamacites, kamahi, kamala, kamalas, kamaloka, kamanichile, kamansi, kamao, kamarezite, kamarupa, kamarupic, kamas, kamass, kamassi, kamavachara, kambal, kamboh, kambou, kame, kameel, kameeldoorn, kameelthorn, kamelaukia, kamelaukion, kamelaukions, kamelkia, kamerad, kames, kami, kamian, kamias, kamichi, kamik, kamika, kamikaze, kamikazes, kamiks, kamis, kamleika, kammalan, kammererite, kammeu, kammina, kamperite, kampong, kampongs, kampseen, kamptomorph, kamptulicon, kampuchea, kampylite, kamseen, kamseens, kamsin, kamsins, kan, kana, kanae, kanaff, kanagi, kanaima, kanaka, kanamono, kanamycin, kanap, kanara, kanarese, kanari, kanas, kanat, kanchil, kand, kande, kandjar, kandol, kane, kaneelhart, kaneh, kanephore, kanephoros, kanes, kang, kanga, kangani, kangany, kangaroo, kangarooer, kangarooing, kangaroolike, kangaroos, kangayam, kangla, kangri, kanji, kanjis, kankedort, kankie, kankrej, kannada, kannen, kannu, kannume, kanone, kanoon, kans, kansan, kansans, kansas, kant, kantar, kantars, kantela, kantele, kanteles, kanteletar, kanten, kantharoi, kantharos, kantian, kantians, kantiara, kantry, kanuka, kanyaw, kanzu, kaoliang, kaoliangs, kaolin, kaolinate, kaoline, kaolines, kaolinic, kaolinisation, kaolinise, kaolinised, kaolinising, kaolinite, kaolinization, kaolinize, kaolinized, kaolinizing, kaolins, kaon, kaons, kapa, kapai, kapas, kapeika, kapelle, kapellmeister, kaph, kaphs, kapok, kapoks, kapote, kapp, kappa, kapparah, kappas, kappe, kappellmeister, kappie, kappland, kapuka, kapur, kaput, kaputt, karabiner, karaburan, karacul, karagan, karaism, karaite, karaka, karakul, karakule, karakuls, karakurt, karamu, karanda, karat, karatas, karate, karateist, karates, karats, karatto, karaya, karbi, karch, kareao, kareau, kareeta, karela, karelian, karen, karewa, karez, karinghota, karite, kariti, karma, karmadharaya, karmas, karmathian, karmic, karmouth, karn, karns, karo, karoo, karoos, karos, kaross, karosses, karou, karpas, karree, karren, karri, karroo, karroos, karrusel, karsha, karst, karstenite, karstic, karsts, kart, kartel, karting, kartings, kartometer, kartos, karts, karuna, karval, karvar, karwar, karyaster, karyatid, karyenchyma, karyochrome, karyochylema, karyocyte, karyogamic, karyogamy, karyokinesis, karyokinetic, karyolitic, karyologic, karyological, karyologically, karyology, karyolymph, karyolysis, karyolytic, karyomere, karyomerite, karyomicrosome, karyomitoic, karyomitome, karyomiton, karyomitosis, karyomitotic, karyon, karyoplasm, karyoplasma, karyoplasmatic, karyoplasmic, karyopyknosis, karyorrhexis, karyoschisis, karyosoma, karyosome, karyosystematics, karyotin, karyotins, karyotype, karyotypic, karyotypical, kas, kasa, kasbah, kasbeke, kascamiol, kaser, kasha, kashas, kasher, kashered, kashering, kashers, kashga, kashi, kashim, kashima, kashira, kashmir, kashmiri, kashmirs, kashrut, kashruth, kashruths, kashruts, kashubian, kasida, kasm, kasolite, kassabah, kassu, kastura, kat, katabases, katabasis, katabatic, katabella, katabolic, katabolically, katabolism, katabolite, katabolize, katabothra, katabothron, katachromasis, katacrotic, katacrotism, katagelophobia, katagenesis, katagenetic, katakana, katakanas, katakinesis, katakinetic, katakinetomer, katakinetomeric, katakiribori, katalase, katalyses, katalysis, katalyst, katalytic, katalyze, katalyzed, katalyzer, katalyzing, katamorphic, katamorphism, katana, kataphoresis, kataphoretic, kataphoric, kataphrenia, kataplasia, kataplectic, kataplexy, katar, katastate, katastatic, katat, katathermometer, katatonia, katatonic, katatype, katchina, katchung, katcina, kath, katha, kathak, kathal, katharevusa, katharine, katharometer, katharses, katharsis, kathartic, kathemoglobin, kathenotheism, katherine, kathisma, kathismata, kathodal, kathode, kathodes, kathodic, katholikoi, katholikos, katholikoses, kathy, kation, kations, katipo, katjepiering, katmon, katogle, katrina, kats, katsunkel, katsup, katuka, katun, katurai, katydid, katydids, katzenjammer, kauch, kauri, kauries, kauris, kaury, kava, kavaic, kavas, kavass, kavasses, kaver, kavika, kaw, kawaka, kawakawa, kawika, kay, kayak, kayaker, kayakers, kayaks, kayan, kayles, kayo, kayoed, kayoes, kayoing, kayos, kays, kayward, kazachki, kazachok, kazatske, kazatski, kazatskies, kazatsky, kazi, kazoo, kazoos, kb, kbar, kbps, kc, kc/s, kcal, kea, keach, keacorn, keap, kearn, keas, keat, keats, keawe, keb, kebab, kebabs, kebar, kebars, kebbie, kebbies, kebbock, kebbocks, kebbuck, kebbucks, kebby, keblah, keblahs, kebob, kebobs, kebyar, kechel, kechumaran, keck, kecked, kecking, keckle, keckled, keckles, keckling, kecks, kecksies, kecksy, kecky, ked, keddah, keddahs, kedge, kedged, kedger, kedgeree, kedgerees, kedges, kedging, kedgy, kedjave, kedlock, kedushah, keech, keef, keefs, keek, keeked, keeker, keekers, keeking, keeks, keel, keelage, keelages, keelback, keelbill, keelbird, keelblock, keelboat, keelboatman, keelboatmen, keelboats, keeldrag, keeled, keeler, keelfat, keelhale, keelhaled, keelhales, keelhaling, keelhaul, keelhauled, keelhauling, keelhauls, keelie, keeling, keelivine, keelless, keelman, keelrake, keels, keelson, keelsons, keelvat, keen, keena, keened, keener, keeners, keenest, keening, keenly, keenness, keennesses, keens, keep, keepable, keeper, keeperess, keepering, keeperless, keepers, keepership, keeping, keepings, keepnet, keeps, keepsake, keepsakes, keepsaky, keepworthy, keerie, keerogue, keeshond, keeshonden, keeshonds, keeslip, keest, keester, keesters, keet, keets, keeve, keeves, kef, keffel, keffiyeh, kefiatoid, kefifrel, kefir, kefiric, kefirs, kefs, keg, kegeler, kegelers, kegful, keggmiengg, kegler, keglers, kegling, keglings, kegs, kehaya, kehillah, kehilloth, kehoeite, keilhauite, keir, keirs, keist, keister, keisters, keita, keitloa, keitloas, kekotene, kekuna, kelchin, kelchyn, keld, kelder, kele, kelebe, kelectome, keleh, kelek, kelep, kelia, kelk, kell, kella, kelleg, kellegk, kellet, kellia, kellick, kellies, kellion, kellock, kellupweed, kelly, kellys, keloid, keloidal, keloids, kelotomies, kelotomy, kelowna, kelp, kelped, kelper, kelpfish, kelpfishes, kelpie, kelpies, kelping, kelps, kelpware, kelpwort, kelpy, kelson, kelsons, kelt, kelter, kelters, keltic, keltics, keltie, kelts, kelty, kelvin, kelvins, kelyphite, kemancha, kemb, kemelin, kemp, kempas, kemperyman, kempite, kemple, kemps, kempster, kempt, kemptken, kempts, kempy, ken, kenaf, kenafs, kenareh, kench, kenches, kend, kendal, kendir, kendna, kendo, kendoist, kendos, kendy, kendyr, kenema, kenlore, kenmark, kenmpy, kennebecker, kennebunker, kenned, kennedy, kennel, kennel's, kenneled, kenneling, kennell, kennelled, kennelling, kennelly, kennelman, kennels, kenner, kennet, kenning, kennings, kenningwort, kenno, kenny, keno, kenogenesis, kenogenetic, kenogenetically, kenogeny, kenophobia, kenos, kenosis, kenosises, kenotic, kenoticism, kenoticist, kenotism, kenotist, kenotoxin, kenotron, kenotrons, kens, kenscoff, kensington, kenspac, kenspeck, kenspeckle, kenspeckled, kent, kentallenite, kente, kentia, kentish, kentle, kentledge, kentrogon, kentrolite, kentuckian, kentuckians, kentucky, kenya, kenyan, kenyans, kenyte, keogenesis, keout, kep, kephalin, kephalins, kephir, kepi, kepis, kepped, keppen, kepping, keps, kept, keracele, keraci, keralite, keramic, keramics, kerana, keraphyllocele, keraphyllous, kerasin, kerasine, kerat, keratalgia, keratectacia, keratectasia, keratectomies, keratectomy, keratin, keratinization, keratinize, keratinized, keratinizing, keratinoid, keratinophilic, keratinose, keratinous, keratins, keratitis, keratoangioma, keratocele, keratocentesis, keratocni, keratoconi, keratoconjunctivitis, keratoconus, keratocricoid, keratode, keratoderma, keratodermia, keratogenic, keratogenous, keratoglobus, keratoglossus, keratohelcosis, keratohyal, keratoid, keratoiritis, keratol, keratoleukoma, keratolysis, keratolytic, keratoma, keratomalacia, keratomas, keratomata, keratome, keratometer, keratometric, keratometry, keratomycosis, keratoncus, keratonosus, keratonyxis, keratophyr, keratophyre, keratoplastic, keratoplasties, keratoplasty, keratorrhexis, keratoscope, keratoscopy, keratose, keratoses, keratosic, keratosis, keratosropy, keratotic, keratotome, keratotomies, keratotomy, keratto, keraulophon, keraulophone, keraunia, keraunion, keraunograph, keraunographic, keraunography, keraunophobia, keraunophone, keraunophonic, keraunoscopia, keraunoscopy, kerb, kerbaya, kerbed, kerbing, kerbs, kerbstone, kerch, kercher, kerchief, kerchief's, kerchiefed, kerchiefs, kerchieft, kerchieves, kerchoo, kerchug, kerchunk, kerectomy, kerel, kerf, kerfed, kerfing, kerflap, kerflop, kerflummox, kerfs, kerfuffle, kerite, kerl, kerman, kermes, kermesic, kermesite, kermess, kermesses, kermis, kermises, kern, kerne, kerned, kernel, kernel's, kerneled, kerneling, kernella, kernelled, kernelless, kernelling, kernelly, kernels, kerner, kernes, kernetty, kerning, kernish, kernite, kernites, kernoi, kernos, kerns, kero, kerogen, kerogens, kerolite, keros, kerosene, kerosenes, kerosine, kerosines, kerplunk, kerria, kerrias, kerrie, kerries, kerrikerri, kerril, kerrite, kerry, kers, kersanne, kersantite, kersey, kerseymere, kerseynette, kerseys, kerslam, kerslosh, kersmash, kerugma, kerugmata, keruing, kerve, kerwham, kerygma, kerygmata, kerygmatic, kerykeion, kerystic, kerystics, kesar, keslep, kesse, kesslerman, kestrel, kestrelkestrels, kestrels, ket, keta, ketal, ketapang, ketatin, ketazine, ketch, ketchcraft, ketches, ketchup, ketchups, ketchy, ketembilla, keten, ketene, ketenes, kethib, kethibh, ketimid, ketimide, ketimin, ketimine, ketine, ketipate, ketipic, ketmie, keto, ketogen, ketogenesis, ketogenetic, ketogenic, ketoheptose, ketohexose, ketoketene, ketol, ketole, ketolyses, ketolysis, ketolytic, ketonaemia, ketone, ketonemia, ketones, ketonic, ketonimid, ketonimide, ketonimin, ketonimine, ketonization, ketonize, ketonuria, ketose, ketoses, ketoside, ketosis, ketosteroid, ketosuccinic, ketotic, ketoxime, kette, ketting, kettle, kettle's, kettlecase, kettledrum, kettledrummer, kettledrums, kettleful, kettlemaker, kettlemaking, kettler, kettles, kettrin, ketty, ketuba, ketubah, ketubahs, ketuboth, ketupa, ketway, ketyl, keup, keuper, keurboom, kevalin, kevazingo, kevel, kevelhead, kevels, kever, kevil, kevils, kevutzah, kevutzoth, keweenawite, kewpie, kex, kexes, kexy, key, keyage, keyaki, keyboard, keyboard's, keyboarded, keyboarder, keyboarding, keyboards, keybutton, keyed, keyhole, keyholes, keying, keyless, keylet, keylock, keyman, keymen, keymove, keynesian, keynote, keynoted, keynoter, keynoters, keynotes, keynoting, keypad, keypad's, keypads, keypress, keypresses, keypunch, keypunched, keypuncher, keypunchers, keypunches, keypunching, keys, keyseat, keyseater, keyserlick, keyset, keysets, keyslot, keysmith, keyster, keysters, keystone, keystoned, keystones, keystroke, keystroke's, keystrokes, keyway, keyways, keywd, keyword, keyword's, keywords, keywrd, kg, kgf, kgr, kha, khaddar, khaddars, khadi, khadis, khafajeh, khagiarite, khahoon, khaiki, khair, khaja, khajur, khakanship, khakham, khaki, khakied, khakilike, khakis, khalal, khalat, khalif, khalifa, khalifas, khalifat, khalifate, khalifs, khalkha, khalsa, khalsah, khamal, khamseen, khamseens, khamsin, khamsins, khan, khanate, khanates, khanda, khandait, khanga, khanjar, khanjee, khankah, khans, khansama, khansamah, khansaman, khanum, khar, kharaj, kharif, kharouba, kharroubah, khartoum, kharua, kharwa, khass, khat, khatib, khatin, khatri, khats, khayal, khazen, khazenim, khazens, kheda, khedah, khedahs, khedas, khediva, khedival, khedivate, khedive, khedives, khediviah, khedivial, khediviate, khella, khellin, khepesh, khesari, khet, khi, khidmatgar, khidmutgar, khilat, khir, khirka, khirkah, khirkahs, khis, khitmatgar, khitmutgar, khmer, khodja, khoja, khojah, khoka, khot, khowar, khrushchev, khu, khubber, khud, khula, khulda, khuskhus, khutba, khutbah, khutuktu, khvat, ki, kiaat, kiabooca, kiack, kiaki, kialee, kialkee, kiang, kiangs, kiaugh, kiaughs, kibbeh, kibber, kibble, kibbled, kibbler, kibblerman, kibbles, kibbling, kibbutz, kibbutzim, kibbutznik, kibe, kibei, kibes, kibitka, kibitz, kibitzed, kibitzer, kibitzers, kibitzes, kibitzing, kibla, kiblah, kiblahs, kiblas, kibosh, kiboshed, kiboshes, kiboshing, kibsey, kiby, kichel, kick, kickable, kickback, kickbacks, kickball, kickboard, kickdown, kicked, kickee, kicker, kickers, kickier, kickiest, kicking, kickish, kickless, kickoff, kickoffs, kickout, kickplate, kicks, kickseys, kickshaw, kickshaws, kicksies, kicksorter, kickstand, kickstands, kicktail, kickup, kickups, kickwheel, kickxia, kicky, kid, kid's, kidang, kidcote, kidded, kidder, kidderminster, kidders, kiddie, kiddier, kiddies, kidding, kiddingly, kiddish, kiddishness, kiddle, kiddo, kiddoes, kiddos, kiddush, kiddushes, kiddushin, kiddy, kidhood, kidlet, kidlike, kidling, kidnap, kidnaped, kidnapee, kidnaper, kidnapers, kidnaping, kidnapped, kidnappee, kidnapper, kidnapper's, kidnappers, kidnapping, kidnapping's, kidnappings, kidnaps, kidney, kidney's, kidneylike, kidneylipped, kidneyroot, kidneys, kidneywort, kids, kidskin, kidskins, kidsman, kidvid, kie, kief, kiefekil, kiefs, kiekie, kiel, kielbasa, kielbasas, kielbasi, kielbasy, kier, kiers, kieselguhr, kieselgur, kieserite, kiesselguhr, kiesselgur, kiesserite, kiester, kiesters, kiestless, kiev, kieye, kif, kifs, kikar, kikawaeo, kike, kikes, kiki, kikoi, kikori, kiku, kikuel, kikumon, kil, kiladja, kilah, kilampere, kilan, kilbrickenite, kildee, kilderkin, kileh, kilerg, kiley, kileys, kilhig, kiliare, kilij, kilim, kilims, kilkenny, kill, killable, killadar, killas, killbuck, killcalf, killcrop, killcu, killdee, killdeer, killdeers, killdees, killed, killeekillee, killeen, killer, killers, killese, killick, killickinnic, killickinnick, killicks, killifish, killifishes, killig, killikinic, killikinick, killing, killingly, killingness, killings, killinite, killjoy, killjoys, killoch, killock, killocks, killogie, killow, kills, killweed, killwort, killy, kiln, kilned, kilneye, kilnhole, kilning, kilnman, kilnrib, kilns, kilnstick, kilntree, kilo, kiloampere, kilobar, kilobars, kilobit, kilobits, kiloblock, kilobuck, kilobyte, kilobytes, kilocalorie, kilocurie, kilocycle, kilocycles, kilodyne, kilogauss, kilograin, kilogram, kilogramme, kilogrammetre, kilograms, kilohertz, kilohm, kilojoule, kiloline, kiloliter, kilolitre, kilolumen, kilom, kilomegacycle, kilometer, kilometers, kilometrage, kilometre, kilometric, kilometrical, kilomole, kilomoles, kilooersted, kiloparsec, kilopoise, kilopound, kilorad, kilorads, kilos, kilostere, kiloton, kilotons, kilovar, kilovolt, kilovoltage, kilovolts, kiloware, kilowatt, kilowatts, kiloword, kilp, kilt, kilted, kilter, kilters, kiltie, kilties, kilting, kiltings, kiltlike, kilts, kilty, kiluck, kim, kimbang, kimberlin, kimberlite, kimbo, kimchee, kimchi, kimigayo, kimmer, kimmeridge, kimnel, kimono, kimonoed, kimonos, kimura, kin, kina, kinabulu, kinaestheic, kinaesthesia, kinaesthesias, kinaesthesis, kinaesthetic, kinaesthetically, kinah, kinase, kinases, kinboot, kinbot, kinbote, kinch, kinchin, kinchinmort, kincob, kind, kindal, kinder, kindergarten, kindergartener, kindergartening, kindergartens, kindergartner, kindergartners, kindest, kindheart, kindhearted, kindheartedly, kindheartedness, kindjal, kindle, kindled, kindler, kindlers, kindles, kindlesome, kindless, kindlessly, kindlier, kindliest, kindlily, kindliness, kindling, kindlings, kindly, kindness, kindnesses, kindred, kindredless, kindredly, kindredness, kindreds, kindredship, kindrend, kinds, kine, kinema, kinemas, kinematic, kinematical, kinematically, kinematics, kinematograph, kinematographer, kinematographic, kinematographical, kinematographically, kinematography, kinemometer, kineplasty, kinepox, kines, kinesalgia, kinescope, kinescoped, kinescopes, kinescoping, kineses, kinesiatric, kinesiatrics, kinesic, kinesically, kinesics, kinesimeter, kinesiologic, kinesiological, kinesiologies, kinesiology, kinesiometer, kinesipathy, kinesis, kinesitherapy, kinesodic, kinestheses, kinesthesia, kinesthesias, kinesthesis, kinesthetic, kinesthetically, kinetic, kinetical, kinetically, kineticism, kineticist, kinetics, kinetin, kinetins, kinetochore, kinetogenesis, kinetogenetic, kinetogenetically, kinetogenic, kinetogram, kinetograph, kinetographer, kinetographic, kinetography, kinetomer, kinetomeric, kinetonema, kinetonucleus, kinetophobia, kinetophone, kinetophonograph, kinetoplast, kinetoplastic, kinetoscope, kinetoscopic, kinetosis, kinetosome, kinfolk, kinfolks, king, kingbird, kingbirds, kingbolt, kingbolts, kingcob, kingcraft, kingcup, kingcups, kingdom, kingdom's, kingdomed, kingdomful, kingdomless, kingdoms, kingdomship, kinged, kingfish, kingfisher, kingfishers, kingfishes, kinghead, kinghood, kinghoods, kinghorn, kinghunter, kinging, kingklip, kingless, kinglessness, kinglet, kinglets, kinglier, kingliest, kinglihood, kinglike, kinglily, kingliness, kingling, kingly, kingmaker, kingmaking, kingpiece, kingpin, kingpins, kingpost, kingposts, kingrow, kings, kingship, kingships, kingside, kingsides, kingsize, kingsman, kingsnake, kingston, kingweed, kingwood, kingwoods, kinhin, kinic, kinin, kininogen, kininogenic, kinins, kink, kinkable, kinkaider, kinkajou, kinkajous, kinkcough, kinked, kinker, kinkhab, kinkhaust, kinkhost, kinkier, kinkiest, kinkily, kinkiness, kinking, kinkle, kinkled, kinkly, kinks, kinksbush, kinky, kinless, kinnery, kinnikinic, kinnikinick, kinnikinnic, kinnikinnick, kinnikinnik, kinnor, kino, kinofluous, kinology, kinone, kinoo, kinoos, kinoplasm, kinoplasmic, kinos, kinospore, kinot, kinotannic, kins, kinsen, kinsfolk, kinship, kinships, kinsman, kinsmanly, kinsmanship, kinsmen, kinspeople, kinswoman, kinswomen, kintar, kintlage, kintra, kintry, kinura, kioea, kionectomies, kionectomy, kionotomies, kionotomy, kiosk, kiosks, kiotome, kiotomies, kiotomy, kiowa, kip, kipage, kipe, kipfel, kippage, kipped, kippeen, kippen, kipper, kippered, kipperer, kippering, kippers, kippin, kipping, kippur, kippy, kips, kipsey, kipskin, kipskins, kipuka, kirbies, kirby, kirghiz, kiri, kirigami, kirigamis, kirimon, kirk, kirker, kirkify, kirking, kirkinhead, kirklike, kirkman, kirkmen, kirks, kirkton, kirktown, kirkward, kirkyard, kirman, kirmess, kirmesses, kirmew, kirn, kirned, kirning, kirns, kirombo, kirpan, kirsch, kirsches, kirschwasser, kirsen, kirtle, kirtled, kirtles, kirve, kirver, kisaeng, kisan, kisang, kischen, kish, kishen, kishka, kishkas, kishke, kishkes, kishon, kishy, kiskadee, kiskatom, kiskatomas, kiskitom, kiskitomas, kislev, kismat, kismats, kismet, kismetic, kismets, kisra, kiss, kissability, kissable, kissableness, kissably, kissage, kissar, kissed, kissel, kisser, kissers, kisses, kissing, kissingly, kissproof, kisswise, kissy, kist, kistful, kistfuls, kists, kistvaen, kiswa, kiswah, kit, kit's, kitab, kitabi, kitabis, kitambilla, kitar, kitbag, kitcat, kitchen, kitchen's, kitchendom, kitchener, kitchenet, kitchenette, kitchenettes, kitchenful, kitchenless, kitchenmaid, kitchenman, kitchenry, kitchens, kitchenward, kitchenwards, kitchenware, kitchenwife, kitcheny, kitchie, kitching, kite, kited, kiteflier, kiteflying, kitelike, kitenge, kiter, kiters, kites, kith, kithara, kitharas, kithe, kithed, kithes, kithing, kithless, kithlessness, kithogue, kiths, kiting, kitish, kitling, kitlings, kitman, kitmudgar, kits, kitsch, kitsches, kitschy, kittar, kitted, kittel, kitten, kitten's, kittendom, kittened, kittenhearted, kittenhood, kittening, kittenish, kittenishly, kittenishness, kittenless, kittenlike, kittens, kittenship, kitter, kittereen, kitthoge, kittie, kitties, kitting, kittisol, kittiwake, kittle, kittled, kittlepins, kittler, kittles, kittlest, kittling, kittlish, kittly, kittock, kittool, kittul, kitty, kittycorner, kittycornered, kittysol, kitysol, kiutle, kiva, kivas, kiver, kivikivi, kivu, kiwach, kiwanian, kiwi, kiwikiwi, kiwis, kiyas, kiyi, kjeldahlization, kjeldahlize, kl, klaberjass, klafter, klaftern, klam, klan, klangfarbe, klanism, klans, klaprotholite, klatch, klatches, klatsch, klatsches, klavern, klaverns, klavier, klaxon, klaxons, kleagle, kleagles, klebsiella, kleeneboc, kleenebok, kleenex, kleig, kleinite, klendusic, klendusity, klendusive, klepht, klephtic, klephtism, klephts, kleptic, kleptistic, kleptomania, kleptomaniac, kleptomaniacal, kleptomaniacs, kleptomanist, kleptophobia, klesha, klezmer, klick, klicket, klieg, klino, klip, klipbok, klipdachs, klipdas, klipfish, kliphaas, klippe, klippen, klipspringer, klismoi, klismos, klister, kln, klockmannite, kloesse, klom, klong, klongs, klooch, kloof, kloofs, klootch, klootchman, klop, klops, klosh, klosse, klowet, kluck, klucker, kludge, kludged, kludges, kludging, klunk, klutz, klutzes, klutzier, klutziest, klutziness, klutzy, klva, klystron, klystrons, km, km/sec, kmel, kmet, kmole, kn, knab, knabble, knack, knackaway, knackebrod, knacked, knacker, knackeries, knackers, knackery, knackier, knackiest, knacking, knackish, knacks, knackwurst, knackwursts, knacky, knag, knagged, knaggier, knaggiest, knaggy, knaidel, knaidlach, knap, knapbottle, knape, knappan, knappe, knapped, knapper, knappers, knapping, knappish, knappishly, knapple, knappy, knaps, knapsack, knapsack's, knapsacked, knapsacking, knapsacks, knapscap, knapscull, knapweed, knapweeds, knar, knark, knarl, knarle, knarred, knarry, knars, knaster, knatch, knatte, knave, knave's, knaveries, knavery, knaves, knaveship, knavess, knavish, knavishly, knavishness, knaw, knawel, knawels, knaydlach, knead, kneadability, kneadable, kneaded, kneader, kneaders, kneading, kneadingly, kneads, knebelite, knee, kneebrush, kneecap, kneecapping, kneecappings, kneecaps, kneed, kneehole, kneeholes, kneeing, kneel, kneeled, kneeler, kneelers, kneelet, kneeling, kneelingly, kneels, kneepad, kneepads, kneepan, kneepans, kneepiece, knees, kneestone, knell, knell's, knelled, knelling, knells, knelt, knet, knetch, knevel, knew, knez, knezi, kniaz, kniazi, knick, knicker, knickerbocker, knickerbocker's, knickerbockered, knickerbockers, knickered, knickers, knickknack, knickknackatory, knickknacked, knickknackery, knickknacket, knickknackish, knickknacks, knickknacky, knicknack, knickpoint, knife, knifeboard, knifed, knifeful, knifeless, knifelike, knifeman, knifeproof, knifer, kniferest, knifers, knifes, knifesmith, knifeway, knifing, knifings, knight, knightage, knighted, knightess, knighthead, knighthood, knighthoods, knighting, knightless, knightlihood, knightlike, knightliness, knightling, knightly, knights, knightship, knightswort, knipperdolling, knish, knishes, knit, knitback, knitch, knits, knitster, knittable, knitted, knitter, knitters, knittie, knitting, knittings, knittle, knitwear, knitwears, knitweed, knitwork, knive, knived, knives, knivey, knob, knob's, knobbed, knobber, knobbier, knobbiest, knobbiness, knobbing, knobble, knobbled, knobbler, knobblier, knobbliest, knobbling, knobbly, knobby, knobkerrie, knobkerry, knoblike, knobs, knobstick, knobstone, knobular, knobweed, knobwood, knock, knockabout, knockaway, knockdown, knockdowns, knocked, knockemdown, knocker, knockers, knocking, knockings, knockless, knockoff, knockoffs, knockout, knockouts, knocks, knockstone, knockup, knockwurst, knockwursts, knoit, knoll, knoll's, knolled, knoller, knollers, knolling, knolls, knolly, knop, knopite, knopped, knopper, knoppie, knoppy, knops, knopweed, knorhaan, knorhmn, knorr, knosp, knosped, knosps, knot, knot's, knotberry, knotgrass, knothead, knothole, knotholes, knothorn, knotless, knotlike, knotroot, knots, knotted, knotter, knotters, knottier, knottiest, knottily, knottiness, knotting, knotty, knotweed, knotweeds, knotwork, knotwort, knout, knouted, knouting, knouts, know, knowability, knowable, knowableness, knowe, knower, knowers, knoweth, knowhow, knowhows, knowing, knowinger, knowingest, knowingly, knowingness, knowings, knowledgable, knowledgableness, knowledgably, knowledge, knowledgeability, knowledgeable, knowledgeableness, knowledgeably, knowledged, knowledgeless, knowledgement, knowledging, known, knownothingism, knowns, knowperts, knows, knox, knoxville, knoxvillite, knub, knubbier, knubbiest, knubbly, knubby, knublet, knuckle, knuckleball, knuckleballer, knucklebone, knucklebones, knuckled, knucklehead, knuckleheaded, knuckleheadedness, knuckleheads, knuckler, knucklers, knuckles, knucklesome, knucklier, knuckliest, knuckling, knuckly, knucks, knuclesome, knuffe, knulling, knur, knurl, knurled, knurlier, knurliest, knurlin, knurling, knurls, knurly, knurry, knurs, knut, knuth, knutty, knyaz, knyazi, knysna, ko, koa, koae, koala, koalas, koali, koan, koans, koas, kob, koban, kobang, kobellite, kobi, kobird, kobold, kobolds, kobong, kobu, kochia, kochliarion, koda, kodak, kodaked, kodaker, kodaking, kodakist, kodakked, kodakking, kodakry, kodiak, kodkod, kodogu, kodro, kodurite, koeberliniaceous, koechlinite, koel, koels, koenenite, koff, koft, kofta, koftgar, koftgari, kogai, kogasin, koggelmannetje, kohekohe, kohemp, kohen, kohens, kohl, kohlrabi, kohlrabies, kohls, kohua, koi, koil, koila, koilanaglyphic, koilon, koilonychia, koimesis, koine, koines, koinon, koinonia, kojang, kojima, kojiri, kokako, kokam, kokama, kokan, kokanee, kokanees, kokerboom, kokia, kokil, kokila, kokio, koklas, koklass, koko, kokobeh, kokoon, kokoona, kokopu, kokoromiko, kokos, kokowai, kokra, koksaghyz, koksagyz, kokstad, koktaite, koku, kokum, kokumin, kokumingun, kola, kolach, kolacky, kolami, kolas, kolattam, kolea, koleroga, kolhoz, kolhozes, kolhozy, kolinski, kolinskies, kolinsky, kolkhos, kolkhoses, kolkhosy, kolkhoz, kolkhozes, kolkhoznik, kolkhozy, kolkoz, kolkozes, kolkozy, kollast, kollaster, koller, kollergang, kolmogorov, kolo, kolobia, kolobion, kolobus, kolokolo, kolos, kolskite, kolsun, koltunna, koltunnor, komarch, komatik, komatiks, kombu, kominuter, komitadji, komitaji, kommandatura, kommetje, kommos, komondor, komondoroc, komondorock, komondorok, komondors, kompeni, kompow, komtok, kon, kona, konak, kondo, konfyt, kong, kongo, kongoni, kongsbergite, kongu, konilite, konimeter, koninckite, konini, koniology, koniophobia, koniscope, konjak, konkani, konohiki, konseal, konstantin, kontakia, kontakion, koodoo, koodoos, kook, kooka, kookaburra, kookeree, kookery, kookie, kookier, kookiest, kookiness, kookri, kooks, kooky, koolah, koolau, kooletah, kooliman, koolokamba, koombar, koomkie, koonti, koopbrief, koorajong, koorhmn, koorka, koosin, kootcha, kootchar, kop, kopec, kopeck, kopecks, kopek, kopeks, kopfring, koph, kophs, kopi, kopis, kopje, kopjes, kopophobia, koppa, koppas, koppen, koppie, koppies, koppite, kops, kor, kora, koradji, korai, korait, korakan, koran, korari, kordax, kore, korea, korean, koreans, korec, koreci, korero, korfball, korhmn, kori, korimako, korin, korma, kornerupine, kornskeppa, kornskeppur, korntonde, korntonder, korntunna, korntunnur, koromika, koromiko, korona, korova, korrel, korrigan, korrigum, kors, korsakoff, korsakow, korumburra, korun, koruna, korunas, koruny, korymboi, korymbos, korzec, kos, kosha, koshare, kosher, koshered, koshering, koshers, kosin, kosmokrator, koso, kosong, kosos, kosotoxin, koss, koswite, kotal, koto, kotoite, kotos, kotow, kotowed, kotower, kotowers, kotowing, kotows, kotschubeite, kottaboi, kottabos, kottigite, kotuku, kotukutuku, kotwal, kotwalee, kotwali, kotyle, kotylos, kou, koulan, koulibiaca, koumis, koumises, koumiss, koumisses, koumys, koumyses, koumyss, koumysses, kouprey, koupreys, kouproh, kourbash, kouroi, kouros, kousin, koussin, kousso, koussos, kouza, kovil, kowbird, kowhai, kowtow, kowtowed, kowtower, kowtowers, kowtowing, kowtows, koyan, koyemshi, kozo, kozuka, kpc, kph, kr, kra, kraal, kraaled, kraaling, kraals, kraft, krafts, kragerite, krageroite, krait, kraits, kraken, krakens, krakowiak, kral, krama, krameria, krameriaceous, kran, krang, krans, krantz, krantzite, krapfen, kras, krasis, krater, kraters, kratogen, kratogenic, kraurite, kraurosis, kraurotic, krausen, krausite, kraut, krauthead, krauts, krautweed, kravers, kreatic, krebs, kreese, kreil, kreis, kreistle, kreitonite, kreittonite, kreitzman, krelos, kremersite, kremlin, kremlinologist, kremlinologists, kremlinology, kremlins, krems, kreng, krennerite, kreosote, krepis, kreplach, kreplech, kreutzer, kreutzers, kreuzer, kreuzers, kriegspiel, krieker, krigia, krill, krills, krimmer, krimmers, krina, kris, krises, krishna, krishnaism, krispies, kriss, krisuvigite, kritarchy, kritrima, krivu, krna, krobyloi, krobylos, krocidolite, krocket, krohnkite, krome, kromeski, kromesky, kromogram, kromskop, krona, krone, kronen, kroner, kronor, kronos, kronur, kroo, kroon, krooni, kroons, krosa, krouchka, kroushka, krs, krubi, krubis, krubut, krubuts, kruller, krullers, krumhorn, krummholz, krummhorn, kryokonite, kryolite, kryolites, kryolith, kryoliths, krypsis, kryptic, krypticism, kryptocyanine, kryptol, kryptomere, krypton, kryptonite, kryptons, ksar, kshatriya, ksi, kt, kthibh, kuan, kuba, kubba, kubong, kubuklion, kuchean, kuchen, kuchens, kudize, kudo, kudos, kudu, kudus, kudzu, kudzus, kue, kueh, kuei, kues, kuffieh, kufic, kufiyeh, kuge, kugel, kugelhof, kuichua, kujawiak, kukang, kukeri, kukoline, kukri, kuku, kukui, kukupa, kula, kulack, kulah, kulaite, kulak, kulaki, kulakism, kulaks, kulan, kulang, kulimit, kulkarni, kullaite, kulm, kulmet, kultur, kulturkampf, kulturs, kumara, kumari, kumbaloi, kumbi, kumbuk, kumhar, kumis, kumiss, kumisses, kumkum, kummel, kummels, kummerbund, kumminost, kumquat, kumquats, kumrah, kumshaw, kumys, kumyses, kunai, kundalini, kung, kunk, kunkur, kunmiut, kunwari, kunzite, kunzites, kupfernickel, kupfferite, kuphar, kupper, kurajong, kurbash, kurbashed, kurbashes, kurbashing, kurchatovium, kurchicine, kurchine, kurd, kurdish, kurdistan, kurgan, kurgans, kurikata, kurmburra, kurn, kurrajong, kursaal, kursch, kurta, kurtas, kurtosis, kurtosises, kuru, kuruma, kurumaya, kurung, kurus, kurvey, kurveyor, kusa, kusam, kusha, kusimanse, kusimansel, kuskite, kuskos, kuskus, kusso, kussos, kusti, kusum, kutch, kutcha, kutta, kuttab, kuttar, kuttaur, kuvasz, kuvaszok, kuwait, kv, kvah, kvar, kvarner, kvas, kvases, kvass, kvasses, kvetch, kvetched, kvetches, kvetching, kvint, kvinter, kvutza, kvutzah, kw, kwacha, kwachas, kwaiken, kwamme, kwan, kwanza, kwarta, kwarterka, kwartje, kwashiorkor, kwatuma, kwaznku, kwazoku, kwela, kwhr, kwintra, ky, kyabuka, kyack, kyacks, kyah, kyak, kyang, kyanise, kyanised, kyanises, kyanising, kyanite, kyanites, kyanization, kyanize, kyanized, kyanizes, kyanizing, kyanol, kyar, kyars, kyat, kyathoi, kyathos, kyats, kyaung, kyd, kye, kyke, kyl, kyle, kylie, kylies, kylikec, kylikes, kylin, kylite, kylix, kyloe, kymation, kymatology, kymbalon, kymnel, kymogram, kymograms, kymograph, kymographic, kymography, kymric, kynurenic, kynurin, kynurine, kyoodle, kyoodled, kyoodling, kyoto, kyphoscoliosis, kyphoscoliotic, kyphoses, kyphosis, kyphotic, kyrial, kyriale, kyrie, kyrielle, kyries, kyrine, kyriologic, kyrios, kyschty, kyschtymite, kyte, kytes, kythe, kythed, kythes, kything, kytoon, kyu, l, l'addition, l'chaim, l'envoy, l'oeil, l's, l'tre, l/w, la, laager, laagered, laagering, laagers, laang, lab, lab's, labaara, labadist, labara, labaria, labarum, labarums, labba, labbella, labber, labby, labdacism, labdacismus, labdanum, labdanums, labefact, labefactation, labefaction, labefied, labefy, labefying, label, labeled, labeler, labelers, labeling, labella, labellate, labelled, labeller, labellers, labelling, labelloid, labellum, labels, labia, labial, labialisation, labialise, labialised, labialising, labialism, labialismus, labiality, labialization, labialize, labialized, labializing, labially, labials, labiate, labiated, labiates, labiatiflorous, labibia, labidometer, labidophorous, labiella, labile, labilities, lability, labilization, labilize, labilized, labilizing, labioalveolar, labiocervical, labiodendal, labiodental, labioglossal, labioglossolaryngeal, labioglossopharyngeal, labiograph, labiogression, labiogutteral, labiolingual, labiomancy, labiomental, labionasal, labiopalatal, labiopalatalize, labiopalatine, labiopharyngeal, labioplasty, labiose, labiotenaculum, labiovelar, labiovelarisation, labiovelarise, labiovelarised, labiovelarising, labiovelarization, labiovelarize, labiovelarized, labiovelarizing, labioversion, labis, labite, labium, lablab, labor, laborability, laborable, laborage, laborant, laboratorial, laboratorially, laboratorian, laboratories, laboratory, laboratory's, labordom, labored, laboredly, laboredness, laborer, laborers, labores, laboress, laborhood, laboring, laboringly, laborings, laborious, laboriously, laboriousness, laborism, laborist, laboristic, laborite, laborites, laborius, laborless, laborous, laborously, laborousness, labors, laborsaving, laborsome, laborsomely, laborsomeness, laboulbeniaceous, labour, labourage, laboured, labouredly, labouredness, labourer, labourers, labouress, labouring, labouringly, labourism, labourist, labourite, labourless, labours, laboursaving, laboursome, laboursomely, labra, labrador, labradorite, labradoritic, labral, labras, labredt, labret, labretifery, labrets, labrid, labroid, labroids, labrosaurid, labrosauroid, labrose, labrum, labrums, labrusca, labrys, labs, laburnum, laburnums, labyrinth, labyrinthal, labyrinthally, labyrinthed, labyrinthian, labyrinthibranch, labyrinthibranchiate, labyrinthic, labyrinthical, labyrinthically, labyrinthiform, labyrinthine, labyrinthitis, labyrinthodon, labyrinthodont, labyrinthodontian, labyrinthodontid, labyrinthodontoid, labyrinths, lac, lacatan, lacca, laccaic, laccainic, laccase, laccic, laccin, laccol, laccolite, laccolith, laccolithic, laccoliths, laccolitic, lace, lacebark, laced, lacedaemonian, laceflower, laceier, laceiest, laceleaf, laceless, lacelike, lacemaker, lacemaking, laceman, lacemen, lacepiece, lacepod, lacer, lacerability, lacerable, lacerant, lacerate, lacerated, lacerately, lacerates, lacerating, laceration, lacerations, lacerative, lacerna, lacernae, lacernas, lacers, lacert, lacertian, lacertid, lacertids, lacertiform, lacertilian, lacertiloid, lacertine, lacertoid, lacertose, lacery, laces, lacet, lacetilian, lacewing, lacewings, lacewoman, lacewomen, lacewood, lacewoods, lacework, laceworker, laceworks, lacey, laceybark, lache, laches, lachesis, lachryma, lachrymable, lachrymae, lachrymaeform, lachrymal, lachrymally, lachrymalness, lachrymary, lachrymation, lachrymator, lachrymatories, lachrymatory, lachrymiform, lachrymist, lachrymogenic, lachrymonasal, lachrymosal, lachrymose, lachrymosely, lachrymosity, lachrymous, lachsa, lacier, laciest, lacily, laciness, lacinesses, lacing, lacings, lacinia, laciniate, laciniated, laciniation, laciniform, laciniola, laciniolate, laciniose, lacinious, lacinula, lacinulas, lacinulate, lacinulose, lacis, lack, lackadaisic, lackadaisical, lackadaisicality, lackadaisically, lackadaisicalness, lackadaisy, lackaday, lackbrained, lackbrainedness, lacked, lacker, lackered, lackerer, lackering, lackers, lackey, lackeydom, lackeyed, lackeying, lackeyism, lackeys, lackeyship, lackies, lacking, lackland, lackluster, lacklusterness, lacklustre, lacklustrous, lacks, lacksense, lackwit, lackwitted, lackwittedly, lackwittedness, lacmoid, lacmus, lacoca, lacolith, laconian, laconic, laconica, laconical, laconically, laconicalness, laconicism, laconicness, laconics, laconicum, laconism, laconisms, laconize, laconized, laconizer, laconizing, lacquer, lacquered, lacquerer, lacquerers, lacquering, lacquerist, lacquers, lacquerwork, lacquey, lacqueyed, lacqueying, lacqueys, lacrimal, lacrimals, lacrimation, lacrimator, lacrimatories, lacrimatory, lacroixite, lacrosse, lacrosser, lacrosses, lacrym, lacs, lactagogue, lactalbumin, lactam, lactamide, lactams, lactant, lactarene, lactarine, lactarious, lactarium, lactary, lactase, lactases, lactate, lactated, lactates, lactating, lactation, lactational, lactationally, lactations, lacteal, lacteally, lacteals, lactean, lactenin, lacteous, lactesce, lactescence, lactescency, lactescenle, lactescense, lactescent, lactic, lacticinia, lactid, lactide, lactiferous, lactiferousness, lactific, lactifical, lactification, lactified, lactiflorous, lactifluous, lactiform, lactifuge, lactify, lactifying, lactigenic, lactigenous, lactigerous, lactim, lactimide, lactinate, lactivorous, lacto, lactobaccilli, lactobacilli, lactobacillus, lactobutyrometer, lactocele, lactochrome, lactocitrate, lactodensimeter, lactoflavin, lactogen, lactogenic, lactoglobulin, lactoid, lactol, lactometer, lactone, lactones, lactonic, lactonization, lactonize, lactonized, lactonizing, lactophosphate, lactoproteid, lactoprotein, lactoscope, lactose, lactoses, lactosid, lactoside, lactosuria, lactothermometer, lactotoxin, lactovegetarian, lactucarium, lactucerin, lactucin, lactucol, lactucon, lactyl, lacuna, lacunae, lacunal, lacunar, lacunaria, lacunaris, lacunars, lacunary, lacunas, lacunate, lacune, lacunes, lacunome, lacunose, lacunosis, lacunosity, lacunule, lacunulose, lacuscular, lacustral, lacustrian, lacustrine, lacwork, lacy, lad, ladakin, ladang, ladanigerous, ladanum, ladanums, ladder, laddered, laddering, ladderless, ladderlike, ladderman, laddermen, ladders, ladderway, ladderwise, laddery, laddess, laddie, laddies, laddikie, laddish, laddock, lade, laded, lademan, laden, ladened, ladening, ladens, lader, laders, lades, ladhood, ladies, ladified, ladify, ladifying, ladin, lading, ladings, ladino, ladinos, ladkin, ladle, ladled, ladleful, ladlefuls, ladler, ladlers, ladles, ladlewood, ladling, ladner, ladron, ladrone, ladrones, ladronism, ladronize, ladrons, lads, lady, lady's, ladybird, ladybirds, ladybug, ladybugs, ladyclock, ladydom, ladyfern, ladyfinger, ladyfingers, ladyfish, ladyfishes, ladyflies, ladyfly, ladyfy, ladyhood, ladyhoods, ladyish, ladyishly, ladyishness, ladyism, ladykiller, ladykin, ladykind, ladykins, ladyless, ladylike, ladylikely, ladylikeness, ladyling, ladylintywhite, ladylove, ladyloves, ladyly, ladypalm, ladypalms, ladysfinger, ladyship, ladyships, ladyslipper, ladysnow, laemodipod, laemodipodan, laemodipodiform, laemodipodous, laemoparalysis, laemostenosis, laen, laender, laeotropic, laeotropism, laeotropous, laertes, laet, laetation, laeti, laetic, laetrile, laevigate, laevo, laevoduction, laevogyrate, laevogyre, laevogyrous, laevolactic, laevorotation, laevorotatory, laevotartaric, laevoversion, laevulin, laevulose, lafayette, laft, lag, lagan, lagans, lagarto, lagen, lagena, lagenae, lagend, lagends, lagenian, lageniform, lageniporm, lager, lagered, lagering, lagers, lagerspetze, lagetto, laggar, laggard, laggardism, laggardly, laggardness, laggards, lagged, laggen, lagger, laggers, laggin, lagging, laggingly, laggings, laggins, laglast, lagly, lagna, lagnappe, lagnappes, lagniappe, lagniappes, lagomorph, lagomorphic, lagomorphous, lagomrph, lagonite, lagoon, lagoon's, lagoonal, lagoons, lagoonside, lagophthalmos, lagophthalmus, lagopode, lagopodous, lagopous, lagopus, lagostoma, lagrangian, lags, laguna, lagunas, lagune, lagunes, lagwort, lah, lahar, lahnda, lahore, lai, laic, laical, laicality, laically, laich, laichs, laicisation, laicise, laicised, laicises, laicising, laicism, laicisms, laicity, laicization, laicize, laicized, laicizer, laicizes, laicizing, laics, laid, laidly, laigh, laighs, laik, lain, lainage, laine, lainer, laiose, lair, lair's, lairage, laird, lairdess, lairdie, lairdly, lairdocracy, lairds, lairdship, laired, lairing, lairless, lairman, lairmen, lairs, lairstone, lairy, laiser, laisse, laissez, lait, laitance, laitances, laith, laithe, laithly, laities, laity, laius, lak, lakarpite, lakatan, lakatoi, lake, lake's, laked, lakefront, lakeland, lakelander, lakeless, lakelet, lakelike, lakemanship, lakeport, lakeports, laker, lakers, lakes, lakeshore, lakeside, lakesides, lakeward, lakeweed, lakey, lakh, lakhs, lakie, lakier, lakiest, lakin, laking, lakings, lakish, lakishness, lakism, lakist, lakke, lakmus, laksa, laky, lalang, lalapalooza, lalaqui, laliophobia, lall, lallan, lalland, lallands, lallans, lallapalooza, lallation, lalled, lalling, lalls, lally, lallygag, lallygagged, lallygagging, lallygags, lalo, laloneurosis, lalopathies, lalopathy, lalophobia, laloplegia, lam, lama, lamaic, lamaism, lamantin, lamany, lamarckian, lamarckism, lamas, lamasary, lamaseries, lamasery, lamastery, lamb, lamb's, lamba, lamback, lambale, lambast, lambaste, lambasted, lambastes, lambasting, lambasts, lambda, lambdacism, lambdas, lambdiod, lambdoid, lambdoidal, lambeau, lambed, lambencies, lambency, lambent, lambently, lamber, lambers, lambert, lamberts, lambes, lambhood, lambie, lambies, lambiness, lambing, lambish, lambitive, lambkill, lambkills, lambkin, lambkins, lambliasis, lamblike, lamblikeness, lambling, lambly, lamboy, lamboys, lambrequin, lambs, lambsdown, lambskin, lambskins, lambsuccory, lamby, lamda, lamdan, lamden, lame, lamebrain, lamebrained, lamebrains, lamed, lamedh, lamedhs, lamedlamella, lameds, lameduck, lamel, lamella, lamellae, lamellar, lamellarly, lamellary, lamellas, lamellate, lamellated, lamellately, lamellation, lamellibranch, lamellibranchiate, lamellicorn, lamellicornate, lamellicornous, lamelliferous, lamelliform, lamellirostral, lamellirostrate, lamelloid, lamellose, lamellosity, lamellule, lamely, lameness, lamenesses, lament, lamentabile, lamentability, lamentable, lamentableness, lamentably, lamentation, lamentation's, lamentational, lamentations, lamentatory, lamented, lamentedly, lamenter, lamenters, lamentful, lamenting, lamentingly, lamentive, lamentory, laments, lamer, lames, lamest, lamester, lamestery, lameter, lametta, lamia, lamiaceous, lamiae, lamias, lamiger, lamiid, lamin, lamina, laminability, laminable, laminae, laminal, laminar, laminaria, laminariaceous, laminarian, laminarin, laminarioid, laminarite, laminary, laminas, laminate, laminated, laminates, laminating, lamination, laminator, laminboard, laminectomy, laming, lamington, laminiferous, laminiform, laminiplantar, laminiplantation, laminitis, laminose, laminous, lamish, lamister, lamisters, lamiter, lamm, lammas, lammed, lammer, lammergeier, lammergeir, lammergeyer, lammie, lamming, lammock, lammy, lamnectomy, lamnid, lamnoid, lamp, lamp's, lampad, lampadaire, lampadaries, lampadary, lampadedromy, lampadephore, lampadephoria, lampadist, lampadite, lampads, lampara, lampas, lampases, lampate, lampatia, lampblack, lampblacked, lampblacking, lamped, lamper, lampern, lampers, lamperses, lampf, lampflower, lampfly, lampful, lamphole, lampic, lamping, lampion, lampions, lampist, lampistry, lampless, lamplet, lamplight, lamplighted, lamplighter, lamplit, lampmaker, lampmaking, lampman, lampmen, lampoon, lampooned, lampooner, lampooners, lampoonery, lampooning, lampoonist, lampoonists, lampoons, lamppost, lampposts, lamprel, lampret, lamprey, lampreys, lampron, lamprophonia, lamprophonic, lamprophony, lamprophyre, lamprophyric, lamprotype, lamps, lampshade, lampshell, lampstand, lampwick, lampworker, lampworking, lampyrid, lampyrids, lampyrine, lams, lamsiekte, lamster, lamsters, lamziekte, lan, lanai, lanais, lanameter, lanarkite, lanas, lanate, lanated, lanaz, lancashire, lancaster, lancasterian, lancastrian, lance, lanced, lancegay, lancegaye, lancejack, lancelet, lancelets, lancelike, lancelot, lancely, lanceman, lancemen, lanceolar, lanceolate, lanceolated, lanceolately, lanceolation, lancepesade, lancepod, lanceprisado, lanceproof, lancer, lancers, lances, lancet, lanceted, lanceteer, lancetfish, lancetfishes, lancets, lancewood, lanch, lancha, lanchara, lanciers, lanciferous, lanciform, lancinate, lancinated, lancinating, lancination, lancing, land, landage, landamman, landammann, landau, landaulet, landaulette, landaus, landblink, landbook, landdrost, landdrosten, lande, landed, lander, landers, landesite, landfall, landfalls, landfang, landfast, landfill, landfills, landflood, landfolk, landform, landforms, landgafol, landgate, landgates, landgravate, landgrave, landgraveship, landgravess, landgraviate, landgravine, landhold, landholder, landholders, landholdership, landholding, landholdings, landimere, landing, landings, landiron, landladies, landlady, landlady's, landladydom, landladyhood, landladyish, landladyship, landleaper, landler, landlers, landless, landlessness, landlike, landline, landlock, landlocked, landlook, landlooker, landloper, landloping, landlord, landlord's, landlordism, landlordly, landlordry, landlords, landlordship, landlouper, landlouping, landlubber, landlubberish, landlubberly, landlubbers, landlubbing, landman, landmark, landmark's, landmarks, landmass, landmasses, landmen, landmil, landmonger, landocracies, landocracy, landocrat, landolphia, landowner, landowner's, landowners, landownership, landowning, landplane, landrace, landrail, landraker, landreeve, landright, lands, landsale, landsat, landscape, landscaped, landscaper, landscapers, landscapes, landscaping, landscapist, landshard, landshark, landship, landsick, landside, landsides, landskip, landskips, landsknecht, landsleit, landslid, landslidden, landslide, landslided, landslides, landsliding, landslip, landslips, landsmaal, landsman, landsmanleit, landsmanshaft, landsmanshaften, landsmen, landspout, landspringy, landstorm, landsturm, landswoman, landtrost, landwaiter, landward, landwards, landwash, landway, landways, landwehr, landwhin, landwire, landwrack, landwreck, landyard, lane, lane's, lanely, lanes, lanesome, lanete, laneway, laney, lang, langaha, langarai, langate, langauge, langbanite, langbeinite, langca, langeel, langel, langi, langiel, langite, langka, langlauf, langlaufer, langlaufers, langlaufs, langle, langley, langleys, langobardic, langoon, langooty, langosta, langouste, langrage, langrages, langrel, langrels, langret, langridge, langsat, langset, langsettle, langshan, langshans, langspiel, langspil, langsyne, langsynes, langteraloo, language, language's, languaged, languageless, languages, languaging, langue, langued, languedoc, languent, langues, languescent, languet, languets, languette, languid, languidly, languidness, languish, languished, languisher, languishers, languishes, languishing, languishingly, languishment, languor, languorment, languorous, languorously, languorousness, languors, langur, langurs, laniard, laniards, laniaries, laniariform, laniary, laniate, lanier, laniferous, lanific, lanifice, laniflorous, laniform, lanigerous, laniiform, lanioid, lanista, lanistae, lanital, lanitals, lank, lanker, lankest, lanket, lankier, lankiest, lankily, lankiness, lankish, lankly, lankness, lanknesses, lanky, lanner, lanneret, lannerets, lanners, lanolated, lanolin, lanoline, lanolines, lanolins, lanose, lanosities, lanosity, lansa, lansat, lansdowne, lanseh, lansfordite, lansing, lansknecht, lanson, lansquenet, lant, lantaca, lantaka, lantana, lantanas, lantanium, lantcha, lanterloo, lantern, lantern's, lanterned, lanternfish, lanternfishes, lanternflower, lanterning, lanternist, lanternleaf, lanternlit, lanternman, lanterns, lanthana, lanthania, lanthanid, lanthanide, lanthanite, lanthanon, lanthanum, lanthopin, lanthopine, lanthorn, lanthorns, lantum, lanuginose, lanuginous, lanuginousness, lanugo, lanugos, lanum, lanx, lanyard, lanyards, lanzknecht, lanzon, lao, laocoon, laodah, laodicean, laos, laotian, laotians, lap, lap's, lapacho, lapachol, lapactic, laparectomy, laparocele, laparocholecystotomy, laparocolectomy, laparocolostomy, laparocolotomy, laparocolpohysterotomy, laparocolpotomy, laparocystectomy, laparocystotomy, laparoelytrotomy, laparoenterostomy, laparoenterotomy, laparogastroscopy, laparogastrotomy, laparohepatotomy, laparohysterectomy, laparohysteropexy, laparohysterotomy, laparoileotomy, laparomyitis, laparomyomectomy, laparomyomotomy, laparonephrectomy, laparonephrotomy, laparorrhaphy, laparosalpingectomy, laparosalpingotomy, laparoscope, laparoscopy, laparosplenectomy, laparosplenotomy, laparostict, laparothoracoscopy, laparotome, laparotomies, laparotomist, laparotomize, laparotomized, laparotomizing, laparotomy, laparotrachelotomy, lapb, lapboard, lapboards, lapcock, lapdog, lapdogs, lapel, lapel's, lapeler, lapelled, lapels, lapful, lapfuls, lapicide, lapidarian, lapidaries, lapidarist, lapidary, lapidate, lapidated, lapidates, lapidating, lapidation, lapidator, lapideon, lapideous, lapides, lapidescence, lapidescent, lapidicolous, lapidific, lapidifical, lapidification, lapidified, lapidifies, lapidify, lapidifying, lapidist, lapidists, lapidity, lapidose, lapies, lapilli, lapilliform, lapillo, lapillus, lapin, lapinized, lapins, lapis, lapises, lapland, laplander, laplanders, lapling, lapon, lapp, lappaceous, lappage, lapped, lapper, lappered, lappering, lappers, lappet, lappeted, lappethead, lappets, lappic, lappilli, lapping, lappish, lapponian, lapps, lapputan, laps, lapsability, lapsable, lapsation, lapse, lapsed, lapser, lapsers, lapses, lapsful, lapsi, lapsibility, lapsible, lapsided, lapsing, lapsingly, lapstone, lapstrake, lapstreak, lapstreaked, lapstreaker, lapsus, laptop, lapulapu, laputan, laputically, lapwing, lapwings, lapwork, laquais, laquear, laquearia, laquearian, laquei, laqueus, lar, lararia, lararia, lararium, larboard, larboards, larbolins, larbowlines, larcenable, larcener, larceners, larcenic, larcenies, larcenish, larcenist, larcenists, larcenous, larcenously, larcenousness, larceny, larch, larchen, larcher, larches, larcin, larcinry, lard, lardacein, lardaceous, larded, larder, larderellite, larderer, larderful, larderie, larderlike, larders, lardier, lardiest, lardiform, lardiner, larding, lardite, lardizabalaceous, lardlike, lardon, lardons, lardoon, lardoons, lardry, lards, lardworm, lardy, lare, lareabell, lares, largamente, largando, large, largebrained, largehanded, largehearted, largeheartedly, largeheartedness, largely, largemouth, largemouthed, largen, largeness, largeour, largeous, larger, larges, largess, largesse, largesses, largest, larget, larghetto, larghettos, larghissimo, larghissimos, largifical, largish, largishness, largition, largitional, largo, largos, largy, lari, lariat, lariated, lariating, lariats, larick, larid, laridine, larigo, larigot, lariid, larikin, larin, larine, larithmic, larithmics, larix, larixin, lark, lark's, larked, larker, larkers, larkier, larkiest, larkiness, larking, larkingly, larkish, larkishly, larkishness, larklike, larkling, larks, larksome, larksomes, larkspur, larkspurs, larky, larlike, larmier, larmoyant, larn, larnakes, larnax, larnyx, laroid, laron, larree, larries, larrigan, larrigans, larrikin, larrikinalian, larrikiness, larrikinism, larrikins, larriman, larrup, larruped, larruper, larrupers, larruping, larrups, larry, lars, larsenite, larum, larums, larva, larvae, larval, larvaria, larvarium, larvariums, larvas, larvate, larvated, larve, larvicidal, larvicide, larvicolous, larviform, larvigerous, larvikite, larviparous, larviposit, larviposition, larvivorous, larvule, laryngal, laryngalgia, laryngeal, laryngeally, laryngean, laryngeating, laryngectomee, laryngectomies, laryngectomize, laryngectomized, laryngectomizing, laryngectomy, laryngemphraxis, laryngendoscope, larynges, laryngic, laryngismal, laryngismus, laryngitic, laryngitis, laryngitus, laryngocele, laryngocentesis, laryngofission, laryngofissure, laryngograph, laryngography, laryngologic, laryngological, laryngologist, laryngology, laryngometry, laryngoparalysis, laryngopathy, laryngopharyngeal, laryngopharynges, laryngopharyngitis, laryngopharynx, laryngopharynxes, laryngophony, laryngophthisis, laryngoplasty, laryngoplegia, laryngorrhagia, laryngorrhea, laryngoscleroma, laryngoscope, laryngoscopic, laryngoscopical, laryngoscopically, laryngoscopies, laryngoscopist, laryngoscopy, laryngospasm, laryngostasis, laryngostenosis, laryngostomy, laryngostroboscope, laryngotome, laryngotomies, laryngotomy, laryngotracheal, laryngotracheitis, laryngotracheoscopy, laryngotracheotomy, laryngotyphoid, laryngovestibulitis, larynx, larynxes, las, lasa, lasagna, lasagnas, lasagne, lasagnes, lasarwort, lascar, lascaree, lascarine, lascars, laschety, lascivient, lasciviently, lascivious, lasciviously, lasciviousness, lase, lased, laser, laser's, laserdisk, laserdisks, laserjet, lasers, laserwort, lases, lash, lashed, lasher, lashers, lashes, lashing, lashingly, lashings, lashins, lashkar, lashkars, lashless, lashlight, lashlite, lashness, lashorn, lasianthous, lasing, lasiocampid, lasiocarpous, lask, lasket, lasking, laspring, lasque, lass, lass's, lasses, lasset, lassie, lassiehood, lassieish, lassies, lassiky, lassitude, lassitudes, lasslorn, lasso, lassock, lassockie, lassoed, lassoer, lassoers, lassoes, lassoing, lassos, lassu, last, lastage, lasted, laster, lasters, lastex, lasting, lastingly, lastingness, lastings, lastjob, lastly, lastness, lastre, lasts, lastspring, lasty, lat, lata, latah, latakia, latakias, latanier, latch, latched, latcher, latches, latchet, latchets, latching, latchkey, latchkeys, latchless, latchman, latchmen, latchstring, latchstrings, late, latebra, latebricole, latecomer, latecomers, latecoming, lated, lateen, lateener, lateeners, lateenrigged, lateens, lateliness, lately, latemost, laten, latence, latencies, latency, latened, lateness, latenesses, latening, latens, latensification, latensified, latensify, latensifying, latent, latentize, latently, latentness, latents, later, latera, laterad, lateral, lateraled, lateraling, lateralis, lateralities, laterality, lateralization, lateralize, lateralized, lateralizing, laterally, laterals, lateran, latericeous, latericumbent, lateriflexion, laterifloral, lateriflorous, laterifolious, laterigrade, laterinerved, laterite, laterites, lateritic, lateritious, lateriversion, laterization, lateroabdominal, lateroanterior, laterocaudal, laterocervical, laterodeviation, laterodorsal, lateroduction, lateroflexion, lateromarginal, lateronuchal, lateroposition, lateroposterior, lateropulsion, laterostigmatal, laterostigmatic, laterotemporal, laterotorsion, lateroventral, lateroversion, latescence, latescent, latesome, latest, latests, lateward, latewhile, latewhiles, latewood, latewoods, latex, latexes, latexosis, lath, latham, lathe, lathed, lathee, latheman, lathen, lather, latherability, latherable, lathered, lathereeve, latherer, latherers, lathering, latheron, lathers, latherwort, lathery, lathes, lathesman, lathesmen, lathhouse, lathi, lathie, lathier, lathiest, lathing, lathings, lathlike, lathreeve, laths, lathwork, lathworks, lathy, lathyric, lathyrism, lathyritic, lati, latian, latibule, latibulize, latices, laticifer, laticiferous, laticlave, laticostate, latidentate, latifolia, latifoliate, latifolious, latifundia, latifundian, latifundio, latifundium, latigo, latigoes, latigos, latimer, latimeria, latin, latinate, latinian, latinism, latinist, latinities, latinity, latinization, latinize, latinized, latinizes, latinizing, latino, latinos, latins, lation, latipennate, latipennine, latiplantar, latirostral, latirostrous, latisept, latiseptal, latiseptate, latish, latissimi, latissimus, latisternal, latitancy, latitant, latitat, latite, latitude, latitude's, latitudes, latitudinal, latitudinally, latitudinarian, latitudinarianism, latitudinarianisn, latitudinarians, latitudinary, latitudinous, lative, latke, latomia, latomy, laton, latonian, latosol, latosolic, latosols, latoun, latrant, latrate, latration, latrede, latreutic, latreutical, latria, latrial, latrially, latrian, latrias, latrine, latrine's, latrines, latro, latrobe, latrobite, latrocinium, latrociny, latron, lats, latten, lattener, lattens, latter, latterkin, latterly, lattermath, lattermint, lattermost, latterness, lattice, lattice's, latticed, latticeleaf, latticelike, lattices, latticewise, latticework, latticicini, latticing, latticinii, latticinio, lattin, lattins, latus, latvia, latvian, latvians, lauan, lauans, laubanite, laud, laudability, laudable, laudableness, laudably, laudanidine, laudanin, laudanine, laudanosine, laudanum, laudanums, laudation, laudative, laudator, laudatorily, laudators, laudatory, laude, lauded, lauder, lauderdale, lauders, laudes, laudian, laudification, lauding, laudist, lauds, laugh, laughability, laughable, laughableness, laughably, laughed, laughee, laugher, laughers, laughful, laughing, laughingly, laughings, laughingstock, laughingstocks, laughs, laughsome, laughter, laughterful, laughterless, laughters, laughworthy, laughy, lauhala, lauia, laulau, laumonite, laumontite, laun, launce, launces, launch, launchable, launched, launcher, launchers, launches, launchful, launching, launchings, launchpad, launchplex, launchways, laund, launder, launderability, launderable, laundered, launderer, launderers, launderette, laundering, launderings, launders, laundress, laundresses, laundries, laundromat, laundromats, laundry, laundrymaid, laundryman, laundrymen, laundryowner, laundrywoman, laundrywomen, launeddas, laur, laura, lauraceous, laurae, lauraldehyde, lauras, laurate, laurdalite, laure, laureal, laureate, laureated, laureates, laureateship, laureateships, laureating, laureation, laurel, laurel's, laureled, laureling, laurelled, laurellike, laurelling, laurels, laurelship, laurelwood, laurence, laurentian, laureole, laurestinus, lauric, laurin, laurinoxylon, laurionite, laurite, laurone, laurotetanine, lauroyl, laurustine, laurustinus, laurvikite, laury, lauryl, laus, lautarite, lautenclavicymbal, lauter, lautite, lautitious, lautu, lauwine, lauwines, lav, lava, lavable, lavabo, lavaboes, lavabos, lavacre, lavadero, lavage, lavages, lavalava, lavalavas, lavalier, lavaliere, lavalieres, lavaliers, lavalike, lavalliere, lavament, lavandera, lavanderas, lavandero, lavanderos, lavandin, lavanga, lavant, lavaret, lavas, lavash, lavatic, lavation, lavational, lavations, lavatorial, lavatories, lavatory, lavatory's, lavature, lave, laveche, laved, laveer, laveered, laveering, laveers, lavement, lavender, lavendered, lavendering, lavenders, lavenite, laver, laveroc, laverock, laverocks, lavers, laverwort, laves, lavette, lavialite, lavic, laving, lavish, lavished, lavisher, lavishers, lavishes, lavishest, lavishing, lavishingly, lavishly, lavishment, lavishness, lavolta, lavrock, lavrocks, lavroffite, lavrovite, lavy, law, law's, lawabidingness, lawbook, lawbreak, lawbreaker, lawbreakers, lawbreaking, lawcourt, lawcraft, lawed, laweour, lawful, lawfullness, lawfully, lawfulness, lawgive, lawgiver, lawgivers, lawgiving, lawine, lawines, lawing, lawings, lawish, lawk, lawks, lawlants, lawless, lawlessly, lawlessness, lawlike, lawmake, lawmaker, lawmakers, lawmaking, lawman, lawmen, lawmonger, lawn, lawn's, lawned, lawner, lawnleaf, lawnlet, lawnlike, lawnmower, lawns, lawny, lawproof, lawrence, lawrencite, lawrencium, lawrightman, lawrightmen, laws, lawsone, lawsonite, lawsuit, lawsuit's, lawsuiting, lawsuits, lawter, lawyer, lawyer's, lawyeress, lawyeresses, lawyering, lawyerism, lawyerlike, lawyerling, lawyerly, lawyers, lawyership, lawyery, lawzy, lax, laxate, laxation, laxations, laxative, laxatively, laxativeness, laxatives, laxator, laxer, laxest, laxiflorous, laxifoliate, laxifolious, laxism, laxist, laxities, laxity, laxly, laxness, laxnesses, lay, layabout, layabouts, layaway, layaways, layback, layboy, laydown, layed, layer, layerage, layerages, layered, layering, layerings, layers, layery, layette, layettes, layfolk, laying, layland, laylight, layloc, laylock, layman, laymanship, laymen, layne, layner, layoff, layoffs, layout, layout's, layouts, layover, layovers, layperson, layrock, lays, layshaft, layship, laystall, laystow, layup, laywoman, laywomen, lazar, lazaret, lazarets, lazarette, lazaretto, lazarettos, lazarist, lazarlike, lazarly, lazarole, lazarone, lazarous, lazars, lazarus, lazary, laze, lazed, lazes, lazied, lazier, lazies, laziest, lazily, laziness, lazinesses, lazing, lazule, lazuli, lazuline, lazulis, lazulite, lazulites, lazulitic, lazurite, lazurites, lazy, lazyback, lazybed, lazybird, lazybone, lazybones, lazyboots, lazyhood, lazying, lazyish, lazylegs, lazyship, lazzarone, lazzaroni, lb, lbf, lbinit, lbs, lbw, lc, lca, lcd, lcm, lconvert, lcsymbol, ld, ldg, ldinfo, le, lea, leach, leachability, leachable, leachate, leachates, leached, leacher, leachers, leaches, leachier, leachiest, leaching, leachman, leachmen, leachy, lead, leadable, leadableness, leadage, leadback, leaded, leaden, leadenhearted, leadenheartedness, leadenly, leadenness, leadenpated, leader, leaderess, leaderette, leaderless, leaders, leadership, leadership's, leaderships, leadeth, leadhillite, leadier, leadiest, leadin, leadiness, leading, leadingly, leadings, leadless, leadline, leadman, leadoff, leadoffs, leadout, leadplant, leadproof, leads, leadsman, leadsmen, leadstone, leadway, leadwood, leadwork, leadworks, leadwort, leadworts, leady, leaf, leafage, leafages, leafbird, leafboy, leafcup, leafdom, leafed, leafen, leafer, leafery, leafgirl, leafhopper, leafhoppers, leafier, leafiest, leafiness, leafing, leafit, leafless, leaflessness, leaflet, leaflet's, leafleteer, leaflets, leaflike, leafmold, leafs, leafstalk, leafstalks, leafwood, leafwork, leafworm, leafworms, leafy, league, leagued, leaguelong, leaguer, leaguered, leaguerer, leaguering, leaguers, leagues, leaguing, leak, leakage, leakage's, leakages, leakance, leaked, leaker, leakers, leakier, leakiest, leakily, leakiness, leaking, leakless, leakproof, leaks, leaky, leal, lealand, leally, lealness, lealties, lealty, leam, leamer, lean, leander, leaned, leaner, leanest, leangle, leaning, leanings, leanish, leanly, leanness, leannesses, leans, leant, leany, leap, leapable, leaped, leaper, leapers, leapfrog, leapfrogged, leapfrogger, leapfrogging, leapfrogs, leapful, leaping, leapingly, leaps, leapt, lear, learier, leariest, learn, learnable, learned, learnedly, learnedness, learner, learners, learnership, learning, learnings, learns, learnt, lears, leary, leas, leasable, lease, leaseback, leased, leasehold, leaseholder, leaseholders, leaseholding, leaseholds, leaseless, leaseman, leasemen, leasemonger, leaser, leasers, leases, leash, leash's, leashed, leashes, leashing, leashless, leasing, leasings, leasow, least, leasts, leastways, leastwise, leat, leath, leather, leatherback, leatherbark, leatherboard, leatherbush, leathercoat, leathercraft, leathered, leatherer, leatherette, leatherfish, leatherfishes, leatherflower, leatherhead, leatherine, leatheriness, leathering, leatherize, leatherjacket, leatherleaf, leatherleaves, leatherlike, leatherlikeness, leathermaker, leathermaking, leathern, leatherneck, leathernecks, leatheroid, leatherroot, leathers, leatherside, leatherware, leatherwing, leatherwood, leatherwork, leatherworker, leatherworking, leathery, leathwake, leatman, leatmen, leave, leaved, leaveless, leavelooker, leaven, leavened, leavening, leavenish, leavenless, leavenous, leavens, leaver, leavers, leaverwood, leaves, leavetaking, leavier, leaviest, leaving, leavings, leavy, leawill, leban, lebanese, lebanon, lebban, lebbek, leben, lebens, lebensraum, lebes, lebhaft, lebkuchen, lebrancho, lecama, lecaniid, lecanine, lecanomancer, lecanomancy, lecanomantic, lecanoraceous, lecanoric, lecanorine, lecanoroid, lecanoscopic, lecanoscopy, lech, lechatelierite, lechayim, lechayims, leche, lecher, lechered, lecherer, lecheries, lechering, lecherous, lecherously, lecherousness, lechers, lechery, leches, lechosa, lechriodont, lechuguilla, lechuguillas, lechwe, lecideaceous, lecideiform, lecideine, lecidioid, lecithal, lecithalbumin, lecithality, lecithic, lecithin, lecithinase, lecithins, lecithoblast, lecithoid, lecithoprotein, leck, lecker, lecontite, lecotropal, lect, lectern, lecterns, lecthi, lectica, lection, lectionaries, lectionary, lections, lectisternium, lector, lectorate, lectorial, lectors, lectorship, lectotype, lectress, lectrice, lectual, lectuary, lecture, lectured, lecturee, lectureproof, lecturer, lecturers, lectures, lectureship, lectureships, lecturess, lecturette, lecturing, lecturn, lecyth, lecythi, lecythid, lecythidaceous, lecythoi, lecythoid, lecythus, led, leda, lede, leden, lederhosen, lederite, ledge, ledged, ledgeless, ledgeman, ledgement, ledger, ledgerdom, ledgered, ledgering, ledgers, ledges, ledget, ledgier, ledgiest, ledging, ledgment, ledgy, ledol, leds, lee, leeangle, leeboard, leeboards, leech, leech's, leechcraft, leechdom, leecheater, leeched, leecher, leechery, leeches, leeching, leechkin, leechlike, leechman, leechwort, leed, leeds, leef, leefang, leefange, leeftail, leeful, leefully, leegatioen, leegte, leek, leekish, leeks, leeky, leelane, leelang, leep, leepit, leer, leered, leerfish, leerier, leeriest, leerily, leeriness, leering, leeringly, leerish, leerness, leeroway, leers, leery, lees, leese, leeser, leeshyy, leesing, leesome, leesomely, leet, leetle, leetman, leetmen, leets, leewan, leeward, leewardly, leewardmost, leewardness, leewards, leeway, leeways, leewill, lefsel, lefsen, left, lefter, leftest, lefties, leftish, leftism, leftisms, leftist, leftist's, leftists, leftments, leftmost, leftness, leftover, leftover's, leftovers, lefts, leftward, leftwardly, leftwards, leftwing, leftwinger, lefty, leg, legacies, legacy, legacy's, legal, legalese, legaleses, legalise, legalised, legalises, legalising, legalism, legalisms, legalist, legalistic, legalistically, legalists, legalities, legality, legalization, legalizations, legalize, legalized, legalizes, legalizing, legally, legalness, legals, legantine, legantinelegatary, legatary, legate, legated, legatee, legatees, legates, legateship, legateships, legati, legatine, legating, legation, legationary, legations, legative, legato, legator, legatorial, legators, legatory, legatos, legature, legatus, legbar, lege, legend, legend's, legenda, legendarian, legendaries, legendarily, legendary, legendic, legendist, legendize, legendized, legendizing, legendless, legendries, legendry, legends, leger, legerdemain, legerdemainist, legerete, legerities, legerity, legers, leges, legge, legged, legger, leggiadrous, leggier, leggiero, leggiest, leggin, legginess, legging, legginged, leggings, leggins, leggy, legharness, leghorn, leghorns, legibilities, legibility, legible, legibleness, legibly, legifer, legific, legion, legion's, legionaries, legionary, legioned, legioner, legionnaire, legionnaires, legionry, legions, legis, legislate, legislated, legislates, legislating, legislation, legislational, legislativ, legislative, legislatively, legislator, legislator's, legislatorial, legislatorially, legislators, legislatorship, legislatress, legislatresses, legislatrices, legislatrix, legislatrixes, legislature, legislature's, legislatures, legist, legister, legists, legit, legitim, legitimacies, legitimacy, legitimate, legitimated, legitimately, legitimateness, legitimating, legitimation, legitimatise, legitimatised, legitimatising, legitimatist, legitimatization, legitimatize, legitimatized, legitimatizing, legitime, legitimisation, legitimise, legitimised, legitimising, legitimism, legitimist, legitimistic, legitimity, legitimization, legitimizations, legitimize, legitimized, legitimizer, legitimizes, legitimizing, legitimum, legits, leglen, legless, leglessness, leglet, leglike, legman, legmen, legoa, legong, legpiece, legpull, legpuller, legpulling, legrete, legroom, legrooms, legrope, legs, legua, leguan, leguleian, leguleious, legume, legumelin, legumen, legumes, legumin, leguminiform, leguminose, leguminous, legumins, legwork, legworks, lehay, lehayim, lehayims, lehmer, lehr, lehrbachite, lehrman, lehrmen, lehrs, lehrsman, lehrsmen, lehua, lehuas, lei, leibnitzian, leicester, leifite, leiger, leighton, leimtype, leiocephalous, leiocome, leiodermatous, leiodermia, leiomyofibroma, leiomyoma, leiomyomas, leiomyomata, leiomyomatous, leiomyosarcoma, leiophyllous, leiotrichine, leiotrichous, leiotrichy, leiotropic, leipzig, leis, leishmania, leishmanial, leishmaniasis, leishmanic, leishmanioid, leishmaniosis, leiss, leister, leistered, leisterer, leistering, leisters, leisurabe, leisurable, leisurably, leisure, leisured, leisureful, leisureless, leisureliness, leisurely, leisureness, leisures, leitmotif, leitmotifs, leitmotiv, leitneriaceous, lek, lekach, lekanai, lekane, lekha, lekker, leks, lekythi, lekythoi, lekythos, lekythus, lelwel, leman, lemanry, lemans, leme, lemel, lemma, lemma's, lemmas, lemmata, lemmatize, lemming, lemmings, lemmitis, lemmoblastic, lemmocyte, lemmon, lemmus, lemnaceous, lemnad, lemnian, lemniscata, lemniscate, lemniscatic, lemnisci, lemniscus, lemnisnisci, lemogra, lemography, lemology, lemon, lemon's, lemonade, lemonades, lemonado, lemonfish, lemonfishes, lemongrass, lemonish, lemonlike, lemons, lemonweed, lemonwood, lemony, lempira, lempiras, lemur, lemures, lemurian, lemurid, lemuriform, lemurine, lemurlike, lemuroid, lemuroids, lemurs, lenad, lenard, lench, lencheon, lend, lendable, lended, lendee, lender, lenders, lending, lends, lene, lenes, leng, lenger, lengest, length, lengthen, lengthened, lengthener, lengtheners, lengthening, lengthens, lengther, lengthful, lengthier, lengthiest, lengthily, lengthiness, lengthly, lengthman, lengths, lengthsman, lengthsmen, lengthsome, lengthsomeness, lengthways, lengthwise, lengthy, leniate, lenience, leniences, leniencies, leniency, lenient, leniently, lenientness, lenify, lenin, leningrad, leninism, leninist, leninists, lenis, lenitic, lenities, lenition, lenitive, lenitively, lenitiveness, lenitives, lenitude, lenity, lennilite, lennoaceous, lennow, leno, lenocinant, lenos, lens, lens's, lense, lensed, lenses, lensless, lenslike, lensman, lensmen, lent, lentamente, lentando, lenten, lenth, lenthways, lentibulariaceous, lentic, lenticel, lenticellate, lenticels, lenticle, lenticonus, lenticula, lenticular, lenticulare, lenticularis, lenticularly, lenticulas, lenticulate, lenticulated, lenticulating, lenticulation, lenticule, lenticulostriate, lenticulothalamic, lentiform, lentigerous, lentigines, lentiginose, lentiginous, lentigo, lentil, lentil's, lentile, lentils, lentiner, lentisc, lentiscine, lentisco, lentiscus, lentisk, lentisks, lentissimo, lentitude, lentitudinous, lentner, lento, lentoid, lentor, lentos, lentous, lenvoi, lenvoy, leo, leodicid, leon, leonard, leonardesque, leonardo, leoncito, leone, leones, leonhardite, leonid, leonine, leoninely, leonines, leonite, leontiasis, leontocephalous, leontodon, leopard, leopard's, leoparde, leopardess, leopardine, leopardite, leopards, leopardskin, leopardwood, leopoldite, leos, leotard, leotards, lep, lepa, lepadid, lepadoid, lepage, lepal, lepargylic, leper, leperdom, lepered, lepero, lepers, lepid, lepidene, lepidin, lepidine, lepidity, lepidly, lepidoblastic, lepidodendraceous, lepidodendrid, lepidodendrids, lepidodendroid, lepidodendroids, lepidoid, lepidolite, lepidomelane, lepidophyllous, lepidophyte, lepidophytic, lepidoporphyrin, lepidopter, lepidoptera, lepidopteral, lepidopteran, lepidopterid, lepidopterist, lepidopterological, lepidopterologist, lepidopterology, lepidopteron, lepidopterous, lepidosaurian, lepidoses, lepidosiren, lepidosirenoid, lepidosis, lepidosteoid, lepidote, lepidotic, lepismoid, lepocyta, lepocyte, leporicide, leporid, leporidae, leporide, leporids, leporiform, leporine, lepospondylous, lepothrix, leppy, lepra, lepralian, lepre, leprechaun, leprechauns, lepric, leprid, leprine, leproid, leprologic, leprologist, leprology, leproma, lepromatous, leprosaria, leprosarium, leprosariums, leprose, leprosed, leproseries, leprosery, leprosied, leprosies, leprosis, leprosity, leprosy, leprotic, leprous, leprously, leprousness, lepry, lepsaria, lepta, leptandra, leptandrin, leptene, leptera, leptid, leptiform, leptinolite, leptite, leptobos, leptocardian, leptocentric, leptocephalan, leptocephali, leptocephalia, leptocephalic, leptocephalid, leptocephaloid, leptocephalous, leptocephalus, leptocephaly, leptocercal, leptochlorite, leptochroa, leptochrous, leptoclase, leptodactyl, leptodactylous, leptodermatous, leptodermous, leptoform, leptokurtic, leptokurtosis, leptology, leptomatic, leptome, leptomedusan, leptomeningeal, leptomeninges, leptomeningitis, leptomeninx, leptometer, leptomonad, lepton, leptonecrosis, leptonema, leptonic, leptons, leptopellic, leptophyllous, leptoprosope, leptoprosopic, leptoprosopous, leptoprosopy, leptorrhin, leptorrhine, leptorrhinian, leptorrhinism, leptorrhiny, leptosomatic, leptosome, leptosomic, leptosperm, leptospira, leptospirae, leptospiral, leptospiras, leptospire, leptospirosis, leptosporangiate, leptostracan, leptostracous, leptotene, leptus, leptynite, lequear, lere, lernaean, lernaeiform, lernaeoid, lerot, lerp, lerret, les, lesbian, lesbianism, lesbians, lesche, lese, lesed, lesion, lesional, lesions, lesiy, leskeaceous, lespedeza, less, lessee, lessees, lesseeship, lessen, lessened, lessener, lessening, lessens, lesser, lesses, lessest, lessive, lessn, lessness, lesson, lesson's, lessoned, lessoning, lessons, lessor, lessors, lest, leste, lester, lestiwarite, lestobioses, lestobiosis, lestobiotic, lestrad, lesya, let, let's, letch, letches, letchy, letdown, letdowns, lete, letgame, lethal, lethalities, lethality, lethalize, lethally, lethals, lethargic, lethargical, lethargically, lethargicalness, lethargies, lethargise, lethargised, lethargising, lethargize, lethargized, lethargizing, lethargus, lethargy, lethe, lethean, lethes, lethied, lethiferous, lethologica, lethy, leto, letoff, letorate, letrist, lets, lett, lettable, letted, letten, letter, lettercard, lettered, letterer, letterers, letteret, letterform, lettergae, lettergram, letterhead, letterheads, lettering, letterings, letterleaf, letterless, letterman, lettermen, lettern, letterpress, letters, letterset, letterspace, letterspaced, letterspacing, letterure, letterweight, letterwood, lettic, lettice, lettiga, letting, lettish, lettrin, lettrure, lettsomite, lettuce, lettuces, letuare, letup, letups, leu, leucaemia, leucaemic, leucaethiop, leucaethiopes, leucaethiopic, leucaniline, leucanthous, leucaugite, leucaurin, leucemia, leucemias, leucemic, leuch, leuchaemia, leuchemia, leuchtenbergite, leucic, leucin, leucine, leucines, leucins, leucism, leucite, leucites, leucitic, leucitis, leucitite, leucitohedron, leucitoid, leucitophyre, leuco, leucobasalt, leucoblast, leucoblastic, leucocarpous, leucochalcite, leucocholic, leucocholy, leucochroic, leucocidic, leucocidin, leucocism, leucocrate, leucocratic, leucocyan, leucocytal, leucocyte, leucocythaemia, leucocythaemic, leucocythemia, leucocythemic, leucocytic, leucocytoblast, leucocytogenesis, leucocytoid, leucocytology, leucocytolysin, leucocytolysis, leucocytolytic, leucocytometer, leucocytopenia, leucocytopenic, leucocytoplania, leucocytopoiesis, leucocytosis, leucocytotherapy, leucocytotic, leucoderma, leucodermatous, leucodermia, leucodermic, leucoencephalitis, leucoethiop, leucogenic, leucoid, leucoindigo, leucoindigotin, leucoline, leucolytic, leucoma, leucomaine, leucomas, leucomatous, leucomelanic, leucomelanous, leucon, leucones, leuconoid, leuconostoc, leucopenia, leucopenic, leucophane, leucophanite, leucophlegmacy, leucophoenicite, leucophore, leucophyllous, leucophyre, leucoplakia, leucoplakial, leucoplast, leucoplastid, leucopoiesis, leucopoietic, leucopus, leucopyrite, leucoquinizarin, leucorrhea, leucorrheal, leucorrhoea, leucorrhoeal, leucoryx, leucosis, leucospermous, leucosphenite, leucosphere, leucospheric, leucostasis, leucosticte, leucosyenite, leucotactic, leucotaxin, leucotaxine, leucotic, leucotome, leucotomies, leucotomy, leucotoxic, leucous, leucoxene, leucyl, leud, leudes, leuds, leuk, leukaemia, leukaemic, leukemia, leukemias, leukemic, leukemics, leukemid, leukemoid, leukoblast, leukoblastic, leukocidic, leukocidin, leukoctyoid, leukocyte, leukocytes, leukocythemia, leukocytic, leukocytoblast, leukocytoid, leukocytopenia, leukocytosis, leukocytotic, leukoderma, leukodystrophy, leukoma, leukomas, leukon, leukons, leukopedesis, leukopenia, leukopenic, leukopoiesis, leukopoietic, leukorrhea, leukorrheal, leukorrhoea, leukorrhoeal, leukoses, leukosis, leukotaxin, leukotaxine, leukotic, leukotomies, leukotomy, leuma, lev, leva, levade, levalloisian, levance, levancy, levant, levanted, levanter, levantera, levanters, levantine, levanting, levanto, levants, levarterenol, levation, levator, levatores, levators, leve, leveche, levee, levee's, leveed, leveeing, levees, leveful, level, leveled, leveler, levelers, levelheaded, levelheadedly, levelheadedness, leveling, levelish, levelism, levelled, leveller, levellers, levellest, levelling, levelly, levelman, levelness, levels, leven, lever, lever's, leverage, leveraged, leverages, leveraging, levered, leverer, leveret, leverets, levering, leverlike, leverman, levers, leverwood, levesel, levet, levi, levi's, leviable, leviathan, leviathans, leviation, levied, levier, leviers, levies, levigable, levigate, levigated, levigates, levigating, levigation, levigator, levin, leviner, levining, levins, levir, levirate, levirates, leviratic, leviratical, leviration, levis, levitant, levitate, levitated, levitates, levitating, levitation, levitational, levitations, levitative, levitator, levite, leviter, levitical, leviticus, levities, levity, levo, levoduction, levoglucose, levogyrate, levogyre, levogyrous, levolactic, levolimonene, levorotary, levorotation, levorotatory, levotartaric, levoversion, levulic, levulin, levulinic, levulins, levulose, levuloses, levulosuria, levy, levying, levyist, levyne, levynite, lew, lewd, lewder, lewdest, lewdly, lewdness, lewdnesses, lewdster, lewing, lewis, lewises, lewisite, lewisites, lewisson, lewissons, lewist, lewnite, lewth, lewty, lex, lexeme, lexemic, lexia, lexic, lexica, lexical, lexicalic, lexicality, lexically, lexicog, lexicographer, lexicographers, lexicographian, lexicographic, lexicographical, lexicographically, lexicographist, lexicography, lexicologic, lexicological, lexicologist, lexicology, lexicon, lexicon's, lexiconist, lexiconize, lexicons, lexicostatistic, lexicostatistical, lexicostatistics, lexigraphic, lexigraphical, lexigraphically, lexigraphy, lexiphanes, lexiphanic, lexiphanicism, lexis, lexological, ley, leyden, leyland, leys, leysing, lf, lg, lgth, lh, lhb, lhd, lherzite, lherzolite, lhiamba, li, liabilities, liability, liability's, liable, liableness, liaise, liaised, liaises, liaising, liaison, liaison's, liaisons, liamba, liana, lianas, liane, lianes, liang, liangle, liangs, lianoid, liar, liar's, liard, liards, liars, lias, liasing, liason, lib, libament, libaniferous, libanophorous, libanotophorous, libant, libard, libate, libated, libating, libation, libational, libationary, libationer, libations, libatory, libbard, libbed, libber, libbers, libbet, libbing, libbra, libecchio, libeccio, libeccios, libel, libelant, libelants, libeled, libelee, libelees, libeler, libelers, libeling, libelist, libelists, libellant, libellary, libellate, libelled, libellee, libellees, libeller, libellers, libelling, libellist, libellous, libellously, libellulid, libelluloid, libelous, libelously, libels, liber, libera, liberal, liberalisation, liberalise, liberalised, liberaliser, liberalising, liberalism, liberalist, liberalistic, liberalites, liberalities, liberality, liberalization, liberalizations, liberalize, liberalized, liberalizer, liberalizes, liberalizing, liberally, liberalness, liberals, liberate, liberated, liberates, liberating, liberation, liberationism, liberationist, liberationists, liberations, liberative, liberator, liberator's, liberators, liberatory, liberatress, liberatrice, liberatrix, liberia, liberian, liberians, liberomotor, libers, libertarian, libertarianism, libertarians, liberticidal, liberticide, liberties, libertinage, libertine, libertines, libertinism, liberty, liberty's, libertyless, liberum, libethenite, libget, libidibi, libidinal, libidinally, libidinist, libidinization, libidinized, libidinizing, libidinosity, libidinous, libidinously, libidinousness, libido, libidos, libinit, libitum, libken, libkin, libr, libra, librae, librairie, libral, librarian, librarian's, librarianess, librarians, librarianship, libraries, librarii, librarious, librarius, library, library's, libraryless, libras, librate, librated, librates, librating, libration, librational, libratory, libre, libretti, librettist, librettists, libretto, librettos, libri, libriform, libris, libroplast, libs, libya, libyan, libyans, licareol, licca, lice, licence, licenceable, licenced, licencee, licencees, licencer, licencers, licences, licencing, licensable, license, licensed, licensee, licensees, licenseless, licenser, licensers, licenses, licensing, licensor, licensors, licensure, licentiate, licentiates, licentiateship, licentiation, licentious, licentiously, licentiousness, licet, lich, licham, lichanos, lichee, lichees, lichen, lichen's, lichenaceous, lichened, lichenian, licheniasis, lichenic, lichenicolous, lichenification, licheniform, lichening, lichenins, lichenise, lichenised, lichenising, lichenism, lichenist, lichenivorous, lichenization, lichenize, lichenized, lichenizing, lichenlike, lichenographer, lichenographic, lichenographical, lichenographist, lichenography, lichenoid, lichenologic, lichenological, lichenologist, lichenology, lichenose, lichenous, lichens, licheny, lichi, lichis, licht, lichted, lichting, lichtly, lichts, lichwake, licit, licitation, licitly, licitness, lick, licked, licker, lickerish, lickerishly, lickerishness, lickerous, lickers, lickety, licking, lickings, lickpenny, licks, lickspit, lickspits, lickspittle, lickspittling, licorice, licorices, licorn, licorne, licorous, licour, lictor, lictorian, lictors, licuri, licury, lid, lid's, lidar, lidars, lidded, lidder, lidderon, lidding, lidflower, lidgate, lidia, lidias, lidicker, lidless, lidlessly, lido, lidocaine, lidos, lids, lie, liebenerite, lieberkuhn, liebfraumilch, liebgeaitor, liebig, liebigite, lieblich, liechtenstein, lied, lieder, liederkranz, lief, liefer, liefest, liefly, liefsome, liege, liegedom, liegeful, liegefully, liegeless, liegely, liegeman, liegemen, lieger, lieges, liegewoman, liegier, lien, lien's, lienable, lienal, lienculi, lienculus, lienectomies, lienectomy, lienee, lienholder, lienic, lienitis, lienocele, lienogastric, lienointestinal, lienomalacia, lienomedullary, lienomyelogenous, lienopancreatic, lienor, lienorenal, lienotoxin, liens, lienteria, lienteric, lienteries, lientery, liepot, lieproof, lieprooflier, lieproofliest, lier, lierne, liernes, lierre, liers, lies, liesh, liespfund, liest, lieu, lieue, lieus, lieut, lieutenancies, lieutenancy, lieutenant, lieutenant's, lieutenantry, lieutenants, lieutenantship, lieve, liever, lievest, lievrite, lif, life, lifeblood, lifeboat, lifeboatman, lifeboatmen, lifeboats, lifebuoy, lifeday, lifedrop, lifeful, lifefully, lifefulness, lifeguard, lifeguards, lifehold, lifeholder, lifehood, lifeleaf, lifeless, lifelessly, lifelessness, lifelet, lifelike, lifelikeness, lifeline, lifelines, lifelong, lifemanship, lifen, lifer, liferent, liferented, liferenter, liferenting, liferentrix, liferoot, lifers, lifesaver, lifesavers, lifesaving, lifeskills, lifesome, lifesomely, lifesomeness, lifespan, lifespans, lifespring, lifestyle, lifestyles, lifetime, lifetime's, lifetimes, lifeward, lifeway, lifeways, lifework, lifeworks, lifey, liflod, lifo, lift, liftable, liftboy, lifted, lifter, lifters, lifting, liftless, liftman, liftmen, liftoff, liftoffs, lifts, lig, ligable, ligament, ligamenta, ligamental, ligamentary, ligamentous, ligamentously, ligaments, ligamentta, ligamentum, ligan, ligand, ligands, ligans, ligas, ligase, ligases, ligate, ligated, ligates, ligating, ligation, ligations, ligative, ligator, ligatory, ligature, ligatured, ligatures, ligaturing, lige, ligeance, liger, liggat, ligge, ligger, light, lightable, lightage, lightboard, lightboat, lightbrained, lighted, lighten, lightened, lightener, lighteners, lightening, lightens, lighter, lighter's, lighterage, lightered, lighterful, lightering, lighterman, lightermen, lighters, lightest, lightface, lightfaced, lightfast, lightfastness, lightfingered, lightfoot, lightfooted, lightful, lightfully, lightfulness, lighthead, lightheaded, lightheadedly, lightheadedness, lighthearted, lightheartedly, lightheartedness, lighthouse, lighthouse's, lighthouseman, lighthouses, lighting, lightings, lightish, lightkeeper, lightless, lightlessness, lightly, lightman, lightmans, lightmanship, lightmen, lightmindedly, lightmindedness, lightmouthed, lightness, lightning, lightning's, lightningbug, lightninged, lightninglike, lightningproof, lightnings, lightplane, lightproof, lightroom, lights, lightscot, lightship, lightships, lightsman, lightsmen, lightsome, lightsomely, lightsomeness, lighttight, lightwards, lightweight, lightweights, lightwood, lightwort, lighty, lightyears, ligitimized, ligitimizing, lignaloes, lignatile, ligne, ligneous, lignes, lignescent, lignicole, lignicoline, lignicolous, ligniferous, lignification, lignifications, lignified, lignifies, ligniform, lignify, lignifying, lignin, lignins, ligninsulphonate, ligniperdous, lignite, lignites, lignitic, lignitiferous, lignitize, lignivorous, lignocaine, lignocellulose, lignocellulosic, lignoceric, lignography, lignone, lignose, lignosity, lignosulfonate, lignosulphite, lignosulphonate, lignous, lignum, lignums, ligroin, ligroine, ligroines, ligroins, ligula, ligulae, ligular, ligulas, ligulate, ligulated, ligule, ligules, liguliflorous, liguliform, ligulin, liguloid, ligure, ligures, ligurian, ligurite, ligurition, ligurrition, ligustrin, liin, lija, likability, likable, likableness, like, likeability, likeable, likeableness, liked, likeful, likehood, likelier, likeliest, likelihead, likelihood, likelihoods, likeliness, likely, likeminded, likemindedness, liken, likened, likeness, likeness's, likenesses, likening, likens, liker, likerish, likerous, likers, likes, likesome, likest, likewalk, likeways, likewise, likewisely, likewiseness, likin, liking, likingly, likings, likker, liknon, likuta, lila, lilac, lilac's, lilaceous, lilacin, lilacky, lilacs, lilacthroat, lilactide, lilas, lilburne, lile, liles, liliaceous, lilial, liliated, lilied, lilies, liliform, lilith, lilium, lill, lillianite, lillibullero, lilliput, lilliputian, lilliputians, lilliputs, lilly, lilt, lilted, lilting, liltingly, liltingness, lilts, lily, lily's, lilyfy, lilyhanded, lilylike, lilywood, lilywort, lim, lima, limace, limacel, limacelle, limaceous, limaciform, limacine, limacines, limacinid, limacoid, limacon, limacons, limail, limaille, liman, limans, limas, limation, limb, limba, limbal, limbas, limbat, limbate, limbation, limbec, limbeck, limbecks, limbed, limber, limbered, limberer, limberest, limberham, limbering, limberly, limberneck, limberness, limbers, limbi, limbic, limbie, limbier, limbiest, limbiferous, limbing, limbless, limbmeal, limbo, limboinfantum, limbos, limbous, limbs, limburger, limburgite, limbus, limbuses, limby, lime, lime's, limeade, limeades, limeberries, limeberry, limebush, limed, limehouse, limekiln, limekilns, limeless, limelight, limelighter, limelights, limelike, limeman, limen, limens, limequat, limer, limerick, limericks, limes, limestone, limestones, limesulfur, limesulphur, limetta, limettin, limewash, limewater, limewood, limewort, limey, limeys, limicoline, limicolous, limier, limiest, limina, liminal, liminary, limine, liminess, liminesses, liming, limit, limitability, limitable, limitableness, limitably, limital, limitanean, limitarian, limitaries, limitary, limitate, limitation, limitation's, limitational, limitations, limitative, limitatively, limited, limitedly, limitedness, limiteds, limiter, limiters, limites, limiting, limitive, limitless, limitlessly, limitlessness, limitor, limitrophe, limits, limity, limivorous, limli, limma, limmata, limmer, limmers, limmock, limmu, limn, limnal, limnanth, limnanthaceous, limned, limner, limners, limnery, limnetic, limniad, limnic, limnimeter, limnimetric, limning, limnite, limnobiologic, limnobiological, limnobiologically, limnobiology, limnobios, limnograph, limnologic, limnological, limnologically, limnologist, limnology, limnometer, limnophil, limnophile, limnophilid, limnophilous, limnophobia, limnoplankton, limnorioid, limns, limo, limoid, limoncillo, limoncito, limonene, limonenes, limoniad, limonin, limonite, limonites, limonitic, limonitization, limonium, limos, limose, limous, limousin, limousine, limousines, limp, limped, limper, limpers, limpest, limpet, limpets, limphault, limpid, limpidity, limpidly, limpidness, limpily, limpin, limpiness, limping, limpingly, limpingness, limpish, limpkin, limpkins, limply, limpness, limpnesses, limps, limpsey, limpsy, limpwort, limpy, limsy, limu, limuli, limulid, limuloid, limuloids, limulus, limurite, limy, lin, lina, linable, linac, linaceous, linacs, linaga, linage, linages, linaloa, linaloe, linalol, linalols, linalool, linalools, linalyl, linamarin, linarite, linch, linchbolt, linchet, linchpin, linchpinned, linchpins, lincloth, lincoln, lincolnesque, lincolnian, lincolniana, lincomycin, lincrusta, lincture, linctus, lind, linda, lindabrides, lindackerite, lindane, lindanes, linden, lindens, linder, lindied, lindies, lindo, lindoite, lindworm, lindy, lindying, line, line's, linea, lineable, lineage, lineaged, lineages, lineal, lineality, lineally, lineament, lineamental, lineamentation, lineaments, lineameter, linear, linearifolius, linearisation, linearise, linearised, linearising, linearities, linearity, linearizable, linearization, linearize, linearized, linearizes, linearizing, linearly, lineary, lineas, lineate, lineated, lineation, lineatum, lineature, linebacker, linebackers, linebacking, linebred, linebreed, linebreeding, linecaster, linecasting, linecut, linecuts, lined, linefeed, linefeeds, lineiform, lineless, linelet, linelike, lineman, linemen, linen, linen's, linendrapers, linener, linenette, linenfold, linenize, linenizer, linenman, linens, linenumber, linenumbers, lineny, lineocircular, lineograph, lineolate, lineolated, lineprinter, liner, linerange, linerless, liners, lines, linesides, linesman, linesmen, linetest, lineup, lineups, linewalker, linework, liney, ling, linga, lingala, lingam, lingams, lingas, lingayat, lingberries, lingberry, lingbird, lingcod, lingcods, linge, lingel, lingenberry, lingence, linger, lingered, lingerer, lingerers, lingerie, lingeries, lingering, lingeringly, lingers, linget, lingier, lingiest, lingism, lingle, lingo, lingoe, lingoes, lingonberries, lingonberry, lingot, lings, lingster, lingtow, lingtowman, lingua, linguacious, linguaciousness, linguadental, linguae, linguaeform, lingual, linguale, lingualis, linguality, lingualize, lingually, linguals, linguanasal, linguatuline, linguatuloid, linguet, linguidental, linguiform, linguine, linguines, linguini, linguinis, linguipotence, linguished, linguist, linguist's, linguister, linguistic, linguistical, linguistically, linguistician, linguistics, linguistry, linguists, lingula, lingulae, lingulate, lingulated, lingulid, linguliferous, linguliform, linguloid, linguodental, linguodistal, linguogingival, linguopalatal, linguopapillitis, linguoversion, lingwort, lingy, linha, linhay, linie, linier, liniest, liniment, liniments, linin, lininess, lining, linings, linins, linitis, liniya, linja, linje, link, linkable, linkage, linkage's, linkages, linkboy, linkboys, linked, linkedit, linkedited, linkediting, linkeditor, linkeditted, linkeditting, linkedness, linker, linkers, linkier, linkiest, linking, linkman, linkmen, links, linksman, linksmen, linksmith, linkster, linkup, linkups, linkwork, linkworks, linky, linn, linnaea, linnaean, linnaeite, linneon, linnet, linnets, linns, lino, linocut, linocuts, linolate, linoleate, linoleic, linolein, linolenate, linolenic, linolenin, linoleum, linoleums, linolic, linolin, linometer, linon, linonophobia, linos, linotype, linotyped, linotyper, linotypes, linotyping, linotypist, linous, linoxin, linoxyn, linpin, linquish, lins, linsang, linsangs, linseed, linseeds, linsey, linseys, linstock, linstocks, lint, lintel, linteled, linteling, lintelled, lintelling, lintels, linten, linter, lintern, linters, lintie, lintier, lintiest, lintless, lintol, lintols, lintonite, lints, lintseed, lintwhite, linty, linum, linums, linwood, liny, linyphiid, liodermia, liomyofibroma, liomyoma, lion, lion's, lionced, lioncel, lionel, lionesque, lioness, lioness's, lionesses, lionet, lionfish, lionfishes, lionheart, lionhearted, lionheartedly, lionheartedness, lionhood, lionisation, lionise, lionised, lioniser, lionisers, lionises, lionising, lionism, lionizable, lionization, lionize, lionized, lionizer, lionizers, lionizes, lionizing, lionlike, lionly, lionne, lionproof, lions, lionship, liotrichine, lip, lip's, lipa, lipacidemia, lipaciduria, lipaemia, lipaemic, liparian, liparid, liparite, liparocele, liparoid, liparomphalus, liparous, lipase, lipases, lipectomies, lipectomy, lipemia, lipemic, lipic, lipid, lipide, lipides, lipidic, lipids, lipin, lipins, lipless, liplet, liplike, lipoblast, lipoblastoma, lipocaic, lipocardiac, lipocele, lipoceratous, lipocere, lipochondroma, lipochrome, lipochromic, lipochromogen, lipoclasis, lipoclastic, lipocyte, lipocytes, lipodystrophia, lipodystrophy, lipoferous, lipofibroma, lipogenesis, lipogenetic, lipogenic, lipogenous, lipogram, lipogrammatic, lipogrammatism, lipogrammatist, lipographic, lipography, lipohemia, lipoid, lipoidaemia, lipoidal, lipoidemia, lipoidic, lipoids, lipolitic, lipolyses, lipolysis, lipolytic, lipoma, lipomas, lipomata, lipomatosis, lipomatous, lipometabolic, lipometabolism, lipomorph, lipomyoma, lipomyxoma, lipopectic, lipopexia, lipophagic, lipophilic, lipophore, lipopod, lipopolysaccharide, lipoprotein, liposarcoma, liposis, liposoluble, liposome, lipostomy, lipothymia, lipothymial, lipothymic, lipothymy, lipotrophic, lipotrophy, lipotropic, lipotropin, lipotropism, lipotropy, lipotype, lipovaccine, lipoxenous, lipoxeny, lipoxidase, lipped, lippen, lippened, lippening, lippens, lipper, lippered, lippering, lipperings, lippers, lippie, lippier, lippiest, lippiness, lipping, lippings, lippitude, lippitudo, lippy, lipread, lipreading, lips, lipsalve, lipsanographer, lipsanotheca, lipse, lipstick, lipsticks, lipuria, lipwork, liq, liquable, liquamen, liquate, liquated, liquates, liquating, liquation, liquefacient, liquefaction, liquefactions, liquefactive, liquefiability, liquefiable, liquefied, liquefier, liquefiers, liquefies, liquefy, liquefying, liquer, liquesce, liquescence, liquescency, liquescent, liquet, liqueur, liqueured, liqueuring, liqueurs, liquid, liquid's, liquidable, liquidambar, liquidamber, liquidate, liquidated, liquidates, liquidating, liquidation, liquidation's, liquidations, liquidator, liquidators, liquidatorship, liquidise, liquidised, liquidising, liquidities, liquidity, liquidization, liquidize, liquidized, liquidizer, liquidizes, liquidizing, liquidless, liquidly, liquidness, liquidogenic, liquidogenous, liquids, liquidus, liquidy, liquified, liquifier, liquifiers, liquifies, liquiform, liquify, liquifying, liquor, liquor's, liquored, liquorer, liquorice, liquoring, liquorish, liquorishly, liquorishness, liquorist, liquorless, liquors, liquory, lir, lira, liras, lirate, liration, lire, lirella, lirellate, lirelliform, lirelline, lirellous, lirioddra, liriodendra, liriodendron, liriodendrons, liripipe, liripipes, liripoop, liroconite, lirot, liroth, lis, lisbon, lisere, lisette, lish, lisiere, lisk, lisle, lisles, lisp, lisp's, lisped, lisper, lispers, lisping, lispingly, lispound, lisps, lispund, liss, lissamphibian, lissencephalic, lissencephalous, lisses, lissoflagellate, lissom, lissome, lissomely, lissomeness, lissomly, lissomness, lissotrichan, lissotrichous, lissotrichy, list, listable, listed, listedness, listel, listels, listen, listenable, listened, listener, listeners, listenership, listening, listenings, listens, lister, listerelloses, listerellosis, listeria, listerian, listeriases, listeriasis, listerioses, listeriosis, listers, listful, listing, listing's, listings, listless, listlessly, listlessness, listred, lists, listwork, listy, liszt, lit, litai, litaneutical, litanies, litany, litanywise, litarge, litas, litation, litatu, litch, litchi, litchis, lite, liter, literacies, literacy, literaehumaniores, literaily, literal, literalisation, literalise, literalised, literaliser, literalising, literalism, literalist, literalistic, literalistically, literalities, literality, literalization, literalize, literalized, literalizer, literalizing, literally, literalminded, literalmindedness, literalness, literals, literarian, literarily, literariness, literary, literaryism, literata, literate, literated, literately, literateness, literates, literati, literatim, literation, literatist, literato, literator, literatos, literature, literature's, literatured, literatures, literatus, literose, literosity, liters, lites, lith, lithaemia, lithaemic, lithagogue, lithangiuria, lithanode, lithanthrax, litharge, litharges, lithate, lithatic, lithe, lithectasy, lithectomy, lithely, lithemia, lithemias, lithemic, litheness, lither, litherly, litherness, lithesome, lithesomeness, lithest, lithi, lithia, lithias, lithiasis, lithiastic, lithiate, lithic, lithically, lithifaction, lithification, lithified, lithify, lithifying, lithiophilite, lithite, lithium, lithiums, lithless, litho, lithobiid, lithobioid, lithocenosis, lithochemistry, lithochromatic, lithochromatics, lithochromatographic, lithochromatography, lithochromic, lithochromography, lithochromy, lithoclase, lithoclast, lithoclastic, lithoclasty, lithoculture, lithocyst, lithocystotomy, lithodesma, lithodialysis, lithodid, lithodomous, lithoed, lithofellic, lithofellinic, lithofracteur, lithofractor, lithog, lithogenesis, lithogenesy, lithogenetic, lithogenous, lithogeny, lithoglyph, lithoglypher, lithoglyphic, lithoglyptic, lithoglyptics, lithograph, lithographed, lithographer, lithographers, lithographic, lithographical, lithographically, lithographing, lithographize, lithographs, lithography, lithogravure, lithoid, lithoidal, lithoidite, lithoing, lithol, litholabe, litholapaxy, litholatrous, litholatry, lithologic, lithological, lithologically, lithologist, lithology, litholysis, litholyte, litholytic, lithomancy, lithomarge, lithometeor, lithometer, lithonephria, lithonephritis, lithonephrotomies, lithonephrotomy, lithontriptic, lithontriptist, lithontriptor, lithopaedion, lithopaedium, lithopedion, lithopedium, lithophagous, lithophane, lithophanic, lithophany, lithophile, lithophilous, lithophone, lithophotography, lithophotogravure, lithophthisis, lithophyl, lithophyll, lithophyllous, lithophysa, lithophysae, lithophysal, lithophyte, lithophytic, lithophytous, lithopone, lithoprint, lithoprinter, lithos, lithoscope, lithosere, lithosian, lithosiid, lithosis, lithosol, lithosols, lithosperm, lithospermon, lithospermous, lithosphere, lithospheric, lithotint, lithotome, lithotomic, lithotomical, lithotomies, lithotomist, lithotomize, lithotomous, lithotomy, lithotony, lithotresis, lithotripsy, lithotriptor, lithotrite, lithotritic, lithotrities, lithotritist, lithotritor, lithotrity, lithotype, lithotyped, lithotypic, lithotyping, lithotypy, lithous, lithoxyl, lithoxyle, lithoxylite, lithsman, lithuania, lithuanian, lithuanians, lithuresis, lithuria, lithy, liti, liticontestation, litigable, litigant, litigants, litigate, litigated, litigates, litigating, litigation, litigationist, litigations, litigator, litigators, litigatory, litigiosity, litigious, litigiously, litigiousness, litiscontest, litiscontestation, litiscontestational, litmus, litmuses, litoral, litorinoid, litotes, litra, litre, litres, lits, litster, litten, litter, litterateur, litterateurs, litteratim, litterbag, litterbug, litterbugs, littered, litterer, litterers, littering, littermate, littermates, litters, littery, little, littleleaf, littleneck, littlenecks, littleness, littler, littles, littlest, littlewale, littlin, littling, littlish, littoral, littorals, littrateur, littress, litu, lituate, litui, lituiform, lituite, lituitoid, lituoline, lituoloid, liturate, liturgic, liturgical, liturgically, liturgician, liturgics, liturgies, liturgiological, liturgiologist, liturgiology, liturgism, liturgist, liturgistic, liturgistical, liturgists, liturgize, liturgy, litus, lituus, litz, livability, livable, livableness, livably, live, liveability, liveable, liveableness, livebearer, liveborn, lived, livedo, livelier, liveliest, livelihead, livelihood, livelihoods, livelily, liveliness, livelong, lively, liven, livened, livener, liveners, liveness, livenesses, livening, livens, liver, liverance, liverberries, liverberry, livered, liverhearted, liverheartedness, liveried, liveries, livering, liverish, liverishness, liverleaf, liverleaves, liverless, liverpool, liverpudlian, livers, liverwort, liverworts, liverwurst, liverwursts, livery, liverydom, liveryless, liveryman, liverymen, lives, livest, livestock, liveth, livetin, livetrap, livetrapped, livetrapping, livetraps, liveware, liveweight, liveyer, livid, lividities, lividity, lividly, lividness, livier, liviers, living, livingless, livingly, livingness, livings, livingstoneite, livish, livishly, livlihood, livor, livraison, livre, livres, livyer, livyers, liwan, lixive, lixivia, lixivial, lixiviate, lixiviated, lixiviating, lixiviation, lixiviator, lixivious, lixivium, lixiviums, liza, lizard, lizard's, lizardfish, lizardfishes, lizardlike, lizards, lizardtail, lizary, lizzie, ll, llama, llamas, llanero, llano, llanos, llareta, llautu, llb, ller, lloyd's, llyn, lm, lm/ft, lm/m, ln, lndg, lnr, lo, loa, loach, loaches, load, loadable, loadage, loaded, loadedness, loaden, loader, loaders, loadinfo, loading, loadings, loadless, loadpenny, loads, loadsome, loadspecs, loadstar, loadstars, loadstone, loadstones, loadum, loaf, loafed, loafer, loaferdom, loaferish, loafers, loafing, loafingly, loaflet, loafs, loaghtan, loaiasis, loam, loamed, loamier, loamiest, loamily, loaminess, loaming, loamless, loams, loamy, loan, loanable, loanblend, loaned, loaner, loaners, loange, loanin, loaning, loanings, loanmonger, loans, loanshark, loansharking, loanshift, loanword, loanwords, loasaceous, loath, loathe, loathed, loather, loathers, loathes, loathful, loathfully, loathfulness, loathing, loathingly, loathings, loathliness, loathly, loathness, loathsome, loathsomely, loathsomeness, loathy, loave, loaves, lob, lobal, lobar, lobate, lobated, lobately, lobation, lobations, lobbed, lobber, lobbers, lobbied, lobbies, lobbing, lobbish, lobby, lobbyer, lobbyers, lobbygow, lobbygows, lobbying, lobbyism, lobbyisms, lobbyist, lobbyists, lobbyman, lobbymen, lobcock, lobcokt, lobe, lobe's, lobectomies, lobectomy, lobed, lobefin, lobefins, lobefoot, lobefooted, lobefoots, lobeless, lobelet, lobelia, lobeliaceous, lobelias, lobelin, lobeline, lobelines, lobellated, lobes, lobfig, lobi, lobiform, lobigerous, lobing, lobiped, loblollies, loblolly, lobo, lobola, lobolo, lobolos, lobopodium, lobos, lobose, lobotomies, lobotomize, lobotomized, lobotomizing, lobotomy, lobs, lobscourse, lobscouse, lobscouser, lobsided, lobster, lobster's, lobstering, lobsterish, lobsterlike, lobsterman, lobsterproof, lobsters, lobstick, lobsticks, lobtail, lobular, lobularly, lobulate, lobulated, lobulation, lobule, lobules, lobulette, lobuli, lobulose, lobulous, lobulus, lobus, lobworm, lobworms, loc, loca, locable, local, locale, localed, locales, localing, localisable, localisation, localise, localised, localiser, localises, localising, localism, localisms, localist, localistic, localists, localite, localites, localities, locality, locality's, localizable, localization, localizations, localize, localized, localizer, localizes, localizing, localled, localling, locally, localness, locals, locanda, locatable, locate, located, locater, locaters, locates, locating, locatio, location, locational, locationally, locations, locative, locatives, locator, locator's, locators, locatum, locellate, locellus, loch, lochaber, lochage, lochagus, lochan, loche, lochetic, lochi, lochia, lochial, lochiocolpos, lochiocyte, lochiometra, lochiometritis, lochiopyra, lochiorrhagia, lochiorrhea, lochioschesis, lochometritis, lochoperitonitis, lochopyra, lochs, lochus, lochy, loci, lociation, lock, lockable, lockage, lockages, lockbox, lockboxes, locked, locker, lockerman, lockermen, lockers, locket, lockets, lockfast, lockful, lockhole, lockian, locking, lockings, lockjaw, lockjaws, lockless, locklet, lockmaker, lockmaking, lockman, locknut, locknuts, lockout, lockout's, lockouts, lockpin, lockram, lockrams, lockrum, locks, locksman, locksmith, locksmithery, locksmithing, locksmiths, lockspit, lockstep, locksteps, lockstitch, lockup, lockup's, lockups, lockwork, locky, lockyer, locn, loco, locodescriptive, locoed, locoes, locofoco, locofocos, locoing, locoism, locoisms, locoman, locomobile, locomobility, locomote, locomoted, locomotes, locomotility, locomoting, locomotion, locomotive, locomotive's, locomotively, locomotiveman, locomotivemen, locomotiveness, locomotives, locomotivity, locomotor, locomotory, locomutation, locos, locoweed, locoweeds, loculament, loculamentose, loculamentous, locular, loculate, loculated, loculation, locule, loculed, locules, loculi, loculicidal, loculicidally, loculose, loculous, loculus, locum, locums, locuplete, locupletely, locus, locusca, locust, locust's, locusta, locustae, locustal, locustberry, locustelle, locustid, locusting, locustlike, locusts, locution, locutionary, locutions, locutor, locutoria, locutories, locutorium, locutorship, locutory, locuttoria, lod, lode, lodeman, lodemanage, loden, lodens, lodes, lodesman, lodesmen, lodestar, lodestars, lodestone, lodestuff, lodge, lodgeable, lodged, lodgeful, lodgeman, lodgement, lodgements, lodgepole, lodger, lodgerdom, lodgers, lodges, lodging, lodginghouse, lodgings, lodgment, lodgments, lodicula, lodicule, lodicules, loe, loed, loeil, loeing, loellingite, loess, loessal, loesses, loessial, loessic, loessland, loessoid, lof, lofstelle, loft, loft's, lofted, lofter, lofters, loftier, loftiest, loftily, loftiness, lofting, loftless, loftman, loftmen, lofts, loftsman, loftsmen, lofty, log, log's, logan, loganberries, loganberry, loganiaceous, loganin, logans, logaoedic, logarithm, logarithm's, logarithmal, logarithmetic, logarithmetical, logarithmetically, logarithmic, logarithmical, logarithmically, logarithmomancy, logarithms, logbook, logbooks, logchip, logcock, loge, logeia, logeion, loges, logeum, loggat, loggats, logged, logger, logger's, loggerhead, loggerheaded, loggerheads, loggers, logget, loggets, loggia, loggias, loggie, loggier, loggiest, loggin, logginess, logging, loggings, loggish, loggy, loghead, logheaded, logia, logic, logic's, logical, logicalist, logicality, logicalization, logicalize, logically, logicalness, logicaster, logician, logician's, logicianer, logicians, logicise, logicised, logicises, logicising, logicism, logicist, logicity, logicize, logicized, logicizes, logicizing, logicless, logics, logie, logier, logiest, logily, login, loginess, loginesses, logins, logion, logions, logis, logistic, logistical, logistically, logistician, logisticians, logistics, logium, logjam, logjams, loglet, loglike, loglog, logman, lognormal, lognormality, lognormally, logo, logocracy, logodaedalus, logodaedaly, logoes, logoff, logogogue, logogram, logogrammatic, logogrammatically, logograms, logograph, logographer, logographic, logographical, logographically, logography, logogriph, logogriphic, logoi, logolatry, logology, logomach, logomacher, logomachic, logomachical, logomachies, logomachist, logomachize, logomachs, logomachy, logomancy, logomania, logomaniac, logometer, logometric, logometrical, logometrically, logopaedics, logopedia, logopedic, logopedics, logophobia, logorrhea, logorrheic, logorrhoea, logos, logothete, logotype, logotypes, logotypies, logotypy, logout, logperch, logperches, logroll, logrolled, logroller, logrolling, logrolls, logs, logship, logway, logways, logwise, logwood, logwoods, logwork, logy, lohan, lohengrin, lohoch, lohock, loiasis, loimic, loimography, loimology, loin, loin's, loincloth, loinclothes, loincloths, loined, loinguard, loins, loir, loiter, loitered, loiterer, loiterers, loitering, loiteringly, loiteringness, loiters, loka, lokacara, lokao, lokaose, lokapala, loke, lokelani, loket, loki, lokiec, lokshen, loli, loll, lollapaloosa, lollapalooza, lollard, lolled, loller, lollers, lollies, lolling, lollingite, lollingly, lollipop, lollipops, lollop, lolloped, lolloping, lollops, lollopy, lolls, lollup, lolly, lollygag, lollygagged, lollygagging, lollygags, lollypop, lollypops, loma, lomastome, lomata, lomatine, lomatinous, lombard, lombardic, lomboy, loment, lomenta, lomentaceous, lomentariaceous, lomentlike, loments, lomentum, lomentums, lomilomi, lomita, lommock, lomonite, lomta, lond, london, londoner, londoners, lone, loneful, lonelier, loneliest, lonelihood, lonelily, loneliness, lonely, loneness, lonenesses, loner, loners, lonesome, lonesomely, lonesomeness, lonesomes, long, longa, longacre, longan, longanamous, longanimities, longanimity, longanimous, longans, longbeak, longbeard, longbill, longboat, longboats, longbow, longbowman, longbows, longcloth, longe, longear, longed, longee, longeing, longer, longeron, longerons, longers, longes, longest, longeval, longeve, longevities, longevity, longevous, longfelt, longfin, longful, longhair, longhaired, longhairs, longhand, longhands, longhead, longheaded, longheadedly, longheadedness, longheads, longhorn, longhorns, longhouse, longicaudal, longicaudate, longicone, longicorn, longies, longilateral, longilingual, longiloquence, longiloquent, longimanous, longimetric, longimetry, longing, longingly, longingness, longings, longinquity, longipennate, longipennine, longirostral, longirostrate, longirostrine, longisection, longish, longitude, longitude's, longitudes, longitudianl, longitudinal, longitudinally, longjaw, longjaws, longleaf, longleaves, longleg, longlegs, longlick, longline, longliner, longlinerman, longlinermen, longlines, longly, longmouthed, longneck, longness, longnesses, longnose, longobard, longpod, longroot, longrun, longs, longshanks, longship, longships, longshore, longshoreman, longshoremen, longshoring, longshot, longshucks, longsighted, longsightedness, longsleever, longsome, longsomely, longsomeness, longspun, longspur, longspurs, longstanding, longsuffering, longtail, longtime, longtimer, longue, longues, longueur, longueurs, longulite, longus, longwall, longway, longways, longwise, longwood, longwool, longword, longwork, longwort, longworth, longyi, lonicera, lonouhard, lonquhard, lontar, loo, loob, loobies, loobily, looby, loobyish, looch, lood, looed, looey, looeys, loof, loofa, loofah, loofahs, loofas, loofie, loofness, loofs, looie, looies, looing, look, lookahead, lookdown, lookdowns, looked, lookee, looker, lookers, looking, lookout, lookouts, looks, lookum, lookup, lookup's, lookups, looky, loom, loomed, loomer, loomery, loomfixer, looming, looms, loon, loonery, looney, loonier, loonies, looniest, looniness, loons, loony, loonybin, loop, loopback, loope, looped, looper, loopers, loopful, loophole, loophole's, loopholed, loopholes, loopholing, loopier, loopiest, looping, loopist, looplet, looplike, loops, loopy, loord, loory, loos, loose, loosebox, loosed, looseleaf, loosely, loosemouthed, loosen, loosened, loosener, looseners, looseness, loosening, loosens, looser, looses, loosest, loosestrife, loosing, loosish, loot, lootable, looted, looten, looter, looters, lootie, lootiewallah, looting, loots, lootsman, lootsmans, loover, lop, lope, loped, lopeman, loper, lopers, lopes, lopeskonce, lopheavy, lophiid, lophin, lophine, lophiodont, lophiodontoid, lophiostomate, lophiostomous, lophobranch, lophobranchiate, lophocalthrops, lophocercal, lophodont, lophophoral, lophophore, lophophorine, lophophytosis, lophostea, lophosteon, lophosteons, lophotriaene, lophotrichic, lophotrichous, loping, lopolith, loppard, lopped, lopper, loppered, loppering, loppers, loppet, loppier, loppiest, lopping, loppy, lops, lopseed, lopsided, lopsidedly, lopsidedness, lopstick, lopsticks, loq, loquacious, loquaciously, loquaciousness, loquacities, loquacity, loquat, loquats, loquence, loquency, loquent, loquently, loquitur, lor, lor', lora, loral, loran, lorandite, lorans, loranskite, loranthaceous, lorarii, lorarius, lorate, lorcha, lord, lordan, lorded, lording, lordings, lordkin, lordless, lordlet, lordlier, lordliest, lordlike, lordlily, lordliness, lordling, lordlings, lordly, lordolatry, lordoma, lordomas, lordoses, lordosis, lordotic, lords, lordship, lordships, lordswike, lordwood, lordy, lore, loreal, lored, lorel, lorelei, loreless, loren, lorenzenite, lores, loretin, lorettoite, lorgnette, lorgnettes, lorgnon, lorgnons, lori, loric, lorica, loricae, loricarian, loricarioid, loricate, loricated, loricates, loricating, lorication, loricoid, lories, lorikeet, lorikeets, lorilet, lorimer, lorimers, loriner, loriners, loring, loriot, loris, lorises, lorisiform, lormery, lorn, lornness, lornnesses, loro, loros, lorries, lorriker, lorry, lors, lorum, lory, losable, losableness, losang, lose, losel, loselism, loselry, losels, losenger, loser, losers, loses, losh, losing, losingly, losings, loss, loss's, lossenite, losser, losses, lossful, lossier, lossiest, lossless, lossproof, lossy, lost, lostling, lostness, lostnesses, lot, lot's, lota, lotah, lotahs, lotan, lotas, lotase, lote, lotebush, lotewood, loth, lothario, lotharios, lothly, lothsome, lotic, lotiform, lotion, lotions, lotium, lotment, loto, lotong, lotophagi, lotophagous, lotophagously, lotor, lotos, lotoses, lotrite, lots, lotted, lotter, lotteries, lottery, lotting, lotto, lottos, lotus, lotuses, lotusin, lotuslike, louch, louche, louchettes, loud, louden, loudened, loudening, loudens, louder, loudering, loudest, loudish, loudishness, loudlier, loudliest, loudly, loudmouth, loudmouthed, loudmouths, loudness, loudnesses, loudspeak, loudspeaker, loudspeaker's, loudspeakers, loudspeaking, louey, lough, lougheen, loughs, louie, louies, louis, louise, louisiana, louisianan, louisianans, louisianian, louisianians, louisine, louisville, louk, loukoum, loukoumi, loulu, loun, lounder, lounderer, lounge, lounged, lounger, loungers, lounges, lounging, loungingly, loungy, loup, loupcervier, loupcerviers, loupe, louped, loupen, loupes, louping, loups, lour, lourd, lourdish, lourdy, loured, lourie, louring, louringly, louringness, lours, loury, louse, louseberries, louseberry, loused, louses, lousewort, lousier, lousiest, lousily, lousiness, lousing, louster, lousy, lout, louted, louter, louther, louting, loutish, loutishly, loutishness, loutre, loutrophoroi, loutrophoros, louts, louty, louvar, louver, louvered, louvering, louvers, louverwork, louvre, louvred, louvres, lovability, lovable, lovableness, lovably, lovage, lovages, lovanenty, lovat, love, loveability, loveable, loveableness, loveably, lovebird, lovebirds, loved, loveday, lovee, loveflower, loveful, lovegrass, lovehood, lovelass, loveless, lovelessly, lovelessness, lovelier, lovelies, loveliest, lovelihead, lovelily, loveliness, loveling, lovelock, lovelocks, lovelorn, lovelornness, lovely, lovemaking, loveman, lovemans, lovemate, lovemonger, lovepot, loveproof, lover, loverdom, lovered, loverhood, lovering, loverless, loverlike, loverliness, loverly, lovers, lovership, loverwise, lovery, loves, lovesick, lovesickness, lovesome, lovesomely, lovesomeness, lovevine, lovevines, loveworth, loveworthy, lovey, lovier, loviers, loving, lovingkindness, lovingly, lovingness, low, lowa, lowable, lowan, lowance, lowball, lowbell, lowborn, lowboy, lowboys, lowbred, lowbrow, lowbrowism, lowbrows, lowdah, lowder, lowdown, lowdowns, lowe, lowed, loweite, lower, lowerable, lowercase, lowerclassman, lowerclassmen, lowered, lowerer, lowering, loweringly, loweringness, lowermost, lowers, lowery, lowes, lowest, lowigite, lowing, lowings, lowish, lowishly, lowishness, lowland, lowlander, lowlanders, lowlands, lowlier, lowliest, lowlife, lowlifer, lowlifes, lowlihead, lowlihood, lowlily, lowliness, lowly, lowman, lowmen, lowmost, lown, lowness, lownesses, lownly, lowrie, lowry, lows, lowse, lowsed, lowser, lowsest, lowsin, lowsing, lowth, lowwood, lowy, lox, loxed, loxes, loxia, loxic, loxing, loxoclase, loxocosm, loxodograph, loxodont, loxodontous, loxodrome, loxodromic, loxodromical, loxodromically, loxodromics, loxodromism, loxodromy, loxolophodont, loxophthalmus, loxosoma, loxotic, loxotomy, loy, loyal, loyaler, loyalest, loyalism, loyalisms, loyalist, loyalists, loyalize, loyally, loyalness, loyalties, loyalty, loyalty's, loyn, lozenge, lozenged, lozenger, lozenges, lozengeways, lozengewise, lozengy, lp, lpm, lr, lrecisianism, lrecl, ls, lsc, lst, lt, ltr, lu, luau, luaus, lub, lubbard, lubber, lubbercock, lubberland, lubberlike, lubberliness, lubberly, lubbers, lube, lubes, lubra, lubric, lubrical, lubricant, lubricant's, lubricants, lubricate, lubricated, lubricates, lubricating, lubrication, lubricational, lubrications, lubricative, lubricator, lubricators, lubricatory, lubricious, lubriciously, lubriciousness, lubricities, lubricity, lubricous, lubrifaction, lubrification, lubrify, lubritorian, lubritorium, lubritory, lucan, lucanid, lucarne, lucarnes, lucban, luce, lucence, lucences, lucencies, lucency, lucent, lucently, lucern, lucernal, lucernarian, lucerne, lucernes, lucerns, luces, lucet, lucia, lucian, lucible, lucid, lucida, lucidae, lucidities, lucidity, lucidly, lucidness, lucifee, lucifer, luciferase, luciferian, luciferin, luciferoid, luciferous, luciferously, luciferousness, lucifers, lucific, luciform, lucifugal, lucifugous, lucigen, lucille, lucimeter, lucina, lucinoid, lucite, lucivee, luck, lucked, lucken, luckful, luckie, luckier, luckies, luckiest, luckily, luckiness, lucking, luckless, lucklessly, lucklessness, luckly, lucks, lucky, lucombe, lucration, lucrative, lucratively, lucrativeness, lucre, lucres, lucretian, lucriferous, lucriferousness, lucrific, lucrify, lucrous, lucrum, luctation, luctiferous, luctiferousness, luctual, lucubrate, lucubrated, lucubrates, lucubrating, lucubration, lucubrations, lucubrator, lucubratory, lucule, luculent, luculently, lucullan, lucullian, lucullite, lucumia, lucumo, lucumony, lucy, lud, ludden, luddite, luddy, ludefisk, ludibrious, ludibry, ludicropathetic, ludicroserious, ludicrosities, ludicrosity, ludicrosplenetic, ludicrous, ludicrously, ludicrousness, ludification, ludlamite, ludo, ludwig, ludwigite, lue, lues, luetic, luetically, luetics, lufberry, lufbery, luff, luffa, luffas, luffed, luffer, luffing, luffs, lug, luge, luger, luges, luggage, luggageless, luggages, luggar, luggard, lugged, lugger, luggers, luggie, luggies, lugging, lughdoan, luging, lugmark, lugs, lugsail, lugsails, lugsome, lugubriosity, lugubrious, lugubriously, lugubriousness, lugubrous, lugworm, lugworms, luhinga, luigini, luigino, lujaurite, lujavrite, lujula, lukan, luke, lukely, lukemia, lukeness, luket, lukeward, lukewarm, lukewarmish, lukewarmly, lukewarmness, lukewarmth, lulab, lulabim, lulabs, lulav, lulavim, lulavs, lull, lullabied, lullabies, lullaby, lullabying, lullay, lulled, luller, lulliloo, lullilooed, lullilooing, lulling, lullingly, lulls, lully, lulu, luluai, lulus, lum, lumachel, lumachella, lumachelle, lumbaginous, lumbago, lumbagos, lumbang, lumbar, lumbarization, lumbars, lumbayao, lumber, lumberdar, lumberdom, lumbered, lumberer, lumberers, lumbering, lumberingly, lumberingness, lumberjack, lumberjacket, lumberjacks, lumberless, lumberly, lumberman, lumbermen, lumbermill, lumbers, lumbersome, lumberyard, lumberyards, lumbocolostomy, lumbocolotomy, lumbocostal, lumbodorsal, lumbodynia, lumbosacral, lumbovertebral, lumbrical, lumbricales, lumbricalis, lumbricid, lumbriciform, lumbricine, lumbricoid, lumbricosis, lumbricus, lumbrous, lumbus, lumen, lumenal, lumens, lumeter, lumina, luminaire, luminal, luminance, luminant, luminare, luminaria, luminaries, luminarious, luminarism, luminarist, luminary, luminate, lumination, luminative, luminator, lumine, lumined, luminesce, luminesced, luminescence, luminescent, luminesces, luminescing, luminiferous, luminificent, lumining, luminism, luminist, luministe, luminists, luminodynamism, luminodynamist, luminologist, luminometer, luminophor, luminophore, luminosities, luminosity, luminous, luminously, luminousness, lumisterol, lumme, lummox, lummoxes, lummy, lump, lumpectomy, lumped, lumpen, lumpenproletariat, lumpens, lumper, lumpers, lumpet, lumpfish, lumpfishes, lumpier, lumpiest, lumpily, lumpiness, lumping, lumpingly, lumpish, lumpishly, lumpishness, lumpkin, lumpman, lumpmen, lumps, lumpsucker, lumpy, lums, lumut, luna, lunacies, lunacy, lunambulism, lunar, lunare, lunaria, lunarian, lunarians, lunarist, lunarium, lunars, lunary, lunas, lunata, lunate, lunated, lunatellus, lunately, lunatic, lunatical, lunatically, lunatics, lunation, lunations, lunatize, lunatum, lunch, lunched, luncheon, luncheon's, luncheoner, luncheonette, luncheonettes, luncheonless, luncheons, luncher, lunchers, lunches, lunchhook, lunching, lunchless, lunchroom, lunchrooms, lunchtime, lundress, lundyfoot, lune, lunel, lunes, lunet, lunets, lunette, lunettes, lung, lungan, lungans, lunge, lunged, lungee, lungees, lungeous, lunger, lungers, lunges, lungfish, lungfishes, lungflower, lungful, lungi, lungie, lunging, lungis, lungless, lungmotor, lungoor, lungs, lungsick, lungworm, lungworms, lungwort, lungworts, lungy, lungyi, lungyis, lunicurrent, lunier, lunies, luniest, luniform, lunisolar, lunistice, lunistitial, lunitidal, lunk, lunker, lunkers, lunkhead, lunkheaded, lunkheads, lunks, lunn, lunoid, lunt, lunted, lunting, lunts, lunula, lunulae, lunular, lunulate, lunulated, lunule, lunules, lunulet, lunulite, luny, lunyie, lupanar, lupanarian, lupanars, lupanin, lupanine, lupe, lupeol, lupeose, lupercal, lupercalia, lupetidin, lupetidine, lupicide, lupiform, lupin, lupinaster, lupine, lupines, lupinin, lupinine, lupinosis, lupinous, lupins, lupis, lupoid, lupoma, lupous, lupulic, lupulin, lupuline, lupulinic, lupulinous, lupulins, lupulinum, lupulone, lupulus, lupus, lupuserythematosus, lupuses, lur, lura, luracan, lural, lurch, lurched, lurcher, lurchers, lurches, lurching, lurchingfully, lurchingly, lurchline, lurdan, lurdane, lurdanes, lurdanism, lurdans, lure, lured, lureful, lurement, lurer, lurers, lures, luresome, lurg, lurgworm, lurid, luridity, luridly, luridness, luring, luringly, lurk, lurked, lurker, lurkers, lurking, lurkingly, lurkingness, lurks, lurky, lurrier, lurries, lurry, luscious, lusciously, lusciousness, luser, lush, lushburg, lushed, lusher, lushes, lushest, lushier, lushiest, lushing, lushly, lushness, lushnesses, lushy, lusitanian, lusk, lusky, lusory, lust, lusted, luster, lustered, lusterer, lustering, lusterless, lusterlessness, lusters, lusterware, lustful, lustfully, lustfulness, lustick, lustier, lustiest, lustihead, lustihood, lustily, lustiness, lusting, lustless, lustly, lustra, lustral, lustrant, lustrate, lustrated, lustrates, lustrating, lustration, lustrational, lustrative, lustratory, lustre, lustred, lustreless, lustres, lustreware, lustrical, lustrification, lustrify, lustrine, lustring, lustrings, lustrous, lustrously, lustrousness, lustrum, lustrums, lusts, lusty, lusus, lususes, lut, lutaceous, lutanist, lutanists, lutany, lutarious, lutation, lute, lute's, lutea, luteal, lutecia, lutecium, luteciums, luted, luteic, lutein, luteinization, luteinize, luteinized, luteinizing, luteins, lutelet, lutemaker, lutemaking, lutenist, lutenists, luteo, luteocobaltic, luteofulvous, luteofuscescent, luteofuscous, luteolin, luteolins, luteolous, luteoma, luteorufescent, luteotrophic, luteotrophin, luteotropic, luteotropin, luteous, luteovirescent, luter, lutes, lutescent, lutestring, lutetium, lutetiums, luteum, luteway, lutfisk, luther, lutheran, lutheranism, lutherans, lutherism, luthern, lutherns, luthier, lutianid, lutianoid, lutidin, lutidine, lutidinic, luting, lutings, lutist, lutists, lutose, lutrin, lutrine, lutulence, lutulent, lux, luxate, luxated, luxates, luxating, luxation, luxations, luxe, luxembourg, luxemburg, luxes, luxive, luxulianite, luxullianite, luxuria, luxuriance, luxuriancy, luxuriant, luxuriantly, luxuriantness, luxuriate, luxuriated, luxuriates, luxuriating, luxuriation, luxurient, luxuries, luxuriety, luxurious, luxuriously, luxuriousness, luxurist, luxurity, luxury, luxury's, luxus, lv, lvalue, lvalues, lvov, lwl, lwm, lwop, lwp, lx, lxx, ly, lyam, lyance, lyard, lyart, lyase, lyases, lyc, lycaenid, lycanthrope, lycanthropia, lycanthropic, lycanthropies, lycanthropist, lycanthropize, lycanthropous, lycanthropy, lycea, lyceal, lycee, lycees, lyceum, lyceums, lych, lychee, lychees, lychnis, lychnises, lychnomancy, lychnoscope, lychnoscopic, lycid, lycine, lycium, lycodoid, lycopene, lycopenes, lycoperdaceous, lycoperdoid, lycoperdon, lycopin, lycopod, lycopode, lycopodiaceous, lycopodium, lycopods, lycorine, lycosid, lyctid, lyddite, lyddites, lydian, lydite, lye, lyencephalous, lyery, lyes, lyfkie, lygaeid, lygus, lying, lyingly, lyings, lyken, lykewake, lym, lymantriid, lymhpangiophlebitis, lymnaean, lymnaeid, lymph, lymphad, lymphadenectasia, lymphadenectasis, lymphadenia, lymphadenitis, lymphadenoid, lymphadenoma, lymphadenomas, lymphadenomata, lymphadenome, lymphadenopathy, lymphadenosis, lymphaemia, lymphagogue, lymphangeitis, lymphangial, lymphangiectasis, lymphangiectatic, lymphangiectodes, lymphangiitis, lymphangioendothelioma, lymphangiofibroma, lymphangiology, lymphangioma, lymphangiomas, lymphangiomata, lymphangiomatous, lymphangioplasty, lymphangiosarcoma, lymphangiotomy, lymphangitic, lymphangitides, lymphangitis, lymphatic, lymphatical, lymphatically, lymphation, lymphatism, lymphatitis, lymphatolysin, lymphatolysis, lymphatolytic, lymphectasia, lymphedema, lymphemia, lymphenteritis, lymphoadenoma, lymphoblast, lymphoblastic, lymphoblastoma, lymphoblastosis, lymphocele, lymphocyst, lymphocystosis, lymphocyte, lymphocytes, lymphocythemia, lymphocytic, lymphocytoma, lymphocytomatosis, lymphocytosis, lymphocytotic, lymphocytotoxin, lymphodermia, lymphoduct, lymphoedema, lymphogenic, lymphogenous, lymphoglandula, lymphogranuloma, lymphogranulomas, lymphogranulomata, lymphogranulomatosis, lymphogranulomatous, lymphographic, lymphography, lymphoid, lymphoidectomy, lymphoidocyte, lymphology, lymphoma, lymphomas, lymphomata, lymphomatoid, lymphomatosis, lymphomatous, lymphomonocyte, lymphomyxoma, lymphopathy, lymphopenia, lymphopenial, lymphopoieses, lymphopoiesis, lymphopoietic, lymphoprotease, lymphorrhage, lymphorrhagia, lymphorrhagic, lymphorrhea, lymphosarcoma, lymphosarcomas, lymphosarcomatosis, lymphosarcomatous, lymphosporidiosis, lymphostasis, lymphotaxis, lymphotome, lymphotomy, lymphotoxemia, lymphotoxin, lymphotrophic, lymphotrophy, lymphous, lymphs, lymphuria, lymphy, lyn, lyncean, lynch, lynchable, lynched, lyncher, lynchers, lynches, lynchet, lynching, lynchings, lyncine, lynn, lynnhaven, lynx, lynx's, lynxes, lynxlike, lyocratic, lyolysis, lyolytic, lyomerous, lyon, lyonetiid, lyonnaise, lyonnesse, lyophil, lyophile, lyophiled, lyophilic, lyophilization, lyophilize, lyophilized, lyophilizer, lyophilizing, lyophobe, lyophobic, lyopomatous, lyotrope, lyotropic, lypemania, lypothymia, lyra, lyraid, lyrate, lyrated, lyrately, lyraway, lyre, lyrebird, lyrebirds, lyreflower, lyreman, lyres, lyretail, lyric, lyrical, lyrically, lyricalness, lyrichord, lyricisation, lyricise, lyricised, lyricises, lyricising, lyricism, lyricisms, lyricist, lyricists, lyricization, lyricize, lyricized, lyricizes, lyricizing, lyricked, lyricking, lyrics, lyrid, lyriform, lyrism, lyrisms, lyrist, lyrists, lys, lysate, lysates, lyse, lysed, lysenkoism, lysergic, lyses, lysidin, lysidine, lysigenic, lysigenous, lysigenously, lysimeter, lysimetric, lysin, lysine, lysines, lysing, lysins, lysis, lysogen, lysogenesis, lysogenetic, lysogenic, lysogenicity, lysogenies, lysogenization, lysogenize, lysogens, lysogeny, lysol, lysolecithin, lysosomal, lysosomally, lysosome, lysosomes, lysozyme, lysozymes, lyssa, lyssas, lyssic, lyssophobia, lyterian, lythe, lythraceous, lytic, lytically, lytta, lyttae, lyttas, lyxose, m, m's, m/s, ma, ma'am, maad, maam, maamselle, maana, maar, maars, maat, mab, mabble, mabela, mabi, mabolo, mabuti, mabyer, mac, macaasim, macaber, macabi, macaboy, macabre, macabrely, macabreness, macabresque, macaco, macacos, macacus, macadam, macadamer, macadamia, macadamise, macadamite, macadamization, macadamize, macadamized, macadamizer, macadamizes, macadamizing, macadams, macague, macan, macana, macao, macaque, macaques, macarism, macarize, macarized, macarizing, macaron, macaroni, macaronic, macaronical, macaronically, macaronicism, macaronics, macaronies, macaronis, macaronism, macaroon, macaroons, macartney, macassar, macauco, macaviator, macaw, macaws, macbeth, maccabaw, maccabaws, maccabean, maccabees, maccaboy, maccaboys, maccaroni, macchia, macchie, macchinetta, macclesfield, macco, maccoboy, maccoboys, maccus, mace, macebearer, maced, macedoine, macedon, macedonia, macedonian, macedonians, macehead, macellum, maceman, macer, macerable, macerate, macerated, macerater, maceraters, macerates, macerating, maceration, macerative, macerator, macerators, macers, maces, macfarlane, mach, machair, machaira, machairodont, machan, machaon, machar, machecoled, macheer, machera, machete, machetes, machi, machiavel, machiavelian, machiavellian, machiavellianism, machiavellians, machiavellist, machicolate, machicolated, machicolating, machicolation, machicolations, machicoulis, machila, machin, machina, machinability, machinable, machinal, machinament, machinate, machinated, machinating, machination, machinations, machinator, machine, machine's, machineable, machined, machineful, machineless, machinelike, machinely, machineman, machinemen, machinemonger, machiner, machineries, machinery, machines, machinification, machinify, machining, machinism, machinist, machinists, machinization, machinize, machinized, machinizing, machinoclast, machinofacture, machinotechnique, machinule, machismo, machismos, machmeter, macho, machopolyp, machos, machree, machrees, machs, machtpolitik, machzor, machzorim, machzors, macies, macilence, macilency, macilent, macing, macintosh, macintoshes, mack, mackallow, mackaybean, mackenboy, mackerel, mackereler, mackereling, mackerels, mackinaw, mackinawed, mackinaws, mackinboy, mackins, mackintosh, mackintoshed, mackintoshes, mackintoshite, mackle, mackled, mackles, macklike, mackling, macks, macle, macled, macles, maclib, maclurin, maco, macoma, maconite, maconne, macquereau, macracanthrorhynchiasis, macradenous, macram, macrame, macrames, macrander, macrandre, macrandrous, macrauchene, macraucheniid, macraucheniiform, macrauchenioid, macrencephalic, macrencephalous, macrencephaly, macrli, macro, macro's, macroaggregate, macroaggregated, macroanalysis, macroanalyst, macroanalytical, macrobacterium, macrobian, macrobiosis, macrobiote, macrobiotic, macrobiotically, macrobiotics, macroblast, macrobrachia, macrocarpous, macrocephali, macrocephalia, macrocephalic, macrocephalism, macrocephalous, macrocephalus, macrocephaly, macrochaeta, macrochaetae, macrocheilia, macrochemical, macrochemically, macrochemistry, macrochiran, macrochiria, macrochiropteran, macrocladous, macroclimate, macroclimatic, macroclimatically, macroclimatology, macrococcus, macrocoly, macroconidial, macroconidium, macroconjugant, macrocornea, macrocosm, macrocosmic, macrocosmical, macrocosmically, macrocosmology, macrocosmos, macrocosms, macrocrystalline, macrocyst, macrocyte, macrocythemia, macrocytic, macrocytosis, macrodactyl, macrodactylia, macrodactylic, macrodactylism, macrodactylous, macrodactyly, macrodiagonal, macrodomatic, macrodome, macrodont, macrodontia, macrodontic, macrodontism, macroeconomic, macroeconomics, macroelement, macroergate, macroevolution, macroevolutionary, macrofarad, macrofossil, macrogamete, macrogametocyte, macrogamy, macrogastria, macroglobulin, macroglobulinemia, macroglobulinemic, macroglossate, macroglossia, macrognathic, macrognathism, macrognathous, macrogonidium, macrograph, macrographic, macrography, macroinstruction, macrolecithal, macrolepidoptera, macrolepidopterous, macrolinguistic, macrolinguistically, macrolinguistics, macrolith, macrology, macromandibular, macromania, macromastia, macromazia, macromelia, macromeral, macromere, macromeric, macromerite, macromeritic, macromesentery, macrometeorological, macrometeorology, macrometer, macromethod, macromole, macromolecular, macromolecule, macromolecule's, macromolecules, macromyelon, macromyelonal, macron, macrons, macronuclear, macronucleate, macronucleus, macronutrient, macropetalous, macrophage, macrophagic, macrophagocyte, macrophagus, macrophotograph, macrophotography, macrophyllous, macrophysics, macrophyte, macrophytic, macropia, macropinacoid, macropinacoidal, macroplankton, macroplasia, macroplastia, macropleural, macropod, macropodia, macropodian, macropodine, macropodous, macroprism, macroprocessor, macroprosopia, macropsia, macropsy, macropteran, macropterous, macroptery, macroptic, macropyramid, macroreaction, macrorhinia, macros, macroscale, macroscelia, macroscian, macroscopic, macroscopical, macroscopically, macrosegment, macroseism, macroseismic, macroseismograph, macrosepalous, macroseptum, macrosmatic, macrosomatia, macrosomatous, macrosomia, macrospecies, macrosphere, macrosplanchnic, macrosporange, macrosporangium, macrospore, macrosporic, macrosporophore, macrosporophyl, macrosporophyll, macrostomatous, macrostomia, macrostructural, macrostructure, macrostyle, macrostylospore, macrostylous, macrosymbiont, macrothere, macrotherioid, macrotherm, macrotia, macrotin, macrotome, macrotone, macrotous, macrourid, macrozoogonidium, macrozoospore, macrura, macrural, macruran, macrurans, macruroid, macrurous, macs, mactation, mactroid, macuca, macula, maculacy, maculae, macular, maculas, maculate, maculated, maculates, maculating, maculation, maculations, macule, maculed, macules, maculicole, maculicolous, maculiferous, maculing, maculocerebral, maculopapular, maculose, macumba, macupa, macupi, macushla, macuta, macute, mad, madafu, madagascar, madagass, madam, madame, madames, madams, madapolam, madapolan, madapollam, madarosis, madarotic, madbrain, madbrained, madcap, madcaply, madcaps, madded, madden, maddened, maddening, maddeningly, maddeningness, maddens, madder, madderish, madders, madderwort, maddest, madding, maddingly, maddish, maddle, maddled, maddock, made, madefaction, madefy, madeira, madeiras, madeleine, madeline, mademoiselle, mademoiselles, madescent, madge, madhab, madhouse, madhouses, madhuca, madia, madid, madidans, madison, madisterium, madling, madly, madman, madmen, madnep, madness, madnesses, mado, madonna, madonnas, madoqua, madrague, madras, madrasah, madrases, madrassah, madrasseh, madre, madreline, madreperl, madreporacean, madreporal, madreporarian, madrepore, madreporian, madreporic, madreporiform, madreporite, madreporitic, madres, madrid, madrier, madrigal, madrigaler, madrigalesque, madrigaletto, madrigalian, madrigalist, madrigals, madrih, madril, madrilene, madroa, madrona, madronas, madrone, madrones, madrono, madronos, mads, madship, madstone, madtom, maduro, maduros, madweed, madwoman, madwomen, madwort, madworts, madzoon, madzoons, mae, maeander, maeandrine, maeandriniform, maeandrinoid, maeandroid, maecenas, maed, maegbot, maegbote, maeing, maelstrom, maelstroms, maenad, maenades, maenadic, maenadically, maenadism, maenads, maenaite, maes, maestive, maestoso, maestosos, maestra, maestri, maestro, maestros, mafey, maffia, maffias, maffick, mafficked, mafficker, mafficking, mafficks, maffioso, maffle, maffler, mafflin, mafia, mafias, mafic, mafiosi, mafioso, mafoo, maftir, maftirs, mafura, mafurra, mag, magadis, magadize, magani, magas, magasin, magazinable, magazinage, magazine, magazine's, magazined, magazinelet, magaziner, magazines, magazinette, magazining, magazinish, magazinism, magazinist, magaziny, magbote, magdalen, magdalene, magdalenes, magdalenian, magdalens, magdaleon, mage, magellan, magenta, magentas, magerful, mages, magged, maggie, magging, maggiore, maggle, maggot, maggot's, maggotiness, maggotpie, maggotry, maggots, maggoty, maghzen, magi, magian, magianism, magic, magical, magicalize, magically, magicdom, magician, magician's, magicians, magicianship, magicked, magicking, magics, magilp, magilps, magiric, magirics, magirist, magiristic, magirological, magirologist, magirology, magism, magister, magisterial, magisteriality, magisterially, magisterialness, magisteries, magisterium, magisters, magistery, magistracies, magistracy, magistral, magistrality, magistrally, magistrand, magistrant, magistrate, magistrate's, magistrates, magistrateship, magistratic, magistratical, magistratically, magistrative, magistrature, magistratus, magma, magmas, magmata, magmatic, magmatism, magna, magnale, magnality, magnalium, magnanerie, magnanime, magnanimities, magnanimity, magnanimous, magnanimously, magnanimousness, magnascope, magnascopic, magnate, magnates, magnateship, magnecrystallic, magnelectric, magneoptic, magnes, magnesia, magnesial, magnesian, magnesias, magnesic, magnesioferrite, magnesite, magnesium, magnet, magneta, magnetic, magnetical, magnetically, magneticalness, magnetician, magnetics, magnetiferous, magnetification, magnetify, magnetimeter, magnetisation, magnetise, magnetised, magnetiser, magnetising, magnetism, magnetism's, magnetisms, magnetist, magnetite, magnetitic, magnetizability, magnetizable, magnetization, magnetize, magnetized, magnetizer, magnetizers, magnetizes, magnetizing, magneto, magnetobell, magnetochemical, magnetochemistry, magnetod, magnetodynamo, magnetoelectric, magnetoelectrical, magnetoelectricity, magnetofluiddynamic, magnetofluiddynamics, magnetofluidmechanic, magnetofluidmechanics, magnetogasdynamic, magnetogasdynamics, magnetogenerator, magnetogram, magnetograph, magnetographic, magnetohydrodynamic, magnetohydrodynamically, magnetohydrodynamics, magnetoid, magnetolysis, magnetomachine, magnetometer, magnetometers, magnetometric, magnetometrical, magnetometrically, magnetometry, magnetomotive, magnetomotivity, magnetomotor, magneton, magnetons, magnetooptic, magnetooptical, magnetooptically, magnetooptics, magnetopause, magnetophone, magnetophonograph, magnetoplasmadynamic, magnetoplasmadynamics, magnetoplumbite, magnetoprinter, magnetoresistance, magnetos, magnetoscope, magnetosphere, magnetospheric, magnetostatic, magnetostriction, magnetostrictive, magnetostrictively, magnetotelegraph, magnetotelephone, magnetotelephonic, magnetotherapy, magnetothermoelectricity, magnetotransmitter, magnetron, magnets, magnicaudate, magnicaudatous, magnifiable, magnific, magnifical, magnifically, magnificat, magnificate, magnification, magnifications, magnificative, magnifice, magnificence, magnificent, magnificently, magnificentness, magnifico, magnificoes, magnificos, magnified, magnifier, magnifiers, magnifies, magnifique, magnify, magnifying, magniloquence, magniloquent, magniloquently, magniloquy, magnipotence, magnipotent, magnirostrate, magnisonant, magnitude, magnitude's, magnitudes, magnitudinous, magnochromite, magnoferrite, magnolia, magnoliaceous, magnolias, magnon, magnum, magnums, magot, magots, magpie, magpied, magpieish, magpies, magrim, mags, magsman, maguari, maguey, magueys, magus, magyar, magyars, maha, mahajan, mahajun, mahal, mahala, mahalamat, mahaleb, mahalla, mahaly, mahant, mahar, maharaj, maharaja, maharajah, maharajahs, maharajas, maharajrana, maharana, maharanee, maharanees, maharani, maharanis, maharao, maharawal, maharawat, maharishi, maharishis, maharmah, maharshi, mahat, mahatma, mahatmaism, mahatmas, mahayana, mahayanist, mahbub, mahdi, mahdism, mahewu, mahican, mahimahi, mahjong, mahjongg, mahjonggs, mahjongs, mahlstick, mahmal, mahmudi, mahoe, mahoes, mahoganies, mahoganize, mahogany, mahogonies, mahogony, mahoitre, maholi, maholtine, mahomet, mahometan, mahometry, mahone, mahonia, mahonias, mahound, mahout, mahouts, mahratta, mahseer, mahsir, mahsur, mahu, mahua, mahuang, mahuangs, mahwa, mahzor, mahzorim, mahzors, maid, maidan, maidchild, maiden, maidenchild, maidenhair, maidenhairs, maidenhairtree, maidenhead, maidenheads, maidenhood, maidenish, maidenism, maidenlike, maidenliness, maidenly, maidens, maidenship, maidenweed, maidhead, maidhood, maidhoods, maidin, maidish, maidishness, maidism, maidkin, maidlike, maidling, maidly, maids, maidservant, maidservants, maidy, maiefic, maieutic, maieutical, maieutics, maigre, maihem, maihems, maiid, mail, mailability, mailable, mailbag, mailbags, mailbox, mailbox's, mailboxes, mailcatcher, mailclad, mailcoach, maile, mailed, mailer, mailers, mailes, mailguard, mailie, mailing, mailings, maill, maille, maillechort, mailless, maillot, maillots, maills, mailman, mailmen, mailplane, mailpouch, mails, mailsack, mailwoman, mailwomen, maim, maimed, maimedly, maimedness, maimer, maimers, maiming, maimon, maims, maimul, main, mainbrace, maine, mainferre, mainframe, mainframe's, mainframes, mainland, mainlander, mainlanders, mainlands, mainline, mainlined, mainliner, mainliners, mainlines, mainlining, mainly, mainmast, mainmasts, mainmortable, mainor, mainour, mainpast, mainpernable, mainpernor, mainpin, mainport, mainpost, mainprise, mainprised, mainprising, mainprisor, mainprize, mainprizer, mains, mainsail, mainsails, mainsheet, mainspring, mainsprings, mainstay, mainstays, mainstream, mainstreams, mainswear, mainsworn, maint, maintain, maintainability, maintainable, maintainableness, maintained, maintainer, maintainers, maintaining, maintainment, maintainor, maintains, maintenance, maintenance's, maintenances, maintenon, maintien, maintop, maintopman, maintopmast, maintopmen, maintops, maintopsail, mainward, maioid, maioidean, maiolica, maiolicas, mair, mairatour, maire, mairie, mairs, maison, maisonette, maisonettes, maist, maister, maistres, maistry, maists, maithuna, maitlandite, maitre, maitres, maitresse, maitrise, maize, maizebird, maizenic, maizer, maizes, majagua, majaguas, majas, majestatic, majestatis, majestic, majestical, majestically, majesticalness, majesticness, majesties, majestious, majesty, majesty's, majestyship, majeure, majidieh, majo, majolica, majolicas, majolist, majoon, major, majora, majorat, majorate, majoration, majordomo, majordomos, majored, majorem, majorette, majorettes, majoring, majoritarian, majoritarianism, majorities, majority, majority's, majorize, majors, majorship, majos, majusculae, majuscular, majuscule, majuscules, makable, makadoo, makahiki, makale, makar, makara, makars, makatea, make, makeable, makebate, makebates, makedom, makefast, makefasts, makefile, makeless, maker, makeready, makeress, makers, makership, makes, makeshift, makeshiftiness, makeshiftness, makeshifts, makeshifty, makeup, makeups, makeweight, makework, makhorka, makhzan, makhzen, maki, makimono, makimonos, making, makings, makluk, mako, makomako, makopa, makos, makoua, makran, makroskelic, maksoorah, makuk, makuta, makutas, makutu, mal, mala, malaanonang, malabar, malabathrum, malabsorption, malacanthid, malacanthine, malacaton, malacca, malaccident, malaceous, malachi, malachite, malacia, malacoderm, malacodermatous, malacodermous, malacoid, malacolite, malacologic, malacological, malacologist, malacology, malacon, malacone, malacophilous, malacophonous, malacophyllous, malacopod, malacopodous, malacopterygian, malacopterygious, malacostracan, malacostracology, malacostracous, malacotic, malactic, maladapt, maladaptation, maladapted, maladaptive, maladdress, malade, maladies, maladive, maladjust, maladjusted, maladjustive, maladjustment, maladjustments, maladminister, maladministered, maladministering, maladministers, maladministration, maladministrative, maladministrator, maladresse, maladroit, maladroitly, maladroitness, maladventure, malady, malady's, malaga, malagash, malagasy, malagma, malaguea, malaguena, malaguenas, malaguetta, malahack, malaise, malaises, malakin, malakon, malalignment, malam, malambo, malamute, malamutes, malander, malandered, malanders, malandrous, malanga, malapaho, malapert, malapertly, malapertness, malaperts, malapi, malapplication, malappointment, malapportioned, malapportionment, malappropriate, malappropriation, malaprop, malapropian, malapropish, malapropism, malapropisms, malapropoism, malapropos, malaprops, malar, malaria, malarial, malarian, malariaproof, malarias, malarin, malarioid, malariologist, malariology, malariotherapy, malarious, malarkey, malarkeys, malarkies, malarky, malaroma, malaromas, malarrangement, malars, malasapsap, malassimilation, malassociation, malate, malates, malathion, malati, malattress, malawi, malawians, malax, malaxable, malaxage, malaxate, malaxation, malaxator, malaxed, malaxerman, malaxermen, malaxing, malay, malaya, malayalam, malayan, malayans, malays, malaysia, malaysian, malaysians, malbehavior, malbrouck, malchite, malconceived, malconduct, malconformation, malconstruction, malcontent, malcontented, malcontentedly, malcontentedness, malcontentism, malcontently, malcontentment, malcontents, malconvenance, malcreated, malcultivation, maldeveloped, maldevelopment, maldigestion, maldirection, maldistribute, maldistribution, maldocchio, maldonite, malduck, male, male's, maleability, malease, maleate, maleates, maleberry, maledicent, maledict, maledicted, maledicting, malediction, maledictions, maledictive, maledictory, maledicts, maleducation, malee, malefaction, malefactions, malefactor, malefactor's, malefactors, malefactory, malefactress, malefactresses, malefeazance, malefic, malefical, malefically, malefice, maleficence, maleficent, maleficently, maleficia, maleficial, maleficiate, maleficiation, maleficio, maleficium, maleic, maleinoid, maleinoidal, malella, malellae, malemiut, malemuit, malemuits, malemute, malemutes, maleness, malenesses, malengin, malengine, malentendu, maleo, maleos, maleruption, males, malesherbiaceous, maletolt, maletote, malevolence, malevolency, malevolent, malevolently, malevolous, malexecution, malfeasance, malfeasant, malfeasantly, malfeasants, malfeasor, malfed, malformation, malformations, malformed, malfortune, malfunction, malfunctioned, malfunctioning, malfunctions, malgovernment, malgr, malgrace, malgrado, malgre, malguzar, malguzari, malheur, malhonest, malhygiene, mali, malic, malice, maliceful, maliceproof, malices, malicho, malicious, maliciously, maliciousness, malicorium, malidentification, malie, maliferous, maliform, malign, malignance, malignancies, malignancy, malignant, malignantly, malignation, maligned, maligner, maligners, malignified, malignify, malignifying, maligning, malignities, malignity, malignly, malignment, maligns, malihini, malihinis, malik, malikadna, malikala, malikana, malikzadi, malimprinted, malinche, maline, malines, malinfluence, malinger, malingered, malingerer, malingerers, malingering, malingers, malingery, malinke, malinowskite, malinstitution, malinstruction, malintent, malinvestment, malism, malison, malisons, malist, malistic, malitia, malkin, malkins, mall, malladrite, mallam, mallanders, mallangong, mallard, mallardite, mallards, malleability, malleabilization, malleable, malleableize, malleableized, malleableizing, malleableness, malleablize, malleablized, malleablizing, malleably, malleal, mallear, malleate, malleated, malleating, malleation, mallecho, malled, mallee, mallees, mallei, malleiferous, malleiform, mallein, malleinization, malleinize, malleli, mallemaroking, mallemuck, mallender, mallenders, malleoincudal, malleolable, malleolar, malleoli, malleolus, mallet, mallet's, malleted, malleting, mallets, malleus, malling, mallophagan, mallophagous, malloseismic, mallow, mallows, mallowwort, malls, mallum, mallus, malm, malmag, malmaison, malmarsh, malmed, malmier, malmiest, malmignatte, malming, malmock, malms, malmsey, malmseys, malmstone, malmy, malnourished, malnourishment, malnutrite, malnutrition, malo, malobservance, malobservation, maloca, malocchio, maloccluded, malocclusion, malocclusions, malodor, malodorant, malodorous, malodorously, malodorousness, malodors, malodour, malojilla, malolactic, malonate, malonic, malonyl, malonylurea, maloperation, malorganization, malorganized, malouah, malpais, malpighiaceous, malpighian, malplaced, malpoise, malposed, malposition, malpractice, malpracticed, malpracticing, malpractioner, malpractitioner, malpraxis, malpresentation, malproportion, malproportioned, malpropriety, malpublication, malreasoning, malrotation, malshapen, malsworn, malt, malta, maltable, maltalent, maltase, maltases, malted, malteds, malter, maltese, maltha, malthas, malthene, malthite, malthouse, malthus, malthusian, malthusianism, maltier, maltiest, maltine, maltiness, malting, maltman, maltobiose, maltodextrin, maltodextrine, maltol, maltols, maltolte, maltose, maltoses, maltreat, maltreated, maltreating, maltreatment, maltreatments, maltreator, maltreats, malts, maltster, maltsters, malturned, maltworm, malty, malum, malunion, malurine, malvaceous, malval, malvasia, malvasian, malvasias, malversation, malverse, malvin, malvoisie, malvolition, malwa, mam, mama, mamaguy, mamaloi, mamamouchi, mamamu, mamas, mamba, mambas, mambo, mamboed, mamboes, mamboing, mambos, mambu, mameliere, mamelon, mamelonation, mameluco, mameluke, mamelukes, mamey, mameyes, mameys, mamie, mamies, mamilla, mamillary, mamillate, mamillated, mamillation, mamlatdar, mamluk, mamluks, mamlutdar, mamma, mamma's, mammae, mammal, mammal's, mammalgia, mammalia, mammalian, mammalians, mammaliferous, mammality, mammalogical, mammalogist, mammalogists, mammalogy, mammals, mammary, mammas, mammate, mammati, mammatocumulus, mammatus, mammectomy, mammee, mammees, mammer, mammered, mammering, mammers, mammet, mammets, mammey, mammeys, mammie, mammies, mammifer, mammifera, mammiferous, mammiform, mammilate, mammilated, mammilla, mammillae, mammillaplasty, mammillar, mammillary, mammillate, mammillated, mammillation, mammilliform, mammilloid, mammilloplasty, mammin, mammitides, mammitis, mammock, mammocked, mammocks, mammodi, mammogen, mammogenic, mammogenically, mammogram, mammographic, mammographies, mammography, mammon, mammondom, mammoni, mammoniacal, mammonish, mammonism, mammonist, mammonistic, mammonite, mammonitish, mammonization, mammonize, mammonolatry, mammons, mammose, mammoth, mammothrept, mammoths, mammotomy, mammotropin, mammula, mammulae, mammular, mammy, mamo, mamona, mamoncillo, mamoncillos, mamoty, mampalon, mampara, mampus, mamry, mamsell, mamushi, mamzer, man, man's, mana, manace, manacing, manacle, manacled, manacles, manacling, manada, manage, manageability, manageable, manageableness, manageably, managed, managee, manageless, management, management's, managemental, managements, manager, manager's, managerdom, manageress, managerial, managerially, managers, managership, managery, manages, managing, manaism, manak, manakin, manakins, manal, manana, mananas, manarvel, manas, manasic, manasseh, manatee, manatees, manati, manatine, manation, manatoid, manavel, manavelins, manavilins, manavlins, manba, manbarklak, manbird, manbot, manbote, manbria, mancala, mancando, manche, manches, manchester, manchet, manchets, manchette, manchild, manchineel, manchu, manchuria, manchurian, manchurians, manchus, mancinism, mancipable, mancipant, mancipare, mancipate, mancipation, mancipative, mancipatory, mancipee, mancipia, mancipium, manciple, manciples, mancipleship, mancipular, mancono, mancus, mand, mandacaru, mandaean, mandala, mandalas, mandalic, mandament, mandamus, mandamuse, mandamused, mandamuses, mandamusing, mandant, mandapa, mandar, mandarah, mandarin, mandarinate, mandarindom, mandarined, mandariness, mandarinic, mandarining, mandarinism, mandarinize, mandarins, mandarinship, mandat, mandataries, mandatary, mandate, mandated, mandatedness, mandatee, mandates, mandating, mandation, mandative, mandator, mandatories, mandatorily, mandatoriness, mandators, mandatory, mandats, mandatum, mandelate, mandelic, manderelle, mandi, mandible, mandibles, mandibula, mandibular, mandibulary, mandibulate, mandibulated, mandibuliform, mandibulohyoid, mandibulomaxillary, mandibulopharyngeal, mandibulosuspensorial, mandil, mandilion, mandingo, mandioca, mandiocas, mandir, mandlen, mandment, mandoer, mandola, mandolas, mandolin, mandoline, mandolinist, mandolinists, mandolins, mandolute, mandom, mandora, mandore, mandorla, mandorlas, mandorle, mandra, mandragora, mandragvn, mandrake, mandrakes, mandrel, mandrels, mandriarch, mandril, mandrill, mandrills, mandrils, mandrin, mandritta, mandruka, mands, mandua, manducable, manducate, manducated, manducating, manducation, manducatory, mandyai, mandyas, mandyases, mandyi, mane, mane's, maned, manege, maneges, maneh, manei, maneless, manent, manequin, manerial, manes, manesheet, maness, manet, maneuver, maneuverability, maneuverable, maneuvered, maneuverer, maneuvering, maneuvers, maneuvrability, maneuvrable, maneuvre, maneuvred, maneuvring, maney, manfish, manful, manfully, manfulness, mang, manga, mangabeira, mangabev, mangabey, mangabeys, mangabies, mangaby, mangal, mangana, manganapatite, manganate, manganblende, manganbrucite, manganeisen, manganese, manganesian, manganesic, manganetic, manganhedenbergite, manganic, manganiferous, manganite, manganium, manganize, manganocalcite, manganocolumbite, manganophyllite, manganosiderite, manganosite, manganostibiite, manganotantalite, manganous, manganpectolite, mange, mangeao, mangeier, mangeiest, mangel, mangelin, mangels, mangelwurzel, manger, manger's, mangerite, mangers, mangery, manges, mangey, mangi, mangier, mangiest, mangily, manginess, mangle, mangled, mangleman, mangler, manglers, mangles, mangling, manglingly, mango, mangoes, mangold, mangolds, mangona, mangonel, mangonels, mangonism, mangonization, mangonize, mangoro, mangos, mangosteen, mangour, mangrass, mangrate, mangrove, mangroves, mangue, mangwe, mangy, manhaden, manhandle, manhandled, manhandler, manhandles, manhandling, manhattan, manhattans, manhead, manhole, manholes, manhood, manhoods, manhours, manhunt, manhunter, manhunting, manhunts, mani, mania, maniable, maniac, maniac's, maniacal, maniacally, maniacs, maniaphobia, manias, manic, manically, manicate, manichaean, manichee, manichord, manichordon, manicole, manicon, manicord, manicotti, manics, maniculatus, manicure, manicured, manicures, manicuring, manicurist, manicurists, manid, manie, manienie, maniere, manifer, manifest, manifesta, manifestable, manifestant, manifestation, manifestation's, manifestational, manifestationist, manifestations, manifestative, manifestatively, manifested, manifestedness, manifester, manifesting, manifestive, manifestly, manifestness, manifesto, manifestoed, manifestoes, manifestos, manifests, manificum, manifold, manifold's, manifolded, manifolder, manifolding, manifoldly, manifoldness, manifolds, manifoldwise, maniform, manify, manihot, manihots, manikin, manikinism, manikins, manila, manilas, manilio, manilla, manillas, manille, manilles, manini, manioc, manioca, maniocas, maniocs, maniple, maniples, manipulability, manipulable, manipular, manipulary, manipulatability, manipulatable, manipulate, manipulated, manipulates, manipulating, manipulation, manipulational, manipulations, manipulative, manipulatively, manipulator, manipulator's, manipulators, manipulatory, manis, manism, manist, manistic, manit, manito, manitoba, manitos, manitou, manitous, manitrunk, manitu, manitus, maniu, manjack, manjak, manjeet, manjel, mank, mankeeper, mankie, mankiller, mankilling, mankin, mankind, mankind's, mankindly, manks, manky, manless, manlessly, manlessness, manlet, manlier, manliest, manlihood, manlike, manlikely, manlikeness, manlily, manliness, manling, manly, manmade, manna, mannaia, mannan, mannans, mannas, manned, mannequin, mannequins, manner, mannerable, mannered, manneredness, mannerhood, mannering, mannerism, mannerisms, mannerist, manneristic, manneristical, manneristically, mannerize, mannerless, mannerlessness, mannerliness, mannerly, manners, mannersome, manness, mannet, mannide, mannie, manniferous, mannified, mannify, mannikin, mannikinism, mannikins, manning, mannire, mannish, mannishly, mannishness, mannitan, mannite, mannites, mannitic, mannitol, mannitols, mannitose, mannoheptite, mannoheptitol, mannoheptose, mannoketoheptose, mannonic, mannopus, mannosan, mannose, mannoses, manny, mano, manoc, manoeuver, manoeuvered, manoeuvering, manoeuvre, manoeuvred, manoeuvreing, manoeuvrer, manoeuvring, manograph, manoir, manometer, manometer's, manometers, manometric, manometrical, manometrically, manometries, manometry, manomin, manor, manor's, manorial, manorialism, manorialize, manors, manorship, manos, manoscope, manostat, manostatic, manpack, manpower, manpowers, manqu, manque, manquee, manqueller, manred, manrent, manroot, manrope, manropes, mans, mansard, mansarded, mansards, manscape, manse, manser, manservant, manses, manship, mansion, mansion's, mansional, mansionary, mansioned, mansioneer, mansionry, mansions, manslaughter, manslaughterer, manslaughtering, manslaughterous, manslaughters, manslayer, manslayers, manslaying, manso, mansonry, manstealer, manstealing, manstopper, manstopping, mansuete, mansuetely, mansuetude, manswear, mansworn, mant, manta, mantal, mantapa, mantappeaux, mantas, manteau, manteaus, manteaux, manteel, mantegar, mantel, mantel's, mantelet, mantelets, manteline, mantelletta, mantellone, mantellshelves, mantelpiece, mantelpieces, mantels, mantelshelf, manteltree, manter, mantes, mantevil, mantic, mantically, manticism, manticora, manticore, mantid, mantids, mantilla, mantillas, mantis, mantises, mantispid, mantissa, mantissa's, mantissas, mantistic, mantle, mantle's, mantled, mantlepiece, mantlepieces, mantlerock, mantles, mantlet, mantletree, mantlets, mantling, mantlings, manto, mantoid, mantologist, mantology, manton, mantra, mantram, mantrap, mantraps, mantras, mantric, mantua, mantuamaker, mantuamaking, mantuan, mantuas, manty, manual, manual's, manualii, manualism, manualist, manualiter, manually, manuals, manuao, manuary, manubaliste, manubria, manubrial, manubriated, manubrium, manubriums, manucaption, manucaptor, manucapture, manucode, manucodiata, manuduce, manuduct, manuduction, manuductive, manuductor, manuductory, manuever, manueverable, manuevered, manuevers, manuf, manufact, manufaction, manufactor, manufactories, manufactory, manufacturable, manufactural, manufacture, manufactured, manufacturer, manufacturer's, manufacturers, manufactures, manufacturess, manufacturing, manuka, manul, manuma, manumea, manumisable, manumise, manumission, manumissions, manumissive, manumit, manumits, manumitted, manumitter, manumitting, manumotive, manuprisor, manurable, manurage, manurance, manure, manured, manureless, manurement, manurer, manurers, manures, manurial, manurially, manuring, manus, manuscript, manuscript's, manuscriptal, manuscription, manuscripts, manuscriptural, manusina, manustupration, manutagi, manutenency, manutergium, manward, manwards, manway, manweed, manwise, manworth, manx, many, manyatta, manyberry, manyfold, manyness, manyplies, manyroot, manysidedness, manyways, manywhere, manywise, manzana, manzanilla, manzanillo, manzanita, manzil, mao, maoism, maoist, maoists, maomao, maori, maoris, maormor, map, map's, mapach, mapache, mapau, maphrian, mapland, maple, maple's, maplebush, mapleface, maplelike, maples, mapmaker, mapmakers, mapmaking, mapo, mappable, mapped, mappemonde, mappen, mapper, mappers, mapping, mapping's, mappings, mappist, mappy, maps, mapwise, maquahuitl, maquereau, maquette, maquettes, maqui, maquillage, maquis, maquisard, mar, mara, marabotin, marabou, marabous, marabout, maraboutism, marabouts, marabunta, marabuto, maraca, maracan, maracas, maracock, marae, marage, maraged, maraging, marah, marais, marajuana, marakapas, maral, maranao, maranatha, marang, maranon, maranta, marantaceous, marantas, marantic, marara, mararie, maras, marasca, marascas, maraschino, maraschinos, marasmic, marasmoid, marasmous, marasmus, marasmuses, maratha, marathi, marathon, marathoner, marathons, marattiaceous, maraud, marauded, marauder, marauders, marauding, marauds, maravedi, maravedis, maray, marbelization, marbelize, marbelized, marbelizing, marble, marbled, marblehead, marbleheader, marblehearted, marbleization, marbleize, marbleized, marbleizer, marbleizes, marbleizing, marblelike, marbleness, marbler, marblers, marbles, marblewood, marblier, marbliest, marbling, marblings, marblish, marbly, marbrinus, marc, marcando, marcantant, marcasite, marcasitic, marcasitical, marcassin, marcatissimo, marcato, marcel, marceline, marcella, marcelled, marceller, marcelling, marcello, marcels, marcescence, marcescent, marcgrave, marcgraviaceous, march, marchand, marchantiaceous, marched, marchen, marcher, marchers, marches, marchesa, marchese, marchesi, marchet, marchetti, marchetto, marching, marchioness, marchionesses, marchite, marchland, marchman, marchmen, marchpane, marcid, marcionism, marcionite, marco, marconi, marconigram, marconigraph, marconigraphy, marcor, marcosian, marcot, marcottage, marcs, mardi, mardy, mare, mare's, mareblob, marechal, marechale, marekanite, maremma, maremmatic, maremme, maremmese, marengo, marennin, mareograph, mares, mareschal, marezzo, marfire, marg, marga, margarate, margaret, margaric, margarin, margarine, margarins, margarita, margaritaceous, margaritae, margarite, margaritic, margaritiferous, margaritomancy, margarodid, margarodite, margarosanite, margaux, margay, margays, marge, marged, margeline, margent, margented, margenting, margents, marges, margin, margin's, marginability, marginal, marginalia, marginality, marginalize, marginally, marginals, marginate, marginated, marginating, margination, margined, marginelliform, marginicidal, marginiform, margining, marginirostral, marginoplasty, margins, margosa, margravate, margrave, margravely, margraves, margravial, margraviate, margravine, marguerite, marguerites, margullie, marhala, maria, mariachi, mariachis, marialite, marian, mariana, marianist, marianna, marianne, marica, maricolous, mariculture, marid, marie, mariengroschen, maries, mariet, marigenous, marigold, marigolds, marigram, marigraph, marigraphic, marihuana, marijuana, marikina, marilyn, marimba, marimbaist, marimbas, marimonda, marina, marinade, marinaded, marinades, marinading, marinal, marinara, marinaras, marinas, marinate, marinated, marinates, marinating, marination, marine, marined, mariner, mariners, marinership, marines, marinheiro, marinist, marinorama, mariola, mariolatry, mariology, marionet, marionette, marionettes, mariposa, mariposas, mariposite, maris, marish, marishes, marishness, marishy, marist, marita, maritage, maritagium, marital, maritality, maritally, mariti, mariticidal, mariticide, maritimal, maritimate, maritime, maritimes, maritorious, mariupolite, marjoram, marjorams, marjorie, mark, marka, markable, markaz, markazes, markdown, markdowns, marked, markedly, markedness, marker, markers, markery, market, marketability, marketable, marketableness, marketably, marketed, marketeer, marketeers, marketer, marketers, marketing, marketings, marketman, marketplace, marketplace's, marketplaces, markets, marketstead, marketwise, markfieldite, markhoor, markhoors, markhor, markhors, marking, markingly, markings, markis, markka, markkaa, markkas, markland, markless, markman, markmen, markmoot, markmote, marks, markshot, marksman, marksmanly, marksmanship, marksmen, markstone, markswoman, markswomen, markup, markups, markweed, markworthy, marl, marlaceous, marlacious, marlberry, marled, marler, marlet, marli, marlier, marliest, marlin, marline, marlines, marlinespike, marlinespikes, marling, marlings, marlingspike, marlins, marlinspike, marlinsucker, marlite, marlites, marlitic, marllike, marlock, marlpit, marls, marly, marm, marmalade, marmalades, marmalady, marmaritin, marmarization, marmarize, marmarized, marmarizing, marmarosis, marmatite, marmelos, marmennill, marmink, marmion, marmit, marmite, marmites, marmolite, marmor, marmoraceous, marmorate, marmorated, marmoration, marmoreal, marmoreally, marmorean, marmoric, marmorize, marmose, marmoset, marmosets, marmot, marmota, marmots, maro, marocain, marok, maronite, maroon, marooned, marooner, marooning, maroons, maroquin, maror, maros, marotte, marouflage, marplot, marplotry, marplots, marprelate, marque, marquee, marquees, marques, marquesan, marquess, marquessate, marquesses, marqueterie, marquetry, marquis, marquisal, marquisate, marquisdom, marquise, marquises, marquisess, marquisette, marquisettes, marquisina, marquisotte, marquisship, marquito, marquois, marraine, marram, marrams, marranism, marranize, marrano, marred, marree, marrer, marrers, marriable, marriage, marriage's, marriageability, marriageable, marriageableness, marriageproof, marriages, married, marriedly, marrieds, marrier, marriers, marries, marring, marrock, marron, marrons, marrot, marrow, marrowbone, marrowbones, marrowed, marrowfat, marrowing, marrowish, marrowless, marrowlike, marrows, marrowsky, marrowskyer, marrowy, marrube, marry, marryer, marrying, marrymuffe, marrys, mars, marsala, marse, marseillais, marseillaise, marseille, marseilles, marses, marsh, marsh's, marshal, marshalate, marshalcies, marshalcy, marshaled, marshaler, marshaless, marshaling, marshall, marshalled, marshaller, marshalling, marshalls, marshalman, marshalment, marshals, marshalsea, marshalship, marshbanker, marshberries, marshberry, marshbuck, marshes, marshfire, marshflower, marshier, marshiest, marshiness, marshite, marshland, marshlander, marshlands, marshlike, marshlocks, marshmallow, marshmallows, marshmallowy, marshman, marshmen, marshs, marshwort, marshy, marsileaceous, marsipobranch, marsipobranchiate, marsoon, marsupia, marsupial, marsupialian, marsupialise, marsupialised, marsupialising, marsupialization, marsupialize, marsupialized, marsupializing, marsupials, marsupian, marsupiate, marsupium, mart, martaban, martagon, martagons, marted, martel, martele, marteline, martellate, martellato, martellement, martello, martellos, martemper, marten, marteniko, martenot, martens, martensite, martensitic, martensitically, martext, martha, martial, martialed, martialing, martialism, martialist, martialists, martiality, martialization, martialize, martialled, martialling, martially, martialness, martials, martian, martians, martiloge, martin, martinet, martineta, martinetish, martinetishness, martinetism, martinets, martinetship, martinez, marting, martingal, martingale, martingales, martini, martinico, martinis, martinmas, martinoe, martins, martite, martlet, martlets, martnet, martrix, marts, martyniaceous, martyr, martyr's, martyrdom, martyrdoms, martyred, martyrer, martyress, martyria, martyries, martyring, martyrisation, martyrise, martyrised, martyrish, martyrising, martyrium, martyrization, martyrize, martyrized, martyrizer, martyrizing, martyrlike, martyrly, martyrolatry, martyrologe, martyrologic, martyrological, martyrologist, martyrologistic, martyrologium, martyrology, martyrs, martyrship, martyrtyria, martyry, maru, marvel, marveled, marveling, marvelled, marvelling, marvellous, marvellously, marvellousness, marvelment, marvelous, marvelously, marvelousness, marvelry, marvels, marver, marvy, marwer, marx, marxian, marxism, marxist, marxists, mary, marybud, maryknoll, maryland, marylander, marylanders, marys, marysole, marzipan, marzipans, mas, masa, masai, masais, masarid, masaridid, masc, mascagnine, mascagnite, mascally, mascara, mascaras, mascaron, maschera, mascle, mascled, mascleless, mascon, mascons, mascot, mascotism, mascotry, mascots, mascotte, mascularity, masculate, masculation, masculine, masculinely, masculineness, masculines, masculinism, masculinist, masculinities, masculinity, masculinization, masculinize, masculinized, masculinizing, masculist, masculofeminine, masculonucleus, masculy, masdeu, maselin, maser, masers, mash, masha, mashak, mashal, mashallah, masham, mashed, mashelton, masher, mashers, mashes, mashgiach, mashgiah, mashgichim, mashgihim, mashie, mashier, mashies, mashiest, mashiness, mashing, mashlam, mashlin, mashloch, mashlum, mashman, mashmen, mashrebeeyah, mashrebeeyeh, mashru, mashy, masjid, masjids, mask, maskable, maskalonge, maskalonges, maskanonge, maskanonges, masked, maskeg, maskegs, maskelynite, masker, maskers, maskery, maskette, maskflower, masking, maskings, maskinonge, maskinonges, masklike, maskmv, maskoid, masks, maslin, masochism, masochist, masochist's, masochistic, masochistically, masochists, mason, mason's, masoned, masoner, masonic, masonically, masoning, masonite, masonried, masonries, masonry, masonrying, masons, masonwork, masooka, masoola, masora, masorete, masque, masquer, masquerade, masqueraded, masquerader, masqueraders, masquerades, masquerading, masquers, masques, mass, massa, massachuset, massachusetts, massacre, massacred, massacrer, massacrers, massacres, massacring, massacrous, massage, massaged, massager, massagers, massages, massageuse, massaging, massagist, massagists, massaranduba, massas, massasauga, masscult, masse, massebah, massecuite, massed, massedly, massedness, massel, masselgem, masser, masses, masseter, masseteric, masseterine, masseters, masseur, masseurs, masseuse, masseuses, massicot, massicotite, massicots, massier, massiest, massif, massifs, massig, massily, massiness, massing, massive, massively, massiveness, massivity, masskanne, massless, masslessness, masslike, massoola, massotherapist, massotherapy, massoy, massula, massy, massymore, mast, mastaba, mastabah, mastabahs, mastabas, mastadenitis, mastadenoma, mastage, mastalgia, mastatrophia, mastatrophy, mastauxe, mastax, mastectomies, mastectomy, masted, master, master's, masterable, masterate, masterdom, mastered, masterer, masterfast, masterful, masterfully, masterfulness, masterhood, masteries, mastering, masterings, masterless, masterlessness, masterlike, masterlily, masterliness, masterling, masterly, masterman, mastermen, mastermind, masterminded, masterminding, masterminds, masterous, masterpiece, masterpiece's, masterpieces, masterproof, masters, mastership, mastersinger, mastersingers, masterstroke, masterwork, masterworks, masterwort, mastery, mastful, masthead, mastheaded, mastheading, mastheads, masthelcosis, mastic, masticability, masticable, masticate, masticated, masticates, masticating, mastication, mastications, masticator, masticatories, masticatory, mastiche, mastiches, masticic, masticot, mastics, masticurous, mastiff, mastiffs, mastigate, mastigia, mastigium, mastigobranchia, mastigobranchial, mastigoneme, mastigophobia, mastigophoran, mastigophore, mastigophoric, mastigophorous, mastigopod, mastigopodous, mastigote, mastigure, masting, mastitic, mastitides, mastitis, mastix, mastixes, mastless, mastlike, mastman, mastmen, mastocarcinoma, mastocarcinomas, mastocarcinomata, mastoccipital, mastochondroma, mastochondrosis, mastodon, mastodonic, mastodons, mastodonsaurian, mastodont, mastodontic, mastodontine, mastodontoid, mastodynia, mastoid, mastoidal, mastoidale, mastoideal, mastoidean, mastoidectomies, mastoidectomy, mastoideocentesis, mastoideosquamous, mastoiditis, mastoidohumeral, mastoidohumeralis, mastoidotomy, mastoids, mastological, mastologist, mastology, mastomenia, mastoncus, mastooccipital, mastoparietal, mastopathies, mastopathy, mastopexy, mastoplastia, mastorrhagia, mastoscirrhus, mastosquamose, mastotomy, mastotympanic, mastras, masts, masturbate, masturbated, masturbates, masturbatic, masturbating, masturbation, masturbational, masturbator, masturbators, masturbatory, mastwood, masty, masu, masurium, masuriums, mat, mat's, matachin, matachina, matachinas, mataco, matadero, matador, matadors, mataeological, mataeologue, mataeology, mataeotechny, matagasse, matagory, matagouri, matai, matajuelo, matalan, matamata, matambala, matamoro, matanza, matapan, matapi, matara, matasano, matax, matboard, match, matchable, matchableness, matchably, matchboard, matchboarding, matchbook, matchbooks, matchbox, matchboxes, matchcloth, matchcoat, matched, matcher, matchers, matches, matchet, matching, matchings, matchless, matchlessly, matchlessness, matchlock, matchlocks, matchmake, matchmaker, matchmakers, matchmaking, matchmark, matchsafe, matchstalk, matchstick, matchwood, matchy, mate, mate's, mated, mategriffon, matehood, matelass, matelasse, mateless, matelessness, mateley, matellasse, matelot, matelotage, matelote, matelotes, matelotte, matelow, mately, matemilk, mater, materfamilias, materia, materiable, material, materialisation, materialise, materialised, materialiser, materialising, materialism, materialist, materialistic, materialistical, materialistically, materialists, materialities, materiality, materialization, materializations, materialize, materialized, materializee, materializer, materializes, materializing, materially, materialman, materialmen, materialness, materials, materiarian, materiate, materiation, materiel, materiels, maternal, maternalise, maternalised, maternalising, maternalism, maternalistic, maternality, maternalize, maternalized, maternalizing, maternally, maternalness, maternities, maternity, maternology, maters, mates, mateship, mateships, matey, mateyness, mateys, matezite, matfellon, matfelon, matgrass, math, matha, mathe, mathematic, mathematical, mathematically, mathematicals, mathematician, mathematician's, mathematicians, mathematicize, mathematics, mathematization, mathematize, mathemeg, mather, mathes, mathesis, mathetic, maths, mathurin, matico, matie, maties, matilda, matildas, matildite, matin, matina, matinal, matindol, matinee, matinees, matiness, matinesses, mating, matings, matins, matipo, matka, matkah, matless, matlo, matlockite, matlow, matmaker, matmaking, matman, matoke, matra, matrace, matrah, matral, matranee, matrass, matrasses, matreed, matres, matriarch, matriarchal, matriarchalism, matriarchate, matriarchic, matriarchical, matriarchies, matriarchist, matriarchs, matriarchy, matric, matrical, matrice, matrices, matricidal, matricide, matricides, matriclan, matriclinous, matricula, matriculable, matriculae, matriculant, matriculants, matricular, matriculate, matriculated, matriculates, matriculating, matriculation, matriculations, matriculator, matriculatory, matriheritage, matriherital, matrilateral, matrilaterally, matriline, matrilineage, matrilineal, matrilineally, matrilinear, matrilinearism, matrilinearly, matrilinies, matriliny, matrilocal, matrilocality, matrimonial, matrimonially, matrimonies, matrimonii, matrimonious, matrimoniously, matrimony, matriotism, matripotestal, matris, matrisib, matrix, matrixes, matrixing, matroclinal, matroclinic, matroclinous, matrocliny, matroid, matron, matronage, matronal, matronhood, matronism, matronize, matronized, matronizing, matronlike, matronliness, matronly, matrons, matronship, matronymic, matross, mats, matster, matsu, matsue, matsuri, matt, matta, mattamore, mattaro, mattboard, matte, matted, mattedly, mattedness, matter, matterate, matterative, mattered, matterful, matterfulness, mattering, matterless, matters, mattery, mattes, matthean, matthew, matti, mattin, matting, mattings, mattins, mattock, mattocks, mattoid, mattoids, mattoir, mattrass, mattrasses, mattress, mattress's, mattresses, matts, mattulla, maturable, maturant, maturate, maturated, maturates, maturating, maturation, maturational, maturations, maturative, mature, matured, maturely, maturement, matureness, maturer, matures, maturescence, maturescent, maturest, maturing, maturish, maturities, maturity, matutinal, matutinally, matutinary, matutine, matutinely, matweed, maty, matza, matzah, matzahs, matzas, matzo, matzoh, matzohs, matzoon, matzoons, matzos, matzot, matzoth, mau, mauby, maucaco, maucauco, maucherite, maud, maudeline, maudle, maudlin, maudlinism, maudlinize, maudlinly, maudlinness, maudlinwort, mauger, maugh, maught, maugrabee, maugre, maukin, maul, maulana, mauled, mauler, maulers, mauley, mauling, mauls, maulstick, maulvi, maumet, maumetries, maumetry, maumets, maun, maunch, maunche, maund, maunder, maundered, maunderer, maunderers, maundering, maunders, maundful, maundies, maunds, maundy, maunge, maungy, maunna, maupassant, mauquahog, mauresque, mauricio, maurist, mauritania, mauritanian, mauritanians, mauser, mausole, mausolea, mausoleal, mausolean, mausoleum, mausoleums, maut, mauther, mauts, mauve, mauvein, mauveine, mauves, mauvette, mauvine, maux, maven, mavens, maverick, mavericks, mavie, mavies, mavin, mavins, mavis, mavises, mavourneen, mavournin, mavrodaphne, maw, mawali, mawbound, mawed, mawger, mawing, mawk, mawkin, mawkingly, mawkish, mawkishly, mawkishness, mawks, mawky, mawmish, mawn, mawp, maws, mawseed, mawsie, mawworm, max, maxi, maxicoat, maxicoats, maxilla, maxillae, maxillar, maxillaries, maxillary, maxillas, maxilliferous, maxilliform, maxilliped, maxillipedary, maxillipede, maxillodental, maxillofacial, maxillojugal, maxillolabial, maxillomandibular, maxillopalatal, maxillopalatine, maxillopharyngeal, maxillopremaxillary, maxilloturbinal, maxillozygomatic, maxim, maxim's, maxima, maximal, maximalist, maximally, maximals, maximate, maximation, maximed, maximin, maximins, maximise, maximised, maximises, maximising, maximist, maximistic, maximite, maximites, maximization, maximize, maximized, maximizer, maximizers, maximizes, maximizing, maxims, maximum, maximumly, maximums, maximus, maxis, maxisingle, maxiskirt, maxixe, maxixes, maxwell, maxwells, may, maya, mayacaceous, mayan, mayans, mayapis, mayapple, mayapples, mayas, maybe, mayberry, maybush, maybushes, maycock, mayday, maydays, mayduke, mayed, mayence, mayest, mayfish, mayfishes, mayflies, mayflower, mayflowers, mayfly, mayhap, mayhappen, mayhaps, mayhem, mayhemmed, mayhemming, mayhems, maying, mayings, mayn't, maynt, mayo, mayonnaise, mayor, mayor's, mayoral, mayorality, mayoralties, mayoralty, mayoress, mayoresses, mayors, mayorship, mayorships, maypole, maypoles, maypop, maypops, mays, maysin, mayst, mayten, maythe, maythes, maytide, mayvin, mayvins, mayweed, mayweeds, maza, mazaedia, mazaedidia, mazaedium, mazagran, mazalgia, mazama, mazame, mazapilite, mazard, mazards, mazarine, mazdaism, mazdoor, mazdur, maze, maze's, mazed, mazedly, mazedness, mazeful, mazel, mazelike, mazement, mazer, mazers, mazes, mazic, mazier, maziest, mazily, maziness, mazinesses, mazing, mazocacothesis, mazodynia, mazolysis, mazolytic, mazopathia, mazopathic, mazopathy, mazopexy, mazourka, mazourkas, mazuca, mazuma, mazumas, mazurka, mazurkas, mazut, mazy, mazzard, mazzards, mb, mbalolo, mbd, mbeuer, mbira, mbiras, mbori, mbps, mc, mccarthyism, mccoy, mcdonald, mcf, mcg, mcphail, md, mdnt, mdse, me, mea, meable, meach, meaching, meacock, meacon, mead, meader, meadow, meadow's, meadowbur, meadowed, meadower, meadowing, meadowink, meadowland, meadowlands, meadowlark, meadowlarks, meadowless, meadows, meadowsweet, meadowsweets, meadowwort, meadowy, meads, meadsman, meadsweet, meadwort, meager, meagerly, meagerness, meagre, meagrely, meagreness, meak, meaking, meal, meal's, mealable, mealberry, mealed, mealer, mealie, mealier, mealies, mealiest, mealily, mealiness, mealing, mealless, mealman, mealmen, mealmonger, mealmouth, mealmouthed, mealock, mealproof, meals, mealtide, mealtime, mealtimes, mealworm, mealworms, mealy, mealybug, mealybugs, mealymouth, mealymouthed, mealymouthedly, mealymouthedness, mealywing, mean, meander, meandered, meanderer, meanderers, meandering, meanderingly, meanders, meandrine, meandriniform, meandrite, meandrous, meandrously, meaned, meaner, meaners, meanest, meanie, meanies, meaning,

meaning's, meaningful, meaningfully, meaningfulness, meaningless, meaninglessly, meaninglessness, meaningly, meaningness, meanings, meanish, meanless, meanly, meanness, meannesses, means, meanspirited, meanspiritedly, meanspiritedness, meant, meantime, meantimes, meantone, meanwhile, meany, mear, mearstone, meas, mease, measle, measled, measledness, measles, measlesproof, measlier, measliest, measly, measondue, measurability, measurable, measurableness, measurably, measurage, measuration, measure, measured, measuredly, measuredness, measureless, measurelessly, measurelessness, measurely, measurement, measurement's, measurements, measurer, measurers, measures, measuring, measuringworm, meat, meat's, meatal, meatball, meatballs, meatbird, meatcutter, meated, meath, meathe, meathead, meatheads, meathook, meathooks, meatic, meatier, meatiest, meatily, meatiness, meatless, meatman, meatmen, meatometer, meatorrhaphy, meatoscope, meatoscopy, meatotome, meatotomy, meats, meature, meatus, meatuses, meatworks, meaty, meaul, meaw, meazle, mebos, mecamylamine, mecate, mecati, mecca, meccano, meccas, mech, mechanal, mechanality, mechanalize, mechanic, mechanic's, mechanical, mechanicalism, mechanicalist, mechanicality, mechanicalization, mechanicalize, mechanically, mechanicalness, mechanician, mechanicochemical, mechanicocorpuscular, mechanicointellectual, mechanicotherapy, mechanics, mechanism, mechanism's, mechanismic, mechanisms, mechanist, mechanistic, mechanistically, mechanists, mechanizable, mechanization, mechanization's, mechanizations, mechanize, mechanized, mechanizer, mechanizers, mechanizes, mechanizing, mechanochemical, mechanochemistry, mechanolater, mechanology, mechanomorphic, mechanomorphically, mechanomorphism, mechanophobia, mechanoreception, mechanoreceptive, mechanoreceptor, mechanotherapeutic, mechanotherapeutics, mechanotherapies, mechanotherapist, mechanotherapists, mechanotheraputic, mechanotheraputically, mechanotherapy, mechant, mechitzah, mechitzoth, mechlin, mechoacan, meck, meckelectomy, meclizine, mecodont, mecometer, mecometry, mecon, meconic, meconidium, meconin, meconioid, meconium, meconiums, meconology, meconophagism, meconophagist, mecopteran, mecopteron, mecopterous, mecrobeproof, mecum, mecums, mecurial, mecurialism, med, medaillon, medaka, medakas, medal, medal's, medaled, medalet, medaling, medalist, medalists, medalize, medallary, medalled, medallic, medallically, medalling, medallion, medallion's, medallioned, medallioning, medallionist, medallions, medallist, medals, meddle, meddlecome, meddled, meddlement, meddler, meddlers, meddles, meddlesome, meddlesomely, meddlesomeness, meddling, meddlingly, mede, medea, medenagan, medevac, medevacs, media, mediacid, mediacies, mediacy, mediad, mediae, mediaeval, mediaevalism, mediaevalist, mediaevalize, mediaevally, medial, medialization, medialize, medialkaline, medially, medials, median, median's, medianic, medianimic, medianimity, medianism, medianity, medianly, medians, mediant, mediants, mediary, medias, mediastina, mediastinal, mediastine, mediastinitis, mediastinotomy, mediastinum, mediate, mediated, mediately, mediateness, mediates, mediating, mediatingly, mediation, mediational, mediations, mediatisation, mediatise, mediatised, mediatising, mediative, mediatization, mediatize, mediatized, mediatizing, mediator, mediatorial, mediatorialism, mediatorially, mediatorious, mediators, mediatorship, mediatory, mediatress, mediatrice, mediatrices, mediatrix, mediatrixes, medic, medic's, medica, medicable, medicably, medicaid, medicaids, medical, medicalese, medically, medicals, medicament, medicamental, medicamentally, medicamentary, medicamentation, medicamentous, medicaments, medicant, medicare, medicares, medicaster, medicate, medicated, medicates, medicating, medication, medications, medicative, medicator, medicatory, medicean, medicinable, medicinableness, medicinal, medicinally, medicinalness, medicinary, medicine, medicine's, medicined, medicinelike, medicinemonger, mediciner, medicines, medicining, medick, medicks, medico, medicobotanical, medicochirurgic, medicochirurgical, medicodental, medicolegal, medicolegally, medicomania, medicomechanic, medicomechanical, medicommissure, medicomoral, medicophysical, medicophysics, medicopsychological, medicopsychology, medicos, medicostatistic, medicosurgical, medicotopographic, medicozoologic, medics, medidia, medidii, mediety, medieval, medievalism, medievalist, medievalistic, medievalists, medievalize, medievally, medievals, medifixed, mediglacial, medii, medille, medimn, medimno, medimnos, medimnus, medina, medine, medino, medio, medioanterior, mediocarpal, mediooccipital, mediocracy, mediocral, mediocre, mediocrely, mediocreness, mediocris, mediocrist, mediocrities, mediocrity, mediocubital, mediodepressed, mediodigital, mediodorsal, mediodorsally, mediofrontal, mediolateral, mediopalatal, mediopalatine, mediopassive, mediopectoral, medioperforate, mediopontine, medioposterior, mediosilicic, mediostapedial, mediotarsal, medioventral, medisance, medisect, medisection, medism, meditabund, meditance, meditant, meditate, meditated, meditatedly, meditater, meditates, meditating, meditatingly, meditatio, meditation, meditationist, meditations, meditatist, meditative, meditatively, meditativeness, meditator, mediterrane, mediterranean, mediterraneous, medithorax, meditullium, medium, medium's, mediumism, mediumistic, mediumization, mediumize, mediumly, mediums, mediumship, medius, medize, medjidie, medjidieh, medlar, medlars, medle, medley, medleyed, medleying, medleys, medlied, medoc, medregal, medrick, medrinacks, medrinacles, medrinaque, medscheat, medula, medulla, medullae, medullar, medullary, medullas, medullate, medullated, medullation, medullispinal, medullitis, medullization, medullose, medullous, medusa, medusae, medusal, medusalike, medusan, medusans, medusas, medusiferous, medusiform, medusoid, medusoids, mee, meebos, meece, meech, meecher, meeching, meed, meedful, meedless, meeds, meek, meeken, meeker, meekest, meekhearted, meekheartedness, meekling, meekly, meekness, meeknesses, meer, meered, meerkat, meerschaum, meerschaums, meese, meet, meetable, meeten, meeter, meeterly, meeters, meeth, meethelp, meethelper, meeting, meetinger, meetinghouse, meetings, meetly, meetness, meetnesses, meets, meg, megaara, megabar, megabars, megabaud, megabit, megabits, megabuck, megabucks, megabyte, megabytes, megacephalia, megacephalic, megacephalous, megacephaly, megacerine, megacerotine, megachilid, megachiropteran, megachiropterous, megacity, megacolon, megacosm, megacoulomb, megacurie, megacycle, megacycles, megadeath, megadeaths, megadont, megadontia, megadontic, megadontism, megadonty, megadynamics, megadyne, megadynes, megaerg, megafarad, megafog, megagamete, megagametophyte, megahertz, megahertzes, megajoule, megakaryoblast, megakaryocyte, megakaryocytic, megalecithal, megaleme, megalerg, megalesthete, megalethoscope, megalith, megalithic, megaliths, megaloblast, megaloblastic, megalocardia, megalocarpous, megalocephalia, megalocephalic, megalocephalous, megalocephaly, megalochirous, megalocornea, megalocyte, megalocytosis, megalodactylia, megalodactylism, megalodactylous, megalodont, megalodontia, megaloenteron, megalogastria, megaloglossia, megalograph, megalography, megalohepatia, megalokaryocyte, megalomania, megalomaniac, megalomaniacal, megalomaniacally, megalomaniacs, megalomanic, megalomelia, megalopa, megalopenis, megalophonic, megalophonous, megalophthalmus, megalopia, megalopic, megalopine, megaloplastocyte, megalopolis, megalopolises, megalopolistic, megalopolitan, megalopolitanism, megalopore, megalops, megalopsia, megalopsychy, megalopteran, megalopterous, megalosaur, megalosaurian, megalosauroid, megalosaurus, megaloscope, megaloscopy, megalosphere, megalospheric, megalosplenia, megalosyndactyly, megaloureter, megamastictoral, megamere, megameter, megametre, megampere, meganucleus, megaparsec, megaphone, megaphoned, megaphones, megaphonic, megaphonically, megaphoning, megaphotographic, megaphotography, megaphyllous, megapod, megapode, megapodes, megapolis, megapolitan, megaprosopous, megapterine, megara, megarad, megarian, megaron, megarons, megasclere, megascleric, megasclerous, megasclerum, megascope, megascopic, megascopical, megascopically, megaseism, megaseismic, megaseme, megasporange, megasporangium, megaspore, megasporic, megasporogenesis, megasporophyll, megass, megasse, megasses, megasynthetic, megathere, megatherian, megatherine, megatherioid, megatherium, megatherm, megathermal, megathermic, megatheroid, megaton, megatons, megatron, megatype, megatypy, megavitamin, megavolt, megavolts, megawatt, megawatts, megaweber, megaword, megawords, megazooid, megazoospore, megbote, megerg, megger, megillah, megillahs, megilloth, megilp, megilph, megilphs, megilps, megmho, megnetosphere, megohm, megohmit, megohmmeter, megohms, megomit, megophthalmus, megotalc, megrim, megrimish, megrims, meguilp, mehalla, mehari, meharis, meharist, mehitzah, mehitzoth, mehmandar, mehtar, mehtarship, meigomian, meiji, meikle, meikles, meile, meiler, mein, meindre, meinie, meinies, meiny, meio, meiobar, meiocene, meionite, meiophylly, meioses, meiosis, meiostemonous, meiotaxy, meiotic, meiotically, meisje, meistersinger, meith, meizoseismal, meizoseismic, mejorana, mekhitarist, mekilta, mekometer, mekong, mel, mela, melaconite, melada, meladiorite, melaena, melaenic, melagabbro, melagra, melagranite, melaleuca, melalgia, melam, melamdim, melamed, melamin, melamine, melamines, melammdim, melammed, melampod, melampode, melampodium, melampyrin, melampyrite, melampyritol, melanaemia, melanaemic, melanagogal, melanagogue, melancholia, melancholiac, melancholiacs, melancholian, melancholic, melancholically, melancholies, melancholily, melancholiness, melancholious, melancholiously, melancholiousness, melancholish, melancholist, melancholize, melancholomaniac, melancholy, melancholyish, melanchthonian, melanconiaceous, melanemia, melanemic, melanesia, melanesian, melanesians, melange, melanger, melanges, melangeur, melanian, melanic, melanics, melaniferous, melanilin, melaniline, melanin, melanins, melanism, melanisms, melanist, melanistic, melanists, melanite, melanites, melanitic, melanization, melanize, melanized, melanizes, melanizing, melano, melanoblast, melanoblastic, melanoblastoma, melanocarcinoma, melanocerite, melanochroi, melanochroic, melanochroite, melanochrous, melanocomous, melanocrate, melanocratic, melanocyte, melanoderm, melanoderma, melanodermia, melanodermic, melanogen, melanogenesis, melanoi, melanoid, melanoidin, melanoids, melanoma, melanomas, melanomata, melanopathia, melanopathy, melanophore, melanoplakia, melanorrhagia, melanorrhea, melanosarcoma, melanosarcomatosis, melanoscope, melanose, melanosed, melanosis, melanosity, melanosome, melanospermous, melanotekite, melanotic, melanotrichous, melanotype, melanous, melanterite, melanthaceous, melanthy, melanure, melanurenic, melanuresis, melanuria, melanuric, melaphyre, melasma, melasmic, melasses, melassigenic, melastomaceous, melastomad, melastome, melatonin, melatope, melaxuma, melba, melbourne, melch, melchite, melchizedek, meld, melded, melder, melders, melding, meldometer, meldrop, melds, mele, meleager, meleagrine, melebiose, melee, melees, melena, melene, melenic, meletin, melezitase, melezitose, meliaceous, melianthaceous, meliatin, melibiose, melic, melicera, meliceric, meliceris, melicerous, melichrous, melicitose, melicoton, melicrate, melicraton, melicratory, melicratum, melilite, melilites, melilitite, melilot, melilots, meline, melinite, melinites, melior, meliorability, meliorable, meliorant, meliorate, meliorated, meliorater, meliorates, meliorating, melioration, meliorations, meliorative, melioratively, meliorator, meliorism, meliorist, melioristic, meliority, meliphagan, meliphagidan, meliphagous, meliphanite, meliponine, melis, melisma, melismas, melismata, melismatic, melismatics, melissa, melissyl, melissylic, melitaemia, melitemia, melithaemia, melithemia, melitis, melitose, melitriose, melittologist, melittology, melituria, melituric, melkhout, mell, mellaginous, mellah, mellate, mellay, melled, melleous, meller, mellic, melliferous, mellific, mellificate, mellification, mellifluate, mellifluence, mellifluent, mellifluently, mellifluous, mellifluously, mellifluousness, mellilita, mellilot, mellimide, melling, mellisonant, mellisugent, mellit, mellita, mellitate, mellite, mellitic, mellitum, mellitus, mellivorous, mellon, mellone, mellonides, mellophone, mellow, mellowed, mellower, mellowest, mellowing, mellowly, mellowness, mellowphone, mellows, mellowy, mells, mellsman, melocoton, melocotoon, melodeon, melodeons, melodia, melodial, melodially, melodias, melodic, melodica, melodical, melodically, melodicon, melodics, melodied, melodies, melodiograph, melodion, melodious, melodiously, melodiousness, melodise, melodised, melodises, melodising, melodism, melodist, melodists, melodium, melodize, melodized, melodizer, melodizes, melodizing, melodractically, melodram, melodrama, melodrama's, melodramas, melodramatic, melodramatical, melodramatically, melodramaticism, melodramatics, melodramatise, melodramatised, melodramatising, melodramatist, melodramatists, melodramatization, melodramatize, melodrame, melody, melody's, melodying, melodyless, meloe, melogram, melograph, melographic, meloid, meloids, melologue, melolonthid, melolonthidan, melolonthine, melomame, melomane, melomania, melomaniac, melomanic, melon, melon's, meloncus, melongena, melongrower, melonist, melonite, melonlike, melonmonger, melonry, melons, melophone, melophonic, melophonist, melopiano, melopianos, meloplast, meloplastic, meloplasties, meloplasty, melopoeia, melopoeic, melos, melosa, melote, melotragedy, melotragic, melotrope, melpell, melpomene, mels, melt, meltability, meltable, meltage, meltages, meltdown, meltdowns, melted, meltedness, melteigite, melter, melters, melteth, melting, meltingly, meltingness, meltith, melton, meltons, melts, meltwater, melungeon, melvie, mem, member, member's, membered, memberless, members, membership, membership's, memberships, membracid, membracine, membral, membrally, membrana, membranaceous, membranaceously, membranal, membranate, membrane, membraned, membraneless, membranelike, membranella, membranelle, membraneous, membranes, membraniferous, membraniform, membranin, membranocalcareous, membranocartilaginous, membranocoriaceous, membranocorneous, membranogenic, membranoid, membranology, membranonervous, membranophone, membranophonic, membranosis, membranous, membranously, membranula, membranule, membrette, membretto, memento, mementoes, mementos, meminna, memnon, memnonian, memo, memo's, memoir, memoire, memoirism, memoirist, memoirs, memorabile, memorabilia, memorability, memorable, memorableness, memorably, memoranda, memorandist, memorandize, memorandum, memorandums, memorate, memoration, memorative, memorda, memoria, memorial, memorialisation, memorialise, memorialised, memorialiser, memorialising, memorialist, memorialization, memorializations, memorialize, memorialized, memorializer, memorializes, memorializing, memorially, memorials, memoried, memories, memorious, memorise, memorist, memoriter, memorizable, memorization, memorize, memorized, memorizer, memorizers, memorizes, memorizing, memory, memory's, memoryless, memorylessness, memos, memphian, memphis, mems, memsahib, memsahibs, men, men's, menaccanite, menaccanitic, menace, menaceable, menaced, menaceful, menacement, menacer, menacers, menaces, menacing, menacingly, menacme, menad, menadic, menadione, menads, menage, menagerie, menageries, menagerist, menages, menald, menaquinone, menarche, menarcheal, menarches, menarchial, menat, mend, mendable, mendacious, mendaciously, mendaciousness, mendacities, mendacity, mended, mendee, mendel, mendelevium, mendelian, mendelianism, mendelianist, mendelism, mendelist, mendelize, mendelssohn, mendelyeevite, mender, menders, mendiant, mendicancies, mendicancy, mendicant, mendicantism, mendicants, mendicate, mendicated, mendicating, mendication, mendicity, mendigo, mendigos, mending, mendings, mendipite, mendment, mendole, mendozite, mends, mendy, mene, meneghinite, menehune, menelaus, menevian, menfolk, menfolks, meng, menhaden, menhadens, menhir, menhirs, menial, menialism, meniality, menially, menialness, menials, menialty, menilite, meningeal, meninges, meningic, meningina, meningioma, meningism, meningismus, meningitic, meningitides, meningitis, meningitophobia, meningocele, meningocephalitis, meningocerebritis, meningococcal, meningococcemia, meningococci, meningococcic, meningococcoci, meningococcus, meningocortical, meningoencephalitic, meningoencephalitis, meningoencephalocele, meningomalacia, meningomyclitic, meningomyelitis, meningomyelocele, meningomyelorrhaphy, meningorachidian, meningoradicular, meningorhachidian, meningorrhagia, meningorrhea, meningorrhoea, meningosis, meningospinal, meningotyphoid, meninting, meninx, meniscal, meniscate, meniscectomy, menisci, menisciform, meniscitis, meniscocytosis, meniscoid, meniscoidal, meniscus, meniscuses, menise, menison, menisperm, menispermaceous, menispermin, menispermine, meniver, menkind, mennom, mennon, mennonist, mennonite, mennonites, mennuet, meno, menognath, menognathous, menologies, menologium, menology, menologyes, menometastasis, menominee, menopausal, menopause, menopausic, menophania, menoplania, menorah, menorahs, menorhynchous, menorrhagia, menorrhagic, menorrhagy, menorrhea, menorrheic, menorrhoea, menorrhoeic, menoschesis, menoschetic, menosepsis, menostasia, menostasis, menostatic, menostaxis, menotyphlic, menow, menoxenia, mens, mensa, mensae, mensal, mensalize, mensas, mensch, menschen, mensches, mense, mensed, menseful, menseless, menservants, menses, menshevik, menshevism, menshevist, mensing, mensis, mensk, menstrua, menstrual, menstruant, menstruate, menstruated, menstruates, menstruating, menstruation, menstruations, menstrue, menstruoos, menstruosity, menstruous, menstruousness, menstruum, menstruums, mensual, mensurability, mensurable, mensurableness, mensurably, mensural, mensuralist, mensurate, mensuration, mensurational, mensurative, menswear, menswears, ment, menta, mentagra, mental, mentalis, mentalism, mentalist, mentalistic, mentalistically, mentalists, mentalities, mentality, mentalization, mentalize, mentally, mentary, mentation, mentery, menthaceous, menthadiene, menthan, menthane, menthe, menthene, menthenes, menthenol, menthenone, menthol, mentholated, menthols, menthone, menthyl, menticide, menticultural, menticulture, mentiferous, mentiform, mentigerous, mentimeter, mentimutation, mention, mentionability, mentionable, mentioned, mentioner, mentioners, mentioning, mentionless, mentions, mentis, mentoanterior, mentobregmatic, mentocondylial, mentohyoid, mentolabial, mentomeckelian, mentoniere, mentonniere, mentonnieres, mentoposterior, mentor, mentor's, mentorial, mentorism, mentors, mentorship, mentum, menu, menu's, menuiserie, menuiseries, menuisier, menuisiers, menuki, menus, meny, menyie, menzie, meow, meowed, meowing, meows, mepacrine, meperidine, mephistopheles, mephitic, mephitical, mephitically, mephitine, mephitis, mephitises, mephitism, meprobamate, meq, mer, meralgia, meraline, merbaby, merbromin, merc, mercal, mercantile, mercantilely, mercantilism, mercantilist, mercantilistic, mercantilists, mercantility, mercaptal, mercaptan, mercaptide, mercaptides, mercaptids, mercapto, mercaptol, mercaptole, mercaptopurine, mercat, mercatoria, mercatorial, mercature, merce, mercement, mercenarian, mercenaries, mercenarily, mercenariness, mercenary, mercenary's, mercer, merceress, merceries, mercerization, mercerize, mercerized, mercerizer, mercerizes, mercerizing, mercers, mercership, mercery, merch, merchandisability, merchandisable, merchandise, merchandised, merchandiser, merchandisers, merchandises, merchandising, merchandize, merchandized, merchandrise, merchandry, merchandy, merchant, merchant's, merchantability, merchantable, merchantableness, merchanted, merchanteer, merchanter, merchanthood, merchanting, merchantish, merchantlike, merchantly, merchantman, merchantmen, merchantries, merchantry, merchants, merchantship, merchet, merci, merciable, merciablely, merciably, mercian, mercies, merciful, mercifully, mercifulness, mercify, merciless, mercilessly, mercilessness, merciment, mercurate, mercuration, mercurial, mercurialisation, mercurialise, mercurialised, mercurialising, mercurialism, mercurialist, mercuriality, mercurialization, mercurialize, mercurialized, mercurializing, mercurially, mercurialness, mercuriamines, mercuriammonium, mercuriate, mercuric, mercurid, mercuride, mercuries, mercurification, mercurified, mercurify, mercurifying, mercurization, mercurize, mercurized, mercurizing, mercurochrome, mercurophen, mercurous, mercury, mercy, mercyproof, merd, merdivorous, merdurinous, mere, mered, merel, merels, merely, merenchyma, merenchymatous, merengue, merengued, merengues, merenguing, merer, meres, meresman, meresmen, merest, merestone, mereswine, meretrices, meretricious, meretriciously, meretriciousness, meretrix, merfold, merfolk, merganser, mergansers, merge, merged, mergence, mergences, merger, mergers, merges, mergh, merging, meriah, mericarp, merice, merida, meridian, meridians, meridie, meridiem, meridienne, meridional, meridionality, meridionally, meril, meringue, meringued, meringues, meringuing, merino, merinos, meriquinoid, meriquinoidal, meriquinone, meriquinonic, meriquinonoid, merises, merisis, merism, merismatic, merismoid, merist, meristele, meristelic, meristem, meristematic, meristematically, meristems, meristic, meristically, meristogenous, merit, meritable, merited, meritedly, meritedness, meriter, meritful, meriting, meritless, meritlessness, meritmonger, meritmongering, meritmongery, meritocracies, meritocracy, meritocrat, meritocratic, meritorious, meritoriously, meritoriousness, meritory, merits, merk, merkhet, merkin, merks, merl, merle, merles, merlette, merligo, merlin, merling, merlins, merlion, merlon, merlons, merls, mermaid, mermaiden, mermaids, merman, mermen, mermithaner, mermithergate, mermithization, mermithized, mermithogyne, mermother, mero, meroblastic, meroblastically, merocele, merocelic, merocerite, meroceritic, merocrine, merocrystalline, merocyte, merodus, merogamy, merogastrula, merogenesis, merogenetic, merogenic, merognathite, merogonic, merogony, merohedral, merohedric, merohedrism, meroistic, meromorphic, meromyarian, meromyosin, merop, meropia, meropias, meropic, meropidan, meroplankton, meroplanktonic, meropodite, meropoditic, merorganization, merorganize, meros, merosomal, merosomatous, merosome, merosthenic, merostomatous, merostome, merostomous, merosymmetrical, merosymmetry, merosystematic, merotomize, merotomy, merotropism, merotropy, merovingian, meroxene, merozoite, merpeople, merribauks, merribush, merrier, merriest, merriless, merrily, merrimack, merriment, merriness, merrow, merrowes, merry, merrymake, merrymaker, merrymakers, merrymaking, merryman, merrymeeting, merrymen, merrythought, merrytrotter, merrywing, merse, mersion, merthiolate, merton, meruit, meruline, merulioid, merv, mervail, merveileux, merveilleux, merwinite, merwoman, merychippus, merycism, merycismus, merycoidodon, merycopotamus, mesa, mesabite, mesaconate, mesaconic, mesad, mesadenia, mesail, mesal, mesalike, mesalliance, mesalliances, mesally, mesameboid, mesange, mesaortitis, mesaraic, mesaraical, mesarch, mesarteritic, mesarteritis, mesas, mesaticephal, mesaticephali, mesaticephalic, mesaticephalism, mesaticephalous, mesaticephaly, mesatipellic, mesatipelvic, mesatiskelic, mesaxonic, mescal, mescaline, mescalism, mescals, meschant, meschantly, mesdames, mesdemoiselles, mese, mesectoderm, meseemed, meseems, mesel, mesela, meseled, meseledness, meselry, mesely, mesem, mesembryanthemum, mesembryo, mesembryonic, mesencephala, mesencephalic, mesencephalon, mesencephalons, mesenchyma, mesenchymal, mesenchymatal, mesenchymatic, mesenchymatous, mesenchyme, mesendoderm, mesenna, mesentera, mesenterial, mesenteric, mesenterical, mesenterically, mesenteries, mesenteriform, mesenteriolum, mesenteritic, mesenteritis, mesenterium, mesenteron, mesenteronic, mesentery, mesentoderm, mesepimeral, mesepimeron, mesepisternal, mesepisternum, mesepithelial, mesepithelium, meseraic, mesethmoid, mesethmoidal, mesh, meshed, meshes, meshier, meshiest, meshing, meshrabiyeh, meshrebeeyeh, meshuga, meshugaas, meshugana, meshugga, meshuggaas, meshuggah, meshuggana, meshuggenah, meshummad, meshwork, meshworks, meshy, mesiad, mesial, mesially, mesian, mesic, mesically, mesilla, mesiobuccal, mesiocervical, mesioclusion, mesiodistal, mesiodistally, mesiogingival, mesioincisal, mesiolabial, mesiolingual, mesion, mesioocclusal, mesiopulpal, mesioversion, mesitine, mesitite, mesityl, mesitylene, mesitylenic, mesivta, mesked, meslen, mesmerian, mesmeric, mesmerical, mesmerically, mesmerisation, mesmerise, mesmeriser, mesmerism, mesmerist, mesmerists, mesmerite, mesmerizability, mesmerizable, mesmerization, mesmerize, mesmerized, mesmerizee, mesmerizer, mesmerizers, mesmerizes, mesmerizing, mesmeromania, mesmeromaniac, mesnage, mesnality, mesnalties, mesnalty, mesne, meso, mesoappendiceal, mesoappendicitis, mesoappendix, mesoarial, mesoarium, mesobar, mesobenthos, mesoblast, mesoblastem, mesoblastema, mesoblastemic, mesoblastic, mesobranchial, mesobregmate, mesocadia, mesocaecal, mesocaecum, mesocardia, mesocardium, mesocarp, mesocarpic, mesocarps, mesocentrous, mesocephal, mesocephalic, mesocephalism, mesocephalon, mesocephalous, mesocephaly, mesochilium, mesochondrium, mesochroic, mesocoele, mesocoelia, mesocoelian, mesocoelic, mesocola, mesocolic, mesocolon, mesocolons, mesocoracoid, mesocranial, mesocranic, mesocratic, mesocuneiform, mesode, mesoderm, mesodermal, mesodermic, mesoderms, mesodic, mesodisilicic, mesodont, mesodontic, mesodontism, mesofurca, mesofurcal, mesogaster, mesogastral, mesogastric, mesogastrium, mesoglea, mesogleal, mesogleas, mesogloea, mesogloeal, mesognathic, mesognathion, mesognathism, mesognathous, mesognathy, mesogyrate, mesohepar, mesohippus, mesokurtic, mesolabe, mesole, mesolecithal, mesolimnion, mesolite, mesolithic, mesologic, mesological, mesology, mesomere, mesomeres, mesomeric, mesomerism, mesometeorological, mesometeorology, mesometral, mesometric, mesometrium, mesomitosis, mesomorph, mesomorphic, mesomorphism, mesomorphous, mesomorphy, mesomyodian, mesomyodous, meson, mesonasal, mesonephric, mesonephridium, mesonephritic, mesonephroi, mesonephros, mesonic, mesonotal, mesonotum, mesons, mesoparapteral, mesoparapteron, mesopause, mesopeak, mesopectus, mesopelagic, mesoperiodic, mesopetalum, mesophil, mesophile, mesophilic, mesophilous, mesophragm, mesophragma, mesophragmal, mesophryon, mesophyl, mesophyll, mesophyllic, mesophyllous, mesophyllum, mesophyls, mesophyte, mesophytic, mesophytism, mesopic, mesoplankton, mesoplanktonic, mesoplast, mesoplastic, mesoplastra, mesoplastral, mesoplastron, mesopleura, mesopleural, mesopleuron, mesoplodont, mesopodia, mesopodial, mesopodiale, mesopodialia, mesopodium, mesopotamia, mesopotamian, mesopotamic, mesoprescutal, mesoprescutum, mesoprosopic, mesopterygial, mesopterygium, mesopterygoid, mesorchial, mesorchium, mesorecta, mesorectal, mesorectta, mesorectum, mesorectums, mesorhin, mesorhinal, mesorhine, mesorhinian, mesorhinism, mesorhinium, mesorhiny, mesorrhin, mesorrhinal, mesorrhine, mesorrhinian, mesorrhinism, mesorrhinium, mesorrhiny, mesosalpinx, mesosaur, mesoscale, mesoscapula, mesoscapular, mesoscutal, mesoscutellar, mesoscutellum, mesoscutum, mesoseismal, mesoseme, mesosiderite, mesosigmoid, mesoskelic, mesosoma, mesosomata, mesosomatic, mesosome, mesosomes, mesosperm, mesosphere, mesospheric, mesospore, mesosporic, mesosporium, mesost, mesostasis, mesosterna, mesosternal, mesosternebra, mesosternebral, mesosternum, mesostethium, mesostomid, mesostyle, mesostylous, mesosuchian, mesotarsal, mesotartaric, mesothelia, mesothelial, mesothelioma, mesothelium, mesotherm, mesothermal, mesothesis, mesothet, mesothetic, mesothetical, mesothoraces, mesothoracic, mesothoracotheca, mesothorax, mesothoraxes, mesothorium, mesotonic, mesotroch, mesotrocha, mesotrochal, mesotrochous, mesotron, mesotronic, mesotrons, mesotrophic, mesotropic, mesotympanic, mesotype, mesovaria, mesovarian, mesovarium, mesoventral, mesoventrally, mesoxalate, mesoxalic, mesoxalyl, mesozoa, mesozoan, mesozoic, mespil, mesprise, mesquin, mesquit, mesquita, mesquite, mesquites, mesquits, mess, message, message's, messaged, messageer, messagery, messages, messaging, messalian, messaline, messan, messans, messe, messed, messeigneurs, messelite, messenger, messenger's, messengers, messengership, messer, messes, messet, messiah, messiahs, messiahship, messianic, messianically, messianism, messias, messidor, messier, messiest, messieurs, messily, messin, messiness, messing, messire, messkit, messman, messmate, messmates, messmen, messor, messroom, messrs, messtin, messuage, messuages, messy, mest, mestee, mestees, mesteno, mester, mesteso, mestesoes, mestesos, mestfull, mestino, mestinoes, mestinos, mestiza, mestizas, mestizo, mestizoes, mestizos, mestlen, mestome, mestranol, mesymnion, met, meta, metabases, metabasis, metabasite, metabatic, metabiological, metabiology, metabiosis, metabiotic, metabiotically, metabismuthic, metabisulphite, metabit, metabits, metabletic, metabola, metabole, metabolian, metabolic, metabolical, metabolically, metabolise, metabolised, metabolising, metabolism, metabolite, metabolites, metabolizability, metabolizable, metabolize, metabolized, metabolizes, metabolizing, metabolon, metabolous, metaboly, metaborate, metaboric, metabranchial, metabrushite, metabular, metacapi, metacarpal, metacarpale, metacarpals, metacarpi, metacarpophalangeal, metacarpus, metacenter, metacentral, metacentre, metacentric, metacentricity, metacercaria, metacercarial, metacetone, metachemic, metachemical, metachemistry, metachlamydeous, metachromasis, metachromatic, metachromatin, metachromatinic, metachromatism, metachrome, metachronal, metachronism, metachronistic, metachrosis, metacinnabar, metacinnabarite, metacircular, metacircularity, metacism, metacismus, metaclase, metacneme, metacoele, metacoelia, metaconal, metacone, metaconid, metaconule, metacoracoid, metacrasis, metacresol, metacromial, metacromion, metacryst, metacyclic, metacymene, metad, metadiabase, metadiazine, metadiorite, metadiscoidal, metadromous, metae, metaethical, metaethics, metafemale, metafluidal, metaformaldehyde, metafulminuric, metagalactic, metagalaxies, metagalaxy, metagaster, metagastric, metagastrula, metage, metagelatin, metagelatine, metagenesis, metagenetic, metagenetically, metagenic, metageometer, metageometrical, metageometry, metages, metagnath, metagnathism, metagnathous, metagnomy, metagnostic, metagnosticism, metagram, metagrammatism, metagrammatize, metagraphic, metagraphy, metagrobolize, metahewettite, metahydroxide, metaigneous, metainfective, metairie, metakinesis, metakinetic, metal, metal's, metalammonium, metalanguage, metalaw, metalbearing, metalbumin, metalcraft, metaldehyde, metaled, metalepses, metalepsis, metaleptic, metaleptical, metaleptically, metaler, metaline, metalined, metaling, metalinguistic, metalinguistically, metalinguistics, metalise, metalised, metalises, metalising, metalism, metalist, metalists, metalization, metalize, metalized, metalizes, metalizing, metall, metallary, metalled, metalleity, metaller, metallic, metallical, metallically, metallicity, metallicize, metallicly, metallics, metallide, metallifacture, metalliferous, metallification, metalliform, metallify, metallik, metallike, metalline, metalling, metallisation, metallise, metallised, metallish, metallising, metallism, metallist, metallization, metallizations, metallize, metallized, metallizing, metallocene, metallochrome, metallochromy, metalloenzyme, metallogenetic, metallogenic, metallogeny, metallograph, metallographer, metallographic, metallographical, metallographically, metallographist, metallography, metalloid, metalloidal, metallometer, metallophobia, metallophone, metalloplastic, metallorganic, metallotherapeutic, metallotherapy, metallurgic, metallurgical, metallurgically, metallurgist, metallurgists, metallurgy, metalmark, metalmonger, metalogic, metalogical, metaloph, metalorganic, metaloscope, metaloscopy, metals, metalsmith, metaluminate, metaluminic, metalware, metalwork, metalworker, metalworkers, metalworking, metalworks, metamale, metamathematical, metamathematician, metamathematics, metamer, metameral, metamere, metameres, metameric, metamerically, metameride, metamerism, metamerization, metamerize, metamerized, metamerous, metamers, metamery, metamitosis, metamorphic, metamorphically, metamorphism, metamorphisms, metamorphize, metamorphopsia, metamorphopsy, metamorphosable, metamorphose, metamorphosed, metamorphoser, metamorphoses, metamorphosian, metamorphosic, metamorphosical, metamorphosing, metamorphosis, metamorphostical, metamorphosy, metamorphotic, metamorphous, metamorphy, metanalysis, metanauplius, metanephric, metanephritic, metanephroi, metanephron, metanephros, metanepionic, metanetwork, metanilic, metaniline, metanitroaniline, metanitrophenol, metanoia, metanomen, metanotal, metanotion, metanotions, metanotum, metantimonate, metantimonic, metantimonious, metantimonite, metantimonous, metanym, metaorganism, metaparapteral, metaparapteron, metapectic, metapectus, metapepsis, metapeptone, metaperiodic, metaph, metaphase, metaphenomenal, metaphenomenon, metaphenylene, metaphenylenediamin, metaphenylenediamine, metaphloem, metaphonical, metaphonize, metaphony, metaphor, metaphor's, metaphoric, metaphorical, metaphorically, metaphoricalness, metaphorist, metaphorize, metaphors, metaphosphate, metaphosphated, metaphosphating, metaphosphoric, metaphosphorous, metaphragm, metaphragma, metaphragmal, metaphrase, metaphrased, metaphrasing, metaphrasis, metaphrast, metaphrastic, metaphrastical, metaphrastically, metaphys, metaphyseal, metaphysic, metaphysical, metaphysically, metaphysician, metaphysicianism, metaphysicians, metaphysicist, metaphysicize, metaphysicous, metaphysics, metaphysis, metaphyte, metaphytic, metaphyton, metaplasia, metaplasis, metaplasm, metaplasmic, metaplast, metaplastic, metapleur, metapleura, metapleural, metapleure, metapleuron, metaplumbate, metaplumbic, metapneumonic, metapneustic, metapodia, metapodial, metapodiale, metapodium, metapolitic, metapolitical, metapolitician, metapolitics, metapophyseal, metapophysial, metapophysis, metapore, metapostscutellar, metapostscutellum, metaprescutal, metaprescutum, metaprotein, metapsychic, metapsychical, metapsychics, metapsychism, metapsychist, metapsychological, metapsychology, metapsychosis, metapterygial, metapterygium, metapterygoid, metarabic, metargon, metarhyolite, metarossite, metarsenic, metarsenious, metarsenite, metarule, metarules, metas, metasaccharinic, metascope, metascutal, metascutellar, metascutellum, metascutum, metasedimentary, metasequoia, metasilicate, metasilicic, metasoma, metasomal, metasomasis, metasomatic, metasomatically, metasomatism, metasomatosis, metasome, metasperm, metaspermic, metaspermous, metastability, metastable, metastably, metastannate, metastannic, metastases, metastasis, metastasize, metastasized, metastasizes, metastasizing, metastatic, metastatical, metastatically, metasternal, metasternum, metasthenic, metastibnite, metastigmate, metastoma, metastomata, metastome, metastrophe, metastrophic, metastyle, metasymbol, metasyntactic, metatantalic, metatarsal, metatarsale, metatarsally, metatarse, metatarsi, metatarsophalangeal, metatarsus, metatarsusi, metatatic, metatatical, metatatically, metataxic, metataxis, metate, metates, metathalamus, metatheology, metatheory, metatheria, metatherian, metatheses, metathesis, metathesise, metathesize, metathetic, metathetical, metathetically, metathoraces, metathoracic, metathorax, metathoraxes, metatitanate, metatitanic, metatoluic, metatoluidine, metatracheal, metatroph, metatrophic, metatrophy, metatungstic, metatype, metatypic, metavanadate, metavanadic, metavariable, metavauxite, metavoltine, metaxenia, metaxite, metaxylem, metaxylene, metayage, metayer, metazoa, metazoal, metazoan, metazoans, metazoea, metazoic, metazoon, mete, metecorn, meted, metegritics, metel, metely, metempiric, metempirical, metempirically, metempiricism, metempiricist, metempirics, metempsychic, metempsychosal, metempsychose, metempsychoses, metempsychosic, metempsychosical, metempsychosis, metempsychosize, metemptosis, metencephala, metencephalic, metencephalla, metencephalon, metencephalons, metensarcosis, metensomatosis, metenteron, metenteronic, meteogram, meteograph, meteor, meteor's, meteorgraph, meteoric, meteorical, meteorically, meteoris, meteorism, meteorist, meteoristic, meteorital, meteorite, meteorites, meteoritic, meteoritical, meteoritics, meteorization, meteorize, meteorlike, meteorogram, meteorograph, meteorographic, meteorography, meteoroid, meteoroidal, meteoroids, meteorol, meteorolite, meteorolitic, meteorologic, meteorological, meteorologically, meteorologist, meteorologists, meteorology, meteoromancy, meteorometer, meteoropathologic, meteoroscope, meteoroscopy, meteorous, meteors, meteorscope, metepa, metepas, metepencephalic, metepencephalon, metepimeral, metepimeron, metepisternal, metepisternum, meter, meterable, meterage, meterages, metered, metergram, metering, meterless, meterman, meterological, meters, metership, meterstick, metes, metestick, metestrus, metewand, meteyard, meth, methacrylate, methacrylic, methadon, methadone, methadons, methaemoglobin, methamphetamine, methanal, methanate, methanated, methanating, methane, methanes, methanoic, methanol, methanolic, methanols, methanolysis, methanometer, methantheline, methaqualone, metheglin, methemoglobin, methemoglobinemia, methemoglobinuria, methenamine, methene, methenyl, mether, methhead, methicillin, methid, methide, methine, methinks, methiodide, methionic, methionine, metho, methobromide, method, method's, methodaster, methodeutic, methodic, methodical, methodically, methodicalness, methodics, methodise, methodised, methodiser, methodising, methodism, methodist, methodist's, methodistic, methodists, methodization, methodize, methodized, methodizer, methodizes, methodizing, methodless, methodological, methodologically, methodologies, methodologist, methodologists, methodology, methodology's, methods, methol, methomania, methone, methotrexate, methought, methoxamine, methoxide, methoxy, methoxybenzene, methoxychlor, methoxyflurane, methoxyl, methronic, meths, methuselah, methyl, methylacetanilide, methylal, methylals, methylamine, methylaniline, methylanthracene, methylase, methylate, methylated, methylating, methylation, methylator, methylbenzene, methylcatechol, methylcholanthrene, methyldopa, methylene, methylenimine, methylenitan, methylethylacetic, methylglycine, methylglycocoll, methylglyoxal, methylheptenone, methylic, methylidyne, methylmalonic, methylnaphthalene, methylol, methylolurea, methylosis, methylotic, methylparaben, methylpentose, methylpentoses, methylphenidate, methylpropane, methyls, methylsulfanol, methyltrinitrobenzene, methyprylon, methysergide, metic, meticulosity, meticulous, meticulously, meticulousness, metier, metiers, metif, meting, metis, metisse, metisses, metochous, metochy, metoestrous, metoestrum, metoestrus, metol, metonic, metonym, metonymic, metonymical, metonymically, metonymies, metonymous, metonymously, metonyms, metonymy, metopae, metope, metopes, metopic, metopion, metopism, metopomancy, metopon, metopons, metoposcopic, metoposcopical, metoposcopist, metoposcopy, metorganism, metosteal, metosteon, metostylous, metoxazine, metoxenous, metoxeny, metra, metralgia, metran, metranate, metranemia, metratonia, metrazol, metre, metrectasia, metrectatic, metrectomy, metrectopia, metrectopic, metrectopy, metrectotmy, metred, metregram, metreless, metreme, metres, metreship, metreta, metrete, metretes, metreza, metria, metric, metric's, metrical, metrically, metricate, metricated, metricates, metricating, metrication, metrician, metricise, metricised, metricising, metricism, metricist, metricity, metricize, metricized, metricizes, metricizing, metrics, metridium, metrification, metrified, metrifier, metrifies, metrify, metrifying, metring, metriocephalic, metrise, metrist, metrists, metritis, metritises, metrizable, metrization, metrize, metrized, metrizing, metro, metrocampsis, metrocarat, metrocarcinoma, metrocele, metroclyst, metrocolpocele, metrocracy, metrocratic, metrocystosis, metrodynia, metrofibroma, metrography, metroliner, metroliners, metrological, metrologically, metrologies, metrologist, metrologue, metrology, metrolymphangitis, metromalacia, metromalacoma, metromalacosis, metromania, metromaniac, metromaniacal, metrometer, metron, metroneuria, metronidazole, metronome, metronomes, metronomic, metronomical, metronomically, metronym, metronymic, metronymy, metroparalysis, metropathia, metropathic, metropathy, metroperitonitis, metrophlebitis, metrophotography, metropole, metropoleis, metropolic, metropolis, metropolises, metropolitan, metropolitanate, metropolitancy, metropolitanism, metropolitanize, metropolitanized, metropolitanship, metropolite, metropolitic, metropolitical, metropolitically, metroptosia, metroptosis, metroradioscope, metrorrhagia, metrorrhagic, metrorrhea, metrorrhexis, metrorthosis, metros, metrosalpingitis, metrosalpinx, metroscirrhus, metroscope, metroscopy, metrostaxis, metrostenosis, metrosteresis, metrostyle, metrosynizesis, metrotherapist, metrotherapy, metrotome, metrotometry, metrotomy, mets, mettar, mettle, mettled, mettles, mettlesome, mettlesomely, mettlesomeness, metump, metumps, metus, metusia, metwand, metze, meu, meubles, meum, meuni, meuniere, meurtriere, meuse, meute, mew, meward, mewed, mewer, mewing, mewl, mewled, mewler, mewlers, mewling, mewls, mews, mexical, mexican, mexicans, mexico, meyerhofferite, mezail, mezair, mezcal, mezcaline, mezcals, mezentian, mezereon, mezereons, mezereum, mezereums, mezo, mezquit, mezquite, mezquites, mezquits, mezuza, mezuzah, mezuzahs, mezuzas, mezuzot, mezuzoth, mezzanine, mezzanines, mezzavoce, mezzo, mezzograph, mezzolith, mezzolithic, mezzos, mezzotint, mezzotinted, mezzotinter, mezzotinting, mezzotinto, mf, mfd, mfg, mfr, mg, mgal, mgd, mgr, mgt, mh, mhg, mho, mhometer, mhorr, mhos, mhz, mi, mia, miacis, miae, miami, miamia, mian, miaou, miaoued, miaouing, miaous, miaow, miaowed, miaower, miaowing, miaows, miargyrite, miarolitic, mias, miascite, miaskite, miasm, miasma, miasmal, miasmas, miasmata, miasmatic, miasmatical, miasmatically, miasmatize, miasmatology, miasmatous, miasmic, miasmology, miasmous, miasms, miauer, miaul, miauled, miauler, miauling, miauls, miauw, miazine, mib, mibound, mibs, mica, micaceous, micacious, micacite, micah, micas, micasization, micasize, micast, micasting, micasts, micate, mication, micawber, micawberism, micawbers, mice, micell, micella, micellae, micellar, micellarly, micelle, micelles, micells, miceplot, micerun, micesource, michael, michaelmas, miche, miched, michelangelo, micher, michery, michigan, miching, micht, mick, mickery, mickey, mickeys, mickies, mickle, micklemote, mickleness, mickler, mickles, micklest, micks, micky, micmac, mico, miconcave, micra, micraco, micracoustic, micraesthete, micramock, micranatomy, micrander, micrandrous, micraner, micranthropos, micrencephalia, micrencephalic, micrencephalous, micrencephalus, micrencephaly, micrergate, micresthete, micrified, micrifies, micrify, micrifying, micro, microaerophile, microaerophilic, microammeter, microampere, microanalyses, microanalysis, microanalyst, microanalytic, microanalytical, microanatomical, microanatomy, microangstrom, microapparatus, microarchitects, microarchitecture, microarchitectures, microbacteria, microbacterium, microbacteteria, microbal, microbalance, microbar, microbarogram, microbarograph, microbars, microbattery, microbe, microbeam, microbeless, microbeproof, microbes, microbial, microbian, microbic, microbicidal, microbicide, microbiologic, microbiological, microbiologically, microbiologies, microbiologist, microbiologists, microbiology, microbion, microbiophobia, microbiosis, microbiota, microbiotic, microbious, microbism, microbium, microblast, microblepharia, microblepharism, microblephary, microbody, microbrachia, microbrachius, microburet, microburette, microburner, microbus, microbuses, microbusses, microcaltrop, microcamera, microcapsule, microcard, microcardia, microcardius, microcards, microcarpous, microcellular, microcentrosome, microcentrum, microcephal, microcephali, microcephalia, microcephalic, microcephalism, microcephalous, microcephalus, microcephaly, microceratous, microchaeta, microchaetae, microcharacter, microcheilia, microcheiria, microchemic, microchemical, microchemically, microchemistry, microchip, microchiria, microchiropteran, microchiropterous, microchromosome, microchronometer, microcinema, microcinematograph, microcinematographic, microcinematography, microcircuit, microcircuitry, microcirculation, microcirculatory, microclastic, microclimate, microclimates, microclimatic, microclimatically, microclimatologic, microclimatological, microclimatologist, microclimatology, microcline, microcnemia, microcoat, micrococcal, micrococci, micrococcic, micrococcocci, micrococcus, microcode, microcoded, microcodes, microcoding, microcoleoptera, microcolon, microcolorimeter, microcolorimetric, microcolorimetrically, microcolorimetry, microcolumnar, microcombustion, microcomputer, microcomputer's, microcomputers, microconidial, microconidium, microconjugant, microconstituent, microcopied, microcopies, microcopy, microcopying, microcoria, microcos, microcosm, microcosmal, microcosmian, microcosmic, microcosmical, microcosmically, microcosmography, microcosmology, microcosmos, microcosms, microcosmus, microcoulomb, microcranous, microcrith, microcryptocrystalline, microcrystal, microcrystalline, microcrystallinity, microcrystallogeny, microcrystallography, microcrystalloscopy, microcultural, microculture, microcurie, microcycle, microcycles, microcyst, microcyte, microcythemia, microcytic, microcytosis, microdactylia, microdactylism, microdactylous, microdensitometer, microdensitometric, microdensitometry, microdentism, microdentous, microdetection, microdetector, microdetermination, microdiactine, microdimensions, microdissection, microdistillation, microdont, microdontia, microdontic, microdontism, microdontous, microdonty, microdose, microdot, microdrawing, microdrive, microdyne, microeconomic, microeconomics, microelectrode, microelectrolysis, microelectronic, microelectronically, microelectronics, microelectrophoresis, microelectrophoretic, microelectrophoretical, microelectrophoretically, microelectroscope, microelement, microencapsulate, microencapsulation, microenvironment, microenvironmental, microerg, microestimation, microeutaxitic, microevolution, microevolutionary, microexamination, microfarad, microfauna, microfaunal, microfelsite, microfelsitic, microfibril, microfibrillar, microfiche, microfiches, microfilaria, microfilarial, microfilm, microfilm's, microfilmable, microfilmed, microfilmer, microfilming, microfilms, microflora, microfloral, microfluidal, microfoliation, microform, microforms, microfossil, microfungal, microfungus, microfurnace, microgalvanometer, microgamete, microgametocyte, microgametophyte, microgamies, microgamy, microgastria, microgastrine, microgauss, microgeological, microgeologist, microgeology, microgilbert, microglia, microglial, microglossia, micrognathia, micrognathic, micrognathous, microgonidial, microgonidium, microgram, microgramme, microgrammes, microgramming, micrograms, microgranite, microgranitic, microgranitoid, microgranular, microgranulitic, micrograph, micrographer, micrographic, micrographical, micrographically, micrographist, micrographs, micrography, micrograver, microgravimetric, microgroove, microgrooves, microgyne, microgyria, microhabitat, microhardness, microhenries, microhenry, microhenrys, microhepatia, microhistochemical, microhistology, microhm, microhmmeter, microhms, microhymenopteron, microimage, microinch, microinjection, microinstruction, microinstruction's, microinstructions, microjoule, microjump, microjumps, microlambert, microlecithal, microlepidopter, microlepidoptera, microlepidopteran, microlepidopterist, microlepidopteron, microlepidopterous, microleukoblast, microlevel, microlite, microliter, microlith, microlithic, microlitic, micrologic, micrological, micrologically, micrologist, micrologue, micrology, microluces, microlux, microluxes, micromania, micromaniac, micromanipulation, micromanipulator, micromanipulators, micromanometer, micromazia, micromeasurement, micromechanics, micromeli, micromelia, micromelic, micromelus, micromembrane, micromeral, micromere, micromeric, micromerism, micromeritic, micromeritics, micromesentery, micrometallographer, micrometallography, micrometallurgy, micrometeorite, micrometeoritic, micrometeorogram, micrometeorograph, micrometeoroid, micrometeorological, micrometeorologist, micrometeorology, micrometer, micrometers, micromethod, micrometric, micrometrical, micrometrically, micrometry, micromho, micromhos, micromicrocurie, micromicrofarad, micromicron, micromil, micromillimeter, micromineralogical, micromineralogy, microminiature, microminiaturization, microminiaturizations, microminiaturize, microminiaturized, microminiaturizing, micromodule, micromolar, micromole, micromorph, micromorphologic, micromorphological, micromorphologically, micromorphology, micromotion, micromotoscope, micromyelia, micromyeloblast, micron, micronemous, micronesia, micronesian, micronesians, micronization, micronize, micronometer, microns, micronuclear, micronucleate, micronuclei, micronucleus, micronutrient, microoperations, microorganic, microorganism, microorganismal, microorganisms, micropalaeontology, micropaleontologic, micropaleontological, micropaleontologist, micropaleontology, micropantograph, microparasite, microparasitic, micropathological, micropathologies, micropathologist, micropathology, micropegmatite, micropegmatitic, micropenis, microperthite, microperthitic, micropetalous, micropetrography, micropetrologist, micropetrology, microphage, microphagocyte, microphagous, microphagy, microphakia, microphallus, microphobia, microphone, microphones, microphonic, microphonics, microphoning, microphonism, microphonograph, microphot, microphotograph, microphotographed, microphotographer, microphotographic, microphotographing, microphotographs, microphotography, microphotometer, microphotometric, microphotometrically, microphotometry, microphotoscope, microphthalmia, microphthalmic, microphthalmos, microphthalmus, microphyll, microphyllous, microphysical, microphysically, microphysics, microphysiography, microphytal, microphyte, microphytic, microphytology, micropia, micropin, micropipet, micropipette, microplakite, microplankton, microplastocyte, microplastometer, micropodal, micropodia, micropodous, micropoecilitic, micropoicilitic, micropoikilitic, micropolariscope, micropolarization, micropopulation, micropore, microporosity, microporous, microporphyritic, microprint, microprobe, microprocedure, microprocedures, microprocessing, microprocessor, microprocessor's, microprocessors, microprogram, microprogram's, microprogrammable, microprogrammed, microprogrammer, microprogramming, microprograms, microprojection, microprojector, micropsia, micropsy, micropterism, micropterous, micropterygid, micropterygious, microptic, micropublisher, micropublishing, micropulsation, micropuncture, micropylar, micropyle, micropyrometer, microradiograph, microradiographic, microradiographical, microradiographically, microradiography, microradiometer, microreaction, microreader, microrefractometer, microreproduction, microrhabdus, microrheometer, microrheometric, microrheometrical, micros, microsaurian, microscale, microsclere, microsclerous, microsclerum, microscopal, microscope, microscope's, microscopes, microscopial, microscopic, microscopical, microscopically, microscopics, microscopies, microscopist, microscopize, microscopopy, microscopy, microsec, microsecond, microsecond's, microseconds, microsection, microsegment, microseism, microseismic, microseismical, microseismicity, microseismograph, microseismology, microseismometer, microseismometrograph, microseismometry, microseme, microseptum, microsiemens, microskirt, microsmatic, microsmatism, microsoftware, microsoma, microsomal, microsomatous, microsome, microsomia, microsomial, microsomic, microsommite, microspace, microspacing, microspecies, microspectrophotometer, microspectrophotometric, microspectrophotometrical, microspectrophotometrically, microspectrophotometry, microspectroscope, microspectroscopic, microspectroscopy, microspermous, microsphaeric, microsphere, microspheric, microspherical, microspherulitic, microsplanchnic, microsplenia, microsplenic, microsporange, microsporanggia, microsporangia, microsporangiate, microsporangium, microspore, microsporiasis, microsporic, microsporidian, microsporocyte, microsporogenesis, microsporophore, microsporophyll, microsporosis, microsporous, microstat, microstate, microstates, microstethoscope, microsthene, microsthenic, microstomatous, microstome, microstomia, microstomous, microstore, microstress, microstructural, microstructure, microstylospore, microstylous, microsublimation, microsurgeon, microsurgeons, microsurgeries, microsurgery, microsurgical, microswitch, microsystems, microtasimeter, microtechnic, microtechnique, microtektite, microtelephone, microtelephonic, microtheos, microtherm, microthermic, microthorax, microtia, microtine, microtines, microtitration, microtome, microtomic, microtomical, microtomist, microtomy, microtonal, microtonality, microtonally, microtone, microtubular, microtubule, microtus, microtypal, microtype, microtypical, microvasculature, microvax, microvaxes, microvillar, microvillous, microvillus, microvolt, microvolume, microvolumetric, microwatt, microwave, microwaves, microweber, microword, microwords, microzoa, microzoal, microzoan, microzoaria, microzoarian, microzoary, microzoic, microzone, microzooid, microzoology, microzoon, microzoospore, microzyma, microzyme, microzymian, micrurgic, micrurgical, micrurgies, micrurgist, micrurgy, miction, micturate, micturated, micturating, micturation, micturition, mid, midafternoon, midair, midairs, midas, midautumn, midaxillary, midband, midbody, midbrain, midbrains, midcarpal, midchannel, midcourse, midday, middays, midden, middens, middenstead, middes, middest, middies, middle, middlebreaker, middlebrow, middlebrowism, middlebrows, middlebuster, middleclass, middled, middlehand, middleland, middleman, middlemanism, middlemanship, middlemen, middlemost, middleness, middler, middlers, middles, middlesail, middlesplitter, middletone, middlewards, middleway, middleweight, middleweights, middlewoman, middlewomen, middling, middlingish, middlingly, middlingness, middlings, middorsal, middy, mide, mideast, midevening, midewin, midewiwin, midfacial, midfield, midfielder, midfields, midforenoon, midfrontal, midgard, midge, midges, midget, midgets, midgety, midgut, midguts, midgy, midheaven, midi, midianite, midicoat, midified, midinette, midinettes, midiron, midirons, midis, midiskirt, midland, midlands, midlandward, midlatitude, midleg, midlegs, midlenting, midline, midlines, midmain, midmandibular, midmonth, midmonthly, midmonths, midmorn, midmorning, midmost, midmosts, midn, midnight, midnightly, midnights, midnoon, midnoons, midocean, midparent, midparentage, midparental, midpit, midpoint, midpoint's, midpoints, midrange, midranges, midrash, midrashic, midrashim, midrashoth, midrib, midribbed, midribs, midriff, midriffs, mids, midscale, midseason, midsection, midsemester, midsentence, midship, midshipman, midshipmanship, midshipmen, midshipmite, midships, midspace, midspaces, midspan, midst, midstead, midstories, midstory, midstout, midstream, midstreet, midstroke, midsts, midstyled, midsummer, midsummerish, midsummers, midsummery, midtap, midtarsal, midterm, midterms, midtown, midtowns, midvein, midventral, midverse, midward, midwatch, midwatches, midway, midways, midweek, midweekly, midweeks, midwest, midwestern, midwesterner, midwesterners, midwestward, midwife, midwifed, midwiferies, midwifery, midwifes, midwifing, midwinter, midwinterly, midwinters, midwintry, midwise, midwived, midwives, midwiving, midyear, midyears, mien, miens, miersite, miff, miffed, miffier, miffiest, miffiness, miffing, miffs, miffy, mig, migale, migg, miggle, miggles, miggs, might, mighted, mightful, mightfully, mightfulness, mightier, mightiest, mightily, mightiness, mightless, mightly, mightn't, mightnt, mights, mighty, mightyhearted, mightyship, miglio, migmatite, migniard, migniardise, migniardize, mignon, mignonette, mignonettes, mignonne, mignonness, mignons, migraine, migraines, migrainoid, migrainous, migrans, migrant, migrants, migrate, migrated, migrates, migrating, migration, migrational, migrationist, migrations, migrative, migrator, migratorial, migrators, migratory, migs, miharaite, mihrab, mijakite, mijl, mijnheer, mijnheerl, mijnheers, mikado, mikadoate, mikadoism, mikados, mike, miked, mikes, mikie, miking, mikra, mikrkra, mikron, mikrons, mikvah, mikvahs, mikveh, mikvehs, mikvoth, mil, mila, milacre, miladi, miladies, miladis, milady, milage, milages, milammeter, milan, milanaise, milanese, milarite, milch, milched, milcher, milchig, milchigs, milchy, mild, milden, mildened, mildening, mildens, milder, mildest, mildew, mildewed, mildewer, mildewing, mildewproof, mildews, mildewy, mildful, mildfulness, mildhearted, mildheartedness, mildish, mildly, mildness, mildnesses, mildred, mile, mile's, mileage, mileages, mileometer, milepost, mileposts, miler, milers, miles, milesian, milesima, milesimo, milesimos, milestone, milestone's, milestones, mileway, milfoil, milfoils, milha, milia, miliaceous, miliarenses, miliarensis, miliaria, miliarial, miliarias, miliarium, miliary, milice, milieu, milieus, milieux, miliola, milioliform, milioline, miliolite, miliolitic, milit, militancy, militant, militantly, militantness, militants, militar, militaries, militarily, militariness, militarisation, militarise, militarised, militarising, militarism, militarist, militaristic, militaristical, militaristically, militarists, militarization, militarize, militarized, militarizes, militarizing, military, militaryism, militaryment, militaster, militate, militated, militates, militating, militation, militia, militiaman, militiamen, militias, militiate, milium, miljee, milk, milkbush, milked, milken, milker, milkeress, milkers, milkfish, milkfishes, milkgrass, milkhouse, milkier, milkiest, milkily, milkiness, milking, milkless, milklike, milkmaid, milkmaid's, milkmaids, milkman, milkmen, milkness, milko, milks, milkshake, milkshed, milkshop, milksick, milksop, milksopism, milksoppery, milksoppiness, milksopping, milksoppish, milksoppishness, milksoppy, milksops, milkstone, milktoast, milkwagon, milkweed, milkweeds, milkwood, milkwoods, milkwort, milkworts, milky, mill, milla, millable, millage, millages, millanare, millard, millboard, millcake, millclapper, millcourse, milldam, milldams, milldoll, mille, milled, millefeuille, millefiore, millefiori, millefleur, millefleurs, milleflorous, millefoliate, millenarian, millenarianism, millenaries, millenarist, millenary, millenia, millenist, millenium, millennia, millennial, millennialism, millennialist, millennialistic, millennially, millennian, millenniarism, millenniary, millennium, millenniums, milleped, millepede, millepeds, millepore, milleporiform, milleporine, milleporite, milleporous, millepunctate, miller, milleress, milleri, millering, millerite, millerole, millers, milles, millesimal, millesimally, millet, millets, millfeed, millful, millhouse, milliad, milliammeter, milliamp, milliampere, milliamperemeter, milliamperes, milliangstrom, milliard, milliardaire, milliards, milliare, milliares, milliarium, milliary, millibar, millibarn, millibars, millicron, millicurie, millidegree, millieme, milliemes, milliequivalent, millier, milliers, millifarad, millifold, milliform, milligal, milligals, milligrade, milligram, milligramage, milligramme, milligrams, millihenries, millihenry, millihenrys, millijoule, millilambert, millile, milliliter, milliliters, millilitre, milliluces, millilux, milliluxes, millime, millimes, millimeter, millimeters, millimetmhos, millimetre, millimetres, millimetric, millimho, millimhos, millimiccra, millimicra, millimicron, millimicrons, millimol, millimolar, millimole, millincost, milline, milliner, millinerial, millinering, milliners, millinery, millines, milling, millings, millinormal, millinormality, millioctave, millioersted, milliohm, milliohms, million, millionaire, millionaire's, millionairedom, millionaires, millionairess, millionairish, millionairism, millionary, millioned, millioner, millionfold, millionism, millionist, millionize, millionnaire, millionocracy, millions, millionth, millionths, milliped, millipede, millipede's, millipedes, millipeds, milliphot, millipoise, milliradian, millirem, millirems, milliroentgen, millisec, millisecond, milliseconds, millisiemens, millistere, millithrum, millivolt, millivoltmeter, millivolts, milliwatt, milliweber, millken, millman, millmen, millnia, millocracy, millocrat, millocratism, millosevichite, millowner, millpond, millponds, millpool, millpost, millrace, millraces, millrind, millrun, millruns, millrynd, mills, millsite, millstock, millstone, millstone's, millstones, millstream, millstreams, milltail, millward, millwheel, millwork, millworker, millworks, millwright, millwrighting, millwrights, milly, milner, milo, milometer, milor, milord, milords, milos, milpa, milpas, milquetoast, milquetoasts, milreis, milrind, mils, milsey, milsie, milt, milted, milter, milters, miltier, miltiest, milting, miltlike, milton, miltonian, miltonic, miltonist, milts, miltsick, miltwaste, milty, milvine, milvinous, milwaukee, milwell, milzbrand, mim, mima, mimamsa, mimbar, mimbars, mimble, mime, mimed, mimeo, mimeoed, mimeograph, mimeographed, mimeographic, mimeographically, mimeographing, mimeographist, mimeographs, mimeography, mimeoing, mimeos, mimer, mimers, mimes, mimesis, mimesises, mimester, mimetene, mimetesite, mimetic, mimetical, mimetically, mimetism, mimetite, mimetites, mimiambi, mimiambic, mimiambics, mimic, mimical, mimically, mimicism, mimicked, mimicker, mimickers, mimicking, mimicries, mimicry, mimics, mimine, miming, miminypiminy, mimir, mimish, mimly, mimmation, mimmed, mimmest, mimming, mimmock, mimmocking, mimmocky, mimmood, mimmoud, mimmouthed, mimmouthedness, mimodrama, mimographer, mimography, mimologist, mimosa, mimosaceous, mimosas, mimosis, mimosite, mimotannic, mimotype, mimotypic, mimp, mimsey, mimsy, mimzy, min, mina, minable, minacious, minaciously, minaciousness, minacities, minacity, minae, minah, minar, minaret, minareted, minarets, minargent, minas, minasragrite, minatnrial, minatorial, minatorially, minatories, minatorily, minatory, minauderie, minaway, minbar, minbu, mince, minced, mincemeat, mincer, mincers, minces, minchah, minchen, minchery, minchiate, mincier, minciers, minciest, mincing, mincingly, mincingness, mincio, mincy, mind, mindblower, minded, mindedly, mindedness, minder, minders, mindful, mindfully, mindfulness, minding, mindless, mindlessly, mindlessness, mindly, minds, mindsickness, mindsight, mine, mineable, mined, minefield, minelayer, minelayers, mineowner, miner, mineragraphic, mineragraphy, mineraiogic, mineral, mineral's, mineralise, mineralised, mineralising, mineralist, mineralizable, mineralization, mineralize, mineralized, mineralizer, mineralizes, mineralizing, mineralocorticoid, mineralogic, mineralogical, mineralogically, mineralogies, mineralogist, mineralogists, mineralogize, mineralogy, mineraloid, minerals, minerologist, minerology, miners, minerva, minerval, minery, mines, minestra, minestrone, minesweeper, minesweepers, minesweeping, minette, minever, mineworker, ming, minge, mingelen, mingie, mingier, mingiest, minginess, mingle, mingleable, mingled, mingledly, minglement, mingler, minglers, mingles, mingling, minglingly, minguetite, mingwort, mingy, minhag, minhagic, minhagim, minhah, mini, miniaceous, miniard, miniate, miniated, miniating, miniator, miniatous, miniature, miniature's, miniatured, miniatureness, miniatures, miniaturing, miniaturist, miniaturistic, miniaturists, miniaturization, miniaturizations, miniaturize, miniaturized, miniaturizes, miniaturizing, minibike, minibikes, minibus, minibuses, minibusses, minicab, minicabs, minicam, minicamera, minicar, minicars, minicomputer, minicomputer's, minicomputers, minidisk, minidisks, minidress, minie, minienize, minification, minified, minifies, minifloppies, minifloppy, minify, minifying, miniken, minikin, minikinly, minikins, minilanguage, minim, minima, minimacid, minimal, minimalism, minimalist, minimalists, minimalkaline, minimally, minimals, minimax, minimaxes, miniment, minimetric, minimi, minimifidian, minimifidianism, minimis, minimisation, minimise, minimised, minimiser, minimises, minimising, minimism, minimistic, minimitude, minimization, minimization's, minimizations, minimize, minimized, minimizer, minimizers, minimizes, minimizing, minims, minimum, minimums, minimus, minimuscular, mining, minings, minion, minionette, minionism, minionly, minions, minionship, minious, minipill, minis, miniscule, miniseries, minish, minished, minisher, minishes, minishing, minishment, miniskirt, miniskirted, miniskirts, ministate, ministates, minister, minister's, ministered, ministeriable, ministerial, ministerialism, ministerialist, ministeriality, ministerially, ministerialness, ministering, ministerium, ministers, ministership, ministrable, ministral, ministrant, ministrants, ministrate, ministration, ministrations, ministrative, ministrator, ministrer, ministress, ministries, ministry, ministry's, ministryship, minisub, minitant, minitrack, minium, miniums, miniver, minivers, minivet, mink, mink's, minkery, minkfish, minkfishes, minkish, minks, minneapolis, minnesinger, minnesingers, minnesong, minnesota, minnesota's, minnesotan, minnesotans, minnie, minniebush, minnies, minning, minnow, minnow's, minnows, minny, mino, minoan, minoize, minometer, minor, minor's, minora, minorage, minorate, minoration, minorca, minorcas, minored, minoress, minoring, minorite, minorities, minority, minority's, minors, minorship, minos, minot, minotaur, minow, mins, minsitive, minster, minsters, minsteryard, minstrel, minstrel's, minstreless, minstrels, minstrelship, minstrelsy, mint, mintage, mintages, mintbush, minted, minter, minters, mintier, mintiest, minting, mintmaker, mintmaking, mintman, mintmark, mintmaster, mints, mintweed, minty, minuend, minuends, minuet, minuetic, minuetish, minuets, minum, minunet, minus, minuscular, minuscule, minuscules, minuses, minutary, minutation, minute, minuted, minutely, minuteman, minutemen, minuteness, minuter, minutes, minutest, minuthesis, minutia, minutiae, minutial, minuting, minutiose, minutious, minutiously, minutissimic, minvend, minverite, minx, minxes, minxish, minxishly, minxishness, minxship, miny, minyan, minyanim, minyans, miocardia, miocene, miolithic, miombo, mioplasmia, mioses, miosis, miothermic, miotic, miotics, mips, miqra, miquelet, miquelets, mir, mirabelle, mirabile, mirabilia, mirabiliary, mirabilis, mirabilite, mirable, mirach, miracicidia, miracidia, miracidial, miracidium, miracle, miracle's, miracled, miraclemonger, miraclemongering, miracles, miracling, miraclist, miracular, miraculist, miraculize, miraculosity, miraculous, miraculously, miraculousness, mirador, miradors, mirage, mirages, miragy, mirandous, mirate, mirbane, mircrobicidal, mird, mirdaha, mirdha, mire, mired, mirepois, mirepoix, mires, miresnipe, mirex, mirexes, miri, miriam, mirid, mirier, miriest, mirific, mirifical, miriki, miriness, mirinesses, miring, mirish, mirk, mirker, mirkest, mirkier, mirkiest, mirkily, mirkiness, mirkish, mirkly, mirkness, mirks, mirksome, mirky, mirled, mirligo, mirliton, mirlitons, mirly, miro, mirror, mirrored, mirroring, mirrorize, mirrorlike, mirrors, mirrorscope, mirrory, mirs, mirth, mirthful, mirthfully, mirthfulness, mirthless, mirthlessly, mirthlessness, mirths, mirthsome, mirthsomeness, mirv, mirvs, miry, miryachit, mirza, mirzas, mis, misaccent, misaccentuation, misaccept, misacception, misaccount, misaccused, misachievement, misacknowledge, misact, misacted, misacting, misacts, misadapt, misadaptation, misadapted, misadapting, misadapts, misadd, misadded, misadding, misaddress, misaddressed, misaddresses, misaddressing, misaddrest, misadds, misadjudicated, misadjust, misadjusted, misadjusting, misadjustment, misadjusts, misadmeasurement, misadminister, misadministration, misadressed, misadressing, misadrest, misadvantage, misadventure, misadventurer, misadventures, misadventurous, misadventurously, misadvertence, misadvice, misadvise, misadvised, misadvisedly, misadvisedness, misadvises, misadvising, misaffect, misaffected, misaffection, misaffirm, misagent, misagents, misaim, misaimed, misaiming, misaims, misalienate, misaligned, misalignment, misalignments, misallegation, misallege, misalleged, misalleging, misalliance, misalliances, misallied, misallies, misallocation, misallot, misallotment, misallotted, misallotting, misallowance, misally, misallying, misalphabetize, misalphabetized, misalphabetizes, misalphabetizing, misalter, misaltered, misaltering, misalters, misanalysis, misanalyze, misanalyzed, misanalyzely, misanalyzing, misandry, misanswer, misanthrope, misanthropes, misanthropi, misanthropia, misanthropic, misanthropical, misanthropically, misanthropies, misanthropism, misanthropist, misanthropists, misanthropize, misanthropos, misanthropy, misapparel, misappear, misappearance, misappellation, misappended, misapplicability, misapplication, misapplied, misapplier, misapplies, misapply, misapplying, misappoint, misappointment, misappraise, misappraised, misappraisement, misappraising, misappreciate, misappreciation, misappreciative, misapprehend, misapprehended, misapprehending, misapprehendingly, misapprehends, misapprehensible, misapprehension, misapprehensions, misapprehensive, misapprehensively, misapprehensiveness, misappropriate, misappropriated, misappropriately, misappropriates, misappropriating, misappropriation, misappropriations, misarchism, misarchist, misarrange, misarranged, misarrangement, misarrangements, misarranges, misarranging, misarray, misarticulate, misarticulated, misarticulating, misarticulation, misascribe, misascription, misasperse, misassay, misassayed, misassaying, misassays, misassent, misassert, misassertion, misassign, misassignment, misassociate, misassociation, misate, misatone, misatoned, misatones, misatoning, misattend, misattribute, misattribution, misaunter, misauthorization, misauthorize, misauthorized, misauthorizing, misaventeur, misaver, misaverred, misaverring, misavers, misaward, misawarded, misawarding, misawards, misbandage, misbaptize, misbear, misbecame, misbecome, misbecoming, misbecomingly, misbecomingness, misbede, misbefall, misbefallen, misbefitting, misbegan, misbeget, misbegetting, misbegin, misbeginning, misbegins, misbegot, misbegotten, misbegun, misbehave, misbehaved, misbehaver, misbehavers, misbehaves, misbehaving, misbehavior, misbehaviour, misbeholden, misbelief, misbeliefs, misbelieve, misbelieved, misbeliever, misbelieving, misbelievingly, misbelove, misbeseem, misbestow, misbestowal, misbestowed, misbestowing, misbestows, misbetide, misbias, misbiased, misbiases, misbiasing, misbiassed, misbiasses, misbiassing, misbill, misbilled, misbilling, misbills, misbind, misbinding, misbinds, misbirth, misbode, misboden, misborn, misbound, misbrand, misbranded, misbranding, misbrands, misbrew, misbuild, misbuilding, misbuilds, misbuilt, misbusy, misbuttoned, misc, miscal, miscalculate, miscalculated, miscalculates, miscalculating, miscalculation, miscalculation's, miscalculations, miscalculator, miscall, miscalled, miscaller, miscalling, miscalls, miscanonize, miscarriage, miscarriageable, miscarriages, miscarried, miscarries, miscarry, miscarrying, miscast, miscasted, miscasting, miscasts, miscasualty, miscategorize, miscategorized, miscategorizing, misce, misceability, miscegenate, miscegenation, miscegenational, miscegenationist, miscegenations, miscegenator, miscegenetic, miscegenist, miscegine, miscellanarian, miscellane, miscellanea, miscellaneal, miscellaneity, miscellaneous, miscellaneously, miscellaneousness, miscellanies, miscellanist, miscellany, miscensure, miscensured, miscensuring, mischallenge, mischance, mischanceful, mischances, mischancy, mischanter, mischaracterization, mischaracterize, mischaracterized, mischaracterizing, mischarge, mischarged, mischarges, mischarging, mischief, mischiefful, mischiefs, mischieve, mischievous, mischievously, mischievousness, mischio, mischoice, mischoose, mischoosing, mischose, mischosen, mischristen, miscibilities, miscibility, miscible, miscipher, miscitation, miscite, miscited, miscites, misciting, misclaim, misclaimed, misclaiming, misclaims, misclass, misclassed, misclasses, misclassification, misclassifications, misclassified, misclassifies, misclassify, misclassifying, misclassing, miscognizable, miscognizant, miscoin, miscoinage, miscoined, miscoining, miscoins, miscollocation, miscolor, miscoloration, miscolored, miscoloring, miscolors, miscolour, miscomfort, miscommand, miscommit, miscommunicate, miscommunication, miscommunications, miscompare, miscomplacence, miscomplain, miscomplaint, miscompose, miscomprehend, miscomprehension, miscomputation, miscompute, miscomputed, miscomputing, misconceit, misconceive, misconceived, misconceiver, misconceives, misconceiving, misconception, misconception's, misconceptions, misconclusion, miscondition, misconduct, misconducted, misconducting, misconfer, misconfidence, misconfident, misconfiguration, misconjecture, misconjectured, misconjecturing, misconjugate, misconjugated, misconjugating, misconjugation, misconjunction, misconnection, misconsecrate, misconsecrated, misconsequence, misconstitutional, misconstruable, misconstrual, misconstruct, misconstruction, misconstructions, misconstructive, misconstrue, misconstrued, misconstruer, misconstrues, misconstruing, miscontent, miscontinuance, misconvenient, misconvey, miscook, miscooked, miscookery, miscooking, miscooks, miscopied, miscopies, miscopy, miscopying, miscorrect, miscorrected, miscorrecting, miscorrection, miscounsel, miscounseled, miscounseling, miscounselled, miscounselling, miscount, miscounted, miscounting, miscounts, miscovet, miscreance, miscreancy, miscreant, miscreants, miscreate, miscreated, miscreating, miscreation, miscreative, miscreator, miscredit, miscredited, miscredulity, miscreed, miscript, miscrop, miscue, miscued, miscues, miscuing, miscultivated, misculture, miscurvature, miscut, miscuts, miscutting, misdate, misdated, misdateful, misdates, misdating, misdaub, misdeal, misdealer, misdealing, misdeals, misdealt, misdecide, misdecision, misdeclaration, misdeclare, misdeed, misdeeds, misdeem, misdeemed, misdeemful, misdeeming, misdeems, misdefine, misdefined, misdefines, misdefining, misdeformed, misdeliver, misdeliveries, misdelivery, misdemean, misdemeanant, misdemeaned, misdemeaning, misdemeanist, misdemeanor, misdemeanors, misdemeanour, misdentition, misdepart, misderivation, misderive, misderived, misderiving, misdescribe, misdescribed, misdescriber, misdescribing, misdescription, misdescriptive, misdesert, misdeserve, misdesignate, misdesire, misdetermine, misdevise, misdevoted, misdevotion, misdiagnose, misdiagnosed, misdiagnoses, misdiagnosing, misdiagnosis, misdiagrammed, misdictated, misdid, misdidived, misdiet, misdight, misdirect, misdirected, misdirecting, misdirection, misdirections, misdirects, misdispose, misdisposition, misdistinguish, misdistribute, misdistribution, misdived, misdivide, misdividing, misdivision, misdo, misdoer, misdoers, misdoes, misdoing, misdoings, misdone, misdoubt, misdoubted, misdoubtful, misdoubting, misdoubts, misdower, misdraw, misdrawing, misdrawn, misdraws, misdread, misdrew, misdrive, misdriven, misdrives, misdriving, misdrove, mise, misease, miseased, miseases, miseat, miseating, miseats, misecclesiastic, misedit, misedited, misediting, misedits, miseducate, miseducated, miseducates, miseducating, miseducation, miseducative, miseffect, misemphasis, misemphasize, misemphasized, misemphasizing, misemploy, misemployed, misemploying, misemployment, misemploys, misencourage, misendeavor, misenforce, misengrave, misenite, misenjoy, misenrol, misenroll, misenrolled, misenrolling, misenrolls, misenrols, misenter, misentered, misentering, misenters, misentitle, misentreat, misentries, misentry, misenunciation, miser, miserabilia, miserabilism, miserabilist, miserabilistic, miserability, miserable, miserableness, miserably, miseration, miserdom, misere, miserected, miserere, misereres, miserhood, misericord, misericorde, misericordia, miseries, miserism, miserliness, miserly, misers, misery, misery's, mises, misesteem, misesteemed, misesteeming, misestimate, misestimated, misestimating, misestimation, misevaluate, misevaluation, misevent, misevents, misexample, misexecute, misexecution, misexpectation, misexpend, misexpenditure, misexplain, misexplained, misexplanation, misexplicate, misexplication, misexposition, misexpound, misexpress, misexpression, misexpressive, misfaith, misfaiths, misfall, misfare, misfashion, misfashioned, misfate, misfather, misfault, misfeasance, misfeasances, misfeasor, misfeasors, misfeature, misfeatured, misfeign, misfield, misfielded, misfielding, misfields, misfigure, misfile, misfiled, misfiles, misfiling, misfire, misfired, misfires, misfiring, misfit, misfit's, misfits, misfitted, misfitting, misfocus, misfocused, misfocusing, misfocussed, misfocussing, misfond, misforgive, misform, misformation, misformed, misforming, misforms, misfortunate, misfortunately, misfortune, misfortune's, misfortuned, misfortuner, misfortunes, misframe, misframed, misframes, misframing, misgauge, misgauged, misgauges, misgauging, misgave, misgesture, misgive, misgiven, misgives, misgiving, misgivingly, misgivinglying, misgivings, misgo, misgotten, misgovern, misgovernance, misgoverned, misgoverning, misgovernment, misgovernor, misgoverns, misgracious, misgrade, misgraded, misgrading, misgraff, misgraffed, misgraft, misgrafted, misgrafting, misgrafts, misgrave, misgrew, misground, misgrounded, misgrow, misgrowing, misgrown, misgrows, misgrowth, misguage, misguaged, misguess, misguessed, misguesses, misguessing, misguggle, misguidance, misguide, misguided, misguidedly, misguidedness, misguider, misguiders, misguides, misguiding, misguidingly, misguise, misgye, mishandle, mishandled, mishandles, mishandling, mishanter, mishap, mishap's, mishappen, mishaps, mishara, mishave, mishear, misheard, mishearing, mishears, miships, mishit, mishits, mishitting, mishmash, mishmashes, mishmee, mishmi, mishmosh, mishmoshes, mishnah, misidentification, misidentifications, misidentified, misidentifies, misidentify, misidentifying, misimagination, misimagine, misimpression, misimprove, misimproved, misimprovement, misimproving, misimputation, misimpute, misincensed, misincite, misinclination, misincline, misinfer, misinference, misinferred, misinferring, misinfers, misinflame, misinform, misinformant, misinformants, misinformation, misinformative, misinformed, misinformer, misinforming, misinforms, misingenuity, misinspired, misinstruct, misinstructed, misinstructing, misinstruction, misinstructions, misinstructive, misinstructs, misintelligence, misintelligible, misintend, misintention, misinter, misinterment, misinterpret, misinterpretable, misinterpretation, misinterpretations, misinterpreted, misinterpreter, misinterpreting, misinterprets, misinterred, misinterring, misinters, misintimation, misiones, misitemized, misjoin, misjoinder, misjoined, misjoining, misjoins, misjudge, misjudged, misjudgement, misjudger, misjudges, misjudging, misjudgingly, misjudgment, misjudgments, miskal, miskals, miskeep, miskeeping, miskeeps, misken, miskenning, miskept, miskill, miskin, miskindle, misknew, misknow, misknowing, misknowledge, misknown, misknows, misky, mislabel, mislabeled, mislabeling, mislabelled, mislabelling, mislabels, mislabor, mislabored, mislaboring, mislabors, mislaid, mislain, mislanguage, mislay, mislayer, mislayers, mislaying, mislays, mislead, misleadable, misleader, misleading, misleadingly, misleadingness, misleads, mislear, misleared, mislearn, mislearned, mislearning, mislearns, mislearnt, misled, misleered, mislen, mislest, mislie, mislies, mislight, mislighted, mislighting, mislights, mislikable, mislike, misliked, misliken, mislikeness, misliker, mislikers, mislikes, misliking, mislikingly, mislin, mislippen, mislit, mislive, mislived, mislives, misliving, mislled, mislocate, mislocated, mislocating, mislocation, mislodge, mislodged, mislodges, mislodging, misluck, misly, mislying, mismade, mismake, mismaking, mismanage, mismanageable, mismanaged, mismanagement, mismanager, mismanages, mismanaging, mismannered, mismanners, mismark, mismarked, mismarking, mismarks, mismarriage, mismarriages, mismarry, mismatch, mismatched, mismatches, mismatching, mismatchment, mismate, mismated, mismates, mismating, mismaze, mismean, mismeasure, mismeasured, mismeasurement, mismeasuring, mismeet, mismeeting, mismeets, mismenstruation, mismet, mismetre, misminded, mismingle, mismosh, mismoshes, mismotion, mismount, mismove, mismoved, mismoves, mismoving, misname, misnamed, misnames, misnaming, misnarrate, misnarrated, misnarrating, misnatured, misnavigate, misnavigated, misnavigating, misnavigation, misnomed, misnomer, misnomered, misnomers, misnumber, misnumbered, misnumbering, misnumbers, misnurture, misnutrition, miso, misobedience, misobey, misobservance, misobserve, misocainea, misocapnic, misocapnist, misocatholic, misoccupied, misoccupy, misoccupying, misogallic, misogamic, misogamies, misogamist, misogamists, misogamy, misogyne, misogynic, misogynical, misogynies, misogynism, misogynist, misogynistic, misogynistical, misogynists, misogynous, misogyny, misohellene, misologies, misologist, misology, misomath, misoneism, misoneist, misoneistic, misopaedia, misopaedism, misopaedist, misopaterist, misopedia, misopedism, misopedist, misopinion, misopolemical, misorder, misordination, misorganization, misorganize, misorganized, misorganizing, misorient, misorientation, misos, misoscopist, misosopher, misosophist, misosophy, misotheism, misotheist, misotheistic, misotramontanism, misotyranny, misoxene, misoxeny, mispackaged, mispacked, mispage, mispaged, mispages, mispagination, mispaging, mispaid, mispaint, mispainted, mispainting, mispaints, misparse, misparsed, misparses, misparsing, mispart, misparted, misparting, misparts, mispassion, mispatch, mispatched, mispatches, mispatching, mispay, mispaying, mispen, mispenned, mispenning, mispens, misperceive, misperceived, misperceiving, misperception, misperform, misperformance, mispersuade, misperuse, misphrase, misphrased, misphrasing, mispick, mispickel, misplace, misplaced, misplacement, misplaces, misplacing, misplant, misplanted, misplanting, misplants, misplay, misplayed, misplaying, misplays, misplead, mispleaded, mispleading, mispleads, misplease, mispled, mispoint, mispointed, mispointing, mispoints, mispoise, mispoised, mispoises, mispoising, mispolicy, misposition, mispossessed, mispractice, mispracticed, mispracticing, mispractise, mispractised, mispractising, mispraise, misprejudiced, mispresent, misprincipled, misprint, misprinted, misprinting, misprints, misprisal, misprise, misprised, mispriser, misprising, misprision, misprisions, misprizal, misprize, misprized, misprizer, misprizes, misprizing, misproceeding, misproduce, misproduced, misproducing, misprofess, misprofessor, mispronounce, mispronounced, mispronouncement, mispronouncer, mispronounces, mispronouncing, mispronunciation, mispronunciations, misproportion, misproportioned, misproportions, misproposal, mispropose, misproposed, misproposing, misproud, misprovide, misprovidence, misprovoke, misprovoked, misprovoking, mispublicized, mispublished, mispunch, mispunctuate, mispunctuated, mispunctuating, mispunctuation, mispurchase, mispurchased, mispurchasing, mispursuit, misput, misputting, misqualified, misqualify, misqualifying, misquality, misquotation, misquotations, misquote, misquoted, misquoter, misquotes, misquoting, misraise, misraised, misraises, misraising, misrate, misrated, misrates, misrating, misread, misreaded, misreader, misreading, misreads, misrealize, misreason, misreceive, misrecital, misrecite, misreckon, misreckoned, misreckoning, misrecognition, misrecognize, misrecollect, misrecollected, misrefer, misreference, misreferred, misreferring, misrefers, misreflect, misreform, misregulate, misregulated, misregulating, misrehearsal, misrehearse, misrehearsed, misrehearsing, misrelate, misrelated, misrelating, misrelation, misreliance, misrelied, misrelies, misreligion, misrely, misrelying, misremember, misremembered, misremembrance, misrender, misrendering, misrepeat, misreport, misreported, misreporter, misreporting, misreports, misreposed, misrepresent, misrepresentation, misrepresentation's, misrepresentations, misrepresentative, misrepresented, misrepresentee, misrepresenter, misrepresenting, misrepresents, misreprint, misrepute, misresemblance, misresolved, misresult, misreward, misrhyme, misrhymed, misrhymer, misrule, misruled, misruler, misrules, misruling, misruly, misrun, miss, missa, missable, missaid, missal, missals, missample, missampled, missampling, missang, missary, missatical, missay, missayer, missaying, missays, misscribed, misscribing, misscript, misseat, misseated, misseating, misseats, missed, misseem, missel, misseldin, missels, missemblance, missend, missending, missends, missense, missenses, missent, missentence, misserve, misservice, misses, misset, missetting, misshape, misshaped, misshapen, misshapenly, misshapenness, misshapes, misshaping, misship, misshipment, misshipped, misshipping, misshod, misshood, missible, missies, missificate, missile, missile's, missileer, missileman, missilemen, missileproof, missilery, missiles, missilries, missilry, missiness, missing, missingly, missiology, mission, missional, missionaries, missionarize, missionary, missionary's, missionaryship, missioned, missioner, missioning, missionization, missionize, missionizer, missions, missis, missises, missish, missishness, mississippi, mississippian, mississippians, missit, missive, missives, missmark, missment, missort, missorted, missorting, missorts, missound, missounded, missounding, missounds, missouri, missourian, missourians, missourite, missout, missouts, misspace, misspaced, misspaces, misspacing, misspeak, misspeaking, misspeaks, misspeech, misspeed, misspell, misspelled, misspelling, misspellings, misspells, misspelt, misspend, misspender, misspending, misspends, misspent, misspoke, misspoken, misstart, misstarted, misstarting, misstarts, misstate, misstated, misstatement, misstatements, misstater, misstates, misstating, misstay, missteer, missteered, missteering, missteers, misstep, misstepping, missteps, misstop, misstopped, misstopping, misstops, misstyle, misstyled, misstyles, misstyling, missuade, missuggestion, missuit, missuited, missuiting, missuits, missummation, missung, missuppose, missupposed, missupposing, missus, missuses, missy, missyish, missyllabication, missyllabification, missyllabified, missyllabify, missyllabifying, mist, mistakable, mistakableness, mistakably, mistake, mistakeful, mistaken, mistakenly, mistakenness, mistakeproof, mistaker, mistakers, mistakes, mistaking, mistakingly, mistakion, mistal, mistassini, mistaste, mistaught, mistbow, mistbows, mistcoat, misteach, misteacher, misteaches, misteaching, misted, mistell, mistelling, mistemper, mistempered, mistend, mistended, mistendency, mistending, mistends, mister, mistered, mistering, misterm, mistermed, misterming, misterms, misters, mistery, mistetch, misteuk, mistfall, mistflower, mistful, misthink, misthinking, misthinks, misthought, misthread, misthrew, misthrift, misthrive, misthrow, misthrowing, misthrown, misthrows, mistic, mistico, mistide, mistier, mistiest, mistify, mistigri, mistigris, mistilled, mistily, mistime, mistimed, mistimes, mistiming, mistiness, misting, mistion, mistitle, mistitled, mistitles, mistitling, mistle, mistless, mistletoe, mistletoes, mistold, mistone, mistonusk, mistook, mistouch, mistouched, mistouches, mistouching, mistrace, mistraced, mistraces, mistracing, mistradition, mistrain, mistral, mistrals, mistranscribe, mistranscribed, mistranscribing, mistranscript, mistranscription, mistranslate, mistranslated, mistranslates, mistranslating, mistranslation, mistreading, mistreat, mistreated, mistreating, mistreatment, mistreats, mistress, mistressdom, mistresses, mistresshood, mistressless, mistressly, mistrial, mistrials, mistrist, mistrow, mistrust, mistrusted, mistruster, mistrustful, mistrustfully, mistrustfulness, mistrusting, mistrustingly, mistrustless, mistrusts, mistry, mistryst, mistrysted, mistrysting, mistrysts, mists, mistune, mistuned, mistunes, mistuning, misture, misturn, mistutor, mistutored, mistutoring, mistutors, misty, mistyish, mistype, mistyped, mistypes, mistyping, mistypings, misunderstand, misunderstandable, misunderstander, misunderstanders, misunderstanding, misunderstanding's, misunderstandingly, misunderstandings, misunderstands, misunderstood, misunderstoodness, misunion, misunions, misura, misusage, misusages, misuse, misused, misuseful, misusement, misuser, misusers, misuses, misusing, misusurped, misvaluation, misvalue, misvalued, misvalues, misvaluing, misventure, misventurous, misviding, misvouch, misvouched, miswandered, misway, miswed, miswedded, misween, miswend, miswern, miswire, miswired, miswiring, miswisdom, miswish, miswoman, misword, misworded, miswording, miswords, misworship, misworshiped, misworshiper, misworshipper, miswrest, miswrit, miswrite, miswrites, miswriting, miswritten, miswrote, miswrought, misy, misyoke, misyoked, misyokes, misyoking, miszealous, miszone, miszoned, miszoning, mit, mit's, mitapsis, mitch, mitchboard, mite, miteproof, miter, mitered, miterer, miterers, miterflower, mitergate, mitering, miters, miterwort, mites, mithan, mither, mithers, mithraic, mithras, mithridate, mithridatic, mithridatise, mithridatised, mithridatising, mithridatism, mithridatize, mithridatized, mithridatizing, miticidal, miticide, miticides, mitier, mitiest, mitigable, mitigant, mitigate, mitigated, mitigatedly, mitigates, mitigating, mitigation, mitigative, mitigator, mitigators, mitigatory, miting, mitis, mitises, mitochondria, mitochondrial, mitochondrion, mitogen, mitogenetic, mitogenic, mitogenicity, mitogens, mitokoromono, mitome, mitomycin, mitoses, mitosis, mitosome, mitotic, mitotically, mitra, mitraille, mitrailleur, mitrailleuse, mitral, mitrate, mitre, mitred, mitreflower, mitrer, mitres, mitrewort, mitriform, mitring, mitsumata, mitsvah, mitsvahs, mitsvoth, mitt, mittatur, mittelhand, mitten, mitten's, mittened, mittenlike, mittens, mittent, mittimus, mittimuses, mittle, mitts, mitty, mitvoth, mity, mitzvah, mitzvahs, mitzvoth, miurus, mix, mixability, mixable, mixableness, mixblood, mixed, mixedly, mixedness, mixen, mixer, mixeress, mixers, mixes, mixhill, mixible, mixilineal, mixing, mixite, mixobarbaric, mixochromosome, mixologies, mixologist, mixology, mixolydian, mixoploid, mixoploidy, mixotrophic, mixt, mixtiform, mixtilineal, mixtilinear, mixtilion, mixtion, mixture, mixture's, mixtures, mixup, mixups, mixy, mizar, mize, mizen, mizenmast, mizens, mizmaze, mizrach, mizrah, mizzen, mizzenmast, mizzenmastman, mizzenmasts, mizzens, mizzentop, mizzentopman, mizzentopmen, mizzle, mizzled, mizzler, mizzles, mizzling, mizzly, mizzonite, mizzy, mk, mks, mkt, mktg, ml, mlange, mlechchha, mlx, mm, mmf, mmfd, mmmm, mn, mna, mnage, mnem, mneme, mnemic, mnemonic, mnemonic's, mnemonical, mnemonicalist, mnemonically, mnemonicon, mnemonics, mnemonism, mnemonist, mnemonization, mnemonize, mnemonized, mnemonizing, mnemosyne, mnemotechnic, mnemotechnical, mnemotechnics, mnemotechnist, mnemotechny, mnesic, mnestic, mniaceous, mnioid, mo, moa, moabite, moabitish, moan, moaned, moanful, moanfully, moanification, moaning, moaningly, moanless, moans, moas, moat, moat's, moated, moathill, moating, moatlike, moats, mob, mob's, mobable, mobbable, mobbed, mobber, mobbers, mobbie, mobbing, mobbish, mobbishly, mobbishness, mobbism, mobbist, mobble, mobby, mobcap, mobcaps, mobed, mobil, mobile, mobiles, mobilia, mobilianer, mobiliary, mobilisable, mobilisation, mobilise, mobilised, mobiliser, mobilises, mobilising, mobilities, mobility, mobilizable, mobilization, mobilizations, mobilize, mobilized, mobilizer, mobilizers, mobilizes, mobilizing, mobilometer, moble, moblike, mobocracies, mobocracy, mobocrat, mobocratic, mobocratical, mobocrats, mobolatry, mobproof, mobs, mobship, mobsman, mobsmen, mobster, mobsters, moc, moca, moccasin, moccasin's, moccasins, moccenigo, mocha, mochas, moche, mochel, mochila, mochilas, mochras, mochudi, mochy, mock, mockable, mockado, mockage, mockbird, mocked, mocker, mockeries, mockernut, mockers, mockery, mocketer, mockful, mockfully, mockground, mocking, mockingbird, mockingbirds, mockingly, mockingstock, mockish, mocks, mockup, mockups, mocmain, moco, mocock, mocomoco, mocuck, mod, modal, modalism, modalist, modalistic, modalities, modality, modality's, modalize, modally, modder, mode, model, model's, modeled, modeler, modelers, modeless, modelessness, modeling, modelings, modelist, modelize, modelled, modeller, modellers, modelling, modelmaker, modelmaking, models, modem, modems, modena, moder, moderant, moderantism, moderantist, moderate, moderated, moderately, moderateness, moderates, moderating, moderation, moderationism, moderationist, moderations, moderatism, moderatist, moderato, moderator, moderatorial, moderators, moderatorship, moderatos, moderatrix, modern, moderne, moderner, modernest, modernicide, modernisation, modernise, modernised, moderniser, modernish, modernising, modernism, modernist, modernistic, modernists, modernities, modernity, modernizable, modernization, modernize, modernized, modernizer, modernizers, modernizes, modernizing, modernly, modernness, moderns, modes, modest, modester, modestest, modesties, modestly, modestness, modesty, modge, modi, modiation, modica, modicity, modicum, modicums, modif, modifiability, modifiable, modifiableness, modifiably, modificability, modificable, modificand, modification, modificationist, modifications, modificative, modificator, modificatory, modified, modifier, modifiers, modifies, modify, modifying, modili, modillion, modiolar, modioli, modiolus, modish, modishly, modishness, modist, modiste, modistes, modistry, modius, modo, modred, mods, modula, modulability, modulant, modular, modularity, modularization, modularize, modularized, modularizes, modularizing, modularly, modulate, modulated, modulates, modulating, modulation, modulations, modulative, modulator, modulator's, modulators, modulatory, module, module's, modules, modulet, moduli, modulize, modulo, modulus, modumite, modus, mody, moe, moeble, moeck, moellon, moerithere, moeritherian, moet, moeurs, mofette, mofettes, moff, moffette, moffettes, moffle, mofussil, mofussilite, mog, mogador, mogadore, mogdad, moggan, mogged, moggies, mogging, moggio, moggy, moghul, mogigraphia, mogigraphic, mogigraphy, mogilalia, mogilalism, mogiphonia, mogitocia, mogo, mogographia, mogos, mogote, mogs, moguey, mogul, moguls, mogulship, moguntine, moha, mohabat, mohair, mohairs, mohalim, mohammed, mohammedan, mohar, moharram, mohatra, mohawk, mohawkite, mohawks, mohegan, mohel, mohels, mohican, mohism, mohnseed, moho, mohock, mohockism, mohoohoo, mohos, mohr, mohur, mohurs, mohwa, moi, moid, moider, moidore, moidores, moier, moiest, moieter, moieties, moiety, moil, moile, moiled, moiler, moilers, moiles, moiley, moiling, moilingly, moils, moilsome, moineau, moio, moir, moira, moirai, moire, moireed, moireing, moires, moirette, moise, moison, moissanite, moist, moisten, moistened, moistener, moisteners, moistening, moistens, moister, moistest, moistful, moistify, moistiness, moistish, moistishness, moistless, moistly, moistness, moisture, moistureless, moistureproof, moistures, moisturize, moisturized, moisturizer, moisturizers, moisturizes, moisturizing, moisty, moit, moither, moitier, moitiest, moity, mojarra, mojarras, mojo, mojos, mokaddam, mokador, mokamoka, moke, mokes, moki, mokihana, mokihi, moko, moksha, mokum, moky, mol, mola, molal, molalities, molality, molar, molariform, molarimeter, molarities, molarity, molars, molary, molas, molasse, molasses, molasseses, molassied, molassy, molave, mold, moldability, moldable, moldableness, moldasle, moldavite, moldboard, moldboards, molded, molder, moldered, moldering, molders, moldery, moldier, moldiest, moldiness, molding, moldings, moldmade, moldproof, molds, moldwarp, moldwarps, moldy, mole, molebut, molecast, molecula, molecular, molecularist, molecularity, molecularly, molecule, molecule's, molecules, molehead, moleheap, molehill, molehillish, molehills, molehilly, moleism, molelike, molendinar, molendinary, molengraaffite, moleproof, moler, moles, moleskin, moleskins, molest, molestation, molestations, molested, molester, molesters, molestful, molestfully, molestie, molesting, molestious, molests, molet, molewarp, moliere, molies, molified, molify, molifying, molilalia, molimen, moliminous, molinary, moline, molinet, moling, molinism, molition, molka, moll, molla, mollah, mollahs, molland, molle, molles, mollescence, mollescent, molleton, mollichop, mollicrush, mollie, mollienisia, mollient, molliently, mollies, mollifiable, mollification, mollified, mollifiedly, mollifier, mollifiers, mollifies, mollify, mollifying, mollifyingly, mollifyingness, molligrant, molligrubs, mollipilose, mollisiose, mollisol, mollities, mollitious, mollitude, molls, mollusc, mollusca, molluscan, molluscans, molluscicidal, molluscicide, molluscivorous, molluscoid, molluscoidal, molluscoidan, molluscoidean, molluscous, molluscousness, molluscs, molluscum, mollusk, molluskan, mollusklike, mollusks, molly, mollycoddle, mollycoddled, mollycoddler, mollycoddlers, mollycoddles, mollycoddling, mollycosset, mollycot, mollyhawk, mollymawk, molman, molmen, molmutian, moloch, molochs, molocker, moloid, moloker, molompi, molosse, molosses, molossian, molossic, molossine, molossoid, molossus, molpe, molrooken, mols, molt, molted, molten, moltenly, molter, molters, molting, molto, molts, moltten, molucca, molvi, moly, molybdate, molybdena, molybdenic, molybdeniferous, molybdenite, molybdenous, molybdenum, molybdic, molybdite, molybdocardialgia, molybdocolic, molybdodyspepsia, molybdomancy, molybdomenite, molybdonosus, molybdoparesis, molybdophyllite, molybdosis, molybdous, molysite, mom, mombin, momble, mome, moment, moment's, momenta, momental, momentally, momentaneall, momentaneity, momentaneous, momentaneously, momentaneousness, momentany, momentarily, momentariness, momentary, momently, momento, momentoes, momentos, momentous, momentously, momentousness, moments, momentum, momentums, momes, momi, momiology, momish, momism, momisms, momist, momma, mommas, momme, mommer, mommet, mommies, mommy, momo, moms, momser, momus, momuses, momzer, mon, mona, monacanthid, monacanthine, monacanthous, monacetin, monach, monachal, monachate, monachism, monachist, monachization, monachize, monacid, monacidic, monacids, monacillo, monacillos, monaco, monact, monactin, monactinal, monactine, monactinellid, monactinellidan, monad, monadal, monadelph, monadelphia, monadelphian, monadelphous, monades, monadic, monadical, monadically, monadiform, monadigerous, monadism, monadisms, monadistic, monadnock, monadology, monads, monaene, monal, monamide, monamine, monamniotic, monander, monandria, monandrian, monandric, monandries, monandrous, monandry, monanthous, monaphase, monapsal, monarch, monarchal, monarchally, monarchess, monarchial, monarchian, monarchianism, monarchianist, monarchianistic, monarchic, monarchical, monarchically, monarchies, monarchism, monarchist, monarchistic, monarchists, monarchize, monarchized, monarchizer, monarchizing, monarchlike, monarcho, monarchomachic, monarchomachist, monarchs, monarchy, monarchy's, monarda, monardas, monarthritis, monarticular, monas, monascidian, monase, monaster, monasterial, monasterially, monasteries, monastery, monastery's, monastic, monastical, monastically, monasticism, monasticize, monastics, monatomic, monatomically, monatomicity, monatomism, monaul, monauli, monaulos, monaural, monaurally, monax, monaxial, monaxile, monaxon, monaxonial, monaxonic, monazine, monazite, monazites, monchiquite, mondain, mondaine, monday, monday's, mondays, monde, mondego, mondes, mondial, mondo, mondos, mondsee, mone, monecian, monecious, monedula, monel, monembryary, monembryonic, monembryony, moneme, monepic, monepiscopacy, monepiscopal, monepiscopus, moner, monera, moneral, moneran, monergic, monergism, monergist, monergistic, moneric, moneron, monerons, monerozoan, monerozoic, monerula, monesia, monest, monestrous, monetarily, monetarism, monetarist, monetarists, monetary, moneth, monetise, monetised, monetises, monetising, monetite, monetization, monetize, monetized, monetizes, monetizing, money, moneyage, moneybag, moneybags, moneychanger, moneychangers, moneyed, moneyer, moneyers, moneyflower, moneygetting, moneygrub, moneygrubber, moneygrubbing, moneying, moneylender, moneylenders, moneylending, moneyless, moneylessness, moneymake, moneymaker, moneymakers, moneymaking, moneyman, moneymonger, moneymongering, moneyocracy, moneys, moneysaving, moneywise, moneywort, mong, mongcorn, mongeese, monger, mongered, mongerer, mongering, mongers, mongery, mongler, mongo, mongoe, mongoes, mongol, mongolia, mongolian, mongolianism, mongolians, mongolic, mongolism, mongoloid, mongoloids, mongols, mongoose, mongooses, mongos, mongrel, mongreldom, mongrelisation, mongrelise, mongrelised, mongreliser, mongrelish, mongrelising, mongrelism, mongrelity, mongrelization, mongrelize, mongrelized, mongrelizing, mongrelly, mongrelness, mongrels, mongst, monheimite, monial, monic, monica, monicker, monickers, monie, monied, monier, monies, moniker, monikers, monilated, monilethrix, moniliaceous, monilial, moniliasis, monilicorn, moniliform, moniliformly, monilioid, moniment, monimiaceous, monimolite, monimostylic, monish, monished, monisher, monishes, monishing, monishment, monism, monisms, monist, monistic, monistical, monistically, monists, monitary, monition, monitions, monitive, monitor, monitored, monitorial, monitorially, monitories, monitoring, monitorish, monitors, monitorship, monitory, monitress, monitrix, monk, monk's, monkbird, monkcraft, monkdom, monkeries, monkery, monkeryies, monkess, monkey, monkeyboard, monkeyed, monkeyface, monkeyfied, monkeyflower, monkeyfy, monkeyfying, monkeyhood, monkeying, monkeyish, monkeyishly, monkeyishness, monkeyism, monkeylike, monkeynut, monkeypod, monkeypot, monkeyrony, monkeyry, monkeys, monkeyshine, monkeyshines, monkeytail, monkfish, monkfishes, monkflower, monkhood, monkhoods, monkish, monkishly, monkishness, monkism, monklike, monkliness, monkly, monkmonger, monks, monkship, monkshood, monkshoods, monmouth, monmouthite, monniker, monnion, monny, mono, monoacetate, monoacetin, monoacid, monoacidic, monoacids, monoalphabetic, monoamid, monoamide, monoamin, monoamine, monoaminergic, monoamino, monoammonium, monoatomic, monoazo, monobacillary, monobase, monobasic, monobasicity, monobath, monoblastic, monoblepsia, monoblepsis, monobloc, monobranchiate, monobromacetone, monobromated, monobromide, monobrominated, monobromination, monobromized, monobromoacetanilide, monobromoacetone, monobutyrin, monocable, monocalcium, monocarbide, monocarbonate, monocarbonic, monocarboxylic, monocardian, monocarp, monocarpal, monocarpellary, monocarpian, monocarpic, monocarpous, monocarps, monocellular, monocentric, monocentrid, monocentroid, monocephalous, monocerco, monocercous, monoceros, monocerous, monochasia, monochasial, monochasium, monochlamydeous, monochlor, monochloracetic, monochloranthracene, monochlorbenzene, monochloride, monochlorinated, monochlorination, monochloro, monochloroacetic, monochlorobenzene, monochloromethane, monochoanitic, monochord, monochordist, monochordize, monochroic, monochromasy, monochromat, monochromate, monochromatic, monochromatically, monochromaticity, monochromatism, monochromator, monochrome, monochromes, monochromic, monochromical, monochromically, monochromist, monochromous, monochromy, monochronic, monochronometer, monochronous, monociliated, monocle, monocled, monocleid, monocleide, monocles, monoclinal, monoclinally, monocline, monoclinian, monoclinic, monoclinism, monoclinometric, monoclinous, monoclonal, monocoelian, monocoelic, monocondylar, monocondylian, monocondylic, monocondylous, monocoque, monocormic, monocot, monocots, monocotyl, monocotyledon, monocotyledonous, monocotyledons, monocracy, monocrat, monocratic, monocratis, monocrats, monocrotic, monocrotism, monocular, monocularity, monocularly, monoculate, monocule, monoculist, monoculous, monocultural, monoculture, monoculus, monocyanogen, monocycle, monocyclic, monocycly, monocystic, monocyte, monocytes, monocytic, monocytoid, monocytopoiesis, monodactyl, monodactylate, monodactyle, monodactylism, monodactylous, monodactyly, monodelph, monodelphian, monodelphic, monodelphous, monodermic, monodic, monodical, monodically, monodies, monodimetric, monodist, monodists, monodize, monodomous, monodont, monodontal, monodram, monodrama, monodramatic, monodramatist, monodrame, monodromic, monodromy, monody, monodynamic, monodynamism, monoecia, monoecian, monoecies, monoecious, monoeciously, monoeciousness, monoecism, monoecy, monoeidic, monoenergetic, monoester, monoestrous, monoethanolamine, monoethylamine, monofil, monofilament, monofilm, monofils, monoflagellate, monoformin, monofuel, monofuels, monogamian, monogamic, monogamies, monogamik, monogamist, monogamistic, monogamists, monogamou, monogamous, monogamously, monogamousness, monogamy, monoganglionic, monogastric, monogene, monogenean, monogeneity, monogeneous, monogenesis, monogenesist, monogenesy, monogenetic, monogenic, monogenically, monogenies, monogenism, monogenist, monogenistic, monogenous, monogeny, monogerm, monoglot, monoglycerid, monoglyceride, monogoneutic, monogonoporic, monogonoporous, monogony, monogram, monogram's, monogramed, monograming, monogramm, monogrammatic, monogrammatical, monogrammed, monogrammic, monogramming, monograms, monograph, monograph's, monographed, monographer, monographers, monographes, monographic, monographical, monographically, monographing, monographist, monographs, monography, monograptid, monogynia, monogynic, monogynies, monogynious, monogynist, monogynoecial, monogynous, monogyny, monohull, monohybrid, monohydrate, monohydrated, monohydric, monohydrogen, monohydroxy, monoicous, monoid, monoketone, monokini, monolater, monolatrist, monolatrous, monolatry, monolayer, monoline, monolingual, monolinguist, monoliteral, monolith, monolithal, monolithic, monolithically, monolithism, monoliths, monolobular, monolocular, monolog, monologian, monologic, monological, monologies, monologist, monologists, monologize, monologized, monologizing, monologs, monologue, monologues, monologuist, monologuists, monology, monomachist, monomachy, monomail, monomania, monomaniac, monomaniacal, monomaniacs, monomanias, monomark, monomastigate, monomeniscous, monomer, monomeric, monomerous, monomers, monometalism, monometalist, monometallic, monometallism, monometallist, monometer, monomethyl, monomethylamine, monomethylated, monomethylic, monometric, monometrical, monomial, monomials, monomict, monomineral, monomineralic, monomolecular, monomolecularly, monomolybdate, monomorphemic, monomorphic, monomorphism, monomorphous, monomyarian, monomyary, mononaphthalene, mononch, mononeural, mononitrate, mononitrated, mononitration, mononitride, mononitrobenzene, mononomial, mononomian, monont, mononuclear, mononucleated, mononucleoses, mononucleosis, mononucleotide, mononychous, mononym, mononymic, mononymization, mononymize, mononymy, monoousian, monoousious, monoparental, monoparesis, monoparesthesia, monopathic, monopathy, monopectinate, monopersonal, monopersulfuric, monopersulphuric, monopetalous, monophagia, monophagism, monophagous, monophagy, monophase, monophasia, monophasic, monophobia, monophoic, monophone, monophonic, monophonically, monophonies, monophonous, monophony, monophotal, monophote, monophthalmic, monophthalmus, monophthong, monophthongal, monophthongization, monophthongize, monophthongized, monophthongizing, monophyletic, monophyleticism, monophyletism, monophylety, monophylite, monophyllous, monophyodont, monophyodontism, monophysite, monopitch, monoplace, monoplacula, monoplacular, monoplaculate, monoplane, monoplanes, monoplanist, monoplasmatic, monoplasric, monoplast, monoplastic, monoplegia, monoplegic, monoploid, monopneumonian, monopneumonous, monopode, monopodes, monopodia, monopodial, monopodially, monopodic, monopodies, monopodium, monopodous, monopody, monopolar, monopolaric, monopolarity, monopole, monopoles, monopolies, monopolisation, monopolise, monopolised, monopoliser, monopolising, monopolism, monopolist, monopolistic, monopolistically, monopolists, monopolitical, monopolizable, monopolization, monopolize, monopolized, monopolizer, monopolizes, monopolizing, monopoloid, monopolous, monopoly, monopoly's, monopolylogist, monopolylogue, monopotassium, monoprionid, monoprionidian, monoprogrammed, monoprogramming, monopropellant, monoprotic, monopsonistic, monopsony, monopsychism, monoptera, monopteral, monopteroi, monopteroid, monopteron, monopteros, monopterous, monoptic, monoptical, monoptote, monoptotic, monopttera, monopylean, monopyrenous, monorail, monorailroad, monorails, monorailway, monorchid, monorchidism, monorchis, monorchism, monorganic, monorhinal, monorhine, monorhinous, monorhyme, monorhymed, monorhythmic, monorime, monos, monosaccharide, monosaccharose, monoschemic, monoscope, monose, monosemic, monosemy, monosepalous, monoservice, monosexualities, monosexuality, monosilane, monosilicate, monosilicic, monosiphonic, monosiphonous, monoski, monosodium, monosomatic, monosomatous, monosome, monosomes, monosomic, monospace, monosperm, monospermal, monospermic, monospermous, monospermy, monospherical, monospondylic, monosporangium, monospore, monospored, monosporiferous, monosporous, monostable, monostele, monostelic, monostelous, monostely, monostich, monostichic, monostichous, monostomatous, monostome, monostomous, monostromatic, monostrophe, monostrophic, monostrophics, monostylous, monosubstituted, monosubstitution, monosulfone, monosulfonic, monosulphide, monosulphone, monosulphonic, monosyllabic, monosyllabical, monosyllabically, monosyllabicity, monosyllabism, monosyllabize, monosyllable, monosyllables, monosyllogism, monosymmetric, monosymmetrical, monosymmetrically, monosymmetry, monosymptomatic, monosynaptic, monosynaptically, monosynthetic, monotelephone, monotelephonic, monotellurite, monotessaron, monothalaman, monothalamian, monothalamic, monothalamous, monothecal, monotheism, monotheist, monotheistic, monotheistical, monotheistically, monotheists, monothelete, monothelious, monothelism, monothelite, monothetic, monotic, monotint, monotints, monotocardiac, monotocardian, monotocous, monotomous, monotonal, monotone, monotones, monotonic, monotonical, monotonically, monotonicity, monotonies, monotonist, monotonize, monotonous, monotonously, monotonousness, monotony, monotremal, monotremata, monotremate, monotrematous, monotreme, monotremous, monotrichate, monotrichic, monotrichous, monotriglyph, monotriglyphic, monotrochal, monotrochian, monotrochous, monotron, monotropaceous, monotrophic, monotropic, monotropically, monotropies, monotropy, monotypal, monotype, monotypes, monotypic, monotypical, monotypous, monoureide, monovalence, monovalency, monovalent, monovariant, monoverticillate, monovoltine, monovular, monoxenous, monoxide, monoxides, monoxime, monoxyla, monoxyle, monoxylic, monoxylon, monoxylous, monozoan, monozoic, monozygotic, monozygous, monroe, monroeism, monrolite, mons, monseigneur, monseignevr, monsia, monsieur, monsieurs, monsieurship, monsignor, monsignore, monsignori, monsignorial, monsignors, monsoon, monsoonal, monsoonish, monsoonishly, monsoons, monspermy, monster, monster's, monsterhood, monsterlike, monsters, monstership, monstrance, monstrances, monstrate, monstration, monstrator, monstricide, monstriferous, monstrification, monstrify, monstrosities, monstrosity, monstrous, monstrously, monstrousness, mont, montabyn, montadale, montage, montaged, montages, montaging, montagnard, montagne, montague, montana, montana's, montanan, montanans, montanas, montane, montanes, montanic, montanin, montanism, montanite, montant, montanto, montbretia, monte, montebrasite, montegre, monteith, monteiths, montem, montera, monterey, montero, monteros, montes, montessori, montessorian, montevideo, montezuma, montgolfier, montgolfiers, montgomery, montgomeryshire, month, month's, monthlies, monthlong, monthly, monthon, months, montia, monticellite, monticle, monticola, monticolae, monticoline, monticulate, monticule, monticuline, monticuliporidean, monticuliporoid, monticulose, monticulous, monticulus, montiform, montigeneous, montilla, montjoy, montjoye, montmartrite, montmorillonite, montmorillonitic, montmorilonite, monton, montpelier, montre, montreal, montross, montroydite, monture, montuvio, monument, monument's, monumental, monumentalise, monumentalised, monumentalising, monumentalism, monumentality, monumentalization, monumentalize, monumentalized, monumentalizing, monumentally, monumentary, monumented, monumenting, monumentless, monumentlike, monuments, monuron, monurons, mony, monzodiorite, monzogabbro, monzonite, monzonitic, moo, moocah, mooch, moocha, mooched, moocher, moochers, mooches, mooching, moochulka, mood, mood's, mooder, moodier, moodiest, moodily, moodiness, moodir, moodish, moodishly, moodishness, moodle, moods, moody, mooed, mooing, mookhtar, mooktar, mool, moola, moolah, moolahs, moolas, moolet, mooley, mooleys, moolings, mools, moolum, moolvee, moolvi, moolvie, moon, moonack, moonal, moonbeam, moonbeams, moonbill, moonblind, moonblink, moonbow, moonbows, mooncalf, mooncalves, mooncreeper, moondog, moondown, moondrop, mooned, mooner, moonery, moonet, mooneye, mooneyes, moonface, moonfaced, moonfall, moonfish, moonfishes, moonflower, moong, moonglade, moonglow, moonhead, moonie, moonier, mooniest, moonily, mooniness, mooning, moonish, moonishly, moonite, moonja, moonjah, moonless, moonlessness, moonlet, moonlets, moonlight, moonlighted, moonlighter, moonlighters, moonlighting, moonlights, moonlighty, moonlike, moonlikeness, moonling, moonlit, moonlitten, moonman, moonmen, moonpath, moonpenny, moonproof, moonquake, moonraker, moonraking, moonrat, moonrise, moonrises, moons, moonsail, moonsails, moonscape, moonscapes, moonseed, moonseeds, moonset, moonsets, moonshade, moonshee, moonshine, moonshined, moonshiner, moonshiners, moonshining, moonshiny, moonshot, moonshots, moonsick, moonsickness, moonsif, moonstone, moonstones, moonstricken, moonstruck, moontide, moonwalk, moonwalker, moonwalking, moonwalks, moonward, moonwards, moonway, moonwort, moonworts, moony, moop, moor, moorage, moorages, moorball, moorband, moorberries, moorberry, moorbird, moorburn, moorburner, moorburning, moorcock, moore, moored, mooress, moorflower, moorfowl, moorfowls, moorhen, moorhens, moorier, mooriest, mooring, moorings, moorish, moorishly, moorishness, moorland, moorlander, moorlands, moorman, moormen, moorn, moorpan, moorpunky, moors, moorsman, moorstone, moortetter, mooruk, moorup, moorwort, moorworts, moory, moos, moosa, moose, mooseberries, mooseberry, moosebird, moosebush, moosecall, mooseflower, moosehood, moosemilk, moosemise, moosetongue, moosewob, moosewood, moosey, moost, moot, mootable, mootch, mooted, mooter, mooters, mooth, mooting, mootman, mootmen, mootness, moots, mootstead, mootsuddy, mootworthy, mop, mopane, mopani, mopboard, mopboards, mope, moped, mopeder, mopeders, mopeds, mopehawk, mopeier, mopeiest, moper, mopers, mopery, mopes, mopey, moph, mophead, mopheaded, mopheadedness, mopier, mopiest, moping, mopingly, mopish, mopishly, mopishness, mopla, moplah, mopoke, mopokes, mopped, mopper, moppers, moppet, moppets, mopping, moppy, mops, mopsey, mopstick, mopsy, mopus, mopuses, mopusses, mopy, moquette, moquettes, mor, mora, morabit, moraceous, morada, morae, morainal, moraine, moraines, morainic, moral, morale, moraler, morales, moralioralist, moralise, moralised, moralises, moralising, moralism, moralisms, moralist, moralistic, moralistically, moralists, moralities, morality, moralization, moralize, moralized, moralizer, moralizers, moralizes, moralizing, moralizingly, moraller, moralless, morally, moralness, morals, moras, morass, morasses, morassic, morassweed, morassy, morat, morate, moration, moratoria, moratorium, moratoriums, moratory, morattoria, moravian, moravite, moray, morays, morbid, morbidezza, morbidities, morbidity, morbidize, morbidly, morbidness, morbiferal, morbiferous, morbific, morbifical, morbifically, morbify, morbility, morbillary, morbilli, morbilliform, morbillous, morbleu, morbose, morbus, morceau, morceaux, morcellate, morcellated, morcellating, morcellation, morcellement, morcha, mord, mordacious, mordaciously, mordacity, mordancies, mordancy, mordant, mordanted, mordanting, mordantly, mordants, mordecai, mordellid, mordelloid, mordenite, mordent, mordents, mordicant, mordicate, mordication, mordicative, mordieu, mordisheen, mordore, mordu, more, moreen, moreens, morefold, moreish, morel, morella, morelle, morelles, morello, morellos, morels, morena, morencite, morendo, moreness, morenita, morenosite, moreover, morepeon, morepork, mores, moresco, moresque, moresques, morfond, morfound, morfounder, morfrey, morg, morga, morgan, morganatic, morganatical, morganatically, morganic, morganite, morganize, morgay, morgen, morgengift, morgens, morgenstern, morglay, morgue, morgues, morian, moribund, moribundity, moribundly, moric, morice, moriche, moriform, morigerate, morigeration, morigerous, morigerously, morigerousness, moriglio, morillon, morin, morindin, morindone, morinel, moringa, moringaceous, moringad, moringuid, moringuoid, morion, morions, morisco, morish, morkin, morling, morlop, mormaer, mormal, mormaor, mormaordom, mormaorship, mormo, mormon, mormonism, mormons, mormorando, mormyr, mormyre, mormyrian, mormyrid, mormyroid, morn, mornay, morne, morned, mornette, morning, morningless, morningly, mornings, morningstar, morningtide, morningward, mornless, mornlike, morns, morntime, mornward, moro, moroc, morocain, moroccan, moroccans, morocco, moroccos, morocota, morological, morologically, morologist, morology, moromancy, moron, moroncy, morone, morones, morong, moronic, moronically, moronism, moronisms, moronities, moronity, moronry, morons, moror, morosaurian, morosauroid, morose, morosely, moroseness, morosis, morosities, morosity, morosoph, moroxite, morph, morphactin, morphallaxes, morphallaxis, morphea, morpheme, morphemes, morphemic, morphemically, morphemics, morphetic, morpheus, morphew, morphgan, morphia, morphias, morphiate, morphic, morphically, morphin, morphinate, morphine, morphines, morphinic, morphinism, morphinist, morphinization, morphinize, morphinomania, morphinomaniac, morphins, morphiomania, morphiomaniac, morphism, morphisms, morphized, morphizing, morpho, morphogeneses, morphogenesis, morphogenetic, morphogenetically, morphogenic, morphogeny, morphographer, morphographic, morphographical, morphographist, morphography, morphol, morpholin, morpholine, morphologic, morphological, morphologically, morphologies, morphologist, morphologists, morphology, morpholoical, morphometric, morphometrical, morphometrically, morphometry, morphon, morphoneme, morphonemic, morphonemics, morphonomic, morphonomy, morphophoneme, morphophonemic, morphophonemically, morphophonemics, morphophyly, morphoplasm, morphoplasmic, morphos, morphoses, morphosis, morphotic, morphotonemic, morphotonemics, morphotropic, morphotropism, morphotropy, morphous, morphrey, morphs, morpion, morpunkee, morra, morral, morrhuate, morrhuin, morrhuine, morrice, morricer, morrion, morrions, morris, morrises, morro, morros, morrow, morrowing, morrowless, morrowmass, morrows, morrowspeech, morrowtide, mors, morsal, morse, morsel, morsel's, morseled, morseling, morselization, morselize, morselled, morselling, morsels, morsing, morsure, mort, mortacious, mortadella, mortal, mortalism, mortalist, mortalities, mortality, mortalize, mortalized, mortalizing, mortally, mortalness, mortals, mortalty, mortalwise, mortancestry, mortar, mortarboard, mortarboards, mortared, mortaring, mortarize, mortarless, mortarlike, mortars, mortarware, mortary, mortbell, mortcloth, mortem, mortersheen, mortgage, mortgage's, mortgageable, mortgaged, mortgagee, mortgagees, mortgager, mortgagers, mortgages, mortgaging, mortgagor, mortgagors, morth, morthwyrtha, mortice, morticed, morticer, mortices, mortician, morticians, morticing, mortier, mortiferous, mortiferously, mortiferousness, mortific, mortification, mortifications, mortified, mortifiedly, mortifiedness, mortifier, mortifies, mortify, mortifying, mortifyingly, mortis, mortise, mortised, mortiser, mortisers, mortises...............

Here marks roughly half-way of
354,984 single words excluding
proper nouns, acronyms, compound
words and phrases, but
including archaic words and
significant variant spellings

Lightning Source UK Ltd.
Milton Keynes UK
UKHW030755280820
368979UK00005B/295